CRIMINAL PROCEDURE:
INVESTIGATION AND RIGHT TO COUNSEL

CRIMINAL PROCEDURE:
INVESTIGATION AND RIGHT TO COUNSEL

Ronald Jay Allen

John Henry Wigmore Professor of Law
Northwestern University

Joseph L. Hoffmann

Harry Pratter Professor of Law
Indiana University — Bloomington

Debra A. Livingston

Paul J. Kellner Professor of Law
Columbia University

William J. Stuntz

Professor of Law
Harvard University

PUBLISHERS

111 Eighth Avenue, New York, NY 10011
www.aspenpublishers.com

Aspen Publishers
Attn: Permissions Department
111 Eighth Avenue
New York, NY 10011-5201

Printed in the United States of America.

1 2 3 4 5 6 7 8 9 0

ISBN 0-7355-5193-6

Library of Congress Cataloging-in-Publication Data

Criminal procedure : investigation and right to counsel/Ronald Jay Allen . . . [et al.].
    p.   cm.
    "[C]ontains the first seven chapters of Comprehensive criminal procedure, 2nd ed., 2005" — Pref.
    Includes bibliographical references.
    ISBN 0-7355-5193-6 (alk. paper)
    1. Criminal procedure — United States — Cases.   2. Criminal justice, Administration of — United States — Cases.   3. Criminal investigation — United States — Cases.   4. Right to counsel — United States — Cases.   I. Allen, Ronald J. (Ronald Jay), 1948–
II. Comprehensive criminal procedure.

KF9618.C75 2005
345.73'056 — dc22

                                                                2005041014

About Aspen Publishers

Aspen Publishers, headquartered in New York City, is a leading information provider for attorneys, business professionals, and law students. Written by pre-eminent authorities, our products consist of analytical and practical information covering both U.S. and international topics. We publish in the full range of formats, including updated manuals, books, periodicals, CDs, and online products.

Our proprietary content is complemented by 2,500 legal databases, containing over 11 million documents, available through our Loislaw division. Aspen Publishers also offers a wide range of topical legal and business databases linked to Loislaw's primary material. Our mission is to provide accurate, timely, and authoritative content in easily accessible formats, supported by unmatched customer care.

To order any Aspen Publishers title, go to *www.aspenpublishers.com* or call 1-800-638-8437.

To reinstate your manual update service, call 1-800-638-8437.

For more information on Loislaw products, go to *www.loislaw.com* or call 1-800-364-2512.

For Customer Care issues, e-mail *CustomerCare@aspenpublishers.com*; call 1-800-234- 1660; or fax 1-800-901-9075.

Aspen Publishers
A Wolters Kluwer Company

To my wife, Julie O'Donnell Allen — R.J.A.

In memory of my mother,
Joanne Matuszak Hoffmann — J.H.

In memory of my grandfather,
Harold Yates DeVenny — D.L.

To Louis Pollak,
mentor and friend — W.S.

Summary of Contents

Contents

PART ONE
THE CRIMINAL PROCESS   1

Chapter 1
Introduction to the Criminal Justice "System"   3

Chapter 2
The Idea of Due Process   77

PART TWO
THE RIGHT TO COUNSEL — THE LINCHPIN OF
CONSTITUTIONAL PROTECTION

Chapter 3
The Right to Counsel and Other Assistance

Chapter 6
The Fifth Amendment 751

Chapter 7
Investigating Complex Crimes   945

Preface

Criminal Procedure: Investigation and Right to Counsel contains the first seven chapters of *Comprehensive Criminal Procedure*, Second Edition, 2005. Many modern American law schools provide two mainstream criminal procedure courses. One course focuses primarily on right to counsel, Fourth Amendment, self-incrimination, and related areas, while the second course focuses primarily on post-arrest, trial, and appellate issues. *Comprehensive Criminal Procedure* provides a set of materials suitable for any criminal procedure course beyond those that focus primarily on state law issues. This book, *Criminal Procedure: Investigation and Right to Counsel*, by contrast, covers all but only the subject matter of the traditional constitutional criminal procedure book. We offer it in this format because of the convenience of a smaller and less expensive set of materials for those offering and taking such a course.

As this book is based on the new second edition of *Comprehensive Criminal Procedure*, a few words, first, about its revision, and, second, about our overall objectives for both books. While we believe that these materials preserve the best parts of their predecessor, we have added material focused on recent developments throughout the book, and have been especially attentive to the effects of the "War on Terror" for criminal procedure doctrine. Post-9/11 developments are taken up in various chapters, and are treated comprehensively in a new and expanded version of Chapter 7 that deals with complex crimes and crimes involving threats to national security. Many other chapters have been thoroughly rewritten, with many new sections, re-edited and reorganized cases, and substitutions of new cases and materials for outdated ones. Of the subject matter of this book, this is especially true of Chapter 5 ("The Fourth Amendment"), which has been almost completely revised, and now includes entirely new discussions on the meaning of both "search" and "seizure," exigent circumstances, searches incident to arrest, the relationship between police discretion and racial profiling, and "special needs," among other topics. Much the same can also be said for Chapter 6 ("The Fifth Amendment"), and, as mentioned, Chapter 7 ("Investigating Complex Crimes").

The book opens with a wide-ranging set of readings about the criminal justice system, combining hard data with expert commentary. The nature of due process adjudication is then introduced, because so much of this field either has been constitutionalized or operates within the shadow of the Constitution. The first major substantive area examined in detail is the right to counsel in Chapter 3. We begin with the right to counsel because it is the linchpin of criminal procedure, obviously so with respect to its constitutional aspects but even more critically so with respect to its statutory and common law aspects. Without adequate counsel, a suspect or defendant is, with rare exceptions, lost. The most elaborate procedural protections courts can devise are of little value to one who neither knows what those protections are nor how they can be used to best advantage.

Following the right to counsel is a chapter chronicling the history of *Boyd v. United States*. We think it fair to say that the Supreme Court of the United States has been reacting to the *Boyd* case for the last century, and that the present law of search and seizure and the right to be free from compelled self-incrimination cannot be understood without a grounding in *Boyd* and its aftermath. This is followed by in-depth examinations of, first, one of the "hottest" areas of criminal procedure today, the Fourth Amendment, followed by a thorough treatment of the Fifth Amendment's self-incrimination clause. The Fifth Amendment materials cover the entire range of relevant issues rather than just the *Miranda* doctrines. There is, in our judgment, often an unfortunate equation between the right to be free from compelled self-incrimination and the prophylactic rules constructed in *Miranda* that actually constitute an exception to the normal requirements of the Fifth Amendment. We carefully sort out these issues in Chapter 6. This book finishes with a study of the problems posed by complex crimes in the completely rewritten Chapter 7.

Criminal procedure is one of the most fascinating and important fields of legal study. More than any other area of law, criminal procedure determines the relationship between government and citizen, and thus defines the legal system's stance toward the demands of autonomy, privacy, and dignity. It often does so through adversarial legal processes. Thus, the study of criminal procedure leads naturally to fundamental problems of reasoning, decision making, and political and social theory, in addition to standard law school questions about the meaning of a constitutional or statutory provision, or the implications of a precedent. The subject demands, and we have tried to bring, intellectual rigor to these materials; we do not shy away from addressing intractable problems. Moreover, much of the present law reflects its past, and thus we have tried to give a picture not only of the law today but also of its history.

In addition to the careful attention given to the historical roots of modern law, we develop four other subthemes while pursuing the overarching theme to this book—that the criminal process significantly forms the boundary between the government and the citizen. First, we draw attention to the real-world implications of alternative regulatory regimes. All too common in this field is the notion that if there is a problem, the courts should remedy it. Often courts are unable to remedy problems, and sometimes their solutions are worse than the initial problems. Second, the subject matter is criminal procedure, but procedure interacts in complex, profound ways with substance. In appraising any procedural matter, especially one involving a judicial determination of a procedural right, the power of legislatures to indirectly eliminate the right through changes in substantive criminal law (or directly through statutory changes to the procedure in question) must be analyzed. Third, much of the modern law of criminal procedure is a direct consequence of the effort to eliminate racial discrimination in the United States, and can be understood only in that context. Last, the implications of limited resources must constantly be kept in mind. All too often neglected is that criminal procedure is instrumental to the construction of a civilized society, and a dollar spent here is a dollar that cannot be spent somewhere else. One can have more expensive criminal procedure or one can have more hospitals, roads, or welfare programs. One cannot, however, have it all.

We have endeavored to keep editing of cases at a minimum, opting at times for textual description over a series of edited excerpts. Editing is unavoidable, however. In all cases and materials reproduced here, we have kept the original footnoting sequence. Wherever our own footnotes might be confused with those of the primary material, our own footnotes are identified by the legend "— EDs." This book contains Supreme Court and lower court cases and legislative materials current through July 2004.

Ronald J. Allen
Joseph L. Hoffmann
Debra A. Livingston
William J. Stuntz

March 2005

Acknowledgments

We are grateful to the following sources for permission to reprint excerpts of their work:

ABA Rule, Rule 1.7 Conflict of Interest: General Rule (as attached) from the ABA Model Rules of Professional Conduct (2001). Copyright © 2001 by the American Bar Association. Reprinted by permission of the American Bar Association. Copies of the ABA Model Rules of Professional Conduct (2001) are available from Service Center, American Bar Association, 750 North Lake Shore Drive, Chicago, IL 60611, 1-800-285-2221.

Francis Allen, Decline of the Rehabilitative Ideal: Penal Policy and Social Purpose, pp. 60-61, 63, 65-66 (1981) Yale University Press. Copyright © 1981 by Yale University Press. Reprinted with permission.

Ronald Allen, Melissa Luttrell, and Anne Kreeger, Clarifying Entrapment, 89 J. Crim. L. & Criminology 407, 413-414, 415-416 (1999). Reprinted by special permission of Northwestern University School of Law, Journal of Criminal Law and Criminology.

Ronald J. Allen and Ross M. Rosenberg, The Fourth Amendment and the Limits of Theory: Local Versus General Theoretical Knowledge, 72 St. John's L. Rev. 1149, 1194, 1197-1200 (1998). Reprinted with permission.

Albert W. Alschuler, Implementing the Criminal Defendant's Right to Trial: Alternatives to the Plea Bargaining System, 50 U. Chi. L. Rev. 931, 932-936, 1048-1050 (1983). Copyright © 1983. Reprinted with permission.

Akhil Reed Amar, The Future of Constitutional Criminal Procedure, 33 Am. Crim. L. Rev. 1123, 1123-1125, 1128-1129, 1132-1134 (1996). Reprinted with permission of the publisher, Georgetown University and American Criminal Law Review (1996).

Anthony Amsterdam, The Supreme Court and the Rights of Suspects in Criminal Cases, 45 N.Y.U. L. Rev. 785, 785-794 (1970). Reprinted with permission of the New York University Law Review.

Anthony Amsterdam, Perspectives on the Fourth Amendment, 58 Minn. L. Rev. 349, 410-411 (1974). Copyright © 1974 by the Minnesota Law Review. Reprinted with permission.

Peter Arenella, *Schmerber* and the Privilege Against Self-Incrimination: A Reappraisal, 20 Am. Crim. L. Rev. 31, 37, 43-45 (1982). Copyright © 1982 by the American Bar Association. Reprinted with permission.

R. Richard Banks, Beyond Profiling: Race, Policing, and the Drug War, 56 Stan. L. Rev. 571, 588-589, 602-603 (2003). Reprinted with permission.

David L. Bazelon, The Realities of *Gideon* and *Argersinger*, 64 Geo. L.J. 811 (1976). Reprinted with permission of the publisher, Georgetown University and Georgetown Law Journal © 1976.

Abraham Blumberg, The Practice of Law as Confidence Game: Organizational Co-optation of a Profession, 1 Law & Soc'y Rev. 15, 18-26, 29-31 (No. 2 1967). Reprinted by permission of the Law and Society Association.

Craig Bradley, Murray v. United States: The Bell Tolls for the Warrant Requirement, 64 Ind. L.J. 907, 917-918 (1989). Reprinted with permission.

William J. Brennan, Jr., State Constitutions and the Protection of Individual Rights, 90 Harv. L. Rev. 489-497 (1977). Copyright © 1977 by The Harvard Law Review Association. Reprinted with permission.

Steven J. Burton, Comment on Empty Ideas: Logical Positivist Analyses of Equality and Rules, 91 Yale L.J. 1136-1141, 1144-1147 (1982). Reprinted by permission of The Yale Law Journal Company and William S. Hein Company from The Yale Law Journal, Vol. 91, pages 1136-1152.

Paul Chevigny, Edge of the Knife, pp. 98-99, 101-102 (1995) New Press. Copyright © 1995. Edge of the Knife: Police Violence in the Americas by Paul Chevigny. Reprinted by permission of The New Press.

Alan M. Dershowitz, excerpt from The Best Defense, pp. xxi-xxii. Copyright © by Alan M. Dershowitz. Used by permission of Random House, Inc.

Christopher L. Eisgruber and Lawrence G. Sager, Civil Liberties in the Dragons' Domain: Negotiating the Blurred Boundary between Domestic Law and Foreign Affairs After 9/11, in Mary L. Dudziak, ed., September 11 in History, 163, 163-164, 166-167 (2003). Copyright 2003, Duke University Press. All rights reserved. Used by permission of the publisher.

Robert Ellickson, Controlling Chronic Misconduct in City Spaces: Of Panhandlers, Skid Rows, and Public-Space Zoning, 105 Yale L.J. 1165, 1247-1248 (1996). Reprinted by permission of The Yale Law Journal Company and William S. Hein Company from The Yale Law Journal, Vol. 105, pages 1165-1248.

Clifford S. Fishman, Interception of Communications in Exigent Circumstances: The Fourth Amendment, Federal Legislation, and the United States Department of Justice, 22 Ga. L. Rev. 1, 5-7, 25, 48-51 (1987). Reprinted with permission.

Charles Fried, Reflections on Crime and Punishment, 30 Suffolk U. L. Rev. 681, 682-683, 685-688, 692-693, 694-695 (1997). Copyright © 1997. Reprinted with permission.

Russell Galloway, The Intruding Eye: A Status Report on the Constitutional Ban Against Paper Searches, 25 Howard L.J. 367, 382-385 (1982). Copyright © 1982 by the Howard Law Journal. Reprinted with permission.

Joseph D. Grano, Ascertaining the Truth, 77 Cornell L. Rev. 1061, 1062-1064 (1992). Copyright © 1992. Reprinted with permission.

Samuel R. Gross and Debra Livingston, Racial Profiling Under Attack, 102 Colum. L. Rev. 1413 (2002).

Philip B. Heymann, Civil Liberties and Human Rights in the Aftermath of September 11, 25 Harv. J.L. & Pub. Pol'y 440, 441-442 (2002).

Pamela Karlan, Discrete and Relational Criminal Representation: The Changing Vision of the Right to Counsel, 105 Harv. L. Rev. 670, 709-710 (1992). Copyright © 1992 by the Harvard Law Review Association. Reprinted with permission.

Randall Kennedy, Race, Crime and the Law, pp. 158-161 (1997) Vintage Books. Copyright © 1997 by Randall Kennedy. Reprinted by permission of Pantheon Books, a division of Random House, Inc.

Michael J. Klarman, The Racial Origins of Modern Criminal Procedure, 99 Mich. L. Rev. 48-97 (2000). Copyright © 2000 by Michigan Law Review.

Stanton D. Krauss, The Life and Times of *Boyd v. United States* (1886-1976), 76 Mich. L. Rev. 184, 212 (1977). Reprinted from Michigan Law Review, 1977. Copyright 1977 by the Michigan Law Review Association. Reprinted with permission.

Wayne LaFave, Jerold Israel, and Nancy King, Criminal Procedure: Criminal Practice Series, Vol. 4, pp. 58-59, Section 13.4(c), 1999, with permission of the West Group.

Barry Latzer, Toward the Decentralization of Criminal Procedure: State Constitutional Law and Selective Incorporation, 87 J. Crim. L. & Criminology 63, 63-66, 68 (1996). Reprinted by special permission of Northwestern University School of Law, Journal of Criminal Law and Criminology.

Andrew Leipold, Why Grand Juries Do Not (and Cannot) Protect the Accused, 80 Cornell L. Rev. 260, 265-267 (1995). Copyright © 1995. Reprinted with permission.

Richard Leo, *Miranda*'s Revenge: Police Interrogation as a Confidence Game, 30 Law & Soc'y Rev. 259 (No. 2 1996). Reprinted with permission of the Law and Society Association.

Lawrence Lessig, Code and Other Laws of Cyberspace, pp. 17, 18, 19, 120, 144-145. Copyright © 1999 by Basic Books, Inc. Reprinted by permission of Basic Books, a member of Perseus Books, L.L.C.

Debra Livingston, Police Discretion and the Quality of Life in Public Places: Courts, Communities, and the New Policing, 97 Colum. L. Rev. 551, 557, 558-561, 621-623, 632-633, 654-657, 670-671 (1997). Copyright © 1997 by Columbia Law Review. Reprinted with permission of the publisher and author.

Debra Livingston, Police, Community Caretaking and the Fourth Amendment, 1998 University of Chicago Legal Forum 261, 278, 273-274. Copyright © 1998 University of Chicago Legal Forum 261. Reprinted with permission.

Debra Livingston, The Unfulfilled Promise of Citizen Review, 1 Ohio St. J. Crim. L. 653, 658-659 (2004). Originally published in the Ohio State Journal of Criminal Law.

Elizabeth F. Loftus, Eyewitness Testimony, p. 60, Harvard University Press, 1996. Copyright © 1996 by Harvard University Press. Reprinted with permission.

Gary Lowenthal, Joint Representation in Criminal Cases: A Critical Appraisal, 64 Va. L. Rev. 939, 941-942 (1978). Reprinted with permission.

Peter Lushing, Testimonial Immunity and the Privilege Against Self-Incrimination: A Study in Isomorphism, 73 J. Crim. L. & Criminology 1690, 1695 (1982). Reprinted by special permission of Northwestern University School of Law, Journal of Criminal Law and Criminology.

Kenneth Mann, Defending White-Collar Crime: A Portrait of Attorneys at Work, Yale University Press, 1985, pp. 6-8, 137-138, 249-250. Copyright © 1985 by Yale University Press. Reprinted with permission.

Gary T. Marx, Undercover: Police Surveillance in America, pp. 22, 33-35, 47. Copyright © 1988 Twentieth Century Fund. Permission granted by the Regents of the University of California and the University of California Press.

Marc Mauer and Tracy Huling, Young Black Americans and the Criminal Justice System: Five Years Later, pp. 7-9, The Sentencing Project (1995). Reprinted with permission of The Sentencing Project.

Note, Formalism, Legal Realism, and Constitutionally Protected Privacy Under the Fourth and Fifth Amendments, 90 Harv. L. Rev. 945, 985-988 (1977). Copyright © 1977 by the Harvard Law Review Association.

Charles E. O'Hara, Fundamentals of Criminal Investigation, Charles C. Thomas, Publisher, 1956, pp. 99, 105-106, 112. Courtesy of Charles C. Thomas, Publisher, Ltd., Springfield, Illinois.

Herbert Packer, The Courts, the Police, and the Rest of Us, 57 J. Crim. L., Criminology & Pol. Sci. 238, 239 (1966). Reprinted by special permission of Northwestern University School of Law, Journal of Criminal Law and Criminology.

Renee Paradis, Carpe Demonstratores: Toward a Bright-Line Rule Governing Seizure in Excessive Force Claims Brought by Demonstrators, 103 Colum. L. Rev. 316, 334-339 (2003). Reprinted by permission.

Frank Read, Lawyers at Lineups: Constitutional Necessity or Avoidable Extravagance? 17 UCLA L. Rev. 339, 388-393 (1969). Reprinted with permission.

Daniel C. Richman, Grand Jury Secrecy: Plugging the Leaks in an Empty Bucket, 36 Am. Crim. L. Rev. 339, 341, 355 (1999). Reprinted with permission of the publisher, Georgetown University and American Criminal Law Review © 1999.

Dorothy E. Roberts, Crime, Race and Reproduction, 67 Tul. L. Rev. 1945, 1945-1947 (1993). Originally published in 67 Tul. L. Rev. 1945-1977 (1993). Reprinted with the permission of the Tulane Law Review Association, which holds the copyright.

Dorothy E. Roberts, Foreword: Race, Vagueness, and the Social Meaning of Order-Maintenance Policing, 89 J. Crim. L. & Criminology 821, 827-828 (1999). Reprinted by special permission of Northwestern University School of Law, Journal of Criminal Law and Criminology.

William A. Schroeder, Warrantless Misdemeanor Arrests and the Fourth Amendment, 58 Mo. L. Rev. 771, 797-801 (1993).

Stephen Schulhofer, Some Kind Words for the Privilege Against Self-Incrimination, 26 Val. U. L. Rev. 311, 329-330 (1991). Copyright © 1991. Reprinted with permission.

Stephen J. Schulhofer, The Enemy Within 60, 68 (2002). Reprinted from The Enemy Within: Intelligence Gathering, Law Enforcement, and Civil Liberties in the Wake of September 11, by Stephen J. Schulhofer with permission from The Century Foundation, Inc. Copyright 2002, New York.

Stephen Schulhofer and David Friedman, Rethinking Indigent Defense: Promoting Effective Representation Through Consumer Sovereignty and Freedom of Choice for All Criminal Defendants, 31 Am. Crim. L. Rev. 73, 93-94 (1993). Reprinted with permission of the publisher, Georgetown University and American Criminal Law Review (1993).

Louis Michael Seidman, Points of Intersection: Discontinuities at the Junction of Criminal Law and the Regulatory State, 7 J. Contemp. Legal Issues 97, 97-98, 100-102, 127 (1996). Reprinted with permission of the author.

David Sklansky, Cocaine, Race and Equal Protection, 47 Stan. L. Rev. 1283-1284, 1322 (1995). Copyright 1995 by Stanford Law Review. Reproduced with permission of Stanford Law Review in the format textbook via Copyright Clearance Center.

David Sklansky, Traffic Stops, Minority Motorists and the Future of the Fourth Amendment, 1997 Sup. Ct. Rev. 271, 300-301. Copyright © 1997 by the University of Chicago Press. Reprinted with permission.

David Sklansky, The Private Police, 46 UCLA L. Rev. 1165, 1175-1176, 1224-1225 (1999). Originally published in 46 UCLA L. Rev. 1165. Copyright 1999, The Regents of the University of California. All rights reserved.

Jerome H. Skolnick and David H. Bayley, The New Blue Line: Police Innovation in Six American Cities, pp. 49-52, Free Press, 1988. Reprinted with the permission of The Free Press, a Division of Simon & Schuster Adult Publishing Group, from The New Blue Line: Police Innovation in Six American Cities by Jerome H. Skolnick and David H. Bayley. Copyright © 1986 by Jerome H. Skolnick and David H. Bayley.

Christopher Slobogin, Why Liberals Should Chuck the Exclusionary Rule, 1999 U. Ill. L. Rev. 363. Copyright © 1999 by The Board of Trustees of the University of Illinois.

Carol S. Steiker, Counter-Revolution in Constitutional Criminal Procedure? Two Audiences, Two Answers, 94 Mich. L. Rev. 2466, 2466-2470, 2536, 2543 (1996). Reprinted from Michigan Law Review, August 1996, Vol. 94, No. 8. Copyright 1996 by The Michigan Law Review Association. Reprinted with permission.

William J. Stuntz, Waiving Rights in Criminal Procedure, 75 Va. L. Rev. 761, 798-799 (1989). Copyright © 1989 by the Virginia Law Review. Reprinted with permission.

William J. Stuntz, Warrants and Fourth Amendment Remedies, 77 Va. L. Rev. 881, 881-883 (1991). Copyright © 1991 by the Virginia Law Review. Reprinted with permission.

William J. Stuntz, Implicit Bargains, Government Power, and the Fourth Amendment, 44 Stan. L. Rev. 553, 555, 584 (1992). Copyright 1992 by Stanford Law Review. Reproduced with permission of Stanford Law Review in the format textbook via Copyright Clearance Center.

William J. Stuntz, Privacy's Problem and the Law of Criminal Procedure, 93 Mich. L. Rev. 1016, 1075-1076 (1995). Reprinted from Michigan Law Review, March 1995, Vol. 93, No. 5. Copyright 1995 by The Michigan Law Review Association.

William J. Stuntz, Substance, Process, and the Civil-Criminal Line, 7 J. Contemp. Legal Issues 1, 14-15 (1996). Reprinted with permission of the author.

William J. Stuntz, The Virtues and Vices of the Exclusionary Rule, 20 Harv. J.L. & Pub. Pol'y 443, 445-446 (1997). Copyright © 1997 by the Harvard Journal of Law and Public Policy. Reprinted with permission.

William J. Stuntz, Local Policing After the Terror, 111 Yale L.J. 2137, 2164-2167 (2002).

Scott E. Sundby, A Return to Fourth Amendment Basics: Undoing the Mischief of *Camara* and *Terry*, 72 Minn. L. Rev. 383, 388-391, 393-394 (1988). Chapter 5, pages 554-555, 556. Reprinted with permission.

Peter Tague, Multiple Representation and Conflicts of Interest in Criminal Cases, 67 Geo. L.J. 1075, 1086-1087, 1094-1095 (1979). Reprinted with permission of the publisher, Georgetown University and Georgetown Law Journal © 1979.

Scott Turow, "Policing the Police: The DA's Job" from Postmortem: The O.J. Simpson Case 189 by Jeffrey Abramson. Copyright © 1996 by Basic Books, Inc. Reprinted by permission of Basic Books, a member of Perseus Books, L.L.C.

Rodney Uphoff, The Criminal Defense Lawyer as Effective Negotiator: A Systemic Approach, 2 Clinical L. Rev. 73-94 (1995). Copyright © 1995. Reprinted with permission.

Silas Wasserstrom and Louis Michael Seidman, The Fourth Amendment as Constitutional Theory, 77 Geo. L.J. 19, 34-35 (1988). Reprinted with permission of the publisher, Georgetown University and Georgetown Law Journal © 1988.

Peter Westen, The Empty Idea of Equality, 95 Harv. L. Rev. 537, 539-540, 543-50 (1982). Copyright © 1982 by the Harvard Law Review Association.

Paul Wice, Chaos in the Courthouse: The Inner Workings of the Urban Criminal Courts, pp. 21-24, 63-65 (1985) Prager Publishers. Copyright © 1985 by Prager Publishers. Reproduced with permission of Greenwood Publishing Group, Inc., Westport, CT.

CRIMINAL PROCEDURE:
INVESTIGATION AND RIGHT TO COUNSEL

PART ONE
THE CRIMINAL PROCESS

Chapter 1

Introduction to the Criminal Justice "System"

A. Introduction

The system of criminal justice America uses to deal with those crimes it cannot prevent and those criminals it cannot deter is not a monolithic, or even a consistent, system. It was not designed or built in one piece at one time. Its philosophic core is that a person may be punished by the Government if, and only if, it has been proved by an impartial and deliberate process that he has violated a specific law. Around that core layer upon layer of institutions and procedures, some carefully constructed and some improvised, some inspired by principle and some by expediency, have accumulated. Parts of the system — magistrates' courts, trial by jury, bail — are of great antiquity. Other parts — juvenile courts, probation and parole, professional policemen — are relatively new. The entire system represents an adaption of the English common law to America's peculiar structure of government, which allows each local community to construct institutions that fill its special needs. Every village, town, county, city and State has its own criminal justice system, and there is a Federal one as well. All of them operate somewhat alike. No two of them operate precisely alike.

> *President's Commission on Law Enforcement and Administration of Justice,*
> *The Challenge of Crime in a Free Society 7 (1967)*

Some of the differences in operation are a result of different formal mechanisms. For example, in the federal system and in approximately two-fifths of the state systems, a defendant cannot be prosecuted for a serious crime unless a grand jury — a group usually composed of 17 to 23 citizens selected from the voter registration lists — has reviewed the evidence and decided to return an indictment or the defendant has waived the right to a grand jury indictment; in other jurisdictions there is no right to a grand jury indictment.[1] In some jurisdictions the

---

1. The Bill of Rights — the first 10 amendments to the federal Constitution — protects citizens against certain actions by the *federal* government. Among these protections are a number of rights applicable to criminal defendants, including the Fifth Amendment right not to be prosecuted for a serious crime in the absence of a grand jury indictment. Over the years the Supreme Court has "incorporated" most of these rights into the due process clause of the Fourteenth Amendment, which restricts the actions of state governments. See Chapter 2, page 77 infra. The federal right to a grand jury indictment is one of the few rights that has not been so incorporated. Thus, states are free to adopt or reject the use of grand juries to screen criminal charges.

authority to decide whether to proceed with a criminal prosecution rests with the local prosecutor; in others the ultimate authority, although rarely exercised, rests with the attorney general. In some jurisdictions the prosecutor's consent is usually required for the issuance of an arrest warrant; in others it is not. However, the Supreme Court has held that a prosecutor's judgment that an arrest warrant should be issued does not satisfy the "independent judicial officer" standard under the Constitution. Generally, judicial approval is required for the dismissal of a serious charge; in some jurisdictions, however, the prosecutor has unilateral discretion to dismiss.

Other, less formal differences contribute even more to variations in the operation of the criminal justice process. For example, the institutional components that constitute the criminal justice system — the police agencies, the public prosecutors, the courts, the correctional departments — each has independent functions, but the operation of each is in part dependent on the operation of the others. They interrelate differently from community to community,[2] and how they interrelate will have an impact on how the entire system operates. Thus, for the most part the prosecutors, the courts, and the correctional officials can deal only with those individuals whom the police arrest. A police officer's decision whether to arrest may in turn be influenced by how the officer believes the other institutional components of the system will respond to a situation. If an officer believes that an individual will be dealt with too leniently, the officer may arrest the individual and not press charges or perhaps not even make the arrest. Samuel Walker, Taming the System 23-24, 39-41 (1993).

Allocation of resources also affects the manner in which the system operates. Limited prosecutorial or judicial resources, for example, will force prosecutors to be more selective in choosing cases with which to proceed. Even allocation of resources within a single component of the criminal justice system has an impact on its operation. For example, at some point fairly early in the process, a member of the prosecutor's staff will review a case to determine whether it is appropriate to proceed with prosecution and, if so, on what charges. Usually the first opportunity to make this decision will be soon after an arrest, and the decision will be based on information contained in a police report. If the information in the report is complete enough to permit an informed decision about prosecution, and if the prosecutor is willing to assign experienced assistants to perform this screening function, cases inappropriate for prosecution can be eliminated from the system early without incurring the cost of proceeding with preliminary hearings or presentation of evidence to the grand jury. On the other hand, if experienced prosecutors are not used for this task or if the quality of initial information from the police is not high, there may be little serious screening of cases by the prosecutor until some later stage in the proceeding.

Even within a single jurisdiction, the order in which the various steps of the criminal justice process occur will depend on how the potential defendant first becomes involved in the system. Typically, for a serious crime there will be an arrest followed by a decision to prosecute. In some situations, however, the

---

2. And there are many communities. There are somewhere on the order of 17,000 police agencies in the United States, and more than 2,000 prosecutorial offices, all with varying resources, concerns, and objectives, and largely subject to no unifying supervision.

decision to prosecute may have been made secretly by the grand jury and prosecutor prior to any attempt to arrest the defendant.[3]

Despite the variations in the operation of the criminal justice process, there are substantial similarities among the federal and various state criminal justice systems with respect to prosecutions for serious criminal violations. Variations both in the formal judicial structure and in the degree of informality with which cases are resolved increase when one focuses on relatively minor crimes. The prosecution of serious criminality in most jurisdictions shares the following characteristics:

1. The initial enforcement responsibility rests with police agencies that have vast discretion in deciding whether to involve individuals in the criminal justice process.

2. The decision whether formally to charge an individual with a crime is the responsibility of a public prosecutor, who also possesses vast discretion.

3. There is some mechanism for screening serious criminal charges to determine whether there is a factual basis for the charge.

4. A criminal defendant is entitled to the assistance of counsel and, if indigent, to have one appointed at public expense if incarceration will result from conviction.

5. The vast majority of defendants participate with prosecutors in negotiating a guilty plea before trial. Most criminal cases are disposed of by negotiated guilty pleas through mechanisms that facilitate negotiation between defendants and prosecutors.

6. A defendant may make various pretrial motions challenging the prosecutor's evidence and the fairness of the criminal process.

7. Successful challenges by a defendant to the prosecution's evidence are often remedied by excluding evidence at trial, in particular in the prosecution's case-in-chief. Exclusion of this evidence does not necessarily mean that the evidence may not be used at other stages of the process, such as in rebuttal or sentencing.

8. Prosecution and defense are occasionally required to share discovery of certain information prior to trial, but nowhere near to the extent found in civil cases.

9. A defendant is entitled to a trial before an impartial judge, to confront and cross-examine opposing witnesses, to present witnesses, to a trial by jury unless the charge is only a "petty offense,"[4] and to an acquittal unless the prosecutor proves each element of the offense beyond a reasonable doubt. All these rights, and others, are waived by guilty pleas.

10. A guilty defendant has the right to address the court prior to sentencing. At sentencing, judges usually have substantial discretion in setting the penalty.

---

3. The grand jury, in addition to performing a screening function, may also act as an investigatory body. Information about an individual's criminal activity may come to light from such an investigation rather than from a citizen complaint or police investigation. On the basis of such information the grand jury may return an indictment prior to the defendant's arrest. Indeed, the arrest may be intentionally delayed for some period of time after the indictment is returned so that the grand jury can complete its investigation without alerting a defendant's confederates.

4. See Duncan v. Louisiana, at page 93 infra.

11. A convicted defendant usually has the right to some form of appellate review.[5]

The criminal justice system is, in a word, complicated. Individual systems themselves are complicated, as the chart below indicates, and in addition, there is no "criminal justice system" in the United States. Rather, there are many overlapping, competing and conflicting, "criminal justice systems" throughout the country. Even within any particular "system," various components may be more in tension with each other than working smoothly toward uniform goals. A substantial part of the subject matter of this course is the commands of the United States Supreme Court that supposedly apply uniformly to these diverse systems, but the effect of any particular command—whether it concerns requirements of warrants, rules about presenting arrested individuals to magistrates, limits on police interrogation, or whatever—obviously will be partly contingent upon the precise contours of the particular system implementing that command. Requiring warrants, for example, will have certain implications in a low-crime, high-resource system, such as the federal system, and quite different implications in a high-crime, low-resource system, such as in many major cities. As you appraise the various opinions of the Court that you will study throughout this semester, and all the other material that is presented, keep this point well in mind.

There are additional points to keep in mind that are especially pertinent to appraising the numerous cases that you will study but that again apply much more generally. There is often a sense in which legal studies tend to focus attention on texts, whether they be cases, statutes, or regulations, and to bring to bear on those texts interpretive methodologies. You will read numerous cases, for example, and one obviously pertinent question will be the fidelity of those cases to the constitutional text. Another will be the logical implications of the various decisions, and so on. These are, to be sure, important questions, but do not neglect that the material you are about to study deals both with real-life human dramas and with the exercise of some of the more extreme forms of power that the state employs. The criminal justice process exists because of crime—people behaving in unlawful and often barbarous ways toward each other. In response to crime, the state is authorized to seize and confine people, strip them of their property and liberty, and even put them to death. And thus another important question, perhaps the single most important question for you to contemplate, is how the texts that you will read relate to these human dramas—whether their commands will be implemented in ways that appropriately respond to both the costs of crime and the costs of law enforcement.

---

5. In many, but not all, jurisdictions the decision to plead guilty is viewed as a waiver of most of the contentions that a defendant might have raised at trial. For example, if a defendant prior to trial moved to exclude a confession on the ground that it was involuntary and if the confession were admitted at the trial, the defendant on appeal could challenge the admissibility of the confession. If the defendant decided to plead guilty after receiving an unfavorable ruling on the pretrial motion to suppress, however, the defendant would not be permitted in many jurisdictions to raise the involuntariness issue on appeal. The defendant, of course, could attack the guilty plea itself as involuntary or claim ineffective assistance of counsel. See generally Lefkowitz v. Newsome, 420 U.S. 283 (1975) (describing New York procedure that permits defendant to raise constitutional claims following guilty plea and holding that existence of such procedure precludes state from relying on guilty plea to foreclose consideration of same constitutional issues in federal habeas corpus proceedings).

BUREAU OF JUSTICE STATISTICS, U.S. DEPARTMENT OF JUSTICE,
A COMPENDIUM OF FEDERAL CRIMINAL JUSTICE STATISTICS, 5 (1998)

System overview

Federal criminal case processing, 1998

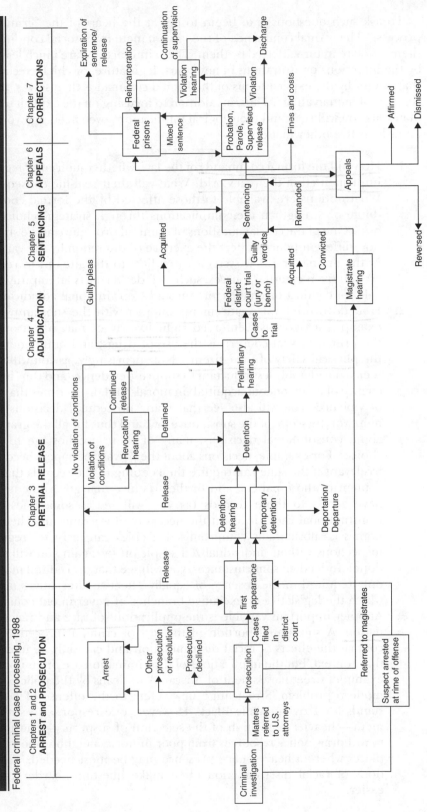

Figure S.1.

To ask such questions is to begin to get at the heart of the "criminal justice process." The formal commands of the law emanate from social conditions, affect them, and are in turn affected by them. These interactions are much less governed by the intentions or aspirations of any court, legislature, or chief executive, or for that matter by the explicit terms of the formal commands themselves, than by the realities of human affairs. Thus, in addition to focusing on the explicit terms of the materials you will read and their logical implications, we encourage you to reflect on at least five other matters:

1. How will the formal commands of the law, whether judicial or legislative, be implemented in the real world? What will their real-life consequences be? What options are available to those affected by the formal commands to dilute or strengthen their implications through strategic choices of their own? One of the crucial questions of criminal procedure at the street level is how different policies affect the exercise of discretion by the various actors in the drama, and how systems can adjust to the attempt to regulate discretion from external sources, such as federal courts attempting to impose rules of conduct on state actors through constitutional adjudication.

2. How do procedural requirements interact with the substantive law? For example, a rigorously enforced right to privacy may mean one thing if the primary social concern is the use of drugs, and quite another if it is the physical safety of the citizenry. Not surprisingly, as you will see, courts seem considerably less reluctant to suppress evidence (and thus increase the chance of an erroneous acquittal) in morals and drug crimes than in crimes of violence. You will also see that many procedural decisions are at the mercy of the scope of the substantive law, and thus for all the grand rhetoric about constitutional decisions, many of them are hostage to legislative choices. For example, decisions about the privacy of papers become largely irrelevant if the state can require the keeping of the records that form the content of those papers, and further require that government inspectors have access to those records (as you will see is sometimes the case). Constitutional rhetoric about the necessity of warrants and the sanctity of homes is substantially compromised if cities can insist on regular safety inspections without individualized suspicion (as again you will see can be done). Indeed, in some instances, you will see that procedural mandates are only required in the absence of equally effective alternatives, alternatives which the legislative or executive branches of government could provide.

3. Another important variable is the implications of race and racial discrimination. A substantial portion of the law of criminal procedure arose to combat the effects of racial discrimination and can only be understood in that context, but the implications of discrimination are often not clear. For example, street harassment of African Americans by the police is a serious modern problem. Street lingo now refers to the offense of DWB, which stands for Driving While Black. However, one response to street harassment — heavier regulation of the selection of suspects — plausibly may be to withdraw police resources from poor minority neighborhoods, just those places where a heavy police presence may be most needed. The implications of racial discrimination often make questions harder rather than easier.

4. What exists today has a long history, and often can be understood only in historical context. As you will see, for example, for close to 100 years the Supreme Court's Fifth Amendment jurisprudence has been reacting to the decision of Boyd v. United States, 116 U.S. 616 (1886), and can only be understood in that light. Moreover, stability and predictability are important variables in all aspects of the law, and criminal procedure is no exception. Consequently, the forms of government and law have an inertial force that staves off change.

5. Last, remember that there are no free lunches. The criminal justice process competes for scarce and limited resources with all other governmental objectives. You may come across situations in your studies that you conclude demand greater resources. A good example may be the overall level of competency of counsel, which may be too low and probably could be raised by the infusion of substantial resources. Another is that both police and prosecutorial discretion exist in substantial part because there is too much crime to handle, given the resources, and therefore both police and prosecutors can pick and choose how to spend their time. But, a dollar spent on providing better counsel or more police and prosecutors is a dollar that cannot be spent somewhere else, either within the criminal justice system, such as on providing speedier or more efficient trials, or outside the criminal justice system, such as on programs to ease the burden of poverty, or the national infrastructure, or student loans, or whatever. Governing involves an endless series of tragic choices in which competing demands must be traded off.

B. Lies, Damned Lies, and Statistics

We present here various statistical snapshots of aspects of the criminal justice system, first from the federal system and then from the states.

BUREAU OF JUSTICE STATISTICS, U.S. DEPARTMENT OF JUSTICE, A COMPENDIUM OF FEDERAL CRIMINAL JUSTICE STATISTICS

1-3 (2002)

The number of suspects investigated by U.S. attorneys increased between 2001 and 2002, from 121,818 to 124,335. About three-quarters of those for which the investigation was concluded were prosecuted — either before a U.S. district court judge (62%) or before a U.S. magistrate (11%) — and 27% of those investigated were not prosecuted by U.S. attorneys.

The number of defendants prosecuted in Federal courts increased slightly between 2001 and 2002, from 86,728 to 90,407.

The number of offenders under Federal correctional supervision increased 77% between 1990 and 2002. At the end of fiscal year 2002, the number of offenders in Federal prison or on community supervision was 250,398 compared to 141,790 during 1990.

At the end of fiscal year 2002, the number of Federal inmates serving a sentence of imprisonment was 143,031. The number under community supervision was 107,367. Over 70% of those under community supervision were on post-incarceration supervised release (73,229) or parole (3,561).

ARREST

During 2002, 124,074 suspects were arrested by Federal law enforcement agencies for violations of Federal law. Twenty-seven percent of those arrested and booked by the U.S. Marshals Service were for drug offenses, 21% for immigration offenses, 18% for supervision violations, 14% for property offenses, 7% for public-order offenses, 6% for weapon offenses, 4% for violent offenses, and 3% to secure and safeguard a material witness.

About 70% of suspects booked by the U.S. Marshals Service were arrested by Department of Justice agencies, while Treasury Department agencies accounted for 12% of all arrests. Within the Department of Justice, the U.S. Marshals Service made 39% of the arrests; the Immigration and Naturalization Service 33%; the Drug Enforcement Administration 14%, and the Federal Bureau of Investigation 13%.

PROSECUTION

During 2002, U.S. attorneys initiated criminal investigations involving 124,335 suspects, and they concluded their investigations of 124,081 suspects. Thirty-one percent of the suspects were investigated for drug, 22% for property, 19% for public order, 14% for immigration, 9% for weapon, and 5% for violent offenses.

Of the suspects in criminal matters concluded, U.S. attorneys prosecuted 76,314 in U.S. district courts and 14,093 were disposed of before U.S. magistrates. During 2002, U.S. attorneys declined 27% of matters concluded.

Suspects in criminal matters involving immigration or drug offenses were more likely to be prosecuted in a U.S. district court (85% and 77%, respectively) than were suspects involved in weapon (70%), violent (54%), property (54%), or public-order offenses (30%). Suspects involved in property offenses (such as fraud), violent offenses, or public-order offenses were more likely to be declined for prosecution (about 40%) than were suspects investigated for weapon (28%), drug (18%), or immigration (3%) offenses.

PRETRIAL RELEASE

Of 78,060 pretrial cases commenced in 2002, 37% of defendants were released after either an initial or detention hearing, while 62% were detained, and less than 1% were dismissed.

During 2002, 45% of the 71,572 defendants who terminated pretrial services were released at some time prior to their criminal trial. Defendants charged with property offenses or public-order offenses were more likely to be released prior to trial (79% and 69%, respectively) than were defendants charged with weapon (43%), drug (41%), violent (35%), or immigration (9%) offenses.

The proportion of defendants released prior to their trial decreased from 62% during 1990 to 45% during 2002.

Defendants having a prior criminal history of serious or violent crimes were less likely to be released than those without a prior criminal history; defendants with a greater number of prior convictions were less likely to be released than those with fewer prior convictions. About 25% of the defendants with a prior violent felony conviction were released before trial, while 61% of defendants with no prior convictions were released. Forty-six percent of defendants with one prior conviction were released, as compared to 37% of defendants having two to four prior convictions and about 28% of defendants having five or more prior convictions.

Eighty-one percent of defendants released prior to trial completed their periods of release without violating the conditions of their release. Nineteen percent of defendants released violated the conditions of their release, and 8% of defendants had their release revoked. Defendants charged with weapon or drug offenses were more likely to commit at least one violation of their conditions of release (31% and 30%, respectively), while defendants charged with weapon or violent offenses were more likely to have their release revoked (13% and 12%, respectively) than were other defendants.

Defendants released during 2002 were more likely to violate the conditions of their pretrial release than those released during 1990. During 2002, 20% of those released at some point prior to trial violated a condition of their release. During 1990, 12% violated their release conditions.

Adjudication

During 2002, 87,727 defendants were charged in Federal courts with a criminal offense, 87% of whom were charged with felonies. Of the defendants charged with felonies, 40% were prosecuted for drug, 21% for property, 17% for immigration, 11% for weapon, 6% for public-order, and 4% for violent offenses.

The number of defendants charged with a felony immigration offense increased by 14% between 2001 and 2002, from 11,504 to 13,101. The number charged with a felony weapon offense increased by 25%, from 6,495 to 8,104.

Criminal cases were concluded against 80,424 defendants during 2002, 87% of whom had been charged with felonies. The proportion of defendants convicted in the Federal courts increased from 81% during 1990 to 89% during 2002. The proportion of convicted defendants who pleaded guilty increased from 87% during 1990 to 96% during 2002.

About 92% of defendants charged with felonies were convicted. The conviction rate was similar for the major offense categories: 95% of defendants charged with immigration offenses, 92% of both drug and violent defendants, 91% of property defendants, 89% of weapon defendants, and 88% of public-order defendants.

Sentencing

Defendants convicted during 2002 were more likely to be sentenced to prison than those convicted during 1990. During 2002, about 75% of defendants were sentenced to prison compared to 60% of those sentenced during 1990.

Ninety-three percent of felony violent offenders received prison terms, as did 92% of felony weapon offenders, 91% of felony drug offenders, 89% of felony immigration offenders, 66% of felony public-order offenders, and 59% of felony property offenders.

**Average Length of Prison Sentences Imposed,
by Offense, October 1, 2001-
September 30, 2002**

Most serious offense of conviction	Average sentence length
All offenses	57.1 mo
Felonies	58.4
Violent offenses	88.5
Property offenses	25.0
Drug offenses	76.0
Public-order offenses	38.5
Weapon offenses	83.9
Immigration offenses	27.9
Misdemeanors	9.8

The 53,682 offenders sentenced to prison received, on average, 57.1 months of imprisonment. Offenders sentenced for felony violent offenses, felony weapon offenses, and felony drug offenses received longer average prison terms (88.5, 83.9, and 76 months, respectively) than those convicted of felony property, immigration, public-order offenses (25, 27.9, and 38.5 months respectively).

While the proportion of defendants sentenced to prison is at an all-time high, average prison sentences have declined from the peak attained during 1992. During 1992, the average prison term imposed was 62.6 months; for violent felony offenders, the average term imposed was 94.8 months; for drug felony offenders, the average term was 84.1 months.

APPEALS

Between 1994 and 2002, the number of appeals received by the U.S. Courts of Appeals remained relatively stable—between about 9,000 and 11,500 annually. However, the proportion of criminal defendants appealing some aspect of their conviction decreased from 21% during 1994 to 16% during 2002.

During 2002, 11,569 criminal appeals were filed, a 3% increase from FY2001 (11,281). Forty-nine percent of the appeals filed challenged both the conviction and sentence imposed. Only 4% of appeals were filed by the Government. Of the 11,695 appeals terminated during 2002, 75% (or 8,770) were terminated on the merits. In 83% of the appeals terminated on the merits, the district court ruling was affirmed, at least in part.

CORRECTIONS

COMMUNITY SUPERVISION

Between 1990 and 2002, the number of offenders on community supervision increased by 27%, from 84,801 during 1990 to 107,367 during 2002. While nearly equal proportions of offenders were serving terms of probation and post-incarceration supervision (parole or supervised release) during 1990, during

2002, over 71% were serving a term of post-incarceration supervision (68% supervised release and 3% parole) while 28% were on probation.

Admissions to Federal Bureau of Prisons, Releases, and Prisoners at Year-End, by Offense, October 1, 2001-September 30, 2002

Most serious offense of conviction	All admissions	All releases	Population at year-end
All offenses	67,877	60,832	143,031
Violent offenses	7.3%	7.7%	9.5%
Property offenses	16.5	18.4	7.1
Drug offenses	42.6	40.6	56.7
Public-order offenses	7.9	8.4	5.6
Weapon offenses	8.3	6.5	9.6
Immigration offenses	17.5	18.3	10.9

Note: Percentages of offenses do not total to 100% due to offenders whose most serious offense of conviction is unknown or indeterminable.

Drug offenders comprised 12% of offenders on probation, 54% of offenders serving terms of supervised release, and 45% of offenders on parole. Property offenders comprised 38% of offenders on probation, 24% of offenders serving terms of supervised release, and 8% of offenders on parole.

A total of 15,116 offenders terminated probation during 2002. Most of these offenders (80%) completed their terms of probation successfully. Twelve percent of probationers terminating supervision during 2002 committed technical violations; 7% committed new crimes.

A total of 27,678 offenders completed terms of supervised release during 2002. Of these offenders, 62% successfully completed their terms without violating conditions of release; 23% committed technical violations; and 13% committed new crimes.

A total of 1,817 offenders completed terms of parole during 2002. Of these offenders, 58% successfully completed their terms without violating conditions of release; 23% committed technical violations; and 13% committed new crimes.

PRISON

Between 1990 and 2002, the number of inmates serving a sentence of imprisonment increased by 151%, from 56,989 during 1990 to 143,031 during 2002.

During 2002, 50,440 prisoners were received by the Bureau of Prisons from U.S. district court commitments. An additional 17,437 prisoners were returned to Federal prison for violating conditions of probation, parole, or supervised release, or were admitted to Federal prison from elsewhere than a U.S. district court.

Drug offenders—who comprised 42% of persons admitted into Federal prison—comprised the largest percentage of persons in prison (57%) at the end of 2002.

During 2002, 44,339 prisoners were released for the first time from Federal prison after commitment by a U.S. district court. Of these, 39,568 were released by standard methods and 4,771 were released by extraordinary means (death, treaty transfer, sentence commutation, or drug treatment). An additional 16,493 prisoners were released from subsequent commitments to Federal prison.

Average time served by Federal offenders increased from 24 months during 1994 to 32 months during 2002. The proportion of the sentence served increased from 65% during 1990 to 91% during 2002.

Violent, weapon, and drug offenders were among those offenders who served the longest prison terms (59 months for violent offenders and 43 months each for weapon and drug offenders).

Average Time to First Release, Standard Releases, by Offense, October 1, 2001-September 30, 2002

Most serious original offense of conviction	Mean time served
All offenses	31.6 mo
Violent offenses	58.8
Property offenses	16.5
Drug offenses	42.9
Public-order offenses	24.8
Weapon offenses	42.9
Immigration offenses	19.2

BRIAN J. OSTROM, NEAL B. KAUDER, & ROBERT C. LAFOUNTAIN, EDITORS, EXAMINING THE WORK OF THE STATE COURTS, 2002: A NATIONAL PERSPECTIVE FROM THE COURT STATISTICS PROJECT

53-86 (2003)

CRIMINAL CASELOADS IN STATE TRIAL COURTS

THE NUMBER OF CRIMINAL CASES IN 2001 WAS JUST OVER 14 MILLION

The vast majority of criminal cases are processed in state rather than in federal courts. The most recent trend in criminal filings shows a decline of about 3 percent since 1998. The trend since 1987 is somewhat recurring, with filings increasing then leveling every three to five years. Overall, the data shows that the number of criminal filings rose by about 2 percent per year.

The recent drop in filings could be related to a number of factors, but the most likely explanations take into account the corresponding drop in crime. More directly, arrest rates, which are predictive of criminal case filings, have been declining since the early 1990s. In fact, 2001 marks the first year in which crime rates have flattened or have begun edging up slightly (depending on type of crime) . . . .

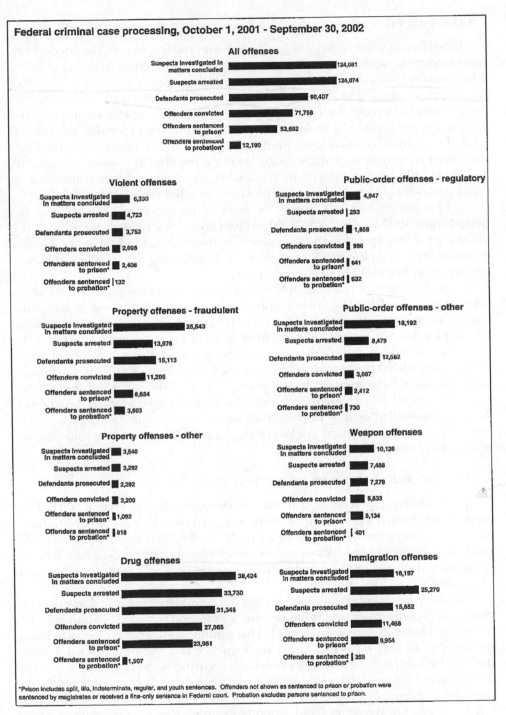

Figure S.2. Compendium of Federal Criminal Justice Statistics (2002).

CLEARANCE RATES REFLECT REDUCTIONS IN A COURT'S PENDING CASELOAD

The success of states in disposing criminal cases reflects, in part, the adequacy of court resources and has implications for the pace of both criminal and civil litigation. Criminal cases consume a disproportionately large chunk of court resources compared to their overall contribution to the total caseload. Constitutional requirements covering the right to counsel ensure that attorneys, judges, and other court personnel will be involved at all stages in the processing of criminal cases. In addition, criminal cases must be disposed under tighter time standards than other types of cases. Finally, courts are often required by constitution, statute, and court rule to give priority to criminal cases. This mandatory attention to criminal cases may result in slower processing of other types of cases.

. . . 17 states cleared 100 percent or more of their criminal caseload for the period from 1999 to 2001. Rhode Island and New York topped the list with the highest clearance rates for all three years. At the other end of the scale, Florida reported the lowest clearance rate of 85 percent, indicating that its courts are likely adding to an inventory of pending cases.

Statewide clearance rates not only reflect a range of management initiatives at the trial court level, but also are influenced by factors such as caseload growth, time standards, and the consistency with which filings and dispositions are measured. Of the 17 states that cleared 100 percent or more of their criminal caseload for the 1999-2001 period, nine experienced a decline in the number of cases filed. All of the 17 states with three-year clearance rates of 100 percent or more have adopted time standards for criminal case processing. Three of the states with high clearance rates (New York, Rhode Island, and West Virginia) have adopted the COSCA/ABA-recommended goal of disposing all felony cases within 180 days from the time of arrest. Time standards for West Virginia and Massachusetts are mandatory, while others are advisory. . . .

VERY FEW CRIMINAL CASES ARE RESOLVED AT TRIAL

Approximately 3 percent of criminal cases were resolved by trial in 2001. Trial rates ranged from 0.9 percent in Vermont to 8 percent in New Mexico. Nationally, jury trials account for 46 percent of all trials. Guilty pleas disposed of about 65 percent of criminal cases. About one criminal case in four is resolved when the prosecutor decides not to continue (nolle prosequi) or all charges are dropped (dismissal).

The plea process is certainly swifter than the formal trial process, and given the growth in criminal caseloads, it has become an integral part of the administration of justice. Those who are in favor of plea bargaining argue that the overwhelming prevalence of guilty pleas provides some evidence that the plea process is more desirable to both sides. Prosecutors benefit by securing high conviction rates without incurring the cost and uncertainty of trial. Defendants presumably prefer the outcome of the negotiation to the exercise of their right to trial or the deal would not be struck. On the other hand, opponents argue that plea bargaining places pressure on defendants to waive their constitutional rights, which results in inconsistent sentencing outcomes and the possibility that innocent people plead guilty rather than risk the chance of a more severe sentence after conviction at trial. Regardless of one's views, it is unlikely that the prevalence of plea bargaining will change in the near future.

FELONY CASELOADS IN STATE TRIAL COURTS

FELONY FILINGS RISE FOR TWO STRAIGHT YEARS — 2000 AND 2001

Felonies are the most serious form of criminal offense, typically punishable by incarceration for a year or more. Felony crimes command a great deal of attention from the general public, impose tremendous burdens on victims (both physical and emotional), and generate substantial costs for taxpayers. In addition, those who work within the criminal justice system know that fluctuations in felony caseloads can have a significant impact on the overall pace of both criminal and civil litigation.

The trend line shows that felony filings grew quickly until 1989, had a slowed growth rate until 1992, and after a brief dip in 1993, resumed an uninterrupted increase until 1998. A 49 percent overall growth in felony filings makes this one of the fastest growing case types (domestic relations cases increased 56 percent over the same time period). These data come from the general jurisdiction trial court systems of the 45 states able to report felony filings for the period 1987 to 2001. . . .

CLEARANCE RATES FELL IN MOST GENERAL JURISDICTION COURTS BETWEEN 1999 AND 2001

. . . Eleven states had clearance rates exceeding 100 percent from 1999 to 2001, likely indicating reductions in pending caseloads. Timely felony case processing continues to be a serious challenge for courts since 26 of 37 states were unable to dispose of as many cases as were filed in the three-year period.

It seems reasonable to speculate that higher clearance rates are related to decreased caseload growth. For example, Alabama, with a high three-year clearance rate of 105, experienced one of the largest declines in population-adjusted filings. . . . Of the remaining 10 states with three-year clearance rates of over 100 percent, four witnessed declines in felony filing rates over the three-year period. At the other end of the spectrum, North Dakota, which has a relatively low three-year clearance rate, experienced the highest growth in filings per 100,000 population.

EXAMINING SERIOUS CRIME

The incidence of violent crime is down. Following a decade of decline, crime rates for some of the most serious criminal offenses are at the lowest levels in a generation. Still, serious crime remains a critical concern to the public and policymakers — and understandably so. High-profile offenses such as murder and kidnapping garner considerable media attention and help shape our general feelings of safety. However, because of the publicity given to notorious criminal cases, it is difficult to gain perspective on larger crime trends and reconcile the news about the drop in crime. . . .

Overall, violent crime victimization was relatively steady between 1973 and 1994, followed by a 47 percent drop between 1994 and 2000.

Victimization rates for all major crime categories are at all-time lows. The declines since the early 1990s also match declines in crimes reported to police.

Rape, robbery, and assault rates all trended downward from 1973 through 2000. The murder trend was fairly even from 1973 through 1991 before dropping steadily through 2000.

Finally, consider the charts on pages 18-21 from Bureau of Justice Statistics, Sourcebook of Criminal Justice Statistics — 2002.

Sourcebook of Criminal Justice Statistics 2002, Table 4.9

Arrests

By offense charged, sex, and age group, United States, 2001 and 2002

(8,787 agencies; 2001 estimated population 177,579,561, 2002 estimated population 179,500,199)

Offense charged	Male Total			Male Under 18 years of age			Female Total			Female Under 18 years of age		
	2001	2002	Percent change	2001	2002	Percent change	2001	2002	Percent change	2001	2002	Percent change
Total[a]	6,541,353	6,540,340	(b)	1,012,899	977,219	−3.5%	1,924,010	1,965,008	2.1%	409,049	401,830	−1.8%
Murder and nonnegligent manslaughter	7,557	7,563	0.1%	710	724	2.0	1,123	952	−15.2	89	87	−2.2
Forcible rape	17,019	17,343	1.9	2,840	2,793	−1.7	206	196	−4.9	43	49	14.0
Robbery	60,195	59,516	−1.1	13,692	13,498	−1.4	6,898	7,007	1.6	1,302	1,358	4.3
Aggravated assault	242,573	240,305	−0.9	30,781	29,513	−4.1	61,138	60,648	−0.8	9,366	9,026	−3.6
Burglary	157,719	158,932	0.8	50,063	48,168	−3.8	25,290	25,230	−0.2	6,955	6,336	−8.9
Larceny-theft	463,925	463,111	−0.2	136,458	131,809	−3.4	270,551	274,001	1.3	87,641	85,613	−2.3
Motor vehicle theft	71,080	73,837	3.9	22,593	21,334	−5.6	14,045	14,612	4.0	4,877	4,576	−6.2
Arson	10,118	8,982	−11.2	5,235	4,741	−9.4	1,925	1,615	−16.1	727	612	−15.8
Violent crime[c]	327,344	324,727	−0.8	46,023	46,528	−3.1	69,365	68,803	−0.8	10,800	10,520	−2.6
Property crime[d]	702,842	704,862	0.3	214,349	206,052	−3.9	311,811	315,458	1.2	100,200	97,137	−3.1
Total Crime Index[e]	1,030,186	1,029,589	−0.1	262,372	252,580	−3.7	381,176	384,261	0.8	111,000	107,657	−3.0
Other assaults	622,322	617,297	−0.8	100,278	100,612	0.3	191,470	195,594	2.2	46,173	47,821	3.6
Forgery and counterfeiting	43,716	43,760	0.1	2,446	2,026	−17.2	29,417	29,212	−0.7	1,392	1,148	−17.5
Fraud	108,347	107,450	−0.8	3,623	3,373	−6.9	90,175	91,268	1.2	1,855	1,711	−7.8
Embezzlement	6,729	6,310	−6.2	706	535	−24.2	6,612	6,291	−4.9	535	391	−26.9
Stolen property; buying, receiving, possessing	69,350	69,215	−0.2	15,148	14,422	−4.8	15,131	15,018	−0.7	2,940	2,687	−8.6
Vandalism	142,512	142,967	0.3	57,962	56,483	−2.6	27,696	28,827	4.1	8,756	8,950	2.2
Weapons; carrying, possessing, etc.	93,886	93,550	−0.4	20,224	19,075	−5.7	8,301	8,126	−2.1	2,325	2,308	−0.7
Prostitution and commercialized vice	16,376	16,575	1.2	260	299	15.0	30,401	30,554	0.5	533	527	−1.1
Sex offenses (except forcible rape end prostitution)	52,118	52,596	0.9	10,509	10,566	0.5	3,971	3,932	−1.0	845	860	1.8
Drug abuse violations	770,247	767,873	−0.3	99,623	92,127	−7.5	169,882	173,969	2.4	19,568	18,532	−5.3
Gambling	3,981	3,841	−3.5	375	441	17.6	585	640	9.4	24	23	−4.2
Offenses against family and children	64,309	65,150	1.3	3,780	3,401	−10.0	19,858	20,982	5.7	2,154	2,162	0.4
Driving under the influence	714,540	724,469	1.4	10,340	10,607	2.6	145,010	154,298	6.4	2,288	2,535	10.8
Liquor laws	301,748	296,394	−1.8	60,992	58,568	−4.0	94,599	95,350	0.8	29,305	29,108	−0.7
Drunkenness	343,540	323,737	−5.8	10,464	9,678	−7.5	54,909	53,117	−3.3	2,817	2,698	−4.2
Disorderly conduct	290,123	284,538	−1.9	75,390	76,639	1.7	94,114	95,013	1.0	32,639	34,355	5.3
Vagrancy	14,448	15,529	7.5	1,284	1,049	−18.3	3,199	3,379	5.6	337	329	−2.4
All other offenses (except traffic)	1,757,527	1,790,117	1.9	181,775	175,355	−3.5	478,468	501,061	4.7	64,527	63,912	−1.0
Suspicion (not included in totals)	1,560	1,981	27.0	421	656	55.8	472	609	29.0	204	277	35.8

Sourcebook of Criminal Justice Statistics 2002, Table 4.9 *(Continued)*

Curfew and loitering law violations	59,527	56,826	−4.5	59,527	56,826	−4.5	28,550	25,177	−5.2	26,550	25,177	−5.2
Runaways	35,821	32,557	−9.1	35,821	32,557	−9.1	52,486	48,939	−6.8	52,486	48,939	−6.8

Note: See Note, table 4.1. This table presents data from all law enforcement agencies submitting complete reports for 12 months in 2001 and 2002 (Source, p. 452). Population figures are estimates calculated from U.S. Census Bureau data. For definitions of offenses, see Appendix 3.

^aDoes not include suspicion.
^bLess than 0.1%.

^cViolent crimes are offenses of murder and nonnegligent manslaughter, forcible rape, robbery, and aggravated assault.
^dProperty crimes are offenses of burglary, larceny-theft, motor vehicle theft, and arson.
^eIncludes arson.

Source: U.S. Department of Justice, Federal Bureau of Investigation, *Crime in the United States, 2002* (Washington, DC: USGPO, 2003), p. 243.

Sourcebook of Criminal Justice Statistics 2002, Table 4.10

Arrests
By offense charged, age group, and race, United States, 2002
(10,370 agencies; 2002 estimated population 205,108,615)

	Total arrests					Percent				
Offense charged	Total	White	Black	American Indian or Alaskan Native	Asian or Pacific Islander	Total	White	Black	American Indian or Alaskan Native	Asian or Pacific Islander
Total	9,797,385	6,923,390	2,633,632	130,636	109,727	100.0%	70.7%	26.9%	1.3%	1.1%
Murder and nonnegligent manslaughter	10,099	4,814	5,047	115	123	100.0	47.7	50.0	1.1	1.2
Forcible rape	20,127	12,766	6,852	240	269	100.0	63.4	34.0	1.2	1.3
Robbery	77,280	34,109	41,837	471	863	100.0	44.1	54.1	0.6	1.1
Aggravated assault	338,850	214,992	115,789	4,069	4,000	100.0	63.4	34.2	1.2	1.2
Burglary	205,873	144,958	56,647	1,992	2,276	100.0	70.4	27.5	1.0	1.1
Larceny-theft	843,066	572,515	246,946	10,345	13,260	100.0	67.9	29.3	1.2	1.6
Motor vehicle theft	107,031	64,625	39,114	1,156	2,136	100.0	60.4	36.5	1.1	2.0
Arson	11,808	9,067	2,537	100	104	100.0	76.8	21.5	0.8	0.9
Violent crime	446,356	266,681	169,525	4,895	5,255	100.0	59.7	38.0	1.1	1.2
Property crime	1,167,778	791,165	345,244	13,593	17,776	100.0	67.7	29.6	1.2	1.5
Total Crime Index	1,614,134	1,057,846	514,769	18,488	23,031	100.0	65.5	31.9	1.1	1.4
Other assaults	919,691	610,946	286,787	12,201	9,757	100.0	66.4	31.2	1.3	1.1
Forgery and counterfeiting	82,882	57,125	24,148	458	1,151	100.0	68.9	29.1	0.6	1.4
Fraud	232,336	157,763	71,538	1,431	1,604	100.0	67.9	30.8	0.6	0.7
Embezzlement	13,379	9,153	3,959	64	203	100.0	68.4	29.6	0.5	1.5
Stolen property; buying, receiving, possessing	91,150	53,535	35,986	611	1,018	100.0	58.7	39.5	0.7	1.1
Vandalism	198,139	150,437	42,757	2,804	2,141	100.0	75.9	21.6	1.4	1.1
Weapons; carrying, possessing, etc.	118,148	73,140	42,810	879	1,319	100.0	61.9	36.2	0.7	1.1
Prostitution and commercialized vice	58,659	33,650	23,455	364	1,190	100.0	57.4	40.0	0.6	2.0
Sex offenses (except forcible rape and prostitution)	67,761	50,378	15,745	680	958	100.0	74.3	23.2	1.0	1.4
Drug abuse violations	1,101,547	728,797	357,725	6,848	8,177	100.0	66.2	32.5	0.6	0.7

Sourcebook of Criminal Justice Statistics 2002, Table 4.10 *(Continued)*

Gambling	7,525	2,033	5,136	38	318	100.0	27.0	68.3	0.5	4.2
Offenses against family and children	97,393	66,440	28,180	1,266	1,507	100.0	68.2	28.9	1.3	1.5
Driving under the influence	1,017,504	893,395	99,548	15,460	9,101	100.0	87.8	9.8	1.5	0.9
Liquor laws	462,215	405,275	41,204	11,397	4,339	100.0	87.7	8.9	2.5	0.9
Drunkenness	412,735	345,448	55,598	9,563	2,126	100.0	83.7	13.5	2.3	0.5
Disorderly conduct	481,932	321,117	149,393	7,883	3,589	100.0	66.6	31.0	1.6	0.7
Vagrancy	19,669	12,223	6,888	419	139	100.0	62.1	35.0	2.1	0.7
All other offenses (except traffic)	2,599,658	1,751,450	778,558	37,377	32,273	100.0	67.4	29.9	1.4	1.2
Suspicion	7,647	4,130	3,128	108	281	100.0	54.0	40.9	1.4	3.7
Curfew and loitering law violations	103,054	70,738	29,717	1,083	1,516	100.0	68.6	28.8	1.1	1.5
Runaways	90,227	68,371	16,603	1,214	4,039	100.0	75.8	18.4	1.3	4.5

Sourcebook of Criminal Justice Statistics 2002, Table 4.10

Arrests
By offense charged, age group, and race, United States, 2002 — Continued

	Arrests of persons under 18 years of age					Percent				
Offense charged	Total	White	Black	American Indian or Alaskan Native	Asian or Pacific Islander	Total	White	Black	American Indian or Alaskan Native	Asian or Pacific Islander
Total	1,620,594	1,158,776	415,854	20,383	25,581	100.0%	71.5%	25.7%	1.3%	1.6%
Murder and nonnegligent manslaughter	972	446	487	23	16	100.0	45.9	50.1	2.4	1.6
Forcible rape	3,355	2,079	1,207	37	32	100.0	62.0	36.0	1.1	1.0
Robbery	17,878	6,895	10,537	91	355	100.0	38.6	58.9	0.5	2.0
Aggravated assault	44,185	26,877	16,217	535	556	100.0	60.8	36.7	1.2	1.3
Burglary	61,754	44,680	15,558	689	827	100.0	72.4	25.2	1.1	1.3
Larceny-theft	248,202	173,910	65,667	3,443	5,182	100.0	70.1	26.5	1.4	2.1
Motor vehicle theft	32,487	18,949	12,428	445	665	100.0	58.3	38.3	1.4	2.0
Arson	5,837	4,711	1,026	48	52	100.0	80.7	17.6	0.8	0.9
Violent crime	66,390	36,297	28,448	686	959	100.0	54.7	42.8	1.0	1.4
Property crime	348,280	242,250	94,679	4,625	6,726	100.0	69.6	27.2	1.3	1.9
Total Crime Index	414,670	278,547	123,127	5,311	7,685	100.0	67.2	29.7	1.3	1.9
Other assaults	168,641	106,119	58,518	1,942	2,062	100.0	62.9	34.7	1.2	1.2
Forgery and counterfeiting	3,644	2,845	711	33	55	100.0	78.1	19.5	0.9	1.5
Fraud	6,418	4,242	2,051	47	78	100.0	66.1	32.0	0.7	1.2
Embezzlement	1,004	696	287	1	20	100.0	69.3	28.6	0.1	2.0
Stolen property; buying, receiving, possessing	18,769	10,612	7,761	134	262	100.0	56.5	41.4	0.7	1.4
Vandalism	75,781	61,373	12,594	919	895	100.0	81.0	16.6	1.2	1.2
Weapons; carrying, possessing, etc.	25,239	16,945	7,751	207	336	100.0	67.1	30.7	0.8	1.3
Prostitution and commercialized vice	1,094	479	597	6	12	100.0	43.8	54.6	0.5	1.1
Sex offenses (except forcible rape and prostitution)	13,857	9,986	3,603	107	161	100.0	72.1	26.0	0.8	1.2
Drug abuse violations	133,494	97,766	33,208	1,152	1,368	100.0	73.2	24.9	0.9	1.0
Gambling	1,114	127	955	0	32	100.0	11.4	85.7	X	2.9

Sourcebook of Criminal Justice Statistics 2002, Table 4.10 *(Continued)*

Offenses against family and children	6,554	4,837	1,541	56	120	100.0	73.8	23.5	0.9	1.8
Driving under the influence	15,155	14,138	628	267	122	100.0	93.3	4.1	1.8	0.8
Liquor laws	105,652	97,372	4,629	2,656	995	100.0	92.2	4.4	2.5	0.9
Drunkenness	13,508	12,155	995	258	100	100.0	90.0	7.4	1.9	0.7
Disorderly conduct	138,847	88,761	47,261	1,708	1,117	100.0	63.9	34.0	1.2	0.8
Vagrancy	1,518	1,147	346	14	11	100.0	75.6	22.8	0.9	0.7
All other offenses (except traffic)	281,184	210,704	62,611	3,261	4,578	100.0	74.9	22.3	1.2	1.6
Suspicion	1,170	816	330	7	17	100.0	69.7	28.2	0.6	1.5
Curfew and loitering law violations	103,054	70,738	29,717	1,083	1,516	100.0	68.6	28.8	1.1	1.5
Runaways	90,227	68,371	16,603	1,214	4,039	100.0	75.8	18.4	1.3	4.5

C. Readings on the Criminal Justice Process

Perceptions of the criminal justice system are as varied as the system itself. Commentators, by virtue of their individual training and experience with the system, inevitably make their observations and evaluations from different perspectives. Moreover, commentators will have, if not different values, at least different priorities that they would like to see reflected in the criminal justice system. The materials in this chapter, without attempting to be comprehensive, offer some important perceptions and insights about the criminal justice system. You, of course, should approach these materials with the same questioning mind and skepticism that you bring to bear on the study of cases.

1. Perspectives on the System as a Whole

HERBERT PACKER, THE COURTS, THE POLICE, AND THE REST OF US

57 J. Crim. L., Criminology & Pol. Sci. 238, 239 (1966)

[T]he kind of criminal process that we have is profoundly affected by a series of competing value choices which, consciously or unconsciously, serve to resolve tensions that arise in the system. These values represent polar extremes which, in real life, are subject to almost infinite modulation and compromise. But the extremes can be identified. The choice, basically, is between what I have termed the Crime Control and the Due Process models. The Crime Control model sees the efficient, expeditious and reliable screening and disposition of persons suspected of crime as the central value to be served by the criminal process. The Due Process model sees that function as limited by and subordinate to the maintenance of the dignity and autonomy of the individual. The Crime Control model is administrative and managerial; the Due Process model is adversary and judicial. The Crime Control model may be analogized to an assembly line, the Due Process model to an obstacle course.[8]

8. The *Crime Control* and *Due Process* concepts admittedly reflect different value choices, and the concepts provide a helpful way to articulate and focus on these value choices. But do they represent two different "models" of the criminal justice system? For a negative answer to this question, see Griffiths, Ideology in Criminal Procedure, or a Third "Model" of the Criminal Process, 79 Yale L.J. 359 (1970). — EDS.

What we have at work today is a situation in which the criminal process as it actually operates in the large majority of cases probably approximates fairly closely the dictates of the Crime Control model. The real-world criminal process tends to be far more administrative and managerial than it does adversary and judicial. Yet, the officially prescribed norms for the criminal process, as laid down primarily by the Supreme Court, are rapidly providing a view that looks more and more like the Due Process model. This development . . . has been in the direction of "judicializing" each stage of the criminal process, of enhancing the capacity of the accused to challenge the operation of the process, and of equalizing the capacity of all persons to avail themselves of the opportunity for challenge so created. . . .

LOUIS MICHAEL SEIDMAN, CRIMINAL PROCEDURE AS THE SERVANT OF POLITICS

12 Const. Commentary 207, 207-211 (1995)

If the Constitution were doing its job, it would obstruct and destabilize our political impulses concerning crime control. Yet today, the Fourth, Fifth and Sixth Amendments function mostly to make us satisfied with a state of affairs that should trouble us deeply.

Here are two facts about American criminal law: The United States has the most elaborate and detailed constitutional protections for criminal defendants of any country in the world. The United States also has the second highest incarceration rate of any country in the world. The relationship between these two facts (if, indeed, there is one at all) is controversial. Some critics of the Fourth, Fifth, and Sixth Amendments argue that they stymie effective law enforcement, thereby encouraging crime and requiring a high incarceration rate. Although this connection is theoretically possible, it is quite implausible. The best data available suggests that criminal procedure protections are doing very little to obstruct successful prosecutions. For example, a tiny percentage of criminal cases are lost or "no papered" because of Fourth Amendment problems. Virtually every empirical study of the impact of *Miranda* suggests that it has not reduced the rate at which suspects confess. The poor quality of criminal defense work has led some distinguished commentators to conclude that counsel now serves primarily as a barrier to the defendant's participation in his own trial. In contrast, some defenders of the Constitution's criminal procedure provisions argue that incarceration rates would be even higher if these protections were unavailable. This claim is similarly implausible. By now, the Fourth Amendment is so riddled with exceptions and limitations that it rarely prevents the police from pursuing any reasonable crime control tactic. Although the Supreme Court continues to insist on the ritualistic reading of *Miranda* warnings, judges have virtually gone out of the business of actually policing the voluntariness of confessions and regularly sanction the sort of coercive tactics that would have led to the suppression of evidence a half century ago. The courts have been satisfied with formal rules requiring the presence of counsel in the courtroom, while tolerating actual courtroom performances that make a mockery of the formal protections. And even when a defendant can demonstrate that the prosecution has violated minimal Fourth, Fifth, and Sixth Amendment protections, the recent evisceration of habeas corpus means that there may be no court available to entertain her claim.

It seems unlikely, then, that the criminal procedure amendments have either exacerbated our crime problem or provided an effective bulwark against police and prosecutorial overreaching. A third possibility is more plausible: constitutional protections intended to make prosecution more difficult instead serve [to] make the prosecutor's job easier.

This reversal of the historic mission of the criminal procedure amendments functions on both the individual and the global level. In individual cases, criminal procedure protections make the punishment we inflict on criminal defendants seem more acceptable. Although the amendments do little to make the prosecutor's job harder, people commonly believe that they obstruct the prosecution of dangerous criminals. Some doubt and ambivalence that might otherwise accompany the use of violent and coercive sanctions is thereby dissipated.

On the global level, criminal procedure protections serve to redirect and exacerbate the popular anger about crime. While crime rates have remained static and even declined slightly in recent years, the rate of incarceration has skyrocketed. There is no easy way to demonstrate that the crime rate would not be higher if we had incarcerated fewer people, but, at a minimum, these statistics demonstrate that the increased rate of incarceration is not caused by an increase in crime. Instead, it seems to be fed by the public perception that crime is out of control and that still more draconian punishments are necessary to deal with it.

Popular misconceptions about criminal procedure protections feed this perception. Because people believe that "legal technicalities" set large numbers of guilty and dangerous criminals free, they think that too many miscreants are escaping punishment. Because they believe that the problem could be brought under control if only the "legal technicalities" were changed, they fail to focus on the bankruptcy of mass-incarceration as a crime fighting strategy.

In the United States today, over one million people are imprisoned, the largest number in our history and the second largest percentage in the world. One out of every 193 adult Americans is behind bars, and the total inmate population is roughly equivalent to that of the city of Phoenix. Despite the absence of any evidence that these extreme measures have helped to control crime, political pressures grow for still more prisons, longer sentences, and more executions.

The criminal procedure amendments have done nothing to slow this decline into barbarism. Instead, they have contributed to an atmosphere that promotes acceptance of a situation that ought to shock us.

JOSEPH D. GRANO, ASCERTAINING THE TRUTH

77 Cornell L. Rev. 1061, 1062-1064 (1992)

Many lawyers and judges sanctimoniously defend our criminal injustice system as essential to individual freedom. Similarly academics, searching for anything or anyone to blame except the individual offenders, often applaud approaches that give offenders second, third, fourth, and even more chances to commit crimes. While these people defend the system, law abiding citizens desert the city's activities, restaurants, and retail merchants.

What accounts for the persistence of the world view illustrated by the misguided academic and judge? To a large extent, I believe it is the attitude of "there but for the grace of God go I," referring unfortunately to the offender rather than the victim. This attitude has its roots in the civil rights movement of the 1960s and in the conventional liberal ideology of the time that equated the typical criminal defendant in one courtroom with the civil rights plaintiff in another. Do not misunderstand me. . . . My argument is not with the civil rights revolution of the 1960s but rather with the distorted vision that saw, and still sees, the criminal offender not as the responsible perpetrator of an evil deed but as an unfortunate victim of a racist and oppressive society.

The view that the blame for crime lies with society rather than with the individual offender did not have much popular appeal even in the 1960s, and it has even less appeal today as crime runs rampant in our cities. Moreover, the "no responsibility" social determinists always have had to confront the rather insurmountable obstacle that the substantive criminal law is premised on a foundation of individual free will and responsibility. The common law requirement of mens rea aptly illustrates this free will foundation.

The procedural system, however, offered an attractive end run for those determined to undermine the substantive law's commitment to individual responsibility. The primary target was the basic notion that the paramount goal (I didn't say the only goal) of sound procedure should be the ascertainment of truth. Individual responsibility and accountability are not easy to achieve in a system that denigrates the importance of discovering the truth. The academics provided the underlying theory; the academics, lawyers, and judges together provided an abundance of truth-defeating procedural rules.

I am not going to review or critique the numerous truth-defeating procedural rules that plague our system. Most of us are familiar with the search and seizure exclusionary rule, with *Miranda* and *Massiah*, with the rule against prosecutorial comment on a defendant's silence, and with the effort to adopt the minority rule on entrapment, which would make the defendant's guilt or innocence irrelevant. We also are familiar with liberalism's continuing, and largely successful, effort to retain these truth-defeating rules. The latest example being the organized drive, spearheaded by the often-wrong ABA, to defeat the Bush Administration's badly needed reforms in the area of habeas corpus.

To facilitate the denigration of the search for truth, the academics who advocated these rules attacked the very concept of truth. We were told, for example, that any emphasis on "truth" must be simplistic, given the "plural forms and multifaceted aspects of that beguiling concept." (I often have wondered what my mother's reaction would have been had I responded to a question about whether I locked my sister in the basement by saying, "Well, the truth is multifaceted and beguiling.")

DOROTHY E. ROBERTS, CRIME, RACE AND REPRODUCTION

67 Tul. L. Rev. 1945, 1945-1947 (1993)

Not only is race used to identify criminals, it is embedded in the very foundation of our criminal law. Race helps to determine who the criminals are, what conduct constitutes a crime, and which crimes society treats most seriously. Today, the states have returned to considering reproduction as a solution to crime;

meanwhile, the federal government is exploring a genetic cause for criminality. Suggestions for applying reproductive techniques to punish crime have gained alarming acceptance. The racial ideology of crime increasingly enlists biology to justify the continued subordination of blacks.

THE CONSTRUCTION OF RACE AND CRIME IN AMERICA

The American criminal justice system has historically served as a means of controlling blacks. This control is accomplished through very concrete means. Local police departments patrol black neighborhoods as if they were occupied territories. The idea of local control of police in black communities seems to most Americans to be as far-fetched as the proverbial fox minding the hen house. Police serve not to protect black citizens, but to protect white citizens from black criminals. It is not surprising that many black Americans view the police with fear, anger, and distrust. The use of criminal justice as a tactic of racial domination is also manifested in the tremendous proportion of black males under correctional supervision. Two recent studies conducted by the National Center on Institutions and Alternatives (NCIA) reveal the enormity of this control. According to the NCIA, on any given day in 1991 in Washington, D.C., forty-two percent of young black males were in jail, on probation or parole, awaiting trial, or being sought on warrants for their arrest. The study suggests that seventy-five percent of black men in the city will be arrested and jailed at least once before reaching age thirty-five. A subsequent study in Baltimore, Maryland, discloses an even higher percentage — over half — of black males under supervision of the criminal justice system. The intimidation, supervision, and imprisonment of blacks in America through law enforcement is one of the most direct means of racial subordination.

The criminal justice system's control of blacks is supported on another level as well. Restraining blacks is justified by a belief system that constructs crime in terms of race and race in terms of crime. The police occupation of black communities and wholesale imprisonment of black citizens does not seem like oppression to the dominant society because it believes that these people are dangerous. It is the racial ideology of crime that sustains continued white domination of blacks in the guise of crime control.

FRANCIS ALLEN, DECLINE OF THE REHABILITATIVE IDEAL: PENAL POLICY AND SOCIAL PURPOSE

60-61, 63, 65-66 (1981)

The last two decades of the twentieth century are not likely to bring full consensus on issues of crime and punishment. Nevertheless, one senses that in the modern decline of the rehabilitative ideal a notable turning point has been reached in American penal policy and, as in other periods of change, both perils and opportunities abound. The shift of perspective of American thought about crime and punishment does not of itself eliminate or even substantially alter the persistent and intractable obstacles to doing penal justice. . . . Much more to the point is the observation that the failures of American criminal justice in the last generation—its insensitivities, corruptions, and inefficiencies; the escalation of violence in American society; the losses in security of life, limb, and possession[—]are failures of a system that as a whole cannot be regarded in any realistic sense as rehabilitative in purpose or effect. The contributions of the rehabilitative ideal to these failures have been at most peripheral.

Much of the attack on penal rehabilitationism ultimately voices broader concerns about the performance of the institutions of criminal justice. Operating a system of pains and penalties under any guise has proved a difficult and unsatisfactory business, and dissatisfactions become increasingly acute as the times encourage doubts and criticisms of governmental action of all sorts and at all levels. Many of the problems of penal rehabilitationism have their analogues in regimes embracing competing goals: just punishment, deterrence, and incapacitation. Thus conceptual difficulties with the notion of rehabilitation are matched by those encountered in efforts to define the concept of punishment proportional to the culpability of offenders. In all regimes, however oriented, the existence, guidance, and containment of discretion is a continuing concern, and in all of them, state power tends continually to impinge on political values.

The meticulous delineation and analysis of policy options has not often characterized American political discourse during the past decade and a half. On the contrary, the political style has been largely one subjecting institutional performances to unremitting attack and articulating an impressive range of dissatisfactions and revulsions. Yet rational penal policy demands that the scrutiny of policy options proceed and that efforts be made to identify the problems characteristic of such alternatives and to inquire which of the old dilemmas are likely to persist.

In recent years, as was noted earlier, a number of groups with widely disparate motives and policy objectives united in an attack on the rehabilitative ideal. One of the strange bed-fellows is that group insisting on increasingly repressive measures in American law enforcement and penology. The extreme law-and-order advocates—the group described as adherents of the war theory of criminal justice [—] constitute one of the important and persistent realities of American political life and one of the principal limiting factors in American penal reform. Although the group rarely attempts coherent or comprehensive statements of position, and the individuals who compose it display great diversity of backgrounds and status, a few generalizations can be made. All of its members are deeply resentful of losses in the quality of American life caused by widespread criminality. Many reflect a kind of nostalgia for an earlier period of American society, real or imagined, when values were clear, the moral consensus was overwhelming, and in which the future was predictable and inviting. Typically such persons believe that modern prisons are country clubs and that American judges are involved in an inexplicable conspiracy to subvert the public order by erecting obstacles to the detection and conviction of the guilty. Repressive regimes both in the prisons and on the streets prove attractive, not only because they are seen as solutions to the crime problem, but also because they express the values of discipline, vigor, and self-confidence largely lacking in contemporary American society.

As a practical program of action the theories of extreme repression are unrealistic, even romantic in nature. Proposals of extreme repression as deliberately adopted policy ignore certain salient features of contemporary American society. Prisons and prisoners today have political constituencies in a sense that was not true in midcentury. One of the consequences of the 1960s was a democratization of punishment. Thousands of middle-class citizens have had experiences in the recent past with arrest, conviction, and incarceration as a result of war protest, civil rights activities, and narcotics offenses. The concept of prisoner-as-alien has little appeal for these groups or for the many in sympathetic association with them. Moreover, members of racial minorities, both in and out of prison, advance political interpretations of crime and punishment strongly antagonistic to policies founded on the war theory of criminal justice. Finally, the interventions of the courts and the judicial concept of prisoners' rights, however narrowly drawn, have proved radically inconsistent with penal regimes of the sort approved by extreme law-and-order advocacy. To achieve the repression proposed by such advocates would involve a significant political transformation of American society, one demanding a much higher tolerance of punitive governmental interventions throughout society than at present exists. No one can say with assurance that such transformations will not occur in the future, but nothing in the present situation, despite the current vogue of capital punishment, suggests that a political consensus supportive of extreme penal repression will soon emerge.

Nor do the prescriptions of radical criminology provide a genuine alternative to the hegemony of the rehabilitative ideal. Indeed, the dogma that the pathologies of criminal justice are the inevitable consequences of an unjust social order is a counsel of despair, at least for those persons not yet ready to man the barricades in an effort to overturn the corrupt and decadent capitalist regime. In short, the position is one that largely abandons the effort at penal reform and amelioration and seeks instead to overturn the structures of power and authority of an unjust social order.

There is, however, another strand of thought which, although rejecting the revolutionary implications of radical criminology, nevertheless associates crime with broader social pathologies — unemployment, family dissolution, bad housing, and the like — and seeks the elimination or lessening of crime by attacks on these conditions. There are probably few persons of liberal political persuasion who do not share this outlook to some degree. But appeals for general social reform do not constitute a penal policy. Indeed, such advocacy of broad social reconstruction may be employed by some as a means to avoid thinking about or involvement in the hard and disagreeable realities of crime and punishment. The advocacy of sweeping social changes primarily because they will reduce crime is rarely sensible. Minimizing crime is a good, but there are other social goals as important; and it is possible that the objectives of crime control may often prove incompatible with other desired ends. Whether and to what extent social reforms reduce the quantum of criminal behavior are far from clear. The system of criminal justice provides a very narrow base from which to launch movements of fundamental social reconstruction, and one may reasonably doubt the competence of criminologists, regardless of the disciplines in which they have been trained, to achieve the brave new world.

It is apparent, then, that one must move to other areas if acceptable options to the hegemony of the rehabilitative ideal are to be found. The weakening of penal rehabilitationism marks a new era in thought about crime and punishment, but it is an era that has as yet produced few theoretical innovations. Rather, the period is one in which old ideas about the ends and means of criminal justice are being treated with a new seriousness. Old concerns about deterring crime, the matching of penalties to culpability, and achieving social defense through the incapacitation of potentially dangerous persons have been revived, and contentions rage over which of these goals should be admitted into a modern system of penal justice and which should be given dominant expression. Disputes surround the questions of whether and how far the decriminalization of conduct now punishable should proceed and the extent penal incarceration can and ought to be avoided in a modern system of penal sanctions.

CAROL S. STEIKER, COUNTER-REVOLUTION IN CONSTITUTIONAL CRIMINAL PROCEDURE? TWO AUDIENCES, TWO ANSWERS

94 Mich. L. Rev. 2466, 2466-2470 (1996)

When Richard M. Nixon ran for president in 1968, he campaigned on a now-familiar "law and order" platform. Among other things, he pledged to appoint Justices to the Supreme Court who would combat the Warren Court's controversial constitutional decisions limiting the power of law enforcement officials to investigate and prosecute crime. When Nixon won the presidency and then almost immediately had the opportunity to replace Chief Justice Earl Warren and three Associate Justices with appointees of his own, it was widely predicted that the major innovations of the Warren Court in constitutional criminal procedure — any list would include *Mapp, Massiah,* and *Miranda* — would not long survive. In the almost thirty years since Nixon's victory, the Supreme Court's pulse-takers have offered periodic updates on the fate of the Warren Court's criminal procedure "revolution" in the Burger and Rehnquist Courts.

The voluminous body of literature formed by these assessments presents something of a puzzle. The unanimity of projection about the future of the Warren Court's criminal procedure soon gave way to widespread disagreement about the nature and extent of the response of the Burger and Rehnquist Courts. On the one hand, many commentators — usually admirers of the Warren Court's handiwork — have lamented over the years about what they view as a wholesale repudiation of the Warren Court's work; their comments are full of words like "retreat," "decline," and "counter-revolution." At the very same time, other commentators — many of them also defenders of the Warren Court — have maintained that these laments are "overstated," and "considerably exaggerated" and that the basic structure of the Warren Court's criminal procedure jurisprudence is firmly "entrenched." As one critic of the Warren Court recently has bemoaned, "The voice that continues to urge repentance [from the Warren Court's criminal procedure] today is truly '[t]he voice of him that crieth in the wilderness.'"

One could attempt to resolve (or repudiate) this puzzling conflict in a variety of ways. One could, for example, attempt to explain disagreement about the nature of change by distinguishing between levels of abstraction — between "doctrinal" and "ideological" change. Or one could note that the difficulties inherent in weighing and measuring any sort of jurisprudential shift are exacerbated greatly in the broad, diffuse, and fact-specific jungle that is constitutional criminal procedure. Or one could ascribe the debate to a dispute over semantics: just how much change, after all, is "revolutionary" or "counter-revolutionary"? Or one simply could write off the more extreme statements on either side of the divide as rhetorical flourishes offered in the spirit of academic "spin control."

I, however, want to resist these temptations to downplay or deny the conflict, because I believe that the debate over continuity and change in constitutional criminal procedure can best be accounted for in an entirely different way — a way that suggests a new kind of critique of the Burger and Rehnquist Courts' criminal procedure jurisprudence. I start with the contention that the Supreme Court has profoundly changed its approach to constitutional criminal procedure since the 1960s at least in the following fairly limited (but obviously important) sense: the Court has clearly become less sympathetic to claims of individual rights and more accommodating to assertions of the need for public order. In the last three decades, the Court has granted review to and found in favor of criminal defendants much less frequently than it did in the heyday of the Warren Court. Thus, at least in Holmes' positivist sense of law as a prediction of what courts will do in fact, the law has changed radically.

The way in which this change has occurred, however, may help explain the academic divide. My contention is that much of this change has occurred quite differently from what was predicted at the close of the Warren Court era. The Burger and Rehnquist Courts have not altered radically — and indeed, occasionally have bolstered — the Warren Court's constitutional norms regarding police practices. The edifice constructed by the Warren Court governing investigative techniques under the Fourth, Fifth, and Sixth Amendments remains surprisingly intact. Rather than redrawing in any drastic fashion the line between constitutional and unconstitutional police conduct, the Supreme Court has revolutionized the consequences of deeming conduct unconstitutional. This revolution has not taken the form of wholesale abolition of the Fourth Amendment's exclusionary rule, or the Fifth or Sixth Amendments' mandates of exclusion; rather, the Court has proliferated a variety of what I would term "inclusionary rules" — rules that permit the use at trial of admittedly unconstitutionally obtained evidence or that let stand criminal convictions based on such evidence. Examples of "inclusionary rules" are the doctrines regarding standing, the good-faith exception to the warrant requirement, the "fruit of the poisonous tree," impeachment, harmless error, and limitations on federal habeas review of criminal convictions.

Thus, for the purposes of my argument, I adapt Professor Meir Dan-Cohen's distinction (which he in turn borrowed from Jeremy Bentham) between "conduct" rules and "decision" rules. Bentham and Dan-Cohen make this distinction in the context of substantive criminal law; for their purposes, "conduct" rules are addressed to the general public in order to guide its behavior (for example, "Let no person steal") and "decision" rules are addressed to public officials in order to guide their decisionmaking about the consequences of violating conduct rules (for example, "Let the judge cause whoever is convicted of stealing to be hanged"). But as any teacher of both substantive and procedural criminal law knows, constitutional criminal procedure is a species of substantive criminal law for cops. Thus, for my purposes, "conduct" rules (my "constitutional norms") are addressed to law enforcement agents regarding the constitutional legitimacy of their investigative practices and "decision" rules (my "inclusionary rules") are addressed to courts regarding the consequences of unconstitutional conduct.

... My primary descriptive claim ... is that the Supreme Court's shift in constitutional criminal procedure from the 1960s to the 1990s has occasioned much more dramatic changes in decision rules than in conduct rules. ... This claim is qualitative rather than quantitative, and comparative rather than absolute. I do not mean to say that the Supreme Court has deployed decision rules more than conduct rules in any strict numerical sense, nor do I contend that constitutional norms have not shifted at all; rather, I argue that the Court's decision-rule cases have diverged far more from the Warren Court's starting point than have its conduct-rule cases. Thus, the dichotomy between decision rules and conduct rules helps to explain the existence of such a deep academic divide. The proponents and debunkers of the "counter-revolution" hypothesis turn out to both be right: the Burger and Rehnquist Courts have accepted to a significant extent the Warren Court's definitions of constitutional "rights" while waging counter-revolutionary war against the Warren Court's constitutional "remedies" of evidentiary exclusion and its federal review and reversal of convictions.

AKHIL REED AMAR, THE FUTURE OF CONSTITUTIONAL CRIMINAL PROCEDURE

33 Am. Crim. L. Rev. 1123, 1123-1125, 1128-1129, 1132-1134 (1996)

As a subfield of constitutional law, constitutional criminal procedure stands as an anomaly. In many other areas of constitutional law, major Marshall Court opinions stand out and continue to frame debate both in courts and beyond. In thinking about judicial review and executive power, we still look to Marbury v. Madison; in pondering the puzzle of jurisdiction-stripping, we go back to Martin v. Hunter's Lessee; in reflecting on the scope of Congress' enumerated powers, and related issues of federalism, we re-examine McCulloch v. Maryland. ... But no comparable Marshall Court landmarks dot the plain of constitutional criminal procedure.

It is often thought that the explanation for this anomaly lies in another Marshall Court landmark, Barron v. Baltimore. Most criminal law, the argument goes, is state law; Murder, rape, robbery, and the like are generally not federal crimes. Under *Barron*, the constitutional criminal procedure rules of the Bill of Rights did not apply against states, and so the Marshall Court predictably heard few cases raising issues of constitutional criminal procedure. *Barron* is indeed part of the story. ...

Then came the Warren Court, which overruled *Barron* and began applying the Fourth, Fifth, and Sixth Amendments directly against states, under the banner of selective incorporation. With many, many more state criminal cases fueling its docket, the Warren Court proceeded to build up, in short order, a remarkable doctrinal edifice of Fourth Amendment, Fifth Amendment, and Sixth Amendment rules — the foundations of modern constitutional criminal procedure.

But these foundations were none too sure. On a lawyerly level, some of the Warren Court's most important criminal procedure pronouncements lacked firm grounding in constitutional text and structure. Key rulings ran counter to early case law both in lower federal courts and in state courts construing analogous provisions of state constitutions. Precisely because so few Marshall Court cases existed, this break with Founding-era understandings was less visible. On key issues, the Warren Court seemed to contradict itself, laying down sweeping rules in some cases that it could not quite live by in other cases. On a political level, many of the Warren Court's constitutional criminal procedure pronouncements did not sit well with the American electorate. The guilty too often seemed to spring free without good reason—and by this time the guilty regularly included murderers, rapists, and robbers and not just federal income tax frauds and customs cheats. In a constitutional democracy, the People, in the long run, usually prevail. Federal judges may be, at times, "insulated" and "countermajoritarian," but majorities elect Presidents, and Presidents, with the advice and consent of Senators, pick federal judges.

And so, with Earl Warren's retirement, and Richard Nixon's election on a "law and order" platform, the Counter-Revolution began. But the foundations of this Counter-Revolution are also none too sure. Like the Warren Court, the Burger and Rehnquist Courts have at times paid little heed to constitutional text, history, and structure and have mouthed rules one day only to ignore them the next. If the Warren Court at times was too easy on the guilty, the Burger and Rehnquist Courts at times have been too hard on the innocent.

Where does all this leave us today? At a crossroads. I submit, the present is a particularly ripe moment for a fundamental rethinking of constitutional criminal procedure, and for a choice among competing visions.

WHERE SHOULD WE GO FROM HERE? CONSTITUTIONAL METHODOLOGY

To begin with, we must distinguish constitutional criminal procedure from criminal procedure generally. Not all sensible rules of criminal procedure can or should be constitutionalized. The Constitution—when read in light of its text, history, and structure, its doctrinal elaboration in precedent, the need for principled judicial standards, and so on—simply may not speak to some issues. This is, of course, one of the reasons we have legislatures—to make sensible policy where the Constitution permits choice. Legislative solutions can be adjusted in the face of new facts or changing values far more easily than can rules that have been read into the Constitution.

Textual argument is, as I have said, a proper starting point for proper constitutional analysis. Sometimes, plain-meaning textual arguments in the end must yield to the weight of other proper constitutional arguments—from history, structure, precedent, practicality, and so on. And so the astonishing thing is not that someone might find the above-catalogued textual points to be outweighed at times by other arguments. Rather, the astonishing thing is that these textual points are almost never made, or even seen. This is true even when the text, carefully read, explains most or all of the leading cases in a given area, or when the text resonates with obvious common sense. In virtually every other area of constitutional law, such a state of affairs is unimaginable. I think it cannot last much longer in the area of constitutional criminal procedure. The field may have evolved as an insular ecosystem unto itself, but global changes in constitutional law discourse must soon affect the atmosphere here, too.

The Constitution seeks to protect the innocent. The guilty, in general, receive procedural protection only as an incidental and unavoidable byproduct of protecting the innocent because of their innocence. Law breaking, as such, is entitled to no legitimate expectation of privacy, and so if a search can detect only law breaking as such, it poses little threat to Fourth Amendment values. By the same token, the exclusionary rule is wrong, as a constitutional rule, precisely because it creates huge windfalls for guilty defendants but gives no direct remedy to the innocent woman wrongly searched. The guiltier you are, the more evidence the police find, the bigger the exclusionary rule windfall; but if the police know you are innocent, and just want to hassle you (because of your race, or politics, or whatever) the exclusionary rule offers exactly zero compensation or deterrence.

Truth and accuracy are vital values. A procedural system that cannot sort the innocent from the guilty will confound any set of substantive laws, however just. And so to throw out highly reliable evidence that can indeed help us separate the innocent from the guilty — and to throw it out by pointing to the Constitution, no less — is constitutional madness. A Constitution proclaimed in the name of We the People should be rooted in enduring values that Americans can recognize as our values. Truth and the protection of innocence are such values. Virtually everything in the Fourth, Fifth, and Sixth Amendments, properly read, promotes, or at least does not betray, these values.

If anyone believes that other nice-sounding, but far less intuitive, ideas are also in the Constitution, the burden of proof should be on him. Here are two examples: (1) "The Constitution requires that government must never profit from its own wrong. Hence, illegally obtained evidence must be excluded." (2) "No man should be compelled to be an instrument of his own destruction. Hence, reliable physical fruits of immunized testimony should be excluded." These sound nice, but where does the Constitution say that? And are we truly willing to live by these as constitutional rules? The first would require that the government return stolen goods to thieves, and illegal drugs to drug-dealers. But this has never been the law. The second would prevent coerced fingerprinting and DNA sampling. This, too, is almost impossible to imagine in practice. By contrast, the innocence-protection rock on which I stand, and the specific Fourth, Fifth, and Sixth Amendment derivations therefrom, are things that we can all live by, without cheating.

WILLIAM J. STUNTZ, THE UNEASY RELATIONSHIP BETWEEN CRIMINAL PROCEDURE AND CRIMINAL JUSTICE

107 Yale L.J. 1, 1-6 (1997)

Most talk about the law of criminal procedure treats that law as a self-contained universe. The picture looks something like this: The Supreme Court says that suspects and defendants have a right to be free from certain types of police or prosecutorial behavior. Police and prosecutors, for the most part, then do as they're told. When they don't, and when the misconduct is tied to criminal convictions, the courts reverse the convictions, thereby sending a message to misbehaving officials. Within the bounds of this picture there is room for a lot of debate about the wisdom or constitutional pedigree of particular doctrines, and the literature is filled with debate of that sort. There is also room for theorizing about the optimal specificity of the rules the Supreme Court creates; the literature contains some of that, though less than it should. Finally, there is room for arguing about remedies — about whether reversing criminal convictions is an appropriate means of getting the police, prosecutors, and trial judges to do what the law says they ought to do. At least in the sphere of Fourth and Fifth Amendment law, a lively debate along those lines exists. But for all their variety, these debates take for granted the same basic picture of the process, a process whose only variables are the rules themselves and the remedies for their violation.

The picture is, of course, wrong. Criminal procedure's rules and remedies are embedded in a larger system, a system that can adjust to those rules in ways other than obeying them. And the rules can in turn respond to the system in a variety of ways, not all of them pleasant. The more one focuses on that dynamic, the more problematic the law of criminal procedure seems.

The heart of the problem is the system's structure. The criminal justice system is dominated by a trio of forces: crime rates, the definition of crime (which of course partly determines crime rates), and funding decisions — how much money to spend on police, prosecutors, defense attorneys, judges, and prisons. These forces determine the ratio of crimes to prosecutors and the ratio of prosecutions to public defenders, and those ratios in turn go far toward determining what the system does and how the system does it. But the law that defines what the criminal process looks like, the law that defines defendants' rights, is made by judges and Justices who have little information about crime rates and funding decisions, and whose incentives to take account of those factors may be perverse. High crime rates make it easy for prosecutors to substitute cases without strong procedural claims for cases with such claims. Underfunding of criminal defense counsel limits the number of procedural claims that can be pressed. Both phenomena make criminal procedure doctrines seem inexpensive to the appellate judges who define those doctrines. Unsurprisingly, given that regulating the criminal justice system has seemed cheap, the courts have done a lot of regulating — more, one suspects, than they would have done in a world where defendants could afford to litigate more often and more aggressively, or where prosecutors could not so easily substitute some cases for others. Criminal procedure is thus distorted by forces its authors probably do not understand.

The distortion runs both ways. As courts have raised the cost of criminal investigation and prosecution, legislatures have sought out devices to reduce those costs. Severe limits on defense funding are the most obvious example, but not the only one. Expanded criminal liability makes it easier for the government to induce guilty pleas, as do high mandatory sentences that serve as useful threats against recalcitrant defendants. And guilty pleas avoid most of the potentially costly requirements that criminal procedure imposes. These strategies would no doubt be politically attractive anyway, but the law of criminal procedure makes them more so. Predictably, underfunding, overcriminalization, and oversentencing have increased as criminal procedure has expanded.

Nor are the law's perverse effects limited to courts and legislatures. Constitutional criminal procedure raises the cost of prosecuting wealthier defendants by giving those defendants more issues to litigate. The result, at the margin, is to steer prosecutors away from such defendants and toward poorer ones. By giving defendants other, cheaper claims to raise, constitutional criminal procedure also raises the cost to defense counsel of investigating and litigating factual claims, claims that bear directly on their clients' innocence or guilt. The result is to steer defense counsel, again at the margin, away from those sorts of claims and toward constitutional issues. More Fourth, Fifth, and Sixth Amendment claims probably mean fewer self-defense claims and mens rea arguments. This turns the standard conservative criticism of the law of criminal procedure on its head. Ever since the 1960s, the right has argued that criminal procedure frees too many of the guilty. The better criticism may be that it helps to imprison too many of the innocent.

It also does little about the concern that, more than anything else, prompted its creation. The post-1960 constitutionalization of criminal procedure arose, in large part, out of the sense that the system was treating black suspects and defendants much worse than white ones. Warren-era constitutional criminal procedure began as a kind of antidiscrimination law. But the criminal justice system is characterized by extraordinary discretion — over the definition of crimes (legislatures can criminalize as much as they wish), over enforcement (police and prosecutors can arrest and charge whom they wish), and over funding (legislatures can allocate resources as they wish). In a system so dominated by discretionary decisions, discrimination is easy, and constitutional law has surprisingly little to say about it.

To some degree, these problems are the product of a particular set of contingent circumstances. Vary the circumstances, and the problems would look quite different. For example, we may someday return to the very low crime-to-prosecutor ratios of the early 1960s, either because crime takes a nosedive or because criminal justice budgets go through the roof (or both). If that happens, prosecutorial discretion will seem less important, for prosecutors will be able to pursue all strong cases and a good number of weak ones. Guilty plea rates will fall as the proportion of contestable cases rises. More trials will mean that the cost of constitutional regulation in this area will become more visible to judges, which might lead the Supreme Court to alter the regulation in important ways. This is just one set of speculations about one possible scenario; other scenarios, pushing prosecutors and courts in very different directions, could easily be spun out. The lesson seems clear: Generalizing is dangerous, for the problems that afflict the system today are the consequence of today's facts and today's law, and both facts and law are certain to change.

Yet some cautious generalizing is still possible. In a legislatively funded system with state-paid prosecutors and defense attorneys, judge-made procedural rights are bound to have some perverse effects, pushing prosecutors and defense attorneys and legislators and even the judges themselves in uncomfortable directions. The effects are impossible to measure, and they will be larger or smaller depending on background circumstances. But they remain real, and inevitable.

It may be that the broad structure of constitutional regulation of criminal justice has it backward, that courts have been not too activist, but activist in the wrong places. The system might be better off today had Warren and his colleagues worried less about criminal procedure, and more about criminal justice.

ALAN DERSHOWITZ, THE BEST DEFENSE

xxi-xxii (1982)

In the process of litigating . . . cases, writing this book and teaching my classes, I have discerned a series of "rules" that seem — in practice — to govern the justice game in America today. Most of the participants in the criminal justice system understand them. Although these rules never appear in print, they seem to control the realities of the process. Like all rules, they are necessarily stated in oversimplified terms. But they tell an important part of how the system operates in practice. Here are some of the key rules of the justice game:

Rule I: Almost all criminal defendants are, in fact, guilty.

Rule II: All criminal defense lawyers, prosecutors and judges understand and believe Rule I.

Rule III: It is easier to convict guilty defendants by violating the Constitution than by complying with it, and in some cases it is impossible to convict guilty defendants without violating the Constitution.

Rule IV: Almost all police lie about whether they violated the Constitution in order to convict guilty defendants.

Rule V: All prosecutors, judges, and defense attorneys are aware of Rule IV.

Rule VI: Many prosecutors implicitly encourage police to lie about whether they violated the Constitution in order to convict guilty defendants.

Rule VII: All judges are aware of Rule VI.

Rule VIII: Most trial judges pretend to believe police officers who they know are lying.

Rule IX: All appellate judges are aware of Rule VIII, yet many pretend to believe the trial judges who pretend to believe the lying police officers.

Rule X: Most judges disbelieve defendants about whether their constitutional rights have been violated, even if they are telling the truth.

Rule XI: Most judges and prosecutors would not knowingly convict a defendant who they believe to be innocent of the crime charged (or a closely related crime).

Rule XII: Rule XI does not apply to members of organized crime, drug dealers, career criminals, or potential informers.

Rule XIII: Nobody really wants justice.

2.   The Distinction between Criminal Procedure, Civil Procedure, and Substantive Criminal Law

WILLIAM J. STUNTZ, SUBSTANCE, PROCESS, AND THE CIVIL-CRIMINAL LINE

7 J. Contemp. Legal Issues 1 (1996)

Criminal procedure is almost completely constitutionalized; civil procedure is not. Meanwhile, the substance of the law of crimes is not very heavily constitutionalized; neither is the substance of the law of everything else. Those substantive restraints that exist—for instance, the First Amendment and equal protection doctrine, not to mention the famous cases that go under the label "substantive due process"—apply, with a few exceptions, to everything the government does. That is, they apply to the civil and criminal spheres alike.

So constitutional law treats the criminal side of the civil-criminal line as special, but only when crafting procedures. When it comes to the rules that regulate primary conduct, constitutional law basically has no civil-criminal line. Legislatures decide what is and is not a crime, just as they decide what (mostly civil) rules apply to sales contracts or securities offerings. Legislatures also decide what procedures apply when civil disputes arise, though they may leave a good deal of that authority to courts as a practical matter. But courts alone decide what the law of criminal procedure looks like, since courts are the system's constitutional lawmakers and criminal procedure is the province of constitutional law.

So the constitution regulates substance in a few significant pockets, but otherwise leaves it alone, and the regulation basically spans the civil-criminal divide. There is no real substantive due process aimed specially at criminal law. Meanwhile, there is some gentle constitutional regulation of the civil process, but the regulation plainly occurs around the edges; the core is governed by non-constitutional law. Only in criminal procedure does constitutional law dominate the field.

There is a standard argument for constitutional criminal procedure's many protections. Arrest, prosecution, and criminal punishment impose huge costs on their targets. The danger is that those costs will be imposed for no reason (i.e., on the whim of some government official) or for a bad reason (e.g., the defendant's race or politics). A large portion of the law of criminal procedure addresses that danger. The requirement of probable cause to justify arrest; the requirement of magistrate review, a preliminary hearing, or grand jury screening to bring a case to trial; the right to counsel at trial and at some pretrial stages; the right to trial by jury; and the beyond-a-reasonable-doubt standard for criminal conviction—all these rights ensure that the government can punish only if it can satisfy a series of neutral decisionmakers of a high probability (increasingly high as one moves from arrest to trial to conviction) that the defendant committed a crime. If the rights work, the specter of punishment for no reason or for evil reasons vanishes.

This happy scenario depends on substantive criminal law doing a good job of separating people who deserve punishment from people who don't. Accuracy is not an end in itself; it matters only if there is something meaningful to be accurate about. The best procedures in the world cannot prevent punishment for the "crime" of being black, or a Rastafarian. In short, good procedural rules require good substantive rules in order to accomplish anything.

That much is no surprise; it is the usual relationship between procedure and substance. But at least in the criminal setting, the relationship is more problematic. Special rules of criminal procedure are not just worthless without substantive limits. The procedural rules may actually be perverse: The procedures themselves give the government an incentive to generate bad substantive rules, as a means of evading or exploiting the differences between the criminal and civil processes. This perversity takes two forms. The first arises from legal boundaries that separate criminal law enforcement from civil law enforcement, boundaries that are almost never litigated yet create important incentives. These boundary rules let the government do things to criminal suspects or defendants that it can't do to civil litigants, thereby creating some incentive to broaden the scope of criminal liability. The second arises from the many rights criminal procedure grants defendants. Safeguarding those rights is, naturally, costly to the government. And broader criminal liability allows the government to escape those costs, both by easing the burden of proving guilt and by easing the task of inducing guilty pleas.

There is a natural dynamic built into our system that leads to overcriminalization. In the absence of substantive limits, broad procedural protections for criminal defendants make that dynamic worse. Meanwhile, the same logic that legitimates constitutional criminal procedure also supports constitutional criminal substance. It follows that the current allocation of authority between constitutional law and legislative power is both unstable and contradictory.

How might the contradiction be resolved? There are two possibilities, both obvious. The system might deregulate criminal procedure, leaving it to the same forces that define criminal law. Or, the system might constitutionalize the borders of criminal law, just as it has done with criminal procedure. That is, constitutional law's line between criminal and civil might be either abolished or extended.

LOUIS MICHAEL SEIDMAN, POINTS OF INTERSECTION: DISCONTINUITIES AT THE JUNCTION OF CRIMINAL LAW AND THE REGULATORY STATE

7 J. Contemp. Legal Issues 97, 97-98, 100-102, 127 (1996)

The law of crime is special. Like an isolated, aboriginal community somehow passed over by the changes all around it, the criminal law has managed to hang onto ancient patterns of thought and behavior. Of course, there is some contact with the outside world. Emissaries from "civilization" produce disruptions when they cross the community's borders. Although these disruptions are real and serious, they remain localized and peripheral. At its core, the criminal law is a living museum that unselfconsciously preserves a rapidly receding past.

. . . [T]he law of crime has managed to remain "formal" in a legal environment dominated by a "regulatory" perspective. Criminal law is preoccupied by discourse about rights, fault, consent, and separate private and public spheres. Much of the rest of the law, in contrast, is frankly utilitarian, regulatory, and collective.

This claim should not be overstated. Civil law is not entirely regulatory in focus, and, conversely, regulatory concepts have had some influence on the criminal law. These qualifications form an important part of my argument. Part of my aim is to demonstrate that formalism has more of a hold over the law in general than many have acknowledged. I also want to demonstrate that regulatory penetration around the peripheries of the criminal law has had a significant disruptive effect.

Still, there are important differences in degree concerning the extent to which regulatory ideas have displaced formalism in different doctrinal areas. The criminal law's central tenets are understandable only in terms of concepts that survive as no more than a deviant counter-tradition in the rest of the law. The upshot is that when standard critical techniques, developed by legal realists in the first third of this century, are applied to criminal law and procedure, they make hash out of the categories that define the doctrine.

Procedural formalism is important to the law's legitimacy because it demonstrates that when judges enforce the law, they are doing something more than simply imposing their will on others. Procedural formalism is not sufficient to legitimate the law, however. Many formalists also believe that the substantive source of law must also be impersonal and legitimate. Formalists who have thought about this substantive vision have often relied on a particular social theory grounded in classical liberalism. Although procedural formalism has had an obvious and important impact on criminal law, it is this substantive social theory that I will emphasize below.

Put crudely, the theory starts with individuals located in a preexisting private sphere—individuals who have separate and, to some degree irreconcilable, desires, life-plans, and beliefs. These individuals, in turn, form a public sphere in order to prevent a war of "all against all." This public sphere is sharply limited. In order to conform to the original bargain that created it, it must remain rigorously neutral as between conflicting individual conceptions of the good and should intervene only when necessary to protect the rights of individuals who continue to decide for themselves how to pursue their lives.

The conventional story is that this social vision was subject to withering assault by the legal realists in the first third of this century and that it collapsed when the Supreme Court effectively overruled Lochner v. New York after 1937. The realist revolt against formalism was, of course, multifaceted, but at a minimum, it entailed a rejection of the freedom of contract ideology thought to mark the boundary between private freedom and public coercion. *Lochner* reflected the view that coercion invading natural and prepolitical private space was justified only when an individual had consented to be bound. Therefore, bakers who contracted to work for longer than ten hours per day did so in an exercise of private freedom and had a right to this choice. Conversely, manufacturers who had not agreed to pay their employers a minimum wage could not be justly coerced into doing so. Because these prohibitions derived from a conception of individual rights ultimately tied to the social contract, instrumental arguments against them premised on maximizing overall welfare were simply beside the point.

The realists attacked this system on two levels. The less radical version of the critique rejected the association between freedom and the private sphere. Individual choice within this sphere was not necessarily free. Instead, it was often coerced by private forces. Government intervention therefore held the potential to increase the realm of freedom by regulating private coercion.

The more radical version rejected the very concepts of public and private or free and coerced. On this view, an antecedent state of nature in which people made free choices in a purely private sphere was a myth. What formalists called "private" was, and had always been, publicly constituted by background laws of property. What formalists called "free will" was, and had always been, situated in a social and political setting that determined the "choices" individuals made.

It followed from both the more radical and the less radical view that the wage contract was not sacrosanct. For less radical realists, it was coerced by the ability of manufacturers to withhold the means of subsistence unless their terms were accepted. On the more radical version, the very conception of a freely assumed obligation was a chimera. Because government was everywhere, choice was always determined by the legal regime, and the only relevant question was the shape of the legal regime that would determine the choice.

. . . Freed from the shackles of a priori reasoning from natural rights, policy managers could redistribute resources and manipulate incentives so as to provide socially optimal outcomes. Under the post-War implicit social contract that dominated American politics until the 1980's, this approach entailed regulation when it made sense on pragmatic grounds to alter market outcomes, social insurance that guaranteed an income floor, and modest redistribution above the floor.

The implications of all this for the criminal law are fairly obvious: Criminal law is simply another form of regulation, to be utilized when the benefits of government intervention outweigh the costs. Following Holmes, a realist's approach to criminal law would, therefore, reject individual consent as a starting point. Under the old, Kantian conception, government coercion was justified only because the criminal, by committing the crime, had freely consented to her own punishment. For realists, this "consent" is as mythical as the consent of workers to the wage contract. The "choices" made by criminals, like all other choices, are conditioned by their surroundings. It does not follow, however, that criminals should not be punished. The moral justification for punishment derives not from free choice, but from the imperatives of social welfare maximization. The key insight is that government inaction is just as likely to limit freedom as government action. The failure to criminalize or punish does not leave individuals free in a preexisting private sphere, any more than government passivity left workers free. Just as workers were coerced by their employers in the absence of government intervention, so too victims of crime are coerced by criminals.

. . . At first blush, many of the "new" rules of criminal procedure announced over the past half century seem to be regulatory in character. For example, although some have tried, it is difficult to justify the rule excluding illegally seized evidence as necessary to enforce the rights of the defendant who benefits from the exclusion. If the rule is justified at all, it is because it provides police officers with useful incentives in the future.

3. Plea Bargaining and Sentencing

ALBERT W. ALSCHULER, IMPLEMENTING THE CRIMINAL DEFENDANT'S RIGHT TO TRIAL: ALTERNATIVES TO THE PLEA BARGAINING SYSTEM

50 U. Chi. L. Rev. 931, 932-936, 1048-1050 (1983)

[P]lea bargaining has come to affect almost every aspect of our criminal justice system from the legislative drafting of substantive offenses through the efforts of correctional officials to rehabilitate convicted offenders.

Even a cursory listing of objections to this practice may consume several paragraphs. Plea bargaining makes a substantial part of an offender's sentence depend, not upon what he did or his personal characteristics, but upon a tactical decision irrelevant to any proper objective of criminal proceedings. In contested cases, it substitutes a regime of split-the-difference for a judicial determination of guilt or innocence and elevates a concept of partial guilt above the requirement that criminal responsibility be established beyond a reasonable doubt. This practice also deprecates the value of human liberty and the purposes of the criminal sanction by treating these things as commodities to be traded for economic savings — savings that, when measured against common social expenditures, usually seem minor.

Plea bargaining leads lawyers to view themselves as judges and administrators rather than as advocates; it subjects them to serious financial and other temptations to disregard their clients' interests; and it diminishes the confidence in attorney-client relationships that can give dignity and purpose to the legal profession and that is essential to the defendant's sense of fair treatment. In addition, this practice makes figureheads of court officials who typically prepare elaborate presentence reports only after the effective determination of sentence through prosecutorial negotiations. Indeed, it tends to make figureheads of judges, whose power over the administration of criminal justice has largely been transferred to people of less experience, who commonly lack the information that judges could secure, whose temperaments have been shaped by their partisan duties, and who have not been charged by the electorate with the important responsibilities that they have assumed. Moreover, plea bargaining perverts both the initial prosecutorial formulation of criminal charges and, as defendants plead guilty to crimes less serious than those that they apparently committed, the final judicial labeling of offenses.

The negotiation process encourages defendants to believe that they have "sold a commodity and that [they have], in a sense, gotten away with something." It sometimes promotes perceptions of corruption. It has led the Supreme Court to a hypocritical disregard of its usual standards of waiver in judging the most pervasive waiver that our criminal justice system permits. The practice of plea bargaining is inconsistent with the principle that a decent society should want to hear what an accused person might say in his defense — and with constitutional guarantees that embody this principle and other professed ideals for the resolution of criminal disputes. . . . However unjust plea bargaining may seem, it has become fashionable to contend that the process is inevitable. Indeed, scholars and practitioners proclaim that "to speak of a plea bargaining-free criminal justice system is to operate in a land of fantasy." They advance two arguments in support of this contention. First, they emphasize the extent of the demon's possession. In view of the overwhelming number of cases that currently are resolved by guilty pleas, they maintain that providing the economic resources necessary to implement the right to trial would be impracticable; their view apparently is that our nation cannot afford to give its criminal defendants their day in court. Second, they suggest that in view of the mutuality of advantage that prosecutors and defense attorneys are likely to perceive in the settlement of criminal cases, any attempt to prohibit this process would be countered by widespread subterfuge. In practice, they argue, the only choice is between a system of negotiated case resolution that is open, honest, and subject to effective regulation and one that has been driven underground.

. . . [O]ne obvious solution to today's excessive dependency on the guilty plea — spending the money necessary to implement our constitutional ideals without shortcuts. Focusing first on felony prosecutions, it argues that the United States could provide three-day jury trials to all felony defendants who reach the trial stage by adding no more than an estimated $850 million to annual criminal justice expenditures. Moreover, it contends that the actual cost of implementing a plea bargaining prohibition would be less than this amount, in part because most cases now resolved through plea bargaining could be tried in less than three days and, even more importantly, because many defendants would plead guilty without bargaining.

. . . [T]he Anglo-American legal system afforded defendants an unfettered right to trial during most of its history and . . . most legal systems of the world apparently survive without plea bargaining today. Nevertheless, every legal system that has managed without plea bargaining has employed a much more expeditious trial procedure than ours.

The impediments to implementation of a plea bargaining prohibition are not worth a fraction of the paralysis that they have prompted. Americans certainly could afford full implementation of the right to jury trial in both felony and misdemeanor prosecutions. Moreover, without additional expenditures, they could allocate existing resources more effectively by simplifying the trial process and making trials more available. Finally, states could easily substitute jury waiver bargaining for plea bargaining. Observers who proclaim that implementation of the right to trial is impossible have perpetrated a remarkable myth—one whose effectiveness depends largely on the "outsider's" fear of being thought naive or utopian and one that any glance outside our own legal system destroys.

At the end of a long investigation of plea bargaining, I confess to some bafflement concerning the insistence of most lawyers and judges that plea bargaining is inevitable and desirable. Perhaps I am wrong in thinking that a few simple precepts of criminal justice should command the unqualified support of fair-minded people:

— that it is important to hear what someone may be able to say in his defense before convicting him of crime;

— that, when he denies his guilt, it is also important to try to determine on the basis of all the evidence whether he is guilty;

— that it is wrong to punish a person, not for what he did, but for asking that the evidence be heard (and wrong deliberately to turn his sentence in significant part on his strategies rather than on his crime);

— and, finally, that it is wrong to alibi departures from these precepts by saying that we do not have the time and money to listen, that most defendants are guilty anyway, that trials are not perfect, that it is all an inevitable product of organizational interaction among stable courtroom work groups, and that any effort to listen would merely drive our failure to listen underground.

From my viewpoint, it is difficult to understand why these precepts are controversial; what is more, I do not understand why the legal profession, far from according them special reverence, apparently values them less than the public in general does. Daniel Webster thought it a matter of definition that "law" would hear before it condemned, proceed upon inquiry, and render judgment only after trial. Apparently the legal profession has lost sight of Webster's kind of law, and, for all the pages that I have written about plea bargaining, the issue in the end may be that simple.

RONALD WRIGHT & MARC MILLER, THE SCREENING/BARGAINING TRADEOFF

55 Stan. L. Rev. 29, 30-35 (2002)

When it comes to plea bargaining, we have created a false dilemma. The dilemma grows out of the central reality of criminal adjudication in the United

States. The vast majority of criminal cases are resolved through guilty pleas rather than trials. Most of those guilty pleas result from negotiations between prosecution and defense.

Scholars, judges, prosecutors, defense lawyers, and politicians have offered only two basic responses to the fact that guilt is mostly resolved through negotiated guilty pleas: They take it or they leave it.

Some take the system more or less as it is. They accept negotiated pleas in the ordinary course of events, either because such a system produces good results or because it is inevitable. They might identify some exceptional cases that create an intolerable risk of convicting innocent defendants, or unusual cases where there are special reasons to doubt the knowing and voluntary nature of the defendant's plea. But the mine run of cases, in this view, must be resolved with a heavy dose of plea bargains and a sprinkling of trials.

Then there are those who leave it, arguing that our system's reliance on negotiated guilty pleas is fundamentally mistaken. Some call for a complete ban. . . . Others, doubting that an outright ban is feasible, still encourage a clear shift to more short trials to resolve criminal charges. Restoring the criminal trial to its rightful place at the center of criminal justice might require major changes in public spending, and it might take a lifetime, but these critics say the monstrosity of the current system demands such a change.

This dilemma about plea bargaining—take it or leave it—is a false one. It is based on a false dichotomy. It errs in assuming that criminal trials are the only alternative to plea bargains. In this erroneous view, fewer plea bargains lead inexorably to more trials; indeed, the whole point in limiting plea bargains is to produce more trials.

[There is] a different choice . . . prosecutorial "screening" as the principal alternative to plea bargains. Of course all prosecutors "screen" when they make any charging decision. By prosecutorial screening we mean a far more structured and reasoned charge selection process than is typical in most prosecutors' offices in this country. The prosecutorial screening system we describe has four interrelated features, all internal to the prosecutor's office: early assessment, reasoned selection, barriers to bargains, and enforcement.

First, the prosecutor's office must make an early and careful assessment of each case, and demand that police and investigators provide sufficient information before the initial charge is filed. Second, the prosecutor's office must file only appropriate charges. Which charges are "appropriate" is determined by several factors. A prosecutor should only file charges that the office would generally want to result in a criminal conviction and sanction. In addition, appropriate charges must reflect reasonably accurately what actually occurred. They are charges that the prosecutor can very likely prove in court. Third, and critically, the office must severely restrict all plea bargaining, and most especially charge bargains. Prosecutors should also recognize explicitly that the screening process is the mechanism that makes such restrictions possible. Fourth, the kind of prosecutorial screening we advocate must include sufficient training, oversight, and other internal enforcement mechanisms to ensure reasonable uniformity in charging and relatively few changes to charges after they have been filed. . . .

Intense prosecutorial screening may produce a small increase in the number of trials, but the more substantial change would likely be an increase in the number of "open" pleas—defendants pleading guilty as charged without any prior negotiated agreement with the prosecutor. . . .

Jurisdictions that implement the screening/bargaining tradeoff will be more honest and more accessible. In hard screening systems, prosecutors will be less likely to "overcharge" or "undercharge." The weakest cases exit early, while those remaining should stand up at trial. A screening-based system should also be more accessible than a system of negotiated pleas, because the public (especially the victims of alleged crimes) will receive clearer and more accurate signals about how the system adjudicates and punishes crimes. The charge is declared publicly from the outset and is easy to evaluate. . . .

We know this practice is viable because it is now operating in a few American jurisdictions, without much controversy and without attracting the attention it deserves. For instance, over the last three decades New Orleans District Attorney Harry Connick has emphasized early screening of cases and has actively discouraged any changes of criminal charges as a result of negotiations after the charges are filed. . . .

[O]ur study of the New Orleans data . . . confirms that a prosecutor can invest serious resources in early evaluation of cases and maintain this practice over the long run. This screening leads to relatively high rates of declination (that is, refusals to prosecute a case after the police recommend charges). When combined with policies discouraging reductions in charges once they are filed, the results are lower levels of negotiated pleas, slightly higher rates of trial, and notably higher rates of open guilty pleas than in typical American jurisdictions. . . .

The screening/bargaining tradeoff should . . . become part of the public, political dialogue about the justice system, especially at election time. The interesting public question should not be the "conviction rate," but rather the "as charged conviction rate." . . . [T]he higher the ratio of "as charged convictions" to "convictions," the more readily a prosecutor should be praised and reelected. A ratio near one — where most convictions are "as charged," *whether they result from guilty pleas or trials* — is the best sign of a healthy, honest, and tough system. The lower the ratio of "as charged convictions" to "convictions" (approaching zero), the more the prosecutor should be criticized for sloppiness, injustice, and obfuscation. A lower ratio might also reflect a prosecutor's undue leniency. . . .

GERARD E. LYNCH, SCREENING VERSUS PLEA BARGAINING: EXACTLY WHAT ARE WE TRADING OFF?

55 Stan. L. Rev. 1399, 1400-1404, 1406-1408 (2003)

In questioning "the traditional plea bargaining/trial tradeoff," and seeking to replace it with a model in which the proper tradeoff is seen as one between plea bargaining and prosecutorial screening, Wright and Miller rather tellingly start with plea bargaining as the baseline system, and ask which of their two alternatives, trials or screening, can best serve as a viable substitute for it. The question seems to be: Can we eliminate plea bargaining without incurring the burden and expense of a vastly increased trial docket? Putting aside for the moment other questions about this formulation, it is readily apparent that asking the question in this way avoids the real reason that plea bargaining is traditionally seen as in opposition to trial: It is the *trial* that is the official baseline system, proclaimed in the Constitution, in all state and federal variations of criminal procedure rules, and in the popular imagination as educated in civics classes and entertained by American media. . . .

Thus, there is a tradeoff between plea bargaining and trials, not merely in the practical sense that (as some have argued and as Wright and Miller dispute) we might not be able to reduce plea bargaining without increasing the number of trials, but in the deeper sense that plea bargaining (and variant systems of agreed disposition) exists in the first place as an alternative to the expense and uncertainty of trials. It is in this sense that I would argue that plea bargaining is best seen as an alternative to a trial system, and that the screening system that appears to operate in New Orleans is simply a variant or refinement of a system of disposition in which the prosecutor, rather than a judge or jury, is the principal adjudicator of guilt and punishment, and the defendant's role is to acquiesce in that determination, rather than to contest it before a neutral adjudicator. . . .

In what sense, then, does the screening system eliminate the defects of a plea bargaining regime? Wright and Miller seem to focus on *bargaining* as the key negative characteristic of adjudication by guilty plea. . . .

. . . "Plea bargaining" is a loaded term. . . . Substantively, it suggests that defendants receive "bargains" — in the sense of discounts — from the presumptively appropriate charge or penalty for their crimes. . . . It is not clear, however, why we should privilege the sentences received by the tiny minority of defendants who go to trial as the "correct" sentences, from which the sentences received by defendants who plead represent an unduly lenient departure. . . . Where almost no one pays the "manufacturer's suggested retail price," and almost everyone buys the item at a "discounted" price, no one really gets a "bargain," and the product's real price is what is actually charged in the marketplace. . . .

But even if we assume for the sake of argument that giving lesser sentences to induce guilty pleas results in sentences that are unduly lenient, Wright and Miller notably do not suggest that defendants who plead guilty in New Orleans receive the same sentences as similar defendants convicted after trial. . . . If . . . defendants who plead guilty receive an imprecise, unannounced, yet roughly predictable sentencing discount from judges in exchange for their waiver of rights, the elimination of "plea bargaining" by prosecutors seems much less significant. There may be reasons why an implicit bargain between defendants and judges who are understood to reward guilty pleas with leniency is preferable to express bargaining with defendants by prosecutors to accomplish the same end. But I suspect few critics of plea bargaining would consider substituting the former system for the latter a major accomplishment.

Procedurally, plea "bargaining" suggests an inappropriate *process* of adjudication, by implying that guilt and punishment are determined by some form of mercantile haggling rather than objective inquiry. But the process of negotiating pleas, in my experience, is not accurately regarded as one of "bargaining," if by that one imagines some simplistic model of haggling over prices. Wright and Miller at times seem implicitly to adopt this model: The prosecutor sets the bid artificially high by overcharging at the outset; the defendant balks and proposes that the charges be dismissed; the parties then settle on a compromise somewhere between these two extremes. The authors . . . seem to regard any reduction from the charged offense as either a sell-out by the prosecutor or an admission that the original charge was merely a bargaining chip. Most plea negotiations, in fact, are primarily discussions of the merits of the case, in which defense attorneys point out legal, evidentiary, or practical weaknesses in the prosecutor's case, or mitigating circumstances that merit mercy, and argue based on these considerations that the defendant is entitled to a more lenient disposition than that originally proposed. . . .

To me, the essence of this practice, and what radically distinguishes it from the adversarial litigation model embodied in textbooks . . . is that the *prosecutor*, rather than a judge or jury, is the central adjudicator of facts (as well as replacing the judge as arbiter of most legal issues and of the appropriate sentence to be imposed). Potential defenses are presented by the defendant and his counsel not in a court, but to a prosecutor, who assesses their factual accuracy and likely persuasiveness to a hypothetical judge or jury, and then decides the charge of which the defendant should be adjudged guilty. Mitigating information, similarly, is argued not to the judge, but to the prosecutor. . . .

. . . Instituting an aggressive screening procedure may significantly improve that process, but only if it implies that prosecutors will reach a more accurate and more just decision, rather than automatically adopting the police view of the appropriate charge or instituting excessive charges in order to bring pressure on defendants to plead. But it hardly constitutes a radical alternative to plea bargaining as actually practiced, and in important ways it merely ratifies and entrenches (or at least, assumes the inevitability of) that practice. . . .

Moreover, certain aspects of the New Orleans screening program endorsed by Wright and Miller . . . may have negative effects on the justice of outcomes. The authors seem to assume, in my opinion unjustifiably, that the charge determined by the prosecutors at an early stage of the case should normally be the charge to which the defendant pleads guilty or that is tried. If the prosecutor is essentially determining guilt, operating as a kind of inquisitorial, administrative adjudicator of the merits of cases, it becomes critical to provide a fair opportunity, within the internal administration process, for the defendant to present evidence, challenge the prosecutor's case, and argue defenses and mitigating circumstances. It is difficult to see how such an opportunity can be provided at the typical screening stage between arrest and charge, before defense counsel can possibly have an adequate opportunity to investigate the case. . . .

. . . The great benefit of Wright and Miller's . . . article is to focus our attention not on lamenting the absence of trials, but on improving the administrative adjudication system (mislabeled plea bargaining) so that it functions better and more fairly. Serious prosecutorial screening to eliminate unjustifiable charges can be a real improvement in the system. Reducing the opportunity for defendants to have meaningful input into the disposition has the opposite effect.

CHARLES FRIED, REFLECTIONS ON CRIME AND PUNISHMENT

30 Suffolk U. L. Rev. 681, 682-683, 685-688, 692-693, 694-695 (1997)

It appears for a number of reasons, including some that do great credit to our commitment to the rule of law and to individual rights, that the United States makes it more difficult than other decent, reasonable democracies to prevent crimes and to apprehend and convict those whose crimes we do not prevent. Once a criminal is convicted in the United States, however, our system subjects the offender to longer sentences in a sometimes degrading regime which is hurtful to criminals and society alike. I do not suggest that prison food, medical care, or amenities are inhumane. . . . In fact, some of our prisons may appear quite astonishingly luxurious to authorities from other countries. Rather, I am more concerned by the failure of some American prison systems to assure the physical safety of its inmates and by the widespread regime of intimidation by stronger, organized inmates against the weaker or less experienced inmates. What we cannot blink away is the astonishing prevalence and tolerance of sexual violence and subjugation particularly among male prisoners. These conditions must be evaluated in the context of the very long sentences served by criminals who will eventually be allowed to leave prison. In short, prison life is too often a terrifying and degrading experience endured by prisoners for unimaginably long periods of time — six, ten, twenty years — after which society expects the released individuals to lead self-sufficient, constructive, and law-abiding lives.

. . . [S]tudies and findings from Florida, Texas, Pennsylvania, Louisiana and Connecticut . . . demonstrate that rape is endemic in the American prison population. In fact, one corrections officer stated that a young inmate's chances of avoiding rape are "almost zero. . . . He'll get raped within the first twenty-four to forty-eight hours. That's almost standard." Furthermore, an investigator observed that ten years ago, when the prison population was far smaller than it is today, there were as many as "eighteen adult males raped every minute" of every day. Moreover, it is common knowledge that an exceptionally large proportion of male prisoners engage in regular homosexual activity, and rape simply becomes the violent alternative to sexual submission. Feminist scholars, including Dworkin, Estrich and MacKinnon, have raised our consciousness about the prevalence of heterosexual rape and the degrading impact that it has upon women. Surely, the homosexual rape prevalent in so many prisons is no less destructive of the souls of its victims. One of the most distressing features of this infernal system is that the prison authorities are aware of the prevalence of prison rape, yet sometimes choose not to intervene and actually discourage complaints. In effect, some prison guards tolerate rape and sexual coercion as a means of making the prison population, particularly the more aggressive and troublesome segment, more manageable.

Thus, the one institution in which we have the almost unlimited right to control the lives of our fellow citizens and which is intended to represent the ultimate commitment to order and personal security, is too often deeply disorderly and ultimately insecure. The lesson for the individuals subjected to this system — including their friends, family members, and everyone else close enough to feel it breathing down their necks — is that our commitment to the moral values of order, lawfulness and security are mere hypocrisy. . . .

This condition of long prison sentences served in often undisciplined, dangerous and degrading circumstances may perhaps be related to the earlier part of our criminal justice system which consists of the methods and procedures by which we seek to prevent crimes, to catch those who commit crimes, and to determine the guilt and punishment of those we catch. The two features I mention make up a system. The United States has elaborate — surely the most elaborate — procedures for determining who will be punished, and yet we also have by far the largest prison population of any industrialized country to which we would care to compare ourselves.

If there is a connection between these two aspects of the system, then it may be seen as an enactment of Cesare Beccaria's formula that the efficacy of punishment is a function of its severity, its swiftness and its certainty. On that hypothesis, if the American criminal justice system has made punishment seem cumbersome, slow and uncertain, then it is only by increasing the severity of the punishment that the public feels that it will get the measure of deterrence to which it merits. I shall call this the Beccaria hypothesis. Such a relationship between the two aspects of the system would also be dynamic, because one effect of such greater severity of penalty would be even greater deployment of those procedures designed to assure the punishment was truly deserved and fairly imposed. . . . These procedural safeguards then contribute to further delays and uncertainties which only increases the public pressure for severity.

4. Some Distributional Consequences of the Criminal Justice System — Race and Drugs

MARC MAUER, YOUNG BLACK AMERICANS AND THE CRIMINAL JUSTICE SYSTEM: FIVE YEARS LATER

7-9 (1995)

We have documented the dramatically high rates of criminal justice control for young black men. In many respects it would be quite surprising if these rates were not high, given the social and economic circumstances and crime rates in their communities.

The growth of the criminal justice system in the past twenty years has coincided with a host of economic disruptions and changes in social policy that have had profound effects on income distribution, employment and family structure. Since the 1970s, many urban areas have witnessed the decline of manufacturing, the expansion of low-wage service industries and the loss of a significant part of the middle class tax base. Real wages have declined for most Americans during this period, with a widening of the gap between rich and poor beginning in the 1980s. For black male high school dropouts in their twenties, annual earnings fell by a full 50 percent from 1973 to 1989. Social service benefits such as mental health services and other supports have generally declined while the social problems that they address have been exacerbated.

The impact of these changes on the African American community has resulted from the intersection of race and class effects. Since African Americans are disproportionately represented in low-income urban communities, the effects of these social ills are intensified. As Douglas Massey and Nancy Denton have illustrated, the persistence of housing segregation exacerbates the difficult life circumstances of these communities, contributing to extremely high rates of unemployment, poor schooling, and high crime rates. Over the years many researchers have examined the extent to which racial disparity within the criminal justice system can be explained by higher crime rates among blacks or other relevant factors. Historically, there can be little doubt about the prominent role played by race in criminal justice processing, given the history of lynching in the

South, the development of chain gangs, and the well documented racial patterns involved in the imposition of the death penalty.

More recently, though, researchers have found that the evidence on these issues is mixed. While some studies have documented specific cases of racially unwarranted outcomes, much research has concluded that, with one significant exception, race plays a relatively minor role in sentencing and incarceration. Michael Tonry's review, for example, concludes that "for nearly a decade there has been a near consensus among scholars and policy analysts that most of the black punishment disproportions result not from racial bias or discrimination within the system but from patterns of black offending and of blacks' criminal records." Similarly, Alfred Blumstein's research has concluded that 76 percent of the racial disparity in prison populations is explained by higher rates of offending among blacks for serious offenses.

But both authors find, as Tonry indicates, that "Drug law enforcement is the conspicuous exception. Blacks are arrested and confined in numbers grossly out of line with their use or sale of drugs." Blumstein concludes that for drug offenses, fully half of the racial disproportions in prison are not explained by higher arrest rates.

While scholars will continue to study the relative influence of race within the criminal justice system, several key issues should not go unaddressed in explaining these disparities. First, as noted above, it is difficult to isolate the relative influence of race and class in public policy and decisionmaking. That is, to the extent that African Americans are overrepresented in the criminal justice system, to what degree is this a function of their being disproportionately low-income?

In its comprehensive examination of the problem of violence, the National Research Council reviewed existing studies of homicide victimization and class. The Council found that among low-income populations blacks had much higher rates of homicide victimization than whites but that among higher income groups, there was essentially no difference. The Council suggests that the more concentrated effects of inner-city poverty may contribute to a more serious breakdown of family and community support than in other low-income neighborhoods.

Studies of sentencing practices reveal that the current offense and the offender's prior record are the most significant factors determining a prison sentence. But if low-income youth are more subject to police scrutiny and have fewer counseling and treatment resources available to them than middle class adolescents, their youthful criminal activities will more likely result in a criminal record that will affect their chances of going to prison later on.

DAVID A. SKLANSKY, COCAINE, RACE AND EQUAL PROTECTION

47 Stan. L. Rev. 1283-1284, 1322 (1995)

Thousands of federal prisoners, including a few I helped prosecute, are currently serving long mandatory sentences for trafficking in crack cocaine. Nine out of ten of them are black. They were sentenced under laws that treat crack offenders far more harshly than the predominantly nonblack defendants caught with the more common, powder form of cocaine. Indeed, since 1986 federal crack defendants have received by law the same sentences imposed on defendants convicted of trafficking in one hundred times as much cocaine powder. Almost without exception, constitutional claims of unequal treatment raised by the crack defendants have been rejected out of hand. . . . What it tells us, I argue, is that there are certain important dimensions of racial injustice our law does not see.

There are many ways to evaluate a set of legal rules, in part because there are many things we want the law to do. The assumption underlying my approach is that one thing we should want legal rules to do is to take into account the important aspects of the situations they address. A set of rules that satisfies this requirement may yet be unfair, unworkable, or otherwise undesirable, but at least it will not be blind to its own major shortcomings. Nor will it tend to blind those who apply it.

These modest boasts, I suggest, cannot be made for equal protection doctrine in its current form. . . . I argue that the crack sentences raise troubling issues of fairness that we should want equal protection doctrine to address. These issues arise, I contend, even under the relatively narrow, process-oriented conception of equality that has dominated equal protection discussions in recent years.

Federal appellate courts have uniformly rejected these challenges, based on a largely mechanical application of the equal protection rules developed by the Supreme Court. I suggest that those rules systematically ignore, and lead judges and others to ignore, much of what is most troubling about the crack sentences: the evidence of at least unconscious racism on the part of Congress, the severity of the disparity between the average sentences imposed on black defendants and those imposed on whites, and the special need to avoid racial bias when meting out criminal punishment.

I offer some tentative thoughts about how equal protection doctrine became so feeble-sighted, and how it could be made more perceptive. Much of the problem . . . may arise from a doctrinal discussion carried out at too high a level of generality. For at least the past two decades the Supreme Court, along with many of its critics, has tended to assume that equal protection doctrine should remain relatively uniform regardless of factual context: the test for unconstitutional inequality in criminal sentencing, for example, should be the same as in civil service promotions. This universalist approach has strong theoretical advantages for constructing equal protection rules for an ideal society. In our real and imperfect society, however, the universalist approach has proved disastrous. It has blocked consideration of equal protection claims that should be taken seriously, and it has stifled the development of our collective understanding of equality.

Inequality tends, notoriously, to be accompanied and sustained by ways of thinking that render it imperceptible to those it benefits, and sometimes also to those it burdens. Many of these ways of thinking have been and remain jurisprudential. But law need not obscure more than it reveals. Indeed, one of the most important functions served on occasion by equal protection law has also been the simplest: identifying inequality and helping to deny it the protection of invisibility.

5. The Police

HERBERT PACKER, THE LIMITS OF THE CRIMINAL SANCTION

283-284 (1968)

The aggressively interventionist character of much of our criminal law thrusts the police into the role of snoopers and harassers. There is simply no way for the police to provide so much as a semblance of enforcement of laws against prostitution, sexual deviance, gambling, narcotics, and the like without widespread and visible intrusion into what people regard as their private lives. . . .

There are three generic types of police investigatory conduct that are so at odds with values of privacy and human dignity that we should resort to them only under the most exigent circumstances. They are physical intrusion, electronic surveillance, and the use of decoys. Although there arguably are circumstances under which each of the three can justifiably be employed, it is safe to say that any use of the criminal sanction that requires consistent use to be made of any of them should be suspect.

JEROME H. SKOLNICK & DAVID H. BAYLEY, COMMUNITY POLICING: ISSUES AND PRACTICES AROUND THE WORLD

49-52 (1988)

One way of comprehending a police department is through a table of organization. Such tables do offer useful, indeed indispensable, information. . . . But however indispensable they might be, tables of organization are limited in the information they offer — they don't tell us anything about the human side of the landscape they describe. The most significant features of police departments — their attitudes, internal divisions, belief systems, traditions, values — cannot be captured by the labelled boxes of a table of organization. . . .

How police officers learn to see the world around them and their role in it has come to be acknowledged by all scholars of police as an indispensable key to understanding the behavior and attitudes of police. "It is a commonplace of the now voluminous sociological literature on police operations and discretion," writes Robert Reiner, "that the rank-and-file officer is the primary determinant of policing where it really counts — on the street."[1] Moreover, . . . there are identifiable commonalities in police culture. . . .

[There is] the perception of *danger* which, although real, is typically magnified. Police officers are sometimes shot at and killed, of course. But the first line of defense against anticipated danger is *suspicion*, the development of a cognitive map of the social world to protect against signs of trouble, offense, and potential threat.

The combination of danger and suspicion leads to a third feature of police culture, namely solidarity or *brotherhood*. Most police tend to socialize with other

---

1. Robert Reiner, The Politics of the Police (Sussex, England: Wheatsheaf Books, 1985), p. 85.

police. . . . There are any number of reasons for police solidarity. One is that police do not work normal hours. As emergency service workers, they often find themselves in the position of having to work nights, weekends, and other odd hours. Police work time is one of the major stresses of police work. When one's days off are Wednesday and Thursday, one becomes a deviant in the social world and is drawn to socialize with others who are similarly situated.

Another reason is that cops don't feel they fit into many worlds they might occupy. Every cop has a story about how they were stared at or otherwise adversely noted at a party or social occasion. This has been a special problem for young police in the 1970's and 1980's, when many of their peers might light up a joint and pass it around at a festive occasion. When faced with this dilemma, young police will find new friends — among police.

A third reason is the policeman's felt need for support from other police. Police are in fact in dangerous or potentially dangerous situations. When cops, looking for drug dealers, walk through a pool hall occupied by unfriendly young men, they depend on their partners for cover and assistance. But, as Mark Baker comments:

> The real reason most police officers socialize exclusively with other police officers is that they just don't trust the people they police — which is everybody who is not a cop. They know the public generally resents their authority and is fickle in its support of police policy and individual police officers. Older officers teach younger ones that it is best to avoid civilians. Civilians will try to "hurt" the cop in the end, they say.[2] . . .

Students of the police have frequently noted the *machismo* qualities in the world of policing.[3] Those who are attracted to the occupation are often very young, in chronological age and in maturity of temperament and judgment. . . . Recruits typically have athletic backgrounds, are sports minded, and are trained in self-defense. It is not uncommon for trainees to bulk the upper body — like football players, through weight lifting — so as to offer a more formidable appearance as a potential adversary in street encounters. They are also trained to handle a variety of offensive weapons, including deadly weapons. They are taught how to disable and kill people with their bare hands. No matter how many warnings may be offered by superiors about limitations on the use of force, its possible use is a central feature of the police role, and of the policemen's perceptions of themselves.

The training and permission in the use of force combined with the youth of police can well inhibit the capacity of a police officer to empathize with the situation of those being policed in ethnically diverse and low-income neighborhoods. . . . Senior officers are . . . less likely to be macho. . . .

When scholars write about the culture of policing, they usually have in mind the street-wise cop who follows a blue code of solidarity with fellow officers. Street-wise officers are likely to be cynical, tough, skeptical of innovation within management. By contrast, management cops tend to project a vision of policing that is more acceptable to the general public. This concept of two contrasting cultures of policing grew out of research conducted in New York City by Ianni and Ianni (1983), who developed a distinction between "street cops" and "management cops."

2. Mark Baker, Cops: Their Lives in Their Own Words (New York: Fawcett, 1985), p. 211.
3. See Robert Reiner, The Politics of the Police, p. 99.

The "street-wise" cop is apt to approve of cutting corners, of throwing weight around on the street, of expressing the qualities of in-group solidarity referred to above. Management cops tend to be more legalistic, rule oriented, rational. . . . [S]ome street cops are hard-boiled cynics who deride innovations in policing as needless and unworkable incursions into the true and eternal role of the cop — the one they were socialized into as recruits by a sometimes venerated field training officer. These "street-wise" police, instead of gradually developing a broader perspective, taking advanced degrees in management, law, or criminal justice and so forth, reinforce their post-recruit identity. Unfortunately, this rein-forcement sometimes develops into a lifelong occupational vision rooted in an abiding, even growing, bitterness that seems impervious to any sort of hope for change or new ideas.

The cynicism typifying these officers may of course also be present at higher levels of management — after all, . . . all American police begin their career as street cops, and the learning that takes place on the street is never outgrown by many. . . . The innovative management cop employs prior street experience to overcome the resistance of the street cop. By contrast, the self-conception of the traditional street cop remains firmly rooted in his earliest training experiences.

Elizabeth Ruess-Ianni summarizes the difference between the two cultures as follows, based on her study of the New York City Police Department:

> In a sense, the management cop culture represents those police who have decided that the old way of running a police department is finished (for a variety of external reasons, such as social pressures, economic realities of the city, increased visibility, minority recruitment, and growth in size that cannot be managed easily in the infor-mal fashion of the old days) and they are "going to get in on the ground floor of something new." They do not, like the street cops, regard community relations, for example, as "Mickey Mouse bullshit," but as something that must be done for poli-tically expedient reasons if not for social ones.[4]

DEBRA LIVINGSTON, POLICE DISCRETION AND THE QUALITY OF LIFE IN PUBLIC PLACES: COURTS, COMMUNITIES, AND THE NEW POLICING

97 Colum. L. Rev. 551, 557, 558-561, 670-671 (1997)

On the whole . . . legal scholars have paid inadequate attention to the reemer-gence of statutes, ordinances, and law enforcement measures aimed at public conduct and, more broadly, the quality of life in public spaces. Moreover, they have virtually ignored the implications of this new focus on quality-of-life concerns for a subject that it profoundly affects — namely, the scope of police discretion in street encounters. This inattention is surprising. After all, the aspiration to con-strain police discretion on the street was in large part what prompted legal scholars over thirty years ago to mount a constitutional attack on the vagueness

---

4. Elizabeth Ruess-Ianni, The Two Cultures of Policing: Street Cops and Management Cops (Brunswick, N.J.: Transaction Books, New Brunswick, 1983), p. 121.

that characterized broadly-worded vagrancy, loitering, breach of peace, and disorderly conduct statutes and ordinances. This scholarly attack helped prompt the
judicial invalidation of many such laws and left police departments with considerably less authority to intervene in street-order problems than citizens often
assumed to be the case.

The ongoing transformation in the philosophy of American policing, from
professional policing to community and problem-oriented policing, will likely
continue to fuel interest, among these scholars, in the "order maintenance" activities of police. Such activities are aimed at preserving what might be termed the
"neighborhood commons": both tangible community resources like parks, streets,
playgrounds, parking lots, and libraries, and the associated intangible interactions
among people, both organized and spontaneous, that take place around these
resources. Proponents of these new policing strategies have increasingly asserted,
as did Jane Jacobs over thirty years ago, that preservation of the neighborhood
commons is essential to the vitality and well-being of American cities. . . .

For legal scholars, this new focus on addressing concerns with the quality of life
in public places raises anew the tension between traditional rule of law concepts
and the order maintenance activities of police. Police intervention to address
neighborhood disorder is different, in kind, from the straightforward investigation, arrest, and prosecution of those who have committed serious crimes. First,
problems of disorder stem not so much from isolated behaviors as from the coming together of certain conditions: the congruence of behavior, its location and
circumstances, its frequency, its intent, and others' reactions. The behavior appropriate in a St. Patrick's Day parade may thus be disruptive on a quiet, residential
street. And while a single person loitering on a street corner is unlikely to threaten
neighborhood life, a street on which many loiter to complete drug transactions,
even apart from their success, is likely to experience decline — to be seen by
many as a place where children should not play, and where those with adequate
resources should choose not to live. But can the police be authorized to intervene
on such a street by dispersing or arresting those loiterers seemingly intent upon
the narcotics trade? And can they be trusted to identify those contexts in which
intervention is appropriate — that is, to distinguish the quiet residential Sunday
morning from St. Patrick's Day on Main Street? Second, police intervention to
address neighborhood order is often invisible to formal legal processes, since
intervention often begins — and ends — with an admonition to "knock it off" or
requests to "quiet down" or "move along." Should police intervene in this way?
Should they intervene except by employing their resources to enforce laws against
serious crime?

Contrary to the implications of some scholarship in the police literature, the
police cannot perform substantial order maintenance tasks without legal authority.
At the same time, the many new laws addressing problems of public disorder, even
those laws that are far more specific than ones struck down in the 1960s and 1970s,
raise many of the same concerns that led courts of that period to invalidate public
order laws for vagueness. Courts have thus been tempted to invoke the open
texture of vagueness review to facially invalidate even reasonably specific public
order laws — a temptation that, when not resisted, retards positive changes in
American policing. While it plays an important role in pruning the legal code
of outright delegations of authority to police to maintain public order as they
deem appropriate, the void-for-vagueness doctrine is itself an inadequate and

even potentially destructive mechanism for constraining police discretion in the performance of order maintenance tasks. Courts cannot "solve" the problem of police discretion by invalidating reasonably specific public order laws—as some have attempted—without seriously impairing legitimate community efforts to enhance the quality of neighborhood life. Nevertheless, because the recent legislative trend does raise many of the same concerns that led courts of the 1960s and 1970s to invalidate vague laws, there is a need for renewed focus upon those political, administrative, and other "subconstitutional" controls that might assist in constraining arbitrary police enforcement. The philosophies of community and problem-oriented policing posit a new way of thinking about police and about the exercise of police discretion that themselves suggest ways in which these controls might work.

Policing, like judging, is a complex task, and the prospects and promise of the new policing reforms must at this juncture be deemed uncertain. Policing is not the simple enforcement of law, though law is important to the police role; policing that ignores the ebb and flow of community life does so only at grave peril to both police and the people for whom they work. But there are real and serious questions here. Can police departments identify those among their number "inclined toward self-directed information gathering and analysis, capable of inventive planning, and motivated to work for long-range solutions," and then use such personnel in problem solving? Can departments walk the tightrope between responsiveness to community concerns and outright deterioration in the ideal of evenhanded enforcement associated with the rule of law? "Perhaps it is better in the long run," as one scholar recently put it, "to say that the law should be equally enforced—even though equal enforcement is often unrealistic—than to say that the law should be used by the police to maintain order acceptable to local communities[.]" But if there is promise in these policing reforms, there is also peril.

Courts have little capacity—very little capacity—to constrain police and to control the discretion that they inevitably exercise on streets, in neighborhoods, in the precincts where patrol officers are given their tours of duty, and in the administrative offices in which police enforcement policies are hammered out. The reforms of the 1960s and 1970s established principles from which no thoughtful person now seeks retreat: that police cannot be delegated authority to maintain order as they see fit and that rules governing the conduct of citizens on the street must set forth intelligible limits on enforcement authority. These reforms, however, could not eliminate the significant discretion that police have in order maintenance tasks, nor could they promote the beneficial exercise of that discretion in ways that might enhance rather than imperil the public life of a community. Interpreted too broadly, the open texture of these constitutional reforms could threaten public order by invalidating the reasonable efforts of communities to regulate matters like unreasonable noise, aggressive panhandling, or loitering on a street corner to solicit customers for the sale of drugs. At the same time, the reforms could not ensure that police departments acted fairly, with restraint, and with an abiding respect for the rights of individuals and for constitutional values. The reforms could not solve the problem of police discretion.

Nor can neighborhoods and their police. But perhaps communities and police departments, prompted by the problems that beset them and the new philosophies that point in a different direction, might take up the task—an ongoing one—of better managing police discretion. . . . There is a dense complexity to the problem of public order with which communities are now grappling and to the enduring problem of controlling the police. Perhaps some views from the bottom up — views that begin with the recognition that neighborhoods and police departments will succeed or fail in their efforts to deal with local problems at the local level, in communities and in neighborhoods, where laws are passed and police policies are pursued — might be in order.

6. The Lawyers and the Trial Courts

PAUL B. WICE, CHAOS IN THE COURTHOUSE: THE INNER WORKINGS OF THE URBAN CRIMINAL COURTS

21-24, 63-65 (1985)

The first problem faced by all cities visited[9] was inadequate staffing. Although particular agencies or institutions within each city's criminal justice system may have differing levels of understaffing, all were handicapped in some degree by personnel shortages. . . . These shortages were documented by federal commission studies in 1967 and 1973.[2] . . .

. . . The judges appeared to be most understaffed at the earlier stages of the adjudicative process — initial appearance, preliminary hearing and arraignment. The arraignment court may also be responsible for deciding pretrial motions, scheduling trials, and conducting pre-sentencing hearings in addition to accepting guilty pleas. By the trial stage, the staffing shortages had generally abated to a tolerable level in most cities. . . .

Closely related to the staffing problems, is the serious backlog of cases. . . .

The most common method criminal courts utilize in dealing with their caseload and delay problems is the practice of plea bargaining. Despite the negative connotations of this term, it describes a negotiating process which has been taking place within our nation's court systems . . . for many decades. A *plea bargain* is simply an agreement between the defendant (with the advice of his attorney) and the prosecutor, that in exchange for a plea of guilty, he will receive favorable consideration by the court. This consideration usually takes the form of being charged with a less serious crime, which will usually result in a lighter sentence or receiving the minimum punishment allowable for the originally-charged offense. The rationale behind this exchange of favors is that the defendant is given the lesser sentence because of his cooperation with the court in choosing not to go to trial and thereby saving the city a great deal of time and expense. . . .

. . . Various studies have indicated that approximately 75 percent of all defendants indicted for felonies plead guilty.[5] . . .

9. This book is based on the study of criminal courts in 15 major jurisdictions over a 12-year period. Chaos in the Courthouse 1. — Eds.

2. President's Commission on Law Enforcement and the Administration of Justice, Task Force Report: The Courts. (Washington, D.C.: Government Printing Office, 1967); National Advisory Commission on Criminal Justice Goals and Standards, Courts. (Washington, D.C.: Government Printing Office, 1973).

5. Pasqual DeVito. An Experiment in the Use of Court Statistics, Judicature. 56 (August/September, 1972), p. 56.

Since nearly two thirds of all defendants accused of committing a felony are indigent, the state is constitutionally obligated to provide the overwhelming majority of defendants with assistance of counsel. In nearly every city visited, the local courts decided to establish a public defender program in order to meet this mandate. . . .

The two alternatives to the public defender plan, for indigent defendants, are either to rely entirely upon an assigned counsel system — privately-appointed members of the bar who are typically paid on a per hour basis — or a mixed system in which the courts have decided to limit the percentage of cases which the local public defender can handle, and reserve the sizable remainder for private attorneys through an assigned counsel system. Large cities rarely find the assigned counsel system cost-effective (although it is most popular in small cities and rural areas). . . .

In most cities, the defendant first notifies the judge of his indigent status and desire to have a court-appointed lawyer at his initial appearance. . . . The judge rarely inquires into the financial capabilities of the defendant. . . . Most judges seem to feel that if a defendant is willing to settle for a public defender, then he is not likely to be in possession of the funds necessary to hire a private attorney. Rarely is a representative from the public defender's office present at this initial appearance, except in an administrative capacity to commence the paperwork. . . .

Two of the major frustrations facing the indigent defendant who is being represented by a public defender are apparent very early in the process. The first, and for many defendants, the most disheartening, is the absence of choice of attorney. . . .

The second frustration, exacerbating the already noted absence of choice, is the assembly-line system of defense in which the indigent defendant may be assisted by a different attorney at nearly every stage of the proceedings up to the arraignment. This means that the indigent will briefly meet with three or four different public defenders for a few minutes before each of his pretrial proceedings. It is also likely that interviews and meetings outside of court may be with an assortment of different public defenders. . . .

For many defendants, the assembly-line style of operation is another indication that the public defender's office is simply an uncaring bureaucracy which is both financially and emotionally subservient to the criminal court judiciary. . . .

Although I am sure that their clientele would vociferously disagree, I do not believe that the quality of public defender services has suffered. After conducting national studies of both public defender programs and private criminal lawyers, I am in agreement with the findings of nearly all of the empirical research which concluded that the ultimate case dispositions are not significantly affected by the type of defense.[31] I still concur with the personal conclusions reached in 1978 that

> although the middle 50 percent of public defenders and private attorneys were operating at similar levels of ability and achieving nearly identical results, there were marked differences at the extremes. Thus it was generally agreed by the criminal lawyers that the top 25 percent of private attorneys were clearly superior to the

---

31. Jean Taylor et al., An Analysis of Defense Counsel in the Processing of Felony Defendants in San Diego, Denver Law Journal (1972), p. 233.

best public defenders, while the bottom 25 percent of the public defenders were believed to be significantly better than the bottom group of private attorneys. [Paul Wice, Criminal Lawyers: An Endangered Species. Beverly Hills, Sage Publications, 1978, p. 201.]

. . . [T]he public defender office may even offer some distinct advantages unavailable to certain private practitioners. Most public defenders have access to their own law libraries, as well as limited use of investigators. Additionally, the public defender is clearly a criminal law specialist. Finally, because of his continual involvement with the prosecutors and judiciary, the public defender can frequently develop a positive working relationship in which the exchange of favors, so necessary to greasing the squeaky wheel of justice, can directly benefit the indigent defendant.

BRUCE JACKSON, LAW AND DISORDER: CRIMINAL JUSTICE IN AMERICA

81 (1984)

Private counsel retained by wealthy clients may assume their clients are innocent, civil rights lawyers representing defendants in politically motivated cases may assume their clients are innocent, but most public defender and court-appointed attorneys — and they handle the greatest bulk of the criminal cases — assume their clients are guilty. "If he's not guilty of this one, he's guilty of one just like it," one public defense lawyer said to me. "He knows it and I know it. Why go up there and argue? Almost everybody in these tanks is guilty of something. Everybody knows that. My job is to see that these people get out of here with as little jail time as possible. You don't win anything in this job because none of these clients are winners." The only time a defendant without funds gets extensive trial and appeal representation is when his case has political aspects and it is picked up by an organization willing to fund it or by an attorney who is not concerned with money. There are not many such organizations and there are not many such attorneys.

Most criminal justice lawyers work as partners with the court and the prosecutors, not as unequivocal representatives of the defendants. The defendants come and go, but the attorney's relationships with the other officers of the court continue for years.

ABRAHAM S. BLUMBERG, THE PRACTICE OF LAW AS CONFIDENCE GAME: ORGANIZATIONAL CO-OPTATION OF A PROFESSION

1 Law & Soc'y Rev. 15, 18-26, 29-31 (No. 2, 1967)

The overwhelming majority of convictions in criminal cases (usually over 90 percent) are not the product of a combative, trial-by-jury process at all, but instead merely involve the sentencing of the individual after a negotiated, bargained-for plea of guilty has been entered. . . .

Organizational goals and discipline impose a set of demands and conditions of practice on the respective professions in the criminal court, to which they respond by abandoning their ideological and professional commitments to the accused client, in the service of these higher claims of the court organization. All court personnel, including the accused's own lawyer, tend to be co-opted to become agent-mediators who help the accused redefine his situation and restructure his perceptions concomitant with a plea of guilty.

Of all the occupational roles in the court the only private individual who is officially recognized as having a special status and concomitant obligations is the lawyer. His legal status is that of "an officer of the court" and he is held to a standard of ethical performance and duty to his client as well as to the court. This obligation is thought to be far higher than that expected of ordinary individuals occupying the various occupational statuses in the court community. However, lawyers, whether privately retained or of the legal-aid, public defender variety, have close and continuing relations with the prosecuting office and the court itself through discreet relations with the judges via their law secretaries or "confidential" assistants. Indeed, lines of communication, influence and contact with those offices, as well as with the Office of the Clerk of the court, Probation Division, and with the press, are essential to present and prospective requirements of criminal law practice. Similarly, the subtle involvement of the press and other mass media in the court's organizational network is not readily discernible to the casual observer. Accused persons come and go in the court system schema, but the structure and its occupational incumbents remain to carry on their respective career, occupational and organizational enterprises. The individual stridencies, tensions, and conflicts a given accused person's case may present to all the participants are overcome, because the formal and informal relations of all the groups in the court setting require it. The probability of continued future relations and interaction must be preserved at all costs.

This is particularly true of the "lawyer regulars" i.e., those defense lawyers, who by virtue of their continuous appearances in behalf of defendants, tend to represent the bulk of a criminal court's non-indigent case workload, and those lawyers who are not "regulars," who appear almost casually in behalf of an occasional client. Some of the "lawyer regulars" are highly visible as one moves about the major urban centers of the nation, their offices line the back streets of the courthouses, at times sharing space with bondsmen. Their political "visibility" in terms of local club house ties, reaching into the judge's chambers and prosecutor's office, are also deemed essential to successful practitioners. . . .

. . . The accused's lawyer has far greater professional, economic, intellectual and other ties to the various elements of the court system than he does to his own client. In short, the court is a closed community.

This is more than just the case of the usual "secrets" of bureaucracy which are fanatically defended from an outside view. Even all elements of the press are zealously determined to report on that which will not offend the board of judges, the prosecutor, probation, legal-aid, or other officials, in return for privileges and courtesies granted in the past and to be granted in the future. Rather than any view of the matter in terms of some variation of a "conspiracy" hypothesis, the simple explanation is one of an ongoing system handling delicate tensions, managing the trauma produced by law enforcement and administration, and requiring almost pathological distrust of "outsiders" bordering on group paranoia.

The hostile attitude toward "outsiders" is in large measure engendered by a defensiveness itself produced by the inherent deficiencies of assembly line justice, so characteristic of our major criminal courts. Intolerably large caseloads of defendants which must be disposed of in an organizational context of limited resources and personnel, potentially subject the participants in the court community to harsh scrutiny from appellate courts, and other public and private sources of condemnation. As a consequence, an almost irreconcilable conflict is posed in terms of intense pressures to process large numbers of cases on the one hand, and the stringent ideological and legal requirements of "due process of law," on the other hand. A rather tenuous resolution of the dilemma has emerged in the shape of a large variety of bureaucratically ordained and controlled "work crimes," short cuts, deviations, and outright rule violations adopted as court practice in order to meet production norms. Fearfully anticipating criticism on ethical as well as legal grounds, all the significant participants in the court's social structure are bound into an organized system of complicity. This consists of a work arrangement in which the patterned, covert, informal breaches, and evasions of "due process" are institutionalized, but are, nevertheless, denied to exist.

These institutionalized evasions will be found to occur to some degree, in all criminal courts. Their nature, scope and complexity are largely determined by the size of the court, and the character of the community in which it is located, e.g., whether it is a large, urban institution, or a relatively small rural county court. In addition, idiosyncratic, local conditions may contribute to a unique flavor in the character and quality of the criminal law's administration in a particular community. However, in most instances a variety of stratagems are employed — some subtle, some crude, in effectively disposing of what are often too large caseloads. A wide variety of coercive devices are employed against an accused-client, couched in a depersonalized, instrumental, bureaucratic version of due process of law, and which are in reality a perfunctory obeisance to the ideology of due process. These include some very explicit pressures which are exerted in some measure by all court personnel, including judges, to plead guilty and avoid trial. In many instances the sanction of a potentially harsh sentence is utilized as the visible alternative to pleading guilty, in the case of recalcitrants. Probation and psychiatric reports are "tailored" to organizational needs, or are at least responsive to the court organization's requirements for the refurbishment of a defendant's social biography, consonant with his new status. A resourceful judge can, through his subtle domination of the proceedings, impose his will on the final outcome of a trial. Stenographers and clerks, in their function as record keepers, are on occasion pressed into service in support of a judicial need to "rewrite" the record of a courtroom event. Bail practices are usually employed for purposes other than simply assuring a defendant's presence on the date of a hearing in connection with his case. Too often, the discretionary power as to bail is part of the arsenal of weapons available to collapse the resistance of an accused person. The foregoing is a most cursory examination of some of the more prominent "short cuts" available to any court organization. . . .

The real key to understanding the role of defense counsel in a criminal case is to be found in the area of the fixing of the fee to be charged and its collection. The problem of fixing and collecting the fee tends to influence to a significant degree the criminal court process itself, and not just the relationship of the lawyer and his client. In essence, a lawyer-client "confidence game" is played. . . . Legal service lends itself particularly well to confidence games. . . .

. . . [M]uch legal activity, whether it is at the lowest or highest "white shoe" law firm levels, is of the brokerage, agent, sales representative, lobbyist type of activity, in which the lawyer acts for someone else in pursuing the latter's interests and designs. The service is intangible. . . .

. . . Defense lawyers condition even the most obtuse clients to recognize that there is a firm interconnection between fee payment and the zealous exercise of professional expertise, secret knowledge, and organizational "connections" in their behalf. Lawyers, therefore, seek to keep their clients in a proper state of tension, and to arouse in them the precise edge of anxiety which is calculated to encourage prompt fee payment. Consequently, the client attitude in the relationship between defense counsel and an accused is in many instances a precarious admixture of hostility, mistrust, dependence, and sycophancy. By keeping his client's anxieties aroused to the proper pitch, and establishing a seemingly causal relationship between a requested fee and the accused's ultimate extrication from his onerous difficulties, the lawyer will have established the necessary preliminary groundwork to assure a minimum of haggling over the fee and its eventual payment.

In varying degrees, as a consequence, all law practice involves a manipulation of the client and a stage management of the lawyer-client relationship so that at least an *appearance* of help and service will be forthcoming. This is accomplished in a variety of ways, often exercised in combination with each other. At the outset, the lawyer-professional employs with suitable variation a measure of sales-puff which may range from an air of unbounding self-confidence, adequacy, and dominion over events, to that of complete arrogance. This will be supplemented by the affectation of a studied, faultless mode of personal attire. In the larger firms, furnishings and office trappings will serve as the backdrop to help in impression management and client intimidation. In all firms, solo or large scale, an access to secret knowledge, and to the seats of power and influence is inferred, or presumed to a varying degree as the basic vendible commodity of the practitioners. . . .

The fee is often collected in stages, each installment usually payable prior to a necessary court appearance required during the course of an accused's career journey. At each stage, in his interviews and communications with the accused, or in addition, with members of his family, if they are helping with the fee payment, the lawyer employs an air of professional confidence and "inside-dopesterism" in order to assuage anxieties on all sides. He makes the necessary bland assurances, and in effect manipulates his client, who is usually willing to do and say the things, true or not, which will help his attorney extricate him. Since the dimensions of what he is essentially selling, organizational influence and expertise, are not technically and precisely measurable, the lawyer can make extravagant claims of influence and secret knowledge with impunity. Thus, lawyers frequently claim to have inside knowledge in connection with information in the hands of the D.A., police, probation officials or to have access to these functionaries. Factually, they often do, and need only to exaggerate the nature of their relationships with them to obtain the desired effective impression upon the client. But, as in the genuine confidence game, the victim who has participated is loathe to do anything which will upset the lesser plea which his lawyer has "conned" him into accepting.

In effect, in his role as double agent, the criminal lawyer performs an extremely vital and delicate mission for the court organization and the accused. Both principals are anxious to terminate the litigation with a minimum of expense and damage to each other. There is no other personage or role incumbent in the total court structure more strategically located, who by training and in terms of his own requirements, is more ideally suited to do so than the lawyer. In recognition of this, judges will cooperate with attorneys in many important ways. For example, they will adjourn the case of an accused in jail awaiting plea or sentence if the attorney requests such action. While explicitly this may be done for some innocuous and seemingly valid reason, the tacit purpose is that pressure is being applied by the attorney for the collection of his fee, which he knows will probably not be forthcoming if the case is concluded. Judges are aware of this tactic on the part of lawyers, who, by requesting an adjournment, keep an accused incarcerated a while longer as a not too subtle method of dunning a client for payment. However, the judges will go along with this, on the ground that important ends are being served. Often, the only end served is to protect a lawyer's fee.

The judge will help an accused's lawyer in still another way. He will lend the official aura of his office and courtroom so that a lawyer can stage manage an impression of an "all out" performance for the accused in justification of his fee. The judge and other court personnel will serve as a backdrop for a scene charged with dramatic fire, in which the accused's lawyer makes a stirring appeal in his behalf. With a show of restrained passion, the lawyer will intone the virtues of the accused and recite the social deprivations which have reduced him to his present state. The speech varies somewhat, depending on whether the accused has been convicted after trial or has pleaded guilty. In the main, however, the incongruity, superficiality, and ritualistic character of the total performance is underscored by a visibly impassive, almost bored reaction on the part of the judge and other members of the court retinue.

Afterward, there is a hearty exchange of pleasantries between the lawyer and district attorney, wholly out of context in terms of the supposed adversary nature of the preceding events. The fiery passion in defense of his client is gone, and the lawyers for both sides resume their offstage relations, chatting amiably and perhaps including the judge in their restrained banter. No other aspect of their visible conduct so effectively serves to put even a casual observer on notice, that these individuals have claims upon each other. These seemingly innocuous actions are indicative of continuing organizational and informal relations, which, in their intricacy and depth, range far beyond any priorities or claims a particular defendant may have. . . .

RODNEY J. UPHOFF, THE CRIMINAL DEFENSE LAWYER AS EFFECTIVE NEGOTIATOR: A SYSTEMIC APPROACH

2 Clinical L. Rev. 73-94 (1995)

I. UNDERSTANDING THE CONTEXT: THE PRESSURE TO PLEA BARGAIN

A. SYSTEMIC PRESSURES TO PLEAD GUILTY . . .

Blumberg undoubtedly is correct that there are criminal defense lawyers of limited ability, zeal or professional commitment who do manipulate their clients into ill-advised plea bargains. Some lawyers do promote their own interests at the expense of their client's best interest. Moreover, Blumberg's analysis highlights the substantial systemic pressures on criminal defense lawyers to behave in a cooperative, non-adversarial manner. And yet, Blumberg's condemnation of criminal defense lawyers as double agents sweeps too broadly. There are simply too many dedicated defense lawyers, too much litigation and too many other variables affecting client decisionmaking to conclude that manipulative, complicitous criminal defense lawyers are the cause of most plea bargaining. . . .

2. The Pressures on Defendants to Plead Guilty

The decision of many defendants to plead guilty is the product of a number of individual forces and systemic factors which have little to do with the behavior of criminal defense lawyers. Indeed, the zeal or even the availability of counsel may have little [effect] on the defendant's decision. Simply put, a significant number of defendants just want to plead guilty. Few criminal defendants, even those who are innocent, actually want to go to trial. Many who are accused of a crime do not even consider going to trial a viable option.

Criminal defendants offer a variety of reasons to explain their reluctance to go to trial and their interest in a plea bargain. Internal as well as external pressures may shape the defendant's attitude. For many defendants, the prospect of actually going through a trial and having to take the witness stand is very intimidating. Fear, embarrassment, or the risk of adverse publicity drives some defendants to negotiate and to avoid trial. Unquestionably, the risk of a jail sentence or the prospects of a harsher sentence also deters many defendants from viewing a trial as a desirable alternative to pleading guilty. For some, a pessimistic or fatalistic mind-set dampens any enthusiasm for going to trial. Standing up to the state by taking a case to trial is similar to taking on city hall, a Sisyphean task few are willing to readily embrace.

Some defendants, of course, have been through the system before and these prior experiences significantly influence their attitude toward plea bargaining. For some, especially defendants of color, their perception that the system is heavily stacked against them adversely affects their view of a trial as a viable option. For other defendants, many criminal cases just do not seem to be "that big a deal" or are "nothing really to worry about." For these defendants, the time and trouble it would take to fight a particular charge is outweighed by the inconvenience the defendant feels. It is easier and quicker simply to plead guilty and to get the matter resolved rather than spend time going to trial even if the charge is baseless or the prosecution's evidence is very weak. Thus, the defendant's attitude about the charge, his or her other responsibilities and time commitments, financial resources, past experiences and perceptions about the criminal justice system all affect the defendant's ability to resist the pressure to enter a negotiated plea.

Some defendants readily admit their guilt and are reluctant to do anything other than acknowledge responsibility for the crime or crimes committed. Sometimes this reaction is fed by the defendant's religious or moral feelings. In other instances, the defendant's "get it over with" attitude is spurred on by concerns that contesting a charge will have a negative effect on the defendant's family, financial situation or employment status. Such defendants may be unaware of or fail to consider the long-term consequences of a hasty decision to plead guilty. . . .

Many defendants, especially those who have already been through the system, recognize that the criminal justice system encourages the resolution of cases through plea bargaining. The prospect of securing a more lenient sentence, in fact, drives many defendants to want to plead guilty. The defendant who received a significant break in an earlier case may be particularly anxious to enter into a plea bargain. Or the defendant may be savvy enough to know that it is advantageous to deal quickly with the police or prosecutor before other potential defendants or coconspirators do. Indeed, a lawyer bent on finding the facts in an initial interview may be brusquely instructed or directed by a seasoned defendant just to "cut a deal." . . .

Notwithstanding counsel's advice, it is often the defendant, not the so-called "double agent" defense lawyer, who is insistent on working out a plea bargain. In many cases defendants simply recognize that our overburdened criminal justice system has been structured to discourage them from going to trial. Too few criminal defendants can really afford to pay the cost of mounting an effective defense. In some jurisdictions, access to appointed counsel, the quality of indigent defenders and the resources provided to support the defense of the indigent affect the extent to which defendants have a meaningful right to go to trial. The unrepresented defendant or the accused able to scrape up only a minimal retainer faces substantial pressure to plead guilty. Take, for example, the defendant who has used his last $500 to bail himself out and to retain counsel. His lawyer threatens to withdraw unless the defendant pays an additional $2,000 for a trial. Rather than fight the charge, the defendant pleads guilty to save the $2,000 fee. Or he accepts the proffered plea bargain because he simply cannot raise any more money. Thus, economic pressures often eliminate the criminal defendant's right to trial as a viable option.

Those pressures intensify for the defendant who is held in jail unable to make bail. Many defendants, especially first offenders, will agree to almost anything to get out of jail. It is all too common for defendants to enter a guilty plea merely as the quickest means to secure their release from jail. Accordingly, defense counsel's ability to secure her client's release on bond is likely to minimize pressure on the defendant to agree to a poor plea bargain, thereby significantly improving counsel's negotiating position.

3. Judicial and Prosecutorial Pressures

Both trial judges and appellate courts contribute to the systemic pressure on defendants to plea bargain. Judges are increasingly under fire by the public and state legislators who clamor for tougher sentences and an end to the "coddling" of criminals. Trial judges, many of whom are elected, cannot grant defendants too many sentencing concessions without being labeled "soft on crime." Yet, overflowing court dockets and prison overcrowding create conflicting pressure on judges to move cases efficiently while still imposing tough sentences. Plea bargaining enables trial judges to resolve large numbers of cases in an orderly, timely fashion that would not be possible if more cases actually went to trial.

Criminal defendants also are discouraged from challenging questionable rulings on suppression issues or taking marginal cases to trial because appellate review often is a lengthy process in which defendants enjoy only limited success. In addition, the expanded application of the harmless error doctrine, the diminution of

the exclusionary rule, the narrowing of the scope of federal habeas corpus relief
and the difficulty of showing ineffective assistance of counsel also encourage defendants to settle their cases. The message sent to defendants and defense lawyers,
whether intended or not, is to cooperate and not litigate.

Trial judges send a similar message to defendants contemplating a trial: go to
trial and if you lose, you will get a stiffer sentence. Even if the defendant is initially
unaware of this reality, defense counsel when discussing the defendant's options
usually will raise this consideration. The uncertainty of success at trial, combined
with the real prospect of a harsher penalty should the defendant lose, makes the
trial option for many defendants a risky gamble. Thus, the defendant's fear of jail
not only may seriously undercut counsel's ability to project a credible threat to go
to trial, but also cripple the client's will to hold out for a better bargain.

Like their indigent defender counterparts, most prosecutors' offices lack sufficient resources to adequately investigate, prepare and try many cases. Prosecutors,
therefore, also are subject to considerable pressure to settle the vast majority of
cases. Unlike defense lawyers, however, prosecutors retain considerable power and
discretion in determining when cases are brought, which cases are dismissed or
pushed and how cases are ultimately settled. Courts have given prosecutors broad
latitude both in the charging decision and in the bargaining process. The prosecutor often can select from a wide range of potential charges growing out of any
criminal episode, which permits the prosecutor to charge one or multiple counts.
In addition, prosecutors generally are free to offer concessions or to threaten
additional punishment to force defendants to accept some negotiated deal.
Prosecutors are well aware of the allure of a "no jail" recommendation and use
it frequently to entice a defendant into a guilty plea in a marginal case, especially if
the offer includes a reduction to a misdemeanor charge. Because a prosecutor's
sentencing recommendations are readily accepted by most judges and the prosecutor is vested with virtually unfettered charging discretion, it is the prosecutor
who really is in the position to dictate the level of punishment meted out to most
defendants. . . .

B. RESISTING THE PRESSURE TO CONFORM

The culture in any particular criminal justice system ultimately influences how
plea bargaining is conducted in that jurisdiction and how many cases actually go to
trial. If in a particular jurisdiction few defense lawyers file motions or take cases to
trial, the pressure on other defense lawyers and defendants to follow suit is much
greater than in a jurisdiction in which defendants regularly exercise their right to
go to trial. A defense lawyer in a jurisdiction in which prosecutors rarely have
to make any concessions because few cases are tried may find it more difficult
to extract reasonable concessions from the prosecutor, even though the state's
case is weak, than defense counsel in a county with a vigorous defense bar. The
prosecutor in a county with a timid defense bar may single out the more zealous
defense lawyer and refuse to provide her clients the kind of concessions generally
provided the more pliant defense lawyers. Defense counsel who stands up to fight
in one case may be concerned that the prosecutor will take it out on her other
clients. . . .

Thus, the conscientious defense lawyer is often in a precarious position.
Defense counsel must attempt to provide zealous representation in a system

geared to the efficient resolution of cases which, for the most part, means entering into negotiated settlements. It is the criminal defense lawyer who vigorously investigates the facts, researches the law, raises appropriate and creative motions, demonstrates a willingness to go to trial and competently handles the trial who is providing the representation demanded by the ethical rules and ABA Standards. Yet, counsel who seeks to gain an advantage for her client in the plea bargaining process by engaging in legitimate tactics—such as filing and aggressively litigating discovery motions, suppression motions, requests for jury instructions, and the like—runs the risk of alienating judges and prosecutors primarily concerned about efficiently disposing of the mass of cases on their crowded dockets. Similarly, a good defense lawyer may want to respond to a prosecutor's inappropriate or unjustified threats in the plea bargaining process by refusing to continue to negotiate and going to trial. She may want to do so not only to secure justice for her individual client but also to demonstrate her willingness to go to trial rather than accept a poor plea bargain. Defense counsel may find herself, however, forced to agree to a poor plea bargain despite her efforts, recommendations and desires because ultimately the choice of accepting a proffered settlement is the client's.

It is important to recognize, then, that it is the defendant's interests, attitude and desires, together with various systemic pressures, that frequently put criminal defense lawyers in a difficult and frustrating position. Defense lawyers all too often find themselves representing an unsympathetic defendant with a lengthy criminal record in a case without any apparent defense. The zealous advocate with a case in which the defendant has little or no leverage confronts a daunting challenge. Many defense lawyers have endured the unpleasant task of going to negotiate on behalf of an unemployed recidivist who simply wants to plead guilty and "bargaining" with a particularly hard-headed prosecutor who is perfectly aware that the state's case is virtually unassailable. In such a case, defense counsel may feel more like a beggar than a bargainer, left with little more than the unenviable chore of imploring a mean-spirited prosecutor to be fair or reasonable. . . .

7. The Supreme Court

ANTHONY AMSTERDAM, THE SUPREME COURT AND THE RIGHTS OF SUSPECTS IN CRIMINAL CASES

45 N.Y.U. L. Rev. 785, 785-794 (1970)

The impression is widespread that decisions of the Supreme Court of the United States during the past decade have vastly enlarged the rights of criminal suspects and defendants. That impression is not wholly unfounded, but the broad form in which it is generally entertained ignores very significant limitations upon what the Supreme Court can do, and what it has in fact done, to create and enforce such rights. . . .

According to Par Lagerkvist,[1] the role of the Pythia or priestess of the Oracle at Delphi was of incomparable grandeur and futility. This young maiden was

_____

1. P. Lagerkvist, The Sibyl (N. Walford transl. 1958).

periodically lashed to a tripod above a noisome abyss, where her god dwelt and from which nauseating odors rose and assaulted her. There, the god entered her body and soul, so that she thrashed madly and uttered inspired, incomprehensible cries. The cries were interpreted by the corps of professional priests of the Oracle, and their interpretations were, of course, for mere mortals the words of the god. The Pythia experienced incalculable ecstasy and degradation; she was viewed with utmost reverence and abhorrence; to her every utterance, enormous importance attached; but, from the practical point of view, what she said did not matter much.

On its tripod atop the system of American criminal justice, the Supreme Court of the United States performs in remarkably Pythian fashion. Occasional ill-smelling cases are wafted up to it by the fortuities of litigation, evoking its inspired and spasmodic reaction. Neither the records nor the issues presented by these cases give the Court a comprehensive view — or even a reliably representative view — of the doings in the dark pit in which criminal suspects, police and the functionaries of the criminal courts wrestle with each other in the sightless ooze. It is not surprising, then, that in these cases the Court should be incapable of announcing judgments which respond coherently to the real problems of the pit. No matter. The significance of the Court's pronouncements — their power to shake the assembled faithful with awful tremors of exultation and loathing — does not depend upon their correspondence with reality. Once uttered, these pronouncements will be interpreted by arrays of lower appellate courts, trial judges, magistrates, commissioners and police officials. *Their* interpretation of the Pythia, for all practical purposes, will become the word of god.

To some extent this Pythian metaphor describes the Supreme Court's functioning in all the fields of law with which the Court deals. But the metaphor has special cogency with regard to the field of criminal procedure and particularly procedure that regulates the rights of suspects in their dealings with police prior to the time of the suspect's first court appearance. Let me explain why this is so and some of the implications of that fact.

First, the Supreme Court, like any other court, lacks the sort of supervisory power over the practices of the police that is possessed by the chief of police or the district attorney. The Court can only review those practices, and thus can only define the rights of suspects subject to those practices, when the practices become an issue in a lawsuit. There are several ways in which police practices may become the subject of a lawsuit. An individual who thinks that he has been mistreated by the police may file a civil action for damages or, in limited circumstances, for an injunction, complaining of false arrest or false imprisonment or assault or the violation of his constitutional rights. But such lawsuits are very rare, and until recently were so rare as to be insignificant, because the obstacles to their maintenance are formidable. Most persons mistreated by the police are marginal types who are quite happy, once out of police clutches, to let well enough alone. Few have the knowledge or resources to obtain the services of a lawyer. Many lawyers who might otherwise be available to them cannot afford to tangle with the police because these lawyers depend upon the good will of the police in other cases (e.g., to protect a divorce client who is being badgered by her estranged husband or to reduce charges against a criminal client) or upon police testimony in other cases (e.g., motor vehicle accident cases) or upon more dubious police services (e.g., referrals).

Juries are not sympathetic to suits against the police; policemen are seldom sufficiently solvent to make verdicts against them worth the trouble to obtain; even fairly solid citizens who sue policemen may have to fear reprisals in the form of traffic tickets, refusals to give needed aid and similar harassments. As a result, civil suits seldom bring police practices under judicial scrutiny. And for reasons too obvious to detail, criminal charges against policemen for mistreatment of citizens are even rarer than civil suits.

So, to date the Supreme Court has had occasion to review the conduct of police almost exclusively in criminal cases where the defendant is the asserted victim of police misconduct. The way in which the issue of police misconduct is presented in such cases almost invariably involves the application of the "exclusionary rule" — that is, an evidentiary rule which disallows the admission against a criminal defendant, at his trial, of certain kinds of evidence obtained in violation of his rights. This exclusionary rule, whose scope and utility in enforcing various constitutional guarantees has been considerably expanded by the Supreme Court in the past decade, is today the principal instrument of judicial control of the police and the principal vehicle for announcement by the courts of the rights of suspects in their dealings with the police.

This last point, in itself, has important implications. Certain police practices (for example, the "booking" and "mugging" of suspects and the assorted minor or major indignities that attend station-house detention of suspects, ranging from the taking of a suspect's belt and shoelaces to vicious beatings) will virtually never become the subjects of judicial scrutiny because they virtually never produce evidence against the suspect. Since there can arise no exclusionary rule challenges to these practices, there have been no significant judicial decisions concerning them; and since (as I shall develop shortly) judicial decisions are almost the only source of legal rights of suspects, suspects do not now have legal rights against or in connection with such practices.

Other police practices (for example, refusing arrested suspects the right to use the telephone or detaining them in pig-sty cells) may or may not come under judicial consideration, depending upon whether they do or do not produce evidentiary consequences such as confessions. For several reasons, judicial control of the latter practices and judicial definition of a suspect's rights in connection with those practices must remain an imprecise, haphazard business. Under the exclusionary rule, judicial attention is focused upon an evidentiary product of the practices rather than upon the practices themselves. For example, a confession will ordinarily be the product of several such practices and of other adventitious circumstances such as the suspect's age and psychological makeup, the nature of police interrogation, etc. Consequently, a judicial ruling admitting or excluding it will seldom give occasion for a clear-cut pronouncement concerning the legality of any one of the underlying practices. Moreover, because these practices themselves are not the focus of the litigation, they will usually be imperfectly explained and explored in the record made before the courts. Courts which pass judgment on them may do so half-sightedly; or, realizing this danger, the courts may strive to avoid passing judgment upon practices that they know they do not understand. The result, once again, is that courts are unable to speak clearly concerning any particular or specific rights of a criminal suspect. Still less are they able to develop systematically any comprehensive canon or register of suspects' rights in the context of the entire range of police practices that affect the suspect.

Second, the Supreme Court of the United States is uniquely unable to take a comprehensive view of the subject of suspects' rights. In part its inability is simply a function of the Court's workload. Saddled with a back-breaking docket and properly occupied with other matters of grave national importance, the Court can only hear three or four cases a year involving the treatment of criminal suspects by the police.

Workload is not the Court's only problem. I have said earlier that fortuities determine which criminal cases reach the Supreme Court. Because police practices are ordinarily challengeable only through the exclusionary rule and because the exclusionary rule ordinarily comes into play only at trial following a plea of not guilty, police treatment of a suspect is effectively insulated against Supreme Court review in that large percentage of criminal convictions (as many as 90 percent in some jurisdictions) that rest upon a guilty plea.

Guilty pleas may be entered for many reasons in cases that involve serious questions of violations of a suspect's rights in the precourt phases. The arguable violations may have had no evidentiary consequences. The prosecution may have sufficient evidence for conviction apart from that obtained through the arguable violations. The defendant may be detained pending trial in default of bail on a charge for which a probationary or "time-served" sentence is likely, so that he will be imprisoned longer awaiting trial on a plea of not guilty than he would as a result of a quick guilty plea. The prosecutor may offer an attractive plea bargain, or the known sentencing practices of the trial judge may promise similar consideration for a guilty plea. Obviously, these factors that determine the entry of a guilty plea do not systematically send to trial a selection of cases which present the courts with any comprehensive set of issues relative to suspects' rights.

Additional selective factors prevent many of the cases that are tried from being appealed or from being carried all the way to the Supreme Court. Factual findings by the trial judge concerning contested police conduct frequently obscure or entirely obstruct the presentation to appellate courts of issues relating to that conduct. A convicted defendant cannot challenge on appeal any treatment by the police that the trial court, crediting incredible police denials, finds did not occur. (For example, suspects invariably "trip" and strike their heads while entering their cells; they are never shoved against the bars by police.) Also, the trial court may admit the police conduct but credit incredible explanations of it. (For example, the humiliating anal examinations to which some suspects are subjected in police stations are justified as "weapons searches" on police testimony that such suspects are known to conceal razor blades between their buttocks.) Finally, the trial court may admit and resolve against the defendant an issue relating to the legality of police conduct, then sentence him so lightly that an appeal is not worthwhile. (Some trial judges will impose light sentences in cases in which they have made dubious evidentiary rulings, thereby "buying off" appeals.) In any event the presentation of a convicted defendant's appeal—still more, the taking of his case to the Supreme Court—depends upon the energy, dedication and painstaking care of his lawyer, commodities understandably scarce on the part of overworked public defenders or private lawyers conscripted without compensation to represent the indigents who constitute the bulk of convicted persons.

For these reasons, the Supreme Court simply never gets to see many of the police practices that raise the most pervasive and significant issues of suspects' rights. The cases which do come to the Court are selected by a process that can only be described as capricious insofar as it may be relied upon to present the Court any opportunity for systematic development of a body of legal rights of individuals in the police, or precourt, phases of criminal proceedings. Therefore, the Court's ability to serve as architect of such a body of rights is woefully slight.

Third, the Court is further disabled by the fact that almost the only law relating to police practices or to suspects' rights is the law that the Court itself makes by its judicial decisions. Statutes and administrative regulations governing these matters are virtually nonexistent. The ubiquitous lack of legislative and executive attention to the problems of police treatment of suspects both forces the Court into the role of lawmaker in this area and makes it virtually impossible for the Court effectively to play that role.

This point has been largely ignored by the Court's conservative critics. The judicial "activism" that they deplore, usually citing the Court's "handcuffing" of the police, has been the almost inevitable consequence of the failure of other agencies of law to assume responsibility for regulating police practices. In most areas of constitutional law the Supreme Court of the United States plays a backstopping role, reviewing the ultimate permissibility of dispositions and policies guided in the first instance by legislative enactments, administrative rules or local common-law traditions. In the area of controls upon the police, a vast abnegation of responsibility at the level of each of these ordinary sources of legal rulemaking has forced the Court to construct *all* the law regulating the everyday functioning of the police. Of course, the Court has responded by being "activist"; it has had to. Its decisions have seemed wildly "liberal" because the only other body of principles operating in the field, against which the Court's principles may be measured, are the principles under which individual policemen act in the absence of any legal restraint.

This same subconstitutional lawlessness which forces the Court to act also prevents it from acting informedly. When the Court reviews the operation of legislation or of administrative regulations or of common-law rules governing, for example, criminal trial procedure, its consideration of the constitutional issues raised is informed and greatly assisted by the very fact that it *is* legislation or a regulation or a rule of some sort that is in question. Because the rule is articulated in more or less general terms, its contour is more or less visible; its relations and interactions with the rules are more or less perceptible, and some of the judgments and policies that underlie or oppose its acceptance are more or less intelligible. However, when the Court reviews conduct, such as police conduct, that is essentially rule-less, it is seriously impeded in understanding the nature, purposes and effects of what it is reviewing. Its view of the questioned conduct is limited to the appearance of the conduct on a particular trial record or records — records which may not even isolate or focus precisely upon that conduct. The Court cannot know whether the conduct before it is typical or atypical, unconnected or connected with a set of other practices or — if there is some connection — what is the comprehensive shape of the set of practices involved, what are their relations, their justifications, their consequences.

Operating thus darkly, the Court is obviously deprived of the ability to make any coherent response to, or to develop any organized regulation of, police conduct. Nor can the Court predict or understand the implications of any rule of constitutional law that it may itself project into this well of shadows. If the Court announces a decision striking down or modifying, for example, some rule of criminal trial practice, it can reasonably foresee how a trial will be conducted following its decision since the decision will operate within a system governed by other visible and predictable rules. But if the Court strikes down a police practice, announces a "right" of a criminal suspect in his dealings with the police, God only knows what the result will be.[10] Out there in the formless void, some adjustment will undoubtedly be made to accommodate the new "right," but what the product of this whole exercise will be remains unfathomable. So, again, the Court is effectively disarmed.

Fourth, when and if the Supreme Court ventures to announce some constitutional right of a suspect, that "right" filters down to the level of flesh and blood suspects only through the refracting layers of lower courts, trial judges, magistrates and police officials. All pronouncements of the Supreme Court undergo this filtering process, but in few other areas of law are the filters as opaque as in the area of suspects' rights.

Let there be no mistake about it. To a mind-staggering extent — to an extent that conservatives and liberals alike who are not criminal trial lawyers simply cannot conceive — the entire system of criminal justice below the level of the Supreme Court of the United States is solidly massed against the criminal suspect. Only a few appellate judges can throw off the fetters of their middle-class backgrounds — the dimly remembered, friendly face of the school crossing guard, their fear of a crowd of "toughs," their attitudes engendered as lawyers before their elevation to the bench by years of service as prosecutors or as private lawyers for honest, respectable business clients — and identify with the criminal suspect instead of with the policeman or with the putative victim of the suspect's theft, mugging, rape or murder. Trial judges still more, and magistrates beyond belief, are functionally and psychologically allied with the police, their co-workers in the unending and scarifying work of bringing criminals to book.

These trial judges and magistrates are the human beings that must find the "facts" when cases involving suspects' rights go into court (that is, when police treatment of a suspect is not conclusively masked behind a guilty plea or ignored by a defense lawyer too overworked or undercompensated to develop the issues adequately). Their factual findings resolve the inevitable conflict between the testimony of the police and the testimony of the suspect — usually a down-and-outer or a bad type, and often a man with a record. The result is about what one would expect. Even when the cases go to court, a suspect's rights as announced by the Supreme Court are something he has, not something he gets.

But, of course, for the reasons mentioned previously, most cases do not go to court. In these cases, the "rights" of the suspect are defined by how the police are willing to treat him. With regard to matters of treatment that have no evidentiary

---

10. One possible result is that prosecutors may offer greater concessions to defendants during plea bargaining. If a bargain is too good to refuse, the defendant may forgo the opportunity to challenge a police practice or assert a constitutional right. To the extent that this occurs, "what the due process revolution will have gained is simply shorter sentences." D. Oaks & W. Lehman, A Criminal Justice System and the Indigent 80 (1968). — Eds.

consequences and hence will not be judicially reviewable in exclusionary rule proceedings, the police have no particular reason to obey the law, even if the Supreme Court has had occasion to announce it. With regard to police practices that may have evidentiary consequences, the police are motivated to obey the law only to the extent that (1) they are more concerned with securing a conviction than with some other police purpose which is served by disobeying the law (in this connection, it is worth noting that police departments almost invariably measure their own efficiency in terms of "clearances by arrest," not by conviction), and (2) they think that they can secure the evidence necessary for conviction within the law.

Police work is hard work; it is righteous work; it is combative work, and competitive. Policemen are undereducated, they are scandalously underpaid, and their personal advancement lies in producing results according to the standards of the police ethic. When they go to the commander's office or to court, their conformity to this ethic is almost always vindicated. Neither their superiors nor the judges whom they know nor the public find it necessary to impede the performance of their duties with fettering rules respecting rights of suspects. If the Supreme Court finds this necessary, it must be that the Court is out of step. So its decisions—which are difficult to understand anyway—cannot really be taken seriously.

This concludes my observations concerning the Supreme Court's power to guarantee rights of criminal suspects in any other than an unworldly sense. The idealist would conclude from what I have said that the priests surrounding the Pythia are unfaithful to their priesthood. The cynic would conclude that the whole damned system is corrupt. I forgo such judgments and conclude only that Supreme Court power to enlarge the rights of suspects is very, very limited. . . .

. . . I do not mean to suggest that Supreme Court decisions respecting suspects' and defendants' rights are unimportant. Like the Pythia's cries, they have vast mystical significance. They state our aspirations. They give a few good priests something to work with. They give some of the faithful the courage to carry on and reason to improve the priesthood instead of tearing down the temple.

Also, they have *some* practical significance. With the Pythia shrieking underground, the priests may pervert the word of god, but they cannot ignore it entirely, nor entirely silence those who offer interpretations of it different from their own. Indeed, fear lest these alternative explanations gain popular support may cause the priests to bend a little in their direction.

So it is worth the effort to examine what the Supreme Court has pronounced concerning suspects' and defendants' rights. . . .[11]

---

11. For more on the relationship between Supreme Court decision making and the operation of the criminal justice system, see Weisberg, Foreword: Criminal Procedure Doctrine: Some Versions of the Skeptical, 76 J. Crim. L. & Criminology 832 (1985). For differing perspectives on the role of the Burger Court in adjudicating the rights of criminal defendants, compare Whitebread, The Burger Court's Counter-Revolution in Criminal Procedure: The Recent Criminal Decisions of the United States Supreme Court, 24 Washburn L.J. 471 (1985), with Israel, Criminal Procedure, the Burger Court, and the Legacy of the Warren Court, 75 Mich. L. Rev. 1319 (1977). See also O'Neill, The Good, The Bad, and the Burger Court: Victim's Rights and a New Model of Criminal Review, 75 J. Crim. L. & Criminology 363 (1984). — EDS.

8. The Role of State Constitutions and State Constitutional Law

WILLIAM J. BRENNAN, JR., STATE CONSTITUTIONS AND
THE PROTECTION OF INDIVIDUAL RIGHTS

90 Harv. L. Rev. 489-497 (1977)

Reaching the biblical summit of three score and ten seems the occasion — or the excuse — for looking back. Forty-eight years ago I entered law school and forty-four years ago was admitted to the New Jersey Bar. In those days of innocence, the preoccupation of the profession, bench and bar, was with questions usually answered by *application* of state common law principles or state statutes. Any necessity to consult federal law was at best episodic. But those were also the grim days of the Depression, and its cure was dramatically to change the face of American law. The year 1933 witnessed the birth of a plethora of new federal laws and new federal agencies developing and enforcing those laws; ones that were to affect profoundly the daily lives of every person in the nation.

In recent years, however, another variety of federal law — that fundamental law protecting all of us from the use of governmental powers in ways inconsistent with American conceptions of human liberty — has dramatically altered the grist of the state courts. Over the past two decades, decisions of the Supreme Court of the United States have returned to the fundamental promises wrought by the blood of those who fought our War between the States, promises which were thereafter embodied in our fourteenth amendment — that the citizens of all our states are also and no less citizens of our United States, that this birthright guarantees our federal constitutional liberties against encroachment by governmental action at any level of our federal system, and that each of us is entitled to due process of law and the equal protection of the laws from our state governments no less than from our national one. Although courts do not today substitute their personal economic beliefs for the judgments of our democratically elected legislatures, Supreme Court decisions under the fourteenth amendment have significantly affected virtually every other area, civil and criminal, of state action. And while these decisions have been accompanied by the enforcement of federal rights by federal courts, they have significantly altered the work of state court judges as well. This is both necessary and desirable under our federal system — state courts no less than federal are and ought to be the guardians of our liberties.

But the point I want to stress here is that state courts cannot rest when they have afforded their citizens the full protections of the federal Constitution. State constitutions, too, are a font of individual liberties, their protections often extending beyond those required by the Supreme Court's interpretation of federal law. The legal revolution which has brought federal law to the fore must not be allowed to inhibit the independent protective force of state law — for without it, the full realization of our liberties cannot be guaranteed.

Of late, however, more and more state courts are construing state constitutional counterparts of provisions of the Bill of Rights as guaranteeing citizens of their states even more protection than the federal provisions, even those identically phrased. This is surely an important and highly significant development for our constitutional jurisprudence and for our concept of federalism. I suppose it was only natural that when during the 1960's our rights and liberties were in the process of becoming increasingly federalized, state courts saw no reason to consider what protections, if any, were secured by state constitutions. It is not easy to pinpoint why state courts are now beginning to emphasize the protections of their states' own bills of rights. It may not be wide of the mark, however, to suppose that these state courts discern, and disagree with, a trend in recent opinions of the United States Supreme Court to pull back from, or at least suspend for the time being, the enforcement of the *Boyd* principle with respect to application of the federal Bill of Rights and the restraints of the due process and equal protection clauses of the fourteenth amendment.

The essential point I am making, of course, is not that the United States Supreme Court is necessarily wrong in its interpretation of the federal Constitution, or that ultimate constitutional truths invariably come prepackaged in the dissents, including my own, from decisions of the Court. It is simply that the decisions of the Court are not, and should not be, dispositive of questions regarding rights guaranteed by counterpart provisions of state law. Accordingly, such decisions are not mechanically applicable to state law issues, and state court judges and the members of the bar seriously err if they so treat them. Rather, state court judges, and also practitioners, do well to scrutinize constitutional decisions by federal courts, for only if they are found to be logically persuasive and well-reasoned, paying due regard to precedent and the policies underlying specific constitutional guarantees, may they properly claim persuasive weight as guideposts when interpreting counterpart state guarantees. I suggest to the bar that, although in the past it might have been safe for counsel to raise only federal constitutional issues in state courts, plainly it would be most unwise these days not also to raise the state constitutional questions.

BARRY LATZER, TOWARD THE DECENTRALIZATION OF CRIMINAL PROCEDURE: STATE CONSTITUTIONAL LAW AND SELECTIVE INCORPORATION

87 J. Crim. L. & Criminology 63, 63-66, 68 (1996)

When one surveys the growing body of criminal procedure cases in which the decision is grounded in a state constitutional provision, a rather startling trend becomes manifest. It is increasingly evident that at some time during the early years of the next century virtually every significant federal constitutional criminal procedure right will have been duplicated or expanded as a matter of state law by the appellate courts of most of the states. That is, the *same* rights that *defendants* now enjoy as a *result of* United States Supreme Court cases construing the federal Bill of Rights, or an even broader state-law-based version of those rights, will be established in most of the states by cases construing state bills of rights. Little if any thought has been given to the implications of this development for constitutional law in the United States, or on the relations between state courts and the United States Supreme Court.

For openers, consider this question: if defendants' rights are protected by state law, why is there a need for redundant federal law? Why provide federal protections where state rights exist, especially in light of the fact that the state rights are as broad or broader? This is in part, of course, a question about the Supreme Court's incorporation policy by which federal rights have been applied to the states through the Fourteenth Amendment Due Process Clause. The stock answer is that together, the federal rights established through incorporation and the rights established through interpretation of state constitutions afford a double-barreled protection for individual rights in America, and we all benefit from such dual assurances. Upon close examination, however, rights-redundancy has distinct disadvantages.

There can be little question that incorporation forced the states to adopt uniform procedures without regard to local needs. In the decades since the 1960s, when the Supreme Court "selectively" incorporated nearly all of the criminal procedure rights in the Bill of Rights, the state courts have had little choice but to give force to these federal procedures (absent broader state rights). No matter how costly, no matter how inefficient, no matter how difficult to implement, no matter how much injustice they might cause, and no matter how inappropriate to local circumstances they might be, the state courts have had to give effect to these federal procedural rights. These disadvantages of incorporation were acknowledged even in the 1960s, but they were believed to be outweighed by one important value: equality. Whatever the disadvantages in stifling state uniqueness, independence, and freedom to experiment, the advantage of uniform treatment of defendants throughout the United States, at least with respect to the fundamental rights of the Bill of Rights, seemed to justify incorporation.

But let us be candid. Incorporation was also predicated upon an assumption — a very negative assumption — about the states, and especially about state courts. The assumption was that some state courts were chronically, and virtually all state courts were occasionally, backward. Without the Supreme Court to stand over them, ready to review and reverse, the state *courts* would fail to provide the minimal rights that all defendants were entitled to at all times. In short, incorporation was motivated by the Mississippi Problem: the assumption that the state bench was, at its worst racist and incompetent, and merely competent most of the time. . . .

[T]he Mississippi Problem is history. . . . [T]he state courts are no longer rights-antediluvians, and . . . therefore an entire set of assumptions underlying incorporation has eroded. The proof of the change in the state courts lies in their eagerness to protect federal constitutional rights, but even more, in the development of state constitutional law. State constitutionalism has not only created rights-redundancy, it has undermined the very reasons for that redundancy. It gives the lie to the assumption that the state bench is rights-backward. Unlike federal constitutional law, which is imposed upon the state courts, state constitutional law is a matter of choice. Whereas state courts must enforce federal procedural rights incorporated into due process, they need not provide equivalent state constitutional rights. State constitutional rights need not be as protective as comparable federal rights, and they certainly do not have to be more protective, as they so often are. State constitutional law epitomizes the change in the attitude and orientation of state judges. It shows that state courts are now every bit as rights-sensitive as the United States Supreme Court, if not more so.

. . . [O]nly those procedures that are both fundamental and required by the Bill of Rights, or are at least demonstrably essential to the implementation of a fundamental right in the Bill of Rights, may be imposed upon the states. Where a procedure is none of the above it is not a proper part of due process and the Supreme Court has no authority to compel the state courts to adopt it. Where a previously incorporated procedure is challenged and it cannot be proven essential to a fundamental right it should be disincorporated, by which I mean that the incorporation decision should be reversed and the procedure should no longer be required by the Fourteenth Amendment Due Process Clause.

Chapter 2
The Idea of Due Process

One of the defining characteristics of the modern state is its monopoly on criminal law enforcement. Government officials, not private individuals, investigate, apprehend, try, and punish criminals. Much of this business is routine and bureaucratic, but some of it is terrifying, and it can be brutal. Suspects' homes and cars must be searched (and the searches can be rough); arrests must be made, sometimes by force; defendants must be incarcerated. Giving the government a monopoly on that kind of power may be necessary, but it is also very dangerous — consider the use of the phrase "police state" to describe less-than-free societies. Police, prosecutors, and the courts can do enormous good: They are the difference between a decent society and an unlivable one. But they can also do enormous harm.

The basic goal of the law of criminal procedure is to limit the harm without too severely limiting the good. In our system, the entity that does most of the limiting is courts. Most of the law of criminal procedure is constitutional, and American constitutional law is largely judge-defined. Which means that judges — and, especially, Supreme Court Justices — are the primary generators of rules for regulating the behavior of police, prosecutors, defense attorneys, and the other actors who administer the criminal process. That explains why books like this one devote so much space to Supreme Court opinions: Those opinions define what Henry Friendly properly labeled our constitutional code of criminal procedure.[1]

All this constitutional regulation begins with the idea of due process: When the state uses its coercive machinery to catch and punish criminals, it must treat people fairly, even the people it wishes to punish. That idea probably underlies the law of criminal procedure in all free societies. In ours, the connection is particularly clear, since the law of criminal procedure begins not only with the idea but with the phrase, "due process of law." The Fifth Amendment bars the federal government from depriving anyone of "life, liberty or property" without it; the Fourteenth Amendment applies that same prohibition to the states. Since the criminal justice system is in the business of depriving people of liberty and property (and occasionally deprives them of life itself), those constitutional bans naturally have their most frequent application to criminal procedure.

That last point deserves emphasis. An enormous amount of ink has been spilled debating the proper meaning of the Due Process Clauses of the Fifth and Fourteenth Amendments — the subject is central to most constitutional law courses. Those debates usually focus on things like economic regulation (see Lochner v.

---

1. See Henry J. Friendly, The Bill of Rights as a Code of Criminal Procedure, 53 Cal. L. Rev. 929 (1965). It should be noted that Friendly thought this constitutional code was a bad development — that it risked stifling reform efforts by other, nonjudicial actors.

New York, 198 U.S. 45 (1905)) and birth control (see Griswold v. Connecticut, 381 U.S. 479 (1965)), abortion (see Roe v. Wade, 410 U.S. 113 (1973)) and gay rights (see Bowers v. Hardwick, 478 U.S. 186 (1986)). But the Due Process Clauses have had their greatest impact not in these places, but in criminal procedure. As of summer 2000, over two million people were incarcerated in the United States. The legal system that put them there is filled with rules that have their origins in the Fourteenth Amendment's Due Process Clause. And the question whether those rules ensure fair punishment begins with the idea of due process.

A Brief History

The relationship between that idea and the American criminal justice system has a long and strange history. Broadly speaking, the history has three phases. The first phase lasts from independence to the passage of the Fourteenth Amendment; the second extends to the 1960s; the third runs to the present.

The first phase is when the criminal justice system as we know it came into being. In 1776 (or 1787 or 1791 — the choice of starting date does not matter here),[2] career public prosecutors basically didn't exist; prosecution was either the crime victim's job, the constable's job, or the job of some private lawyer serving as a temporary public advocate. Police forces didn't exist either; constables and sheriffs performed their law enforcement task largely through the aid of private parties.[3] There seems to have been no plea bargaining — the best history of that topic to date puts its origins in the early nineteenth century.[4] Criminal law, the body of rules that define the elements of crimes, had little meaning, since juries could decide what the law was on an ad hoc basis.[5] And imprisonment for crime was rare; penitentiaries were still a half-century in the future.[6] Many of the most basic, taken-for-granted features of contemporary criminal justice were absent at the time of the Founding — indeed, they were unimaginable.

By 1868, the year the Fourteenth Amendment was ratified, all that had changed, and changed dramatically. Public prosecutors, police forces, plea bargains, and prisons were all common. Criminal law was defined by a mix of courts and legislatures, just as it is today. The criminal justice system of 1868 — an interlocking set of public institutions that managed large numbers of cases and administered punishment to large numbers of people — would be quite recognizable to us today, for the system then and the system now share most basic features.

2. Independence was declared in 1776, the convention that produced our Constitution was held in 1787, and the Bill of Rights was ratified in 1791. Whichever of these is the relevant date, the statements in the text hold true.

3. See generally Peter Charles Hoffer, Law and People in Colonial America 80-89 (1992).

4. See George Fisher, Plea Bargaining's Triumph, 109 Yale L.J. 857 (2000).

5. See, e.g., William E. Nelson, The Eighteenth-Century Background of John Marshall's Constitutional Jurisprudence, 76 Mich. L. Rev. 904 (1978).

6. At the time of the Founding, penitentiaries were first being used in England. See George Fisher, The Birth of the Prison Retold, 104 Yale L.J. 1235 (1994). The widespread use of incarceration in America began only in the 1820s and 1830s. See David J. Rothman, Perfecting the Prison: United States, 1789-1865, in The Oxford History of the Prison 100 (Norval Morris & David J. Rothman eds., 1998).

In other words, when the Constitution (including the Bill of Rights) was written, no criminal justice system in the modern sense existed. Constitutional norms came first; the system came later. Given that timing, it would hardly be surprising if there were some tension between the norms and the system.

All the more so, since the criminal justice system evolved in the nineteenth century with basically no input from constitutional law. The Bill of Rights included a number of rules that were specifically about criminal procedure — the Fifth Amendment's ban on double jeopardy, requirement of indictment by grand jury, and privilege against self-incrimination, the Sixth Amendment's rights to counsel and trial by jury, the Eighth Amendment's ban on cruel and unusual punishments. But like the rest of the Bill of Rights, those criminal procedure rules applied only to the federal government. See Barron v. Baltimore, 32 U.S. 243 (1833). And the federal government did very, very little in the way of criminal law enforcement — as late as 1904, the federal government incarcerated only 1,641 people, a mere 3% of the number of state prisoners. See Margaret Werner Cahalan, Historical Corrections Statistics in the United States, 1850–1984, at 29 tbl. 3-2 (1986). State constitutions seem not to have played any particular role either, perhaps because criminal appeals were still so unusual.[7] The criminal justice system that emerged in the nineteenth century was generated from the bottom up, not from the top down; institutions like public prosecutors and police forces sprang up locally without any overall design and without any constitutional regulation. The same was true of practices like plea bargaining.

Enter the Fourteenth Amendment. The Fourteenth Amendment's ban on deprivations of life, liberty, or property without due process of law, unlike the similar ban in the Fifth Amendment, applied to the *states*. Then as now, the states are the locus of the huge majority of criminal law enforcement. Thus, though there is no reason to believe its authors viewed it this way, the Fourteenth Amendment's Due Process Clause amounted to a textual invitation to courts to define some limits on the newly emerged criminal justice system, by defining what a fair criminal process must entail.

Beginning with Hurtado v. California, 110 U.S. 516 (1884), reprinted at page 80 infra, the Supreme Court began accepting that invitation; for the next 75 years, the Court engaged in the business of placing constitutional limits on the criminal process, with the limits anchored in due process. The results are described in the notes following *Hurtado*. For now, it is enough to note that the limits were both few and vague. By 1960, there were at most a handful of things state criminal justice systems were clearly not allowed to do — they could not run mob-dominated trials;[8] they could not pay judges by the conviction;[9] they could not beat confessions out of suspects[10] — but otherwise, they were subject only to the amorphous notion that whatever they did had to comply with "fundamental fairness," which seemed to permit anything that did not "shock the conscience" of the judiciary. What any of that meant was a mystery, apparently even to the Justices, but what it did *not* mean was a substantial body of law regulating the criminal process. There

7. See, e.g., Francis A. Allen, *Griffin v. Illinois:* Antecedents and Aftermath, 25 U. Chi. L. Rev. 151, 154 (1957) (calling criminal appeals "a modern innovation"). For an argument that appeals in criminal cases were more widespread in the eighteenth and nineteenth centuries, see Marc M. Arkin, Rethinking the Constitutional Right to a Criminal Appeal, 39 UCLA L. Rev. 503 (1992).

8. Moore v. Dempsey, 261 U.S. 86 (1923).

9. Tumey v. Ohio, 273 U.S. 510 (1927).

10. Brown v. Mississippi, 297 U.S. 278 (1936).

was a law of due process in 1960, but it barely deserved the label "law," and it hardly ensured a fair process.

The 1960s at least remedied the first of those two deficiencies: At the end of that decade, we had, for the first time, a large law of constitutional criminal procedure. The 1960s saw a series of major reforms in the criminal justice system, and the reforms were both based on federal constitutional law and driven by the Supreme Court. But these reforms had a different constitutional basis than the sporadic limits the Court had imposed between 1884 and 1960. For the most part, as it sought to rein in what it saw as an abusive criminal justice system, Earl Warren's Supreme Court relied not on due process but on the Bill of Rights. Limits on search and seizure and police interrogation, the right to counsel, the privilege against self-incrimination, the ban on double jeopardy, the right to jury trial—these became the foundations of American criminal procedure, and each has spawned its own elaborate body of law. These bodies of law will occupy the bulk of this large book. But the words "due process" rarely appear in the cases that define these constitutional rules; instead, the relevant piece of constitutional text comes from the Fourth, Fifth, or Sixth Amendments. In effect, the Supreme Court decided that defining due process was impossible, so it turned to the enterprise of defining the more specific guarantees of the Bill of Rights. But the point of those guarantees is itself due process; the goal remains to define criminal procedure in a way that ensures fair treatment for the millions of people who pass through the criminal justice system's large net. The basic question that so bothered the Court from 1884 to 1960—What are the conditions of a fair criminal process?—has not so much been answered as recast, and perhaps avoided.

In short, for roughly its first century, our nation had no law of constitutional criminal procedure. For roughly the next 80 years, the Supreme Court tried, and largely failed, to define a law of criminal procedure built on the phrase "due process of law." For the 40 years after that, down to the present, the phrase "due process of law" has faded in importance; a huge, nearly comprehensive law of criminal procedure has been built on the various provisions of the Bill of Rights. But the idea of due process still lurks in the background, posing the basic question any criminal process must face: Is this fair?

A. Defining Due Process

HURTADO v. CALIFORNIA

Writ of Error to the Supreme Court of California
110 U.S. 516 (1884)

MR. JUSTICE MATTHEWS delivered the opinion of the Court. [Hurtado was charged and convicted of first-degree murder. He was charged by information, not indictment; that is, no grand jury ever considered his case. He argued that the absence of grand jury indictment for a serious crime violated the Fourteenth Amendment's guarantee of due process.]

. . . The proposition of law we are asked to affirm is that an indictment or presentment by a grand jury, as known to the common law of England, is essential to that "due process of law," when applied to prosecutions for felonies, which is secured and guaranteed by [the Fourteenth Amendment to] the Constitution of the United States, and which accordingly it is forbidden to the States respectively to dispense with in the administration of criminal law. . . .

. . . [I]t is maintained on behalf of the plaintiff in error that the phrase "due process of law" is equivalent to "law of the land," as found in the 29th chapter of Magna Charta; that by immemorial usage it has acquired a fixed, definite, and technical meaning; that it refers to and includes, not only the general principles of public liberty and private right, which lie at the foundation of all free government, but the very institutions which, venerable by time and custom, have been tried by experience and found fit and necessary for the preservation of those principles. . . .

This, it is argued, furnishes an indispensable test of what constitutes "due process of law"; that any proceeding otherwise authorized by law, which is not thus sanctioned by usage, or which supersedes and displaces one that is, cannot be regarded as due process of law.

But this inference is unwarranted. The real [principle] is, that a process of law, which is not otherwise forbidden, must be taken to be due process of law, if it can show the sanction of settled usage both in England and in this country; but it by no means follows that nothing else can be due process of law. . . . [T]o hold that such a characteristic is essential to due process of law, would be to deny every quality of the law but its age, and to render it incapable of progress or improvement. It would be to stamp upon our jurisprudence the unchangeableness attributed to the laws of the Medes and Persians. . . .

The Constitution of the United States was ordained, it is true, by descendants of Englishmen, who inherited the traditions of English law and history; but it was made for an undefined and expanding future, and for a people gathered and to be gathered from many nations and of many tongues. . . . There is nothing in Magna Charta, rightly construed as a broad charter of public right and law, which ought to exclude the best ideas of all systems and of every age; and as it was the characteristic principle of the common law to draw its inspiration from every fountain of justice, we are not to assume that the sources of its supply have been exhausted. On the contrary, we should expect that the new and various experiences of our own situation and system will mould and shape it into new and not less useful forms. . . .

We are to construe this phrase in the Fourteenth Amendment by the [usage] of the Constitution itself. The same words are contained in the Fifth Amendment. That article makes specific and express provision for perpetuating the institution of the grand jury, so far as relates to prosecutions for the more aggravated crimes under the laws of the United States. It declares that:

> "No person shall be held to answer for a capital or otherwise infamous crime, unless on a presentment or indictment of a grand jury, except in cases arising in the land or naval forces, or in the militia when in actual service in time of war or public danger; nor shall any person be subject for the same offence to be twice put in jeopardy of life or limb; nor shall he be compelled in any criminal case to be a witness against himself." [It then immediately adds]: "Nor be deprived of life, liberty, or property, without due process of law."

According to a recognized canon of interpretation, especially applicable to formal and solemn instruments of constitutional law, we are forbidden to assume, without clear reason to the contrary, that any part of this most important amendment is superfluous. The natural and obvious inference is, that in the sense of the Constitution, "due process of law" was not meant or intended to include . . . the institution and procedure of a grand jury in any case. The conclusion is equally irresistible, that when the same phrase was employed in the Fourteenth Amendment to restrain the action of the States, it was used in the same sense and with no greater extent; and that if in the adoption of that amendment it had been part of its purpose to perpetuate the institution of the grand jury in all the States, it would have embodied, as did the Fifth Amendment, express declarations to that effect. Due process of law in the latter refers to that law of the land which derives its authority from the legislative powers conferred upon Congress by the Constitution of the United States, exercised within the limits therein prescribed, and interpreted according to the principles of the common law. In the Fourteenth Amendment, by parity of reason, it refers to that law of the land in each State, which derives its authority from the inherent and reserved powers of the State, exerted within the limits of those fundamental principles of liberty and justice which lie at the base of all our civil and political institutions, and the greatest security for which resides in the right of the people to make their own laws, and alter them at their pleasure. . . .

But it is not to be supposed that these legislative powers are absolute and despotic, and that the amendment prescribing due process of law is too vague and indefinite to operate as a practical restraint. It is not every act, legislative in form, that is law. Law is something more than mere will exerted as an act of power. It must be not a special rule for a particular person or a particular case, but, in the language of Mr. Webster, in his familiar definition, "the general law, a law which hears before it condemns, which proceeds upon inquiry, and renders judgment only after trial," so "that every citizen shall hold his life, liberty, property and immunities under the protection of the general rules which govern society," and thus excluding, as not due process of law, acts of attainder, bills of pains and penalties, acts of confiscation, acts reversing judgments, and acts directly transferring one man's estate to another, legislative judgments and decrees, and other similar special, partial and arbitrary exertions of power under the forms of legislation. Arbitrary power, enforcing its edicts to the injury of the persons and property of its subjects, is not law, whether manifested as the decree of a personal monarch or of an impersonal multitude. . . . The enforcement of these limitations by judicial process is the device of self-governing communities to protect the rights of individuals and minorities, as well against the power of numbers, as against the violence of public agents transcending the limits of lawful authority, even when acting in the name and wielding the force of the government. . . .

It follows that any legal proceeding enforced by public authority, whether sanctioned by age and custom, or newly devised in the discretion of the legislative power, in furtherance of the general public good, which regards and preserves these principles of liberty and justice, must be held to be due process of law. . . .

Tried by these principles, we are unable to say that the substitution for a presentment or indictment by a grand jury of the proceeding by information, after examination and commitment by a magistrate, certifying to the probable guilt of the defendant, with the right on his part to the aid of counsel, and to the cross-examination of the witnesses produced for the prosecution, is not due process of law. . . .

Mr. Justice Harlan, dissenting.

. . . [I]t is said that the framers of the Constitution did not suppose that due process of law necessarily required for a capital offence the institution and procedure of a grand jury, else they would not in the same amendment prohibiting the deprivation of life, liberty, or property, without due process of law, have made specific and express provision for a grand jury where the crime is capital or otherwise infamous. . . .

This line of argument, it seems to me, would lead to results which are inconsistent with the vital principles of republican government. If the presence in the Fifth Amendment of a specific provision for grand juries in capital cases, alongside the provision for due process of law . . . is held to prove that "due process of law" did not . . . require a grand jury in capital cases, inexorable logic would require it to be, likewise, held that the right not to be put twice in jeopardy of life and limb for the same offence, nor compelled in a criminal case to testify against one's self — rights and immunities also specifically recognized in the Fifth Amendment — were not protected by that [same] due process of law. . . . More than that, other amendments of the Constitution proposed at the same time, expressly recognize the right of persons to just compensation for private property taken for public use; their right, when accused of crime, to be informed of the nature and cause of the accusation against them, and to a speedy and public trial, by an impartial jury of the State and district wherein the crime was committed; to be confronted by the witnesses against them; and to have compulsory process for obtaining witnesses in their favor. Will it be claimed that these rights were not secured by the "law of the land" or by "due process of law," as declared and established at the foundation of our government? Are they to be excluded from the enumeration of the fundamental principles of liberty and justice, and, therefore, not embraced by "due process of law"? If the argument of my brethren be sound, those rights — although universally recognized at the establishment of our institutions as secured by that due process of law which for centuries had been the foundation of Anglo-Saxon liberty — were not deemed by our fathers as essential in the due process of law prescribed by our Constitution; because, — such seems to be the argument — had they been regarded as involved in due process of law they would not have been specifically and expressly provided for. . . .

Still further, it results from the doctrines of the opinion — if I do not misapprehend its scope — that the clause of the Fourteenth Amendment forbidding the deprivation of life or liberty without due process of law, would not be violated by a State regulation, dispensing with petit juries in criminal cases, and permitting a person charged with a crime involving life to be tried before a single judge, or even a justice of the peace, upon a rule to show cause why he should not be hanged. . . .

. . . My sense of duty constrains me to dissent from this interpretation of the supreme law of the land.

Mr. Justice Field did not take part in the decision of this case.

NOTES ON THE MEANING OF "DUE PROCESS OF LAW" IN CRIMINAL CASES

1. *Hurtado* was the Supreme Court's first extended discussion of what "due process of law" means for criminal procedure. How well did the Court do? Do

the majority and dissenting opinions reflect the kinds of concerns you would expect to see? Do the opinions make you think better or worse of the idea of giving the Supreme Court the power to define the rules that govern the criminal process?

In answering these questions, it helps to have some more information about the issue in *Hurtado*. The question before the Court was whether California was required to proceed by indictment in capital cases. To translate, the question was whether murder defendants like Hurtado (and perhaps defendants in other felony cases) were constitutionally entitled to a judgment by a grand jury that they should be charged, as a prerequisite to going to trial. How one answers that question, in turn, might plausibly depend on one's sense of what grand juries do, how they function. Consider the following description of contemporary grand jury practice in federal cases:[11]

> The operation of a typical federal grand jury is straightforward. A pool of citizens is summoned at random from the judicial district where the jury will sit. From the group of qualified people who appear, twenty-three are chosen to serve on the jury. The jurors sit for an indefinite period not to exceed eighteen months; the number of days per month when they must actually appear depends on the prosecutor's case load. A district court judge administers the oath and gives the jurors general instructions about their duties. This marks the end of the judge's formal involvement in the process. From that point forward, the prosecutor dictates the course of the proceedings.
>
> The most striking feature of grand jury hearings is their secrecy. The press and public are barred from the proceedings, as are suspects and their counsel. Even judges are not allowed in the grand jury room; attendance is limited to the prosecutor, the jurors, the court reporter, and the single witness being questioned. Those who participate in the hearing are sworn to secrecy, and the court may use its contempt powers to ensure that this silence is maintained even after the case is resolved.
>
> Once in session, the grand jury's primary task is to review the cases presented to it by the government. The prosecutor calls and questions witnesses, and presents documentary evidence related to the crime in question. Unlike trial jurors, grand jurors may ask questions of the witness and may discuss the case with the prosecutor as evidence is submitted. After the case is presented, the prosecutor asks the jurors to vote to return an indictment accusing the defendant of a specific crime that the prosecutor believes is supported by the evidence. The jurors then deliberate in private. If at least twelve agree that there is probable cause to believe that the suspect committed the crime, the grand jury returns a "true bill" that, when signed by the prosecutor, becomes the indictment. If the grand jury concludes that the evidence is insufficient, it returns a "no bill" (or "no true bill"), and any preliminary charges filed against the suspect are dismissed.
>
> By traditional trial standards, a grand jury is allowed to consider a surprising, even shocking, mix of evidence. . . . The Rules of Evidence do not apply, so the prosecutor can ask leading questions and pursue matters that would be considered irrelevant if presented at trial. The decision of which evidence to present is also in the prosecutor's hands: the suspect has no right to testify in his own defense, and if he does testify, is not allowed to bring counsel with him into the grand jury room. The suspect may not put on contrary evidence, is not given access to the testimony of his accusers until

---

11. This description is reprinted at pages 1079-1080 infra as part of the consideration of grand juries as screening devices.

the trial begins, and indeed, may not even be told he is being investigated. The result . . . is that grand jurors hear only what the prosecution wants them to hear. . . .

Andrew Leipold, Why Grand Juries Do Not (And Cannot) Protect the Accused, 80 Cornell L. Rev. 260, 265-267 (1995) (footnotes omitted). As the title of Leipold's article suggests, it is not clear how this process protects criminal defendants. On the contrary, its chief use today seems to be as a device the government uses to obtain information — hence the widespread use of grand jury subpoenas in white-collar criminal investigations.

Of course, white-collar criminal practice was well in the future when *Hurtado* was decided, and grand jury practice was no doubt different in some respects in 1884 than it is today. But the essential point — prosecutorial control over the information grand jurors receive — would have been true then as now. Given that point, is there any serious argument for constitutionally requiring grand juries? What could Justice Harlan have been worrying about?

2. Both Justice Matthews and Justice Harlan offered coherent, fairly well developed interpretations of due process. Justice Matthews construes "due process of law" with special emphasis on the words "of law"; the result is a constitutional requirement of legality and nonarbitrariness. Justice Harlan sees due process as incorporating the list of protections that appear in the Bill of Rights; the result of this view is to transfer interpretive questions from the Fourteenth Amendment to the more particular guarantees of the Fourth, Fifth, and Sixth Amendments. Though these positions competed with each other in *Hurtado*, each has prevailed in its own sphere over the years. (Harlan's argument has won the greater victory, as the next main case shows.) In addition to these two interpretations, two other views of due process in criminal cases have won judicial favor from time to time. Some cases treat due process as a guarantee of accurate procedures, meaning procedures that minimize the risk that innocent defendants will be convicted of crime. And some cases define "due process" as "fundamental fairness," which turns out to be a term defined more by judicial intuition than by any analytic structure.

Each of these four strands — due process as the rule of law, due process as the Bill of Rights, due process as accuracy, and due process as "fundamental fairness" — survives in the law of due process today. Oddly, none of the four views seems to have much to do with any of the others. That strange fact has its origins in cases from early in the twentieth century. For in the decades following *Hurtado*, the Supreme Court saw a wide range of cases challenging one or another aspect of state criminal procedure, but as it decided those cases the Court did not follow a consistent path. Rather, the Court seized on whichever of the four approaches mentioned in the preceding paragraph seemed most applicable to the issue at hand (and whichever was able to attract a majority of the Court). Cases taking one approach usually made no mention of cases taking another, and at some times the Court seemed unaware that some of the approaches even existed. The upshot is that today, there are (at least) four meanings of due process in criminal cases, and there is no obvious answer to the question why one meaning prevails in one kind of case and another in a different kind of case.

The material that follows briefly traces the development of each of those four meanings. As you read it, ask yourself whether one or another of these approaches seems clearly superior to the others, or (alternatively) whether the law is better off with strands of each.

The Rule of Law. The following passage in Justice Matthews's opinion in *Hurtado* offers a good summary of what is meant by the "rule of law":

> It is not every act, legislative in form, that is law. Law is something more than mere will exerted as an act of power. It must be not a special rule for a particular person or a particular case, but, in the language of Mr. Webster, in his familiar definition, "the general law, a law which hears before it condemns, which proceeds upon inquiry, and renders judgment only after trial," . . . and thus excluding, as not due process of law, acts of attainder, bills of pains and penalties, acts of confiscation, acts reversing judgments, and acts directly transferring one man's estate to another, legislative judgments and decrees, and other similar special, partial and arbitrary exertions of power under the forms of legislation. Arbitrary power, enforcing its edicts to the injury of the persons and property of its subjects, is not law, whether manifested as the decree of a personal monarch or of an impersonal multitude. . . .

For a good contemporary statement of the same principle, see John C. Jeffries, Jr., Legality, Vagueness, and the Construction of Penal Statutes, 71 Va. L. Rev. 189, 212 (1985):

> The rule of law signifies the constraint of arbitrariness in the exercise of government power. In the context of the penal law, it means that the agencies of official coercion should, to the extent feasible, be guided by rules — that is, by openly acknowledged, relatively stable, and generally applicable statements of proscribed conduct. The evils to be retarded are caprice and whim, the misuse of government power for private ends, and the unacknowledged reliance on illegitimate criteria of selection. The goals to be advanced are regularity and evenhandedness in the administration of justice and accountability in the use of government power.

This idea of ensuring that criminal punishment is according to law and not "mere will" requires, at the least, that crimes be defined generally rather than (as Matthews put it) as a "special rule for a particular person or a particular case." That much is easy. Legislatures cannot make it a crime to *be* Hurtado, nor can they wait until Hurtado acts and then criminalize whatever he has done.

More importantly as a practical matter, the rule-of-law idea might be thought to require that legislatures define crimes with some specificity, that vague criminal statutes be deemed unconstitutional. Jeffries states the basic argument well:

> The power to define a vague law is effectively left to those who enforce it, and those who enforce the penal law characteristically operate in settings of secrecy and informality, often punctuated by a sense of emergency, and rarely constrained by self-conscious generalization of standards. In such circumstances, the wholesale delegation of discretion naturally invites its abuse, and an important first step in constraining that discretion is the invalidation of indefinite laws.

Id. at 215.

For a long period following *Hurtado,* this idea lay mostly dormant. Vagueness doctrine existed, but it was mostly used as an adjunct to First Amendment law, a way to invalidate laws that might chill protected speech. See Note, The Void-for-Vagueness Doctrine in the Supreme Court, 109 U. Pa. L. Rev. 67 (1960). Beginning in the early 1970s, though, the Supreme Court began to apply vagueness doctrine to strike down statutes that seemed to criminalize ordinary street behavior. Thus, in Coates v. Cincinnati, 402 U.S. 611 (1971), the Court invalidated an ordinance that forbade conduct "annoying to persons passing by." In Papachristou v. Jacksonville, 405 U.S. 156 (1972), the Court struck down a vagrancy law that criminalized, inter alia, "rogues and vagabonds," "habitual loafers," and "persons wandering or strolling around from place to place without any lawful purpose or object." More recently, in Chicago v. Morales, 527 U.S. 41 (1999), the Court invalidated a local ordinance that prohibited loitering by two or more people, at least one of whom was a "street gang member." *Morales* is excerpted at page 609 infra.

Cases like *Coates*, *Papachristou*, and *Morales* are all applications of Justice Matthews's rule-of-law view of due process. Are the applications sound? Does the rule-of-law idea go farther? Suppose a given jurisdiction forbids knowing possession of marijuana. Suppose further that there have been no prosecutions for this offense for several years and that marijuana possession is fairly common in some communities. Under these circumstances, would an arrest or prosecution for marijuana possession violate the rule of law? Does the answer depend on why the defendant was selected for arrest and prosecution? Is that something courts will be able to uncover?

More generally, is the rule-of-law ideal a good basis for constitutional regulation of the criminal justice system generally? Consider how one might apply the ideal to, say, police brutality. Is the problem with excessive police violence that the violence is lawless? Or is it something else?

The Bill of Rights. The Fourth Amendment forbids unreasonable searches and seizures. The Fifth Amendment requires indictment by grand jury for "capital, or otherwise infamous crime[s]," and bans double jeopardy and compelled self-incrimination. The Sixth Amendment grants defendants "the right to a speedy and public trial, by an impartial jury," as well as the right to be informed of the charges, to be confronted with opposing witnesses, to have "compulsory process for obtaining witnesses in his favor," and to have "the Assistance of Counsel for his defence."

As Justice Harlan's dissent in *Hurtado* shows, one longstanding reading of due process in criminal cases is that it incorporates all these rights. That position was rejected in *Hurtado* and for a long time afterward: In 1908, the Court declined to incorporate the privilege against self-incrimination into due process, see Twining v. New Jersey, 211 U.S. 78 (1908); three decades later, the Court similarly declined to incorporate the prohibition against double jeopardy into due process. See Palko v. Connecticut, 302 U.S. 319 (1937). But beginning in the middle of the twentieth century, the Court reversed course. In Wolf v. Colorado, 338 U.S. 25 (1949), the Court concluded that the Fourth Amendment's ban on unreasonable searches and seizures applied to the states through the Due Process Clause. (Though the Court waited until 1961 to apply the exclusionary rule to the states. See Mapp v. Ohio, 367 U.S. 643 (1961), reprinted at page 336.) And in the 1960s, a series of decisions incorporated every one of the rights listed in the preceding paragraph except for the right to a grand jury. *Hurtado* still stands, but today it stands alone — everywhere else, the argument of the first Justice Harlan has prevailed. Duncan v. Louisiana, the next main case, discusses this development.

There is a lively debate about the historical accuracy of incorporation — about the question whether the authors and ratifiers of the Fourteenth Amendment intended to apply the Bill of Rights to state and local governments. For the classic arguments on each side, see Charles Fairman, Does the Fourteenth Amendment Incorporate the Bill of Rights? The Original Understanding, 2 Stan. L. Rev. 5 (1949) (against incorporation); William Winslow Crosskey, Charles Fairman, "Legislative History," and the Constitutional Limitations on State Authority, 22 U. Chi. L. Rev. 1 (1954) (for incorporation). That debate is, to say the least, not easily summarized.

Putting historical questions aside, what is the case, either principled or pragmatic, for reading "due process" as meaning, roughly, "that process which complies with the Bill of Rights"? One possible answer is that compliance with the Bill of Rights will generate a fair criminal process. But it would be surprising if that were true. Recall that the Bill of Rights arose out of a legal system that had none of the basic institutions of contemporary American criminal justice. For the Framers to have accurately anticipated the conditions of a fair criminal process today, they would have to have accurately anticipated district attorneys' offices and police forces, plea bargaining and prison systems. That kind of foresight seems, literally, incredible. It seems more likely that some Bill of Rights protections improve the criminal process, others make that process worse, and still others make no real difference. That hardly sounds like a recipe for sound constitutional regulation.

And there is another difficulty. One might imagine that due process of law flows out of some principle, that constitutional regulation of the criminal process is in pursuit of some definable goal. The rule of law is a plausible candidate for such a goal or principle, as is accuracy. But the Bill of Rights is not. There is no obvious unifying principle to the disparate set of protections in the Fourth, Fifth, and Sixth Amendments. That makes it hard to see how the phrase "due process of law" has room to hold all those protections.

Accuracy (and Race). In a series of decisions in the 1920s and 1930s, the Supreme Court overturned convictions of black defendants in Southern state courts in circumstances where there was good reason to believe the defendants were innocent. Michael Klarman describes four such cases:

> . . . [All of the cases] involved southern black criminal defendants convicted and sentenced to death after egregiously unfair trials. In Moore v. Dempsey,[5] the Supreme Court interpreted the Due Process Clause of the Fourteenth Amendment to forbid criminal convictions obtained through mob-dominated trials. In Powell v. Alabama,[6] the Court ruled that the Due Process Clause requires state appointment of counsel in capital cases and overturned convictions where defense counsel had been appointed the morning of trial. In Norris v. Alabama,[7] the Court reversed a conviction under the Equal Protection Clause where blacks had been intentionally excluded from juries. To reach that result, the Court had to revise the critical "subconstitutional"[8] rules that previously had made such claims nearly impossible to prove. In Brown v. Mississippi,[9] the Court construed the Due Process Clause to forbid criminal convictions based on confessions extracted through torture.

5. 261 U.S. 86 (1923).
6. 287 U.S. 45 (1932).
7. 294 U.S. 587 (1935).
8. By "subconstitutional" rules, I mean not the substantive liability standards, but rather the all-important rules bearing on standards of proof, standards of appellate review, and access to federal court. For a fuller discussion, see Michael J. Klarman, The *Plessy* Era, 1998 Sup. Ct. Rev. 303, 376-78.
9. 297 U.S. 278 (1936).

These four decisions arose from three distinct episodes. In *Moore*, six black defendants appealed death sentences imposed for a murder allegedly committed in connection with the infamous race riot in Phillips County, Arkansas in the fall of 1919.[10] Phillips was a typical deep South cotton county with a black majority of approximately three-to-one. According to the local black community, the cause of the racial altercation that culminated in the *Moore* litigation was the brutal suppression by whites of an effort by black sharecroppers after World War I to form a tenant farmers' union and to seek legal redress for their landlords' peonage practices. The white community, on the contrary, charged that the cause of the conflagration was a black conspiracy to murder white planters throughout the county. An initial altercation in which whites shot into a black union meeting at a church and blacks returned the gunfire, killing a white man, quickly escalated into mayhem. Marauding whites, some of whom flocked to Phillips County from adjoining states and enjoyed the assistance of federal troops ostensibly employed to quell the disturbance, went on a rampage against blacks, tracking them down through the rural county, and killing (on one estimate) as many as 250 of them. Seventy-nine blacks (and no whites) were prosecuted as a result of the riot; twelve received the death penalty for murder; and six were involved in the appeal to the United States Supreme Court in Moore v. Dempsey. The Court reversed their convictions on the ground that mob-dominated trial proceedings violated the Due Process Clause.

The second and third race-based criminal procedure cases of the interwar period, Powell v. Alabama and Norris v. Alabama, both arose out of the famous Scottsboro Boys episode.[11] Nine black youths, ranging in age from thirteen to twenty, impoverished, illiterate, and transient, were charged with raping two young white women, alleged to be prostitutes, on a freight train in northern Alabama in the spring of 1931. They were tried in a mob-dominated atmosphere, and eight of the defendants received the death penalty. The state supreme court reversed one of these death sentences on the ground that the defendant was too young to be executed under state law and affirmed the other seven. The United States Supreme Court twice reversed the Scottsboro Boys' convictions — the first time on the ground that they had been denied the right to counsel, and the second time on the ground that blacks had been intentionally excluded from the grand jury that indicted them and the trial jury that convicted them.

Fourth and finally, in Brown v. Mississippi the Supreme Court reversed the death sentences of three black sharecroppers convicted of murdering their white landlord.[12] The principal evidence against the defendants was their own confessions, extracted through torture. The Supreme Court ruled that convictions so obtained violated the Due Process Clause of the Fourteenth Amendment.

These four cases arose out of three quite similar episodes. Southern black defendants were charged with serious crimes against whites — either rape or murder. All three sets of defendants nearly were lynched before their cases could be brought to trial. In all three episodes, mobs comprised of hundreds or even thousands of whites surrounded the courthouse during the trial, demanding that the defendants be turned over for a swift execution. No change of venue was granted in these cases (except in the retrial of the Scottsboro Boys). Lynchings were avoided only through the presence of state militiamen armed with machine guns surrounding the courthouse. There was a

10. The most detailed treatment of *Moore* is Richard C. Cortner, A Mob Intent on Death: The NAACP and the Arkansas Riot Cases (1988). A briefer description appears in O. A. Rogers, Jr., The Elaine Race Riots of 1919, 19 Ark. Hist. Q. 142 (1960).

11. For extensive treatment of the Scottsboro Boys episode, see Dan T. Carter, Scottsboro: A Tragedy of the American South (rev. ed. 1979) and James Goodman, Stories of Scottsboro (1994).

12. The most complete treatment is Richard C. Cortner, A "Scottsboro" Case in Mississippi: The Supreme Court and *Brown v. Mississippi* (1986).

serious doubt — not just with the aid of historical hindsight, but at the time of the trial — as to whether any of the defendants was in fact guilty of the crime charged. The defendants in *Moore* and *Brown* were tortured into confessing. In all three cases, defense lawyers were appointed either the day of or the day preceding trial, with no adequate opportunity to consult with their clients, to interview witnesses, or to prepare a defense strategy. Trials took place quickly after the alleged crimes in order to avoid a lynching — less than a week afterwards in *Brown*, twelve days in *Powell*, and a month in *Moore*. The trials were completed within a matter of hours (forty-five minutes in *Moore*), and the juries, from which blacks were intentionally excluded in all three cases, deliberated for only a matter of minutes before imposing death sentences.[13]

Michael J. Klarman, The Racial Origins of Modern Criminal Procedure, 99 Mich. L. Rev. 48, 50-52 (2000).

As Klarman argues in his article, these cases are as much about race as about criminal procedure. But they gave rise to an idea that goes beyond race — the idea that due process should ensure accurate procedures, procedures that would prevent conviction of innocent defendants. Thus, the problem with the mob-dominated trial in *Moore*, with the absence of any real defense counsel in *Powell*, and with the beating-induced confession in *Brown* was the same: All tended to lead to conviction and punishment without regard to whether the defendants were guilty.

From roughly 1940 to 1960, this strand of due process produced two major lines of cases. First, indigent criminal defendants were entitled to appointed counsel if there were "special circumstances" that made it impossible for them to represent themselves. See Betts v. Brady, 316 U.S. 455 (1942). Obviously, this standard required a good deal of ad hoc evaluation of the nature of the case in order to decide whether appointed counsel was really necessary. The second line of cases held, following Brown v. Mississippi, that involuntary confessions were inadmissible. That standard prompted a good deal of litigation in the 1940s and 1950s; one of the themes running through those cases was the need to ensure that confessions were truthful. See, e.g., Stein v. New York, 346 U.S. 156, 182 (1953) ("The tendency of the innocent . . . to risk remote results of a false confession rather than suffer immediate pain is so strong that judges long ago found it necessary to . . . treat[ ] any confession made concurrently with torture or threat of brutality as too untrustworthy to be received as evidence of guilt.").

Since 1960, due-process-as-accuracy has produced a variety of doctrines. Under Brady v. Maryland, 373 U.S. 83 (1963), and its progeny, the prosecution must turn over exculpatory evidence to the defense. (This requirement is discussed in Chapter 11.) Under Drope v. Missouri, 420 U.S. 162 (1975), defendants cannot be made to stand trial unless they are competent to assist in their own defense.

13. On Scottsboro, see Carter, supra note 11, chs. 1-2; Goodman, supra note 11, chs. 1-2. On *Moore*, see Cortner, *Mob*, supra note 10, ch. 1. On *Brown*, see Cortner, *Brown*, supra note 12, chs. 1-2. The Scottsboro Boys certainly were innocent of the crimes charged, as revealed in a subsequent recantation by one of the alleged victims. Their innocence should have been reasonably clear at the trial both from the medical evidence and from the conflicting testimony of the prosecution's witnesses. See Brief for Petitioners at 28-30, Powell v. Alabama, 287 U.S. 45 (1932) (Nos. 98-100), reprinted in 27 Landmark Briefs and Arguments of the Supreme Court of the United States: Constitutional Law 291, 324-326 (Philip B. Kurland & Gerhard Casper eds. 1975); Carter, supra, at 27-30, 227-28, 232. The *Brown* defendants possibly were innocent, and the State surely lacked sufficient evidence to convict them apart from their tortured [confessions]. See Brown v. State, 161 So. 465, 471 (Miss. 1935) (Griffith, J., dissenting). The *Moore* defendants at most were guilty of being present when the lethal shots were fired, and not even clearly of this. See Cortner, *Mob*, supra note 10, 124-25. . . .

(This line of cases is discussed in Medina v. California, at page 100 infra.) Ake v. Oklahoma, 470 U.S. 168 (1985), holds that in some cases the court must appoint a mental health expert to assist in the preparation of a defendant's insanity claim.

Are these rules adequate to ensure a fair process? Is there anything beyond accuracy that needs constitutional protection?

"Fundamental Fairness." The last of the four strands is the hardest to describe, because it boils down to little more than judicial intuition. In a series of cases going back to the first decade of the twentieth century, the Supreme Court has decided whether due process requires a given practice by asking whether the practice is somehow basic to a decent criminal justice system — whether it is the sort of protection any free society ought to provide. The Court has used different phrases to capture this approach at different times; today the phrase of choice is "fundamental fairness." What is meant by that phrase (or by its earlier substitutes) is not clear; it seems to be a stand-in for a generalized sense that some kinds of government conduct are outrageous (never mind why) or that some procedures are essential (never mind for what).

An early example of this approach is Twining v. New Jersey, 211 U.S. 78 (1908). Twining's jury was told it could draw adverse inferences from his failure to take the witness stand; Twining's claim was that this violated the privilege against self-incrimination, which, he argued, applied to New Jersey through the Fourteenth Amendment's Due Process Clause. The Court's analysis is captured by the following strange sentence: "We have to consider whether the right is so fundamental in due process that a refusal of the right is a denial of due process." Id. at 107. The Court's answer was no. In Palko v. Connecticut, 302 U.S. 319 (1937), the Court gave the same answer when asked whether the prohibition against double jeopardy was sufficiently "fundamental." (Palko was tried and convicted of second-degree murder; he successfully appealed the conviction; the state then retried him and this time convicted him of capital murder and sentenced him to death.) Justice Cardozo, speaking for the majority, explained the line between those procedures required by due process and those not:

> There emerges the perception of a rationalizing principle which gives . . . a proper order and coherence. The right to trial by jury and the immunity from prosecution except as the result of an indictment may have value and importance. Even so, they are not of the very essence of a scheme of ordered liberty. To abolish them is not to violate a "principle of justice so rooted in the traditions and conscience of our people as to be ranked as fundamental." Snyder v. Massachusetts, [291 U.S. 97,] 105. Few would be so narrow or provincial as to maintain that a fair and enlightened system of justice would be impossible without them. What is true of jury trials and indictments is true also, as the cases show, of the immunity from compulsory self-incrimination. Twining v. New Jersey, supra. This too might be lost, and justice still be done. . . . Justice . . . would not perish if the accused were subject to a duty to respond to orderly inquiry. . . .
>   . . . Is that kind of double jeopardy to which the statute has subjected [the defendant] a hardship so acute and shocking that our polity will not endure it? Does it violate those "fundamental principles of liberty and justice which lie at the base of all our civil and political institutions"? Hebert v. Louisiana, [272 U.S. 312]. The answer surely must be "no."

One is tempted to ask, "why not?"

This sort of analysis reached its nadir in Rochin v. California, 342 U.S. 165 (1952). The Court recounted the facts in *Rochin* as follows:

Having "some information that [the petitioner here] was selling narcotics," three deputy sheriffs of the County of Los Angeles, on the morning of July 1, 1949, made for the two-story dwelling house in which Rochin lived with his mother, common-law wife, brothers and sisters. Finding the outside door open, they entered and then forced open the door to Rochin's room on the second floor. Inside they found petitioner sitting partly dressed on the side of the bed, upon which his wife was lying. On a "night stand" beside the bed the deputies spied two capsules. When asked "Whose stuff is this?" Rochin seized the capsules and put them in his mouth. A struggle ensued, in the course of which the three officers "jumped upon him" and attempted to extract the capsules. The force they applied proved unavailing against Rochin's resistance. He was handcuffed and taken to a hospital. At the direction of one of the officers a doctor forced an emetic solution through a tube into Rochin's stomach against his will. This "stomach pumping" produced vomiting. In the vomited matter were found two capsules which proved to contain morphine.

In a stunningly uninformative opinion by Justice Frankfurter, the Court concluded that the stomach pumping violated due process:

The vague contours of the Due Process Clause do not leave judges at large. We may not draw on our merely personal and private notions and disregard the limits that bind judges in their judicial function. Even though the concept of due process of law is not final and fixed, these limits are derived from considerations that are fused in the whole nature of our judicial process. These are considerations deeply rooted in reason and in the compelling traditions of the legal profession. The Due Process Clause places upon this Court the duty of exercising a judgment, within the narrow confines of judicial power in reviewing State convictions, upon interests of society pushing in opposite directions. . . .

. . . [T]hat does not make due process of law a matter of judicial caprice. The faculties of the Due Process Clause may be indefinite and vague, but the mode of their ascertainment is not self-willed. In each case "due process of law" requires an evaluation based on a disinterested inquiry pursued in the spirit of science, on a balanced order of facts exactly and fairly stated, on the detached consideration of conflicting claims, on a judgment not ad hoc and episodic but duly mindful of reconciling the needs both of continuity and of change in a progressive society.

Applying these general considerations to the circumstances of the present case, we are compelled to conclude that the proceedings by which this conviction was obtained do more than offend some fastidious squeamishness or private sentimentalism about combatting crime too energetically. This is conduct that shocks the conscience. Illegally breaking into the privacy of the petitioner, the struggle to open his mouth and remove what was there, the forcible extraction of his stomach's contents — this course of proceeding by agents of government to obtain evidence is bound to offend even hardened sensibilities. They are methods too close to the rack and the screw to permit of constitutional differentiation.

342 U.S. at 170-172. Is Justice Frankfurter saying anything more than that he thinks the police behaved very badly? Does he say why?

Rochin-style due process analysis survives today, at least in a few outposts. A good modern example is Darden v. Wainwright, 477 U.S. 168 (1986). *Darden* was a capital murder case; in his closing argument, the prosecutor called the defendant an "animal," said "he shouldn't be out of his cell unless he has a leash on him," and expressed the wish that someone could have "blown his head off" before he had committed the crime. The Court held that the argument was improper, but not improper enough to amount to a violation of due process:

> . . . The relevant question is whether the prosecutors' comments "so infected the trial with unfairness as to make the resulting conviction a denial of due process." Donnelly v. DeChristoforo, 416 U.S. 637 (1974). . . .
>
> Under this standard of review, we agree with the reasoning of every court to consider these comments that they did not deprive petitioner of a fair trial. The prosecutors' argument did not manipulate or misstate the evidence, nor did it implicate other specific rights of the accused such as the right to counsel or the right to remain silent. . . . The trial court instructed the jurors several times that their decision was to be made on the basis of the evidence alone, and that the arguments of counsel were not evidence. The weight of the evidence against petitioner was heavy . . . [reducing] the likelihood that the jury's decision was influenced by argument. . . . For these reasons, we agree with the District Court below that "Darden's trial was not perfect—few are—but neither was it fundamentally unfair."

477 U.S. at 181-183. So the search in *Rochin* was shocking, while the prosecutor's argument in *Darden* was not (though it was close). Why are some things shocking and others not? Is there any content to these cases? Does the idea of fundamental fairness seem empty?

B. *Incorporation*

DUNCAN v. LOUISIANA

Appeal from the Supreme Court of Louisiana
391 U.S. 145 (1968)

MR. JUSTICE WHITE delivered the opinion of the Court.

Appellant, Gary Duncan, was convicted of simple battery in the Twenty-fifth Judicial District Court of Louisiana. Under Louisiana law simple battery is a misdemeanor, punishable by a maximum of two years' imprisonment and a $300 fine. Appellant sought trial by jury, but because the Louisiana Constitution grants jury trials only in cases in which capital punishment or imprisonment at hard labor may be imposed, the trial judge denied the request. Appellant was convicted and sentenced to serve 60 days in the parish prison and pay a fine of $150. [The conviction was affirmed on appeal.] . . .

Appellant was 19 years of age when tried. While driving on Highway 23 in Plaquemines Parish on October 18, 1966, he saw two younger cousins engaged in a conversation by the side of the road with four white boys. Knowing his cousins, Negroes who had recently transferred to a formerly all-white high school, had reported the occurrence of racial incidents at the school, Duncan stopped the car, got out, and approached the six boys. At trial the white boys and a white onlooker testified, as did appellant and his cousins. The testimony was in dispute on many points, but the witnesses agreed that appellant and the white boys spoke to each other, that appellant encouraged his cousins to break off the encounter and enter his car, and that appellant was about to enter the car himself for the purpose of driving away with his cousins. The whites testified that just before getting in the car appellant slapped Herman Landry, one of the white boys, on the elbow. The Negroes testified that appellant had not slapped Landry, but had merely touched him. The trial judge concluded that the State had proved beyond a reasonable doubt that Duncan had committed simple battery, and found him guilty.

The Fourteenth Amendment denies the States the power to "deprive any person of life, liberty, or property, without due process of law." In resolving conflicting claims concerning the meaning of this spacious language, the Court has looked increasingly to the Bill of Rights for guidance; many of the rights guaranteed by the first eight Amendments to the Constitution have been held to be protected against state action by the Due Process Clause of the Fourteenth Amendment. That clause now protects the right to compensation for property taken by the State;[4] the rights of speech, press, and religion covered by the First Amendment;[5] the Fourth Amendment rights to be free from unreasonable searches and seizures and to have excluded from criminal trials any evidence illegally seized;[6] the right guaranteed by the Fifth Amendment to be free of compelled self-incrimination;[7] and the Sixth Amendment rights to counsel,[8] to a speedy[9] and public[10] trial, to confrontation of opposing witnesses,[11] and to compulsory process for obtaining witnesses.[12]

The test for determining whether a right extended by the Fifth and Sixth Amendments with respect to federal criminal proceedings is also protected against state action by the Fourteenth Amendment has been phrased in a variety of ways in the opinions of this Court. The question has been asked whether a right is among those "fundamental principles of liberty and justice which lie at the base of all our civil and political institutions," Powell v. Alabama, 287 U.S. 45, 67 (1932); whether it is "basic in our system of jurisprudence," In re Oliver, 333 U.S. 257, 273 (1948); and whether it is "a fundamental right, essential to a fair trial," Gideon v. Wainwright, 372 U.S. 335, 343-344 (1963). The claim before us is that the right to trial by jury guaranteed by the Sixth Amendment meets these tests. The position of Louisiana, on the other hand, is that the Constitution imposes upon the States no duty to give a jury trial in any criminal case, regardless of the seriousness of the crime or the size of the punishment which may be imposed. Because we believe that trial by jury in criminal cases is fundamental to the American scheme of justice, we hold that the Fourteenth Amendment guarantees a right of jury trial in all criminal cases which — were they to be tried in a federal court — would come within the Sixth Amendment's guarantee.[14] Since we consider the appeal before us

4. Chicago, B. & Q. R. Co. v. Chicago, 166 U.S. 226 (1897).
5. See, e.g., Fiske v. Kansas, 274 U.S. 380 (1927).
6. See Mapp v. Ohio, 367 U.S. 643 (1961).
7. Malloy v. Hogan, 378 U.S. 1 (1964).
8. Gideon v. Wainwright, 372 U.S. 335 (1963).
9. Klopfer v. North Carolina, 386 U.S. 213 (1967).
10. In re Oliver, 333 U.S. 257 (1948).
11. Pointer v. Texas, 380 U.S. 400 (1965).
12. Washington v. Texas, 388 U.S. 14 (1967).

14. In one sense recent cases applying provisions of the first eight Amendments to the States represent a new approach to the "incorporation" debate. Earlier the Court can be seen as having asked, when inquiring into whether some particular procedural safeguard was required of a State, if a civilized system could be imagined that would not accord the particular protection. For example, Palko v. Connecticut, 302 U.S. 319, 325 (1937), stated: "The right to trial by jury and the immunity from prosecution except

to be such a case, we hold that the Constitution was violated when appellant's demand for jury trial was refused.

The history of trial by jury in criminal cases has been frequently told. It is sufficient for present purposes to say that by the time our Constitution was written, jury trial in criminal cases had been in existence in England for several centuries and carried impressive credentials traced by many to Magna Carta. Its preservation and proper operation as a protection against arbitrary rule were among the major objectives of the revolutionary settlement which was expressed in the Declaration and Bill of Rights of 1689. . . . Jury trial came to America with English colonists, and received strong support from them. Royal interference with the jury trial was deeply resented. . . . The Declaration of Independence stated solemn objections to the King's . . . "depriving us in many cases, of the benefits of Trial by Jury." . . . The Constitution itself, in Art. III, §2, commanded: "The Trial of all Crimes, except in Cases of Impeachment, shall be by Jury; and such Trial shall be held in the State where the said Crimes shall have been committed." . . .

The constitutions adopted by the original States guaranteed jury trial. Also, the constitution of every State entering the Union thereafter in one form or another protected the right to jury trial in criminal cases. Even such skeletal history is impressive support for considering the right to jury trial in criminal cases to be fundamental to our system of justice. . . .

Jury trial continues to receive strong support. The laws of every State guarantee a right to jury trial in serious criminal cases; no State has dispensed with it; nor are there significant movements under way to do so. . . .

. . . The guarantees of jury trial in the Federal and State Constitutions reflect a profound judgment about the way in which law should be enforced and justice administered. A right to jury trial is granted to criminal defendants in order to prevent oppression by the Government. Those who wrote our constitutions knew

---

as the result of an indictment may have value and importance. Even so, they are not of the very essence of a scheme of ordered liberty. . . . Few would be so narrow or provincial as to maintain that a fair and enlightened system of justice would be impossible without them." The recent cases, on the other hand, have proceeded upon the valid assumption that state criminal processes are not imaginary and theoretical schemes but actual systems bearing virtually every characteristic of the common-law system that has been developing contemporaneously in England and in this country. The question thus is whether given this kind of system a particular procedure is fundamental—whether, that is, a procedure is necessary to an Anglo-American regime of ordered liberty. It is this sort of inquiry that can justify the conclusions that state courts must exclude evidence seized in violation of the Fourth Amendment, Mapp v. Ohio, 367 U.S. 643 (1961); that state prosecutors may not comment on a defendant's failure to testify, Griffin v. California, 380 U.S. 609 (1965); and that criminal punishment may not be imposed for the status of narcotics addiction, Robinson v. California, 370 U.S. 660 (1962). Of immediate relevance for this case are the Court's holdings that the States must comply with certain provisions of the Sixth Amendment, specifically that the States may not refuse a speedy trial, confrontation of witnesses, and the assistance, at state expense if necessary, of counsel. See cases cited in nn. 8-12, supra. Of each of these determinations that a constitutional provision originally written to bind the Federal Government should bind the States as well it might be said that the limitation in question is not necessarily fundamental to fairness in every criminal system that might be imagined but is fundamental in the context of the criminal processes maintained by the American States.

. . . A criminal process which was fair and equitable but used no juries is easy to imagine. It would make use of alternative guarantees and protections which would serve the purposes that the jury serves in the English and American systems. Yet no American State has undertaken to construct such a system. Instead, every American State, including Louisiana, uses the jury extensively, and imposes very serious punishments only after a trial at which the defendant has a right to a jury's verdict. In every State, including Louisiana, the structure and style of the criminal process—the supporting framework and the subsidiary procedures—are of the sort that naturally complement jury trial, and have developed in connection with and in reliance upon jury trial.

from history and experience that it was necessary to protect against unfounded criminal charges brought to eliminate enemies and against judges too responsive to the voice of higher authority. . . . Providing an accused with the right to be tried by a jury of his peers gave him an inestimable safeguard against the corrupt or over-zealous prosecutor and against the compliant, biased, or eccentric judge. If the defendant preferred the common-sense judgment of a jury to the more tutored but perhaps less sympathetic reaction of the single judge, he was to have it. Beyond this, the jury trial provisions in the Federal and State Constitutions reflect a fundamental decision about the exercise of official power — a reluctance to entrust plenary powers over the life and liberty of the citizen to one judge or to a group of judges. . . . The deep commitment of the Nation to the right of jury trial in serious criminal cases as a defense against arbitrary law enforcement qualifies for protection under the Due Process Clause of the Fourteenth Amendment, and must therefore be respected by the States.

. . . We are aware of the long debate, especially in this century, among those who write about the administration of justice, as to the wisdom of permitting untrained laymen to determine the facts in civil and criminal proceedings. . . . [A]t the heart of the dispute have been express or implicit assertions that juries are incapable of adequately understanding evidence or determining issues of fact, and that they are unpredictable, quixotic, and little better than a roll of dice. Yet, the most recent and exhaustive study of the jury in criminal cases concluded that juries do understand the evidence and come to sound conclusions in most of the cases presented to them and that when juries differ with the result at which the judge would have arrived, it is usually because they are serving some of the very purposes for which they were created and for which they are now employed.[26]

The State of Louisiana urges that holding that the Fourteenth Amendment assures a right to jury trial will cast doubt on the integrity of every trial conducted without a jury. Plainly, this is not the import of our holding. . . . We would not assert . . . that every criminal trial — or any particular trial — held before a judge alone is unfair or that a defendant may never be as fairly treated by a judge as he would be by a jury. Thus we hold no constitutional doubts about the practices, common in both federal and state courts, of accepting waivers of jury trial and prosecuting petty crimes without extending a right to jury trial. However, the fact is that in most places more trials for serious crimes are to juries than to a court alone; a great many defendants prefer the judgment of a jury to that of a court. Even where defendants are satisfied with bench trials, the right to a jury trial very likely serves its intended purpose of making judicial or prosecutorial unfairness less likely.

Louisiana's final contention is that even if it must grant jury trials in serious criminal cases, the conviction before us is valid and constitutional because here the petitioner was tried for simple battery and was sentenced to only 60 days in the parish prison. . . . It is doubtless true that there is a category of petty crimes or offenses which is not subject to the Sixth Amendment jury trial provision and should not be subject to the Fourteenth Amendment jury trial requirement here applied to the States. . . . In the case before us the Legislature of Louisiana has made simple battery a criminal offense punishable by imprisonment for up to two years and a fine. The question, then, is whether a crime carrying such a penalty is an offense which Louisiana may insist on trying without a jury. . . .

26. [Citing Harry Kalven, Jr., & Hans Zeisel, The American Jury (1966).]

. . . In the federal system, petty offenses are defined as those punishable by no more than six months in prison and a $500 fine. In 49 of the 50 States crimes subject to trial without a jury, which occasionally include simple battery, are punishable by no more than one year in jail. Moreover, in the late 18th century in America crimes triable without a jury were for the most part punishable by no more than a six-month prison term, although there appear to have been exceptions to this rule. We need not, however, settle in this case the exact location of the line between petty offenses and serious crimes. It is sufficient for our purposes to hold that a crime punishable by two years in prison is, based on past and contemporary standards in this country, a serious crime and not a petty offense. Consequently, appellant was entitled to a jury trial and it was error to deny it. . . .

[The concurring opinion of Justice Black, joined by Justice Douglas, and the dissenting opinion of Justice Harlan, joined by Justice Stewart, are omitted.]

NOTES ON *DUNCAN* AND THE INCORPORATION OF THE BILL OF RIGHTS

1. *Duncan*'s facts, at least as the Court recounts them, suggest a racially rigged proceeding, do they not? In this respect, *Duncan* looks like Moore v. Dempsey, 261 U.S. 86 (1923), Powell v. Alabama, 287 U.S. 45 (1932), and Brown v. Mississippi, 297 U.S. 278 (1936)—earlier cases in which the Court overturned convictions of black defendants in proceedings that seemed racially rigged. (*Moore*, *Powell*, and *Brown* are discussed at pages 88-91 supra.)

In none of these cases did the Court treat the legal issue as one of race discrimination. Instead, the Court's rulings were general, mandating or prohibiting certain procedures across the board—no mob-dominated trials in *Moore*, no uncounseled convictions in capital cases in *Powell*, no involuntary confessions in *Brown*, no denial of jury trial in *Duncan*. This has been a longstanding pattern in the law of constitutional criminal procedure. A great deal of the law covered in books like this one arises out of cases like *Duncan*—cases in which the real concern seems to be race-based injustice. Yet the law almost always deals with that concern indirectly, by regulating procedures that have little to do with race.

Why the indirection? Why not say Duncan's conviction was discriminatory, and leave it at that? One answer is that regulating discrimination directly would have led the Court, and the judiciary, into some very large and complex thickets. Suppose in a given jurisdiction, black Americans constitute 10 percent of the population but 25 percent of those arrested and convicted of crimes. Does that suggest discrimination? It might. But it might mean instead that the black population of that jurisdiction is disproportionately poor, and hence disproportionately involved in (and victimized by) crime. Indeed, the *absence* of a racial disproportion might be a sign of discrimination. Consider: In South Carolina in 1950—the deep South, during the heyday of Jim Crow—the imprisoned felon population was slightly *whiter* than the population as a whole. Compare Federal Bureau of Prisons, National Prisoner Statistics: Prisoners in State and Federal Institutions—1950, at 55 tbl. 21 (1954) (prison population nearly two-thirds white) with U.S. Department of Commerce, Statistical Abstract of the United States–1953, at 36 tbl. 25 (overall population 61 percent white). South Carolina in 1950 was not running a color-blind criminal justice system. The more plausible possibility is that local police forces and local prosecutors were neglecting to investigate and prosecute crimes *against* blacks. Since most crime is intra-racial, that tendency would naturally lead to fewer black prisoners. For a good discussion of this two-sided nature of discrimination in the criminal justice system, see Randall Kennedy, Race, Crime, and the Law (1997). All of which means that it is much harder than one might think to draw the line between racist law enforcement and law enforcement that is trying as best it can to advance the interests of the communities it serves.

Spotting clear cases of discrimination, like *Duncan*, may be easy. But once the easy cases are put aside, discrimination becomes much more subtle—which is not to say it is less real or less substantial—and much harder for courts to identify. Should the focus be on discrimination against black suspects? Black crime victims? Should courts be in the business of allocating police and prosecutorial resources across different racial communities? These questions, and others equally hard, would have to be faced if the Court sought to attack the criminal justice system's race problems directly.

None of this is to say that the Court's approach in *Duncan*, or in earlier cases like *Moore, Powell*, and *Brown*, was right. Perhaps we would be better off if race were addressed more directly in the law of criminal procedure. Whatever the right answer to that question is, the Supreme Court's usual strategy has been to sidestep—and to regulate procedures aggressively on *non*-racial grounds.

2. Notice one key difference between *Duncan* and most of the pre-incorporation due process cases. In the older due process cases, the Court almost always responded to apparent injustices with standards that required case-by-case development and application. Brown v. Mississippi, 297 U.S. 278 (1936), barred the use of involuntary confessions, but left open what voluntariness meant. Betts v. Brady, 316 U.S. 455 (1942), required use of appointed counsel where special circumstances suggested a particular need, but left undefined what those circumstances were. In *Duncan*, by contrast, the Court established a hard-and-fast rule. At the least, the Court said, any crime punishable by two years in prison triggers the right to a jury; the Court hinted that any crime punishable by more than six months would do so as well. (The hint was soon confirmed by Baldwin v. New York, 399 U.S. 66 (1970).) Why the shift from standards to rules? What would a standard (as opposed to a rule) look like in *Duncan*?

3. The move from standards to rules is one of the most important effects of incorporation; in one area after another, the Court of the 1960s and 1970s created a large body of detailed legal rules where previously constitutional law had said little more than "be fair." Examples include the right to jury trial in *Duncan*, covered in more detail in Chapter 12, the detailed rules governing the Fourth Amendment's warrant requirement (and exceptions thereto) covered in Chapter 5, the rules governing application of the Fifth Amendment's privilege against self-incrimination to police interrogation, covered in Chapter 6, or the rules defining the ban on double jeopardy, the subject of Chapter 14. In each of these areas, pre-incorporation constitutional law either said nothing at all or offered only a vague prohibition of extreme misconduct. Constitutional law today says a great deal, and a great deal of it is in the form of rules.

As that description suggests, there are two other changes that went alongside the move from standards to rules. Before incorporation, constitutional law regulated the criminal process very lightly. After incorporation, it regulates much more extensively. Constitutional law today goes far toward defining the criminal process — it is not a marginal presence in criminal procedure; on the contrary, it *dominates* criminal procedure. So constitutional regulation has become much more intrusive — much larger — as it has become much more rule-like. The last of these three changes is the most obvious. Incorporation shifts the constitutional focus from the Due Process Clause to the various criminal procedure provisions of the Bill of Rights. Instead of construing the phrase "due process of law," courts today are more likely to be interpreting phrases like "the assistance of counsel," or "compelled to be a witness against himself," or "unreasonable searches and seizures."

These three changes — from standards to rules, from light regulation to heavy regulation, from due process to the Bill of Rights — happened together. Is that anything more than an accident? Couldn't the Supreme Court have crafted a law of due process that was more rule-like? That regulated criminal procedure more extensively? As you study subsequent chapters in this book, consider this question: How might the law differ if it were based on due process and not on some provision of the Fourth, Fifth, or Sixth Amendment?

4. One common complaint about pre-incorporation due process cases is the absence of any clear, agreed-upon value being advanced. In some cases the Court seemed concerned with ensuring accurate trials; in other cases it was more concerned with preserving the rule of law; in still others it was concerned with something the Justices found impossible to articulate, capturing it in labels like "fundamental fairness" or "shocks the conscience." Incorporation seems, at first blush, to solve that problem, by anchoring the Court's criminal procedure decisions in more definite pieces of constitutional text. The right to a jury, the right to counsel, the privilege against self-incrimination — all these things seem clearer than "due process of law."

But that clarity may be an illusion. Think about *Duncan* and the right to jury trial. What is the point of that right? There are several possible answers. Juries could be designed to ensure accuracy — the idea here would be that a single judge is more likely to convict an innocent defendant than are 12 citizens. Or juries could be designed as a democratic check on the judiciary. Here the image is of juries as mini-legislatures, supervising the behavior of police, prosecutors, and judges. Yet a third possibility is suggested by the facts in *Duncan*: Juries could be a way to ensure that racial or ethnic minorities are punished with the consent of their peers. That might translate into juries that always have black or Latino members when judging black or Latino defendants.

These possibilities lead to very different visions of the right. If accuracy is the point, the right to a jury ought to be available, at the least, for all serious crimes — as *Duncan* holds. If preserving a democratic check on the courts is the point, perhaps juries ought to be required in *all* criminal trials (and perhaps *trials* should be required, since plea bargains are hidden from the public). If ensuring minority representation is the point, maybe the right to a jury ought to be available to black defendants like Duncan, but not to the white teenagers with whom Duncan was allegedly fighting.

In short, the Court must, at least tacitly, decide what the right to a jury is *about* in order to decide what that right entails. Answering that question may be no easier than answering the question what due process is about. And with incorporation, the question is repeated for every Bill of Rights provision. What is the point of banning "unreasonable searches and seizures"? Privacy protection? Protecting against police coercion? Something else? What about the privilege against self-incrimination — is it a protection for the guilty, or for the innocent? Does it protect freedom of thought, or does it only limit the government's ability to twist people's arms? Is the right to counsel a means of ensuring equality between rich and poor defendants, or a tool for generating accurate results? Because of incorporation, the law of criminal procedure must answer all these questions. And the questions are just as difficult as the question the Due Process Clause poses: What does it mean to treat people fairly?

C. The Residual Due Process Clause

What is left of due process in criminal cases apart from the Bill of Rights? Consider the following case.

MEDINA v. CALIFORNIA

Certiorari to the Supreme Court of California
505 U.S. 437 (1992)

JUSTICE KENNEDY delivered the opinion of the Court.

It is well established that the Due Process Clause of the Fourteenth Amendment prohibits the criminal prosecution of a defendant who is not competent to stand trial. Drope v. Missouri, 420 U.S. 162 (1975); Pate v. Robinson, 383 U.S. 375 (1966). The issue in this case is whether the Due Process Clause permits a State to require a defendant who alleges incompetence to stand trial to bear the burden of proving so by a preponderance of the evidence.

In 1984, petitioner Teofilo Medina, Jr., stole a gun from a pawnshop in Santa Ana, California. In the weeks that followed, he held up two gas stations, a drive-in dairy, and a market, murdered three employees of those establishments, attempted to rob a fourth employee, and shot at two passers-by who attempted to follow his getaway car. Petitioner was . . . charged with a number of criminal offenses, including three counts of first-degree murder. Before trial, petitioner's counsel moved for a competency hearing . . . on the ground that he was unsure whether petitioner had the ability to participate in the criminal proceedings against him.

Under California law, "[a] person cannot be tried or adjudged to punishment while such person is mentally incompetent." Cal. Penal Code Ann. §1367 (West 1982). A defendant is mentally incompetent "if, as a result of mental disorder or developmental disability, the defendant is unable to understand the nature of the criminal proceedings or to assist counsel in the conduct of a defense in a rational manner." Ibid. The statute establishes a presumption that the defendant is competent, and the party claiming incompetence bears the burden of proving that the defendant is incompetent by a preponderance of the evidence. . . .

The trial court granted the motion for a hearing and the preliminary issue of petitioner's competence to stand trial was tried to a jury. Over the course of the 6-day hearing, in addition to lay testimony, the jury heard conflicting expert testimony about petitioner's mental condition. The Supreme Court of California gives this summary:

> "Dr. Gold, a psychiatrist who knew defendant while he was in the Arizona prison system, testified that defendant was a paranoid schizophrenic and was incompetent to assist his attorney at trial. Dr. Echeandia, a clinical psychologist at the Orange County jail, doubted the accuracy of the schizophrenia diagnosis, and could not express an opinion on defendant's competence to stand trial. Dr. Sharma, a psychiatrist, likewise expressed doubts regarding the schizophrenia diagnosis and leaned toward a finding of competence. Dr. Pierce, a psychologist, believed defendant was schizophrenic, with impaired memory and hallucinations, but nevertheless was competent to stand trial. Dr. Sakurai, a jail psychiatrist, opined that although defendant suffered from depression, he was competent, and that he may have been malingering. Dr. Sheffield, who treated defendant for knife wounds he incurred in jail, could give no opinion on the competency issue." 51 Cal. 3d 870, 880, 799 P.2d 1282, 1288 (1990).

During the competency hearing, petitioner engaged in several verbal and physical outbursts. On one of these occasions, he overturned the counsel table.

. . . The jury found petitioner competent to stand trial. A new jury was empaneled for the criminal trial, and . . . found [petitioner] guilty of all three counts of first-degree murder and a number of lesser offenses. . . . A sanity hearing was held, and the jury found that petitioner was sane at the time of the offenses. At the penalty phase, the jury found that the murders were premeditated and deliberate and returned a verdict of death. The trial court imposed the death penalty for the murder convictions and sentenced petitioner to a prison term for the remaining offenses. . . . [The California Supreme Court affirmed.]

Petitioner argues that our decision in Mathews v. Eldridge, 424 U.S. 319 (1976), provides the proper analytical framework for determining whether California's allocation of the burden of proof in competency hearings comports with due process. We disagree. In *Mathews*, we articulated a three-factor test for evaluating procedural due process claims which requires a court to consider

> "first, the private interest that will be affected by the official action; second, the risk of an erroneous deprivation of such interest through the procedures used, and the probable value, if any, of additional or substitute procedural safeguards; and finally, the Government's interest, including the function involved and the fiscal and administrative burdens that the additional or substitute procedural requirement would entail." Id., at 335.

In our view, the *Mathews* balancing test does not provide the appropriate framework for assessing the validity of state procedural rules which, like the one at bar, are part of the criminal process. . . .

In the field of criminal law, we "have defined the category of infractions that violate 'fundamental fairness' very narrowly" based on the recognition that, "beyond the specific guarantees enumerated in the Bill of Rights, the Due Process Clause has limited operation." Dowling v. United States, 493 U.S. 342, 352 (1990). The Bill of Rights speaks in explicit terms to many aspects of criminal procedure, and the expansion of those constitutional guarantees under the open-ended rubric of the Due Process Clause invites undue interference with both considered legislative judgments and the careful balance that the Constitution strikes between liberty and order. As we said in Spencer v. Texas, 385 U.S. 554, 564 (1967), "it has never been thought that [decisions under the Due Process Clause] establish this Court as a rule-making organ for the promulgation of state rules of criminal procedure."

Mathews itself involved a due process challenge to the adequacy of administrative procedures established for the purpose of terminating Social Security disability benefits, and the *Mathews* balancing test was first conceived to address due process claims arising in the context of administrative law. . . .

The proper analytical approach, and the one that we adopt here, is that set forth in Patterson v. New York, 432 U.S. 197 (1977), which was decided one year after *Mathews*. In *Patterson*, we rejected a due process challenge to a New York law which placed on a criminal defendant the burden of proving the affirmative defense of extreme emotional disturbance. Rather than relying upon the *Mathews* balancing test, however, we reasoned that a narrower inquiry was more appropriate:

> "It goes without saying that preventing and dealing with crime is much more the business of the States than it is of the Federal Government, and that we should not lightly construe the Constitution so as to intrude upon the administration of justice by the individual States. Among other things, it is normally 'within the power of the State to regulate procedures under which its laws are carried out, including the burden of producing evidence and the burden of persuasion,' and its decision in this regard is not subject to proscription under the Due Process Clause unless 'it offends some principle of justice so rooted in the traditions and conscience of our people as to be ranked as fundamental.' Speiser v. Randall, 357 U.S. 513, 523 (1958)." Patterson v. New York, 432 U.S. at 201-202.

As *Patterson* suggests, because the States have considerable expertise in matters of criminal procedure and the criminal process is grounded in centuries of common-law tradition, it is appropriate to exercise substantial deference to legislative judgments in this area. The analytical approach endorsed in *Patterson* is thus far less intrusive than that approved in *Mathews*.

Based on our review of the historical treatment of the burden of proof in competency proceedings, the operation of the challenged rule, and our precedents, we cannot say that the allocation of the burden of proof to a criminal defendant to prove incompetence "offends some principle of justice so rooted in the traditions and conscience of our people as to be ranked as fundamental." Patterson v. New York, 432 U.S. at 202 (internal quotation marks omitted). Historical practice is probative of whether a procedural rule can be characterized as fundamental. See In re Winship, 397 U.S. 358, 361 (1970). The rule that a criminal defendant who is incompetent should not be required to stand trial has deep roots in our common-law heritage. Blackstone acknowledged that a defendant "who became 'mad' after the commission of an offense should not be arraigned for it 'because he is not able to plead to it with that advice and caution that he ought,' " and "if he became 'mad' after pleading, he should not be tried, 'for how can he make his defense?' " Drope v. Missouri, 420 U.S. at 171 (quoting 4 W. Blackstone, Commentaries *24); accord, 1 M. Hale, Pleas of the Crown *34-*35.

By contrast, there is no settled tradition on the proper allocation of the burden of proof in a proceeding to determine competence. . . . Contemporary practice, while of limited relevance to the due process inquiry, demonstrates that there remains no settled view of where the burden of proof should lie. . . . Some States have enacted statutes that, like §1369(f), place the burden of proof on the party raising the issue. E.g., Conn. Gen. Stat. §54-56d(b) (1991); Pa. Stat. Ann., Tit. 50, §7403(a) (Purdon Supp. 1991). A number of state courts have said that the burden of proof may be placed on the defendant to prove incompetence. E.g., Wallace v. State, 248 Ga. 255, 258-259, 282 S.E.2d 325, 330 (1981); State v. Aumann, 265 N.W.2d 316, 319-320 (Iowa 1978); State v. Chapman, 104 N.M. 324, 327-328, 721 P.2d 392, 395-396 (1986); Barber v. State, 757 S.W.2d 359, 362-363 (Tex. Crim. App. 1988) (en banc). Still other state courts have said that the burden rests with the prosecution. E.g., Diaz v. State, 508 A.2d 861, 863-864 (Del. 1986); Commonwealth v. Crowley, 393 Mass. 393, 400-401, 471 N.E.2d 353, 357-358 (1984); State v. Bertrand, 123 N.H. 719, 727-728, 465 A.2d 912, 916 (1983); State v. Jones, 406 N.W.2d 366, 369-370 (S.D. 1987).

Discerning no historical basis for concluding that the allocation of the burden of proving incompetence to the defendant violates due process, we turn to consider whether the rule transgresses any recognized principle of "fundamental fairness" in operation. . . .

Under California law, the allocation of the burden of proof to the defendant will affect competency determinations only in a narrow class of cases where the evidence is in equipoise; that is, where the evidence that a defendant is competent is just as strong as the evidence that he is incompetent. Our cases recognize that a defendant has a constitutional right "not to be tried while legally incompetent," and that a State's "failure to observe procedures adequate to protect a defendant's right not to be tried or convicted while incompetent to stand trial deprives him of his due process right to a fair trial." Drope v. Missouri, 420 U.S. at 172, 173. Once a State provides a defendant access to procedures for making a competency evaluation, however, we perceive no basis for holding that due process further requires the State to assume the burden of vindicating the defendant's constitutional right by persuading the trier of fact that the defendant is competent to stand trial.

Petitioner relies upon federal- and state-court decisions which have said that the allocation of the burden of proof to the defendant in these circumstances is inconsistent with the rule of Pate v. Robinson, 383 U.S. at 384, where we held that a defendant whose competence is in doubt cannot be deemed to have waived his right to a competency hearing. . . . In our view, the question whether a defendant whose competence is in doubt may waive his right to a competency hearing is quite different from the question whether the burden of proof may be placed on the defendant once a hearing is held. The rule announced in *Pate* was driven by our concern that it is impossible to say whether a defendant whose competence is in doubt has made a knowing and intelligent waiver of his right to a competency hearing. Once a competency hearing is held, however, the defendant is entitled to the assistance of counsel, and psychiatric evidence is brought to bear on the question of the defendant's mental condition. Although an impaired defendant might be limited in his ability to assist counsel in demonstrating incompetence, the defendant's inability to assist counsel can, in and of itself, constitute probative evidence of incompetence, and defense counsel will often have the best-informed view of the defendant's ability to participate in his defense. While reasonable minds may differ as to the wisdom of placing the burden of proof on the defendant in these circumstances, we believe that a State may take such factors into account in making judgments as to the allocation of the burden of proof. . . .

Petitioner argues that psychiatry is an inexact science, and that placing the burden of proof on the defendant violates due process because it requires the defendant to "bear the risk of being forced to stand trial as a result of an erroneous finding of competency." Brief for Petitioner 8. . . . The Due Process Clause does not, however, require a State to adopt one procedure over another on the basis that it may produce results more favorable to the accused. See, e.g., Patterson v. New York, 432 U.S. at 208 ("Due process does not require that every conceivable step be taken, at whatever cost, to eliminate the possibility of convicting an innocent person"). Consistent with our precedents, it is enough that the State affords the criminal defendant on whose behalf a plea of incompetence is asserted a reasonable opportunity to demonstrate that he is not competent to stand trial.

Petitioner further contends that the burden of proof should be placed on the State because we have allocated the burden to the State on a variety of other issues that implicate a criminal defendant's constitutional rights. E.g., Colorado v. Connelly, 479 U.S. 157, 168-169 (1986) (waiver of *Miranda* rights); Nix v. Williams, 467 U.S. 431, 444-445, n.5 (1984) (inevitable discovery of evidence obtained by unlawful means); United States v. Matlock, 415 U.S. 164, 177-178, n.14 (1974) (voluntariness of consent to search); Lego v. Twomey, 404 U.S. 477, 489 (1972) (voluntariness of confession). The decisions upon which petitioner relies, however, do not control the result here, because they involved situations where the government sought to introduce inculpatory evidence obtained by virtue of a waiver of, or in violation of, a defendant's constitutional rights. In such circumstances, allocating the burden of proof to the government furthers the objective of "deterring lawless conduct by police and prosecution." Ibid. No such purpose is served by allocating the burden of proof to the government in a competency hearing.

In light of our determination that the allocation of the burden of proof to the defendant does not offend due process, it is not difficult to dispose of petitioner's challenge to the presumption of competence imposed by §1369(f). . . . [I]n essence, the challenged presumption is a restatement of the burden of proof, and it follows from what we have said that the presumption does not violate the Due Process Clause.

Nothing in today's decision is inconsistent with our long-standing recognition that the criminal trial of an incompetent defendant violates due process. Rather, our rejection of petitioner's challenge to §1369(f) is based on a determination that the California procedure is "constitutionally adequate" to guard against such results, Drope v. Missouri, 420 U.S. at 172, and reflects our considered view that "traditionally, due process has required that only the most basic procedural safeguards be observed; more subtle balancing of society's interests against those of the accused has been left to the legislative branch," Patterson v. New York, 432 U.S. at 210. . . .

JUSTICE O'CONNOR, with whom JUSTICE SOUTER joins, concurring in the judgment.

I concur in the judgment of the Court, but I reject its intimation that the balancing of equities is inappropriate in evaluating whether state criminal procedures amount to due process. . . . The balancing of equities that Mathews v. Eldridge [, 424 U.S. 319 (1976),] outlines remains a useful guide in due process cases.

In *Mathews*, however, we did not have to address the question of how much weight to give historical practice; in the context of modern administrative procedures, there was no historical practice to consider. . . . While I agree with the Court that historical pedigree can give a procedural practice a presumption of constitutionality, the presumption must surely be rebuttable.

. . . Against the historical status quo, I read the Court's opinion to allow some weight to be given countervailing considerations of fairness in operation, considerations much like those we evaluated in *Mathews*. Any less charitable reading of the Court's opinion would put it at odds with many of our criminal due process cases, in which we have required States to institute procedures that were neither required at common law nor explicitly commanded by the text of the Constitution. See, e.g., Griffin v. Illinois [, 351 U.S. 12 (1956)] (due process right to trial transcript on appeal); Brady v. Maryland, 373 U.S. 83 (1963) (due process right to discovery of exculpatory evidence); Sheppard v. Maxwell, 384 U.S. 333 (1966) (due process right to protection from prejudicial publicity and courtroom disruptions); Chambers v. Mississippi, 410 U.S. 284 (1973) (due process right to introduce certain evidence); Gagnon v. Scarpelli, 411 U.S. 778 (1973) (due process right to hearing and counsel before probation revoked); Ake v. Oklahoma [, 470 U.S. 68 (1985)] (due process right to psychiatric examination when sanity is significantly in question).

In determining whether the placement of the burden of proof is fundamentally unfair, relevant considerations include: whether the government has superior access to evidence; whether the defendant is capable of aiding in the garnering and evaluation of evidence on the matter to be proved; and whether placing the burden of proof on the government is necessary to help enforce a further right, such as the right to be presumed innocent, the right to be free from self-incrimination, or the right to be tried while competent.

After balancing the equities in this case, I agree with the Court that the burden of proof may constitutionally rest on the defendant. . . . [T]he competency determination is based largely on the testimony of psychiatrists. The main concern of the prosecution, of course, is that a defendant will feign incompetence in order to avoid trial. If the burden of proving competence rests on the government, a defendant will have less incentive to cooperate in psychiatric investigations, because an inconclusive examination will benefit the defense, not the prosecution. A defendant may also be less cooperative in making available friends or family who might have information about the defendant's mental state. States may therefore decide that a more complete picture of a defendant's competence will be obtained if the defense has the incentive to produce all the evidence in its possession. The potentially greater overall access to information provided by placing the burden of proof on the defense may outweigh the danger that, in close cases, a marginally incompetent defendant is brought to trial. Unlike the requirement of a hearing or a psychiatric examination, placing the burden of proof on the government will not necessarily increase the reliability of the proceedings. The equities here, then, do not weigh so much in petitioner's favor as to rebut the presumption of constitutionality that the historical toleration of procedural variation creates. . . .

[The dissenting opinion of Justice Blackmun, joined by Justice Stevens, is omitted.]

NOTES AND QUESTIONS

1. The Supreme Court first held, squarely, that due process requires a hearing on the defendant's competence to stand trial in cases where competence is plausibly at issue in Pate v. Robinson, 383 U.S. 375 (1966). In that case, the state conceded the existence of the legal right but argued that the defendant had waived it. The Court rejected the argument out of hand, saying only that "it is contradictory to argue that a defendant may be incompetent, and yet knowingly or intelligently 'waive' his right to have the court determine his capacity to stand trial." Id. at 384. Is that right? Does the presence of competent defense counsel affect the waiver issue?

Pate left the law of competence to stand trial in an uncertain state. Drope v. Missouri, 420 U.S. 162 (1975), resolved some of the uncertainty. The defendant in *Drope* had a history of mental illness. During his rape trial he tried unsuccessfully to kill himself; the trial court ruled that the trial could continue in the defendant's absence, and he was convicted. No inquiry into the defendant's competence to stand trial was conducted. A unanimous Court concluded that due process was violated:

> It has long been accepted that a person whose mental condition is such that he lacks the capacity to understand the nature and object of the proceedings against him, to consult with counsel, and to assist in preparing his defense may not be subjected to a trial. Thus, Blackstone wrote that one who became "mad" after the commission of an offense should not be arraigned for it "because he is not able to plead to it with that advice and caution that he ought." Similarly, if he became "mad" after pleading, he should not be tried, "for how can he make his defense?" 4 W. Blackstone, Commentaries *24. . . . Accordingly, as to federal cases, we have approved a test of incompetence which seeks to ascertain whether a criminal defendant " 'has sufficient present ability to consult with his lawyer with a reasonable degree of rational understanding — and whether he has a rational as well as factual understanding of the proceedings against him.' " Dusky v. United States, 362 U.S., at 402.
>
> In Pate v. Robinson, 383 U.S. 375 (1966), we held that the failure to observe procedures adequate to protect a defendant's right not to be tried or convicted while incompetent to stand trial deprives him of his due process right to a fair trial. . . . [T]he Court did not prescribe a general standard with respect to the nature or quantum of evidence necessary to require resort to an adequate procedure. Rather, it noted that under the Illinois statute a hearing was required where the evidence raised a " 'bona fide doubt' " as to a defendant's competence, and the Court concluded "that the evidence introduced on Robinson's behalf entitled him to a hearing on this issue." 383 U.S., at 385. . . .
>
> In the present case . . . , [the question is] whether, in light of what was then known, the failure to make further inquiry into petitioner's competence to stand trial, denied him a fair trial. . . .
>
> Notwithstanding the difficulty of making evaluations of the kind required in these circumstances, we conclude that the record reveals a failure to give proper weight to the information suggesting incompetence which came to light during trial. . . .
>
> The import of our decision in Pate v. Robinson is that evidence of a defendant's irrational behavior, his demeanor at trial, and any prior medical opinion on competence to stand trial are all relevant in determining whether further inquiry is required, but that even one of these factors standing alone may, in some circumstances, be sufficient. There are, of course, no fixed or immutable signs which invariably indicate

the need for further inquiry to determine fitness to proceed; the question is often a difficult one in which a wide range of manifestations and subtle nuances are implicated. That they are difficult to evaluate is suggested by the varying opinions trained psychiatrists can entertain on the same facts.

. . . Petitioner's absence [from much of his trial] bears on the analysis in two ways: first, it was due to an act which suggests a rather substantial degree of mental instability contemporaneous with the trial; second, as a result of petitioner's absence the trial judge and defense counsel were no longer able to observe him in the context of the trial and to gauge from his demeanor whether he was able to cooperate with his attorney and to understand the nature and object of the proceedings against him.

Even when a defendant is competent at the commencement of his trial, a trial court must always be alert to circumstances suggesting a change that would render the accused unable to meet the standards of competence to stand trial. Whatever the relationship between mental illness and incompetence to stand trial, in this case the bearing of the former on the latter was sufficiently likely that, in light of the evidence of petitioner's behavior including his suicide attempt, and there being no opportunity without his presence to evaluate that bearing in fact, the correct course was to suspend the trial until such an evaluation could be made. . . .

420 U.S. at 172-175, 179-181. *Drope* was an easy case: defense counsel had moved for a hearing on competence prior to trial, and moved for a continuance when his client attempted suicide. What if no such motion is made?

The question is not merely hypothetical. The usual consequence of a finding of incompetence to stand trial is not that the defendant goes free — rather, the state is likely to initiate some form of civil commitment proceeding. Civil commitment statutes generally authorize holding defendants in custody as long as they are a danger to themselves or to others. For some defendants, that may mean a de facto life sentence, which may be considerably worse than the prison term the defendant faces if he is convicted of a crime. Notice what this means: Competence to stand trial is unlike most criminal procedure issues. Ordinarily, defendants have a strong incentive to raise valid procedural claims. In the case of competence, a rational defendant may wish to ignore the issue. Of course, if the defendant is arguably incompetent, he is not likely to *be* rational. But his lawyer is. What should defense counsel do if her client (i) may well be incompetent to stand trial, (ii) faces a brief prison term if convicted, and (iii) faces a long stay in a state-run mental institution if civilly committed? How does your answer to this question bear on the burden-of-proof issue in *Medina*?

2. During the same Term as *Medina*, the Court decided Riggins v. Nevada, 504 U.S. 127 (1992). In *Riggins*, following a sparse evidentiary hearing, the trial court permitted the forced medication of the defendant with an antipsychotic drug. The trial court's order "gave no indication of the court's rationale." In reversing, the Court, per Justice O'Connor, opined:

Although we have not had occasion to develop substantive standards for judging forced administration of such drugs in the trial or pretrial settings, Nevada certainly would have satisfied due process if the prosecution had demonstrated and the District Court had found that treatment with antipsychotic medication was medically appropriate and, considering less intrusive alternatives, essential for the sake of Riggins' own safety or the safety of others. Similarly, the State might have been able to justify medically appropriate, involuntary treatment with the drug by establishing that it could not obtain an adjudication of Riggins' guilt or innocence by using less intrusive means.

. . . We have no occasion to finally prescribe such substantive standards . . . , since the District Court allowed the administration of Mellaril to continue without making *any* determination of the need for this course or *any* findings about reasonable alternatives. The court's laconic order denying Riggins' motion did not adopt the State's view, which was that continued administration of Mellaril was required to ensure that the defendant could be tried; in fact, the hearing testimony casts considerable doubt on that argument. Nor did the order indicate a finding that safety considerations or other compelling concerns outweighed Riggins' interest in freedom from unwanted antipsychotic drugs.

504 U.S. at 135-136. Is *Riggins* consistent with *Medina*?

3. In Cooper v. Oklahoma, 517 U.S. 348 (1996), the Court confronted a state statute that required defendants to prove incompetence by clear and convincing evidence. The Court found that rule, unlike the burden-of-proof rule in *Medina*, violated due process:

The question we address today is quite different from the question posed in *Medina*. Petitioner's claim requires us to consider whether a State may proceed with a criminal trial after the defendant has demonstrated that he is more likely than not incompetent. Oklahoma does not contend that it may require the defendant to prove incompetence beyond a reasonable doubt. The State maintains, however, that the clear and convincing standard provides a reasonable accommodation of the opposing interests of the State and the defendant. We are persuaded, by both traditional and modern practice and the importance of the constitutional interest at stake, that the State's argument must be rejected.

"Historical practice is probative of whether a procedural rule can be characterized as fundamental," *Medina*, 505 U.S. at 446. In this case, unlike in *Medina*, there is no indication that the rule Oklahoma seeks to defend has any roots in prior practice. Indeed, it appears that a rule significantly more favorable to the defendant has had a long and consistent application. . . .

[The Court then discussed a series of cases suggesting that the traditional common law rule required only proof of incompetence by a preponderance of the evidence.]

Contemporary practice demonstrates that the vast majority of jurisdictions remain persuaded that the heightened standard of proof imposed on the accused in Oklahoma is not necessary to vindicate the State's interest in prompt and orderly disposition of criminal cases. Only 4 of the 50 States presently require the criminal defendant to prove his incompetence by clear and convincing evidence. None of the remaining 46 jurisdictions imposes such a heavy burden on the defendant. Indeed, a number of States place no burden on the defendant at all, but rather require the prosecutor to prove the defendant's competence to stand trial once a question about competency has been credibly raised. The situation is no different in federal court. Congress has directed that the accused in a federal prosecution must prove incompetence by a preponderance of the evidence. 18 U.S.C. §4241. . . .

The near-uniform application of a standard that is more protective of the defendant's rights than Oklahoma's clear and convincing evidence rule supports our conclusion that the heightened standard offends a principle of justice that is deeply "rooted in the traditions and conscience of our people." *Medina*, 505 U.S. at 445 (internal quotation marks omitted).

517 U.S. at 355-356, 360-362. After *Cooper*, states may force defendants to prove incompetence, but not by more than a preponderance. Does this seem like a sensible splitting of the difference, or like an arbitrary splitting of constitutional hairs?

Perhaps *Medina* and *Cooper*, taken together, represent a sound pragmatic judgment — that defendants are better able to gather evidence of incompetence than the government is to prove competence, *but* that a "clear and convincing" burden would risk too many incompetent defendants going to trial. But is there any principled basis for drawing the line where *Medina* and *Cooper* draw it?

This is a persistent problem in criminal procedure. Protections for defendants' rights constantly involve questions of degree — infinite protection is impossible, so protection must be rationed, graded. And there is rarely any obvious reason to choose this degree of protection rather than something a little more, or a little less. More than most areas of law, criminal procedure may be in the business of splitting differences, and splitting differences rarely seems principled.

4. Notice the *Medina* Court's statement that the Mathews v. Eldridge test for due process, the test used in civil cases, is not to be used in criminal procedure. Instead, the Court says in *Medina*, "because the States have considerable expertise in matters of criminal procedure and the criminal process is grounded in centuries of common-law tradition, it is appropriate to exercise substantial deference to legislative judgments in this area."

Does this statement seem strange? One would ordinarily think of criminal procedure as deserving greater constitutional regulation than the civil process. Yet the *Medina* Court seems to flip the two categories. Why?

The reason, the Court says, is the Bill of Rights: "The Bill of Rights speaks in explicit terms to many aspects of criminal procedure, and the expansion of those constitutional guarantees under the open-ended rubric of the Due Process Clause invites undue interference with both considered legislative judgments and the careful balance that the Constitution strikes between liberty and order." The idea resembles a kind of constitutional displacement, with the Bill of Rights occupying the relevant constitutional space, leaving very little space left over for an expansive reading of due process.

What do you think of that idea? Does it affect your view of incorporation? Decisions like *Duncan* plainly offered greater protection to criminal defendants in some respects; the reasoning in *Medina* suggests those decisions may have led to reduced protection in other areas.

5. What kind of protection is appropriate when suspected terrorists are detained by military personnel? Should they receive the kind of due process that criminal defendants receive? Less? More? The claimant in Hamdi v. Rumsfeld, 124 S. Ct. 2633 (2004), was a United States citizen who had been detained — initially in Afghanistan and later at the Naval Brigs in Norfolk, Virginia, and Charleston, South Carolina — for more than two years as an alleged "enemy combatant" in the war against "forces hostile to the United States or coalition partners" in Afghanistan; Hamdi sought judicial review of the legality of his detention through a writ of habeas corpus.

There was no majority opinion in *Hamdi*. Justice O'Connor, writing for herself, Chief Justice Rehnquist, and Justices Kennedy and Breyer, found the government's initial detention lawful in view of Congress's enactment (one week after September 11, 2001) of the Authorization for Use of Military Force (AUMF), which authorized the President to use "all necessary and appropriate force" against "nations, organizations, or persons" associated with the September 11 terrorist attacks. But Justice O'Connor rejected the government's broad claim that Hamdi could be held indefinitely, without formal charges or proceedings, until such time as the government decides—in whatever fashion it chooses—whether and/or when to grant Hamdi access to counsel or any other form of legal process. At the same time, Justice O'Connor also rejected Hamdi's argument that he should be entitled to full-fledged habeas corpus review of the legality of his detention. According to Justice O'Connor:

> . . . The ordinary mechanism that we use for balancing such serious competing interests, and for determining the procedures that are necessary to ensure that a citizen is not "deprived of life, liberty or property, without due process of law," . . . is the test that we articulated in Mathews v. Eldridge, 424 U.S. 319 (1976). . . . It is beyond question that substantial interests lie on both sides of the scale in this case. . . . [A]s critical as the Government's interest may be in detaining those who actually pose an immediate threat to the national security of the United States during ongoing international conflict, history and common sense teach us that an unchecked system of detention carries the potential to become a means for oppression and abuse of others who do not present that sort of threat. . . . We reaffirm today the fundamental nature of a citizen's right to be free from involuntary confinement by his own government without due process of law, and we weigh the opposing governmental interests against the curtailment of liberty that such confinement entails. . . .
>
> We therefore hold that a citizen-detainee seeking to challenge his classification as an enemy combatant must receive notice of the factual basis for his classification, and a fair opportunity to rebut the Government's factual assertions before a neutral decisionmaker. . . . These essential constitutional promises may not be eroded.
>
> At the same time, the exigencies of the circumstances may demand that, aside from these core elements, enemy combatant proceedings may be tailored to alleviate their uncommon potential to burden the Executive at a time of ongoing military conflict. Hearsay, for example, may need to be accepted as the most reliable available evidence from the Government in such a proceeding. Likewise, the Constitution would not be offended by a presumption in favor of the Government's evidence, so long as that presumption remained a rebuttable one and fair opportunity for rebuttal were provided. . . .
>
> In sum, while the full protections that accompany challenges to detentions in other settings may prove unworkable and inappropriate in the enemy-combatant setting, the threats to military operations posed by a basic system of independent review are not so weighty as to trump a citizen's core rights to challenge meaningfully the Government's case and to be heard by an impartial adjudicator. . . .
>
> There remains the possibility that the standards we have articulated could be met by an appropriately authorized and properly constituted military tribunal. . . . In the absence of such a process, however, a court that receives a petition for a writ of habeas corpus from an alleged enemy combatant must itself ensure that the minimum requirements of due process are achieved. . . .

124 S. Ct. 2646-2651.

Justice Souter, joined by Justice Ginsburg, concurred in part, dissented in part, and concurred in the judgment remanding Hamdi's case to the habeas court for further review, thus providing the necessary additional votes for that judgment. Justice Souter disagreed with Justice O'Connor's initial conclusion that the AUMF authorizes the government's detention of "enemy combatants" who, like Hamdi, are American citizens. Therefore, according to Justice Souter, Hamdi should be entitled to immediate release from custody, and should not even have to litigate—under *any* standard—the question whether he is an "enemy combatant." Nevertheless, because only three other Justices shared that view, Justice Souter proceeded to join Justice O'Connor's opinion to the extent that it at least afforded Hamdi an opportunity to present evidence, in a neutral forum, to show that he is not an "enemy combatant." Justice Souter explained that this fulfilled "the need to give practical effect to the conclusions of eight members of the Court rejecting the Government's position," but stressed that, by doing so, he did not "adopt the plurality's resolution of constitutional issues that I would not reach."

Justice Scalia, joined by Justice Stevens, dissented on the ground that the government has only two lawful choices, in the case of an American citizen believed to be an "enemy combatant" and detained within the United States: either charge him with a crime (such as treason), or suspend the writ of habeas corpus as authorized by the Suspension Clause, Article I, §9, cl. 2 of the Constitution. According to Justice Scalia, the broad sweep of American history (as well as several hundred years of English history before it) establishes that "criminal process was viewed as the primary means — and the only means absent congressional action suspending the writ — not only to punish traitors, but to incapacitate them." Thus, "Hamdi is entitled to a habeas decree requiring his release unless (1) criminal proceedings are promptly brought, or (2) Congress has suspended the writ of habeas corpus" (which no one in *Hamdi* claimed that Congress has done).

Finally, Justice Thomas, also in dissent, argued that the government's position should have been upheld, because "[t]his detention falls squarely within the Federal Government's war powers, and we lack the expertise and capacity to second-guess that decision."

Which of the various positions in *Hamdi* seems most faithful to the ideals of due process? Notice Justice Scalia's argument that the law of criminal procedure ought to apply, so long as the detention is on American soil and the detainee is an American citizen. If, someday, that argument prevails, and if the government contends that the law of criminal procedure insufficiently protects society's interest in combatting domestic terrorism, what should courts do? Should criminal procedure rules be relaxed across the board? Relaxed only in terrorism cases? Or should "justice be done, though the heavens fall"?

6. Return to the interpretive question that lies at the heart of *Hamdi, Medina, Duncan, Hurtado*, and a host of other due process cases: What values does due process protect? In criminal cases, one's answer probably begins with accuracy: Above all else, the criminal process should be designed to ensure that innocent defendants are not convicted and punished. How well does American criminal procedure protect against punishment of innocent defendants? Perhaps not very well:

> . . . As the scope of various constitutional protections has continued to expand [in the years since incorporation], judicial review targeted at potential errors on the merits — at cases where the wrong person was convicted — has been surprisingly muted. When, for example, the Supreme Court established constitutional sufficiency-of-the-evidence review in 1979, Justice Stevens predicted that federal judges would be swamped by the resulting additional work. The flood of new work never materialized, in part because appellate treatment of the relevant claims has been so perfunctory. Ineffective assistance doctrine, created in the 1970s and 1980s, has regulated conflicts of interest much more rigorously than it has regulated attorney decisions not to make plausible factual arguments. The Court's 1985 decision in Ake v. Oklahoma, requiring appointment of mental health experts to assist in preparing a criminal defense, has

had few ripple effects, remaining basically restricted to the very small pool of insanity defense claims that go to trial.

Most strikingly, as the Supreme Court and lower appellate courts have developed standards of review for different kinds of constitutional claims, the courts consistently have adopted more favorable standards of review for *non*-guilt-related claims than for those claims most likely to be tied to guilt and innocence. The erroneous denial of Fourth Amendment and *Miranda* claims must be harmless beyond a reasonable doubt for the government to escape reversal on appeal. But a defendant making an ineffective-assistance-of-counsel claim (again, outside of conflicts of interest, which may be least tied to guilt or innocence and which require no showing of prejudice at all) must show a reasonable probability—substantially more than a reasonable doubt—that counsel's error or errors caused the defendant's conviction. The same tougher standard applies to claims that the government wrongfully withheld material exculpatory evidence. Nonconstitutional claims of newly discovered evidence . . . must meet an even tougher standard: The new evidence must not only have been unavailable at the time of trial but must also prove that the result reached at trial was probably wrong.

William J. Stuntz, The Uneasy Relationship Between Criminal Procedure and Criminal Justice, 107 Yale L.J. 1, 61-62 (1997). Perhaps incorporation of the Bill of Rights has yielded not so much *expansion* of defendants' rights as the *displacement* of some rights by others. Is the trade worth it? Has the Bill of Rights distracted attention from the system's central job: separation of the guilty from the innocent? Or is that not the system's central job?

PART TWO

THE RIGHT TO COUNSEL — THE LINCHPIN OF CONSTITUTIONAL PROTECTION

Chapter 3
The Right to Counsel and Other Assistance

A. The Constitutional Requirements

1. The Right to the Assistance of Counsel at Trial

In all criminal prosecutions, the accused shall enjoy the right . . . to have the Assistance of Counsel for his defence.

U.S. Const. amend. VI

It never has been doubted by this court, or any other so far as we know, that notice and hearing are preliminary steps essential to the passing of an enforceable judgment, and that they, together with a legally competent tribunal having jurisdiction of the case, constitute basic elements of the constitutional requirement of due process of law. . . .

What, then, does a hearing include? Historically and in practice, in our own country at least, it has always included the right to the aid of counsel when desired and provided by the party asserting the right. The right to be heard would be, in many cases, of little avail if it did not comprehend the right to be heard by counsel. Even the intelligent and educated layman has small and sometimes no skill in the science of law. If charged with crime, he is incapable, generally, of determining for himself whether the indictment is good or bad. He is unfamiliar with the rules of evidence. Left without the aid of counsel he may be put on trial without a proper charge, and convicted upon incompetent evidence, or evidence irrelevant to the issue or otherwise inadmissible. He lacks both the skill and knowledge adequately to prepare his defense, even though he have a perfect one. He requires the guiding hand of counsel at every step in the proceedings against him. Without it, though he be not guilty, he faces the danger of conviction because he does not know how to establish his innocence. If that be true of men of intelligence, how much more true is it of the ignorant and illiterate, or those of feeble intellect. If in any case, civil or criminal, a state or federal court were arbitrarily to refuse to hear a party by counsel, employed by and appearing for him, it reasonably may not be doubted that such a refusal would be a denial of a hearing, and, therefore, of due process in the constitutional sense.

Justice Sutherland, for the Court, in Powell v. Alabama,
287 U.S. 45, 68-69 (1932)

The meaning and scope of the Sixth Amendment right to counsel in criminal proceedings have been contested, for the most part, in the context of the right of an indigent to have counsel appointed and financed by the state. As the preceding quotation from *Powell* indicates, the right to be heard by retained counsel has never been seriously questioned in the United States. Quite early in our history, we rejected the English common law that denied accused felons the right to the assistance of retained counsel. For a discussion of the history of the right to counsel, see Note, An Historical Argument for the Right to Counsel during Police Interrogation, 73 Yale L.J. 1000, 1018-1034 (1964).

However, we proved to be much less solicitous of the plight of the indigent. In capital cases, federal law required the appointment of counsel, 1 Stat. 118 (1790), and a number of states followed a similar path. Nonetheless, it was not until *Powell* that the Supreme Court held that in capital cases Fourteenth Amendment due process is violated by state action that in effect denied a defendant access to effective assistance of counsel. Moreover, *Powell* appeared to be limited to those cases in which the defendant is "incapable adequately of making his own defense because of ignorance, feeble-mindedness, illiteracy, or the like." *Powell*, 287 U.S. at 71. The Court did hold, however, that the state's "duty is not discharged by an assignment [of counsel] at such a time or under such circumstances as to preclude the giving of effective aid in the preparation and trial of the case." Id.

Powell, in essence, created a *special circumstances rule* — effective assistance, or an adequate opportunity to obtain it, must be provided in capital cases if defendants are unable to represent themselves adequately. This special circumstances rule was transmuted into a "flat" requirement of counsel in capital cases at least by 1961 in Hamilton v. Alabama, 368 U.S. 52 (1961), in large measure due to the awesome finality of capital punishment. See Yale Kamisar, Betts v. Brady Twenty Years Later: The Right to Counsel and Due Process Values, 61 Mich. L. Rev. 219, 255 (1962). But see id. at 255-260 (arguing that sentence is immaterial to need for counsel).

In noncapital cases a special circumstances rule also developed that required the appointment of counsel only when the absence of counsel would result in a "trial . . . offensive to the common and fundamental ideas of fairness and right." Betts v. Brady, 316 U.S. 455, 473 (1942). In *Betts*, the Court, over a sharp and prescient dissent by Justice Black, held that due process does not demand the appointment of counsel for indigent defendants in every state case because "the furnishing of counsel in all cases whatever" is *not* "dictated by natural, inherent and fundamental principles of justice." Id. at 464.

Four years prior to *Betts*, the Supreme Court held that the Sixth Amendment required the appointment of counsel in noncapital federal criminal prosecutions. In doing so, the Court commented:

> The Sixth Amendment stands as a constant admonition that if the constitutional safeguards it provides be lost, justice will not "still be done." It embodies a realistic recognition of the obvious truth that the average defendant does not have the professional legal skill to protect himself when brought before a tribunal with power to take his life or liberty, wherein the prosecution is presented by experienced and learned counsel. That which is simple, orderly and necessary to the lawyer, to the untrained layman may appear intricate, complex and mysterious.

Johnson v. Zerbst, 304 U.S. 458, 462-463 (1938).

But if "justice cannot be done" in all federal prosecutions and state capital cases without the assistance of counsel, and if, in state noncapital cases, the right to counsel "when desired and provided by the party asserting the right" is something that the party "requires . . . at every step," in order to minimize the chance of an erroneous conviction,[1] how could the *Betts* "special circumstances rule" be maintained? How could it be that justice *could* be done in a state but not in a federal prosecution when an indigent is tried without counsel? And how does the absence of wealth minimize the need for counsel's guiding hand whether in a capital or noncapital case? Prior to *Gideon*, in short, had not the Court *already concluded*, even if it had still to be articulated, that the absence of counsel was itself a "special circumstance"?[2]

GIDEON v. WAINWRIGHT

Certiorari to the Supreme Court of Florida
372 U.S. 335 (1963)

MR. JUSTICE BLACK delivered the opinion of the Court.

Petitioner was charged in a Florida state court with having broken and entered a poolroom with intent to commit a misdemeanor. This offense is a felony under Florida law. Appearing in court without funds and without a lawyer, petitioner asked the court to appoint counsel for him, whereupon the following colloquy took place:

> *The Court:*   Mr. Gideon, I am sorry, but I cannot appoint Counsel to represent you in this case. Under the laws of the State of Florida, the only time the Court can appoint Counsel to represent a Defendant is when that person is charged with a capital offense. I am sorry, but I will have to deny your request to appoint Counsel to defend you in this case.
> *The Defendant:*   The United States Supreme Court says I am entitled to be represented by Counsel.

Put to trial before a jury, Gideon conducted his defense about as well as could be expected from a layman. He made an opening statement to the jury, cross-examined the State's witnesses, presented witnesses in his own defense, declined to testify himself, and made a short argument "emphasizing his innocence to the charge contained in the Information filed in this case." The jury returned a

---

1. Indeed, the Supreme Court had gone so far as to say that a defendant's right to be heard by retained counsel was "unqualified." Chandler v. Fretag, 348 U.S. 3, 9 (1954). The reason for this conclusion surely was the Court's recognition of the significance of counsel. Id. at 9-10. But the very same "significance" that results in a conclusion of an unqualified right to be heard by retained counsel obviously highlights the untenable plight of the indigent unable to obtain counsel. This, too, appears to have contributed to the Court's willingness to reconsider *Betts*.

2. From 1950 until *Gideon*, the Supreme Court found a "special circumstance" requiring the appointment of counsel in every case that it heard that raised the issue. By 1962, the standard had apparently become "potential prejudice," a standard that will virtually always be met. Chewning v. Cunningham, 368 U.S. 443 (1962).

verdict of guilty, and petitioner was sentenced to serve five years in the state prison. . . . Since 1942, when Betts v. Brady, 316 U.S. 455, was decided by a divided Court, the problem of a defendant's federal constitutional right to counsel in a state court has been a continuing source of controversy and litigation in both state and federal courts. To give this problem another review here, we granted certiorari. Since Gideon was proceeding in forma pauperis, we appointed counsel to represent him and requested both sides to discuss in their briefs and oral arguments the following: "Should this Court's holding in Betts v. Brady . . . be reconsidered?" . . .

I

The facts upon which Betts claimed that he had been unconstitutionally denied the right to have counsel appointed to assist him are strikingly like the facts upon which Gideon here bases his federal constitutional claim. Betts was indicted for robbery in a Maryland state court. On arraignment, he told the trial judge of his lack of funds to hire a lawyer and asked the court to appoint one for him. Betts was advised that it was not the practice in that county to appoint counsel for indigent defendants except in murder and rape cases. He then pleaded not guilty, had witnesses summoned, cross-examined the State's witnesses, examined his own, and chose not to testify himself. He was found guilty by the judge, sitting without a jury, and sentenced to eight years in prison. Like Gideon, Betts sought release by habeas corpus, alleging that he had been denied the right to assistance of counsel in violation of the Fourteenth Amendment. Betts was denied any relief, and on review this Court affirmed. It was held that a refusal to appoint counsel for an indigent defendant charged with a felony did not necessarily violate the Due Process Clause of the Fourteenth Amendment, which for reasons given the Court deemed to be the only applicable federal constitutional provision. The Court said:

> Asserted denial [of due process] is to be tested by an appraisal of the totality of facts in a given case. That which may, in one setting, constitute a denial of fundamental fairness, shocking to the universal sense of justice, may, in other circumstances, and in the light of other considerations, fall short of such denial. [316 U.S. at 462.]

Treating due process as "a concept less rigid and more fluid than those envisaged in other specific and particular provisions of the Bill of Rights," the Court held that refusal to appoint counsel under the particular facts and circumstances in the *Betts* case was not so "offensive to the common and fundamental ideas of fairness" as to amount to a denial of due process. Since the facts and circumstances of the two cases are so nearly indistinguishable, we think the Betts v. Brady holding if left standing would require us to reject Gideon's claim that the Constitution guarantees him the assistance of counsel. Upon full reconsideration we conclude that Betts v. Brady should be overruled.

II

The Sixth Amendment provides, "In all criminal prosecutions, the accused shall enjoy the right . . . to have the Assistance of Counsel for his defence." We have construed this to mean that in federal courts counsel must be provided for defendants unable to employ counsel unless the right is competently and intelligently waived.[3] Betts argued that this right is extended to indigent defendants in state courts by the Fourteenth Amendment. In response the Court stated that, while the Sixth Amendment laid down "no rule for the conduct of the States, the question recurs whether the constraint laid by the Amendment upon the national courts expresses a rule so fundamental and essential to a fair trial, and so, to due process of law, that it is made obligatory upon the States by the Fourteenth Amendment." 316 U.S., at 465. In order to decide whether the Sixth Amendment's guarantee of counsel is of this fundamental nature, the court in *Betts* set out and considered "[r]elevant data on the subject . . . afforded by constitutional and statutory provisions subsisting in the colonies and the States prior to the inclusion of the Bill of Rights in the national Constitution, and in the constitutional, legislative, and judicial history of the States to the present date." 316 U.S., at 465. On the basis of this historical data the Court concluded that "appointment of counsel is not a fundamental right, essential to a fair trial." 316 U.S., at 471. It was for this reason the *Betts* Court refused to accept the contention that the Sixth Amendment's guarantee of counsel for indigent federal defendants was extended to or, in the words of that Court, "made obligatory upon the States by the Fourteenth Amendment." Plainly, had the Court concluded that appointment of counsel for an indigent criminal defendant was "a fundamental right, essential to a fair trial," it would have held that the Fourteenth Amendment requires appointment of counsel in a state court, just as the Sixth Amendment requires in a federal court.

We think the Court in *Betts* had ample precedent for acknowledging that those guarantees of the Bill of Rights which are fundamental safeguards of liberty immune from federal abridgment are equally protected against state invasion by the Due Process Clause of the Fourteenth Amendment. This same principle was recognized, explained, and applied in Powell v. Alabama, 287 U.S. 45 (1932), a case upholding the right of counsel, where the Court held that despite sweeping language to the contrary in Hurtado v. California, 110 U.S. 516 (1884), the Fourteenth Amendment "embraced" those "'fundamental principles of liberty and justice which lie at the base of all our civil and political institutions,'" even though they had been "specifically dealt with in another part of the federal Constitution." 287 U.S., at 67. In many cases other than *Powell* and *Betts*, this Court has looked to the fundamental nature of original Bill of Rights guarantees to decide whether the Fourteenth Amendment makes them obligatory on the States. Explicitly recognized to be of this "fundamental nature" and therefore made immune from state invasion by the Fourteenth, or some part of it, are the First Amendment's freedoms of speech, press, religion, assembly, association, and petition for redress of grievances. For the same reason, though not always in precisely the same terminology, the Court has made obligatory on the States the Fifth Amendment's command that private property shall not be taken for public use without just compensation, the Fourth Amendment's prohibition of unreasonable searches and seizures, and the Eighth's ban on cruel and unusual punishment. On the other hand, this Court in Palko v. Connecticut, 302 U.S. 319 (1937), refused to hold that the Fourteenth Amendment made the double jeopardy provision of the Fifth Amendment obligatory on the States. In so refusing, however, the

---

3. Johnson v. Zerbst, 304 U.S. 458 (1938).

Court, speaking through Mr. Justice Cardozo, was careful to emphasize that "immunities that are valid as against the federal government by force of the specific pledges of particular amendments have been found to be implicit in the concept of ordered liberty, and thus, through the Fourteenth Amendment, become valid as against the states" and that guarantees "in their origin . . . effective against the federal government alone" had by prior cases "been taken over from the earlier articles of the federal bill of rights and brought within the Fourteenth Amendment by a process of absorption." 302 U.S., at 324-325, 326.

We accept Betts v. Brady's assumption, based as it was on our prior cases, that a provision of the Bill of Rights which is "fundamental and essential to a fair trial" is made obligatory upon the States by the Fourteenth Amendment. We think the Court in *Betts* was wrong, however, in concluding that the Sixth Amendment's guarantee of counsel is not one of these fundamental rights. Ten years before Betts v. Brady, this Court, after full consideration of all the historical data examined in *Betts*, had unequivocally declared that "the right to the aid of counsel is of this fundamental character." Powell v. Alabama, 287 U.S. 25, 68 (1932). . . . And again in 1938 this Court said:

> [The assistance of counsel] is one of the safeguards of the Sixth Amendment deemed necessary to insure fundamental human rights of life and liberty. . . . The Sixth Amendment stands as a constant admonition that if the constitutional safeguards it provides be lost, justice will not "still be done." [Johnson v. Zerbst, 304 U.S. 458, 462 (1938).] . . .

In light of these and many other prior decisions of this Court, it is not surprising that the *Betts* Court, when faced with the contention that "one charged with crime, who is unable to obtain counsel, must be furnished counsel by the State," conceded that "[e]xpressions in the opinions of this court lend color to the argument. . . ." 316 U.S., at 462-463. The fact is that in deciding as it did — that "appointment of counsel is not a fundamental right, essential to a fair trial" — the Court in Betts v. Brady made an abrupt break with its own well-considered precedents. In returning to these old precedents, sounder we believe than the new, we but restore constitutional principles established to achieve a fair system of justice. Not only these precedents but also reason and reflection require us to recognize that in our adversary system of criminal justice, any person haled into court, who is too poor to hire a lawyer, cannot be assured a fair trial unless counsel is provided for him. This seems to us to be an obvious truth. Governments, both state and federal, quite properly spend vast sums of money to establish machinery to try defendants accused of crime. Lawyers to prosecute are everywhere deemed essential to protect the public's interest in an orderly society. Similarly, there are few defendants charged with crime, few indeed, who fail to hire the best lawyers they can get to prepare and present their defenses. That government hires lawyers to prosecute and defendants who have the money hire lawyers to defend are the strongest indications of the widespread belief that lawyers in criminal courts are necessities, not luxuries. The right of one charged with crime to counsel may not be deemed fundamental and essential to fair trials in some countries, but it is in ours. From the very beginning, our state and national constitutions and laws have laid great emphasis on procedural and substantive safeguards designed to assure fair trials before impartial tribunals in which every defendant stands equal before the law. This noble idea cannot be realized if the poor man charged with crime has to face his accusers without a lawyer to assist him. . . . The Court in Betts v. Brady departed from the sound wisdom upon which the Court's holding in Powell v. Alabama rested. Florida, supported by two other States, has asked that Betts v. Brady be left intact. Twenty-two states, as friends of the Court, argue that *Betts* was "an anachronism when handed down" and that it should now be overruled. We agree.

Reversed.

MR. JUSTICE DOUGLAS, concurring.

While I join the opinion of the Court, a brief historical resume of the relation between the Bill of Rights and the first section of the Fourteenth Amendment seems pertinent. Since the adoption of that Amendment, ten Justices have felt that it protects from infringement by the States the privileges, protections, and safeguards granted by the Bill of Rights. . . . Unfortunately it has never commanded a Court. Yet, happily, all constitutional questions are always open. And what we do today does not foreclose the matter.

My Brother Harlan is of the view that a guarantee of the Bill of Rights that is made applicable to the States by reason of the Fourteenth Amendment is a lesser version of that same guarantee as applied to the Federal Government. Mr. Justice Jackson shared that view. But that view has not prevailed[4] and rights protected against state invasion by the Due Process Clause of the Fourteenth Amendment are not watered-down versions of what the Bill of Rights guarantees.

MR. JUSTICE CLARK, concurring in the result.

That the Sixth Amendment requires appointment of counsel in "all criminal prosecutions" is clear, both from the language of the Amendment and from this Court's interpretation. . . . It is equally clear from the above cases, all decided after *Betts* . . . that the Fourteenth Amendment requires such appointment in all prosecutions for capital crimes. The Court's decision today, then, does no more than erase a distinction which has no basis in logic and an increasingly eroded basis in authority. In Kinsella v. United States ex rel. Singleton, 361 U.S. 234 (1960), we specifically rejected any constitutional distinction between capital and noncapital offenses as regards congressional power to provide for court-martial trials of civilian dependents of armed forces personnel. Having previously held that civilian dependents could not constitutionally be deprived of the protections of Article III and the Fifth and Sixth Amendments in capital cases, Reid v. Covert, 354 U.S. 1 (1957), we held that the same result must follow in noncapital cases. . . .

I must conclude here, as in *Kinsella*, supra, that the Constitution makes no distinction between capital and noncapital cases. The Fourteenth Amendment requires due process of law for the deprival of "liberty" just as for deprival of "life," and there cannot constitutionally be a difference in the quality of the process based merely upon a supposed difference in the sanction involved. How can the Fourteenth Amendment tolerate a procedure which it condemns in capital cases on the ground that deprival of liberty may be less onerous than deprival of life—a value judgment not universally accepted—or that only the latter deprival is

4. The cases are collected by Mr. Justice Black in Speiser v. Randall, 357 U.S. 513, 530. And see Eaton v. Price, 364 U.S. 263, 274-276.

irrevocable? I can find no acceptable rationalization for such a result, and I therefore concur in the judgment of the Court.

Mr. Justice Harlan, concurring.

I agree that Betts v. Brady should be overruled, but consider it entitled to a more respectful burial than has been accorded, at least on the part of those of us who were not on the Court when that case was decided.

I cannot subscribe to the view that Betts v. Brady represented "an abrupt break with its own well-considered precedents." . . . In 1932, in Powell v. Alabama, . . . a capital case, this Court declared that under the particular facts there presented — "the ignorance and illiteracy of the defendants, their youth, the circumstances of public hostility . . . and above all that they stood in deadly peril of their lives" (287 U.S., at 71) — the state court had a duty to assign counsel for the trial as a necessary requisite of due process of law. It is evident that these limiting facts were not added to the opinion as an afterthought; they were repeatedly emphasized, see 287 U.S., at 52, 57-58, 71, and were clearly regarded as important to the result.

Thus when this Court, a decade later, decided Betts v. Brady, it did no more than to admit of the possible existence of special circumstances in noncapital as well as capital trials, while at the same time insisting that such circumstances be shown in order to establish a denial of due process. The right to appointed counsel had been recognized as being considerably broader in federal prosecutions, see Johnson v. Zerbst, 304 U.S. 458, but to have imposed these requirements on the States would indeed have been "an abrupt break" with the almost immediate past. The declaration that the right to appointed counsel in state prosecutions, as established in Powell v. Alabama, was not limited to capital cases was in truth not a departure from, but an extension of, existing precedent. The principles declared in *Powell* and in *Betts*, however, have had a troubled journey throughout the years that have followed first the one case and then the other. Even by the time of the *Betts* decision, dictum in at least one of the Court's opinions had indicated that there was an absolute right to the services of counsel in the trial of state capital cases.[1] Such dicta continued to appear in subsequent decisions,[2] and any lingering doubts were finally eliminated by the holding of Hamilton v. Alabama, 368 U.S. 52.

In noncapital cases, the "special circumstances" rule has continued to exist in form while its substance has been substantially and steadily eroded. In the first decade after *Betts*, there were cases in which the Court found special circumstances to be lacking, but usually by a sharply divided vote. However, no such decision has been cited to us, and I have found none, after Quicksall v. Michigan, 339 U.S. 660, decided in 1950. At the same time, there have been not a few cases in which special circumstances were found in little or nothing more than the "complexity" of the legal questions presented, although those questions were often of only routine difficulty. The Court has come to recognize, in other words, that the mere existence of a serious criminal charge constituted in itself special circumstances requiring the services of counsel at trial. In truth the Betts v. Brady rule is no longer a reality.

---

1. Avery v. Alabama, 308 U.S. 444, 445.
2. E.g., Bute v. Illinois, 333 U.S. 640, 674; Uveges v. Pennsylvania, 335 U.S. 437, 441.

This evolution, however, appears not to have been fully recognized by many state courts, in this instance charged with the front-line responsibility for the enforcement of constitutional rights. To continue a rule which is honored by this Court only with lip service is not a healthy thing and in the long run will do disservice to the federal system.

The special circumstances rule has been formally abandoned in capital cases, and the time has now come when it should be similarly abandoned in noncapital cases, at least as to offenses which, as the one involved here, carry the possibility of a substantial prison sentence. (Whether the rule should extend to *all* criminal cases need not now be decided.) This indeed does no more than to make explicit something that has long since been foreshadowed in our decisions.

In agreeing with the Court that the right to counsel in a case such as this should now be expressly recognized as a fundamental right embraced in the Fourteenth Amendment, I wish to make a further observation. When we hold a right or immunity, valid against the Federal Government, to be "implicit in the concept of ordered liberty" and thus valid against the States, I do not read our past decisions to suggest that by so holding, we automatically carry over an entire body of federal law and apply it in full sweep to the States. Any such concept would disregard the frequently wide disparity between the legitimate interests of the States and of the Federal Government, the divergent problems that they face, and the significantly different consequences of their actions.

. . . In what is done today I do not understand the Court to depart from the principles laid down in Palko v. Connecticut, 302 U.S. 319, or to embrace the concept that the Fourteenth Amendment "incorporates" the Sixth Amendment as such.

On these premises I join in the judgment of the Court.

NOTES AND QUESTIONS

1. In one sense the result in *Gideon* appears to have been inevitable. Even if there are cases that could be tried fairly without defense counsel, one cannot determine from the record in uncounseled cases which ones would have benefited from counsel. Records that look good on appeal might have looked quite different had counsel been present. Indeed, *Betts* is such a case. Each of the courts that reviewed the record in *Betts* concluded that Betts had not been prejudiced by the absence of counsel. In an insightful analysis of the factual setting of *Betts*, Professor Kamisar demonstrated quite forcefully that a competent lawyer may very well have had an impact on the outcome of the trial. Yale Kamisar, The Right to Counsel and the Fourteenth Amendment: A Dialogue on "The Most Pervasive Right" of an Accused, 30 U. Chi. L. Rev. 1, 42-56 (1962). Consider just one of the many points Professor Kamisar made. One of the witnesses at trial, Bollinger, identified Betts at the jailhouse, as well as a coat, dark glasses, and a handkerchief allegedly worn by Betts during the robbery in question. *But:*

> *What* coat? *Whose* dark glasses and handkerchief? . . .
> Is it possible that the coat Bollinger "identified" at the jail was simply one the police procured from somebody other than Betts — pursuant to Bollinger's own description of the dark gray, bagged-pocketed coat the man wore who robbed him?

Even if a coat were offered in evidence, "objects or things offered in evidence do not generally identify themselves." The object must be shown to have some connection with Betts. Not only was this not done; no coat was ever offered in evidence. . . .

As for the other items, there was testimony by the state that "smoked glasses were put on Betts' eyes and a handkerchief around his neck like the man was supposed to have had that did the holding up." But once again, no handkerchief or glasses were offered in evidence. Presumably, Betts owned a handkerchief or two, but once again, the state failed to establish that he even owned a pair of dark glasses. One alibi witness who was asked about this on cross simply did "not know," and the matter was dropped.

Why did the state fail to offer any of these items in evidence? Why was one of Betts' own witnesses cross-examined, albeit casually, about the defendant's ownership of a dark gray overcoat and smoked glasses? If the state had possessed these items, why would it have asked such questions? Although the matter is not free from doubt — because neither trial judge nor prosecutor seemed to care much and Betts evidently failed to realize how this would weaken the state's case — it is difficult to avoid the conclusion that the following "bootstraps" operation occurred: Bollinger described to the police the various items the robber was supposed to have worn; the police simply went out, begged or borrowed the requisite coat, glasses and handkerchief, and slapped them on Betts; Bollinger then made his identification, based largely on the coat, glasses and handkerchief the police had put on Betts.

2. Even if it is true that defense counsel normally is of value, does it follow that the result in *Gideon* is constitutionally mandated? There is no requirement that the state provide everything that is useful or of value to defendants. Thus, there must be some other criteria that determine what the state must provide. To what extent, for example, should constitutional analysis be informed by general practice in the states? By the "intent of the Framers" of the relevant constitutional provisions? By the cost to government of a decision one way or the other? By what is "fair" or "just"? If notions of fairness or justice are to play a role, how does one determine what those words mean?

3. Regardless of the scope of words such as "fairness" or "justice," there probably would be general agreement that any practice that generated a relatively high risk of erroneous convictions is "unfair," as the absence of counsel most likely does. Why was that not emphasized more in *Gideon*? Justice Black's opinion for the Court in *Gideon* primarily asserted that *Betts* was an abrupt change from its precedents and thus was wrong, although the excerpt from *Powell* at the beginning of this section was quoted but not developed. Is that adequate? If a court decides to overrule a case, how can it go about it? How *should* it go about it, or does it matter? For an interesting discussion, see Jerold Israel, Gideon v. Wainwright: The "Art" of Overruling, [1963] Sup. Ct. Rev. 211. Does the method employed in the majority opinion explain, at least in part, why the concurrences were written to what was a unanimous judgment?

4. What are *Gideon*'s consequences? At one level, the answer seems easy: Presumably the system functions better and more accurately when defendants have lawyers than when they must fend for themselves. But the answer may be more complicated than first appears. Defense lawyers make criminal trials more elaborate and hence more expensive. The state presumably must bear that cost. Yet the state need not hold a trial in order to obtain a conviction: Most

convictions—in the neighborhood of 90 percent by most estimates—are the result of guilty pleas, not criminal trials. And the more costly trials are to the state, the more the state may be willing to pay, in the form of reduced charges or sentences, in order to get the defendant to plead guilty. These "payments" are, of course, the centerpiece of plea bargaining. The point is that *Gideon*, like other defense rights that raise the expense of criminal prosecution, may significantly improve the criminal trial process, but it may also lead to a system in which fewer defendants actually use that process. Which is better—a careful and expensive trial process coupled with lots of guilty pleas, or a more casual trial process that is used by more defendants?

NOTES ON THE SCOPE OF THE *GIDEON* RIGHT TO COUNSEL

1. What was the judgment in *Gideon*, apart from the overruling of *Betts*? What, in other words, is the scope of the right to counsel imposed on the states by *Gideon*? Must counsel be appointed in every criminal case? Every felony? What about trials of misdemeanors with a jury, or when a somewhat complicated issue may be contested? The Supreme Court first faced that question in Argersinger v. Hamlin, 407 U.S. 25 (1972):

> Petitioner, an indigent, was charged in Florida with carrying a concealed weapon, an offense punishable by imprisonment up to six months, a $1,000 fine, or both. The trial was to a judge, and petitioner was unrepresented by counsel. He was sentenced to serve 90 days in jail, and brought this habeas corpus action in the Florida Supreme Court, alleging that, being deprived of his right to counsel, he was unable as an indigent layman properly to raise and present to the trial court good and sufficient defenses to the charge for which he stands convicted. The Florida Supreme Court by a four-to-three decision, in ruling on the right to counsel, followed the line we marked out in Duncan v. Louisiana, 391 U.S. 145, 159, as respects the right to trial by jury and held that the right to court-appointed counsel extends only to trials "for non-petty offenses punishable by more than six months imprisonment." . . . We reverse.

In rejecting the analogy to trial by jury, the Court noted:

> The right to trial by jury, also guaranteed by the Sixth Amendment by reason of the Fourteenth, was limited by Duncan v. Louisiana to trials where the potential punishment was imprisonment for six months or more. But . . . the right to trial by jury has a different genealogy and is brigaded with a system of trial to a judge alone. As stated in *Duncan:*
>
>> Providing an accused with the right to be tried by a jury of his peers gave him an inestimable safeguard against the corrupt or overzealous prosecutor and against the compliant, biased, or eccentric judge. If the defendant preferred the common-sense judgment of a jury to the more tutored but perhaps less sympathetic reaction of the single judge, he was to have it. Beyond this, the jury trial provisions in the Federal and State Constitutions reflect a fundamental decision about the exercise of official power—a reluctance to entrust plenary powers over the life and liberty of the citizen to one judge or to a group of judges. Fear of unchecked power, so typical of our State and Federal Governments in other respects, found expression in the criminal law in this insistence upon community participation in the determination of guilt or innocence. The deep commitment of the Nation to the right of jury trial in serious criminal cases as a defense against arbitrary law enforcement qualifies for protection under the Due Process Clause of the Fourteenth Amendment, and must therefore be respected by the States. [391 U.S., at 156.]

While there is historical support for limiting the "deep commitment" to trial by jury to "serious criminal cases,"[2] there is no such support for a similar limitation on the right to assistance of counsel:

> Originally, in England, a person charged with treason or felony was denied the aid of counsel, except in respect of legal questions which the accused himself might suggest. At the same time parties in civil cases and persons accused of misdemeanors were entitled to the full assistance of counsel. . . . [It] appears that in at least twelve of the thirteen colonies the rule of the English common law, in the respect now under consideration, had been definitively rejected and the right to counsel fully recognized in all criminal prosecutions, save that in one or two instances the right was limited to capital offenses or to the more serious crimes. . . . [Powell v. Alabama, 287 U.S. 45, 60 and 64-65.]

The Sixth Amendment thus extended the right to counsel beyond its common-law dimensions. But there is nothing in the language of the Amendment, its history, or in the decisions of this Court, to indicate that it was intended to embody a retraction of the right in petty offenses wherein the common law previously did require that counsel be provided. . . .

We reject, therefore, the premise that since prosecutions for crimes punishable by imprisonment for less than six months may be tried without a jury, they may also be tried without a lawyer. . . .

The requirement of counsel may well be necessary for a fair trial even in a petty-offense prosecution. We are by no means convinced that legal and constitutional questions involved in a case that actually leads to imprisonment even for a brief period are any less complex than when a person can be sent off for six months or more. . . .

We hold, therefore, that absent a knowing and intelligent waiver, no person may be imprisoned for any offense, whether classified as petty, misdemeanor, or felony, unless he was represented by counsel at his trial. . . .

Justice Powell concurred in the result, but expressed doubts about the breadth of the decision. . . .

I am in accord with the Court that an indigent accused's need for the assistance of counsel does not mysteriously evaporate when he is charged with an offense punishable by six months or less. . . . Many petty offenses will also present complex legal and factual issues that may not be fairly tried if the defendant is not assisted by counsel. Even in relatively simple cases, some defendants, because of ignorance or some other handicap, will be incapable of defending themselves. The consequences of a misdemeanor conviction, whether they be a brief period served under the sometimes deplorable conditions found in local jails or the effect of a criminal record on employability, are frequently of sufficient magnitude not to be casually dismissed by the label "petty."

Serious consequences also may result from convictions not punishable by imprisonment. Stigma may attach to a drunken-driving conviction or a hit-and-run escapade. Losing one's driver's license is more serious for some individuals than a brief stay in jail. . . . When the deprivation of property rights and interests is of sufficient consequences,[11] denying the assistance of counsel to indigents who are incapable of defending themselves is a denial of due process.

2. See Felix Frankfurter & Thomas G. Corcoran, Petty Offenses and the Constitutional Guaranty of Trial by Jury, 39 Harv. L. Rev. 917, 980-982 (1926). . . .

11. A wide range of civil disabilities may result from misdemeanor convictions, such as forfeiture of public office (State ex rel. Stinger v. Kruger, 280 Mo. 293, 217 S.W. 310 (1919)); disqualification for a licensed profession (Cal. Bus. & Prof. Code §3094 (1962) (optometrists); N.C. Gen. Stat. §93A-4(b)

. . . Due process, perhaps the most fundamental concept in our law, embodies principles of fairness rather than immutable line drawing as to every aspect of a criminal trial. While counsel is often essential to a fair trial, this is by no means a universal fact. Some petty offense cases are complex; others are exceedingly simple. As a justification for furnishing counsel to indigents accused of felonies, the Court noted, "That government hires lawyers to prosecute and defendants who have the money hire lawyers to defend are the strongest indications of the widespread belief that lawyers in criminal courts are necessities, not luxuries."[12] Yet government often does not hire lawyers to prosecute petty offenses; instead the arresting police officer presents the case. Nor does every defendant who can afford to do so hire lawyers to defend petty charges. Where the possibility of a jail sentence is remote and the probable fine seems small, or where the evidence of guilt is overwhelming, the costs of assistance of counsel may exceed the benefits.[13] It is anomalous that the Court's opinion today will extend the right of appointed counsel to indigent defendants in cases where the right to counsel would rarely be exercised by nonindigent defendants. . . .

The Fifth and Fourteenth Amendments guarantee that property, as well as life and liberty, may not be taken from a person without affording him due process of law. The majority opinion suggests no constitutional basis for distinguishing between deprivations of liberty and property. In fact, the majority suggests no reason at all for drawing this distinction. The logic it advances for extending the right to counsel to all cases in which the penalty of any imprisonment is imposed applies equally well to cases in which other penalties may be imposed. Nor does the majority deny that some "nonjail" penalties are more serious than brief jail sentences. . . .

There are thousands of statutes and ordinances which authorize imprisonment for six months or less, usually as an alternative to a fine. These offenses include some of the most trivial of misdemeanors, ranging from spitting on the sidewalk to certain traffic offenses. They also include a variety of more serious misdemeanors. This broad spectrum of petty-offense cases daily floods the lower criminal courts. The rule laid down today will confront the judges of each of these courts with an awkward dilemma. If counsel is not appointed or knowingly waived, no sentence of imprisonment for any duration may be imposed. The judge will therefore be forced to decide in advance of trial — and without hearing the evidence — whether he will forgo entirely his judicial discretion to impose some sentence of imprisonment and abandon his responsibility to consider the full range of punishments established by the legislature. His alternatives, assuming the availability of counsel, will be to appoint counsel and retain the discretion vested in him by law, or to abandon this discretion in advance and proceed without counsel. . . .

I would hold that the right to counsel in petty-offense cases is not absolute but is one to be determined by the trial courts exercising a judicial discretion on a case-by-case basis. The determination should be made before the accused formally pleads; many petty cases are resolved by guilty pleas in which the assistance of counsel may be required.

(1965) (real estate brokers)), and loss of pension rights (Fla. Stat. Ann. §185.18(3) (1966) (police disability pension denied when injury is result of participation in fights, riots, civil insurrections, or while committing crime); Ind. Ann. Stat. §28-4616 (1948) (teacher convicted of misdemeanor resulting in imprisonment); Pa. Stat. Ann., Tit. 53 §39323 (Supp. 1972-1973) and §65599 (1957) (conviction of crime or misdemeanor)). See generally Project, The Collateral Consequences of a Criminal Conviction, 23 Vand. L. Rev. 929 (1970).

12. Gideon v. Wainwright, 372 U.S., at 344.

13. In petty offenses, there is much less plea negotiation than in serious offenses. See Report by the President's Commission of Law Enforcement and Administration of Justice, The Challenge of Crime in a Free Society (hereinafter Challenge) 134 (1967). Thus, in cases where the evidence of guilt is overwhelming, the assistance of counsel is less essential to obtain a lighter sentence.

It is impossible, as well as unwise, to create a precise and detailed set of guidelines for judges to follow in determining whether the appointment of counsel is necessary to assure a fair trial. Certainly three general factors should be weighed. First, the court should consider the complexity of the offense charged. . . .

Second, the court should consider the probable sentence that will follow if a conviction is obtained. The more serious the likely consequences, the greater is the probability that a lawyer should be appointed. . . .

Third, the court should consider the individual factors peculiar to each case. These, of course, would be the most difficult to anticipate. One relevant factor would be the competency of the individual defendant to present his own case. The attitude of the community toward a particular defendant or particular incident would be another consideration. . . .

2. In light of *Argersinger* what procedures should a trial judge follow before deciding whether to appoint counsel? Should the judge request something on the order of a presentence investigation? Without such information, how can an intelligent decision be reached concerning the appropriate sanctions? Should the judge also take into account the likelihood of conviction? How can that be done *before* trial, and at what cost? The financial burden can perhaps be minimized by simply asking the prosecutor to relate the basis of the charge, but should the trial judge be exposed to a one-sided summary of the case prior to trial? Does the answer to that depend in part on whether there is a jury?

3. Under Duncan v. Louisiana, 391 U.S. 145 (1968), criminal defendants have a Sixth Amendment right to a jury trial in cases where the crime charged is punishable by more than six months' imprisonment. The Supreme Court in *Argersinger* rejected as too constrictive the analogy, embraced by the Florida Supreme Court, that the scope of the Sixth Amendment right to counsel should be measured in the same way as the jury trial right. But while the Court gave with the left hand, did it take away with the right? In those jurisdictions that extend the right to a jury to petty offenses (those punishable by six months or less), does the invocation of that right carry with it a constitutional right to counsel? The problem extends beyond petty cases. Consider the plight of an individual charged with a misdemeanor, conviction for which will cause unpleasant collateral consequences to the defendant, loss of a driver's license, for example. If, after hearing a summary of the case and perhaps the defendant's record, the trial judge decides not to appoint counsel, the defendant must choose between self-representation before a jury or permitting the judge, who has already heard a one-sided presentation of the case, to sit as a fact finder. Do you see a way to avoid this dilemma?

In Lewis v. United States, 518 U.S. 322 (1996), the Court concluded that a defendant does not have a constitutional right to trial by jury when prosecuted in a single proceeding for multiple petty offenses, even if the possible aggregate prison term exceeds six months. In an interesting passage, however, the Court suggested that other factors may be relevant to determining whether an offense is "petty" for purposes of the Sixth Amendment: "An offense carrying a maximum prison term of six months or less is presumed petty, unless the legislature has authorized additional statutory penalties so severe as to indicate that the legislature considered the offense serious." For a critical analysis of *Lewis*, see Colleen P. Murphy, The Narrowing of the Entitlement to Criminal Jury Trial, [1997] Wis. L. Rev. 133.

4. Consider Justice Powell's *Argersinger* concurrence. Why does he wish to resurrect the *Betts* special circumstances rule? Are you convinced or unpersuaded? Which is likely to be more difficult, to determine whether imprisonment may be the preferred sanction if the defendant is guilty or to determine, without the aid of defense counsel, whether a case is sufficiently complex as to require the assistance of counsel? Note further that Justice Powell asserts that "Due Process . . . embodies principles of fairness rather than immutable line drawing." How helpful is that? How do you determine what is "fair" without "drawing a line" between that and what is "unfair"?

5. To introduce the excerpt from *Argersinger*, we asked what you thought the holding in *Gideon* is. What do you think the holding in *Argersinger* is? Does *Argersinger* supplement, or modify, *Gideon*? Does counsel need to be appointed in a felony case in which the judge determines before trial not to sentence the defendant to a term of imprisonment? If so, why? What is the significance of labeling one offense a felony and another a misdemeanor? How do aggravated misdemeanors fit into the taxonomy? See, e.g., Iowa Crim. Code §903.1 (aggravated misdemeanor punishable by two-year imprisonment). The Court in Scott v. Illinois, 440 U.S. 367 (1979), addressed some of these issues:

> We granted certiorari in this case to resolve a conflict among state and lower federal courts regarding the proper application of our decision in Argersinger v. Hamlin. . . . Scott was convicted of theft and fined $50 after a bench trial in the Circuit Court of Cook County, Ill. . . . The applicable Illinois statute set the maximum penalty for such an offense at a $500 fine or one year in jail, or both. The petitioner argues that a line of this Court's cases culminating in Argersinger v. Hamlin, . . . requires state provision of counsel whenever imprisonment is an authorized penalty . . . .
>
> Although the intentions of the *Argersinger* Court are not unmistakably clear from its opinion, we conclude today that *Argersinger* did indeed delimit the constitutional right to appointed counsel in state criminal proceedings. Even were the matter res nova, we believe that the central premise of *Argersinger* — that actual imprisonment is a penalty different in kind from fines or the mere threat of imprisonment — is eminently sound and warrants adoption of actual imprisonment as the line defining the constitutional right to appointment of counsel. *Argersinger* has proved workable, whereas any extension would create confusion and impose unpredictable, but necessarily substantial, costs on 50 quite diverse States.[5] We therefore hold that the Sixth and Fourteenth Amendments to the United States Constitution require only that no indigent criminal defendant be sentenced to a term of imprisonment unless the State has afforded him the right to assistance of appointed counsel in his defense. The judgement of the Supreme Court of Illinois is accordingly affirmed.

Justice Brennan dissented:

> In my view petitioner could prevail in this case without extending the right to counsel beyond what was assumed to exist in *Argersinger*. Neither party in that case questioned

---

5. Unfortunately, extensive empirical work has not been done. That which exists suggests that the requirements of *Argersinger* have not proved to be unduly burdensome. See, e.g., B. Ingraham, The Impact of *Argersinger* — One Year Later, 8 Law & Soc. Rev. 615 (1974). That some jurisdictions have had difficulty implementing *Argersinger* is certainly not an argument for extending it. S. Krantz, C. Smith, D. Rossman, P. Froyd & J. Hoffman, Right to Counsel in Criminal Cases 1-18 (1976).

the existence of the right to counsel in trials involving "non-petty" offenses punishable by more than six months in jail. The question the Court addressed was whether the right applied to some "petty" offenses to which the right to jury trial did not extend. The Court's reasoning in applying the right to counsel in the case before it—that the right to counsel is more fundamental to a fair proceeding than the right to jury trial and that the historical limitations on the jury trial right are irrelevant to the right to counsel—certainly cannot support a standard for the right to counsel that is more restrictive than the standard for granting a right to jury trial. . . . *Argersinger* thus established a "two dimensional" test for the right to counsel: the right attaches to any "nonpetty" offense punishable by more than six months in jail and in addition to any offense where actual incarceration is likely regardless of the maximum authorized penalty. See Duke, The Right to Appointed Counsel: *Argersinger* and Beyond, 12 Am. Crim. L. Rev. 601 (1975).

The offense of "theft" with which Scott was charged is certainly not a "petty" one. It is punishable by a sentence of up to one year in jail. Unlike many traffic or other "regulatory" offenses, it carries the moral stigma associated with common-law crimes traditionally recognized as indicative of moral depravity. The State indicated at oral argument that the services of a professional prosecutor were considered essential to the prosecution of this offense. . . . Likewise, nonindigent defendants charged with this offense would be well advised to hire the "best lawyers they can get." Scott's right to the assistance of appointed counsel is thus plainly mandated by the logic of the Court's prior cases, including *Argersinger* itself.

. . . Not only is the "actual imprisonment" standard unprecedented as the exclusive test, but also the problems inherent in its application demonstrate the superiority of an "authorized imprisonment" standard that would require the appointment of counsel for indigents accused of any offense for which imprisonment for any time is authorized.

First, the "authorized imprisonment" standard more faithfully implements the principles of the Sixth Amendment identified in *Gideon*. The procedural rules established by state statutes are geared to the nature of the potential penalty for an offense, not to the actual penalty imposed in particular cases. The authorized penalty is also a better predictor of the stigma and other collateral consequences that attach to conviction of an offense. With the exception of *Argersinger*, authorized penalties have been used consistently by this Court as the true measures of the seriousness of offenses. . . . Imprisonment is a sanction particularly associated with criminal offenses; trials of offenses punishable by imprisonment accordingly possess the characteristics found by *Gideon* to require the appointment of counsel. By contrast, the "actual imprisonment" standard, as the Court's opinion in this case demonstrates, denies the right to counsel in criminal prosecutions to accuseds who suffer the severe consequences of prosecution other than imprisonment.

Second, the "authorized imprisonment" test presents no problems of administration. It avoids the necessity for time-consuming consideration of the likely sentence in each individual case before trial and the attendant problems of inaccurate predictions, unequal treatment, and apparent and actual bias. . . .

Finally, the "authorized imprisonment" test ensures that courts will not abrogate legislative judgments concerning the appropriate range of penalties to be considered for each offense. . . .

The apparent reason for the Court's adoption of the "actual imprisonment" standard for all misdemeanors is concern for the economic burden that an "authorized imprisonment" standard might place on the States. But, with all respect, that concern is both irrelevant and speculative.

This Court's role in enforcing constitutional guarantees for criminal defendants cannot be made dependent on the budgetary decisions of state governments. . . .

6. Does *Scott* dramatically change the prior understanding of the scope of the Sixth Amendment? *Argersinger* referred explicitly to "the trial of a misdemeanor," thus apparently leaving intact the general understanding that *Gideon* requires the appointment of counsel for indigents in all felony cases. Is that understanding consistent with *Scott*? If the only constitutional criterion is actual imprisonment, then presumably it should apply to misdemeanors and felonies alike. Nevertheless, lower courts have mostly assumed since *Scott* that felonies are governed by *Gideon*'s across-the-board requirement of appointment of counsel. In an offhand statement in a footnote, the Supreme Court accepted that view. Nichols v. United States, 511 U.S. 738, 743 n. 9 (1994) ("In felony cases, in contrast to misdemeanor charges, the Constitution requires that an indigent defendant be offered appointed counsel unless that right is intelligently and competently waived.") (citing *Gideon*).

Also, is it now clear that the right to counsel and the right to trial by jury are entirely independent and that invocation of a right to a jury trial is not a "special circumstance" that initiates a right to counsel? And is it also now clear that there is no longer any form of a "special circumstances" rule?

7. Or is there a better way to read *Scott*? If you read *Scott* broadly, it fundamentally reworks the meaning of the Sixth Amendment, but can it also be read more narrowly, as essentially refining *Argersinger*'s treatment of less serious criminal cases? Read more narrowly, would the aftermath of *Scott* contain a series of principles, any one of which would be adequate to require counsel in any particular case? What are those principles? In this regard, consider the implications of United States v. Nachtigal, 507 U.S. 1 (1993), in which the court of appeals held that a jury trial was required even though maximum punishment did not exceed six months. The Court summarily reversed but in doing so emphasized the importance of Blanton v. North Las Vegas, 489 U.S. 538 (1989), which implies that factors other than length of sentence may be relevant to the right to a jury trial. If that is so, can factors other than imprisonment be relevant to the right to counsel?

8. How do you know whether to read *Scott* broadly or narrowly? Is the Court's opinion enlightening? Of what significance, for example, is the Court's reluctance to extend already extended lines? Its various references to social costs or a lack of available lawyers? For an excellent discussion of these and related issues, see Lawrence Herman & Charles A. Thompson, Scott v. Illinois and the Right to Counsel: A Decision in Search of a Doctrine?, 17 Am. Crim. L. Rev. 71 (1979).

9. How cogent is the majority's emphasis on imprisonment as the controlling factor? Criminal conviction apparently has a stigmatizing effect on the defendant, and there are other, more tangible collateral consequences that can follow from conviction, such as the loss of various kinds of licenses or of the right to vote. Did the Court adequately address these kinds of consequences? Indeed, did the Court address these at all? How should they be addressed?

10. The most serious collateral consequence that can flow from a criminal conviction is a dramatically increased sentence for a subsequent criminal conviction. In Baldasar v. Illinois, 446 U.S. 222 (1980), the Court reviewed the constitutionality of a statute that converted a second conviction for misdemeanor theft (property worth less than $150) into a felony with enhanced punishment. Baldasar was convicted of the first offense without counsel, and the question before the Court was whether the uncounseled conviction could trigger the enhancement

provisions after the second, counseled conviction. By a 5–4 vote, the Court said no, though no single opinion commanded a majority.

In Nichols v. United States, 511 U.S. 738 (1994), the Court returned to this issue. In 1983, Nichols was convicted of driving under the influence, a misdemeanor, for which he was fined but not jailed. He was not represented in the DUI proceeding. In 1990 Nichols was convicted on federal drug charges, and under the federal sentencing guidelines, the earlier, uncounseled DUI conviction led to an addition of roughly two years to his federal prison sentence. The Supreme Court upheld the sentence. In an opinion by Chief Justice Rehnquist, one of the dissenters in *Baldasar*, the Court concluded that *Baldasar* should be overruled, and that uncounseled convictions could henceforth be used to enhance sentences for subsequent crimes. The Court reasoned that this was the only position that was "consistent with the traditional understanding of the sentencing process, which we have often recognized as less exacting than the process of establishing guilt":

> As a general proposition, a sentencing judge "may appropriately conduct an inquiry broad in scope, largely unlimited either as to the kind of information he may consider, or the source from which it may come." (U.S. v. Tucker, 404 U.S. 443, 448) . . . "Traditionally, sentencing judges have considered a wide variety of factors in addition to evidence of guilt in determining what sentence to impose on a convicted defendant." (Wisconsin v. Mitchell, 508 U.S. 476, 485) . . . One such important factor, as recognized by state recidivism statutes and the criminal history component of the Sentencing Guidelines, is a defendant's prior convictions. Sentencing courts have not only taken into consideration a defendant's prior convictions, but have also considered a defendant's past criminal behavior, even if no conviction resulted from that behavior. We have upheld the constitutionality of considering such previous conduct in Williams v. New York, 337 U.S. 241 (1949). . . . [And] in McMillan v. Pennsylvania, 477 U.S. 79 (1986) . . . we held that the state could consider, as a sentence enhancement factor, visible possession of a firearm during the felonies of which defendant was found guilty.
>
> Thus, consistently with due process, petitioner in the present case could have been sentenced more severely based simply on evidence of the underlying conduct which gave rise to the previous DUI offense. And the state need prove such conduct only by a preponderance of the evidence. Surely, then, it must be constitutionally permissible to consider a prior uncounseled misdemeanor conviction based on the same conduct where that conduct must be proven beyond a reasonable doubt.

511 U.S. 747-748. Justice Blackmun, joined by Justices Stevens and Ginsburg, dissented, arguing that the Court's position squarely conflicted with *Scott*. According to Justice Blackmun, *Scott* stands for the proposition that Nichols's uncounseled DUI conviction may not be "used as the basis for any incarceration, not even a 1-day jail sentence," id. at 754 (Blackmun, J., dissenting), much less the two years of additional time Nichols had to serve.

Which position in *Nichols* is more faithful to *Scott*? Which position is more faithful to *Gideon*? What you are beginning to see is that such questions are often quite difficult to answer. Constitutional principles can arise in cases in virtually limitless ways. Any single case applies those principles to the facts of that case, but their applicability to some other case with different facts can be unpredictable. The right to counsel area is a good example of this because of the enormous complexity involved in the various ways that states can sanction offenders, and the numerous variables that can affect the decision to sanction. One sees in the path forward from *Gideon* the implications of this dynamic. Rather than laying down immutable principles to then be faithfully applied in a straightforward fashion, the Court is engaged in a common law process of building up a system of precedent sensitive to the factual nuances of the cases that arise. Some recent scholarship suggests that this may be generally true with respect to the Court's constitutional criminal procedure jurisprudence. See, e.g., Ronald J. Allen & Ross M. Rosenberg, The Fourth Amendment and the Limits of Theory: Local Versus General Theoretical Knowledge, 72 St. John's L. Rev. 1149 (1998); Ronald J. Allen & M. Kristin Mace, The Self-Incrimination Clause Explained and Its Future Predicted, 94 J. Crim. L. & Criminology 243 (2004); Craig M. Bradley, The Uncertainty Principle in the Supreme Court, 1986 Duke L.J. 1. With that thought in mind, consider the following case.

ALABAMA v. SHELTON

Certiorari to the Alabama Supreme Court
535 U.S. 654 (2002)

JUSTICE GINSBURG delivered the opinion of the Court.

This case concerns the Sixth Amendment right of an indigent defendant charged with a misdemeanor punishable by imprisonment, fine, or both, to the assistance of court-appointed counsel. Two prior decisions control the Court's judgment. First, in Argersinger v. Hamlin, 407 U.S. 25 (1972), this Court held that defense counsel must be appointed in any criminal prosecution, "whether classified as petty, misdemeanor, or felony," id., at 37, "that actually leads to imprisonment even for a brief period," id., at 33. Later, in Scott v. Illinois, 440 U.S. 367, 373-374 (1979), the Court drew the line at "actual imprisonment," holding that counsel need not be appointed when the defendant is fined for the charged crime, but is not sentenced to a term of imprisonment.

Defendant-respondent LeReed Shelton, convicted of third-degree assault, was sentenced to a jail term of 30 days, which the trial court immediately suspended, placing Shelton on probation for two years. The question presented is whether the Sixth Amendment right to appointed counsel, as delineated in *Argersinger* and *Scott*, applies to a defendant in Shelton's situation. We hold that a suspended sentence that may "end up in the actual deprivation of a person's liberty" may not be imposed unless the defendant was accorded "the guiding hand of counsel" in the prosecution for the crime charged. *Argersinger*, 407 U.S., at 40.

I

After representing himself at a bench trial in the District Court of Etowah County, Alabama, Shelton was convicted of third-degree assault, a class A misdemeanor carrying a maximum punishment of one year imprisonment and a $2000 fine. He invoked his right to a new trial before a jury in Circuit Court, where he again appeared without a lawyer and was again convicted. The court repeatedly warned Shelton about the problems self-representation entailed, but at no time offered him assistance of counsel at state expense.

The Circuit Court sentenced Shelton to serve 30 days in the county prison. As authorized by Alabama law, however, the court suspended that sentence and placed Shelton on two years' unsupervised probation, conditioned on his payment of court costs, a $500 fine, reparations of $25, and restitution in the amount of $516.69.

Shelton appealed his conviction and sentence on Sixth Amendment grounds. . . . A suspended sentence, the [Alabama Court of Criminal Appeals] concluded, does not trigger the Sixth Amendment right to appointed counsel unless there is "evidence in the record that the [defendant] has actually been deprived of liberty." Because Shelton remained on probation, the court held that he had not been denied any Sixth Amendment right at trial.

The Supreme Court of Alabama reversed the Court of Criminal Appeals in relevant part. . . . In the Alabama high court's view, a suspended sentence constitutes a "term of imprisonment" within the meaning of *Argersinger* and *Scott* even though incarceration is not immediate or inevitable. And because the State is constitutionally barred from activating the conditional sentence, the Alabama court concluded, "the threat itself is hollow and should be considered a nullity." Accordingly, the court affirmed Shelton's conviction and the monetary portion of his punishment, but invalidated "that aspect of his sentence imposing 30 days of suspended jail time." By reversing Shelton's suspended sentence, the State informs us, the court also vacated the two-year term of probation.

Courts have divided on the Sixth Amendment question presented in this case. Some have agreed with the decision below that appointment of counsel is a constitutional prerequisite to imposition of a conditional or suspended prison sentence. . . . Others have rejected that proposition. . . . We granted certiorari to resolve the conflict.

II

. . . Applying the "actual imprisonment" rule to the case before us, we take up first the [following] question . . . : Where the State provides no counsel to an indigent defendant, does the Sixth Amendment permit activation of a suspended sentence upon the defendant's violation of the terms of probation? We conclude that it does not. A suspended sentence is a prison term imposed for the offense of conviction. Once the prison term is triggered, the defendant is incarcerated not for the probation violation, but for the underlying offense. The uncounseled conviction at that point "results in imprisonment," Nichols [v. United States, 511 U.S. 738, 746 (1994)]; it "ends up in the actual deprivation of a person's liberty," *Argersinger*, 407 U.S., at 40. This is precisely what the Sixth Amendment, as interpreted in *Argersinger* and *Scott*, does not allow.

Amicus[3] resists this reasoning primarily on two grounds. First, he attempts to align this case with our decisions in *Nichols* and Gagnon v. Scarpelli, 411 U.S. 778 (1973). . . .

Nichols presented the question whether the Sixth Amendment barred consideration of a defendant's prior uncounseled misdemeanor conviction in determining his sentence for a subsequent felony offense. 511 U.S. at 740. [We

---

3. Oddly, when this case got to the Supreme Court, Alabama refused to defend its own statute, so the Court appointed Professor Charles Fried as amicus to defend that position. — EDS.

concluded that] "an uncounseled misdemeanor conviction, valid under *Scott* because no prison term was imposed, is also valid when used to enhance punishment at a subsequent conviction." Id., at 749. In *Gagnon*, the question was whether the defendant, who was placed on probation pursuant to a suspended sentence for armed robbery, had a due process right to representation by appointed counsel at a probation revocation hearing. 411 U.S., at 783. We held that counsel was not invariably required in parole or probation revocation proceedings; we directed, instead, a "case-by-case approach" turning on the character of the issues involved. Id., at 788-791.

Considered together, amicus contends, *Nichols* and *Gagnon* establish this principle: Sequential proceedings must be analyzed separately for Sixth Amendment purposes, and only those proceedings "resulting in *immediate* actual imprisonment" trigger the right to state-appointed counsel, id., at 13 (emphasis added). Thus, the defendant in *Nichols* had no right to appointed counsel in the DUI proceeding because he was not immediately imprisoned at the conclusion of that proceeding. The uncounseled DUI, valid when imposed, did not later become invalid because it was used to enhance the length of imprisonment that followed a separate and subsequent felony proceeding. Just so here, amicus contends: Shelton had no right to appointed counsel in the Circuit Court because he was not incarcerated immediately after trial; his conviction and suspended sentence were thus valid and could serve as proper predicates for actual imprisonment at a later hearing to revoke his probation.

Gagnon and *Nichols* do not stand for the broad proposition amicus would extract from them. The dispositive factor in those cases was not whether incarceration occurred immediately or only after some delay. Rather, the critical point was that the defendant had a recognized right to counsel when adjudicated guilty of the felony offense for which he was imprisoned. . . . Unlike this case, in which revocation of probation would trigger a prison term imposed for a misdemeanor of which Shelton was found guilty without the aid of counsel, the sentences imposed in *Nichols* and *Gagnon* were for felony convictions—a federal drug conviction in *Nichols*, and a state armed robbery conviction in *Gagnon*—for which the right to counsel is unquestioned. . . .

Thus, neither *Nichols* nor *Gagnon* altered or diminished *Argersinger*'s command that "no person may be imprisoned *for any offense* . . . unless he was represented by counsel at his trial," 407 U.S. at 37 (emphasis added). Far from supporting amicus' position, *Gagnon* and *Nichols* simply highlight that the Sixth Amendment inquiry trains on the stage of the proceedings corresponding to Shelton's Circuit Court trial, where his guilt was adjudicated, eligibility for imprisonment established, and prison sentence determined. . . .

Amicus also contends that "practical considerations clearly weigh against" the extension of the Sixth Amendment appointed-counsel right to a defendant in Shelton's situation. He cites figures suggesting that although conditional sentences are commonly imposed, they are rarely activated. Tr. of Oral Arg. 20-21 (speculating that "hundreds of thousands" of uncounseled defendants receive suspended sentences, but only "thousands" of that large number are incarcerated upon violating the terms of their probation). Based on these estimations, amicus argues that a rule requiring appointed counsel in every case involving a suspended sentence would unduly hamper the States' attempts to impose effective probationary punishment. A more "workable solution," he contends, would permit imposition of a suspended sentence on an uncounseled defendant and require appointment of counsel, if at all, only at the probation revocation stage, when incarceration is imminent.

. . . [But] the sole issue at the [probation revocation] hearing . . . is whether the defendant breached the terms of probation. . . . The validity or reliability of the underlying conviction is beyond attack. . . .

We think it plain that a hearing so timed and structured cannot compensate for the absence of trial counsel, for it does not even address the key Sixth Amendment inquiry: whether the adjudication of guilt corresponding to the prison sentence is sufficiently reliable to permit incarceration. Deprived of counsel when tried, convicted, and sentenced, and unable to challenge the original judgment at a subsequent probation revocation hearing, a defendant in Shelton's circumstances faces incarceration on a conviction that has never been subjected to "the crucible of meaningful adversarial testing," United States v. Cronic, 466 U.S. 648, 656 (1984). The Sixth Amendment does not countenance this result.

In a variation on amicus' position, the dissent would limit review in this case to the question whether the *imposition* of Shelton's suspended sentence required appointment of counsel, answering that question "plainly no" because such a step "does not deprive a defendant of his personal liberty." Only if the sentence is later activated, the dissent contends, need the Court "ask whether the procedural safeguards attending the imposition of [Shelton's] sentence comply with the Constitution."

Severing the analysis in this manner makes little sense. One cannot assess the constitutionality of imposing a suspended sentence while simultaneously walling off the procedures that will precede its activation. The dissent imagines a set of safeguards Alabama might provide at the probation revocation stage sufficient to cure its failure to appoint counsel prior to sentencing, including, perhaps, "complete retrial of the misdemeanor violation with assistance of counsel." But there is no cause for speculation about Alabama's procedures; they are established by Alabama statute and decisional law, and they bear no resemblance to those the dissent invents in its effort to sanction the prospect of Shelton's imprisonment on an uncounseled conviction. Assessing the issue before us in light of actual circumstances, we do not comprehend how the procedures Alabama in fact provides at the probation revocation hearing could bring Shelton's sentence within constitutional bounds.

. . . Most jurisdictions already provide a state-law right to appointed counsel more generous than that afforded by the Federal Constitution. All but 16 States, for example, would provide counsel to a defendant in Shelton's circumstances, either because he received a substantial fine or because state law authorized incarceration for the charged offense or provided for a maximum prison term of one year. There is thus scant reason to believe that a rule conditioning imposition of a suspended sentence on provision of appointed counsel would affect existing practice in the large majority of the States. And given the current commitment of most jurisdictions to affording court-appointed counsel to indigent misdemeanants while simultaneously preserving the option of probationary punishment, we do not share amicus' concern that other States may lack the capacity and resources to do the same.

Moreover, even if amicus is correct that "some courts and jurisdictions at least cannot bear" the costs of the rule we confirm today, those States need not abandon probation or equivalent measures as viable forms of punishment. Although they may not attach probation to an imposed and suspended prison sentence, States unable or unwilling routinely to provide appointed counsel to misdemeanants in Shelton's situation are not without recourse to another option capable of yielding a similar result.

That option is pretrial probation, employed in some form by at least 23 States. [Citations are omitted.] Under such an arrangement, the prosecutor and defendant agree to the defendant's participation in a pretrial rehabilitation program, which includes conditions typical of post-trial probation. The adjudication of guilt and imposition of sentence for the underlying offense then occur only if and when the defendant breaches those conditions. . . .

Like the regime urged by amicus, this system reserves the appointed-counsel requirement for the "small percentage" of cases in which incarceration proves necessary, thus allowing a State to "supervise a course of rehabilitation" without providing a lawyer every time it wishes to pursue such a course, *Gagnon*, 411 U.S., at 784. Unlike amicus' position, however, pretrial probation also respects the constitutional imperative that "no person may be imprisoned for any offense . . . unless he was represented by counsel at his trial," *Argersinger*, 407 U.S., at 37. . . .

Satisfied that Shelton is entitled to appointed counsel at the critical stage when his guilt or innocence of the charged crime is decided and his vulnerability to imprisonment is determined, we affirm the judgment of the Supreme Court of Alabama.

It is so ordered.

JUSTICE SCALIA, with whom THE CHIEF JUSTICE, JUSTICE KENNEDY, and JUSTICE THOMAS join, dissenting.

. . . Respondent's 30-day suspended sentence, and the accompanying 2-year term of probation, are invalidated for lack of appointed counsel even though respondent has not suffered, and may never suffer, a deprivation of liberty. The Court holds that the suspended sentence violates respondent's Sixth Amendment right to counsel because it "*may* 'end up in the actual deprivation of [respondent's] liberty,' " ante (emphasis added), *if* he someday violates the terms of probation, *if* a court determines that the violation merits revocation of probation, and *if* the court determines that no other punishment will "adequately protect the community from further criminal activity" or "avoid depreciating the seriousness of the violation," Ala. Code §15-22-54(d)(4). And to all of these contingencies there must yet be added, before the Court's decision makes sense, an element of rank speculation. Should all these contingencies occur, the Court speculates, the Alabama Supreme Court would mechanically apply its decisional law applicable to routine probation revocation (which establishes procedures that the Court finds inadequate) rather than adopt special procedures for situations that raise constitutional questions in light of *Argersinger* and *Scott*. . . .

But that question is not the one before us, and the Court has no business offering an advisory opinion on its answer. We are asked to decide whether "imposition of a suspended or conditional sentence in a misdemeanor case invoke[s] a defendant's Sixth Amendment right to counsel." Pet. for Cert. i. Since *imposition* of a suspended sentence does not deprive a defendant of his personal liberty, the answer to that question is plainly no. In the future, *if and when* the State of Alabama seeks to imprison respondent on the previously suspended sentence, we can ask whether the procedural safeguards attending the imposition of that sentence comply with the Constitution. But that question is *not* before us now. . . .

. . . Surely the procedures attending reimposition of a suspended sentence would be adequate if they required, upon the defendant's request, complete retrial of the misdemeanor violation with assistance of counsel. By what right does the Court deprive the State of that option? It may well be a sensible option, since most defendants will be induced to comply with the terms of their probation by the mere threat of a retrial that could send them to jail, and since the expense of those rare, counseled retrials may be much less than the expense of providing counsel initially in all misdemeanor cases that bear a possible sentence of imprisonment. And it may well be that, in some cases, even procedures short of complete retrial will suffice.

Our prior opinions placed considerable weight on the practical consequences of expanding the right to appointed counsel beyond cases of actual imprisonment. See, e.g., *Scott*, 440 U.S., at 373 (any extension of *Argersinger* would "impose unpredictable, but necessarily substantial, costs on 50 quite diverse States"); see also *Argersinger*, 407 U.S., at 56-62 (Powell, J., concurring in result) (same). Today, the Court gives this consideration the back of its hand. Its observation that "[a]ll but 16 States" already appoint counsel for defendants like respondent, is interesting but quite irrelevant, since today's holding is not confined to *defendants like respondent*. Appointed counsel must henceforth be offered before *any* defendant can be awarded a suspended sentence, no matter how short. Only 24 States have announced a rule of this scope.[4] Thus, the Court's decision imposes a large, new burden on a majority of the States, including some of the poorest. . . . That burden consists not only of the cost of providing state-paid counsel in cases of such insignificance that even financially prosperous defendants sometimes forgo the expense of hired counsel; but also the cost of enabling courts and prosecutors to respond to the "over-lawyering" of minor cases. Nor should we discount the burden placed on the minority 24 States that currently provide counsel: that they keep their current disposition forever in place, however imprudent experience proves it to be.

Today's imposition upon the States finds justification neither in the text of the Constitution, nor in the settled practices of our people, nor in the prior jurisprudence of this Court. I respectfully dissent.

---

4. Ten of the thirty-four States cited by the Court do not offer appointed counsel in all cases where a misdemeanor defendant might suffer a suspended sentence. Six States guarantee counsel only when the authorized penalty is at least three or six months' imprisonment. [There follows a series of citations, and a detailed explanation of the exceptions that apply to misdemeanor cases in the other four states to which JUSTICE SCALIA refers.] . . .

The Court asserts that the burden of today's decision on these jurisdictions is small because the "circumstances in which [they] currently allow prosecution of misdemeanors without appointed counsel are quite *narrow*." (emphasis added). But the narrowness of the range of circumstances covered says nothing about the number of suspended-sentence cases covered. Misdemeanors punishable by less than six months' imprisonment may be a narrow category, but it may well include the vast majority of cases in which (precisely *because* of the minor nature of the offense) a suspended sentence is imposed. There is simply nothing to support the Court's belief that few offenders are prosecuted for crimes in which counsel is not already provided. . . .

NOTES AND QUESTIONS

1. The subject of *Shelton* is the scope of the *Gideon* right to state-paid counsel for indigent defendants. The Court decided that the scope of that right is broad — broader, by some measures, than most states previously provided. Why? Is there a rationale for the *Gideon* right that explains *Shelton*, but that also explains why the right does not extend to misdemeanor cases where neither incarceration nor the threat of it is part of the defendant's sentence?

2. Why isn't it good enough, as the dissenters suggest, to give Shelton an elaborate process, *with* counsel, if and when his probation is revoked? What do you think about the majority's asserted justification for precluding Alabama from trying to develop such a process, if and when it is needed?

3. In the Supreme Court, Alabama also argued for an alternative, creative way around the Sixth Amendment problem: Enforce the conditions of probation through contempt proceedings for failure to abide by those conditions, which could in turn lead to jail or prison as long as defense counsel is provided at the time of the contempt proceeding. The Court did not address this argument, as it had not been presented below.

If the state's contempt argument loses, *Shelton* has potentially large effects on the prosecution of low-grade misdemeanors. At least in a few states, it is common to prosecute such cases, and impose probation or a suspended sentence, without offering counsel to defendants. This amounts to an order to the defendant to keep his nose clean — if he fails to do so, he can go to jail; otherwise, his conviction will carry no significant penalty. Most defendants faced with that threat do keep their noses clean; only a very small minority of suspended sentences are ever imposed and a similarly small minority of probations are revoked. After *Shelton*, though, the state must provide counsel in all these cases, even the ones (the great majority) where the defendant is never incarcerated — or else the state must abandon its threat. Perhaps the state will do just that. But abandoning the threat of jail might make the misdemeanor proceeding pointless: Remember that we're talking about indigent defendants (other defendants can, of course, hire counsel for themselves), so significant fines are not available as a deterrent to further crimes. The obvious alternative is to see that many more misdemeanor defendants get lawyers — but also that many more misdemeanor defendants go directly to jail.

2. Further Emanations of the Right to Counsel — Counsel on Appeal and Other Forms of Assistance

Seven years prior to *Gideon*, in Griffin v. Illinois, 351 U.S. 12 (1956), the Court rendered a decision with enormous implications that nonetheless remained dormant for the most part until the day *Gideon* was decided. It was not *Gideon* that resurrected *Griffin*, however; rather, it was *Gideon*'s companion case, Douglas v. California, 372 U.S. 353 (1963). In *Griffin*, the Court struck down an Illinois statute that denied free transcripts of trial proceedings to indigents in circumstances in which a transcript was necessary for an appeal under Illinois law. A four-person plurality, with Justice Frankfurter concurring, concluded that the Constitution prohibits a state from structuring an appellate process that has the effect of denying an effective review to indigents while permitting it to those with financial means.

If all *Griffin* stood for is that a state may not deny access to an important process on the basis of wealth, it still would have been an important decision interpreting the due process requirement of fairness in the criminal process, but not a particularly startling one. The plurality, however, did not stop at the point of access as a requirement of fairness. Instead, the plurality suggested that the real issue in *Griffin* was not access but any discrimination between the rich and the poor. Indeed, the opinion went so far as to say: "There can be no equal justice when the kind of trial a man gets depends on the amount of money he has." Were that to be taken literally, fundamental changes in the criminal process would have to be brought about, for a defendant of means is better off in myriad ways than a person without substantial funds.

Douglas v. California gave the appearance of beginning to take literally the dicta of *Griffin*. Petitioners in *Douglas* were convicted and appealed as of right to the California Court of Appeal. On appeal, petitioners requested, and were denied, the assistance of appellate counsel. However, the denial came only after the court of appeal, following the applicable California rule of criminal procedure, made an independent investigation of the record to determine whether the assistance of counsel would be helpful to the petitioner or the court. Thus, petitioners were not denied access to the appellate process; they were only denied state-financed assistance after a determination was made that such assistance would be futile. Nonetheless, the Court found the California procedure unconstitutional, in large part on the basis of *Griffin*. Consequently, *Griffin*, as modified by *Douglas*, no longer appeared to be limitable to questions of access if indeed it ever was.

The limits of *Douglas*, however, are unclear. Read broadly, it would seem to require the extirpation of all differences resulting from the financial condition of defendants. However, it is difficult to tell from the opinions in *Douglas* how broadly to read it, because the underlying rationale of the decision is not adequately specified. As in *Griffin*, the decision could have been based either upon some notion of fairness that was now seen to extend beyond questions of access or, by contrast, upon the requirement of equal treatment. The greater the reliance on equal treatment as the operative principle, however, the more difficult it becomes to draw limits on the reach of *Douglas*. And indeed in the years following *Douglas*, the Court appeared to interpret *Douglas* as providing an equality principle that was extended in a series of cases, and each succeeding case heightened the perceived tension between the equality principle and the other possible explanation for *Douglas*—fundamental fairness. This process culminated in the following case.

ROSS v. MOFFITT

Certiorari to the United States Court of Appeals for the Fourth Circuit
417 U.S. 600 (1974)

MR. JUSTICE REHNQUIST delivered the opinion of the Court.

We are asked in this case to decide whether Douglas v. California, . . . which requires appointment of counsel for indigent state defendants on their first appeal as of right, should be extended to require counsel for discretionary state appeals and for applications for review in this Court. The Court of Appeals for the Fourth

Circuit held that such appointment was required by the Due Process and Equal Protection Clauses of the Fourteenth Amendment. . . .

II

This Court, in the past 20 years, has given extensive consideration to the rights of indigent persons on appeal. In Griffin v. Illinois, 351 U.S. 12 (1956), the first of the pertinent cases, the Court had before it an Illinois rule allowing a convicted criminal defendant to present claims of trial error to the Supreme Court of Illinois only if he procured a transcript of the testimony adduced at his trial. No exception was made for the indigent defendant, and thus one who was unable to pay the cost of obtaining such a transcript was precluded from obtaining appellate review of asserted trial error. . . . The Court in *Griffin* held that this discrimination violated the Fourteenth Amendment.

Succeeding cases invalidated similar financial barriers to the appellate process, at the same time reaffirming the traditional principle that a State is not obliged to provide any appeal at all for criminal defendants. McKane v. Durston, 153 U.S. 684 (1894). The cases encompassed a variety of circumstances but all had a common theme. For example, Lane v. Brown, 372 U.S. 477 (1963), involved an Indiana provision declaring that only a public defender could obtain a free transcript of a hearing on a coram nobis application. If the public defender declined to request one, the indigent prisoner seeking to appeal had no recourse. In Draper v. Washington, 372 U.S. 487 (1963), the State permitted an indigent to obtain a free transcript of the trial at which he was convicted only if he satisfied the trial judge that his contentions on appeal would not be frivolous. The appealing defendant was in effect bound by the trial court's conclusions in seeking to review the determination of frivolousness, since no transcript or its equivalent was made available to him. In Smith v. Bennett, 365 U.S. 708 (1961), Iowa had required a filing fee in order to process a state habeas corpus application by a convicted defendant, and in Burns v. Ohio, 360 U.S. 252 (1959), the State of Ohio required a $20 filing fee in order to move the Supreme Court of Ohio for leave to appeal from a judgment of the Ohio Court of Appeals affirming a criminal conviction. Each of these state-imposed financial barriers to the adjudication of a criminal defendant's appeal was held to violate the Fourteenth Amendment.

The decisions discussed above stand for the proposition that a State cannot arbitrarily cut off appeal rights for indigents while leaving open avenues of appeal for more affluent persons. In Douglas v. California, 372 U.S. 353 (1963), however, a case decided the same day as *Lane*, supra, and *Draper*, supra, the Court departed somewhat from the limited doctrine of the transcript and fee cases and undertook an examination of whether an indigent's access to the appellate system was adequate. The Court in *Douglas* concluded that a State does not fulfill its responsibility toward indigent defendants merely by waiving its own requirements that a convicted defendant procure a transcript or pay a fee in order to appeal, and held that the State must go further and provide counsel for the indigent on his first appeal as of right. It is this decision we are asked to extend today.

Petitioners in *Douglas*, each of whom had been convicted by a jury on 13 felony counts, took appeals as of right to the California District Court of Appeal. No filing fee was exacted of them, no transcript was required in order to present their arguments to the Court of Appeal, and the appellate process was therefore open to them. Petitioners, however, claimed that they not only had the right to make use of the appellate process, but were also entitled to court-appointed and state-compensated counsel because they were indigent. The California appellate court examined the trial record on its own initiative, following the then-existing rule in California, and concluded that " 'no good whatever could be served by appointment of counsel.' " 372 U.S., at 355. It therefore denied petitioners' request for the appointment of counsel.

This Court held unconstitutional California's requirement that counsel on appeal would be appointed for an indigent only if the appellate court determined that such appointment would be helpful to the defendant or to the court itself. The Court noted that under this system an indigent's case was initially reviewed on the merits without the benefit of any organization or argument by counsel. By contrast, persons of greater means were not faced with the preliminary "ex parte examination of the record," id., at 356, but had their arguments presented to the court in fully briefed form. The Court noted, however, that its decision extended only to initial appeals as of right, and went on to say:

> We need not now decide whether California would have to provide counsel for an indigent seeking a discretionary hearing from the California Supreme Court after the District Court of Appeal has sustained his conviction . . . or whether counsel must be appointed for an indigent seeking review of an appellate affirmance of his conviction in this Court by appeal as of right or by petition for a writ of certiorari which lies within the Court's discretion. But it is appropriate to observe that a State can, consistently with the Fourteenth Amendment, provide for differences so long as the result does not amount to a denial of due process or an "invidious discrimination." Williamson v. Lee Optical Co., 348 U.S. 483, 489; Griffin v. Illinois, supra, p. 18. Absolute equality is not required; lines can be and are drawn and we often sustain them. Id., at 356-357.

The precise rationale for the *Griffin* and *Douglas* lines of cases has never been explicitly stated, some support being derived from the Equal Protection Clause of the Fourteenth Amendment, and some from the Due Process Clause of that Amendment.[8] Neither Clause by itself provides an entirely satisfactory basis for the result reached, each depending on a different inquiry which emphasizes different factors. "Due process" emphasizes fairness between the State and the individual dealing with the State, regardless of how other individuals in the same situation may be treated. "Equal protection," on the other hand, emphasizes disparity in treatment by a State between classes of individuals whose situations are arguably indistinguishable. We will address these issues separately in the succeeding sections.

---

8. The Court of Appeals in this case, for example, examined both possible rationales, stating: "If the holding [in *Douglas*] be grounded on the equal protection clause, inequality in the circumstances of these cases is as obvious as it was in the circumstances of *Douglas*. If the holding in *Douglas* were grounded on the Due Process Clause, and Mr. Justice Harlan in dissent thought the discourse should have been in these terms, due process encompasses elements of equality. There simply cannot be due process of the law to a litigant deprived of all professional assistance when other litigants, similarly situated, are able to obtain professional assistance and to be benefited by it. The same concepts of fairness and equality, which require counsel in a first appeal of right, require counsel in other and subsequent discretionary appeals." 483 F.2d, at 655.

III

Recognition of the due process rationale in *Douglas* is found both in the Court's opinion and in the dissenting opinion of Mr. Justice Harlan. The Court in *Douglas* stated that "[w]hen an indigent is forced to run this [gauntlet] of a preliminary showing of merit, the right to appeal does not comport with fair procedure." 372 U.S., at 357. Mr. Justice Harlan thought that the due process issue in *Douglas* was the only one worthy of extended consideration, remarking: "The real question in this case, I submit, and the only one that permits of satisfactory analysis, is whether or not the state rule, as applied in this case, is consistent with the requirements of fair procedure guaranteed by the Due Process Clause." Id., at 363.

We do not believe that the Due Process Clause requires North Carolina to provide respondent with counsel on his discretionary appeal to the State Supreme Court. At the trial stage of a criminal proceeding, the right of an indigent defendant to counsel is fundamental and binding upon the States by virtue of the Sixth and Fourteenth Amendments. Gideon v. Wainwright, 372 U.S. 335 (1963). But there are significant differences between the trial and appellate stages of a criminal proceeding. The purpose of the trial stage from the State's point of view is to convert a criminal defendant from a person presumed innocent to one found guilty beyond a reasonable doubt. To accomplish this purpose, the State employs a prosecuting attorney who presents evidence to the court, challenges any witnesses offered by the defendant, argues rulings of the court, and makes direct arguments to the court and jury seeking to persuade them of the defendant's guilt. Under these circumstances "reason and reflection require us to recognize that in our adversary system of criminal justice, any person haled into court, who is too poor to hire a lawyer, cannot be assured a fair trial unless counsel is provided for him." Id., at 344.

By contrast, it is ordinarily the defendant, rather than the State, who initiates the appellate process, seeking not to fend off the efforts of the State's prosecutor but rather to overturn a finding of guilt made by a judge or jury below. The defendant needs an attorney on appeal not as a shield to protect him against being "haled into court" by the State and stripped of his presumption of innocence, but rather as a sword to upset the prior determination of guilt. This difference is significant for, while no one would agree that the State may simply dispense with the trial stage of proceedings without a criminal defendant's consent, it is clear that the State need not provide any appeal at all. McKane v. Durston, 153 U.S. 684 (1894). The fact that an appeal *has* been provided does not automatically mean that a State then acts unfairly by refusing to provide counsel to indigent defendants at every stage of the way. Douglas v. California, supra. Unfairness results only if indigents are singled out by the State and denied meaningful access to the appellate system because of their poverty. That question is more profitably considered under an equal protection analysis.

IV

Language invoking equal protection notions is prominent both in *Douglas* and in other cases treating the rights of indigents on appeal. The Court in *Douglas*, for example, stated: "[W]here the merits of *the one and only appeal* an indigent has as of right are decided without benefit of counsel, we think an unconstitutional line has been drawn between rich and poor." 372 U.S., at 357. (Emphasis in original.) . . .

. . . Despite the tendency of all rights "to declare themselves absolute to their logical extreme,"[9] there are obviously limits beyond which the equal protection analysis may not be pressed without doing violence to principles recognized in other decisions of this Court. The Fourteenth Amendment "does not require absolute equality or precisely equal advantages," San Antonio Independent School District v. Rodriguez, 411 U.S. 1, 24 (1973), nor does it require the State to "equalize economic conditions." Griffin v. Illinois, 351 U.S., at 23 (Frankfurter, J., concurring). It does require that the state appellate system be "free of unreasoned distinctions," Rinaldi v. Yeager, 384 U.S. 305, 310 (1966), and that indigents have an adequate opportunity to present their claims fairly within the adversary system. Griffin v. Illinois, supra; Draper v. Washington, 372 U.S. 487 (1963). The State cannot adopt procedures which leave an indigent defendant "entirely cut off from any appeal at all," by virtue of his indigency, Lane v. Brown, 372 U.S., at 481, or extend to such indigent defendants merely a "meaningless ritual" while others in better economic circumstances have a "meaningful appeal." Douglas v. California, supra, at 358. The question is not one of absolutes, but one of degrees. In this case we do not believe that the Equal Protection Clause, when interpreted in the context of these cases, requires North Carolina to provide free counsel for indigent defendants seeking to take discretionary appeals to the North Carolina Supreme Court, or to file petitions for certiorari in this Court.

A

The North Carolina appellate system, as are the appellate systems of almost half the States, is multitiered, providing for both an intermediate Court of Appeals and a Supreme Court. . . . In criminal cases, an appeal as of right lies directly to the Supreme Court in all cases which involve a sentence of death or life imprisonment, while an appeal of right in all other criminal cases lies to the Court of Appeals. . . .

The statute governing discretionary appeals to the Supreme Court is N.C. Gen. Stat. §7A-31 (1969). This statute provides, in relevant part, that "[i]n any cause in which appeal has been taken to the Court of Appeals . . . the Supreme Court may in its discretion, on motion of any party to the cause or on its own motion, certify the cause for review by the Supreme Court, either before or after it has been determined by the Court of Appeals." The statute further provides that "[i]f the cause is certified for transfer to the Supreme Court after its determination by the Court of Appeals, the Supreme Court reviews the decision of the Court of Appeals." . . .

Appointment of counsel for indigents in North Carolina is governed by N.C. Gen. Stat. §§7A-450 et seq. (1969 and Supp. 1973). These provisions . . . have generally been construed to limit the right to appointed counsel in criminal cases to direct appeals taken as of right. Thus North Carolina has followed the mandate of Douglas v. California, supra, and authorized appointment of counsel for a convicted defendant appealing to the intermediate Court of Appeals, but has not gone beyond *Douglas* to provide for appointment of counsel for a defendant

9. Hudson County Water Co. v. McCarter, 209 U.S. 349, 355 (1908).

who seeks either discretionary review in the Supreme Court of North Carolina or a writ of certiorari here.

B

The facts show that respondent . . . received the benefit of counsel in examining the record of his trial and in preparing an appellate brief on his behalf for the state Court of Appeals. Thus, prior to his seeking discretionary review in the State Supreme Court, his claims had "once been presented by a lawyer and passed upon by an appellate court." Douglas v. California, 372 U.S. at 356. We do not believe that it can be said, therefore, that a defendant in respondent's circumstances is denied meaningful access to the North Carolina Supreme Court simply because the State does not appoint counsel to aid him in seeking review in that court. At that stage he will have, at the very least, a transcript or other record of trial proceedings, a brief on his behalf in the Court of Appeals setting forth his claims of error, and in many cases an opinion by the Court of Appeals disposing of his case. These materials, supplemented by whatever submission respondent may make pro se, would appear to provide the Supreme Court of North Carolina with an adequate basis for its decision to grant or deny review.

We are fortified in this conclusion by our understanding of the function served by discretionary review in the North Carolina Supreme Court. The critical issue in that court, as we perceive it, is not whether there has been "a correct adjudication of guilt" in every individual case, see Griffin v. Illinois, 351 U.S., at 18, but rather whether "the subject matter of the appeal has significant public interest," whether "the cause involves legal principles of major significance to the jurisprudence of the State," or whether the decision below is in probable conflict with a decision of the Supreme Court. The Supreme Court may deny certiorari even though it believes that the decision of the Court of Appeals was incorrect, see Peaseley v. Virginia Iron, Coal & Coke Co., 282 N.C. 585, 194 S.E.2d 133 (1973), since a decision which appears incorrect may nevertheless fail to satisfy any of the criteria discussed above. Once a defendant's claims of error are organized and presented in a lawyerlike fashion to the Court of Appeals, the justices of the Supreme Court of North Carolina who make the decision to grant or deny discretionary review should be able to ascertain whether his case satisfies the standards established by the legislature for such review.

This is not to say, of course, that a skilled lawyer, particularly one trained in the somewhat arcane art of preparing petitions for discretionary review, would not prove helpful to any litigant able to employ him. An indigent defendant seeking review in the Supreme Court of North Carolina is therefore somewhat handicapped in comparison with a wealthy defendant who has counsel assisting him in every conceivable manner at every stage in the proceeding. But both the opportunity to have counsel prepare an initial brief in the Court of Appeals and the nature of discretionary review in the Supreme Court of North Carolina make this relative handicap far less than the handicap borne by the indigent defendant denied counsel on his initial appeal as of right in *Douglas*. And the fact that a particular service might be of benefit to an indigent defendant does not mean that the service is constitutionally required. The duty of the State under our cases is not to duplicate the legal arsenal that may be privately retained by a criminal defendant in a continuing effort to reverse his conviction, but only to assure the indigent defendant an adequate opportunity to present his claims fairly in the context of the State's appellate process. We think respondent was given that opportunity under the existing North Carolina system.

V

Much of the discussion in the preceding section is equally relevant to the question of whether a State must provide counsel for a defendant seeking review of his conviction in this Court. North Carolina will have provided counsel for a convicted defendant's only appeal as of right, and the brief prepared by that counsel together with one and perhaps two North Carolina appellate opinions will be available to this Court in order that it may decide whether or not to grant certiorari. This Court's review, much like that of the Supreme Court of North Carolina, is discretionary and depends on numerous factors other than the perceived correctness of the judgment we are asked to review.

There is also a significant difference between the source of the right to seek discretionary review in the Supreme Court of North Carolina and the source of the right to seek discretionary review in this Court. The former is conferred by the statutes of the State of North Carolina, but the latter is granted by statute enacted by Congress. Thus the argument relied upon in the *Griffin* and *Douglas* cases, that the State having once created a right of appeal must give all persons an equal opportunity to enjoy the right, is by its terms inapplicable. The right to seek certiorari in this Court is not granted by any State, and exists by virtue of federal statute with or without the consent of the State whose judgment is sought to be reviewed.

The suggestion that a State is responsible for providing counsel to one petitioning this Court simply because it initiated the prosecution which led to the judgment sought to be reviewed is unsupported by either reason or authority. It would be quite as logical under the rationale of *Douglas* and *Griffin,* and indeed perhaps more so, to require that the Federal Government or this Court furnish and compensate counsel for petitioners who seek certiorari here to review state judgments of conviction. Yet this Court has followed a consistent policy of denying applications for appointment of counsel by persons seeking to file jurisdictional statements or petitions for certiorari in this Court. See, e.g., Drumm v. California, 373 U.S. 947 (1963). . . . In the light of these authorities, it would be odd, indeed, to read the Fourteenth Amendment to impose such a requirement on the States, and we decline to do so.

VI

We do not mean by this opinion to in any way discourage those States which have, as a matter of legislative choice, made counsel available to convicted defendants at all stages of judicial review. Some States which might well choose to do so as a matter of legislative policy may conceivably find that other claims for public funds within or without the criminal justice system preclude the implementation of such a policy at the present time. North Carolina, for example, while it does not provide counsel to indigent defendants seeking discretionary review on appeal, does provide counsel for indigent prisoners in several situations where such appointments are not required by any constitutional decision of this Court. Our reading of the

Fourteenth Amendment leaves these choices to the State, and respondent was denied no right secured by the Federal Constitution when North Carolina refused to provide counsel to aid him in obtaining discretionary appellate review.

The judgment of the Court of Appeals' holding to the contrary is reversed.

MR. JUSTICE DOUGLAS, with whom MR. JUSTICE BRENNAN and MR. JUSTICE MARSHALL concur, dissenting.

I would affirm the judgment below because I am in agreement with the opinion of Chief Judge Haynsworth for a unanimous panel in the Court of Appeals. 483 F.2d 650. . . .

Chief Judge Haynsworth could find "no logical basis for differentiation between appeals of right and permissive review procedures in the context of the Constitution and the right to counsel." 483 F.2d, at 653. More familiar with the functioning of the North Carolina criminal justice system than are we, he concluded that "in the context of constitutional questions arising in criminal prosecutions, permissive review in the state's highest court may be predictably the most meaningful review the conviction will receive." Ibid. The North Carolina Court of Appeals, for example, will be constrained in diverging from an earlier opinion of the State Supreme Court, even if subsequent developments have rendered the earlier Supreme Court decision suspect. "[T]he state's highest court remains the ultimate arbiter of the rights of its citizens." Ibid.

Chief Judge Haynsworth also correctly observed that the indigent defendant proceeding without counsel is at a substantial disadvantage relative to wealthy defendants represented by counsel when he is forced to fend for himself in seeking discretionary review from the State Supreme Court or from this Court. It may well not be enough to allege error in the courts below in layman's terms; a more sophisticated approach may be demanded. . . . Furthermore, the lawyer who handled the first appeal in a case would be familiar with the facts and legal issues involved in the case. It would be a relatively easy matter for the attorney to apply his expertise in filing a petition for discretionary review to a higher court, or to advise his client that such a petition would have no chance of succeeding.

Douglas v. California was grounded on concepts of fairness and equality. The right to seek discretionary review is a substantial one, and one where a lawyer can be of significant assistance to an indigent defendant. It was correctly perceived below that the "same concepts of fairness and equality, which require counsel in a first appeal of right, require counsel in other and subsequent discretionary appeals." Id., at 655.

NOTES AND QUESTIONS

1. How convincing is the Court's argument in *Ross* that a lawyer will generally not materially advance a defendant's interests during a discretionary appeal process, especially given the nature of discretionary reviews? Does that view adequately reflect the realities of criminal litigation? Reconsider Justice Douglas's dissent, supra. Even if discretionary reviewing courts sit to hear cases of "significant public interest," cases "in probable conflict" with applicable precedent, or cases involving "legal principles of major significance to the jurisprudence" of the jurisdictions, why should a person of means have a better chance of

having his case heard than an indigent? What, in short, should be the limits of the state's responsibility to offset the constraints of poverty? Consider the following:

One of the prime objectives of the civilized administration of justice is to render the poverty of the litigant an irrelevancy. While this is true of the entire range of judicial administration, the interests involved make the attainment of this objective peculiarly urgent in the administration of criminal justice. The interests sought to be protected by the enforcement of criminal statutes involve no less than the order and internal security of the community. At the same time, the administration of criminal justice raises fundamental problems as to the relations of the individual to the state; for it is in the criminal law that the most stringent sanctions at the disposal of government are sought to be imposed on the individual. Here government proposes to deprive the individual of his property, his liberty, and even, on occasion his life. . . .

It should be understood that governmental obligation to deal effectively with problems of poverty in the administration of criminal justice does not rest or depend upon some hypothetical obligation of government to indulge in acts of public charity. It does not presuppose a general commitment on the part of the federal government to relieve impoverished persons of the consequences of limited means, whenever or however manifested. It does not even presuppose that government is always required to take into account the means of the citizen when dealing directly with its citizens. Few would maintain that in disposing of surplus property, for example, government is required to set prices at such levels that all citizens are rendered equally able to buy.

The obligation of government in the criminal cases rests on wholly different considerations and reflects principles of much more limited application. The essential point is that the problems of poverty with which this Report is concerned arise in a process *initiated* by government for the achievement of basic governmental purposes. It is, moreover, a process that has as one of its consequences the imposition of severe disabilities on the persons proceeded against. Duties arise from action. When a course of conduct, however legitimate, entails the possibility of serious injury to persons, a duty on the actor to avoid the reasonably avoidable injuries is ordinarily recognized. When government chooses to exert its powers in the criminal area, its obligation is surely no less than that of taking reasonable measures to eliminate those factors that are irrelevant to just administration of the law but which, nevertheless, may occasionally affect determinations of the accused's liability or penalty. While government may not be required to relieve the accused of his poverty, it may properly be required to minimize the influence of poverty on its administration of justice.

The Committee, therefore, conceives the obligation of government less as an undertaking to eliminate "discrimination" against a class of accused persons and more as a broad commitment by government to rid its processes of all influences that tend to defeat the ends a system of justice is intended to serve. Such a concept of "equal justice" does not confuse equality of treatment with identity of treatment. We assume that government must be conceded flexibility in devising its measures and that reasonable classifications are permitted. The crucial question is, has government done all that can reasonably be required of it to eliminate those factors that inhibit the proper and effective assertion of grounds relevant to the criminal liability of the accused or to the imposition of sanctions and disabilities on the accused at all stages of the criminal process?

. . . It is not only the interests of accused persons that require attention be given to the problems of poverty in criminal-law administration. Other and broader social interests are involved. We believe that the problems considered in this Report concern no less than the proper functioning of the rule of law in the criminal area and that, therefore, the interests and welfare of all citizens are in issue. . . .

The essence of the adversary system is challenge. The survival of our system of criminal justice and the values which it advances depends upon a constant, searching, and creative questioning of official decisions and assertions of authority at all stages of the process. The proper performance of the defense function is thus as vital to the health of the system as the performance of the prosecuting and adjudicatory functions. It follows that insofar as the financial status of the accused impedes vigorous and proper challenges, it constitutes a threat to the viability of the adversary system. We believe that the system is imperiled by the large numbers of accused persons unable to employ counsel or to meet even modest bail requirements and by the large, but indeterminate, numbers of persons, able to pay some part of the costs of defense, but unable to finance a full and proper defense. Persons suffering such disabilities are incapable of providing the challenges that are indispensable to satisfactory operation of the system. The loss to the interests of accused individuals, occasioned by these failures, are great and apparent. It is also clear that a situation in which persons are required to contest a serious accusation but are denied access to the tools of contest is offensive to fairness and equity. Beyond these considerations, however, is the fact that the conditions produced by the financial incapacity of the accused are detrimental to the proper functioning of the system of justice and that the loss in vitality of the adversary system, thereby occasioned, significantly endangers the basic interests of a free community.

Report of the Attorney General's Committee on Poverty and Administration of Criminal Justice 8-11 (1963).

2. Assuming that the Court is correct that it is helpful to distinguish "fairness" from "equality," what does "fairness" seem to mean to the Court in the context of *Ross*? What are the word's parameters and, more important, how were they reached? Can the Court be serious, for example, when it says "unfairness results only if indigents are singled out by the State and denied meaningful access to the appellate system because of their poverty"? Why should access be the sole criterion of fairness? What role should other values play, such as reliability in factfinding or concern for basic notions of human dignity? Indeed, if access is the primary criterion, does *Ross* substantially undercut *Douglas*? If not, what does the word *access* mean, and why is not that meaning as applicable to the petitioner in *Ross* as it was to those in *Douglas*?

3. Maybe the problem is not what the meaning of "access" or "fairness" but instead with the meaning of "equality." Do "fairness" and "access" differ from "equality" in a meaningful or useful way? Consider the following exchange.

PETER WESTEN, THE EMPTY IDEA OF EQUALITY, 95 HARV. L. REV. 537, 539-540, 543-545, 545-550 (1982): Equality is commonly perceived to differ from rights and liberties. . . .

I believe that this contrasting of rights and equality is fundamentally misconceived. It is based on a misunderstanding, both in law and in morals, about the role of equality in ethical discourse. To avoid possible misunderstanding, let me emphasize what I mean by equality and rights. By "equality" I mean the proposition in law and morals that "people who are alike should be treated alike" and its correlative, that "people who are unalike should be treated unalike." Equality thus includes all statements to the effect that the reason one person should be treated in a certain way is that he is "like" or "equal to" or "similar to" or "identical to" or "the same as" another who receives such treatment. "Rights," by contrast, means all claims that can justly be made by or on behalf of an individual or group of individuals to some condition or power — except claims that "people who are alike be treated alike." . . .

The proposition that "likes should be treated alike" is said to be a universal moral truth — a truth that can "be intuitively known with perfect clearness and certainty." Why? What is the connection between the fact that people are alike and the normative conclusion that they ought to be treated alike? How can one move from an "is" to an "ought"?

The answer can be found in the component parts of the equality formula. The formula "people who are alike should be treated alike" involves two components: (1) a determination that two people are alike; and (2) a moral judgment that they ought to be treated alike. The determinative component is the first. Once one determines that two people are alike for purposes of the equality principle, one knows how they ought to be treated. To understand why this is so — that is, to understand how (1) works — one must understand what kind of determination (1) is. One must know precisely what it means to say for purposes of equality that two persons are alike.

First, "people who are alike" might mean people who are alike in every respect. The trouble is that no two people are alike in every respect. The only things that are completely alike in every respect are immaterial symbols and forms, such as ideal numbers and geometric figures, which are not themselves the subject of morals.

Second, "people who are alike" may mean people, who, though not alike in every respect, are alike in some respects. Unfortunately, while the previous definition excludes every person in the world, the present definition includes every person and thing because all people and things are alike in some respect; and one is left with the morally absurd proposition that "all people and things should be treated alike."

Third, "people who are alike" may refer to people who are *morally* alike in a certain respect. The latter interpretation successfully avoids the philosophical hurdle of deriving an "ought" from an "is." It starts with a normative determination that two people are alike in a morally significant respect and moves to a normative conclusion that the two should be treated alike. Instead of deriving an "ought" from an "is," it derives an "ought" from an "ought." However, categories of morally alike objects do not exist in nature; moral alikeness is established only when people define categories. To say that people are morally alike is therefore to articulate a moral standard of treatment — a standard or rule specifying certain treatment for certain people — by reference to which they are, and thus are to be treated, alike. . . . Just as no categories of "like" people exist in nature, neither do categories of "like" treatment exist; treatments can be alike only in reference to some moral rule. Thus, to say that people who are morally alike in a certain respect "should be treated alike" means that they should be treated in accord with the moral rule by which they are determined to be alike. Hence "likes should be treated alike" means that people for whom a certain treatment is prescribed by a standard should all be given the treatment prescribed by the standard. Or, more simply, people who by a rule should be treated alike should by the rule be treated alike.

So there it is: Equality is entirely "[c]ircular." It tells us to treat like people alike; but when we ask who "like people" are, we are told they are "people who should be treated alike." Equality is an empty vessel with no substantive moral content of its own. Without moral standards, equality remains meaningless, a formula that can have nothing to say about how we should act. With such standards, equality becomes superfluous, a formula that can do nothing but repeat what we already know. As Bernard Williams observed, "when the statement of equality ceases to claim more than is warranted, it rather rapidly reaches the point where it claims less than is interesting." . . . Relationships of equality (and inequality) are derivative, secondary relationships; they are logically posterior, not anterior, to rights. To say that two persons are the same in a certain respect is to presuppose a rule—a prescribed standard for treating them—that both fully satisfy. Before such a rule is established, no standard of comparison exists. After such a rule is established, equality between them is a "logical consequence" of the established rule. They are then "equal" in respect of the rule because that is what equal means: "Equally" means " 'according to one and the same rule.' " They are also then entitled to equal treatment under the rule because that is what possessing a rule means: "To conform to a rule is (tautologically) to apply it to the cases to which it applies." To say that two people are "equal" and entitled to be treated "equally" is to say that they both fully satisfy the criteria of a governing rule of treatment. It says nothing at all about the content or wisdom of the governing rule. . . .

It might be thought that, while relationships of equality logically follow substantive definitions of right, equality may also precede definitions of right. Thus, it might be thought that a substantive right of persons to be treated with human respect is itself a product of an antecedent judgment that all persons are equal. That is not so. To see why, consider how one would go about deciding whether monstrously deformed neonates or human embryos or stroke victims in irreversible comas should be treated as "persons" for purposes of the right to respect. In trying to make the decision, one gets nowhere by intoning that all persons are equal, because the very question is whether the three candidates are indeed "persons" within the meaning of the rule. Nor does it do any good to say that likes should be treated alike, because the very question is whether the three candidates are indeed alike for purposes of human respect. Rather, one must first identify the trait that entitles anyone to be treated with respect and then ascertain empirically whether the trait appears in one or more of the three candidates.[40] If the candidates possess the relevant trait, they become "persons" within the meaning of the rule and hence entitled to respect. If they lack the relevant trait, they are not "persons," not equal to persons, and not to be treated like persons for purposes of the rule.

---

40. The issue of the empirical basis for moral traits has caused some confusion. Some commentators, believing that relationships of equality must be grounded in some verifiable traits, tend to conclude that equality is entirely empirical. . . . others, believing that an "ought" cannot be inferred from an "is," tend to conclude that moral notions of equality have no empirical basis.

. . . In fact, both contending camps are correct. Statements of moral and legal equality do have an empirical base, because otherwise one would have no way of distinguishing those creatures who are equal from those who are not. . . . Yet at the same time, statements of moral or legal equality also presuppose a normative element. . . . In short, statements of equality presuppose the presence of empirical traits that we decide ought to carry certain moral consequences.

STEVEN BURTON, COMMENT ON "EMPTY IDEAS": LOGICAL POSITIVIST ANALYSES OF EQUALITY AND RULES, 91 YALE L.J. 1136-1141, 1144-1147 (1982): In a recent article in the Harvard Law Review, Professor Peter Westen directs his considerable capacity for logical analysis at the idea of equality. Professor Westen asserts and defends "two propositions: (1) that statements of equality logically entail (and necessarily collapse into) simpler statements of rights; and (2) that the additional step of transforming simple statements of rights into statements of equality not only involves unnecessary work but also engenders profound conceptual confusion." Therefore, he says, equality is an "empty idea" that "should be banished from moral and legal discourse as an explanatory norm."

Many, no doubt, will wish to defend equality as a concept with independent content, at least in some situations. This Comment takes a different tack. "Statements of rights" (rules) are the heroes of Professor Westen's story, though they are spared the scrutiny lavished on equality. He seems to regard rules as suitable norms for explanatory moral and legal discourse — norms that in themselves are independent of equality, imbued with content, and comparatively simple to apply without confusion.[4] Using methods of logical analysis similar to those Westen used to criticize equality, this Comment will demonstrate that rules collapse into equality and also are empty, in the sense that Westen regards equality as empty. By the logical positivist method of analysis, both equality and rules must be banished from explanatory legal and moral discourse, a move that would render such discourse impossible. The alternative is to reject that method of analysis because it proves too much, and to retain both equality and rules as instruments of thought and argument. . . .

Now the assumption seems to be that "the terms of the rule *dictate* that it be applied," and that they do so by an intellectual process that does not depend of necessity on considerations of equality, or on other norms that are vulnerable to the criticisms made of equality.[13] Though Professor Westen did not undertake to analyze the logic of rules in his paper, such an analysis is necessary to the soundness of his thesis, which appeals to the meaningfulness and analytical simplicity of rules as contrasted with equality. We would have two choices if the idea of substantive rights, determined by the language of rules, were as empty as, and collapsed into, the idea of equality. We could conclude that rules also should be "banished from moral and legal discourse as an explanatory norm," or that neither

4. . . . Professor Westen might regard substantive rights as empty ideas analytically, but useful ones nonetheless. Cf. Westen at 579 n. 147. ("Some formal concepts [such as rights] are quite handy, even indispensible [*sic*].") He argues that equality as a form of analysis is not useful, id. at 577-592, largely because "people do not realize that [equality] is derivative [from substantive rights], and not realizing it, they allow equality to distort the substance of their decisionmaking." Id. at 592. It would seem to be at least equally so that "people" often do not realize that statements of substantive rights themselves are empty of content in the same sense, and allow the so-called plain meanings of such statements to distort their decision making. Westen offers no empirical grounds for concluding that equality causes more confusion than rules. Cf. infra Note 14 (such grounds might support Westen's position if rights did not collapse into equality); Note 50 (like equality, rules hide their incompleteness).

13. To summarize, the principal criticisms were (1) that statements of equality have no substantive content *of their own*, but depend on norms outside equality *itself*, id. at 553, 566, 571-572, 574, 577-778, 580-881; (2) that equality is a wholly normative concept, lacking the identification of empirical traits, the presence of which would entitle a person to the treatment claimed, id. at 544-547, 549; and (3) that application of the equality norm requires logically illicit moves between "is" and "ought," id. at 544-545. To justify banishing equality while retaining rules requires at least that rules be different from and better than equality by the same criteria.

concept should be banished because the method of analysis yielding such an absurd result is inappropriate. . . .

It is simply wrong, however, to suggest that substantive rights can be determined in any case without reference to a person's normative relationship to other rightsholders, at least if the statement is meant to convey what is involved in legal reasoning. Let us consider the right of free speech. The general terms of the First Amendment appear on their face to be simple to apply: "Congress shall make no law . . . abridging the freedom of speech. . . . " We will apply this general proscription to two particular cases, which will serve as illustrations throughout the remainder of this Part.

Imagine that a state has made it a crime to hang the Governor in effigy, and that a state has made it a crime to hang any person, including the Governor. It will be seen that the Supreme Court could not reach conclusions as to the validity of these laws without considering the normative relationship of (1) hanging the Governor or (2) hanging the Governor in effigy to other activities that enjoy (or do not enjoy) First Amendment protection. The Court must determine whether hanging the Governor in effigy or in the flesh is in some important aspect "like" such other activities—for example, (3) making a public speech criticizing the Governor or (4) hanging one's spouse. Because "the terms of the rule" do not "dictate" which aspect of each activity is *important*, arguments based on the rule collapse into arguments by analogy, which themselves are claims to equal treatment under the law. . . .

. . . In the analysis of reasoning, analogies necessarily appeal to the principle that "like cases should be treated alike"—the equality principle—and are vulnerable to the criticisms Westen makes of equality, to the same extent. . . .

To separate rules from equality completely, one who would adopt Professor Westen's position seems forced to regard legal reasoning as fundamentally deductive, rather than purposive, inductive, or analogical in character. Only a logical positivist model of legal reasoning can purport to explain rules and rights independently of equality or other similarly vulnerable norms. Thus, in the hypothetical free speech cases, a statement of the state's general duty of behavior (the rule) would stand as the major premise of a syllogism. A statement of the state's treatment of the person (the facts) would stand as the minor premise. Whether the state acted in accord with its duty would depend on whether the rule logically entailed the facts.

That this is Professor Westen's view of all defensible legal reasoning seems a fair interpretation of his expressions in this work, despite the facial implausibility of such a mechanical model. To repeat, he says that "[t]o decide whether a person's speech rights are violated, one *juxtaposes* the state's general duty of behavior against the state's particular treatment of the person to determine whether the state treats the person in *accord* with its prescribed duty." He emphasizes that equality between two persons "is a 'logical consequence' of the established rule." Thus, "[r]elationships of equality are derivative, secondary relationships; they are logically posterior, not anterior, to rights." . . .

I suggest that the two Governor-hanging cases are clear because we engage in analogical reasoning. We posit a clear case of protected speech (a lecture criticizing the Governor's policies) and a clear case of murder (killing one's spouse). In the light of the values underlying the First Amendment, we regard hanging the Governor in effigy as more like the first case, and hanging the Governor as more like the second. And we regard all four cases as easy ones. Of course, no two of the four cases are alike in all respects, and all four cases are alike in some respects. We make a normative judgment as to what respects are the important ones.

That judgment, however, is not a logical consequence of the terms of the First Amendment, which cannot be applied in a particular case without recourse to such analogies. For example, all four cases are "expression" in some respect, while none of the four cases is "expression" in all respects; and all are "anti-social behaviors" in some but not all respects. To apply the rule, we must make judgments about which respects are important in each case. The judgment of importance in applying a rule, like the judgment of similarity in using an analogy, depends on unspecified values outside the rule itself, and involves us in analytical problems of moving from "ought" to "is" when we apply the rule. Professor Westen therefore errs in stating that the conclusions are the "logical consequences" of the rule — not normative judgments but logically deduced from a "given." Where are the "given" rules that distinguish the Governor-hanging cases?

To test the point further, let us posit some rules (really meta-rules) that stand on a different logical plane and tell us how to apply the enacted rules: (1) The First Amendment shall not invalidate state statutes if the statutes are necessary to protect a compelling state interest; and (2) a constitutional provision shall be construed according to the intention of the Framers or according to its purpose. It should be observed that both of the meta-rules are judge-made and consequently partake of the problems of common-law rules, making the process of applying enacted rules wholly dependent on analogical reasoning in the same manner. But let us pass over that problem and inquire whether these rules can be applied without engaging in reasoning by analogy — without using the equality principle to determine substantive rights.

The logic of the so-called "compelling state interest" test is fairly transparent. To say that the First Amendment invalidates a state statute unless the statute is necessary to protect a compelling state interest is logically reducible to saying something like: Freedom of expression is more important than a state statute unless the state statute is more important than freedom of expression. Again, what do we mean by "important"? Surely nothing follows as a "logical consequence" in any real-world case from "important" as the key term in the major premise of a syllogism. Neither "compelling state interest" nor "importance" are things that exist in nature (observables), nor can they be reduced analytically to necessary and sufficient conditions that are observable without deriving an "is" from an "ought." They are normative concepts. As such, they beg the question whether application of a state murder statute to one who hung the Governor, or a state statute against hanging the Governor in effigy, should be invalidated by the First Amendment: It should if it should. One might offer another rule to tell us, as a "logical consequence," what a compelling state interest is — a meta-meta-rule — but it should be apparent that this tack leads to an infinite regress of no small significance.

The logic of construing a constitutional provision according to the intention of the Framers or according to its purpose could lead us into a similar regress. Neither "intention" nor "purpose" are observables, if we state them in the abstract. We can say that the Framers intended the First Amendment to protect "expression" or "political expression," though they said "speech" or that this was the purpose of the text. The problems of knowing such things, with the assurance necessary to exclude de novo normative judgments, are well-known. And even if we knew that the Framers had such an intention or purpose, we still do not know that hanging the Governor in effigy and in the flesh are not both "expression," or neither "expression," or one "expression" and the other not, or the other "expression" and the one not, so far as the logical consequences of the meta-rule take us. Again, we need a meta-meta-rule and are off into the darkness of a regress.

Alternatively, the purpose or intention (of "freedom of speech" or of "compelling state interest") can be stated in the particular. To do so, however, is to state a case, be it hypothetical or historical. To say merely that the evil before the minds of the Framers was, for example, suppression of the political opposition is again abstract, a negative version of the statement analyzed in the preceding paragraph. We must have a *case,* such as what happened to Zenger, or what Zenger did. As "general propositions do not decide concrete cases," however, "[c]oncrete decisions do not make law." What Zenger did can be described in narrow terms and limited to the press, or in broad terms and expanded to cover all thought and action. Another meta-meta-rule seems necessary to tell us what the rule of the *Zenger* case is, unless we break the regress by shifting from deduction to analogy. Then, we might say, hanging the Governor in effigy is like what Zenger did but hanging the Governor is not, and all might agree.

Of course, shifting from deduction to analogy (equality) does not solve our problems as analysts of legal reasoning. The problem identified by Professor Westen and others—identifying normative grounds for purposes of determining whether cases are alike or unalike—is no small problem. It is not solved, however, by shifting from equality to rules, which also depend on unspecified values outside the rules themselves. Thus, if rules are given the same kind of intensive logical analysis that Westen gives to equality, they too stand empty and collapse into equality. This logical analysis of rules and equality drives us back and forth between the two in a regress, as when we stand between the barber's mirrors. . . .

The debate over the nature of equality has a long philosophical history, but it also has an immediate practical significance. The notion that like cases should be treated alike has a strong rational and emotional pull; but without substantive determinations of what counts in determining "like cases," the commitment to treating like cases alike appears empty. Consider a concrete example. What does it mean to provide equal medical insurance to males and females? Does it violate equality to cover pregnancy, since that provides a benefit that only females can take advantage of? Or does it violate equality by excluding a major health issue from coverage, and where no analogous issue is excluded for males? Or consider pension benefits on the assumption that the life expectancy of males is shorter than females. Should males and females be paid the same monthly benefits or instead an amount that actuarially will result in equal payouts over the lives of both? These examples point out what is at stake in the Weston/Burton debate: Before one can analyze "equality," one needs to know what counts for the analysis. For an extended development of this idea, see Amartya Sen, Inequality Reexamined (1992).

Return to the criminal procedure battleground on which this debate is fought: the scope of the right to counsel and other assistance. One consequence of granting the right to state-paid counsel and other forms of assistance, whether at trial or on appeal or anywhere else, is to reduce the likelihood of errors that favor the state. Innocent Gideons are less likely to be convicted in a regime that gives them help. The flip side of this proposition is equally clear: Denying state assistance raises the risk of errors that favor the state. The decision to extend or contract the *Gideon* right is a decision about whether to tolerate a higher risk of error in the state's favor. And of course it is also a decision about how much lowering the risk of wrongful conviction is worth.

Your views about that decision—and thus your views about the equality versus fairness debate explored above—might depend on just what issues are on the table. If the question is whether Gideon in fact broke into the poolroom as the state charged, there would be widespread agreement that any substantial risk of error in the state's favor is unacceptable. But suppose the question is whether a police officer read the *Miranda* warnings correctly before questioning the defendant, or whether an officer had probable cause to search the trunk of the defendant's car, or whether the prosecutor's peremptory challenges were prompted by racial stereotypes. Should the system be willing to tolerate a higher risk of error for questions like these than for issues that bear more directly on guilt and innocence? In practice, it does: The burden of persuasion on issues of the sort just mentioned is usually a preponderance of the evidence, while guilt must be proved beyond a reasonable doubt. Errors on some issues are treated as less important than errors on others.

Perhaps this divide, between issues on which errors in the state's favor are seen as intolerable and issues for which that is not so, suggests why the Court's right-to-counsel jurisprudence might be unsatisfying. The right to counsel, like burdens of persuasion, is in part about allocating the risk of error. With burden-of-proof law, we allocate that risk issue by issue; the burden can be assigned differently on different issues in the same proceeding. The right to counsel cannot work that way as a practical matter. Defendants either receive state-paid counsel on discretionary state appeals or they do not: No one suggests giving defendants counsel with respect to sufficiency-of-the-evidence claims but not with respect to challenges to evidentiary rulings. The result may be that the right to counsel must always go too far or not far enough, since wherever the right is granted (or denied), it affects a range of issues, some of which are more important to resolve correctly than others.

What do you think?

NOTES AND QUESTIONS ON FAIRNESS, EQUALITY, AND THE RIGHT TO COUNSEL

Every act the government takes, and every institution that it structures, can raise the intertwined questions of fairness and equality. The following notes highlight the myriad ways this question comes up in the right to counsel context.

1. Recall that Douglas v. California, supra page 139, held that a criminal defendant has the right to counsel—under the Fourteenth Amendment, not the Sixth

Amendment—on his first appeal as of right. Evitts v. Lucey, 469 U.S. 387 (1985), addressed the related question "whether the Due Process Clause of the Fourteenth Amendment guarantees the criminal defendant the effective assistance of counsel on such an appeal." In other words, does the right to counsel carry with it the corresponding right to have that counsel perform to an acceptable level? At trial, where the *Gideon* right to counsel applies, the answer is clearly yes, as we will explore later in this chapter. What about on appeal?

In *Evitts,* the Court, in an opinion by Justice Brennan, held that the answer to this question is also yes:

> Almost a century ago, the Court held that the Constitution does not require States to grant appeals as of right to criminal defendants seeking to review alleged trial court errors. McKane v. Durston, 153 U.S. 684 (1894). Nonetheless, if a State has created appellate courts as "an integral part of the . . . system for finally adjudicating the guilt or innocence of a defendant," Griffin v. Illinois, 351 U.S., at 18, the procedures used in deciding appeals must comport with the demands of the Due Process and Equal Protection Clauses of the Constitution. . . .
>
> The two lines of cases . . . recognizing the right to counsel on a first appeal as of right and . . . recognizing that the right to counsel at trial includes a right to effective assistance of counsel . . . are dispositive of respondent's claim. In bringing an appeal as of right from his conviction, a criminal defendant is attempting to demonstrate that the conviction, and the consequent drastic loss of liberty, is unlawful. To prosecute the appeal, a criminal appellant must face an adversary proceeding that—like a trial—is governed by intricate rules that to a layperson would be hopelessly forbidding. An unrepresented appellant—like an unrepresented defendant at trial—is unable to protect the vital interests at stake. . . .
>
> A first appeal as of right therefore is not adjudicated in accord with due process of law if the appellant does not have the effective assistance of an attorney.[7] . . .
>
> The right to an appeal would be unique among state actions if it could be withdrawn without consideration of applicable due process norms. For instance, although a State may choose whether it will institute any given welfare program, it must operate whatever programs it does establish subject to the protections of the Due Process Clause. See Goldberg v. Kelly, 397 U.S. 254, 262 (1970). . . . In short, when a State opts to act in a field where its action has significant discretionary elements, it must nonetheless act in accord with the dictates of the Constitution—and, in particular, in accord with the Due Process Clause. . . .
>
> According to the petitioners, the constitutional requirements recognized in *Griffin, Douglas,* and the cases that followed had their source in the Equal Protection Clause, and not the Due Process Clause, of the Fourteenth Amendment. In support of this contention, petitioners point out that all of the cases in the *Griffin* line have involved claims by indigent defendants that they have the same right to a decision on the merits of their appeal as do wealthier defendants who are able to afford lawyers, transcripts, or the other prerequisites of a fair adjudication on the merits. As such, petitioners claim, the cases all should be understood as equal protection cases challenging the constitutional validity of the distinction made between rich and poor criminal defendants. Petitioners conclude that if the Due Process Clause permits criminal appeals as of right to be forfeited because the appellant has no transcript or no attorney, it surely permits such appeals to be forfeited when the appellant has an attorney who is unable to assist in prosecuting the appeal.

7. As Ross v. Moffitt, 417 U.S. 600 (1974), held, the considerations governing a discretionary appeal are somewhat different. Of course, the right to effective assistance of counsel is dependent on the right to counsel itself. . . .

Petitioners' argument rests on a misunderstanding of the diverse sources of our holdings in this area. In Ross v. Moffitt, we held that "[t]he precise rationale for the *Griffin* and *Douglas* lines of cases has never been explicitly stated, some support being derived from the Equal Protection Clause of the Fourteenth Amendment, and some from the Due Process Clause of that Amendment." This rather clear statement in *Ross* that the Due Process Clause played a significant role in prior decisions is well supported by the cases themselves. . . .

Justice Rehnquist, in dissent, responded:

There is no constitutional requirement that a State provide an appeal at all. . . . McKane v. Durston, 153 U.S. 684, 687 (1894). If a State decides to confer a right of appeal, it is free to do so "upon such terms as in its wisdom may be deemed proper." Id., at 687-688. . . . Proper analysis of our precedents would indicate that apart from the Equal Protection Clause, which respondent has not invoked in this case, there cannot be a constitutional right to *counsel* on appeal, and that, therefore, even under the logic of the Court there cannot be derived a constitutional right to *effective assistance of counsel* on appeal.

According to Justice Rehnquist, in other words, the defendant must take the "bitter with the sweet" — having no constitutional right to an appeal at all, due process cannot be violated when the state chooses to give him an appeal, but then precludes him from complaining about his appellate lawyer's alleged ineffectiveness. Nor can this be an equal protection violation, because the state's rule applies to all appellate lawyers — whether retained or appointed — the same way.

2. Can *Ross* and *Evitts* be reconciled? Can *Ross* be reconciled with Mayer v. City of Chicago, 404 U.S. 189 (1971)? In *Mayer,* the Court held that a state must provide an indigent defendant, free of charge, with a record of sufficient completeness to permit proper consideration of his claims on appeal, even though such a record is *not,* unlike in *Griffin,* a condition precedent for an appeal.

One interesting aspect of *Mayer* was the state's argument that *Griffin* should not be extended to cases in which the relevant sentence is a fine rather than imprisonment. The Court, per Justice Brennan, responded:

The city of Chicago urges another distinction to set this case apart from *Griffin* and its progeny. The city notes that the defendants in all the transcript cases previously decided by this Court were sentenced to some term of confinement. Where the accused, as here, is not subject to imprisonment, but only a fine, the city suggests that his interest in a transcript is outweighed by the State's fiscal and other interests in not burdening the appellate process. This argument misconceives the principle of *Griffin.* . . . Griffin does not represent a balance between the needs of the accused and the interests of society; its principle is a flat prohibition against pricing indigent defendants out of as effective an appeal as would be available to others able to pay their own way. The invidiousness of the discrimination that exists when criminal procedures are made available only to those who can pay is not erased by any differences in the sentences that may be imposed. The State's fiscal interest is, therefore, irrelevant.

We add that even approaching the problem in the terms the city suggests hardly yields the answer the city tenders. The practical effects of conviction of even petty offenses of the kind involved here are not to be minimized. A fine may bear as heavily on an indigent accused as forced confinement. The collateral consequences of conviction may be even more serious, as when (as was apparently a possibility in this case) the impecunious medical student finds himself barred from the practice of medicine because of a conviction he is unable to appeal for lack of funds. Moreover, the State's long-term interest would not appear to lie in making access to appellate processes from even its most inferior courts depend upon the defendant's ability to pay. It has been aptly said: "[F]ew citizens ever have contact with the higher courts. In the main, it is the police and the lower court Bench and Bar that convey the essence of our democracy to the people. Justice, if it can be measured, must be measured by the experience the average citizen has with the police and the lower courts."[7] Arbitrary denial of appellate review of proceedings of the State's lowest trial courts may save the State some dollars and cents, but only at the substantial risk of generating frustration and hostility toward its courts among the most numerous consumers of justice. . . .

Id. at 196-199.

In M.L.B. v. S.L.J., 519 U.S. 102 (1996), a Mississippi Chancery Court terminated a mother's parental rights, and the mother appealed. Her appeal was dismissed because she could not pay the record preparation fees as required by a Mississippi statute. The Court held that the statute violated the equal protection and due process clauses of the Fourteenth Amendment: "We hold that, just as a state may not block an indigent petty offender's access to an appeal afforded others [see *Mayer*], so Mississippi may not deny M.L.B. because of her poverty, appellate review of the sufficiency of the evidence on which the trial court found her unfit to remain a parent." This is the furthest extension of *Mayer* to date. In *M.L.B.*, Justice Thomas in a strong dissent argues that *Mayer* was wrongly decided and should be overruled.

3. Compare *Mayer* to *Scott*, page 129. *Griffin* and its progeny reflect the basic need for legal assistance. Why, then, should a defendant be better off on appeal than at trial? Or does that misconstrue the basic thrust of *Griffin*? Are its referents outside the policies that inform the Sixth Amendment right to counsel? If so, where are they?

Not surprisingly, equality and/or fairness peters out at various points (like in *Ross* itself). In United States v. MacCollom, 426 U.S. 317 (1976), the Court sustained the constitutionality of 28 U.S.C. §753(f), which provides a free transcript to indigent prisoners asserting a claim under 28 U.S.C. §2255 (the statute that provides federal prisoners with the right to challenge their convictions in a separate, collateral proceeding similar to a habeas corpus petition) only if the trial judge certifies that the asserted claim is not frivolous and that the transcript is necessary. Had the defendant directly appealed his conviction, a free transcript would have been provided by direction of law; but the defendant did not appeal the conviction. In disposing of the defendant's claim, Justice Rehnquist, writing for a four-Justice plurality, argued:

Respondent chose to forgo his opportunity for direct appeal with its attendant unconditional free transcript. This choice affects his later equal protection claim as well as his due process claim. Equal protection does not require the Government to furnish to the indigent a delayed duplicate of a right of appeal with attendant free transcript

---

7. Patrick V. Murphy, The Role of the Police in Our Modern Society, 26 The Record of the Association of the Bar of the City of New York 292, 293 (1971).

which it offered in the first instance, even though a criminal defendant of means might well decide to purchase such a transcript in pursuit of relief under §2255. The basic question is one of adequacy of respondent's access to procedures for review of his conviction, Ross v. Moffitt, supra, and it must be decided in the light of avenues which respondent chose not to follow as well as those he now seeks to widen. We think it enough at the collateral-relief stage that Congress has provided that the transcript be paid for by public funds if one demonstrates to a district judge that his §2255 claim is not frivolous, and that the transcript is needed to decide the issue presented.

426 U.S. at 325-326.

Justice Brennan, joined by Justice Marshall, was unconvinced:

> . . . the plurality's opinion today that respondent may be required to show more than indigency before being entitled to his trial transcript for purposes of collateral review is a plain departure from *Griffin* and its progeny.
>
> The denial in this case is particularly egregious, for one of respondent's claims on the merits is that he was denied effective assistance of counsel. Substantiation of such a claim is virtually impossible without the aid of a trial transcript. Yet the plurality denigrates respondent's claim as a "naked allegation." . . . Essentially, therefore, he is denied a transcript for making an unsubstantiated allegation, an allegation that obviously he cannot establish without a transcript.
>
> . . . The Constitution demands that respondent, despite his indigency, be afforded the same opportunity for collateral review of his conviction as the nonindigent. . . .
>
> The plurality's reliance . . . upon Ross v. Moffitt . . . is patently misplaced. Th[e] quotation from *Ross,* read in context, speaks not merely to equality of opportunity in the overall criminal process, but also to equality of opportunity at any stage of the process where the validity of the defendant's restraint or conviction is the primary consideration.

Id. at 332-333.

Consider also the per curiam decision of Wainwright v. Torna, 455 U.S. 586 (1982):

> Respondent is in custody pursuant to several felony convictions. The Florida Supreme Court dismissed an application for a writ of certiorari, on the ground that the application was not filed timely. . . . A petition for rehearing and clarification was later denied. . . .
>
> In Ross v. Moffitt, . . . this Court held that a criminal defendant does not have a constitutional right to counsel to pursue discretionary state appeals or applications for review in this Court. Respondent does not contest the finding of the District Court that he had no absolute right to appeal his convictions to the Florida Supreme Court. Since respondent had no constitutional right to counsel, he could not be deprived of the effective assistance of counsel by his retained counsel's failure to file the application timely.[4] The District Court was correct in dismissing the petition.

---

4. Respondent was not denied due process of law by the fact that counsel deprived him of his right to petition the Florida Supreme Court for review. Such deprivation — even if implicating a due process interest — was caused by his counsel, and not by the State. Certainly, the actions of the Florida Supreme Court in dismissing an application for review that was not filed timely did not deprive respondent of due process of law.

The motion of respondent for leave to proceed in forma pauperis is granted. The petition for writ of certiorari is granted and the judgment of the Court of Appeals is therefore reversed.

It is so ordered.

4. Indigency may also affect the nature of the sanction imposed on conviction. In Williams v. Illinois, 399 U.S. 235 (1970), the Court held a statute unconstitutional that permitted the maximum jail sentence to be increased if the defendant failed to pay the fine that was also imposed, when the reason for the failure to pay was the defendant's indigency. Subsequently, in Tate v. Short, 401 U.S. 395 (1971), the Court struck down a statute that permitted a sentence of a fine to be converted into a jail sentence where the defendant was unable to pay the fine. Consider the following passage from the *Tate* opinion:

> Our opinion in *Williams* stated the premise of this conclusion in saying that "the Equal Protection Clause of the Fourteenth Amendment requires that the statutory ceiling placed on imprisonment for any substantive offense be the same for all defendants irrespective of their economic status." 399 U.S., at 244. Since Texas has legislated a "fines only" policy for traffic offenses, that statutory ceiling cannot, consistently with the Equal Protection clause, limit the punishment to payment of the fine if one is able to pay it, yet convert the fine into a prison term for an indigent defendant without the means to pay his fine. Imprisonment in such a case is not imposed to further any penal objective of the State. It is imposed to augment the state's revenues but obviously does not serve that purpose; the defendant cannot pay because he is indigent and his imprisonment, rather than aiding collection of the revenue, saddles the State with the cost of feeding and housing him for the period of his imprisonment.
>
> There are, however, other alternatives to which the State may constitutionally resort to serve its concededly valid interest in enforcing payment of fines. We repeat our observation in *Williams* in that regard, 399 U.S., at 244-245 (footnotes omitted):
>
> "The State is not powerless to enforce judgments against those financially unable to pay a fine; indeed, a different result would amount to inverse discrimination since it would enable an indigent to avoid both the fine and imprisonment for nonpayment whereas other defendants must always suffer one or the other conviction.
>
> "It is unnecessary for us to canvass the numerous alternatives to which the State by legislative enactment — or judges within the scope of their authority — may resort in order to avoid imprisoning an indigent beyond the statutory maximum for involuntary nonpayment of a fine or court costs. Appellant has suggested several plans, some of which are already utilized in some States, while others resemble those proposed by various studies. The State is free to choose from among the variety of solutions already proposed and, of course, it may devise new ones."[5]
>
> We emphasize that our holding today does not suggest any constitutional infirmity in imprisonment of a defendant with the means to pay a fine who refuses or neglects to do so. Nor is our decision to be understood as precluding imprisonment as an enforcement method when alternative means are unsuccessful despite the defendant's reasonable efforts to satisfy the fines by those means; the determination of the

5. Several States have a procedure for paying fines in installments. E.g., Cal. Penal Code §1205 (1970) (misdemeanors); Del. Code Ann., Tit. 11, §4332(c) (Supp. 1968); Md. Ann. Code, Art. 38, §4(a)(2) (Supp. 1970); Mass. Gen. Laws Ann., c.279, §1A (1959); N.Y. Code Crim. Proc. §470-d(1)(b) (Supp. 1970); Pa. Stat. Ann., Tit. 19, §953 (1964); Wash. Rev. Code §9.92.070. . . .

constitutionality of imprisonment in that circumstance must await the presentation of a concrete case. . . .

401 U.S. at 395-401.

In light of *Tate* and *Williams,* under what circumstances may a state take the financial condition of the defendant into account in sentencing?

In Bearden v. Georgia, 461 U.S. 660 (1983), the Court considered whether a state may sentence a defendant to compulsory, and useful, labor to "work off" a fine:

> The question in this case is whether the Fourteenth Amendment prohibits a State from revoking an indigent defendant's probation for failure to pay a fine and restitution. Its resolution involves a delicate balance between the acceptability, and indeed wisdom, of considering all relevant factors when determining an appropriate sentence for an individual and the impermissibility of imprisoning a defendant solely because of his lack of financial resources. We conclude that the trial court erred in automatically revoking probation because petitioner could not pay his fine, without determining that petitioner had not made sufficient bona fide efforts to pay or that adequate alternative forms of punishment did not exist. We therefore reverse the judgment of the Georgia Court of Appeals upholding the revocation of probation, and remand for a new sentencing determination. . . .
>
> We hold . . . that in revocation proceedings for failure to pay a fine or restitution, a sentencing court must inquire into the reasons for the failure to pay. If the probationer willfully refused to pay or failed to make sufficient bona fide efforts legally to acquire the resources to pay, the court may revoke probation and sentence the defendant to imprisonment within the authorized range of its sentencing authority. If the probationer could not pay despite sufficient bona fide efforts to acquire the resources to do so, the court must consider alternate measures of punishment other than imprisonment. Only if alternate measures are not adequate to meet the State's interests in punishment and deterrence may the court imprison a probationer who has made sufficient bona fide efforts to pay. To do otherwise would deprive the probationer of his conditional freedom simply because, through no fault of his own, he cannot pay the fine. Such a deprivation would be contrary to the fundamental fairness required by the Fourteenth Amendment. . . .[12]

JUSTICE WHITE concurred:

We deal here with the recurring situation where a person is convicted under a statute that authorizes fines or imprisonment or both, as well as probation. The defendant is

_____

12. As our holding makes clear, we agree with Justice White that poverty does not insulate a criminal defendant from punishment or necessarily prevent revocation of his probation for inability to pay a fine. We reject as impractical, however, the approach suggested by Justice White. He would require a "good-faith effort" by the sentencing court to impose a term of imprisonment "roughly equivalent" to the fine and restitution that the defendant failed to pay. Even putting to one side the question of judicial "good faith," we perceive no meaningful standard by which a sentencing or reviewing court could assess whether a prison sentence has an equivalent sting to the original fine. Under our holding the sentencing court must focus on criteria typically considered daily by sentencing courts throughout the land in probation revocation hearings: whether the defendant has demonstrated sufficient efforts to comply with the terms of probation and whether nonimprisonment alternatives are adequate to satisfy the State's interests in punishment and deterrence. Nor is our requirement that the sentencing court consider alternative forms of punishment a "novel" requirement. In both *Williams* and *Tate,* the Court emphasized the availability of alternate forms of punishment in holding that indigents could not be subjected automatically to imprisonment.

then fined and placed on probation, one of the conditions of which is that he pay the fine and make restitution. In such a situation, the Court takes as a given that the state has decided that imprisonment is inappropriate because it is unnecessary to achieve its penal objectives. But that is true only if the defendant pays the fine and makes restitution and thereby suffers the financial penalty that such payment entails. Had the sentencing judge been quite sure that the defendant could not pay the fine, I cannot believe that the court would not have imposed some jail time or that either the Due Process or Equal Protection Clause of the Constitution would prevent such imposition.

Poverty does not insulate those who break the law from punishment. When probation is revoked for failure to pay a fine, I find nothing in the Constitution to prevent the trial court from revoking probation and imposing a term of imprisonment if revocation does not automatically result in the imposition of a long jail term and if the sentencing court makes a good-faith effort to impose a jail sentence that in terms of the state's sentencing objectives will be roughly equivalent to the fine and restitution that the defendant failed to pay. See Wood v. Georgia, 450 U.S. 261, 284-287 (White, J., dissenting).

The Court holds, however, that if a probationer cannot pay the fine for reasons not of his own fault, the sentencing court must at least consider alternative measures of punishment other than imprisonment, and may imprison the probationer only if the alternative measures are deemed inadequate to meet the State's interests in punishment and deterrence. . . . There is no support in our cases or, in my view, the Constitution, for this novel requirement.

The Court suggests, . . . that if the sentencing court rejects nonprison alternatives as "inadequate," it is "impractical" to impose a prison term roughly equivalent to the fine in terms of achieving punishment goals. Hence, I take it, that had the trial court in this case rejected nonprison alternatives, the sentence it imposed would be constitutionally impregnable. Indeed, there would be no bounds on the length of the imprisonment that could be imposed, other than those imposed by the Eighth Amendment. But Williams v. Illinois, 399 U.S. 235 (1970) and Tate v. Short, 401 U.S. 395 (1971), stand for the proposition that such "automatic" conversion of a fine into a jail term is forbidden by the Equal Protection Clause, and by so holding, the Court in those cases was surely of the view that there is a way of converting a fine into a jail term that is not "automatic." In building a superstructure of procedural steps that sentencing courts must follow, the Court seems to forget its own concern about imprisoning an indigent person for failure to pay a fine.

In this case, in view of the long prison term imposed, the state court obviously did not find that the sentence was "a rational and necessary trade-off to punish the individual who possessed no accumulated assets," Williams v. Illinois, supra, 399 U.S., at 265 (Harlan, J., concurring). Accordingly, I concur in the judgment.

5. The practical meaning of the right to counsel depends on how indigent defendants are given lawyers and on how the lawyers are paid. There are several different methods. Most densely populated areas use public defender offices. These offices consist of full-time attorneys who do nothing but indigent defense; the offices are usually funded by an annual government appropriation. If the appropriation is low and the caseload high, the results can be staggering: Caseloads in some offices ranged as high as 400 felonies per attorney per year; other offices report caseloads of up to 1,200 misdemeanors per attorney per year. Richard Klein & Robert Spangenberg, The Indigent Defense Crisis (American Bar Association Section on Criminal Justice 1993).

Where public defender offices do not exist, indigent defendants are usually assigned counsel. The pay scale is typically low, although there have been significant improvements in many jurisdictions over the past decade. Not so, however, in Virginia:

> In addition to having non-waiveable per-case maximums, Virginia has the lowest per-case maximum fee for non-capital cases in the country. In 2002, the maximum allowable fee for a felony punishable by more than 20 years was set at $1,235 and for all other felonies $445. However, the statutory amounts authorized in the legislative code were not completely funded in Virginia's budget. Thus, in Circuit Court, the actual amount paid for felony cases with a sentence of more than 20 years was $1,096 . . . and for felonies up to 20 years, the actual amount paid was $395. . . .

The Spangenberg Group, State and County Expenditures for Indigent Defense Services in Fiscal Year 2002, at p. 27 (available online at: *http://www.abanet.org/legalservices/downloads/sclaid/indigentdefense/indigentdefexpend2003.pdf*). Similar problems exist in Illinois ($1,250 maximum fee for a noncapital case), Maryland ($1,000 maximum), Mississippi ($1,000 maximum, not subject to waiver, plus overhead expenses at a presumptive rate of $25 per hour), and New Jersey (hourly rate of $25 per hour out-of-court, or $30 per hour in-court), among others. The Spangenberg Group, Rates of Compensation Paid to Court-Appointed Counsel in Non-Capital Felony Cases at Trial: A State-by-State Overview (August 2003), available online at: *http://www.abanet.org/legalservices/downloads/sclaid/indigentdefense/compensationratesnoncapital2003.pdf.*

> . . . When compensation is on an hourly basis, judges or court administrators always review fee claims, and they often reduce fees, sometimes in a way that the attorneys consider arbitrary. In any event, there is usually a cap on total compensation payable. . . .
> . . . Finally, some jurisdictions regard indigent defense as a "pro bono" obligation, and appointed counsel, usually conscripts rather than volunteers, receive no compensation at all. Although the no-compensation approach is exceptional, flat fees or fee caps are so low in many jurisdictions that hourly compensation in cases that go to trial is virtually nil.

Stephen J. Schulhofer & David D. Friedman, Rethinking Indigent Defense: Promoting Effective Representation through Consumer Sovereignty and Freedom of Choice for All Criminal Defendants, 31 Am. Crim. L. Rev. 73, 93-94 (1993) (footnotes omitted).

There have been some challenges to the constitutionality of such regimes, but not many successful ones. For a notable exception, see State v. Peart, 621 So. 2d 780 (La. 1993). In *Peart,* the Louisiana Supreme Court concluded that indigent defendants in New Orleans were frequently being deprived of effective assistance of counsel due to the extremely high caseloads that public defenders were required to carry. Id. at 788-790. The court held that henceforth defendants in that district would have a rebuttable presumption that counsel was ineffective, at least until the funding problem was rectified. Id. at 790-792. *Peart* was decided under Louisiana law, though the content of Louisiana's requirement of effective assistance was not obviously different from the content of the federal law requirement.

Bruce Green offers a different angle on this problem, by emphasizing how underfunding of indigent defense tends to push defense counsel to violate their ethical obligation to defend their clients properly:

> Most criminal defendants in the United States cannot afford to pay for a lawyer's services, and as a result their lawyers are government funded. Unfortunately, some state and local governments drastically under-fund indigent defense services. Criminal defense lawyers serving in these jurisdictions typically carry grossly excessive caseloads and are therefore severely restricted in how much time they can devote to individual clients. . . .
>
> . . . [T]he under-funding of indigent defense also raises a serious and inadequately recognized problem of professional ethics: the systemic neglect of indigent defendants by their appointed lawyers. The legal profession's ethics rules establish standards for representation. However, many lawyers for indigent defendants engage in a practice that systematically violates these professional norms. They do not serve all their clients with "diligence" and "thoroughness," conduct "adequate preparation," or give matters the "required attention." Such criminal defense lawyers do not keep clients "reasonably informed," do not "comply with [their clients'] reasonable requests for information," do not consult with clients about how the lawyer will pursue their objectives, and do not explain matters to clients so that they can make "informed decisions."[4]

Bruce A. Green, Criminal Neglect: Indigent Defense from a Legal Ethics Perspective, 52 Emory L.J. 1169, 1169-1170 (2003).

6. It can hardly be a surprise to find that the right to state-paid counsel doesn't mean much unless the state appropriates an adequate amount to pay for it. Yet in the 41 years since *Gideon* was decided, the Supreme Court has made no move to require adequate funding. Why not? The answer may have more to do with timing than with any constitutional principle. If adequate funding for indigent defense were to arise out of litigation, the litigation would likely take the form of a class-action lawsuit by criminal defendants (or perhaps by their lawyers), seeking to enjoin the state both to provide an appropriate level of resources to local public defenders' offices and to offer an appropriate pay scale to separately appointed counsel. In 1963, when *Gideon* was decided, the era of large-scale institutional injunction litigation had not yet begun. No one even imagined the kind of lawsuits just described.

The late 1960s and 1970s saw a boom in class actions seeking complex injunctions against government agencies (they became known as "structural injunctions"). Plaintiffs in a number of these cases succeeded—meaning that a number of federal courts issued injunctions that directed government officials to manage their agencies in particular ways; most of those edicts also required the expenditure of large amounts of money. But those cases were brought by parents of public-school children seeking the busing of students to achieve racial balance, or by inmates of state prisons or local jails seeking improvements in the conditions of their incarceration. No similar suits were brought by criminal defendants seeking better funding for defense counsel. By the time *those* claims began to arise, in the late 1980s and 1990s, structural injunctions had gone out of fashion; the Supreme Court had cut back on judges' authority to issue broad orders to government agencies—especially when those orders required those agencies to spend large amounts of money. For the classic example of this new, more restrictive

---

4. The quoted language appears at Model Rules of Professional Conduct 1.1., 1.2, 1.3, and 1.4 (2002). — EDS.

attitude, see Missouri v. Jenkins, 515 U.S. 70 (1995), where the Court overturned a broad injunctive order aimed at reforming the Kansas City school system. Given that attitude, it is not exactly surprising that Sixth Amendment funding claims have not enjoyed much success.

In other words, underfunding-of-indigent-defense claims simply arrived at the courthouse too late. If those claims had arisen in 1970 or 1975, they might have won the day: States might have been required to establish the kinds of institutional arrangements and budget practices that would ensure adequate provision of defense counsel to indigents. But because structural injunctions were tried elsewhere — schools and prisons — and found wanting, courts have been loath to use them to enforce Sixth Amendment rights.

7. Statutes in various jurisdictions provide for the furnishing of aid to indigents, other than counsel and transcripts, that may assist in the preparation for trial or be useful at trial itself, e.g., investigative aids or expert evaluation and testimony. In federal litigation, the relevant statute is 18 U.S.C. §3006A, which also provides for the appointment of counsel on habeas "in the interests of justice" in cases not involving the death penalty.[5]

In Ake v. Oklahoma, 470 U.S. 68 (1985), the Court held that when an indigent defendant "demonstrates to the trial judge that his sanity at the time of the offense is to be a significant factor at trial, the State must, at a minimum, assure the defendant access to a competent psychiatrist who will conduct an appropriate examination and assist in evaluation, preparation, and presentation of the defense." 470 U.S. at 83. In emphasizing that a defendant must have access to the "basic tools of an adequate defense," id. at 77, the Court further held that a defendant must have access to psychiatric expertise if his future dangerousness is relevant as an aggravating factor in a capital sentencing proceeding.

8. The Supreme Court has extended, in certain respects, the analysis developed in the *Griffin/Douglas* line of cases to civil suits. The Court, for example, struck down a state filing fee that restricted the access of indigents to a divorce proceeding in Boddie v. Connecticut, 401 U.S. 371 (1971). In Little v. Streater, 452 U.S. 1 (1981), the Court held that the appellant, the putative father in a paternity suit, was denied due process when the state refused to fund potentially dispository blood-grouping tests that the appellant could not afford. However, on the same day *Little* was decided, the Court held in Lassiter v. Department of Social Services of Durham County, 452 U.S. 18 (1981), that failure to appoint counsel for indigent

---

5. As for death penalty cases, the Anti-Drug Abuse Act of 1988, 21 U.S.C.A. §§848(q) and 848(r) (West 1994 & Supp. 1998), requires the appointment of counsel for indigent prisoners seeking to set aside a death sentence in federal habeas corpus proceedings (under either 28 U.S.C. §2254, for state prisoners, or 28 U.S.C. §2255, for federal prisoners). The Court, in McFarland v. Scott, 512 U.S. 849 (1994), held that appointment of counsel under this statute can be made prior to the actual filing of the habeas corpus petition, i.e., upon the prisoner's filing of a motion seeking counsel to help with the preparation of a habeas corpus petition. In the Anti-Terrorism and Effective Death Penalty Act of 1996 (AEDPA), Congress added a section to the federal habeas corpus statute that allows states to "opt in" to a new system providing accelerated habeas procedures for capital cases. No state has qualified, so far, for these procedures. The qualifications include the requirement that the state must provide qualified counsel in state postconviction proceedings for indigent prisoners seeking to set aside a death sentence. See 28 U.S.C. §2261. The statute further provides: "The ineffectiveness or incompetence of counsel during State or Federal post-conviction proceedings in a capital case shall not be a ground for relief in a [federal habeas corpus] proceeding arising under section 2254." See 28 U.S.C. §2261(e); death-row inmates get a broader statutory right to appointed counsel, but cannot challenge counsel's effectiveness. No court has yet ruled on this provision's legality.

parents in a state-initiated proceeding to terminate parental status did not violate due process. For a discussion, see The Supreme Court, 1980 Term: Indigents' Rights to State Funding in Civil Actions, 95 Harv. L. Rev. 132 (1981). For a discussion of the general problem of providing indigents access to legal services, see Note, Court Appointment of Attorneys in Civil Cases: The Constitutionality of Uncompensated Legal Assistance, 81 Colum. L. Rev. 366 (1981). By contrast, as noted in Note 1, page 159 supra, the right to appeal a decision terminating parental rights cannot be conditioned upon the parent's ability to pay a record preparation fee. M.L.B. v. S.L.J., 519 U.S. 102 (1996).

9. The Court has upheld certain limitations on retained counsel. In Walters v. National Ass'n. of Radiation Survivors, 473 U.S. 305 (1985), the Court upheld a federal statute that limits to $10 the fee that may be paid counsel representing a veteran seeking benefits from the Veterans Administration, remarking: "Simple factual questions are capable of resolution in a nonadversarial context, and it is less than crystal clear why *lawyers* must be available to identify possible errors in *medical* judgment." Id. at 330. Citing *Walters,* the Court in Washington v. Harper, 494 U.S. 210 (1990), found no violation of due process in a state statute permitting the decision to give state prisoners antipsychotic drugs to be made by medical personnel and without judicial involvement or counsel for the prisoner. The Seventh Circuit concluded that a college student is not entitled to legal representation at a disciplinary hearing, even though the result of the hearing could be suspension or dismissal. According to the court, the University did not violate the student's rights by excluding the lawyer from the hearing. Osteen v. Henley, 13 F.3d 221 (7th Cir. 1993).

The Supreme Court also held that 28 U.S.C. §1915(d), which authorizes a federal district court to "request" counsel to represent an indigent person in a civil action, does not authorize a court to require an attorney to accept such an assignment. However, the Court did not discuss whether federal district courts possess an inherent power to require such representation; the Court limited its discussion to the question of statutory interpretation. Mallard v. United States District Court for the Southern District of Iowa, 490 U.S. 296 (1989).

3. Critical Stages of the Proceeding

The Supreme Court has held that the right to counsel applies at every critical stage of a criminal prosecution, Coleman v. Alabama, 399 U.S. 1 (1970), which raises two issues—what is a "criminal prosecution," and which of its stages are "critical"? It is now well settled that a "criminal prosecution" begins for purposes of right to counsel when adversary judicial proceedings have been begun, and that it continues throughout the sentencing process. Thus, the criminal prosecution begins at the initial appearance or any formal charging process such as the filing of an indictment or information (whichever comes first), Brewer v. Williams, 430 U.S. 387 (1977), and it continues until the final determination by the trial judge of the sentence to be imposed. Mempa v. Rhay, 389 U.S. 128 (1967) (right to counsel applicable at probation revocation hearing at which judge imposed sentence).

What makes a stage "critical" is somewhat more problematic. The word apparently refers to any formal interaction between the defendant and the state that could adversely affect the defendant's ability effectively to exercise a legal right. Thus, preliminary hearings, *Coleman,* supra, initial appearances, *Brewer,* supra, and arraignments, Hamilton v. Alabama, 368 U.S. 52 (1961), are *critical* stages of a criminal prosecution, but ex parte proceedings that will not adversely affect a defendant's legal rights, such as warrant procedures (discussed in Chapter 5), are not. Moreover, the concept of a "critical stage" also extends to any *informal* meeting between the defendant and a representative of the state that is designed or is likely to elicit incriminating information from the defendant (discussed in Chapter 6).[6]

The Sixth Amendment is not applicable past the point of sentencing. In Morrissey v. Brewer, 408 U.S. 471 (1972), the Court held that parole revocation is not a part of a criminal prosecution but that due process nonetheless mandates certain procedural protections. In Gagnon v. Scarpelli, 411 U.S. 778 (1973), the Court held that one of those protections is right to counsel at parole or probation revocation proceedings where, unlike *Mempa*, sentence was not imposed at the hearing and where there are "special circumstances." The special circumstances calling for counsel exist whenever the probationer or parolee makes a request for counsel, based on a timely and colorable claim (i) that he has not committed the alleged violation of the conditions upon which he is at liberty; or (ii) that, even if the violation is a matter of public record and is uncontested, there are substantial reasons which justified or mitigated the violation and make revocation inappropriate, and that the reasons are complex or otherwise difficult to develop or present. Id. at 790. The Court has also determined that a prisoner has a right to be heard in prison disciplinary hearings that could adversely affect his liberty interests, but not necessarily with the assistance of counsel. Wolff v. McDonnell, 418 U.S. 539 (1974). For a discussion, see David A. Harris, The Constitution and Truth Seeking: A New Theory on Expert Services for Indigent Defendants, 83 J. Crim. L. & Criminology 469 (1992). Curiously enough, the Court in *Gagnon* made a point of emphasizing that it was *not* deciding anything about the scope of the right to be heard by retained counsel in revocation proceedings. 411 U.S. at 783 n. 6. Counsel need not be appointed for inmates placed in administrative segregation as a result of crimes committed while incarcerated, unless adversary judicial proceedings are initiated against the inmates. United States v. Gouveia, 467 U.S. 180 (1984).

Given these limitations on the scope of the right to counsel, not surprisingly the Court has also held that it does not extend to habeas corpus/collateral attack proceedings (which are discussed in Chapter 15, infra). Pennsylvania v. Finley, 481 U.S. 551 (1987) (Sixth Amendment right not applicable on habeas); Murray v. Giarratano, 492 U.S. 1, 10 (1989) (no due process right to counsel on access to courts theory in habeas).

B. *Effective Assistance of Counsel*

1. The Meaning of Effective Assistance

The mere appointment of counsel does not satisfy the constitutional guarantee of right to counsel. Indeed, the trial court in Powell v. Alabama appointed counsel

---

6. If an interrogation of a suspect occurs prior to the initiation of adversarial proceedings, however, the accused's protections rest on the Fifth Amendment right to be free from compelled self-incrimination; under *Miranda*, the right to counsel serves as a prophylactic rule to protect the self-incrimination right (discussed in Chapter 6 infra).

but in such a way as to preclude the giving of effective aid in the preparation and trial of the case. The concern for effectiveness has been a consistent thread running through the Supreme Court's cases, as evidenced by the rhetoric in McMann v. Richardson, 397 U.S. 759 (1970) ("if the right to counsel guaranteed by the Constitution is to serve its purpose, defendants cannot be left to the mercies of incompetent counsel," id. at 771).

In order to ensure the conditions under which effective assistance is likely to be obtained, the Supreme Court has rendered a series of decisions prohibiting certain forms of interference with the attorney-client relationship. An attorney may not be prohibited from conferring with the client during an overnight recess that falls between direct examination and cross-examination. Geders v. United States, 425 U.S. 80 (1976). A lawyer may not be denied the right to give a closing summation in a nonjury trial. Herring v. New York, 422 U.S. 853 (1975). The state may not prohibit the attorney from eliciting the client's testimony on direct examination, Ferguson v. Georgia, 365 U.S. 570 (1961), nor may the state restrict the attorney's choice as to when to put the defendant on the stand, Brooks v. Tennessee, 406 U.S. 605 (1972). There are limits on the Court's solicitude for criminal defendants, however. In Perry v. Leeke, 488 U.S. 272 (1989), the Court held that the trial court did not err by ordering the defendant not to consult with his lawyer during a 15-minute recess that followed immediately his direct examination and preceded cross-examination.

Outside of these, and similar, relatively narrow areas, during much of the nation's history the lower courts almost uniformly adopted the "mockery of justice" standard to test claims of ineffectiveness under which ineffectiveness was found only in such shocking circumstances as to reduce the trial to a farce or charade. Even inebriated counsel often was insufficient cause to find lack of effectiveness.

The mockery of justice standard seems inordinately low, but there are some justifications for it. The higher the level of scrutiny, the greater is the impetus on the part of the trial judge to intervene in derogation of basic premises of the adversary system. Moreover, intervention may occur at a point of what appears to be problematic action by counsel but in fact is an integral part of a trial strategy known only to counsel. Also, the more active trial judges become, the more they are implicitly or explicitly critical of the bar that practices before them; and the more active appellate courts become, the more critical they become of the trial judges.

Beginning around 1970, a large proportion of the states, and most of the federal circuits, replaced the mockery of justice standard with one that requires counsel to possess and exercise the legal competence customarily found in the jurisdiction. For an early and influential example, see Moore v. United States, 432 F.2d 730 (3d Cir. 1970). Two developments stimulated this change. The first was the Supreme Court's legitimation of plea bargaining in 1970. See Chapter 10, infra. If pleas were now to receive greater protection against challenge, then the legal advice received by an accused assumes greater importance. Moreover, one of the challenges to a guilty plea that could not be deemed waived by it is the very advice that led to the plea in the first instance, which has the effect of focusing greater attention on the competency of counsel throughout the plea negotiations. The second development that stimulated a greater concern for the competency of counsel was the Supreme Court's tightening of habeas corpus (recently furthered by Congress). As avenues to relief for habeas petitioners have narrowed, the incentive to relitigate those closed avenues under the rubric of right to counsel has grown.

The Supreme Court finally turned to these issues in:

STRICKLAND v. WASHINGTON

Certiorari to the United States Court of Appeals for the Eleventh Circuit
466 U.S. 668 (1984)

JUSTICE O' CONNOR delivered the opinion of the Court.

This case requires us to consider the proper standards for judging a criminal defendant's contention that the Constitution requires a conviction or death sentence to be set aside because counsel's assistance at the trial or sentencing was ineffective.

I

A

During a ten-day period in September 1976, respondent planned and committed three groups of crimes, which included three brutal stabbing murders, torture, kidnapping, severe assaults, attempted murders, attempted extortion, and theft. After his two accomplices were arrested, respondent surrendered to police and voluntarily gave a lengthy statement confessing to the third of the criminal episodes. The State of Florida indicted respondent for kidnapping and murder and appointed an experienced criminal lawyer to represent him.

Counsel actively pursued pretrial motions and discovery. He cut his efforts short, however, and he experienced a sense of hopelessness about the case, when he learned that, against his specific advice, respondent had also confessed to the first two murders. By the date set for trial, respondent was subject to indictment for three counts of first degree murder and multiple counts of robbery, kidnapping for ransom, breaking and entering and assault, attempted murder, and conspiracy to commit robbery. Respondent waived his right to a jury trial, again acting against counsel's advice, and pleaded guilty to all charges, including the three capital murder charges.

In the plea colloquy, respondent told the trial judge that, although he had committed a string of burglaries, he had no significant prior criminal record and that at the time of his criminal spree he was under extreme stress caused by his inability to support his family. . . . He also stated, however, that he accepted responsibility for the crimes. . . . The trial judge told respondent that he had "a great deal of respect for people who are willing to step forward and admit their responsibility" but that he was making no statement at all about his likely sentencing decision. . . .

Counsel advised respondent to invoke his right under Florida law to an advisory jury at his capital sentencing hearing. Respondent rejected the advice and waived the right. He chose instead to be sentenced by the trial judge without a jury recommendation.

In preparing for the sentencing hearing, counsel spoke with respondent about his background. He also spoke on the telephone with respondent's wife and mother, though he did not follow up on the one unsuccessful effort to meet with them. He did not otherwise seek out character witnesses for respondent. . . . Nor did he request a psychiatric examination, since his conversations with his client gave no indication that respondent had psychological problems. . . .

Counsel decided not to present and hence not to look further for evidence concerning respondent's character and emotional state. That decision reflected trial counsel's sense of hopelessness about overcoming the evidentiary effect of respondent's confessions to the gruesome crimes. . . . It also reflected the judgment that it was advisable to rely on the plea colloquy for evidence about respondent's background and about his claim of emotional stress: The plea colloquy communicated sufficient information about these subjects, and by [forgoing] the opportunity to present new evidence on these subjects, counsel prevented the State from cross-examining respondent on his claim and from putting on psychiatric evidence of its own. . . .

Counsel also excluded from the sentencing hearing other evidence he thought was potentially damaging. He successfully moved to exclude respondent's "rap sheet." . . . Because he judged that a presentence report might prove more detrimental than helpful, as it would have included respondent's criminal history and thereby undermined the claim of no significant history of criminal activity, he did not request that one be prepared. . . .

At the sentencing hearing, counsel's strategy was based primarily on the trial judge's remarks at the plea colloquy as well as on his reputation as a sentencing judge who thought it important for a convicted defendant to own up to his crime. Counsel argued that respondent's remorse and acceptance of responsibility justified sparing him from the death penalty. . . . Counsel also argued that respondent had no history of criminal activity and that respondent committed the crimes under extreme mental or emotional disturbance, thus coming within the statutory list of mitigating circumstances. He further argued that respondent should be spared death because he had surrendered, confessed, and offered to testify against a co-defendant and because respondent was fundamentally a good person who had briefly gone badly wrong in extremely stressful circumstances. The State put on evidence and witnesses largely for the purpose of describing the details of the crimes. Counsel did not cross-examine the medical experts who testified about the manner of death of respondent's victims. . . .

. . . The trial judge found numerous aggravating circumstances and no (or a single comparatively insignificant) mitigating circumstance. With respect to each of the three convictions for capital murder, the trial judge concluded: "A careful consideration of all matters presented to the court impels the conclusion that there are insufficient mitigating circumstances . . . to outweigh the aggravating circumstances." He therefore sentenced respondent to death on each of the three counts of murder and to prison terms for the other crimes. The Florida Supreme Court upheld the convictions and sentences on direct appeal. . . .

C

Respondent next filed a petition for a writ of habeas corpus in the United States District Court for the Southern District of Florida.

The District Court held an evidentiary hearing to inquire into trial counsel's efforts to investigate and to present mitigating circumstances. Respondent offered the affidavits and reports he had submitted in the state collateral proceedings; he also called his trial counsel to testify. The State of Florida, over respondent's objection, called the trial judge to testify. [The court denied the petition for a writ of habeas corpus.]

On appeal, . . . the Court of Appeals stated that the Sixth Amendment right to assistance of counsel accorded criminal defendants a right to "counsel reasonably likely to render and rendering reasonably effective assistance given the totality of the circumstances." The court remarked in passing that no special standard applies in capital cases such as the one before it: the punishment that a defendant faces is merely one of the circumstances to be considered in determining whether counsel was reasonably effective. The court then addressed respondent's contention that his trial counsel's assistance was not reasonably effective because counsel breached his duty to investigate nonstatutory mitigating circumstances.

The court agreed that the Sixth Amendment imposes on counsel a duty to investigate, because reasonably effective assistance must be based on professional decisions and informed legal choices can be made only after investigation of options. The court observed that counsel's investigatory decisions must be assessed in light of the information known at the time of the decisions, not in hindsight, and that "[t]he amount of pretrial investigation that is reasonable defies precise measurement." Nevertheless, putting guilty-plea cases to one side, the court attempted to classify cases presenting issues concerning the scope of the duty to investigate before proceeding to trial.

If there is only one plausible line of defense, the court concluded, counsel must conduct a "reasonably substantial investigation" into that line of defense, since there can be no strategic choice that renders such an investigation unnecessary. The same duty exists if counsel relies at trial on only one line of defense, although others are available. In either case, the investigation need not be exhaustive. It must include "an independent examination of the facts, circumstances, pleadings and laws involved." The scope of the duty, however, depends on such facts as the strength of the government's case and the likelihood that pursuing certain leads may prove more harmful than helpful.

If there is more than one plausible line of defense, the court held, counsel should ideally investigate each line substantially before making a strategic choice about which lines to rely on at trial. If counsel conducts such substantial investigations, the strategic choices made as a result "will seldom if ever" be found wanting. Because advocacy is an art and not a science, and because the adversary system requires deference to counsel's informed decisions, strategic choices must be respected in these circumstances if they are based on professional judgment.

If counsel does not conduct a substantial investigation into each of several plausible lines of defense, assistance may nonetheless be effective. Counsel may not exclude certain lines of defense for other than strategic reasons. Limitations of time and money, however, may force early strategic choices, often based solely on conversations with the defendant and a review of the prosecution's evidence. Those strategic choices about which lines of defense to pursue are owed deference commensurate with the reasonableness of the professional judgments on which they are based. Thus, "when counsel's assumptions are reasonable given the totality of the circumstances and when counsel's strategy represents a reasonable choice based upon those assumptions, counsel need not investigate lines of defense that he has chosen not to employ at trial." Among the factors relevant to deciding whether particular strategic choices are reasonable are the experience of the attorney, the inconsistency of unpursued and pursued lines of defense, and the potential for prejudice from taking an unpursued line of defense. . . .

The Court of Appeals thus laid down the tests to be applied in the Eleventh Circuit in challenges to convictions on the ground of ineffectiveness of counsel. . . . Summarily rejecting respondent's claims other than ineffectiveness of counsel, the court accordingly reversed the judgment of the District Court and remanded the case. On remand, the court finally ruled, the state trial judge's testimony, though admissible "to the extent that it contains personal knowledge of historical facts or expert opinion," was not to be considered admitted into evidence to explain the judge's mental processes in reaching his sentencing decision. . . .

D

Petitioners, who are officials of the State of Florida, filed a petition for a writ of certiorari seeking review of the decision of the Court of Appeals. The petition presents a type of Sixth Amendment claim that this Court has not previously considered in any generality. . . . With the exception of Cuyler v. Sullivan [see page 200, infra] which involved a claim that counsel's assistance was rendered ineffective by a conflict of interest, the Court has never directly and fully addressed a claim of "actual ineffectiveness" of counsel's assistance in a case going to trial. . . .

II . . .

In giving meaning to the requirement [of effective assistance of counsel,] we must take its purpose — to ensure a fair trial — as the guide. The benchmark for judging any claim of ineffectiveness must be whether counsel's conduct so undermined the proper functioning of the adversarial process that the trial cannot be relied on as having produced a just result.

The same principle applies to a capital sentencing proceeding such as that provided by Florida law. We need not consider the role of counsel in an ordinary sentencing, which may involve informal proceedings and standardless discretion in the sentencer, and hence may require a different approach to the definition of constitutionally effective assistance. . . .

III

A convicted defendant's claim that counsel's assistance was so defective as to require reversal of a conviction or death sentence has two components. First, the defendant must show that counsel's performance was deficient. This requires showing that counsel made errors so serious that counsel was not functioning as the "counsel" guaranteed the defendant by the Sixth Amendment. Second, the defendant must show that the deficient performance prejudiced the defense. This requires showing that counsel's errors were so serious as to deprive the defendant of a fair trial, a trial whose result is reliable. Unless a defendant makes both showings, it cannot be said that the conviction or death sentence resulted from a breakdown in the adversary process that renders the result unreliable.

A

As all the Federal Courts of Appeals have now held, the proper standard for attorney performance is that of reasonably effective assistance. . . . When a convicted defendant complains of the ineffectiveness of counsel's assistance, the defendant must show that counsel's representation fell below an objective standard of reasonableness.

More specific guidelines are not appropriate. The Sixth Amendment refers simply to "counsel," not specifying particular requirements of effective assistance. It relies instead on the legal profession's maintenance of standards sufficient to justify the law's presumption that counsel will fulfill the role in the adversary process that the Amendment envisions. . . . The proper measure of attorney performance remains simply reasonableness under prevailing professional norms.

Representation of a criminal defendant entails certain basic duties. Counsel's function is to assist the defendant, and hence counsel owes the client a duty of loyalty, a duty to avoid conflicts of interest. . . . From counsel's function as assistant to the defendant derive the overarching duty to advocate the defendant's cause and the more particular duties to consult with the defendant on important decisions and to keep the defendant informed of important developments in the course of the prosecution. Counsel also has a duty to bring to bear such skill and knowledge as will render the trial a reliable adversarial testing process. . . .

These basic duties neither exhaustively define the obligations of counsel nor form a checklist for judicial evaluation of attorney performance. In any case presenting an ineffectiveness claim, the performance inquiry must be whether counsel's assistance was reasonable considering all the circumstances. Prevailing norms of practice as reflected in American Bar Association standards and the like, e.g., ABA Standards for Criminal Justice 4-1.1 to 4-8.6 (2d ed. 1980) ("The Defense Function"), are guides to determining what is reasonable, but they are only guides. No particular set of detailed rules for counsel's conduct can satisfactorily take account of the variety of circumstances faced by defense counsel or the range of legitimate decisions regarding how best to represent a criminal defendant. Any such set of rules would interfere with the constitutionally protected independence of counsel and restrict the wide latitude counsel must have in making tactical decisions. . . . Indeed, the existence of detailed guidelines for representation could distract counsel from the overriding mission of vigorous advocacy of the defendant's cause. Moreover, the purpose of the effective assistance guarantee of the Sixth Amendment is not to improve the quality of legal representation, although that is a goal of considerable importance to the legal system. The purpose is simply to ensure that criminal defendants receive a fair trial.

Judicial scrutiny of counsel's performance must be highly deferential. It is all too tempting for a defendant to second-guess counsel's assistance after conviction or adverse sentence, and it is all too easy for a court, examining counsel's defense after it has proved unsuccessful, to conclude that a particular act or omission of counsel was unreasonable. . . . A fair assessment of attorney performance requires that every effort be made to eliminate the distorting effects of hindsight, to reconstruct the circumstances of counsel's challenged conduct, and to evaluate the conduct from counsel's perspective at the time. Because of the difficulties inherent in making the evaluation, a court must indulge a strong presumption that counsel's conduct falls within the wide range of reasonable professional assistance. . . . There are countless ways to provide effective assistance in any given case. Even the best criminal defense attorneys would not defend a particular client in the same way. See Gary Goodpaster, The Trial for Life: Effective Assistance of Counsel in Death Penalty Cases, 58 N.Y.U. L. Rev. 299, 343 (1983).

The availability of intrusive post-trial inquiry into attorney performance or of detailed guidelines for its evaluation would encourage the proliferation of ineffectiveness challenges. Criminal trials resolved unfavorably to the defendant would increasingly come to be followed by a second trial, this one of counsel's unsuccessful defense. Counsel's performance and even willingness to serve could be adversely affected. Intensive scrutiny of counsel and rigid requirements for acceptable assistance could dampen the ardor and impair the independence of defense counsel, discourage the acceptance of assigned cases, and undermine the trust between attorney and client.

Thus, a court deciding an actual ineffectiveness claim must judge the reasonableness of counsel's challenged conduct on the facts of the particular case, viewed as of the time of counsel's conduct. A convicted defendant making a claim of ineffective assistance must identify the acts or omissions of counsel that are alleged not to have been the result of reasonable professional judgment. The court must then determine whether, in light of all the circumstances, the identified acts or omissions were outside the wide range of professionally competent assistance. In making that determination, the court should keep in mind that counsel's function, as elaborated in prevailing professional norms, is to make the adversarial testing process work in the particular case. At the same time, the court should recognize that counsel is strongly presumed to have rendered adequate assistance and made all significant decisions in the exercise of reasonable professional judgment.

These standards require no special amplification in order to define counsel's duty to investigate, the duty at issue in this case. As the Court of Appeals concluded, strategic choices made after thorough investigation of law and facts relevant to plausible options are virtually unchallengeable; and strategic choices made after less than complete investigation are reasonable precisely to the extent that reasonable professional judgments support the limitations on investigation. In other words, counsel has a duty to make reasonable investigations or to make a reasonable decision that makes particular investigations unnecessary. In any ineffectiveness case, a particular decision not to investigate must be directly assessed for reasonableness in all the circumstances, applying a heavy measure of deference to counsel's judgments.

The reasonableness of counsel's actions may be determined or substantially influenced by the defendant's own statements or actions. Counsel's actions are usually based, quite properly, on informed strategic choices made by the defendant and on information supplied by the defendant. In particular, what investigation decisions are reasonable depends critically on such information. For example, when the facts that support a certain potential line of defense are generally known to counsel because of what the defendant has said, the need for further investigation may be considerably diminished or eliminated altogether. And when a defendant has given counsel reason to believe that pursuing certain investigations would be fruitless or even harmful, counsel's failure to pursue those investigations may not later be challenged as unreasonable. In short, inquiry into counsel's conversations with the defendant may be critical to a proper assessment of counsel's investigation decisions, just as it may be critical to a proper assessment of counsel's other litigation decisions. . . .

B

An error by counsel, even if professionally unreasonable, does not warrant setting aside the judgment of a criminal proceeding if the error had no effect on the judgment. . . . The purpose of the Sixth Amendment guarantee of counsel is to ensure that a defendant has the assistance necessary to justify reliance on the outcome of the proceeding. Accordingly, any deficiencies in counsel's performance must be prejudicial to the defense in order to constitute ineffective assistance under the Constitution.

In certain Sixth Amendment contexts, prejudice is presumed. Actual or constructive denial of the assistance of counsel altogether is legally presumed to result in prejudice. So are various kinds of state interference with counsel's assistance. . . . Prejudice in these circumstances is so likely that case by case inquiry into prejudice is not worth the cost. Moreover, such circumstances involve impairments of the Sixth Amendment right that are easy to identify and, for that reason and because the prosecution is directly responsible, easy for the government to prevent.

One type of actual ineffectiveness claim warrants a similar, though more limited, presumption of prejudice. In Cuyler v. Sullivan, 446 U.S., at 345-350, the Court held that prejudice is presumed when counsel is burdened by an actual conflict of interest. In those circumstances, counsel breaches the duty of loyalty, perhaps the most basic of counsel's duties. . . .

Conflict of interest claims aside, actual ineffectiveness claims alleging a deficiency in attorney performance are subject to a general requirement that the defendant affirmatively prove prejudice. The government is not responsible for, and hence not able to prevent, attorney errors that will result in reversal of a conviction or sentence. Attorney errors come in an infinite variety and are as likely to be utterly harmless in a particular case as they are to be prejudicial. They cannot be classified according to likelihood of causing prejudice. Nor can they be defined with sufficient precision to inform defense attorneys correctly just what conduct to avoid. Representation is an art, and an act or omission that is unprofessional in one case may be sound or even brilliant in another. Even if a defendant shows that particular errors of counsel were unreasonable, therefore, the defendant must show that they actually had an adverse effect on the defense.

It is not enough for the defendant to show that the errors had some conceivable effect on the outcome of the proceeding. Virtually every act or omission of counsel would meet that test, . . . and not every error that conceivably could have influenced the outcome undermines the reliability of the result of the proceeding. Respondent suggests requiring a showing that the errors "impaired the presentation of the defense." That standard, however, provides no workable principle. Since any error, if it is indeed an error, "impairs" the presentation of the defense, the proposed standard is inadequate because it provides no way of deciding what impairments are sufficiently serious to warrant setting aside the outcome of the proceeding.

On the other hand, we believe that a defendant need not show that counsel's deficient conduct more likely than not altered the outcome in the case. This outcome-determinative standard has several strengths. It defines the relevant inquiry in a way familiar to courts, though the inquiry, as is inevitable, is anything but precise. The standard also reflects the profound importance of finality in criminal proceedings. Moreover, it comports with the widely used standard for assessing motions for new trial based on newly discovered evidence. . . . Nevertheless, the standard is not quite appropriate.

Even when the specified attorney error results in the omission of certain evidence, the newly discovered evidence standard is not an apt source from which to draw a prejudice standard for ineffectiveness claims. The high standard for newly discovered evidence claims presupposes that all the essential elements of a presumptively accurate and fair proceeding were present in the proceeding whose result is challenged. . . . An ineffective assistance claim asserts the absence of one of the crucial assurances that the result of the proceeding is reliable, so finality concerns are somewhat weaker and the appropriate standard of prejudice should be somewhat lower. The result of a proceeding can be rendered unreliable, and hence the proceeding itself unfair, even if the errors of counsel cannot be shown by a preponderance of the evidence to have determined the outcome.

Accordingly, the appropriate test for prejudice finds its roots in the test for materiality of exculpatory information not disclosed to the defense by the prosecution, United States v. Agurs, 427 U.S., at 104, 112-113, and in the test for materiality of testimony made unavailable to the defense by Government deportation of a witness, United States v. Valenzuela-Bernal, 458 U.S., at 872-874. The defendant must show that there is a reasonable probability that, but for counsel's unprofessional errors, the result of the proceeding would have been different. A reasonable probability is a probability sufficient to undermine confidence in the outcome.

In making the determination whether the specified errors resulted in the required prejudice, a court should presume, absent challenge to the judgment on grounds of evidentiary insufficiency, that the judge or jury acted according to law. An assessment of the likelihood of a result more favorable to the defendant must exclude the possibility of arbitrariness, whimsy, caprice, "nullification," and the like. A defendant has no entitlement to the luck of a lawless decisionmaker, even if a lawless decision cannot be reviewed. The assessment of prejudice should proceed on the assumption that the decisionmaker is reasonably, conscientiously, and impartially applying the standards that govern the decision. It should not depend on the idiosyncracies of the particular decisionmaker, such as unusual propensities toward harshness or leniency. Although these factors may actually have entered into counsel's selection of strategies and, to that limited extent, may thus affect the performance inquiry, they are irrelevant to the prejudice inquiry. Thus, evidence about the actual process of decision, if not part of the record of the proceeding under review, and evidence about, for example, a particular judge's sentencing practices, should not be considered in the prejudice determination.

The governing legal standard plays a critical role in defining the question to be asked in assessing the prejudice from counsel's errors. When a defendant challenges a conviction, the question is whether there is a reasonable probability that, absent the errors, the fact-finder would have had a reasonable doubt respecting guilt. When a defendant challenges a death sentence such as the one at issue in this case, the question is whether there is a reasonable probability that, absent the errors, the sentencer — including an appellate court, to the extent it independently reweighs the evidence — would have concluded that the balance of aggravating and mitigating circumstances did not warrant death.

In making this determination, a court hearing an ineffectiveness claim must consider the totality of the evidence before the judge or jury. Some of the factual findings will have been unaffected by the errors, and factual findings that were affected will have been affected in different ways. Some errors will have had a pervasive effect on the inferences to be drawn from the evidence, altering the entire evidentiary picture, and some will have had an isolated, trivial effect. Moreover, a verdict or conclusion only weakly supported by the record is more likely to have been affected by the errors than one with overwhelming record support. Taking the unaffected findings as a given, and taking due account of the effect of the errors on the remaining findings, a court making the prejudice inquiry must ask if the defendant has met the burden of showing that the decision reached would reasonably likely have been different absent the errors.

IV

A number of practical considerations are important for the application of the standards we have outlined. Most important, in adjudicating a claim of actual ineffectiveness of counsel, a court should keep in mind that the principles we have stated do not establish mechanical rules. Although those principles should guide the process of decision, the ultimate focus of inquiry must be on the fundamental fairness of the proceeding whose result is being challenged. In every case the court should be concerned with whether, despite the strong presumption of reliability, the result of the particular proceeding is unreliable because of a break-down in the adversarial process that our system counts on to produce just results. . . .

Although we have discussed the performance component of an ineffectiveness claim prior to the prejudice component, there is no reason for a court deciding an ineffective assistance claim to approach the inquiry in the same order or even to address both components of the inquiry if the defendant makes an insufficient showing on one. In particular, a court need not determine whether counsel's performance was deficient before examining the prejudice suffered by the defendant as a result of the alleged deficiencies. The object of an ineffectiveness claim is not to grade counsel's performance. If it is easier to dispose of an ineffectiveness claim on the ground of lack of sufficient prejudice, which we expect will often be so, that course should be followed. Courts should strive to ensure that ineffectiveness claims not become so burdensome to defense counsel that the entire criminal justice system suffers as a result.

The principles governing ineffectiveness claims should apply in federal collateral proceedings as they do on direct appeal or in motions for a new trial. As indicated by the "cause and prejudice" test for overcoming procedural waivers of claims of error, the presumption that a criminal judgment is final is at its strongest in collateral attacks on that judgment. . . . An ineffectiveness claim, however, as our articulation of the standards that govern decision of such claims makes clear, is an attack on the fundamental fairness of the proceeding whose result is challenged. Since fundamental fairness is the central concern of the writ of habeas corpus, . . . no special standards ought to apply to ineffectiveness claims made in habeas proceedings.

Finally, in a federal habeas challenge to a state criminal judgment, a state court conclusion that counsel rendered effective assistance is not a finding of fact binding on the federal court to the extent stated by 28 U.S.C. §2254(d). Ineffectiveness is not a question of "basic, primary, or historical fac[t]." Rather, like the question whether multiple representation in a particular case gave rise to a conflict of interest, it is a mixed question of law and fact. . . . Although state court findings of fact made in the course of deciding an ineffectiveness claim are subject to the deference requirement of §2254(d), and although District Court findings are subject to the clearly erroneous standard of Fed. R. Civ. Proc. 52(a), both the performance and prejudice components of the ineffectiveness inquiry are mixed questions of law and fact.

V . . .

Application of the governing principles is not difficult in this case. The facts as described above, . . . make clear that the conduct of respondent's counsel at and before respondent's sentencing proceeding cannot be found unreasonable. They also make clear that, even assuming the challenged conduct of counsel was unreasonable, respondent suffered insufficient prejudice to warrant setting aside his death sentence.

With respect to the performance component, the record shows that respondent's counsel made a strategic choice to argue for the extreme emotional distress mitigating circumstance and to rely as fully as possible on respondent's acceptance of responsibility for his crimes. Although counsel understandably felt hopeless about respondent's prospects, . . . nothing in the record indicates, as one possible reading of the District Court's opinion suggests . . . that counsel's sense of hopelessness distorted his professional judgment. Counsel's strategy choice was well within the range of professionally reasonable judgments, and the decision not to seek more character or psychological evidence than was already in hand was likewise reasonable.

The trial judge's views on the importance of owning up to one's crimes were well known to counsel. The aggravating circumstances were utterly overwhelming. Trial counsel could reasonably surmise from his conversations with respondent that character and psychological evidence would be of little help. Respondent had already been able to mention at the plea colloquy the substance of what there was to know about his financial and emotional troubles. Restricting testimony on respondent's character to what had come in at the plea colloquy ensured that contrary character and psychological evidence and respondent's criminal history, which counsel had successfully moved to exclude, would not come in. On these facts, there can be little question, even without application of the presumption of adequate performance, that trial counsel's defense, though unsuccessful, was the result of reasonable professional judgment.

With respect to the prejudice component, the lack of merit of respondent's claim is even more stark. The evidence that respondent says his trial counsel should have offered at the sentencing hearing would barely have altered the sentencing profile presented to the sentencing judge. As the state courts and District Court found, at most this evidence shows that numerous people who knew respondent thought he was generally a good person and that a psychiatrist and a psychologist believed he was under considerable emotional stress that did not rise to the level of extreme disturbance. Given the overwhelming aggravating factors, there is no reasonable probability that the omitted evidence would have changed the conclusion that the aggravating circumstances outweighed the mitigating circumstances and, hence, the sentence imposed. Indeed, admission of the evidence respondent now offers might even have been harmful to his case: his "rap sheet" would probably have been admitted into evidence, and the psychological reports would have directly contradicted respondent's claim that the mitigating circumstance of extreme emotional disturbance applied to his case.

Our conclusions on both the prejudice and performance components of the ineffectiveness inquiry do not depend on the trial judge's testimony at the District Court hearing. We therefore need not consider the general admissibility of that testimony, although, as noted . . . , that testimony is irrelevant to the prejudice inquiry. Moreover, the prejudice question is resolvable, and hence the ineffectiveness claim can be rejected, without regard to the evidence presented at the District Court hearing. The state courts properly concluded that the ineffectiveness claim was meritless without holding an evidentiary hearing.

Failure to make the required showing of either deficient performance or sufficient prejudice defeats the ineffectiveness claim. Here there is a double failure. More generally, respondent has made no showing that the justice of his sentence was rendered unreliable by a breakdown in the adversary process caused by deficiencies in counsel's assistance. Respondent's sentencing proceeding was not fundamentally unfair.

We conclude, therefore, that the District Court properly declined to issue a writ of habeas corpus. The judgment of the Court of Appeals is accordingly reversed.

JUSTICE MARSHALL, dissenting. . . .

I

The opinion of the Court revolves around two holdings. First, the majority ties the constitutional minima of attorney performance to a simple "standard of reasonableness." . . . Second, the majority holds that only an error of counsel that has sufficient impact on a trial to "undermine confidence in the outcome" is grounds for overturning a conviction. . . . I disagree with both of these rulings.

A

My objection to the performance standard adopted by the Court is that it is so malleable that, in practice, it will either have no grip at all or will yield excessive variation in the manner in which the Sixth Amendment is interpreted and applied by different courts. To tell lawyers and the lower courts that counsel for a criminal defendant must behave "reasonably" and must act like "a reasonably competent attorney," . . . is to tell them almost nothing. In essence, the majority has instructed judges called upon to assess claims of ineffective assistance of counsel to advert to their own intuitions regarding what constitutes "professional" representation, and has discouraged them from trying to develop more detailed standards governing the performance of defense counsel. In my view, the Court has thereby not only abdicated its own responsibility to interpret the Constitution, but also impaired the ability of the lower courts to exercise theirs.

The debilitating ambiguity of an "objective standard of reasonableness" in this context is illustrated by the majority's failure to address important issues concerning the quality of representation mandated by the Constitution. It is an unfortunate but undeniable fact that a person of means, by selecting a lawyer and paying him enough to ensure he prepares thoroughly, usually can obtain better representation than that available to an indigent defendant, who must rely on appointed counsel, who, in turn, has limited time and resources to devote to a given case. Is a "reasonably competent attorney" a reasonably competent adequately paid retained lawyer or a reasonably competent appointed attorney? It is also a fact that the quality of representation available to ordinary defendants in different parts of the country varies significantly. Should the standard of performance mandated by the Sixth Amendment vary by locale? The majority offers no clues as to the proper responses to these questions. . . .

The opinion of the Court of Appeals in this case represents one sound attempt to develop particularized standards designed to ensure that all defendants receive effective legal assistance. . . . By refusing to address the merits of these proposals, and indeed suggesting that no such effort is worthwhile, the opinion of the Court, I fear, will stunt the development of constitutional doctrine in this area.

B

I object to the prejudice standard adopted by the Court for two independent reasons. *First,* it is often very difficult to tell whether a defendant convicted after a trial in which he was ineffectively represented would have fared better if his lawyer had been competent. Seemingly impregnable cases can sometimes be dismantled by good defense counsel. On the basis of a cold record, it may be impossible for a reviewing court confidently to ascertain how the government's evidence and arguments would have stood up against rebuttal and cross-examination by a shrewd, well prepared lawyer. The difficulties of estimating prejudice after the fact are exacerbated by the possibility that evidence of injury to the defendant may be missing from the record precisely because of the incompetence of defense counsel. In view of all these impediments to a fair evaluation of the probability that the outcome of a trial was affected by ineffectiveness of counsel, it seems to me senseless to impose on a defendant whose lawyer has been shown to have been incompetent the burden of demonstrating prejudice.

Second and more fundamentally, the assumption on which the Court's holding rests is that the only purpose of the constitutional guarantee of effective assistance of counsel is to reduce the chance that innocent persons will be convicted. In my view, the guarantee also functions to ensure that convictions are obtained only through fundamentally fair procedures. The majority contends that the Sixth Amendment is not violated when a manifestly guilty defendant is convicted after a trial in which he was represented by a manifestly ineffective attorney. I cannot agree. Every defendant is entitled to a trial in which his interests are vigorously and conscientiously advocated by an able lawyer. A proceeding in which the defendant does not receive meaningful assistance in meeting the forces of the state does not, in my opinion, constitute due process. . . .

III

The majority suggests that, "[f]or purposes of describing counsel's duties," a capital sentencing proceeding "need not be distinguished from an ordinary trial." I cannot agree.

The Court has repeatedly acknowledged that the Constitution requires stricter adherence to procedural safeguards in a capital case than in other cases. . . .

In my view, a person on death row, whose counsel's performance fell below constitutionally acceptable levels, should not be compelled to demonstrate a "reasonable probability" that he would have been given a life sentence if his lawyer had been competent . . . ; if the defendant can establish a significant chance that the outcome would have been different, he surely should be entitled to a redetermination of his fate. . . .

IV

The views expressed in the preceding section oblige me to dissent from the majority's disposition of the case before us. It is undisputed that respondent's trial counsel made virtually no investigation of the possibility of obtaining testimony from respondent's relatives, friends, or former employers pertaining to respondent's character or background. Had counsel done so, he would have found several persons willing and able to testify that, in their experience, respondent was a responsible, nonviolent man, devoted to his family, and active in the affairs of his church. . . . Respondent contends that his lawyer could have and should have used that testimony to "humanize" respondent, to counteract the impression conveyed by the trial that he was little more than a cold-blooded killer. Had this evidence been admitted, respondent argues, his chances of obtaining a life sentence would have been significantly better.

Measured against the standards outlined above, respondent's contentions are substantial. Experienced members of the death-penalty bar have long recognized the crucial importance of adducing evidence at a sentencing proceeding that establishes the defendant's social and familial connections. . . . The State makes a colorable — though in my view not compelling — argument that defense counsel in this case might have made a reasonable "strategic" decision not to present such evidence at the sentencing hearing on the assumption that an unadorned acknowledgement of respondent's responsibility for his crimes would be more likely to appeal to the trial judge, who was reputed to respect persons who accepted responsibility for their actions. But however justifiable such a choice might have been after counsel had fairly assessed the potential strength of the mitigating evidence available to him, counsel's failure to make any significant effort to find out what evidence might be garnered from respondent's relatives and acquaintances surely cannot be described as "reasonable." Counsel's failure to investigate is particularly suspicious in light of his candid admission that respondent's confessions and conduct in the course of the trial gave him a feeling of "hopelessness" regarding the possibility of saving respondent's life. . . .

That the aggravating circumstances implicated by respondent's criminal conduct were substantial . . . does not vitiate respondent's constitutional claim; judges and juries in cases involving behavior at least as egregious have shown mercy, particularly when afforded an opportunity to see other facets of the defendant's personality and life. Nor is respondent's contention defeated by the possibility that the material his counsel turned up might not have been sufficient to establish a *statutory* mitigating circumstance under Florida law; Florida sentencing judges and the Florida Supreme Court sometimes refuse to impose death sentences in cases "in which, even though *statutory* mitigating circumstances do not outweigh statutory aggravating circumstances, the addition of nonstatutory mitigating circumstances tips the scales in favor of life imprisonment." Barclay v. Florida, 463 U.S. 939, 964 (Stevens, J., concurring in the judgment) (emphasis in original).

If counsel had investigated the availability of mitigating evidence, he might well have decided to present some such material at the hearing. If he had done so, there is a significant chance that respondent would have been given a life sentence. In my view, those possibilities, conjoined with the unreasonableness of counsel's failure to investigate, are more than sufficient to establish a violation of the Sixth Amendment and to entitle respondent to a new sentencing proceeding.

I respectfully dissent.

NOTES AND QUESTIONS

1. The majority and dissent disagree on the role of the defendant's probable guilt and whether the purported error likely would have affected the outcome. What do you think of the dissenters' argument that these factors are largely irrelevant? What is the significance of these two points? Is all well that ends well, or not? Does the majority's position overestimate the value of stability and finality or the minority's underestimate it?

2. Note that the *Strickland* majority has a complicated view of the question whether hindsight is appropriate in these cases. The Court states explicitly that attorney performance must *not* be judged in hindsight; lawyers' judgments are to be assessed according to how those judgments appeared at the time they were made. But the prejudice standard *is* applied with hindsight: The defendant cannot obtain relief unless he shows it is reasonably likely that his attorney's errors altered the outcome. This two-pronged approach rules out two kinds of claims. The first was mentioned in the preceding note: a claim by a defendant whose lawyer behaved incompetently but who would have been convicted (or, as in *Strickland*, sentenced to death) regardless. The second is a claim by a defendant whose lawyer made a reasonable (or perhaps only marginally negligent) mistake that cost her client the case. Justice Marshall's dissent in *Strickland* essentially argues that the defendant in the first case should get relief. Doesn't the second case deserve relief even more? What does that say about the relationship between attorney incompetence and prejudice, and about the role of the ineffective-assistance doctrine?

3. There are several categories where *Strickland*'s prejudice standard does not operate, because the Court has held that prejudice is presumed. These include: actual or constructive denial of counsel (as in *Gideon* or *Powell*); certain kinds of state interference with counsel (such as, e.g., refusing to allow counsel to meet with the defendant during an overnight recess, see Geders v. United States, 425 U.S. 80 (1976); and some situations involving attorney conflicts of interest, see infra, at page 196.

In United States v. Cronic, 466 U.S. 648 (1984), a companion case to *Strickland*, the Court defined one more "presumed prejudice" category: where "counsel failed to function in any meaningful sense as the government's adversary." What do you think that means?

The *Cronic* category potentially could have become very significant, but its scope has turned out to be quite limited. In Bell v. Cone, 535 U.S. 685 (2002), the Court explained *Cronic* as follows:

> In *Cronic*, we considered whether the Court of Appeals was correct in reversing a defendant's conviction under the Sixth Amendment without inquiring into counsel's actual performance or requiring the defendant to show the effect it had on the trial. We determined that the court had erred and remanded to allow the claim to be considered under *Strickland*'s test. In the course of deciding this question, we identified three situations implicating the right to counsel that involved circumstances "so likely to prejudice the accused that the cost of litigating their effect in a particular case is unjustified." [466 U.S.,] at 658-659.
>
> First and "[m]ost obvious" was the "complete denial of counsel." Id. at 659. A trial would be presumptively unfair, we said, where the accused is denied the presence of counsel at "a critical stage," id. at 659, a phrase we used . . . to denote a step of a criminal proceeding, such as arraignment, that held significant consequences for the accused. Second, we posited that a similar presumption was warranted if "counsel entirely fails to subject the prosecution's case to meaningful adversarial testing." [Id.] at 659. Finally, we said that in cases like Powell v. Alabama, 287 U.S. 45 (1932), where counsel is called upon to render assistance under circumstances where competent counsel very likely could not, the defendant need not show that the proceedings were affected. *Cronic*, supra, at 659-662.

The defendant in *Bell* was convicted of robbery and capital murder, and sentenced to death. At the sentencing proceeding, defense counsel cross-examined government witnesses but called no defense witnesses, referring instead to the evidence introduced at trial in support of defendant's insanity claim. Defense counsel also waived closing argument, ostensibly to avoid giving the prosecutor a chance to argue in rebuttal. Defendant argued that this amounted to a "fail[ure] to subject the prosecution's case to meaningful adversarial testing," and so amounted to ineffective assistance of counsel without regard to whether there was any prejudice. With only Justice Stevens dissenting, the Court disagreed:

> . . . When we spoke in *Cronic* of the possibility of presuming prejudice based on an attorney's failure to test the prosecutor's case, we indicated that the attorney's failure must be complete. . . . Here, respondent's argument is not that his counsel failed to oppose the prosecution throughout the sentencing proceeding as a whole, but that his counsel failed to do so at specific points. For purposes of distinguishing between the rule of *Strickland* and that of *Cronic*, this difference is not of degree but of kind. . . .
>
> We hold, therefore, that the state correctly identified the principles announced in *Strickland* as those governing the analysis of respondent's claim.

Given the analysis in *Bell*, one suspects that successful *Cronic* claims will be rare. Lower-court cases generally confirm this observation: The number of reported *Strickland* claims is enormous — *Strickland* claims are probably the single largest category of criminal procedure claims — while the number of *Cronic* claims is very small.

4. *Strickland* involved a capital sentencing hearing, and the Court concluded that such hearings should not be treated differently from trials on the merits for purposes of effective assistance of counsel. Are you convinced? Should counsel at capital sentencing hearings be held to a higher standard than counsel at trial? For discussions, see Stephen B. Bright, Counsel for the Poor: The Death Sentence Not for the Worst Crime But for the Worst Lawyer, 103 Yale L.J. 1835 (1994); and Welsh S. White, Effective Assistance of Counsel in Capital Cases: The Evolving Standard of Care, [1993] U. Ill. L. Rev. 323 (both answering "yes").

Consider Williams v. Taylor, 529 U.S. 362 (2000). As in *Strickland,* the defendant in *Williams* was convicted of capital murder; also as in *Strickland,* Williams's ineffective-assistance claim focused on what defense counsel did, and failed to do, at the subsequent capital sentencing proceeding:

> The evidence offered by Williams's trial counsel at the sentencing hearing consisted of the testimony of Williams' mother, two neighbors, and a taped excerpt from a statement by a psychiatrist. One of the neighbors had not been previously interviewed by defense counsel, but was noticed by counsel in the audience during the proceedings and asked to testify on the spot. The three witnesses briefly described Williams as a "nice boy" and not a violent person. The recorded psychiatrist's testimony did little more than relate Williams's statement during an examination that in the course of one of his earlier robberies, he had removed the bullets from a gun so as not to injure anyone.
>
> In his cross-examination of the prosecution witnesses, Williams' counsel repeatedly emphasized the fact that Williams had initiated the contact with the police that enabled them to solve the murder and to identify him as the perpetrator of the recent assaults, as well as the car thefts. In closing argument, Williams' counsel characterized Williams' confessional statements as "dumb," but asked the jury to give weight to the fact that he had "turned himself in, not on one crime but on four . . . that the [police otherwise] would not have solved." The weight of defense counsel's closing, however, was devoted to explaining that it was difficult to find a reason why the jury should spare Williams' life.

Id. at 1500. That is what Williams's lawyer did; here is the Court's account of what he failed to do:

> . . . [Counsel] failed to conduct an investigation that would have uncovered extensive records graphically describing Williams' nightmarish childhood, not because of any strategic calculation but because they incorrectly thought that state law barred access to such records. Had they done so, the jury would have learned that Williams' parents had been imprisoned for the criminal neglect of Williams and his siblings, that Williams had been severely and repeatedly beaten by his father, that he had been committed to the custody of the social services bureau for two years during his parents' incarceration (including one stint in an abusive foster home), and then, after his parents were released from prison, had been returned to his parents' custody.
>
> Counsel failed to introduce available evidence that Williams was "borderline mentally retarded" and did not advance beyond sixth grade in school. They failed to seek prison records recording Williams' commendations for helping to crack a prison drug ring and for returning a guard's missing wallet, or the testimony of prison officials who described Williams as among the inmates "least likely to act in a violent, dangerous or provocative way." Counsel failed even to return the phone call of a certified public accountant who had offered to testify that he had visited Williams frequently

when Williams was incarcerated as part of a prison ministry program, that Williams "seemed to thrive in a more regimented and structured environment," and that Williams was proud of the carpentry degree he earned while in prison.

Of course, not all of the additional evidence was favorable to Williams. The juvenile records revealed that he had been thrice committed to the juvenile system — for aiding and abetting larceny when he was 11 years old, for pulling a false fire alarm when he was 12, and for breaking and entering when he was 15. But as the Federal District Court correctly observed, the failure to introduce the . . . voluminous amount of evidence that did speak in Williams' favor was not justified by a tactical decision to focus on Williams' voluntary confession. Whether or not those omissions were sufficiently prejudicial to have affected the outcome of sentencing, they clearly demonstrate that trial counsel did not fulfill their obligation to conduct a thorough investigation of the defendant's background. . . .

Id. at 1514-1515. And here is the Court's analysis of prejudice in *Williams*:

We are also persuaded . . . that counsel's unprofessional service prejudiced Williams within the meaning of *Strickland*. . . .

. . . Williams turned himself in, alerting police to a crime they otherwise would never have discovered, expressing remorse for his actions, and cooperating with the police after that. While this, coupled with the prison records and guard testimony, may not have overcome a finding of future dangerousness, the graphic description of Williams' childhood, filled with abuse and privation, or the reality that he was "borderline mentally retarded," might well have influenced the jury's appraisal of his moral culpability. The circumstances recited in his several confessions are consistent with the view that in each case his violent behavior was a compulsive reaction rather than the product of cold-blooded premeditation. Mitigating evidence unrelated to dangerousness may alter the jury's selection of penalty, even if it does not undermine or rebut the prosecution's death-eligibility case. . . .

Id. at 1515-1516. Is the Court's analysis in *Williams* consistent with *Strickland*? Is it consistent with the kind of analysis one would use with a claim that counsel behaved incompetently at trial?

In Wiggins v. Smith, 539 U.S. 510 (2003), the Court, by a 7–2 majority, similarly found both inadequate performance and prejudice based on a capital defense lawyer's failure to investigate mitigating evidence. In an interesting twist, the Court did not rest its decision on the complete failure of investigation, as counsel had done some, but instead found that the scope of investigation was inadequate. What do you think of this? On the one hand, the level of competence in many death penalty trials and sentencing hearings is appallingly low, and thus any boost given to it is plausibly defensible. On the other hand, does this permit, indeed as a matter of constitutional law mandate, every decision that counsel makes concerning the allocation of time and resources to investigative efforts to be second-guessed by the federal courts, thus further increasing the instability of decisions?

5. In Roe v. Flores-Ortega, 528 U.S. 470 (2000), the Court considered the implications of *Strickland* for postsentencing advice concerning the right to appeal and the necessity for the timely filing of a notice of appeal. The filing deadline had passed, and the facts were ambiguous as to whether counsel had consulted with the client about the appellate process or advised him of his need to file the notice of

appeal. The Court held that the *Strickland* standards applied, and that, with respect to the performance prong, flat rules concerning consultation were not constitutionally justifiable. Nonetheless, the Court opined that "[I]f counsel has consulted with the defendant, the question of deficient performance is easily answered: Counsel performs in a professionally unreasonable manner only by failing to follow the defendant's express instructions with respect to an appeal." What if counsel had not consulted with the client? Again, no flat rules exist, according to the Court, but: "We instead hold that counsel has a constitutionally imposed duty to consult with the defendant about an appeal where there is reason to think either (1) that a rational defendant would want to appeal (for example, because there are nonfrivolous grounds for appeal, or (2) that this particular defendant reasonably demonstrated to counsel that he was interested in appealing." As to prejudice, if the failure to consult deprives an individual of the right to appeal, prejudice will be presumed if the defendant demonstrates "that there is a reasonable probability that, but for counsel's deficient failure to consult with him about an appeal, he would have timely appealed."

6. In Hill v. Lockhart, 477 U.S. 52 (1985), the defendant alleged that his guilty plea was involuntary as a result of ineffective assistance of counsel because he received erroneous information about his parole eligibility from his counsel. Counsel advised the defendant that he would have to serve one-third of his time before he would be eligible for parole, whereas in fact he had to serve one-half of his time as a result of a previous conviction, of which counsel was apparently not informed by the defendant. In applying *Strickland* to this case, the Court concluded that "in order to satisfy the 'prejudice' requirement, the defendant must show that there is a reasonable probability that, but for counsel's errors, he would not have pleaded guilty and would have insisted on going to trial."

Hill says that *Strickland*'s prejudice standard means the same thing in guilty plea cases as in cases that go to trial. But there is a kind of outcome effect in guilty plea cases that has no analogue for cases that go to trial. Many, perhaps most, guilty pleas are the product of bargaining. It is likely that in many of these cases attorney errors will not affect whether the defendant will plead guilty, but *will* affect the terms of the plea agreement — the charge, the prosecutor's sentencing recommendation, and so forth. Under *Hill*, those sorts of outcome effects apparently don't count, because the defendant cannot show that but for the attorney error he "would not have pleaded guilty and would have insisted on going to trial." Is that the right result? Is it consistent with *Strickland*? *Hill* is considered in greater detail in Chapter 10 infra.

7. In Cuyler v. Sullivan, 446 U.S. 335 (1980), the Court held that ineffective assistance by retained counsel violated the constitutional right to counsel, thus disposing of the issue whether there is "state action" in such circumstances. Nonetheless, whatever the "state action" is in criminal cases generally, it is inadequate to permit an indigent to sue appointed counsel under 42 U.S.C. §1983 for damages resulting from allegedly ineffective assistance in derogation of the defendant's right to counsel. In Polk County v. Dodson, 454 U.S. 312 (1981), the Court held that an attorney engaged in representing a client does not act "under color of state law." Therefore, §1983 is not applicable. *Sullivan* is considered further at page 200 infra.

FURTHER NOTES ON THE PREJUDICE STANDARD

1. What is the lawyer's responsibility when dealing with possibly perjurious testimony? In Nix v. Whiteside, 475 U.S. 157 (1986), the defendant (Whiteside) was charged with murder. Initially, he told his court-appointed lawyer (Robinson) that he stabbed the victim while the victim was reaching for a gun. Upon further questioning, however, he admitted that he had not actually seen a gun. No gun was found at the crime scene, and none of the other witnesses reported seeing a gun. About one week before the trial, Whiteside told Robinson that he had seen something "metallic" in the victim's hand. He added, "If I don't say I saw a gun I'm dead." Robinson informed Whiteside that this would be perjury, and that he would not assist in it. Robinson told Whiteside that if he insisted on perjuring himself, Robinson would advise the trial court about the perjury, impeach Whiteside's testimony, and withdraw from Whiteside's representation.

The Court split 5–4 on the application of *Strickland*'s performance prong to Robinson's conduct, with the dissent critical of Robinson for essentially "judging" his own client, but the majority finding Robinson's conduct acceptable under prevailing professional norms:

> . . . Considering Robinson's representation of respondent in light of the accepted norms of professional conduct, we discern no failure to adhere to reasonable professional standards that would in any sense make out a deprivation of the Sixth Amendment right to counsel. Whether Robinson's conduct is seen as a successful attempt to dissuade his client from committing the crime of perjury, or whether seen as a "threat" to withdraw from representation and disclose the illegal scheme, Robinson's representation of Whiteside falls well within accepted standards of professional conduct and the range of reasonable professional conduct acceptable under *Strickland*. . . .
>
> Whatever the scope of a constitutional right to testify, it is elementary that such a right does not extend to testifying *falsely*. In Harris v. New York, we assumed the right of an accused to testify "in his own defense, or to refuse to do so" and went on to hold that "that privilege cannot be construed to include the right to commit perjury. Having voluntarily taken the stand, petitioner was under an obligation to speak truthfully. . . ." 401 U.S., at 225. In *Harris* we held the defendant could be impeached by prior contrary statements which had been ruled inadmissible under Miranda v. Arizona. *Harris* and other cases make it crystal clear that there is no right whatever—constitutional or otherwise—for a defendant to use false evidence. . . .
>
> Robinson's admonitions to his client can in no sense be said to have forced respondent into an *impermissible* choice between his right to counsel and his right to testify as he proposed for there was no *permissible* choice to testify falsely. For defense counsel to take steps to persuade a criminal defendant to testify truthfully, or to withdraw, deprives the defendant of neither his right to counsel nor the right to testify truthfully. In United States v. Havens we made clear that "when defendants testify, they must testify truthfully or suffer the consequences." When an accused proposes to resort to perjury or to produce false evidence, one consequence is the risk of withdrawal of counsel.

All nine Justices agreed, however, that whether or not Robinson's performance was adequate, Whiteside could not have suffered "prejudice," within the meaning of *Strickland*. According to the majority:

> We hold that, as a matter of law, counsel's conduct complained of here cannot establish the prejudice required for relief under the second strand of the *Strickland*

inquiry. . . . The *Strickland* Court noted that the "benchmark" of an ineffective assistance claim is the fairness of the adversary proceeding, and that in judging prejudice and the likelihood of a different outcome, "[a] defendant has no entitlement to the luck of a lawless decisionmaker." . . .

In his attempt to evade the prejudice requirement of *Strickland,* Whiteside relies on cases involving conflicting loyalties of counsel. [See, e.g.,] Cuyler v. Sullivan, 446 U.S. 335 (1980). . . . Here, there was indeed a "conflict," but of a quite different kind; it was one imposed on the attorney by the client's proposal to commit the crime of fabricating testimony without which, as he put it, "I'm dead." . . . If a "conflict" between a client's proposal and counsel's ethical obligation gives rise to a presumption that counsel's assistance was prejudicially ineffective, every guilty criminal's conviction would be suspect if the defendant had sought to obtain an acquittal by illegal means. Can anyone doubt what practices and problems would be spawned by such a rule and what volumes of litigation it would generate?

Whether he was persuaded or compelled to desist from perjury, Whiteside has no valid claim that confidence in the result of his trial has been diminished by his desisting from the contemplated perjury. Even if we were to assume that the jury might have believed his perjury, it does not follow that Whiteside was prejudiced. . . .

Whiteside's attorney treated Whiteside's proposed perjury in accord with professional standards, and since Whiteside's truthful testimony could not have prejudiced the result of his trial, the Court of Appeals was in error to direct the issuance of a writ of habeas corpus and must be reversed.

2. What effect did *Nix* have on the meaning of *Strickland*'s "prejudice" requirement? The one proposition that all nine Justices agreed on in *Nix* was that the failure to use perjured testimony cannot satisfy that requirement. Why not? Preventing client perjury can of course affect the outcome of a case — indeed, affecting the outcome is presumably the entire point of the perjury. Yet all the Justices were prepared to hold that even if attorney Robinson's performance violated constitutional standards, and apparently even if his performance led to Whiteside's conviction, Whiteside suffered no Sixth Amendment prejudice. This position suggests that *Strickland* prejudice requires more than that attorney ineffectiveness have an effect on the outcome of the case; it requires the *right kind* of outcome effect.

What kind of outcome effect counts? The idea seems to be that preventing perjured testimony by the defendant is not the sort of thing that leads to an unjust result, regardless of what one thinks of defense counsel's conduct. But what does "unjust" mean in this context? Must a defendant show a reasonable probability that he is innocent?

3. In Kimmelman v. Morrison, 477 U.S. 365 (1986), decided the same Term as *Nix,* the Court "decline[d] to hold either that the guarantee of effective assistance of counsel belongs solely to the innocent or that it attaches only to matters affecting the determination of actual guilt." Id. at 380. If innocence and guilt are not the focus, what is?

Neil Morrison was charged with rape. A key piece of evidence was a bedsheet seized from Morrison's apartment in the course of an apparently illegal search. Morrison's lawyer did not file a timely motion to suppress the bedsheet and accompanying test results; the evidence came in, and Morrison was convicted. The Supreme Court then held that Morrison had satisfied *Strickland*'s performance prong, and remanded for factual findings on prejudice; the prejudice discussion suggests that if Morrison's Fourth Amendment claim would have won, and if there is a reasonable probability that admitting the bedsheet changed the outcome, *Strickland*'s prejudice requirement would be satisfied. *Kimmelman*, 477 U.S. at 387-390. Justice Powell, joined by Chief Justice Burger and Justice Rehnquist, wrote separately, arguing that "the admission of illegally seized but reliable evidence does not lead to an unjust or fundamentally unfair verdict," id. at 396, and thus that there could be no Sixth Amendment prejudice in a case of this sort. (Powell nevertheless concurred in the Court's judgment, on the ground that the argument just noted was not raised by the government at any stage of the litigation.)

As Powell noted, there was no claim in *Kimmelman* that the bedsheet, along with lab tests performed on it, was anything other than reliable evidence. How is the admission of reliable evidence different from the exclusion of unreliable evidence, which is essentially what happened in *Nix*? Is there any definition of *Strickland* prejudice that makes sense of both *Nix* and *Kimmelman*? *Kimmelman* itself does not offer any answer: neither Powell's opinion nor the *Kimmelman* majority mentions *Nix*. Does the answer lie in the nature of legal representation, that it is one thing to have an advocate who will ensure that the game is played by the rules but quite another to have one who declines to follow them?

4. What are the implications of Lockhart v. Fretwell, 506 U.S. 364 (1993)? In *Lockhart,* the defendant was convicted and sentenced to death for a robbery-murder. One of the aggravating factors found by the jury at the capital sentencing proceeding was that the murder had been committed for pecuniary gain. This essentially duplicated the finding by the same jury at the guilt phase of the proceeding: Fretwell was convicted of felony murder, and the underlying felony was robbery. Under then-governing Eighth Circuit law, this duplication was constitutionally impermissible, so that Fretwell would have been legally entitled to have his death sentence overturned. But defense counsel did not object to the pecuniary gain aggravating factor. Fretwell claimed that this oversight amounted to ineffective assistance. By the time his ineffective assistance claim was litigated on habeas, however, an intervening Supreme Court case had caused the Eighth Circuit to change its rule, so that duplicative aggravating factors became permissible. In other words, Fretwell would have won his case (and thereby avoided a death sentence) had his attorney made the right argument at the time he was sentenced, but because of the delay, the same argument lost on habeas review (and would still lose, if it were raised today).

Both sides agreed that defense counsel's performance fell below *Strickland*'s standard, so the litigation focused on prejudice. The Supreme Court, in an opinion by Chief Justice Rehnquist, held that the prejudice requirement had not been met, even though his lawyer's error had probably affected the outcome of Fretwell's capital sentencing proceeding:

> . . . [A]n analysis focussing solely on mere outcome determination, without attention to whether the result of the proceeding was fundamentally unfair or unreliable, is defective. To set aside a conviction or sentence solely because the outcome would have been different but for counsel's error may grant the defendant a windfall to which the law does not entitle him.
>
> Our decision in Nix v. Whiteside makes this very point. The respondent in that case argued that he received ineffective assistance because his counsel refused to

cooperate in presenting perjured testimony. Obviously, had the respondent presented false testimony to the jury, there might have been a reasonable probability that the jury would not have returned a verdict of guilty. Sheer outcome determination, however, was not sufficient to make out a claim under the Sixth Amendment. We held that "as a matter of law, counsel's conduct . . . cannot establish the prejudice required for relief under the second strand of the *Strickland* inquiry." 475 U.S., at 175. The touchstone of an ineffective assistance claim is the fairness of the adversary proceeding, and "in judging prejudice and the likelihood of a different outcome, '[a] defendant has no entitlement to the luck of a lawless decisionmaker.' " Ibid. (quoting *Strickland,* 466 U.S., at 695).

506 U.S. at 370.

The Court concluded that "[t]he result of the sentencing proceeding in the present case was neither unfair nor unreliable." Id. Interestingly, though *Nix* was extensively cited and discussed, *Kimmelman* was hardly mentioned.

What does "prejudice" mean now? Is there a difference between being deprived of an unjustified windfall and the failure to get the advantage of the benefits the law bestows?

5. In another recent foray into this area, Williams v. Taylor [for the facts of *Williams,* see Note 4, supra page 185], the Court discussed the relationship among *Strickland, Lockhart,* and *Nix*:

> The Virginia Supreme Court erred in holding that our decision in Lockhart v. Fretwell modified or in some way supplanted the rule set down in *Strickland.* It is true that while the *Strickland* test provides sufficient guidance for resolving virtually all ineffective-assistance-of-counsel claims, there are situations in which the overriding focus on fundamental fairness may affect the analysis. Thus, on the one hand, as *Strickland* itself explained, there are a few situations in which prejudice may be presumed. And, on the other hand, there are also situations in which it would be unjust to characterize the likelihood of a different outcome as legitimate "prejudice." Even if a defendant's false testimony might have persuaded the jury to acquit him, it is not fundamentally unfair to conclude that he was not prejudiced by counsel's interference with his intended perjury. Nix v. Whiteside.
>
> Similarly, in *Lockhart,* we concluded that, given the overriding interest in fundamental fairness, the likelihood of a different outcome attributable to an incorrect interpretation of the law should be regarded as a potential "windfall" to the defendant rather than the legitimate "prejudice" contemplated by our opinion in *Strickland.* . . . Because the ineffectiveness of Fretwell's counsel had not deprived him of any substantive or procedural right to which the law entitled him, we held that his claim did not satisfy the "prejudice" component of the *Strickland* test.
>
> Cases such as Nix v. Whiteside and Lockhart v. Fretwell do not justify a departure from a straightforward application of *Strickland* when the ineffectiveness of counsel does deprive the defendant of a substantive or procedural right to which the law entitles him. In the instant case, it is undisputed that Williams had a right — indeed, a constitutionally protected right — to provide the jury with the mitigating evidence that his trial counsel either failed to discover or failed to offer.

Are *Nix* and *Lockhart* now limited to their facts? Is the argument Justice Powell made in *Kimmelman* now dead?

6. Does Williams v. Taylor represent a change in direction in the Court's interpretation of *Strickland* prejudice? Consider Glover v. United States, 531 U.S. 198

(2001), where in a unanimous opinion delivered by Justice Kennedy the Court considered the kinds of errors in sentencing proceedings that might be deemed prejudicial enough to support an ineffective-assistance claim:

> The issue presented rests upon the initial assumption, which we accept for analytic purposes, that the trial court erred in a Sentencing Guidelines determination after petitioner's conviction of a federal offense. The legal error, petitioner alleges, increased his prison sentence by at least 6 months and perhaps by 21 months. We must decide whether this would be "prejudice" under Strickland v. Washington, 466 U.S. 668 (1984). The Government is not ready to concede error in the sentencing determination but now acknowledges that if an increased prison term did flow from an error the petitioner has established *Strickland* prejudice. In agreement with the Government and petitioner on this point, we reverse and remand for further proceedings. . . .

> [After his conviction was final, defendant filed a motion to correct his sentence, alleging ineffective assistance of counsel as the reason for the error]. The District Court denied Glover's motion [for resentencing], determining that under Seventh Circuit precedent an increase of 6 to 21 months in a defendant's sentence was not significant enough to amount to prejudice for purposes of Strickland v. Washington. . . .

> It appears the Seventh Circuit drew the substance of its no-prejudice rule from our opinion in Lockhart v. Fretwell. *Lockhart* holds that in some circumstances a mere difference in outcome will not suffice to establish prejudice. The Seventh Circuit extracted from this holding the rule at issue here, which denies relief when the increase in sentence is said to be not so significant as to render the outcome of sentencing unreliable or fundamentally unfair. The Court explained last Term that our holding in Lockhart does not supplant the *Strickland* analysis. The Seventh Circuit was incorrect to rely on *Lockhart* to deny relief to persons attacking their sentence who might show deficient performance in counsel's failure to object to an error of law affecting the calculation of a sentence because the sentence increase does not meet some baseline standard of prejudice. Authority does not suggest that a minimal amount of additional time in prison cannot constitute prejudice. Quite to the contrary, our jurisprudence suggests that any amount of actual jail time has Sixth Amendment significance. Compare Argersinger v. Hamlin, 407 U.S. 25 (1972) (holding that the assistance of counsel must be provided when a defendant is tried for a crime that results in a sentence of imprisonment), with Scott v. Illinois, 440 U.S. 367 (1979) (holding that a criminal defendant has no Sixth Amendment right to counsel when his trial does not result in a sentence of imprisonment). Our decisions on the right to jury trial in a criminal case do not suggest that there is no prejudice in the circumstances here. Those cases have limited the right to jury trial to offenses where the potential punishment was imprisonment for six months or more. See *Argersinger,* supra, at 29 (citing Duncan v. Louisiana, 391 U.S. 145 (1968)). But they do not control the question whether a showing of prejudice, in the context of a claim for ineffective assistance of counsel, requires a significant increase in a term of imprisonment.

> The Seventh Circuit's rule is not well considered in any event, because there is no obvious dividing line by which to measure how much longer a sentence must be for the increase to constitute substantial prejudice. Indeed, it is not even clear if the relevant increase is to be measured in absolute terms or by some fraction of the total authorized sentence. Although the amount by which a defendant's sentence is increased by a particular decision may be a factor to consider in determining

whether counsel's performance in failing to argue the point constitutes ineffective assistance, under a determinate system of constrained discretion such as the Sentencing Guidelines it cannot serve as a bar to a showing of prejudice. We hold that the Seventh Circuit erred in engrafting this additional requirement onto the prejudice branch of the *Strickland* test. This is not a case where trial strategies, in retrospect, might be criticized for leading to a harsher sentence. Here we consider the sentencing calculation itself, a calculation resulting from a ruling which, if it had been error, would have been correctable on appeal. We express no opinion on the ultimate merits of Glover's claim because the question of deficient performance is not before us, but it is clear that prejudice flowed from the asserted error in sentencing. . . .

After *Glover,* it would appear that any effect on the length of a prison or jail term constitutes *Strickland* prejudice. How does that square with the way trial errors are analyzed? Suppose defense counsel in *Glover* had made a mistake at Glover's trial; suppose further that the mistake had raised the odds of Glover's conviction by, say, 1 percent. Glover was then convicted. Presumably, counsel's error would not satisfy *Strickland*'s prejudice prong, because it did not raise a "reasonable probability" that, but for the error, the outcome would have been different.

Now suppose Glover's counsel's error cost Glover one extra month in prison — that, but for the error, Glover would have been sentenced to 83 months, instead of the 84-month sentence he actually received. Why does that extra month amount to prejudice, when adding 1 percent to the odds of conviction doesn't? And if the latter premise is wrong — if even a small increase in the odds of conviction does amount to prejudice — what is left of the "reasonable probability" standard? Perhaps these questions misconceive what is at stake in these cases. Perhaps the question to ask is whether the change in the probability of guilt plausibly could affect the conclusion of guilt beyond a reasonable doubt. If so, the error would be prejudicial; if not, it would not be. This harmonizes the line of cases, although it is by no means clear that this is what the Court had in mind.

Note, incidentally, that *Glover*-type ineffectiveness claims would seem to be plausible only where the defendant is deprived, as a result of his lawyer's mistake, of a particular sentence (or sentencing range) to which he is legally entitled. This, in turn, is likely to be true only where the sentence is determinate, as opposed to broadly discretionary. Otherwise, it would be very difficult for the reviewing court to say that the lawyer's mistake made a "reasonable probability" of a difference in the sentencing outcome. For more on determinate sentencing and its consequences, see infra, Chapter 13.

FURTHER NOTES ON THE PERFORMANCE STANDARD

1. What is wrong with articulating a basic checklist of obligations for counsel and enforcing it in an appropriate fashion? The first suggestion of that idea was Joseph D. Grano, The Right to Counsel: Collateral Issues Affecting Due Process, 54 Minn. L. Rev. 1175, 1248 (1970). Judge David L. Bazelon developed Grano's suggestion in his article, The Realities of *Gideon* and *Argersinger,* 64 Geo. L.J. 811 (1976). Consider his proposed list, id. at 837-838:

PRELIMINARY HEARING _____

Date

_____

Comments

_____
_____
_____
_____
_____

	Official Records	*Obtained**
1.	Complaint	_____
2.	Bail Agency form	_____
3.	Narcotics Treatment Ad. report	_____
4.	Arrest warrant (affidavit)	_____
5.	Search warrant (affidavit)	_____
6.	Defendant's record	_____
7.	PD 251	_____
8.	PD 252, 253, 254	_____
9.	PD 163	_____
10.	Other _____	_____

	Statements	*Obtained**
1.	Written	_____
2.	Oral	_____
3.	Co-defendant	_____

	Scientific Exams	AUSA *Requested*	*Obtained**
1.	Mental	_____	_____
2.	Fingerprints	_____	_____
3.	Blood	_____	_____
4.	Semen	_____	_____
5.	Hair	_____	_____
6.	Fiber	_____	_____
7.	Pathologist	_____	_____
8.	Ballistics	_____	_____
9.	Chemist report	_____	_____
10.	Handwriting	_____	_____
11.	Other _____	_____	_____

	Police Officer Witnesses	*Name & Precinct*	*Interview Obtained**
1.	Arresting Officer	_____	_____
2.	Mobile Crime Lab	_____	_____
3.	Invest. Officer	_____	_____
4.	Line-Up Officer	_____	_____
5.	Search Officer	_____	_____
6.	Confession Officer	_____	_____

	Other Witnesses	*Name & Address*	*Interview Obtained**
1.	Victim	_____	_____
2.	Eyewitnesses	_____	_____
3.	Other	_____	_____

Motions to be Filed (check) Comments

_____1. Suppression of Tangible Object _____

_____

_____2. Suppression of Statements _____

_____

_____3. Identification _____

_____

_____4. Severance _____

_____

_____5. Notice of Alibi _____

_____

_____6. Notice of Insanity Defense _____

_____

_____7. Mental Competency Exam _____

_____

_____8. Bond Review _____

_____

_____9. Other _____

_____

Defendant's Version of Events _____

_____

_____

_____

_____

I hereby certify that the case referred to in the above work-sheet has been completely investigated and information contained therein and attached thereto is accurate to the best of my knowledge.

Date _____ *Attorney's Signature* _____

*Attached is a copy of all statements, oral or written, obtained by counsel, all documents, reports, interviews, and other materials received in the preparation of this case. A completed time sheet is also to be maintained for purposes of administrative records.

2. The attorney performance standard adopted by *Strickland* rejects the idea of adopting a checklist of this sort. Instead, the Court adopts a reasonableness standard. But "reasonableness" in this context seems to mean something other than ordinary negligence: The Court's discussion suggests something more like a gross negligence standard. Why such a deferential approach? Why not hold defense counsel to a tougher standard? What would the consequences of doing so be for the independence of defense counsel, the attorney-client relationship, and functions of an adversary system?

2.   Multiple Representation

A special problem of effective assistance arises in cases in which a lawyer represents more than one client in either joint or separate proceedings. The difficulty results from the potential conflict of interest among the defendants. In separate trials of accomplices, for example, a lawyer will have to choose whether to call certain potentially exculpating witnesses at the first trial. If the lawyer chooses not to call the witnesses, the defense in the present case will be impaired in order to protect the defense in the later trial. If, on the other hand, the witnesses are called, the defense at the first trial will be bolstered at the cost to the defense at the second trial of exposing to the prosecution the contents of the defendant's case. Moreover, it is the lawyer, who owes the duty of essentially undivided allegiance to the client, who will have to make the choices. Obviously, the necessity of making such choices compromises the faithful discharge of the duty and may impact adversely on the client's interests.

The problems are exacerbated in joint proceedings. Consider the following passage from Gary T. Lowenthal, Joint Representation in Criminal Cases: A Critical Appraisal, 64 Va. L. Rev. 939, 941-942 (1978):

> An attorney appeared in a municipal court for the purpose of requesting a reduction of bail for four defendants jointly charged with possession of a large cache of drugs seized from a communal house. Referring to the first of his clients, the lawyer stated: "This defendant should be released on his own recognizance, Your Honor, because he has no rap sheet. Obviously he is not a hardened criminal and should not be locked up with others who are." When the second defendant's case was called, counsel argued: "No drugs were found in this defendant's bedroom, Your Honor. His chance for an acquittal is great and consequently it is highly likely that he will show up for trial." On behalf of the third defendant, the lawyer began to argue that his client had lived in the area all of his life. The judge interrupted the lawyer, asking him if any drugs had been seized from the bedroom of defendant number three. The lawyer responded. "No comment, Your Honor." The judge countered with the remark: "I suppose that this client also has a prior record, making him a hardened criminal," evoking the response that although the defendant had a prior record, he certainly was not a hardened criminal. The fourth defendant then interrupted the proceedings by eagerly requesting to be represented by the public defender.[11] . . .

---

11. This incident occurred in March 1972, before Judge Jacqueline Taber in Department Six of the Oakland-Piedmont Municipal Court, Oakland, California, when I was an Assistant Public Defender for Alameda County, California. See Letter from Judge Jacqueline Taber to Gary T. Lowenthal (Oct. 23, 1978) (copy on file with the Virginia Law Review Association). It is the most vivid of many such incidents that prompted me to write this article.

The episode related above illustrates a circumstance of the criminal process that is essential to an understanding of joint representation in practice. Decisionmakers exercise considerable discretion in evaluating and comparing defendants at every stage of a criminal case. The government, for example, has substantial leeway in determining which charges, if any, to file against an accused; a judge or magistrate may consider a broad range of factors when predicting whether a defendant will appear in court if released on bail; the prosecutor's discretion in plea bargaining is almost unlimited in most jurisdictions; a trier of fact is free to ignore the evidence in acquitting the defendant; and a judge or jury is expected to differentiate among convicted offenders to arrive at an appropriate sentence for each. At each step in the process, a defendant's appearance, attitude, and background, as well as the extent of his culpability, will influence decisionmakers. As a result, a lawyer's effectiveness in representing a client will depend in virtually every case on how well he can manipulate these factors to the advantage of the client. Thus the lawyer must differentiate his client from others charged with the same or similar conduct and emphasize those attributes of his client that will have a favorable effect on the prosecutor, judge, or jury.

As Professor Lowenthal proceeds to point out in great detail, the ability of the lawyer to distinguish one client from another is greatly compromised in cases of joint representation. Yet joint representation may offer advantages at times. As Justice Frankfurter noted: "Joint representation is a means of insuring against reciprocal recrimination. A common defense often gives strength against a common attack." Glasser v. United States, 315 U.S. 60, 92 (1942) (Frankfurter, J., dissenting). The question thus arises whether there are circumstances that render joint representation so defective as to violate the right to counsel, and at least where joint representation is forced on defendants, the answer is yes.

The seminal decision is Glasser v. United States, supra, which is concisely summarized in the second major Supreme Court opinion analyzing these problems, Holloway v. Arkansas, 435 U.S. 475 (1978):

> More than 35 years ago, in Glasser v. United States, 315 U.S. 60 (1942), this Court held that by requiring an attorney to represent two codefendants whose interests were in conflict the District Court had denied one of the defendants his Sixth Amendment right to the effective assistance of counsel. In that case the Government tried five codefendants in a joint trial for conspiracy to defraud the United States. Two of the defendants, Glasser and Kretske, were represented initially by separate counsel. On the second day of trial, however, Kretske became dissatisfied with his attorney and dismissed him. The District Judge thereupon asked Glasser's attorney, Stewart, if he would also represent Kretske. Stewart responded by noting a possible conflict of interests: His representation of both Glasser and Kretske might lead the jury to link the two men together. Glasser also made known that he objected to the proposal. The District Court nevertheless appointed Stewart, who continued as Glasser's retained counsel, to represent Kretske. Both men were convicted.
>
>   Glasser contended in this Court that Stewart's representation at trial was ineffective because of a conflict between the interests of his two clients. This Court held that "the 'assistance of counsel' guaranteed by the Sixth Amendment contemplates that such assistance be untrammeled and unimpaired by a court order requiring that one lawyer should simultaneously represent conflicting interests." Id., at 70. The record disclosed that Stewart failed to cross-examine a Government witness whose testimony linked Glasser with the conspiracy and failed to object to the admission of arguably inadmissible evidence. This failure was viewed by the Court as a result of Stewart's desire to protect Kretske's interests, and was thus "indicative of Stewart's struggle to serve two

masters. . . . " Id., at 75. After identifying this conflict of interests, the Court declined to inquire whether the prejudice flowing from it was harmless and instead ordered Glasser's conviction reversed.

In *Holloway*, the Court reversed a conviction on the basis of *Glasser* in circumstances that effectively highlight the difficulties of joint. In *Holloway*, a single public defender was appointed to represent three co-defendants. Counsel moved the court to appoint separate counsel because of a possibility of conflict of interest. He later renewed his motion "on the grounds that one or two of the defendants may testify and, if they do, then I will not be able to cross-examine them because I have received confidential information from them." To which, the trial court responded: "I don't know why you wouldn't," and denied the motion. 435 U.S. at 478. Now, consider the following dialogue:

> On the second day of trial, after the prosecution had rested its case, Hall [trial counsel] advised the court that, against his recommendation, all three defendants had decided to testify. He then stated:
>
>> Now, since I have been appointed, I had previously filed a motion asking the Court to appoint a separate attorney for each defendant because of a possible conflict of interest. This conflict will probably be now coming up since each one of them wants to testify.
>>
>> *The Court:* That's all right; let them testify. There is no conflict of interest. Every time I try more than one person in this court each one blames it on the other one.
>>
>> *Mr. Hall:* I have talked to each one of these defendants, and I have talked to them individually, not collectively.
>>
>> *The Court:* Now talk to them collectively.

The court then indicated satisfaction that each petitioner understood the nature and consequences of his right to testify on his own behalf, whereupon Hall observed:

>> I am in a position now where I am more or less muzzled as to any cross-examination.
>>
>> *The Court:* You have no right to cross-examine your own witness.
>>
>> *Mr. Hall:* Or to examine them.
>>
>> *The Court:* You have a right to examine them, but have no right to cross-examine them. The prosecuting attorney does that.
>>
>> *Mr. Hall:* If one [defendant] takes the stand, somebody needs to protect the other two's interest while that one is testifying, and I can't do that since I have talked to each one individually.
>>
>> *The Court:* Well, you have talked to them, I assume, individually and collectively, too. They all say they want to testify. I think it's perfectly alright [*sic*] for them to testify if they want to, or not. It's their business. . . . Each defendant said he wants to testify, and there will be no cross-examination of these witnesses, just a direct examination by you.
>>
>> *Mr. Hall:* Your Honor, I can't even put them on direct examination because if I ask them —
>>
>> *The Court:* (Interposing) You can just put them on the stand and tell the Court that you have advised them of their rights and they want to testify;

then you tell the man to go ahead and relate what he wants to. That's all you need to do.

Holloway took the stand on his own behalf, testifying that during the time described as the time of the robbery he was at his brother's home. His brother had previously given similar testimony. When Welch, a codefendant, took the witness stand, the record shows Hall advised him, as he had Holloway, that "I cannot ask you any questions that might tend to incriminate any one of the three of you. . . . Now, the only thing I can say is tell these ladies and gentlemen of the jury what you know about this case." Welch responded that he did not "have any kind of speech ready for the jury or anything. I thought I was going to be questioned." When Welch denied, from the witness stand, that he was at the restaurant the night of the robbery, Holloway interrupted, asking:

> Your Honor, are we allowed to make an objection?
> *The Court:*   No, sir. Your counsel will take care of any objections.
> *Mr. Hall:*   Your Honor, that is what I am trying to say. I can't cross-examine them.
> *The Court:*   You proceed like I tell you to, Mr. Hall. You have no right to cross-examine your own witness anyhow. [Id. at 478-480.]

Because of the actions of the trial court in *Holloway,* the Supreme Court reversed, but its opinion is unenlightening in several crucial respects, as is summarized by Professor Peter Tague in Multiple Representation and Conflicts of Interest in Criminal Cases, 67 Geo. L.J. 1075, 1086-1087 (1979):

> The decisions in both *Glasser* and *Holloway,* however, begged the crucial issue of identifying what acts or omissions by a trial judge "force" counsel on an unwilling defendant. Although the remarkable insensitivity of the Arkansas trial judge made the Court's decision to reverse understandable, the Court left the role of counsel and of the trial court undefined. What must counsel do to trigger the trial court's obligation to inquire? Is it enough if counsel identifies the nature of the conflict in generic terms, as Hall had done, or must counsel identify the relevant disciplinary rules or facts that create the conflict? With respect to counsel's obligation to identify the conflict, for example, the Court said that Hall could have explained the conflict more clearly, but did not indicate what other information would have proven helpful or how far Hall could have gone without violating the attorney-client privilege. Further, must the trial court accept counsel's claim that a conflict exists or may it probe to satisfy itself that a conflict does exist? If the trial court may inquire, may it question the defendants as well as counsel? On these points, the Court vacillated. Although it approved accepting counsel's claim and appointing separate counsel without inquiry, it did not "preclude" inquiry into the sufficiency of counsel's representations. If the court can inquire, what does it do if met with counsel's refusal to amplify his claim on the ground of privilege? Similarly, the Court did not address whether the trial court could evaluate the conflict, as stated by counsel or as inferred by the court, to determine if it was de minimis on the facts of the given case and therefore did not require separate counsel.

How many of those questions did the Court answer two years later?

CUYLER v. SULLIVAN

Certiorari to the United States Court of Appeals for the Third Circuit
446 U.S. 335 (1980)

MR. JUSTICE POWELL delivered the opinion of the Court.

I

Respondent John Sullivan was indicted with Gregory Carchidi and Anthony DiPasquale for the first-degree murders of John Gorey and Rita Janda. The victims, a labor official and his companion, were shot to death in Gorey's second-story office at the Philadelphia headquarters of Teamsters' Local 107. Francis McGrath, a janitor, saw the three defendants in the building just before the shooting. They appeared to be awaiting someone, and they encouraged McGrath to do his work on another day. McGrath ignored their suggestions. Shortly afterward, Gorey arrived and went to his office. McGrath then heard what sounded like firecrackers exploding in rapid succession. Carchidi, who was in the room where McGrath was working, abruptly directed McGrath to leave the building and to say nothing. McGrath hastily complied. When he returned to the building about 15 minutes later, the defendants were gone. The victims' bodies were discovered the next morning.

Two privately retained lawyers, G. Fred DiBona and A. Charles Peruto, represented all three defendants throughout the state proceedings that followed the indictment. Sullivan had different counsel at the medical examiner's inquest, but he thereafter accepted representation from the two lawyers retained by his codefendants because he could not afford to pay his own lawyer.[1] At no time did Sullivan or his lawyers object to the multiple representation. Sullivan was the first defendant to come to trial. The evidence against him was entirely circumstantial, consisting primarily of McGrath's testimony. At the close of the Commonwealth's case, the defense rested without presenting any evidence. The jury found Sullivan guilty and fixed his penalty at life imprisonment. . . . Sullivan's codefendants, Carchidi and DiPasquale, were acquitted at separate trials.

Sullivan then petitioned for collateral relief. . . . He alleged, among other claims, that he had been denied effective assistance of counsel because his defense lawyers represented conflicting interests. In five days of hearings, the Court of Common Pleas heard evidence from Sullivan, Carchidi, Sullivan's lawyers, and the judge who presided at Sullivan's trial.

DiBona and Peruto had different recollections of their roles at the trials of the three defendants. DiBona testified that he and Peruto had been "associate counsel" at each trial. . . . Peruto recalled that he had been chief counsel for Carchidi and DiPasquale, but that he merely had assisted DiBona in Sullivan's trial. DiBona and Peruto also gave conflicting accounts of the decision to rest Sullivan's defense. DiBona said he had encouraged Sullivan to testify even though the Commonwealth had presented a very weak case. Peruto remembered that he had not "want[ed] the

---

1. DiBona and Peruto were paid in part with funds raised by friends of the three defendants. The record does not disclose the source of the balance of their fee, but no part of the money came from either Sullivan or his family. See United States ex rel. Sullivan v. Cuyler, 593 F.2d 512, 518, and n. 7 (C.A.3 1979).

defense to go on because I thought we would only be exposing the [defense] witnesses for the other two trials that were coming up."... Sullivan testified that he had deferred to his lawyers' decision not to present evidence for the defense. But other testimony suggested that Sullivan preferred not to take the stand because cross-examination might have disclosed an extramarital affair. Finally, Carchidi claimed he would have appeared at Sullivan's trial to rebut McGrath's testimony about Carchidi's statement at the time of the murders.

The Court of Common Pleas ... did not pass directly on the claim that defense counsel had a conflict of interest, but it found that counsel fully advised Sullivan about his decision not to testify.... All other claims for collateral relief were rejected or reserved for consideration in the new appeal.

The Pennsylvania Supreme Court affirmed both Sullivan's original conviction and the denial of collateral relief....

Having exhausted his state remedies, Sullivan sought habeas corpus relief in the United States District Court for the Eastern District of Pennsylvania. The petition was referred to a Magistrate, who found that Sullivan's defense counsel had represented conflicting interests. The District Court, however, accepted the Pennsylvania Supreme Court's conclusion that there had been no multiple representation. The court also found that, assuming there had been multiple representation, the evidence adduced in the state postconviction proceeding revealed no conflict of interest....

The Court of Appeals for the Third Circuit reversed.... We granted certiorari to consider recurring issues left unresolved by Holloway v. Arkansas. We now vacate and remand....

IV

We come ... to Sullivan's claim that he was denied the effective assistance of counsel guaranteed by the Sixth Amendment because his lawyers had a conflict of interest. The claim raises two issues expressly reserved in Holloway v. Arkansas, 435 U.S., at 483-484. The first is whether a state trial judge must inquire into the propriety of multiple representation even though no party lodges an objection. The second is whether the mere possibility of a conflict of interest warrants the conclusion that the defendant was deprived of his right to counsel.

A

In *Holloway,* a single public defender represented three defendants at the same trial. The trial court refused to consider the appointment of separate counsel despite the defense lawyer's timely and repeated assertions that the interests of his clients conflicted. This Court recognized that a lawyer forced to represent codefendants whose interests conflict cannot provide the adequate legal assistance required by the Sixth Amendment. Given the trial court's failure to respond to timely objections, however, the Court did not consider whether the alleged conflict actually existed. It simply held that the trial court's error unconstitutionally endangered the right to counsel.

Holloway requires state trial courts to investigate timely objections to multiple representation. But nothing in our precedents suggests that the Sixth Amendment requires state courts themselves to initiate inquiries into the propriety of multiple representation in every case.[10] Defense counsel have an ethical obligation to avoid conflicting representations and to advise the court promptly when a conflict of interest arises during the course of trial. Absent special circumstances, therefore, trial courts may assume either that multiple representation entails no conflict or that the lawyer and his clients knowingly accept such risk of conflict as may exist. Indeed, as the Court noted in *Holloway,* trial courts necessarily rely in large measure upon the good faith and good judgment of defense counsel. "An 'attorney representing two defendants in a criminal matter is in the best position professionally and ethically to determine when a conflict of interest exists or will probably develop in the course of a trial.'" Unless the trial court knows or should have known that a particular conflict exists, the court need not initiate an inquiry.

Nothing in the circumstances of this case indicates that the trial court had a duty to inquire whether there was a conflict of interest. The provision of separate trials for Sullivan and his codefendants significantly reduced the potential for a divergence in their interests. No participant in Sullivan's trial ever objected to the multiple representation. DiBona's opening argument for Sullivan outlined a defense compatible with the view that none of the defendants was connected with the murders. . . . The opening argument also suggested that counsel was not afraid to call witnesses whose testimony might be needed at the trials of Sullivan's codefendants. . . . Finally, as the Court of Appeals noted, counsel's critical decision to rest Sullivan's defense was on its face a reasonable tactical response to the weakness of the circumstantial evidence presented by the prosecutor. On these facts, we conclude that the Sixth Amendment imposed upon the trial court no affirmative duty to inquire into the propriety of multiple representation.

B

Holloway reaffirmed that multiple representation does not violate the Sixth Amendment unless it gives rise to a conflict of interest. Since a possible conflict inheres in almost every instance of multiple representation, a defendant who objects to multiple representation must have the opportunity to show that potential conflicts impermissibly imperil his right to a fair trial. But unless the trial court fails to afford such an opportunity, a reviewing court cannot presume that the possibility for conflict has resulted in ineffective assistance of counsel. Such a presumption would preclude multiple representation even in cases where "[a] common defense . . . gives strength against a common attack."

In order to establish a violation of the Sixth Amendment, a defendant who raised no objection at trial must demonstrate that an actual conflict of interest adversely affected his lawyer's performance. In Glasser v. United States, for example, the

---

10. In certain cases, proposed Federal Rule of Criminal Procedure 44(c) provides that the federal district courts "shall promptly inquire with respect to . . . joint representation and shall personally advise each defendant of his right to the effective assistance of counsel, including separate representation." See also ABA Project on Standards for Criminal Justice, Function of the Trial Judge §3.4(b) (App. Draft 1972).

Several Courts of Appeals already invoke their supervisory power to require similar inquiries. As our promulgation of Rule 44(c) suggests, we view such an exercise of the supervisory power as a desirable practice. See generally William W. Schwarzer, Dealing with Incompetent Counsel — The Trial Judge's Role, 93 Harv. L. Rev. 633, 653-654 (1980).

Although some Circuits have said explicitly that the Sixth Amendment does not require an inquiry into the possibility of conflicts, a recent opinion in the Second Circuit held otherwise, Colon v. Fogg, 603 F.2d 403, 407 (1979).

record showed that defense counsel failed to cross-examine a prosecution witness whose testimony linked Glasser with the crime, and failed to resist the presentation of arguably inadmissible evidence. The Court found that both omissions resulted from counsel's desire to diminish the jury's perception of a codefendant's guilt. Indeed, the evidence of counsel's "struggle to serve two masters [could not] seriously be doubted." Since this actual conflict of interest impaired Glasser's defense, the Court reversed his conviction.

Dukes v. Warden, 406 U.S. 250 (1972), presented a contrasting situation. Dukes pleaded guilty on the advice of two lawyers, one of whom also represented Dukes' codefendants on an unrelated charge. Dukes later learned that this lawyer had sought leniency for the codefendants by arguing that their cooperation with the police induced Dukes to plead guilty. Dukes argued in this Court that his lawyer's conflict of interest had infected his plea. We found "nothing in the record . . . which would indicate that the alleged conflict resulted in ineffective assistance of counsel and did in fact render the plea in question involuntary and unintelligent." Since Dukes did not identify an actual lapse in representation, we affirmed the denial of habeas corpus relief.

Glasser established that unconstitutional multiple representation is never harmless error. Once the Court concluded that Glasser's lawyer had an actual conflict of interest, it refused "to indulge in nice calculations as to the amount of prejudice" attributable to the conflict. The conflict itself demonstrated a denial of the "right to have the effective assistance of counsel." 315 U.S., at 76. Thus, a defendant who shows that a conflict of interest actually affected the adequacy of his representation need not demonstrate prejudice in order to obtain relief. But until a defendant shows that his counsel actively represented conflicting interests, he has not established the constitutional predicate for his claim of ineffective assistance. . . .

C

The Court of Appeals granted Sullivan relief because he had shown that the multiple representation in this case involved a possible conflict of interest. We hold that the possibility of conflict is insufficient to impugn a criminal conviction. In order to demonstrate a violation of his Sixth Amendment rights, a defendant must establish that an actual conflict of interest adversely affected his lawyer's performance. Sullivan believes he should prevail even under this standard. He emphasizes Peruto's admission that the decision to rest Sullivan's defense reflected a reluctance to expose witnesses who later might have testified for the other defendants. The petitioner, on the other hand, points to DiBona's contrary testimony and to evidence that Sullivan himself wished to avoid taking the stand. Since the Court of Appeals did not weigh these conflicting contentions under the proper legal standard, its judgment is vacated and the case is remanded for further proceedings consistent with this opinion.

So ordered.

MR. JUSTICE MARSHALL, concurring in part and dissenting in part. . . .

I believe . . . that the potential for conflict of interest in representing multiple defendants is "so grave," see ABA Project on Standards for Criminal Justice, Defense Function, Standard 4-3.5(b) (App. Draft, 2d ed. 1979), that whenever two or more defendants are represented by the same attorney the trial judge must make a preliminary determination that the joint representation is the product of the defendants' informed choice. I therefore [think] . . . that the trial court has a duty to inquire whether there is multiple representation, to warn defendants of the possible risks of such representation, and to ascertain that the representation is the result of the defendants' informed choice.

I dissent from the Court's formulation of the proper standard for determining whether multiple representation has violated the defendant's right to the effective assistance of counsel. The Court holds that in the absence of an objection at trial, the defendant must show "that an actual conflict of interest adversely affected his lawyer's performance." . . . If the Court's holding would require a defendant to demonstrate that his attorney's trial performance differed from what it would have been if the defendant had been the attorney's only client, I believe it is inconsistent with our previous cases. Such a test is not only unduly harsh, but incurably speculative as well. The appropriate question under the Sixth Amendment is whether an actual, relevant conflict of interests existed during the proceedings. If it did, the conviction must be reversed. Since such a conflict was present in this case, I would affirm the judgment of the Court of Appeals.

Our cases make clear that every defendant has a constitutional right to "the assistance of an attorney unhindered by a conflict of interests." Holloway v. Arkansas, 435 U.S. 475, 483, n. 5 (1978). "[T]he 'assistance of counsel' guaranteed by the Sixth Amendment contemplates that such assistance be untrammeled and unimpaired by a court order requiring that one lawyer shall simultaneously represent conflicting interests." Glasser v. United States, 315 U.S. 60, 70 (1942). If "[t]he possibility of the inconsistent interests of [the clients] was brought home to the court" by means of an objection at trial, id., at 71, the court may not require joint representation. But if no objection was made at trial, the appropriate inquiry is whether a conflict actually existed during the course of the representation.

Because it is the simultaneous representation of conflicting interests against which the Sixth Amendment protects a defendant, he need go no further than to show the existence of an actual conflict. An actual conflict of interests negates the unimpaired loyalty a defendant is constitutionally entitled to expect and receive from his attorney.

Moreover, a showing that an actual conflict adversely affected counsel's performance is not only unnecessary, it is often an impossible task. As the Court emphasized in *Holloway:*

> [I]n a case of joint representation of conflicting interests the evil — it bears repeating — is in what the advocate finds himself compelled to *refrain* from doing. . . . It may be possible in some cases to identify from the record the prejudice resulting from an attorney's failure to undertake certain trial tasks, but even with a record of the sentencing hearing available it would be difficult to judge intelligently the impact of a conflict on the attorney's representation of a client. And to assess the impact of a conflict of interests on the attorney's options, tactics, and decisions in plea negotiations would be virtually impossible. 435 U.S., at 490-491.

Accordingly, in *Holloway* we emphatically rejected the suggestion that a defendant must show prejudice in order to be entitled to relief. For the same reasons, it would usually be futile to attempt to determine how counsel's conduct would have been different if he had not been under conflicting duties. . . .

NOTES AND QUESTIONS

1. After *Sullivan*, what are the consequences of making, as compared to *not* making, a pretrial objection to joint representation?

2. What does it mean that "a defendant who shows that a conflict of interest actually affected the adequacy of his representation need not demonstrate prejudice in order to obtain relief"?

3. In Burger v. Kemp, 483 U.S. 776 (1987), the Court held that an actual conflict of interest was not present in the following circumstances: Two law partners represented two codefendants in a capital murder case. One of the partners wrote the appellate briefs for both defendants. The brief filed on Burger's behalf did not make a "lesser culpability" argument (i.e., argue that Burger was the less culpable of the killers); Burger argued that that omission showed an actual conflict that adversely affected counsel's representation. The Court concluded that the "decision to forgo this [argument] had a sound strategic basis," and found that if there were any conflict, it had not affected the representation Burger received.

4. Reconsider the discussion of *Sullivan* in *Strickland*, page 176 supra. Does *Sullivan* apply to every conflict of interest, or only those involving multiple representations? The circuit courts have split on the question. For a discussion, see Brent Coverdale, *Cuyler* versus *Strickland:* The Proper Standard for Self-Interested Conflicts of Interest, 47 U. Kan. L. Rev. 209 (1998).

In *Sullivan*, the trial judge had no good reason to suspect the potential conflict. What should the standard of effective assistance be when the trial judge was or should have been aware of a potential conflict? Should there be a duty to inquire? In the absence of inquiry, should prejudice be presumed if counsel has any conflict whatsoever? Ought there to be different standards for active representation of conflicted interests as compared to a conflict that may emerge from the prior representation of a different person? The Supreme Court addressed a number of these questions in Mickens v. Taylor, 535 U.S. 162 (2002):

> In 1993, a Virginia jury convicted petitioner Mickens of the premeditated murder of Timothy Hall during or following the commission of an attempted forcible sodomy. Finding the murder outrageously and wantonly vile, it sentenced petitioner to death. In June 1998, Mickens filed a petition for writ of habeas corpus . . . in the United States District Court for the Eastern District of Virginia, alleging, inter alia, that he was denied effective assistance of counsel because one of his court-appointed attorneys had a conflict of interest at trial. Federal habeas counsel had discovered that petitioner's lead trial attorney, Bryan Saunders, was representing Hall (the victim) on assault and concealed-weapons charges at the time of the murder. Saunders had been appointed to represent Hall, a juvenile, on March 20, 1992, and had met with him once for 15 to 30 minutes some time the following week. Hall's body was discovered on March 30, 1992, and four days later a juvenile court judge dismissed the charges against him, noting on the docket sheet that Hall was deceased. The one-page docket sheet also listed Saunders as Hall's counsel. On April 6, 1992, the same judge appointed Saunders to represent petitioner. Saunders did not disclose to the court, his co-counsel, or petitioner that he had previously represented Hall. Under Virginia law, juvenile case files are confidential and may not generally be disclosed without a court order, but petitioner learned about Saunders' prior representation when a clerk mistakenly produced Hall's file to federal habeas counsel.

On these facts, the Defendant argued for automatic reversal whenever a trial judge knew or should have known of a potential conflict, but failed to inquire into it. The Court, per Justice Scalia, disagreed:

> Petitioner's proposed rule of automatic reversal when there existed a conflict that did not affect counsel's performance, but the trial judge failed to make the *Sullivan*-mandated inquiry, makes little policy sense. [T]he rule applied when the trial judge is not aware of the conflict (and thus not obligated to inquire) is that prejudice will be presumed only if the conflict has significantly affected counsel's performance— thereby rendering the verdict unreliable, even though *Strickland* prejudice cannot be shown. The trial court's awareness of a potential conflict neither renders it more likely that counsel's performance was significantly affected nor in any other way renders the verdict unreliable. Nor does the trial judge's failure to make the *Sullivan*-mandated inquiry often make it harder for reviewing courts to determine conflict and effect, particularly since those courts may rely on evidence and testimony whose importance only becomes established at the trial.
>
> Nor, finally, is automatic reversal simply an appropriate means of enforcing *Sullivan*'s mandate of inquiry. Despite [the dissent's] belief that there must be a threat of sanction (to-wit, the risk of conferring a windfall upon the defendant) in order to induce "resolutely obdurate" trial judges to follow the law, we do not presume that judges are as careless or as partial as those police officers who need the incentive of the exclusionary rule. And in any event, the *Sullivan* standard, which requires proof of effect upon representation but (once such effect is shown) presumes prejudice, already creates an "incentive" to inquire into a potential conflict. In those cases where the potential conflict is in fact an actual one, only inquiry will enable the judge to avoid all possibility of reversal by either seeking waiver or replacing a conflicted attorney. We doubt that the deterrence of "judicial dereliction" that would be achieved by an automatic reversal rule is significantly greater.
>
> Since this was not a case in which (as in *Holloway*) counsel protested his inability simultaneously to represent multiple defendants; and since the trial court's failure to make the *Sullivan*-mandated inquiry does not reduce the petitioner's burden of proof; it was at least necessary, to void the conviction, for petitioner to establish that the conflict of interest adversely affected his counsel's performance. The Court of Appeals having found no such effect, the denial of habeas relief must be affirmed.

Having said all that, the majority went on to announce that perhaps it was all dicta in that the Court was assuming but not deciding that *Sullivan* applied in the first place:

> Lest today's holding be misconstrued, we note that the only question presented was the effect of a trial court's failure to inquire into a potential conflict upon the *Sullivan* rule that deficient performance of counsel must be shown. The case was presented and argued on the assumption that (absent some exception for failure to inquire) *Sullivan* would be applicable—requiring a showing of defective performance, but not requiring in addition (as *Strickland* does in other ineffectiveness-of-counsel cases), a showing of probable effect upon the outcome of trial. That assumption was not unreasonable in light of the holdings of Courts of Appeals, which have applied *Sullivan* "unblinkingly" to "all kinds of alleged attorney ethical conflicts," Beets v. Scott, 65 F.3d 1258, 1266 (C.A.5 1995) (en banc). They have invoked the Sullivan standard not only when (as here) there is a conflict rooted in counsel's obligations to *former* clients, but even when

representation of the defendant somehow implicates counsel's personal or financial interests, including a book deal, a job with the prosecutor's office, the teaching of classes to Internal Revenue Service agents, a romantic "entanglement" with the prosecutor, or fear of antagonizing the trial judge.

It must be said, however, that the language of *Sullivan* itself does not clearly establish, or indeed even support, such expansive application. "[U]ntil," it said, "a defendant shows that his counsel *actively represented* conflicting interests, he has not established the constitutional predicate for his claim of ineffective assistance." 446 U.S., at 350 (emphasis added). Both *Sullivan* itself, and *Holloway,* stressed the high probability of prejudice arising from multiple concurrent representation, and the difficulty of proving that prejudice. See also Geer, Representation of Multiple Criminal Defendants: Conflicts of Interest and the Professional Responsibilities of the Defense Attorney, 62 Minn. L. Rev. 119, 125-140 (1978); Lowenthal, Joint Representation in Criminal Cases: A Critical Appraisal, 64 Va. L. Rev. 939, 941-950 (1978). Not all attorney conflicts present comparable difficulties. Thus, the Federal Rules of Criminal Procedure treat concurrent representation and prior representation differently, requiring a trial court to inquire into the likelihood of conflict whenever jointly charged defendants are represented by a single attorney (Rule 44(c)), but not when counsel previously represented another defendant in a substantially related matter, even where the trial court is aware of the prior representation.

Perhaps because the Court was so badly splintered, with Stevens, Souter, Breyer, and Ginsburg dissenting, Justice Kennedy wrote a separate concurrence emphasizing that "At petitioner's request, the District Court conducted an evidentiary hearing on the conflict claim and issued a thorough opinion, which found that counsel's brief representation of the victim had no effect whatsoever on the course of petitioner's trial." Stevens, Breyer, and Ginsburg all expressed concerns that, regardless of actual prejudice, the events in this case did not satisfy the appearance of justice, especially in a capital case. Justice Souter went further and claimed that the majority had misapplied the cases to effect a change in the law:

> The different burdens on the *Holloway* and *Sullivan* defendants are consistent features of a coherent scheme for dealing with the problem of conflicted defense counsel; a prospective risk of conflict subject to judicial notice is treated differently from a retrospective claim that a completed proceeding was tainted by conflict, although the trial judge had not been derelict in any duty to guard against it. When the problem comes to the trial court's attention before any potential conflict has become actual, the court has a duty to act prospectively to assess the risk and, if the risk is not too remote, to eliminate it or to render it acceptable through a defendant's knowing and intelligent waiver. This duty is something more than the general responsibility to rule without committing legal error; it is an affirmative obligation to investigate a disclosed possibility that defense counsel will be unable to act with uncompromised loyalty to his client. It was the judge's failure to fulfill that duty of care to enquire further and do what might be necessary that the *Holloway* Court remedied by vacating the defendant's subsequent conviction. The error occurred when the judge failed to act, and the remedy restored the defendant to the position he would have occupied if the judge had taken reasonable steps to fulfill his obligation. But when the problem of conflict comes to judicial attention not prospectively, but only after the fact, the defendant must show an actual conflict with adverse consequence to him in order to get relief. Fairness requires nothing more, for no judge was at fault in allowing a trial to proceed even though fraught with hidden risk.

In light of what the majority holds today, it bears repeating that, in this coherent scheme established by *Holloway* and *Sullivan,* there is nothing legally crucial about an objection by defense counsel to tell a trial judge that conflicting interests may impair the adequacy of counsel's representation. Counsel's objection in *Holloway* was important as a fact sufficient to put the judge on notice that he should enquire. In most multiple-representation cases, it will take just such an objection to alert a trial judge to prospective conflict, and the *Sullivan* Court reaffirmed that the judge is obliged to take reasonable prospective action whenever a timely objection is made. But the Court also indicated that an objection is not required as a matter of law: "Unless the trial court knows or reasonably should know that a particular conflict exists, the court need not initiate an enquiry." The Court made this clear beyond cavil 10 months later when Justice Powell, the same Justice who wrote the *Sullivan* opinion, explained in Wood v. Georgia that *Sullivan* "mandates a reversal when the trial court has failed to make an inquiry even though it 'knows or reasonably should know that a particular conflict exists.'" 450 U.S., at 272, n. 18 (emphasis in original).

Since the District Court in this case found that the state judge was on notice of a prospective potential conflict, this case calls for nothing more than the application of the prospective notice rule announced and exemplified by *Holloway* and confirmed in *Sullivan* and *Wood*. The remedy for the judge's dereliction of duty should be an order vacating the conviction and affording a new trial.

Justice Souter's reliance on Wood v. Georgia is a bit peculiar, as the actual holding in the case sent the case back to the district court to make the *Sullivan* inquiry. In a passage unremarked by Justice Souter, the *Wood* Court said: "On the record before us, we cannot be sure whether counsel was influenced in his basic strategic decisions by the interests of his employer who hired him. If this was the case, the due process rights of petitioners were not respected." 450 U.S. at 272.

Regardless who wins the game of parsing prior opinions, what should the respective burdens be in cases like this? If a defendant makes no objection to his or her representation, why should there be any after-the-fact review that does not, at a minimum, focus on some prejudice to the defendant's case? For that matter, why shouldn't the defendant meet the *Strickland* burden of showing a reasonable probability that the conflicted representation might have affected the outcome in the case? Why is it the trial court's, or the prosecutor's, responsibility to police the relationship between defense counsel and client? Reversals of reliable convictions impose substantial costs. A plausibly erroneous, or just different, outcome may justify such costs, but do you think the "appearance of justice" does? And what, exactly, are the demands of "the appearance of justice"? Wouldn't Souter's proposed approach create perverse incentives for defendants to proceed with conflicted representation? If there is an acquittal, the case is over; if there is a conviction, there may be a substantial chance of a reversal and a second bite of the apple. Bear in mind that there are other possible means of regulation in cases like this, including sanctions on the lawyer. After all, it is the lawyer and the client that create these problems; shouldn't they have the incentive to correct them rather than to benefit from them?

5. What result under *Sullivan* if a defendant, in full knowledge of a potential conflict, waives the right not to have separate counsel, and subsequently the potential conflict is actualized? In this regard, consider Rule 44(c) of the Federal Rules of Criminal Procedure, which is cited in footnote 10 of *Sullivan* and which has since

gone into effect (with some recent stylistic changes):

Rule 44. Right to and Appointment of Counsel

(a) Right to Appointed Counsel. A defendant who is unable to obtain counsel is entitled to have counsel appointed to represent the defendant at every stage of the proceeding from initial appearance through appeal, unless the defendant waives this right.

(b) Appointment Procedure. Federal law and local court rules govern the procedure for implementing the right to counsel.

(c) Inquiry Into Joint Representation.

(1) Joint Representation. Joint representation occurs when:

(A) two or more defendants have been charged jointly under Rule 8(b) or have been joined for trial under Rule 13; and

(B) the defendants are represented by the same counsel, or counsel who are associated in law practice.

(2) Court's Responsibilities in Cases of Joint Representation. The court must promptly inquire about the propriety of joint representation and must personally advise each defendant of the right to the effective assistance of counsel, including separate representation. Unless there is good cause to believe that no conflict of interest is likely to arise, the court must take appropriate measures to protect each defendant's right to counsel.

In an insightful analysis of Rule 44(c) prior to its effective date, Professor Tague commented:

If the rule values the assistance of conflict-free representation above the right to choose one's attorney, it has three distressing omissions. First, the rule orders the "court" to make an inquiry about possible conflicts whenever defendants "are charged pursuant to Rule 8(b) or have been joined for trial pursuant to Rule 13." Does the rule apply only after the defendants have been indicted or an information has been filed in district court? Is there then no obligation to inquire at any earlier stage, such as at the presentment or the preliminary hearing? The rule's reference to the "court" as the inquiring entity supports this apparent restriction. Rule 44(a) distinguishes between the "court" and the magistrate who usually appoints counsel at the presentment and presides at the preliminary hearing. A magistrate could appoint a single attorney whose representation would continue at least until arraignment on the indictment. Indeed, the Advisory Committee implies that separate counsel need not be initially appointed for each defendant. This limitation is unfortunate. The rule recognizes the importance of the inquiry even if the defendants decide to plead guilty before trial. Many defendants seek to plead guilty before they are indicted, because the defendants frequently obtain a more favorable plea bargain if they plead early in the process. A guilty plea might bury a glaring conflict that infected the plea bargaining for the codefendants.

Second, the rule does not appear to cover cases like Dukes v. Warden, in which a defendant, charged alone in one proceeding, is a codefendant in a second proceeding and one attorney represents defendants in both proceedings. The rule's reference to Rules 8(b) and 13 suggests that the court is not under any obligation even if it knows of the separate indictments. The rule also would appear to apply if the codefendants are severed under Rule 14.

Third, the rule fails to provide adequate guidelines for review of a postconviction attack based on conflict. The Committee indicates that although a trial court's failure to make a Rule 44(c) inquiry will not necessarily result in reversal, an appellate court is more likely to find that a conflict existed in this instance. Further, because conflicts that were not apparent initially may surface later in the proceeding, even an adequate initial inquiry does not preclude reversal on conflict grounds. If the trial court makes an inadequate inquiry or none at all, the appellate court would still face the problem of defining and allocating the burden of proving the existence of a conflict. The proposed rule thus fails to solve one of the major problems of multiple representation.

Peter Tague, Multiple Representation and Conflicts of Interest in Criminal Cases, 67 Geo. L.J. 1075, 1094-1095 (1979).

These limitations led Professor Tague to conclude that the Rule should be further amended to require the appointment of separate counsel for all indigents and to require that nonindigents at least discuss the matter with separate counsel. Second, if defendants insist on joint representation, they should have to establish an intelligent waiver. Other commentators have concluded that there should be a flat prohibition against joint representation. Gary T. Lowenthal, Joint Representation in Criminal Cases: A Critical Appraisal, 64 Va. L. Rev. 939, 986 (1978). How would you work out these conflicting concerns of autonomy and procedural fairness?

6. The general view seems to be that a client may waive the right to conflict-free representation. See, e.g., United States v. Curcio, 680 F.2d 881 (2d Cir. 1982). However, in Wheat v. United States, 486 U.S. 153 (1988), the Court held that trial courts do not have to accept defendants' waivers of conflict-free representation, notwithstanding the presumption in favor of counsel of choice. In part the Court was motivated by the fact that the courts of appeals have indicated a willingness to entertain ineffective-assistance-of-counsel claims by defendants who have specifically waived the right to conflict-free representation.

7. What about the *government's* interest in separate counsel? Consider the following argument concerning *Wheat,* the case just mentioned:

> In *Wheat,* there are two reasons why the coconspirators might have wished to use Iredale [the defendants' attorney] as common counsel. The first, offered by the defendants, is unobjectionable: The defendants believed Iredale to be a very good attorney, better than the likely alternatives. But the second is troubling. If the three defendants in question were guilty, they may well have faced a classic prisoners' dilemma: It may have been in each individual's interest to "sell out" to the government and implicate his colleagues, but may have been far better for all if all either lied or remained silent. Common counsel may have removed the dilemma by facilitating the enforcement of an agreement not to finger each other. Obtaining the testimony of one conspirator against others may require careful negotiation with the would-be witness. If all the conspirators have the same lawyer, the government is, in effect, able to deal with one defendant only by dealing with all.

William J. Stuntz, Waiving Rights in Criminal Procedure, 75 Va. L. Rev. 761, 798-799 (1989). On the other hand, if the government's interests count, what is to prevent the government from objecting to common counsel solely in order to get an unusually strong defense lawyer out of the case, at least with respect to some of the defendants? There is some reason to believe that that is what happened in *Wheat.* See Pamela S. Karlan, Discrete and Relational Criminal Representation: The Changing Vision of the Right to Counsel, 105 Harv. L. Rev. 670, 687 n. 79 (1992) (noting that Iredale was reportedly an exceptionally good lawyer).

See also Bruce A. Green, "Through a Glass, Darkly": How the Court Sees Motions to Disqualify Criminal Defense Lawyers, 89 Colum. L. Rev. 1201 (1989) (criticizing *Wheat*).

Are there any situations in which defendants should simply be barred from proceeding with conflicted counsel? Some courts are saying yes. For example, in United States v. Fulton, 5 F.3d 605 (2d Cir. 1993), during trial the government disclosed that a government witness presently on the stand had alleged that he had illegally imported heroin for Fulton's defense counsel. The court informed the defendant that this injected the defense counsel's interests into the trial, and further that counsel would not be able to cross-examine the witness on these matters, because to do so would reveal confidences of a former client. The client nonetheless wished to proceed with counsel and to waive the conflict. The court of appeals reversed the ensuing conviction on the ground that "no rational defendant would knowingly and intelligently be represented by a lawyer whose conduct was guided largely by a desire for self-preservation." How could the court know what "largely" guided defense counsel? What do you think of the equation of this choice with the inability to make a knowing and intelligent waiver? More importantly, why, absent a showing of prejudice, should a defendant be insulated from the consequences of such choices, even if you think such a choice is problematic? For that matter, is even prejudice sufficient to require reversal? Unless the defendant is truly incompetent, and not just made a decision that ex post looks like it didn't work out, why shouldn't the defendant be stuck with the consequences of his or her choices? Had Fulton been acquitted, he would have walked, regardless of his lack of a "knowing and intelligent" waiver. Following a conviction, what justifies forcing the state to go through the time, expense, and risk, of another trial?

The Second Circuit extended the *Fulton* holding in the infamous case of United States v. Schwarz, 283 F.3d 76 (2d Cir. 2002) dealing with various defendants and charges "brought related to the events surrounding the brutal assault on Abner Louima in the early hours of August 9, 1997, while he was in custody at the 70th Police Precinct in Brooklyn, New York, and its aftermath." Following two jury trials, the defendants were convicted. One of them, Schwarz, appealed on the ground that his defense counsel had unwaivable conflicts. The facts, according to the court, were:

> Shortly after the assault on Louima in August 1997, the law firm that represented the Policeman's Benevolent Association ("PBA"), the police officers' union, hired Stephen Worth and Stuart London as trial counsel to represent Schwarz and Bruder respectively. Both attorneys were hired as outside conflict counsel to avoid any conflicts of interest that might arise if the PBA's regular retained law firm were to represent multiple defendants. Worth's and London's fees were to be paid by the PBA.
>
> In February 1998, after Schwarz had been indicted by the federal grand jury, Worth, London, and some other attorneys formed a law firm, Worth, Longworth & Bamundo, LLP (the "Worth firm"). In May 1998, the Worth firm entered into a two-year $10 million retainer agreement with the PBA (the "PBA retainer") to represent all police officers in administrative, disciplinary, and criminal matters as well as to provide them with civil legal representation. After entering into the PBA retainer, Worth and London agreed to continue their representation of Schwarz and Bruder without charging further fees beyond the PBA retainer.
>
> Shortly after learning of the formation of the Worth firm and its agreement with the PBA, the government wrote a letter to the district court dated May 28, 1998, to

advise it of potential conflicts of interest arising from the joint representation of Schwarz and Bruder by partners in the same law firm and from the Worth firm's PBA retainer. The government urged the district court to conduct a hearing pursuant to United States v. Curcio, 680 F.2d 881 (2d Cir. 1982).

Worth, on behalf of himself and London, wrote a letter to the district court dated June 17, 1998, to provide details concerning these issues. The letter asserted that no substitution of counsel was needed, in part because the Worth firm had not represented any PBA officials or delegates that had been called to testify before the grand jury, and in part because "[t]here is no de facto conflict between the respective defenses of Officer Schwarz and Officer Bruder. In fact, it was and is our intention to move for separate trials . . . because Officer Bruder can offer testimony which is exculpatory in nature." Worth's letter informed the court that Schwarz and Bruder had been advised about the potential conflicts and were prepared to waive their right to conflict-free counsel. . . .

Schwarz and Bruder submitted identical affidavits stating that they understood the potential conflicts raised by being represented by attorneys from the same law firm and that they agreed "that our separate and joint defenses to these charges are such that one defendant's defense will have no impact on the other defendant's defense, since there is no inconsistency in our defenses. In fact the defenses dovetail with each other." Both defendants asserted that they wanted to keep Worth and London as their counsel. The affidavits made no mention of any potential conflicts that might arise in connection with the PBA retainer.

The government, Worth, and London filed additional letters with the district court fleshing out the areas of potential conflict. These letters focused primarily on the dangers of two defendants being represented by the same law firm and on potential conflicts that might arise if PBA officials and delegates were called as witnesses at the trial. With respect to the latter, the Government expressed the view that "the Worth firm's representation of both the instant defendants and the PBA represents an actual conflict [that] cannot be waived." Worth and London argued that disqualification of the attorneys without a Curcio hearing would violate Schwarz's and Bruder's Sixth Amendment right to counsel of their choice. They also urged that there was no unwaivable conflict, stating that "if this Court's concern focuses on the relationship of the PBA with the various defendants and witnesses, that concern is illusory" because there was no showing that the government would call any PBA witnesses and, in any event, the law firm had not and would not represent any other PBA witnesses or parties. Thus, the only conflict presented, they argued, arose from the joint representation of Schwarz and Bruder by the Worth firm — a conflict that could be waived by the defendants.

On September 11, 1998, with the first trial still several months away, the district judge held a hearing in which he advised Schwarz and Bruder regarding the risks presented by the potential conflicts. The district judge told Schwarz and Bruder that while he could not foresee all of the potential conflicts that might arise, some of the potential conflicts with respect to the joint representation of Schwarz and Bruder by the same law firm included that (1) defense counsel might not offer independent advice concerning the benefits of taking a plea bargain or testifying in court because it would be detrimental to "the other one of you"; (2) "[t]here may be some defense that could be made or evidence offered that helps one of you but hurts the other one"; (3) the attorney may not be able to independently judge whether to cross-examine or impeach a witness that "helps one of you but hurts the other one" or whether to offer reputation evidence or argue "that one of you is less [culpable] than the other one"; and (4) defense counsel might inadvertently or deliberately reveal confidences covered by the attorney-client privilege to his partner representing the other defendant.

In describing conflicts that might arise in connection with the PBA retainer, the district judge noted that the PBA and its president, Lou Matarazzo, who had signed the PBA retainer, were defendants in a civil suit that had been filed by Louima. Louima's suit alleged a conspiracy among the PBA (through its agents), Matarazzo, and the criminal defendants to injure Louima and to cover up the conspiracy, and raised claims of negligent supervision and monitoring. The district judge informed Schwarz and Bruder that what occurred in the criminal case could have a significant effect on the civil case and that the testimony in the criminal case would be relevant to the civil case. Id. at 12-13. The district judge also told the two defendants that the PBA's and Matarazzo's interests might differ from those of Schwarz and Bruder in, for example, pleading guilty, testifying, or cross-examining witnesses, and that these different interests might affect counsel's ability to offer advice that was in the defendants' best interests. Id. The district judge concluded his advice by observing that "it would be unrealistic to suppose that the beneficiaries of a ten-million-dollar contract, which evidently the firm hopes will be renewed in the year 2000, would be indifferent to the welfare of the PBA." Id. at 13. Following the hearing, the district court issued an order scheduling a *Curcio* hearing, appointing independent counsel to advise Schwarz and Bruder, and prohibiting the Worth firm from representing the PBA or any of its members other than Schwarz and Bruder in the Louima civil suit.

At the *Curcio* hearing, the government once again took the position that the conflict resulting from the PBA retainer was so serious that it could not be waived. Hr'g Tr. dated Sept. 16, 1998, at 4. The district court then addressed each defendant individually, including the following colloquy with Schwarz:

> *The Court:* Mr. Schwarz, tell me what you see here as inconsistencies between your case and Mr. Bruder's case.
>
> *Defendant Schwarz:* I understand that with this case, there may be some potential conflicts of interest, one being that my attorney and Mr. Bruder's attorney are now with the same firm. This is a conflict in that one defendant may receive a better defense at the expense of the other defendant.
>
> I'm also aware of the contract that my attorney has with the PBA. I know that there's another conflict with that, in that the government may call other police officers who are a member of the PBA or even PBA officials. There's a concern that possibly my attorney may have another agenda and may not be vigorous in his cross-examination of these witnesses.
>
> I'm also aware of in the calling of witnesses with this potential conflict, with the two lawyers in the same firm. If they call a witness who — my lawyer may be reluctant to call a witness who may be able to help me but who in his testimony may be harmful to the other defendant. I understand that there could be a conflict in that.
>
> Other conflict issues were if the government were to offer some type of plea to one defendant, that would probably be harmful to the other defendant. Also, if there were a guilty conviction, another conflict may be that my attorney may be reluctant, if he was trying to plead for some type of leniency, he may be reluctant to try to shift blame on to the other defendant in this case. . . .
>
> *The Court:* Do you want to keep your lawyer?
>
> *Defendant Schwarz:* Yes, sir.

After the independent counsel appointed by the district court on behalf of Schwarz told the court that he had advised Schwarz of all of these conflicts and believed Schwarz understood them, the court accepted Schwarz's waiver of the right to conflict-free counsel and permitted Worth to continue representing Schwarz, while Worth's partner London was permitted to continue representing Bruder.

In a peculiar opinion on the issue whether Schwarz had waived the conflict, the court said:

> The waiver given by Schwarz at the *Curcio* hearing would defeat his claim of ineffective assistance of counsel unless it is determined that (1) the conflict with respect to the PBA retainer was so severe as to be unwaivable, or (2) the *Curcio* waiver by Schwarz was not knowing and intelligent with respect to the specific conflict that led to the lapse in Worth's representation. We need not decide whether Schwarz's waiver was knowing and intelligent because we conclude that the actual conflict that Schwarz's attorney faced was unwaivable. . . .
>
> Although the particular conflict at issue in *Fulton* belonged to that narrow category of conflicts that we have deemed to be per se violations of the Sixth Amendment right to counsel, *Fulton*'s rationale with respect to when an attorney's self-interest renders a conflict unwaivable is equally applicable to the unusual facts of this case. As noted above, Worth's representation of Schwarz was in conflict not only with his ethical obligation to the PBA as his client, but also with his own substantial self-interest in the two-year, $10 million retainer agreement his newly formed firm had entered into with the PBA. Like the conflict in *Fulton,* Worth's conflict "so permeate[d] the defense that no meaningful waiver could be obtained." *Fulton,* 5 F.3d at 613. We must assume that, under such circumstances, the distinct possibility existed that, at each point the conflict was felt, Worth would sacrifice Schwarz's interests for those of the PBA. Indeed, we think it likely that these very concerns motivated the government to argue to the district court at the *Curcio* hearing that the conflict created by the PBA retainer could not be waived. Thus, we conclude that the conflict between Worth's representation of Schwarz, on the one hand, and his ethical obligation to the PBA as his client and his self interest in the PBA retainer, on the other, was so severe that no rational defendant in Schwarz's position would have knowingly and intelligently desired Worth's representation. Cf. id. ("[N]o rational defendant would knowingly and intelligently be represented by a lawyer whose conduct was guided largely by a desire for self-preservation."); cf. also United States v. Arrington, 867 F.2d 122, 129 (2d Cir. 1989) (upholding district court's disqualification of attorney "saddled" with serious conflict where allowing waiver would have required defendant to "forego[] the presentation of . . . evidence that would [have been] of great assistance").
>
> In sum, we hold that Schwarz's counsel suffered an actual conflict, that the conflict adversely affected his counsel's representation, and that the conflict was unwaivable. Accordingly, we are required to vacate Schwarz's conviction in the first trial and remand for a new trial.

"In sum," hasn't this court held that it needn't decide if the waiver in this case was knowing and intelligent because under these facts it could never be knowing and intelligent? Review the colloquy with the defendant reproduced above. Did the court take this peculiar tack because plainly this was a knowing and intelligent waiver? Why sacrifice the interests in effective law enforcement through a reversal of a conviction in a case like this rather than sanction the lawyers — if indeed there is any problem?

8. If there is a claim of conflict of interest, should the defense be forced to divulge the confidential information upon which the claim is premised? See United States v. Young, 644 F.2d 1008 (4th Cir. 1981). Should counsel be allowed to withdraw when it appears that a former client would testify against the present client? See United States v. Morando, 628 F.2d 535 (9th Cir. 1980).

C. Some Implications of the Right to Counsel

1. The Right to Proceed Pro Se

Somewhat counterintuitively, rights do not necessarily mean one also has the right to dispense with the right. The right to trial by jury, for example, does not mean a defendant has a right to a bench trial. The Court dealt with the right to forgo counsel — the right to proceed pro se — in the following case.

FARETTA v. CALIFORNIA

Certiorari to the Court of Appeal of California, Second Appellate District
422 U.S. 806 (1975)

MR. JUSTICE STEWART delivered the opinion of the Court.

The question before us now is whether a defendant in a state criminal trial has a constitutional right to proceed *without* counsel when he voluntarily and intelligently elects to do so. Stated another way, the question is whether a State may constitutionally hale a person into its criminal courts and there force a lawyer upon him, even when he insists that he wants to conduct his own defense. It is not an easy question, but we have concluded that a State may not constitutionally do so.

I

Anthony Faretta was charged with grand theft in an information filed in the Superior Court of Los Angeles County, Cal. At the arraignment, the Superior Court Judge assigned to preside at the trial appointed the public defender to represent Faretta. Well before the date of trial, however, Faretta requested that he be permitted to represent himself. Questioning by the judge revealed that Faretta had once represented himself in a criminal prosecution, that he had a high school education, and that he did not want to be represented by the public defender because he believed that the office was "very loaded down with . . . a heavy case load." The judge responded that he believed Faretta was "making a mistake" and emphasized that in further proceedings Faretta would receive no special favors. Nevertheless, after establishing that Faretta wanted to represent himself and did not want a lawyer, the judge, in a "preliminary ruling," accepted Faretta's waiver of the assistance of counsel. The judge indicated, however, that he might reverse this ruling if it later appeared that Faretta was unable adequately to represent himself.

Several weeks thereafter, but still prior to trial, the judge sua sponte held a hearing to inquire into Faretta's ability to conduct his own defense, and questioned him specifically about both the hearsay rule and the state law governing the challenge of potential jurors. After consideration of Faretta's answers, and observation of his demeanor, the judge ruled that Faretta had not made an intelligent and knowing waiver of his right to the assistance of counsel, and also ruled that Faretta had no constitutional right to conduct his own defense. The judge, accordingly, reversed his earlier ruling permitting self-representation and again appointed the public defender to represent Faretta. Faretta's subsequent request for leave to act as cocounsel was rejected, as were his efforts to make certain motions in his own behalf.[5] Throughout the subsequent trial, the judge required that Faretta's defense be conducted only through the appointed lawyer from the public defender's office. At the conclusion of the trial, the jury found Faretta guilty as charged, and the judge sentenced him to prison.

The California Court of Appeal, relying upon a then-recent California Supreme Court decision that had expressly decided the issue, affirmed the trial judge's ruling that Faretta had no federal or state constitutional right to represent himself.[7] Accordingly, the appellate court affirmed Faretta's conviction. A petition for rehearing was denied without opinion, and the California Supreme Court denied review. We granted certiorari.

II

In the federal courts, the right of self-representation has been protected by statute since the beginnings of our Nation. Section 35 of the Judiciary Act of 1789, 1 Stat. 73, 92, enacted by the First Congress and signed by President Washington one day before the Sixth Amendment was proposed, provided that "in all the courts of the United States, the parties may plead and manage their own causes personally or by the assistance of . . . counsel." The right is currently codified in 28 U.S.C. §1654.

With few exceptions, each of the several States also accords a defendant the right to represent himself in any criminal case. The Constitutions of 36 States explicitly confer that right. Moreover, many state courts have expressed the view that the right is also supported by the Constitution of the United States.

This Court has more than once indicated the same view. In Adams v. United States ex rel. McCann, 317 U.S. 269, 279, the Court recognized that the Sixth Amendment right to the assistance of counsel implicitly embodies a "correlative right to dispense with a lawyer's help." The defendant in that case, indicted for federal mail fraud violations, insisted on conducting his own defense without benefit of counsel. He also requested a bench trial and signed a waiver of his right to trial by jury. The prosecution consented to the waiver of a jury, and the waiver was accepted by the court. The defendant was convicted, but the Court of Appeals reversed the conviction on the ground that a person accused of a felony could not competently waive his right to trial by jury except upon the advice of a lawyer. This Court reversed and reinstated the conviction, holding that "an accused, in the exercise of a free and intelligent choice, and with the considered approval of the court, may waive trial by jury, and so likewise may he competently and intelligently waive his Constitutional right to assistance of counsel." Id., at 275.

The *Adams* case does not, of course, necessarily resolve the issue before us. It held only that "the Constitution does not force a lawyer upon a defendant." Id., at 279.[12] Whether the Constitution forbids a State from forcing a lawyer upon a

5. Faretta also urged without success that he was entitled to counsel of his choice, and three times moved for the appointment of a lawyer other than the public defender. These motions, too, were denied.

7. The Court of Appeal also held that the trial court had not "abused its discretion in concluding that Faretta had not made a knowing and intelligent waiver of his right to be represented by counsel," since "Faretta did not appear aware of the possible consequences of waiving the opportunity for skilled and experienced representation at trial."

12. The holding of *Adams* was reaffirmed in a different context in Carter v. Illinois, 329 U.S. 173, 174-175, where the Court again adverted to the right of self-representation: "Neither the historic

defendant is a different question. But the Court in *Adams* did recognize, albeit in dictum, an affirmative right of self-representation:

> The right to assistance of counsel and the *correlative right to dispense with a lawyer's help* are not legal formalisms. They rest on considerations that go to the substance of an accused's position before the law. . . .
>
> . . . What were contrived as protections for the accused should not be turned into fetters. . . . To deny an accused a choice of procedure in circumstances in which he, though a layman, is as capable as any lawyer of making an intelligent choice, is to impair the worth of great Constitutional safeguards by treating them as empty verbalisms.
>
> . . . When the administration of the criminal law . . . is hedged about as it is by the Constitutional safeguards for the protection of an accused, to deny him in the exercise of his free choice the right to dispense with some of these safeguards . . . is to imprison a man in his privileges and call it the Constitution.

In other settings as well, the Court has indicated that a defendant has a constitutionally protected right to represent himself in a criminal trial. For example, in Snyder v. Massachusetts, 291 U.S. 97, the Court held that the Confrontation Clause of the Sixth Amendment gives the accused a right to be present at all stages of the proceedings where fundamental fairness might be thwarted by his absence. This right to "presence" was based upon the premise that the "defense may be made easier if the accused is permitted to be present at the examination of jurors or the summing up of counsel, *for it will be in his power*, if present, to give advice or suggestion or *even to supersede his lawyers altogether and conduct the trial himself.*" Id., at 106 (emphasis added). And in Price v. Johnston, 334 U.S. 266, the Court, in holding that a convicted person had no absolute right to argue his own appeal, said this holding was in "sharp contrast" to his "recognized privilege of conducting his own defense at the trial."

The United States Courts of Appeals have repeatedly held that the right of self-representation is protected by the Bill of Rights. . . .

This Court's past recognition of the right of self-representation, the federal-court authority holding the right to be of constitutional dimension, and the state constitutions pointing to the right's fundamental nature form a consensus not easily ignored. "[T]he mere fact that a path is a beaten one," Mr. Justice Jackson once observed, "is a persuasive reason for following it."[13] We confront here a nearly universal conviction, on the part of our people as well as our courts, that forcing a lawyer upon an unwilling defendant is contrary to his basic right to defend himself if he truly wants to do so.

III

This consensus is soundly premised. The right of self-representation finds support in the structure of the Sixth Amendment, as well as in the English and colonial jurisprudence from which the Amendment emerged.

---

conception of Due Process nor the vitality it derives from progressive standards of justice denies a person *the right to defend himself* or to confess guilt. Under appropriate circumstances the Constitution requires that counsel be tendered; it does not require that under all circumstances counsel be forced upon a defendant." (Emphasis added.) See also Moore v. Michigan, 355 U.S. 155, 161.

13. Robert H. Jackson, Full Faith and Credit — The Lawyer's Clause of the Constitution, 45 Col. L. Rev. 1, 26 (1945).

A . . .

The Sixth Amendment does not provide merely that a defense shall be made for the accused; it grants to the accused personally the right to make his defense. It is the accused, not counsel, who must be "informed of the nature and cause of the accusation," who must be "confronted with the witnesses against him," and who must be accorded "compulsory process for obtaining witnesses in his favor." Although not stated in the Amendment in so many words, the right to self-representation — to make one's own defense personally — is thus necessarily implied by the structure of the Amendment.[15] The right to defend is given directly to the accused; for it is he who suffers the consequences if the defense fails.

The counsel provision supplements this design. It speaks of the "assistance" of counsel, and an assistant, however expert, is still an assistant. The language and spirit of the Sixth Amendment contemplate that counsel, like the other defense tools guaranteed by the Amendment, shall be an aid to a willing defendant — not an organ of the State interposed between an unwilling defendant and his right to defend himself personally. To thrust counsel upon the accused, against his considered wish, thus violates the logic of the Amendment. In such a case, counsel is not an assistant, but a master;[16] and the right to make a defense is stripped of the personal character upon which the Amendment insists. It is true that when a defendant chooses to have a lawyer manage and present his case, law and tradition may allocate to the counsel the power to make binding decisions of trial strategy in many areas. Cf. Henry v. Mississippi, 379 U.S. 443, 451; Brookhart v. Janis, 384 U.S. 1, 7-8; Fay v. Noia, 372 U.S. 391, 439. This allocation can only be justified, however, by the defendant's consent, at the outset, to accept counsel as his representative. An unwanted counsel "represents" the defendant only through a tenuous and unacceptable legal fiction. Unless the accused has acquiesced in such representation, the

15. This Court has often recognized the constitutional stature of rights that, though not literally expressed in the document, are essential to due process of law in a fair adversary process. It is now accepted, for example, that an accused has a right to be present at all stages of the trial where his absence might frustrate the fairness of the proceedings, Snyder v. Massachusetts, 291 U.S. 97; to testify on his own behalf, see Harris v. New York, 401 U.S. 222, 225; Brooks v. Tennessee, 406 U.S. 605, 612; cf. Ferguson v. Georgia, 365 U.S. 570; and to be convicted only if his guilt is proved beyond a reasonable doubt, In re Winship, 397 U.S. 358; Mullaney v. Wilbur, 421 U.S. 684.

The inference of rights is not, of course, a mechanical exercise. In Singer v. United States, 380 U.S. 24, the Court held that an accused has no right to a bench trial, despite his capacity to waive his right to a jury trial. In so holding, the Court stated that "[t]he ability to waive a constitutional right does not ordinarily carry with it the right to insist upon the opposite of that right." Id., at 34-35. But that statement was made only *after* the Court had concluded that the Constitution does not affirmatively protect any right to be tried by a judge. Recognizing that an implied right must arise independently from the design and history of the constitutional text, the Court searched for, but could not find, any "indication that the colonists considered the ability to waive a jury trial to be [of] equal importance to the right to demand one." Id., at 26. Instead, the Court could locate only "isolated instances" of a right to trial by judge, and concluded that these were "clear departures from the common law." Ibid.

We follow the approach of *Singer* here. Our concern is with an *independent* right of self-representation. We do not suggest that this right arises mechanically from a defendant's power to waive the right to the assistance of counsel. See supra, at 814-815. On the contrary, the right must be independently found in the structure and history of the constitutional text.

16. Such a result would sever the concept of counsel from its historic roots. The first lawyers were personal friends of the litigant, brought into court by him so that he might "take 'counsel' with them" before pleading. 1 F. Pollock & F. Maitland, The History of English Law 211 (2d ed. 1909). Similarly, the first "attorneys" were personal agents, often lacking any professional training, who were appointed by those litigants who had secured royal permission to carry on their affairs through a representative, rather than personally. Id., at 212-213.

defense presented is not the defense guaranteed him by the Constitution, for, in a very real sense, it is not *his* defense.

B

The Sixth Amendment, when naturally read, thus implies a right of self-representation. This reading is reinforced by the Amendment's roots in English legal history. [The Court proceeded to an examination of English legal history, concluding that the "common law rule has evidently always been that 'no person charged with a criminal offense can have counsel forced upon him against his will.'"]

C

In the American Colonies the insistence upon a right of self-representation was, if anything, more fervent than in England. . . . [After a lengthy examination of the colonial experience, the Court concluded that] there is no evidence that the colonists and the Framers ever doubted the right of self-representation, or imagined that this right might be considered inferior to the right of assistance of counsel. To the contrary, the colonists and the Framers, as well as their English ancestors, always conceived of the right to counsel as an "assistance" for the accused, to be used at his option, in defending himself. The Framers selected in the Sixth Amendment a form of words that necessarily implies the right of self-representation. That conclusion is supported by centuries of consistent history.

IV

There can be no blinking the fact that the right of an accused to conduct his own defense seems to cut against the grain of this Court's decisions holding that the Constitution requires that no accused can be convicted and imprisoned unless he has been accorded the right to the assistance of counsel. . . . For it is surely true that the basic thesis of those decisions is that the help of a lawyer is essential to assure the defendant a fair trial. And a strong argument can surely be made that the whole thrust of those decisions must inevitably lead to the conclusion that a State may constitutionally impose a lawyer upon even an unwilling defendant.

But it is one thing to hold that every defendant, rich or poor, has the right to the assistance of counsel, and quite another to say that a State may compel a defendant to accept a lawyer he does not want. The value of state-appointed counsel was not unappreciated by the Founders, yet the notion of compulsory counsel was utterly foreign to them. And whatever else may be said of those who wrote the Bill of Rights, surely there can be no doubt that they understood the inestimable worth of free choice.

It is undeniable that in most criminal prosecutions defendants could better defend with counsel's guidance than by their own unskilled efforts. But where the defendant will not voluntarily accept representation by counsel, the potential advantage of a lawyer's training and experience can be realized, if at all, only imperfectly. To force a lawyer on a defendant can only lead him to believe that the law contrives against him. Moreover, it is not inconceivable that in some rare instances, the defendant might in fact present his case more effectively by conducting his own defense. Personal liberties are not rooted in the law of averages. The right to defend is personal. The defendant, and not his lawyer or the State, will bear the personal consequences of a conviction. It is the defendant, therefore, who must be free personally to decide whether in his particular case counsel is to his advantage. And although he may conduct his own defense ultimately to his own detriment, his choice must be honored out of "that respect for the individual which is the lifeblood of the law." Illinois v. Allen, 397 U.S. 337, 350-351 (Brennan, J., concurring).[46]

V

When an accused manages his own defense, he relinquishes, as a purely factual matter, many of the traditional benefits associated with the right to counsel. For this reason, in order to represent himself, the accused must "knowingly and intelligently" [forgo] those relinquished benefits. Johnson v. Zerbst, 304 U.S., at 464-465. Cf. Von Moltke v. Gillies, 332 U.S. 708, 723-724 (plurality opinion of Black, J.). Although a defendant need not himself have the skill and experience of a lawyer in order competently and intelligently to choose self-representation, he should be made aware of the dangers and disadvantages of self-representation, so that the record will establish that "he knows what he is doing and his choice is made with eyes open." Adams v. United States ex rel. McCann, 317 U.S., at 279.

Here, weeks before trial, Faretta clearly and unequivocally declared to the trial judge that he wanted to represent himself and did not want counsel. The record affirmatively shows that Faretta was literate, competent, and understanding, and that he was voluntarily exercising his informed free will. The trial judge had warned Faretta that he thought it was a mistake not to accept the assistance of counsel, and that Faretta would be required to follow all the "ground rules" of trial procedure. We need make no assessment of how well or poorly Faretta had mastered the intricacies of the hearsay rule and the California code provisions that govern challenges of potential jurors on voir dire. For his technical legal knowledge, as such, was not relevant to an assessment of his knowing exercise of the right to defend himself.

In forcing Faretta, under these circumstances, to accept against his will a state-appointed public defender, the California courts deprived him of his constitutional right to conduct his own defense. Accordingly, the judgment before us is vacated, and the case is remanded for further proceedings not inconsistent with this opinion.

It is so ordered.

---

46. We are told that many criminal defendants representing themselves may use the courtroom for deliberate disruption of their trials. But the right of self-representation has been recognized from our beginnings by federal law and by most of the States, and no such result has thereby occurred. Moreover, the trial judge may terminate self-representation by a defendant who deliberately engages in serious and obstructionist misconduct. See Illinois v. Allen, 397 U.S. 337. Of course, a State may—even over objection by the accused—appoint a "standby counsel" to aid the accused if and when the accused requests help, and to be available to represent the accused in the event that termination of the defendant's self-representation is necessary. See United States v. Dougherty, 154 U.S. App. D.C. 76, 87-89, 473 F.2d 1113, 1124-1126.

The right of self-representation is not a license to abuse the dignity of the courtroom. Neither is it a license not to comply with relevant rules of procedural and substantive law. Thus, whatever else may or may not be open to him on appeal, a defendant who elects to represent himself cannot thereafter complain that the quality of his own defense amounted to a denial of "effective assistance of counsel."

MR. CHIEF JUSTICE BURGER, with whom MR. JUSTICE BLACKMUN and MR. JUSTICE REHNQUIST join, dissenting.

This case . . . is another example of the judicial tendency to constitutionalize what is thought "good." That effort fails on its own terms here, because there is nothing desirable or useful in permitting every accused person, even the most uneducated and inexperienced, to insist upon conducting his own defense to criminal charges. Moreover, there is no constitutional basis for the Court's holding, and it can only add to the problems of an already malfunctioning criminal justice system. I therefore dissent.

I

The most striking feature of the Court's opinion is that it devotes so little discussion to the matter which it concedes is the core of the decision, that is, discerning an independent basis in the Constitution for the supposed right to represent oneself in a criminal trial.[2] . . . Its ultimate assertion that such a right is tucked between the lines of the Sixth Amendment is contradicted by the Amendment's language and its consistent judicial interpretation.

As the Court seems to recognize . . . the conclusion that the rights guaranteed by the Sixth Amendment are "personal" to an accused reflects nothing more than the obvious fact that it is he who is on trial and therefore has need of a defense. But neither that nearly trivial proposition nor the language of the Amendment, which speaks in uniformly mandatory terms, leads to the further conclusion that the right to counsel is merely supplementary and may be dispensed with at the whim of the accused. Rather, this Court's decisions have consistently included the right to counsel as an integral part of the bundle making up the larger "right to a defense as we know it." . . .

The reason for this hardly requires explanation. The fact of the matter is that in all but an extraordinarily small number of cases an accused will lose whatever defense he may have if he undertakes to conduct the trial himself. . . . Obviously, [the necessity of counsel to guarantee a fair trial does] not vary depending upon whether the accused actively desires to be represented by counsel or wishes to proceed pro se. Nor is it accurate to suggest, as the Court seems to later in its opinion, that the quality of his representation at trial is a matter with which only the accused is legitimately concerned. . . . Although we have adopted an adversary system of criminal justice, . . . the prosecution is more than an ordinary litigant, and the trial judge is not simply an automaton who insures that technical rules are adhered to. Both are charged with the duty of insuring that justice, in the broadest sense of that term, is achieved in every criminal trial. . . . That goal is ill-served, and the integrity of and public confidence in the system are undermined, when an easy conviction is obtained due to the defendant's ill-advised decision to waive counsel. The damage thus inflicted is not mitigated by the lame explanation that the defendant simply availed himself of the "freedom" "to go to jail under his own banner. . . ." United States ex rel. Maldonado v. Denno, 348 F.2d 12, 15 (C.A.2 1965). The system of criminal justice should not be available as an instrument of self-destruction.

---

2. The Court deliberately, and in my view properly, declines to characterize this case as one in which the defendant was denied a fair trial. . . .

In short, both the "spirit and the logic" of the Sixth Amendment are that every person accused of crime shall receive the fullest possible defense; in the vast majority of cases this command can be honored only by means of the expressly guaranteed right to counsel, and the trial judge is in the best position to determine whether the accused is capable of conducting his defense. True freedom of choice and society's interest in seeing that justice is achieved can be vindicated only if the trial court retains discretion to reject any attempted waiver of counsel and insist that the accused be tried according to the Constitution. This discretion is as critical an element of basic fairness as a trial judge's discretion to decline to accept a plea of guilty. See Santobello v. New York, 404 U.S. 257, 262 (1971).

II

The Court's attempt to support its result by collecting dicta from prior decisions is no more persuasive than its analysis of the Sixth Amendment. Considered in context, the cases upon which the Court relies to "beat its path" either lead it nowhere or point in precisely the opposite direction.

In Adams v. United States ex rel. McCann, 317 U.S. 269 (1942), and Carter v. Illinois, 329 U.S. 173 (1946), the defendants had competently waived counsel but later sought to renounce actions taken by them while proceeding pro se. In both cases this Court upheld the convictions, holding that neither an uncounseled waiver of jury trial nor an uncounseled guilty plea is inherently defective under the Constitution. The language which the Court so carefully excises from those opinions relates, not to an affirmative right of self-representation, but to the consequences of waiver.[4] In Adams, for example, Mr. Justice Frankfurter was careful to point out that his reference to a defendant's "correlative right to dispense with a lawyer's help" meant only that "[h]e may waive his Constitutional right to assistance of counsel." But, as the Court recognizes, the power to waive a constitutional right does not carry with it the right to insist upon its opposite.

Similarly, in Carter the Court's opinion observed that the Constitution "does not require that under all circumstances counsel be forced upon a defendant," citing Adams, 329 U.S., at 174-175 (emphasis added). I, for one, find this statement impossible to square with the Court's present holding that an accused is absolutely entitled to dispense with a lawyer's help under all conditions. Thus, although Adams and Carter support the Court's conclusion that a defendant who represents himself may not thereafter disaffirm his deliberate trial decisions, . . . they provide it no comfort regarding the primary issue in this case.[5] . . .

In short, what the Court represents as a well-traveled road is in reality a constitutional trail which it is blazing for the first time today, one that has not even been hinted at in our previous decisions. Far from an interpretation of the Sixth Amendment, it is a perversion of the provision to which we gave full meaning in Gideon v. Wainwright and Argersinger v. Hamlin.

4. Indeed, the portion of the Court's quotation which warns against turning constitutional protections into "fetters" refers to the right to trial by jury, not the right to counsel. See Adams v. United States ex rel. McCann, 317 U.S. 269, 279 (1942). This Court has, of course, squarely held that there is no constitutional right to dispense with a jury. Singer v. United States, 380 U.S. 24 (1965).

5. No more relevant is Snyder v. Massachusetts, 291 U.S. 97 (1934). The reference in that case to an accused's "power . . . to supersede his lawyers" simply helped explain why his defense might "be made easier" if he were "permitted to be present at the examination of jurors or the summing up of counsel. . . ." Id., at 106. . . .

III

. . . Piecing together shreds of English legal history and early state constitutional and statutory provisions, without a full elaboration of the context in which they occurred or any evidence that they were relied upon by the drafters of our Federal Constitution, creates more questions than it answers and hardly provides the firm foundation upon which the creation of new constitutional rights should rest. We are well reminded that this Court once employed an exhaustive analysis of English and colonial practices regarding the right to counsel to justify the conclusion that it was fundamental to a fair trial and, less than 10 years later, used essentially the same material to conclude that it was not. Compare Powell v. Alabama, 287 U.S., at 60-65, with Betts v. Brady, 316 U.S. 455, 465-471 (1942).

As if to illustrate this point, the single historical fact cited by the Court which would appear truly relevant to ascertaining the meaning of the Sixth Amendment proves too much. As the Court points out, . . . §35 of the Judiciary Act of 1789 provided a statutory right to self-representation in federal criminal trials. The text of the Sixth Amendment, which expressly provides only for a right to counsel, was proposed the day after the Judiciary Act was signed. It can hardly be suggested that the Members of the Congress of 1789, then few in number, were unfamiliar with the Amendment's carefully structured language, which had been under discussion since the 1787 Constitutional Convention. And it would be most remarkable to suggest, had the right to conduct one's own defense been considered so critical as to require constitutional protection, that it would have been left to implication. Rather, under traditional canons of construction, *inclusion* of the right in the Judiciary Act and its *omission* from the constitutional amendment drafted at the same time by many of the same men, supports the conclusion that the omission was intentional.

There is no way to reconcile the idea that the Sixth Amendment impliedly guaranteed the right of an accused to conduct his own defense with the contemporaneous action of the Congress in passing a statute explicitly giving that right. If the Sixth Amendment created a right to self-representation it was unnecessary for Congress to enact any statute on the subject at all. In this case, therefore, history ought to lead judges to conclude that the Constitution leaves to the judgment of legislatures, and the flexible process of statutory amendment, the question whether criminal defendants should be permitted to conduct their trials pro se.

. . . And the fact that we have not hinted at a contrary view for 185 years is surely entitled to some weight in the scales.[6] . . .

IV

Society has the right to expect that, when courts find new rights implied in the Constitution, their potential effect upon the resources of our criminal justice system will be considered. However, such considerations are conspicuously absent from the Court's opinion in this case.

It hardly needs repeating that courts at all levels are already handicapped by the unsupplied demand for competent advocates, with the result that it often takes far

---

6. The fact that Congress has retained a statutory right to self-representation suggests that it has also assumed that the Sixth Amendment does not guarantee such a right. See 28 U.S.C. §1654.

longer to complete a given case than experienced counsel would require. If we were to assume that there will be widespread exercise of the newly discovered constitutional right to self-representation, it would almost certainly follow that there will be added congestion in the courts and that the quality of justice will suffer. Moreover, the Court blandly assumes that once an accused has elected to defend himself he will be bound by his choice and not be heard to complain of it later. . . . This assumption ignores the role of appellate review, for the reported cases are replete with instances of a convicted defendant being relieved of a deliberate decision even when made *with the advice of counsel*. See Silber v. United States, 370 U.S. 717 (1962). It is totally unrealistic, therefore, to suggest that an accused will always be held to the consequences of a decision to conduct his own defense. Unless, as may be the case, most persons accused of crime have more wit than to insist upon the dubious benefit that the Court confers today, we can expect that many expensive and good-faith prosecutions will be nullified on appeal for reasons that trial courts are now deprived of the power to prevent.[7]

MR. JUSTICE BLACKMUN, with whom THE CHIEF JUSTICE and MR. JUSTICE REHNQUIST join, dissenting.

. . . I note briefly the procedural problems that, I suspect, today's decision will visit upon trial courts in the future. Although the Court indicates that a pro se defendant necessarily waives any claim he might otherwise make of ineffective assistance of counsel, . . . the opinion leaves open a host of other procedural questions. Must every defendant be advised of his right to proceed pro se? If so, when must that notice be given? Since the right to assistance of counsel and the right to self-representation are mutually exclusive, how is the waiver of each right to be measured? If a defendant has elected to exercise his right to proceed pro se, does he still have a constitutional right to assistance of standby counsel? How soon in the criminal proceeding must a defendant decide between proceeding by counsel or pro se? Must he be allowed to switch in midtrial? May a violation of the right to self-representation ever be harmless error? Must the trial court treat the pro se defendant differently than it would professional counsel? I assume that many of these questions will be answered with finality in due course. Many of them, however, such as the standards of waiver and the treatment of the pro se defendant, will haunt the trial of every defendant who elects to exercise his right to self-representation. The procedural problems spawned by an absolute right to self-representation will far outweigh whatever tactical advantage the defendant may feel he has gained by electing to represent himself.

If there is any truth to the old proverb that "one who is his own lawyer has a fool for a client," the Court by its opinion today now bestows a *constitutional* right on one to make a fool of himself.

NOTES AND QUESTIONS

1. Who wins the historical argument in *Faretta* centering on the intent of the framers of the Sixth Amendment? Which way does the statutory history cut?

---

7. Some of the damage we can anticipate from a defendant's ill-advised insistence on conducting his own defense may be mitigated by appointing a qualified lawyer to sit in the case as the traditional "friend of the court." The Court does not foreclose this option. . . .

2. If a defendant's right to proceed pro se is violated, what should be the remedy?

3. Pro se representation is quite uncommon, and thus is not a large practical problem for the legal system. Moreover, the few defendants who elect to proceed pro se are systematically convicted in short order, largely because, precisely as the dissenters in *Faretta* predicted, such individuals typically are incompetent to conduct their defense. One famous case involved Colin Ferguson, the "Long Island Railroad Shooter," who entered a commuter rail car and began shooting passengers, killing 6 and wounding 19 more. He proceeded pro se, causing much anguish by cross-examining the surviving victims, and was quickly convicted. People v. Ferguson 670 N.Y.S.2d 327 (N.Y.A.D. 2 Dept. 1998).

Another such case involves the "twentieth hijacker," Zacarias Moussaoui, who was accused of being involved in the plot leading to the destruction of the World Trade Center on Sept. 11, 2001. He, too, exercised his right to proceed pro se, but in a curious twist his decision worked for a while to his advantage. We say "for a while," because the trial judge eventually tired of his behavior and revoked his right to proceed pro se, largely on the ground that he was not playing the game anywhere near appropriately. The interesting twist, though, came from his insistence on interviewing prisoners in custody of the United States whom he asserted might provide him exculpatory evidence. For its part, the U.S. Government claimed these individuals were security assets and allowing Moussaoui access to them would compromise national security. The District Judge ordered that adequate access be provided, which might have meant personal meetings between Moussaoui (acting as his own lawyer) and the individuals in custody. Had things played out in that fashion, this might have put the government to the choice of allowing such access or dismissing charges against, and freeing, Moussaoui. As it turned out, the Fourth Circuit determined that substitutions for live access could be fashioned, and ordered it done. The entire story is laid out in United States v. Moussaoui, 365 F.3d 292 (4th Cir. 2004); 382 F.3d 453 (4th Cir. 2004).

4. For another good example of the dangers (and maybe the benefits?) of self-representation, consider the case of Adam Martin, accused — together with two of his brothers — with robbing several banks along I-35 in Austin, Texas. Adam chose to represent himself. At a pretrial hearing, he subpoenaed his brother, Michael (who was already serving time after pleading guilty to one of the robberies), and asked him to state whether Adam had committed any crimes. To which Michael replied: "Yeah. You were with me on four different bank robberies, Adam, you know that."

At trial, things did not get better for Adam. His cross-examination of Michael (by now, a prosecution witness) included bizarre questions about Michael's nicknames, his religion, and the time the two brothers spent together in jail. At one point, Adam asked Michael, "Do you fear me in any way?" Michael responded, "I've seen you do people bad ways," and told how Adam had attacked people with knives and was once involved with organized crime. When Adam noted that "I haven't been convicted of it," Michael replied, "That doesn't mean it's not true."

Adam was convicted on all charges. Afterwards, he explained: "The right to defend yourself in this country is one of the greatest rights you have." He also said that he considered disrupting the trial, but decided not to do so because he feared that it might jeopardize the rights of future pro se litigants. See Steven Kreytak, "Eldest of Three Bank-Robbing Brothers Guilty; "I-35 Robber," Who Acted as

Own Attorney, Not Surprised at Verdict," Austin American-Statesman, August 19, 2004, p. A1.

5. Interestingly, given the general parameters of Sixth Amendment doctrine, a convicted defendant does not have the right to dispense with the assistance of counsel on appeal. In Martinez v. Court of Appeal of California, 528 U.S. 152 (2000), the Court said:

> We are not aware of any historical consensus establishing a right of self-representation on appeal. We might, nonetheless, paraphrase *Faretta* and assert: No State or Colony ever forced counsel upon a convicted appellant, and no spokesman ever suggested that such a practice would be tolerable or advisable. Such negative historical evidence was meaningful to the *Faretta* Court, because the fact that the "[dog] had not barked" arguably demonstrated that early lawmakers intended to preserve the "long-respected right of self-representation" at trial. Historical silence, however, has no probative force in the appellate context because there simply was no long-respected right of self-representation on appeal. In fact, the right of appeal itself is of relatively recent origin.
>
> Appeals as of right in federal courts were nonexistent for the first century of our Nation, and appellate review of any sort was rarely allowed. The States, also, did not generally recognize an appeal as of right until Washington became the first to constitutionalize the right explicitly in 1889. There was similarly no right to appeal in criminal cases at common law, and appellate review of any sort was "limited" and "rarely used." Thus, unlike the inquiry in *Faretta,* the historical evidence does not provide any support for an affirmative constitutional right to appellate self-representation.
>
> The *Faretta* majority's reliance on the structure of the Sixth Amendment is also not relevant. The Sixth Amendment identifies the basic rights that the accused shall enjoy in "all criminal prosecutions." They are presented strictly as rights that are available in preparation for trial and at the trial itself. The Sixth Amendment does not include any right to appeal. As we have recognized, "[t]he right of appeal, as we presently know it in criminal cases, is purely a creature of statute." *Abney,* 431 U.S., at 656. It necessarily follows that the Amendment itself does not provide any basis for finding a right to self-representation on appeal. . . . Indeed, none of our many cases safeguarding the rights of an indigent appellant has placed any reliance on either the Sixth Amendment or on *Faretta.*
>
> Finally, the *Faretta* majority found that the right to self-representation at trial was grounded in part in a respect for individual autonomy. This consideration is, of course, also applicable to an appellant seeking to manage his own case. As we explained in *Faretta,* at the trial level "[t]o force a lawyer on a defendant can only lead him to believe that the law contrives against him." On appellate review, there is surely a similar risk that the appellant will be skeptical of whether a lawyer, who is employed by the same government that is prosecuting him, will serve his cause with undivided loyalty. Equally true on appeal is the related observation that it is the appellant personally who will bear the consequences of the appeal.
>
> In light of our conclusion that the Sixth Amendment does not apply to appellate proceedings, any individual right to self-representation on appeal based on autonomy principles must be grounded in the Due Process Clause. Under the practices that prevail in the Nation today, however, we are entirely unpersuaded that the risk of either disloyalty or suspicion of disloyalty is a sufficient concern to conclude that a constitutional right of self-representation is a necessary component of a fair appellate proceeding. We have no doubt that instances of disloyal representation are rare. In both trials and appeals there are, without question, cases in which counsel's performance is ineffective.

Even in those cases, however, it is reasonable to assume that counsel's performance is more effective than what the unskilled appellant could have provided for himself.

No one, including Martinez and the *Faretta* majority, attempts to argue that as a rule pro se representation is wise, desirable or efficient.[10] Although we found in *Faretta* that the right to defend oneself at trial is "fundamental" in nature, 422 U.S., at 817, it is clear that it is representation by counsel that is the standard, not the exception. See Patterson v. Illinois, 487 U.S. 285, 307 (1988) (noting the "strong presumption against" waiver of right to counsel). Our experience has taught us that "a pro se defense is usually a bad defense, particularly when compared to a defense provided by an experienced criminal defense attorney."[11]

. . . Even at the trial level . . . , the government's interest in ensuring the integrity and efficiency of the trial at times outweighs the defendant's interest in acting as his own lawyer. . . . In the appellate context, the balance between the two competing interests surely tips in favor of the State. The status of the accused defendant, who retains a presumption of innocence throughout the trial process, changes dramatically when a jury returns a guilty verdict. . . . In the words of the *Faretta* majority, appellate proceedings are simply not a case of "hal[ing] a person into its criminal courts."

Note that *Martinez* was a 9–0 decision, with eight Justices joining the majority opinion. Does some of the language in *Martinez* suggest that the Court may be ready to rethink the balance that was struck in *Faretta* between autonomy and the integrity of the trial?

NOTES ON COMPETENCY AND WAIVER

1. Is there, or ought there to be, a requirement of competency to waive counsel, separate from the issues of competency to proceed to trial and an intelligent waiver? The New York Court of Appeals answered the question negatively in the aptly named case of People v. Reason, 37 N.Y.2d 351 (1975). According to the court, "it would be difficult to say that a standard which was designed to determine whether a defendant was capable of defending himself, is inadequate when he chooses to conduct his own defense." Id. at 354. The court consequently affirmed defendant's convictions of murder and attempted murder. Bearing in mind the limits of anecdotal data, consider the decision in *Reason* in light of the following excerpts from Mr. Reason's opening and closing to the jury:

> *The Court:* The order of business before the Court now, Mr. Reason, is your opening statement. Will you proceed and make it properly?
> *The Defendant:* I will try to prove the existence of the dead, reincarnation of the realm of Todis, . . . Hays, . . . Hell, the underworld and the hushed truth of society based upon the entities of which our way of life is based. Fighting among themselves even for possession of the living and the dead and the association of whatever rationality or religion.
>
> I will prove an angel, demon, a devil and a soul. Paradoxically I will introduce proof of police corruption, political control of government, criminal

---

10. Some critics argue that the right to proceed pro se at trial in certain cases is akin to allowing the defendant to waive his right to a fair trial. See, e.g., United States v. Farhad, 190 F.3d 1097, 1106-1107 (CA9 1999) (Reinhardt, J., concurring specially), *cert. pending*, No. 99-7127.

11. Decker, The Sixth Amendment Right to Shoot Oneself in the Foot: An Assessment of the Guarantee of Self-Representation Twenty Years after Faretta, 6 Seton Hall Const. L. J. 483, 598 (1996).

affairs according to certain arbitrations, abiding the way of life for a particular entity of homage of their dues for the bargaining of their souls. . . .

I will prove or I will disprove Christ as our God, saints, the devil and let these entities of the power to take human life and due — there is many deeply religious people that say it was the will of God who in many instances — it isn't always the will of God, but the will of other entities or as we read at the bottom of insurance contracts except by acts of God, sometimes by those acts of men too, by means of what may be considered a spiritual sort seemingly to have been of natural causes and often some that would have died by the cause of another is used as an instrument to die; that the other would be subject to the instrument of society such as fate, destiny, pre-destiny. But history is an accepted fact as disorderly as it may be which I will also attempt to prove, and historically men have proved, prayed to something of a greater competency, to Jehovah, Brahma, Ghatama, God and others. They believe, practice and perform rituals of sorcery, Budabo, witchcraft, Christianity, black magic, occult, Bubanza, . . . soothsayers, fortune tellers and priests. . . .

I will introduce the defendant's bad character to show his good intention or expose his entire criminal record, acts of his criminal importance, accomplishments, activities and disciplinary reports be considered. . . .

[In closing, the defendant argued in part:]

The issue of the dead belonged to God. It's in the bible. Each of the dead belong to God. God seeks the past. Life gives birth to time, time is passed, just passed, time passed, just passed. Anticipate time. Time is past. Hour has already been. I wrote right here, I would like to repeat that and I would, I would like to repeat that.

A long time ago, anticipating this, I would like to repeat that.

The issue of the dead belong of God. God seeks what is passed. Life gives birth to time. Time is past. We set time ahead of us confusing time and motion with duration. We are towards a delusion, perhaps, create illusion of a present that don't really exist; create instantaneous occurring successions on the same pattern offset by the evolving sun as time though it made difference to the sun how fast — (Unintelligible).

Now, look at that, you people. I wrote it for you people. Memorized the whole thing if I had the time. This is not only pedantics, I quote Corinthian, Chapter 13, 8th Verse.

In Godinez v. Moran, 509 U.S. 389 (1993), the Supreme Court embraced the basic conclusion of the *Reason* court on the competency issue, holding that competency to waive the right to counsel, as well as to plead guilty, is measured by the same standard as competency to stand trial. That standard was established in Dusky v. United States, 420 U.S. 162 (1960): whether the defendant has "sufficient present ability to consult with his lawyer with a reasonable degree of rational understanding" and has "a rational as well as factual understanding of the proceedings against him." The *Godinez* Court added:

A finding that a defendant is competent to stand trial, however, is not all that is necessary before he may be permitted to plead guilty or waive his right to counsel. In addition to determining that a defendant who seeks to plead guilty or waive counsel is competent, a trial court must satisfy itself that the waiver of his constitutional rights is knowing and voluntary. Parke v. Raley, 506 U.S. 20, 28-29 (1992) (guilty plea); *Faretta,* supra, at 835 (waiver of counsel). In this sense there *is* a "heightened" standard for pleading guilty and for waiving the right to counsel, but it is not a heightened standard of *competence.*[12]

This two-part inquiry is what we had in mind in [Westbrook v. Arizona, 384 U.S. 150 (1966) (per curiam)]. When we distinguished between "competence to stand trial" and "competence to waive [the] constitutional right to the assistance of counsel," 384 U.S., at 150, we were using "competence to waive" as a shorthand for the "intelligent and competent waiver" requirement of Johnson v. Zerbst. This much is clear from the fact that we quoted that very language from *Zerbst* immediately after noting that the trial court had not determined whether the petitioner was competent to waive his right to counsel. See 384 U.S., at 150 (" 'This protecting duty imposes the serious and weighty responsibility upon the trial judge of determining whether there is an intelligent and competent waiver by the accused' ") (quoting Johnson v. Zerbst, 304 U.S., at 465. Thus, *Westbrook* stands only for the unremarkable proposition that when a defendant seeks to waive his right to counsel, a determination that he is competent to stand trial is not enough; the waiver must also be intelligent and voluntary before it can be accepted.

The Court also noted that states could choose to impose a higher standard of competency than the one mandated by *Dusky,* which merely established the due process minimum standard.

Can such a higher standard of competency be applied to a *Faretta* situation, in which the defendant has a *constitutional right* to waive counsel? The Seventh Circuit, in an opinion by Judge Posner, has said yes:

It is one thing for a defendant to have sufficient mentation to be able to follow the trial proceedings with the aid of a lawyer, and another to be able to represent himself; and while Brooks clearly had the former, he seems equally clearly to have lacked the latter, if we may judge from his wild behavior and incomprehensible outbursts during the trial. And if he was incompetent to conduct his own defense, this is evidence that his decision to waive counsel was not "knowing and intelligent," as all waivers must be in order to be legally effective . . . , Johnson v. Zerbst, 304 U.S. 458, 464-465 (1938). . . . A waiver of counsel would make no sense from the defendant's standpoint if he knew he was incompetent to defend himself (unless his intent was to disrupt the trial — in which event it would not be an exercise of the right recognized by *Faretta*); and so senseless a waiver could only with difficulty be regarded as knowing and intelligent. That appears to be this case. . . .

[E]ven if the standards for competence to stand trial and for competence to waive the right of counsel are the same, the existence of an effective waiver need not be automatically deduced from a finding that the defendant is competent to stand trial. This would be obvious if having determined that the defendant was competent to stand trial the judge had asked the defendant whether he wanted a lawyer but had not explained the consequences of going to trial without one. A judge who, having explained the consequences, finds that the defendant doesn't understand them is

12. The focus of a competency inquiry is the defendant's mental capacity; the question is whether he has the ability to understand the proceedings. . . . The purpose of the "knowing and voluntary" inquiry, by contrast, is to determine whether the defendant actually does understand the significance and consequences of a particular decision and whether the decision is uncoerced. See *Faretta,* supra, at 835 (defendant waiving counsel must be "made aware of the dangers and disadvantages of self-representation, so that the record will establish that 'he knows what he is doing and his choice is made with eyes open' "). . . .

entitled to conclude that although competent to stand trial, the defendant has not made an effective waiver of his right to counsel and therefore may not represent himself. This result is consistent with *Godinez*.

Wisconsin, as this case illustrates, has set a higher standard for waivers of the *Faretta* right than for competence to stand trial. . . . Because being competent to stand trial and having waived the right to counsel do not require the same information, and because the former competence does not imply an effective waiver in all cases, we do not think that Wisconsin's approach violates the rule of *Godinez*.

Brooks v. McCaughtry, 380 F.3d 1009 (7th Cir. 2004).

2. What does it mean that a waiver of counsel must be "knowing and intelligent"? Is that phrase internally inconsistent? If not, what are its referents? The Court in *Faretta* asserts that "technical knowledge" is not even relevant to the inquiry and implies that on being convicted a technically incompetent individual may not assert ineffectiveness as a grounds for relief. How realistic is that? How would you react as a judge to a case in which an untrained person unknowingly forwent a potentially dispositive defense? See United States v. Weninger, 624 F.2d 163 (10th Cir. 1980), disallowing a defense of ineffectiveness from a defendant who proceeded pro se at trial. Do you think the *Weninger* approach will be universally followed by the courts? If you were a judge, how could you avoid *Faretta*'s limitation on claiming error due to incompetency in a case where you believed the pro se representation to have been incompetent and led to a false conviction, but in which no other legally adequate ground for reversal existed? Might you stretch other legal rules to reach the right result? That is exactly what a number of courts have done, according to Sarah L. Allen, Faretta: Self-Representation, or Legal Misrepresentation?, 90 Iowa L. Rev. (forthcoming 2005). The author searched for cases involving pro se representation, that involved reversals of convictions, and in which there were dissents, the idea being that dissents might signal a majority stretching the law. A number of such cases were found with majority opinions fairly plainly stretching other legal rules to compensate for the inability to reverse on competency grounds.

3. Should a waiver of the Sixth Amendment right to counsel ever be allowed without first appointing counsel to discuss the matter with the defendant?

What about the closely related situation where a defendant seeks to waive his right to counsel and plead guilty without the advice of counsel? Does the Constitution require that such a defendant be informed specifically by the trial judge, prior to entering the plea, that by virtue of waiving his right to counsel (1) he may wind up overlooking a viable defense, and (2) he may make an unwise decision about entering the plea? In Iowa v. Tovar, 124 S. Ct. 1379 (2004), the Court rejected the claim that such warnings are essential to an intelligent and knowing waiver of the right to counsel, holding that in such a situation the Constitution requires knowledge of only the nature of charges, the right to be counseled about the plea, and the range of allowable punishments. *Tovar* is discussed in greater detail, infra, in Chapter 10.

Are some of the difficulties predicted by the dissenters in *Faretta* reflected in the next case?

McKASKLE v. WIGGINS

Certiorari to the United States Court of Appeals for the Fifth Circuit
465 U.S. 168 (1984)

JUSTICE O'CONNOR delivered the opinion of the Court.

In Faretta v. California, 422 U.S. 806 (1975), this Court recognized a defendant's Sixth Amendment right to conduct his own defense. The Court also held that a trial court may appoint "standby counsel" to assist the pro se defendant in his defense. Today we must decide what role standby counsel who is present at trial over the defendant's objection may play consistent with the protection of the defendant's *Faretta* rights.

I

Carl Edwin Wiggins was convicted of robbery and sentenced to life imprisonment as a recidivist. His conviction was set aside because of a defective indictment. When Wiggins was retried he was again convicted and sentenced to life imprisonment. Standby counsel were appointed to assist Wiggins at both trials. Wiggins now challenges counsel's participation in his second trial.

Prior to the first trial, a hearing was held on Wiggins' motion to proceed pro se. The court granted the motion, but simultaneously appointed two attorneys to act as standby counsel. Wiggins initially objected to their presence. Shortly thereafter, however, counsel asked Wiggins how they should conduct themselves at trial, and Wiggins expressly requested that they bring appropriate objections directly to the attention of the court, without first consulting him. After the trial, newly appointed counsel discovered that the original indictment was defective, and a new trial was granted.

On April 16, 1973, about two months before the second trial began, Wiggins filed a request for appointed counsel, stating that he wished to rescind his earlier waiver of counsel. The next day Wiggins filled out and signed a form captioned "Petition for Appointment of Counsel and Order Thereon." The trial court appointed Benjamin Samples. About a month later Wiggins filed an additional request for counsel. Five days later Wiggins filled out another appointment of counsel form, and the trial court appointed R. Norvell Graham.

Wiggins' wishes respecting appointed counsel remained volatile as his second trial approached. When pretrial proceedings began on June 4, 1973, Wiggins announced that he would be defending himself pro se; he then firmly requested that counsel not be allowed to interfere with Wiggins' presentations to the court. Wiggins reaffirmed his desire to proceed pro se on the following morning, June 5, and objected even to the court's insistence that counsel remain available for consultation. The trial began later that day, and shortly thereafter Wiggins interrupted his cross-examination of a witness to consult with Graham off the record. Still later, Wiggins expressly agreed to allow Graham to conduct voir dire of another witness.

Wiggins started the next day of trial, June 6, with a request that the trial not proceed in Samples' absence from the courtroom. Later that morning Wiggins requested that counsel not be allowed to assist or interrupt, but a short while after Wiggins interrupted his own cross-examination of a witness to confer with Samples off the record. When the trial reconvened in the afternoon, Wiggins agreed to proceed in Samples' absence. After Samples returned, however, Wiggins again interrupted his own cross-examination of a witness to confer with him. Later Wiggins insisted that counsel should not initiate private consultations with Wiggins. Before the end of the day Wiggins once again found occasion to interrupt his own examination of a witness to confer with Samples.

On the following day, June 7, Wiggins agreed that Graham would make Wiggins' opening statement to the jury. On June 8, Wiggins was once again willing to have the trial proceed in the absence of one of his standby counsel. Following his conviction, Wiggins moved for a new trial. At the July 31 hearing on Wiggins' motion, Wiggins denounced the services standby counsel had provided. He insisted that they had unfairly interfered with his presentation of his defense.

After exhausting direct appellate and state habeas review Wiggins filed a petition for federal habeas corpus relief. He argued that standby counsel's conduct deprived him of his right to present his own defense, as guaranteed by *Faretta*. The District Court denied the habeas petition, but the Court of Appeals for the Fifth Circuit reversed. Wiggins v. Estelle, 681 F.2d 266, rehearing denied, 691 F.2d 213 (C.A.5 1982). The Court of Appeals held that Wiggins' Sixth Amendment right of self-representation was violated by the unsolicited participation of overzealous standby counsel:

> [T]he rule that we establish today is that court-appointed standby counsel is "to be seen, but not heard." By this we mean that he is not to compete with the defendant or supersede his defense. Rather, his presence is there for advisory purposes only, to be used or not used as the defendant sees fit.

We do not accept the Court of Appeals' rule, and reverse its judgment.

II . . .

B

. . . A defendant's right to self-representation plainly encompasses certain specific rights to have his voice heard. The pro se defendant must be allowed to control the organization and content of his own defense, to make motions, to argue points of law, to participate in voir dire, to question witnesses, and to address the court and the jury at appropriate points in the trial. The record reveals that Wiggins was in fact accorded all of these rights.

III

Wiggins claims, and the Court of Appeals agreed, that the pro se defendant may insist on presenting his own case wholly free from interruption or other uninvited involvement by standby counsel. . . .

In our view, both *Faretta*'s logic and its citation of the *Dougherty* case indicate that no absolute bar on standby counsel's unsolicited participation is appropriate or was intended. The right to appear pro se exists to affirm the dignity and autonomy of the accused and to allow the presentation of what may, at least occasionally, be the accused's best possible defense. Both of these objectives can be achieved without categorically silencing standby counsel.

In determining whether a defendant's *Faretta* rights have been respected, the primary focus must be on whether the defendant had a fair chance to present his case in his own way. *Faretta* itself dealt with the defendant's affirmative right to participate, not with the limits on standby counsel's additional involvement. The specific rights to make his voice heard that Wiggins was plainly accorded, form the core of a defendant's right of self-representation.

We recognize, nonetheless, that the right to speak for oneself entails more than the opportunity to add one's voice to a cacophony of others. As Wiggins contends, the objectives underlying the right to proceed pro se may be undermined by unsolicited and excessively intrusive participation by standby counsel. In proceedings before a jury the defendant may legitimately be concerned that multiple voices "for the defense" will confuse the message the defendant wishes to convey, thus defeating *Faretta*'s objectives.[7] Accordingly, the *Faretta* right must impose some limits on the extent of standby counsel's unsolicited participation.[8]

First, the pro se defendant is entitled to preserve actual control over the case he chooses to present to the jury. This is the core of the *Faretta* right. If standby counsel's participation over the defendant's objection effectively allows counsel to make or substantially interfere with any significant tactical decisions, or to control the questioning of witnesses, or to speak *instead* of the defendant on any matter of importance, the *Faretta* right is eroded.

Second, participation by standby counsel without the defendant's consent should not be allowed to destroy the jury's perception that the defendant is representing himself. The defendant's appearance in the status of one conducting his own defense is important in a criminal trial, since the right to appear pro se exists to affirm the accused's individual dignity and autonomy. In related contexts the courts have recognized that a defendant has a right to be present at all important stages of trial, Snyder v. Massachusetts, that he may not normally be forced to appear in court in shackles or prison garb, Estelle v. Williams, and that he has a right to present testimony in his own behalf, see Harris v. New York; Brooks v. Tennessee. Appearing before the jury in the status of one who is defending himself may be equally important to the pro se defendant. From the jury's perspective, the message conveyed by the defense may depend as much on the messenger as on the message itself. From the defendant's own point of view, the right to appear pro se can lose much of its importance if only the lawyers in the courtroom know that the right is being exercised.

7. A pro se defendant must generally accept any unsolicited help or hindrance that may come from the judge who chooses to call and question witnesses, from the prosecutor who faithfully exercises his duty to present evidence favorable to the defense, from the plural voices speaking "for the defense" in a trial of more than one defendant, or from an amicus counsel appointed to assist the court, see Brown v. United States, 105 U.S. App. D.C. 77, 83, 264 F.2d 363, 369 (C.A.D.C. 1959) (Judge Burger, concurring in part).

8. Since the right of self-representation is a right that when exercised usually increases the likelihood of a trial outcome unfavorable to the defendant, its denial is not amenable to "harmless error" analysis. The right is either respected or denied; its deprivation cannot be harmless. As a corollary, however, a defendant who exercises his right to appear pro se "cannot thereafter complain that the quality of his own defense amounted to a denial of 'effective assistance of counsel.'" *Faretta*, 422 U.S., at 834 n. 46. Moreover, the defendant's right to proceed pro se exists in the larger context of the criminal trial designed to determine whether or not a defendant is guilty of the offense with which he is charged. The trial judge may be required to make numerous rulings reconciling the participation of standby counsel with a pro se defendant's objection to that participation; nothing in the nature of the *Faretta* right suggests that the usual deference to "judgment calls" on these issues by the trial judge should not obtain here as elsewhere.

IV

Participation by standby counsel outside the presence of the jury engages only the first of these two limitations. A trial judge, who in any event receives a defendant's original *Faretta* request and supervises the protection of the right throughout the trial, must be considered capable of differentiating the claims presented by a pro se defendant from those presented by standby counsel. . . . Accordingly, the appearance of a pro se defendant's self-representation will not be unacceptably undermined by counsel's participation outside the presence of the jury.

Thus, *Faretta* rights are adequately vindicated in proceedings outside the presence of the jury if the pro se defendant is allowed to address the court freely on his own behalf and if disagreements between counsel and the pro se defendant are resolved in the defendant's favor whenever the matter is one that would normally be left to the discretion of counsel.

. . . [W]e are satisfied that counsel's participation outside the presence of the jury fully satisfied the first standard we have outlined. Wiggins was given ample opportunity to present his own position to the court on every matter discussed. He was given time to think matters over, to explain his problems and concerns informally, and to speak to the judge off the record. Standby counsel participated actively, but for the most part in an orderly manner. The one instance of overbearing conduct by counsel was a direct result of Wiggins' own indecision as to who would question the witness on voir dire. Wiggins was given abundant opportunity to argue his contentions to the court.

Equally important, all conflicts between Wiggins and counsel were resolved in Wiggins' favor. The trial judge repeatedly explained to all concerned that Wiggins' strategic choices, not counsel's, would prevail.

. . . Not every motion made by Wiggins was granted, but in no instance was counsel's position adopted over Wiggins' on a matter that would normally be left to the defense's discretion.

V

Participation by standby counsel in the presence of the jury is more problematic. It is here that the defendant may legitimately claim that excessive involvement by counsel will destroy the appearance that the defendant is acting pro se. This, in turn, may erode the dignitary values that the right to self-representation is intended to promote and may undercut the defendant's presentation to the jury of his own most effective defense. Nonetheless, we believe that a categorical bar on participation by standby counsel in the presence of the jury is unnecessary.

A . . .

The record in this case reveals that Wiggins' pro se efforts were undermined primarily by his own, frequent changes of mind regarding counsel's role. Early in the trial Wiggins insisted he wished to proceed entirely without assistance, but shortly thereafter he expressly agreed that counsel should question a witness on voir dire. Wiggins objected vehemently to some of counsel's motions, but warmly embraced others. Initially Wiggins objected to standby counsel's presence; later he refused to allow the trial to proceed in their absence; in the end he agreed that counsel would make a closing statement for the defense. The only two long appearances by counsel at Wiggins' trial, one before the jury and one outside its presence, were both initiated with Wiggins' express approval. In these circumstances it is very difficult to determine how much of counsel's participation was in fact contrary to Wiggins' desires of the moment.

Faretta does not require a trial judge to permit "hybrid" representation of the type Wiggins was actually allowed. But if a defendant is given the opportunity and elects to have counsel appear before the court or jury, his complaints concerning counsel's subsequent unsolicited participation lose much of their force. A defendant does not have a constitutional right to choreograph special appearances by counsel. Once a pro se defendant invites or agrees to any substantial participation by counsel, subsequent appearances by counsel must be presumed to be with the defendant's acquiescence, at least until the defendant expressly and unambiguously renews his request that standby counsel be silenced.

B

Faretta rights are also not infringed when standby counsel assists the pro se defendant in overcoming routine procedural or evidentiary obstacles to the completion of some specific task, such as introducing evidence or objecting to testimony, that the defendant has clearly shown he wishes to complete. Nor are they infringed when counsel merely helps to ensure the defendant's compliance with basic rules of courtroom protocol and procedure. In neither case is there any significant interference with the defendant's actual control over the presentation of his defense. The likelihood that the defendant's appearance in the status of one defending himself will be eroded is also slight, and in any event it is tolerable. A defendant does not have a constitutional right to receive personal instruction from the trial judge on courtroom procedure. Nor does the Constitution require judges to take over chores for a pro se defendant that would normally be attended to by trained counsel as a matter of course. . . .

Accordingly, we make explicit today what is already implicit in *Faretta:* A defendant's Sixth Amendment rights are not violated when a trial judge appoints standby counsel — even over the defendant's objection — to relieve the judge of the need to explain and enforce basic rules of courtroom protocol or to assist the defendant in overcoming routine obstacles that stand in the way of the defendant's achievement of his own clearly indicated goals. Participation by counsel to steer a defendant through the basic procedures of trial is permissible even in the unlikely event that it somewhat undermines the pro se defendant's appearance of control over his own defense. . . .

C

Putting aside participation that was either approved by Wiggins or attendant to routine clerical or procedural matters, counsel's unsolicited comments in front of the jury were infrequent and for the most part innocuous. On two occasions Graham interrupted a witness's answer to a question put by Wiggins. The first interruption was trivial. When the second was made the jury was briefly excused and subsequently given a cautionary instruction as requested by Graham. Wiggins made no objection. Standby counsel also moved for a mistrial three times in the presence of the jury. Each motion was in response to allegedly prejudicial questions or comments by the prosecutor. Wiggins did not comment on the first motion, but he opposed the following two. All three motions were immediately denied by the trial court. Regrettably, counsel used profanity to express his exasperation on the second occasion.[15] Finally, counsel played an active role at the punishment phase of the trial. The record supplies no explanation for the sudden change in this regard. Wiggins made no objection to counsel's participation in this phase of the trial. We can only surmise that by then Wiggins had concluded that appearing pro se was not in his best interests.

The statements made by counsel during the guilt phase of the trial, in the presence of the jury and without Wiggins' express consent, occupy only a small portion of the transcript. Most were of an unobjectionable, mechanical sort. While standby counsel's participation at Wiggins' trial should not serve as a model for future trials, we believe that counsel's involvement fell short of infringing on Wiggins' *Faretta* rights. Wiggins unquestionably maintained actual control over the presentation of his own defense at all times.

We are also persuaded that Wiggins was allowed to appear before the jury in the status of one defending himself. At the outset the trial judge carefully explained to the jury that Wiggins would be appearing pro se. Wiggins, not counsel, examined prospective jurors on voir dire, cross-examined the prosecution's witnesses, examined his own witnesses, and made an opening statement for the defense. Wiggins objected to the prosecutor's case at least as often as did counsel. If Wiggins' closing statement to the jury had to compete with one made by counsel, it was only because Wiggins agreed in advance to that arrangement.

By contrast, counsel's interruptions of Wiggins or witnesses being questioned by Wiggins in the presence of the jury were few and perfunctory. Most of counsel's uninvited comments were directed at the prosecutor. Such interruptions present little threat to a defendant's *Faretta* rights, at least when the defendant's view regarding those objections has not been clearly articulated. On the rare occasions that disagreements between counsel and Wiggins were aired in the presence of the jury the trial judge consistently ruled in Wiggins' favor. This was a pattern more likely to reinforce than to detract from the appearance that Wiggins was controlling his own defense. The intrusions by counsel at Wiggins' trial were simply not substantial or frequent enough to have seriously undermined Wiggins' appearance before the jury in the status of one representing himself.

VI

Faretta affirmed the defendant's constitutional right to appear on stage at his trial. We recognize that a pro se defendant may wish to dance a solo, not a pas de deux.

---

15. *Mr. Graham:* Objection, Your Honor. The district attorney is testifying.
   The Court: Don't lead.
   Mr. Graham: I ask the Court to instruct the jury to disregard the remarks of counsel as not being testimony in the case.
   The Court: The Court will instruct the jury to disregard the last statement made by Mr. Rodriguez.
   Mr. Graham: Notwithstanding the Court's instruction, I am sure it is so prejudicial as to require a mistrial.
   Defendant: No, Your Honor. I object to a mistrial. I object to counsel—
   The Court: I denied the motion for mistrial. Overruled.
   Mr. Graham: Jesus Christ. . . .

Standby counsel must generally respect that preference. But counsel need not be excluded altogether, especially when the participation is outside the presence of the jury or is with the defendant's express or tacit consent. The defendant in this case was allowed to make his own appearances as he saw fit. In our judgment counsel's unsolicited involvement was held within reasonable limits.

The judgment of the Court of Appeals is therefore reversed.

JUSTICE BLACKMUN concurs in the result.

JUSTICE WHITE, with whom JUSTICE BRENNAN and JUSTICE MARSHALL join, dissenting. . . .

. . . The Court concludes, on the basis of its examination of the record, that Wiggins was afforded "a fair chance to present his case in his own way," and that "counsel's unsolicited involvement was held within reasonable limits." It arrives at this conclusion by applying a two-part test that, in my judgment, provides little or no guidance for counsel and trial judges, imposes difficult, if not impossible, burdens on appellate courts, and undoubtedly will lead to the swift erosion of defendants' constitutional right to proceed pro se.

Under the Court's new test, it is necessary to determine whether the pro se defendant retained "actual control over the case he [chose] to present to the jury," and whether standby counsel's participation "destroyed the jury's perception that the defendant [was] representing himself." Although this test purports to protect all of the values underlying our holding in Faretta, it is unclear whether it can achieve this result.

As long as the pro se defendant is allowed his say, the first prong of the Court's test accords standby counsel at a bench trial or any proceeding outside the presence of a jury virtually untrammeled discretion to present any factual or legal argument to which the defendant does not object. The limits placed on counsel's participation in this context by the "actual control" test are more apparent than real. First, counsel may not "make or substantially interfere with any significant tactical decisions." Unless counsel directly overrides a defendant's strategy in the presence of the judge, however, it is apparent that courts will be almost wholly incapable of assessing the subtle and not-so-subtle effects of counsel's participation on the defense. Second, the Court suggests that conflicts between the pro se defendant and standby counsel on "matter[s] that would normally be left to the defense's discretion," id., at 953, will be resolved in the defendant's favor. But many disagreements will not produce direct conflicts requiring a trial court to choose one position over another. Under the Court's opinion, the burden apparently will fall on the pro se defendant to comprehend counsel's submissions and to create conflicts for the trial court to resolve. If applied this way, the Court's test surely will prove incapable of safeguarding the interest in individual autonomy from which the Faretta right derives.

Although the Court is more solicitous of a pro se defendant's interests when standby counsel intervenes before a jury, the test's second prong suffers from similar shortcomings. To the extent that trial and appellate courts can discern the point at which counsel's unsolicited participation substantially undermines a pro se defendant's appearance before the jury, a matter about which I harbor substantial doubts, their decisions will, to a certain extent, "affirm the accused's individual dignity and autonomy." But they will do so incompletely, for in focusing on how the jury views the defendant, the majority opinion ignores Faretta's emphasis on the defendant's own perception of the criminal justice system, Faretta v. California, supra, 422 U.S., at 834, and implies that the Court actually adheres to the result-oriented harmless error standard it purports to reject. . . .

In short, I believe that the Court's test is unworkable and insufficiently protective of the fundamental interests we recognized in *Faretta*. . . .

NOTES AND QUESTIONS

1. Should a defendant be permitted to act as cocounsel with appointed or retained counsel? What may be gained or lost by that? For a discussion of a case of joint representation, see Angela Yvonne Davis, If They Come in the Morning (1971). "Hybrid representation" is typically disallowed. United States v. Olson, 576 F.2d 1267 (8th Cir. 1978); Wright v. Estelle, 572 F.2d 1071 (5th Cir. 1978); Burney v. State, 244 Ga. 33, 257 S.E.2d 543 (1979).

2. If an individual has the right to proceed pro se as an implication of basic demands of human dignity, should the person also have the right, if indigent, to choose who shall be appointed counsel if the person wishes to have counsel appointed? The general view is that there is no such right, the leading case being Drumgo v. Superior Court, 8 Cal. 3d 930, 506 P.2d 1007, 106 Cal. Rptr. 631 (1973). Five years after *Drumgo*, the California Supreme Court held that failure to respect an indigent's choice of counsel may amount to an abuse of discretion by the trial court when there are objective circumstances making the defendant's request reasonable. Harris v. Superior Court, 19 Cal. 3d 786, 567 P.2d 750, 140 Cal. Rptr. 318 (1977). The objective circumstances found persuasive in *Harris* were that the counsel the defendants desired to be appointed represented the defendants in related matters and were intimately acquainted with the factual and legal matters likely to be relevant to the present litigation. Moreover, counsel appointed by the trial court were essentially ignorant of the case.

In Morris v. Slappy, 461 U.S. 1 (1983), the Court held that the Sixth Amendment did not guarantee a "meaningful relationship" between attorney and client. Therefore, it was not error to refuse to grant a continuance to allow one public defender, whom the defendant desired as counsel, rather than another to try the case. The primary issue, according to the Court, was whether the attorney who actually tried the case did so competently.

3. May counsel "waive" the honor of representing an indigent defendant? The problem arises primarily after conviction, when counsel is of the view that an appeal would be fruitless. In Anders v. California, 386 U.S. 738 (1967), the Court held that an attorney who wishes to withdraw from a case after conviction on the grounds that an appeal would be wholly frivolous may request permission to do so but must file a brief referring to anything in the record that might support an appeal. The relevant court is then to decide whether to permit withdrawal. Requiring counsel to write a brief in support of what counsel believes to be a wholly frivolous appeal may seem curious, but there are cases in which such briefs have led to reversals. Paul D. Carrington, Daniel J. Meador, & Maurice Rosenberg, Justice on Appeal 77 (1976). In McCoy v. Court of Appeals of Wisconsin, District 1, 486 U.S. 429 (1988), the Court upheld a Wisconsin statute that required counsel writing *Anders* briefs to include a discussion of why the issues raised in the brief lacked merit. The Court reaffirmed *Anders* in Penson v. Ohio, 488 U.S. 75 (1988),

holding that it was error to fail to appoint counsel to brief and argue any claim that a court of appeals finds to be colorable, even if problematic. The Court also held that Strickland v. Washington does not apply in this context, for otherwise *Anders* would be virtually overruled.

In the Court's most recent foray into the *Anders* thicket, it held that the *Anders* requirements are really not requirements at all but merely one method by which to ensure that a state's procedure "afford adequate and effective appellate review to indigent's appeal [so that] an indigent's appeal will be resolved in a way that is related to the merit of that appeal." Smith v. Robbins, 528 U.S. 259 (2000). This, according to the Court, is the central obligation imposed by the *Griffin/Douglas* line of cases. The Court described the procedures upheld in *Smith*:

> [C]ounsel, upon concluding that an appeal would be frivolous, files a brief with the appellate court that summarizes the procedural and factual history of the case, with citations of the record. He also attests that he has reviewed the record, explained his evaluation of the case to his client, provided the client with a copy of the brief, and informed the client of his right to file a pro se supplemental brief. He further requests that the court independently examine the record for arguable issues. Unlike under the *Anders* procedure, counsel . . . neither explicitly states that his review has led him to conclude that an appeal would be frivolous (although that is considered implicit) nor requests leave to withdraw. Instead, he is silent on the merits of the case and expresses his availability to brief any issues on which the court might desire briefing.
>
> The appellate court . . . must "conduct a review of the entire record," regardless of whether the defendant has filed a pro se brief. . . . If the appellate court, after its review of the record pursuant to *Wende*, also finds the appeal to be frivolous, it may affirm. If, however, it finds an arguable (i.e., nonfrivolous) issue, it orders briefing on that issue.

In Pennsylvania v. Finley, 481 U.S. 551 (1987), the Supreme Court concluded that an indigent does not have either an equal protection or a due process right to appointed counsel in postconviction proceedings and thus has no right to insist that the *Anders* procedures for withdrawal of appointed counsel be followed when the state nonetheless had provided counsel. The Court rejected the argument that Evitts v. Lucey, page 157 supra, mandated that whenever a state supplies counsel, due process is implicated in such a manner that demands the *Anders* procedures.

The Court has protected the access of prisoners to the courts, however. In Johnson v. Avery, 393 U.S. 483 (1969), the Court held that prisoners without counsel could not be denied the aid of literate prisoners in filing habeas corpus motions. The Court based its holding primarily on its belief that some prisoners would be effectively denied access to the courts if they were unable at least to secure the aid of other, literate prisoners in filing these motions. Similarly, in Bounds v. Smith, 430 U.S. 817 (1977), the Court held a state had to provide prisoners either with adequate law libraries or with adequate legal assistance to facilitate prisoners' requests for postconviction relief. In Lewis v. Casey, 518 U.S. 343 (1996), the Court held that *Bounds* did not create a right to a law library or legal assistance, but is limited to the right of access to the courts. The Court disavowed statements in *Bounds* that prisoners must be able to discover grievances and to litigate effectively once in court. The Court also held that to give systemic relief, the district court has to find system-wide problems, not just one or two instances of adverse consequences, which had not been established.

Is *Finley* inconsistent with Bounds v. Smith in the context of death penalty litigation? Given the complexity of death penalty litigation and the stringent time constraints under which it is done, does a person on death row have a Sixth Amendment right to counsel because without counsel a prisoner on death row is effectively barred from competently litigating any claims for error that may be present in the case? No, said the Court in Murray v. Giarratano, 492 U.S. 1 (1989). A four-member plurality (Chief Justice Rehnquist, White, O'Connor, and Scalia) held that *Bounds* was limited to an adequate law library (or legal assistance instead of a law library). Justice Kennedy concurred on the ground that

> [t]he requirement of access can be satisfied in various ways. . . . While Virginia has not adopted procedures for securing representation that are as far reaching as those available in other States, no prisoner on death row in Virginia has been unable to obtain counsel to represent him in post-conviction proceedings, and Virginia's prison system is staffed with institutional lawyers to assist in preparing petitions for post-conviction relief. I am not prepared to say that this scheme violates the Constitution.

4. In the context of representation at trial, it is a given that the ultimate decision on defense strategy belongs to the defendant (although good defense attorneys probably rarely, if ever, have much difficulty persuading a defendant to go along with the lawyer's view of sound strategy). But on appeal, there are limits to the defendant's ability to control counsel.

In Jones v. Barnes, 463 U.S. 745 (1983), the Court rejected the defendant's assertion that "counsel has a constitutional duty to raise every nonfrivolous issue requested by the defendant":

> Experienced advocates since time beyond memory have emphasized the importance of winnowing out weaker arguments on appeal and focusing on one central issue if possible, or at most on a few key issues. Justice Jackson, after observing appellate advocates for many years, stated:
>
> > One of the first tests of a discriminating advocate is to select the question, or questions, that he will present orally. Legal contentions, like the currency, depreciate through over-issue. The mind of an appellate judge is habitually receptive to the suggestion that a lower court committed an error. But receptiveness declines as the number of assigned errors increases. Multiplicity hints at lack of confidence in any one. . . . [E]xperience on the bench convinces me that multiplying assignments of error will dilute and weaken a good case and will not save a bad one. [Jackson, Advocacy before the United States Supreme Court, 25 Temple L.Q. 115, 119 (1951).]
>
> Justice Jackson's observation echoes the advice of countless advocates before him and since. An authoritative work on appellate practice observes:
>
> > Most cases present only one, two, or three significant questions. . . . Usually, . . . if you cannot win on a few major points, the others are not likely to help, and to attempt to deal with a great many in the limited number of pages allowed for briefs will mean that none may receive adequate attention. The effect of adding weak arguments will be to dilute the force of the stronger ones. [R. Stern, Appellate Practice in the United States 266 (1981).]
>
> There can hardly be any question about the importance of having the appellate advocate examine the record with a view to selecting the most promising issues for review. This has assumed a greater importance in an era when oral argument is strictly limited in most courts — often to as little as 15 minutes — and when page limits on

briefs are widely imposed. See, e.g., Fed. Rules App. Proc. 28(g); McKinney's 1982 New York Rules of Court §§670.17(g)(2), 670.22. Even in a court that imposes no time or page limits, however, the new per se rule laid down by the Court of Appeals is contrary to all experience and logic. A brief that raises every colorable issue runs the risk of burying good arguments — those that, in the words of the great advocate John W. Davis, "go for the jugular," Davis, The Argument of an Appeal, 26 A.B.A.J. 895, 897 (1940) — in a verbal mound made up of strong and weak contentions. See generally, e.g., John C. Godbold, Twenty Pages and Twenty Minutes — Effective Advocacy on Appeal, 30 Sw. L.J. 801 (1976).

This Court's decision in *Anders,* far from giving support to the new per se rule announced by the Court of Appeals [that all nonfrivolous issues raised by the client must be argued by the attorney], is to the contrary. *Anders* recognized that the role of the advocate "requires that he support his client's appeal to the best of his ability." 386 U.S., at 744. Here the appointed counsel did just that. For judges to second-guess reasonable professional judgments and impose on appointed counsel a duty to raise every "colorable" claim suggested by a client would disserve the very goal of vigorous and effective advocacy that underlies *Anders.* Nothing in the Constitution or our interpretation of that document requires such a standard.[7]

2. The Implications of Forfeiture Statutes

CAPLIN & DRYSDALE, CHARTERED v. UNITED STATES

Certiorari to the United States Court of Appeals for the Fourth Circuit
491 U.S. 617 (1989)

JUSTICE WHITE delivered the opinion of the Court.

We are called on to determine whether the federal drug forfeiture statute includes an exemption for assets that a defendant wishes to use to pay an attorney who conducted his defense in the criminal case where forfeiture was sought. Because we determine that no such exemption exists, we must decide whether that statute, so interpreted, is consistent with the Fifth and Sixth Amendments. We hold that it is.

I

In January 1985, Christopher Reckmeyer was charged in a multicount indictment with running a massive drug importation and distribution scheme. The scheme was alleged to be a continuing criminal enterprise (CCE), in violation of 21 U.S.C. §848 (1982 ed., Supp. V). Relying on a portion of the CCE statute that authorizes forfeiture to the government of "property constituting, or derived from . . . proceeds . . . obtained" from drug-law violations,[1] the indictment sought

---

7. The only question presented by this case is whether a criminal defendant has a constitutional right to have appellate counsel raise every nonfrivolous issue that the defendant requests. The availability of federal habeas corpus to review claims that counsel declined to raise is not before us, and we have no occasion to decide whether counsel's refusal to raise requested claims would constitute "cause" for a petitioner's default within the meaning of Wainwright v. Sykes, 433 U.S. 72 (1977). See also Engle v. Isaac, 456 U.S. 107, 128 (1982).

1. The forfeiture statute provides, in relevant part, that any person convicted of a particular class of criminal offenses: "shall forfeit to the United States, irrespective of any provision of State law — " (1) any

forfeiture of specified assets in Reckmeyer's possession. At this time, the District Court entered a restraining order forbidding Reckmeyer to transfer any of the listed assets that were potentially forfeitable.

Sometime earlier, Reckmeyer had retained petitioner, a law firm, to represent him in the ongoing grand jury investigation which resulted in the January 1985 indictments. Notwithstanding the restraining order, Reckmeyer paid the firm $25,000 for preindictment legal services a few days after the indictment was handed down; this sum was placed by petitioner in an escrow account. Petitioner continued to represent Reckmeyer following the indictment.

On March 7, 1985, Reckmeyer moved to modify the District Court's earlier restraining order to permit him to use some of the restrained assets to pay petitioner's fees; Reckmeyer also sought to exempt from any postconviction forfeiture order the assets that he intended to use to pay petitioner. However, one week later, before the District Court could conduct a hearing on this motion, Reckmeyer entered a plea agreement with the Government. Under the agreement, Reckmeyer pleaded guilty to the drug-related CCE charge, and agreed to forfeit all of the specified assets listed in the indictment. The day after Reckmeyer's plea was entered, the District Court denied his earlier motion to modify the restraining order, concluding that the plea and forfeiture agreement rendered irrelevant any further consideration of the propriety of the court's pretrial restraints. Subsequently, an order forfeiting virtually all of the assets in Reckmeyer's possession was entered by the District Court in conjunction with his sentencing.

After this order was entered, petitioner filed a petition under 21 U.S.C. §853(n) (1982 ed., Supp. V), which permits third parties with an interest in forfeited property to ask the sentencing court for an adjudication of their rights to that property; specifically, §853(n)(6)(B) gives a third party who entered into a bona fide transaction with a defendant a right to make claims against forfeited property, if that third party was "at the time of [the transaction] reasonably without cause to believe that the [defendant's assets were] subject to forfeiture." Petitioner claimed an interest in $170,000 of Reckmeyer's assets, for services it had provided Reckmeyer in conducting his defense; petitioner also sought the $25,000 being held in the escrow account, as payment for preindictment legal services. Petitioner argued alternatively that assets used to pay an attorney were exempt from forfeiture under §853, and if not, the failure of the statute to provide such an exemption rendered it unconstitutional. The District Court granted petitioner's claim for a share of the forfeited assets.

A panel of the Fourth Circuit affirmed, finding that—while §853 contained no statutory provision authorizing the payment of attorneys' fees out of forfeited assets—the statute's failure to do so impermissibly infringed a defendant's Sixth Amendment right to the counsel of his choice. The Court of Appeals agreed to hear the case en banc, and reversed. All the judges of the Fourth Circuit agreed that the language of the CCE statute acknowledged no exception to its forfeiture

---

property constituting, or derived from, any proceeds the person obtained, directly or indirectly, as the result of such violation. . . .

"The court, in imposing sentence on such person, shall order, in addition to any other sentence imposed . . . that the person forfeit to the United States all property described in this subsection." 21 U.S.C. §853 (1982 ed., Supp. V). There is no question here that the offenses respondent was accused of in the indictment fell within the class of crimes triggering this forfeiture provision.

requirement that would recognize petitioner's claim to the forfeited assets. A majority found this statutory scheme constitutional; four dissenting judges, however, agreed with the panel's view that the statute so-construed violated the Sixth Amendment.

Petitioner sought review of the statutory and constitutional issues raised by the Court of Appeals' holding. We granted certiorari, and now affirm.

II

Petitioner's first submission is that the statutory provision that authorizes pretrial restraining orders on potentially forfeitable assets in a defendant's possession grants district courts equitable discretion to determine when such orders should be imposed. This discretion should be exercised under "traditional equitable standards," petitioner urges, including a "weigh[ing] of the equities and competing hardships on the parties"; under this approach, a court "must invariably strike the balance so as to allow a defendant [to pay] . . . for bona fide attorneys fees," petitioner argues. Petitioner further submits that once a district court so exercises its discretion, and fails to freeze assets that a defendant then uses to pay an attorney, the statute's provision for recapture of forfeitable assets transferred to third parties, may not operate on such sums.

Petitioner's argument, as it acknowledges, is based on the view of the statute expounded by Judge Winter of the Second Circuit in his concurring opinion in that Court of Appeals' en banc decision, United States v. Monsanto, 852 F.2d 1400, 1405-1411 (1988). We reject this interpretation of the statute today in our decision in United States v. Monsanto [491 U.S. 600 (1989)], which reverses the Second Circuit's holding in that case. As we explain in our *Monsanto* decision, whatever discretion §853(e) provides district court judges to refuse to enter pretrial restraining orders, it does not extend as far as petitioner urges — nor does the exercise of that discretion "immunize" nonrestrained assets from subsequent forfeiture under §853(c), if they are transferred to an attorney to pay legal fees. Thus, for the reasons provided in our opinion in *Monsanto*, we reject petitioner's statutory claim.

III

We therefore address petitioner's constitutional challenges to the forfeiture law. Petitioner contends that the statute infringes on criminal defendants' Sixth Amendment right to counsel of choice, and upsets the "balance of power" between the government and the accused in a manner contrary to the Due Process Clause of the Fifth Amendment. We consider these contentions in turn.

A

Petitioner's first claim is that the forfeiture law makes impossible, or at least impermissibly burdens, a defendant's right "to select and be represented by one's preferred attorney." Wheat v. United States, 486 U.S. 153, 159 (1988). Petitioner does not, nor could it defensibly do so, assert that impecunious defendants have a Sixth Amendment right to choose their counsel. The amendment guarantees defendants in criminal cases the right to adequate representation, but those who do not have the means to hire their own lawyers have no cognizable complaint so long as they are adequately represented by attorneys appointed by the courts. "[A] defendant may not insist on representation by an attorney he cannot afford." *Wheat,* supra, at 159. Petitioner does not dispute these propositions. Nor does the Government deny that the Sixth Amendment guarantees a defendant the right to be represented by an otherwise qualified attorney whom that defendant can afford to hire, or who is willing to represent the defendant even though he is without funds. Applying these principles to the statute in question here, we observe that nothing in §853 prevents a defendant from hiring the attorney of his choice, or disqualifies any attorney from serving as a defendant's counsel. Thus, unlike *Wheat,* this case does not involve a situation where the Government has asked a court to prevent a defendant's chosen counsel from representing the accused. Instead, petitioner urges that a violation of the Sixth Amendment arises here because of the forfeiture, at the instance of the Government, of assets that defendants intend to use to pay their attorneys.

Even in this sense, of course, the burden the forfeiture law imposes on a criminal defendant is limited. The forfeiture statute does not prevent a defendant who has nonforfeitable assets from retaining any attorney of his choosing. Nor is it necessarily the case that a defendant who possesses nothing but assets the Government seeks to have forfeited will be prevented from retaining counsel of choice. Defendants like Reckmeyer may be able to find lawyers willing to represent them, hoping that their fees will be paid in the event of acquittal, or via some other means that a defendant might come by in the future. The burden placed on defendants by the forfeiture law is therefore a limited one.

Nonetheless, there will be cases where a defendant will be unable to retain the attorney of his choice, when that defendant would have been able to hire that lawyer if he had access to forfeitable assets, and if there was no risk that fees paid by the defendant to his counsel would later be recouped under §853(c).[4] It is in these cases, petitioner argues, that the Sixth Amendment puts limits on the forfeiture statute.

This submission is untenable. Whatever the full extent of the Sixth Amendment's protection of one's right to retain counsel of his choosing, that protection does not go beyond "the individual's right to spend his own money to obtain the advice and assistance of . . . counsel." A defendant has no Sixth Amendment right to spend another person's money for services rendered by an attorney, even if those funds are the only way that that defendant will be able to retain the attorney of his choice. A robbery suspect, for example, has no Sixth Amendment right to use funds he has stolen from a bank to retain an attorney to defend him if he is apprehended. The money, though in his possession is not rightfully his; the government does not violate the Sixth Amendment if it seizes the robbery proceeds, and refuses to permit the defendant to use them to pay for his defense. . . .

Petitioner seeks to distinguish such cases for Sixth Amendment purposes by arguing that the bank's claim to robbery proceeds rests on "pre-existing property

---

4. That section of the statute, which includes the so-called "relation back" provision, states: "All right, title, and interest in property described in [§853] vests in the United States upon the commission of the act giving rise to forfeiture under this section. Any such property that is subsequently transferred to a person other than the defendant may be the subject of a special verdict of forfeiture and thereafter shall be forfeited to the United States, unless the transferee [establishes his entitlement to such property pursuant to §853(n)]." 21 U.S.C. §853(c) (1982 ed., Supp. V).

rights," while the Government's claim to forfeitable assets rests on a "penal statute" which embodies the "fictive property-law concept of . . . relation-back" and is merely "a mechanism for preventing fraudulent conveyances of the defendant's assets, not . . . a device for determining true title to property." Brief for Petitioner 40-41. In light of this, petitioner contends, the burden placed on defendant's Sixth Amendment rights by the forfeiture statute outweighs the Government's interest in forfeiture.

The premises of petitioner's constitutional analysis are unsound in several respects. First, the property rights given the Government by virtue of the forfeiture statute are more substantial than petitioner acknowledges. In §853(c), the so-called "relation-back" provision, Congress dictated that "[a]ll right, title and interest in property" obtained by criminals via the illicit means described in the statute "vests in the United States upon the commission of the act giving rise to forfeiture." As Congress observed when the provision was adopted, this approach, known as the "taint theory," is one that "has long been recognized in forfeiture cases," including the decision in United States v. Stowell, 133 U.S. 1 (1890). In *Stowell*, the Court explained the operation of a similar forfeiture provision (for violations of the Internal Revenue Code) as follows:

> "As soon [as the possessor of the forfeitable asset committed the violation] of the internal revenue laws, the forfeiture under those laws took effect, and (though needing judicial condemnation to perfect it) operated from that time as a statutory conveyance to the United States of all the right, title, and interest then remaining in the [possessor]; and was as valid and effectual, against all the world, as a recorded deed. The right so vested in the United States could not be defeated or impaired by any subsequent dealings of the . . . [possessor]." *Stowell*, supra, at 19.

In sum, §853(c) reflects the application of the long-recognized and lawful practice of vesting title to any forfeitable assets, in the United States, at the time of the criminal act giving rise to forfeiture. Concluding that Reckmeyer cannot give good title to such property to petitioner because he did not hold good title is neither extraordinary or novel. Nor does petitioner claim, as a general proposition that the relation-back provision is unconstitutional, or that Congress cannot, as a general matter, vest title to assets derived from the crime in the Government, as of the date of the criminal act in question. Petitioner's claim is that whatever part of the assets that is necessary to pay attorney's fees cannot be subjected to forfeiture. But given the Government's title to Reckmeyer's assets upon conviction, to hold that the Sixth Amendment creates some right in Reckmeyer to alienate such assets, or creates a right on petitioner's part to receive these assets, would be peculiar.

There is no constitutional principle that gives one person the right to give another's property to a third party, even where the person seeking to complete the exchange wishes to do so in order to exercise a constitutionally protected right. While petitioner and its supporting amici attempt to distinguish between the expenditure of forfeitable assets to exercise one's Sixth Amendment rights, and expenditures in the pursuit of other constitutionally protected freedoms, there is no such distinction between, or hierarchy among, constitutional rights. If defendants have a right to spend forfeitable assets on attorney's fees, why not on exercises of the right to speak, practice one's religion, or travel? The full exercise of these rights, too, depends in part on one's financial wherewithal; and forfeiture, or even the threat of forfeiture, may similarly prevent a defendant from enjoying these rights as fully as he might otherwise. Nonetheless, we are not about to recognize an antiforfeiture exception for the exercise of each such right; nor does one exist for the exercise of Sixth Amendment rights, either.

Petitioner's "balancing analysis" to the contrary rests substantially on the view that the Government has only a modest interest in forfeitable assets that may be used to retain an attorney. Petitioner takes the position that, in large part, once assets have been paid over from client to attorney, the principal ends of forfeiture have been achieved: dispossessing a drug dealer or racketeer of the proceeds of his wrongdoing. We think that this view misses the mark for three reasons.

First, the Government has a pecuniary interest in forfeiture that goes beyond merely separating a criminal from his ill-gotten gains; that legitimate interest extends to recovering *all* forfeitable assets, for such assets are deposited in a Fund that supports law-enforcement efforts in a variety of important and useful ways. The sums of money that can be raised for law-enforcement activities this way are substantial,[6] and the Government's interest in using the profits of crime to fund these activities should not be discounted.

Second, the statute permits "rightful owners" of forfeited assets to make claims for forfeited assets before they are retained by the government. The Government's interest in winning undiminished forfeiture thus includes the objective of returning property, in full, to those wrongfully deprived or defrauded of it. Where the Government pursues this restitutionary end, the government's interest in forfeiture is virtually indistinguishable from its interest in returning to a bank the proceeds of a bank robbery; and a forfeiture-defendant's claim of right to use such assets to hire an attorney, instead of having them returned to their rightful owners, is not more persuasive than a bank robber's similar claim.

Finally, as we have recognized previously, a major purpose motivating congressional adoption and continued refinement of the RICO and CCE forfeiture provisions has been the desire to lessen the economic power of organized crime and drug enterprises. This includes the use of such economic power to retain private counsel. As the Court of Appeals put it: "Congress has already underscored the compelling public interest in stripping criminals such as Reckmeyer of their undeserved economic power, and part of that undeserved power may be the ability to command high-priced legal talent." The notion that the government has a legitimate interest in depriving criminals of economic power, even insofar as that power is used to retain counsel of choice, may be somewhat unsettling. But when a defendant claims that he has suffered some substantial impairment of his Sixth Amendment rights by virtue of the seizure or forfeiture of assets in his possession, such a complaint is no more than the reflection of "the harsh reality that the quality of a criminal defendant's representation frequently may turn on his ability to retain the best counsel money can buy." Again, the Court of Appeals put it aptly: "The modern day Jean Valjean must be satisfied with appointed counsel. Yet the drug merchant claims that his possession of huge sums of money . . . entitles him to something more. We reject this contention, and any

6. For example, just one of the assets which Reckmeyer agreed to forfeit, a parcel of land known as "Shelburne Glebe," see App. 57 (forfeiture order), was recently sold by federal authorities for $5.8 million. Washington Post, May 10, 1989, p. D1, cols. 1-4. The proceeds of the sale will fund federal, state, and local law enforcement activities.

notion of a constitutional right to use the proceeds of crime to finance an expensive defense."[7]

It is our view that there is a strong governmental interest in obtaining full recovery of all forfeitable assets, an interest that overrides any Sixth Amendment interest in permitting criminals to use assets adjudged forfeitable to pay for their defense. Otherwise, there would be an interference with a defendant's Sixth Amendment rights whenever the government freezes or takes some property in a defendant's possession before, during or after a criminal trial. So-called "jeopardy assessments" — IRS seizures of assets to secure potential tax liabilities, see 26 U.S.C. §6861 — may impair a defendant's ability to retain counsel in a way similar to that complained of here. Yet these assessments have been upheld against constitutional attack. . . . Moreover, petitioner's claim to a share of the forfeited assets postconviction would suggest that the government could never impose a burden on assets within a defendant's control that could be used to pay a lawyer.[9] Criminal defendants, however, are not exempted from federal, state, and local taxation simply because these financial levies may deprive them of resources that could be used to hire an attorney.

We therefore reject petitioner's claim of a Sixth Amendment right of criminal defendants to use assets that are the government's — assets adjudged forfeitable, as Reckmeyer's were — to pay attorneys' fees, merely because those assets are in their possession.[10]

---

7. We also reject the contention, advanced by amici, see, e.g., Brief for Amicus Curiae of the American Bar Association as Amicus Curiae 20-22, and accepted by some courts considering claims like petitioner's, see, e.g., United States v. Rogers, 602 F. Supp. 1332, 1349-1350 (Col. 1985), that a type of "per se" ineffective assistance of counsel results — due to the particular complexity of RICO or drug-enterprise cases — when a defendant is not permitted to use assets in his possession to retain counsel of choice, and instead must rely on appointed counsel. If such an argument were accepted, it would bar the trial of indigents charged with such offenses, because those persons would have to rely on appointed counsel — which this view considers per se ineffective.

If appointed counsel is ineffective in a particular case, a defendant has resort to the remedies discussed in Strickland v. Washington, 466 U.S. 668 (1984). But we cannot say that the Sixth Amendment's guarantee of effective assistance of counsel is a guarantee of a privately-retained counsel in every complex case, irrespective of a defendant's ability to pay.

9. A myriad of other law-enforcement mechanisms operate in a manner similar to IRS jeopardy assessments, and might also be subjected to Sixth Amendment invalidation if petitioner's claim were accepted. See Kathleen F. Brickey, Attorneys' Fee Forfeitures, 36 Emory L.J. 761, 770-772 (1987).

10. Petitioner advances three additional reasons for invalidating the forfeiture statute, all of which concern possible ethical conflicts created for lawyers defending persons facing forfeiture of assets in their possession.

Petitioner first notes the statute's exemption from forfeiture of property transferred to a bona fide purchaser who was "reasonably without cause to believe that the property was subject to forfeiture." 21 U.S.C. §853(n)(6)(B). This provision, it is said, might give an attorney an incentive not to investigate a defendant's case as fully as possible, so that the lawyer can invoke it to protect from forfeiture any fees he has received. Yet given the requirement that any assets which the Government wishes to have forfeited must be specified in the indictment, see Fed. Rule Crim. Proc. 7(c)(2), the only way a lawyer could be a beneficiary of §853(n)(6)(B) would be to fail to read the indictment of his client. In this light, the prospect that a lawyer might find himself in conflict with his client, by seeking to take advantage of §853(n)(6)(B), amounts to very little. Petitioner itself concedes that such a conflict will, as a practical matter, never arise: A defendant's "lawyer . . . could not demonstrate that he was 'reasonably without cause to believe that the property was subject to forfeiture,'" petitioner concludes at one point. Brief for Petitioner 31.

The second possible conflict arises in plea bargaining: Petitioner posits that a lawyer may advise a client to accept an agreement entailing a more harsh prison sentence but no forfeiture — even where contrary to the client's interests — in an effort to preserve the lawyer's fee. Following such a strategy, however, would surely constitute ineffective assistance of counsel. We see no reason why our cases such as Strickland v. Washington are inadequate to deal with any such ineffectiveness where it arises. In any

B

Petitioner's second constitutional claim is that the forfeiture statute is invalid under the Due Process Clause of the Fifth Amendment because it permits the Government to upset the "balance of forces between the accused and his accuser." We are not sure that this contention adds anything to petitioner's Sixth Amendment claim, because, while "[t]he Constitution guarantees a fair trial through the Due Process Clauses . . . it defines the basic elements of a fair trial largely through the several provisions of the Sixth Amendment." We have concluded above that the Sixth Amendment is not offended by the forfeiture provisions at issue here. Even if, however, the Fifth Amendment provides some added protection not encompassed in the Sixth Amendment's more specific provisions, we find petitioner's claim based on the Fifth Amendment unavailing.

Forfeiture provisions are powerful weapons in the war on crime; like any such weapons, their impact can be devastating when used unjustly. But due process claims alleging such abuses are cognizable only in specific cases of prosecutorial misconduct (and petitioner has made no such allegation here) or when directed to a rule that is inherently unconstitutional. "The fact that the . . . Act might operate unconstitutionally under some conceivable set of circumstances is insufficient to render it . . . invalid," United States v. Salerno, 481 U.S. 739, 745 (1987). Petitioner's claim — that the power available to prosecutors under the statute could be abused — proves too much, for many tools available to prosecutors can be misused in a way that violates the rights of innocent persons. As the Court of Appeals put it, in rejecting this claim when advanced below: "Every criminal law carries with it the potential for abuse, but a potential for abuse does not require a finding of facial invalidity."

We rejected a claim similar to petitioner's last Term, in Wheat v. United States, 486 U.S. 153 (1988). In *Wheat,* the petitioner argued that permitting a court to disqualify a defendant's chosen counsel because of conflicts of interest — over that defendant's objection to the disqualification — would encourage the government to "manufacture" such conflicts to deprive a defendant of his chosen attorney. While acknowledging that this was possible, we declined to fashion the per se constitutional rule petitioner sought in *Wheat,* instead observing that "trial courts are undoubtedly aware of [the] possibility" of abuse, and would have to "take it into consideration," when dealing with disqualification motions.

A similar approach should be taken here. The Constitution does not forbid the imposition of an otherwise permissible criminal sanction, such as forfeiture,

---

event, there is no claim that such conduct occurred here, nor could there be, as Reckmeyer's plea agreement included forfeiture of virtually every asset in his possession.

Finally, petitioner argues that the forfeiture statute, in operation, will create a system akin to "contingency fees" for defense lawyers: Only a defense lawyer who wins acquittal for his client will be able to collect his fees, and contingent fees in criminal cases are generally considered unethical. See ABA Model Rules of Professional Conduct, Rule 1.5(d)(2) (1983); ABA Model Code of Professional Responsibility DR 2-106(C) (1979). But there is no indication here that petitioner, or any other firm, has actually sought to charge a defendant on a contingency basis; rather the claim is that a law firm's prospect of collecting its fee may turn on the outcome at trial. This, however, may often be the case in criminal defense work. Nor is it clear why permitting contingent fees in criminal cases — if that is what the forfeiture statute does — violates a criminal defendant's Sixth Amendment rights. The fact that a federal statutory scheme authorizing contingency fees — again, if that is what Congress has created in §853 (a premise we doubt) — is at odds with model disciplinary rules or state disciplinary codes hardly renders the federal statute invalid.

merely because in some cases prosecutors may abuse the processes available to them, e.g., by attempting to impose them on persons who should not be subjected to that punishment. Cases involving particular abuses can be dealt with individually by the lower courts, when (and if) any such cases arise.

IV

For the reasons given above, we find that petitioner's statutory and constitutional challenges to the forfeiture imposed here are without merit. The judgment of the Court of Appeals is therefore affirmed.

JUSTICE BLACKMUN, with whom JUSTICE BRENNAN, JUSTICE MARSHALL, and JUSTICE STEVENS join, dissenting.

Those jurists who have held forth against the result the majority reaches in these cases have been guided by one core insight; that it is unseemly and unjust for the Government to beggar those it prosecutes in order to disable their defense at trial. The majority trivializes "the burden the forfeiture law imposes on a criminal defendant." Instead, it should heed the warnings of our district court judges, whose day-to-day exposure to the criminal-trial process enables them to understand, perhaps far better than we, the devastating consequences of attorney's fee forfeiture for the integrity of our adversarial system of justice. . . .

The criminal forfeiture statute we consider today could have been interpreted to avoid depriving defendants of the ability to retain private counsel — and should have been so interpreted, given the grave "constitutional and ethical problems" raised by the forfeiture of funds used to pay legitimate counsel fees.

II

The majority has decided otherwise, however, and for that reason is compelled to reach the constitutional issue it could have avoided. But the majority pauses hardly long enough to acknowledge "the Sixth Amendment's protection of one's right to retain counsel of his choosing," let alone to explore its "full extent." Instead, it moves rapidly from the observation that "a defendant may not insist on representation by an attorney he cannot afford," Wheat v. United States, 486 U.S. 153, 161 (1988), to the conclusion that the Government is free to deem the defendant indigent by declaring his assets "tainted" by criminal activity the Government has yet to prove. That the majority implicitly finds the Sixth Amendment right to counsel of choice so insubstantial that it can be outweighed by a legal fiction demonstrates, still once again, its "apparent unawareness of the function of the independent lawyer as a guardian of our freedom."

A

Over 50 years ago, this Court observed: "It is hardly necessary to say that the right to counsel being conceded, a defendant should be afforded a fair opportunity to secure counsel of his own choice." Powell v. Alabama, 287 U.S. 45, 53 (1932). For years, that proposition was settled; the controversial question was whether the defendant's right to use his own funds to retain his chosen counsel was the outer limit of the right protected by the Sixth Amendment. The Court's subsequent decisions have made clear that an indigent defendant has the right to appointed counsel, and that the Sixth Amendment guarantees at least minimally effective assistance of counsel. But while court appointment of effective counsel plays a crucial role in safeguarding the fairness of criminal trials, it has never defined the outer limits of the Sixth Amendment's demands. The majority's decision in this case reveals that it has lost track of the distinct role of the right to counsel of choice in protecting the integrity of the judicial process, a role that makes "the right to be represented by privately retained counsel . . . the primary, preferred component of the basic right" protected by the Sixth Amendment.

The right to retain private counsel serves to foster the trust between attorney and client that is necessary for the attorney to be a truly effective advocate. Not only are decisions crucial to the defendant's liberty placed in counsel's hands, but the defendant's perception of the fairness of the process, and his willingness to acquiesce in its results, depend upon his confidence in his counsel's dedication, loyalty, and ability. When the Government insists upon the right to choose the defendant's counsel for him, that relationship of trust is undermined: Counsel is too readily perceived as the Government's agent rather than his own. Indeed, when the Court in *Faretta* held that the Sixth Amendment prohibits a court from imposing appointed counsel on a defendant who prefers to represent himself, its decision was predicated on the insight that "[t]o force a lawyer on a defendant can only lead him to believe that the law contrives against him."

The right to retain private counsel also serves to assure some modicum of equality between the Government and those it chooses to prosecute. The Government can be expected to "spend vast sums of money . . . to try defendants accused of crime," Gideon v. Wainwright, 372 U.S., at 344, and of course will devote greater resources to complex cases in which the punitive stakes are high. Precisely for this reason, "there are few defendants charged with crime, few indeed, who fail to hire the best lawyers they can get to prepare and present their defenses." Ibid. But when the Government provides for appointed counsel, there is no guarantee that levels of compensation and staffing will be even average. Where cases are complex, trials long, and stakes high, that problem is exacerbated. Over the long haul, the result of lowered compensation levels will be that talented attorneys will "decline to enter criminal practice. . . . This exodus of talented attorneys could devastate the criminal defense bar." Bruce J. Winick, Forfeiture of Attorneys' Fees under RICO and CCE and the Right to Counsel of Choice: the Constitutional Dilemma and How to Avoid It, 43 U. Miami L. Rev. 765, 781 (1989). Without the defendant's right to retain private counsel, the Government too readily could defeat its adversaries simply by outspending them.

The right to privately chosen and compensated counsel also serves broader institutional interests. The "virtual socialization of criminal defense work in this country" that would be the result of a widespread abandonment of the right to retain chosen counsel, too readily would standardize the provision of criminal-defense services and diminish defense counsel's independence. There is a place in our system of criminal justice for the maverick and the risk-taker, for approaches that might not fit into the structured environment of a public defender's office, or that might displease a judge whose preference for nonconfrontational styles of advocacy might influence the judge's appointment decisions. There is also a place for the employment of "specialized defense counsel" for technical and complex cases. The choice of counsel is the primary means for the defendant to establish the kind of defense he will put forward. Only a healthy, independent defense bar can be expected to meet the demands of the varied circumstances faced by criminal defendants. . . .

In sum, our chosen system of criminal justice is built upon a truly equal and adversarial presentation of the case, and upon the trust that can exist only when counsel is independent of the Government. Without the right, reasonably exercised, to counsel of choice, the effectiveness of that system is imperilled.

B

Had it been Congress' express aim to undermine the adversary system as we know it, it could hardly have found a better engine of destruction than attorney's fee forfeiture. The main effect of forfeitures under the Act, of course, will be to deny the defendant the right to retain counsel, and therefore the right to have his defense designed and presented by an attorney he has chosen and trusts.[14] If the Government restrains the defendant's assets before trial, private counsel will be unwilling to continue or to take on the defense. Even if no restraining order is entered, the possibility of forfeiture after conviction will itself substantially diminish the likelihood that private counsel will agree to take the case. The "message [to private counsel] is 'Do not represent this defendant or you will lose your fee.' That being the kind of message lawyers are likely to take seriously, the defendant will find it difficult or impossible to secure representation." United States v. Badalamenti, 614 F. Supp., at 196.

The resulting relationship between the defendant and his court-appointed counsel will likely begin in distrust, and be exacerbated to the extent that the defendant perceives his new-found "indigency" as a form of punishment imposed by the Government in order to weaken his defense. If the defendant had been represented by private counsel earlier in the proceedings, the defendant's sense that the Government has stripped him of his defense will be sharpened by the concreteness of his loss. Appointed counsel may be inexperienced and undercompensated and, for that reason, may not have adequate opportunity or resources to deal with the special problems presented by what is likely to be a complex trial. The already scarce resources of a public defender's office will be stretched to the limit. Facing a lengthy trial against a better-armed adversary, the temptation to recommend a guilty plea will be great. The result, if the defendant is convicted, will be a sense, often well grounded, that justice was not done.

Even if the defendant finds a private attorney who is "so foolish, ignorant, beholden or idealistic as to take the business," the attorney-client relationship will be undermined by the forfeiture statute. Perhaps the attorney will be willing to violate ethical norms by working on a contingent fee basis in a criminal case.

---

14. There is reason to fear that, in addition to depriving a defendant of counsel of choice, there will be circumstances in which the threat of forfeiture will deprive the defendant of any counsel. If the Government chooses not to restrain transfers by employing §853(e)(1), it is likely that the defendant will not qualify as "indigent" under the Criminal Justice Act. Potential private counsel will be aware of the threat of forfeiture, and, as a result, will likely refuse to take the case. Although it is to be hoped that a solution will be developed for a defendant who "falls between the cracks" in this manner, there is no guarantee that accommodation will be made in an orderly fashion, and that trial preparation will not be substantially delayed because of the difficulties in securing counsel.

But if he is not—and we should question the integrity of any criminal-defense attorney who would violate the ethical norms of the profession by doing so— the attorney's own interests will dictate that he remain ignorant of the source of the assets from which he is paid. Under §853(c), a third-party transferee may keep assets if "the transferee establishes . . . that he is a bona fide purchaser for value of such property who at the time of purchase was reasonably without cause to believe that the property was subject to forfeiture under this section." The less an attorney knows, the greater the likelihood that he can claim to have been an "innocent" third party. The attorney's interest in knowing nothing is directly adverse to his client's interest in full disclosure. The result of the conflict may be a less vigorous investigation of the defendant's circumstances, leading in turn to a failure to recognize or pursue avenues of inquiry necessary to the defense. Other conflicts of interest are also likely to develop. The attorney who fears for his fee will be tempted to make the Government's waiver of fee-forfeiture the sine qua non for any plea agreement, a position which conflicts with his client's best interests.

Perhaps most troubling is the fact that forfeiture statutes place the Government in the position to exercise an intolerable degree of power over any private attorney who takes on the task of representing a defendant in a forfeiture case. The decision whether to seek a restraining order rests with the prosecution, as does the decision whether to waive forfeiture upon a plea of guilty or a conviction at trial. The Government will be ever tempted to use the forfeiture weapon against a defense attorney who is particularly talented or aggressive on the client's behalf— the attorney who is better than what, in the Government's view, the defendant deserves. The spectre of the Government's selectively excluding only the most talented defense counsel is a serious threat to the equality of forces necessary for the adversarial system to perform at its best. An attorney whose fees are potentially subject to forfeiture will be forced to operate in an environment in which the Government is not only the defendant's adversary, but also his own.

The long-term effects of the fee-forfeiture practice will be to decimate the private criminal-defense bar. As the use of the forfeiture mechanism expands to new categories of federal crimes and spreads to the States, only one class of defendants will be free routinely to retain private counsel: the affluent defendant accused of a crime that generates no economic gain. As the number of private clients diminishes, only the most idealistic and the least skilled of young lawyers will be attracted to the field, while the remainder seek greener pastures elsewhere.

In short, attorney's-fee forfeiture substantially undermines every interest served by the Sixth Amendment right to chosen counsel, on the individual and institutional levels, over the short term and the long haul. . . .

III

In my view, the Act as interpreted by the majority is inconsistent with the intent of Congress, and seriously undermines the basic fairness of our criminal-justice system. That a majority of this Court has upheld the constitutionality of the Act as so interpreted will not deter Congress, I hope, from amending the Act to make clear that Congress did not intend this result. This Court has the power to declare the Act constitutional, but it cannot thereby make it wise.

NOTES AND QUESTIONS

1. Does *Caplin & Drysdale* differ from most of the other cases in this chapter? Most of the Sixth Amendment cases the Supreme Court has decided have involved discrete "one shot" criminal episodes. Powell v. Alabama and Gideon v. Wainwright are obvious examples. *Caplin & Drysdale,* by contrast, involved a complex criminal enterprise, a "massive drug importation and distribution scheme," in the Court's words. What is the proper conceptual framework in such cases? Consider the following argument:

> One might view the ability to purchase lawyers' services as very much like the ability to acquire any other market commodity. Just as we strip Reckmeyer . . . of the ability to buy fancy houses, so, too, we deny [him] the right to hire fancy lawyers.
>
> But there is an alternative conception . . . under which lawyers are a very different kind of good. Under this conception, economic power serves as an *instrumentality* of criminal activity as well as a *proceed* from it. The complex criminal enterprise's wealth gives the enterprise opportunities for criminal activity that poorer entities do not have and gives it opportunities to evade liability that less affluent criminals lack. If the outcome of a criminal proceeding is positively correlated to the caliber of counsel appearing on a defendant's behalf, and if the caliber of counsel is positively related to the ability to retain the best counsel money can buy — both common assumptions — then the economic power acquired by a complex enterprise may enable the enterprise to stay in business by avoiding convictions and forfeitures. Economic power not only constitutes a *benefit* to the criminal; it also lessens her *costs* (because it lowers the probability that she will be detected or successfully prosecuted). The power to buy fancy lawyers may in fact be *worse* than the power to buy fancy houses, because the latter does not facilitate the commission of further crimes as the former can.

Pamela S. Karlan, Discrete and Relational Criminal Representation: The Changing Vision of the Right to Counsel, 105 Harv. L. Rev. 670, 709-710 (1992). If Professor Karlan is right, does that mean Sixth Amendment law should treat lawyers in organized crime cases differently than in more run-of-the-mill criminal cases?

2. What happens to a defendant who cannot pay for a lawyer because all his assets are potentially forfeitable? Presumably the defendant is forced to take appointed counsel. The Court seems to think that is not so bad: After all, it is the same representation that tens of thousands of other defendants receive. Or is it? Reread Note 5 at page 163, concerning the ways in which appointed counsel are paid. Remember that the *Caplin & Drysdale* problem is more likely to arise in conspiracy and large-scale drug distribution cases than in cases of ordinary "street crime." Such cases are likely to be expensive and time-consuming to investigate and try — perhaps a good deal more expensive than the average criminal case. Might the low pay scales, fee caps, and high caseloads of appointed criminal defense attorneys have a different effect on attorney representation in conspiracy cases than in more straightforward criminal cases? If so, what would the effect be? How can the law respond to it?

3. Various criminal statutes allow or mandate forfeiture of a defendant's assets upon conviction, and courts regularly order forfeiture of funds and property used for attorney fees. In addition to RICO, dealt with in *Caplin & Drydale*, and the Continuing Criminal Enterprise Act, dealt with a companion case to *Caplin & Drydale*, United States v. Monsanto, 491 U.S. 600, 615 (1989), the Comprehensive

Forfeiture Act of 1984, Pub. L. No. 98-473, tit. II, ch. III, §§301-323, 98 Stat. 2040, also provides for forfeiture, but does not explicitly include attorney fees. These acts all have a "relation back" clause, which vests the government's interest in property subject to forfeiture as of the time of the crime. This prevents the defendant from avoiding forfeiture by transferring property to a third party, and is the primary vehicle for seizing assets already given to an attorney for fees. Courts may take action to prevent the loss of forfeitable property and to give notice to persons who may have interests in the property. Third parties may seek to preserve their interests in otherwise forfeitable property. There are, for example, "innocent owner" provisions designed to protect individuals who engage in good faith transactions with a person subsequently convicted of crimes involving forfeiture.

In applying these statutes, courts have not been terribly forgiving. For example, in United States v. 1977 Porsche Carrera 911 VIN 9117201924 License No. 459 DWR, 748 F. Supp. 1180 (W.D. Texas, 1990), in concluding that an automobile allegedly given in partial payment for services was forfeitable nonetheless, the court said:

> If a lawyer receives property under suspicious circumstances, he has a duty to investigate further into the origin of the property in order to establish that he has not been "willfully blind" as to the illegal nature of the property. This Court is of the opinion that even in a case in which a lawyer is truly ignorant of any wrongdoing at the precise moment of acquisition of the property, but subsequently learns within a reasonable period (here, a period as short as a few days) that the property is proceeds or has been used to facilitate a crime, that lawyer should not be considered an "innocent owner" . . .
>
> The Court is aware of the hardships this may impose on criminal defense lawyers, but such burden is contemplated by the asset forfeiture provisions, which aim to prevent criminals from using the proceeds of their illegal activities to obtain "the best defense counsel that money can buy." Of course, the Government also has responsibilities under the forfeiture provisions. For instance, the Government has a duty to initiate forfeiture proceedings within a reasonable period of time. It would be inequitable for the Government to wait several months or a year to initiate such proceedings until a lawyer has spent many hours in the preparation of a defense on behalf of his client. In this case, however, seizure was effected on May 18, 1989, only seventeen days after the oral contract for legal services was allegedly made. Moreover, the Claimant received more than sufficient actual notice that the Respondent was subject to forfeiture before he performed any significant legal services on behalf of Saxon Hatchett. Such information came, at the latest, one day after the contract was made. In the Court's opinion, the Claimant assumed the risk of forfeiture under these circumstances, and he has failed to establish the "innocence" required under the [statute] . . . Any other result would require that the Court view the facts of this case with "willful blindness."

4. If requiring the forfeiture of assets that would otherwise have been used to pay for counsel does not violate any of the defendant's rights, what about searching a lawyer pursuant to a warrant while the lawyer's client is testifying before a grand jury? No, said the Court in Conn v. Gabbert, 526 U.S. 286 (1999), at least insofar as the due process clause is concerned. Whether such a search might be unreasonable under the Fourth Amendment was not decided.

5. How about charging the attorney with a crime? The line between receiving legitimate fees and illegal money laundering may not be perfectly clear. Whether

clear or not, various attorneys have been indicted for their alleged involvement in criminal conspiracies that often involve allegations of money laundering. For an example, see United States v. Abbell, 963 F. Supp. 1178 (S.D. Fla., 1997).

D.   The Sixth Amendment Applied: Lineups, Showups, and Photographic Arrays

A particularly important problem with potential right to counsel implications is identifications through lineups, showups, and photographic arrays. In United States v. Wade, 388 U.S. 218 (1967), the Court held that the Sixth Amendment was violated by a postindictment lineup held in the absence of counsel:

> [T]he confrontation compelled by the State between the accused and the victim or witnesses to a crime to elicit identification evidence is peculiarly riddled with innumerable dangers and variable factors which might seriously, even crucially, derogate from a fair trial. The vagaries of eyewitness identification are well-known; the annals of criminal law are rife with instances of mistaken identification.[6] . . . A major factor contributing to the high incidence of miscarriage of justice from mistaken identification has been the degree of suggestion inherent in the manner in which the prosecution presents the suspect to witnesses for pretrial identification. A commentator has observed that "[t]he influence of improper suggestion upon identifying witnesses probably accounts for more miscarriages of justice than any other single factor—perhaps it is responsible for more such errors than all other factors combined." Patrick M. Wall, Eye-Witness Identification in Criminal Cases 26. Suggestion can be created intentionally or unintentionally in many subtle ways.[7] And the dangers for the suspect are particularly grave when the witness' opportunity for observation was insubstantial, and thus his susceptibility to suggestion the greatest.
>
> Moreover, "[i]t is a matter of common experience that, once a witness has picked out the accused at the line-up, he is not likely to go back on his word later on, so that in practice the issue of identity may (in the absence of other relevant evidence) for all practical purposes be determined there and then, before the trial."[8]
>
> The pretrial confrontation for purpose of identification may take the form of a lineup, also known as an "identification parade" or "showup," as in the present case, or presentation of the suspect alone to the witness, as in Stovall v. Denno. It is obvious that risks of suggestion attend either form of confrontation and increase the dangers inhering in eyewitness identification. But as is the case with secret interrogations, there is serious difficulty in depicting what transpires at lineups and other forms of identification confrontations. . . . [T]he defense can seldom reconstruct the manner and mode of lineup identification for judge or jury at trial. Those participating in a lineup with the accused may often be police officers; in any event, the participants' names are rarely recorded or divulged at trial. The impediments to an objective observation are increased when the victim is the witness. Lineups are prevalent in

6. Borchard, Convicting the Innocent; Frank & Frank, Not Guilty; Wall, Eye-Witness Identification in Criminal Cases. . . .

7. See Patrick M. Wall, supra, n. 6, at 26-65; Daniel E. Murray, The Criminal Lineup at Home and Abroad, 1966 Utah L. Rev. 610; David Napley, Problems of Effecting the Presentation of the Case for a Defendant, 66 Col. L. Rev. 94, 98-99 (1966). . . .

8. Glanville Williams & H. A. Hammelmann, Identification Parades, Part I, [1963] Crim. L. Rev. 479, 482.

rape and robbery prosecutions and present a particular hazard that a victim's understandable outrage may excite vengeful or spiteful motives. In any event, neither witnesses nor lineup participants are apt to be alert for conditions prejudicial to the suspect. And if they were, it would likely be of scant benefit to the suspect since neither witnesses nor lineup participants are likely to be schooled in the detection of suggestive influences.[13] Improper influences may go undetected by a suspect, guilty or not, who experiences the emotional tension which we might expect in one being confronted with potential accusers. Even when he does observe abuse, if he has a criminal record he may be reluctant to take the stand and open up the admission of prior convictions. Moreover, any protestations by the suspect of the fairness of the lineup made at trial are likely to be in vain; the jury's choice is between the accused's unsupported version and that of the police officers present. In short, the accused's inability to reconstruct at trial any unfairness that occurred at the lineup may deprive him of his only opportunity meaningfully to attack the credibility of the witness' courtroom identification. . . .

No substantial countervailing policy considerations have been advanced against the requirement of the presence of counsel. Concern is expressed that the requirement will forestall prompt identifications and result in obstruction of the confrontations. As for the first, we note that in the two cases in which the right to counsel is today held to apply, counsel had already been appointed and no argument is made in either case that notice to counsel would have prejudicially delayed the confrontations. Moreover, we leave open the question whether the presence of substitute counsel might not suffice where notification and presence of the suspect's own counsel would result in prejudicial delay. And to refuse to recognize the right to counsel for fear that counsel will obstruct the course of justice is contrary to the basic assumptions upon which this Court has operated in Sixth Amendment cases. . . . In our view counsel can hardly impede legitimate law enforcement; on the contrary, for the reasons expressed, law enforcement may be assisted by preventing the infiltration of taint in the prosecution's identification evidence. That result cannot help the guilty avoid conviction but can only help assure that the right man has been brought to justice.

Legislative or other regulations, such as those of local police departments, which eliminate the risks of abuse and unintentional suggestion at lineup proceedings and the impediments to meaningful confrontation at trial may also remove the basis for regarding the stage as "critical." But neither Congress nor the federal authorities have seen fit to provide a solution. What we hold today "in no way creates a constitutional straitjacket which will handicap sound efforts at reform, nor is it intended to have this effect." Miranda v. Arizona, [384 U.S. 436] at 467. . . .

We come now to the question whether the denial of Wade's motion to strike the courtroom identification by the bank witnesses at trial because of the absence of his counsel at the lineup required, as the Court of Appeals held, the grant of a new trial at which such evidence is to be excluded. We do not think this disposition can be justified without first giving the Government the opportunity to establish by clear and convincing evidence that the in-court identifications were based upon observations of the suspect other than the lineup identification.

. . . Where, as here, the admissibility of evidence of the lineup identification itself is not involved, a per se rule of exclusion of courtroom identification would

13. An additional impediment to the detection of such influences by participants, including the suspect, is the physical conditions often surrounding the conduct of the lineup. In many, lights shine on the stage in such a way that the suspect cannot see the witness. See Gilbert v. United States, 366 F.2d 923 (C.A. 9th Cir. 1966). In some a one-way mirror is used and what is said on the witness' side cannot be heard. . . .

be unjustified.[32] . . . A rule limited solely to the exclusion of testimony concerning identification at the lineup itself, without regard to admissibility of the courtroom identification, would render the right to counsel an empty one. The lineup is most often used, as in the present case, to crystallize the witnesses' identification of the defendant for future reference. We have already noted that the lineup identification will have that effect. The State may then rest upon the witnesses' unequivocal courtroom identification, and not mention the pretrial identification as part of the State's case at trial. Counsel is then in the predicament in which Wade's counsel found himself—realizing that possible unfairness at the lineup may be the sole means of attack upon the unequivocal courtroom identification, and having to probe in the dark in an attempt to discover and reveal unfairness, while bolstering the government witness' courtroom identification by bringing out and dwelling upon his prior identification. Since counsel's presence at the lineup would equip him to attack not only the lineup identification but the courtroom identification as well, limiting the impact of violation of the right to counsel to exclusion of evidence only of identification at the lineup itself disregards a critical element of that right.

We think it follows that the proper test to be applied in these situations is that quoted in Wong Sun v. United States, 371 U.S. 471, 488, " '[W]hether, granting establishment of the primary illegality, the evidence to which instant objection is made has been come at by exploitation of that illegality or instead by means sufficiently distinguishable to be purged of the primary taint.' Maguire, Evidence of Guilt 221 (1959)." . . . Application of this test in the present context requires consideration of various factors; for example, the prior opportunity to observe the alleged criminal act, the existence of any discrepancy between any prelineup description and the defendant's actual description, any identification prior to lineup of another person, the identification by picture of the defendant prior to the lineup, failure to identify the defendant on a prior occasion, and the lapse of time between the alleged act and the lineup identification. It is also relevant to consider those facts which, despite the absence of counsel, are disclosed concerning the conduct of the lineup.[33] On the record now before us we cannot make the determination whether the in-court identifications had an independent origin. This was not an issue at trial, although there is some evidence relevant to a determination. That inquiry is most properly made in the District Court. We therefore think the appropriate procedure to be followed is to vacate the conviction pending a hearing to determine whether the in-court identifications had an independent source, or whether, in any event, the introduction of the evidence was harmless error, Chapman v. California, 386 U.S. 18, and for the District Court to reinstate the conviction or order a new trial, as may be proper. . . .

In the companion case of Gilbert v. California, 388 U.S. 263 (1967), the Court held that a per se exclusionary rule was applicable to out-of-court identification made in violation of the suspect's right to counsel. In the other companion case, Stovall v. Denno, 388 U.S. 293 (1967), the Court held that

32. We reach a contrary conclusion in Gilbert v. California, supra, as to the admissibility of the witness' testimony that he also identified the accused at the lineup.

33. Thus it is not the case that "[i]t matters not how well the witness knows the suspect, whether the witness is the suspect's mother, brother, or long-time associate, and no matter how long or well the witness observed the perpetrator at the scene of the crime." Such factors will have an important bearing upon the true basis of the witness' in-court identification. . . .

Wade was to be applied only to lineups or showups occurring after the decision in *Wade* but that prior lineups could be tested by a due process standard, as we discuss below.

To what should the *Wade* rules apply? To any lineup? After all, the existence of an indictment is irrelevant to the dangers identified in *Wade*. To any identification procedures, such as photographic arrays? What would the impact of such conclusions be on the police? The Court first addressed such issues just five years after *Wade* in Kirby v. Illinois, 406 U.S. 682 (1972), which involved preindictment lineup:

I

In a line of constitutional cases in this Court stemming back to the Court's landmark opinion in Powell v. Alabama, it has been firmly established that a person's Sixth and Fourteenth Amendment right to counsel attaches only at or after the time that adversary judicial proceedings have been initiated against him. . . .

This is not to say that a defendant in a criminal case has a constitutional right to counsel only at the trial itself. The *Powell* case makes clear that the right attaches at the time of arraignment, and the Court has recently held that it exists also at the time of a preliminary hearing. Coleman v. Alabama. . . . But the point is that, while members of the Court have differed as to existence of the right to counsel in the contexts of some of the above cases, *all* of those cases have involved points of time at or after the initiation of adversary judicial criminal proceedings—whether by way of formal charge, preliminary hearing, indictment, information, or arraignment. . . .

The initiation of judicial criminal proceedings is far from a mere formalism. It is the starting point of our whole system of adversary criminal justice. For it is only then that the government has committed itself to prosecute, and only then that the adverse positions of government and defendant have solidified. It is then that a defendant finds himself faced with the prosecutorial forces of organized society, and immersed in the intricacies of substantive and procedural criminal law. It is this point, therefore, that marks the commencement of the "criminal prosecutions" to which alone the explicit guarantees of the Sixth Amendment are applicable. . . .

In this case we are asked to import into a routine police investigation an absolute constitutional guarantee historically and rationally applicable only after the onset of formal prosecutorial proceedings. We decline to do so. Less than a year after *Wade* and *Gilbert* were decided, the Court explained the rule of those decisions as follows: "The rationale of those cases was that an accused is entitled to counsel at any 'critical stage of the *prosecution*,' and that a post-indictment lineup is such a 'critical stage.' " We decline to depart from that rationale today by imposing a per se exclusionary rule upon testimony concerning an identification that took place long before the commencement of any prosecution whatever.

II

What has been said is not to suggest that there may not be occasions during the course of a criminal investigation when the police do abuse identification procedures. Such abuses are not beyond the reach of the Constitution. As the Court pointed out in *Wade* itself, it is always necessary to "scrutinize *any* pretrial confrontation. . . ." The Due Process Clause of the Fifth and Fourteenth Amendments forbids a lineup that is unnecessarily suggestive and conducive to irreparable mistaken identification. When a person has not been formally charged with a criminal offense, *Stovall* strikes the appropriate constitutional balance between the right of a suspect to be protected from prejudicial procedures and the interest of society in the prompt and purposeful investigation of an unsolved crime.

We omit the dissents in *Kirby* that make the obvious point that *Wade* and *Kirby* are impossible to reconcile on *Wade*'s rationale. Of course, they are easy to reconcile on *Kirby*'s rationale. Which strikes you as more persuasive, as more rational, as more appropriate?

Can the police arrange a noncustodial, surreptitious viewing of the accused? Does it matter when it would occur — pre- or postindictment? Does a defendant have a right to a pretrial lineup? Most courts have held that it is a matter left to the trial judge's discretion, see, e.g., People v. Baines, 30 Cal. 3d 143, 635 P.2d 455, 177 Cal. Rptr. 861 (1981), but consider the implications of Moore v. Illinois, 434 U.S. 220 (1977), in which the defendant was identified by the complaining witness at a preliminary hearing at which he was not represented by counsel. The defendant was convicted and appealed on the grounds that his identification at the preliminary hearing violated *Wade*. The Court of Appeals was unpersuaded, but the Supreme Court reversed:

> The Court of Appeals . . . read *Kirby* as holding that evidence of a corporeal identification conducted in the absence of defense counsel must be excluded only if the identification is made after the defendant is *indicted*. . . . Such a reading cannot be squared with *Kirby* itself, which held that an accused's rights under *Wade* and *Gilbert* attach to identifications conducted "at or after the initiation of adversary judicial criminal proceedings," including proceedings instituted "by way of formal charge [or] preliminary hearing." 406 U.S., at 689. The prosecution in this case was commenced under Illinois law when the victim's complaint was filed in court. The purpose of the preliminary hearing was to determine whether there was probable cause to bind petitioner over to the grand jury and to set bail. Petitioner had the right to oppose the prosecution at that hearing by moving to dismiss the charges and to suppress the evidence against him. He faced counsel for the State, who elicited the victim's identification, summarized the State's other evidence against petitioner, and urged that the State be given more time to marshal its evidence. It is plain that "the government ha[d] committed itself to prosecute," and that petitioner found "himself faced with the prosecutorial forces of organized society, and immersed in the intricacies of substantive and procedural criminal law." *Kirby*. The State candidly concedes that this preliminary hearing marked the "initiation of adversary judicial criminal proceedings" against petitioner, . . . and it hardly could contend otherwise. The Court of Appeals therefore erred in holding that petitioner's rights under *Wade* and *Gilbert* had not yet attached at the time of the preliminary hearing.
>
> The Court of Appeals also suggested that *Wade* and *Gilbert* did not apply here because the "in-court identification could hardly be considered a line-up." . . . The meaning of this statement is not entirely clear. If the court meant that a one-on-one identification procedure, as distinguished from a lineup, is not subject to the counsel requirement, it was mistaken. Although *Wade* and *Gilbert* both involved lineups, *Wade* clearly contemplated that counsel would be required in both situations: "The pretrial

confrontation for purpose of identification may take the form of a lineup . . . or presentation of the suspect alone to the witness. . . . It is obvious that risks of suggestion attend either form of confrontation. . . ." Indeed, a one-on-one confrontation generally is thought to present greater risks of mistaken identification than a lineup. E.g., Patrick M. Wall, Eye-Witness Identification in Criminal Cases 27-40 (1965); Glanville Williams & H. A. Hammelmann, Identification Parades — I, Crim. L. Rev. 479, 480-481 (1963). There is no reason, then, to hold that a one-on-one identification procedure is not subject to the same requirements as a lineup.

If the court believed that petitioner did not have a right to counsel at this identification procedure because it was conducted in the course of a judicial proceeding, we do not agree. The reasons supporting *Wade*'s holding that a corporeal identification is a critical stage of a criminal prosecution for Sixth Amendment purposes apply with equal force to this identification. It is difficult to imagine a more suggestive manner in which to present a suspect to a witness for their critical first confrontation than was employed in this case. The victim, who had seen her assailant for only 10 to 15 seconds, was asked to make her identification after she was told that she was going to view a suspect, after she was told his name and heard it called as he was led before the bench, and after she heard the prosecutor recite the evidence believed to implicate petitioner. Had petitioner been represented by counsel, some or all of this suggestiveness could have been avoided.[5] . . .

Could an attorney in *Moore* have required that the complaining witness first view the accused in a lineup?

A number of police departments responded to *Wade* by promulgating rules to govern lineups that were designed to ensure counsel's presence. Do you think counsel is an absolute requirement, or could lineups be conducted with sufficient safeguards to make counsel unnecessary? For a discussion, see Frank T. Read, Lawyers at Lineups: Constitutional Necessity or Avoidable Extravagance?, 17 UCLA L. Rev. 339 (1969). Recognizing that the Court in *Wade* implied that regulation designed to offset the potential for prejudice at lineups and to preserve a defendant's right to confrontation at trial could supplant the requirement of counsel emanating from *Wade*, Professor Read proposed the following Model Regulation, id. at 388-393:

Proposed Regulation of Eyewitness Identification Procedures

(1) *Restrictions on Identification*

(a) Restrictions on Police. No law enforcement officer shall conduct a lineup or otherwise attempt, by having a witness view or hear the voice of an arrested person, to secure the identification of an arrested person as a person involved in a crime unless such identification procedure is authorized by this regulation. . . .

---

5. For example, counsel could have requested that the hearing be postponed until a lineup could be arranged at which the victim would view petitioner in a less suggestive setting. Short of that, counsel could have asked that the victim be excused from the courtroom while the charges were read and the evidence against petitioner was recited, and that petitioner be seated with other people in the audience when the victim attempted an identification. Counsel might have sought to cross-examine the victim to test her identification before it hardened. Because it is in the prosecution's interest as well as the accused's that witnesses' identifications remain untainted, we cannot assume that such requests would have been in vain. Such requests ordinarily are addressed to the sound discretion of the court; we express no opinion as to whether the preliminary hearing court would have been required to grant any such requests.

(b) Restrictions on Witnesses. No witness at trial shall hereafter be permitted to identify a criminal defendant as the person involved in a crime unless the prosecution has first shown, to the Court's satisfaction, and in the absence of the jury:

(1) That the witness was sufficiently acquainted with the defendant before the alleged offense to make recognition then likely; or

(2) That the witness' recognition of the defendant arose from an independent origin or source under circumstances other than that the police or other authorities were attempting to elicit identification; or

(3) That all pertinent provisions of this regulation were followed by police in conducting eyewitness confrontation or lineup identification procedures. . . .

(2) *Required Procedures*

A lineup or identification procedure is authorized only if there has been compliance with the following rules:

(a) No person participating in any police lineup or other identification procedure and no person present at such lineup or identification procedure shall do any act or say any thing which shall directly, indirectly, or impliedly suggest to or influence any identifying witness to make or not to make a particular identification, or which suggests to or influences any identifying witness to believe or suspect that any member or members of the group standing [in] the lineup has been arrested for the offense in question or for any offense.

(b) The officer conducting any police lineup or identification proceeding shall take all steps necessary to guarantee that any identification or failure to identify shall be the product of the free choice of the identifying witness based on the independent recollection or recognition of such witness. . . .

(c) All police lineups or identification proceedings shall be composed of a minimum of five persons, in addition to the suspect, and these additional five or more persons shall be of the same general age, sex, race and general physical characteristics as the suspect and be required to wear clothing similar to that worn by the suspect. . . .

(d) All body movements, gestures or verbal statements that may be necessary shall be done one time only by each person participating in the lineup and shall be repeated only at the express request of the identifying witness. . . .

(e) The suspect may select his own position in any police lineup or identification procedure and may change his position after each identifying witness has completed his viewing. . . .

(f) Under no circumstances shall any identifying witness be allowed to see a suspect or any member of the lineup in custody or otherwise prior to the lineup or identification procedure and no interrogation of the suspect or any member of the lineup group shall occur in the presence of an identifying witness. . . .

(g) Two (2) or more identifying witnesses shall not view the same lineup or identification procedure in each other's presence nor shall they be permitted to communicate with each other before completion of all attempted identifications by all witnesses. . . .

(h) Prior to viewing the lineup, an identifying witness shall be required to give a description of the person or persons responsible for the crime in question and such description shall be written and signed or otherwise verified and a copy of such description and all other descriptions that may have been given to the police prior to the lineup shall be made available to defense counsel. . . .

(i) Any identifying witness may remain unseen or masked when viewing the lineup or identification procedure. . . .

(j) The officer conducting any police lineup or identification proceeding shall record the names and addresses of persons participating in the lineup or identification, including the suspect or defendant, the others standing in the lineup group with the suspect or defendant, the police officers present, any person representing the suspect, and any independent observers; provided however, that names of identifying witnesses shall not be required to be disclosed; a copy of said list of names and addresses so recorded shall be furnished to defense counsel.

(k) A full record of all statements made by the identifying witness regarding the identification shall be made by voice recording, or, if no such recording equipment is available, a complete transcript of all statements made by the identifying witness regarding the identification shall be made; a copy of such voice recording or transcript shall be made available to defense counsel.

(l) A visual recording of the conduct of the lineup or identification procedure shall be made by videotape or other appropriate moving picture-type process, or, if no such videotape or moving picture type equipment is available, a minimum of one good quality color photograph of the entire group included in the lineup which was viewed by the identifying witness shall be taken and a copy of such photograph shall be made available to defense counsel. . . .

(3) *Urgent Necessity*

In cases of urgent necessity, as where a witness is dying at the scene of the crime, an identification confrontation shall be lawful with only such compliance with subsections a, b, j, k, and l of section 2, above, as may be reasonable under the circumstances. . . .

Prof. Read's proposal anticipated the work that would be done by psychologists decades later. See Note 4, infra page 273.

How do the principles of *Wade* and *Kirby* apply to photographic arrays? That question was addressed in United States v. Ash, 413 U.S. 300 (1973):

II . . .

[The history of the right to counsel] suggests that the core purpose of the counsel guarantee was to assure "Assistance" at trial, when the accused was confronted with both the intricacies of the law and the advocacy of the public prosecutor. Later developments have led this Court to recognize that "Assistance" would be less than meaningful if it were limited to the formal trial itself. . . .

The function of counsel in rendering "Assistance" continued at the lineup under consideration in *Wade* and its companion cases. Although the accused was not confronted there with legal questions, the lineup offered opportunities for prosecuting authorities to take advantage of the accused. Counsel was seen by the Court as being more sensitive to, and aware of, suggestive influences than the accused himself, and as better able to reconstruct the events at trial. Counsel present at lineup would be able to remove disabilities of the accused in precisely the same fashion that counsel compensated for the disabilities of the layman at trial. Thus, the Court mentioned that the accused's memory might be dimmed by "emotional tension," that the accused's credibility at trial would be diminished by his status as defendant, and that the accused might be unable to present his version effectively without giving up his privilege against compulsory self-incrimination. United States v. Wade. It was in order to compensate for these deficiencies that the Court found the need for the assistance of counsel.

This review of the history and expansion of the Sixth Amendment counsel guarantee demonstrates that the test utilized by the Court has called for examination of the event in order to determine whether the accused required aid in coping with legal problems or assistance in meeting his adversary. . . .

IV

A substantial departure from the historical test would be necessary if the Sixth Amendment were interpreted to give Ash a right to counsel at the photographic identification in this case. Since the accused himself is not present at the time of the photographic display, and asserts no right to be present, no possibility arises that the accused might be misled by his lack of familiarity with the law or overpowered by his professional adversary. Similarly, the counsel guarantee would not be used to produce equality in a trial-like adversary confrontation. Rather, the guarantee was used by the Court of Appeals to produce confrontation at an event that previously was not analogous to an adversary trial.

Even if we were willing to view the counsel guarantee in broad terms as a generalized protection of the adversary process, we would be unwilling to go so far as to extend the right to a portion of the prosecutor's trial-preparation interviews with witnesses. Although photography is relatively new, the interviewing of witnesses before trial is a procedure that predates the Sixth Amendment. In England in the 16th and 17th centuries counsel regularly interviewed witnesses before trial. 9 W. Holdsworth, History of English Law 226-228 (1926). The traditional counterbalance in the American adversary system for these interviews arises from the equal ability of defense counsel to seek and interview witnesses himself.

That adversary mechanism remains as effective for a photographic display as for other parts of pretrial interviews.[10] No greater limitations are placed on defense counsel in constructing displays, seeking witnesses, and conducting photographic identifications than those applicable to the prosecution.[11] Selection of the picture of a person other than the accused, or the inability of a witness to make any selection, will be useful to the defense in precisely the same manner that the selection of a picture of the defendant would be useful to the prosecution.[12] In this very case, for example, the initial tender of the photographic display was by Bailey's counsel, who sought to demonstrate that the witness had failed to make a photographic identification. Although we do not suggest that equality of access to photographs removes all potential for abuse, it does remove any inequality in the adversary process itself and thereby fully satisfies the historical spirit of the Sixth Amendment's counsel guarantee.

10. Duplication by defense counsel is a safeguard that normally is not available when a formal confrontation occurs. Defense counsel has no statutory authority to conduct a preliminary hearing, for example, and defense counsel will generally be prevented by practical considerations from conducting his own lineup. Even in some confrontations, however, the possibility of duplication may be important. The Court noted this in holding that the taking of handwriting exemplars did not constitute a "critical stage": "If, for some reason, an unrepresentative exemplar is taken, this can be brought out and corrected through the adversary process at trial since the accused can make an unlimited number of additional exemplars for analysis and comparison by government and defense handwriting experts." Gilbert v. California.

11. We do not suggest, of course, that defense counsel has any greater freedom than the prosecution to abuse the photographic identification. Evidence of photographic identifications conducted by the defense may be excluded as unreliable under the same standards that would be applied to unreliable identifications conducted by the Government.

12. The Court of Appeals deemed it significant that a photographic identification is admissible as substantive evidence, whereas other parts of interviews may be introduced only for impeachment. . . . In this case defense counsel for Bailey introduced the inability to identify, and that was received into evidence. Thus defense counsel still received benefits equivalent to those available to the prosecution. Although defense counsel may be concerned that repeated photographic displays containing the accused's picture as the only common characteristic will tend to promote identification of the accused, the defense has other balancing devices available to it, such as the use of a sufficiently large number of photographs to counteract this possibility.

The argument has been advanced that requiring counsel might compel the police to observe more scientific procedures or might encourage them to utilize corporeal rather than photographic displays. This Court has recognized that improved procedures can minimize the dangers of suggestion. Simmons v. United States. Commentators have also proposed more accurate techniques.[15]

Pretrial photographic identifications, however, are hardly unique in offering possibilities for the actions of the prosecutor unfairly to prejudice the accused. Evidence favorable to the accused may be withheld; testimony of witnesses may be manipulated; the results of laboratory tests may be contrived. In many ways the prosecutor, by accident or by design, may improperly subvert the trial. The primary safeguard against abuses of this kind is the ethical responsibility of the prosecutor,[16] who, as so often has been said, may "strike hard blows" but not "foul ones." If that safeguard fails, review remains available under due process standards. . . .

We are not persuaded that the risks inherent in the use of photographic displays are so pernicious that an extraordinary system of safeguards is required.

We hold, then, that the Sixth Amendment does not grant the right to counsel at photographic displays conducted by the Government for the purpose of allowing a witness to attempt an identification of the offender.

Justices Brennan, Marshall, and Douglas dissented:

. . . As the Court of Appeals recognized, "the dangers of mistaken identification . . . set forth in Wade are applicable in large measure to photographic as well as corporeal identifications." To the extent that misidentification may be attributable to a witness' faulty memory or perception, or inadequate opportunity for detailed observation during the crime, the risks are obviously as great at a photographic display as at a lineup. But "[b]ecause of the inherent limitations of photography, which presents its subject in two dimensions rather than the three dimensions of reality, . . . a photographic identification, even when properly obtained, is clearly inferior to a properly obtained corporeal identification." Patrick M. Wall, Eye-Witness Identification in Criminal Cases 70 (1965). Indeed, noting "the hazards of initial identification by photograph," we have expressly recognized that "a corporeal identification . . . is normally more accurate" than a photographic identification. Simmons v. United States.[9] Thus, in this sense at least, the dangers of misidentification are even greater at a photographic display than at a lineup.

Moreover, as in the lineup situation, the possibilities for impermissible suggestion in the context of a photographic display are manifold. Such suggestion, intentional, or unintentional, may derive from three possible sources. First, the photographs

15. E.g., Patrick M. Wall, Eye-Witness Identification in Criminal Cases 77-85 (1965); Nathan R. Sobel, supra, n. 14, at 309-310; Comment, 56 Iowa L. Rev. 408, 420-421 (1970).

16. Throughout a criminal prosecution the prosecutor's ethical responsibility extends, of course, to supervision of any continuing investigation of the case. By prescribing procedures to be used by his agents and by screening the evidence before trial with a view to eliminating unreliable identifications, the prosecutor is able to minimize abuse in photographic displays even if they are conducted in his absence.

9. See also Nathan R. Sobel, Assailing the Impermissible Suggestion: Evolving Limitations on the Abuse of Pre-Trial Criminal Identification Methods, 38 Brooklyn L. Rev. 261, 264, 296 (1971); Glanville Williams & H. A. Hammelmann, Identification Parades, [1955] Crim. L. Rev. 525, 531; Comment, Photographic Identification: The Hidden Persuader, 56 Iowa L. Rev. 408, 419 (1970); Note, Pretrial Photographic Identification — A "Critical Stage" of Criminal Proceedings?, 21 Syracuse L. Rev. 1235, 1241 (1970). Indeed, recognizing the superiority of corporeal to photographic identifications, English courts have long held that once the accused is in custody, pre-lineup photographic identification is "indefensible" and grounds for quashing the conviction. See also Patrick M. Wall, Eye-Witness Identification in Criminal Cases 71 (1965).

themselves might tend to suggest which of the pictures is that of the suspect. For example, differences in age, pose, or other physical characteristics of the persons represented, and variations in the mounting, background, lighting, or markings of the photographs all might have the effect of singling out the accused.

Second, impermissible suggestion may inhere in the manner in which the photographs are displayed to the witness. The danger of misidentification is, of course, "increased if the police display to the witness . . . the pictures of several persons among which the photograph of a single such individual recurs or is in some way emphasized." And, if the photographs are arranged in an asymmetrical pattern, or if they are displayed in a time sequence that tends to emphasize a particular photograph, "any identification of the photograph which stands out from the rest is no more reliable than an identification of a single photograph, exhibited alone." P. Wall, supra, at 81.

Third, gestures or comments of the prosecutor at the time of the display may lead an otherwise uncertain witness to select the "correct" photograph. For example, the prosecutor might "indicate to the witness that [he has] other evidence that one of the persons pictured committed the crime,"[11] and might even point to a particular photograph and ask whether the person pictured "looks familiar." More subtly, the prosecutor's inflection, facial expressions, physical motions, and myriad other almost imperceptible means of communication might tend, intentionally or unintentionally, to compromise the witness' objectivity. Thus, as is the case with lineups, "[i]mproper photographic identification procedures, . . . by exerting a suggestive influence upon the witnesses, can often lead to an erroneous identification. . . ." Patrick M. Wall, supra, at 89.[12] And "[r]egardless of how the initial misidentification comes about, the witness thereafter is apt to retain in his memory the image of the photograph rather than of the person actually seen. . . ." Simmons v. United States. As a result, " 'the issue of identity may (in the absence of other relevant evidence) for all practical purposes be determined there and then, before the trial.' " United States v. Wade. . . .

Moreover, as with lineups, the defense can "seldom reconstruct" at trial the mode and manner of photographic identification. It is true, of course, that the photographs used at the pretrial display might be preserved for examination at trial. But "it may also be said that a photograph can preserve the record of a lineup; yet this does not justify a lineup without counsel." Indeed, in reality, preservation of the photographs affords little protection to the unrepresented accused. For, although retention of the photographs may mitigate the dangers of misidentification due to the suggestiveness of the photographs themselves, it cannot in any sense reveal to defense counsel the more subtle, and therefore more dangerous, suggestiveness that might derive from the manner in which the photographs were displayed or any accompanying comments or gestures. Moreover, the accused cannot rely upon the witnesses themselves to

---

11. Simmons v. United States, supra, at 383.

12. The Court maintains that "the ethical responsibility of the prosecutor" is in itself a sufficient "safeguard" against impermissible suggestion at a photographic display. . . . The same argument might, of course, be made with respect to lineups. Moreover, it is clear that the "prosecutor" is not always present at such pretrial displays. Indeed, in this very case, one of the four eyewitnesses was shown the color photographs on the morning of trial by an agent of the FBI, *not* in the presence of the "prosecutor." And even though "the ethical responsibility of the prosecutor" might be an adequate "safeguard" against *intentional* suggestion, it can hardly be doubted that a "prosecutor" is, after all, only human. His behavior may be fraught with wholly *unintentional* and indeed unconscious nuances that might effectively suggest the "proper" response. See Patrick M. Wall, supra, n. 9, at 26-65; David Napley, Problems of Effecting the Presentation of the Case for a Defendant, 66 Col. L. Rev. 94, 98–99 (1966); Glanville Williams & H. A. Hammelmann, Identification Parades — I, [1963] Crim. L. Rev. 479, 483. And, of course, as *Wade* itself makes clear, unlike other forms of unintentional prosecutorial "manipulation," even unintentional suggestiveness at an identification procedure involves serious risks of "freezing" the witness' mistaken identification and creates almost insurmountable obstacles to reconstruction at trial.

expose these latter sources of suggestion, for the witnesses are not "apt to be alert for conditions prejudicial to the suspect. And if they were, it would likely be of scant benefit to the suspect" since the witnesses are hardly "likely to be schooled in the detection of suggestive influences." Id., at 230.

Finally, and *unlike* the lineup situation, the accused himself is not even present at the photographic identification, thereby reducing the likelihood that irregularities in the procedures will ever come to light. Indeed, in *Wade*, the Government itself observed:[14]

> When the defendant is present — as he is during a lineup — he may personally observe the circumstances, report them to his attorney, and (if he chooses to take the stand) testify about them at trial. . . . [I]n the absence of an accused, on the other hand, there is no one present to verify the fairness of the interview or to report any irregularities. If the prosecution were tempted to engage in "sloppy or biased or fraudulent" conduct . . . , it would be far more likely to do so when the accused is absent than when he himself is being "used."

Thus, the difficulties of reconstructing at trial an uncounseled photographic display are at least equal to, and possibly greater than, those involved in reconstructing an uncounseled lineup.[15] And, as the Government argued in *Wade*, in terms of the need for counsel, "[t]here is no meaningful difference between a witness' pretrial identification from photographs and a similar identification made at a lineup." For, in both situations "the accused's inability effectively to reconstruct at trial any unfairness that occurred at the [pretrial identification] may deprive him of his only opportunity meaningfully to attack the credibility of the witness' courtroom identification." United States v. Wade, supra, at 231-232. As a result, both photographic and corporeal identifications create grave dangers that an innocent defendant might be convicted simply because of his inability to expose a tainted identification. This being so, considerations of logic, consistency, and, indeed, fairness compel the conclusion that a pretrial photographic identification, like a pretrial corporeal identification, is a "critical stage of the prosecution at which [the accused is] 'as much entitled to such aid [of counsel] . . . as at the trial itself.'" Id., at 237, quoting Powell v. Alabama, 287 U.S., at 57.

---

14. Brief for United States 24-25 in United States v. Wade, No. 334, O.T. 1966.

15. The Court's assertion, . . . that these difficulties of reconstruction are somehow minimized because the defense can "duplicate" a photographic identification reflects a complete misunderstanding of the issues in this case. Aside from the fact that lineups can also be "duplicated," the Court's assertion is wholly inconsistent with the underlying premises of both *Wade* and *Gilbert*. For, unlike the Court today, the Court in both of those decisions recognized a critical difference between "systematized or scientific analyzing of the accused's fingerprints, blood sample, clothing, hair, and the like," on the one hand, and eyewitness identification, on the other. In essence, the Court noted in *Wade* and *Gilbert* that, in the former situations, the accused can preserve his right to a fair trial simply by "duplicating" the tests of the Government, thereby enabling him to expose any errors in the Government's analysis. Such "duplication" is possible, however, *only* because the accused's tests can be made *independently* of those of the Government — that is, any errors in the Government's analyses cannot affect the reliability of the accused's tests. That simply is not the case, however, with respect to eyewitness identifications, whether corporeal or photographic. Due to the "freezing effect" recognized in *Wade*, once suggestion has tainted the identification, its mark is virtually indelible. For once a witness has made a mistaken identification, "'he is not likely to go back on his word later on.'" United States v. Wade. As a result, any effort of the accused to "duplicate" the initial photographic display will almost necessarily lead to a reaffirmation of the initial misidentification.

The Court's related assertion, that "equality of access" to the results of a Government conducted photographic display "remove[s] any inequality in the adversary process," . . . is similarly flawed. For due to the possibilities for suggestion, intentional or unintentional, the so-called "equality of access" is, in reality, skewed sharply in favor of the prosecution.

How responsive is *Ash* to the real problem of photographic identification? The Supreme Court did not purport to determine the extent to which due process analysis is relevant to photographic arrays, an issue apparently settled by Manson v. Braithwaite, which is discussed below. Inappropriate suggestiveness is the central problem, however. Consider the following from Randolph N. Jonakait, Reliable Identification: Could the Supreme Court Tell in *Manson v. Braithwaite?*, 52 U. Colo. L. Rev. 511, 523-525 (1981):

Untrustworthy identifications will be admitted if the courts do not understand what criteria truly indicate reliability. Untrustworthy identifications will also be admitted if courts cannot discern suggestive identification procedures. Scientific studies indicate that two prevalent identification procedures, looking at mugshots and lineups, are often suggestive.[47] One of the reasons for their suggestiveness relates to the psychological phenomenon of unconscious transference: A face seen in one situation is mistakenly remembered to have been seen in another. In one study, two or three days after a staged crime, witnesses looked at mugshots. Some of the pictures were of

---

47. Suggestiveness, of course, not only affects identifications; it can affect many areas of litigation. For example, the suggestiveness of questioning by police officers investigating a crime or lawyers preparing a witness for trial can alter a witness's memory of an event. Thus, in one set of experiments, subjects were shown a film of a moving automobile. Some were then asked, "How fast was the white sports car going while traveling along the country road?" Others were asked, "How fast was the white sports car going when it passed the barn while traveling along the country road?" No barn was visible in the film. A week later, all the subjects were asked whether they remembered seeing a barn in the movie. Of those given the misinformation, 17 percent remembered the nonexistent structure, while only 3 percent who had been asked the neutral question said they saw it. E. Loftus, [Eyewitness Testimony (1979)] at 60.

Questioning does not have to be this blatant to produce a similar effect. One set of subjects who had viewed a film of a car accident was asked to estimate the speed of the cars when they "smashed." The other set was asked to give the speed when they "hit." Later, all subjects were tested on their memory of seeing broken glass in the collision. Nearly 33 percent of those whose question included the word "smashed" reported broken glass; only 14 percent of the other set did. No broken glass was evident in the film.

Limitations on these distortions have been discovered. For instance, the memory can be affected mainly about peripheral items, not central items. Furthermore, once a witness resists blatantly false information, his resistance to other misleading suggestions also increases. The timing of the suggestive questioning also affects the distortion. The greater the lapse of time between the perception and the suggestion, the greater the likelihood of memory alteration. If the suggestion occurs shortly after the perception, both the memory of the event and the suggestion will fade. Loftus summarizes: "Longer retention intervals lead to worse performance, consistent information improves performance, and misleading information that is given immediately after an event has less of an impact on the memory than misleading information that is delayed until just prior to the test. Apparently, giving the event information a chance to fade in memory makes it easier to introduce misleading information." In practical terms, then, the greatest danger is not with the police investigating immediately after a crime, but with attorneys preparing witnesses for trial.

The mere wording of a question designed to elicit recall, however, can affect the recollection given. For instance, one half of a group of subjects was asked how "tall" a person was and gave an average answer of "seventy-nine inches." The other half was asked how "short." The average answer to that question was "sixty-nine inches." Similarly, how "long" was a movie brought the reply, "130 minutes;" how short, "100 minutes." Of course, leading questions are controlled in court, but not before. The time before trial is the crucial period. Once an answer is stamped upon one's memory, subsequent attempts to recall the memory may not elicit the original memory, but only the response to an earlier question.

These studies, of course, only begin to provide the information needed to make litigation more just. Current data merely indicate some factors tending to cause inaccurate memories; it does not reveal whether a memory has been distorted in particular instances. See A. D. Yarmey, [The Psychology of Eyewitness Identification (1979)] at 73. The studies do, however, provide guidance to those desirous of the fullest, most reliable recollections. Loftus suggests that the investigator interested in getting the most complete and accurate story should first solicit a free narrative and then follow up with questions to fill in the gaps.

"criminals" from the event, while others were of people the witnesses had never before seen. Four or five days after the photos were inspected, a corporeal lineup was held. "18 percent of the persons in the lineup who had never been seen before were mistakenly identified. However, if a person's mugshot had been seen in the interim, this percentage rose to 29 percent."[48]

It frequently happens in criminal cases that a few days after a crime the witnesses thumb through pictures and are later asked to make identifications from a lineup. Unconscious transference might cause an innocent person to be positively identified in a lineup simply because his picture was in police files. Several things can be done to protect against this effect. For instance, if a suspect is identified at a lineup and his picture was viewed earlier by the witness who did not identify that picture as depicting the criminal, the identification procedure should be regarded as suggestive. No determination about this unconscious transference can be made, however, if there is no way to ascertain what pictures the witness saw. Often the witness looks through large books or file drawers of photos, and the police usually have no records of what is in those books or drawers. By the time an identification is challenged in court, no one can discover whether the witness saw a picture of the defendant before the lineup identification. The starting point, then, should be to require police to keep accurate records of the mugshots shown to witnesses.

Some of the suggestiveness of showing pictures can be lessened by the use of control people. After a description is obtained from a witness, pictures of people who fit the description but who could not have committed the crime — police officers, for example — should be inserted with the other pictures to be viewed. At a subsequent lineup, the control people as well as the suspects should be present in the lineup. This would not eliminate false identifications, but it might lessen the chance of unconscious transference.

As mentioned above, the Court has held that due process can be violated by the introduction of unreliable identification evidence. The Court's fullest treatment of the due process test came in Manson v. Braithwaite, 432 U.S. 98 (1977):

Stovall v. Denno, 388 U.S. 293 (1967), decided in 1967, concerned a petitioner who had been convicted in a New York court of murder. He was arrested the day following the crime and was taken by the police to a hospital where the victim's wife, also wounded in the assault, was a patient. After observing Stovall and hearing him speak, she identified him as the murderer. She later made an in-court identification. On federal habeas, Stovall claimed the identification testimony violated his Fifth, Sixth, and Fourteenth Amendment rights. The District Court dismissed the petition, and the Court of Appeals, en banc, affirmed. This Court also affirmed. On the identification issue, the Court reviewed the practice of showing a suspect singly for purposes of identification, and the claim that this was so unnecessarily suggestive and conducive to irreparable mistaken identification that it constituted a denial of due process of law. The Court noted that the practice "has been widely condemned," 388 U.S., at 302, but it concluded that "a claimed violation of due process of law in the conduct of a confrontation depends on the totality of the circumstances surrounding it." Ibid. In that case, showing Stovall to the victim's spouse "was imperative." . . .

Neil v. Biggers, 409 U.S. 188 (1972), decided in 1972, concerned a respondent who had been convicted in a Tennessee court of rape, on evidence consisting in part of the victim's visual and voice identification of Biggers at a station-house showup seven months after the crime. The victim had been in her assailant's presence for some time

48. E. Loftus, supra . . . at 151.

and had directly observed him indoors and under a full moon outdoors. She testified that she had "no doubt" that Biggers was her assailant. She previously had given the police a description of the assailant. She had made no identification of others presented at previous showups, lineups, or through photographs. On federal habeas, the District Court held that the confrontation was so suggestive as to violate due process. The Court of Appeals affirmed. This Court reversed on that issue, and held that the evidence properly had been allowed to go to the jury. The Court reviewed *Stovall* and certain later cases where it had considered the scope of due process protection against the admission of evidence derived from suggestive identification procedures, namely, Simmons v. United States; Foster v. California; and Coleman v. Alabama.[8] The Court concluded that general guidelines emerged from these cases "as to the relationship between suggestiveness and misidentification." The "admission of evidence of a showup without more does not violate due process." The Court expressed concern about the lapse of seven months between the crime and the confrontation and observed that this "would be a seriously negative factor in most cases." The "central question," however, was "whether under the 'totality of the circumstances' the identification was reliable even though the confrontation procedure was suggestive." Applying that test, the Court found "no substantial likelihood of misidentification. The evidence was properly allowed to go to the jury."

Biggers well might be seen to provide an unambiguous answer to the question before us: The admission of testimony concerning a suggestive and unnecessary identification procedure does not violate due process so long as the identification possesses sufficient aspects of reliability.[9] In one passage, however, the Court

8. *Simmons* involved photographs, mostly group ones, shown to bankteller victims who made in-court identifications. The Court discussed the "chance of misidentification," 390 U.S., at 383; declined to prohibit the procedure "either in the exercise of our supervisory power or, still less, as a matter of constitutional requirement," id., at 384; and held that each case must be considered on its facts and that a conviction would be set aside only if the identification procedure "was so impermissibly suggestive as to give rise to a very substantial likelihood of irreparable misidentification." Id. The out-of-court identification was not offered. Mr. Justice Black would have denied Simmons' due process claim as frivolous. Id., at 395-396.

Foster concerned repeated confrontations between a suspect and the manager of an office that had been robbed. At a second lineup, but not at the first and not at a personal one-to-one confrontation, the manager identified the suspect. At trial he testified as to this and made an in-court identification. The Court reaffirmed the *Stovall* standard and then concluded that the repeated confrontations were so suggestive as to violate due process. The case was remanded for the state courts to consider the question of harmless error.

In *Coleman* a plurality of the Court was of the view that the trial court did not err when it found that the victim's in-court identifications did not stem from a lineup procedure so impermissibly suggestive as to give rise to a substantial likelihood of misidentification. 399 U.S., at 5-6.

9. Mr. Justice Marshall argues in dissent that our cases have "established two different due process tests for two very different situations." . . . Pretrial identifications are to be covered by *Stovall*, which is said to require exclusion of evidence concerning unnecessarily suggestive pretrial identifications without regard to reliability. In-court identifications, on the other hand, are to be governed by *Simmons* and admissibility turns on reliability. The Court's cases are sorted into one category or the other. *Biggers*, which clearly adopts the reliability of the identification as the guiding factor in the admissibility of both pretrial and in-court identifications, is condemned for mixing the two lines and for adopting a uniform rule.

Although it must be acknowledged that our cases are not uniform in their emphasis, they hardly suggest the formal structure the dissent would impose on them. If our cases truly established two different rules, one might expect at some point at least passing reference to the fact. There is none. And if *Biggers* departed so grievously from the past cases, it is surprising that there was not at least some mention of the point in Mr. Justice Brennan's dissent. In fact, the cases are not so readily sorted as the dissent suggests. Although *Foster* involved both in-court and out-of-court identifications, the Court seemed to apply only a single standard for both. And although *Coleman* involved only an in-court identification, the plurality cited *Stovall* for the guiding rule that the claim was to be assessed on the "totality of the surrounding circumstances." 399 U.S., at 4. Thus, *Biggers* is not properly seen as a departure from the past cases, but as a synthesis of them.

observed that the challenged procedure occurred pre-Stovall and that a strict rule would make little sense with regard to a confrontation that preceded the Court's first indication that a suggestive procedure might lead to the exclusion of evidence. One perhaps might argue that, by implication, the Court suggested that a different rule could apply post-*Stovall*. The question before us, then, is simply whether the *Biggers* analysis applies to post-*Stovall* confrontations as well to those pre-*Stovall*. . . .

IV

Petitioner at the outset acknowledges that "the procedure in the instant case was suggestive [because only one photograph was used] and unnecessary" [because there was no emergency or exigent circumstance]. The respondent, in agreement with the Court of Appeals, proposes a per se rule of exclusion that he claims is dictated by the demands of the Fourteenth Amendment's guarantee of due process. He rightly observes that this is the first case in which this Court has had occasion to rule upon strictly post-*Stovall* out-of-court identification evidence of the challenged kind.

Since the decision in *Biggers*, the Courts of Appeals appear to have developed at least two approaches to such evidence. See Charles A. Pulaski, Jr., Neil v. Biggers: The Supreme Court Dismantles the *Wade* Trilogy's Due Process Protection, 26 Stan. L. Rev. 1097, 1111-1114 (1974). The first, or per se approach, employed by the Second Circuit in the present case, focuses on the procedures employed and requires exclusion of the out-of-court identification evidence, without regard to reliability, whenever it has been obtained through unnecessarily [suggestive] confrontation procedures.[10] The justifications advanced are the elimination of evidence of uncertain reliability, deterrence of the police and prosecutors, and the stated "fair assurance against the awful risks of misidentification."

The second, or more lenient, approach is one that continues to rely on the totality of the circumstances. It permits the admission of the confrontation evidence if, despite the suggestive aspect, the out-of-court identification possesses certain features of reliability. Its adherents feel that the per se approach is not mandated by the Due Process Clause of the Fourteenth Amendment. This second approach, in contrast to the other, is ad hoc and serves to limit the societal costs imposed by a sanction that excludes relevant evidence from consideration and evaluation by the trier of fact.

The respondent here stresses . . . the need for deterrence of improper identification practice, a factor he regards as preeminent. Photographic identification, it is said, continues to be needlessly employed. He notes that the legislative regulation "the Court had hoped [United States v.] Wade would engender" has not been forthcoming. He argues that a totality rule cannot be expected to have a significant deterrent impact; only a strict rule of exclusion will have direct and immediate impact on law enforcement agents. Identification evidence is so convincing to the jury that sweeping exclusionary rules are required. Fairness of the trial is threatened by suggestive confrontation evidence, and thus, it is said, an exclusionary rule has an established constitutional predicate.

There are, of course, several interests to be considered and taken into account. The driving force behind . . . *Wade*, . . . *Gilbert* . . . and *Stovall*, all decided on the same day, was the Court's concern with the problems of eyewitness identification. Usually the

---

10. Although the per se approach demands the exclusion of testimony concerning unnecessarily suggestive identifications, it does permit the admission of testimony concerning a subsequent identification, including an in-court identification, if the subsequent identification is determined to be reliable. 527 F.2d, at 367. The totality approach, in contrast, is simpler: If the challenged identification is reliable, then testimony as to it and any identification in its wake is admissible.

witness must testify about an encounter with a total stranger under circumstances of emergency or emotional stress. The witness' recollection of the stranger can be distorted easily by the circumstances or by later actions of the police. Thus, *Wade* and its companion cases reflect the concern that the jury not hear eyewitness testimony unless that evidence has aspects of reliability. It must be observed that both approaches before us are responsive to this concern. The per se rule, however, goes too far since its application automatically and peremptorily, and without consideration of alleviating factors, keeps evidence from the jury that is reliable and relevant.

The second factor is deterrence. Although the per se approach has the more significant deterrent effect, the totality approach also has an influence on police behavior. The police will guard against unnecessarily suggestive procedures under the totality rule, as well as the per se one, for fear that their actions will lead to the exclusion of identifications as unreliable.

The third factor is the effect on the administration of justice. Here the per se approach suffers serious drawbacks. Since it denies the trier reliable evidence, it may result, on occasion, in the guilty going free. Also, because of its rigidity, the per se approach may make error by the trial judge more likely than the totality approach. And in those cases in which the admission of identification evidence is error under the per se approach but not under the totality approach — cases in which the identification is reliable despite an unnecessarily suggestive identification procedure — reversal is a Draconian sanction. Certainly, inflexible rules of exclusion that may frustrate rather than promote justice have not been viewed recently by this Court with unlimited enthusiasm. . . .

It is true, as has been noted, that the Court in *Biggers* referred to the pre-*Stovall* character of the confrontation in that case. But that observation was only one factor in the judgmental process. It does not translate into a holding that post-*Stovall* confrontation evidence automatically is to be excluded.

The standard, after all, is that of fairness as required by the Due Process Clause of the Fourteenth Amendment. . . . *Stovall,* with its reference to "the totality of the circumstances," and *Biggers,* with its continuing stress on the same totality, did not, singly or together, establish a strict exclusionary rule or new standard of due process. Judge Leventhal, although speaking pre-*Biggers* and of a pre-*Wade* situation, correctly has described *Stovall* as protecting an *evidentiary* interest and, at the same time, as recognizing the limited extent of that interest in our adversary system.[14]

We therefore conclude that reliability is the linchpin in determining the admissibility of identification testimony for both pre- and post-*Stovall* confrontations. The factors to be considered are set out in *Biggers.* These include the opportunity of the witness to view the criminal at the time of the crime, the witness' degree of attention, the accuracy of his prior description of the criminal, the level of certainty demonstrated at the confrontation, and the time between the crime and the confrontation. Against these factors is to be weighed the corrupting effect of the suggestive identification itself.

---

14. "In essence what the *Stovall* due process right protects is an evidentiary interest. . . .

"It is part of our adversary system that we accept at trial much evidence that has strong elements of untrustworthiness — an obvious example being the testimony of witnesses with a bias. While identification testimony is significant evidence, such testimony is still only evidence, and unlike the presence of counsel, is not a factor that goes to the very heart — the 'integrity' — of the adversary process.

"Counsel can both cross-examine the identification witnesses and argue in summation as to factors causing doubts as to the accuracy of the identification — including reference to both any suggestibility in the identification procedure and any countervailing testimony such as alibi." Clemons v. United States, 133 U.S. App. D.C. 27, 48, 408 F.2d 1230, 1251 (1968) (concurring opinion) (footnote omitted), cert. denied, 394 U.S. 964 (1969).

NOTES AND QUESTIONS

1. The commentary on the Supreme Court's identification decisions consistently criticizes the Court for being overly sanguine about the ability of jurors to assess the limitations of eyewitness testimony. One developing strategy to assist the jury in this regard is to employ experts—usually psychologists—to testify to the limits of human perception, memory, etc. as well as to the potential for suggestiveness such encounters possess. The courts have not been very receptive to such evidence, although a few courts have admitted it. For a discussion of the cases, and an argument for admission, see Steven P. Grossman, Suggestive Identifications: The Supreme Court's Due Process Test Fails to Meet Its Own Criteria, 11 U. Balt. L. Rev. 53 (1981). A few cases have held that exclusion of expert testimony on the limits of eyewitness identifications was an abuse of discretion. See, e.g., State v. Chapple, 135 Ariz. 281, 660 P.2d 1208 (1983); People v. McDonald, 37 Cal. 3d 351 (1884). *Chapple* was subsequently limited to its facts. State v. Poland, 144 Ariz. 388, 698 P.2d 183 (1985). These cases did not precipitate an avalanche, and "[a]t this point in time, the admission of expert psychological testimony on eyewitness memory appears to be the exception rather than the rule." Steven Penrod, Solomon M. Fulero, & Brian L. Cutler, Expert Psychological Testimony on Eyewitness Reliability before and after *Daubert*: The State of the Law and the Science 229, 230 (1995). This is for two reasons. First, the science has not produced the clear-cut answers most amenable to judicial use. For a discussion, see Rogers Elliott, Expert Testimony about Eyewitness Identification, 17 L. & Hum. Behav. 423 (1993). Second, the critical question is not human foibles in eyewitness identification but whether expert testimony will positively contribute to accurate verdicts. That is not easy to establish. For a discussion, see Michael McCloskey & Howard E. Egeth, Eyewitness Identification: What Can a Psychologist Tell a Jury?, 38 Am. Psychol. 550 (1983).

2. The national concern over false confessions has generated a lot of psychological work on both the operation of memory and the ability of individuals to make reliable identifications. False identifications often play a role in erroneous convictions. For a discussion, see Jim Dwyer, Peter Neufeld & F. Barry Scheck, Actual Innocence: Five Days to Execution and Other Dispatches from the Wrongly Convicted (2000). For a good discussion of the complexity of memory that can lead to false identifications, see Ralph N. Haber & Lyn Haber, Experiencing, Remembering and Report Events, 6 Psy. Pub. Pol. & L. 1057 (2000). A particular problem is cross-racial identifications, which are systematically more difficult to make than own-race identifications. Christian A. Meissner & John C. Brigham, Eyewitness Identification: Thirty Years of Investigating the Own-Race Bias in Memory for Faces: A Meta-Analytic Review, 7 Psy. Pub. Pol. & L. 3 (2001). Similarly, identifications by children are often influenced by their susceptibility to suggestiveness. M. Bruck & J. Ceci, The Description of Children's Suggestibility, in Nancy L. Stein et al. (eds.), Memory for Everyday and Emotional Events (1997).

3. Another possible response to the problem of identification is to provide for special jury instructions. See State v. Green, 86 N.J. 281, 430 A.2d 914 (1981), reversing for the failure of the trial court to give such instructions. Compare Illinois Pattern Jury Instruction (Criminal) 3.15, which recommends leaving the matter to the argument of counsel. In Joseph D. Grano, *Kirby, Biggers,* and *Ash*: Do Any Constitutional Safeguards Remain against the Danger of Convicting the

Innocent?, 72 Mich. L. Rev. 717, 796-797 (1974), Professor Grano suggests the following:

> Because of the scientifically proven dangers of mistaken identification, the law has established certain rules for the conduct of identification procedures. One of the most significant dangers is that the identification procedure will itself mislead the witness into identifying the wrong person. For example, when the police present only one person to the witness, they magnify the risk of mistake. The witness, though perfectly honest, is likely to be misled into believing that the police must have captured the right person if they are presenting him . . . for identification. A much safer procedure is to conduct a lineup, where the witness is tested by being forced to pick the defendant from a group of men. Because lineups are much more reliable, . . . the police [should not] conduct . . . one-man showups when a lineup can be held. In this case, the police, without justifiable excuse, [did so]. In doing this, they unnecessarily increased the risk of mistaken identification. In evaluating the identification evidence in this case, you should consider this . . . and the unnecessary risk it caused.

4. For a thorough discussion of the relevant science and its application to eyewitness identification procedures, see Gary L. Wells, Mark Small, Steven Penrod, Roy S. Malpass, Solomon M. Fulero, & C. A. E. Brimacombe, Eyewitness Identification Procedures: Recommendations for Lineups and Photospreads, 22 L. & Hum. Behav. 603 (1998). Wells et al. made the following recommendations:

1. The person conducting a lineup should not know who is accused;
2. The person making an identification should be told that perhaps the suspect is not in the lineup;
3. The suspect should look like everyone else in the lineup; and
4. Statements of confidence from those identifying should be obtained.

5. In this area, as in others, state courts of last resort are extending procedural protections to defendants as a matter of state law that exceed the federal constitutional requirements. See, e.g., People v. Adams, 440 N.Y.S.2d 902 (N.Y. 1981) (forbidding the admission of testimony concerning an unnecessarily suggestive identification, but also applying harmless-error analysis); People v. Bustamonte, 634 P.2d 927, 177 Cal. Rptr. 576 (1981) (extending right to counsel to preindictment lineups).

6. Does *Manson* keep out only what normal evidentiary rules would exclude as irrelevant in any event? Conversely, does *Manson* constitutionalize the relevancy rule? Why should unreliable identification evidence be treated differently from any other unreliable, inculpating evidence?

PART THREE

THE RIGHT TO BE LET ALONE — AN EXAMINATION OF THE FOURTH AND FIFTH AMENDMENTS AND RELATED AREAS

Chapter 4

The Rise and Fall of Boyd v. United States

... Boyd v. United States [is] a case that will be remembered as long as civil liberty lives in the United States.

> *Justice Brandeis, dissenting, in*
> *Olmstead v. United States,*
> *277 U.S. 438, at 474 (1928)*

... *Boyd* is dead.

> *Stanton D. Krauss, The Life and Times of*
> *Boyd v. United States (1886-1976),*
> *76 Mich. L. Rev. 184, 212 (1977)*
> *(hereinafter cited as* Krauss)

It is a trivial exercise in two different senses to learn what the law "is." Law is in a constant state of change. Thus, to "know" the law is to know only what was, not what is. Similarly, legal principles are in large measure conclusions or labels applied to a synthesis of competing interests, considerations, and developments that themselves change over time. To understand the principles, one must understand their etiologies and implications, not just their logical relationships. As Oliver Wendell Holmes put it in The Common Law (1881):

> It is something to show that the consistency of a system requires a particular result, but it is not all. The life of the law has not been logic: it has been experience. The felt necessities of the time, the prevalent moral and political theories, intuitions of public policy, avowed or unconscious, even the prejudices which judges share with their fellow-men, have had a good deal more to do than the syllogism in determining the rules by which men should be governed. The law embodies the story of a nation's development through many centuries, and it cannot be dealt with as if it contained only the axioms and corollaries of a book of mathematics. In order to know what it is, we must know what it has been, and what it tends to become. We must alternately consult history and existing theories of legislation. But the most difficult labor will be to understand the combination of the two into new products at every stage. The substance of the law at any given time pretty nearly corresponds, so far as it goes, with what is then understood to be convenient; but its form and machinery, and the degree to which it is able to work out desired results, depend very much upon its past. ...

. . . In [using history to explicate legal principles, however,] there are two errors equally to be avoided both by writer and reader. One is that of supposing, because an idea seems very familiar and natural to us, that it has always been so. Many things which we take for granted have had to be laboriously fought out or thought out in past times. The other mistake is the opposite one of asking too much of history. We start with man full grown. It may be assumed that the earliest barbarian whose practices are to be considered, had a good many of the same feelings and passions as ourselves.

Id. at 1-2.

The necessity of understanding the source of contemporary developments in order to understand, and more importantly to evaluate, the developments themselves is nowhere more evident than in the areas of the Fourth and Fifth amendments. The starting point is the following case.

BOYD v. UNITED STATES

Error to the United States District Court for the Southern District of New York
116 U.S. 616 (1886)

MR. JUSTICE BRADLEY delivered the opinion of the Court.

This was an information filed by the District Attorney of the United States in the District Court for the Southern District of New York, in July, 1884, in a cause of seizure and forfeiture of property, against thirty-five cases of plate glass, seized by the collector as forfeited to the United States, under §12 of the "Act to amend the customs revenue laws, and to repeal moieties," passed June 22, 1874, 18 Stat. 186.

It is declared by that section that any owner, importer, consignee, &c., who shall, with intent to defraud the revenue, make, or attempt to make, any entry of imported merchandise, by means of any fraudulent or false invoice, affidavit, letter or paper, or by means of any false statement, written or verbal, or who shall be guilty of any wilful act or omission by means whereof the United States shall be deprived of the lawful duties, or any portion thereof, accruing upon the merchandise, or any portion thereof, embraced or referred to in such invoice, affidavit, letter, paper, or statement, or affected by such act or omission, shall for each offence be fined in any sum not exceeding $5000 nor less than $50, or be imprisoned for any time not exceeding two years, or both; and, in addition to such fine, such merchandise shall be forfeited.

The charge was that the goods in question were imported into the United States to the port of New York, subject to the payment of duties; and that the owners or agents of said merchandise, or other person unknown, committed the alleged fraud, which was described in the words of the statute. The plaintiffs in error entered a claim for the goods, and pleaded that they did not become forfeited in manner and form as alleged. On the trial of the cause it became important to show the quantity and value of the glass contained in twenty-nine cases previously imported. To do this the district attorney offered in evidence an order made by the District Judge under §5 of the same act of June 22, 1874, directing notice under seal of the court to be given to the claimants, requiring them to produce the invoice of the twenty-nine cases. The claimants, in obedience to the notice, but objecting to its validity and to the constitutionality of the law, produced the invoice; and when it was offered in evidence by the district attorney they objected to its reception on the ground that, in a suit for forfeiture, no evidence can be compelled from the claimants themselves, and also that the statute, so far as it compels production of evidence to be used against the claimants is unconstitutional and void.

The evidence being received, and the trial closed, the jury found a verdict for the United States, condemning the thirty-five cases of glass which were seized, and judgment of forfeiture was given. This judgment was affirmed by the Circuit Court, and the decision of that court is now here for review. . . .

The 5th section of the act of June 22, 1874, under which this order was made, is in the following words, to wit:

> In all suits and proceedings other than criminal arising under any of the revenue laws of the United States, the attorney representing the government, whenever in his belief any business book, invoice, or paper belonging to, or under the control of, the defendant or claimant, will tend to prove any allegation made by the United States, may make a written motion, particularly describing such book, invoice, or paper, and setting forth the allegation which he expects to prove; and thereupon the court in which suit or proceeding is pending may, at its discretion, issue a notice to the defendant or claimant to produce such book, invoice, or paper in court, at a day and hour to be specified in said notice, which, together with a copy of said motion, shall be served formally on the defendant or claimant by the United States marshal by delivering to him a certified copy thereof, or otherwise serving the same as original notices of suit in the same court are served; and if the defendant or claimant shall fail or refuse to produce such book, invoice, or paper in obedience to such notice, the allegations stated in the said motion shall be taken as confessed, unless his failure or refusal to produce the same shall be explained to the satisfaction of the court. And if produced the said attorney shall be permitted, under the direction of the court, to make examination (at which examination the defendant, or claimant, or his agent, may be present) of such entries in said book, invoice, or paper as relate to or tend to prove the allegation aforesaid, and may offer the same in evidence on behalf of the United States. But the owner of said books and papers, his agent or attorney, shall have, subject to the order of the court, the custody of them, except pending their examination in court as aforesaid.

This section was passed in lieu of the 2d section of the act of March 2, 1867, . . . which section of said last-mentioned statute authorized the district judge, on complaint and affidavit that any fraud on the revenue had been committed by any person interested or engaged in the importation of merchandise, to issue his warrant to the marshal to enter any premises where any invoices, books, or papers were deposited relating to such merchandise, and take possession of such books and papers and produce them before said judge, to be subject to his order, and allowed to be examined by the collector, and to be retained as long as the judge should deem necessary.

The section last recited was passed in lieu of the 7th section of the act of March 3, 1863, . . . 12 Stat. 737. The 7th section of this act was in substance the same as the 2d section of the act of 1867, except that the warrant was to be directed to the collector instead of the marshal. It was the first legislation of the kind that ever appeared on the statute book of the United States, and, as seen from its date, was adopted at a period of great national excitement, when the powers of the government were subjected to a severe strain to protect the national existence.

The clauses of the Constitution, to which it is contended that these laws are repugnant, are the Fourth and Fifth Amendments. The Fourth declares, "The right of the people to be secure in their persons, houses, papers, and effects, against unreasonable searches and seizures, shall not be violated, and no warrants shall issue, but upon probable cause, supported by oath or affirmation, and particularly describing the place to be searched, and the persons or things to be seized." The Fifth Article, amongst other things, declares that no person "shall be compelled in any criminal case to be a witness against himself."

But, in regard to the Fourth Amendment, it is contended that, whatever might have been alleged against the constitutionality of the acts of 1863 and 1867, that of 1874, under which the order in the present case was made, is free from constitutional objection, because it does not authorize the search and seizure of books and papers, but only requires the defendant or claimant to produce them. That is so; but it declares that if he does not produce them, the allegations which it is affirmed they will prove shall be taken as confessed. This is tantamount to compelling their production; for the prosecuting attorney will always be sure to state the evidence expected to be derived from them as strongly as the case will admit of. It is true that certain aggravating incidents of actual search and seizure, such as forcible entry into a man's house and searching amongst his papers, are wanting, and to this extent the proceeding under the act of 1874 is a mitigation of that which was authorized by the former acts; but it accomplishes the substantial object of those acts in forcing from a party evidence against himself. It is our opinion, therefore, that a compulsory production of a man's private papers to establish a criminal charge against him, or to forfeit his property, is within the scope of the Fourth Amendment to the Constitution, in all cases in which a search and seizure would be; because it is a material ingredient, and effects the sole object and purpose of search and seizure.

The principal question, however, remains to be considered. Is a search and seizure, or, what is equivalent thereto, a compulsory production of a man's private papers, to be used in evidence against him in a proceeding to forfeit his property for alleged fraud against the revenue laws — is such a proceeding for such a purpose an "*unreasonable* search and seizure" within the meaning of the Fourth Amendment of the Constitution? or, is it a legitimate proceeding? It is contended by the counsel for the government, that it is a legitimate proceeding, sanctioned by long usage, and the authority of judicial decision. No doubt long usage, acquiesced in by the courts, goes a long way to prove that there is some plausible ground or reason for it in the law, or in the historical facts which have imposed a particular construction of the law favorable to such usage. . . . But we do not find any long usage, or any contemporary construction of the Constitution, which would justify any of the acts of Congress now under consideration. As before stated, the act of 1863 was the first act in this country, and, we might say, either in this country or in England, so far as we have been able to ascertain, which authorized the search and seizure of a man's private papers, or the compulsory production of them, for the purpose of using them in evidence against him in a criminal case, or in a proceeding to enforce the forfeiture of his property. Even the act under which the obnoxious writs of assistance were issued did not go as far as this, but only authorized the examination of ships and vessels, and persons found therein, for the purpose of finding goods prohibited to be imported or exported, or on which the duties were not paid, and to enter into and search any suspected vaults, cellars, or warehouses for such goods. The search for and seizure of stolen or forfeited goods, or goods liable to duties and concealed to avoid the payment thereof, are totally different things from a search for and seizure of a man's private books and papers for the purpose of obtaining information therein contained, or of using them as evidence against him. The two things differ *toto coelo*. In the one case, the government is entitled to the possession of the property; in the other it is not. The seizure of stolen goods is authorized by the common law; and the seizure of goods forfeited for a breach of the revenue laws, or concealed to avoid the duties payable on them, has been authorized by English statutes for at least two centuries past; and the like seizures have been authorized by our own revenue acts from the commencement of the government. The first statute passed by Congress to regulate the collection of duties, the act of July 31, 1789, 1 Stat. 29, 43, contains provisions to this effect. As this act was passed by the same Congress which proposed for adoption the original amendments to the Constitution, it is clear that the members of that body did not regard searches and seizures of this kind as "unreasonable," and they are not embraced within the prohibition of the amendment. So, also, the supervision authorized to be exercised by officers of the revenue over the manufacture or custody of excisable articles, and the entries thereof in books required by law to be kept for their inspection, are necessarily excepted out of the category of unreasonable searches and seizures. So, also, the laws which provide for the search and seizure of articles and things which it is unlawful for a person to have in his possession for the purpose of issue or disposition, such as counterfeit coin, lottery tickets, implements of gambling, &c., are not within this category. Many other things of this character might be enumerated. The entry upon premises, made by a sheriff or other officer of the law, for the purpose of seizing goods and chattels by virtue of a judicial writ, such as an attachment, a sequestration, or an execution, is not within the prohibition of the Fourth or Fifth Amendment, or any other clause of the Constitution; nor is the examination of a defendant under oath after an ineffectual execution, for the purpose of discovering secreted property or credits, to be applied to the payment of a judgment against him, obnoxious to those amendments.

But, when examined with care, it is manifest that there is a total unlikeness of these official acts and proceedings to that which is now under consideration. In the case of stolen goods, the owner from whom they were stolen is entitled to their possession; and in the case of excisable or dutiable articles, the government has an interest in them for the payment of the duties thereon, and until such duties are paid has a right to keep them under observation, or to pursue and drag them from concealment; and in the case of goods seized on attachment or execution, the creditor is entitled to their seizure in satisfaction of his debt; and the examination of a defendant under oath to obtain a discovery of concealed property or credits is a proceeding merely civil to effect the ends of justice, and is no more than what the court of chancery would direct on a bill for discovery. Whereas, by the proceeding now under consideration, the court attempts to extort from the party his private books and papers to make him liable for a penalty or to forfeit his property.

In order to ascertain the nature of the proceedings intended by the Fourth Amendment to the Constitution under the terms "unreasonable searches and seizures," it is only necessary to recall the contemporary or then recent history of the controversies on the subject, both in this country and in England. The practice had obtained in the colonies of issuing writs of assistance to the revenue officers, empowering them, in their discretion, to search suspected places for smuggled goods, which James Otis pronounced "the worst instrument of arbitrary power, the most destructive of English liberty, and the fundamental principles of law, that ever was found in an English law book"; since they placed "liberty of every man in the hands of every petty officer."* This was in February, 1761, in Boston, and the famous debate in which it occurred was perhaps the most prominent event which inaugurated the resistance of the colonies to the oppressions of the mother country. "Then and there," said John Adams, "then and there was the first scene of the first act of opposition to the arbitrary claims of Great Britain. Then and there the child Independence was born."

These things, and the events which took place in England immediately follow-ing the argument about writs of assistance in Boston, were fresh in the memories of those who achieved our independence and established our form of gov-ernment. . . . Prominent and principal among these was the practice of issuing general warrants by the Secretary of State, for searching private houses for the discovery and seizure of books and papers that might be used to convict their owner of the charge of libel. . . . The case . . . which will always be celebrated as being the occasion of Lord Camden's memorable discussion of the subject, was that of Entick v. Carrington and Three Other King's Messengers, reported at length in 19 Howell's State Trials, 1029.[1] The action was trespass for entering the plaintiff's dwelling-house in November, 1762, and breaking open his desks, boxes, &c., and searching and examining his papers. The jury rendered a special verdict, and the case was twice solemnly argued at the bar. Lord Camden pro-nounced the judgment of the court in Michaelmas Term, 1765, and the law as expounded by him has been regarded as settled from that time to this, and his great judgment on that occasion is considered as one of the landmarks of English liberty. It was welcomed and applauded by the lovers of liberty in the colonies as well as in the mother country. It is regarded as one of the permanent monuments of the British Constitution, and is quoted as such by the English authorities on that subject down to the present time.

As every American statesman, during our revolutionary and formative period as a nation, was undoubtedly familiar with this monument of English freedom, and considered it as the true and ultimate expression of constitutional law, it may be confidently asserted that its propositions were in the minds of those who framed the Fourth Amendment to the Constitution, and were considered as sufficiently explanatory of what was meant by unreasonable searches and seizures. We think, therefore, it is pertinent to the present subject of discussion to quote somewhat largely from this celebrated judgment.

---

* Note by the Court. — Cooley's Constitutional Limitations, 301-303, (5th ed. 368, 369). A very full and interesting account of this discussion will be found in the works of John Adams, vol. 2, Appendix A, pp. 523-525; vol. 10, pp. 183, 233, 244, 256, &c., and in Quincy's Reports, pp. 469-482: and see Paxton's Case, do. 51-57, which was argued in November of the same year (1761). An elaborate history of the writs of assistance is given in the Appendix to Quincy's Reports, above referred to, written by Horace Gray, Jr., Esq., now a member of this court.

1. For a discussion of *Entick* and its background, see Russell W. Galloway, Jr., The Intruding Eye: A Status Report on the Constitutional Ban against Paper Searches, 25 How. L.J. 367 (1982). — EDS.

After describing the power claimed by the Secretary of State for issuing general search warrants, and the manner in which they were executed, Lord Camden says:

Such is the power, and, therefore, one would naturally expect that the law to warrant it should be clear in proportion as the power is exorbitant. If it is law, it will be found in our books; if it is not to be found there, it is not law.

The great end for which men entered into society was to secure their property. That right is preserved sacred and incommunicable in all instances where it has not been taken away or abridged by some public law for the good of the whole. The cases where this right of property is set aside by positive law are various. Distresses, executions, forfeitures, taxes, &c., are all of this description, wherein every man by common consent gives up that right for the sake of justice and the general good. By the laws of England, every invasion of private property, be it ever so minute, is a trespass. No man can set his foot upon my ground without my license, but he is liable to an action though the damage be nothing; which is proved by every declaration in trespass where the defendant is called upon to answer for bruising the grass and even treading upon the soil. If he admits the fact, he is bound to show, by way of justification, that some positive law has justified or excused him. The justification is submitted to the judges, who are to look into the books, and see if such a justification can be maintained by the text of the statute law, or by the principles of the common law. If no such excuse can be found or produced, the silence of the books is an authority, against the defendant, and the plaintiff must have judgment. According to this reasoning, it is now incumbent upon the defendants to show the law by which this seizure is warranted. If that cannot be done, it is a trespass.

Papers are the owner's goods and chattels; they are his dearest property; and are so far from enduring a seizure, that they will hardly bear an inspection; and though the eye cannot by the laws of England be guilty of a trespass, yet where private papers are removed and carried away the secret nature of those goods will be an aggravation of the trespass, and demand more considerable damages in that respect. Where is the written law that gives any magistrate such a power? I can safely answer, there is none; and, therefore, it is too much for us, without such authority, to pronounce a practice legal which would be subversive of all the comforts of society.

But though it cannot be maintained by any direct law, yet it bears a resemblance, as was urged, to the known case of search and seizure for stolen goods. I answer that the difference is apparent. In the one, I am permitted to seize my own goods, which are placed in the hands of a public officer, till the felon's conviction shall entitle me to restitution. In the other, the party's own property is seized before and without conviction, and he has no power to reclaim his goods, even after his innocence is declared by acquittal. . . .

Then, after showing that these general warrants for search and seizure of papers originated with the Star Chamber, and never had any advocates in Westminster Hall except Chief Justice Scroggs and his associates, Lord Camden proceeds to add:

Lastly, it is urged as an argument of utility, that such a search is a means of detecting offenders by discovering evidence. I wish some cases had been shown, where the law forceth evidence out of the owner's custody by process. There is no process against papers in civil causes. It has been often tried, but never prevailed. Nay, where the adversary has by force or fraud got possession of your own proper evidence, there is no way to get it back but by action. In the criminal law such a proceeding was never heard of; and yet there are some crimes, such, for instance, as murder, rape, robbery, and house-breaking, to say nothing of forgery and perjury, that are more atrocious than libelling. But our law has provided no paper-search in these cases to help forward the conviction. Whether this proceedeth from the gentleness of the law towards criminals, or from a consideration that such a power would be more pernicious to the innocent than useful to the public, I will not say. It is very certain that the law obligeth no man to accuse himself; because the necessary means of compelling self-accusation, falling upon the innocent as well as the guilty, would be both cruel and unjust; and it would seem, that search for evidence is disallowed upon the same principle. Then, too, the innocent would be confounded with the guilty.

After a few further observations, his Lordship concluded thus: "I have now taken notice of everything that has been urged upon the present point; and upon the whole we are all of opinion, that the warrant to seize and carry away the party's papers in the case of a seditious libel, is illegal and void."*

The principles laid down in this opinion affect the very essence of constitutional liberty and security. They reach farther than the concrete form of the case then before the court, with its adventitious circumstances; they apply to all invasions on the part of the government and its employees of the sanctity of a man's home and the privacies of life. It is not the breaking of his doors, and the rummaging of his drawers, that constitutes the essence of the offence; but it is the invasion of his indefeasible right of personal security, personal liberty and private property, where that right has never been forfeited by his conviction of some public offence, — it is the invasion of this sacred right which underlies and constitutes the essence of Lord Camden's judgment. Breaking into a house and opening boxes and drawers are circumstances of aggravation; but any forcible and compulsory extortion of a man's own testimony or of his private papers to be used as evidence to convict him of crime or to forfeit his goods, is within the condemnation of that judgment. In this regard the Fourth and Fifth Amendments run almost into each other.

Can we doubt that when the Fourth and Fifth Amendments to the Constitution of the United States were penned and adopted, the language of Lord Camden was relied on as expressing the true doctrine on the subject of searches and seizures, and as furnishing the true criteria of the reasonable and "unreasonable" character of such seizures? Could the men who proposed those amendments, in the light of Lord Camden's opinion, have put their hands to a law like those of March 3, 1863, and March 2, 1867, before recited? If they could not, would they have approved the 5th section of the act of June 22, 1874, which was adopted as a substitute for the previous laws? It seems to us that the question cannot admit of a doubt. They never would have approved of them. The struggles against arbitrary power in which they had been engaged for more than twenty years, would have been too deeply engraved in their memories to have allowed them to approve of such insidious disguises of the old grievance which they had so deeply abhorred. . . .

Reverting then to the peculiar phraseology of this act, and to the information in the present case, which is founded on it, we have to deal with an act which expressly excludes criminal proceedings from its operation (though embracing civil suits for penalties and forfeitures), and with an information not technically a

---

* Note by the Court. — See further as to searches and seizures, Story on the Constitution, §§1901, 1902, and notes; Cooley's Constitutional Limitations, 299, (5th ed. 365); Sedgwick on Stat. and Const. Law, 2d ed. 498; Wharton Com. on Amer. Law, §560; Robinson v. Richardson, 13 Gray, 454.

criminal proceeding, and neither, therefore, within the literal terms of the Fifth Amendment to the Constitution any more than it is within the literal terms of the Fourth. Does this relieve the proceedings or the law from being obnoxious to the prohibitions of either? We think not; we think they are within the spirit of both.

We have already noticed the intimate relation between the two amendments. They throw great light on each other. For the "unreasonable searches and seizures" condemned in the Fourth Amendment are almost always made for the purpose of compelling a man to give evidence against himself, which in criminal cases is condemned in the Fifth Amendment; and compelling a man "in a criminal case to be a witness against himself," which is condemned in the Fifth Amendment, throws light on the question as to what is an "unreasonable search and seizure" within the meaning of the Fourth Amendment. And we have been unable to perceive that the seizure of a man's private books and papers to be used in evidence against him is substantially different from compelling him to be a witness against himself. We think it is within the clear intent and meaning of those terms. We are also clearly of opinion that proceedings instituted for the purpose of declaring the forfeiture of a man's property by reason of offences committed by him, though they may be civil in form, are in their nature criminal. In this very case, the ground of forfeiture as declared in the 12th section of the act of 1874, on which the information is based, consists of certain acts of fraud committed against the public revenue in relation to imported merchandise, which are made criminal by the statute; and it is declared, that the offender shall be fined not exceeding $5000 nor less than $50, or be imprisoned not exceeding two years, or both; and in addition to such fine such merchandise shall be forfeited. These are the penalties affixed to the criminal acts; the forfeiture sought by this suit being one of them. If an indictment had been presented against the claimants, upon conviction the forfeiture of the goods could have been included in the judgment. If the government prosecutor elects to waive an indictment, and to file a civil information against the claimants — that is, civil in form — can he by this device take from the proceeding its criminal aspect and deprive the claimants of their immunities as citizens, and extort from them a production of their private papers, or, as an alternative, a confession of guilt? This cannot be. The information, though technically a civil proceeding, is in substance and effect a criminal one. . . . As, therefore, suits for penalties and forfeitures incurred by the commission of offences against the law, are of this quasi-criminal nature, we think that they are within the reason of criminal proceedings for all the purposes of the Fourth Amendment of the Constitution, and of that portion of the Fifth Amendment which declares that no person shall be compelled in any criminal case to be a witness against himself; and we are further of opinion that a compulsory production of the private books and papers of the owner of goods sought to be forfeited in such a suit is compelling him to be a witness against himself, within the meaning of the Fifth Amendment to the Constitution, and is the equivalent of a search and seizure — and an unreasonable search and seizure — within the meaning of the Fourth Amendment. Though the proceeding in question is divested of many of the aggravating incidents of actual search and seizure, yet, as before said, it contains their substance and essence, and effects their substantial purpose. It may be that it is the obnoxious thing in its mildest and least repulsive form; but illegitimate and unconstitutional practices get their first footing in that way, namely, by silent approaches and slight deviations from legal modes of procedure. This can only be obviated by adhering to the rule that constitutional provisions for the security of person and property should be liberally construed. A close and literal construction deprives them of half their efficacy, and leads to gradual depreciation of the right, as if it consisted more in sound than in substance. It is the duty of courts to be watchful for the constitutional rights of the citizen, and against any stealthy encroachments thereon. Their motto should be *obsta principiis*. We have no doubt that the legislative body is actuated by the same motives; but the vast accumulation of public business brought before it sometimes prevents it on a first presentation, from noticing objections which become developed by time and the practical application of the objectionable law. . . .

We think that the notice to produce the invoice in this case, the order by virtue of which it was issued, and the law which authorized the order, were unconstitutional and void, and that the inspection by the district attorney of said invoice, when produced in obedience to said notice, and its admission in evidence by the court, were erroneous and unconstitutional proceedings. We are of opinion, therefore, that

The judgment of the Circuit Court should be reversed, and the cause remanded, with directions to award a new trial.

MR. JUSTICE MILLER, with whom was THE CHIEF JUSTICE, concurring.

I concur in the judgment of the court, reversing that of the Circuit Court, and in so much of the opinion of this court as holds the 5th section of the act of 1874 void as applicable to the present case.

I am of opinion that this is a criminal case within the meaning of that clause of the Fifth Amendment to the Constitution of the United States which declares that no person "shall be compelled in any criminal case to be a witness against himself."

And I am quite satisfied that the effect of the act of Congress is to compel the party on whom the order of the court is served to be a witness against himself. The order of the court under the statute is in effect a subpoena duces tecum, and, though the penalty for the witness's failure to appear in court with the criminating papers is not fine and imprisonment, it is one which may be made more severe, namely, to have charges against him of a criminal nature, taken for confessed, and made the foundation of the judgment of the court. That this is within the protection which the Constitution intended against compelling a person to be a witness against himself, is, I think, quite clear.

But this being so, there is no reason why this court should assume that the action of the court below, in requiring a party to produce certain papers as evidence on the trial, authorizes an unreasonable search or seizure of the house, papers, or effects of that party.

There is in fact no search and no seizure authorized by the statute. No order can be made by the court under it which requires or permits anything more than service of notice on a party to the suit. . . .

Nothing in the nature of a search is here hinted at. Nor is there any seizure, because the party is not required at any time to part with the custody of the papers. They are to be produced in court, and, when produced, the United States attorney is permitted, under the direction of the court, to make examination in presence of the claimant, and may offer in evidence such entries in the books, invoices, or papers as relate to the issue. The act is careful to say that "the owner of said books and papers, his agent or attorney, shall have, subject to the order of the court, the custody of them, except pending their examination in court as aforesaid." . . .

The things . . . forbidden [by the Fourth Amendment] are two — search and seizure. And not all searches nor all seizures are forbidden, but only those that are unreasonable. Reasonable searches, therefore, may be allowed, and if the thing sought be found, it may be seized.

But what search does this statute authorize? If the mere service of a notice to produce a paper to be used as evidence, which the party can obey or not as he chooses is a search, then a change has taken place in the meaning of words, which has not come within my reading, and which I think was unknown at the time the Constitution was made. The searches meant by the Constitution were such as led to seizure when the search was successful. But the statute in this case uses language carefully framed to forbid any seizure under it, as I have already pointed out.

While the framers of the Constitution had their attention drawn, no doubt, to the abuses of this power of searching private houses and seizing private papers, as practiced in England, it is obvious that they only intended to restrain the abuse, while they did not abolish the power. Hence it is only *unreasonable* searches and seizures that are forbidden, and the means of securing this protection was by abolishing searches under warrants, which were called general warrants, because they authorized searches in any place, for any thing.

This was forbidden, while searches founded on affidavits, and made under warrants which described the thing to be searched for, the person and place to be searched, are still permitted.

I cannot conceive how a statute aptly framed to require the production of evidence in a suit by mere service of notice on the party, who has that evidence in his possession, can be held to authorize an unreasonable search or seizure, when no seizure is authorized or permitted by the statute.

I am requested to say that THE CHIEF JUSTICE concurs in this opinion.

NOTES AND QUESTIONS

1. Does the decision in *Boyd* rest on concerns of privacy, desire to protect a person's papers, or an expansive view of the incriminating pressures that are inappropriate for a government to bring to bear on an individual? To what extent do these concerns interrelate? Does it matter which concern *Boyd* primarily is based on? Can you tell from the opinions in *Boyd* how these questions might be answered?

Thirty-five years after *Boyd*, the Court in Gouled v. United States, 255 U.S. 298 (1921), returned to these issues. *Gouled* applied *Boyd* to a search and seizure pursuant to a warrant that produced documents of the defendant, later used at trial over objection. In finding the Fourth Amendment violated by the search and seizure, and the use of the evidence at trial in violation of the Fifth, the Court said:

> Although search warrants have thus been used in many cases ever since the adoption of the Constitution, and although their use has been extended from time to time to meet new cases within the old rules, nevertheless it is clear that, at common law and as the result of . . . *Boyd* . . . they may not be used as a means of gaining access to a man's house or office and papers solely for the purpose of making search to secure evidence to be

used against him in a criminal or penal proceeding, but that they may be resorted to only when a primary right to such search and seizure may be found in the interest which the public or the complainant may have in the property to be seized, or in the right to the possession of it, or when a valid exercise of the police power renders possession of the property by the accused unlawful and provides that it may be taken. *Boyd Case*, pp. 623, 624.

There is no special sanctity in papers, as distinguished from other forms of property, to render them immune from search and seizure, if only they fall within the scope of the principles of the cases in which other property may be seized, and if they be adequately described in the affidavit and warrant. . . .

Is the Court's last sentence about the lack of "special sanctity in papers" significant? Consider the following passage:

This passing remark, which was not without support in *Boyd*, reflected the common-sense judgment that, if the government's appropriation of an individual's documents as mere evidence is wrongful because it makes him "the unwilling source" of incrimination evidence, the same must be true of the seizure of any of his other possessions. Its effect, however, was to transform the paper-search rule of *Boyd* into a broader rule under which the search for or seizure of any item as "mere evidence" was proscribed. In this roundabout way, the fourth amendment in fact became the protector of privacy.

Krauss, page 277 supra, at 190.

2. What is the significance of property for the "intimate relationship" of the Fourth and Fifth amendments that is so important to *Boyd*? Consider the following passage:

Justice Bradley offered no positive definition of "the indefeasible right of personal security, personal liberty and private property" that he considered to be at the core of the intimate relation between the two amendments. It is clear, however, that confidentiality was not the interest that the Court sought to protect. Whether the Boyds had kept the invoice a secret to the world or whether they had made its contents a matter of public knowledge was irrelevant; either way, the government's action was illegal. But, perhaps because the opinion was couched in such sweeping language, the positive nature of the fundamental right was unclear.

Later courts[20] interpreted *Boyd* as identifying the privilege against self-incrimination as the concept at the heart of the intimate relation. Viewing an individual's papers as an extension of his "self," adherents of this view treated the unreasonable search clause of the fourth amendment as an extension of the fifth amendment. On this theory, the amendments, taken together, define the ultimate scope of each person's right not to be compelled to serve as the source of evidence against himself.

But this guarantee that a person's papers are free from official inspection was absolute only in theory. The *Boyd* majority had to reconcile its doctrine with traditional practices. Historically, the government had been allowed to require recordkeeping

---

20. See, e.g., Olmstead v. United States, 277 U.S. 438 (1928), . . . Brown v. Walker, 161 U.S. 591 (1896).

In holding that an individual who has been granted immunity may be compelled to testify against himself, the majority in *Brown* must have concluded that *Boyd* had been solely concerned with protecting the individual from compelled self-incrimination. The four dissenting justices, on the other hand, cited *Boyd* in support of the proposition that, because the Constitution grants the individual an *absolute* right to remain silent, testimony compelled under a grant of immunity is subject to constitutional attack.

with regard to certain goods, such as those subject to duties, in which it had some property interest, and those records had always been deemed seizable. The Court in *Boyd* incorporated this tradition into its constitutional theory by proclaiming the seizure of documents to be inherently unconstitutional only when they were taken as mere evidence and by granting that, on the basis of its property interest in such goods, the government had a superior right to the corresponding records. Because any such record did not truly belong to the accused, it could not be viewed as an extension of his "self"; thus, its use against him did not constitute a compelled self-incrimination. This accommodation to tradition did not seem to compromise the general paper-search rule significantly. The rule attached to all documents in an individual's possession to which he had a superior claim of right. Consequently, although it was not viewed as having been designed to protect property rights per se, the scope of the privilege embodied in the unreasonable search clause came to be defined in terms of the law of property. In that respect, the doctrine contained the seeds of its own destruction.

Krauss, page 277 supra, at 188-189.

3. The initial stage of the assault on *Boyd* is accurately summarized by Krauss, supra, at 191-195:

Over the years, the Court grew increasingly dissatisfied with interpreting the unreasonable search clause in terms of property interests. This dissatisfaction had several possible sources. Traditional views of the sanctity of property were quickly giving way to the demand for increasing governmental control over its ownership, use, and disposition. The view that a fundamental right to privacy exists, espoused in the famous article by Brandeis and Warren,[35] was gaining acceptance. This concept was defined in terms of a basic right "to be left alone,"[36] rather than in terms of the technicalities of English property law. Finally, perhaps the Court simply was not content with the results that would have been entailed by strict adherence to the mere evidence rule as it had been propounded in *Boyd* and expanded by *Gouled*.

Where strict adherence would not interfere with governmental regulation of economic activity, the rule was duly applied. . . .

Where the mere evidence rule interfered with governmental regulation of economic activity, however, it was modified or "refined." In a group of cases involving subpoenas directed to business organizations, the Court refused to include such associations within the class of entities protected by the fifth amendment privilege. In Hale v. Henkel,[38] the Court held that the privilege does not apply to corporations. Thus, an agent cannot refuse to answer questions or to comply with a subpoena duces tecum[39] on the ground that the corporation might be incriminated. Moreover, because the documents are in the custody of and are being subpoenaed from the corporate entity rather than from the agent, the agent cannot refuse to comply on the ground that compliance might incriminate him.[40] . . . Of the decisions that considered *Boyd* during this period

35. Warren & Brandeis, The Right to Privacy, 4 Harv. L. Rev. 193 (1890).
36. Olmstead v. United States, 277 U.S. 438, 478 (1928) (Brandeis, J., dissenting).
38. 201 U.S. 43 (1906).
39. The order involved in the *Boyd* case differed from a subpoena duces tecum only in the penalty imposed for noncompliance. *Hale* held that the paper-search rule enunciated in *Boyd* applied as well to subpoenas duces tecum.
40. In Wilson v. United States, 221 U.S. 361 (1911), the writ was directed to the corporation. In Dreier v. United States, 221 U.S. 394 (1911), it was directed to the agent. In both cases the Court held that the self-incrimination clause did not allow the agent to refuse to comply with the subpoena. It was later held, however, that the custodian of an organization's "missing" documents can refuse to answer questions about their whereabouts when to do so would incriminate him. Curcio v. United States, 354 U.S. 118, 125 (1957).

of retreat, perhaps Shapiro v. United States[43] had the greatest impact on the individual's ability to shield the details of his life from the government. In that case the Court enunciated the "required records" doctrine, under which no person can invoke the fourth or fifth amendment to justify refusal to comply with a facially valid subpoena compelling the production of records that the person is legally required to keep. This decision represented a complete rejection of the fundamental limitations that the Court in *Boyd* had placed on the government's power to compel the production of records kept pursuant to its command. The Court in effect recognized the power of the legislature to acquire any and all information it wants from an individual.[44]

The Court also narrowed the scope of the protection provided by the mere evidence rule in Marron v. United States.[45] In that case the Court distinguished between property that is merely evidence of a crime and property used in the commission of a crime.[46] Whereas *Gouled* had allowed the seizure of an instrumentality of a crime only insofar as it was contraband, *Marron* allowed the seizure of *any* such instrumentality. Because even papers can be characterized as instrumentalities of crime,[47] *Marron* represented a serious threat to the zone of protection established by *Boyd* and broadened by *Gouled*.[48]

To the extent that the decisions following *Boyd* and *Gouled* reduced the obstacles to governmental seizure of an individual's property, they also narrowed his effective zone of privacy. A conflict arose within the Court over this development. Although the dispute concerned the fundamental nature of the rights protected by the fourth and fifth amendments, it took the form of a debate over the "real" meaning of *Boyd*. On the one hand, proponents of the traditional interpretation of *Boyd* believed that the core of the "intimate relation" between the amendments was the privilege against self-incrimination. Since the key question to these Justices was whether the evidence belonged to the defendant, they found the government's increasing power to intrude into the life of the individual to be constitutionally permissible so long as the exercise of that power was consistent with the rules of property law. On the other hand, advocates of a revisionist interpretation of *Boyd* argued that the true concern of the framers of the fourth and fifth amendments was the protection of a fundamental right of privacy. . . .

This revisionist interpretation of the "intimate relation" first appeared as a fully articulated doctrine in Justice Brandeis' dissent in Olmstead v. United States.[52] That case concerned the applicability of the fourth amendment to warrantless wiretapping by government agents. The majority, which was as eager to facilitate the government's efforts to combat crime as it had been a year earlier in *Marron*, analyzed the issue in terms of the privilege against self-incrimination,[53] whose parameters were

43. 335 U.S. 1 (1948).

44. Congress eventually exercised this authority to require the keeping of records to aid its fight against crime, as well as its regulation of economic activity. On the basis of this "required records" doctrine, the Court has sanctioned congressional enactments that have intruded substantially upon personal privacy. See United States v. Miller, 425 U.S. 435, 447 (1976) (Brennan, J., dissenting); California Bankers Assn. v. Shultz, 416 U.S. 21, 93 (1974) (Marshall, J., dissenting). But see Grosso v. United States, 390 U.S. 62 (1968); Marchetti v. United States, 390 U.S. 39 (1968).

45. 275 U.S. 192 (1927).

46. The Court in *Marron* did not attempt to explain its holding in terms of a superior title theory. A possible rationale for the decision is that, by using an object to commit a crime, the criminal has forfeited it to the state.

47. In *Marron*, the Court treated records maintained in an establishment where liquor was sold as instrumentalities. *Gouled* had also recognized that papers might be used as instrumentalities of crime. See 255 U.S. at 309.

48. For a discussion of the ingenuity of prosecutors in characterizing different types of property as instrumentalities, see Comment, The Search and Seizure of Private Papers: Fourth and Fifth Amendment Considerations, 6 Loy. L.A. L. Rev. 274, 282-283 (1973).

52. 277 U.S. 438 (1928).

53. See 277 U.S. at 462-463.

determined by property law. Finding that speech is not property within the context of the fourth amendment, they concluded that wiretapping infringed upon an interest protected by the fourth amendment, and thereby the fifth, only if it involved trespassing upon the accused's tangible property. Justice Brandeis' dissent, however, argued that the majority opinion was based on the false premise that the fourth amendment had been designed either to perpetuate antiquated notions of English property law or to bolster the privilege against self-incrimination.[54] In Justice Brandeis' view, at the heart of *Entick*, *Boyd*, and *Gouled* was the premise that the amendment had been designed to protect a fundamental "right to be left alone".[55] "Every unjustifiable intrusion by the Government upon the private life of the individual, whatever the means employed, must be deemed a violation of the Fourth Amendment. And the use, as evidence in a criminal proceeding, of facts ascertained by such intrusion must be deemed a violation of the Fifth."[56] Although Justice Brandeis had lost the battle in *Olmstead*, by the second half of the twentieth century he had won the war. The theory that his dissenting opinion espoused eventually became the official position of the Court.[57] Moreover, during this period it became clear that the mere evidence rule had outlived its usefulness. The criteria for determining whether an object was immune from seizure had become so structured that the rule no longer served as a bulwark for the privilege against self-incrimination. Furthermore, the rule was at odds with public opinion, as it frustrated the popular demand for law and order that was increasing along with the crime rate. Although Justice Brandeis had identified the right of privacy as the basic interest to be protected, he had indicated neither the manner in which this protection would be ensured nor the extent to which the law derived from *Boyd* would have to be repudiated. The Court undertook this task in three cases decided three decades after *Olmstead*: Schmerber v. California,[58] Warden v. Hayden,[59] and Berger v. New York.[60] . . .

SCHMERBER v. CALIFORNIA

Certiorari to the Appellate Department of the Superior Court of California,
County of Los Angeles
384 U.S. 757 (1966)

MR. JUSTICE BRENNAN delivered the opinion of the Court.

Petitioner was convicted in Los Angeles Municipal Court of the criminal offense of driving an automobile while under the influence of intoxicating liquor. He had been arrested at a hospital while receiving treatment for injuries suffered in an accident involving the automobile that he had apparently been driving. At the direction of a police officer, a blood sample was then withdrawn from petitioner's body by a physician at the hospital. The chemical analysis of this sample revealed a

54. Justice Brandeis advocated a privacy rationale for the Fifth Amendment, also. See text at Note 56 infra.

55. 277 U.S. at 478.

56. 277 U.S. at 478-479.

57. Regarding the Fourth Amendment, see, e.g., Wolf v. Colorado, 338 U.S. 25, 27 (1949) ("The security of one's privacy against arbitrary intrusion by the police . . . is at the core of the Fourth Amendment."). Regarding the Fifth Amendment, see, e.g., Griswold v. Connecticut, 381 U.S. 479, 484 (1965) ("The Fifth Amendment in its Self-Incrimination Clause enables the citizen to create a zone of privacy which government may not force him to surrender to his detriment.").

58. 384 U.S. 757 (1966).

59. 387 U.S. 294 (1967). [Other aspects of *Warden* are discussed in Chapter 5 infra—EDS.]

60. 388 U.S. 41 (1967). [Other aspects of *Berger* are considered in Chapter 7 infra—EDS.]

percent by weight of alcohol in his blood at the time of the offense which indicated intoxication, and the report of this analysis was admitted in evidence at the trial. Petitioner objected to receipt of this evidence of the analysis on the ground that the blood had been drawn despite his refusal, on the advice of his counsel, to consent to the test. He contended that in that circumstance the withdrawal of the blood and the admission of the analysis in evidence denied him due process of law under the Fourteenth Amendment, as well as specific guarantees of the Bill of Rights secured against the States by that Amendment: his privilege against self-incrimination under the Fifth Amendment; his right to counsel under the Sixth Amendment; and his right not to be subjected to unreasonable searches and seizures in violation of the Fourth Amendment. The Appellate Department of the California Superior Court rejected these contentions and affirmed the conviction. . . .

II.   THE PRIVILEGE AGAINST SELF-INCRIMINATION CLAIM

. . . We . . . must now decide whether the withdrawal of the blood and admission in evidence of the analysis involved in this case violated petitioner's privilege. We hold that the privilege protects an accused only from being compelled to testify against himself, or otherwise provide the State with evidence of a testimonial or communicative nature,[5] and that the withdrawal of blood and use of the analysis in question in this case did not involve compulsion to these ends.

It could not be denied that in requiring petitioner to submit to the withdrawal and chemical analysis of his blood the State compelled him to submit to an attempt to discover evidence that might be used to prosecute him for a criminal offense. He submitted only after the police officer rejected his objection and directed the physician to proceed. The officer's direction to the physician to administer the test over petitioner's objection constituted compulsion for the purposes of the privilege. The critical question, then, is whether petitioner was thus compelled "to be a witness against himself."[6]

If the scope of the privilege coincided with the complex of values it helps to protect, we might be obliged to conclude that the privilege was violated. In

---

5. A dissent suggests that the report of the blood test was "testimonial" or "communicative," because the test was performed in order to obtain the testimony of others, communicating to the jury facts about petitioner's condition. Of course, all evidence received in court is "testimonial" or "communicative" if these words are thus used. But the Fifth Amendment relates only to acts on the part of the person to whom the privilege applies, and we use these words subject to the same limitations. A nod or head-shake is as much a "testimonial" or "communicative" act in this sense as are spoken words. But the terms as we use them do not apply to evidence of acts noncommunicative in nature as to the person asserting the privilege, even though, as here, such acts are compelled to obtain the testimony of others.

6. Many state constitutions, including those of most of the original Colonies, phrase the privilege in terms of compelling a person to give "evidence" against himself. But our decision cannot turn on the Fifth Amendment's use of the word "witness." "[A]s the manifest purpose of the constitutional provisions, both of the States and of the United States, is to prohibit the compelling of testimony of a self-incriminating kind from a party or a witness, the liberal construction which must be placed upon constitutional provisions for the protection of personal rights would seem to require that the constitutional guaranties, however differently worded, should have as far as possible the same interpretation. . . ." Counselman v. Hitchcock, 142 U.S. 547, 584-585. 8 Wigmore, Evidence §2252 (McNaughton rev. 1961).

Miranda v. Arizona, [discussed in Chapter 6 infra] the Court said of the interests protected by the privilege:

> All these policies point to one overriding thought: the constitutional foundation underlying the privilege is the respect a government — state or federal — must accord to the dignity and integrity of its citizens. To maintain a "fair state-individual balance," to require the government "to shoulder the entire load," . . . to respect the inviolabilty of the human personality, our accusatory system of criminal justice demands that the government seeking to punish an individual produce the evidence against him by its own independent labors, rather than by the cruel, simple expedient of compelling it from his own mouth.

The withdrawal of blood necessarily involves puncturing the skin for extraction, and the percent by weight of alcohol in that blood, as established by chemical analysis, is evidence of criminal guilt. Compelled submission fails on one view to respect the "inviolability of the human personality." Moreover, since it enables the State to rely on evidence forced from the accused, the compulsion violates at least one meaning of the requirement that the State procure the evidence against an accused "by its own independent labors."

As the passage in *Miranda* implicitly recognizes, however, the privilege has never been given the full scope which the values it helps to protect suggest. History and a long line of authorities in lower courts have consistently limited its protection to situations in which the State seeks to submerge those values by obtaining the evidence against an accused through "the cruel, simple expedient of compelling it from his own mouth. . . . In sum, the privilege is fulfilled only when the person is guaranteed the right 'to remain silent unless he chooses to speak in the unfettered exercise of his own will.'" Ibid. The leading case in this Court is Holt v. United States, 218 U.S. 245. There the question was whether evidence was admissible that the accused, prior to trial and over his protest, put on a blouse that fitted him. It was contended that compelling the accused to submit to the demand that he model the blouse violated the privilege. Mr. Justice Holmes, speaking for the Court, rejected the argument as "based upon an extravagant extension of the Fifth Amendment," and went on to say:

> [T]he prohibition of compelling a man in a criminal court to be witness against himself is a prohibition of the use of physical or moral compulsion to extort communications from him, not an exclusion of his body as evidence when it may be material. The objection in principle would forbid a jury to look at a prisoner and compare his features with a photograph in proof.

It is clear that the protection of the privilege reaches an accused's communications, whatever form they might take, and the compulsion of responses which are also communications, for example, compliance with a subpoena to produce one's papers. Boyd v. United States, 116 U.S. 616. On the other hand, both federal and state courts have usually held that it offers no protection against compulsion to submit to fingerprinting, photographing, or measurements, to write or speak for identification, to appear in court, to stand, to assume a stance, to walk, or to make a particular gesture. The distinction which has emerged, often expressed in different ways, is that the privilege is a bar against compelling "communications" or "testimony," but that compulsion which makes a suspect or accused the source of "real or physical evidence" does not violate it.

Although we agree that this distinction is a helpful framework for analysis, we are not to be understood to agree with past applications in all instances. There will be many cases in which such a distinction is not readily drawn. Some tests seemingly directed to obtain "physical evidence," for example, lie detector tests measuring changes in body function during interrogation, may actually be directed to eliciting responses which are essentially testimonial. To compel a person to submit to testing in which an effort will be made to determine his guilt or innocence on the basis of physiological responses, whether willed or not, is to evoke the spirit and history of the Fifth Amendment. Such situations call to mind the principle that the protection of the privilege "is as broad as the mischief against which it seeks to guard."

In the present case, however, no such problem of application is presented. Not even a shadow of testimonial compulsion upon or enforced communication by the accused was involved either in the extraction or in the chemical analysis. Petitioner's testimonial capacities were in no way implicated; indeed, his participation, except as a donor, was irrelevant to the results of the test, which depend on chemical analysis and on that alone.[9] Since the blood test evidence, although an incriminating product of compulsion, was neither petitioner's testimony nor evidence relating to some communicative act or writing by the petitioner, it was not inadmissible on privilege grounds.

III. The Right to Counsel Claim

This conclusion also answers petitioner's claim that, in compelling him to submit to the test in face of the fact that his objection was made on the advice of counsel, he was denied his Sixth Amendment right to the assistance of counsel. Since petitioner was not entitled to assert the privilege, he has no greater right because counsel erroneously advised him that he could assert it. His claim is strictly limited to the failure of the police to respect his wish, reinforced by counsel's advice, to be left inviolate. No issue of counsel's ability to assist petitioner in respect of any rights he did possess is presented. The limited claim thus made must be rejected.

IV. The Search and Seizure Claim . . .

The overriding function of the Fourth Amendment is to protect personal privacy and dignity against unwarranted intrusion by the State. . . .

The values protected by the Fourth Amendment thus substantially overlap those the Fifth Amendment helps to protect. History and precedent have required that we today reject the claim that the Self-Incrimination Clause of the Fifth Amendment requires the human body in all circumstances to be held inviolate against state

---

9. This conclusion would not necessarily govern had the State tried to show that the accused had incriminated himself when told that he would have to be tested. Such incriminating evidence may be an unavoidable by-product of the compulsion to take the test, especially for an individual who fears the extraction or opposes it on religious grounds. If it wishes to compel persons to submit to such attempts to discover evidence, the State may have to forgo the advantage of any *testimonial* products of administering the test — products which would fall within the privilege. Indeed, there may be circumstances in which the pain, danger, or severity of an operation would almost inevitably cause a person to prefer confession to undergoing the "search," and nothing we say today should be taken as establishing the permissibility of compulsion in that case. But no such situation is presented in this case. . . .

expeditions seeking evidence of crime. But if compulsory administration of a blood test does not implicate the Fifth Amendment, it plainly involves the broadly conceived reach of a search and seizure under the Fourth Amendment. That Amendment expressly provides that "[t]he right of the people to be secure in their *persons*, houses, papers, and effects, against unreasonable searches and seizures, shall not be violated. . . ." (Emphasis added.) It could not reasonably be argued, and indeed respondent does not argue, that the administration of the blood test in this case was free of the constraints of the Fourth Amendment. Such testing procedures plainly constitute searches of "persons," within the meaning of that Amendment.

Because we are dealing with intrusions into the human body rather than with state interferences with property relationships or private papers — "houses, papers, and effects" — we write on a clean slate. Limitations on the kinds of property which may be seized under warrant,[10] as distinct from the procedures for search and the permissible scope of search,[11] are not instructive in this context. We begin with the assumption that once the privilege against self-incrimination has been found not to bar compelled intrusions into the body for blood to be analyzed for alcohol content, the Fourth Amendment's proper function is to constrain, not against all intrusions as such, but against intrusions which are not justified in the circumstances, or which are made in an improper manner. In other words, the questions we must decide in this case are whether the police were justified in requiring petitioner to submit to the blood test, and whether the means and procedures employed in taking his blood respected relevant Fourth Amendment standards of reasonableness.

In this case, as will often be true when charges of driving under the influence of alcohol are pressed, these questions arise in the context of an arrest made by an officer without a warrant. Here, there was plainly probable cause for the officer to arrest petitioner and charge him with driving an automobile while under the influence of intoxicating liquor. The police officer who arrived at the scene shortly after the accident smelled liquor on petitioner's breath, and testified that petitioner's eyes were "bloodshot, watery, sort of a glassy appearance." The officer saw petitioner again at the hospital, within two hours of the accident. There he noticed similar symptoms of drunkenness. He thereupon informed petitioner "that he was under arrest and that he was entitled to the services of an attorney, and that he could remain silent, and that anything that he told me would be used against him in evidence." . . .

Although the facts which established probable cause to arrest in this case also suggested the required relevance and likely success of a test of petitioner's blood for alcohol, the question remains whether the arresting officer was permitted to draw these inferences himself, or was required instead to procure a warrant before proceeding with the test. Search warrants are ordinarily required for searches of dwellings, and, absent an emergency, no less could be required where intrusions

10. See, e.g., Gouled v. United States, 255 U.S. 298; Boyd v. United States, 116 U.S. 616; contra, People v. Thayer, 63 Cal. 2d 635, 408 P.2d 108 (1965); State v. Bisaccia, 45 N.J. 504, 213 A.2d 185 (1965); Note, Evidentiary Searches: The Rule and the Reason, 54 Geo. L.J. 593 (1966).

11. See, e.g., Silverman v. United States, 365 U.S. 505; Abel v. United States, 362 U.S. 217, 235; United States v. Rabinowitz, 339 U.S. 56.

into the human body are concerned. . . . The importance of informed, detached and deliberate determinations of the issue whether or not to invade another's body in search of evidence of guilt is indisputable and great.

The officer in the present case, however, might reasonably have believed that he was confronted with an emergency, in which the delay necessary to obtain a warrant, under the circumstances, threatened "the destruction of evidence," Preston v. United States, 376 U.S. 364, 367. We are told that the percentage of alcohol in the blood begins to diminish shortly after drinking stops, as the body functions to eliminate it from the system. Particularly in a case such as this, where time had to be taken to bring the accused to a hospital and to investigate the scene of the accident, there was no time to seek out a magistrate and secure a warrant. Given these special facts, we conclude that the attempt to secure evidence of blood-alcohol content in this case was an appropriate incident to petitioner's arrest.

Similarly, we are satisfied that the test chosen to measure petitioner's blood-alcohol level was a reasonable one. Extraction of blood samples for testing is a highly effective means of determining the degree to which a person is under the influence of alcohol. . . .

Finally, the record shows that the test was performed in a reasonable manner. Petitioner's blood was taken by a physician in a hospital environment according to accepted medical practices. We are thus not presented with the serious questions which would arise if a search involving use of a medical technique, even of the most rudimentary sort, were made by other than medical personnel or in other than a medical environment—for example, if it were administered by police in the privacy of the stationhouse. To tolerate searches under these conditions might be to invite an unjustified element of personal risk of infection and pain.

We thus conclude that the present record shows no violation of petitioner's right under the Fourth and Fourteenth Amendments to be free of unreasonable searches and seizures. It bears repeating, however, that we reach this judgment only on the facts of the present record. The integrity of an individual's person is a cherished value of our society. That we today hold that the Constitution does not forbid the States minor intrusions into an individual's body under stringently limited conditions in no way indicates that it permits more substantial intrusions, or intrusions under other conditions.

Affirmed. . . .

Mr. Chief Justice Warren, dissenting.

While there are other important constitutional issues in this case, I believe it is sufficient for me to reiterate my dissenting opinion in Breithaupt v. Abram, 352 U.S. 432, 440, [which upheld a conviction based in part on an analysis of blood extracted from an unconscious suspect] as the basis on which to reverse this conviction.

Mr. Justice Black with whom Mr. Justice Douglas joins, dissenting.

I would reverse petitioner's conviction. . . . I disagree with the Court's holding that California did not violate petitioner's constitutional right against self-incrimination when it compelled him, against his will, to allow a doctor to puncture his blood vessels in order to extract a sample of blood and analyze it for alcoholic content, and then used that analysis as evidence to convict petitioner of a crime.

The Court admits that "the State compelled [petitioner] to submit to an attempt to discover evidence [in his blood] that might be [and was] used to prosecute him for a criminal offense." To reach the conclusion that compelling a person to give his blood to help the State convict him is not equivalent to compelling him to be a witness against himself strikes me as quite an extraordinary feat. The Court, however, overcomes what had seemed to me to be an insuperable obstacle to its conclusion by holding that

> . . . the privilege protects an accused only from being compelled to testify against himself, or otherwise provide the State with evidence of a testimonial or communicative nature, and that the withdrawal of blood and use of the analysis in question in this case did not involve compulsion to these ends.

I cannot agree that this distinction and reasoning of the Court justify denying petitioner his Bill of Rights' guarantee that he must not be compelled to be a witness against himself.

In the first place it seems to me that the compulsory extraction of petitioner's blood for analysis so that the person who analyzed it could give evidence to convict him had both a "testimonial" and a "communicative nature." The sole purpose of this project which proved to be successful was to obtain "testimony" from some person to prove that petitioner had alcohol in his blood at the time he was arrested. And the purpose of the project was certainly "communicative" in that the analysis of the blood was to supply information to enable a witness to communicate to the court and jury that petitioner was more or less drunk.

I think it unfortunate that the Court rests so heavily for its very restrictive reading of the Fifth Amendment's privilege against self-incrimination on the words "testimonial" and "communicative." These words are not models of clarity and precision as the Court's rather labored explication shows. Nor can the Court, so far as I know, find precedent in the former opinions of this Court for using these particular words to limit the scope of the Fifth Amendment's protection. . . .

It concedes, as it must so long as Boyd v. United States stands, that the Fifth Amendment bars a State from compelling a person to produce papers he has that might tend to incriminate him. It is a strange hierarchy of values that allows the State to extract a human being's blood to convict him of a crime because of the blood's content but proscribes compelled production of his lifeless papers. Certainly there could be few papers that would have any more "testimonial" value to convict a man of drunken driving than would an analysis of the alcoholic content of a human being's blood introduced in evidence at a trial for driving while under the influence of alcohol. In such a situation blood, of course, is not oral testimony given by an accused but it can certainly "communicate" to a court and jury the fact of guilt.

The Court itself . . . expresses its own doubts, if not fears, of its own shadowy distinction between compelling "physical evidence" like blood which it holds does not amount to compelled self-incrimination, and "eliciting responses which are essentially testimonial." And in explanation of its fears the Court goes on to warn that

> To compel a person to submit to testing [by lie detectors for example] in which an effort will be made to determine his guilt or innocence on the basis of physiological

responses, whether willed or not, is to evoke the spirit and history of the Fifth Amendment. Such situations call to mind the principle that the protection of the privilege "is as broad as the mischief against which it seeks to guard." Counselman v. Hitchcock, 142 U.S. 547, 562.

A basic error in the Court's holding and opinion is its failure to give the Fifth Amendment's protection against compulsory self-incrimination the broad and liberal construction that *Counselman* and other opinions of this Court have declared it ought to have.

The liberal construction given the Bill of Rights' guarantee in Boyd v. United States, supra, . . . makes that one among the greatest constitutional decisions of this Court. . . . The Court today departs from the teachings of *Boyd*. Petitioner Schmerber has undoubtedly been compelled to give his blood "to furnish evidence against himself," yet the Court holds that this is not forbidden by the Fifth Amendment. With all deferences I must say that the Court here gives the Bill of Rights' safeguard against compulsory self-incrimination a construction that would generally be considered too narrow and technical even in the interpretation of an ordinary commercial contract. . . . How can it reasonably be doubted that the blood test evidence was not in all respects the actual equivalent of "testimony" taken from petitioner when the result of the test was offered as testimony, was considered by the jury as testimony, and the jury's verdict of guilt rests in part on that testimony? The refined, subtle reasoning and balancing process used here to narrow the scope of the Bill of Rights' safeguard against self-incrimination provides a handy instrument for further narrowing of that constitutional protection, as well as others, in the future. Believing with the Framers that these constitutional safeguards broadly construed by independent tribunals of justice provide our best hope for keeping our people free from governmental oppression, I deeply regret the Court's holding. . . .

Mr. Justice Douglas, dissenting.

I adhere to the views of The Chief Justice in his dissent in Breithaupt v. Abram, 352 U.S. 432, 440, and to the views I stated in my dissent in that case (id., 442) and add only a word. We are dealing with the right of privacy which, since the *Breithaupt* case, we have held to be within the penumbra of some specific guarantees of the Bill of Rights. Griswold v. Connecticut, 381 U.S. 479. Thus, the Fifth Amendment marks "a zone of privacy" which the Government may not force a person to surrender. Id., 484. Likewise the Fourth Amendment recognizes that right when it guarantees the right of the people to be secure "in their persons." Ibid. No clearer invasion of this right of privacy can be imagined than forcible bloodletting of the kind involved here.

Mr. Justice Fortas, dissenting.

I would reverse. In my view, petitioner's privilege against self-incrimination applies. I would add that, under the Due Process Clause, the State, in its role as prosecutor, has no right to extract blood from an accused or anyone else, over his protest. As prosecutor, the State has no right to commit any kind of violence upon the person, or to utilize the results of such a tort, and the extraction of blood, over protest, is an act of violence. Cf. Chief Justice Warren's dissenting opinion in Breithaupt v. Abram, 352 U.S. 432, 440.

WARDEN, MARYLAND PENITENTIARY v. HAYDEN

Certiorari to the United States Court of Appeals for the Fourth Circuit
387 U.S. 294 (1967)

MR. JUSTICE BRENNAN delivered the opinion of the Court.

We review in this case the validity of the proposition that there is under the Fourth Amendment a "distinction between merely evidentiary materials, on the one hand, which may not be seized either under the authority of a search warrant or during the course of a search incident to arrest, and on the other hand, those objects which may validly be seized including the instrumentalities and means by which a crime is committed, the fruits of crime such as stolen property, weapons by which escape of the person arrested might be effected, and property the possession of which is a crime."[1]

A Maryland court sitting without a jury convicted respondent of armed robbery. Items of his clothing, a cap, jacket, and trousers, among other things, were seized during a search of his home, and were admitted in evidence without objection. After unsuccessful state court proceedings, he sought and was denied federal habeas corpus relief in the District Court for Maryland. A divided panel of the Court of Appeals for the Fourth Circuit reversed. The Court of Appeals believed that Harris v. United States, 331 U.S. 145, 154, sustained the validity of the search, but held that respondent was correct in his contention that the clothing seized was improperly admitted in evidence because the items had "evidential value only" and therefore were not lawfully subject to seizure. We granted certiorari. We reverse. . . .

[The Court disposed of the validity of the search. For a discussion, see page 466 infra.]

We come, then, to the question whether, even though the search was lawful, the Court of Appeals was correct in holding that the seizure and introduction of the items of clothing violated the Fourth Amendment because they are "mere evidence." The distinction made by some of our cases between seizure of items of evidential value only and seizure of instrumentalities, fruits, or contraband has been criticized by courts and commentators. The Court of Appeals, however, felt "obligated to adhere to it." We today reject the distinction as based on premises no longer accepted as rules governing the application of the Fourth Amendment.[8] . . .

Nothing in the language of the Fourth Amendment supports the distinction between "mere evidence" and instrumentalities, fruits of crime, or contraband. On its face, the provision assures the "right of the people to be secure in their persons, houses, papers, and effects . . . ," without regard to the use to which any of these things are applied. This "right of the people" is certainly unrelated to the "mere

---

1. Harris v. United States, 331 U.S. 145, 154; see also Gouled v. United States, 255 U.S. 298; United States v. Lefkowitz, 285 U.S. 452, 465-466; United States v. Rabinowitz, 339 U.S. 56, 64, n. 6; Abel v. United States, 362 U.S. 217, 234-235.

8. This Court has approved the seizure and introduction of items having only evidential value without, however, considering the validity of the distinction rejected today. See Schmerber v. California, 384 U.S. 757; Cooper v. California, 386 U.S. 58.

evidence" limitation. Privacy is disturbed no more by a search directed to a purely evidentiary object than it is by a search directed to an instrumentality, fruit, or contraband. A magistrate can intervene in both situations, and the requirements of probable cause and specificity can be preserved intact. Moreover, nothing in the nature of the property seized as evidence renders it more private than property seized, for example, as an instrumentality; quite the opposite may be true. Indeed, the distinction is wholly irrational, since, depending on the circumstances, the same "papers and effects" may be "mere evidence" in one case and "instrumentality" in another.

In Gouled v. United States, the Court said that search warrants "may not be used as a means of gaining access to a man's house or office and papers solely for the purpose of making search to secure evidence to be used against him in a criminal or penal proceeding. . . ." The Court derived from Boyd v. United States, supra, the proposition that warrants "may be resorted to only when a primary right to such search and seizure may be found in the interest which the public or the complainant may have in the property to be seized, or in the right to the possession of it, or when a valid exercise of the police power renders possession of the property by the accused unlawful and provides that it may be taken," 255 U.S., at 309; that is, when the property is an instrumentality or fruit of crime, or contraband. Since it was "impossible to say, on the record . . . that the Government had any interest" in the papers involved "other than as evidence against the accused . . . ," "to permit them to be used in evidence would be, in effect, as ruled in the *Boyd Case*, to compel the defendant to become a witness against himself." Id., at 311.

The items of clothing involved in this case are not "testimonial" or "communicative" in nature, and their introduction therefore did not compel respondent to become a witness against himself in violation of the Fifth Amendment. This case thus does not require that we consider whether there are items of evidential value whose very nature precludes them from being the object of a reasonable search and seizure.

The Fourth Amendment ruling in *Gouled* was based upon the dual, related premises that historically the right to search for and seize property depended upon the assertion by the Government of a valid claim of superior interest, and that it was not enough that the purpose of the search and seizure was to obtain evidence to use in apprehending and convicting criminals. . . .

The premise that property interests control the right of the Government to search and seize has been discredited. Searches and seizures may be "unreasonable" within the Fourth Amendment even though the Government asserts a superior property interest at common law. We have recognized that the principal object of the Fourth Amendment is the protection of privacy rather than property, and have increasingly discarded fictional and procedural barriers rested on property concepts. . . . And with particular relevance here, we have given recognition to the interest in privacy despite the complete absence of a property claim by suppressing the very items which at common law could be seized with impunity: stolen goods, Henry v. United States, 361 U.S. 98; instrumentalities, Beck v. Ohio, 379 U.S. 89; McDonald v. United States, supra; and contraband, Trupiano v. United States, 334 U.S. 699; Aguilar v. Texas, 378 U.S. 108.

The premise in *Gouled* that government may not seize evidence simply for the purpose of proving crime has likewise been discredited. The requirement that the Government assert in addition some property interest in material it seizes has long been a fiction,[11] obscuring the reality that government has an interest in solving crime. *Schmerber* settled the proposition that it is reasonable, within the terms of the Fourth Amendment, to conduct otherwise permissible searches for the purpose of obtaining evidence which would aid in apprehending and convicting criminals. The requirements of the Fourth Amendment can secure the same protection of privacy whether the search is for "mere evidence" or for fruits, instrumentalities or contraband. . . .

The rationale most frequently suggested for the rule preventing the seizure of evidence is that "limitations upon the fruit to be gathered tend to limit the quest itself." But privacy "would be just as well served by a restriction on search to the even-numbered days of the month. . . . And it would have the extra advantage of avoiding hair-splitting questions. . . ." Kaplan, [Search and Seizure: A No-Man's Land in the Criminal Law, 49 Cal. L. Rev. 474,] at 479. The "mere evidence" limitation has spawned exceptions so numerous and confusion so great, in fact, that it is questionable whether it affords meaningful protection. But if its rejection does enlarge the area of permissible searches, the intrusions are nevertheless made after fulfilling the probable cause and particularity requirements of the Fourth Amendment and after the intervention of "a neutral and detached magistrate. . . ." The Fourth Amendment allows intrusions upon privacy under these circumstances, and there is no viable reason to distinguish intrusions to secure "mere evidence" from intrusions to secure fruits, instrumentalities, or contraband.

The judgment of the Court of Appeals is reversed.

MR. JUSTICE BLACK concurs in the result.

MR. JUSTICE FORTAS, with whom THE CHIEF JUSTICE joins, concurring.

While I agree that the Fourth Amendment should not be held to require exclusion from evidence of the clothing as well as the weapons and ammunition found by the officers during the search, I cannot join in the majority's broad — and in my judgment, totally unnecessary — repudiation of the so-called "mere evidence" rule.

Our Constitution envisions that searches will ordinarily follow procurement by police of a valid search warrant. Such warrants are to issue only on probable cause, and must describe with particularity the persons or things to be seized. There are exceptions to this rule. Searches may be made incident to a lawful arrest, and — as today's decision indicates — in the course of "hot pursuit." But searches under each of these exceptions have, until today, been confined to those essential to fulfill the purpose of the exception: that is, we have refused to permit use of

11. At common law the Government did assert a superior property interest when it searched lawfully for stolen property, since the procedure then followed made it necessary that the true owner swear that his goods had been taken. But no such procedure need be followed today; the Government may demonstrate probable cause and lawfully search for stolen property even though the true owner is unknown or unavailable to request and authorize the Government to assert his interest. As to instrumentalities, the Court in *Gouled* allowed their seizure, not because the Government had some property interest in them (under the ancient, fictitious forfeiture theory), but because they could be used to perpetrate further crime. 255 U.S., at 309. The same holds true, of course, for "mere evidence"; the prevention of crime is served at least as much by allowing the Government to identify and capture the criminal, as it is by allowing the seizure of his instrumentalities. Finally, contraband is indeed property in which the Government holds a superior interest, but only because the Government decides to vest such an interest in itself. And while there may be limits to what may be declared contraband, the concept is hardly more than a form through which the Government seeks to prevent and deter crime.

articles the seizure of which could not be strictly tied to and justified by the exigencies which excused the warrantless search. The use in evidence of weapons seized in a "hot pursuit" search or search incident to arrest satisfies this criterion because of the need to protect the arresting officers from weapons to which the suspect might resort. The search for and seizure of fruits are, of course, justifiable on independent grounds: The fruits are an object of the pursuit or arrest of the suspect, and should be restored to their true owner. The seizure of contraband has been justified on the ground that the suspect has not even a bare possessory right to contraband. . . .

In the present case, the articles of clothing admitted into evidence are not within any of the traditional categories which describe what materials may be seized, either with or without a warrant. The restrictiveness of these categories has been subjected to telling criticism, and although I believe that we should approach expansion of these categories with the diffidence which their imposing provenance commands, I agree that the use of identifying clothing worn in the commission of a crime and seized during "hot pursuit" is within the spirit and intendment of the "hot pursuit" exception to the search-warrant requirement. That is because the clothing is pertinent to identification of the person hotly pursued as being, in fact, the person whose pursuit was justified by connection with the crime. I would frankly place the ruling on that basis. I would not drive an enormous and dangerous hole in the Fourth Amendment to accommodate a specific and, I think, reasonable exception.

As my Brother Douglas notes, post, opposition to general searches is a fundamental of our heritage and of the history of Anglo-Saxon legal principles. Such searches, pursuant to "writs of assistance," were one of the matters over which the American Revolution was fought. The very purpose of the Fourth Amendment was to outlaw such searches, which the Court today sanctions. I fear that in gratuitously striking down the "mere evidence" rule, which distinguished members of this Court have acknowledged as essential to enforce the Fourth Amendment's prohibition against general searches, the Court today needlessly destroys, root and branch, a basic part of liberty's heritage.

MR. JUSTICE DOUGLAS, dissenting.

We start with the Fourth Amendment. . . .

This constitutional guarantee, . . . has been thought, until today, to have two faces of privacy:

(1) One creates a zone of privacy that may not be invaded by the police through raids, by the legislators through laws, or by magistrates through the issuance of warrants.

(2) A second creates a zone of privacy that may be invaded either by the police in hot pursuit or by a search incident to arrest or by a warrant issued by a magistrate on a showing of probable cause. . . .

This is borne out by what happened in the Congress. In the House the original draft read as follows:

The right of the people to be secured in their persons, houses, papers, and effects, shall not be violated by warrants issuing without probable cause, supported by oath or affirmation, and not particularly describing the place to be searched and the persons or things to be seized. 1 Annals of Cong. 754.

That was amended to read "The right of the people to be secured in their persons, houses, papers, and effects, against unreasonable seizures and searches," etc. Ibid. Mr. Benson, Chairman of a Committee of Three to arrange the amendments, objected to the words "by warrants issuing" and proposed to alter the amendment so as to read "and no warrant shall issue." Ibid. But Benson's amendment was defeated. Ibid. And if the story had ended there, it would be clear that the Fourth Amendment touched only the form of the warrants and the manner of their issuance. But when the Benson Committee later reported the Fourth Amendment to the House, it was in the form he had earlier proposed and was then accepted. 1 Annals of Cong. 779. The Senate agreed. Senate Journal August 25, 1789.

Thus it is clear that the Fourth Amendment has two faces of privacy, a conclusion emphasized by Nelson B. Lasson, The History and Development of the Fourth Amendment to the United States Constitution 103 (1937):

> As reported by the Committee of Eleven and corrected by Gerry, the Amendment was a one-barrelled affair, directed apparently only to the essentials of a valid warrant. The general principle of freedom from unreasonable search and seizure seems to have been stated only by way of premise, and the positive inhibition upon action by the Federal Government limited consequently to the issuance of warrants without probable cause, etc. That Benson interpreted it in this light is shown by his argument that although the clause was good as far as it went, *it was not sufficient*, and by the change which he advocated to obviate this objection. The provision as he proposed it contained *two* clauses. The general right of security from unreasonable search and seizure was given a sanction of its own and the amendment thus intentionally given a broader scope. That the prohibition against "unreasonable searches" was intended, accordingly, to cover something other than the form of the warrant is a question no longer left to implication to be derived from the phraseology of the Amendment. . . .

. . . Our question is whether the Government, though armed with a proper search warrant or though making a search incident to an arrest, may seize, and use at the trial, testimonial evidence, whether it would otherwise be barred by the Fifth Amendment or would be free from such strictures. The teaching of *Boyd* is that such evidence, though seized pursuant to a lawful search, is inadmissible. . . .

We have, to be sure, breached that barrier, Schmerber v. California, 384 U.S. 757, being a conspicuous example. But I dissented then and renew my opposing view at this time. That which is taken from a person without his consent and used as testimonial evidence violates the Fifth Amendment.

That was the holding in *Gouled;* and that was the line of authority followed by Judge Simon Sobeloff, writing for the Court of Appeals for reversal in this case. 363 F.2d 647. As he said, even if we assume that the search was lawful, the articles of clothing seized were of evidential value only and under *Gouled* could not be used at the trial against petitioner. As he said, the Fourth Amendment guarantees the right of the people to be secure "in their persons, houses, papers, and effects, against unreasonable searches and seizures." Articles of clothing are covered as well as papers. Articles of clothing may be of evidential value as much as documents or papers.

Judge Learned Hand stated a part of the philosophy of the Fourth Amendment in United States v. Poller, 43 F.2d 911, 914:

> [I]t is only fair to observe that the real evil aimed at by the Fourth Amendment is the search itself, that invasion of a man's privacy which consists in rummaging about among his effects to secure evidence against him. If the search is permitted at all, perhaps it does not make so much difference what is taken away, since the officers will ordinarily not be interested in what does not incriminate, and there can be no sound policy in protecting what does. Nevertheless, limitations upon the fruit to be gathered tend to limit the quest itself. . . .

The right of privacy protected by the Fourth Amendment relates in part of course to the precincts of the home or the office. But it does not make them sanctuaries where the law can never reach. . . . A policeman in "hot pursuit" or an officer with a search warrant can enter any house, any room, any building, any office. The privacy of those *places* is of course protected against invasion except in limited situations. The full privacy protected by the Fourth Amendment is, however, reached when we come to books, pamphlets, papers, letters, documents, and other personal effects. Unless they are contraband or instruments of the crime, they may not be reached by any warrant nor may they be lawfully seized by the police who are in "hot pursuit." By reason of the Fourth Amendment the police may not rummage around among these personal effects, no matter how formally perfect their authority may appear to be. They may not seize them. If they do, those articles may not be used in evidence. Any invasion whatsoever of those personal effects is "unreasonable" within the meaning of the Fourth Amendment. That is the teaching of Entick v. Carrington, Boyd v. United States, and Gouled v. United States. . . .

The constitutional philosophy is, I think, clear. The personal effects and possessions of the individual (all contraband and the like excepted) are sacrosanct from prying eyes, from the long arm of the law, from any rummaging by police. Privacy involves the choice of the individual to disclose or to reveal what he believes, what he thinks, what he possesses. The article may be a nondescript work of art, a manuscript of a book, a personal account book, a diary, invoices, personal clothing, jewelry, or whatnot. Those who wrote the Bill of Rights believed that every individual needs both to communicate with others and to keep his affairs to himself. That dual aspect of privacy means that the individual should have the freedom to select for himself the time and circumstances when he will share his secrets with others and decide the extent of that sharing. This is his prerogative not the States'. The Framers, who were as knowledgeable as we, knew what police surveillance meant and how the practice of rummaging through one's personal effects could destroy freedom. . . .

The third case in which the Court considered the extent to which "the law derived from *Boyd* would have to be repudiated" was Berger v. New York, 388 U.S. 41 (1967):

> We . . . turn to New York's statute to determine the basis of the search and seizure authorized by it upon the order of a state supreme court justice, a county judge or

general sessions judge of New York County. Section 813-a authorizes the issuance of an "ex parte order for eavesdropping" upon "oath or affirmation of a district attorney, or of the attorney-general or of an officer above the rank of sergeant of any police department of the state or of any political subdivision thereof. . . ." The oath must state "that there is reasonable ground to believe that evidence of crime may be thus obtained, and particularly describing the person or persons whose communications, conversations or discussions are to be overheard or recorded and the purpose thereof, and . . . identifying the particular telephone number or telegraph line involved." The judge "may examine on oath the applicant and any other witness he may produce and shall satisfy himself of the existence of reasonable grounds for the granting of such application." The order must specify the duration of the eavesdrop — not exceeding two months unless extended — and "(a)ny such order together with the papers upon which the application was based, shall be delivered to and retained by the applicant as authority for the eavesdropping authorized therein." . . .

The Fourth Amendment commands that a warrant issue not only upon probable cause supported by oath or affirmation, but also "particularly describing the place to be searched, and the persons or things to be seized." New York's statute lacks this particularization. It merely says that a warrant may issue on reasonable ground to believe that evidence of crime may be obtained by the eavesdrop. It lays down no requirement for particularity in the warrant as to what specific crime has been or is being committed, nor "the place to be searched," or "the persons or things to be seized" as specifically required by the Fourth Amendment. The need for particularity and evidence of reliability in the showing required when judicial authorization of a search is sought is especially great in the case of eavesdropping. By its very nature eavesdropping involves an intrusion on privacy that is broad in scope. As was said in Osborn v. United States, 385 U.S. 32 (1966), the "indiscriminate use of such devices in law enforcement raises grave constitutional questions under the Fourth and Fifth Amendments," and imposes "a heavier responsibility on this Court in its supervision of the fairness of procedures. . . ." At 329, n. 7. There, two judges acting jointly authorized the installation of a device on the person of a prospective witness to record conversations between him and an attorney for a defendant then on trial in the United States District Court. The judicial authorization was based on an affidavit of the witness setting out in detail previous conversations between the witness and the attorney concerning the bribery of jurors in the case. The recording device was, as the Court said, authorized "under the most precise and discriminate circumstances, circumstances which fully met the 'requirement of particularity'" of the Fourth Amendment. The Court was asked to exclude the evidence of the recording of the conversations seized pursuant to the order on constitutional grounds, Weeks v. United States, 232 U.S. 383 (1914), or in the exercise of supervisory power, McNabb v. United States, 318 U.S. 332 (1943). The Court refused to do so finding that the recording, although an invasion of the privacy protected by the Fourth Amendment, was admissible because of the authorization of the judges, based upon "a detailed factual affidavit alleging the commission of a specific criminal offense directly and immediately affecting the administration of justice . . . for the narrow and particularized purpose of ascertaining the truth of the affidavit's allegations." The invasion was lawful because there was sufficient proof to obtain a search warrant to make the search for the limited purpose outlined in the order of the judges. Through these "precise and discriminate" procedures the order authorizing the use of the electronic device afforded similar protections to those that are present in the use of conventional warrants authorizing the seizure of tangible evidence. Among other safeguards, the order described the type of conversation sought with particularity, thus indicating the specific objective of the Government in entering the constitutionally protected area and the limitations placed upon the officer executing the warrant.

Under it the officer could not search unauthorized areas; likewise, once the property sought, and for which the order was issued, was found the officer could not use the order as a passkey to further search. In addition, the order authorized one limited intrusion rather than a series or a continuous surveillance. And, we note that a new order was issued when the officer sought to resume the search and probable cause was shown for the succeeding one. Moreover, the order was executed by the officer with dispatch, not over a prolonged and extended period. In this manner no greater invasion of privacy was permitted than was necessary under the circumstances. Finally the officer was required to and did make a return on the order showing how it was executed and what was seized. Through these strict precautions the danger of an unlawful search and seizure was minimized.

By contrast, New York's statute lays down no such "precise and discriminate" requirements. Indeed, it authorizes the "indiscriminate use" of electronic devices as specifically condemned in *Osborn*. "The proceeding by search warrant is a drastic one," Sgro v. United States, 287 U.S. 206 (1932), and must be carefully circumscribed so as to prevent unauthorized invasions of "the sanctity of a man's home and the privacies of life." Boyd v. United States, 116 U.S. 616, 630. New York's broadside authorization rather than being "carefully circumscribed" so as to prevent unauthorized invasions of privacy actually permits general searches by electronic devices, the truly offensive character of which was first condemned in Entick v. Carrington, 19 How. St. Tr. 1029, and which were then known as "general warrants." The use of the latter was a motivating factor behind the Declaration of Independence. In view of the many cases commenting on the practice it is sufficient here to point out that under these "general warrants" customs officials were given blanket authority to conduct general searches for goods imported to the Colonies in violation of the tax laws of the Crown. The Fourth Amendment's requirement that a warrant "particularly describ(e) the place to be searched, and the persons or things to be seized," repudiated these general warrants and "makes general searches . . . impossible and prevents the seizure of one thing under a warrant describing another. As to what is to be taken, nothing is left to the discretion of the officer executing the warrant." Marron v. United States, 275 U.S. 192, 196 (1927).

We believe the statute here is equally offensive. First, as we have mentioned, eavesdropping is authorized without requiring belief that any particular offense has been or is being committed; nor that the "property" sought, the conversations, be particularly described. The purpose of the probable cause requirement of the Fourth Amendment, to keep the state out of constitutionally protected areas until it has reason to believe that a specific crime has been or is being committed, is thereby wholly aborted. Likewise the statute's failure to describe with particularity the conversations sought gives the officer a roving commission to "seize" any and all conversations. It is true that the statute requires the naming of "the person or persons whose communications, conversations or discussions are to be overheard or recorded. . . ." But this does no more than identify the person whose constitutionally protected area is to be invaded rather than "particularly describing" the communications, conversations, or discussions to be seized. As with general warrants this leaves too much to the discretion of the officer executing the order. Secondly, authorization of eavesdropping for a two-month period is the equivalent of a series of intrusions, searches, and seizures pursuant to a single showing of probable cause. Prompt execution is also avoided. During such a long and continuous (24 hours a day) period the conversations of any and all persons coming into the area covered by the device will be seized indiscriminately and without regard to their connection with the crime under investigation. Moreover, the statute permits, and there were authorized here, extensions of the original two-month period—presumably for two months each—on a mere showing that such extension is "in the public interest." Apparently the original grounds on which the eavesdrop order was initially issued also form the basis of the renewal. This we believe insufficient without a showing of present probable cause for the continuance of the eavesdrop. Third, the statute places no termination date on the eavesdrop once the conversation sought is seized. This is left entirely in the discretion of the officer. Finally, the statute's procedure, necessarily because its success depends on secrecy, has no requirement for notice as do conventional warrants, nor does it overcome this defect by requiring some showing of special facts. On the contrary, it permits uncontested entry without any showing of exigent circumstances. Such a showing of exigency, in order to avoid notice would appear more important in eavesdropping, with its inherent dangers, than that required when conventional procedures of search and seizure are utilized. Nor does the statute provide for a return on the warrant thereby leaving full discretion in the officer as to the use of seized conversations of innocent as well as guilty parties. In short, the statute's blanket grant of permission to eavesdrop is without adequate judicial supervision or protective procedures.

NOTES AND QUESTIONS

1. What is left of the theoretical underpinnings of *Boyd* and *Gouled* after *Schmerber, Hayden*, and *Berger*? Is it conceivable that the "paper search" component of *Boyd* survived these cases? Is the seizure of spoken words in any crucial respect different from the seizure of private papers? Is it true that the "mere evidence" rule is insupportable? Consider the following passage from Russell W. Galloway, Jr., The Intruding Eye: A Status Report on the Constitutional Ban against Paper Searches, 25 How. L.J. 367, 382-385 (1982):

[T]he mere evidence rule was a rational method for protecting privacy. When searches and seizures are limited to contraband, fruits and instrumentalities, the only persons who may be searched, in most instances, are criminals. Normally, only the criminals themselves possess contraband, fruits or instrumentalities. In contrast, innocent people (so-called "third parties") frequently possess evidence that may tie some *other* person to a crime. Thus, the mere evidence rule ensures that the government will not be able to invade the privacy of innocent third parties. Moreover, evidence searches often result in much more serious invasions of personal privacy. Rarely will a person's private papers contain contraband, fruits or instrumentalities. Yet searches for evidence of crime lead easily and directly into private paper where descriptions of prior acts and statements may be recorded side by side with the most intimate details of private life and thought. A search for a stolen television, for example, will normally be far less intrusive than a search for written statements concerning the suspect's whereabouts on the night the television was stolen. For reasons such as these, Learned Hand described the policy underlying the mere evidence rule as follows: "Limitations upon the fruit to be gathered tend to limit the quest itself."[70] . . .

The reasons given for the repudiation of the mere evidence rule are unconvincing. The absence of explicit reference to the mere evidence rule in the fourth amendment means little in light of the Court's insistence that *Entick* was in the forefront of the framers' minds when they banned unreasonable searches.[78] The Court's assurances notwithstanding, evidence searches tend to disturb privacy *much more deeply* than

70. United States v. Poller, 43 F.2d 911, 914 (2d Cir. 1930).
78. See, e.g., Boyd v. United States, 116 U.S. 616, 626-627 (1886), which stated: "As every American statesm[a]n, during our revolutionary and formative period as a nation, was undoubtedly familiar with

searches for contraband, fruits and instrumentalities. One need only consider, for example, that neither extended electronic surveillance, one of the most insidious invasions of privacy, nor the reading of most private papers would be possible if the mere evidence rule had been retained. The mere evidence rule was definitely not an irrational restriction like "a restriction on search to even-numbered days." The mere evidence rule was a rational limitation which operated to restrict searches of innocent third parties and to ban the most intrusive invasions of private papers and conversations.

Boyd continues to generate favorable commentary. See, e.g., Richard A. Nagareda, "Compulsion to Be a Witness" and the Resurrection of *Boyd*, 74 N.Y.U. L. Rev. 1575 (1999); Eric Schnapper, Unreasonable Searches and Seizures of Papers, 71 Va. L. Rev. 869 (1985). But see Samuel A. Alito, Jr., Documents and the Privilege against Self Incrimination, 48 U. Pitt. L. Rev. 27 (1986).

2. Although the Court struck down the statute in *Berger*, did it essentially write its replacement? Is that replacement statute true to the message of *Boyd*? Should it have been? These and other issues are considered in Chapter 5 infra.

3. The Court continued its reconstruction of *Boyd* in Fisher v. United States, 425 U.S. 391 (1976), and Andresen v. Maryland, 427 U.S. 463 (1976). In *Fisher*, the Court upheld a summons that directed the defendants' attorneys to produce documents prepared by defendants' accountants and turned over to the attorneys for purposes of obtaining legal advice. After determining that the materials would be privileged in the hands of the attorney, as a result of the attorney-client privilege, only if the Fifth Amendment protected the materials when they were in the possession of the client, the Court proceeded to discuss its understanding of the Fourth and the Fifth Amendments:

It is true that the Court has often stated that one of the several purposes served by the constitutional privilege against compelled testimonial self-incrimination is that of protecting personal privacy. . . . But the Court has never suggested that every invasion of privacy violates the privilege. Within the limits imposed by the language of the Fifth Amendment, which we necessarily observe, the privilege truly serves privacy interests; but the Court has never on any ground, personal privacy included, applied the Fifth Amendment to prevent the otherwise proper acquisition or use of evidence which, in the Court's view, did not involve compelled testimonial self-incrimination of some sort.[5]

The proposition that the Fifth Amendment protects private information obtained without compelling self-incriminating testimony is contrary to the clear statements of this Court that under appropriate safeguards private incriminating statements of an accused may be overheard and used in evidence, if they are not compelled at the time they were uttered, . . . Berger v. New York; . . . and that disclosure of private information may be compelled if immunity removes the risk of incrimination. If the Fifth Amendment protected generally against the obtaining of private information from a

---

[Entick v. Carrington] . . . , and considered it as the true and ultimate expression of constitutional law, it may be confidently asserted that its propositions were in the minds of those who framed the Fourth Amendment to the Constitution, and were considered as sufficiently explanatory of what was meant by unreasonable searches and seizures."

5. There is a line of cases in which the Court stated that the Fifth Amendment was offended by the use in evidence of documents or property seized in violation of the Fourth Amendment. . . . In any event the predicate for those cases, lacking here, was a violation of the Fourth Amendment.

man's mouth or pen or house, its protections would presumably not be lifted by probable cause and a warrant or by immunity. The privacy invasion is not mitigated by immunity; and the Fifth Amendment's strictures, unlike the Fourth's, are not removed by showing reasonableness. The Framers addressed the subject of personal privacy directly in the Fourth Amendment. They struck a balance so that when the State's reason to believe incriminating evidence will be found becomes sufficiently great, the invasion of privacy becomes justified and a warrant to search and seize will issue. They did not seek in still another Amendment — the Fifth — to achieve a general protection of privacy but to deal with the more specific issue of compelled self-incrimination.

We cannot cut the Fifth Amendment completely loose from the moorings of its language, and make it serve as a general protector of privacy — a word not mentioned in its text and a concept directly addressed in the Fourth Amendment. We adhere to the view that the Fifth Amendment protects against "compelled self-incrimination, not [the disclosure of] private information." United States v. Nobles, 422 U.S. 225, 233 n. 7 (1975).

Insofar as private information not obtained through compelled self-incriminating testimony is legally protected, its protection stems from other sources[6] — the Fourth Amendment's protection against seizures without warrant or probable cause and against subpoenas which suffer from "too much indefiniteness or breadth in the things required to be 'particularly described,'" Oklahoma Press Pub. Co. v. Walling, 327 U.S. 186, 208 (1946); or evidentiary privileges such as the attorney-client privilege.[7]

425 U.S. at 399-401.

In light of its general understanding of the amendments, the only Fifth Amendment problem the Court could see with a summons to produce documents prepared by someone else (here the accountants) had to do with the testimonial components of production itself.

A subpoena served on a taxpayer requiring him to produce an accountant's workpapers in his possession without doubt involves substantial compulsion. But it does not compel oral testimony; nor would it ordinarily compel the taxpayer to restate, repeat, or affirm the truth of the contents of the documents sought. Therefore, the Fifth Amendment would not be violated by the fact alone that the papers on their face might incriminate the taxpayer, for the privilege protects a person only against being incriminated by his own compelled testimonial communications. Schmerber v. California, supra. . . . The accountant's workpapers are not the taxpayer's. They were not prepared by the taxpayer, and they contain no testimonial declarations by him. Furthermore, as far as this record demonstrates, the preparation of all of the papers sought in these cases was wholly voluntary, and they cannot be said to contain compelled testimonial evidence, either of the taxpayers or of anyone else.[11] The

6. In Couch v. United States, 409 U.S. 322 (1973), on which taxpayers rely for their claim that the Fifth Amendment protects their "legitimate expectation of privacy," the Court differentiated between the things protected by the Fourth and Fifth Amendments. "We hold today that no Fourth or Fifth Amendment claim can prevail where, as in this case, there exists no legitimate expectation of privacy and no semblance of governmental compulsion against the person of the accused." Id., at 336.

7. The taxpayers and their attorneys have not raised arguments of a Fourth Amendment nature before this Court and could not be successful if they had. The summonses are narrowly drawn and seek only documents of unquestionable relevance to the tax investigation. Special problems of privacy which might be presented by subpoena of a personal diary, United States v. Bennett, 409 F.2d 888, 897 (CA2 1969) (Friendly, J.), are not involved here.

First Amendment values are also plainly not implicated in these cases.

11. The fact that the documents may have been written by the person asserting the privilege is insufficient to trigger the privilege, Wilson v. United States, 221 U.S. 361, 378 (1911). And, unless the

taxpayer cannot avoid compliance with the subpoena merely by asserting that the item of evidence which he is required to produce contains incriminating writing, whether his own or that of someone else.

The act of producing evidence in response to a subpoena nevertheless has communicative aspects of its own, wholly aside from the contents of the papers produced. Compliance with the subpoena tacitly concedes the existence of the papers demanded and their possession or control by the taxpayer. It also would indicate the taxpayer's belief that the papers are those described in the subpoena. Curcio v. United States, 354 U.S. 118, 125 (1957). The elements of compulsion are clearly present, but the more difficult issues are whether the tacit averments of the taxpayer are both "testimonial" and "incriminating" for purposes of applying the Fifth Amendment. These questions perhaps do not lend themselves to categorical answers; their resolution may instead depend on the facts and circumstances of particular cases or classes thereof. In light of the records now before us, we are confident that however incriminating the contents of the accountant's workpapers might be, the act of producing them—the only thing which the taxpayer is compelled to do—would not itself involve testimonial self-incrimination.

It is doubtful that implicitly admitting the existence and possession of the papers rises to the level of testimony within the protection of the Fifth Amendment. The papers belong to the accountant, were prepared by him, and are the kind usually prepared by an accountant working on the tax returns of his client. Surely the Government is in no way relying on the "truthtelling" of the taxpayer to prove the existence of or his access to the documents. 8 Wigmore §2264, p. 380. The existence and location of the papers are a foregone conclusion and the taxpayer adds little or nothing to the sum total of the Government's information by conceding that he in fact has the papers. Under these circumstances by enforcement of the summons "no constitutional rights are touched. The question is not of testimony but of surrender." In re Harris, 221 U.S. 274, 279 (1911). . . .

As for the possibility that responding to the subpoena would authenticate the workpapers, production would express nothing more than the taxpayer's belief that the papers are those described in the subpoena. The taxpayer would be no more competent to authenticate the accountant's workpapers or reports by producing them than he would be to authenticate them if testifying orally. The taxpayer did not prepare the papers and could not vouch for their accuracy. The documents would not be admissible in evidence against the taxpayer without authenticating testimony. Without more, responding to the subpoena in the circumstances before us would not appear to represent a substantial threat of self-incrimination. Moreover, in [a series of cases] the custodian of corporate, union, or partnership books or those of a bankrupt business was ordered to respond to a subpoena for the business' books even though doing so involved a "representation that documents produced are those demanded by the subpoena," Curcio v. United States, 354 U.S., at 125.

425 U.S. at 409-413.

Justice Brennan concurred, but made the point that the Fifth Amendment in his view would protect against the production of private papers that were unrelated to

---

Government has compelled the subpoenaed person to write the document, cf. Marchetti v. United States, 390 U.S. 39 (1968); Grosso v. United States, 390 U.S. 62 (1968), the fact that it was written by him is not controlling with respect to the Fifth Amendment issue. Conversations may be seized and introduced in evidence under proper safeguards, . . . Berger v. New York, 388 U.S. 41 (1967); . . . if not compelled. In the case of a documentary subpoena the only thing compelled is the act of producing the document and the compelled act is the same as the one performed when a chattel or document not authored by the producer is demanded. McCormick §128, p. 269.

the defendant's business activities. Justice Marshall also concurred, primarily on the ground that *Fisher* would not modify the scope of the protections previously afforded by the Court's decisions:

> I am hopeful that the Court's new theory, properly understood and applied, will provide substantially the same protection as our prior focus on the contents of the documents. The Court recognizes, as others have argued, that the act of production can verify the authenticity of the documents produced. But the promise of the Court's theory lies in its innovative discernment that production may also verify the documents' very existence and present possession by the producer. This expanded recognition of the kinds of testimony inherent in production not only rationalizes the cases, but seems to me to afford almost complete protection against compulsory production of our most private papers.
>
> Thus, the Court's rationale provides a persuasive basis for distinguishing between the corporate document cases and those involving the papers of private citizens. Since the existence of corporate record books is seldom in doubt, the verification of their existence, inherent in their production, may fairly be termed not testimonial at all. On the other hand, there is little reason to assume the present existence and possession of most private papers, and certainly not those Mr. Justice Brennan places at the top of his list of documents that the privilege should protect. . . . Indeed, there would appear to be a precise inverse relationship between the private nature of the document and the permissibility of assuming its existence. Therefore, under the Court's theory, the admission through production that one's diary, letters, prior tax returns, personally maintained financial records, or cancelled checks exist would ordinarily provide substantial testimony. The incriminating nature of such an admission is clear, for while it may not be criminal to keep a diary, or write letters or checks, the admission that one does and that those documents are still available may quickly — or simultaneously — lead to incriminating evidence. If there is a "real danger" of such a result, that is enough under our cases to make such testimony subject to the claim of privilege. Thus, in practice, the Court's approach should still focus upon the private nature of the papers subpoenaed and protect those about which *Boyd* and its progeny were most concerned.
>
> The Court's theory will also limit the prosecution's ability to use documents secured through a grant of immunity. If authentication that the document produced is the document demanded were the only testimony inherent in production, immunity would be a useful tool for obtaining written evidence. So long as a document obtained under an immunity grant could be authenticated through other sources, as would often be possible, reliance on the immunized testimony — the authentication — and its fruits would not be necessary, and the document could be introduced. The Court's recognition that the act of production also involves testimony about the existence and possession of the subpoenaed documents mandates a different result. Under the Court's theory, if the document is to be obtained the immunity grant must extend to the testimony that the document is presently in existence. Such a grant will effectively shield the contents of the document, for the contents are a direct fruit of the immunized testimony — that the document exists — and cannot usually be obtained without reliance on that testimony. Accordingly, the Court's theory offers substantially the same protection against procurement of documents under grant of immunity that our prior cases afford.
>
> In short, while the Court sacrifices our pragmatic, if somewhat ad hoc, content analysis for what might seem an unduly technical focus on the act of production itself, I am far less pessimistic than Mr. Justice Brennan that this new approach signals the end of Fifth Amendment protection for documents we have long held to be

privileged. I am not ready to embrace the approach myself, but I am confident in the ability of the trial judges who must apply this difficult test in the first instance to act with sensitivity to our traditional concerns in this uncertain area. . . .

425 U.S. at 432-434.

In *Andresen*, the Court dealt with the issue left open in *Fisher* — the production of a person's private papers — but approached it from a different perspective. The defendant was convicted on various counts of fraud. At trial, the government relied on personal business papers of the defendant that were seized under the authority of a search warrant. Some of the documents seized included memoranda handwritten by the defendant. According to the Court, this raised "the issue whether the introduction into evidence of a person's business records, seized during a search of his offices, violates the Fifth Amendment's command."

> The question . . . is whether the seizure of these business records, and their admission into evidence at his trial, compelled petitioner to testify against himself in violation of the Fifth Amendment. This question may be said to have been reserved in Warden v. Hayden . . .
>
> In the very recent case of Fisher v. United States, the Court held that an attorney's production, pursuant to a lawful summons, of his client's tax records in his hands did not violate the Fifth Amendment privilege of the taxpayer "because enforcement against a taxpayer's lawyer would not 'compel' the taxpayer to do anything — and certainly would not compel him to be a 'witness' against himself." . . . [7]
>
> Similarly, in this case, petitioner was not asked to say or to do anything. The records seized contained statements that petitioner had voluntarily committed to writing. The search for and seizure of these records were conducted by law enforcement personnel. Finally, when these records were introduced at trial, they were authenticated by a handwriting expert, not by petitioner. Any compulsion of petitioner to speak, other than the inherent psychological pressure to respond at trial to unfavorable evidence, was not present.
>
> This case thus falls within the principle stated by Mr. Justice Holmes: "A party is privileged from producing the evidence but not from its production." Johnson v. United States, 228 U.S. 457, 458 (1913). This principle recognizes that the protection afforded by the Self-Incrimination Clause of the Fifth Amendment "adheres basically to the person, not to information that may incriminate him." Couch v. United States, 409 U.S., at 328. Thus, although the Fifth Amendment may protect an individual from complying with a subpoena for the production of his personal records in his possession because the very act of production may constitute a compulsory authentication of incriminating information, see Fisher v. United States, supra, a seizure of the same materials by law enforcement officers differs in a crucial respect — the individual against whom the search is directed is not required to aid in the discovery, production, or authentication of incriminating evidence. . . .
>
> We find a useful analogy to the Fifth Amendment question in those cases that deal with the "seizure" of oral communications. As the Court has explained, "[t]he constitutional

---

7. Petitioner relies on the statement in *Couch* that "possession bears the closest relationship to personal compulsion forbidden by the Fifth Amendment," 409 U.S., at 331, in support of his argument that possession of incriminating evidence itself supplies the predicate for invocation of the privilege. *Couch*, of course, was concerned with the production of documents pursuant to a summons directed to the accountant where there might have been a possibility of compulsory self-incrimination by the principal's implicit or explicit "testimony" that the documents were those identified in the summons. The risk of authentication is not present where the documents are seized pursuant to a search warrant.

privilege against self-incrimination . . . is designed to prevent the use of legal process to force from the lips of the accused individual the evidence necessary to convict him or to force him to produce and authenticate any personal documents or effects that might incriminate him." Bellis v. United States, 417 U.S., at 88. The significant aspect of this principle was apparent and applied in Hoffa v. United States, where the Court rejected the contention that an informant's "seizure" of the accused's conversation with him, and his subsequent testimony at trial concerning that conversation, violated the Fifth Amendment. The rationale was that, although the accused's statements may have been elicited by the informant for the purpose of gathering evidence against him, they were made voluntarily. We see no reasoned distinction to be made between the compulsion upon the accused in that case and the compulsion in this one. In each, the communication, whether oral or written, was made voluntarily. The fact that seizure was contemporaneous with the communication in *Hoffa* but subsequent to the communication here does not affect the question whether the accused was compelled to speak.

Finally we do not believe that permitting the introduction into evidence of a person's business records seized during an otherwise lawful search would offend or undermine any of the policies undergirding the privilege. Murphy v. Waterfront Comm'n, 378 U.S. 52, 55 (1964).[8]

In this case, petitioner, at the time he recorded his communication, at the time of the search, and at the time the records were admitted at trial, was not subjected to "the cruel trilemma of self-accusation, perjury or contempt." Indeed, he was never required to say or to do anything under penalty of sanction. Similarly, permitting the admission of the records in question does not convert our accusatorial system of justice into an inquisitorial system. "The requirement of specific charges, their proof beyond a reasonable doubt, the protection of the accused from confessions extorted through whatever form of police pressures, the right to a prompt hearing before a magistrate, the right to assistance of counsel, to be supplied by government when circumstances make it necessary, the duty to advise an accused of his constitutional rights — these are all characteristics of the accusatorial system and manifestations of its demands." Watts v. Indiana, 338 U.S. 49, 54 (1949). None of these attributes is endangered by the introduction of business records "independently secured through skillful investigation." Ibid. Further, the search for and seizure of business records pose no danger greater than that inherent in every search that evidence will be "elicited by inhumane treatment and abuses." 378 U.S., at 55. In this case, the statements seized were voluntarily committed to paper before the police arrived to search for them, and petitioner was not treated discourteously during the search. Also, the "good cause" to "disturb," ibid., petitioner was independently determined by the judge who issued the warrants; and the State bore the burden of executing them. Finally, there is no chance, in this case, of petitioner's statements being self-deprecatory and untrustworthy because they were extracted from him — they were already in existence and had been made voluntarily.

We recognize, of course, that the Fifth Amendment protects privacy to some extent. However, "the Court has never suggested that every invasion of privacy violates the

---

8. "The privilege against self-incrimination . . . reflects many of our fundamental values and most noble aspirations: our unwillingness to subject those suspected of crime to the cruel trilemma of self-accusation, perjury or contempt; our preference for an accusatorial rather than an inquisitorial system of criminal justice; our fear that self-incriminating statements will be elicited by inhumane treatment and abuses; our sense of fair play which dictates 'a fair state-individual balance by requiring the government to leave the individual alone until good cause is shown for disturbing him and by requiring the government in its contest with the individual to shoulder the entire load' . . . ; our respect for the inviolability of the human personality and of the right of each individual 'to a private enclave where he may lead a private life' . . . ; our distrust of self-deprecatory statements; and our realization that the privilege, while sometimes 'a shelter to the guilty,' is often 'a protection to the innocent.' "

privilege." Fisher v. United States, 425 U.S., at 399. Indeed, we recently held that unless incriminating testimony is "compelled," any invasion of privacy is outside the scope of the Fifth Amendment's protection, saying that "the Fifth Amendment protects against 'compelled self-incrimination, not [the disclosure of] private information.'" Id., at 401. Here, as we have already noted, petitioner was not compelled to testify in any manner.

Accordingly, we hold that the search of an individual's office for business records, their seizure, and subsequent introduction into evidence do not offend the Fifth Amendment's proscription that "[n]o person . . . shall be compelled in any criminal case to be a witness against himself."

427 U.S. at 471-477.

4. What does *Fisher* protect? Frankly, the answer to that question is not altogether clear. Some of its opacity is eliminated by recognizing that, generally speaking, production of any tangible item may communicate two different types of information. The item may speak for itself, as writings do, and as other kinds of items may (a gun which can be tested by ballistics experts, for example). This is precisely the kind of information that the Court found not to be protected by the Fifth Amendment because its creation was not compelled. The second type of information communicated by the act of production has to do with the object itself rather than its contents. By producing an object, one admits that it exists, that it is genuine, and that one believes it to be the item requested by the government. By admitting such matters, the person producing the object would provide the government sufficient information to authenticate it under normal evidentiary rules. Unlike the contents, this information is compelled and thus is protected by the Fifth Amendment.

The difficulty is that the two aspects of information discussed above are paradigm cases, but in the real world they exist as variables. Sometimes the government knows what is in a writing and who possesses it, and sometimes the government possesses virtually no information on either score. How the "act of production" rationale is supposed to apply in the complex manifestations of these two variables that are generated in real life is unclear.

Fisher may seem to be indifferent to whether the government knows the contents of a writing. After all, that is just what the Court said is not protected by the Fifth Amendment. Nonetheless, there is an intimate connection between knowing the contents and knowing of the existence of a document, a matter that the Court found to be protected. Indeed, in one sense only if the government already knows of the contents of a document can it know of the existence of the document. If the government does not know the contents of a document, producing it admits that it exists and contains whatever it contains, information that the government would not previously have possessed. And of course, if the government already knew what the document contains, in many cases the government would not need it. There is thus often tension between the government's claim that it knows of the existence of a document and that it needs it. How the "act of production" rationale resolves this tension is not clear.

5. After *Fisher* and *Andresen*, may the state obtain, in any fashion, a diary that it has probable cause to believe would incriminate the diary's owner and possessor? Should it be able to do so? Consider the following passage from Note, Formalism,

Legal Realism, and Constitutionally Protected Privacy under the Fourth and Fifth Amendments, 90 Harv. L. Rev. 945, 985-988 (1977):

> The conclusion that the fourth and fifth amendments should protect absolutely a core of one's expressions and effects is impelled by the moral and symbolic need to recognize and defend the private aspect of personality.
>
> Belief in the uniqueness of each individual is one of the fundamental moral tenets of Western society. Such uniqueness inheres in being human and is not an entitlement to be granted or withheld by the state. In fact, one of the primary purposes of law is to ensure respect for this belief by preserving each person's right to a private life free from unwanted intrusion and disclosure. Justice Brandeis saw this as the purpose underlying the fourth amendment:
>
> > The makers of our Constitution undertook to secure conditions favorable to the pursuit of happiness. They recognized the significance of man's spiritual nature, of his feelings and of his intellect. . . . They sought to protect Americans in their beliefs, their thoughts, their emotions and their sensations. They conferred, as against the Government, the right to be let alone. . . .[247]
>
> A record of one's private beliefs and emotions tells a good deal about the person. Similarly, when one intimately and privately shares such thoughts and feelings with others he reveals much of the inner person he is.[248] Such experiences may include the exchange of letters, tapes, or phone conversations as well as actual gathering and conversation. Just as recognition of the relationship between private reflection, socialization, and personality has led the Court to block legislative attempts to control intimate private conduct,[249] interference with the private life by search or subpoena should be proscribed under the fourth and fifth amendments rather than tolerated as a necessary incident of criminal law enforcement. The privacy value should not suffer abridgement simply because there is reason to believe a person is involved in criminal activity.

Consider the following excerpt that proposes that the "paper search" rule of *Boyd* can be seen to survive *Fisher* as a function of the First Amendment. If that point is recognized, the author suggests, the present state of the law provides reasonable protection for the central concerns expressed in *Boyd*.

> Properly read, Fisher v. United States stands for the proposition that no defendant may be compelled to authenticate evidence. Although this holding narrows the application of the self-incrimination clause, it adequately protects the rights of criminal defendants if the prohibitions of other amendments and evidentiary rules are properly applied. The implicit authentication doctrine of the fifth amendment prevents defendants from being forced to verify the case against them. The protection of the fourth amendment applicable to subpoenas duces tecum prohibits authorities from wholesale rummaging through a citizen's papers. Finally, the first amendment can prevent the government from probing into a defendant's most personal papers. Specific amendments answer specific concerns. Drawing on all of them, courts can forge a broad constitutional protection for all citizens' rights.

247. Olmstead v. United States, 277 U.S. 438, 478 (1928) (Brandeis, J., dissenting).

248. Charles Fried, Privacy, 77 Yale L.J. 475, 477-478 (1968). See also Griswold v. Connecticut, 381 U.S. 479, 486 (1965).

249. Roe v. Wade, 410 U.S. 113 (1973) (abortion); Eisenstadt v. Baird, 405 U.S. 438 (1972) (contraceptives for unmarried persons); Stanley v. Georgia, 394 U.S. 557 (1969) (private possession of obscene material); Griswold v. Connecticut, 381 U.S. 479 (1965) (right of marital privacy).

Note, The Rights of Criminal Defendants and the Subpoena Duces Tecum: The Aftermath of *Fisher v. United States*, 95 Harv. L. Rev. 683, 701, 702 (1982).

The author of the Krauss quotation at the beginning of the chapter, page 277 supra, although not considering the First Amendment issue, views the state of the law considerably less sanguinely:

> In light of *Andresen* and *Fisher*, *Boyd* is dead. No zone of privacy now exists that the government cannot enter to take an individual's property for the purpose of obtaining incriminating information. In most cases, the zone can be entered by the issuance of a subpoena; in the rest, it can be breached by a search warrant. . . . The words of the Constitution can legitimately be understood in many ways. Precedent and history can be used to support divergent readings. Ultimately, the difference between the various interpretations given to the Constitution can be traced to disagreements on policy.
>
> So it is with *Boyd*. That case reflected the belief of a majority of the Justices then constituting the Supreme Court that the individual's interest in the rights that the privilege against self-incrimination was designed to safeguard was more important than the government's interest in convicting criminals. The Court protected those rights as completely as possible, though it could have read the Constitution as compelling less. At least seven members of that Court shared the views expressed in the *Boyd* opinion:
>
>> Though the proceeding in question is divested of many of the aggravating effects of actual search and seizure, yet, as before said, it contains their substance and essence, and effects their essential purpose. It may be that it is the obnoxious thing in its mildest and least repulsive form, but illegitimate and unconstitutional practices get their first footing in that way, namely, by silent approaches and slight deviations from legal modes of procedure. This can only be obviated by adhering to the rule that constitutional provisions for the security of person and property should be liberally construed. A close and literal construction of them deprives them of half their efficacy, and leads to gradual depreciation of the right, as if it consisted more in sound than in substance. It is the duty of courts to be watchful for the constitutional rights of the citizen, and guard against any stealthy encroachments thereon. Their motto should be *obsta principiis*.[138]
>
> The Burger Court has rejected *Boyd* because it no longer considers those values to be paramount; it is more impressed by the government's interest in combatting crime. In *Couch*, Justice Powell captured the spirit of the current Court: "It is important, in applying constitutional principles, to interpret them in light of the fundamental interests of personal liberty they were meant to serve. Respect for these principles is eroded when they leap their proper bounds to interfere with the legitimate interest of society in enforcement of its laws and collection of the revenues."[139] Accordingly, *Boyd* is dead. But the Court refuses to take the final step of overruling it.
>
> Justice Brandeis once called *Boyd* "a case that will be remembered as long as civil liberty lives in the United States."[140] At least it deserves a decent burial.

Krauss, 76 Mich. L. Rev. at 211-212.

To which view do you subscribe, and why? The trend is to permit even diaries to be seized by the government. A juvenile was convicted of murder on the basis of her diary, for example. See "Dear Diary" teen convicted of murder, Chicago Tribune, Sunday, June 12, 1993, sec. 1, at 8. The possible demise of *Boyd* has

138. 116 U.S. at 635.
139. Couch v. United States, 409 U.S. 322, 336 (1973).
140. Olmstead v. United States, 277 U.S. 438, 474 (Brandeis, J., dissenting).

not been universally decried. See Robert S. Gerstein, The Demise of *Boyd:* Self-Incrimination and Private Papers in the Burger Court, 27 UCLA L. Rev. 343 (1979), arguing that *Boyd* obscured the rationale of the Fifth Amendment's concern for autonomy, and Henry J. Friendly, The Fifth Amendment Tomorrow: The Case for Constitutional Change, 37 U. Cin. L. Rev. 671 (1968), arguing that *Boyd* should be overruled.

The circuits are split on whether the Fifth Amendment provides any protection for the contents of private papers such as diaries. For a discussion, see In re Grand Jury Subpoena Duces Tecum Dated October 29, 1992, 1 F.3d 87 (2d Cir. 1993). In Senate Select Committee on Ethics v. Senator Bob Packwood, 845 F. Supp. 17 (D.D.C. 1994), the United States District Court for the District of Columbia enforced a Senatorial subpoena against Senator Packwood requiring the production of personal diaries relevant to an ethics investigation. Both the United States Court of Appeals for the District of Columbia Circuit and the Supreme Court refused to stay the order pending appeal. Senator Packwood resigned rather than comply, and thus the order was not considered further on appeal. In 1992, prosecutors were allowed to use a defendant's personal diary to prove he sent a letter bomb. Moody v. United States, 977 F.2d 1425 (11th Cir. 1992). In Canada, an appellate court has upheld an order to turn over a diary. Vickers v. Rondpre, Nos. CA017117, CA017354 (C. App. for British Columbia July 13, 1993). However, the Ninth Circuit has held that a subpoena for a diary could violate the Fifth Amendment. In re Grand Jury Proceedings, 759 F.2d 1418 (9th Cir. 1985).

6. In light of *Schmerber* and the other cases we have been considering, the Court has held that individuals can be required to give voice exemplars, United States v. Wade, page 255 supra; and handwriting exemplars, Gilbert v. California, page 257 supra. In such cases, an individual is normally subpoenaed to appear. The Court has held that subpoenas do not need to meet the probable cause standard of the Fourth Amendment. Rather, they must call for relevant material and not be unduly burdensome. The author argues that one solution for fears of overly broad subpoenas, as well as for fears concerning the demise of *Boyd*, is to require a higher than normal standard for obtaining private papers. There are, however, due process limits on the extraction of evidence from a suspect's body. In Rochin v. California, 342 U.S. 165 (1952), the Court reversed a conviction for possession of drugs that was based in part on evidentiary use of morphine tablets obtained by forcibly injecting an emetic into the defendant, over his objection, causing him to vomit up the capsules.

In Pennsylvania v. Muniz, 496 U.S. 582 (1990), the Court concluded that the incriminating inferences from a suspect's inability to perform sobriety tests were admissible on the *Wade/Gilbert* ground that there was no testimonial compulsion. *Muniz* is excerpted in Chapter 6 at pages 784-786.

7. If the defendant can be forced to yield information concerning his or her physical characteristics, should the defendant have the right to present such information in the defense case without waiving Fifth Amendment rights? Yes, say most courts. See, e.g., United States v. Bay, 748 F.2d 1344 (9th Cir. 1984).

8. Has the Supreme Court finally buried *Boyd*? Perhaps the reports of its demise are premature. In United States v. Doe, 465 U.S. 605 (1984), the Court concluded that "the Fifth Amendment privilege against compelled self-incrimination applies to the business records of a sole proprietorship," including *Fisher*'s authentication/

act of production doctrine, and affirmed the lower courts' findings that the act of production in this case would be incriminating.

By contrast, in a curious opinion in Braswell v. United States, 487 U.S. 99 (1988), a five-to-four majority of the Court addressed the question

> whether the custodian of corporate records may resist a subpoena for such records on the ground that the act of production would incriminate him in violation of the Fifth Amendment. We conclude that he may not. . . .
>
> There is no question but that the contents of the subpoenaed business records are not privileged. See *Doe*, supra; Fisher v. United States. Similarly, petitioner asserts no self-incrimination claim on behalf of the corporations; it is well established that such artificial entities are not protected by the Fifth Amendment. Petitioner instead relies solely upon the argument that his act of producing the documents has independent testimonial significance, which would incriminate him individually, and that the Fifth Amendment prohibits government compulsion of that act. The bases for this argument are extrapolated from the decisions of this Court in *Fisher* and *Doe*. . . .
>
> Had petitioner conducted his business as a sole proprietorship, *Doe* would require that he be provided the opportunity to show that his act of production would entail testimonial self-incrimination. But petitioner has operated his business through the corporate form, and we have long recognized that for purposes of the Fifth Amendment, corporations and other collective entities are treated differently from individuals. This doctrine — known as the collective entity rule — has a lengthy and distinguished pedigree [which the Court proceeded to discuss, citing cases such as Wilson v. United States, 221 U.S. 361 (1911), United States v. White, 322 U.S. 694 (1944), and Bellis v. United States, 417 U.S. 85 (1974)]. . . .
>
> The plain mandate of these decisions is that without regard to whether the subpoena is addressed to the corporation, or as here, to the individual in his capacity as a custodian, a corporate custodian such as petitioner may not resist a subpoena for corporate records on Fifth Amendment grounds. Petitioner argues, however, that this rule falls in the wake of Fisher v. United States, and United States v. Doe. In essence, petitioner's argument is as follows: In response to Boyd v. United States, with its privacy rationale shielding personal books and records, the Court developed the collective entity rule, which declares simply that corporate records are not private and therefore are not protected by the Fifth Amendment. The collective entity decisions were concerned with the contents of the documents subpoenaed, however, and not with the act of production. In *Fisher* and *Doe*, the Court moved away from the privacy based collective entity rule, replacing it with a compelled testimony standard under which the contents of business documents are never privileged but the act of producing the documents may be. Under this new regime, the act of production privilege is available without regard to the entity whose records are being sought. . . .
>
> To be sure, the holding in *Fisher* — later reaffirmed in *Doe* — embarked upon a new course of Fifth Amendment analysis. We cannot agree, however, that it rendered the collective entity rule obsolete. The agency rationale undergirding the collective entity decisions, in which custodians asserted that production of entity records would incriminate them personally, survives. . . . [T]he Court has consistently recognized that the custodian of corporate or entity records holds those documents in a representative rather than a personal capacity. Artificial entities such as corporations may act only through their agents, and a custodian's assumption of his representative capacity leads to certain obligations, including the duty to produce corporate records on proper demand by the Government. Under those circumstances, the custodian's act of production is not deemed a personal act, but rather an act of the corporation. Any claim of Fifth Amendment privilege asserted by the agent would

be tantamount to a claim of privilege by the corporation — which of course possesses no such privilege. . . .

Although a corporate custodian is not entitled to resist a subpoena on the ground that his act of production will be personally incriminating, we do think certain consequences flow from the fact that the custodian's act of production is one in his representative rather than personal capacity. Because the custodian acts as a representative, the act is deemed one of the corporation and not the individual. Therefore, the Government concedes, as it must, that it may make no evidentiary use of the "individual act" against the individual. For example, in a criminal prosecution against the custodian, the Government may not introduce into evidence before the jury the fact that the subpoena was served upon and the corporation's documents were delivered by one particular individual, the custodian. The Government has the right, however, to use the corporation's act of production against the custodian. The Government may offer testimony — for example, from the process server who delivered the subpoena and from the individual who received the records — establishing that the corporation produced the records subpoenaed. The jury may draw from the corporation's act of production the conclusion that the records in question are authentic corporate records, which the corporation possessed, and which it produced in response to the subpoena. And if the defendant held a prominent position within the corporation that produced the records, the jury may, just as it would had someone else produced the documents, reasonably infer that he had possession of the documents or knowledge of their contents. Because the jury is not told that the defendant produced the records, any nexus between the defendant and the documents results solely from the corporation's act of production and other evidence in the case.[11] . . .

NOTES AND QUESTIONS ON *BRASWELL*

1. What do you think of a jurisprudence that gives details of enterprise law substantial constitutional significance? Perhaps the problem lies in *Fisher*. Does it stand for something too complicated to be administered? Professor Heidt thinks perhaps so. Robert Heidt, The Fifth Amendment Privilege and Documents — Cutting *Fisher*'s Tangled Line, 49 Mo. L. Rev. 439 (1984). See also Kevin R. Reitz, Clients, Lawyers and the Fifth Amendment: The Need for a Projected Privilege, 41 Duke L.J. 572 (1991). A substantial literature is being produced that examines the relationship between the Fifth Amendment and demands for the production of documents. See, e.g., Robert P. Mosteller, Simplifying Subpoena Law: Taking the Fifth Amendment Seriously, 73 Va. L. Rev. 1 (1987); Note, Fifth Amendment Privilege for Producing Corporate Documents, 84 Mich. L. Rev. 1544 (1986).

2. The corporation in *Braswell* was basically a one-man operation, much like the sole proprietorship in *Doe*. Yet the Fifth Amendment applies to the subpoena in

---

11. We reject the suggestion that the limitation on the evidentiary use of the custodian's act of production is the equivalent of constructive use immunity barred under our decision in *Doe*, 465 U.S., at 616-617. Rather, the limitation is a necessary concomitant of the notion that a corporate custodian acts as an agent and not an individual when he produces corporate records in response to a subpoena addressed to him in his representative capacity.

We leave open the question whether the agency rationale supports compelling a custodian to produce corporate records when the custodian is able to establish, by showing for example that he is the sole employee and officer of the corporation, that the jury would inevitably conclude that he produced the records.

Doe but not to the one in *Braswell*. Why, exactly? Does the *Braswell* Court offer a satisfying answer?

Consider a different answer. Suppose the privilege *did* apply to subpoenas for corporate documents. Now suppose that the government issues a subpoena for documents in a corporate vice-president's file cabinet. The documents technically incriminate the corporate vice-president, but only technically. On the other hand, if they come to light, the documents are sure to send the CEO to prison. Might the vice-president be tempted to decline to produce the documents, allegedly on the ground that they incriminate him (but really in order to save the CEO's hide)? Such assertions of the privilege, nominally due to fear of self-incrimination but actually designed to avoid incriminating someone else, would be very common indeed if corporate documents were covered by the privilege. As for the application of the collective entity to one-person corporations like the one in *Braswell*: if *Braswell* came out the other way, how would courts draw the line between corporations that count as corporations for purposes of the privilege and corporations that are treated like sole proprietorships?

3. Reread the last of the quoted paragraphs from the *Braswell* majority opinion. Before that paragraph, the Court had explained that Braswell did not enjoy any Fifth Amendment protection when responding to a subpoena for corporate documents. But then, the Court goes on to say that, maybe, Braswell's act of producing the documents could not be used against him personally — which suggests that he does enjoy Fifth Amendment protection after all. What gives?

4. Why can individuals be required to turn over but not to testify about documents? According to the *Fisher* line of cases, the act of production is, or at least can be, testimonial. If any particular act is testimonial, what coherent theory allows that form of testimony to be compelled but provides protection for some other form of testimony? If a rose by any other name would smell as sweet, why isn't testimony protected no matter what the label?

5. Reconsider note 6, page 317 supra. Why doesn't the act of production rationale apply to such matters as voice and handwriting exemplars?

6. *Doe* and *Braswell* are important criminal procedure cases, but they are more than that: because the scope of the subpoena power is so important to the administration of a variety of regulatory statutes, they have an impact on the law that undergirds the regulatory state. What difference do you think that makes in the Court's reasoning, and its results?

The point may be broader. If there is one constant in the modern state, it is the need for information. Whether on tax forms, in OSHA or EPA inspections, in SEC investigations, or through the various ways government employers monitor their employees, the government is constantly inspecting otherwise private places or requiring citizens to produce (or to step aside and let the government uncover) otherwise private information. Presumably the privacy value that underlies *Boyd* applies to information gathering *outside* the criminal process — after all, the privacy intrusion does not depend on whether it is a police officer or an IRS agent who is doing the looking. Does this mean that any attempt to seriously protect privacy would place severe limits on government activities that we have come to accept as routine? Does that explain *Boyd*'s checkered history? Does it imply that constitutional protection of individual privacy is necessarily linked with pro-"laissez-faire" constitutional law? The answer to each of these questions is 'yes,' according to

William J. Stuntz, Privacy's Problem and the Law of Criminal Procedure, 93 Mich.
L. Rev. 1016, 1030-1034, 1050-1054 (1995):

Law enforcement, civil or criminal, depends on information. That information is often "private" in the sense that it rests in the hands of someone who would like it kept secret. This description fits almost all incriminating evidence in the hands of a criminal defendant, information that sometimes cannot be extracted due to the Fifth Amendment. Much of the information the system needs is also "private" in a more meaningful sense. It is of a type that many people, not just a particular litigant, might care about keeping secret. A cocaine dealer may be convicted because of drugs found in his bedroom closet; even those who comply with the drug laws wish to keep people out of their bedroom closets. A fraud conviction may depend on evidence of a large bank deposit on a given date; even wholly honest citizens value the secrecy of their bank transactions.

Fourth Amendment law purports to protect most information that is private in this second sense. . . .

If one starts with this definition of private, protecting private information outside the criminal context would have huge substantive effects, especially if the information is protected absolutely—without any provision for disclosure in response to a showing of relevance or need or cause. . . . [I]n any system that seeks to do more than pro forma regulation of business or finance or that tries to police the distribution of guns or drugs, absolute protection of private information is unacceptable unless private is defined so narrowly as to make the enterprise pointless. Much criminal law enforcement, and an even larger category of civil regulation, would be impossible. . . .

That, in a nutshell, is the substantive problem with protecting the kinds of privacy interests we claim to protect in search and seizure cases. Wherever the regulatory state engages in any form of compelled information gathering (and it does so everywhere), there is an enormous cost to taking privacy interests seriously: doing so requires judicial judgments about whether one regulatory path is more reasonable than another. That sounds uncomfortably close to the regime that the Supreme Court sought to bury a half-century ago [as it began the process of limiting *Boyd*'s reach]. . . .

Had the cases continued along the path [of a broad reading of *Boyd*], *Boyd* might have come to play much the same role in constitutional law, and perhaps the same villain's role in constitutional theory, that Lochner v. New York and its ilk came to play. Government regulation required lots of information, and *Boyd* came dangerously close to giving regulated actors a blanket entitlement to nondisclosure. It is hard to see how modern health, safety, environmental, or economic regulation would be possible in such a regime.

As it happened, the cases did not continue along *Boyd*'s path. Beginning in the first decade of this century, *Boyd* was effectively cabined, so much so that its implications for the world outside criminal justice have been largely forgotten. Hale v. Henkel held that corporations have no privilege against self-incrimination and receive only slight protection against unreasonable searches and seizures. Marron v. United States held that instrumentalities of crime could be seized without violating the Fourth or Fifth Amendments, and also that documents could be instrumentalities. Shapiro v. United States held that the privilege was not violated by asking someone to produce "required records"—meaning any records that the government ordered him to keep—no matter how incriminating the records' contents might be. These cases left *Boyd* largely inapplicable to the burgeoning world of government regulation. The records in *Boyd* itself were probably instrumentalities under *Marron*, and the documents sought in the various ICC cases of the 1890s might well have been judged "required records" by the standards used a half-century later.

The Court did not explain its position in these cases in privacy terms. By and large, it justified the outcomes by political necessity. *Hale*, which arose out of a grand jury investigation of antitrust violations, is the clearest example. The argument for a corporate privilege was strong: Wigmore, then the foremost expert on the privilege's scope and meaning, thought it applied to corporations as it did to individuals. That was the position the Court had taken with respect to the Due Process Clause, and like that clause the Fifth Amendment privilege applied to "any person." Moreover, the privacy interest in corporate documents was at least as plausible as *Boyd*'s privacy interest in his invoices. Even if a corporation could not "feel" privacy intrusions, its shareholders and employees could; as with due process claims, corporate assertion of the privilege against self-incrimination was a way of protecting the flesh-and-blood people whose money and labor made the corporation run. *Hale* rejected all these arguments in a peremptory paragraph, stating that "the privilege claimed would practically nullify" the Sherman Act.

In other words, *Boyd*-style privacy protection was not compatible with activist government, because government cannot be very activist if it cannot force people to tell it things. Cases like *Hale* resolved the conflict by yielding ground—preserving privacy protection, but only within boundaries that themselves had nothing whatever to do with privacy. Privacy's substantive shadow was kept within acceptable bounds, but only by fiat.

Professor Stuntz both accurately captures the consistent reduction in the significance of the *Boyd* case and identifies its cause in the demands of the modern bureaucratic state. Perhaps the single most remarkable aspect of these developments has been their consistency. With the exception of a few ambiguous paragraphs scattered throughout the cases concerning the potential scope of immunity following responses to subpoenas, the Supreme Court has consistently cut back the potential scope of *Boyd*-like claims. Has that process come to an end? Consider the Court's most recent foray into this area.

UNITED STATES v. HUBBELL

Certiorari to the United States Court of Appeals for the District of Columbia Circuit
530 U.S. 27 (2000)

JUSTICE STEVENS delivered the opinion of the Court.

The two questions presented concern the scope of a witness' protection against compelled self-incrimination: (1) whether the Fifth Amendment privilege protects a witness from being compelled to disclose the existence of incriminating documents that the Government is unable to describe with reasonable particularity; and (2) if the witness produces such documents pursuant to a grant of immunity, whether 18 U.S.C. §6002 prevents the Government from using them to prepare criminal charges against him.[2]

---

2. Section 6002 provides: "Whenever a witness refuses, on the basis of his privilege against self-incrimination, to testify or provide other information in a proceeding before or ancillary to—

I

This proceeding arises out of the second prosecution of respondent, Webster Hubbell, commenced by the Independent Counsel appointed in August 1994 to investigate possible violations of federal law relating to the Whitewater Development Corporation. The first prosecution was terminated pursuant to a plea bargain. In December 1994, respondent pleaded guilty to charges of mail fraud and tax evasion arising out of his billing practices as a member of an Arkansas law firm from 1989 to 1992, and was sentenced to 21 months in prison. In the plea agreement, respondent promised to provide the Independent Counsel with "full, complete, accurate, and truthful information" about matters relating to the Whitewater investigation.

The second prosecution resulted from the Independent Counsel's attempt to determine whether respondent had violated that promise. In October 1996, while respondent was incarcerated, the Independent Counsel served him with a subpoena duces tecum calling for the production of 11 categories of documents before a grand jury sitting in Little Rock, Arkansas. On November 19, he appeared before the grand jury and invoked his Fifth Amendment privilege against self-incrimination. In response to questioning by the prosecutor, respondent initially refused "to state whether there are documents within my possession, custody, or control responsive to the Subpoena." Thereafter, the prosecutor produced an order, which had previously been obtained from the District Court pursuant to 18 U.S.C. §6003(a),[3] directing him to respond to the subpoena and granting him immunity "to the extent allowed by law."[4] Respondent then produced 13,120 pages of documents and records and responded to a series of questions that established that those were all of the documents in his custody or control that were responsive to the commands in the subpoena, with the exception of a few documents he claimed were shielded by the attorney-client and attorney work-product privileges.

The contents of the documents produced by respondent provided the Independent Counsel with the information that led to this second prosecution. On April 30, 1998, a grand jury in the District of Columbia returned a 10-count indictment charging respondent with various tax-related crimes and mail and wire fraud. The District Court dismissed the indictment relying, in part, on the ground that the Independent Counsel's use of the subpoenaed documents violated §6002 because all of the evidence he would offer against respondent at trial derived

---

"(1) a court or grand jury of the United States,
"(2) an agency of the United States, or
"(3) either House of Congress, a joint committee of the two Houses, or a committee or a subcommittee of either House,
    "and the person presiding over the proceeding communicates to the witness an order issued under this title, the witness may not refuse to comply with the order on the basis of his privilege against self-incrimination; but no testimony or other information compelled under the order (or any information directly or indirectly derived from such testimony or other information) may be used against the witness in any criminal case, except a prosecution for perjury, giving a false statement, or otherwise failing to comply with the order."

3. Section 6003(a) authorizes a district court to issue an order requiring an "individual to give testimony or provide other information which he refuses to give or provide on the basis of his privilege against self-incrimination." The effect of such an order is covered by §6002, quoted in n. 2, supra.

4. In re Grand Jury Proceedings, No. GJ-96-3 (E.D. Ark., Nov. 14, 1996), App. 60-61.

either directly or indirectly from the testimonial aspects of respondent's immunized act of producing those documents.[6] Noting that the Independent Counsel had admitted that he was not investigating tax-related issues when he issued the subpoena, and that he had "'learned about the unreported income and other crimes from studying the records' contents,'" the District Court characterized the subpoena as "the quintessential fishing expedition."

The Court of Appeals vacated the judgment and remanded for further proceedings. The majority concluded that the District Court had incorrectly relied on the fact that the Independent Counsel did not have prior knowledge of the contents of the subpoenaed documents. The question the District Court should have addressed was the extent of the Government's independent knowledge of the documents' existence and authenticity, and of respondent's possession or control of them. It explained:

> On remand, the district court should hold a hearing in which it seeks to establish the extent and detail of the [G]overnment's knowledge of Hubbell's financial affairs (or of the paperwork documenting it) on the day the subpoena issued. It is only then that the court will be in a position to assess the testimonial value of Hubbell's response to the subpoena. Should the Independent Counsel prove capable of demonstrating with reasonable particularity a prior awareness that the exhaustive litany of documents sought in the subpoena existed and were in Hubbell's possession, then the wide distance evidently traveled from the subpoena to the substantive allegations contained in the indictment would be based upon legitimate intermediate steps. To the extent that the information conveyed through Hubbell's compelled act of production provides the necessary linkage, however, the indictment deriving therefrom is tainted.

In the opinion of the dissenting judge, the majority failed to give full effect to the distinction between the contents of the documents and the limited testimonial significance of the act of producing them. In his view, as long as the prosecutor could make use of information contained in the documents or derived therefrom without any reference to the fact that respondent had produced them in response to a subpoena, there would be no improper use of the testimonial aspect of the immunized act of production. In other words, the constitutional privilege and the statute conferring use immunity would only shield the witness from the use of any information resulting from his subpoena response "beyond what the prosecutor would receive if the documents appeared in the grand jury room or in his office unsolicited and unmarked, like manna from heaven."

On remand, the Independent Counsel acknowledged that he could not satisfy the "reasonable particularity" standard prescribed by the Court of Appeals and entered into a conditional plea agreement with respondent. In essence, the agreement provides for the dismissal of the charges unless this Court's disposition of the case makes it reasonably likely that respondent's "act of production immunity" would not pose a significant bar to his prosecution. The case is not moot, however, because the agreement also provides for the entry of a guilty plea and a sentence that will not include incarceration if we should reverse and issue an opinion that is

---

6. As an independent basis for dismissal, the District Court also concluded that the Independent Counsel had exceeded his jurisdiction under the Ethics in Government Act of 1978, as amended by the Independent Counsel Reauthorization Act of 1994, 28 U.S.C. §§591-599. That holding was reversed by the Court of Appeals and is not at issue here.

sufficiently favorable to the Government to satisfy that condition. Despite that agreement, we granted the Independent Counsel's petition for a writ of certiorari in order to determine the precise scope of a grant of immunity with respect to the production of documents in response to a subpoena. We now affirm. . . .

IV

The Government correctly emphasizes that the testimonial aspect of a response to a subpoena duces tecum does nothing more than establish the existence, authenticity, and custody of items that are produced. We assume that the Government is also entirely correct in its submission that it would not have to advert to respondent's act of production in order to prove the existence, authenticity, or custody of any documents that it might offer in evidence at a criminal trial; indeed, the Government disclaims any need to introduce any of the documents produced by respondent into evidence in order to prove the charges against him. It follows, according to the Government, that it has no intention of making improper "use" of respondent's compelled testimony.

The question, however, is not whether the response to the subpoena may be introduced into evidence at his criminal trial. That would surely be a prohibited "use" of the immunized act of production. But the fact that the Government intends no such use of the act of production leaves open the separate question whether it has already made "derivative use" of the testimonial aspect of that act in obtaining the indictment against respondent and in preparing its case for trial. It clearly has.

It is apparent from the text of the subpoena itself that the prosecutor needed respondent's assistance both to identify potential sources of information and to produce those sources. See Appendix, infra. Given the breadth of the description of the 11 categories of documents called for by the subpoena, the collection and production of the materials demanded was tantamount to answering a series of interrogatories asking a witness to disclose the existence and location of particular documents fitting certain broad descriptions. The assembly of literally hundreds of pages of material in response to a request for "any and all documents reflecting, referring, or relating to any direct or indirect sources of money or other things of value received by or provided to" an individual or members of his family during a 3-year period, is the functional equivalent of the preparation of an answer to either a detailed written interrogatory or a series of oral questions at a discovery deposition. Entirely apart from the contents of the 13,120 pages of materials that respondent produced in this case, it is undeniable that providing a catalog of existing documents fitting within any of the 11 broadly worded subpoena categories could provide a prosecutor with a "lead to incriminating evidence," or "a link in the chain of evidence needed to prosecute."

Indeed, the record makes it clear that that is what happened in this case. The documents were produced before a grand jury sitting in the Eastern District of Arkansas in aid of the Independent Counsel's attempt to determine whether respondent had violated a commitment in his first plea agreement. The use of those sources of information eventually led to the return of an indictment by a grand jury sitting in the District of Columbia for offenses that apparently are unrelated to that plea agreement. What the District Court characterized as a "fishing expedition" did produce a fish, but not the one that the Independent Counsel expected to hook. It is abundantly clear that the testimonial aspect of respondent's act of producing subpoenaed documents was the first step in a chain of evidence that led to this prosecution. The documents did not magically appear in the prosecutor's office like "manna from heaven." They arrived there only after respondent asserted his constitutional privilege, received a grant of immunity, and — under the compulsion of the District Court's order — took the mental and physical steps necessary to provide the prosecutor with an accurate inventory of the many sources of potentially incriminating evidence sought by the subpoena. It was only through respondent's truthful reply to the subpoena[23] that the Government received the incriminating documents of which it made "substantial use . . . in the investigation that led to the indictment." Brief for United States 3.

For these reasons, we cannot accept the Government's submission that respondent's immunity did not preclude its derivative use of the produced documents because its "possession of the documents [was] the fruit only of a simple physical act — the act of producing the documents." It was unquestionably necessary for respondent to make extensive use of "the contents of his own mind" in identifying the hundreds of documents responsive to the requests in the subpoena. The assembly of those documents was like telling an inquisitor the combination to a wall safe, not like being forced to surrender the key to a strongbox. The Government's anemic view of respondent's act of production as a mere physical act that is principally non-testimonial in character and can be entirely divorced from its "implicit" testimonial aspect so as to constitute a "legitimate, wholly independent source" (as required by *Kastigar*) for the documents produced simply fails to account for these realities.

In sum, we have no doubt that the constitutional privilege against self-incrimination protects the target of a grand jury investigation from being compelled to answer questions designed to elicit information about the existence of sources of potentially incriminating evidence. That constitutional privilege has the same application to the testimonial aspect of a response to a subpoena seeking discovery of those sources. Before the District Court, the Government arguably conceded that respondent's act of production in this case had a testimonial aspect that entitled him to respond to the subpoena by asserting his privilege against self-incrimination. See 167 F.3d, at 580 (noting District Court's finding that "Hubbell's compelled act of production required him to make communications as to the existence, possession, and authenticity of the subpoenaed documents"). On appeal and again before this Court, however, the Government has argued that the communicative aspect of respondent's act of producing ordinary business records is insufficiently "testimonial" to support a claim of privilege because the existence and possession of such records by any businessman is a "foregone conclusion" under our decision in Fisher v. United States. This argument both misreads *Fisher* and ignores our subsequent decision in United States v. Doe, 465 U.S. 605 (1984).

---

23. See William J. Stuntz, Self-Incrimination and Excuse, 88 Colum. L. Rev. 1227, 1228-1229, 1256-1259, 1277-1279 (1988) (discussing the conceptual link between truth-telling and the privilege in the document production context); Samuel A. Alito, Jr., Documents and the Privilege Against Self-Incrimination, 48 U. Pitt. L. Rev. 27, 47 (1986); 8 J. Wigmore, Evidence §2264, p. 379 (J. McNaughton rev. 1961) (describing a subpoena duces tecum as "process relying on [the witness's] moral responsibility for truthtelling").

... *Fisher* involved summonses seeking production of working papers prepared by the taxpayers' accountants that the IRS knew were in the possession of the taxpayers' attorneys. In rejecting the taxpayers' claim that these documents were protected by the Fifth Amendment privilege, we stated:

> "It is doubtful that implicitly admitting the existence and possession of the papers rises to the level of testimony within the protection of the Fifth Amendment. The papers belong to the *accountant*, were prepared by him, and are the kind usually prepared by an accountant working on the tax returns of his client. Surely the Government is in no way relying on the "truthtelling" of the *taxpayer* to prove the existence of or his access to the documents. . . . The existence and location of the papers are a foregone conclusion and the taxpayer adds little or nothing to the sum total of the Government's information by conceding that he in fact has the papers." 425 U.S. at 411 (emphases added).

Whatever the scope of this "foregone conclusion" rationale, the facts of this case plainly fall outside of it. While in *Fisher* the Government already knew that the documents were in the attorneys' possession and could independently confirm their existence and authenticity through the accountants who created them, here the Government has not shown that it had any prior knowledge of either the existence or the whereabouts of the 13,120 pages of documents ultimately produced by respondent. The Government cannot cure this deficiency through the over-broad argument that a businessman such as respondent will always possess general business and tax records that fall within the broad categories described in this subpoena. The *Doe* subpoenas also sought several broad categories of general business records, yet we upheld the District Court's finding that the act of producing those records would involve testimonial self-incrimination. Given our conclusion that respondent's act of production had a testimonial aspect, at least with respect to the existence and location of the documents sought by the Government's subpoena, respondent could not be compelled to produce those documents without first receiving a grant of immunity under §6003. As we construed §6002 in *Kastigar*, such immunity is co-extensive with the constitutional privilege. *Kastigar* requires that respondent's motion to dismiss the indictment on immunity grounds be granted unless the Government proves that the evidence it used in obtaining the indictment and proposed to use at trial was derived from legitimate sources "wholly independent" of the testimonial aspect of respondent's immunized conduct in assembling and producing the documents described in the subpoena. The Government, however, does not claim that it could make such a showing. Rather, it contends that its prosecution of respondent must be considered proper unless someone — presumably respondent — shows that "there is some substantial relation between the compelled testimonial communications implicit in the act of production (as opposed to the act of production standing alone) and some aspect of the information used in the investigation or the evidence presented at trial." Brief for United States 9. We could not accept this submission without repudiating the basis for our conclusion in *Kastigar* that the statutory guarantee of use and derivative-use immunity is as broad as the constitutional privilege itself. This we are not prepared to do.

Accordingly, the indictment against respondent must be dismissed. The judgment of the Court of Appeals is affirmed.

It is so ordered.

APPENDIX TO OPINION OF THE COURT

On October 31, 1996, upon application by the Independent Counsel, a subpoena was issued commanding respondent to appear and testify before the grand jury of the United States District Court for the Eastern District of Arkansas on November 19, 1996, and to bring with him various documents described in a "Subpoena Rider" as follows:

"A. Any and all documents reflecting, referring, or relating to any direct or indirect sources of money or other things of value received by or provided to Webster Hubbell, his wife, or children from January 1, 1993 to the present, including but not limited to the identity of employers or clients of legal or any other type of work.

"B. Any and all documents reflecting, referring, or relating to any direct or indirect sources of money or other things of value received by or provided to Webster Hubbell, his wife, or children from January 1, 1993 to the present, including but not limited to billing memoranda, draft statements, bills, final statements, and/or bills for work performed or time billed from January 1, 1993 to the present.

"C. Copies of all bank records of Webster Hubbell, his wife, or children for all accounts from January 1, 1993 to the present, including but not limited to all statements, registers and ledgers, cancelled checks, deposit items, and wire transfers.

"D. Any and all documents reflecting, referring, or relating to time worked or billed by Webster Hubbell from January 1, 1993 to the present, including but not limited to original time sheets, books, notes, papers, and/or computer records.

"E. Any and all documents reflecting, referring, or relating to expenses incurred by and/or disbursements of money by Webster Hubbell during the course of any work performed or to be performed by Mr. Hubbell from January 1, 1993 to the present.

"F. Any and all documents reflecting, referring, or relating to Webster Hubbell's schedule of activities, including but not limited to any and all calendars, daytimers, time books, appointment books, diaries, records of reverse telephone toll calls, credit card calls, telephone message slips, logs, other telephone records, minutes, databases, electronic mail messages, travel records, itineraries, tickets for transportation of any kind, payments, bills, expense backup documentation, schedules, and/or any other document or database that would disclose Webster Hubbell's activities from January 1, 1993 to the present.

"G. Any and all documents reflecting, referring, or relating to any retainer agreements or contracts for employment of Webster Hubbell, his wife, or his children from January 1, 1993 to the present.

"H. Any and all tax returns and tax return information, including but not limited to all W-2s, form 1099s, schedules, draft returns, work papers, and backup documents filed, created or held by or on behalf of Webster Hubbell, his wife, his children, and/or any business in which he, his wife, or his children holds or has held an interest, for the tax years 1993 to the present.

"I. Any and all documents reflecting, referring, or relating to work performed or to be performed or on behalf of the City of Los Angeles, California, the Los Angeles Department of Airports or any other Los Angeles municipal Governmental entity, Mary Leslie, and/or Alan S. Arkatov, including but not limited to correspondence, retainer agreements, contracts, time sheets, appointment calendars, activity calendars, diaries, billing statements, billing memoranda, telephone records, telephone message slips, telephone credit card statements, itineraries, tickets for transportation, payment records, expense receipts, ledgers, check registers, notes, memoranda, electronic mail, bank deposit items, cashier's checks, traveler's checks, wire transfer records and/or other records of financial transactions.

"J. Any and all documents reflecting, referring, or relating to work performed or to be performed by Webster Hubbell, his wife, or his children on the recommendation, counsel or other influence of Mary Leslie and/or Alan S. Arkatov, including but not limited to correspondence, retainer agreements, contracts, time sheets, appointment calendars, activity calendars, diaries, billing statements, billing memoranda, telephone records, telephone message slips, telephone credit card statements, itineraries, tickets for transportation, payment records, expense receipts, ledgers, check registers, notes, memoranda, electronic mail, bank deposit items, cashier's checks, traveler's checks, wire transfer records and/or other records of financial transactions.

"K. Any and all documents related to work performed or to be performed for or on behalf of Lippo Ltd. (formerly Public Finance (H.K.) Ltd.), the Lippo Group, the Lippo Bank, Mochtar Riady, James Riady, Stephen Riady, John Luen Wai Lee, John Huang, Mark W. Grobmyer, C. Joseph Giroir, Jr., or any affiliate, subsidiary, or corporation owned or controlled by or related to the aforementioned entities or individuals, including but not limited to correspondence, retainer agreements, contracts, time sheets, appointment calendars, activity calendars, diaries, billing statements, billing memoranda, telephone records, telephone message slips, telephone credit card statements, itineraries, tickets for transportation, payment records, expense receipts, ledgers, check registers, notes, memoranda, electronic mail, bank deposit items, cashier's checks, traveler's checks, wire transfer records and/or other records of financial transactions."

JUSTICE THOMAS, with whom JUSTICE SCALIA joins, concurring.

Our decision today involves the application of the act-of-production doctrine, which provides that persons compelled to turn over incriminating papers or other physical evidence pursuant to a subpoena duces tecum or a summons may invoke the Fifth Amendment privilege against self-incrimination as a bar to production only where the act of producing the evidence would contain "testimonial" features. I join the opinion of the Court because it properly applies this doctrine, but I write separately to note that this doctrine may be inconsistent with the original meaning of the Fifth Amendment's Self-Incrimination Clause. A substantial body of evidence suggests that the Fifth Amendment privilege protects against the compelled production not just of incriminating testimony, but of any incriminating evidence. In a future case, I would be willing to reconsider the scope and meaning of the Self-Incrimination Clause. . . .

This Court has not always taken the approach to the Fifth Amendment that we follow today. The first case interpreting the Self-Incrimination Clause — Boyd v. United States — was decided, though not explicitly, in accordance with the understanding that "witness" means one who gives evidence [whether in testimonial form or otherwise]. In *Boyd*, this Court unanimously held that the Fifth Amendment protects a defendant against compelled production of books and papers. And the Court linked its interpretation of the Fifth Amendment to the common-law understanding of the self-incrimination privilege.

But this Court's decision in Fisher v. United States rejected this understanding, permitting the Government to force a person to furnish incriminating physical evidence and protecting only the "testimonial" aspects of that transfer. In so doing, *Fisher* not only failed to examine the historical backdrop to the Fifth Amendment, it also required—as illustrated by extended discussion in the opinions below in this case—a difficult parsing of the act of responding to a subpoena duces tecum.

None of the parties in this case has asked us to depart from *Fisher*, but in light of the historical evidence that the Self-Incrimination Clause may have a broader reach than *Fisher* holds, I remain open to a reconsideration of that decision and its progeny in a proper case.[6]

CHIEF JUSTICE REHNQUIST dissents and would reverse the judgment of the Court of Appeals in part, for the reasons given by Judge Williams in his dissenting opinion in that court, 167 F.3d 552, 597 (C.A.D.C. 1999).

NOTES AND QUESTIONS

1. In a passage not reproduced in the excerpt from the *Hubbell* case, the Court purported not to call into question its previous cases dealing with the interaction of the Fifth Amendment and the demands of the regulatory state:

> [E]ven though the act may provide incriminating evidence, a criminal suspect may be compelled to put on a shirt, to provide a blood sample or handwriting exemplar, or to make a recording of his voice. The act of exhibiting such physical characteristics is not the same as a sworn communication by a witness that relates either express or implied assertions of fact or belief. Similarly, the fact that incriminating evidence may be the byproduct of obedience to a regulatory requirement, such as filing an income tax return, maintaining required records, or reporting an accident, does not clothe such required conduct with the testimonial privilege. More relevant to this case is the settled proposition that a person may be required to produce specific documents even though they contain incriminating assertions of fact or belief because the creation of those documents was not "compelled" within the meaning of the privilege.

2. Has the Court nonetheless created a derivative evidence rule with a potential scope as broad as the most robust reading of *Boyd* might generate? The Court found Hubbell's rights to have been violated because "[i]t was unquestionably necessary for respondent to make extensive use of 'the contents of his own mind' in identifying the hundreds of documents responsive to the requests in the subpoena." Does it matter whether "extensive use" of the contents of the mind is required rather than only minimal use, or is it any use of the contents of the mind that matters? Is there a distinction, and if so what is it, between the use, extensive or not, of the "contents" of the mind and other uses of the mind? Can you make sense of the idea that the "contents" of a person's mind are not employed when, for example, the person responds to a request to put on a

---

6. To hold that the Government may not compel a person to produce incriminating evidence (absent an appropriate grant of immunity) does not necessarily answer the question whether (and, if so, when) the Government may secure that same evidence through a search or seizure. The lawfulness of such actions, however, would be measured by the Fourth Amendment rather than the Fifth.

shirt or provide a handwriting exemplar? It is easy to make a distinction between a person who is forcibly robed in a shirt against his will and one who through the exercise of will puts on the shirt, but do you think that is the distinction the Court is getting at? If so, how could it possibly apply to giving voice or handwriting exemplars?

3. In *Hubbell*, the Court says that "[t]he assembly of those documents was like telling an inquisitor the combination to a wall safe, not like being forced to surrender the key to a strongbox." What might the difference be? Again, there is a clear difference between forbidding a person from interfering with another person's taking possession of a key in plain sight and demanding that a person turn over a key not in plain sight, but that does not seem to capture the Court's point, does it? The Court seems to think there is a difference between forcing a person to disclose the location of a key and forcing the person to disclose the numbers to the combination. What, exactly, is the difference? It cannot simply be the difference between an act and a statement. That is precisely the distinction the Court rejected in *Hubbell* when it asserted that the assembling of the documents called for by the subpoena was the "functional equivalent of the preparation of an answer to either a detailed written interrogatory or a series of oral questions at a discovery deposition" and therefore within the protections of the Fifth Amendment.

4. Under what circumstances could the Government demand that papers be turned over and still use their contents to prosecute an individual? The Court says that *Hubbell* differs from *Fisher* precisely because in *Fisher* "the Government already knew that the documents were in the attorneys' possession and could independently confirm their existence and authenticity through the accountants who created them, [while] here the Government has not shown that it had any prior knowledge of either the existence or the whereabouts of the 13,120 pages of documents ultimately produced by the respondent." However, there was no claim in *Fisher* that the Government knew the contents of the documents. Had the Government known the contents, it most likely would not have needed the documents. In respect of the contents of the documents, then, are not the two cases quite similar? What distinguishes them is precisely that the Government did not know of the existence and location of the documents in Hubbell's case. Those were communicated by Hubbell both in the act of production and in his responses before the Grand Jury, but the Government agreed that it could not make use of any of those compelled communications. Moreover, the contents of the documents were not derived from these compelled communications, even though the Government's knowledge was. Why did that not satisfy whatever rights Hubbell possessed?

5. For one effort to answer these various questions, see Ronald J. Allen & Kristin Mace, The Fifth Amendment Explained and Its Future Predicted, 94 J. Crim. L. & Crim. 243-294 (2004), who argue that the future of the Fifth Amendment prong of *Boyd* will be determined by how the tension between *Hubbell* and *Fisher* is resolved. *Fisher* seemed to indicate that the contents and makeup of papers turned over were not derivative fruits of the act of production and that merely responding to a subpoena was not necessarily incriminating for the purposes of the Fifth Amendment. *Hubbell* casts doubt on both propositions. Thus, future cases will need to resolve the scope of derivative fruits doctrine and whether any cognition at all in responding to a subpoena triggers the Fifth Amendment, or instead whether "extensive" cognition is required [See note 4, supra].

6. Whatever the answers turn out to be to these puzzles concerning the meaning of *Hubbell*, remember that the case deals only with the Fifth Amendment branch of the *Boyd* jurisprudence; the Fourth Amendment branch remains untouched. Thus, if a search warrant could have issued for these same documents, the government would have had an alternative route to obtaining them. As you shall see, that depends on whether the government had probable cause to seize the documents as evidence of some crime and whether they could be described with sufficient "particularity" to satisfy the Fourth Amendment. One cannot tell from the case itself whether either requirement could have been satisfied. It is interesting, but by no means dispositive of these matters, to note that what Hubbell was eventually indicted for had nothing to do with the investigation that generated the subpoena in the first place.

——————————————

Whether *Boyd* should be extolled or vilified, its ideal continues to exert a powerful hold on the legal imagination. As the following chapters show, the goal of privacy protection is far from dead in the law of criminal procedure. Notwithstanding the repeated claims of its demise, *Boyd* still casts a large shadow.

Chapter 5

The Fourth Amendment

The Fourth Amendment plays two key roles in the American legal order. The first is as the law's chief source of privacy protection. The Fourth Amendment's domain extends to "all invasions on the part of the government and its employees of the sanctity of a man's home and the privacies of life"—so the Supreme Court said in 1886: four years *before* Samuel Warren and Louis Brandeis penned the essay widely credited with making privacy a central concept in American law. See Boyd v. United States, 116 U.S. 616, 630 (1886); Samuel D. Warren & Louis D. Brandeis, The Right of Privacy, 4 Harv. L. Rev. 193 (1890). For most of American history, that privacy protection was aspirational only; it had little practical relevance. Only federal officials were bound by *Boyd* to respect the sanctity of homes and "the privacies of life," since the Fourth Amendment applied only to the federal government—and the federal government's criminal law enforcement apparatus was quite small. Local police agencies were much more likely to invade individual privacy, and those agencies were subject to no serious legal regulation, constitutional or otherwise. That state of affairs changed in 1961, when the Supreme Court held that the Fourth Amendment's exclusionary rule applied in state and federal cases alike. Mapp v. Ohio, 367 U.S. 643 (1961). *Mapp* gave Fourth Amendment law its teeth. *Boyd* ensured that the law *Mapp* enforced was grounded in privacy.

The second role Fourth Amendment law plays concerns not the interest being protected but rather the actors being regulated. The Fourth Amendment applies to all government actors, but it is almost always enforced against police officers. It is not too much to say that the Fourth Amendment functions as a kind of tort law for the police, the chief source of legal regulation of criminal law enforcement. Since there are more than 13 million arrests each year, and 750,000 police officers working for local, state, or federal governments, the task of regulating police is obviously important—it seems fair to say that *some* regulation of policing is essential to any free society.

And legal regulation of police searches and arrests consists mostly of Fourth Amendment regulation. There is a state law of search and seizure, but until the last generation it was very thin; the number of reported state cases discussing search and seizure claims before 1961 was trivially small. Today, most state-law search and seizure cases arise under state constitutional provisions that parallel the federal Fourth Amendment; the arguments and holdings in those cases tend to track arguments that appear in Fourth Amendment cases. And police training programs, which once (again, before 1961) ignored training in the law, now offer elaborate instruction in legal rules—meaning, mostly, Fourth Amendment rules.

All of this is quite different from the state of affairs that prevails elsewhere in federal constitutional law. Most of constitutional law defines outer bounds within which the government may operate; the rules that define ordinary government operations are nonconstitutional. For the people who run public schools or government hospitals, constitutional law is a secondary concern; it has little to do with the day-to-day business of those institutions. For police, Fourth Amendment law is the primary source of legal restraint; it regulates ordinary, run-of-the-mill interactions between officers and suspects.

These two roles — protecting individual privacy and regulating the police — may be more important in the twenty-first century than ever before. Advances in information technology place privacy at greater risk than in an age when police used eyes and ears rather than computer programs to monitor suspects. Yet, in an age of terrorism, police *need* to do a lot of monitoring: the costs of regulating the police badly may be measured in lives lost, perhaps thousands of them. One question you should keep in mind, as you study the materials in this chapter, is whether the law regulates wisely — whether privacy is adequately protected without disabling the police from guarding public safety.

Text and History

One of the large stories of the past generation in constitutional law is the revival of attention to the constitutional text and the original intent of the men who wrote and ratified it. This revival has been less pronounced in Fourth Amendment law than in some other areas; even so, text-and-history arguments appear frequently in the materials that follow, and a few initial comments might be helpful.

The text of the Fourth Amendment is uncomplicated:

> The right of the people to be secure in their persons, houses, papers, and effects, against unreasonable searches and seizures, shall not be violated, and no warrants shall issue, but upon probable cause, supported by oath or affirmation, and particularly describing the place to be searched, and the persons or things to be seized.

Notice that the first clause of the Amendment defines the prohibition — no "unreasonable searches and seizures." The second clause places some restrictions on the issuance of warrants, the most important being the requirement of probable cause. The relationship between the two clauses is, on the face of the text, unclear; it will be explored in detail in section C infra. For now, it is enough to say that the conventional reading of the text, the one adopted in nearly all Supreme Court opinions until recently, treats probable cause and a warrant as defining the usual conditions for a "reasonable" search or seizure. Today, the trend is to treat reasonableness as a freestanding concept, not necessarily anchored to warrants or probable cause. The results of that trend are explored in section D infra.

This relatively simple text has a relatively simple history. Though there are serious debates about some aspects of the story, most scholars agree on the basic outlines. The Fourth Amendment arose out of a trio of famous eighteenth-century cases, two from England and one from the colonies. The less famous of the two English cases was Entick v. Carrington, 19 Howell's State Trials 1029 (C.P. 1765), which is discussed at length in the opinion in Boyd v. United States, page 278 supra. Entick was an English pamphleteer critical of the King's ministers. As part of a seditious libel investigation, a warrant was issued authorizing Entick's arrest and the seizure of all his books and papers. The warrant was carried out; Entick sued for trespass, and he won a verdict of 300 pounds. The other English case was Wilkes v. Wood, 19 Howell's State Trials 1153 (C.P. 1763). Wilkes was likewise a pamphleteer, and also a well-known Member of Parliament, perhaps the most popular man in England in his day. He too was a critic of the government, and he too was rewarded with arrest, search of his home, and the seizure of his books and papers (some 49 of Wilkes's friends received the same treatment). All these searches and seizures were made pursuant to a warrant that neither named suspects nor specified places to be searched. Like Entick, Wilkes and a number of his friends sued for trespass and won; in Wilkes's case the verdict was 1,000 pounds, a considerable sum at the time. Both *Entick* and *Wilkes* won renown in the American colonies in the years leading up to the American Revolution; the judge who presided over both their trials, Lord Camden, was a colonial hero for whom a number of American cities and counties were named.

The third case arose in colonial Massachusetts, where customs inspectors were seeking to crack down on the smuggling that then dominated Boston's economy. To aid them in that task, inspectors used "writs of assistance," which were issued by the King and which authorized the inspectors both to draft assistance (hence the name of the writs) and to search any place where smuggled goods might be concealed. In 1761 in *The Writs of Assistance Case*, James Otis argued, on behalf of some of the smugglers, that these writs conveyed no legal authority. Otis lost, but according to John Adams, his argument was the beginning of the Revolution—in Adams's words, "Then and there was the child Independence born."

Whatever else the Fourth Amendment was about, it was probably designed to enact the results in *Entick* and *Wilkes* and to overturn the result in *The Writs of Assistance Case*. Notice that none of the three cases involved a typical instance of criminal law enforcement: These were not investigations of murders, rapes, or robberies. Indeed, two of the three cases—*Entick* and *Wilkes*—arose out of investigations that could not happen today, because they would be clear violations of the *First* Amendment. (Had English law had an equivalent to our First Amendment and had the searches in *Entick* and *Wilkes* therefore not happened, the Fourth Amendment might not exist.) Notice too that the officials who conducted the searches in these cases were not ordinary police officers—in *Entick* and *Wilkes*, they were "messengers," special agents of the Crown; in *The Writs of Assistance Case*, they were customs inspectors. That is no accident; ordinary police officers did not exist, either in eighteenth-century England or in the colonies. The first police force was established in London in 1829; American police forces were born, one by one, between that date and about 1870. Thus, the Fourth Amendment—the prime source of legal restraint for the police—was written before the police existed, at least in anything like the form they take today. That fact might lead one to be cautious when seeking to determine the "original understanding" of various contemporary Fourth Amendment issues.

Remedy and Right

Of course, today Fourth Amendment litigation overwhelmingly involves challenges to searches and seizures conducted by the police in the course of investigating or enforcing ordinary criminal prohibitions — homicide, rape, theft, and, especially, drug violations. The large majority of those challenges occur in criminal cases, as defendants seek to suppress evidence they claim the police seized in violation of the Fourth Amendment.

There are other remedies for Fourth Amendment violations — they are explored in section F infra — but the dominant one, the one that is invoked most often by far, is the exclusionary rule. Motions to suppress illegally seized physical evidence are filed in 5 percent of criminal cases (defendants win 17 percent of those motions). See Peter F. Nardulli, The Societal Cost of the Exclusionary Rule: An Empirical Assessment, [1983] Am. Bar Found. Res. J. 595, 595-96. Even if only a quarter of all arrests produce a criminal case, that would mean roughly 175,000 suppression motions per year, nationwide. The number of civil lawsuits against police for Fourth Amendment violations is, at most, a few thousand per year. The number of criminal prosecutions is a few dozen.

That may have a large effect on the substance of Fourth Amendment law. The exclusionary rule shapes the kinds of Fourth Amendment cases judges see. All exclusionary rule claims seek to suppress incriminating evidence; if no incriminating evidence is found, there is nothing for the defendant to exclude. Thus, judges see the cases where the police find cocaine in the car, not the cases where they find nothing. Perhaps that affects the way judges think about car searches. You should consider, as you read the cases that follow, how the presence of the exclusionary rule might have affected judicial perceptions about different kinds of searches, and how those perceptions might have affected the various Fourth Amendment doctrines those cases discuss.

We begin the chapter with a brief consideration of the exclusionary rule, because it is so important to so many features of Fourth Amendment law. The chapter then turns to the substance of Fourth Amendment law — what the Fourth Amendment requires of the police or the other officials to whom it applies — and then returns, in section F, to a more detailed consideration of the exclusionary rule and other remedies for Fourth Amendment violations.

A. The Exclusionary Rule

MAPP v. OHIO

Appeal from the Supreme Court of Ohio
367 U.S. 643 (1961)

MR. JUSTICE CLARK delivered the opinion of the Court.

Appellant stands convicted of knowingly having had in her possession and under her control certain lewd and lascivious books, pictures, and photographs in violation of §2905.34 of Ohio's Revised Code.[2] . . . [T]he Supreme Court of

---

2. The statute provides in pertinent part that

"No person shall knowingly . . . have in his possession or under his control an obscene, lewd, or lascivious book [or] . . . picture. . . .

   "Whoever violates this section shall be fined not less than two hundred nor more than two thousand dollars or imprisoned not less than one nor more than seven years, or both."

Ohio found that her conviction was valid though "based primarily upon the introduction in evidence of lewd and lascivious books and pictures unlawfully seized
during an unlawful search of defendant's home. . . . "

On May 23, 1957, three Cleveland police officers arrived at appellant's residence in that city pursuant to information that "a person [was] hiding out in the
home, who was wanted for questioning in connection with a recent bombing, and
that there was a large amount of policy paraphernalia being hidden in the home."
Miss Mapp and her daughter by a former marriage lived on the top floor of the
two-family dwelling. Upon their arrival at that house, the officers knocked on the
door and demanded entrance but appellant, after telephoning her attorney,
refused to admit them without a search warrant. They advised their headquarters
of the situation and undertook a surveillance of the house.

The officers again sought entrance some three hours later when four or more
additional officers arrived on the scene. When Miss Mapp did not come to the
door immediately, at least one of the several doors to the house was forcibly
opened[3] and the policemen gained admittance. Meanwhile Miss Mapp's attorney
arrived, but the officers, having secured their own entry, and continuing in their
defiance of the law, would permit him neither to see Miss Mapp nor to enter the
house. It appears that Miss Mapp was halfway down the stairs from the upper floor
to the front door when the officers, in this highhanded manner, broke into the
hall. She demanded to see the search warrant. A paper, claimed to be a warrant,
was held up by one of the officers. She grabbed the "warrant" and placed it in her
bosom. A struggle ensued in which the officers recovered the piece of paper and as
a result of which they handcuffed appellant because she had been "belligerent" in
resisting their official rescue of the "warrant" from her person. Running rough-
shod over appellant, a policeman "grabbed" her, "twisted [her] hand," and she
"yelled [and] pleaded with him" because "it was hurting." Appellant, in handcuffs,
was then forcibly taken upstairs to her bedroom where the officers searched a
dresser, a chest of drawers, a closet and some suitcases. They also looked into a
photo album and through personal papers belonging to the appellant. The search
spread to the rest of the second floor including the child's bedroom, the living
room, the kitchen and a dinette. The basement of the building and a trunk found
therein were also searched. The obscene materials for possession of which she was
ultimately convicted were discovered in the course of that widespread search.

At the trial no search warrant was produced by the prosecution, nor was the
failure to produce one explained or accounted for. At best, "There is, in the
record, considerable doubt as to whether there ever was any warrant for the search
of defendant's home." 170 Ohio St., at 430, 166 N.E.2d, at 389. The Ohio
Supreme Court believed a "reasonable argument" could be made that the conviction should be reversed "because the 'methods' employed to obtain the
[evidence] . . . were such as to offend a sense of justice," but the court found
determinative the fact that the evidence had not been taken "from defendant's
person by the use of brutal or offensive physical force against defendant."

The State says that even if the search were made without authority, or otherwise
unreasonably, it is not prevented from using the unconstitutionally seized

3. A police officer testified that "we did pry the screen door to gain entrance"; the attorney on the
scene testified that a policeman "tried . . . to kick in the door" and then "broke the glass in the door and
somebody reached in and opened the door and let them in"; the appellant testified that "The back door
was broken."

evidence at trial, citing Wolf v. Colorado, 338 U.S. 25 (1949), in which this Court did indeed hold "that in a prosecution in a State court for a State crime the Fourteenth Amendment does not forbid the admission of evidence obtained by an unreasonable search and seizure." On this appeal, . . . it is urged once again that we review that holding.[4]

Seventy-five years ago, in Boyd v. United States, 116 U.S. 616, 630 (1886), considering the Fourth and Fifth Amendments as running "almost into each other" on the facts before it, this Court held that the doctrines of those Amendments "apply to all invasions on the part of the government and its employes of the sanctity of a man's home and the privacies of life." . . . The Court noted that "constitutional provisions for the security of person and property should be liberally construed. . . . It is the duty of courts to be watchful for the constitutional rights of the citizen, and against any stealthy encroachments thereon." . . . Less than 30 years after Boyd, this Court, in Weeks v. United States, 232 U.S. 383 (1914), stated that "the Fourth Amendment . . . put the courts of the United States and Federal officials, in the exercise of their power and authority, under limitations and restraints." . . . Specifically dealing with the use of the evidence unconstitutionally seized, the Court concluded:

> If letters and private documents can thus be seized and held and used in evidence against a citizen accused of an offense, the protection of the Fourth Amendment declaring his right to be secure against such searches and seizures is of no value, and, so far as those thus placed are concerned, might as well be *stricken from* the Constitution. . . .

Finally, the Court in that case clearly stated that use of the seized evidence involved "a denial of the constitutional rights of the accused." . . .

In 1949, 35 years after *Weeks* was announced, this Court, in Wolf v. Colorado, supra, . . . discussed the effect of the Fourth Amendment upon the States through the operation of the Due Process Clause of the Fourteenth Amendment. . . . [A]fter declaring that the "security of one's privacy against arbitrary intrusion by the police" is "implicit in 'the concept of ordered liberty' and as such enforceable against the States through the Due Process Clause," and announcing that it "stoutly adhere[d]" to the *Weeks* decision, the Court decided that the *Weeks* exclusionary rule would not then be imposed upon the States as "an essential ingredient of the right." The Court's reasons for not considering essential to the right to privacy, as a curb imposed upon the States by the Due Process Clause, that which decades before had been posited as part and parcel of the Fourth Amendment's limitation upon federal encroachment of individual privacy, were bottomed on factual considerations. . . .

The Court in *Wolf* first stated that "the contrariety of views of the States" on the adoption of the exclusionary rule of *Weeks* was "particularly impressive"; and, in this connection, that it could not "brush aside the experience of States which deem the incidence of such conduct by the police too slight to call for a deterrent remedy . . . by overriding the [States'] relevant rules of evidence." While in 1949,

---

4. Other issues have been raised on this appeal but, in the view we have taken of the case, they need not be decided. Although appellant chose to urge what may have appeared to be the surer ground for favorable disposition and did not insist that *Wolf* be overruled, the amicus curiae, who was also permitted to participate in the oral argument, did urge the Court to overrule *Wolf*.

prior to the *Wolf* case, almost two-thirds of the States were opposed to the use of the exclusionary rule, now, despite the *Wolf* case, more than half of those since passing upon it, by their own legislative or judicial decision, have wholly or partly adopted or adhered to the *Weeks* rule. Significantly, among those now following the rule is California, which, according to its highest court, was "compelled to reach that conclusion because other remedies have completely failed to secure compliance with the constitutional provisions. . . . " People v. Cahan, 44 Cal. 2d 434, 445, 282 P.2d 905, 911 (1955). In connection with this California case, we note that the second basis elaborated in *Wolf* in support of its failure to enforce the exclusionary doctrine against the States was that "other means of protection" have been afforded "the right to privacy." 338 U.S., at 30. The experience of California that such other remedies have been worthless and futile is buttressed by the experience of other States. . . .

Likewise, time has set its face against what *Wolf* called the "weighty testimony" of People v. Defore, 242 N.Y. 13, 150 N.E. 585 (1926). There Justice (then Judge) Cardozo, rejecting adoption of the *Weeks* exclusionary rule in New York, had said that "the Federal rule as it stands is either too strict or too lax." 242 N.Y., at 22, 150 N.E., at 588. However, the force of that reasoning has been largely vitiated by later decisions of this Court. These include the recent discarding of the "silver platter" doctrine which allowed federal judicial use of evidence seized in violation of the Constitution by state agents, Elkins v. United States, [364 U.S. 206 (1960)]; the relaxation of the formerly strict requirements as to standing to challenge the use of evidence thus seized, so that now the procedure of exclusion . . . is available to anyone even "legitimately on [the] premises" unlawfully searched, Jones v. United States, 362 U.S. 257, 266-267 (1960); and, finally, the formulation of a method to prevent state use of evidence unconstitutionally seized by federal agents, Rea v. United States, 350 U.S. 214 (1956). . . .

It, therefore, plainly appears that the factual considerations supporting the failure of the *Wolf* Court to include the *Weeks* exclusionary rule when it recognized the enforceability of the right to privacy against the States in 1949, while not basically relevant to the constitutional consideration, could not, in any analysis, now be deemed controlling.

. . . Today we once again examine *Wolf*'s constitutional documentation of the right to privacy free from unreasonable state intrusion, and, after its dozen years on our books, are led by it to close the only courtroom door remaining open to evidence secured by official lawlessness in flagrant abuse of that basic right, reserved to all persons as a specific guarantee against that very same unlawful conduct. We hold that all evidence obtained by searches and seizures in violation of the Constitution is, by that same authority, inadmissible in a state court.

Since the Fourth Amendment's right of privacy has been declared enforceable against the States through the Due Process Clause of the Fourteenth, it is enforceable against them by the same sanction of exclusion as is used against the Federal Government. Were it otherwise, then just as without the *Weeks* rule the assurance against unreasonable federal searches and seizures would be "a form of words," valueless and undeserving of mention in a perpetual charter of inestimable human liberties, so too, without that rule the freedom from state invasions of privacy would be so ephemeral and so neatly severed from its conceptual nexus with the freedom from all brutish means of coercing evidence as not to merit this Court's high regard as a freedom "implicit in the concept of ordered liberty." . . . [T]he admission of the new constitutional right by *Wolf* could not consistently tolerate denial of its most important constitutional privilege, namely, the exclusion of the evidence which an accused had been forced to give by reason of the unlawful seizure. To hold otherwise is to grant the right but in reality to withhold its privilege and enjoyment. Only last year the Court itself recognized that the purpose of the exclusionary rule "is to deter — to compel respect for the constitutional guaranty in the only effectively available way — by removing the incentive to disregard it." Elkins v. United States, supra, at 217. . . .

Moreover, our holding that the exclusionary rule is an essential part of both the Fourth and Fourteenth Amendments is not only the logical dictate of prior cases, but it also makes very good sense. There is no war between the Constitution and common sense. Presently, a federal prosecutor may make no use of evidence illegally seized, but a State's attorney across the street may, although he supposedly is operating under the enforceable prohibitions of the same Amendment. Thus the State, by admitting evidence unlawfully seized, serves to encourage disobedience to the Federal Constitution which it is bound to uphold. Moreover, as was said in *Elkins*, "the very essence of a healthy federalism depends upon the avoidance of needless conflict between state and federal courts." 364 U.S., at 221. . . . In nonexclusionary States, federal officers, being human, were . . . invited to and did, as our cases indicate, step across the street to the State's attorney with their unconstitutionally seized evidence. Prosecution on the basis of that evidence was then had in a state court in utter disregard of the enforceable Fourth Amendment. If the fruits of an unconstitutional search had been inadmissible in both state and federal courts, this inducement to evasion would have been sooner eliminated. . . .

There are those who say, as did Justice (then Judge) Cardozo, that under our constitutional exclusionary doctrine "the criminal is to go free because the constable has blundered." People v. Defore, 242 N.Y., at 21, 150 N.E., at 587. In some cases this will undoubtedly be the result. But, as was said in *Elkins*, "there is another consideration — the imperative of judicial integrity." 364 U.S., at 222. The criminal goes free, if he must, but it is the law that sets him free. Nothing can destroy a government more quickly than its failure to observe its own laws, or worse, its disregard of the charter of its own existence. As Mr. Justice Brandeis, dissenting, said in Olmstead v. United States, 277 U.S. 438, 485 (1928): "Our Government is the potent, the omnipresent teacher. For good or for ill, it teaches the whole people by its example. . . . If the Government becomes a lawbreaker, it breeds contempt for law; it invites every man to become a law unto himself; it invites anarchy." Nor can it lightly be assumed that, as a practical matter, adoption of the exclusionary rule fetters law enforcement. Only last year this Court expressly considered that contention and found that "pragmatic evidence of a sort" to the contrary was not wanting. Elkins v. United States, supra, at 218. The Court noted that

> The federal courts themselves have operated under the exclusionary rule of *Weeks* for almost half a century; yet it has not been suggested either that the Federal Bureau of Investigation has thereby been rendered ineffective, or that the administration of criminal justice in the federal courts has thereby been disrupted. Moreover, the experience of the states is impressive. . . . The movement towards the rule of exclusion has been halting but seemingly inexorable. Id., at 218-219.

The ignoble shortcut to conviction left open to the State tends to destroy the entire system of constitutional restraints on which the liberties of the people rest. Having once recognized that the right to privacy embodied in the Fourth Amendment is enforceable against the States, and that the right to be secure against rude invasions of privacy by state officers is, therefore, constitutional in origin, we can no longer permit that right to remain an empty promise. Because it is enforceable in the same manner and to like effect as other basic rights secured by the Due Process Clause, we can no longer permit it to be revocable at the whim of any police officer who, in the name of law enforcement itself, chooses to suspend its enjoyment. Our decision, founded on reason and truth, gives to the individual no more than that which the Constitution guarantees him, to the police officer no less than that to which honest law enforcement is entitled, and, to the courts, that judicial integrity so necessary in the true administration of justice. . . .

MR. JUSTICE BLACK, concurring.

. . . I am . . . not persuaded that the Fourth Amendment, standing alone, would be enough to bar the introduction into evidence against an accused of papers and effects seized from him in violation of its commands. For the Fourth Amendment does not itself contain any provision expressly precluding the use of such evidence, and I am extremely doubtful that such a provision could properly be inferred from nothing more than the basic command against unreasonable searches and seizures. . . . [But] when the Fourth Amendment's ban against unreasonable searches and seizures is considered together with the Fifth Amendment's ban against compelled self-incrimination, a constitutional basis emerges which not only justifies but actually requires the exclusionary rule.

The close interrelationship between the Fourth and Fifth Amendments, as they apply to this problem, has long been recognized and, indeed, was expressly made the ground for this Court's holding in Boyd v. United States. There the Court fully discussed this relationship and declared itself "unable to perceive that the seizure of a man's private books and papers to be used in evidence against him is substantially different from compelling him to be a witness against himself." . . . In the final analysis, it seems to me that the *Boyd* doctrine, though perhaps not required by the express language of the Constitution strictly construed, is amply justified from an historical standpoint, soundly based in reason, and entirely consistent with what I regard to be the proper approach to interpretation of our Bill of Rights. . . .

MR. JUSTICE DOUGLAS, concurring.

. . . This criminal proceeding started with a lawless search and seizure. The police entered a home forcefully, and seized documents that were later used to convict the occupant of a crime. . . .

The only remaining remedy, if exclusion of the evidence is not required, is an action of trespass by the homeowner against the offending officer. . . . The truth is that trespass actions against officers who make unlawful searches and seizures are mainly illusory remedies.

Without judicial action making the exclusionary rule applicable to the States, Wolf v. Colorado in practical effect reduced the guarantee against unreasonable searches and seizures to "a dead letter," as Mr. Justice Rutledge said in his dissent. See 338 U.S., at 47.

[*Wolf*] was decided in 1949. The immediate result was a storm of constitutional controversy which only today finds its end. I believe that this is an appropriate case in which to put an end to the asymmetry which *Wolf* imported into the law. It is an appropriate case because the facts it presents show — as would few other cases — the casual arrogance of those who have the untrammelled power to invade one's home and to seize one's person. . . .

Memorandum of MR. JUSTICE STEWART.

. . . I express no view as to the merits of the constitutional issue which the Court today decides. I would, however, reverse the judgment in this case, because I am persuaded that the provision of §2905.34 of the Ohio Revised Code, upon which the petitioner's conviction was based, is, in the words of Mr. Justice Harlan, not "consistent with the rights of free thought and expression assured against state action by the Fourteenth Amendment."

MR. JUSTICE HARLAN, whom MR. JUSTICE FRANKFURTER and MR. JUSTICE WHITTAKER join, dissenting.

In overruling the *Wolf* case the Court, in my opinion, has forgotten the sense of judicial restraint which, with due regard for stare decisis, is one element that should enter into deciding whether a past decision of this Court should be overruled. Apart from that I also believe that the *Wolf* rule represents sounder Constitutional doctrine than the new rule which now replaces it. . . .

At the heart of the majority's opinion in this case is the following syllogism: (1) the rule excluding in federal criminal trials evidence which is the product of an illegal search and seizure is "part and parcel" of the Fourth Amendment; (2) *Wolf* held that the "privacy" assured against federal action by the Fourth Amendment is also protected against state action by the Fourteenth Amendment; and (3) it is therefore "logically and constitutionally necessary" that the *Weeks* exclusionary rule should also be enforced against the States.

This reasoning ultimately rests on the unsound premise that because *Wolf* carried into the States, as part of "the concept of ordered liberty" embodied in the Fourteenth Amendment, the principle of "privacy" underlying the Fourth Amendment, it must follow that whatever configurations of the Fourth Amendment have been developed in the particularizing federal precedents are likewise to be deemed a part of "ordered liberty," and as such are enforceable against the States. For me, this does not follow at all. . . .

I would not impose upon the States this federal exclusionary remedy. The reasons given by the majority for now suddenly turning its back on *Wolf* seem to me notably unconvincing.

First, it is said that "the factual grounds upon which *Wolf* was based" have since changed, in that more States now follow the *Weeks* exclusionary rule than was so at the time *Wolf* was decided. While that is true, a recent survey indicates that at present one-half of the States still adhere to the common-law non-exclusionary rule, and one, Maryland, retains the rule as to felonies. But in any case surely all this is beside the point, as the majority itself indeed seems to recognize. Our concern here, as it was in *Wolf*, is not with the desirability of that rule but only with the question whether the States are Constitutionally free to follow it or not as they may themselves determine, and the relevance of the disparity of views among the States on this point lies simply in the fact that the judgment involved is a debatable one. . . .

The preservation of a proper balance between state and federal responsibility in the administration of criminal justice demands patience on the part of those who might like to see things move faster among the States in this respect. Problems of criminal law enforcement vary widely from State to State. One State, in considering the totality of its legal picture, may conclude that the need for embracing the *Weeks* rule is pressing because other remedies are unavailable or inadequate to secure compliance with the substantive Constitutional principle involved. Another, though equally solicitous of Constitutional rights, may choose to pursue one purpose at a time, allowing all evidence relevant to guilt to be brought into a criminal trial, and dealing with Constitutional infractions by other means. Still another may consider the exclusionary rule too rough-and-ready a remedy, in that it reaches only unconstitutional intrusions which eventuate in criminal prosecution of the victims. Further, a State after experimenting with the *Weeks* rule for a time may, because of unsatisfactory experience with it, decide to revert to a non-exclusionary rule. And so on. . . .

[W]e are told that imposition of the *Weeks* rule on the States makes "very good sense," in that it will promote recognition by state and federal officials of their "mutual obligation to respect the same fundamental criteria" in their approach to law enforcement, and will avoid "needless conflict between state and federal courts.". . .

An approach which regards the issue as one of achieving procedural symmetry or of serving administrative convenience surely disfigures the boundaries of this Court's functions in relation to the state and federal courts. . . . Here we review state procedures whose measure is to be taken not against the specific substantive commands of the Fourth Amendment but under the flexible contours of the Due Process Clause. I do not believe that the Fourteenth Amendment empowers this Court to mould state remedies effectuating the right to freedom from "arbitrary intrusion by the police" to suit its own notions of how things should be done, as, for instance, the California Supreme Court did in People v. Cahan, 44 Cal. 2d 434, 282 P.2d 905, with reference to procedures in the California courts or as this Court did in *Weeks* for the lower federal courts.

A state conviction comes to us as the complete product of a sovereign judicial system. Typically a case will have been tried in a trial court, tested in some final appellate court, and will go no further. In the comparatively rare instance when a conviction is reviewed by us on due process grounds we deal then with a finished product in the creation of which we are allowed no hand, and our task, far from being one of over-all supervision, is, speaking generally, restricted to a determination of whether the prosecution was Constitutionally fair. The specifics of trial procedure, which in every mature legal system will vary greatly in detail, are within the sole competence of the States. I do not see how it can be said that a trial becomes unfair simply because a State determines that evidence may be considered by the trier of fact, regardless of how it was obtained, if it is relevant to the one issue with which the trial is concerned, the guilt or innocence of the accused. Of course, a court may use its procedures as an incidental means of pursuing other ends than the correct resolution of the controversies before it. Such indeed is the *Weeks* rule, but if a State does not choose to use its courts in this way, I do not believe that this Court is empowered to impose this much-debated procedure on local courts, however efficacious we may consider the *Weeks* rule to be as a means of securing Constitutional rights. . . .

I regret that I find so unwise in principle and so inexpedient in policy a decision motivated by the high purpose of increasing respect for Constitutional rights. But in the last analysis I think this Court can increase respect for the Constitution only if it rigidly respects the limitations which the Constitution places upon it, and respects as well the principles inherent in its own processes. In the present case I think we exceed both, and that our voice becomes only a voice of power, not of reason.

NOTES AND QUESTIONS

1. *Mapp* has an unusual history. It was litigated as a *First* Amendment case; the Fourth Amendment was barely mentioned in the parties' briefs and in the oral argument. The First Amendment question was whether Ohio could criminalize possession of obscene materials in one's home — a serious question that potentially involved both the bounds of obscenity and the question whether criminal law must distinguish between conduct inside and outside one's dwelling. Mapp's First Amendment argument prevailed eight years later, in Stanley v. Georgia, 394 U.S. 557 (1969), in which the Court struck down a Georgia statute similar to the Ohio statute under which Mapp was convicted.

Does Mapp's First Amendment claim strengthen her Fourth Amendment argument? Does the exclusionary rule seem more palatable in cases in which the crime is substantively questionable? Recall that the Fourth Amendment arose out of seditious libel investigations, which would be unconstitutional today and might have seemed substantively questionable even in the eighteenth century. See Entick v. Carrington, 19 Howell's State Trials 1029 (C.P. 1765); Wilkes v. Wood, 19 Howell's State Trials 1153 (C.P. 1763). For an extended discussion of this point, see William J. Stuntz, The Substantive Origins of Criminal Procedure, 105 Yale L.J. 393 (1995).

2. If the nature of the crime in *Mapp* strengthens the argument for an exclusionary rule, might a more serious crime offer a reason for limiting the rule? Why not hold that illegally seized evidence is inadmissible — unless the evidence was seized in a homicide investigation, or in an investigation of terrorist networks?

3. What is the relationship between the exclusionary remedy and the Fourth Amendment right? Is the remedy *part of* the right? Or is it merely a means by which the right is protected? Justice Clark's opinion for the Court in *Mapp* was ambiguous on these questions. Not so Justice Black — notice the emphasis he places on Boyd v. United States, 116 U.S. 616 (1886), which married the Fourth Amendment to the Fifth Amendment's privilege against self-incrimination. The exclusionary rule was, in a sense, the progeny of that marriage. The use of compelled self-incriminating testimony in court was and is a clear violation of the privilege — the privilege was not merely a ban on the compulsion, but also on *the evidentiary use* of that compulsion. If the Fourth Amendment is seen as a kind of adjunct of the Fifth, then the exclusionary rule is a natural part of the Fourth Amendment right.

4. On the other hand, the Fourth Amendment's text reads differently than the text of the Fifth Amendment. Which leads to one of the most common criticisms of *Mapp*: that the Court's decision runs contrary to the text, since the Fourth Amendment nowhere states that it is to be enforced by an exclusionary rule. See, e.g., Akhil Reed Amar, Fourth Amendment First Principles, 107 Harv. L. Rev. 757 (1994). Of course, the Fourth Amendment does not say anything about other remedies, either. One of the problems the Court faced in *Weeks* and *Wolf* and *Mapp* was how to enforce a prohibition that specifies no means of enforcement. One possibility is to use tort suits, which was roughly the approach the common law took at the time the Fourth Amendment was ratified. But as Justice Douglas's opinion notes, these common law remedies were, in practice, close to nonexistent at the time of *Mapp*: One nationwide survey of judges, prosecutors, defense lawyers, and police chiefs found that 76 percent were unaware of *any* civil suits against police officers for illegal searches or seizures. See Stuart S. Nagel, Law and Society: Testing the Effects of Excluding Illegally Seized Evidence, [1965] Wis. L. Rev. 283. Should the Court be bound by common law remedies in that setting, or should it be free to craft appropriate remedies of its own?

5. Consider the arguments in the majority opinion. One is that differences in federal and state rules were an invitation to evasion by police at both levels of government. The idea is that local police would search illegally and then hand the evidence over to federal agents, and federal agents would return the favor in other cases. Yet that problem is surely solvable without *Mapp*. Indeed, the Court had already solved it, by holding both that federal prosecutors could not use evidence illegally obtained by state officials, Elkins v. United States, 364 U.S. 206 (1960), and that federal agents could not hand over to state prosecutors the fruits of the agents' illegal searches, Rea v. United States, 350 U.S. 214 (1956).

6. Another reason the majority gave for the result in *Mapp* was "the imperative of judicial integrity." In what sense does admission of illegally obtained evidence conflict with judicial integrity? Might judicial integrity actually cut the other way? Imagine a robbery case in which the stolen goods were found on the defendant immediately after the robbery but suppressed because the search that uncovered them was unconstitutional. At trial, the prosecution puts on testimony of witnesses who placed the defendant near the scene of the robbery, but no one can actually identify the defendant as the robber. The defense, naturally, points out the weaknesses in the government's case. The judge, prosecutor, defense attorney, and defendant all know the defendant was caught red-handed. But the jury doesn't. And the defense is, at least indirectly, striving to persuade the jury that the defendant didn't rob the store, while the defendant, both lawyers, and the judge know he did. Is that process characterized by integrity?

This point highlights a basic problem with the exclusionary rule, and with the Court's integrity argument. On the one hand, one can say, with Justice Clark, that admitting illegally obtained evidence seems to condone the illegality. On the other hand, suppressing it produces a kind of fraud on the fact finder. At the least, concern for the system's integrity seems to be present on both sides of the scale, does it not?

7. The integrity of the system is at issue in another respect. The exclusionary rule is enforced in suppression hearings, in which the most common witnesses are the defendant and the police officer(s) who conducted the search. Defendants tend not to be the most credible of witnesses, because they have a strong motive to lie, in

order to exclude the incriminating evidence. The more serious the crime—and most cases involve crimes much more serious than Mapp's (which is not a crime at all anymore)—the stronger that motive, and hence the less credible the defendant. The officer, meanwhile, will tend naturally to be more credible: He may have some incentive to lie as well, but that incentive is less strong than the defendant's, and the officer, unlike the defendant, is not seeking to suppress incriminating evidence. This swearing match creates both the opportunity and the temptation for police perjury, or so it would seem.

Morgan Cloud summarizes the evidence on police perjury as follows:

> . . . The empirical studies on the subject suggest that perjured testimony is common, particularly in drug prosecutions. These studies indicate that police officers commit perjury most often to avoid suppression of evidence and to fabricate probable cause, knowing that judges "may 'wink' at obvious police perjury in order to admit incriminating evidence." . . .
>
> Of course, this does not mean that all police officers lie under oath, or that most officers lie, or that even some officers lie all the time. But these empirical studies substantiate the subjective belief common among lawyers, judges, and police officers that police perjury occurs—and frequently enough to be a significant problem for the justice system. We know it exists, but it is impossible to determine with any precision how often it occurs, or how often officers "get away with it."

Morgan Cloud, The Dirty Little Secret, 43 Emory L.J. 1311, 1312-1313 (1994). As Christopher Slobogin notes, the exclusionary rule is at least partly responsible:

> The most obvious explanation for all of this lying is a desire to see the guilty brought to "justice." As law enforcement officers, the police do not want a person they know to be a criminal to escape conviction simply because of a "technical" violation of the Constitution [or] a procedural formality. . . .

Christopher Slobogin, Testilying: Police Perjury and What to Do About It, 67 U. Colo. L. Rev. 1037, 1044 (1996). Is this a persuasive argument against the exclusionary rule, or is it merely an argument that the legal system should do a better job of judging the credibility of police testimony? Is that possible given an exclusionary rule?

8. A third argument the Court makes for the exclusionary rule is deterrence. Though this argument was not dominant in *Mapp*, it has become the dominant argument for the exclusionary rule; over the past three decades, the Supreme Court has repeatedly stated that the rule exists *solely* in order to deter violations of the Fourth Amendment. See, e.g., United States v. Leon, 468 U.S. 897 (1984). (*Leon* is reprinted at page 683 infra.) There is a large literature on the subject. For a good summary, see Christopher Slobogin, Why Liberals Should Chuck the Exclusionary Rule, [1999] U. Ill. L. Rev. 363. Slobogin concludes that the evidence is mixed, and not terribly informative:

> No one is going to win the empirical debate over whether the exclusionary rule deters the police from committing a significant number of illegal searches and seizures. Most of the studies of the rule suggest that it forces police to pay more attention to the Fourth Amendment than they would without any sanction for illegal searches. At the same time, virtually all the studies also suggest that, for many police officers,

concern over the rule is not a significant influence when contemplating a search or seizure. In short, we do not know how much the rule deters. . . .

We probably never will. . . . Observations of police in action, interviews, and questionnaires are probably the best source of data we have. Even here, however, there are significant problems. Observational studies to date have been anecdotal in nature, interviews may be tainted by underreporting of misbehavior, and conclusions drawn from hypothetical questions [e.g., asking police officers whether they would search in a given fact situation] are plagued by the external validity problem familiar to all social scientists who try to draw generalizations . . . from laboratory studies. . . .

. . . [T]hus, one is left with two plausible points of view. . . . Those who favor the rule can reasonably assert that officers who know illegally seized evidence will be excluded cannot help but try to avoid illegal searches because they will have nothing to gain from them. . . . Just as reasonably, those who oppose the rule can point out that its most direct consequence is imposed on the prosecutor rather than the cop, that police know and count on the fact that the rule is rarely applied (for both legal and not-so-legal reasons), and that the rule cannot affect searches and seizures the police believe will not result in prosecution.

Id. at 368-372.

As Slobogin rightly notes, the exclusionary rule matters only if (i) incriminating evidence is found, and (ii) the government wishes to charge the defendant with a crime that the evidence tends to prove. When the police know beforehand that one or both these conditions will be absent, they have no reason to fear application of the exclusionary rule.

That is no small point. Twenty-seven percent of felony arrestees are never convicted of anything, usually because the charges against them were voluntarily dismissed. Sourcebook of Criminal Justice Statistics — 2002, at tbl. 5.57 (available at *www.albany.edu/sourcebook*). Another 20 percent are convicted (usually by guilty plea) but serve no prison or jail time. See id. at tbl. 5.59. Keep in mind that these are *felony* arrestees; the percentages are higher for misdemeanor arrests. In that kind of world, officers will often care little about evidence to be used in formal adjudications; rather, they will search in order to seize drugs and guns and dispose of them, or to harass or inconvenience suspects, or to "send a message" to gang members on the street, or for some other reason having nothing to do with criminal prosecution. The exclusionary rule provides no deterrent to those kinds of searches. And those may be the kinds of searches (at least when illegal) that most need deterring.

Plus, of course, when the police behave violently, when they strike or shoot suspects, they are typically not searching for evidence. Consequently, excessive police use of force rarely gives rise to an exclusionary rule claim. The exclusionary rule thus does not contribute to the deterrence of excessive force; other remedies must do that job. All of which says that the exclusionary rule's deterrent benefits are limited, at best.

9. On the other hand, the exclusionary rule's costs seem fairly low. In United States v. Leon, 468 U.S. 897 (1984), the Supreme Court noted studies showing that only 1 or 2 percent of felony arrestees escape punishment because of the exclusionary rule (the figure rises to between 3 and 7 percent when one considers only felony drug arrests). See id. at 907 n. 6.

10. Oddly, one of the exclusionary rule's great virtues may be that it does not deter too *much*. The idea here is that some sort of damages remedy (the usual

alternative to exclusion) would overdeter, and that the exclusionary rule solves that overdeterrence problem:

> . . . Police are paid on salary, not by the arrest or search. This is a good thing: given the enormous scope of criminal liability in our system, we rely heavily on the police to exercise discretion not to search and arrest. This system of payment, coupled with this degree of discretion, is a recipe for overdeterrence. Officers gain little from the marginal legal search, so if they lose something substantial from the marginal illegal one, they may choose simply to search much less often and thereby reduce their exposure.
>
> . . . [Similarly, if] an officer faces serious loss whenever he makes a bad arrest, he will make fewer bad arrests, but also many fewer good ones. The same is true, only more so, if the law threatens the officer with jail for constitutional violations. The social costs of this overdeterrence are surely high: they can be measured by murders and rapes and drug deals that would not have happened if their perpetrators had been put away.
>
> The temptation is to solve this problem by making the government, rather than the individual police officer, bear the immediate costs of legal liability. Unfortunately, that move solves nothing. Most police work for local governments, and most local governments operate under serious budget constraints. The effect of governmental damages liability for police misconduct mimics the effect of making individual officers pay damages: the locality has an incentive to reduce its liability by reducing the level of policing. And police work is redistributive. Because crime tends to be concentrated in poor neighborhoods, the people who get the biggest benefits from police work do not pay the biggest tax bills. So the government cannot respond to a rise in the cost of police services (which is what broader damages liability means) by charging the beneficiaries of those services more. Just as a government faced with large damages liability for running a municipal pool, which serves poor residents but is paid for by rich ones, may simply close the pool, a government faced with large damages liability for the police may simply reduce the police presence in areas likeliest to give rise to lawsuits. This is overdeterrence writ large.
>
> In a system faced with these problems, suppressing evidence looks like a godsend. Suppression is restitutionary: the officer loses the very thing he gained from the illegal search, and no more. That largely takes care of overdeterrence. And because the rule does not seriously overdeter, courts need not reserve it for the worst constitutional violations. Instead, the exclusionary rule can be applied across the board to the mass of illegal searches and seizures, without fear that doing so will lead officers to stop searching altogether. This gives courts the chance to define just where the constitutional line falls, to develop a working body of law in this area that tells police [what] they should and should not do. These virtues—the ability to deter without overdeterring, coupled with the ability to define the law—are very substantial indeed.

William J. Stuntz, The Virtues and Vices of the Exclusionary Rule, 20 Harv. J.L. & Pub. Pol'y 443, 445-446 (1997). For a contrary argument, suggesting that carefully crafted damages remedies against local governments would work better than the exclusionary rule, see Slobogin, Why Liberals Should Chuck the Exclusionary Rule, 1999 U. Ill. L. Rev. 363, discussed in Note 8 supra.

11. Return to the facts of *Mapp*. What remedy do you think would fairly compensate her for the harm caused by the illegal search? What remedy do you think would have deterred the officers from behaving as they did?

B. The Scope of the Fourth Amendment

1. The Meaning of "Searches"

a. The Relationship between Privacy and Property

KATZ v. UNITED STATES

Certiorari to the United States Court of Appeals for the Ninth Circuit
389 U.S. 347 (1967)

MR. JUSTICE STEWART delivered the opinion of the Court.

The petitioner was convicted in the District Court for the Southern District of California under an eight-count indictment charging him with transmitting wagering information by telephone from Los Angeles to Miami and Boston in violation of a federal statute. At trial the Government was permitted, over the petitioner's objection, to introduce evidence of the petitioner's end of telephone conversations, overheard by FBI agents who had attached an electronic listening and recording device to the outside of the public telephone booth from which he had placed his calls. In affirming his conviction, the Court of Appeals rejected the contention that the recordings had been obtained in violation of the Fourth Amendment, because "[t]here was no physical entrance into the area occupied by [the petitioner]." We granted certiorari in order to consider the constitutional questions thus presented.

The petitioner had phrased those questions as follows:

"A. Whether a public telephone booth is a constitutionally protected area so that evidence obtained by attaching an electronic listening recording device to the top of such a booth is obtained in violation of the right to privacy of the user of the booth.

"B. Whether physical penetration of a constitutionally protected area is necessary before a search and seizure can be said to be violative of the Fourth Amendment to the United States Constitution."

We decline to adopt this formulation of the issues. In the first place the correct solution of Fourth Amendment problems is not necessarily promoted by incantation of the phrase "constitutionally protected area." Secondly, the Fourth Amendment cannot be translated into a general constitutional "right to privacy." That Amendment protects individual privacy against certain kinds of governmental intrusion, but its protections go further, and often have nothing to do with privacy at all.[4] Other provisions of the Constitution protect personal privacy from other forms of governmental invasion.[5] But the protection of a person's *general*

---

4. "The average man would very likely not have his feelings soothed any more by having his property seized openly than by having it seized privately and by stealth. . . . And a person can be just as much, if not more, irritated, annoyed and injured by an unceremonious public arrest by a policeman as he is by a seizure in the privacy of his office or home." Griswold v. State of Connecticut, 381 U.S. 479, 509 (dissenting opinion of Mr. Justice Black).

5. The First Amendment, for example, imposes limitations upon governmental abridgment of "freedom to associate and privacy in one's associations." NAACP v. State of Alabama, 357 U.S. 449,

right to privacy — his right to be let alone by other people — is, like the protection
of his property and of his very life, left largely to the law of the individual States.

Because of the misleading way the issues have been formulated, the parties have
attached great significance to the characterization of the telephone booth from
which the petitioner placed his calls. The petitioner has strenuously argued that
the booth was a "constitutionally protected area." The Government has maintained with equal vigor that it was not.[8] But this effort to decide whether or not
a given "area," viewed in the abstract, is "constitutionally protected" deflects attention from the problem presented by this case.[9] For the Fourth Amendment
protects people, not places. What a person knowingly exposes to the public,
even in his own home or office, is not a subject of Fourth Amendment protection.
But what he seeks to preserve as private, even in an area accessible to the public,
may be constitutionally protected. The Government stresses the fact that the telephone booth from which the petitioner made his calls was constructed partly of
glass, so that he was as visible after he entered it as he would have been if he had
remained outside. But what he sought to exclude when he entered the booth was
not the intruding eye — it was the uninvited ear. He did not shed his right to do so
simply because he made his calls from a place where he might be seen. No less
than an individual in a business office, in a friend's apartment, or in a taxicab, a
person in a telephone booth may rely upon the protection of the Fourth
Amendment. One who occupies it, shuts the door behind him, and pays the toll
that permits him to place a call is surely entitled to assume that the words he utters
into the mouthpiece will not be broadcast to the world. To read the Constitution
more narrowly is to ignore the vital role that the public telephone has come to play
in private communication.

The Government contends, however, that the activities of its agents in this case
should not be tested by Fourth Amendment requirements, for the surveillance
technique they employed involved no physical penetration of the telephone
booth from which the petitioner placed his calls. It is true that the absence of
such penetration was at one time thought to foreclose further Fourth
Amendment inquiry, Olmstead v. United States, 277 U.S. 438, 457, 464, 466;
Goldman v. United States, 316 U.S. 129, 134-136, for that Amendment was
thought to limit only searches and seizures of tangible property.[13] But "[t]he
premise that property interests control the right of the Government to search
and seize has been discredited." Warden v. Hayden, 387 U.S. 294, 304. Thus,
although a closely divided Court supposed in *Olmstead* that surveillance without
any trespass and without the seizure of any material object fell outside the ambit of

---

462. The Third Amendment's prohibition against the unconsented peacetime quartering of soldiers
protects another aspect of privacy from governmental intrusion. To some extent, the Fifth Amendment
too "reflects the Constitution's concern for . . . ' . . . the right of each individual "to a private enclave
where he may lead a private life."'" Tehan v. Shott, 382 U.S. 406, 416. Virtually every governmental
action interferes with personal privacy to some degree. The question in each case is whether that
interference violates a command of the United States Constitution.

8. In support of their respective claims, the parties have compiled competing lists of "protected
areas" for our consideration. It appears to be common ground that a private home is such an area but
that an open field is not.

9. It is true that this Court has occasionally described its conclusions in terms of "constitutionally
protected areas," but we have never suggested that this concept can serve as a talismanic solution to
every Fourth Amendment problem.

13. We do not deal in this case with the law of detention or arrest under the Fourth Amendment.

the Constitution, we have since departed from the narrow view on which that decision rested. Indeed, we have expressly held that the Fourth Amendment governs not only the seizure of tangible items, but extends as well to the recording of oral statements, overheard without any "technical trespass under . . . local property law." Silverman v. United States, 365 U.S. 505, 511. Once this much is acknowledged, and once it is recognized that the Fourth Amendment protects people — and not simply "areas" — against unreasonable searches and seizures, it becomes clear that the reach of that Amendment cannot turn upon the presence or absence of a physical intrusion into any given enclosure.

We conclude that the underpinnings of *Olmstead* and *Goldman* have been so eroded by our subsequent decisions that the "trespass" doctrine there enunciated can no longer be regarded as controlling. The Government's activities in electronically listening to and recording the petitioner's words violated the privacy upon which he justifiably relied while using the telephone booth and thus constituted a "search and seizure" within the meaning of the Fourth Amendment. The fact that the electronic device employed to achieve that end did not happen to penetrate the wall of the booth can have no constitutional significance.

The question remaining for decision, then, is whether the search and seizure conducted in this case complied with constitutional standards. In that regard, the Government's position is that its agents acted in an entirely defensible manner: They did not begin their electronic surveillance until investigation of the petitioner's activities had established a strong probability that he was using the telephone in question to transmit gambling information to persons in other States, in violation of federal law. Moreover, the surveillance was limited, both in scope and in duration, to the specific purpose of establishing the contents of the petitioner's unlawful telephonic communications. The agents confined their surveillance to the brief periods during which he used the telephone booth,[14] and they took great care to overhear only the conversations of the petitioner himself.[15]

Accepting this account of the Government's actions as accurate, it is clear that this surveillance was so narrowly circumscribed that a duly authorized magistrate, properly notified of the need for such investigation, specifically informed of the basis on which it was to proceed, and clearly apprised of the precise intrusion it would entail, could constitutionally have authorized, with appropriate safeguards, the very limited search and seizure that the Government asserts in fact took place. . . .

. . . Yet the inescapable fact is that this restraint was imposed by the agents themselves, not by a judicial officer. They were not required, before commencing the search, to present their estimate of probable cause for detached scrutiny by a neutral magistrate. They were not compelled, during the conduct of the search itself, to observe precise limits established in advance by a specific court order. Nor were they directed, after the search had been completed, to notify the authorizing

14. Based upon their previous visual observations of the petitioner, the agents correctly predicted that he would use the telephone booth for several minutes at approximately the same time each morning. The petitioner was subjected to electronic surveillance only during this predetermined period. Six recordings, averaging some three minutes each, were obtained and admitted in evidence. They preserved the petitioner's end of conversations concerning the placing of bets and the receipt of wagering information.

15. On the single occasion when the statements of another person were inadvertently intercepted, the agents refrained from listening to them.

magistrate in detail of all that had been seized. In the absence of such safeguards, this Court has never sustained a search upon the sole ground that officers reasonably expected to find evidence of a particular crime and voluntarily confined their activities to the least intrusive means consistent with that end. Searches conducted without warrants have been held unlawful "notwithstanding facts unquestionably showing probable cause," Agnello v. United States, 269 U.S. 20, 33, for the Constitution requires "that the deliberate, impartial judgment of a judicial officer . . . be interposed between the citizen and the police. . . . " Wong Sun v. United States, 371 U.S. 471, 481-482. "Over and again this Court has emphasized that the mandate of the [Fourth] Amendment requires adherence to judicial processes," United States v. Jeffers, 342 U.S. 48, 51, and that searches conducted outside the judicial process, without prior approval by judge or magistrate, are per se unreasonable under the Fourth Amendment — subject only to a few specifically established and well-delineated exceptions.

It is difficult to imagine how any of those exceptions could ever apply to the sort of search and seizure involved in this case. . . .

The Government does not question these basic principles. Rather, it urges the creation of a new exception to cover this case. It argues that surveillance of a telephone booth should be exempted from the usual requirement of advance authorization by a magistrate upon a showing of probable cause. We cannot agree. Omission of such authorization

> "bypasses the safeguards provided by an objective predetermination of probable cause, and substitutes instead the far less reliable procedure of an after-the-event justification for the . . . search, too likely to be subtly influenced by the familiar shortcomings of hindsight judgment." Beck v. State of Ohio, 379 U.S. 89, 96.

And bypassing a neutral predetermination of the *scope* of a search leaves individuals secure from Fourth Amendment violations "only in the discretion of the police." Id., at 97.

These considerations do not vanish when the search in question is transferred from the setting of a home, an office, or a hotel room to that of a telephone booth. Wherever a man may be, he is entitled to know that he will remain free from unreasonable searches and seizures. The government agents here ignored "the procedure of antecedent justification . . . that is central to the Fourth Amendment," a procedure that we hold to be a constitutional precondition of the kind of electronic surveillance involved in this case. Because the surveillance here failed to meet that condition, and because it led to the petitioner's conviction, the judgment must be reversed.

It is so ordered.

MR. JUSTICE MARSHALL took no part in the consideration or decision of this case. [The concurring opinions of Justice Douglas and Justice White are omitted.]

MR. JUSTICE HARLAN, concurring.

I join the opinion of the Court, which I read to hold only (a) that an enclosed telephone booth is an area where, like a home, and unlike a field, a person has a constitutionally protected reasonable expectation of privacy; (b) that electronic as well as physical intrusion into a place that is in this sense private may constitute a violation of the Fourth Amendment; and (c) that the invasion of a constitutionally protected area by federal authorities is, as the Court has long held, presumptively unreasonable in the absence of a search warrant.

As the Court's opinion states, "the Fourth Amendment protects people, not places." The question, however, is what protection it affords to those people. Generally, as here, the answer to that question requires reference to a "place." My understanding of the rule that has emerged from prior decisions is that there is a twofold requirement, first that a person have exhibited an actual (subjective) expectation of privacy and, second, that the expectation be one that society is prepared to recognize as "reasonable." Thus a man's home is, for most purposes, a place where he expects privacy, but objects, activities, or statements that he exposes to the "plain view" of outsiders are not "protected" because no intention to keep them to himself has been exhibited. On the other hand, conversations in the open would not be protected against being overheard, for the expectation of privacy under the circumstances would be unreasonable.

The critical fact in this case is that "[o]ne who occupies [a telephone booth], shuts the door behind him, and pays the toll that permits him to place a call is surely entitled to assume" that his conversation is not being intercepted. The point is not that the booth is "accessible to the public" at other times, but that it is a temporarily private place whose momentary occupants' expectations of freedom from intrusion are recognized as reasonable.

In Silverman v. United States, 365 U.S. 505, we held that eavesdropping accomplished by means of an electronic device that penetrated the premises occupied by petitioner was a violation of the Fourth Amendment. That case established that interception of conversations reasonably intended to be private could constitute a "search and seizure," and that the examination or taking of physical property was not required. This view of the Fourth Amendment was followed in Wong Sun v. United States, 371 U.S. 471, at 485, and Berger v. New York, 388 U.S. 41, at 51. In *Silverman* we found it unnecessary to re-examine Goldman v. United States, 316 U.S. 129, which had held that electronic surveillance accomplished without the physical penetration of petitioner's premises by a tangible object did not violate the Fourth Amendment. This case requires us to reconsider *Goldman*, and I agree that it should now be overruled.[*] Its limitation on Fourth Amendment protection is, in the present day, bad physics as well as bad law, for reasonable expectations of privacy may be defeated by electronic as well as physical invasion. . . .

MR. JUSTICE BLACK, dissenting. . . .

My basic objection is twofold: (1) I do not believe that the words of the Amendment will bear the meaning given them by today's decision, and (2) I do not believe that it is the proper role of this Court to rewrite the Amendment in order "to bring it into harmony with the times" and thus reach a result that many people believe to be desirable.

While I realize that an argument based on the meaning of words lacks the scope, and no doubt the appeal, of broad policy discussions and philosophical discourses

---

[*] I also think that the course of development evinced by *Silverman*, supra, *Wong Sun*, supra, *Berger*, supra, and today's decision must be recognized as overruling Olmstead v. United States, 277 U.S. 438, which essentially rested on the ground that conversations were not subject to the protection of the Fourth Amendment.

on such nebulous subjects as privacy, for me the language of the Amendment is the crucial place to look in construing a written document such as our Constitution. . . . The first clause protects "persons, houses, papers, and effects, against unreasonable searches and seizures. . . . " These words connote the idea of tangible things with size, form, and weight, things capable of being searched, seized, or both. The second clause of the Amendment still further establishes its Framers' purpose to limit its protection to tangible things by providing that no warrants shall issue but those "particularly describing the place to be searched, and the persons or things to be seized." A conversation overheard by eavesdropping, whether by plain snooping or wiretapping, is not tangible and, under the normally accepted meanings of the words, can neither be searched nor seized. In addition the language of the second clause indicates that the Amendment refers not only to something tangible so it can be seized but to something already in existence so it can be described. Yet the Court's interpretation would have the Amendment apply to overhearing future conversations which by their very nature are nonexistent until they take place. How can one "describe" a future conversation, and, if one cannot, how can a magistrate issue a warrant to eavesdrop one in the future? It is argued that information showing what is expected to be said is sufficient to limit the boundaries of what later can be admitted into evidence; but does such general information really meet the specific language of the Amendment which says "particularly describing"? Rather than using language in a completely artificial way, I must conclude that the Fourth Amendment simply does not apply to eavesdropping.

Tapping telephone wires, of course, was an unknown possibility at the time the Fourth Amendment was adopted. But eavesdropping (and wiretapping is nothing more than eavesdropping by telephone) was . . . "an ancient practice which at common law was condemned as a nuisance. 4 Blackstone, Commentaries 168. . . . " [Berger v. New York], 388 U.S., at 45. There can be no doubt that the Framers were aware of this practice, and if they had desired to outlaw or restrict the use of evidence obtained by eavesdropping, I believe that they would have used the appropriate language to do so in the Fourth Amendment. They certainly would not have left such a task to the ingenuity of language-stretching judges. . . .

The first case to reach this Court which actually involved a clear-cut test of the Fourth Amendment's applicability to eavesdropping through a wiretap was, of course, *Olmstead*, supra. In holding that the interception of private telephone conversations by means of wiretapping was not a violation of the Fourth Amendment, this Court, speaking through Mr. Chief Justice Taft, examined the language of the Amendment and found, just as I do now, that the words could not be stretched to encompass overheard conversations:

> "The Amendment itself shows that the search is to be of material things — the person, the house, his papers or his effects. The description of the warrant necessary to make the proceeding lawful, is that it must specify the place to be searched and the person or *things* to be seized. . . .
> "Justice Bradley in the *Boyd* case [116 U.S. 616 (1886)] and Justice Clark[e] in [Gouled v. United States, 255 U.S. 298 (1921)] said that the Fifth Amendment and the Fourth Amendment were to be liberally construed to effect the purpose of the

framers of the Constitution in the interest of liberty. But that can not justify enlargement of the language employed beyond the possible practical meaning of houses, persons, papers, and effects, or so to apply the words search and seizure as to forbid hearing or sight." [277 U.S., at 464-465.]

Goldman v. United States, 316 U.S. 129, is an even clearer example of this Court's traditional refusal to consider eavesdropping as being covered by the Fourth Amendment. There federal agents used a detectaphone, which was placed on the wall of an adjoining room, to listen to the conversation of a defendant carried on in his private office and intended to be confined within the four walls of the room. This Court, referring to *Olmstead*, found no Fourth Amendment violation. . . .

Since I see no way in which the words of the Fourth Amendment can be construed to apply to eavesdropping, that closes the matter for me. In interpreting the Bill of Rights, I willingly go as far as a liberal construction of the language takes me, but I simply cannot in good conscience give a meaning to words which they have never before been thought to have and which they certainly do not have in common ordinary usage. I will not distort the words of the Amendment in order to "keep the Constitution up to date" or "to bring it into harmony with the times." It was never meant that this Court have such power, which in effect would make us a continuously functioning constitutional convention.

With this decision the Court has completed, I hope, its rewriting of the Fourth Amendment, which started only recently when the Court began referring incessantly to the Fourth Amendment not so much as a law against *unreasonable* searches and seizures as one to protect an individual's privacy. By clever word juggling the Court finds it plausible to argue that language aimed specifically at searches and seizures of things that can be searched and seized may, to protect privacy, be applied to eavesdropped evidence of conversations that can neither be searched nor seized. Few things happen to an individual that do not affect his privacy in one way or another. Thus, by arbitrarily substituting the Court's language, designed to protect privacy, for the Constitution's language, designed to protect against unreasonable searches and seizures, the Court has made the Fourth Amendment its vehicle for holding all laws violative of the Constitution which offend the Court's broadest concept of privacy. . . .

The Fourth Amendment protects privacy only to the extent that it prohibits unreasonable searches and seizures of "persons, houses, papers, and effects." No general right is created by the Amendment so as to give this Court the unlimited power to hold unconstitutional everything which affects privacy. Certainly the Framers, well acquainted as they were with the excesses of governmental power, did not intend to grant this Court such omnipotent lawmaking authority as that. The history of governments proves that it is dangerous to freedom to repose such powers in courts.

For these reasons I respectfully dissent.

NOTES AND QUESTIONS

1. *Katz* is the leading case on the question what constitutes a "search" for Fourth Amendment purposes. Notice that the immediate effect of *Katz* was to expand the Fourth Amendment's scope by rejecting the notions: (1) that the Amendment is

concerned only with the search or seizure of tangible property; and (2) that the Amendment only applies to surveillance techniques involving the physical penetration of protected spaces. Broadly, *Katz* continued the reconstruction of Boyd v. United States, 116 U.S. 616 (1886), detailed in the last chapter. But notice that even as it reworked the very scope of the Amendment (and seemingly in the direction of bringing more within the Fourth Amendment's concern), *Katz* offered no comprehensive test of Fourth Amendment coverage, nor any general theory by which questions of coverage might be resolved. As one scholar puts it: "In the end, the basis of the *Katz* decision seems to be that the fourth amendment protects those interests that may justifiably claim fourth amendment protection." Anthony G. Amsterdam, Perspectives on the Fourth Amendment, 58 Minn. L. Rev. 349, 385 (1974).

2. Or is this conclusion too harsh? The *Katz* Court does, after all, make *some* things clear. First, neither a property interest in a given space nor physical trespass of that space is the sine qua non of a Fourth Amendment "search." And while Justice Stewart's majority opinion offered no robust theory to support those conclusions, the opinion plainly seems motivated by some conception of privacy. (Notwithstanding disclaimers like "the Fourth Amendment cannot be translated into a general constitutional 'right to privacy'" and that "the protection of a person's *general* right to privacy — his right to be let alone by other people — is, like the protection of his property . . . , left largely to the law of the individual States.")

Justice Stewart's opinion did not long define the law in this area; Justice Harlan's two-prong formula soon became the Court's test for determining whether a "search" had taken place: "My understanding of the rule that has emerged from prior decisions is that there is a twofold requirement, first that a person have exhibited an actual (subjective) expectation of privacy and second, that the expectation be one that society is prepared to recognize as 'reasonable.'" If a search takes place only when the Government intrudes on an individual's reasonable expectation of privacy, it would seem that some animating theory of privacy is necessary — if only to ground questions about the Fourth Amendment's scope. What might this theory of privacy be?

3. But perhaps this is the point. The Court invoked privacy to resolve a Fourth Amendment coverage question, but it didn't really develop any articulated statement of what this Fourth Amendment privacy might mean. Was this necessarily a failing? Consider the argument in Ronald J. Allen & Ross M. Rosenberg, The Fourth Amendment and the Limits of Theory: Local Versus General Theoretical Knowledge, 72 St. John's L. Rev. 1149 (1998). Allen and Rosenberg draw on the distinction, made famous by Friederich Hayek, between "made" and "grown" orders. "Made" orders are created by some plan or design. "Grown" orders, by contrast, arise spontaneously without central coordination. Allen and Rosenberg argue that Fourth Amendment law, a "grown" order, is ill-suited to overarching theory but that it more properly evolves incrementally, in a process not unlike the evolution of the common law:

> Made orders usually possess a limited number of variables, and thus those variables may be manipulated in order to produce predictable outcomes. If the woodlot suffers a drought, watering will promote growth. If the soil becomes too acidic, it can be treated. . . . Spontaneous orders are extremely complex; introducing reforms into spontaneous systems leads to much more unpredictable consequences. Introducing

a new vine as ground cover around the periphery of the forest may result in the forest's destruction as the vine, freed from its natural enemies, grows out of control and chokes out all other plant forms. Unintended, unanticipated consequences are much more likely to result from the introduction of change into a spontaneous order. . . .

In essence, the Fourth Amendment is . . . a grown, spontaneous system. . . . [I]t has too many variables to yield its essence to logical analysis designed to generate decision algorithms. Its subject matter encompasses virtually every human action and interaction imaginable, . . . from public statements to private thoughts recorded in a secret diary, from the affairs of the homeless to those of Dow Chemical, from participating in illegal [drug] markets . . . to illegal restraints of trade. . . . The beliefs of the [academic] commentators, in short, that . . . the Fourth Amendment or privacy will reduce to simple variables, a simple theory, is unjustified. Some things are just more complicated than that.

Are we, then, simply at the mercy of an uncontrollable monster? No. . . . [C]autious, incremental change, with a sensitive awareness of the need for close monitoring and adjustment can be done with a reasonable prospect of favorable outcomes — as the common law demonstrates so well. Adjustments can come from other sources besides the courts, of course. Whatever the sources, we suggest this is the path to take. . . .

Id. at 1197-1200 (footnotes omitted). If Allen and Rosenberg are right, questions of the Fourth Amendment's coverage might best be approached incrementally, and without the aid of any overly articulated theory of what constitutes the privacy subject to Fourth Amendment regulation. Perhaps incrementalism ensures that the Court's conception of privacy can adapt to changes in culture and technology — the sorts of change evident in *Katz* itself, where the Court grapples with a surveillance technique unknown to the Framers.

4. While the specific holding in *Katz* expanded the scope of the Fourth Amendment's concerns, numerous commentators have observed that its methodology may have led the Court to restrict the definition of "searches" in subsequent cases. Professor Colb has argued, for instance, that since *Katz* was decided, the Court's overall methodology for defining the Fourth Amendment search has "steadily eroded privacy in specific cases, and conceptually promisc[s] to eliminate it altogether." Sherry F. Colb, What is a Search? Two Conceptual Flaws in Fourth Amendment Doctrine and Some Hints of a Remedy, 55 Stan. L. Rev. 119, 121 (2002). If Colb is right (a question you will be better able to answer after considering *Katz*'s progeny) would a more developed theory of Fourth Amendment privacy have helped avoid this result? Was (and is) the Supreme Court situated to provide such a theory?

5. Be aware that one issue lurking just beneath the surface in *Katz* is the degree to which Fourth Amendment regulation should be uniform, with a single set of legal requirements to govern all searches and seizures, or graduated, with greater or lesser regulation depending on the nature and degree of the privacy intrusion at stake. Until fairly recently, Fourth Amendment law followed the first, "all-or-nothing" approach to the regulation of policing. Thus, if a particular police action constituted a "search" or a "seizure," then (at least presumptively) it had to be based on probable cause and authorized by a judicial warrant. As Professor Amsterdam noted some years ago, this approach to the Fourth Amendment strains the process of drawing the Amendment's boundary lines: "Police practices that cry for some form of constitutional control but not the control of a warrant or a probable cause requirement must be dubbed 'searches' and overrestricted or

dubbed something other than searches and left completely unrestricted." It would be both

> easier and more likely for a court to say that a patrolman's shining of a flashlight into the interior of a parked car was a "search" if that conclusion did not encumber the flashlight with a warrant requirement but simply required, for example, that the patrolman "be able to point to specific and articulable facts" supporting a reasonable inference that something in the car required his attention.

Amsterdam, Perspectives on the Fourth Amendment, 58 Minn. L. Rev. at 393. But does this mean that a "graduated approach" to the Fourth Amendment—an approach in which the Amendment would impose lesser or greater restraints on searches and seizures in proportion to their intrusiveness or the nature of the interests they invade—would be preferable? We take up this question in more detail later. For now, consider Professor Amsterdam's famous conclusion that despite the advantages such an approach would have for the process of defining the Fourth Amendment's coverage

> . . . the graduated model . . . [would] convert[ ] the fourth amendment into one immense Rorschach blot. . . . [P]resent law is a positive paragon of simplicity compared to what a graduated fourth amendment would produce. The varieties of police behavior and of the occasions that call it forth are so innumerable that their reflection in a general sliding scale approach could only produce more slide than scale.

Id. at 393-394.

6. *Katz* determined that a physical trespass is not *necessary* to invoke Fourth Amendment protections. But as it turns out, neither is such a trespass automatically *sufficient* to ensure that a given police activity constitutes a search. Long before *Katz*, the Court established an "open fields" doctrine which held that police entry and search of open fields involves no Fourth Amendment intrusion even if officers intrude on privately owned land. Hester v. United States, 265 U.S. 57 (1924). This doctrine was reaffirmed post-*Katz* in Oliver v. United States, 466 U.S. 170 (1984). Oliver and Thornton were charged with drug offenses for cultivating marijuana. Oliver was growing marijuana on his farm, in a field located more than a mile from his house; Thornton's marijuana was growing in two patches in the woods behind his house. Both locations were highly secluded, and both were posted with "No Trespassing" signs. In each case, police officers discovered the marijuana as the result of a warrantless entry onto and inspection of the property. Justice Powell wrote the opinion for the Court concluding that the officers' trespass did not constitute a search:

> The rule announced in Hester v. United States was founded upon the explicit language of the Fourth Amendment. That Amendment indicates with some precision the places and things encompassed by its protections. As Justice Holmes explained for the Court in his characteristically laconic style: "[T]he special protection accorded by the Fourth Amendment to the people in their 'persons, houses, papers, and effects,' is not extended to the open fields. The distinction between the latter and the house is as old as the common law." . . .

This interpretation of the Fourth Amendment's language is consistent with the understanding of the right to privacy expressed in our Fourth Amendment jurisprudence. Since Katz v. United States, 389 U.S. 347 (1967), the touchstone of Amendment analysis has been the question whether a person has a "constitutionally protected reasonable expectation of privacy." Id., at 360 (Harlan, J., concurring). . . .

No single factor determines whether an individual legitimately may claim under the Fourth Amendment that a place should be free of government intrusion not authorized by warrant. In assessing the degree to which a search infringes upon individual privacy, the Court has given weight to such factors as the intention of the Framers . . . , the uses to which the individual has put a location, and our societal understanding that certain areas deserve the most scrupulous protection from government invasion. . . .

In this light, the rule of Hester v. United States, supra, that we reaffirm today, may be understood as providing that an individual may not legitimately demand privacy for activities conducted out of doors in fields, except in the area immediately surrounding the home. This rule is true to the conception of the right to privacy embodied in the Fourth Amendment. The Amendment reflects the recognition of the Framers that certain enclaves should be free from arbitrary government interference. For example, the Court since the enactment of the Fourth Amendment has stressed "the overriding respect for the sanctity of the home that has been embedded in our traditions since the origins of the Republic." Payton v. New York, [445 U.S. 573, 601 (1980)].

In contrast, open fields do not provide the setting for those intimate activities that the Amendment is intended to shelter from government interference or surveillance. There is no societal interest in protecting the privacy of those activities, such as the cultivation of crops, that occur in open fields. Moreover, as a practical matter these lands usually are accessible to the public and the police in ways that a home, an office, or commercial structure would not be. . . .

Nor is the government's intrusion upon an open field a "search" in the constitutional sense because that intrusion is a trespass at common law. The existence of a property right is but one element in determining whether expectations of privacy are legitimate. . . .

Id. at 176-179, 183.

Is Justice Powell's textual argument at all persuasive in light of *Katz*? Justice Marshall, joined by Justices Brennan and Stevens, dissented in *Oliver*, specifically noting that neither the telephone booth in *Katz* nor the conversation conducted therein could fairly be described as a "person, house, paper, or effect" — and yet the *Katz* Court held the Fourth Amendment to apply. But setting this problem aside, what about the majority's analysis of the privacy interests at stake in open fields? The Court rejected a case-by-case approach to the open fields doctrine, noting that police officers should not have to guess before every intrusion "whether landowners had erected fences sufficiently high, posted a sufficient number of warning signs, or located contraband in an area sufficiently secluded to establish a right of privacy." Id. at 181. But is it so clear that even such marked efforts to protect privacy in land outside the immediate confines of the home should be inadequate to establish a Fourth Amendment interest? What happened to the first prong of Justice Harlan's two-prong test? See William C. Heffernan, Fourth Amendment Privacy Interests, 92 J. Crim. L. & Criminology 1, 36 (2001/2002).

7. The open fields doctrine distinguishes between open fields and "curtilage"—the area surrounding the home where reasonable privacy expectations receive Fourth Amendment protection. In United States v. Dunn, 480 U.S. 294 (1987), the Court considered this distinction and concluded that a barn located approximately 50 yards from a fence surrounding the defendant's residence was outside the curtilage and in an open field. In *Dunn*, Drug Enforcement Administration agents had to cross several barbed-wire fences on the defendant's 200-acre ranch to reach the barn. They also had to pass through a wooden fence that enclosed the front portion of the barn in order to get close enough to look inside and observe what appeared to be a drug laboratory. The agents entered the ranch several times before eventually obtaining a warrant, searching the barn, and seizing amphetamines and materials used in the manufacture of controlled substances. The Court concluded that these warrantless entries did not violate Dunn's Fourth Amendment rights because the officers had entered only on open fields, not the curtilage.[1]

The Court reasoned that "curtilage questions should be resolved with particular reference to four factors: the proximity of the area claimed to be curtilage to the home, whether the area is included within an enclosure surrounding the home, the nature of the uses to which the area is put and the steps taken by the resident to protect the area from observations by the people passing by." Id. at 301. The Court rejected the government's argument that it should adopt a bright-line rule that the curtilage extends no farther than the nearest fence surrounding a fenced house, noting that "[a]pplication of the Government's 'first fence rule' might lead to diminished Fourth Amendment protection in those cases where a structure lying outside a home's enclosed fence" is nevertheless used for those intimate activities associated with the home. Id. at 301 n. 4. Does this mean police after *Dunn* must in every case guess how far the curtilage extends? Isn't this precisely the sort of inquiry the Court sought to avoid in *Oliver*? If so, why are questions about the extent of the home's curtilage treated differently from questions about whether a given tract of land constitutes an open field?

8. Police do not always inspect open fields (not to mention curtilage) by walking across them. Sometimes they fly. In California v. Ciraolo, 476 U.S. 207 (1986), police inspected the backyard of a house while flying in a fixed-wing aircraft at 1,000 feet. They discovered marijuana growing there. While recognizing that the yard was within the curtilage of the home and that a fence shielded the yard from street observation, the Court nevertheless held that the aerial surveillance did not constitute a search: "In an age where private and commercial flight in the public airways is routine, it is unreasonable for respondent to expect that his marijuana plants were constitutionally protected from being observed with the naked eye from an altitude of 1,000 feet." Id. at 215. *Ciraolo* set the stage for the next case, where the Justices further explored what constitutes a reasonable expectation of privacy when police officers fly overhead.

---

1. The Court assumed without deciding that Dunn had a protectable interest in the barn itself, but reasoned that prior to obtaining the warrant, the officers never intruded on this interest because they did not enter the barn, but only "stood outside the curtilage of the house and in the open fields upon which the barn was constructed, and peered into the barn's open front." Id. at 304.

FLORIDA v. RILEY

Certiorari to the Supreme Court of Florida
488 U.S. 445 (1989)

JUSTICE WHITE announced the judgment of the Court and delivered an opinion, in which THE CHIEF JUSTICE, JUSTICE SCALIA, and JUSTICE KENNEDY joined.

On certification to it by a lower state court, the Florida Supreme Court addressed the following question: "Whether surveillance of the interior of a partially covered greenhouse in a residential backyard from the vantage point of a helicopter located 400 feet above the greenhouse constitutes a 'search' for which a warrant is required under the Fourth Amendment. . . . " 511 So. 2d 282 (1987). The court answered the question in the affirmative, and we granted the State's petition for certiorari challenging that conclusion.

Respondent Riley lived in a mobile home located on five acres of rural property. A greenhouse was located 10 to 20 feet behind the mobile home. Two sides of the greenhouse were enclosed. The other two sides were not enclosed but the contents of the greenhouse were obscured from view from surrounding property by trees, shrubs, and the mobile home. The greenhouse was covered by corrugated roofing panels, some translucent and some opaque. At the time relevant to this case, two of the panels, amounting to approximately 10% of the roof area, were missing. A wire fence surrounded the mobile home and the greenhouse, and the property was posted with a "DO NOT ENTER" sign.

This case originated with an anonymous tip to the Pasco County Sheriff's office that marijuana was being grown on respondent's property. When an investigating officer discovered that he could not see the contents of the greenhouse from the road, he circled twice over respondent's property in a helicopter at the height of 400 feet. With his naked eye, he was able to see through the openings in the roof and one or more of the open sides of the greenhouse and to identify what he thought was marijuana growing in the structure. A warrant was obtained based on these observations, and the ensuing search revealed marijuana growing in the greenhouse. Respondent was charged with possession of marijuana under Florida law. . . .

We agree with the State's submission that our decision in California v. Ciraolo, 476 U.S. 207 (1986), controls this case. There, acting on a tip, the police inspected the backyard of a particular house while flying in a fixed-wing aircraft at 1,000 feet. With the naked eye the officers saw what they concluded was marijuana growing in the yard. A search warrant was obtained on the strength of this airborne inspection, and marijuana plants were found. . . . We [held] that the inspection was not a search subject to the Fourth Amendment. We recognized that the yard was within the curtilage of the house, that a fence shielded the yard from observation from the street, and that the occupant had a subjective expectation of privacy. We held, however, that such an expectation was not reasonable and not one "that society is prepared to honor." Id., at 214. . . . "In an age where private and commercial flight in the public airways is routine, it is unreasonable for respondent to expect that his marijuana plants were constitutionally protected from being observed with the naked eye from an altitude of 1,000 feet. The Fourth Amendment simply does not require the police traveling in the public airways at this altitude to obtain a warrant in order to observe what is visible to the naked eye." Id., at 215.

We arrive at the same conclusion in the present case. In this case, as in *Ciraolo*, the property surveyed was within the curtilage of respondent's home. Riley no doubt intended and expected that his greenhouse would not be open to public inspection, and the precautions he took protected against ground-level observation. Because the sides and roof of his greenhouse were left partially open, however, what was growing in the greenhouse was subject to viewing from the air. . . .

Nor on the facts before us, does it make a difference for Fourth Amendment purposes that the helicopter was flying at 400 feet when the officer saw what was growing in the greenhouse through the partially open roof and sides of the structure. We would have a different case if flying at that altitude had been contrary to law or regulation. But helicopters are not bound by the lower limits of the navigable airspace allowed to other aircraft. Any member of the public could legally have been flying over Riley's property in a helicopter at the altitude of 400 feet and could have observed Riley's greenhouse. The police officer did no more. This is not to say that an inspection of the curtilage of a house from an aircraft will always pass muster under the Fourth Amendment simply because the plane is within the navigable airspace specified by law. But it is of obvious importance that the helicopter in this case was *not* violating the law, and there is nothing in the record or before us to suggest that helicopters flying at 400 feet are sufficiently rare in this country to lend substance to respondent's claim that he reasonably anticipated that his greenhouse would not be subject to observation from that altitude. Neither is there any intimation here that the helicopter interfered with respondent's normal use of the greenhouse or of other parts of the curtilage. As far as this record reveals, no intimate details connected with the use of the home or curtilage were observed, and there was no undue noise, and no wind, dust, or threat of injury. In these circumstances, there was no violation of the Fourth Amendment. . . .

JUSTICE O'CONNOR, concurring in the judgment. . . .

Observations of curtilage from helicopters at very low altitudes are not perfectly analogous to ground-level observations from public roads or sidewalks. While in both cases the police may have a legal right to occupy the physical space from which their observations are made, the two situations are not necessarily comparable in terms of whether expectations of privacy from such vantage points should be considered reasonable. Public roads, even those less traveled by, are clearly demarked public thoroughfares. Individuals who seek privacy can take precautions, tailored to the location of the road, to avoid disclosing private activities to those who pass by. They can build a tall fence, for example, and thus ensure private enjoyment of the curtilage without risking public observation from the road or sidewalk. If they do not take such precautions, they cannot reasonably expect privacy from public observation. In contrast, even individuals who have taken effective precautions to ensure against ground-level observations cannot block off all conceivable aerial views of their outdoor patios and yards without entirely giving up their enjoyment of those areas. . . . The fact that a helicopter could conceivably observe the curtilage at virtually any altitude or angle, without violating FAA regulations, does not in itself mean that an individual has no reasonable expectation of privacy from such observation.

In determining whether Riley had a reasonable expectation of privacy from aerial observation, the relevant inquiry after *Ciraolo* is not whether the helicopter was where it had a right to be under FAA regulations. Rather, consistent with *Katz*, we must ask whether the helicopter was in the public airways at an altitude at which members of the public travel with sufficient regularity that Riley's expectation of privacy from aerial observation was not "one that society is prepared to recognize as 'reasonable.'" Katz [v. United States, 389 U.S. 347, 361 (1967)]. . . .

In my view, the defendant must bear the burden of proving that his expectation of privacy was a reasonable one, and thus that a "search" within the meaning of the Fourth Amendment even took place. . . .

Because there is reason to believe that there is considerable public use of airspace at altitudes of 400 feet and above, and because Riley introduced no evidence to the contrary before the Florida courts, I conclude that Riley's expectation that his curtilage was protected from naked-eye aerial observation from that altitude was not a reasonable one. However, public use of altitudes lower than that — particularly public observations from helicopters circling over the curtilage of a home — may be sufficiently rare that police surveillance from such altitudes would violate reasonable expectations of privacy, despite compliance with FAA air safety regulations.

JUSTICE BRENNAN, with whom JUSTICE MARSHALL and JUSTICE STEVENS, join, dissenting. . . .

. . . Under the plurality's exceedingly grudging Fourth Amendment theory, the expectation of privacy is defeated if a single member of the public could conceivably position herself to see into the area in question without doing anything illegal. It is defeated whatever the difficulty a person would have in so positioning herself, and however infrequently anyone would in fact do so. In taking this view the plurality ignores the very essence of *Katz*. . . .

In California v. Ciraolo, 476 U.S. 207 (1986), we held that whatever might be observed from the window of an airplane flying at 1,000 feet could be deemed unprotected by any reasonable expectation of privacy. That decision was based on the belief that airplane traffic at that altitude was sufficiently common that no expectation of privacy could inure in anything on the ground observable with the naked eye from so high. . . . Seizing on a reference in *Ciraolo* to the fact that the police officer was in a position "where he ha[d] a right to be," ibid., today's plurality professes to find this case indistinguishable because FAA regulations do not impose a minimum altitude requirement on helicopter traffic; thus, the officer in this case too made his observations from a vantage point where he had a right to be.

It is a curious notion that the reach of the Fourth Amendment can be so largely defined by administrative regulations issued for purposes of flight safety. It is more curious still that the plurality relies to such an extent on the legality of the officer's act, when we have consistently refused to equate police violation of the law with infringement of the Fourth Amendment.[3] But the plurality's willingness to end its inquiry when it finds that the officer was in a position he had a right

3. In *Oliver v. United States*, 466 U.S. 170 (1984), for example, we held that police officers who trespassed upon posted and fenced private land did not violate the Fourth Amendment, despite the fact that their action was subject to criminal sanctions. We noted that the interests vindicated by the Fourth Amendment were not identical with those served by the common law of trespass.

to be in is misguided for an even more fundamental reason. Finding determinative the fact that the officer was where he had a right to be is, at bottom, an attempt to analogize surveillance from a helicopter to surveillance by a police officer standing on a public road and viewing evidence of crime through an open window or a gap in a fence. In such a situation, the occupant of the home may be said to lack any reasonable expectation of privacy in what can be seen from that road — even if, in fact, people rarely pass that way.

The police officer positioned 400 feet above Riley's backyard was not, however, standing on a public road. The vantage point he enjoyed was not one any citizen could readily share. His ability to see over Riley's fence depended on his use of a very expensive and sophisticated piece of machinery to which few ordinary citizens have access. In such circumstances it makes no more sense to rely on the legality of the officer's position in the skies than it would to judge the constitutionality of the wiretap in *Katz* by the legality of the officer's position outside the telephone booth. . . . The question before us must be not whether the police were where they had a right to be, but whether public observation of Riley's curtilage was so commonplace that Riley's expectation of privacy in his backyard could not be considered reasonable. . . .

What separates me from JUSTICE O'CONNOR is essentially an empirical matter concerning the extent of public use of the airspace at that altitude, together with the question of how to resolve that issue. I do not think the constitutional claim should fail simply because "there is reason to believe" that there is "considerable" public flying this close to earth or because Riley "introduced no evidence to the contrary before the Florida courts." . . .

If, however, we are to resolve the issue by considering whether the appropriate party carried its burden of proof, I again think that Riley must prevail. Because the State has greater access to information concerning customary flight patterns and because the coercive power of the State ought not be brought to bear in cases in which it is unclear whether the prosecution is a product of an unconstitutional, warrantless search, the burden of proof properly rests with the State and not with the individual defendant. The State quite clearly has not carried this burden. . . .

JUSTICE BLACKMUN, dissenting.

The question before the Court is whether the helicopter surveillance over Riley's property constituted a "search" within the meaning of the Fourth Amendment. Like JUSTICE BRENNAN, JUSTICE MARSHALL, JUSTICE STEVENS, and JUSTICE O'CONNOR, I believe that answering this question depends upon whether Riley has a "reasonable expectation of privacy" that no such surveillance would occur, and does not depend upon the fact that the helicopter was flying at a lawful altitude under FAA regulations. A majority of this Court thus agrees to at least this much. . . .

[B]ecause I believe that private helicopters rarely fly over curtilages at an altitude of 400 feet, I would impose upon the prosecution the burden of proving contrary facts necessary to show that Riley lacked a reasonable expectation of privacy. Indeed, I would establish this burden of proof for any helicopter surveillance case in which the flight occurred below 1,000 feet — in other words, for any aerial surveillance case not governed by the Court's decision in California v. Ciraolo, 476 U.S. 207 (1986).

In this case, the prosecution did not meet this burden of proof, as JUSTICE BRENNAN notes. This failure should compel a finding that a Fourth Amendment search occurred. But because our prior cases gave the parties little guidance on the burden of proof issue, I would remand this case to allow the prosecution an opportunity to meet this burden. . . .

NOTES AND QUESTIONS

1. The plurality doesn't quite say that the question whether Riley had a reasonable expectation of privacy in his greenhouse turns solely on the applicable FAA regulations; indeed, Justice White specifically rejects that position. But doesn't the plurality's methodology suggest that the mere *possibility* of lawful public observation, rather than its frequency or its likelihood, can render a subjective expectation of privacy unreasonable? As Professor Simmons points out, "Although it is now possible for law enforcement officials — or the general public — to fly in the air and observe the activities in private backyards, the practice is hardly considered routine and commonplace." Ric Simmons, From *Katz* to *Kyllo*: A Blueprint for Adapting the Fourth Amendment to Twenty-first Century Technologies, 53 Hastings L.J. 1303, 1333 (2002). Moreover, shouldn't the reasonableness of Riley's privacy expectation be determined, not by the prevalence of helicopters nationwide, but by the situation in his own rural community? (Parenthetically, who should bear the burden of establishing just how common it is for helicopters to hover at 400 feet in Pasco County?) On the other hand, do we want a body of Fourth Amendment law in which the very meaning of a search might vary from place to place?

2. Because of *Riley* and *Ciraolo*, most aerial surveillance of a home's curtilage is outside the scope of Fourth Amendment concern, while physical invasion of the curtilage is still likely to be held a "search." Does this make any sense? After all, if the Fourth Amendment protects reasonable expectations of privacy, what difference does the police method of intrusion make, so long as equivalent personal information is (or is not) disclosed? See id. at 1306 (arguing that courts should disregard the method of search in applying the *Katz* test and consider "only the result of the search — the type of information that was acquired.") In this connection, consider Bond v. United States, 529 U.S. 334 (2000). In *Bond*, a Border Patrol official who had boarded a bus to check the immigration status of its passengers squeezed the soft luggage that passengers had placed in overhead storage as he walked the bus aisle. His suspicions aroused by a "brick-like" object that he felt in one of the bags, the officer eventually obtained consent to open the bag and discovered a "brick" of methamphetamine. Chief Justice Rehnquist, writing for the Court, concluded that the officer's manipulation of the exterior of the bag constituted a search:

> . . . [T]he Government asserts that by exposing his bag to the public, petitioner lost a reasonable expectation that his bag would not be physically manipulated. The Government relies on our decisions in California v. Ciraolo, [476 U.S. 207 (1986)], and Florida v. Riley, 488 U.S. 445 (1989), for the proposition that matters open to public observation are not protected by the Fourth Amendment. . . .
>
> But *Ciraolo* and *Riley* are different from this case because they involved only visual, as opposed to tactile, observation. Physically invasive inspection is simply more intrusive than purely visual inspection. . . .

Our Fourth Amendment analysis embraces two questions. First, we ask whether the individual, by his conduct, has exhibited an actual expectation of privacy. . . . Here, petitioner sought to preserve privacy by using an opaque bag and placing that bag directly above his seat. Second, we inquire whether the individual's expectation of privacy is "one that society is prepared to recognize as reasonable." When a bus passenger places a bag in an overhead bin, he expects that other passengers or bus employees may move it for one reason or another. . . . He does not expect that other passengers or bus employees will, as a matter of course, feel the bag in an exploratory manner. But this is exactly what the agent did here. . . .

529 U.S. at 337-339. Is the animating vision of privacy in *Katz* starting to look a little complicated? After all, as Justice Breyer pointed out in a dissent joined by Justice Scalia, it is hardly unusual for overhead luggage to be pushed, pulled, prodded and squeezed by people attempting to make room for another parcel. Indeed, "[t]he comparative likelihood that strangers will give bags in an overhead compartment a hard squeeze" does seem far greater than the likelihood that strangers will look down at fenced-in property from an aircraft. 529 U.S. at 341.

Citing *Bond*, Professor Taslitz notes that "[t]he Court does sometimes . . . shift privacy analyses from a probability assessment (combined with a normative one heavily weighing the state's crime control needs) to an affective assessment (combined with a normative focus on how to weigh the emotional harms suffered by the affected individuals)." Andrew E. Taslitz, The Fourth Amendment in the Twenty-first Century: Technology, Privacy, and Human Emotions, 65 Law and Contemp. Prob. 125, 149-150 (2002). But does the majority capture anything fundamental with its distinction between "physically invasive" and "purely visual" inspections? (And on the subject of visual inspections, wasn't it irrelevant in *Katz* that the telephone booth was partly constructed of glass? How does that square with *Bond*?) Contrary to the majority's "affective" analysis, the dissent strongly contended that "[w]hether tactile manipulation (say, of the exterior of luggage) is more intrusive or less intrusive than visual observation (say, through a lighted window) necessarily depends on the particular circumstances." Isn't this correct?

3. Finally, consider United States v. Place, 462 U.S. 695 (1983). Federal narcotics agents suspected that two suitcases in the possession of Raymond Place, a deplaning passenger at LaGuardia Airport, contained narcotics. The officers exposed the suitcases to a "sniff test" by a narcotics detection dog. When the dog reacted positively to one of the suitcases, the officers obtained a search warrant for the bag and discovered that it contained cocaine. The Supreme Court, in an opinion by Justice O'Connor, determined that the "sniff test" was not a Fourth Amendment "search":

A "canine sniff" by a well-trained narcotics detection dog . . . does not require opening the luggage. It does not expose noncontraband items that otherwise would remain hidden from public view, as does, for example, an officer's rummaging through the contents of the luggage. Thus, the manner in which information is obtained through this investigative technique is much less intrusive than a typical search. Moreover, the sniff discloses only the presence or absence of narcotics, a contraband item. Thus, despite the fact that the sniff tells the authorities something about the contents of the luggage, the information obtained is limited. . . .

In these respects, the canine sniff is sui generis. We are aware of no other investigative procedure that is so limited both in the manner in which the information is obtained and in the content of the information revealed by the procedure. Therefore, we conclude that the particular course of investigation that the agents intended to pursue here — exposure of respondent's luggage, which was located in a public place, to a trained canine — did not constitute a "search" within the meaning of the Fourth Amendment.

Id. at 707. What notion of privacy is at work in *Place*? Is the idea that no one can have a reasonable expectation of privacy in criminal activity? Every state's criminal code has hundreds of separate offenses; the federal criminal code has thousands. The large majority of these crimes go almost entirely unenforced. As a practical matter, there may be a great deal of technically criminal behavior that most people would regard as "private" in the ordinary sense of that word. On the other hand, Place's crime was not spitting on the sidewalk. And if the dog was well-trained, passengers without drugs in their suitcases had nothing to fear from this tactic.

On yet *another* hand, physical manipulation of the exterior of a bag likewise reveals a limited amount of information. Is it obvious that the "search" in *Bond* was more intrusive than the dog sniff in *Place*? Is the need for Fourth Amendment regulation of police activity more apparent in one case than in the other?

4. One more thought on Fourth Amendment privacy. As it turns out, much law enforcement investigation involves seeking out the cooperation of witnesses. A suspect's friends and neighbors may be located and interviewed. Perhaps an employer or a relative has relevant information. Most of these witnesses work cooperatively with police; such interactions rarely involve "searches," as Fourth Amendment law construes the term. Yet police investigation of this sort can raise enormous privacy concerns — at least insofar as we conceive of privacy (which can mean many things) as the safeguarding of personal information. Is it a problem that police investigation of this type falls largely outside of Fourth Amendment control? You may want to reconsider this question after you have examined the materials in the next subsection.

b. "Knowingly Expose[d] to the Public"

Recall the *Katz* majority's admonition that "[w]hat a person knowingly exposes to the public, even in his own home or office, is not a subject of Fourth Amendment protection." Katz v. United States, 389 U.S. at 351. This idea has played a central role in shaping the Court's post-*Katz* decisionmaking — and in a direction that some view as placing too much police investigative activity outside Fourth Amendment constraints. The Court's critics may be right or wrong. But to understand the case law and how it is developed, it is centrally important to grapple with this idea of "knowing exposure."

We begin with the sensitive subject of undercover agents and informants. Prior to *Katz*, the Court decided several cases involving the Fourth Amendment's application to the use of undercover agents and informants who engaged in communications with suspects, some of which were either secretly recorded or transmitted to back-up law enforcement personnel. In Hoffa v. United States, 385 U.S. 293, 302 (1966), the Court held that the successful efforts of an informant to obtain the confidence of a suspect and to elicit statements from him involved only "a wrongdoer's misplaced belief that a person to whom he voluntarily confide[d] his wrongdoing [would] not reveal it" — and so "no interest legitimately protected by the Fourth Amendment." Accord, Lewis v. United States, 385 U.S. 206 (1966). The Court had earlier held that neither the recording of statements elicited by an undercover agent, see Lopez v. United States, 373 U.S. 427 (1963), nor the transmission of a suspect's statements to a nearby police officer via a secret microphone hidden on an informant's person, see On Lee v. United States, 343 U.S. 747 (1952), violated the Fourth Amendment. In the next case, the Court addressed the question whether its decision in *Katz* — with its newfound focus on reasonable expectations of privacy — affected these results.

UNITED STATES v. WHITE

Certiorari to the United States Court of Appeals for the Seventh Circuit
401 U.S. 745 (1971)

MR. JUSTICE WHITE announced the judgment of the Court and an opinion in which the CHIEF JUSTICE, MR. JUSTICE STEWART, and MR. JUSTICE BLACKMUN joined.

In 1966, respondent James A. White was tried and convicted under two consolidated indictments charging various illegal transactions in narcotics. . . . The issue before us is whether the Fourth Amendment bars from evidence the testimony of governmental agents who related certain conversations which had occurred between defendant White and a government informant, Harvey Jackson, and which the agents overheard by monitoring the frequency of a radio transmitter carried by Jackson and concealed on his person. On four occasions the conversations took place in Jackson's home; each of these conversations was overheard by an agent concealed in a kitchen closet with Jackson's consent and by a second agent outside the house using a radio receiver. Four other conversations — one in respondent's home, one in a restaurant, and two in Jackson's car — were overheard by the use of radio equipment. The prosecution was unable to locate and produce Jackson at the trial and the trial court overruled objections to the testimony of the agents who conducted the electronic surveillance. The jury returned a guilty verdict and defendant appealed. . . .

Our problem is not what the privacy expectations of particular defendants in particular situations may be or the extent to which they may in fact have relied on the discretion of their companions. Very probably, individual defendants neither know nor suspect that their colleagues have gone or will go to the police or are carrying recorders or transmitters. Otherwise, conversation would cease and our problem with these encounters would be nonexistent or far different from those now before us. Our problem, in terms of the principles announced in *Katz*, is what expectations of privacy are constitutionally "justifiable" — what expectations the Fourth Amendment will protect in the absence of a warrant. So far, the law permits the frustration of actual expectations of privacy by permitting authorities to use the testimony of those associates who for one reason or another have determined to turn to the police, as well as by authorizing the use of informants in the manner exemplified by *Hoffa* and *Lewis*.[2] If the law gives no protection to the wrongdoer

2. Justice White described *Hoffa* and *Lewis* earlier in the opinion as follows:

Hoffa . . . , which was left undisturbed by *Katz*, held that however strongly a defendant may trust an apparent colleague, his expectations in this respect are not protected by the Fourth

whose trusted accomplice is or becomes a police agent, neither should it protect him when that same agent has recorded or transmitted the conversations which are later offered in evidence to prove the State's case.

Inescapably, one contemplating illegal activities must realize and risk that his companions may be reporting to the police. If he sufficiently doubts their trustworthiness, the association will very probably end or never materialize. But if he has no doubts, or allays them, or risks what doubt he has, the risk is his. In terms of what his course will be, what he will or will not do or say, we are unpersuaded that he would distinguish between probable informers on the one hand and probable informers with transmitters on the other. Given the possibility or probability that one of his colleagues is cooperating with the police, it is only speculation to assert that the defendant's utterances would be substantially different or his sense of security any less if he also thought it possible that the suspected colleague is wired for sound. At least there is no persuasive evidence that the difference in this respect between the electronically equipped and the unequipped agent is substantial enough to require discrete constitutional recognition, particularly under the Fourth Amendment which is ruled by fluid concepts of "reasonableness."

Nor should we be too ready to erect constitutional barriers to relevant and probative evidence which is also accurate and reliable. An electronic recording will many times produce a more reliable rendition of what a defendant has said than will the unaided memory of a police agent. It may also be that with the recording in existence it is less likely that the informant will change his mind, less chance that threat or injury will suppress unfavorable evidence and less chance that cross-examination will confound the testimony. Considerations like these obviously do not favor the defendant, but we are not prepared to hold that a defendant who has no constitutional right to exclude the informer's unaided testimony nevertheless has a Fourth Amendment privilege against a more accurate version of the events in question.

It is thus untenable to consider the activities and reports of the police agent himself, though acting without a warrant, to be a "reasonable" investigative effort and lawful under the Fourth Amendment but to view the same agent with a recorder or transmitter as conducting an "unreasonable" and unconstitutional search and seizure. Our opinion is currently shared by Congress and the Executive Branch, Title III, Omnibus Crime Control and Safe Streets Act of 1968, 82 Stat. 212, 18 U.S.C. §2510 et seq. (1964 ed., Supp. V), and the American Bar Association. Project on Standards for Criminal Justice, Electronic Surveillance §4.1 (Approved Draft 1971). It is also the result reached by prior cases in this Court. . . .

The judgment of the Court of Appeals is reversed.[3]

Amendment when it turns out that the colleague is a government agent regularly communicating with the authorities. . . . No warrant to "search and seize" is required in such circumstances, nor is it when the Government sends to defendant's home a secret agent who conceals his identity and makes a purchase of narcotics from the accused, *Lewis.* . . . — EDS.

3. The Court had earlier held in Desist v. United States, 394 U.S. 244 (1969), that *Katz* would not be applied retroactively to electronic surveillance predating the *Katz* decision. Since the activity in *White* occurred prior to that decision, Justice White's plurality opinion relied on *Desist* as an independent basis for affirming the conviction. Justice Brennan believed that *Katz* required overruling both *On Lee* and *Lopez* but concurred with the four-justice plurality on the retroactivity issue. — EDS.

MR. JUSTICE BLACK concurs in the judgment of the Court for the reasons set forth in his dissent in Katz v. United States.

[The concurring opinion of Justice Brennan is omitted.]

MR. JUSTICE DOUGLAS, dissenting.

The issue in this case is clouded and concealed by the very discussion of it in legalistic terms. What the ancients knew as "eavesdropping," we now call "electronic surveillance"; but to equate the two is to treat man's first gunpowder on the same level as the nuclear bomb. Electronic surveillance is the greatest leveler of human privacy ever known. How most forms of it can be held "reasonable" within the meaning of the Fourth Amendment is a mystery. To be sure, the Constitution and Bill of Rights are not to be read as covering only the technology known in the 18th century. Otherwise its concept of "commerce" would be hopeless when it comes to the management of modern affairs. At the same time the concepts of privacy which the Founders enshrined in the Fourth Amendment vanish completely when we slavishly allow an all-powerful government, proclaiming law and order, efficiency, and other benign purposes, to penetrate all the walls and doors which men need to shield them from the pressures of a turbulent life around them and give them the health and strength to carry on. . . .

Monitoring, if prevalent, certainly kills free discourse and spontaneous utterances. Free discourse — a First Amendment value — may be frivolous or serious, humble or defiant, reactionary or revolutionary, profane or in good taste; but it is not free if there is surveillance. Free discourse liberates the spirit, though it may produce only froth. The individual must keep some facts concerning his thoughts within a small zone of people. At the same time he must be free to pour out his woes or inspirations or dreams to others. He remains the sole judge as to what must be said and what must remain unspoken. This is the essence of the idea of privacy implicit in the First and Fifth Amendments as well as in the Fourth. . . .

MR. JUSTICE HARLAN, dissenting. . . .

The plurality opinion . . . [adopts] the following reasoning: if A can relay verbally what is revealed to him by B (as in Lewis and Hoffa), or record and later divulge it (as in Lopez), what difference does it make if A conspires with another to betray B by contemporaneously transmitting to the other all that is said? The contention is, in essence, an argument that the distinction between third-party monitoring and other undercover techniques is one of form and not substance. The force of the contention depends on the evaluation of two separable but intertwined assumptions: first, that there is no greater invasion of privacy in the third-party situation, and, second, that uncontrolled consensual surveillance in an electronic age is a tolerable technique of law enforcement, given the values and goals of our political system.

The first of these assumptions takes as a point of departure the so-called "risk analysis" approach of Lewis, and Lopez, and to a lesser extent On Lee, or the expectations approach of Katz. While these formulations represent an advance over the unsophisticated trespass analysis of the common law, they too have their limitations and can, ultimately, lead to the substitution of words for analysis. The analysis must, in my view, transcend the search for subjective expectations or legal attribution of assumptions of risk. Our expectations, and the risks we assume, are in large part reflections of laws that translate into rules the customs and values of the past and present.

Since it is the task of the law to form and project, as well as mirror and reflect, we should not, as judges, merely recite the expectations and risks without examining the desirability of saddling them upon society. The critical question, therefore, is whether under our system of government, as reflected in the Constitution, we should impose on our citizens the risks of the electronic listener or observer without at least the protection of a warrant requirement.

This question must, in my view, be answered by assessing the nature of a particular practice and the likely extent of its impact on the individual's sense of security balanced against the utility of the conduct as a technique of law enforcement. For those more extensive intrusions that significantly jeopardize the sense of security which is the paramount concern of Fourth Amendment liberties, I am of the view that more than self-restraint by law enforcement officials is required and at the least warrants should be necessary.

The impact of the practice of third-party bugging, must, I think, be considered such as to undermine that confidence and sense of security in dealing with one another that is characteristic of individual relationships between citizens in a free society. It goes beyond the impact on privacy occasioned by the ordinary type of "informer" investigation upheld in *Lewis* and *Hoffa*. The argument of the plurality opinion, to the effect that it is irrelevant whether secrets are revealed by the mere tattletale or the transistor, ignores the differences occasioned by third-party monitoring and recording which insures full and accurate disclosure of all that is said, free of the possibility of error and oversight that inheres in human reporting.

Authority is hardly required to support the proposition that words would be measured a good deal more carefully and communication inhibited if one suspected his conversations were being transmitted and transcribed. Were third-party bugging a prevalent practice, it might well smother that spontaneity — reflected in frivolous, impetuous, sacrilegious, and defiant discourse — that liberates daily life. Much off-hand exchange is easily forgotten and one may count on the obscurity of his remarks, protected by the very fact of a limited audience, and the likelihood that the listener will either overlook or forget what is said, as well as the listener's inability to reformulate a conversation without having to contend with a documented record.[24] All these values are sacrificed by a rule of law that permits official monitoring of private discourse limited only by the need to locate a willing assistant. . . .

Finally, it is too easy to forget — and, hence, too often forgotten — that the issue here is whether to interpose a search warrant procedure between law enforcement

---

24. From the same standpoint it may also be thought that electronic recording by an informer of a face-to-face conversation with a criminal suspect, as in *Lopez*, should be differentiated from third-party monitoring, as in *On Lee* and the case before us, in that the latter assures revelation to the Government by obviating the possibility that the informer may be tempted to renege in his undertaking to pass on to the Government all that he has learned. While the continuing vitality of *Lopez* is not drawn directly into question by this case, candor compels me to acknowledge that the views expressed in this opinion may impinge upon that part of the reasoning in *Lopez* which suggested that a suspect has no right to anticipate unreliable testimony. I am now persuaded that such an approach misconceives the basic issue, focusing, as it does, on the interests of a particular individual rather than evaluating the impact of a practice on the sense of security that is the true concern of the Fourth Amendment's protection of privacy. Distinctions do, however, exist between *Lopez*, where a known Government agent uses a recording device, and this case which involves third-party overhearing. However unlikely that the participant recorder will not play his tapes, the fact of the matter is that in a third-party situation the intrusion is instantaneous. Moreover, differences in the prior relationship between the investigator and the suspect may provide a focus for future distinctions.

agencies engaging in electronic eavesdropping and the public generally. By casting its "risk analysis" solely in terms of the expectations and risks that "wrongdoers" or "one contemplating illegal activities" ought to bear, the plurality opinion, I think, misses the mark entirely. *On Lee* does not simply mandate that criminals must daily run the risk of unknown eavesdroppers prying into their private affairs; it subjects each and every law-abiding member of society to that risk. The very purpose of interposing the Fourth Amendment warrant requirement is to redistribute the privacy risks throughout society in a way that produces the results the plurality opinion ascribes to the *On Lee* rule. Abolition of *On Lee* would not end electronic eavesdropping. It would prevent public officials from engaging in that practice unless they first had probable cause to suspect an individual of involvement in illegal activities and had tested their version of the facts before a detached judicial officer. . . .

[The dissenting opinion of JUSTICE MARSHALL is omitted.]

NOTES AND QUESTIONS

1. According to the plurality opinion in *White*, it makes no sense to recognize a Fourth Amendment privilege against the use at trial of an accurate version of one's conversation — a version secretly tape-recorded or transmitted by an informant—when there is no Fourth Amendment privilege barring the informant from testifying to his recollection of the conversation. But this argument begs the question whether the Court took a wrong turn in *Hoffa* and *Lewis*. The basis for the holdings in these "unbugged agent" cases was that persons assume the risk that their trusted colleagues may be or may become government agents. But should we have to assume this risk? At least when the government places a covert agent in our midst to cajole us into talking, isn't it "constitutionally justifiable" to impose the requirement of a warrant based on probable cause?

In part, the answer may depend on which metaphor one chooses. Current doctrine tends to emphasize the comparison between the undercover agent and a gossipy friend, the idea being that, just as we all bear the risk that our friends will repeat things they've heard us say, so suspects bear the risk that people they trust (including successful undercover agents) will betray that trust. An alternative comparison is between the undercover agent and a spy. Like spies (and unlike gossipy friends), undercover agents are not who they pretend to be — they are not friends who talk too much but rather are more like enemies who pretend to be friends. Do we really bear the risk of spies in our ordinary lives? If not, should we bear the risk of police spies? Why should the Fourth Amendment reach a transmitting device placed on a telephone booth but not one placed on a person charged with following the suspect and eliciting potentially incriminating statements?

2. Perhaps the results in cases like *Hoffa*, *Lewis*, and *White* stem from the recognition that certain crimes cannot be investigated effectively without using covert agents and that the warrant and probable cause requirements would unduly frustrate their use. Professor Philip Heymann has argued that undercover operations are most important to the investigation of crimes that cannot be readily observed and reported by witnesses and that will not be reported by participants or victims. See Philip Heymann, Understanding Criminal Investigations, 22 Harv. J. Legis.

315, 325-327, 331-334 (1985). Narcotics trafficking and the bribery of public officials, for instance, involve willing participants and infrequently produce victims who notice they have been harmed. Similarly, the intimidation of witnesses makes it difficult to investigate crimes like loan sharking or extortion. Requiring an overly rigorous form of factual justification prior to use of a covert agent "could altogether eliminate the use of undercover operations in even the most pressing situations." Id. at 332.

Assume for the moment that Heymann is right. (He probably is.) How much weight should courts give this kind of government need? If the investigation of some but not all crimes requires covert methods, should Fourth Amendment law differ according to the kinds of crime police investigate? Whatever the best answer in theory, historically Fourth Amendment law does seem to have responded to law enforcement needs, and law enforcement needs are in part a function of what crimes the police investigate. For now, note three points: First, some crimes by their nature require much more in the way of privacy intrusion to investigate than others. Second, as Heymann's article emphasizes, those crimes often (though not always) involve consensual transactions. Third and finally, our society devotes a great deal of energy and resources to attacking drug crime, which primarily consists of consensual transactions. Given those three points, perhaps the outcome in *White* should seem unsurprising.

3. The plurality opinion in *White* cites Title III of the Omnibus Crime Control and Safe Streets Act of 1968, which is treated in more detail in Chapter 7. In the wake of *Katz* and also Berger v. New York, 388 U.S. 41 (1967), which held New York's wiretap statute to be unconstitutional,[4] Congress enacted Title III to establish procedures for the use of electronic eavesdropping by law enforcement that would be consistent with the Court's holdings. After its enactment, most states passed their own statutes patterned on Title III's provisions. Today, Title III and similar state statutes, along with more recently enacted laws like the Electronic Communications Privacy Act of 1986, regulate not only the use of traditional wiretaps and the electronic surveillance of oral communications, but also the interception of electronic communications such as e-mail. Most of these statutes, however, do not apply to the recording or third-party surveillance of a communication when one of the parties to the communication consents — hence, they play little role in regulating police use of undercovers and informants.

4. Finally, notice that by the time *White* was decided, Justice Harlan, the author of the "reasonable expectations" approach, was already expressing reservations about any analytic framework for Fourth Amendment coverage questions — including his own — that might lead to the "substitution of words for analysis." Whatever you may think about the result in *White*, doesn't it suggest that Justice Harlan's caution may be well taken? Does *White*'s methodology amount to a conclusion that the "knowing exposure" of one's words to another forfeits the protections of the Fourth Amendment if that other elects to betray us? Doesn't this mean, in practice, that we secure Fourth Amendment protection for what we choose to say only by saying nothing? Is this approach to defining the Fourth Amendment's scope consistent with any robust account of the privacy interests that the Amendment should protect? Ponder the *Katz* Court's statement that "[w]hat a person knowingly exposes to the public" cannot be the subject of

---

4. *Berger* is discussed in Chapter 4 at pages 304-307.

Fourth Amendment protection as you read the following case. Is the next case an example of how a legal formula can take on a life of its own?

CALIFORNIA v. GREENWOOD

Certiorari to the Court of Appeal of California, Fourth Appellate District
486 U.S. 35 (1988)

JUSTICE WHITE delivered the opinion of the Court. . . .

In early 1984, Investigator Jenny Stracner of the Laguna Beach Police Department received information indicating that respondent Greenwood might be engaged in narcotics trafficking. . . . On April 6, 1984, Stracner asked the neighborhood's regular trash collector to pick up the plastic garbage bags that Greenwood had left on the curb in front of his house and to turn the bags over to her without mixing their contents with garbage from other houses. The trash collector cleaned his truck bin of other refuse, collected the garbage bags from the street in front of Greenwood's house, and turned the bags over to Stracner. The officer searched through the rubbish and found items indicative of narcotics use. She recited the information that she had gleaned from the trash search in an affidavit in support of a warrant to search Greenwood's home.

Police officers encountered both respondents at the house later that day when they arrived to execute the warrant. The police discovered quantities of cocaine and hashish during their search of the house. Respondents were arrested on felony narcotics charges. They subsequently posted bail.

The police continued to receive reports of many late-night visitors to the Greenwood house. On May 4, Investigator Robert Rahaeuser obtained Greenwood's garbage from the regular trash collector in the same manner as had Stracner. The garbage again contained evidence of narcotics use.

Rahaeuser secured another search warrant for Greenwood's home based on the information from the second trash search. The police found more narcotics and evidence of narcotics trafficking when they executed the warrant. Greenwood was again arrested.

The Superior Court dismissed the charges against respondents on the authority of *People v. Krivda*, 5 Cal. 3d 357 (1971), which held that warrantless trash searches violate the Fourth Amendment. . . . The court found that the police would not have had probable cause to search the Greenwood home without the evidence obtained from the trash searches.

The Court of Appeal affirmed. . . .

The California Supreme Court denied the State's petition for review of the Court of Appeal's decision. We granted certiorari, and now reverse.

The warrantless search and seizure of the garbage bags left at the curb outside the Greenwood house would violate the Fourth Amendment only if respondents manifested a subjective expectation of privacy in their garbage that society accepts as objectively reasonable. Respondents do not disagree with this standard.

They assert, however, that they had, and exhibited, an expectation of privacy with respect to the trash that was searched by the police: The trash, which was placed on the street for collection at a fixed time, was contained in opaque plastic bags, which the garbage collector was expected to pick up, mingle with the trash of others, and deposit at the garbage dump. The trash was only temporarily on the street, and there was little likelihood that it would be inspected by anyone.

It may well be that respondents did not expect that the contents of their garbage bags would become known to the police or other members of the public. An expectation of privacy does not give rise to Fourth Amendment protection, however, unless society is prepared to accept that expectation as objectively reasonable.

Here, we conclude that respondents exposed their garbage to the public sufficiently to defeat their claim to Fourth Amendment protection. It is common knowledge that plastic garbage bags left on or at the side of a public street are readily accessible to animals, children, scavengers, snoops,[4] and other members of the public. Moreover, respondents placed their refuse at the curb for the express purpose of conveying it to a third party, the trash collector, who might himself have sorted through respondents' trash or permitted others, such as the police, to do so. . . .

[A]s we have held, the police cannot reasonably be expected to avert their eyes from evidence of criminal activity that could have been observed by any member of the public. Hence, "[w]hat a person knowingly exposes to the public, even in his own home or office, is not a subject of Fourth Amendment protection." Katz v. United States. . . .

The judgment of the California Court of Appeal is therefore reversed. . . .

It is so ordered.

JUSTICE KENNEDY took no part in the consideration or decision of this case.

JUSTICE BRENNAN, with whom JUSTICE MARSHALL joins, dissenting.

Every week for two months, and at least once more a month later, the Laguna Beach police clawed through the trash that respondent Greenwood left in opaque, sealed bags on the curb outside his home. Complete strangers minutely scrutinized their bounty, undoubtedly dredging up intimate details of Greenwood's private life and habits. The intrusions proceeded without a warrant, and no court before or since has concluded that the police acted on probable cause to believe Greenwood was engaged in any criminal activity. . . .

The Framers of the Fourth Amendment understood that "unreasonable searches" of "paper[s] and effects" — no less than "unreasonable searches" of "person[s] and houses" — infringe privacy. . . . [S]o long as a package is "closed against inspection," the Fourth Amendment protects its contents, "wherever they may be," and the police must obtain a warrant to search it just "as is required when papers are subjected to search in one's own household." . . .

Our precedent . . . leaves no room to doubt that had respondents been carrying their personal effects in opaque, sealed plastic bags — identical to the ones they placed on the curb — their privacy would have been protected from warrantless police intrusion. . . .

---

4. Even the refuse of prominent Americans has not been invulnerable. In 1975, for example, a reporter for a weekly tabloid seized five bags of garbage from the sidewalk outside the home of Secretary of State Henry Kissinger. Washington Post, July 9, 1975, p. A1, col. 8. A newspaper editorial criticizing this journalistic "trashpicking" observed that "[e]vidently . . . 'everybody does it.'" Washington Post, July 10, 1975, p. A18, col. 1. We of course do not, as the dissent implies, "bas[e] [our] conclusion" that individuals have no reasonable expectation of privacy in their garbage on this "sole incident." Post, at 51.

Respondents deserve no less protection just because Greenwood used the bags to discard rather than to transport his personal effects. Their contents are not inherently any less private, and Greenwood's decision to discard them, at least in the manner in which he did, does not diminish his expectation of privacy.

A trash bag, like [other containers we have addressed,] "is a common repository for one's personal effects" and, even more than many of them, is "therefore . . . inevitably associated with the expectation of privacy." . . . A single bag of trash testifies eloquently to the eating, reading, and recreational habits of the person who produced it. A search of trash, like a search of the bedroom, can relate intimate details about sexual practices, health, and personal hygiene. Like rifling through desk drawers or intercepting phone calls, rummaging through trash can divulge the target's financial and professional status, political affiliations and inclinations, private thoughts, personal relationships, and romantic interests. It cannot be doubted that a sealed trash bag harbors telling evidence of the "intimate activity associated with the 'sanctity of a man's home and the privacies of life,' " which the Fourth Amendment is designed to protect.

The Court properly rejects the State's attempt to distinguish trash searches from other searches on the theory that trash is abandoned and therefore not entitled to an expectation of privacy. As the author of the Court's opinion observed last Term, a defendant's "property interest [in trash] does not settle the matter for Fourth Amendment purposes, for the reach of the Fourth Amendment is not determined by state property law." [California v. Rooney, 483 U.S. 307, 320 (1987)] (WHITE, J., dissenting). In evaluating the reasonableness of Greenwood's expectation that his sealed trash bags would not be invaded, the Court has held that we must look to "understandings that are recognized and permitted by society." Most of us, I believe, would be incensed to discover a meddler — whether a neighbor, a reporter, or a detective — scrutinizing our sealed trash containers to discover some detail of our personal lives. That was, quite naturally, the reaction to the sole incident on which the Court bases its conclusion that "snoops" and the like defeat the expectation of privacy in trash. When a tabloid reporter examined then-Secretary of State Henry Kissinger's trash and published his findings, Kissinger was "really revolted" by the intrusion and his wife suffered "grave anguish." N.Y. Times, July 9, 1975, p. A1, col. 8. The public response roundly condemning the reporter demonstrates that society not only recognized those reactions as reasonable, but shared them as well. . . .

That is not to deny that isolated intrusions into opaque, sealed trash containers occur. When, acting on their own, "animals, children, scavengers, snoops, [or] other members of the public," *actually* rummage through a bag of trash and expose its contents to plain view, "police cannot reasonably be expected to avert their eyes from evidence of criminal activity that could have been observed by any member of the public." . . .

Had Greenwood flaunted his intimate activity by strewing his trash all over the curb for all to see, or had some nongovernmental intruder invaded his privacy and done the same, I could accept the Court's conclusion that an expectation of privacy would have been unreasonable. Similarly, had police searching the city dump run across incriminating evidence that, despite commingling with the trash of others, still retained its identity as Greenwood's, we would have a different case. But all that Greenwood "exposed . . . to the public," were the exteriors of several opaque, sealed containers. . . .

The mere *possibility* that unwelcome meddlers *might* open and rummage through the containers does not negate the expectation of privacy in their contents any more than the possibility of a burglary negates an expectation of privacy in the home; or the possibility of a private intrusion negates an expectation of privacy in an unopened package; or the possibility that an operator will listen in on a telephone conversation negates an expectation of privacy in the words spoken on the telephone. "What a person . . . seeks to preserve as private, *even in an area accessible to the public*, may be constitutionally protected." *Katz*, 389 U.S., at 351-352. We have therefore repeatedly rejected attempts to justify a State's invasion of privacy on the ground that the privacy is not absolute. See Chapman v. United States, 365 U.S. 610, 616-617 (1961) (search of a house invaded tenant's Fourth Amendment rights even though landlord had authority to enter house for some purposes); Stoner v. California, 376 U.S. 483, 487-490 (1964) (implicit consent to janitorial personnel to enter motel room does not amount to consent to police search of room); O'Connor v. Oretega, 480 U.S. 709, 717 (1987) (a government employee has a reasonable expectation of privacy in his office, even though "it is the nature of government offices that others — such as fellow employees, supervisors, consensual visitors, and the general public — may have frequent access to an individual's office"). . . .

Nor is it dispositive that "respondents placed their refuse at the curb for the express purpose of conveying it to a third party, . . . who might himself have sorted through respondents' trash or permitted others, such as the police, to do so." In the first place, Greenwood can hardly be faulted for leaving trash on his curb when a county ordinance commanded him to do so, Orange County Code §4-3-45(a) (1986) (must "remov[e] from the premises at least once each week" all "solid waste created, produced or accumulated in or about [his] dwelling house"), and prohibited him from disposing of it in any other way, see Orange County Code §3-3-85 (1988) (burning trash is unlawful). . . . More importantly, even the voluntary relinquishment of possession or control over an effect does not necessarily amount to a relinquishment of a privacy expectation in it. Were it otherwise, a letter or package would lose all Fourth Amendment protection when placed in a mailbox or other depository with the "express purpose" of entrusting it to the postal officer or a private carrier; those bailees are just as likely as trash collectors (and certainly have greater incentive) to "sor[t] through" the personal effects entrusted to them, "or permi[t] others, such as police to do so." Yet, it has been clear for at least 110 years that the possibility of such an intrusion does not justify a warrantless search by police in the first instance.

In holding that the warrantless search of Greenwood's trash was consistent with the Fourth Amendment, the Court paints a grim picture of our society. It depicts a society in which local authorities may command their citizens to dispose of their personal effects in the manner least protective of the "sanctity of [the] home and the privacies of life," Boyd v. United States, 116 U.S., at 630, and then monitor them arbitrarily and without judicial oversight — a society that is not prepared to recognize as reasonable an individual's expectation of privacy in the most private of personal effects sealed in an opaque container and disposed of in a manner designed to commingle it imminently and inextricably with the trash of others. The American society with which I am familiar . . . is more dedicated to individual liberty and more sensitive to intrusions on the sanctity of the home than the Court is willing to acknowledge.

I dissent.

NOTES AND QUESTIONS

1. What do you think? Does *Greenwood* represent a defensible approach to privacy protection, or does it, as Justice Harlan cautioned in *White*, substitute words for analysis? Be aware that the Court has invoked the concept of "knowing exposure" in a number of cases to limit the Fourth Amendment's coverage. Thus, a bank depositor has no protectible Fourth Amendment interest in the bank's microfilms of his checks, deposit slips, and other financial records related to his account because he "takes the risk, in revealing his affairs to another, that the information will be conveyed by that person to the Government." United States v. Miller, 424 U.S. 435, 443 (1976). Similarly, the telephone company's installation at its offices pursuant to police request of a pen register to record the numbers dialed on an individual's telephone raises no Fourth Amendment concern because individuals "voluntarily convey[ ] numerical information to the telephone company and 'expose[ ]' that information . . . in the ordinary course of business." Smith v. Maryland, 442 U.S. 735, 744 (1979).

2. Whether these results are defensible, there are a number of questions about the Court's approach in these and similar cases. As Professor Heffernan has said, the cases seem to suggest that we have privacy expectations only in contexts where we demonstrate "eternal vigilance" against others: "[E]ven the slightest exposure of an item to the public can defeat a privacy claim." William C. Heffernan, Fourth Amendment Privacy Interests, 92 J. Crim. L. & Criminology 1, 38-40 (2001/2002). But Heffernan argues that our actual experiences with what is "public" and what is "private" don't lead us to be eternally vigilant against the scrutiny of others, but instead to rely on "an expectation that outsiders will exercise forbearance with respect to personal matters." Think of all our limited, special-purpose revelations of private information: "[P]eople who take steps to ensure that the public does not have access to their financial records nonetheless routinely rely on bank officials to process their checks and deposits." Id. at 39. If we expose things to others all the time on the expectation that these others will respect our privacy, does this suggest a problem with the Court's framework?

3. For that matter, do we have any choice but to make such special-purpose revelations? We may "knowingly" reveal our deposit information to the bank and the numbers we dial to the telephone company, but are such revelations in any sense voluntary — at least assuming we want to live in the complex and interdependent society that we call our own? Note Justice Brennan's observation that Greenwood was required by law to leave his garbage at the curb. Shouldn't the law entitle Greenwood to rely on the garbage collector's rectitude about personal information that his garbage might disclose — particularly given his limited options for trash disposal?

4. Professor Coombs has argued that cases like *Greenwood*, *Miller*, and *Smith* reflect a narrow, individualistic conception of privacy that is deeply contrary to reality: "Much of what is important in human life takes place in a situation of shared privacy. The important events in our lives are shared with a chosen group of others; they do not occur in isolation, nor are they open to the entire world." Mary I. Coombs, Shared Privacy and the Fourth Amendment, or the Rights of Relationships, 75 Cal. L. Rev. 1593 (1987). Though the Court has viewed such "sharing" as proof of the absence of reasonable privacy expectations, it is not clear that citizens view privacy in the same way. The survey participants in one

empirical study, for instance, considered the government perusal of bank records to be highly intrusive. See Christopher Slobogin & Joseph E. Schumacher, Reasonable Expectations of Privacy and Autonomy in Fourth Amendment Cases: An Empirical Look at "Understandings Recognized and Permitted by Society," 42 Duke L.J. 727, 740 (1993).

c. Privacy and Technology

When the Fourth Amendment was written and ratified, the chief tools used for "searches" were the constable's eyes and a lantern. There were no listening devices; eavesdropping was done with the human ear, not wires or bugs. Today, a great many searches are still performed by the unaided eyes and ears of a police officer. But a great many make use of surveillance techniques and technologies that no one imagined in 1791. You have already encountered some of those technologies: telephones and "bugs" in *Katz*, the helicopter in *Riley*, the wire worn by the informant in *White*. What happens when the technology is more advanced? In the years since *Katz*, the Supreme Court has made plain that anything that a suspect "knowingly exposes" to the public is exposed to the police as well. But how are courts to measure what is, and isn't, "exposed"? Is it anything any member of the public could see or hear with the most advanced surveillance technology available? Anything the *police* can see or hear with the most advanced technology available to *them*?

We begin with electronic tracking devices. In United States v. Knotts, 460 U.S. 276 (1983), the Court held that no search took place when police monitored a beeper attached to a drum of chloroform, a chemical commonly used for the manufacture of illegal drugs, to track the movements of a car they knew to be carrying the drum. The Court concluded that a person travelling in a car on public thoroughfares has no reasonable expectation of privacy in his movements from one place to the next because he "voluntarily convey[s] to anyone who want[s] to look the fact that he [is] travelling over particular roads in a particular direction, the fact of whatever stops he ma[kes], and the fact of his final destination when he exit[s] from public roads onto private property." Id. at 281-282. Is this a sound application of the "knowingly exposed" principle? Does it seem right that we have no reasonable expectation of privacy in our movements from place to place? Or do we reasonably possess some measure of privacy in public places — if only by virtue of our anonymity and the inattention of others? The next case, also involving the use of an electronic tracking device, provided the Court with a second opportunity to pursue this and related issues only one year after *Knotts* was decided.

UNITED STATES v. KARO

Certiorari to the United States Court of Appeals for the Tenth Circuit
468 U.S. 705 (1984)

JUSTICE WHITE delivered the opinion of the Court.

In United States v. Knotts, 460 U.S. 276 (1983), we held that the warrantless monitoring of an electronic tracking device ("beeper") inside a container of chemicals did not violate the Fourth Amendment when it revealed no information that could not have been obtained through visual surveillance. In this case, we are called upon to address two questions left unresolved in *Knotts*: (1) whether installation of a beeper in a container of chemicals with the consent of the original owner constitutes a search or seizure within the meaning of the Fourth Amendment when the container is delivered to a buyer having no knowledge of the presence of the beeper, and (2) whether monitoring of a beeper falls within the ambit of the Fourth Amendment when it reveals information that could not have been obtained through visual surveillance.

In August 1980 Agent Rottinger of the Drug Enforcement Administration (DEA) learned that respondents James Karo, Richard Horton, and William Harley had ordered 50 gallons of ether from Government informant Carl Muehlenweg of Graphic Photo Design in Albuquerque, N.M. Muehlenweg told Rottinger that the ether was to be used to extract cocaine from clothing that had been imported into the United States. . . . With Muehlenweg's consent, agents substituted their own can containing a beeper for one of the cans in the shipment and then had all 10 cans painted to give them a uniform appearance.

On September 20, 1980, agents saw Karo pick up the ether from Muehlenweg. They then followed Karo to his house using visual and beeper surveillance. At one point later that day, agents determined by using the beeper that the ether was still inside the house, but they later determined that it had been moved undetected to Horton's house, where they located it using the beeper. . . . Two days later, agents discovered that the ether had once again been moved, and, using the beeper, they located it at the residence of Horton's father. The next day, the beeper was no longer transmitting from Horton's father's house, and agents traced the beeper to a commercial storage facility. . . .

Using the beeper, agents traced the beeper can to another self-storage facility three days later. Agents detected the smell of ether coming from locker 15 and learned from the manager that Horton and Harley had rented that locker using an alias the same day that the ether had been removed from the first storage facility. The agents . . . obtained consent from the manager of the facility to install a closed-circuit video camera in a locker that had a view of locker 15. On February 6, 1981, agents observed, by means of the video camera, Gene Rhodes and an unidentified woman removing the cans from the locker and loading them onto the rear bed of Horton's pickup truck. Using both visual and beeper surveillance agents tracked the truck to Rhodes' residence where it was parked in the driveway. Agents then observed Rhodes and a woman bringing boxes and other items from inside the house and loading the items into the trunk of an automobile. Agents did not see any cans being transferred from the pickup.

At about 6 p.m. on February 6, the car and the pickup left the driveway and traveled along public highways to Taos. During the trip, the two vehicles were under both physical and electronic surveillance. When the vehicles arrived at a house in Taos rented by Horton, Harley, and Michael Steele, the agents did not maintain tight surveillance for fear of detection. When the vehicles left the Taos residence, agents determined, using the beeper monitor, that the beeper can was still inside the house. Again on February 7, the beeper revealed that the ether can was still on the premises. At one point, agents noticed that the windows of the house were wide open on a cold windy day, leading them to suspect that the ether was being used. On February 8, the agents applied for and obtained a warrant to search the Taos residence based in part on information derived through use of the beeper. The warrant was executed on February 10, 1981, and Horton, Harley, Steele, and Evan Roth were arrested, and cocaine and laboratory equipment were seized. . . .

. . . It is clear that the actual placement of the beeper into the can violated no one's Fourth Amendment rights. The can into which the beeper was placed belonged at the time to the DEA, and by no stretch of the imagination could it be said that respondents then had any legitimate expectation of privacy in it. The ether and the original 10 cans, on the other hand, belonged to, and were in the possession of, Muehlenweg, who had given his consent to any invasion of those items that occurred. Thus, even if there had been no substitution of cans and the agents had placed the beeper into one of the original 10 cans, Muehlenweg's consent was sufficient to validate the placement of the beeper in the can.

The Court of Appeals . . . did not hold that the actual placement of the beeper into the ether can violated the Fourth Amendment. Instead, it held that the violation occurred at the time the beeper-laden can was transferred to Karo. . . .

Not surprisingly, the Court of Appeals did not describe the transfer as either a "search" or a "seizure," for plainly it is neither. . . . The mere transfer to Karo of a can containing an unmonitored beeper infringed no privacy interest. It conveyed no information that Karo wished to keep private, for it conveyed no information at all. To be sure, it created a *potential* for an invasion of privacy, but we have never held that potential, as opposed to actual, invasions of privacy constitute searches for purposes of the Fourth Amendment. . . .

We likewise do not believe that the transfer of the container constituted a seizure. . . . Although the can may have contained an unknown and unwanted foreign object, it cannot be said that anyone's possessory interest was interfered with in a meaningful way. At most, there was a technical trespass on the space occupied by the beeper. The existence of a physical trespass is only marginally relevant to the question of whether the Fourth Amendment has been violated, however, for an actual trespass is neither necessary nor sufficient to establish a constitutional violation. . . .

Here, there is no gainsaying that the beeper was used to locate the ether in a specific house in Taos, N.M., and that that information was in turn used to secure a warrant for the search of the house. . . . This case thus presents the question whether the monitoring of a beeper in a private residence, a location not open to visual surveillance, violates the Fourth Amendment rights of those who have a justifiable interest in the privacy of the residence. . . . [W]e think that it does.

At the risk of belaboring the obvious, private residences are places in which the individual normally expects privacy free of governmental intrusion not authorized by a warrant, and that expectation is plainly one that society is prepared to recognize as justifiable . . . In this case, had a DEA agent thought it useful to enter the Taos residence to verify that the ether was actually in the house and had he done so surreptitiously and without a warrant, there is little doubt that he would have engaged in an unreasonable search within the meaning of the Fourth Amendment. For purposes of the Amendment, the result is the same where, without a warrant, the Government surreptitiously employs an electronic device to obtain information that it could not have obtained by observation from outside the curtilage of the house. The beeper tells the agent that a particular article is actually located at a particular time in the private residence and is in the possession of the person or persons whose residence is being watched. Even if visual surveillance has revealed that the article to which the beeper is attached has entered the house, the later monitoring not only verifies the officers' observations but also establishes that the article remains on the premises. . . .

The monitoring of an electronic device such as a beeper is, of course, less intrusive than a full-scale search, but it does reveal a critical fact about the interior of the premises that the Government is extremely interested in knowing and that it could not have otherwise obtained without a warrant. The case is thus not like *Knotts*, for there the beeper told the authorities nothing about the interior of Knotts' cabin. . . .

We cannot accept the Government's contention that it should be completely free from the constraints of the Fourth Amendment to determine by means of an electronic device, without a warrant and without probable cause or reasonable suspicion, whether a particular article — or a person, for that matter — is in an individual's home at a particular time. Indiscriminate monitoring of property that has been withdrawn from public view would present far too serious a threat to privacy interests in the home to escape entirely some sort of Fourth Amendment oversight. . . .

[B]y maintaining the beeper the agents verified that the ether was actually located in the Taos house and that it remained there while the warrant was sought. This information was obtained without a warrant and would therefore be inadmissible at trial against those with privacy interests in the house. . . . That information, which was included in the warrant affidavit, would also invalidate the warrant for the search of the house if it proved to be critical to establishing probable cause for the issuance of the warrant. . . .

It requires only a casual examination of the warrant affidavit . . . to conclude that the officers could have secured the warrant without relying on the beeper to locate the ether in the house sought to be searched. The affidavit recounted the months-long tracking of the evidence, including the visual and beeper surveillance of Horton's pickup on its trip from Albuquerque to the immediate vicinity of the Taos residence; its departure a short time later without the ether; its later return to the residence; and the visual observation of the residence with its windows open on a cold night.

This leaves the question whether any part of this additional information contained in the warrant affidavit was itself the fruit of a Fourth Amendment violation. . . .

. . . On the initial leg of its journey, the ether came to rest in Karo's house where it was monitored; it then moved in succession to two other houses . . . before it was moved first to a locker in one public warehouse and then to a locker in another. . . . On September 6, the ether was removed from the second storage facility and transported to Taos.

Assuming for present purposes that prior to its arrival at the second warehouse the beeper was illegally used to locate the ether . . . we are confident that such use of the beeper does not taint its later use in locating the ether and tracking it to Taos. The movement of the ether from the first warehouse was undetected, but by monitoring the beeper the agents discovered that it had been moved to the second storage facility. No prior monitoring of the beeper contributed to this discovery; using the beeper for this purpose was thus untainted by any possible prior illegality. Furthermore, the beeper informed the agents only that the ether was somewhere in the warehouse; it did not identify the specific locker in which the ether was located. Monitoring the beeper revealed nothing about the contents of the locker . . . and hence was not a search of that locker. The locker was identified only when agents traversing the public parts of the facility found that the smell of ether was coming from a specific locker.

The agents set up visual surveillance of that locker, and on September 6, they observed Rhodes and a female remove the ether and load it into Horton's pickup truck. The truck moved over the public streets and was tracked by beeper to Rhodes' house, where it was temporarily parked. At about 6 p.m. the truck was observed departing and was tracked visually and by beeper to the vicinity of the house in Taos. Because locating the ether in the warehouse was not an illegal search — and because the ether was seen being loaded into Horton's truck, which then traveled the public highways — it is evident that under *Knotts* there was no violation of the Fourth Amendment. . . . Under these circumstances, it is clear that the warrant affidavit, after striking the facts about monitoring the beeper while it was in the Taos residence, contained sufficient untainted information to furnish probable cause for the issuance of the search warrant. . . .

The judgment of the Court of Appeals is accordingly reversed.

[Justice O'Connor's opinion, joined by Justice Rehnquist, concurring in part and concurring in the judgment, is omitted.]

JUSTICE STEVENS, with whom JUSTICE BRENNAN and JUSTICE MARSHALL join, concurring in part and dissenting in part.

The beeper is a species of radio transmitter. Mounted inside a container, it has much in common with a microphone mounted on a person. It reveals the location of the item to which it is attached — the functional equivalent of a radio transmission saying "Now I am at _____."

. . . In my opinion the surreptitious use of a radio transmitter — whether it contains a microphone or merely a signalling device — on an individual's personal property is both a seizure and a search within the meaning of the Fourth Amendment. . . .

[T]he Court correctly concludes that when beeper surveillance reveals the location of property that has been concealed from public view, it constitutes a "search" within the meaning of the Fourth Amendment. . . . However, I find it necessary to write separately because I believe the Fourth Amendment's reach is somewhat broader. . . .

The attachment of the beeper, in my judgment, constituted a "seizure." The owner of property, of course, has a right to exclude from it all the world, including the Government, and a concomitant right to use it exclusively for his own purposes. When the Government attaches an electronic monitoring device to that property, it infringes that exclusionary right. . . . Surely such an invasion is an "interference" with possessory rights; the right to exclude, which attached as soon as the can respondents purchased was delivered, had been infringed. That interference is also "meaningful"; the character of the property is profoundly different when infected with an electronic bug than when it is entirely germ free. . . .

The Court has developed a relatively straightforward test for determining what expectations of privacy are protected by the Fourth Amendment with respect to the possession of personal property. If personal property is in the plain view of the public, the possession of the property is in no sense "private" and hence is unprotected: "What a person knowingly exposes to the public, even in his own home or office, is not a subject of Fourth Amendment protection." Katz v. United States, 389 U.S. 347, 351 (1967). When a person's property is concealed from public view, however, then the fact of his possession is private and the subject of Fourth Amendment protection. . . .

United States v. Knotts, 460 U.S. 276 (1983), illustrates this approach. There, agents watched as a container of chloroform in which they had placed a beeper was delivered to Knotts' codefendant and placed in his car. They then used the beeper to track the car's movements on a single trip through a public place. Used in this way the beeper did not disclose that the codefendant was in possession of the property; the agents already knew that. It revealed only the route of a trip through areas open to the public, something that was hardly concealed from public view. . . .

In this case, the beeper enabled the agents to learn facts that were not exposed to public view. In *Knotts* the agents already saw the codefendant take possession of chloroform, and therefore the beeper accomplished no more than following the codefendant without the aid of the beeper would have. Here, once the container went into Karo's house, the agents thereafter learned who had the container and where it was only through use of the beeper. The beeper alone told them when the container was taken into private residences and storage areas, and when it was transported from one place to another.

The Court recognizes that concealment of personal property from public view gives rise to Fourth Amendment protection when it writes: "Indiscriminate monitoring of property that has been withdrawn from public view would present far too serious a threat to privacy interests in the home to escape entirely some sort of Fourth Amendment oversight." This protection is not limited to times when the beeper was in a home. The beeper also revealed when the can of ether had been moved. When a person drives down a public thoroughfare in a car with a can of ether concealed in the trunk, he is not exposing to public view the fact that he is in possession of a can of ether; the can is still "withdrawn from public view" and hence its location is entitled to constitutional protection. . . . In this case it was only the beeper that enabled the agents to discover where the can was once it had been concealed in Karo's house. . . .

The agents did not know who was in possession of the property or where it was once it entered Karo's house. From that moment on it was concealed from view. Because the beeper enabled the agents to learn the location of property otherwise concealed from public view, it infringed a privacy interest protected by the Fourth Amendment. . . .

Accordingly, I respectfully dissent.

NOTES AND QUESTIONS

1. The *Karo* Court distinguishes between the use of a beeper to obtain information that at least in theory could have been obtained by an officer's visual observations from a lawful vantage point, and the use of a beeper to obtain information from within a private residence that could not have been so observed. We will explore privacy interests in the home in some detail in the next case. For now,

what about the principle established in *Knotts* and followed in *Karo*? Does the Court shortchange the privacy interests we have in our public movements — privacy interests that may today be at risk with the development of new technologies? "Intelligent transportation systems" that rely on features like electronic toll collection have already added to the information available to law enforcement about the movement of people in public spaces. Professor Weisberg has opined that various automatic tracking systems may one day "permit the state to know everywhere you have driven and when — every road you have taken, every toll you have paid, every gas station you have patronized." Robert Weisberg, IVHS, Legal Privacy, and the Legacy of Dr. Faustus, 11 Santa Clara Computer & High Tech. I.J. 75, 76 (1995). Granted, the Court noted in *Knotts* that if the 24-hour surveillance of citizens by law enforcement authorities ever becomes a problem, "there will be time enough then to determine whether different constitutional principles may be applicable." United States v. Knotts, 460 U.S. 276, 284 (1983). But developing technology may have brought us closer to this possibility than the Court ever deemed likely in the 1980s, when *Knotts* and *Karo* were decided.

2. In fact, we may be there already. Think about the growing use of surveillance cameras in this country — cameras that record the faces we have "knowingly exposed" in the name of reassuring us about the safety of public places. Consider the British experience with such cameras. In the 1990s, fears of terrorism prompted the British to install cameras in public places on a wide scale — so that by one estimate, there are at least 4.2 million surveillance cameras in the United Kingdom, each keeping a watchful public eye. Professor Rosen recently described the prevalence of these cameras in the City of London:

> As I filed through customs at Heathrow Airport, there were cameras concealed in domes in the ceiling. There were cameras pointing at the ticket counters, at the escalators, and at the tracks as I waited for the Heathrow Express to Paddington Station. When I got out at Paddington, there were cameras on the platform and cameras on the pillars in the main terminal. Cameras followed me as I walked from the main station to the underground, and there were cameras at each of the stations on the way to King's Cross. Outside King's Cross, there were cameras trained on the bus stand and the taxi stand and the sidewalk, and still more cameras in the station. There were cameras on the backs of buses to record people who crossed into the wrong traffic lane. Throughout Britan today, there are speed cameras and redlight cameras, cameras in lobbies and elevators, in hotels and restaurants, in nursery schools and high schools. There are even cameras in hospitals. . . . By one estimate, the average Briton is now photographed by more than 300 separate cameras from 30 separate CCTV networks in a single day.

Jeffrey Rosen, The Naked Crowd 36-37 (2004). According to Rosen, the British cameras, though initially justified as a counterterrorism measure, have come to serve a variety of other purposes. They provide the record supporting the ban of disorderly persons from shopping malls. They monitor and deter "unconventional" behavior in public places. See id. at 38. Rosen predicts that in the not distant future, when such cameras are able to feed digital images to a central monitoring station where images can be analyzed with face and behavioral-recognition software, "the possibilities of Panopticon will suddenly become very real." Already there is evidence that the close monitoring of young men, especially young men of color, has produced a backlash: "CCTV is far less popular among black men than among British men as a whole." Id. at 49. Rosen argues that the cameras in Britain are "a powerful inducement toward social conformity." They represent "ways of putting people in their place, of deciding who gets in and who stays out" — as when the one-time shoplifter or miscreant finds herself permanently barred from a public establishment. In this way, Rosen says, the cameras "are in tension with values of equality. They are ways of . . . limiting people's movement and restricting their opportunities." Id. at 51.

In the wake of 9/11, there are many who claim that greater use of such technology is important in the United States. Does this possibility raise Fourth Amendment privacy concerns that suggest a need to depart from the approach of cases like *Knotts* and *Karo*? Or is this about privacy at all? Note that at least part of Rosen's argument against such cameras is that they are in tension with American society's supposed openness to perpetual reinvention of the self. New digital technologies may make it possible for people to be "followed throughout life by their past misdeeds," see id. at 52 — to be instantly identified as a check bouncer, for instance, on entry into a supermarket. But is this a Fourth Amendment privacy concern? Aren't those who live in small towns also unable to leave their past misdeeds behind — at least without moving to another place?

On the other hand, as Professor Slobogin has observed, we probably do expect some degree of anonymity in public, as we walk into a bar or an AA meeting; as we pick out a video or order deli food. See Christopher Slobogin, Public Privacy: Camera Surveillance of Public Places and the Right to Anonymity, 72 Miss. L.J. 213, 238-239 (2002). The small town police officer who is familiar with community residents' pasts, moreover, knows the *people* he polices — not just their "digital dossiers," to borrow Professor Solove's phrase. See Daniel J. Solove, Digital Dossiers and the Dissipation of Fourth Amendment Privacy, 75 S. Cal. L. Rev. 1083, 1095 (2002) (noting that technological advance has made possible near instant access to "a horde of aggregated bits of information combined to reveal a portrait of who we are based on what we buy, the organizations we belong to, how we navigate the Internet, and which shows and videos we watch").

3. Even the use of a precision aerial mapping camera that enhances what the eye alone can see will not necessarily render police surveillance of outdoor movements subject to Fourth Amendment constraints. In Dow Chemical Co. v. United States, 476 U.S. 227, 238 (1986), the Court observed that "surveillance of private property by using highly sophisticated surveillance equipment not generally available to the public, such as satellite technology, might be constitutionally proscribed absent a warrant." Noting that the area subject to surveillance in the case before it was more like an open field than the curtilage of a home, however, the Court concluded that the use of an aerial mapping camera to take photographs of the open areas of a chemical plant from altitudes of 1,200, 3,000, and 12,000 feet did not bring Fourth Amendment protections into play. See id. at 239.

But as *Karo* itself illustrates, the Court has sharply distinguished between the use of technology to track public movements and its use to glean information from inside the home. Consider whether this sharp distinction makes sense as you read the following case.

KYLLO v. UNITED STATES

Certiorari to the United States Court of Appeals for the Ninth Circuit
533 U.S. 27 (2001)

JUSTICE SCALIA delivered the opinion of the Court. . . .

In 1991 Agent William Elliott of the United States Department of the Interior came to suspect that marijuana was being grown in the home belonging to petitioner Danny Kyllo, part of a triplex on Rhododendron Drive in Florence, Oregon. Indoor marijuana growth typically requires high-intensity lamps. In order to determine whether an amount of heat was emanating from petitioner's home consistent with the use of such lamps, at 3:20 a.m. on January 16, 1992, Agent Elliott and Dan Haas used an Agema Thermovision 210 thermal imager to scan the triplex. Thermal imagers detect infrared radiation, which virtually all objects emit but which is not visible to the naked eye. The imager converts radiation into images based on relative warmth—black is cool, white is hot, shades of gray connote relative differences; in that respect, it operates somewhat like a video camera showing heat images. The scan of Kyllo's home took only a few minutes and was performed from the passenger seat of Agent Elliott's vehicle across the street from the front of the house and also from the street in back of the house. The scan showed that the roof over the garage and a side wall of petitioner's home were relatively hot compared to the rest of the home and substantially warmer than neighboring homes in the triplex. Agent Elliott concluded that petitioner was using halide lights to grow marijuana in his house, which indeed he was. Based on tips from informants, utility bills, and the thermal imaging, a Federal Magistrate Judge issued a warrant authorizing a search of petitioner's home, and the agents found an indoor growing operation involving more than 100 plants. Petitioner was indicted on one count of manufacturing marijuana. . . . He unsuccessfully moved to suppress the evidence seized from his home and then entered a conditional guilty plea.

The Court of Appeals for the Ninth Circuit remanded the case for an evidentiary hearing regarding the intrusiveness of thermal imaging. On remand the District Court found that the Agema 210 "is a non-intrusive device which emits no rays or beams and shows a crude visual image of the heat being radiated from the outside of the house"; it "did not show any people or activity within the walls of the structure"; "[t]he device used cannot penetrate walls or windows to reveal conversations or human activities"; and "[n]o intimate details of the home were observed." Based on these findings, the District Court upheld the validity of the warrant that relied in part upon the thermal imaging, and reaffirmed its denial of the motion to suppress. A divided Court of Appeals initially reversed, but that opinion was withdrawn and the panel (after a change in composition) affirmed. . . . We granted certiorari. . . .

The present case involves officers on a public street engaged in more than naked-eye surveillance of a home. We have previously reserved judgment as to how much technological enhancement of ordinary perception from such a vantage point, if any, is too much. While we upheld enhanced aerial photography of an industrial complex in *Dow Chemical*, we noted that we found "it important that this is *not* an area immediately adjacent to a private home, where privacy expectations are most heightened," 476 U.S., at 237, n. 4 (emphasis in original).

It would be foolish to contend that the degree of privacy secured to citizens by the Fourth Amendment has been entirely unaffected by the advance of technology. For example . . . the technology enabling human flight has exposed to public view (and hence, we have said, to official observation) uncovered portions of the house and its curtilage that once were private. See *Ciraolo*, [476 U.S.], at 215. The question we confront today is what limits there are upon this power of technology to shrink the realm of guaranteed privacy.

The *Katz* test — whether the individual has an expectation of privacy that society is prepared to recognize as reasonable — has often been criticized as circular, and hence subjective and unpredictable. While it may be difficult to refine *Katz* when the search of areas such as telephone booths . . . or even the curtilage and uncovered portions of residences is at issue, in the case of the search of the interior of homes — the prototypical and hence most commonly litigated area of protected privacy — there is a ready criterion, with roots deep in the common law, of the minimal expectation of privacy that *exists*, and that is acknowledged to be *reasonable*. . . . We think that obtaining by sense-enhancing technology any information regarding the interior of the home that could not otherwise have been obtained without physical "intrusion into a constitutionally protected area" constitutes a search — at least where (as here) the technology in question is not in general public use. This assures preservation of that degree of privacy against government that existed when the Fourth Amendment was adopted. On the basis of this criterion, the information obtained by the thermal imager in this case was the product of a search.

The Government maintains, however, that the thermal imaging must be upheld because it detected "only heat radiating from the external surface of the house." The dissent makes this its leading point, contending that there is a fundamental difference between what it calls "off-the-wall" observations and "through-the-wall surveillance." But just as a thermal imager captures only heat emanating from a house, so also a powerful directional microphone picks up only sound emanating from a house — and a satellite capable of scanning from many miles away would pick up only visible light emanating from a house. We rejected such a mechanical interpretation of the Fourth Amendment in *Katz*, where the eavesdropping device picked up only sound waves that reached the exterior of the phone booth. Reversing that approach would leave the homeowner at the mercy of advancing technology — including imaging technology that could discern all human activity in the home. While the technology used in the present case was relatively crude, the rule we adopt must take account of more sophisticated systems that are already in use or in development. . . .

The Government also contends that the thermal imaging was constitutional because it did not "detect private activities occurring in private areas." It points out that in *Dow Chemical* we observed that the enhanced aerial photography did not reveal any "intimate details." 476 U.S., at 238. *Dow Chemical*, however, involved enhanced aerial photography of an industrial complex, which does not share the Fourth Amendment sanctity of the home. . . . In the home, our cases show, *all* details are intimate details, because the entire area is held safe from prying government eyes. . . .

Limiting the prohibition of thermal imaging to "intimate details" would not only be wrong in principle; it would be impractical in application. . . . To begin with, there is no necessary connection between the sophistication of the surveillance equipment and the "intimacy" of the details that it observes — which means that one cannot say (and the police cannot be assured) that use of the relatively crude equipment at issue here will always be lawful. The Agema Thermovision 210 might disclose, for example, at what hour each night the lady of the house takes her daily sauna and bath — a detail that many would consider "intimate"; and a much more sophisticated system might detect nothing more intimate than the fact that someone left a closet light on. We could not, in other words, develop a rule approving only that through-the-wall surveillance which identifies objects no smaller than 36 by 36 inches, but would have to develop a jurisprudence specifying which home activities are "intimate" and which are not. And even when (if ever) that jurisprudence were fully developed, no police officer would be able to know *in advance* whether his through-the-wall surveillance picks up "intimate" details — and thus would be unable to know in advance whether it is constitutional. . . .

We have said that the Fourth Amendment draws "a firm line at the entrance to the house." That line, we think, must be not only firm but also bright — which requires clear specification of those methods of surveillance that require a warrant. While it is certainly possible to conclude from the videotape of the thermal imaging that occurred in this case that no "significant" compromise of the homeowner's privacy has occurred, we must take the long view, from the original meaning of the Fourth Amendment forward. . . . Where, as here, the Government uses a device that is not in general public use, to explore details of the home that would previously have been unknowable without physical intrusion, the surveillance is a "search" and is presumptively unreasonable without a warrant. . . .

JUSTICE STEVENS, with whom THE CHIEF JUSTICE, JUSTICE O'CONNOR, and JUSTICE KENNEDY join, dissenting. . . .

While the Court "take[s] the long view" and decides this case based largely on the potential of yet-to-be-developed technology that might allow "through-the-wall surveillance," this case involves nothing more than off-the-wall surveillance by law enforcement officers to gather information exposed to the general public from the outside of petitioner's home. All that the infrared camera did in this case was passively measure heat emitted from the exterior surfaces of petitioner's home; all that those measurements showed were relative differences in emission levels, vaguely indicating that some areas of the roof and outside walls were warmer than others. . . . [N]o details regarding the interior of petitioner's home were revealed. . . .

Indeed, the ordinary use of the senses might enable a neighbor or passerby to notice the heat emanating from a building, particularly if it is vented, as was the case here. Additionally, any member of the public might notice that one part of a house is warmer than another part or a nearby building if, for example, rainwater evaporates or snow melts at different rates across its surfaces. . . .

Thus, the notion that heat emissions from the outside of a dwelling are a private matter implicating the protections of the Fourth Amendment (the text of which guarantees the right of the people "to be secure *in* their . . . houses" against unreasonable searches and seizures (emphasis added)) is not only unprecedented but also quite difficult to take seriously. Heat waves, like aromas that are generated in a kitchen, or in a laboratory or opium den, enter the public domain if and when they leave a building. A subjective expectation that they would remain private is not only implausible but also surely not "one that society is prepared to recognize as 'reasonable.'" *Katz*, 389 U.S., at 361 (Harlan, J., concurring).

To be sure, the homeowner has a reasonable expectation of privacy concerning what takes place within the home, and the Fourth Amendment's protection against physical invasions of the home should apply to their functional equivalent. But the equipment in this case did not penetrate the walls of petitioner's home, and while it did pick up "details of the home" that were exposed to the public, it did not obtain "any information regarding the *interior* of the home." In the Court's own words, based on what the thermal imager "showed" regarding the outside of petitioner's home, the officers "concluded" that petitioner was engaging in illegal activity inside the home. It would be quite absurd to characterize their thought processes as "searches," regardless of whether they inferred (rightly) that petitioner was growing marijuana in his house, or (wrongly) that "the lady of the house [was taking] her daily sauna and bath." . . . For the first time in its history, the Court assumes that an inference can amount to a Fourth Amendment violation.

Notwithstanding the implications of today's decision, there is a strong public interest in avoiding constitutional litigation over the monitoring of emissions from homes, and over the inferences drawn from such monitoring. . . . [P]ublic officials should not have to avert their senses or their equipment from detecting emissions in the public domain such as excessive heat, traces of smoke, suspicious odors, odorless gases, airborne particulates, or radioactive emissions, any of which could identify hazards to the community. In my judgment, monitoring such emissions with "sense-enhancing technology," and drawing useful conclusions from such monitoring, is an entirely reasonable public service.

On the other hand, the countervailing privacy interest is at best trivial. After all, homes generally are insulated to keep heat in, rather than to prevent the detection of heat going out, and it does not seem to me that society will suffer from a rule requiring the rare homeowner who both intends to engage in uncommon activities that produce extraordinary amounts of heat, and wishes to conceal that production from outsiders, to make sure that the surrounding area is well insulated. . . .

Instead of trying to answer the question whether the use of the thermal imager in this case was even arguably unreasonable, the Court has fashioned a rule that is intended to provide essential guidance for the day when "more sophisticated systems" gain the "ability to 'see' through walls and other opaque barriers." . . . In my judgment, the Court's new rule is at once too broad and too narrow, and is not justified by the Court's explanation for its adoption. . . .

Despite the Court's attempt to draw a line that is "not only firm but also bright," the contours of its new rule are uncertain because its protection apparently dissipates as soon as the relevant technology is "in general public use." Yet how much use is general public use is not even hinted at by the Court's opinion, which makes the somewhat doubtful assumption that the thermal imager used in this case does not satisfy that criterion. In any event, putting aside its lack of clarity, this criterion is somewhat perverse because it seems likely that the threat to privacy will grow, rather than recede, as the use of intrusive equipment becomes more readily available. . . .

The application of the Court's new rule to "any information regarding the interior of the home," is also unnecessarily broad. If it takes sensitive equipment to detect an odor that identifies criminal conduct and nothing else, the fact that the odor emanates from the interior of a home should not provide it with constitutional protection. The criterion, moreover, is too sweeping in that information "regarding" the interior of a home apparently is not just information obtained through its walls, but also information concerning the outside of the building that could lead to (however many) inferences "regarding" what might be inside. Under that expansive view, I suppose, an officer using an infrared camera to observe a man silently entering the side door of a house at night carrying a pizza might conclude that its interior is now occupied by someone who likes pizza, and by doing so the officer would be guilty of conducting an unconstitutional "search" of the home.

Because the new rule applies to information regarding the "interior" of the home, it is too narrow as well as too broad. Clearly, a rule that is designed to protect individuals from the overly intrusive use of sense-enhancing equipment should not be limited to a home. If such equipment did provide its user with the functional equivalent of access to a private place — such as, for example, the telephone booth involved in *Katz*, or an office building — then the rule should apply to such an area as well as to a home. See *Katz*, 389 U.S., at 351 ("[T]he Fourth Amendment protects people, not places"). . . .

The two reasons advanced by the Court as justifications for the adoption of its new rule are both unpersuasive. First, the Court suggests that its rule is compelled by our holding in *Katz*, because in that case, as in this, the surveillance consisted of nothing more than the monitoring of waves emanating from a private area into the public domain. Yet there are critical differences between the cases. In *Katz*, the electronic listening device attached to the outside of the phone booth allowed the officers to pick up the content of the conversation inside the booth, making them the functional equivalent of intruders because they gathered information that was otherwise available only to someone inside the private area; it would be as if, in this case, the thermal imager presented a view of the heat-generating activity inside petitioner's home. By contrast, the thermal imager here disclosed only the relative amounts of heat radiating from the house; it would be as if, in *Katz*, the listening device disclosed only the relative volume of sound leaving the booth, which presumably was discernible in the public domain. Surely, there is a significant difference between the general and well-settled expectation that strangers will not have direct access to the contents of private communications, on the one hand, and the rather theoretical expectation that an occasional homeowner would even care if anybody noticed the relative amounts of heat emanating from the walls of his house, on the other. It is pure hyperbole for the Court to suggest that refusing to extend the holding of *Katz* to this case would leave the homeowner at the mercy of "technology that could discern all human activity in the home."

Second, the Court argues that the permissibility of "through-the-wall surveillance" cannot depend on a distinction between observing "intimate details" such as "the lady of the house [taking] her daily sauna and bath," and noticing only "the nonintimate rug on the vestibule floor" or "objects no smaller than 36 by 36 inches." This entire argument assumes, of course, that the thermal imager in this case could or did perform "through-the-wall surveillance" that could identify any detail "that would previously have been unknowable without physical intrusion." In fact, the device could not and did not enable its user to identify either the lady of the house, the rug on the vestibule floor, or anything else inside the house, whether smaller or larger than 36 by 36 inches. Indeed, the vague thermal images of petitioner's home that are reproduced in the Appendix were submitted by him to the District Court as part of an expert report raising the question whether the device could even take "accurate, consistent infrared images" of the *outside* of his house. But even if the device could reliably show extraordinary differences in the amounts of heat leaving his home, drawing the inference that there was something suspicious occurring inside the residence — a conclusion that officers far less gifted than Sherlock Holmes would readily draw — does not qualify as "through-the-wall surveillance," much less a Fourth Amendment violation.

Although the Court is properly and commendably concerned about the threats to privacy that may flow from advances in the technology available to the law enforcement profession, it has unfortunately failed to heed the tried and true counsel of judicial restraint. Instead of concentrating on the rather mundane issue that is actually presented by the case before it, the Court has endeavored to craft an all-encompassing rule for the future. It would be far wiser to give legislators an unimpeded opportunity to grapple with these emerging issues rather than to shackle them with prematurely devised constitutional constraints.

I respectfully dissent.

NOTES AND QUESTIONS

1. Does the distinction between "through-the-wall" and "off-the-wall" surveillance sound familiar? Is the majority correctly declining to resurrect a version of the trespass requirement so soundly rejected in *Katz*?

2. Maybe so. But at the same time, the majority's emphasis on the location of the police activity — on the special sanctity of the home — seems in tension with the *Katz* Court's admonition that "the Fourth Amendment protects people, not places." Professor Sklansky has pointed out that *Katz* "seemed to promise a Fourth Amendment that was less tied to specific locations, and therefore somehow more modern." The Justices in the years since *Katz*, "keep renewing that promise, but . . . have never figured out how to make good on it." David A. Sklansky, Back to the Future: *Kyllo, Katz*, and Common Law, 72 Miss. L.J. 143, 160 (2002). From this perspective, *Kyllo* is but one of a number of more recent cases in which the Court, with Justice Scalia in the lead, has looked to the past in an effort to anchor Fourth Amendment law — to free it from the indeterminacy that characterizes its efforts to answer the question, "What is a search?"

3. To be clear, the *Kyllo* Court's emphasis on the special sanctity of the home is in no way unique. "Ever since *Katz*, the Supreme Court has repeatedly reaffirmed two basic propositions about the Fourth Amendment. The first is that the protection the Amendment provides is independent of location. The second is that the Amendment provides special protection to the home." Id. at 190. The Court in *Kyllo* invokes the second of these two inconsistent propositions and promises, with regard to the interior of homes, the "preservation of that degree of privacy . . . that existed when the Fourth Amendment was adopted" — at least insofar as the general public use of technology that can glean information from the home does not become a problem. But do heightened protections for the home make sense? Consider the following:

Of course there are costs to treating the home differently than other places. If privacy receives more protection in the home than elsewhere, it necessarily follows that leaving one's home means losing some privacy — that the price of full privacy is not going out. That price might impair rather than foster a free and vibrant society. Moreover, the price is not visited equally on everyone, because not all homes are equivalent. . . . [R]ich people have bigger and more comfortable homes than poor people; it is therefore much easier for rich people than for poor people to stay home when engaged in activities they wish to keep private. Granting homes more privacy than other places therefore tilts Fourth Amendment protection in favor of the rich and against the poor. . . .

Sklansky, 72 Miss. L.J. at 192. Of course, as Professor Sklansky goes on to say, all this is not to suggest that advocates for greater privacy need necessarily view the result in *Kyllo* negatively: "[T]here is little reason to believe that erasing the boundary between the home and the street would give streets as much privacy as homes, instead of giving homes as little privacy as streets." Id. at 193. But *Kyllo*'s emphasis on the privacy interest in homes may give short shrift to other places (including cyberspace) where privacy interests are high and the Court has not yet developed a Fourth Amendment framework for dealing with new technologies.

4. Consider another angle on the search in *Kyllo*. *Kyllo* is an example of what one might call "white-collar drug investigations" — police investigation of drug networks that cater to middle- or upper-class customers. Most drug arrests and drug prosecutions fall into a different category; they occur not on places like Rhododendron Drive in Florence, Oregon, but on rough street corners in high-crime urban neighborhoods. And note one other important fact about these "blue-collar" drug cases: disproportionately, the search targets, arrestees, and defendants those cases generate are African Americans.

Kyllo makes white-collar drug investigations a little more costly than they otherwise might be. At the margin, that is likely to shift police resources away from those investigations and toward more blue-collar drug cases. In other words, part of the cost of increased privacy protection for homes is that police attention will tend to be diverted elsewhere, to spaces where Fourth Amendment regulation is more lax — like urban street corners. See William J. Stuntz, The Distribution of Fourth Amendment Privacy, 67 Geo. Wash. L. Rev. 1265, 1274-1287 (1999). Is that wise criminal justice policy?

5. What about the Court's approach to advancing technology? Should Fourth Amendment analysis turn on whether "the technology in question is not in general public use"? And how is "general public use" to be determined? Presumably if the device in question is available in the local Wal-Mart, its use does not trigger the Fourth Amendment. What about an Internet catalogue? As publicly available technology advances, constitutionally protected privacy will diminish. Is that result right as a matter of constitutional law?

6. *Kyllo* was decided before 9/11; it's interesting to speculate if it might have come out differently if the Court had in mind a hypothetical investigation into chemical weapons manufacture rather than the marijuana case before it. Perhaps the dissent may have a point in taking the majority to task for abandoning basic tenets of judicial restraint — not to mention the cautious, incremental style of Fourth Amendment adjudication endorsed by Allen and Rosenberg and discussed in Note 3 on page 356. After all, if technological advances produced a wholly unobtrusive, non-invasive scanner that could detect from the street whether explosives or chemical weapons were being unlawfully stored in a home — without

revealing anything else — is it so obvious that the use of such a device should trigger Fourth Amendment protections? Does the test enunciated in *Kyllo* necessarily reject the reasoning of *Place*, the canine sniff case discussed in Note 3 on page 366, at least as that reasoning might apply to information about the home?

7. Your view of the majority's approach might depend on the consequences of subjecting a given law enforcement activity to Fourth Amendment regulation. Recall the discussion in Note 5 on page 357 about whether Fourth Amendment law follows the graduated or "all-or-nothing" approach to the regulation of police activity. In a graduated regime, it may not matter so much that use of a noninvasive scanner that might detect chemical weapons is covered by the Fourth Amendment, provided that law enforcement agents acting consistently with the Amendment's requirements can nevertheless employ the scanner in most circumstances. If the consequence of Fourth Amendment regulation is essentially to render the scanner useless for the detection of such activity, however (if subjecting the scanner to Fourth Amendment constraints means deciding that it can be used only when a warrant for physical entry into the home could also be obtained), that might be a different matter.

2. The Meaning of "Seizures"

FLORIDA v. BOSTICK

Certiorari to the Supreme Court of Florida
501 U.S. 429 (1991)

JUSTICE O'CONNOR delivered the opinion of the Court. . . .

In this case, two officers discovered cocaine when they searched a suitcase belonging to Terrance Bostick. The underlying facts of the search are in dispute, but the Florida Supreme Court . . . stated explicitly the factual premise for its decision:

> " 'Two officers, complete with badges, insignia and one of them holding a recognizable zipper pouch, containing a pistol, boarded a bus bound from Miami to Atlanta during a stopover in Fort Lauderdale. Eyeing the passengers, the officers, admittedly without articulable suspicion, picked out the defendant passenger and asked to inspect his ticket and identification. The ticket, from Miami to Atlanta, matched the defendant's identification and both were immediately returned to him as unremarkable. However, the two police officers persisted and explained their presence as narcotics agents on the lookout for illegal drugs. In pursuit of that aim, they then requested the defendant's consent to search his luggage. Needless to say, there is a conflict in the evidence about whether the defendant consented to the search of the second bag in which the contraband was found and as to whether he was informed of his right to refuse consent. However, any conflict must be resolved in favor of the state, it being a question of fact decided by the trial judge.' "

Two facts are particularly worth noting. First, the police specifically advised Bostick that he had the right to refuse consent. Bostick appears to have disputed the point, but, as the Florida Supreme Court noted explicitly, the trial court resolved this evidentiary conflict in the State's favor. Second, at no time did the officers threaten Bostick with a gun. The Florida Supreme Court indicated that one officer carried a zipper pouch containing a pistol—the equivalent of carrying a gun in a holster—but the court did not suggest that the gun was ever removed from its pouch, pointed at Bostick, or otherwise used in a threatening manner. . . .

The sole issue presented for our review is whether a police encounter on a bus of the type described above necessarily constitutes a "seizure" within the meaning of the Fourth Amendment. . . .

Our cases make it clear that a seizure does not occur simply because a police officer approaches an individual and asks a few questions. So long as a reasonable person would feel free "to disregard the police and go about his business," the encounter is consensual. . . . The encounter will not trigger Fourth Amendment scrutiny unless it loses its consensual nature. The Court made precisely this point in Terry v. Ohio, 392 U.S. 1, 19, n. 16 (1968): "Obviously, not all personal intercourse between policemen and citizens involves 'seizures' of persons. Only when the officer, by means of physical force or show of authority, has in some way restrained the liberty of a citizen may we conclude that a 'seizure' has occurred." . . .

There is no doubt that if this same encounter had taken place before Bostick boarded the bus or in the lobby of the bus terminal, it would not rise to the level of a seizure. The Court has dealt with similar encounters in airports and has found them to be "the sort of consensual encounter[s] that implicat[e] no Fourth Amendment interest." We have stated that even when officers have no basis for suspecting a particular individual, they may generally ask questions of that individual, ask to examine the individual's identification, and request consent to search his or her luggage—as long as the police do not convey a message that compliance with their requests is required.

Bostick insists that this case is different because it took place in the cramped confines of a bus. A police encounter is much more intimidating in this setting, he argues, because police tower over a seated passenger and there is little room to move around. Bostick claims to find support in language from Michigan v. Chesternut, 486 U.S. 567, 573 (1988), and other cases, indicating that a seizure occurs when a reasonable person would believe that he or she is not "free to leave." Bostick maintains that a reasonable bus passenger would not have felt free to leave under the circumstances of this case because there is nowhere to go on a bus. Also, the bus was about to depart. Had Bostick disembarked, he would have risked being stranded and losing whatever baggage he had locked away in the luggage compartment.

The Florida Supreme Court found this argument persuasive, so much so that it adopted a per se rule prohibiting the police from randomly boarding buses as a means of drug interdiction. The state court erred, however, in focusing on whether Bostick was "free to leave" rather than on the principle that those words were intended to capture. . . .

[T]he mere fact that Bostick did not feel free to leave the bus does not mean that the police seized him. Bostick was a passenger on a bus that was scheduled to depart. He would not have felt free to leave the bus even if the police had not been present. Bostick's movements were "confined" in a sense, but this was the natural result of his decision to take the bus; it says nothing about whether or not the police conduct at issue was coercive. . . .

. . . Accordingly, the "free to leave" analysis on which Bostick relies is inapplicable. In such a situation, the appropriate inquiry is whether a reasonable person would feel free to decline the officers' requests or otherwise terminate the encounter. This formulation follows logically from prior cases and breaks no new ground. We have said before that the crucial test is whether, taking into account all of the circumstances surrounding the encounter, the police conduct would "have communicated to a reasonable person that he was not at liberty to ignore the police presence and go about his business." *Chesternut*, supra, 486 U.S., at 569. Where the encounter takes place is one factor, but it is not the only one. . . .

The facts of this case . . . leave some doubt whether a seizure occurred. Two officers walked up to Bostick on the bus, asked him a few questions, and asked if they could search his bags. As we have explained, no seizure occurs when police ask questions of an individual, ask to examine the individual's identification, and request consent to search his or her luggage — so long as the officers do not convey a message that compliance with their requests is required. Here, the facts recited by the Florida Supreme Court indicate that the officers did not point guns at Bostick or otherwise threaten him and that they specifically advised Bostick that he could refuse consent.

Nevertheless, we refrain from deciding whether or not a seizure occurred in this case. The trial court made no express findings of fact, and the Florida Supreme Court rested its decision on a single fact — that the encounter took place on a bus — rather than on the totality of the circumstances. We remand so that the Florida courts may evaluate the seizure question under the correct legal standard. We do reject, however, Bostick's argument that he must have been seized because no reasonable person would freely consent to a search of luggage that he or she knows contains drugs. This argument cannot prevail because the "reasonable person" test presupposes an *innocent* person. . . .

We adhere to the rule that, in order to determine whether a particular encounter constitutes a seizure, a court must consider all the circumstances surrounding the encounter to determine whether the police conduct would have communicated to a reasonable person that the person was not free to decline the officers' requests or otherwise terminate the encounter. That rule applies to encounters that take place on a city street or in an airport lobby, and it applies equally to encounters on a bus. . . .

The judgment of the Florida Supreme Court is reversed, and the case is remanded for further proceedings not inconsistent with this opinion.

It is so ordered.

JUSTICE MARSHALL, with whom JUSTICE BLACKMUN and JUSTICE STEVENS join, dissenting. . . .

At issue in this case is a "new and increasingly common tactic in the war on drugs": the suspicionless police sweep of buses in interstate or intrastate travel. . . .

These sweeps are conducted in "dragnet" style. The police admittedly act without an "articulable suspicion" in deciding which buses to board and which passengers to approach for interviewing.[1] . . .

1. . . . It does not follow, however, that the approach of passengers during a sweep is completely random. Indeed, at least one officer who routinely confronts interstate travelers candidly admitted that

To put it mildly, these sweeps "are inconvenient, intrusive, and intimidating." They occur within cramped confines, with officers typically placing themselves in between the passenger selected for an interview and the exit of the bus. Because the bus is only temporarily stationed at a point short of its destination, the passengers are in no position to leave as a means of evading the officers' questioning. Undoubtedly, such a sweep holds up the progress of the bus. Thus, this "new and increasingly common tactic," burdens the experience of traveling by bus with a degree of governmental interference to which, until now, our society has been proudly unaccustomed. . . .

The question for this Court, then, is whether the suspicionless, dragnet-style sweep of buses in intrastate and interstate travel is consistent with the Fourth Amendment. The majority suggests that this latest tactic in the drug war is perfectly compatible with the Constitution. I disagree.

I have no objection to the manner in which the majority frames the test for determining whether a suspicionless bus sweep amounts to a Fourth Amendment "seizure." . . . What I cannot understand is how the majority can possibly suggest an affirmative answer to this question. . . .

. . . Two officers boarded the Greyhound bus on which respondent was a passenger while the bus, en route from Miami to Atlanta, was on a brief stop to pick up passengers in Fort Lauderdale. The officers made a visible display of their badges and wore bright green "raid" jackets bearing the insignia of the Broward County Sheriff's Department; one held a gun in a recognizable weapons pouch. . . . Once on board, the officers approached respondent, who was sitting in the back of the bus, identified themselves as narcotics officers and began to question him. One officer stood in front of respondent's seat, partially blocking the narrow aisle through which respondent would have been required to pass to reach the exit of the bus.

As far as is revealed by facts on which the Florida Supreme Court premised its decision, the officers did not advise respondent that he was free to break off this "interview." Inexplicably, the majority repeatedly stresses the trial court's implicit finding that the police officers advised respondent that he was free to refuse permission to search his travel bag. This aspect of the exchange between respondent and the police is completely irrelevant to the issue before us. For as the State concedes, and as the majority purports to "accept," *if* respondent was unlawfully seized when the officers approached him and initiated questioning, the resulting search was likewise unlawful no matter how well advised respondent was of his right to refuse it. Consequently, the issue is not whether a passenger in respondent's position would have felt free to deny consent to the search of his bag, but whether such a passenger — without being apprised of his rights — would have felt free to terminate the antecedent encounter with the police.

Unlike the majority, I have no doubt that the answer to this question is no. Apart from trying to accommodate the officers, respondent had only two options.

---

race is a factor influencing his decision whom to approach. See United States v. Williams, No. 1:89CR0135 (ND Ohio, June 13, 1989), p. 3 ("Detective Zaller testified that the factors initiating the focus upon the three young black males in this case included: (1) that they were young and black. . . ."), aff'd, No. 89-4083 (CA6, Oct. 19, 1990), p. 7 (the officers "knew that the couriers, more often than not, were young black males"), vacated and remanded, 500 U.S. 901 (1991). Thus, the basis of the decision to single out particular passengers during a suspicionless sweep is less likely to be *inarticulable* than *unspeakable*.

First, he could have remained seated while obstinately refusing to respond to the officers' questioning. But in light of the intimidating show of authority that the officers made upon boarding the bus, respondent reasonably could have believed that such behavior would only arouse the officers' suspicions and intensify their interrogation. . . .

Second, respondent could have tried to escape the officers' presence by leaving the bus altogether. But because doing so would have required respondent to squeeze past the gun-wielding inquisitor who was blocking the aisle of the bus, this hardly seems like a course that respondent reasonably would have viewed as available to him. . . .

Even if respondent had perceived that the officers would *let* him leave the bus, moreover, he could not reasonably have been expected to resort to this means of evading their intrusive questioning. For so far as respondent knew, the bus's departure from the terminal was imminent. Unlike a person approached by the police on the street or at a bus or airport terminal after reaching his destination, a passenger approached by the police at an intermediate point in a long bus journey cannot simply leave the scene and repair to a safe haven to avoid unwanted probing by law-enforcement officials. The vulnerability that an intrastate or interstate traveler experiences when confronted by the police outside of his "own familiar territory" surely aggravates the coercive quality of such an encounter. . . .

Rather than requiring the police to justify the coercive tactics employed here, the majority blames respondent for his own sensation of constraint. . . . Thus, in the majority's view, because respondent's "freedom of movement was restricted by a factor independent of police conduct — i.e., by his being a passenger on a bus" — respondent was not seized for purposes of the Fourth Amendment.

This reasoning borders on sophism and trivializes the values that underlie the Fourth Amendment. Obviously, a person's "voluntary decision" to place himself in a room with only one exit does not authorize the police to force an encounter upon him by placing themselves in front of the exit. . . . By consciously deciding to single out persons who have undertaken interstate or intrastate travel, officers who conduct suspicionless, dragnet-style sweeps put passengers to the choice of cooperating or of exiting their buses and possibly being stranded in unfamiliar locations. It is exactly because this "choice" is no "choice" at all that police engage in this technique.

In my view, the Fourth Amendment clearly condemns the suspicionless, dragnet-style sweep of intrastate or interstate buses. Withdrawing this particular weapon from the government's drug-war arsenal would hardly leave the police without any means of combatting the use of buses as instrumentalities of the drug trade. The police would remain free, for example, to approach passengers whom they have a reasonable, articulable basis to suspect of criminal wrongdoing. Alternatively, they could continue to confront passengers without suspicion so long as they took simple steps, like advising the passengers confronted of their right to decline to be questioned, to dispel the aura of coercion and intimidation that pervades such encounters.

I dissent.

Eleven years later, the Court considered another case involving bus interdiction.

UNITED STATES v. DRAYTON

Certiorari to the United States Court of Appeals for the Eleventh Circuit
536 U.S. 194 (2002)

JUSTICE KENNEDY delivered the opinion of the Court.

The Fourth Amendment permits police officers to approach bus passengers at random to ask questions and to request their consent to searches, provided a reasonable person would understand that he or she is free to refuse. Florida v. Bostick, 501 U.S. 429 (1991). This case requires us to determine whether officers must advise bus passengers during these encounters of their right not to cooperate.

On February 4, 1999, respondents Christopher Drayton and Clifton Brown, Jr., were traveling on a Greyhound bus en route from Ft. Lauderdale, Florida, to Detroit, Michigan. The bus made a scheduled stop in Tallahassee, Florida. The passengers were required to disembark so the bus could be refueled and cleaned. As the passengers reboarded, the driver checked their tickets and then left to complete paperwork inside the terminal. As he left, the driver allowed three members of the Tallahassee Police Department to board the bus as part of a routine drug and weapons interdiction effort. The officers were dressed in plain clothes and carried concealed weapons and visible badges.

Once onboard Officer Hoover knelt on the driver's seat and faced the rear of the bus. He could observe the passengers and ensure the safety of the two other officers without blocking the aisle or otherwise obstructing the bus exit. Officers Lang and Blackburn went to the rear of the bus. Blackburn remained stationed there, facing forward. Lang worked his way toward the front of the bus, speaking with individual passengers as he went. He asked the passengers about their travel plans and sought to match passengers with luggage in the overhead racks. To avoid blocking the aisle, Lang stood next to or just behind each passenger with whom he spoke.

According to Lang's testimony, passengers who declined to cooperate with him or who chose to exit the bus at any time would have been allowed to do so without argument. In Lang's experience, however, most people are willing to cooperate. Some passengers go so far as to commend the police for their efforts to ensure the safety of their travel. Lang could recall five to six instances in the previous year in which passengers had declined to have their luggage searched. It also was common for passengers to leave the bus for a cigarette or a snack while the officers were on board. Lang sometimes informed passengers of their right to refuse to cooperate. On the day in question, however, he did not.

Respondents were seated next to each other on the bus. Drayton was in the aisle seat, Brown in the seat next to the window. Lang approached respondents from the rear and leaned over Drayton's shoulder. He held up his badge long enough for respondents to identify him as a police officer. With his face 12-to-18 inches away from Drayton's, Lang spoke in a voice just loud enough for respondents to hear:

> "I'm Investigator Lang with the Tallahassee Police Department. We're conducting bus interdiction [*sic*], attempting to deter drugs and illegal weapons being transported on the bus. Do you have any bags on the bus?"

Both respondents pointed to a single green bag in the overhead luggage rack. Lang asked, "Do you mind if I check it?," and Brown responded, "Go ahead." Lang handed the bag to Officer Blackburn to check. The bag contained no contraband.

Officer Lang noticed that both respondents were wearing heavy jackets and baggy pants despite the warm weather. In Lang's experience drug traffickers often use baggy clothing to conceal weapons or narcotics. The officer thus asked Brown if he had any weapons or drugs in his possession. And he asked Brown: "Do you mind if I check your person?" Brown answered, "Sure," and cooperated by leaning up in his seat, pulling a cell phone out of his pocket, and opening up his jacket. Lang reached across Drayton and patted down Brown's jacket and pockets, including his waist area, sides, and upper thighs. In both thigh areas, Lang detected hard objects similar to drug packages detected on other occasions. Lang arrested and handcuffed Brown. Officer Hoover escorted Brown from the bus.

Lang then asked Drayton, "Mind if I check you?" Drayton responded by lifting his hands about eight inches from his legs. Lang conducted a patdown of Drayton's thighs and detected hard objects similar to those found on Brown. He arrested Drayton and escorted him from the bus. A further search revealed that respondents had duct-taped plastic bundles of powder cocaine between several pairs of their boxer shorts. . . .

The District Court determined that the police conduct was not coercive and respondents' consent to the search was voluntary. . . .

The Court of Appeals for the Eleventh Circuit reversed and remanded with instructions to grant respondents' motions to suppress. The court held that this disposition was compelled by its previous decisions in United States v. Washington, 151 F.3d 1354 (1998), and United States v. Guapi, 144 F.3d 1393 (1998). Those cases had held that bus passengers do not feel free to disregard police officers' requests to search absent "some positive indication that consent could have been refused."

We granted certiorari. The respondents, we conclude, were not seized and their consent to the search was voluntary; and we reverse. . . .

The Court has addressed on a previous occasion the specific question of drug interdiction efforts on buses. . . .

. . . *Bostick* first made it clear that for the most part per se rules are inappropriate in the Fourth Amendment context. The proper inquiry necessitates a consideration of "all the circumstances surrounding the encounter." The Court noted next that the traditional rule, which states that a seizure does not occur so long as a reasonable person would feel free "to disregard the police and go about his business," California v. Hodari D., 499 U.S. 621, 628 (1991), is not an accurate measure of the coercive effect of a bus encounter. . . . The proper inquiry "is whether a reasonable person would feel free to decline the officers' requests or otherwise terminate the encounter." Finally, the Court rejected Bostick's argument that he must have been seized because no reasonable person would consent to a search of luggage containing drugs. The reasonable person test, the Court explained, is objective and "presupposes an *innocent* person."

In light of the limited record, *Bostick* refrained from deciding whether a seizure occurred. The Court, however, identified two factors "particularly worth noting" on remand. First, although it was obvious that an officer was armed, he did not remove the gun from its pouch or use it in a threatening way. Second, the officer advised the passenger that he could refuse consent to the search.

Relying upon this latter factor, the Eleventh Circuit has adopted what is in effect a per se rule that evidence obtained during suspicionless drug interdiction efforts aboard buses must be suppressed unless the officers have advised passengers of their right not to cooperate and to refuse consent to a search. . . .

. . . The Court of Appeals erred in adopting this approach.

Applying the *Bostick* framework to the facts of this particular case, we conclude that the police did not seize respondents when they boarded the bus and began questioning passengers. The officers gave the passengers no reason to believe that they were required to answer the officers' questions. When Officer Lang approached respondents, he did not brandish a weapon or make any intimidating movements. He left the aisle free so that respondents could exit. He spoke to passengers one by one and in a polite, quiet voice. Nothing he said would suggest to a reasonable person that he or she was barred from leaving the bus or otherwise terminating the encounter.

There were ample grounds for the District Court to conclude that "everything that took place between Officer Lang and [respondents] suggests that it was cooperative" and that there "was nothing coercive [or] confrontational" about the encounter. There was no application of force, no intimidating movement, no overwhelming show of force, no brandishing of weapons, no blocking of exits, no threat, no command, not even an authoritative tone of voice. It is beyond question that had this encounter occurred on the street, it would be constitutional. The fact that an encounter takes place on a bus does not on its own transform standard police questioning of citizens into an illegal seizure. . . .

Respondents make much of the fact that Officer Lang displayed his badge. In *Florida v. Rodriguez*, 469 U.S., at 5-6, however, the Court rejected the claim that the defendant was seized when an officer approached him in an airport, showed him his badge, and asked him to answer some questions. Likewise, in INS v. Delgado, 466 U.S. 210, 212-213 (1984), the Court held that Immigration and Naturalization Service (INS) agents' wearing badges and questioning workers in a factory did not constitute a seizure. And while neither Lang nor his colleagues were in uniform or visibly armed, those factors should have little weight in the analysis. Officers are often required to wear uniforms and in many circumstances this is cause for assurance, not discomfort. Much the same can be said for wearing sidearms. That most law enforcement officers are armed is a fact well known to the public. The presence of a holstered firearm thus is unlikely to contribute to the coerciveness of the encounter absent active brandishing of the weapon.

Officer Hoover's position at the front of the bus also does not tip the scale in respondents' favor. Hoover did nothing to intimidate passengers, and he said nothing to suggest that people could not exit and indeed he left the aisle clear. . . .

Finally, the fact that in Officer Lang's experience only a few passengers have refused to cooperate does not suggest that a reasonable person would not feel free to terminate the bus encounter. In Lang's experience it was common for passengers to leave the bus for a cigarette or a snack while the officers were questioning passengers. And of more importance, bus passengers answer officers' questions and otherwise cooperate not because of coercion but because the passengers know that their participation enhances their own safety and the safety of those around them. "While most citizens will respond to a police request, the fact that people do so, and do so without being told they are free not to respond, hardly eliminates the consensual nature of the response." *Delgado*, supra, at 216.

Drayton contends that even if Brown's cooperation with the officers was consensual, Drayton was seized because no reasonable person would feel free to terminate the encounter with the officers after Brown had been arrested. The Court of Appeals did not address this claim; and in any event the argument fails. The arrest of one person does not mean that everyone around him has been seized by police. If anything, Brown's arrest should have put Drayton on notice of the consequences of continuing the encounter by answering the officers' questions. . . .

We turn now from the question whether respondents were seized to whether they were subjected to an unreasonable search, i.e., whether their consent to the suspicionless search was involuntary. In circumstances such as these, where the question of voluntariness pervades both the search and seizure inquiries, the respective analyses turn on very similar facts. And, as the facts above suggest, respondents' consent to the search of their luggage and their persons was voluntary. Nothing Officer Lang said indicated a command to consent to the search. Rather, when respondents informed Lang that they had a bag on the bus, he asked for their permission to check it. And when Lang requested to search Brown and Drayton's persons, he asked first if they objected, thus indicating to a reasonable person that he or she was free to refuse. . . .

The Court has rejected in specific terms the suggestion that police officers must always inform citizens of their right to refuse when seeking permission to conduct a warrantless consent search. "While knowledge of the right to refuse consent is one factor to be taken into account, the government need not establish such knowledge as the sine qua non of an effective consent." Nor do this Court's decisions suggest that even though there are no per se rules, a presumption of invalidity attaches if a citizen consented without explicit notification that he or she was free to refuse to cooperate. . . .

In a society based on law, the concept of agreement and consent should be given a weight and dignity of its own. Police officers act in full accord with the law when they ask citizens for consent. It reinforces the rule of law for the citizen to advise the police of his or her wishes and for the police to act in reliance on that understanding. When this exchange takes place, it dispels inferences of coercion. . . .

JUSTICE SOUTER, with whom JUSTICE STEVENS and JUSTICE GINSBURG join, dissenting.

Anyone who travels by air today submits to searches of the person and luggage as a condition of boarding the aircraft. It is universally accepted that such intrusions are necessary to hedge against risks that, nowadays, even small children understand. The commonplace precautions of air travel have not, thus far, been justified for ground transportation, however, and no such conditions have been placed on passengers getting on trains or buses. There is therefore an air of unreality about the Court's explanation that bus passengers consent to searches of their luggage to "enhanc[e] their own safety and the safety of those around them." Nor are the other factual assessments underlying the Court's conclusion in favor of the Government more convincing.

The issue we took to review is whether the police's examination of the bus passengers, including respondents, amounted to a suspicionless seizure under the Fourth Amendment. If it did, any consent to search was plainly invalid as a product of the illegal seizure.

Florida v. Bostick, 501 U.S. 429 (1991), established the framework for determining whether the bus passengers were seized in the constitutional sense. . . .

Before applying the standard in this case, it may be worth getting some perspective from different sets of facts. A perfect example of police conduct that supports no colorable claim of seizure is the act of an officer who simply goes up to a pedestrian on the street and asks him a question. A pair of officers questioning a pedestrian, without more, would presumably support the same conclusion. Now consider three officers, one of whom stands behind the pedestrian, another at his side toward the open sidewalk, with the third addressing questions to the pedestrian a foot or two from his face. Finally, consider the same scene in a narrow alley. On such barebones facts, one may not be able to say a seizure occurred, even in the last case, but one can say without qualification that the atmosphere of the encounters differed significantly from the first to the last examples. In the final instance there is every reason to believe that the pedestrian would have understood, to his considerable discomfort, what Justice Stewart described as the "threatening presence of several officers," United States v. Mendenhall, 446 U.S. 544, 554 (1980) (opinion of Stewart, J.). The police not only carry legitimate authority but also exercise power free from immediate check, and when the attention of several officers is brought to bear on one civilian the imbalance of immediate power is unmistakable. We all understand this, as well as we understand that a display of power rising to Justice Stewart's "threatening" level may overbear a normal person's ability to act freely, even in the absence of explicit commands or the formalities of detention. As common as this understanding is, however, there is little sign of it in the Court's opinion. . . .

[F]or reasons unexplained, the driver with the tickets entitling the passengers to travel had yielded his custody of the bus and its seated travelers to three police officers, whose authority apparently superseded the driver's own. The officers took control of the entire passenger compartment, one stationed at the door keeping surveillance of all the occupants, the others working forward from the back. With one officer right behind him and the other one forward, a third officer accosted each passenger at quarters extremely close and so cramped that as many as half the passengers could not even have stood to face the speaker. None was asked whether he was willing to converse with the police or to take part in the enquiry. Instead the officer said the police were "conducting bus interdiction," in the course of which they "would like . . . cooperation." The reasonable inference was that the "interdiction" was not a consensual exercise, but one the police would carry out whatever the circumstances; that they would prefer "cooperation" but would not let the lack of it stand in their way. There was no contrary indication that day, since no passenger had refused the cooperation requested, and there was no reason for any passenger to believe that the driver would return and the trip resume until the police were satisfied. The scene was set and an atmosphere of obligatory participation was established by this introduction. Later requests to search prefaced with "Do you mind . . ." would naturally have been understood in the terms with which the encounter began.

It is very hard to imagine that either Brown or Drayton would have believed that he stood to lose nothing if he refused to cooperate with the police, or that he had any free choice to ignore the police altogether. No reasonable passenger could have believed that, only an uncomprehending one. . . . While I am not prepared to say that no bus interrogation and search can pass the *Bostick* test without a warning that passengers are free to say no, the facts here surely required more from the officers than a quiet tone of voice. A police officer who is certain to get his way has no need to shout. . . .

NOTES AND QUESTIONS

1. What role does the meaning of "seizures" play in the protection of Fourth Amendment privacy? At first blush, doesn't a governmental seizure suggest that *liberty* — not privacy — is at stake? But if privacy is the "right to be let alone," as Justice Brandeis famously said, then perhaps privacy is more at issue than might first appear to be the case. After all, what is more basic to the right to be let alone than the right not to have a police officer in your face?

2. But does the Court's definition of the concept of seizure adequately protect this right? In United States v. Mendenhall, 446 U.S. 544 (1980), Justice Stewart gave examples of factors the presence of which might suggest that a given police-citizen encounter constitutes a "seizure" for Fourth Amendment purposes. These factors include "the threatening presence of several officers, the display of a weapon by an officer, some physical touching of the person of the citizen, or the use of language or tone of voice indicating that compliance with the officer's request might be compelled." Id. at 554. Yet even if none of the factors just listed is present, does the average person when approached by a police officer feel free to terminate the encounter — whether or not it occurs on a bus? Isn't the seizure test in fact a legal fiction premised on the view that effective law enforcement requires that police be entitled to trade upon the pressure to cooperate that citizens feel?

3. Perhaps that last question is unfair. Some police-citizen encounters are surely voluntary. The friendly cop on the beat doesn't exist solely in fiction, and many people do in fact want to cooperate with the police. The legal problem is distinguishing consensual encounters from the nonconsensual kind. But if this is the problem, why isn't the solution the one rejected in *Drayton* — namely, imposing a requirement that police advise citizens of their right to go about their business by ending the conversation? What is the source of the Court's hostility to this per se rule — at least in the context of bus encounters like those in *Bostick* and *Drayton*? Note that in the oral argument in *Drayton*, the Government asserted that police activity of the type in *Bostick* and *Drayton* is particularly important "in today's environment with respect to the protection of passengers in the Nation's public transportation system." How big a role might such considerations have played in the result in this post-9/11 case?

4. According to the *Bostick* Court, consensual police-citizen encounters are those that a reasonable person in the citizen's shoes would feel free to terminate. Should race factor into this "reasonable person" test? Professor Maclin has argued that "the dynamics surrounding an encounter between a police officer and a black male are quite different from those that surround an encounter between an officer and the so-called average, reasonable person." Tracey Maclin, "Black and Blue Encounters" — Some Preliminary Thoughts about Fourth Amendment Seizures: Should Race Matter?, 26 Val. U. L. Rev. 243, 250 (1991). He contends that the race of the individual stopped

should be considered in assessing the coerciveness of a police encounter:

> My position simply recognizes that, for most black men, the typical police confronta-
> tion is not a consensual encounter. Black men simply do not trust police officers to respect
> their rights. Although many black men *know* of their right to walk away from a police
> encounter, I submit that most do not trust the police to respect their decision to do so.

Id. at 272. A reasonable person test that does not take account of race, in Maclin's
view, "runs the risk that majoritarian values and perceptions of police practices will
go unchallenged." Id. at 274. Do you agree? Should the *Bostick* Court have taken
into account that "many black men like Bostick are unlikely to challenge or resist
the requests of armed drug agents who appear, unannounced, inside a bus aisle
seeking permission to search for illegal drugs"? Id. at 278.

5. In Brower v. County of Inyo, 489 U.S. 593 (1989), the Court dealt with the
question whether police officers had "seized" Brower when the stolen car he was
driving crashed into a police roadblock that was set up to stop him, resulting in his
death. *Brower* was a federal civil rights action brought by Brower's heirs, who
claimed that the use of the roadblock violated Brower's Fourth Amendment rights.
According to the complaint:

> [R]espondents (1) caused an 18-wheel tractor-trailer to be placed across both lanes of
> a two-lane highway in the path of Brower's flight, (2) "effectively concealed" this
> roadblock by placing it behind a curve and leaving it unilluminated, and (3) posi-
> tioned a police car, with its headlights on, between Brower's oncoming vehicle and the
> truck, so that Brower would be "blinded" on his approach.

Id. at 594.

The Ninth Circuit affirmed the district court's dismissal of the plaintiffs' Fourth
Amendment claim, concluding that there had been no "seizure." The Supreme
Court reversed. After observing that the Fourth Amendment is not implicated
when a suspect being chased by the police suddenly loses control of his car and
crashes, Justice Scalia's opinion for the Court stated:

> Violation of the Fourth Amendment requires an intentional acquisition of physical
> control. A seizure occurs even when an unintended person or thing is the object of the
> detention or taking, but the detention or taking itself must be wilful. This is implicit in
> the word "seizure," which can hardly be applied to an unknowing act. . . .
>
> Thus, if a parked and unoccupied police car slips its brake and pins a passenger
> against a wall, it is likely that a tort has occurred, but not a violation of the Fourth
> Amendment. And the situation would not change if the passerby happened, by lucky
> chance, to be a serial murderer for whom there was an outstanding arrest warrant —
> even if, at the time he was pinned, he was in the process of running away from two
> pursuing constables. It is clear, in other words, that a Fourth Amendment seizure does
> not occur whenever there is a governmentally caused termination of an individual's
> freedom of movement (the innocent passerby), nor even whenever there is a govern-
> mentally caused and governmentally *desired* termination of an individual's freedom of
> movement (the fleeing felon), but only when there is a governmental termination of
> freedom of movement *through means intentionally applied*. . . .
>
> [It is not] possible in determining whether there has been a seizure in a case such as
> this, to distinguish between a roadblock that is designed to give the oncoming driver

the option of a voluntary stop (e.g., one at the end of a long straightaway), and a roadblock that is designed precisely to produce a collision (e.g., one located just around a bend). In determining whether the means that terminates the freedom of movement is the very means that the government intended we cannot draw too fine a line, or we will be driven to saying that one is not seized who has been stopped by the accidental discharge of a gun with which he was meant only to be bludgeoned, or by a bullet in the heart that was meant only for the leg. We think it enough for a seizure that a person be stopped by the very instrumentality set in motion or put in place in order to achieve that result. . . .

This is not to say that the precise character of the roadblock is irrelevant. . . . [For §1983 liability], the seizure must be "unreasonable." Petitioners can claim the right to recover for Brower's death only because the unreasonableness they allege consists precisely of setting up the roadblock in such manner as to be likely to kill him. This should be contrasted with the situation that would obtain if the sole claim of unreasonableness were that there was no probable cause for the stop. In that case, if Brower had had the opportunity to stop voluntarily at the roadblock, but had negligently or intentionally driven into it, then, because of lack of proximate causality, respondents, though responsible for depriving him of his freedom of movement, would not be liable for his death. Thus, the circumstances of this roadblock, including the allegation that the headlights were used to blind the oncoming driver, may yet determine the outcome of this case.

Id. at 596-599 (emphasis original).

In an opinion concurring in the judgment, Justice Stevens, joined by Justices Brennan, Marshall, and Blackmun, observed: "[T]here is no dispute that the roadblock was intended to stop the decedent. Decision in the case before us is thus not advanced by pursuing a hypothetical inquiry concerning whether an unintentional act might also violate the Fourth Amendment." Id. at 601.

6. *Bostick* and *Drayton* both involved suspects who at least partially cooperated with police, and who later argued that a reasonable person in their position would not have felt free to do otherwise. California v. Hodari D., 499 U.S. 621 (1991), concerned the Fourth Amendment's application to a case in which the suspect seeks to avoid an encounter with the police. It specifically addressed the question whether a suspect who attempts to run away from police is seized when police pursue him.

The suspect in *Hodari D.* fled at the sight of an approaching police car. Officer Pertoso pursued the suspect on foot. Just before tackling him and bringing him to the ground, Officer Pertoso observed Hodari toss away a small object that turned out to be crack cocaine. Hodari argued that this evidence should be suppressed because he was unlawfully seized at the moment he saw Officer Pertoso running toward him. In an opinion by Justice Scalia, the Supreme Court determined that Hodari was not seized within the meaning of the Fourth Amendment at the time he discarded the cocaine:

> As this case comes to us, the only issue presented is whether, at the time he dropped the drugs, Hodari had been "seized" within the meaning of the Fourth Amendment. If so, respondent argues, the drugs were the fruit of that seizure and the evidence concerning them was properly excluded. If not, the drugs were abandoned by Hodari and lawfully recovered by the police, and the evidence should have been admitted. . . .
>
> We have long understood that the Fourth Amendment's protection against "unreasonable . . . seizures" includes seizure of the person. From the time of the founding to the present, the word "seizure" has meant a "taking possession," 2 N.

Webster, An American Dictionary of the English Language 67 (1828). For most purposes at common law, the word connoted not merely grasping, or applying physical force to, the animate or inanimate object in question, but actually bringing it within physical control. A ship still fleeing, even though under attack, would not be considered to have been seized as a war prize. Cf. The Josefa Segunda, 10 Wheat. 312, 325-326 (1825). A res capable of manual delivery was not seized until "tak[en] into custody." Pelham v. Rose, 9 Wall. 103, 106 (1870). To constitute an arrest, however — the quintessential "seizure of the person" under our Fourth Amendment jurisprudence — the mere grasping or application of physical force with lawful authority, whether or not it succeeded in subduing the arrestee, was sufficient. See, e.g., Whitehead v. Keyes, 85 Mass. 495, 501 (1862) ("[A]n officer effects an arrest of a person whom he has authority to arrest, by laying his hand on him for the purpose of arresting him, though he may not succeed in stopping and holding him"). . . .

To say that an arrest is effected by the slightest application of physical force, despite the arrestee's escape, is not to say that for Fourth Amendment purposes there is a *continuing* arrest during the period of fugitivity. If, for example, Pertoso had laid his hands upon Hodari to arrest him, but Hodari had broken away and had *then* cast away the cocaine, it would hardly be realistic to say that that disclosure had been made during the course of an arrest. The present case, however, is even one step further removed. It does not involve the application of any physical force; Hodari was untouched by Officer Pertoso at the time he discarded the cocaine. His defense relies instead upon the proposition that a seizure occurs "when the officer, by means of physical force or *show of authority*, has in some way restrained the liberty of a citizen." Terry v. Ohio, 392 U.S. 1, 19, n. 16 (1968) (emphasis added). Hodari contends (and we accept as true for purposes of this decision) that Pertoso's pursuit qualified as a "show of authority" calling upon Hodari to halt. The narrow question before us is whether, with respect to a show of authority as with respect to application of physical force, a seizure occurs even though the suspect does not yield. We hold that it does not.

The language of the Fourth Amendment, of course, cannot sustain respondent's contention. The word "seizure" readily bears the meaning of a laying on of hands or application of physical force to restrain movement, even when it is ultimately unsuccessful. ("She seized the purse-snatcher, but he broke out of her grasp.") It does not remotely apply, however, to the prospect of a policeman yelling "Stop, in the name of the law!" at a fleeing form that continues to flee. . . . Nor can the result respondent wishes to achieve be produced — indirectly, as it were — by suggesting that Pertoso's uncomplied-with show of authority was a common-law arrest, and then appealing to the principle that all common-law arrests are seizures. An arrest requires *either* physical force (as described above) *or*, where that is absent, *submission* to the assertion of authority. . . .

We do not think it desirable, even as a policy matter, to stretch the Fourth Amendment beyond its words and beyond the meaning of arrest, as respondent urges. Street pursuits always place the public at some risk, and compliance with police orders to stop should therefore be encouraged. Only a few of those orders, we must presume, will be without adequate basis, and since the addressee has no ready means of identifying the deficient ones it almost invariably is the responsible course to comply. Unlawful orders will not be deterred, moreover, by sanctioning through the exclusionary rule those of them that are *not* obeyed. Since policemen do not command "Stop!" expecting to be ignored, or give chase hoping to be outrun, it fully suffices to apply the deterrent to their genuine, successful seizures. . . .

Id. at 623-627.

As Justice Stevens pointed out in a dissent joined by Justice Marshall, the Court's reliance on common law precedents in *Hodari D.* is at odds with the

Court's approach to Fourth Amendment interpretation in *Katz*: "Significantly, in the *Katz* opinion, the Court repeatedly used the word 'seizure' to describe the process of recording sounds that could not possibly have been the subject of a common-law seizure." 499 U.S. at 634. Is there any more reason for the Court to look to the common law in this context than in the context of electronic surveillance? Why or why not?

7. The last point may relate to a broader question. How much should the Court be influenced in its approach to Fourth Amendment interpretation by the reality we discussed at the start of this chapter—namely, that Fourth Amendment law functions as a chief source of legal regulation of police? The dissenters also argued that by hinging the timing of a seizure on the citizen's reaction, rather than on the officer's conduct, the majority deprived police of the ability to determine in advance whether contemplated conduct implicated the Fourth Amendment— presumably undercutting the ability to implement appropriate training around the legal standard. Because of the range of possible responses to a police show of authority and the time that may elapse between a show of authority (like the sound of sirens accompanied by a patrol car's flashing lights) and the complete submission of the citizen, the dissenters further contended that the majority's approach "can only create uncertainty and generate litigation." Id. at 643-644. Do you agree with these criticisms? If so, what weight should factors such as these have in the Court's approach to Fourth Amendment interpretation?

8. *Brower*'s emphasis on seizure as the "intentional acquisition of physical control" and *Hodari D.*'s distinction between "seizure by physical force" and by "show of authority plus submission" may raise as many questions as they answer. Consider one recent discussion of the problems inherent in applying seizure standards developed in criminal investigations to a very different context— confrontations between police and protestors:

> [A]t large-scale public street demonstrations police are acting in their public order function and are not primarily concerned with making arrests. Dozens or hundreds of officers confront hundreds or thousands of demonstrators. . . . Where force is used, it is usually in service of a dispersal order. . . . Rarely are all or even most demonstrators actually arrested for failing to disperse; police intent in using force is to clear the streets quickly by making demonstrators leave, rather than to detain and arrest them.
>
> . . . [M]any of the methods used by police in handling recent large-scale demonstrations present added difficulties in determining when their use constitutes a seizure of their targets. . . . [W]eaponry includes less-lethal munitions such as rubber, plastic, foam, and wooden bullets and bean bag rounds; chemical irritants such as tear gas and pepper spray; and other assorted devices, including concussion grenades, more colorfully known as "flash-bang devices." . . .
>
> . . . [I]t is unclear whether less-lethal munitions that do not hit their mark will implicate *Hodari D.*'s per se physical force rule, or instead constitute a show of authority. . . .
>
> Chemical irritants such as mace and pepper spray present two difficulties: Does use of these gaseous agents constitute a "touching" of citizens by police . . . ? If so, are only direct targets of the irritant "touched," or are members of a crowd over whom the gas merely "wafted" also touched? . . .
>
> Those demonstrators who cannot avail themselves of *Hodari D.*'s per se rule for physical force must proceed under a theory of show of authority, and face a difficult road to seizure. . . .
>
> If courts were to . . . hold that police use of less-lethal weapons against demonstrators to enforce a dispersal order constitutes a show of police authority sufficient to

seize, demonstrators would still need to "submit" to that authority to be seized under California v. Hodari D. What would submission look like in such a case? Holding one's ground? Running away as quickly as possible—i.e., doing precisely what Hodari D. did, but also what police want demonstrators to do? . . .

Hodari D.'s statement that the slightest touching with lawful authority constitutes an arrest currently represents the best chance of demonstrators . . . to establish seizure and receive Fourth Amendment review of police action against them. If *Hodari D.* is taken at its word, it seems likely that demonstrators who were directly touched by rubber bullets and chemical irritants were seized. . . . *Hodari D.*'s word, however, is relatively untested, and the Court's earlier decision in Brower v. County of Inyo and subsequent lower court readings of *Hodari D.* that identify a requirement of officer intent to arrest cast into further doubt its viability.

In *Brower* the Court held that a seizure by physical force is "an intentional acquisition of physical control." . . . *Brower* and similar formulations of seizure can be read to indicate that where one avenue of movement is denied to a citizen, she is not seized, but where all avenues of movement are denied to her, she is. Whereas touching a suspect is usually an attempt or a prelude to denying freedom of movement to the suspect, in the case of demonstrators, the touching is an attempt to deny only one avenue of movement—e.g., continuing a march, or remaining in a particular area. . . .

. . . This is essentially the overarching problem demonstrators face under current law: whereas arrest, the "quintessential 'seizure of the person,'" involves an attempt to subdue and detain the subject, a dispersal order involves an attempt to mobilize the subject by force. . . . It is uncertain whether a touching without intent to seize will be a seizure, or the targets of force not touched by the force will be seized.

Renee Paradis, Carpe Demonstratores: Towards a Bright-Line Rule Governing Seizure in Excessive Force Claims Brought by Demonstrators, 103 Colum. L. Rev. 316, 334-339 (2003). Should the definition of "seizures" be context-specific? Does the same definition work in *Hodari D., Brower,* and police dispersal of a public demonstration? Does the difficulty of defining "seizures" cast doubt on the enterprise of using Fourth Amendment law as the primary tool for regulating the police?

3.   To Whom Does the Fourth Amendment Apply?

UNITED STATES v. VERDUGO-URQUIDEZ

Certiorari to the United States Court of Appeals for the Ninth Circuit
494 U.S. 259 (1990)

CHIEF JUSTICE REHNQUIST delivered the opinion of the Court.

The question presented by this case is whether the Fourth Amendment applies to the search and seizure by United States agents of property that is owned by a nonresident alien and located in a foreign country. We hold that it does not.

Respondent Rene Martin Verdugo-Urquidez is a citizen and resident of Mexico. He is believed by the United States Drug Enforcement Agency (DEA) to be one of the leaders of a large and violent organization in Mexico that smuggles narcotics into the United States. . . . [T]he Government obtained a warrant for his arrest on August 3, 1985. In January 1986, Mexican police officers . . .

apprehended Verdugo-Urquidez in Mexico and transported him to the United States Border Patrol station in Calexico, California. There, United States marshals arrested respondent and eventually moved him to a correctional center in San Diego, California, where he remains incarcerated pending trial.

Following respondent's arrest, Terry Bowen, a DEA agent assigned to the Calexico DEA office, decided to arrange for searches of Verdugo-Urquidez's Mexican residences located in Mexicali and San Felipe. Bowen believed that the searches would reveal evidence related to respondent's alleged narcotics trafficking activities and his involvement in the kidnaping and torture-murder of DEA Special Agent Enrique Camarena Salazar (for which respondent subsequently has been convicted in a separate prosecution.) Bowen telephoned Walter White, the Assistant Special Agent in charge of the DEA office in Mexico City, and asked him to seek authorization for the search from the Director General of the Mexican Federal Judicial Police (MFJP). . . . White eventually contacted the Director General, who authorized the searches and promised the cooperation of Mexican authorities. Thereafter, DEA agents working in concert with officers of the MFJP searched respondent's properties in Mexicali and San Felipe and seized certain documents. . . .

The District Court granted respondent's motion to suppress evidence seized during the searches, concluding that the Fourth Amendment applied to the searches and that the DEA agents had failed to justify searching respondent's premises without a warrant. A divided panel of the Court of Appeals for the Ninth Circuit affirmed. . . .

. . . We granted certiorari.

Before analyzing the scope of the Fourth Amendment, we think it significant to note that it operates in a different manner than the Fifth Amendment, which is not at issue in this case. The privilege against self-incrimination . . . is a fundamental trial right of criminal defendants. Although conduct by law enforcement officials prior to trial may ultimately impair that right, a constitutional violation occurs only at trial. The Fourth Amendment functions differently. It prohibits "unreasonable searches and seizures" whether or not the evidence is sought to be used in a criminal trial, and a violation of the Amendment is "fully accomplished" at the time of an unreasonable governmental intrusion. For purposes of this case, therefore, if there were a constitutional violation, it occurred solely in Mexico. . . .

The Fourth Amendment provides:

> "The right of the people to be secure in their persons, houses, papers, and effects, against unreasonable searches and seizures, shall not be violated, and no Warrants shall issue, but upon probable cause, supported by Oath or affirmation, and particularly describing the place to be searched, and the persons or things to be seized."

That text, by contrast with the Fifth and Sixth Amendments, extends its reach only to "the people." Contrary to the suggestion of amici curiae that the Framers used this phrase "simply to avoid [an] awkward rhetorical redundancy," "the people" seems to have been a term of art employed in select parts of the Constitution. The Preamble declares that the Constitution is ordained and established by "the People of the United States." The Second Amendment protects "the right of the people to keep and bear Arms," and the Ninth and Tenth Amendments provide that certain rights and powers are retained by and reserved to "the people."

See also U.S. Const., Amdt. 1 ("Congress shall make no law . . . abridging . . . *the right of the people* peaceably to assemble") (emphasis added); Art. I, §2, cl. 1 ("The House of Representatives shall be composed of Members chosen every second Year *by the People of the several States*") (emphasis added). While this textual exegesis is by no means conclusive, it suggests that "the people" protected by the Fourth Amendment, and by the First and Second Amendments, and to whom rights and powers are reserved in the Ninth and Tenth Amendments, refers to a class of persons who are part of a national community or who have otherwise developed sufficient connection with this country to be considered part of that community. The language of these Amendments contrasts with the words "person" and "accused" used in the Fifth and Sixth Amendments regulating procedure in criminal cases.

What we know of the history of the drafting of the Fourth Amendment also suggests that its purpose was to restrict searches and seizures which might be conducted by the United States in domestic matters. The Framers originally decided not to include a provision like the Fourth Amendment, because they believed the National Government lacked power to conduct searches and seizures. See C. Warren, The Making of the Constitution 508-509 (1928); The Federalist No. 84, p. 513 (C. Rossiter ed. 1961) (A. Hamilton); 1 Annals of Cong. 437 (1789) (statement of J. Madison). Many disputed the original view that the Federal Government possessed only narrow delegated powers over domestic affairs, however, and ultimately felt an Amendment prohibiting unreasonable searches and seizures was necessary. . . . The driving force behind the adoption of the Amendment . . . was widespread hostility among the former colonists to the issuance of writs of assistance empowering revenue officers to search suspected places for smuggled goods, and general search warrants permitting the search of private houses, often to uncover papers that might be used to convict persons of libel. See Boyd v. United States, 116 U.S. 616, 625-626 (1886). The available historical data show, therefore, that the purpose of the Fourth Amendment was to protect the people of the United States against arbitrary action by their own Government; it was never suggested that the provision was intended to restrain the actions of the Federal Government against aliens outside of the United States territory.

There is likewise no indication that the Fourth Amendment was understood by contemporaries of the Framers to apply to activities of the United States directed against aliens in foreign territory or in international waters. Only seven years after the ratification of the Amendment, French interference with American commercial vessels engaged in neutral trade triggered what came to be known as the "undeclared war" with France. In an Act to "protect the Commerce of the United States" in 1798, Congress authorized President Adams to "instruct the commanders of the public armed vessels which are, or which shall be employed in the service of the United States, to subdue, seize and take any armed French vessel, which shall be found within the jurisdictional limits of the United States, or elsewhere, on the high seas." §1 of An Act Further to Protect the Commerce of the United States, ch. 68, 1 Stat. 578. . . . Congress also gave the President power to grant to the owners of private armed ships and vessels of the United States "special commissions," which would allow them "the same license and authority. . . ." §2, 1 Stat. 579. Under the latter provision, 365 private armed vessels were commissioned before March 1, 1799, see G. Allen, Our Naval War with France 59 (1967); together, these enactments resulted in scores of seizures of foreign vessels under congressional authority. . . . [I]t was never suggested that the Fourth Amendment restrained the authority of Congress or of United States agents to conduct operations such as this.

The global view taken by the Court of Appeals of the application of the Constitution is also contrary to this Court's decisions in the *Insular Cases*, which held that not every constitutional provision applies to governmental activity even where the United States has sovereign power. See, e.g., Balzac v. Porto Rico, 258 U.S. 298 (1922) (Sixth Amendment right to jury trial inapplicable in Puerto Rico); Ocampo v. United States, 234 U.S. 91(1914) (Fifth Amendment grand jury provision inapplicable in Philippines); Dorr v. United States, 195 U.S. 138 (1904) (jury trial provision inapplicable in Philippines); Hawaii v. Mankichi, 190 U.S. 197 (1903) (provisions on indictment by grand jury and jury trial inapplicable in Hawaii); Downes v. Bidwell, 182 U.S. 244 (1901) (Revenue Clauses of Constitution inapplicable to Puerto Rico). In *Dorr*, we declared the general rule that in an unincorporated territory—one not clearly destined for statehood— Congress was not required to adopt "a system of laws which shall include the right of trial by jury, and that *the Constitution does not, without legislation and of its own force, carry such right to territory so situated.*" 195 U.S., at 149 (emphasis added). Only "fundamental" constitutional rights are guaranteed to inhabitants of those territories. If that is true with respect to territories ultimately governed by Congress, respondent's claim that the protections of the Fourth Amendment extend to aliens in foreign nations is even weaker. . . .

Indeed, we have rejected the claim that aliens are entitled to Fifth Amendment rights outside the sovereign territory of the United States. In Johnson v. Eisentrager, 339 U.S. 763 (1950), the Court held that enemy aliens arrested in China and imprisoned in Germany after World War II could not obtain writs of habeas corpus in our federal courts on the ground that their convictions for war crimes had violated the Fifth Amendment and other constitutional provisions. The *Eisentrager* opinion acknowledged that in some cases constitutional provisions extend beyond the citizenry; "[t]he alien . . . has been accorded a generous and ascending scale of rights as he increases his identity with our society." Id., at 770. But our rejection of extraterritorial application of the Fifth Amendment was emphatic. . . . If such is true of the Fifth Amendment, which speaks in the relatively universal term of "person," it would seem even more true with respect to the Fourth Amendment, which applies only to "the people."

To support his all-encompassing view of the Fourth Amendment, respondent points to language from the plurality opinion in Reid v. Covert, 354 U.S. 1 (1957). *Reid* involved an attempt by Congress to subject the wives of American servicemen to trial by military tribunals without the protection of the Fifth and Sixth Amendments. . . . *Reid* . . . decided that United States citizens stationed abroad could invoke the protection of the Fifth and Sixth Amendments. . . . Since respondent is not a United States citizen, he can derive no comfort from the *Reid* holding.

Verdugo-Urquidez also relies on a series of cases in which we have held that aliens enjoy certain constitutional rights. See, e.g., Plyler v. Doe, 457 U.S. 202, 211-212 (1982) (illegal aliens protected by Equal Protection Clause); Kwong Hai Chew v. Colding, 344 U.S. 590, 596 (1953) (resident alien is a "person" within the meaning of the Fifth Amendment); Bridges v. Wixon, 326 U.S. 135, 148 (1945) (resident aliens have First Amendment rights); Russian Volunteer Fleet v. United States, 282 U.S. 481 (1931) (Just Compensation Clause of Fifth Amendment); Wong

Wing v. United States, 163 U.S. 228, 238 (1896) (resident aliens entitled to Fifth and Sixth Amendment rights); Yick Wo v. Hopkins, 118 U.S. 356, 369 (1886) (Fourteenth Amendment protects resident aliens). These cases, however, establish only that aliens receive constitutional protections when they have come within the territory of the United States and developed substantial connections with this country. . . .

JUSTICE STEVENS' concurrence in the judgment takes the view that even though the search took place in Mexico, it is nonetheless governed by the requirements of the Fourth Amendment because respondent was "lawfully present in the United States . . . even though he was brought and held here against his will." But this sort of presence — lawful but involuntary — is not of the sort to indicate any substantial connection with our country. The extent to which respondent might claim the protection of the Fourth Amendment if the duration of his stay in the United States were to be prolonged — by a prison sentence, for example — we need not decide. When the search of his house in Mexico took place, he had been present in the United States for only a matter of days. . . .

The Court of Appeals found some support for its holding in our decision in INS v. Lopez-Mendoza, 468 U.S. 1032 (1984), where a majority of Justices assumed that the Fourth Amendment applied to illegal aliens in the United States. . . . The question presented for decision in *Lopez-Mendoza* was limited to whether the Fourth Amendment's exclusionary rule should be extended to civil deportation proceedings; it did not encompass whether the protections of the Fourth Amendment extend to illegal aliens in this country. . . . Our statements in *Lopez-Mendoza* are therefore not dispositive of how the Court would rule on a Fourth Amendment claim by illegal aliens in the United States if such a claim were squarely before us. Even assuming such aliens would be entitled to Fourth Amendment protections, their situation is different from respondent's. The illegal aliens in *Lopez-Mendoza* were in the United States voluntarily and presumably had accepted some societal obligations; but respondent had no voluntary connection with this country that might place him among "the people" of the United States. . . .

Not only are history and case law against respondent, but . . . the result of accepting his claim would have significant and deleterious consequences for the United States in conducting activities beyond its boundaries. The rule adopted by the Court of Appeals would apply not only to law enforcement operations abroad, but also to other foreign policy operations which might result in "searches or seizures." The United States frequently employs Armed Forces outside this country — over 200 times in our history — for the protection of American citizens or national security. Congressional Research Service, Instances of Use of United States Armed Forces Abroad, 1798-1989 (E. Collier ed. 1989). Application of the Fourth Amendment to those circumstances could significantly disrupt the ability of the political branches to respond to foreign situations involving our national interest. Were respondent to prevail, aliens with no attachment to this country might well bring actions for damages to remedy claimed violations of the Fourth Amendment in foreign countries or in international waters. . . . The Members of the Executive and Legislative Branches are sworn to uphold the Constitution, and they presumably desire to follow its commands. But the Court of Appeals' global view of its applicability would plunge them into a sea of uncertainty as to what might be reasonable in the way of searches and seizures conducted abroad. Indeed, the Court of Appeals held that absent exigent circumstances, United States agents could not effect a "search or seizure" for law enforcement purposes in a foreign country without first obtaining a warrant — which would be a dead letter outside the United States — from a magistrate in this country. Even if no warrant were required, American agents would have to articulate specific facts giving them probable cause to undertake a search or seizure if they wished to comply with the Fourth Amendment as conceived by the Court of Appeals.

We think that the text of the Fourth Amendment, its history, and our cases discussing the application of the Constitution to aliens and extraterritorially require rejection of respondent's claim. At the time of the search, he was a citizen and resident of Mexico with no voluntary attachment to the United States, and the place searched was located in Mexico. Under these circumstances, the Fourth Amendment has no application. . . .

The judgment of the Court of Appeals is accordingly
Reversed.

JUSTICE KENNEDY, concurring.

I agree that no violation of the Fourth Amendment has occurred and that we must reverse the judgment of the Court of Appeals. Although some explanation of my views is appropriate given the difficulties of this case, I do not believe they depart in fundamental respects from the opinion of the Court, which I join. . . .

. . . I cannot place any weight on the reference to "the people" in the Fourth Amendment as a source of restricting its protections. With respect, I submit these words do not detract from its force or its reach. Given the history of our Nation's concern over warrantless and unreasonable searches, explicit recognition of "the right of the people" to Fourth Amendment protection may be interpreted to underscore the importance of the right, rather than to restrict the category of persons who may assert it. The restrictions that the United States must observe with reference to aliens beyond its territory or jurisdiction depend, as a consequence, on general principles of interpretation, not on an inquiry as to who formed the Constitution or a construction that some rights are mentioned as being those of "the people."

I take it to be correct, as the plurality opinion in Reid v. Covert sets forth, that the Government may act only as the Constitution authorizes, whether the actions in question are foreign or domestic. See 354 U.S., at 6. But this principle is only a first step in resolving this case. The question before us then becomes what constitutional standards apply when the Government acts, in reference to an alien, within its sphere of foreign operations. . . .

The conditions and considerations of this case would make adherence to the Fourth Amendment's warrant requirement impracticable and anomalous. . . . If the search had occurred in a residence within the United States, I have little doubt that the full protections of the Fourth Amendment would apply. But that is not this case. The absence of local judges or magistrates available to issue warrants, the differing and perhaps unascertainable conceptions of reasonableness and privacy that prevail abroad, and the need to cooperate with foreign officials all indicate that the Fourth Amendment's warrant requirement should not apply in Mexico as it does in this country. For this reason, in addition to the other persuasive justifications stated by the Court, I agree that no violation of the Fourth Amendment has occurred in the case before us. . . .

JUSTICE STEVENS, concurring in the judgment.

In my opinion aliens who are lawfully present in the United States are among those "people" who are entitled to the protection of the Bill of Rights, including the Fourth Amendment. Respondent is surely such a person even though he was brought and held here against his will. . . . I do agree, however, with the Government's submission that the search conducted by the United States agents with the approval and cooperation of the Mexican authorities was not "unreasonable" as that term is used in the first Clause of the Amendment. I do not believe the Warrant Clause has any application to searches of noncitizens' homes in foreign jurisdictions because American magistrates have no power to authorize such searches. I therefore concur in the Court's judgment.

JUSTICE BRENNAN, with whom JUSTICE MARSHALL joins, dissenting. . . .

Particularly in the past decade, our Government has sought, successfully, to hold foreign nationals criminally liable under federal laws for conduct committed entirely beyond the territorial limits of the United States that nevertheless has effects in this country. Foreign nationals must now take care not to violate our drug laws, our antitrust laws, our securities laws, and a host of other federal criminal statutes. The enormous expansion of federal criminal jurisdiction outside our Nation's boundaries has led one commentator to suggest that our country's three largest exports are now "rock music, blue jeans, and United States law." Grundman, The New Imperialism: The Extraterritorial Application of United States Law, 14 Int'l Law. 257, 257 (1980).

The Constitution is the source of Congress' authority to criminalize conduct, whether here or abroad, and of the Executive's authority to investigate and prosecute such conduct. But the same Constitution also prescribes limits on our Government's authority to investigate, prosecute, and punish criminal conduct, whether foreign or domestic. . . .

The Fourth Amendment guarantees the right of "the people" to be free from unreasonable searches and seizures. . . . According to the majority, the term "the people" refers to "a class of persons who are part of a national community or who have otherwise developed sufficient connection with this country to be considered part of that community." The Court admits that "the people" extends beyond the citizenry, but leaves the precise contours of its "sufficient connection" test unclear. . . .

What the majority ignores, however, is the most obvious connection between Verdugo-Urquidez and the United States: he was investigated and is being prosecuted for violations of United States law and may well spend the rest of his life in a United States prison. The "sufficient connection" is supplied not by Verdugo-Urquidez, but by the Government. Respondent is entitled to the protections of the Fourth Amendment because our Government, by investigating him and attempting to hold him accountable under United States criminal laws, has treated him as a member of our community for purposes of enforcing our laws. He has become, quite literally, one of the governed. . . .

. . . If we expect aliens to obey our laws, aliens should be able to expect that we will obey our Constitution when we investigate, prosecute, and punish them. . . .

Mutuality is essential to ensure the fundamental fairness that underlies our Bill of Rights. Foreign nationals investigated and prosecuted for alleged violations of United States criminal laws are just as vulnerable to oppressive Government behavior as are United States citizens investigated and prosecuted for the same alleged violations. . . .

Mutuality also serves to inculcate the values of law and order. By respecting the rights of foreign nationals, we encourage other nations to respect the rights of our citizens. Moreover, as our Nation becomes increasingly concerned about the domestic effects of international crime, we cannot forget that the behavior of our law enforcement agents abroad sends a powerful message about the rule of law to individuals everywhere. . . .

Finally, when United States agents conduct unreasonable searches, whether at home or abroad, they disregard our Nation's values. For over 200 years, our country has considered itself the world's foremost protector of liberties. The privacy and sanctity of the home have been primary tenets of our moral, philosophical, and judicial beliefs. . . . How can we explain to others—and to ourselves—that these long cherished ideals are suddenly of no consequence when the door being broken belongs to a foreigner? . . .

The Court . . . relies on a series of cases dealing with the application of criminal procedural protections outside of the United States to conclude that "not every constitutional provision applies to governmental activity even where the United States has sovereign power." None of these cases, however, purports to read the phrase "the people" as limiting the protections of the Fourth Amendment to those with "sufficient connection" to the United States, and thus none gives content to the majority's analysis. The cases shed no light on the question whether respondent—a citizen of a nonenemy nation being tried in a United States federal court—is one of "the people" protected by the Fourth Amendment.

The majority mischaracterizes Johnson v. Eisentrager, 339 U.S. 763 (1950), as having "rejected the claim that aliens are entitled to Fifth Amendment rights outside the sovereign territory of the United States." In *Johnson*, 21 German nationals were convicted of engaging in continued military activity against the United States after the surrender of Germany and before the surrender of Japan in World War II. The Court held that "the Constitution does not confer a right of personal security or an immunity from military trial and punishment upon an *alien enemy* engaged in the hostile service of a government at war with the United States." 339 U.S., at 785 (emphasis added). . . . The Court rejected the German nationals' efforts to obtain writs of habeas corpus not because they were foreign nationals, but because they were enemy soldiers.

The *Insular Cases* are likewise inapposite. The *Insular Cases* all concerned whether accused persons enjoyed the protections of certain rights in criminal prosecutions brought by territorial authorities in territorial courts. These cases were limited to their facts long ago, see Reid v. Covert, 354 U.S., at 14 (plurality opinion) ("[I]t is our judgment that neither the cases nor their reasoning should be given any further expansion"), and they are of no analytical value when a criminal defendant seeks to invoke the Fourth Amendment in a prosecution by the Federal Government in a federal court.

The majority's rejection of respondent's claim to Fourth Amendment protection is apparently motivated by its fear that application of the Amendment to law enforcement searches against foreign nationals overseas "could significantly disrupt the ability of the political branches to respond to foreign situations involving our national interest." The majority's doomsday scenario—that American Armed Forces conducting a mission to protect our national security with no law enforcement objective "would have to articulate specific facts giving them probable cause to undertake a search or seizure," — is fanciful. . . . Accepting respondent as one of "the governed" . . . hardly requires the Court to accept enemy aliens in wartime as among "the governed" entitled to invoke the protection of the Fourth Amendment. See Johnson v. Eisentrager, supra.

Moreover, with respect to non-law-enforcement activities not directed against enemy aliens in wartime but nevertheless implicating national security, doctrinal exceptions to the general requirements of a warrant and probable cause likely would be applicable more frequently abroad, thus lessening the purported tension between the Fourth Amendment's strictures and the Executive's foreign affairs power. . . .

Because the Fourth Amendment governs the search of respondent's Mexican residences, the District Court properly suppressed the evidence found in that search because the officers conducting the search did not obtain a warrant. . . .

[T]he Warrant Clause [is not] inapplicable merely because a warrant from a United States magistrate could not "authorize" a search in a foreign country. Although this may be true as a matter of international law, it is irrelevant to our interpretation of the Fourth Amendment. As a matter of United States constitutional law, a warrant serves the same primary function overseas as it does domestically: it assures that a neutral magistrate has authorized the search and limited its scope. The need to protect those suspected of criminal activity from the unbridled discretion of investigating officers is no less important abroad than at home. . . .

JUSTICE BLACKMUN, dissenting.

I cannot accept the Court of Appeals' conclusion, echoed in some portions of JUSTICE BRENNAN's dissent, that the Fourth Amendment governs every action by an American official that can be characterized as a search or seizure. American agents acting abroad generally do not purport to exercise *sovereign* authority over the foreign nationals with whom they come in contact. The relationship between these agents and foreign nationals is therefore fundamentally different from the relationship between United States officials and individuals residing within this country.

I am inclined to agree with JUSTICE BRENNAN, however, that when a foreign national is held accountable for purported violations of United States criminal laws, he has effectively been treated as one of "the governed" and therefore is entitled to Fourth Amendment protections. . . . In any event, as JUSTICE STEVENS notes, respondent was lawfully (though involuntarily) within this country at the time the search occurred. Under these circumstances I believe that respondent is entitled to invoke protections of the Fourth Amendment. I agree with the Government, however, that an American magistrate's lack of power to authorize a search abroad renders the Warrant Clause inapplicable to the search of a noncitizen's residence outside this country.

The Fourth Amendment nevertheless requires that the search be "reasonable." And when the purpose of a search is the procurement of evidence for a criminal prosecution, we have consistently held that the search, to be reasonable, must be based upon probable cause. Neither the District Court nor the Court of Appeals addressed the issue of probable cause, and I do not believe that a reliable determination could be made on the basis of the record before us. I therefore would vacate the judgment of the Court of Appeals and remand the case for further proceedings.

NOTES AND QUESTIONS

1. Notice how the Court's opinion distinguishes the Fifth Amendment privilege against self-incrimination from the Fourth Amendment's ban on unreasonable searches and seizures. Are you persuaded by the distinction?

Notwithstanding the alleged difference between those two constitutional protections, the principle of *Verdugo-Urquidez* appears to apply equally to the Fifth Amendment context. The defendant in Balsys v. United States, 524 U.S. 666 (1998), was a Lithuanian immigrant suspected of involvement in Nazi war crimes during World War II. In a deportation proceeding, Balsys was asked about his activities during the war, and he "took the Fifth." Balsys claimed that his answers might lead to criminal liability in Lithuania, Germany, and Israel—but not in the United States. The Supreme Court held that the privilege does not apply to risks of criminal liability in other countries. Are *Verdugo-Urquidez* and *Balsys* consistent? If not, which one is right?

2. Consider the position that Justices Stevens and Blackmun take: the Fourth Amendment applies in *Verdugo-Urquidez*, but the requirement of a warrant issued by a neutral and detached magistrate does not. Why not apply the warrant requirement? Justice Stevens says the answer is that "American magistrates have no power to authorize" searches like the one in *Verdugo-Urquidez*. Why not? If the American Constitution required a warrant from an American magistrate as a condition to such a search, presumably American magistrates would have the relevant authority. What is Justice Stevens' concern?

3. One possible solution to the problem in *Verdugo-Urquidez* would be to hold that the Fourth Amendment applies, but that its content depends on foreign law. If under Mexican law the search is reasonable and appropriate, then the Fourth Amendment is satisfied. If not, it isn't—and evidence obtained in the search is inadmissible. Why does the Court not take that approach?

4. One way to put the issue in *Verdugo-Urquidez* is this: Does the Fourth Amendment follow the government, or does it follow the citizenry? Does it apply to all relevant actions by American government officials? Or does it apply to all invasions of the relevant interests when those interests are held by American citizens or others who are entitled to the protection of American law? Which is the right answer? On the one hand, Fourth Amendment law is precisely about putting limits on government intrusions into liberty and privacy; if those limits are wise, why not impose them wherever and whenever the government acts? On the other hand, shouldn't this be a matter for Mexican law to sort out, since the search was of a Mexican citizen's property on Mexican soil? On yet another hand—this sounds a bit like Tevye in "Fiddler on the Roof"; at some point, one runs out of hands—if the enforcement mechanism is exclusion, then shouldn't the legal restriction depend on the court system in which the defendant is prosecuted? If our government wants to use our courts, then it should obey our Fourth Amendment. If it wants to use Mexican courts and the Mexicans agree, then application of Mexican law is appropriate. What is wrong with *that* answer?

5. Chief Justice Rehnquist devotes a substantial fraction of his majority opinion to the implications of a contrary holding for America's military. Those implications are even more substantial now than they were at the time of *Verdugo-Urquidez*. In an age of terrorism, international police work is both common and very important, and it often involves military and intelligence services as well as police agencies — both ours and those of other countries. There are obvious reasons not to impose the Fourth Amendment on an Army unit seeking to maintain order in a battle zone in Iraq or Afghanistan. One possible response is to hold the police to Fourth Amendment standards — here and abroad — but to exempt the military from those standards. Yet that solution has its own problems. If, say, FBI agents operating overseas are bound by a strict set of constitutional rules and the military is not, the FBI will have a substantial incentive to hand off problems to the armed services in order to avoid application of constitutional restrictions. Is that a healthy state of affairs? Is there any way out of this problem?

6. Notice that the law remains uncertain even after *Verdugo-Urquidez*. Five Justices joined in the majority opinion, but Justice Kennedy — one of the five — seems to disavow the majority's analysis limiting Fourth Amendment protections to members of the national community and those who have developed sufficient connection with it. So, there are five votes for an opinion that says that the Fourth Amendment does not apply, and four votes for the proposition that it does — but one of the five basically agrees with the four. Ironically given the *Verdugo-Urquidez* Court's discussion of the Fifth Amendment privilege, the Fourth Amendment may turn out to have more extraterritorial reach than the Fifth.

7. At least one district court has taken the majority opinion in *Verdugo-Urquidez* at its word. Consider United States v. Esparza-Mendoza, 265 F. Supp. 1254 (D. Utah 2003). Esparza-Mendoza illegally entered the United States from Mexico in 1996. He was convicted of a felony narcotics charge in Utah in 1999 and was subsequently deported. At the time of his deportation, Esparza-Mendoza was instructed that he was not to re-enter the United States and that it would constitute a crime under U.S. law to do so. At some later point, he nevertheless returned.

In 2002, Esparza-Mendoza came into contact with a police officer when his girlfriend and her sister had a loud dispute that resulted in neighbors calling the police. The officer on the scene directed Esparza-Mendoza to provide identification; he was eventually discovered to be unlawfully in the United States and was charged with illegal reentry. Esparza-Mendoza claimed that his Fourth Amendment rights had been violated by the officer who had required him to identify himself. The District Court concluded that the Fourth Amendment did not apply:

> It is hard to see how Esparza-Mendoza has sufficient connection to this country to be regarded as one of "the People" to whom the Fourth Amendment extends. Indeed, Esparza-Mendoza will doubtlessly be deported when he is released from prison. He has managed to illegally enter Utah and, by virtue of that fact alone, he is entitled to those rights which follow from mere presence in this country. But he lacks entitlement to those rights which come from being a member of American society — including Fourth Amendment rights.

265 F. Supp. 2d at 1271 (holding that Esparza-Mendoza, as a previously deported felon, lacked sufficient connection to the United States to assert a Fourth

Amendment claim). We said at the start of this chapter that the Fourth Amendment operates as a chief source of legal regulation of police in the United States. If the Fourth Amendment is inapplicable to Esparza-Mendoza's encounter with police, what law *does* apply?

8. Note that in United States v. Bin Laden, 126 F. Supp. 2d 264 (S.D.N.Y. 2000), the prosecution of several al Qaeda participants in the August 1998 bombings of the United States Embassies in Nairobi, Kenya and Dar es Salaam, Tanzania, Judge Sand determined that Wadih El Hage, an American citizen, was entitled to assert Fourth Amendment claims arising from the search of his residence in Kenya and also the electronic surveillance of his telephones. (These searches were conducted by the United States for foreign intelligence purposes and occurred long before the embassy bombings.) Citing *Verdugo-Urquidez*, however, the District Court ultimately determined that the Warrant Clause should not apply to the collection of foreign intelligence abroad because "the power of the Executive to conduct foreign intelligence collection would be significantly frustrated by the imposition of a warrant requirement in this context." 126 F. Supp. 2d at 277. Judge Sand adopted a foreign intelligence exception to the warrant requirement for those searches targeting foreign powers or their agents which are conducted abroad and ultimately denied El-Hage's motion to suppress.

Is Judge Sand right? Is his position consistent with *Verdugo-Urquidez*?

C. Probable Cause and Warrants

The last section dealt with the Fourth Amendment's scope. Some kinds of police observation amount to "searches," and some don't. In some police-citizen encounters the citizen is "seized," and in some he isn't. If no "search" or "seizure" has taken place, the Fourth Amendment does not apply.

What happens when the Fourth Amendment *does* apply? That question breaks down into two others: (1) To what standard are the police held — in other words, how much or what kind of justification must they have in order to search or seize? (2) And who decides whether that justification is present — a magistrate in a warrant proceeding before the search or seizure takes place, or a trial judge in a suppression hearing after the fact? Fourth Amendment law has a traditional answer to each of these questions. The presumptive standard that applies to police searches and seizures is probable cause. The presumptive decisionmaker is a neutral magistrate, in advance of the search or seizure. Sometimes these two requirements are relaxed, but the strong presumption, again according to Fourth Amendment tradition, is that searches and seizures must be supported by probable cause and must be authorized by a warrant.

Notice that these two requirements are different and separable. Probable cause is a substantive standard: it defines the level of suspicion police must have before they search or seize someone or some thing. The warrant requirement is a rule of procedure: it determines the method by which probable cause or some other substantive standard is to be applied. One could have searches supported by probable cause but without a warrant; one could also have searches authorized by a warrant but without probable cause — in fact, both these scenarios exist in Fourth Amendment law (though the second is rare). But the classical starting point for Fourth Amendment analysis joins the two; unless the case falls within one or another recognized exception, the police must meet both the substantive hurdle and the procedural one.

Most Fourth Amendment decisions take the probable cause requirement for granted, as though its justification were too obvious to bother spelling out. But probable cause has not always been the dominant standard in Fourth Amendment cases. Under Boyd v. United States, 116 U.S. 616 (1886), it appeared that in most cases, there was no standard at all — if the Fourth Amendment applied, the police conduct was forbidden. (*Boyd*'s rise and fall are described in Chapter 4.) That sounds extreme, and perhaps it is. But it is the surest way to protect individual privacy: define a zone of private life, and declare that the government may not invade it. The probable cause standard presupposes that the government *can* invade one's privacy — as long as it has a good enough reason. Strangely, there is no developed body of literature defending the proposition that probable cause *is* a good enough reason.

The warrant requirement has received a good deal more attention, from judges and academics alike. The standard justification was best and most famously put by Justice Jackson in Johnson v. United States, 333 U.S. 10, 13-14 (1948):

> The point of the Fourth Amendment, which often is not grasped by zealous officers, is not that it denies law enforcement the support of the usual inferences which reasonable men draw from evidence. Its protection consists in requiring that those inferences be drawn by a neutral and detached magistrate instead of being judged by the officer engaged in the often competitive enterprise of ferreting out crime. Any assumption that evidence sufficient to support a magistrate's disinterested determination to issue a search warrant will justify the officers in making a search without a warrant would reduce the Amendment to a nullity and leave the people's homes secure only in the discretion of police officers.

Notwithstanding this stirring language, the presumption that police must have a warrant before searching was never as strong as it appeared. There have always been enough exceptions that a large fraction, probably a large majority, of searches and seizures have fallen outside the scope of the warrant requirement, and a smaller but still substantial fraction fall outside the requirement of probable cause as well. Nevertheless, courts continue to talk as though both probable cause and a warrant are presumptively required — though that talk is much less frequent than it once was — so it makes sense to start with the meaning of those two requirements.

The Text (Again)

The idea that Fourth Amendment analysis begins with the probable cause and warrant requirements is long-standing, but it has also long been under attack. One line of attack stems from the Fourth Amendment's text:

> The right of the people to be secure in their persons, houses, papers, and effects, against unreasonable searches and seizures, shall not be violated, and no warrants shall issue, but upon probable cause, supported by oath or affirmation, and particularly describing the place to be searched, and the persons or things to be seized.

Notice that the first clause, which contains the basic prohibition of "unreasonable searches and seizures," mentions neither probable cause nor warrants. The second clause mentions both, but it expressly *requires* only that "no warrants shall issue, but upon probable cause." Nowhere does the text say that warrants themselves are ever required. Nor does it say that probable cause is to be the ordinary standard for searches and seizures.

In an influential discussion that surveyed the background and historical development of Fourth Amendment law, Telford Taylor — his chief reputation was as a prosecutor at the Nuremberg war crimes trials — argued that this text was plainly designed to limit warrants, not to require them. Telford Taylor, Two Studies in Constitutional Interpretation 23-50 (1969). Taylor noted that in the eighteenth century cases that gave rise to the Fourth Amendment, general warrants (including, in the colonies, the infamous writs of assistance) were used as a means of authorizing searches that would have been illegal under the common law. Accordingly, Taylor argued, the Framers sought to limit this abuse of warrants. By requiring warrants and probable cause, Taylor maintained, the Supreme Court had "stood the Fourth Amendment on its head."[5]

Taylor's argument suggests that neither the warrant process nor the probable cause standard ought to govern in ordinary search and seizure cases. Five years after Taylor's argument, Anthony Amsterdam offered the following response:

> The Court's construction of the amendment as embodying an overriding preference for search warrants is supportable, in my view, because the Court is obliged to give an internally coherent reading to the unreasonableness clause and the warrant clause as expressions of repudiation of the general warrant. In this view, the fourth amendment condemns searches conducted under general warrants and writs of assistance as "unreasonable." It also forbids unreasonable warrantless searches. That is all the amendment says about warrantless searches, and the word "unreasonable" is hardly self-illuminating. Surely then the Court has done right to seek some part of the meaning of an "unreasonable" warrantless search by asking what the condemnation of general warrants and writs implies about the nature of "unreasonable" searches and seizures. . . .
>
> The framers of the fourth amendment accepted specific warrants as reasonable: the second clause of the amendment tells us so. Therefore, the objectionable feature of general warrants and writs must be their indiscriminate character. Warrants are not to issue indiscriminately: that is the office of the probable cause requirement. Nor may indiscriminate searches be made under them: that is why particularity of description of the persons or things to be seized is demanded. . . .
>
> Indiscriminate searches or seizures might be thought to be bad for either or both of two reasons. The first is that they expose people and their possessions to interferences by government when there is no good reason to do so. The concern here is against

---

5. Taylor, supra, at 23-24. Akhil Amar has expanded on Taylor's historical analysis, reaching the same basic conclusion: that the Fourth Amendment was intended to be read as requiring neither probable cause nor warrants (Taylor's chief focus was the warrant requirement, but his, and Amar's, argument applies to both). See Akhil Reed Amar, Fourth Amendment First Principles, 107 Harv. L. Rev. 757 (1994). More recently, some scholars have suggested that the history is more complicated than Taylor and Amar believed — and that warrants may have been used in the eighteenth century as they are today, as a tool for protecting individuals from unjustified searches. See Morgan Cloud, Searching Through History; Searching for History, 63 U. Chi. L. Rev. 1707 (1996); Thomas Y. Davies, Recovering the Original Fourth Amendment, 98 Mich. L. Rev. 547 (1999); Tracey Maclin, The Central Meaning of the Fourth Amendment, 35 Wm. & Mary L. Rev. 197 (1993).

unjustified searches and seizures. . . . The second is that indiscriminate searches and seizures are conducted at the discretion of executive officials, who may act despotically and capriciously in the exercise of the power to search and seize. This latter concern runs against *arbitrary* searches and seizures. . . .

Anthony G. Amsterdam, Perspectives on the Fourth Amendment, 58 Minn. L. Rev. 349, 410-411 (1974). The best way to protect against arbitrary and unjustified searches, Amsterdam maintained, is to require probable cause and a warrant whenever feasible.

The choice between these two readings — Taylor's, with its focus on reasonableness, with probable cause and warrants a kind of textual afterthought; and Amsterdam's, with probable cause and warrants serving to define what reasonableness means — is the central choice in Fourth Amendment law today. The merits of that choice obviously depend, in part, on what probable cause means and on what the warrant process entails.

The following two subsections take up those two issues. Subsection 3 in this section then deals with cases in which probable cause is the governing standard but warrants are not required. The next section, section D, takes up those cases in which the probable cause and warrant requirements have both been held inapplicable, and a (usually softer) "reasonableness" standard applies instead.

1. The Probable Cause Standard

Courts have had trouble finding a working definition of probable cause. In Brinegar v. United States, 338 U.S. 160 (1949), the Supreme Court said, unhelpfully, that a police officer has probable cause to arrest when "the facts and circumstances within [the officers'] knowledge and of which they had reasonably trustworthy information [are] sufficient in themselves to warrant a man of reasonable caution in the belief that an offense has been or is being committed." Id. at 175-176 (quotation omitted). What that definition means depends, obviously, on how it is applied. And in the Supreme Court, it has been applied most often in cases involving the police use of informants. Consider the facts and holdings of the following three cases, the first involving a police officer's bare hunch, the second and third involving informants' tips.

In Nathanson v. United States, 290 U.S. 41 (1933), a police officer, in support of an application for a search warrant for illegal liquor, swore out an affidavit that stated simply that the officer "has cause to suspect and does believe that certain merchandise," namely illegal liquor, "is now deposited and contained within the premises of J.J. Nathanson." Id. at 44. The warrant was issued and the search carried out. The Court unanimously found the search illegal, saying:

> Under the Fourth Amendment, an officer may not properly issue a warrant to search a private dwelling unless he can find probable cause therefor from facts or circumstances presented to him under oath or affirmation. Mere affirmance of belief or suspicion is not enough.

Id. at 47.

In Draper v. United States, 358 U.S. 307 (1958), an informant named Hereford "from time to time gave information" to federal agent Marsh about narcotics violations; "Hereford was paid small sums of money" for the information. According to Marsh, these tips had consistently been accurate.

> . . . Hereford told Marsh that James Draper . . . recently had taken up abode at a stated address in Denver and "was peddling narcotics to several addicts" in that city. Four days later, on September 7, Hereford told Marsh "that Draper had gone to Chicago the day before . . . by train [and] that he was going to bring back three ounces of heroin [and] that he would return to Denver either on the morning of the 8th of September or the morning of the 9th of September also by train." Hereford also gave Marsh a detailed physical description of Draper and of the clothing he was wearing, and said that he would be carrying "a tan zipper bag," and that he habitually "walked real fast."
>
> On the morning of September 8, Marsh and a Denver police officer went to the Denver Union Station and kept watch over all incoming trains from Chicago, but they did not see anyone fitting the description that Hereford had given. Repeating the process on the morning of September 9, they saw a person, having the exact physical attributes and wearing the precise clothing described by Hereford, alight from an incoming Chicago train and start walking "fast" toward the exit. He was carrying a tan zipper bag in his right hand and the left was thrust in his raincoat pocket. Marsh, accompanied by the police officer, . . . stopped and arrested him. They then searched him and found . . . two "envelopes containing heroin" clutched in his left hand in his raincoat pocket, and found [a] syringe in the tan zipper bag. . . .

Id. at 309-310. The Supreme Court found that Marsh had probable cause to support the arrest; the accompanying search was a permissible search incident to arrest. (See pages 531-552 infra for discussion of searches incident to arrest.)

In Spinelli v. United States, 393 U.S. 410 (1969), FBI agents obtained a warrant to search the defendant's apartment based on an affidavit containing these allegations:

1. The FBI had kept track of Spinelli's movements on five days during the month of August 1965. On four of these occasions, Spinelli was seen crossing one of two bridges leading from Illinois into St. Louis, Missouri, between 11 a.m. and 12:15 p.m. On four of the five days, Spinelli was also seen parking his car in a lot used by residents of an apartment house at 1108 Indian Circle Drive in St. Louis, between 3:30 p.m. and 4:45 p.m. On one day, Spinelli was followed further and seen to enter a particular apartment in the building.
2. An FBI check with the telephone company revealed that this apartment contained two telephones listed under the name of Grace P. Hagen, and carrying the numbers WYdown 4-0029 and WYdown 4-0136.
3. The application stated that "William Spinelli is known to this affiant and to federal law enforcement agents and local law enforcement agents as a bookmaker, an associate of bookmakers, a gambler, and an associate of gamblers."
4. Finally, it was stated that the FBI "has been informed by a confidential reliable informant that William Spinelli is operating a handbook and accepting wagers and disseminating wagering information by means of the telephones which have been assigned the numbers WYdown 4-0029 and WYdown 4-0136."

Id. at 413-414. Writing for the Court, Justice Harlan analyzed the affidavit as follows:

> There can be no question that the last item mentioned, detailing the informant's tip, has a fundamental place in this warrant application. Without it, probable cause could not be established. The first two items reflect only innocent-seeming activity and data. Spinelli's travels to and from the apartment building and his entry into a particular apartment on one occasion could hardly be taken as bespeaking gambling activity; and there is surely nothing unusual about an apartment containing two separate telephones. Many a householder indulges himself in this petty luxury. Finally, the allegation that Spinelli was "known" to the affiant and to other federal and local law enforcement officers as a gambler and an associate of gamblers is but a bald and unilluminating assertion of suspicion that is entitled to no weight in appraising the magistrate's decision. Nathanson v. United States, 290 U.S. 41, 46 (1933).

Id. at 414. Justice Harlan went on to note the circular quality of the government's argument: "[T]he Government claims that the informant's tip gives a suspicious color to the FBI's reports detailing Spinelli's innocent-seeming conduct and that, conversely, the FBI's surveillance corroborates the informant's tip, thereby entitling it to more weight." He rejected that "totality of the circumstances" approach, in favor of "a more precise analysis" of informants' tips that emphasizes both the informant's reliability and the basis of his knowledge:

> Applying these principles to the present case, we first consider the weight to be given the informer's tip when it is considered apart from the rest of the affidavit. It is clear that a Commissioner could not credit it without abdicating his constitutional function. Though the affiant swore that his confidant was "reliable," he offered the magistrate no reason in support of this conclusion. Perhaps even more important is the fact that . . . [t]he tip does not contain a sufficient statement of the underlying circumstances from which the informer concluded that Spinelli was running a bookmaking operation. We are not told how the FBI's source received his information — it is not alleged that the informant personally observed Spinelli at work or that he had ever placed a bet with him. Moreover, if the informant came by the information indirectly, he did not explain why his sources were reliable. In the absence of a statement detailing the manner in which the information was gathered, it is especially important that the tip describe the accused's criminal activity in sufficient detail that the magistrate may know that he is relying on something more substantial than a casual rumor circulating in the underworld or an accusation based merely on an individual's general reputation.
>
> . . . Such an inference cannot be made in the present case. Here, the only facts supplied were that Spinelli was using two specified telephones and that these phones were being used in gambling operations. This meager report could easily have been obtained from an offhand remark heard at a neighborhood bar. . . .
>
> We conclude, then, that in the present case the informant's tip — even when corroborated to the extent indicated — was not sufficient to provide the basis for a finding of probable cause. This is not to say that the tip was so insubstantial that it could not properly have counted in the magistrate's determination. Rather, it needed some further support. When we look to the other parts of the application, however, we find nothing alleged which would permit the suspicions engendered by the informant's report to ripen into a judgment that a crime was probably being committed. As we have already seen, the allegations detailing the FBI's surveillance of Spinelli and its investigation of the telephone company records contain no

suggestion of criminal conduct when taken by themselves — and they are not endowed with an aura of suspicion by virtue of the informer's tip. Nor do we find that the FBI's reports take on a sinister color when read in light of common knowledge that book-making is often carried on over the telephone and from premises ostensibly used by others for perfectly normal purposes. . . . All that remains to be considered is the flat statement that Spinelli was "known" to the FBI and others as a gambler. But just as a simple assertion of police suspicion is not itself a sufficient basis for a magistrate's finding of probable cause, we do not believe it may be used to give additional weight to allegations that would otherwise be insufficient.

Id. at 416-419.

Draper and *Spinelli* seemed to point in opposite directions. The next case appeared to resolve the tension.

ILLINOIS v. GATES

Certiorari to the Supreme Court of Illinois
462 U.S. 213 (1983)

JUSTICE REHNQUIST delivered the opinion of the Court.

Respondents Lance and Susan Gates were indicted for violation of state drug laws after police officers, executing a search warrant, discovered marihuana and other contraband in their automobile and home. Prior to trial the Gateses moved to suppress evidence seized during this search. . . .

II

. . . A chronological statement of events usefully introduces the issues at stake. Bloomingdale, Ill., is a suburb of Chicago located in Du Page County. On May 3, 1978, the Bloomingdale Police Department received by mail an anonymous handwritten letter which read as follows:

This letter is to inform you that you have a couple in your town who strictly make their living on selling drugs. They are Sue and Lance Gates, they live on Greenway, off Bloomingdale Rd. in the condominiums. Most of their buys are done in Florida. Sue his wife drives their car to Florida, where she leaves it to be loaded up with drugs, then Lance flys down and drives it back. Sue flys back after she drops the car off in Florida. May 3 she is driving down there again and Lance will be flying down in a few days to drive it back. At the time Lance drives the car back he has the trunk loaded with over $100,000.00 in drugs. Presently they have over $100,000.00 worth of drugs in their basement.

They brag about the fact they never have to work, and make their entire living on pushers.

I guarantee if you watch them carefully you will make a big catch. They are friends with some big drugs dealers, who visit their house often.

Lance & Susan Gates
Greenway
in Condominiums

The letter was referred by the Chief of Police of the Bloomingdale Police Department to Detective Mader, who decided to pursue the tip. Mader learned, from the office of the Illinois Secretary of State, that an Illinois driver's license had been issued to one Lance Gates, residing at a stated address in Bloomingdale.

He contacted a confidential informant, whose examination of certain financial records revealed a more recent address for the Gateses, and he also learned from a police officer assigned to O'Hare Airport that "L. Gates" had made a reservation on Eastern Airlines Flight 245 to West Palm Beach, Fla., scheduled to depart from Chicago on May 5 at 4:15 p.m.

Mader then made arrangements with an agent of the Drug Enforcement Administration for surveillance of the May 5 Eastern Airlines flight. The agent later reported to Mader that Gates had boarded the flight, and that federal agents in Florida had observed him arrive in West Palm Beach and take a taxi to the nearby Holiday Inn. They also reported that Gates went to a room registered to one Susan Gates and that, at 7 o'clock the next morning, Gates and an unidentified woman left the motel in a Mercury bearing Illinois license plates and drove northbound on an interstate highway frequently used by travelers to the Chicago area. In addition, the DEA agent informed Mader that the license plate number on the Mercury was registered to a Hornet station wagon owned by Gates. The agent also advised Mader that the driving time between West Palm Beach and Bloomingdale was approximately 22 to 24 hours.

Mader signed an affidavit setting forth the foregoing facts, and submitted it to a judge of the Circuit Court of Du Page County, together with a copy of the anonymous letter. The judge of that court thereupon issued a search warrant for the Gateses' residence and for their automobile. . . .

At 5:15 a.m. on March 7, only 36 hours after he had flown out of Chicago, Lance Gates, and his wife, returned to their home in Bloomingdale, driving the car in which they had left West Palm Beach some 22 hours earlier. The Bloomingdale police were awaiting them, searched the trunk of the Mercury, and uncovered approximately 350 pounds of marihuana. A search of the Gateses' home revealed marihuana, weapons, and other contraband. The Illinois Circuit Court ordered suppression of all these items, on the ground that the affidavit submitted to the Circuit Judge failed to support the necessary determination of probable cause to believe that the Gateses' automobile and home contained the contraband in question. This decision was affirmed in turn by the Illinois Appellate Court, and by a divided vote of the Supreme Court of Illinois.

The Illinois Supreme Court concluded — and we are inclined to agree — that, standing alone, the anonymous letter sent to the Bloomingdale Police Department would not provide the basis for a magistrate's determination that there was probable cause to believe contraband would be found in the Gateses' car and home. The letter provides virtually nothing from which one might conclude that its author is either honest or his information reliable; likewise, the letter gives absolutely no indication of the basis for the writer's predictions regarding the Gateses' criminal activities. Something more was required, then, before a magistrate could conclude that there was probable cause to believe that contraband would be found in the Gateses' home and car.

. . . In holding that the affidavit in fact did not contain sufficient additional information to sustain a determination of probable cause, the Illinois court applied a "two-pronged test," derived from our decision in Spinelli v. United States, 393 U.S. 410 (1969). The Illinois Supreme Court . . . understood *Spinelli* as requiring that the anonymous letter satisfy each of two independent requirements before it could be relied on. According to this view, the letter, as supplemented by Mader's affidavit, first had to adequately reveal the "basis of knowledge" of the letterwriter — the particular means by which he came by the information given in his report. Second, it had to provide facts sufficiently establishing either the "veracity" of the affiant's informant, or, alternatively, the "reliability" of the informant's report in this particular case.

. . . [T]he "veracity" prong was not satisfied because, "[there] was simply no basis [for] conclud[ing] that the anonymous person [who wrote the letter to the Bloomingdale Police Department] was credible." . . . In addition, the letter gave no indication of the basis of its writer's knowledge of the Gateses' activities. . . . Thus, [the court] concluded that no showing of probable cause had been made.

We agree with the Illinois Supreme Court that an informant's "veracity," "reliability," and "basis of knowledge" are all highly relevant in determining the value of his report. We do not agree, however, that these elements should be understood as entirely separate and independent requirements to be rigidly exacted in every case. . . . Rather, as detailed below, they should be understood simply as closely intertwined issues that may usefully illuminate the common-sense, practical question whether there is "probable cause" to believe that contraband or evidence is located in a particular place.

III

. . . Perhaps the central teaching of our decisions bearing on the probable-cause standard is that it is a "practical, nontechnical conception." Brinegar v. United States, 338 U.S. 160, 176 (1949). "In dealing with probable cause, . . . as the very name implies, we deal with probabilities. These are not technical; they are the factual and practical considerations of everyday life on which reasonable and prudent men, not legal technicians, act." Id., at 175. . . .

As these comments illustrate, probable cause is a fluid concept — turning on the assessment of probabilities in particular factual contexts — not readily, or even usefully, reduced to a neat set of legal rules. Informants' tips doubtless come in many shapes and sizes from many different types of persons. . . .

. . . [T]he "two-pronged test" directs analysis into two largely independent channels — the informant's "veracity" or "reliability" and his "basis of knowledge." There are persuasive arguments against according these two elements such independent status. Instead, they are better understood as relevant considerations in the totality-of-the-circumstances analysis that traditionally has guided probable-cause determinations: a deficiency in one may be compensated for, in determining the overall reliability of a tip, by a strong showing as to the other, or by some other indicia of reliability.

If, for example, a particular informant is known for the unusual reliability of his predictions of certain types of criminal activities in a locality, his failure, in a particular case, to thoroughly set forth the basis of his knowledge surely should not serve as an absolute bar to a finding of probable cause based on his tip. Likewise, if an unquestionably honest citizen comes forward with a report of criminal activity — which if fabricated would subject him to criminal liability — we have found rigorous scrutiny of the basis of his knowledge unnecessary. Adams v. Williams, [407 U.S. 143 (1972)]. Conversely, even if we entertain some doubt as to an informant's motives, his explicit and detailed description of alleged wrongdoing, along with a statement that the event was observed firsthand, entitles his tip to greater weight than might otherwise be the case. . . .

As early as Locke v. United States, 7 Cranch 339, 348 (1813), Chief Justice Marshall observed, in a closely related context: "[The] term 'probable cause,' according to its usual acceptation, means less than evidence which would justify condemnation. . . . It imports a seizure made under circumstances which warrant suspicion." More recently, we said that "the *quanta* . . . of proof" appropriate in ordinary judicial proceedings are inapplicable to the decision to issue a warrant. *Brinegar*, 338 U.S., at 173. Finely tuned standards such as proof beyond a reasonable doubt or by a preponderance of the evidence, useful in formal trials, have no place in the magistrate's decision. While an effort to fix some general, numerically precise degree of certainty corresponding to "probable cause" may not be helpful, it is clear that "only the probability, and not a prima facie showing, of criminal activity is the standard of probable cause." *Spinelli*, 393 U.S., at 419. . . .

Finally, . . . [t]he strictures that inevitably accompany the "two-pronged test" cannot avoid seriously impeding the task of law enforcement. If, as the Illinois Supreme Court apparently thought, that test must be rigorously applied in every case, anonymous tips would be of greatly diminished value in police work. Ordinary citizens, like ordinary witnesses, generally do not provide extensive recitations of the basis of their everyday observations. Likewise, as the Illinois Supreme Court observed in this case, the veracity of persons supplying anonymous tips is by hypothesis largely unknown, and unknowable. As a result, anonymous tips seldom could survive a rigorous application of either of the *Spinelli* prongs. Yet, such tips, particularly when supplemented by independent police investigation, frequently contribute to the solution of otherwise "perfect crimes." While a conscientious assessment of the basis for crediting such tips is required by the Fourth Amendment, a standard that leaves virtually no place for anonymous citizen informants is not.

For all these reasons, we conclude that it is wiser to abandon the "two-pronged test" established by . . . *Spinelli*.[11] In its place we reaffirm the totality-of-the-circumstances analysis that traditionally has informed probable-cause determinations. The task of the issuing magistrate is simply to make a practical, common-sense decision whether, given all the circumstances set forth in the affidavit before him, including the "veracity" and "basis of knowledge" of persons supplying hearsay information, there is a fair probability that contraband or evidence of a crime will be found in a particular place. And the duty of a reviewing court is simply to ensure that the magistrate had a "substantial basis for . . . conclud[ing]" that probable cause existed. Jones v. United States, 362 U.S., at 271. . . .

Our earlier cases illustrate the limits beyond which a magistrate may not venture in issuing a warrant. A sworn statement of an affiant that "he has cause to suspect and does believe" that liquor illegally brought into the United States is located on certain premises will not do. Nathanson v. United States, 290 U.S. 41 (1933). . . . An officer's statement that "[a]ffiants have received reliable information from a credible person and do believe" that heroin is stored in a home, is likewise inadequate. Aguilar v. Texas, 378 U.S. 108 (1964). As in *Nathanson*, this is

11. . . . Whether the allegations submitted to the magistrate in *Spinelli* would, under the view we now take, have supported a finding of probable cause, we think it would not be profitable to decide. There are so many variables in the probable-cause equation that one determination will seldom be a useful "precedent" for another. Suffice it to say that while we in no way abandon *Spinelli*'s concern for the trustworthiness of informers and for the principle that it is the magistrate who must ultimately make a finding of probable cause, we reject the rigid categorization suggested by some of its language.

a mere conclusory statement that gives the magistrate virtually no basis at all for making a judgment regarding probable cause. Sufficient information must be presented to the magistrate to allow that official to determine probable cause; his action cannot be a mere ratification of the bare conclusions of others. In order to ensure that such an abdication of the magistrate's duty does not occur, courts must continue to conscientiously review the sufficiency of affidavits on which warrants are issued. But when we move beyond the "bare bones" affidavits present in cases such as *Nathanson* and *Aguilar*, this area simply does not lend itself to a prescribed set of rules, like that which had developed from *Spinelli*. Instead, the flexible, common-sense standard articulated [above] better serves the purposes of the Fourth Amendment's probable-cause requirement.

IV

Our decisions applying the totality-of-the-circumstances analysis outlined above have consistently recognized the value of corroboration of details of an informant's tip by independent police work. . . .

Our decision in Draper v. United States, 358 U.S. 307 (1959), . . . is the classic case on the value of corroborative efforts of police officials. There, an informant named Hereford reported that Draper would arrive in Denver on a train from Chicago on one of two days, and that he would be carrying a quantity of heroin. The informant also supplied a fairly detailed physical description of Draper, and predicted that he would be wearing a light colored raincoat, brown slacks, and black shoes, and would be walking "real fast." Id., at 309. Hereford gave no indication of the basis for his information.[12]

On one of the stated dates police officers observed a man matching this description exit a train arriving from Chicago; his attire and luggage matched Hereford's report and he was walking rapidly. We explained in *Draper* that, by this point in his investigation, the arresting officer "had personally verified every facet of the information given him by Hereford except whether petitioner had accomplished his mission and had the three ounces of heroin on his person or in his bag. And surely, with every other bit of Hereford's information being thus personally verified, [the officer] had 'reasonable grounds' to believe that the remaining unverified bit of Hereford's information — that Draper would have the heroin with him — was likewise true," id., at 313.

The showing of probable cause in the present case was fully as compelling as that in *Draper*. Even standing alone, the facts obtained through the independent investigation of Mader and the DEA at least suggested that the Gateses were involved in drug trafficking. In addition to being a popular vacation site, Florida is well known as a source of narcotics and other illegal drugs. Lance Gates' flight to West Palm Beach, his brief, overnight stay in a motel, and apparent immediate return north to Chicago in the family car, conveniently awaiting him in

12. The tip in *Draper* might well not have survived the rigid application of the "two-pronged test" that developed following *Spinelli*. The only reference to Hereford's reliability was that he had "been engaged as a 'special employee' of the Bureau of Narcotics at Denver for about six months, and from time to time gave information to [the police for] small sums of money, and that [the officer] had always found the information given by Hereford to be accurate and reliable." 358 U.S., at 309. Likewise, the tip gave no indication of how Hereford came by his information. At most, the detailed and accurate predictions in the tip indicated that, however Hereford obtained his information, it was reliable.

West Palm Beach, is as suggestive of a prearranged drug run, as it is of an ordinary vacation trip.

In addition, the judge could rely on the anonymous letter, which had been corroborated in major part by Mader's efforts—just as had occurred in *Draper*.[13] The Supreme Court of Illinois reasoned that *Draper* involved an informant who had given reliable information on previous occasions, while the honesty and reliability of the anonymous informant in this case were unknown to the Bloomingdale police. While this distinction might be an apt one at the time the Police Department received the anonymous letter, it became far less significant after Mader's independent investigative work occurred. The corroboration of the letter's predictions that the Gateses' car would be in Florida, that Lance Gates would fly to Florida in the next day or so, and that he would drive the car north toward Bloomingdale all indicated, albeit not with certainty, that the informant's other assertions also were true. "[B]ecause an informant is right about some things, he is more probably right about other facts," *Spinelli*, 393 U.S., at 427 (WHITE, J., concurring)—including the claim regarding the Gateses' illegal activity. This may well not be the type of "reliability" or "veracity" necessary to satisfy some views of the "veracity prong" of *Spinelli*, but we think it suffices for the practical, common-sense judgment called for in making a probable-cause determination. . . .

Finally, the anonymous letter contained a range of details relating not just to easily obtained facts and conditions existing at the time of the tip, but to future actions of third parties ordinarily not easily predicted. The letterwriter's accurate information as to the travel plans of each of the Gateses was of a character likely obtained only from the Gateses themselves, or from someone familiar with their not entirely ordinary travel plans. If the informant had access to accurate information of this type a magistrate could properly conclude that it was not unlikely that he also had access to reliable information of the Gateses' alleged illegal activities. Of course, the Gateses' travel plans might have been learned from a talkative neighbor or travel agent. . . . But, as discussed previously, probable cause does not demand the certainty we associate with formal trials. It is enough that there was a fair probability that the writer of the anonymous letter had obtained his entire story either from the Gateses or someone they trusted. And corroboration of major portions of the letter's predictions provides just this probability. It is apparent, therefore, that the judge issuing the warrant had a "substantial basis for . . . conclud[ing]" that probable cause to search the Gateses' home and car existed. . . .

JUSTICE WHITE, concurring in the judgment.

. . . Abandoning the "two-pronged test" of . . . Spinelli v. United States, 393 U.S. 410 (1969), the Court upholds the validity of the warrant under a new "totality of the circumstances" approach. Although I agree that the warrant should be upheld, I reach this conclusion in accordance with [*Spinelli*'s] framework.

13. The Illinois Supreme Court thought that the verification of details contained in the anonymous letter in this case amounted only to "[t]he corroboration of innocent activity," and that this was insufficient to support a finding of probable cause. We are inclined to agree, however, with the observation of Justice Moran in his dissenting opinion that "[i]n this case, just as in *Draper*, seemingly innocent activity became suspicious in light of the initial tip." And it bears noting that *all* of the corroborating detail established in *Draper* was of entirely innocent activity . . . .

For present purposes, the . . . *Spinelli* rules can be summed up as follows. First, an affidavit based on an informant's tip, standing alone, cannot provide probable cause for issuance of a warrant unless the tip includes information that apprises the magistrate of the informant's basis for concluding that the contraband is where he claims it is (the "basis of knowledge" prong), *and* the affiant informs the magistrate of his basis for believing that the informant is credible (the "veracity" prong). *Spinelli*, supra, at 412-413, 416. Second, if a tip fails under either or both of the two prongs, probable cause may yet be established by independent police investigatory work that corroborates the tip to such an extent that it supports "both the inference that the informer was generally trustworthy and that he made his charge . . . on the basis of information obtained in a reliable way." *Spinelli*, supra, at 417. . . .

In the present case, it is undisputed that the anonymous tip, by itself, did not furnish probable cause. The question is whether those portions of the affidavit describing the results of the police investigation of the respondents, when considered in light of the tip, "would permit the suspicions engendered by the informant's report to ripen into a judgment that a crime was probably being committed." *Spinelli*, supra, at 418. . . .

[T]he proper focus should be on whether the actions of the suspects, whatever their nature, give rise to an inference that the informant is credible and that he obtained his information in a reliable manner.

Thus, in Draper v. United States, 358 U.S. 307 (1959), an informant stated on September 7 that Draper would be carrying narcotics when he arrived by train in Denver on the morning of September 8 or September 9. The informant also provided the police with a detailed physical description of the clothes Draper would be wearing when he alighted from the train. The police observed Draper leaving a train on the morning of September 9, and he was wearing the precise clothing described by the informant. The Court held that the police had probable cause to arrest Draper at this point, even though the police had seen nothing more than the totally innocent act of a man getting off a train carrying a briefcase. . . . The fact that the informant was able to predict, two days in advance, the exact clothing Draper would be wearing dispelled the possibility that his tip was just based on rumor . . . . Probably Draper had planned in advance to wear these specific clothes so that an accomplice could identify him. A clear inference could therefore be drawn that the informant was either involved in the criminal scheme himself or that he otherwise had access to reliable, inside information.

As in *Draper*, the police investigation in the present case satisfactorily demonstrated that the informant's tip was as trustworthy as one that would alone satisfy [*Spinelli*]. The tip predicted that Sue Gates would drive to Florida, that Lance Gates would fly there a few days after May 3, and that Lance would then drive the car back. After the police corroborated these facts,[23] the judge could reasonably have inferred, as he apparently did, that the informant, who had specific knowledge of these unusual travel plans, did not make up his story and that he obtained his information in a reliable way. It is theoretically possible, as respondents insist, that the tip could have been supplied by a "vindictive travel agent" and that the Gateses' activities, although unusual, might not have been unlawful. But [our cases]

---

23. JUSTICE STEVENS is correct that one of the informant's predictions proved to be inaccurate. However, . . . an informant need not be infallible.

do not require that certain guilt be established before a warrant may properly be issued. . . .

The Court agrees that the warrant was valid, but, in the process of reaching this conclusion, it overrules the [*Spinelli* test] and replaces [it] with a "totality of the circumstances" standard. . . . [B]ecause I am inclined to believe that, when applied properly, the [*Spinelli*] rules play an appropriate role in probable-cause determinations, and because the Court's holding may foretell an evisceration of the probable-cause standard, I do not join the Court's holding.

The Court reasons that the "veracity" and "basis of knowledge" tests are not independent, and that a deficiency as to one can be compensated for by a strong showing as to the other. Thus, a finding of probable cause may be based on a tip from an informant "known for the unusual reliability of his predictions" or from "an unquestionably honest citizen," even if the report fails thoroughly to set forth the basis upon which the information was obtained. If this is so, then it must follow a fortiori that the "affidavit of an officer, known by the magistrate to be honest and experienced, stating that [contraband] is located in a certain building" must be acceptable. *Spinelli*, 393 U.S., at 424 (WHITE, J., concurring). It would be quixotic if a similar statement from an honest informant, but not one from an honest officer, could furnish probable cause. But we have repeatedly held that the unsupported assertion or belief of an officer does not satisfy the probable-cause requirement. See, e.g., Nathanson v. United States, 290 U.S. 41 (1933). Thus, this portion of today's holding can be read as implicitly rejecting the teachings of these prior holdings. . . .

[Justice Brennan's dissenting opinion, joined by Justice Marshall, is omitted.]

JUSTICE STEVENS, with whom JUSTICE BRENNAN joins, dissenting.

The fact that Lance and Sue Gates made a 22-hour nonstop drive from West Palm Beach, Florida, to Bloomingdale, Illinois, only a few hours after Lance had flown to Florida provided persuasive evidence that they were engaged in illicit activity. That fact, however, was not known to the judge when he issued the warrant to search their home.

What the judge did know at that time was that the anonymous informant had not been completely accurate in his or her predictions. The informant had indicated that "Sue . . . drives their car to Florida *where she leaves it to be loaded up with drugs. . . . Sue fl[ies] back after she drops the car off in Florida.*" Yet Detective Mader's affidavit reported that she "left the West Palm Beach area driving the Mercury northbound."

The discrepancy between the informant's predictions and the facts known to Detective Mader is significant for three reasons. First, it cast doubt on the informant's hypothesis that the Gates already had "over [$100,000] worth of drugs in their basement." The informant had predicted an itinerary that always kept one spouse in Bloomingdale, suggesting that the Gates did not want to leave their home unguarded because something valuable was hidden within. That inference obviously could not be drawn when it was known that the pair was actually together over a thousand miles from home.

Second, the discrepancy made the Gates' conduct seem substantially less unusual than the informant had predicted it would be. It would have been odd if, as predicted, Sue had driven down to Florida on Wednesday, left the car, and flown right back to Illinois. But the mere facts that Sue was in West Palm Beach with the car, that she was joined by her husband at the Holiday Inn on Friday, and that the couple drove north together the next morning[3] are neither unusual nor probative of criminal activity.

Third, the fact that the anonymous letter contained a material mistake undermines the reasonableness of relying on it as a basis for making a forcible entry into a private home. . . .

NOTES AND QUESTIONS

1. Some aspects of the Court's decision in *Gates* bear on the warrant process, but for the most part the opinion is about the meaning of probable cause. At least officially, probable cause means the same thing in warrant and non-warrant cases. Keep that in mind as you read the notes that follow; except where otherwise noted, the questions and issues raised apply whether or not the officer got a warrant.

2. For every search or arrest where the probable cause standard applies, the question arises: What must the police have probable cause to believe?

For arrests, the answer is: that the defendant committed a crime. For searches, the answer is: that the police will find evidence of crime in the place being searched. Nominally, the standard does not vary according to the seriousness of the crime. Note that in *Gates*, there is no language to the effect that, because the police were looking for marijuana rather than for evidence of, say, multiple murders, a higher level of probability is needed to justify the search. On the contrary, as far as the Supreme Court is concerned, probable cause appears to mean the same thing regardless of what crime the police are investigating.

Why should that be so? Doesn't the state have a much stronger interest in investigating some crimes than others? The Gateses had a great deal of marijuana in their basement, but it was, after all, marijuana, not a set of plans to blow up a large public building. Shouldn't that matter to the governing Fourth Amendment standard?

It probably does matter, at least in practice. Magistrates likely apply at least slightly different standards when issuing warrants to search for evidence of different sorts of crimes (imagine if the police in *Gates* had been asking to search for a few marijuana cigarettes instead of the large quantities at issue). But those differences go unacknowledged in the doctrine, and presumably they vary from courthouse to courthouse and crime to crime.

3. Variation in the practical meaning of "probable cause" is especially likely given the way *Gates* defines the standard. The Court in *Gates* rejects *Spinelli*'s two-part test in part because it was too technical, too legally complicated; in the place of *Spinelli* the Court puts a consider-all-the-circumstances, "commonsense" inquiry. That amounts to a decision not to have a detailed law of probable cause, with different tests for different sorts of cases, and with some fact patterns resolved categorically either in favor of or against the police. Probable cause, after *Gates*, seems to be fact-specific, not susceptible to detailed legal analysis. (Note that the next main case may modify that conclusion, at least slightly.) Is that sensible?

---

3. Detective Mader's affidavit hinted darkly that the couple had set out upon "that interstate highway commonly used by travelers to the Chicago area." But the same highway is also commonly used by travelers to Disney World, Sea World, and Ringling Brothers and Barnum and Bailey Circus World. It is also the road to Cocoa Beach, Cape Canaveral, and Washington, D.C. I would venture that each year dozens of perfectly innocent people fly to Florida, meet a waiting spouse, and drive off together in the family car.

4. Notice one consequence of keeping the law of probable cause to a minimum: it permits local variation. This obviously makes the kind of decisions mentioned in Note 2 more likely. It also makes more likely a system in which probable cause is applied more stringently in a given city than in its suburbs (or vice versa)—just as negligence in personal injury litigation is likely to mean different things to juries in neighboring jurisdictions. The more this sort of thing happens, the more Fourth Amendment law amounts to a series of local liability rules, rather than one standard to which police must adhere everywhere.

Second, keeping the law of probable cause to a minimum reduces the power of appellate courts. Under *Spinelli*, state and federal appellate courts decided a host of probable cause cases, developing variations and permutations on the famous two-part test. Since *Gates*, the appellate case law has been less substantial. Appellate judges seem to have less power over the meaning of probable cause. Magistrates and trial judges have more. Is *that* sensible?

Perhaps so. It is often hard to tell whether a given set of facts creates a probability that evidence of crime will be found in a given place; as with many things, experience in making and observing such decisions will likely produce better decisions. Magistrates and trial judges, who must decide on warrant applications and suppression hearings, make such decisions with great frequency. Appellate judges do not. Perhaps the probable cause standard is in safer hands after *Gates* than before it.

5. Much of what the Court has had to say about the meaning of probable cause has come in cases involving informants' tips. Why would that be so?

It would *not* be so if informants could easily be brought before the magistrate for questioning. Presumably they cannot, because they are unwilling to disclose their identities other than to the officers with whom they deal. One author of a leading study of warrants noted that magistrates very rarely insist on disclosure of the informant's identity. The same author notes: "In each of the cases in which the court [did order] that the informant be produced, the prosecution dismissed the charges, rather than comply." L. Paul Sutton, Getting Around the Fourth Amendment, in Carl B. Klockars & Stephen D. Mastrofski eds., Thinking About Police 433, 441 (2d ed. 1991).

If informants cannot be made to submit to questioning, magistrates and judges have two choices: decide to believe them or decide not to. How should that choice be made? Consider the following four scenarios:

> Anonymous Informant tells Officer that once a week, Suspect flies to Florida, loads up a trailer with bags of white powder, and then drives the trailer to Suspect's house in Illinois, where he unloads the contents of the trailer into his basement. Officer then observes Suspect do the things Anonymous Informant described.
>
> Anonymous Informant tells Officer that Suspect will, at 7:30 p.m. next Tuesday, be standing at a particular intersection downtown, that Suspect will be wearing a blue suit, red polka-dot tie, black tassled loafers, and a tan trench coat and will be carrying a briefcase. Anonymous Informant further tells Officer that the briefcase will contain cocaine. Officer confirms that Suspect is indeed in the place described, wearing the clothes described, carrying a briefcase, on Tuesday at 7:30 p.m.
>
> Anonymous Informant tells Officer that Suspect has cocaine in his house. Anonymous Informant has always supplied good information in the past—his tips have always been right. But he offers no supporting data.

There is no informant. Officer tells Magistrate that Suspect has cocaine in his house. Officer says he can't explain why he believes this, but he reminds Magistrate that he (Officer) has never been wrong about such things in the past.

In the first scenario, the information supplied suggests guilt; the officer's observations confirm the information, so it makes no difference whether the informant is trustworthy or not. The second scenario resembles *Draper*: The informant has supplied information with plenty of detail, but none of the information gives rise to a substantial inference of crime. The case for finding probable cause rests on the tip, which is to say it rests on trusting the informant. The argument for trusting the informant is, roughly, this: Since he knew so much about the details of Suspect's movements and choice of clothing, he must have known about Suspect's illegal activities. Since he was right about the former, he must be right about the latter. *Gates* approves of findings of probable cause based on that sort of reasoning.

Scenario #3 is a case that would have failed under *Spinelli*, but might succeed after *Gates*. (Should it?) The strong track record presumably suggests that the informant is highly credible, and *Gates* suggests that a strong showing of either credibility or basis of the informant's knowledge can compensate for a weak showing of the other.

Which leads to scenario #4. Here, there is no probable cause under *Nathanson*. Why? If informants with good track records are trustworthy, why aren't officers with good track records? After all, the informants are themselves likely involved with crime; the officers aren't (one hopes). Is there any principled way to answer this question without doing away with informants?

6. Given that the law does, in some circumstances, trust informants but not police officers, might that tempt some officers to concoct phony "informants"? What, if anything, can the law do to minimize that temptation?

7. Very little data exists on the success rate of police searches. Data on warrantless searches is close to nonexistent, and the best data on warrants probably comes from a study sponsored by the National Center for State Courts in the early 1980s. See Richard Van Duizend, L. Paul Sutton, & Charlotte A. Carter, The Search Warrant Process: Preconceptions, Perceptions, Practices (1985). The NCSC study showed two things that might bear on one's evaluation of *Gates*, and of how the law should treat informants' tips. First, informants' tips seem to be closely tied to drug investigations. Warrant applications that rely on informants' tips overwhelmingly arise in drug cases—in the seven jurisdictions studied, the percentages range from 55 to 96; five of the seven percentages were 75 or higher. See id. at 33 tbl. 14. And, the other side of the coin, warrant applications in drug investigations overwhelmingly rely on informants' tips—those percentages range from 44 to 93, with six of the seven jurisdictions exceeding 70 percent. See id. at 34 tbl. 15. These numbers suggest, unsurprisingly, that informants' tips may be particularly important to the penetration of drug markets; such tips may matter a good deal less when investigating other crimes.

Second, searches pursuant to warrants usually uncover evidence: In the cases covered by the NCSC study, evidence was seized more than 90 percent of the time, and at least some evidence listed in the warrant was seized 86 percent of the time. See id. at 38 tbl. 21. (The authors of the study note skeptically: "The reader is reminded that these percentages are probably inflated for at least some of the cities" because of the failure to keep consistent records of searches that do not turn up evidence. Id. at 38.) The data do not answer the question whether informants' tips make warrant applications more accurate, though it is worth noting that the jurisdiction where police relied on informants' tips most frequently (71 percent of warrants were based on them) also had the lowest success rate (76 percent of searches uncovered evidence listed in the warrant). See id. at 33 tbl. 13, 38 tbl. 21.

8. In a portion of *Gates* not excerpted above, the Court emphasized the deference that appellate courts are to give decisions by magistrates to issue warrants:

> A magistrate's "determination of probable cause should be paid great deference by reviewing courts." *Spinelli*, supra, at 419. "A grudging or negative attitude by reviewing courts toward warrants," [United States v. Ventresca, 380 U.S. 102, 108 (1965)], is inconsistent with the Fourth Amendment's strong preference for searches conducted pursuant to a warrant; "courts should not invalidate warrant[s] by interpreting affidavit[s] in a hypertechnical, rather than a commonsense, manner." Id., at 109.
>
> If the affidavits submitted by police officers are subjected to the type of scrutiny some courts have deemed appropriate, police might well resort to warrantless searches, with the hope of relying on consent or some other exception to the Warrant Clause that might develop at the time of the search. In addition, the possession of a warrant by officers conducting an arrest or search greatly reduces the perception of unlawful or intrusive police conduct, by assuring "the individual whose property is searched or seized of the lawful authority of the executing officer, his need to search, and the limits of his power to search." United States v. Chadwick, 433 U.S. 1, 9 (1977). Reflecting this preference for the warrant process, the traditional standard for review of an issuing magistrate's probable-cause determination has been that so long as the magistrate had a "substantial basis for . . . conclud[ing]" that a search would uncover evidence of wrongdoing, the Fourth Amendment requires no more. Jones v. United States, 362 U.S. 257, 271 (1960). . . .

This language suggests that deference is reserved for warrants, that in cases where police search without a warrant the decision of the trial judge on the defendant's motion to suppress need not receive deference. That suggestion was confirmed, in a way, by the next case.

ORNELAS v. UNITED STATES

Certiorari to the United States Court of Appeals for the Seventh Circuit
517 U.S. 690 (1996)

CHIEF JUSTICE REHNQUIST delivered the opinion of the Court.

Petitioners each pleaded guilty to possession of cocaine with intent to distribute. They reserved their right to appeal the District Court's denial of their motion to suppress the cocaine found in their car. The District Court had found reasonable suspicion to stop and question petitioners as they entered their car, and probable cause to remove one of the interior panels where a package containing two kilograms of cocaine was found. The Court of Appeals opined that the finding[] of . . . probable cause to search should be reviewed "deferentially," and "for clear error." We hold that the ultimate question[] of . . . probable cause to make a warrantless search should be reviewed de novo.

The facts are not disputed. In the early morning of a December day in 1992, Detective Michael Pautz, a 20-year veteran of the Milwaukee County Sheriff's Department with 2 years specializing in drug enforcement, was conducting drug-interdiction surveillance in downtown Milwaukee. Pautz noticed a 1981 two-door Oldsmobile with California license plates in a motel parking lot. The car attracted Pautz's attention for two reasons: because older model, two-door General Motors cars are a favorite with drug couriers because it is easy to hide things in them; and because California is a "source State" for drugs. Detective Pautz radioed his dispatcher to inquire about the car's registration. The dispatcher informed Pautz that the owner was either Miguel Ledesma Ornelas or Miguel Ornelas Ledesma from San Jose, California; Pautz was unsure which name the dispatcher gave. Detective Pautz checked the motel registry and learned that an Ismael Ornelas accompanied by a second man had registered at 4 a.m., without reservations.

Pautz called for his partner, Donald Hurrle, a detective with approximately 25 years of law enforcement experience, assigned for the past 6 years to the drug enforcement unit. When Hurrle arrived at the scene, the officers contacted the local office of the Drug Enforcement Administration (DEA) and asked DEA personnel to run the names Miguel Ledesma Ornelas and Ismael Ornelas through the Narcotics and Dangerous Drugs Information System (NADDIS), a federal database of known and suspected drug traffickers. Both names appeared in NADDIS. The NADDIS report identified Miguel Ledesma Ornelas as a heroin dealer from El Centro, California, and Ismael Ornelas, Jr., as a cocaine dealer from Tucson, Arizona. The officers then summoned Deputy Luedke. . . . Detective Hurrle informed Luedke of what they knew and together they waited.

Sometime later, petitioners emerged from the motel and got into the Oldsmobile. Detective Hurrle approached the car, identified himself as a police officer, and inquired whether they had any illegal drugs or contraband. Petitioners answered "No." Hurrle then asked for identification and was given two California driver's licenses bearing the names Saul Ornelas and Ismael Ornelas. Hurrle asked them if he could search the car and petitioners consented. The men appeared calm, but Ismael was shaking somewhat. Deputy Luedke, who over the past nine years had searched approximately 2,000 cars for narcotics, searched the Oldsmobile's interior. He noticed that a panel above the right rear passenger armrest felt somewhat loose and suspected that the panel might have been removed and contraband hidden inside. Luedke would testify later that a screw in the doorjam adjacent to the loose panel was rusty, which to him meant that the screw had been removed at some time. Luedke dismantled the panel and discovered two kilograms of cocaine. Petitioners were arrested.

Petitioners filed pretrial motions to suppress, alleging that the police officers violated their Fourth Amendment rights when . . . Deputy Luedke searched inside the panel without a warrant.[1] . . .

_____

1. Petitioners also alleged that they had not given their consent to search the interior of the car. The Magistrate Judge rejected this claim, finding that the record "clearly establishe[d] consent to search the Oldsmobile" and that "neither [petitioner] placed any restrictions on the areas the officers could search." The Magistrate ruled that this consent did not give the officers authority to search inside the panel, however, because under Seventh Circuit precedent the police may not dismantle the car body during an otherwise valid search unless the police have probable cause to believe the car's panels contain narcotics. We assume correct the Circuit's limitation on the scope of consent only for purposes of this decision.

. . . The District Court thought that the model, age, and source-State origin of the car, and the fact that two men traveling together checked into a motel at 4 o'clock in the morning without reservations, formed a drug-courier profile and that this profile together with the NADDIS reports . . . became probable cause when Deputy Luedke found the loose panel. Accordingly, the court ruled that the cocaine need not be excluded.

The Court of Appeals reviewed deferentially the District Court's [probable cause determination]; it would reverse only upon a finding of "clear error." . . . With respect to the probable-cause finding, . . . the court remanded the case for a determination on whether Luedke was credible when testifying about the loose panel. [On remand, the hearing Magistrate found Luedke's testimony credible, the District Court accepted that finding and again found probable cause for the search, and the Seventh Circuit "held that determination not clearly erroneous."] . . .

. . . ["Probable cause" is a] common-sense, nontechnical conception[ ] that deal[s] with "the factual and practical considerations of everyday life on which reasonable and prudent men, not legal technicians, act." Illinois v. Gates, 462 U.S. 213, 231 (1983). As such, the standard [is] "not readily, or even usefully, reduced to a neat set of legal rules." *Gates*, supra, at 232. We have described . . . - probable cause to search as existing where the known facts and circumstances are sufficient to warrant a man of reasonable prudence in the belief that contraband or evidence of a crime will be found, see *Gates*, supra, at 238. We have cautioned that . . . [this standard is a] fluid concept[ ] that [takes its] substantive content from the particular contexts in which the [standard is] assessed. *Gates*, supra, at 232. . . .

The principal components of a determination of . . . probable cause will be the events which occurred leading up to the stop or search, and then the decision whether these historical facts, viewed from the standpoint of an objectively reasonable police officer, amount to . . . probable cause. The first part of the analysis involves only a determination of historical facts, but the second is a mixed question of law and fact: "[T]he historical facts are admitted or established, the rule of law is undisputed, and the issue is whether the facts satisfy the [relevant] statutory [or constitutional] standard, or to put it another way, whether the rule of law as applied to the established facts is or is not violated." Pullman-Standard v. Swint, 456 U.S. 273, 289, n. 19 (1982).

We think independent appellate review of . . . ultimate determinations of . . . probable cause is consistent with the position we have taken in past cases. We have never, when reviewing a probable-cause . . . determination ourselves, expressly deferred to the trial court's determination. See, e.g., Brinegar [v. United States, 338 U.S. 160 (1949)] (rejecting District Court's conclusion that the police lacked probable cause). A policy of sweeping deference would permit, "[i]n the absence of any significant difference in the facts," "the Fourth Amendment's incidence [to] tur[n] on whether different trial judges draw general conclusions that the facts are sufficient or insufficient to constitute probable cause." *Brinegar*, supra, at 171. Such varied results would be inconsistent with the idea of a unitary system of law. This, if a matter-of-course, would be unacceptable.

In addition, the legal rules for probable cause . . . acquire content only through application. Independent review is therefore necessary if appellate courts are to maintain control of, and to clarify, the legal principles.

Finally, de novo review tends to unify precedent and will come closer to providing law enforcement officers with a defined "set of rules which, in most instances, makes it possible to reach a correct determination beforehand as to whether an invasion of privacy is justified in the interest of law enforcement." New York v. Belton, 453 U.S. 454, 458 (1981). . . .

The Court of Appeals, in adopting its deferential standard of review here, reasoned that de novo review for warrantless searches would be inconsistent with the "great deference" paid when reviewing a decision to issue a warrant, see Illinois v. Gates, 462 U.S. 213 (1983). We cannot agree. The Fourth Amendment demonstrates a "strong preference for searches conducted pursuant to a warrant," *Gates*, supra, at 236, and the police are more likely to use the warrant process if the scrutiny applied to a magistrate's probable-cause determination to issue a warrant is less than that for warrantless searches. Were we to eliminate this distinction, we would eliminate the incentive.

We therefore hold that as a general matter determinations of . . . probable cause should be reviewed de novo on appeal. Having said this, we hasten to point out that a reviewing court should take care both to review findings of historical fact only for clear error and to give due weight to inferences drawn from those facts by resident judges and local law enforcement officers.

A trial judge views the facts of a particular case in light of the distinctive features and events of the community; likewise, a police officer views the facts through the lens of his police experience and expertise. The background facts provide a context for the historical facts, and when seen together yield inferences that deserve deference. For example, . . . Milwaukee . . . is unlikely to have been an overnight stop selected at the last minute by a traveler coming from California to points east. The 85-mile width of Lake Michigan blocks any further eastward progress. And while the city's salubrious summer climate and seasonal attractions bring many tourists at that time of year, the same is not true in December. Milwaukee's average daily high temperature in that month is 31 degrees and its average daily low is 17 degrees; the percentage of possible sunshine is only 38 percent. It is a reasonable inference that a Californian stopping in Milwaukee in December is either there to transact business or to visit family or friends. The background facts, though rarely the subject of explicit findings, inform the judge's assessment of the historical facts.

In a similar vein, our cases have recognized that a police officer may draw inferences based on his own experience in deciding whether probable cause exists. To a layman the sort of loose panel below the back seat armrest in the automobile involved in this case may suggest only wear and tear, but to Officer Luedke, who had searched roughly 2,000 cars for narcotics, it suggested that drugs may be secreted inside the panel. An appeals court should give due weight to a trial court's finding that the officer was credible and the inference was reasonable.

We vacate the judgments and remand the case to the Court of Appeals to review de novo the District Court's determinations that the officer had reasonable suspicion and probable cause in this case. . . .

[Justice Scalia's dissenting opinion is omitted.]

NOTES AND QUESTIONS

1. Given the definition of probable cause offered by *Gates*, how much does the standard of review matter? If probable cause determinations are always

fact-specific, appellate decisions are unlikely to have broad legal implications. And if probable cause determinations almost always rest on credibility judgments (and deference is still owed to district court findings of fact, including credibility judgments), there will rarely be reason for reversal.

On the other hand, perhaps the standard of review matters, but in a more subtle fashion than one might think. Consider the following argument:

> . . . Ornelas and his co-defendant won in the Supreme Court, and the case was widely reported as a victory for criminal defendants. But the matter is not so simple.
>
> . . . Immediately after holding that determinations of probable cause . . . should generally receive de novo review, the Court in *Ornelas* "hasten[ed] to point out" that appellate courts "should take care . . . to give due weight to the inferences drawn by resident judges and local law enforcement officers." This instruction is not simply inconsistent with true de novo review; it is inconsistent in a way that gives the prose-cution a leg up. A deferential standard of review like "clear error," the standard initially applied by the court of appeals in *Ornelas*, gives weight to the judgments of the trial court, but not to those of the officers involved in the case. By rejecting a "clear error" standard in favor of a "de novo with due weight" standard, the Court in effect declared that police officers should receive as much deference as trial judges. Taken as a whole, then, *Ornelas* may make appellate review of suppression rulings appreciably more hospitable to law enforcement.

David A. Sklansky, Traffic Stops, Minority Motorists, and the Future of the Fourth Amendment, 1997 Sup. Ct. Rev. 271, 300-301.

2. The probable cause determination in *Ornelas* rested heavily on the loose panel in the defendant's car. The meaning of that loose panel depends on a pair of empirical questions: How many similarly loose panels hide drugs? How many don't? Hard data on those questions do not exist; the best one can do is to draw inferences from one's own experience and intuitions and from the testimony of police witnesses. Whose inferences are likely to be more accurate—the trial judge's, or the appellate panel's?

Perhaps trial judges do a better job of making such determinations—after all, the trial judge is more likely to have seen similar cases before than is the appellate court—but it may be that *neither* trial *nor* appellate judges have the knowledge base necessary to do a good job of making determinations like the one in *Ornelas*. If so, probable cause determinations like that one boil down to the question whether the judge should trust the police officer. The "due weight" language in the Court's opinion (see the preceding note) suggests that the legally correct answer to that question is ordinarily yes.

3. Trusting police officers does not sound like a recipe for careful judicial review. But what is the alternative? If courts undertake a searching, careful review of officers' testimony in cases like *Ornelas*, police officers might respond by embel-lishing, by adding "facts" until probable cause becomes clear. Courts are not necessarily in a good position to combat this tactic, for just as they may not know what inferences to draw from a loose panel in an automobile, they may not know when officers are embellishing and when they are telling the truth.

And from the officers' perspective, embellishment—perjury—may seem more defensible than one might first suspect. Consider Jerome Skolnick's account of the following episode, involving an officer who sees a "known addict" on the street.

> When approached, . . . the suspect turned around and backed off to the police car, with his left hand closed. The officer asked the man to open his fist. Instead, the man quickly brought his hand to his mouth . . . .

Jerome Skolnick, Justice Without Trial 210 (3d ed. 1994). Did the officer have probable cause at this point? The officer thought so, though he also thought a judge would likely disagree. Skolnick's account continues:

> As the police officer said:
>> It's awfully hard to explain to a judge what I mean when I testify that I saw a furtive movement. . . . I can testify as to the character of the neighborhood, my knowledge that the man was an addict, and all that stuff, but what I mean is that when I see a hype move the way that guy moved, I *know* he's trying to get rid of something. [Emphasis supplied by the speaker.]
>
> I asked the police officer if he had ever been wrong in this kind of judgment, and he replied that he had but felt that he was right often enough to justify a search, even when lacking evidence to arrest the suspect.

Id. at 211. In the incident just described, the officer in Skolnick's account was right: The suspect swallowed a marijuana cigarette.

Police officers will often be better at identifying criminal behavior than at analyzing or explaining how the identification process works. The result may be that judges — or at least some judges — undervalue police hunches. Would it be surprising if even ordinarily honest officers tended to exaggerate or twist the facts in response? Yet if judges respond by deferring to officers' hunches, what is left of the probable cause standard? Is there any way out of this box?

4. "Probable cause" cases generally raise two kinds of issues. The first is the level of probability that a given kind of evidence can be found at a particular place. The second is how that level of probability should be apportioned among the individuals at the scene — or, to put it more simply, who is a suspect and who is a mere bystander. Consider the following case.

MARYLAND v. PRINGLE

Certiorari to the Court of Appeals of Maryland
540 U.S. 366 (2003)

CHIEF JUSTICE REHNQUIST delivered the opinion of the Court.

. . . At 3:16 a.m. on August 7, 1999, a Baltimore County Police officer stopped a Nissan Maxima for speeding. There were three occupants in the car: Donte Partlow, the driver and owner, respondent Pringle, the front-seat passenger, and Otis Smith, the back-seat passenger. The officer asked Partlow for his license and registration. When Partlow opened the glove compartment to retrieve the vehicle registration, the officer observed a large amount of rolled-up money in the glove compartment. The officer returned to his patrol car with Partlow's license and registration to check the computer system for outstanding violations. The computer check did not reveal any violations. The officer returned to the stopped car, had Partlow get out, and issued him an oral warning.

After a second patrol car arrived, the officer asked Partlow if he had any weapons or narcotics in the vehicle. Partlow indicated that he did not. Partlow then consented to a search of the vehicle. The search yielded $763 from the glove compartment and five plastic glassine baggies containing cocaine from behind the back-seat armrest. When the officer began the search the armrest was in the upright position flat against the rear seat. The officer pulled down the armrest and found the drugs, which had been placed between the armrest and the back seat of the car.

The officer questioned all three men about the ownership of the drugs and money, and told them that if no one admitted to ownership of the drugs he was going to arrest them all. The men offered no information regarding the ownership of the drugs or money. All three were placed under arrest and transported to the police station.

Later that morning, Pringle . . . gave an oral and written confession in which he acknowledged that the cocaine belonged to him, that he and his friends were going to a party, and that he intended to sell the cocaine or "[u]se it for sex." Pringle maintained that the other occupants of the car did not know about the drugs, and they were released.

The trial court denied Pringle's motion to suppress his confession as the fruit of an illegal arrest, holding that the officer had probable cause to arrest Pringle. A jury convicted Pringle of possession with intent to distribute cocaine and possession of cocaine. He was sentenced to 10 years' incarceration without the possibility of parole . . . .

The Court of Appeals of Maryland, by divided vote, reversed, holding that, absent specific facts tending to show Pringle's knowledge and dominion or control over the drugs, "the mere finding of cocaine in the back armrest when [Pringle] was a front seat passenger in a car being driven by its owner is insufficient to establish probable cause for an arrest for possession." 370 Md. 525, 545, 805 A.2d 1016, 1027 (2002). We granted certiorari, and now reverse.

. . . Maryland law authorizes police officers to execute warrantless arrests . . . for felonies committed in an officer's presence or where an officer has probable cause to believe that a felony has been committed or is being committed in the officer's presence. A warrantless arrest of an individual in a public place for a felony, or a misdemeanor committed in the officer's presence, is consistent with the Fourth Amendment if the arrest is supported by probable cause. United States v. Watson, 423 U.S. 411, 424 (1976); see Atwater v. Lago Vista, 532 U.S. 318, 354 (2001) (stating that "[i]f an officer has probable cause to believe that an individual has committed even a very minor criminal offense in his presence, he may, without violating the Fourth Amendment, arrest the offender").

It is uncontested in the present case that the officer, upon recovering the five plastic glassine baggies containing suspected cocaine, had probable cause to believe a felony had been committed. The sole question is whether the officer had probable cause to believe that Pringle committed that crime.

The long-prevailing standard of probable cause protects "citizens from rash and unreasonable interferences with privacy and from unfounded charges of crime," while giving "fair leeway for enforcing the law in the community's protection." Brinegar v. United States, 338 U.S. 160, 176 (1949). On many occasions, we have reiterated that the probable-cause standard is a " 'practical, nontechnical conception' " that deals with " 'the factual and practical considerations of everyday life on which reasonable and prudent men, not legal technicians, act.'" Illinois v. Gates, 462 U.S. 213, 231 (1983) (quoting *Brinegar, supra*, at 175-176). "[P]robable cause is a fluid concept—turning on the assessment of probabilities in particular factual contexts—not readily, or even usefully, reduced to a neat set of legal rules." *Gates*, 462 U.S., at 232.

The probable-cause standard is incapable of precise definition or quantification into percentages because it deals with probabilities and depends on the totality of the circumstances. See ibid.; *Brinegar*, 338 U.S., at 175. We have stated, however, that "[t]he substance of all the definitions of probable cause is a reasonable ground for belief of guilt," ibid., and that the belief of guilt must be particularized with respect to the person to be searched or seized, Ybarra v. Illinois, 444 U.S. 85, 91 (1979). In Illinois v. Gates, we noted:

> "As early as Locke v. United States, 11 U.S. 339 (1813), Chief Justice Marshall observed, in a closely related context: '[T]he term "probable cause," according to its usual acceptation, means less than evidence which would justify condemnation. . . . It imports a seizure made under circumstances which warrant suspicion.' More recently, we said that 'the *quanta* . . . of proof' appropriate in ordinary judicial proceedings are inapplicable to the decision to issue a warrant. *Brinegar*, 338 U.S., at 173. Finely tuned standards such as proof beyond a reasonable doubt or by a preponderance of the evidence, useful in formal trials, have no place in the [probable-cause] decision." 462 U.S., at 235.

To determine whether an officer had probable cause to arrest an individual, we examine the events leading up to the arrest, and then decide "whether these historical facts, viewed from the standpoint of an objectively reasonable police officer, amount to" probable cause, *Ornelas, supra*, at 696.

In this case, Pringle was one of three men riding in a Nissan Maxima at 3:16 a.m. There was $763 of rolled-up cash in the glove compartment directly in front of Pringle. Five plastic glassine baggies of cocaine were behind the back-seat armrest and accessible to all three men. Upon questioning, the three men failed to offer any information with respect to the ownership of the cocaine or the money.

We think it an entirely reasonable inference from these facts that any or all three of the occupants had knowledge of, and exercised dominion and control over, the cocaine. Thus a reasonable officer could conclude that there was probable cause to believe Pringle committed the crime of possession of cocaine, either solely or jointly.

Pringle's attempt to characterize this case as a guilt-by-association case is unavailing. His reliance on Ybarra v. Illinois, supra, and United States v. Di Re, 332 U.S. 581 (1948), is misplaced. In *Ybarra*, police officers obtained a warrant to search a tavern and its bartender for evidence of possession of a controlled substance. Upon entering the tavern, the officers conducted patdown searches of the customers present in the tavern, including Ybarra. Inside a cigarette pack retrieved from Ybarra's pocket, an officer found six tinfoil packets containing heroin. We stated:

> "[A] person's mere propinquity to others independently suspected of criminal activity does not, without more, give rise to probable cause to search that person. Where the standard is probable cause, a search or seizure of a person must be supported by probable cause particularized with respect to that person. This requirement cannot be undercut or avoided by simply pointing to the fact that coincidentally there exists

probable cause to search or seize another or to search the premises where the person may happen to be." 444 U.S., at 91.

We held that the search warrant did not permit body searches of all of the tavern's patrons and that the police could not pat down the patrons for weapons, absent individualized suspicion. Id., at 92.

This case is quite different from *Ybarra*. Pringle and his two companions were in a relatively small automobile, not a public tavern. In Wyoming v. Houghton, 526 U.S. 295 (1999), we noted that "a car passenger—unlike the unwitting tavern patron in *Ybarra*—will often be engaged in a common enterprise with the driver, and have the same interest in concealing the fruits or the evidence of their wrong-doing." Id., at 304-305. Here we think it was reasonable for the officer to infer a common enterprise among the three men. The quantity of drugs and cash in the car indicated the likelihood of drug dealing, an enterprise to which a dealer would be unlikely to admit an innocent person with the potential to furnish evidence against him.

In *Di Re*, a federal investigator had been told by an informant, Reed, that he was to receive counterfeit gasoline ration coupons from a certain Buttitta at a particular place. The investigator went to the appointed place and saw Reed, the sole occupant of the rear seat of the car, holding gasoline ration coupons. There were two other occupants in the car: Buttitta in the driver's seat and Di Re in the front passenger's seat. Reed informed the investigator that Buttitta had given him counterfeit coupons. Thereupon, all three men were arrested and searched. After noting that the officers had no information implicating Di Re and no information pointing to Di Re's possession of coupons, unless presence in the car warranted that inference, we concluded that the officer lacked probable cause to believe that Di Re was involved in the crime. 332 U.S., at 592-594. We said "[a]ny inference that everyone on the scene of a crime is a party to it must disappear if the Government informer singles out the guilty person." Id., at 594. No such singling out occurred in this case; none of the three men provided information with respect to the ownership of the cocaine or money.

We hold that the officer had probable cause to believe that Pringle had committed the crime of possession of a controlled substance. Pringle's arrest therefore did not contravene the Fourth and Fourteenth Amendments. Accordingly, the judgment of the Court of Appeals of Maryland is reversed, and the case is remanded for further proceedings not inconsistent with this opinion.

NOTES AND QUESTIONS

1. Notice that *Pringle* was unanimous: to the Court, this was an easy case. Does the probable cause inquiry seem easy to you?

2. Consider Ybarra v. Illinois, 444 U.S. 85 (1979), one of the cases discussed in *Pringle*. The police had a warrant to search the Aurora Tap Bar in Aurora, Illinois, and its bartender, a young white male named Greg, for drugs. "[S]even or eight" police officers went to the bar to execute the warrant. Id. at 88. According to Justice Stewart's majority opinion, this is what happened next:

> . . . One of the officers then proceeded to pat down each of the 9 to 13 customers present in the tavern, while the remaining officers engaged in an extensive search of the premises.

The police officer who frisked the patrons found the appellant, Ventura Ybarra, in front of the bar standing by a pinball machine. In his first patdown of Ybarra, the officer felt what he described as "a cigarette pack with objects in it." He did not remove this pack from Ybarra's pocket. Instead, he moved on and proceeded to pat down other customers. After completing this process the officer returned to Ybarra and frisked him once again. This second search of Ybarra took place approximately 2 to 10 minutes after the first. The officer relocated and retrieved the cigarette pack from Ybarra's pants pocket. Inside the pack he found six tinfoil packets containing a brown powdery substance which later turned out to be heroin.

Id. at 88-89. The Court found the search of Ybarra unconstitutional. Justice Stewart explained:

> There is no reason to suppose that, when the search warrant was issued on March 1, 1976, the authorities had probable cause to believe that any person found on the premises of the Aurora Tap Tavern, aside from "Greg," would be violating the law. . . .
>
> Not only was probable cause to search Ybarra absent at the time the warrant was issued, it was still absent when the police executed the warrant. Upon entering the tavern, the police did not recognize Ybarra and had no reason to believe that he had committed, was committing, or was about to commit any offense under state or federal law. Ybarra made no gestures indicative of criminal conduct, made no movements that might suggest an attempt to conceal contraband, and said nothing of a suspicious nature to the police officers. In short, the agents knew nothing in particular about Ybarra, except that he was present, along with several other customers, in a public tavern at a time when the police had reason to believe that the bartender would have heroin for sale.
>
> It is true that the police possessed a warrant based on probable cause to search the tavern in which Ybarra happened to be at the time the warrant was executed. But, a person's mere propinquity to others independently suspected of criminal activity does not, without more, give rise to probable cause to search that person. Where the standard is probable cause, a search or seizure of a person must be supported by probable cause particularized with respect to that person. This requirement cannot be undercut or avoided by simply pointing to the fact that coincidentally there exists probable cause to search or seize another or to search the premises where the person may happen to be. The Fourth and Fourteenth Amendments protect the "legitimate expectations of privacy" of persons, not places.

Id. at 90-91. Notice that a portion of the preceding paragraph is quoted in the Court's opinion in *Pringle*. Does the quoted passage read differently in context? Is *Pringle* consistent with *Ybarra*?

3. Perhaps the key distinction is that Pringle was in a car, and Ybarra was in a bar. (Sounds like "if it doesn't fit, you must acquit.") Should public businesses be treated differently than social gatherings? Or, perhaps the problem is simple numbers: there were three people riding in Pringle's car, and "nine to thirteen" customers in the Aurora Tap Tavern, including Ybarra. If that is the distinction, where is the dividing line? Between three and four? Eight and nine? Twelve and thirteen?

4. Suppose that several police officers conduct a raid on a mosque, after having received a tip stating that the mosque is the site of terrorist activity. Assume that the tip satisfies Illinois v. Gates, 462 U.S. 213 (1983). May the police search anyone in the mosque? Everyone? No one?

2. The Warrant "Requirement"

The Supreme Court has so often expressed a preference for searches and seizures pursuant to warrant that the superiority of warrants over after-the-fact sanctions for Fourth Amendment violations is widely taken for granted. In fact, the Fourth Amendment's warrant "requirement" is something of a puzzle:

> First, its very existence seems odd. Legal standards are usually enforced through after-the-fact review. . . . Potential tortfeasors do not ordinarily seek judicial permission to engage in risky conduct; they decide how to behave in light of the governing law and (if things work out badly) defend themselves in litigation later. It is not clear why search and seizure law should work differently. Suppression hearings and damages actions offer readily available means of reviewing police decisions after the fact. And there is no obvious reason why police officers cannot both understand the legal signals these decisions provide and translate those signals into behavior on the street. Finally, after-the-fact review in suppression hearings or damage suits is both adversarial and in-depth, while review of warrant applications by magistrates is ex parte and cursory, so that one would expect that the ex post decisions better protect individuals' interests. . . .
>
> . . . The Supreme Court . . . claims that the warrant requirement is the centerpiece of the law of search and seizure, and that pre-screening by neutral and detached magistrates is the heart of citizens' protection against police overreaching. But the same Court regularly narrows the range of cases to which the warrant requirement applies. . . . [T]he critics are, if anything worse. On the one hand, they argue that the Court should substantially broaden the scope of the warrant requirement, in order to protect citizens' privacy in the many cases that are now left to the supposed vagaries of after-the-fact review. But the same critics often contend that magistrates are rubber stamps who cannot be trusted to do a sound job of deciding whether probable cause exists in particular cases, and hence should receive little deference from district courts in suppression hearings. This position seems odd, to say the least: if magistrates do a poor job of deciding whether probable cause exists, it is unclear why anyone should want them to do so more often, or indeed at all.

William J. Stuntz, Warrants and Fourth Amendment Remedies, 77 Va. L. Rev. 881, 881-883 (1991).

Stuntz argues that in an exclusionary rule system, the preference for warrants may address two problems: that judges' after-the-fact probable cause determinations may be biased by knowledge that incriminating evidence has been found, and that police in suppression hearings may subvert Fourth Amendment standards by testifying falsely — something they are less able to do when required to state the relevant facts before evidence is found. This still leaves the puzzle, however, as to why *magistrates* review warrant applications:

> The [warrant] requirement is premised on the assumption that officials engaged in the "often competitive enterprise of ferreting out crime" cannot be relied upon to give appropriate weight to privacy costs. But there is surely no a priori reason that police officers must necessarily be unconcerned about the legal protection of fourth amendment rights. Conversely, there is no a priori reason why magistrates, who are also law enforcement officers of a sort, should be especially sensitive to such rights. . . .
>
> Imagine a police department in which a senior, well-respected officer is told that his function is to review warrants to ensure that they are supported by probable cause.

Is there reason to doubt that, once informed of his role, he would do a less effective job than a magistrate? . . .

Of course, modern police departments do not have such officers. Ironically, this failure is attributable, at least in part, to the Court's insistence that they cannot assign officers to this role. The Court's pessimistic assumptions about police behavior thus become self-fulfilling prophecies. . . .

Silas J. Wasserstrom & Louis Michael Seidman, The Fourth Amendment as Constitutional Theory, 77 Geo. L.J. 19, 34-35 (1988).

Thus, the arguments for a warrant preference rule may be both more subtle and more complicated than is sometimes assumed. Returning to the Fourth Amendment's text for a moment, however, it clearly contemplates the existence of some warrant process. Indeed, the text goes to some lengths to impose conditions on the issuance of warrants beyond the basic probable cause requirement. Thus, probable cause must be "supported by Oath or affirmation." Warrants must particularly describe "the place to be searched, and the persons or things to be seized." The Court has added that the magistrate who issues a warrant must be "neutral and detached." Johnson v. United States, 333 U.S. 10, 14 (1946). In addition, state and federal statutes, local codes, and local rules of court commonly specify procedures for warrants—requiring that search warrants be executed within a specified period of time, for instance, or mandating daytime execution in the absence of special reasons for proceeding at night. All this may suggest a high degree of formality in the warrant process, but don't be fooled—in fact there is considerably less formality in the process than one might suppose.

The Oath or Affirmation Requirement

The oath or affirmation requirement is often satisfied by specifying the facts giving rise to probable cause in a police officer's affidavit that is attached to the warrant application—though oral statements may also be sworn. In some places, affiant police officers appear personally before the magistrate. Other places expressly authorize telephonic search warrant procedures that dispense with any personal appearance requirement.

It is important that the circumstances giving rise to probable cause be adequately presented to the magistrate. In Whiteley v. Warden, 401 U.S. 560, 565 n. 8 (1971), the Court concluded that facially insufficient affidavits "cannot be rehabilitated by testimony concerning information possessed by the affiant when he sought the warrant but not disclosed to the issuing magistrate." A defendant may challenge a facially *sufficient* affidavit after the fact, however, when it is shown to contain false statements. "Negligent" or "innocent" falsehoods will not invalidate a warrant. But if a defendant can establish that the affidavit contained perjured statements or false statements made in reckless disregard of their truth, and provided the affidavit's remaining content is not sufficient to establish probable cause, the search warrant will be voided and the fruits of the search excluded. Franks v. Delaware, 438 U.S. 154, 155-156 (1978).

The NCSC research team that examined the search warrant application process in seven cities in the early 1980s, see page 436 supra, found that in most places warrant affidavits "were often barely distinguishable from one another: extensive and critical portions of many affidavits were rendered in 'boilerplate' recitations of informant reliability, information trustworthiness, and probable cause to believe certain specified contraband was in the possession of the accused at the place indicated." L. Paul Sutton, Getting Around the Fourth Amendment, in Carl B. Klockars & Stephen D. Mastrofski eds., Thinking About Police 433, 440-441 (2d ed. 1991). This raises the question how seriously officers take the warrant preparation process. One magistrate interviewed in connection with the study recounted the following exchange stemming from the magistrate's having asked an officer/affiant about a specific statement in the affidavit that contradicted a statement the officer made orally:

> *Officer:* Well, I didn't write that statement.
> *Magistrate:* But you signed it! And that concerns me. You know, you could potentially open yourself up to a nice lawsuit if you're going to issue warrants that you haven't read and you don't know what's contained within the four corners of those warrants.
> *Officer:* All I'm doing is relying on my best information and belief.
> *Magistrate:* But your best information and belief is more than what's in here!

Id. at 442. One way to avoid scenarios like this is to use prosecutors to screen warrant applications, in the hope that those applications will both be more informative and contain fewer errors. From the perspective of the police officer, however, prosecutorial screening may simply mean more needless delay. Consider one officer's view of the typical reception he received when seeking help from the district attorney's office in obtaining a warrant:

> There could be three or four attorneys over there right now who don't have court or who don't have anything going on. But if you say that I have a search warrant that needs to be done, they panic. . . . So, I've been told, "Wait until so-and-so gets back from court and he'll do it for you."

Id. at 435. Another officer echoed these sentiments:

> If you really pressure them, they maybe they can grab somebody on his way back from court or something and he may want to do it, but you have really interrupted his day. . . . [T]hat's the distinct impression you get. Very rarely do you just call and say, "I need a search warrant. We just got the information. Can I come see one of you? and they say, "Yeah, come see Mr. Smith. He's here; he'll be waiting for you."

Id. at 436.

The Magistrate

The Supreme Court has had several occasions to interpret the "neutral and detached magistrate" requirement. In Coolidge v. New Hampshire, 403 U.S. 443 (1971), the Court found the requirement to be violated by a procedure in which a state attorney general issued a search warrant in the course of a murder investigation that he was conducting. The Court has also refused to uphold a warrant process in which the magistrate received a fee for issuing warrants but not for refusing them. See Connally v. Georgia, 429 U.S. 245 (1977). In the view of some commentators, however, the Court may have done little else to ensure that the review of warrant applications by magistrates is meaningful:

> The validity of the Court's procedural structure rests on the empirical claim that "neutral and detached" magistrates do a better job of assessing the law enforcement/privacy tradeoff than do police officers. But the "rubber stamp" quality of magistrate review of warrant applications is an open scandal, and the Court has done little to show that it takes its own procedures seriously. On the contrary, it has failed to impose minimal standards to ensure that magistrates understand the meaning of probable cause.

Silas J. Wasserstrom & Louis Michael Seidman, The Fourth Amendment as Constitutional Theory, 77 Geo. L.J. 19, 34 (1988). In Shadwick v. City of Tampa, 407 U.S. 345, 350-352 (1972), the Court upheld a warrant process in which clerks without law degrees were permitted to issue arrest warrants for municipal ordinance violations, noting that "[c]ommunities may have sound reasons for delegating the responsibility of issuing warrants to competent personnel other than judges or lawyers."

The process by which warrants are issued, moreover, can be quite perfunctory. Consider again what the NCSC team heard from interested parties during its study:

> In virtually every jurisdiction we studied, representatives of all perspectives (police, judiciary, prosecution, and defense) suggested that at least some of the judges with whom they had contact were sometimes remiss in their review of warrant applications. Characterizations of this delinquency ranged from sympathetic concern (usually on the part of law enforcement) to biting sarcasm (on the part of the offending party's judicial brethren). We must have been told by at least one person in each of the jurisdictions studied that "There are some judges who will sign anything."

L. Paul Sutton, Getting Around the Fourth Amendment, in Carl B. Klockars & Stephen D. Mastrofski eds., Thinking About Police 433, 439 (2d ed. 1991).

Officers interviewed for the study also noted "considerable variation . . . not only in terms of judges' interpretation of the evidence required to meet the probable cause standard but also in terms of judges' attitudes about whether certain crimes ought even to be enforced." Id. at 436. In the words of one law enforcement official:

> If [the judge] feels comfortable with the area of law — say narcotics law — [then he] doesn't treat you like a pain. . . . He will show some desire, some willingness to work [with you], look at the thing, ask you some questions, professionally discuss the thing. [Conversely,] there are those judges obviously who don't believe that strongly in taking a hard-line approach to narcotics enforcement. I think that is reflected in their attitudes when we come in to get search warrants.

Id. at 437.

Perfunctory review of warrant applications by some magistrates and variation among magistrates in the standards they apply to such review create opportunities for "judge shopping" by police. Such opportunities in turn might suggest that the warrant application process imposes few real restraints on law enforcement. Lest you too easily conclude from all this that the process is not meaningful, however, it's worth recalling that searches pursuant to warrants usually uncover evidence — over 90 percent of the time, according to the NCSC research. See page 436 supra. This figure at least suggests that police often target the right places in their warrant applications. Do you think this is a consequence of the warrant process? Or is it merely coincident with it? For an argument that the key benefit of the warrant process may be the inconvenience it poses for the police — that searches pursuant to warrants tend to succeed because police officers don't want to spend hours waiting to see a magistrate only to engage in a fruitless search — see Donald Dripps, Living with *Leon*, 95 Yale L.J. 906 (1986).

The Particularity Requirement

The Fourth Amendment's text requires that warrants "particularly describ[e] the place to be searched, and the persons or things to be seized." With respect to the place searched, the Supreme Court has said that the description should be particular enough to permit an officer "with reasonable effort [to] ascertain and identify the place intended." Steele v. United States, 267 U.S. 498, 503 (1925). When a seemingly adequate description of the premises turns out to be so ambiguous that police have no idea which premises to search, the particularity requirement is not satisfied and police may not proceed. If police possess information that clarifies the ambiguity or if it is reasonably clear what portion of the warrant description is in error, however, a search of the "proper" premises may be permitted.

What if the police search the wrong place? In Maryland v. Garrison, 480 U.S. 79 (1987), police had probable cause to search the third-floor apartment of Lawrence McWebb. Without realizing that the third floor contained two apartments, they obtained a warrant to search "'the premises known as 2036 Park Avenue third floor apartment.'" The police entered the wrong apartment and seized contraband there before discovering their error. The Court first determined that the warrant was valid when issued, based on the information that the police disclosed to the magistrate, or had a duty to discover and disclose. The validity of the search of the apartment "depend[ed] on whether the officers' failure to realize the overbreadth of the warrant was objectively reasonable"; after reviewing the facts, the Court determined that the officers' mistake satisfied this standard. Id. at 88.

The particularity requirement for items sought to be seized serves several purposes. First, it supports the probable cause requirement: if the police cannot specify what they are looking for, the factual basis for their suspicions is likely weak. Second, it limits the legitimate scope of searches both spatially and temporally. (Thus, if police are searching only for stolen paintings, they may not look in desk drawers or other places too small to contain them. Once the paintings are found, the search must end.) Finally, the particularity requirement helps to ensure that people will not be wrongly deprived of their property. Note, however, that in Andresen v. Maryland, 427 U.S. 463 (1976), the Court upheld warrants that, after listing a long series of specific documents to be seized, also authorized the seizure of "other fruits, instrumentalities and evidence of crime at (this) time unknown."

The Court construed the phrase to refer to the specific crime under investigation and held that so construed, its inclusion did not render the warrants fatally general. Note, too, that the particularity requirement does not mean that police are absolutely precluded from seizing other items not mentioned in the warrant application. See pages 479-489 infra for a discussion of the plain view doctrine.

The Execution of Warrants

Not only do warrants and warrant applications raise Fourth Amendment issues; so may the manner in which warrants are "executed" — in other words, the manner in which searches pursuant to warrants are carried out. One set of questions involves the scope of the "knock and announce" requirement. That requirement may be unique in Fourth Amendment jurisprudence: all four of the Supreme Court decisions that have established and defined it were unanimous.

In Wilson v. Arkansas, 514 U.S. 927 (1995), the Supreme Court held that absent some law enforcement interest establishing the reasonableness of an unannounced intrusion, the Fourth Amendment requires police to knock and announce themselves before entering premises to execute a warrant. Richards v. Wisconsin, 520 U.S. 385 (1997), raised the question whether *Wilson* mandated a case-by-case inquiry, or whether some cases might categorically permit "no-knock" entries. The Wisconsin Supreme Court had ruled that such entries were automatically permissible whenever police executed search warrants in felony drug investigations. Writing for the Court, Justice Stevens rejected this per se rule:

> [T]he Wisconsin rule contains considerable overgeneralization. For example, while drug investigation frequently does pose special risks to officer safety and the preservation of evidence, not every drug investigation will pose these risks to a substantial degree. For example, a search could be conducted at a time when the only individuals present in a residence have no connection with the drug activity and thus will be unlikely to threaten officers or destroy evidence. Or the police could know that the drugs being searched for were of a type or in a location that made them impossible to destroy quickly. . . . Wisconsin's blanket rule impermissibly insulates these cases from judicial review.

Id. at 393. Justice Stevens' opinion concluded that "[i]n order to justify a 'no-knock' entry, the police must have a reasonable suspicion that knocking and announcing their presence, under the particular circumstances, would be dangerous or futile, or that it would inhibit the effective investigation of the crime by, for example, allowing the destruction of evidence."

In United States v. Ramirez, 523 U.S. 65 (1998), the Court made clear that this standard applies even when the officers must damage property to make their unannounced entry. Chief Justice Rehnquist's opinion for the Court cautioned, however, that "[t]he general touchstone of reasonableness . . . governs the method of execution of the warrant. Excessive or unnecessary destruction of property in the course of a search may violate the Fourth Amendment, even though the entry itself is lawful and the fruits of the search not subject to suppression." Id. at 71. The Court revisited the "knock and announce" requirement yet again in the next case, and the Justices again found themselves unanimous.

UNITED STATES v. BANKS

Certiorari to the United States Court of Appeals for the Ninth Circuit
540 U.S. 31 (2003)

JUSTICE SOUTER delivered the opinion of the Court.

Officers executing a warrant to search for cocaine in respondent Banks's apartment knocked and announced their authority. The question is whether their 15-to-20-second wait before a forcible entry satisfied the Fourth Amendment. . . . We hold that it did.

With information that Banks was selling cocaine at home, North Las Vegas Police Department officers and Federal Bureau of Investigation agents got a warrant to search his two-bedroom apartment. As soon as they arrived there, about 2 o'clock on a Wednesday afternoon, officers posted in front called out "police search warrant" and rapped hard enough on the door to be heard by officers at the back door. There was no indication whether anyone was home, and after waiting for 15 to 20 seconds with no answer, the officers broke open the front door with a battering ram. Banks was in the shower and testified that he heard nothing until the crash of the door, which brought him out dripping to confront the police. The search produced weapons, crack cocaine, and other evidence of drug dealing.

In response to drug and firearms charges, Banks moved to suppress evidence, arguing that the officers executing the search warrant waited an unreasonably short time before forcing entry, and so violated . . . the Fourth Amendment. . . . The District Court denied the motion, and Banks pleaded guilty, reserving his right to challenge the search on appeal.

A divided panel of the Ninth Circuit reversed . . . In assessing the reasonableness of the execution of the warrant, the panel majority set out a nonexhaustive list of "factors that an officer reasonably should consider" in deciding when to enter premises identified in a warrant, after knocking and announcing their presence but receiving no express acknowledgment:

"(a) size of the residence; (b) location of the residence; (c) location of the officers in relation to the main living or sleeping areas of the residence; (d) time of day; (e) nature of the suspected offense; (f) evidence demonstrating the suspect's guilt; (g) suspect's prior convictions and, if any, the type of offense for which he was convicted; and (h) any other observations triggering the senses of the officers that reasonably would lead one to believe that immediate entry was necessary."

The majority also defined four categories of intrusion after knock and announcement, saying that the classification "aids in the resolution of the essential question whether the entry made herein was reasonable under the circumstances":

"(1) entries in which exigent circumstances exist and non-forcible entry is possible, permitting entry to be made simultaneously with or shortly after announcement; (2) entries in which exigent circumstances exist and forced entry by destruction of property is required, necessitating more specific inferences of exigency; (3) entries in which no exigent circumstances exist and non-forcible entry is possible, requiring an explicit refusal of admittance or a lapse of a significant amount of time; and (4) entries in which no exigent circumstances exist and forced entry by destruction of property is required, mandating an explicit refusal of admittance or a lapse of an even more substantial amount of time."

The panel majority put the action of the officers here in the last category, on the understanding that they destroyed the door without hearing anything to suggest a refusal to admit even though sound traveled easily through the small apartment. . . .

We granted certiorari to consider how to go about applying the standard of reasonableness to the length of time police with a warrant must wait before entering without permission after knocking and announcing their intent in a felony case. We now reverse. . . .

The Fourth Amendment says nothing specific about formalities in exercising a warrant's authorization, speaking to the manner of searching as well as to the legitimacy of searching at all simply in terms of the right to be "secure . . . against unreasonable searches and seizures." Although the notion of reasonable execution must therefore be fleshed out, we have done that case by case, largely avoiding categories and protocols for searches. . . .

In Wilson v. Arkansas, 514 U.S. 927 (1995), we held that the common law knock-and-announce principle is one focus of the reasonableness enquiry; and we subsequently decided that although the standard generally requires the police to announce their intent to search before entering closed premises, the obligation gives way when officers "have a reasonable suspicion that knocking and announcing their presence, under the particular circumstances, would be dangerous or futile, or . . . would inhibit the effective investigation of the crime by, for example, allowing the destruction of evidence," Richards v. Wisconsin, 520 U.S. 385, 394 (1997). . . .

Since most people keep their doors locked, entering without knocking will normally do some damage, a circumstance too common to require a heightened justification when a reasonable suspicion of exigency already justifies an unwarned entry. We have accordingly held that police in exigent circumstances may damage premises so far as necessary for a no-knock entrance without demonstrating the suspected risk in any more detail than the law demands for an unannounced intrusion simply by lifting the latch. United States v. Ramirez, 523 U.S. 65, 70-71 (1998). Either way, it is enough that the officers had a reasonable suspicion of exigent circumstances.

. . . Although the police concededly arrived at Banks's door without reasonable suspicion of facts justifying a no-knock entry, they argue that announcing their presence started the clock running toward the moment of apprehension that Banks would flush away the easily disposable cocaine, prompted by knowing the police would soon be coming in. . . .

Banks does not, of course, deny that exigency may develop in the period beginning when officers with a warrant knock to be admitted, and the issue comes down to whether it was reasonable to suspect imminent loss of evidence after the 15 to 20 seconds the officers waited prior to forcing their way. Though . . . this call is a close one, we think that after 15 or 20 seconds without a response, police could fairly suspect that cocaine would be gone if they were reticent any longer. . . .

[E]ach of [Banks's] reasons for saying that 15 to 20 seconds was too brief rests on a mistake about the relevant enquiry: the fact that he was actually in the shower and did not hear the officers is not to the point, and the same is true of the claim that it might have taken him longer than 20 seconds if he had heard the knock and headed straight for the door. As for the shower, it is enough to say that the facts known to the police are what count in judging reasonable waiting time, and there is no indication that the police knew that Banks was in the shower. . . .

And the argument that 15 to 20 seconds was too short for Banks to have come to the door ignores the very risk that justified prompt entry. True, if the officers were to justify their timing here by claiming that Banks's failure to admit them fairly suggested a refusal to let them in, Banks could at least argue that no such suspicion can arise until an occupant has had time to get to the door, a time that will vary with the size of the establishment, perhaps five seconds to open a motel room door, or several minutes to move through a townhouse. In this case, however, the police claim exigent need to enter, and the crucial fact in examining their actions is not time to reach the door but the particular exigency claimed. On the record here, what matters is the opportunity to get rid of cocaine, which a prudent dealer will keep near a commode or kitchen sink. . . . That is, when circumstances are exigent because a pusher may be near the point of putting his drugs beyond reach, it is imminent disposal, not travel time to the entrance, that governs when the police may reasonably enter; since the bathroom and kitchen are usually in the interior of a dwelling, not the front hall, there is no reason generally to peg the travel time to the location of the door, and no reliable basis for giving the proprietor of a mansion a longer wait than the resident of a bungalow, or an apartment like Banks's. And 15 to 20 seconds does not seem an unrealistic guess about the time someone would need to get in a position to rid his quarters of cocaine. . . .

Our emphasis on totality analysis necessarily rejects positions taken on each side of this case. *Ramirez*, for example, cannot be read with the breadth the Government espouses, as "reflect[ing] a general principle that the need to damage property in order to effectuate an entry to execute a search warrant should not be part of the analysis of whether the entry itself was reasonable." . . . One point in making an officer knock and announce . . . is to give a person inside the chance to save his door. That is why, in the case with no reason to suspect an immediate risk of frustration or futility in waiting at all, the reasonable wait time may well be longer when police make a forced entry, since they ought to be more certain the occupant has had time to answer the door. . . . Police seeking a stolen piano may be able to spend more time to make sure they really need the battering ram.

On the other side, we disapprove of the Court of Appeals's four-part scheme for vetting knock-and-announce entries. To begin with, the demand for enhanced evidence of exigency before a door can reasonably be damaged by a warranted no-knock intrusion was already bad law before the Court of Appeals decided this case. In *Ramirez* (a case from the Ninth Circuit), we rejected an attempt to subdivide felony cases by accepting "mild exigency" for entry without property damage, but requiring "more specific inferences of exigency" before damage would be reasonable. The Court of Appeals did not cite *Ramirez*.

. . . Here . . . the Court of Appeals's overlay of a categorical scheme on the general reasonableness analysis threatens to distort the "totality of the circumstances" principle, by replacing a stress on revealing facts with resort to pigeonholes. Attention to cocaine rocks and pianos tells a lot about the chances of their respective disposal and its bearing on reasonable time. Instructions couched in terms like "significant amount of time," and "an even more substantial amount of time," tell very little.

. . . Absent exigency, the police must knock and receive an actual refusal or wait out the time necessary to infer one. But in a case like this, where the officers knocked and announced their presence, and forcibly entered after a reasonable suspicion of exigency had ripened, their entry satisfied . . . the Fourth Amendment, even without refusal of admittance.

The judgment of the Court of Appeals is reversed.

So ordered.

NOTES AND QUESTIONS

1. In a portion of the opinion not excerpted here, the *Banks* Court justifies its preference for case-by-case articulation of the notion of reasonable execution (not to mention its evident hostility to the Ninth Circuit's preference for developing "categories and protocols for searches"). According to the Court:

> We have treated reasonableness as a function of the facts of cases so various that no template is likely to produce sounder results than examining the totality of circumstances in a given case; it is too hard to invent categories without giving short shrift to details that turn out to be important in a given instance, and without inflating marginal ones.

Is this persuasive? Or does the refusal to articulate knock-and-announce "rules" — not to mention rules for other aspects of conducting a search — amount to nothing more than unjustified deference to the police?

2. Cases like *Banks* stand for the proposition that when the Supreme Court defines the standard as "reasonableness under all the circumstances," it wants no more definition than that. *Banks* is thus singing the same tune as Illinois v. Gates, 462 U.S. 213 (1983), where the Court replaced the elaborate rule structure of Spinelli v. United States, 393 U.S. 410 (1969), with a "fair probability" test — to be judged (naturally) based on all the circumstances.

In *Banks* as in *Gates*, the difference between the determinate rule structure and the vague standard may not, in the end, prove to be large. As they make their reasonableness determinations, courts are free to take account of the same factors the Ninth Circuit took account of. The chief difference is likely to be *who* takes account of those factors. If Fourth Amendment law conformed to the Ninth Circuit's wishes, appellate courts would exercise a great deal of power in knock-and-announce cases — just as they exercised a great deal of power in probable cause cases when *Spinelli* defined the law of probable cause. Under *Banks*, trial courts are likely to have a lot of leeway in determining whether the officers behaved reasonably in breaking down defendants' doors. Just as trial courts have a good deal of leeway in defining "probable cause" under *Gates*.

3. Compare *Banks* to *Richards*. In *Richards*, the Court rejected a per se rule allowing no-knock entries in felony drug cases. The officers in *Banks* had no reasonable suspicion of facts justifying a no-knock entry at the time they arrived on the scene. But 15 seconds after knocking (even if it takes longer than that to get to the door) they are permitted to break in, due principally to the ease with which narcotics may be disposed of. Are these results — both reached unanimously — consistent?

4. The Court's knock-and-announce cases recognize that law enforcement interests might establish the reasonableness of an unannounced entry. What about an unannounced and covert entry in which notice of the search is delayed? Conventional search warrants are executed "overtly." A resident may be present during the search; in any event, notice of the search is left behind. Courts have recognized circumstances, however, in which "sneak-and-peek" warrants may be upheld. See, e.g., United States v. Villegas, 899 F.2d 1324, 1337 (2d Cir. 1990) (permitting delayed notice upon "good reason").

The USA PATRIOT Act (United and Strengthening America by Providing Appropriate Tools Required to Intercept and Obstruct Terrorism Act) of 2001, Pub. L. No. 107-56, 115 Stat. 272, enacted in the wake of September 11 for the stated purposed of enabling government officials to protect against similar attacks, included a uniform statutory standard for the issuance of delayed notice search warrants, or so-called "sneak-and-peek" warrants, in *all* federal cases — not just those involving terrorism. 18 U.S.C. §3103a(b) provides that as to search warrants

> to search for or seize any property or material that constitutes evidence of a criminal offense in violation of the laws of the United States, any notice required, or that may be required, to be given may be delayed if (1) the court finds reasonable cause to believe that providing immediate notification of the execution of the warrant may have an adverse result;[6] (2) the warrant prohibits the seizure of any tangible property . . . except where the court finds reasonable necessity for the seizure; and (3) the warrant provides for the giving of such notice within a reasonable period of its execution, which period may thereafter be extended by the court for good cause shown.

In a report to Congress regarding the USA PATRIOT Act's implementation, the Justice Department indicated that as of April 1, 2003, it had requested and received a judicial order delaying notice of the execution of a warrant on 47 occasions. Courts have authorized delays as short as one day and as long as 90 days and have also permitted delays of unspecified duration, until indictments have been unsealed. (Note that the Government may also seek extensions of the period of delayed notice.) As of April 1, 2003, the Justice Department had received judicial authorization for a seizure in connection with a delayed notification warrant on 14 occasions. Courts found that seizures were necessary in these "sneak and peek" cases: "(1) to prevent jeopardizing the investigation by protecting the safety of confidential informants; (2) to prevent compromising an investigation by preventing the removal or destruction of evidence; and/or (3) to seize controlled substances that are inherently dangerous to the community."[7] Do so-called "sneak-and-peek" warrants raise special concerns beyond those associated with the normal warrant procedure? Why or why not?

5. Sometimes the execution of a warrant raises *First* Amendment concerns. Zurcher v. Stanford Daily, 436 U.S. 547 (1978), raised the question whether First Amendment concerns limit the use of warrants to search newspaper offices.

---

6. An adverse result is defined to include endangering the life or physical safety of an individual; flight from prosecution; evidence tampering; witness intimidation; or otherwise seriously jeopardizing an investigation or unduly delaying a trial. — EDS.

7. Sensenbrenner/Conyers Release Justice Department Oversight Answers Regarding USA PATRIOT Act and War on Terrorism, p. 10 (May 20, 2003).

Officers had probable cause to believe that a photographer with the *Stanford Daily* had taken photographs of demonstrators who had attacked police. The officers sought and received a warrant to search the student newspaper's office, and the search was carried out. The Court refused to impose special limits on the use of warrants in this context, noting that "if the requirements of specificity and reasonableness are properly applied, policed, and observed," no occasion would arise for officers "to rummage at large in newspaper files or to intrude into or to deter normal editorial and publication decisions." Id. at 566. The next case addresses the propriety of "media ride-alongs" in which reporters accompany police as they perform their duties and, as we will see, sometimes gain access to private places.

WILSON v. LAYNE

Certiorari to the United States Court of Appeals for the Fourth Circuit
526 U.S. 603 (1999)

CHIEF JUSTICE REHNQUIST delivered the opinion of the Court.

While executing an arrest warrant in a private home, police officers invited representatives of the media to accompany them. We hold that such a "media ride-along" does violate the Fourth Amendment. . . .

In early 1992, the Attorney General of the United States approved "Operation Gunsmoke," a special national fugitive apprehension program in which United States Marshals worked with state and local police to apprehend dangerous criminals. The "Operation Gunsmoke" policy statement explained that the operation was to concentrate on "armed individuals wanted on federal and/or state and local warrants for serious drug and other violent felonies." This effective program ultimately resulted in over 3,000 arrests in 40 metropolitan areas.

One of the dangerous fugitives identified as a target of "Operation Gunsmoke" was Dominic Wilson, the son of petitioners Charles and Geraldine Wilson. Dominic Wilson had violated his probation on previous felony charges of robbery, theft, and assault with intent to rob, and the police computer listed "caution indicators" that he was likely to be armed, to resist arrest, and to "assaul[t] police." The computer also listed his address as 909 North StoneStreet Avenue in Rockville, Maryland. Unknown to the police, this was actually the home of petitioners, Dominic Wilson's parents. Thus, in April 1992, the Circuit Court for Montgomery County issued three arrest warrants for Dominic Wilson, one for each of his probation violations. The warrants were each addressed to "any duly authorized peace officer," and commanded such officers to arrest him and bring him "immediately" before the Circuit Court to answer an indictment as to his probation violation. The warrants made no mention of media presence or assistance.

In the early morning hours of April 16, 1992, a Gunsmoke team of Deputy United States Marshals and Montgomery County Police officers assembled to execute the Dominic Wilson warrants. The team was accompanied by a reporter and a photographer from the Washington Post, who had been invited by the Marshals to accompany them on their mission as part of a Marshals Service ride-along policy.

At around 6:45 a.m., the officers, with media representatives in tow, entered the dwelling at 909 North StoneStreet Avenue in the Lincoln Park neighborhood of Rockville. Petitioners Charles and Geraldine Wilson were still in bed when they heard the officers enter the home. Petitioner Charles Wilson, dressed only in a pair of briefs, ran into the living room to investigate. Discovering at least five men in street clothes with guns in his living room, he angrily demanded that they state their business, and repeatedly cursed the officers. Believing him to be an angry Dominic Wilson, the officers quickly subdued him on the floor. Geraldine Wilson next entered the living room to investigate, wearing only a nightgown. She observed her husband being restrained by the armed officers.

When their protective sweep was completed, the officers learned that Dominic Wilson was not in the house, and they departed. During the time that the officers were in the home, the Washington Post photographer took numerous pictures. The print reporter was also apparently in the living room observing the confrontation between the police and Charles Wilson. At no time, however, were the reporters involved in the execution of the arrest warrant. The Washington Post never published its photographs of the incident.

Petitioners sued the law enforcement officials in their personal capacities for money damages. . . . They contended that the officers' actions in bringing members of the media to observe and record the attempted execution of the arrest warrant violated their Fourth Amendment rights. The District Court denied respondents' motion for summary judgment on the basis of qualified immunity.

On interlocutory appeal to the Court of Appeals, a divided panel reversed and held that respondents were entitled to qualified immunity. The case was twice reheard en banc, where a divided Court of Appeals again upheld the defense of qualified immunity. The Court of Appeals declined to decide whether the actions of the police violated the Fourth Amendment. . . .

Recognizing a split among the Circuits on this issue, we granted certiorari in this case . . . and now affirm the Court of Appeals, although by different reasoning.

. . . We now turn to the Fourth Amendment question.

In 1604, an English court made the now-famous observation that "the house of every one is to him as his castle and fortress, as well for his defence against injury and violence, as for his repose." *Semayne's Case*, 5 Co. Rep. 91a, 91b, 77 Eng. Rep. 194, 195 (K.B.). In his Commentaries on the Laws of England, William Blackstone noted that

> "the law of England has so particular and tender a regard to the immunity of a man's house, that it stiles it his castle, and will never suffer it to be violated with impunity: agreeing herein with the sentiments of an[c]ient Rome. . . . For this reason no doors can in general be broken open to execute any civil process; though, in criminal causes, the public safety supersedes the private." 4 Commentaries 223 (1765-1769).

The Fourth Amendment embodies this centuries-old principle of respect for the privacy of the home. . . .

Here, of course, the officers had . . . a warrant, and they were undoubtedly entitled to enter the Wilson home in order to execute the arrest warrant for Dominic Wilson. But it does not necessarily follow that they were entitled to bring a newspaper reporter and a photographer with them. In Horton v. California, 496 U.S. 128, 140 (1990), we held "[i]f the scope of the search exceeds that permitted by the terms of a validly issued warrant or the character of the relevant exception from the warrant requirement, the subsequent seizure is unconstitutional without more." While this does not mean that every police action while inside a home must be explicitly authorized by the text of the warrant, see Michigan v. Summers, 452 U.S. 692, 705 (1981) (Fourth Amendment allows temporary detainer of homeowner while police search the home pursuant to warrant), the Fourth Amendment does require that police actions in execution of a warrant be related to the objectives of the authorized intrusion.

Certainly the presence of reporters inside the home was not related to the objectives of the authorized intrusion. Respondents concede that the reporters did not engage in the execution of the warrant, and did not assist the police in their task. The reporters therefore were not present for any reason related to the justification for police entry into the home — the apprehension of Dominic Wilson.

This is not a case in which the presence of the third parties directly aided in the execution of the warrant. Where the police enter a home under the authority of a warrant to search for stolen property, the presence of third parties for the purpose of identifying the stolen property has long been approved by this Court and our common-law tradition.

Respondents argue that the presence of the Washington Post reporters in the Wilsons' home nonetheless served a number of legitimate law enforcement purposes. They first assert that officers should be able to exercise reasonable discretion about when it would "further their law enforcement mission to permit members of the news media to accompany them in executing a warrant." But this claim ignores the importance of the right of residential privacy at the core of the Fourth Amendment. It may well be that media ride-alongs further the law enforcement objectives of the police in a general sense, but that is not the same as furthering the purposes of the search. Were such generalized "law enforcement objectives" themselves sufficient to trump the Fourth Amendment, the protections guaranteed by that Amendment's text would be significantly watered down.

Respondents next argue that the presence of third parties could serve the law enforcement purpose of publicizing the government's efforts to combat crime, and facilitate accurate reporting on law enforcement activities. There is certainly language in our opinions interpreting the First Amendment which points to the importance of "the press" in informing the general public about the administration of criminal justice. . . . No one could gainsay the truth of these observations, or the importance of the First Amendment in protecting press freedom from abridgment by the government. But the Fourth Amendment also protects a very important right, and in the present case it is in terms of that right that the media ride-alongs must be judged.

Surely the possibility of good public relations for the police is simply not enough, standing alone, to justify the ride-along intrusion into a private home. And even the need for accurate reporting on police issues in general bears no direct relation to the constitutional justification for the police intrusion into a home in order to execute a felony arrest warrant.

Finally, respondents argue that the presence of third parties could serve in some situations to minimize police abuses and protect suspects, and also to protect the safety of the officers. While it might be reasonable for police officers to themselves videotape home entries as part of a "quality control" effort to ensure that the rights of homeowners are being respected, or even to preserve evidence, such a situation is significantly different from the media presence in this case. The Washington Post reporters in the Wilsons' home were working on a story for their own purposes. They were not present for the purpose of protecting the officers, much less the Wilsons. A private photographer was acting for private purposes, as evidenced in part by the fact that the newspaper and not the police retained the photographs. Thus, although the presence of third parties during the execution of a warrant may in some circumstances be constitutionally permissible, the presence of *these* third parties was not.

. . . We hold that it is a violation of the Fourth Amendment for police to bring members of the media or other third parties into a home during the execution of a warrant when the presence of the third parties in the home was not in aid of the execution of the warrant.[8] . . .

[Justice Stevens' opinion concurring in part and dissenting in part is omitted.]

NOTES AND QUESTIONS

1. You may recall that when defining "searches," the Supreme Court has usually taken an all-or-nothing approach to privacy protection — so that, for example, the selective disclosure of one's bank records to the bank or one's garbage to the disposal company is enough to defeat the reasonableness of any privacy expectation that one might claim with regard to these items. See supra, at 374-379. In Wilson v. Layne, by contrast, we see that once the Fourth Amendment is triggered (and there is no doubt that the entry into the Wilsons' home constituted a "search"), even authorized intrusions onto Fourth Amendment privacy do not make that privacy go away: the fact that a search of the home was constitutional does not mean that *this* search was *carried out* constitutionally. Police actions in executing a warrant must be "related to the objectives of the authorized intrusion" — and opening up the Wilson home for media scrutiny fell outside the objectives of the search. Whatever else that approach is, it isn't all-or-nothing. Does this difference between *Wilson* and the "search" cases make sense?

2. Is *Wilson* uniquely about the home? Not according to a recent Second Circuit case that invoked the reasoning in *Wilson* to impose Fourth Amendment limits on the common "perp walk." The perp walk, according to the Second Circuit, "is a widespread police practice in New York City in which the suspected perpetrator of a crime, after being arrested, is 'walked' in front of the press so that he can be photographed or filmed." In Lauro v. Charles, 219 F.3d 202, 203 (2d Cir. 2000), in an opinion by Judge Calabresi, the Second Circuit held that "staged" perp walks, serving no law enforcement purpose, "exacerbate[] the seizure of the arrestee unreasonably and therefore violate[] the Fourth Amendment." In *Lauro*, the arrestee, already in the precinct, was walked outside the station house, placed in an unmarked police car, driven around the block, removed from the car, and then walked back into the station house so that a television crew from Fox 5

---

8. In a portion of the opinion not excerpted here, the Court went on to conclude that at the time of the media ride-along at issue, the officers' conduct did not violate "clearly established" Fourth Amendment law — so that the officers were entitled to qualified immunity and the Wilsons were not entitled to a monetary award. Justice Stevens dissented from this portion of the Court's opinion. The doctrine of qualified immunity is discussed infra at pages 729-737. — EDS.

News could film the walk. The *Lauro* Court determined that this staged walk implicated Lauro's protected privacy interest in not being "displayed to the world, against his will, in handcuffs, and in a posture connoting guilt." Id. at 212, n. 7. The panel took pains to note, however, that its holding did not reach cases "in which there is a legitimate law enforcement justification for transporting a subject. . . . Nor do we reach the question of whether, in those circumstances, it would be proper for the police to notify the media ahead of time that a suspect is to be transported."

3. A later Second Circuit panel limited *Lauro*'s impact, at least partly on the view that perp walks serve serious law enforcement purposes: "The image of the accused being led away to contend with the justice system powerfully communicates government efforts to thwart the criminal element, and it may deter others from attempting similar crimes." Caldarola v. County of Westchester, 343 F.3d 570, 572-573 (2d Cir. 2003). In *Caldarola*, investigators established cases against a number of corrections officers for receiving disability benefits on the basis of fraudulent job injury claims. The corrections officers were directed to report to headquarters, where they were formally placed under arrest and then videotaped as they were walked to cars in the parking lot for transportation to the police station. Investigators subsequently held a press conference to publicize the investigation; during the press conference, investigators played the videotape and distributed copies. (They also alerted the media that the arrestees were pending arraignment; camera crews were able to film the corrections officers as they ascended the steps of the courthouse.)

The *Caldarola* panel determined that the Fourth Amendment was implicated by the Government's acts of coordinating the arrests, videotaping the post-arrest walk, and disseminating the videotape; the Circuit Court determined, however, that these actions were reasonable and served legitimate law enforcement purposes such as informing the public and enhancing the transparency of the criminal justice system. The panel distinguished *Lauro* on the ground that the perp walk there was wholly staged; the coordinated nature of the arrests in *Caldarola*, the Court of Appeals concluded, did not defeat the law enforcement justification for transporting the arrestees. "Because there was a minimal expectation of privacy in the parking lot," the panel concluded, "and the conduct of the arresting officers did not unreasonably exceed the scope of what was necessary to effectuate the arrest and to otherwise serve legitimate government purposes," there was no Fourth Amendment injury. Do you agree? Should *Wilson* have required a more searching examination of the investigators' actions in *Caldarola*? Or was the Second Circuit right to conclude that the corrections officers' privacy expectations in the Department of Corrections parking lot were "minimal and not comparable to that of an individual in his home. . . . "? Id. at 577.

3. "Exceptions" to the Warrant "Requirement"

Katz v. United States, 389 U.S. 347, 357 (1967), describes the scope of the warrant requirement this way: "[S]earches conducted outside the judicial process, without prior approval by judge or magistrate, are per se unreasonable under the Fourth Amendment—subject only to a few specifically established and well-delineated exceptions." As this language suggests, when courts decide whether a warrant is or is not required, the issue usually is framed in terms of the bounds of one or another exception to the warrant requirement. Taken individually, these exceptions may seem narrow enough. Cumulatively, the exceptions may be the rule — and warrants the real exception.

a. Exigent Circumstances

MINCEY v. ARIZONA

Certiorari to the Supreme Court of Arizona
437 U.S. 385 (1978)

MR. JUSTICE STEWART delivered the opinion of the Court.

On the afternoon of October 28, 1974, undercover police officer Barry Headricks of the Metropolitan Area Narcotics Squad knocked on the door of an apartment in Tucson, Ariz., occupied by the petitioner, Rufus Mincey. Earlier in the day, Officer Headricks had allegedly arranged to purchase a quantity of heroin from Mincey and had left, ostensibly to obtain money. On his return he was accompanied by nine other plainclothes policemen and a deputy county attorney. The door was opened by John Hodgman, one of three acquaintances of Mincey who were in the living room of the apartment. Officer Headricks slipped inside and moved quickly into the bedroom. Hodgman attempted to slam the door in order to keep the other officers from entering, but was pushed back against the wall. As the police entered the apartment, a rapid volley of shots was heard from the bedroom. Officer Headricks emerged and collapsed on the floor. When other officers entered the bedroom they found Mincey lying on the floor, wounded and semiconscious. Officer Headricks died a few hours later in the hospital.

The petitioner was indicted for murder, assault, and three counts of narcotics offenses. He was tried at a single trial and convicted on all the charges. At his trial and on appeal, he contended that evidence used against him had been unlawfully seized from his apartment without a warrant. . . . The Arizona Supreme Court . . . held that the warrantless search of a homicide scene is permissible under the Fourth and Fourteenth Amendments. . . .

The first question presented is whether the search of Mincey's apartment was constitutionally permissible. After the shooting, the narcotics agents, thinking that other persons in the apartment might have been injured, looked about quickly for other victims. They found a young woman wounded in the bedroom closet and Mincey apparently unconscious in the bedroom, as well as Mincey's three acquaintances (one of whom had been wounded in the head) in the living room. Emergency assistance was requested, and some medical aid was administered to Officer Headricks. But the agents refrained from further investigation, pursuant to a Tucson Police Department directive that police officers should not investigate incidents in which they are involved. They neither searched further nor seized any evidence; they merely guarded the suspects and the premises.

Within 10 minutes, however, homicide detectives who had heard a radio report of the shooting arrived and took charge of the investigation. They supervised the removal of Officer Headricks and the suspects, trying to make sure that the scene was disturbed as little as possible, and then proceeded to gather evidence. Their search lasted four days, during which period the entire apartment was searched, photographed, and diagrammed. The officers opened drawers, closets, and cupboards, and inspected their contents; they emptied clothing pockets; they dug bullet fragments out of the walls and floors; they pulled up sections of the carpet and removed them for examination. Every item in the apartment was closely examined and inventoried, and 200 to 300 objects were seized. In short, Mincey's apartment was subjected to an exhaustive and intrusive search. No warrant was ever obtained.

The petitioner's pretrial motion to suppress the fruits of this search was denied after a hearing. Much of the evidence introduced against him at trial (including photographs and diagrams, bullets and shell casings, guns, narcotics, and narcotics paraphernalia) was the product of the four-day search of his apartment. On appeal, the Arizona Supreme Court reaffirmed previous decisions in which it had held that the warrantless search of the scene of a homicide is constitutionally permissible. . . .

We cannot agree. The Fourth Amendment proscribes all unreasonable searches and seizures, and it is a cardinal principle that "searches conducted outside the judicial process, without prior approval by judge or magistrate, are per se unreasonable under the Fourth Amendment—subject only to a few specifically established and well-delineated exceptions." Katz v. United States, 389 U.S. 347, 357. The Arizona Supreme Court did not hold that the search of the petitioner's apartment fell within any of the exceptions to the warrant requirement previously recognized by this Court, but rather that the search of a homicide scene should be recognized as an additional exception.

Several reasons are advanced by the State to meet its "burden . . . to show the existence of such an exceptional situation" as to justify creating a new exception to the warrant requirement. See Vale v. Louisiana, [399 U.S. 30,] 34. None of these reasons, however, persuades us of the validity of the generic exception delineated by the Arizona Supreme Court.

The first contention is that the search of the petitioner's apartment did not invade any constitutionally protected right of privacy. See Katz v. United States, supra. This argument appears to have two prongs. On the one hand, the State urges that by shooting Officer Headricks, Mincey forfeited any reasonable expectation of privacy in his apartment. . . . [T]his reasoning would impermissibly convict the suspect even before the evidence against him was gathered. On the other hand, the State contends that the police entry to arrest Mincey was so great an invasion of his privacy that the additional intrusion caused by the search was constitutionally irrelevant. But this claim is hardly tenable in light of the extensive nature of this search. . . .

The State's second argument in support of its categorical exception to the warrant requirement is that a possible homicide presents an emergency situation demanding immediate action. We do not question the right of the police to respond to emergency situations. Numerous state and federal cases have recognized that the Fourth Amendment does not bar police officers from making warrantless entries and searches when they reasonably believe that a person within is in need of immediate aid. Similarly, when the police come upon the scene of a homicide they may make a prompt warrantless search of the area to see if there are other victims or if a killer is still on the premises. . . .

But a warrantless search must be "strictly circumscribed by the exigencies which justify its initiation," Terry v. Ohio, [392 U.S. 1,] 25-26, and it simply cannot be contended that this search was justified by any emergency threatening life or limb.

All the persons in Mincey's apartment had been located before the investigating homicide officers arrived there and began their search. And a four-day search that included opening dresser drawers and ripping up carpets can hardly be rationalized in terms of the legitimate concerns that justify an emergency search.

Third, the State points to the vital public interest in the prompt investigation of the extremely serious crime of murder. No one can doubt the importance of this goal. But the public interest in the investigation of other serious crimes is comparable. If the warrantless search of a homicide scene is reasonable, why not the warrantless search of the scene of a rape, a robbery, or a burglary? "No consideration relevant to the Fourth Amendment suggests any point of rational limitation of such a doctrine." Chimel v. California, [395 U.S. 752, 766 (1969)].

Moreover, the mere fact that law enforcement may be made more efficient can never by itself justify disregard of the Fourth Amendment. The investigation of crime would always be simplified if warrants were unnecessary. But the Fourth Amendment reflects the view of those who wrote the Bill of Rights that the privacy of a person's home and property may not be totally sacrificed in the name of maximum simplicity in enforcement of the criminal law. For this reason, warrants are generally required to search a person's home or his person unless "the exigencies of the situation" make the needs of law enforcement so compelling that the warrantless search is objectively reasonable under the Fourth Amendment. McDonald v. United States, 335 U.S. 451, 456. See, e.g., Warden v. Hayden, 387 U.S. 294, 298-300 ("hot pursuit" of fleeing suspect); Schmerber v. California, 384 U.S. 757, 770-771 (imminent destruction of evidence).

Except for the fact that the offense under investigation was a homicide, there were no exigent circumstances in this case. . . . There was no indication that evidence would be lost, destroyed, or removed during the time required to obtain a search warrant. Indeed, the police guard at the apartment minimized that possibility. And there is no suggestion that a search warrant could not easily and conveniently have been obtained. We decline to hold that the seriousness of the offense under investigation itself creates exigent circumstances of the kind that under the Fourth Amendment justify a warrantless search. . . .

It may well be that the circumstances described by the Arizona Supreme Court would usually be constitutionally sufficient to warrant a search of substantial scope. But the Fourth Amendment requires that this judgment in each case be made in the first instance by a neutral magistrate. . . .

In sum, we hold that the "murder scene exception" created by the Arizona Supreme Court is inconsistent with the Fourth and Fourteenth Amendments—that the warrantless search of Mincey's apartment was not constitutionally permissible simply because a homicide had recently occurred there. . . .

[The concurring opinion of Justice Marshall, joined by Justice Brennan, and the opinion by Justice Rehnquist concurring in part and dissenting in part, are omitted.]

NOTES ON EXIGENT CIRCUMSTANCES

1. *Mincey* was recently reaffirmed in Flippo v. West Virginia, 528 U.S. 11 (1999) (per curiam). The facts in *Flippo* are as follows:

> One night in 1996, petitioner and his wife were vacationing at a cabin in a state park. After petitioner called 911 to report that they had been attacked, the police

arrived to find petitioner waiting outside the cabin, with injuries to his head and legs. After questioning him, an officer entered the building and found the body of petitioner's wife, with fatal head wounds. The officers closed off the area, took petitioner to the hospital, and searched the exterior and environs of the cabin for footprints or signs of forced entry. When a police photographer arrived at about 5:30 a.m., the officers reentered the building and proceeded to "process the crime scene." Brief in Opposition 5. For over 16 hours, they took photographs, collected evidence, and searched through the contents of the cabin. According to the trial court, "at the crime scene, the investigating officers found on a table in Cabin 13, among other things, a briefcase, which they, in the ordinary course of investigating a homicide, opened, wherein they found and seized various photographs and negatives."

The Court unanimously concluded that the contents of the briefcase should be suppressed.

What is accomplished by insisting that the officers in *Mincey* or *Flippo* get a warrant? There is not the slightest doubt that a warrant would have been issued; indeed, there is not the slightest doubt that a warrant to search the scene of a homicide would *always* be issued. Is requiring a warrant therefore a waste of time?

2. The basic idea of exigent circumstances is easy: Officers should not be required to get a warrant when they can't feasibly do so. That simple principle gives rise to at least four kinds of cases. *Mincey* and *Flippo* are one: In those cases, the officers were legally in the defendant's dwelling without a warrant — they had exigent circumstances enough to justify entry — but their warrantless searches lasted too long. *Mincey* and *Flippo* stand for the proposition that the warrantless search must end, roughly, when the exigency ends. The other three kinds of exigent circumstances claims arise more often than the issue in *Mincey* and *Flippo*; the next three notes deal with each in turn.

3. *Fleeing suspects*. The facts in Warden v. Hayden, 387 U.S. 294 (1967), illustrate this category:

> About 8 a.m. on March 17, 1962, an armed robber entered the business premises of the Diamond Cab Company in Baltimore, Maryland. He took some $363 and ran. Two cab drivers in the vicinity, attracted by shouts of "Holdup," followed the man to 2111 Cocoa Lane. One driver notified the company dispatcher by radio that the man was a Negro about 5' 8" tall, wearing a light cap and dark jacket, and that he had entered the house on Cocoa Lane. The dispatcher relayed the information to police who were proceeding to the scene of the robbery. Within minutes, police arrived at the house in a number of patrol cars.

Id. at 297. The officers proceeded to search the house, finding the man, two guns, and the jacket and cap the man had been wearing. The Court concluded that this was a valid warrantless search:

> The Fourth Amendment does not require police officers to delay in the course of an investigation if to do so would gravely endanger their lives or the lives of others. Speed here was essential, and only a thorough search of the house for persons and weapons could have insured that Hayden was the only man present and that the police had control of all weapons which could be used against them or to effect an escape.

Id. at 298-299.

4. *Destruction of evidence.* Perhaps the most common kind of exigent circumstance is the fear that, if officers do not search immediately, evidence will be destroyed. In Mendez v. Colorado, 986 P.2d 285 (Colo. 1999), two police officers, while on an unrelated call, smelled "a strong odor of burning marijuana" coming from a hotel room. The officers summoned the hotel manager, instructed the manager to open the door with a master key, and entered. Once inside, they discovered the defendant in the process of flushing marijuana down the toilet; they also discovered small amounts of both marijuana and cocaine. The Colorado Supreme Court held that the smell of marijuana smoke justified dispensing with a warrant: "This odor indicated that evidence of a crime, that is, possession of marijuana, was in the process of being burned and thereby destroyed. As such, we conclude that there was a very real and substantial likelihood that contraband would continue to be destroyed before a warrant could be obtained to search the motel room." Justice Hobbs dissented, noting that possession of small amounts of marijuana was a "non-jailable offense" in Colorado, punishable by no more than a $100 fine; under those circumstances, the threat of destruction of evidence was not enough to justify a warrantless entry.

The officers in United States v. Dickerson, 195 F.3d 1183 (10th Cir. 1999), had a "knock-and-announce" warrant to search the defendant's house for evidence of crack distribution; before they could carry out that warrant they encountered the defendant outside the house and, after a noisy struggle with the defendant and several of his friends, arrested him. The officers then entered the house without any announcement, meaning that the entry was not authorized by the warrant. The government argued exigent circumstances: The noise from the arrest could be heard inside, and there might be other people in the house (there were, as it turned out) destroying evidence if the officers delayed entering. The court accepted the government's argument and found the entry legal.

In light of *Mendez* and *Dickerson*, consider the "knock and talk" procedure followed by police in Milwaukee:

> . . . [I]n a "knock and talk," the police approach a house or apartment in which they suspect drug dealing is occurring. They listen outside the door for a brief period of time, and then they knock on the door and attempt to persuade whoever answers to give them permission to enter. If consent is forthcoming, they enter and interview the occupants of the place; if it is not, they try to see from their vantage point at the door whether drug paraphernalia or contraband is in plain view. If it is, then they make a warrantless entry.

United States v. Johnson, 170 F.3d 908 (7th Cir. 1999). Is the warrantless entry justified? Not in *Johnson*. There, the police went to an apartment door and listened for a brief time; just when the officers were about to knock on the door, the defendant opened it. They asked consent to enter the apartment, and the defendant refused. One of the officers claimed he saw a woman throw down a crack pipe inside the apartment, but that testimony was disbelieved by the trial court. The officers then frisked the defendant (still standing in the doorway) and entered the apartment, where they found two guns and small quantities of cocaine. The Seventh Circuit Court of Appeals found, over a spirited dissent by Judge Easterbrook, that the frisk and entry were illegal — though the court went out of its way to state: "We do not hold today that the 'knock and talk' technique is automatically unconstitutional."

When would a "knock and talk" entry be permissible? If the officer's testimony about the crack pipe in *Johnson* were believable, would *that* entry be permissible?

5. *"Community caretaking"*[9] *and the Simpson search*. Sometimes police need to enter a home or building quickly, with no time to obtain a warrant, for reasons that have nothing to do with catching criminals or finding evidence:

> Police routinely receive calls from friends, neighbors, relatives, and employers expressing concern about people who have not been heard from over a period of time. These people are often elderly and the callers are often fearful that the missing person may be ill or even dead. Police must respond to such calls, but absent unusual circumstances, they in no way conceive of them as implicating law enforcement objectives. Patrol officers typically visit the person's residence (often after some delay) and they knock on the door. All is well if the person answers. But what if there is no response?

Debra Livingston, Police, Community Caretaking, and the Fourth Amendment, 1998 U. Chi. Legal F. 261, 278. Suppose, in such a case, the police enter, find no one inside, but discover a large quantity of drugs. Are the drugs admissible? The same issue arises in cases in which the police seek to protect not personal safety but property: Neighbors report a possible burglary; the police show up, find a window or door open but no one home; they enter, and find evidence of crime by the homeowners.

As Livingston's article recounts, courts have been fairly quick to find exigent circumstances in such cases. But as the scenarios just described suggest, sometimes the issue is not just exigency but probable cause as well. Officers entering the house of an elderly couple at the instigation of concerned neighbors may have no reason to believe they will uncover evidence of crime inside. Officers checking out the scene of a burglary may have some suspicion that the burglar is still inside, but that suspicion may fall far short of probable cause. Should the officers be permitted to enter — and, if they find anything, to use it — anyway? Livingston says yes:

> Community caretaking intrusions are unlike searches and seizures for the purpose of locating evidence or suspects in several important ways. First, the absence of a law enforcement motive often mitigates the harms associated with intrusions on privacy for the purpose of criminal investigation. Thus, when police enter the home of an elderly woman to ensure that she is not injured within, their "search" does not "damage reputation or manifest official suspicion." Nor is it as intrusive as the normal search for evidence on such premises — a search which criminal investigators will pursue throughout the home until the evidence is found or determined not to be present.
>
> Similarly, the potential for overzealousness is often reduced when police serve community caretaking, as opposed to law enforcement ends. Motivated by the desire to make felony arrests, police may be tempted to search a warehouse based on mere suspicion that evidence will be found within. This temptation is less likely to be present, however, when police answer complaints about noxious odors or barking dogs. . . .

Id. at 273-274. Are you persuaded?

---

9. This phrase is taken from Cady v. Dombrowski, 413 U.S. 433, 441 (1973).

One possible concern in "community caretaking" cases is that police might pretend to be seeking to help victims in order to establish exigency or even exempt themselves from the probable cause requirement. Consider the facts underlying the most famous suppression hearing of the past decade (millennium?), the hearing on O.J. Simpson's motion to suppress the bloody glove found in a search of the grounds of his residence — the glove matched one found at the scene of the murders — several hours after the bodies of Nicole Brown Simpson and Ronald Goldman had been found:

> Detectives Philip Vannatter and Mark Fuhrman testified that they and two other detectives traveled to Mr. Simpson's home on Rockingham Avenue to inform him of the murder so he could make arrangements for his children.
>
> The detectives testified that after getting no response to the buzzer at the gate, and following their discovery of a small spot of blood on Mr. Simpson's Bronco, which was on the street, they jumped the wall because they feared for Mr. Simpson's safety. It was after this adventure in low-rent rappelling . . . that Detective Fuhrman says he found the famous bloody glove.

Scott Turow, Policing the Police: The DA's Job, in Postmortem: The O.J. Simpson Case 189 (Jeffrey Abramson ed. 1996). This search was conducted without a warrant. The police claimed exigency, based on their concern that Simpson himself might have been a victim. As Vannatter put it, "I was concerned that something had occurred there, whether I had a second murder scene, whether I had someone injured, whether I had someone that was stalking Mr. Simpson and his wife, whatever." Jeffrey Toobin, The Run of His Life: The People v. O.J. Simpson 141 (1996) (quoting Vannatter's testimony). As with most "community caretaking" cases, this exigency argument prevailed.

According to Scott Turow, that was a mistake:

> . . . [T]he detectives' explanation as to why they were at the house is hard to believe. At the time of the [hearing on the suppression motion], before the DNA results had come in, the bloody glove, which matched one found at the crime scene, was the foremost evidence against Mr. Simpson. So the police were under tremendous pressure to explain their actions in a way that would legally excuse them for violating Mr. Simpson's rights and allow the glove to be introduced as evidence.
>
> Thus the dubious claim about fearing for Mr. Simpson's safety. Four police detectives were not needed to carry a message about Nicole Simpson's death. These officers undoubtedly knew what Justice Department statistics indicate: that half of the women murdered in the United States are killed by their husbands or boyfriends. Simple probabilities made Mr. Simpson a suspect.
>
> Also, Mark Fuhrman had been called to the Simpson residence years earlier when Mr. Simpson was abusing his wife. Thus Mr. Simpson was more than the usual suspect husband; he had a known propensity to do violence to his wife. Of course, he is also one of the most exceptional physical talents of his generation, a member of the relatively small class of human beings capable of murdering two persons at once and of wielding a knife with sufficient power to virtually decapitate someone.
>
> If veteran police detectives did not arrive at the gate of Mr. Simpson's home thinking he might have committed these murders, then they should have been fired.

Turow, supra, at 189-190. Notice that if the officers were seeking not to protect Simpson but to gather evidence against him, it would have been hard to claim exigency: Several hours had passed since the bodies had been discovered—clearly enough time to have obtained a warrant. If, on the other hand, the officers were indeed worried about Simpson's safety, that delay was not a problem—they could easily enough say that their concern was triggered by finding the blood spot on Simpson's Bronco.

Simpson's case suggests that community caretaking arguments may tend to involve hard credibility judgments, with cases turning on police officers' motive—were they trying to protect the homeowner whose house they entered, or were they trying to build a case against him? Fourth Amendment law is generally structured so as to make police motive irrelevant, precisely in order to avoid such credibility judgments. Should the law take that posture in cases like Simpson's? A court could conclude, after all, that Vannatter's and Fuhrman's subjective beliefs do not matter, that the question is whether, based on the objective circumstances at the time of the search, Simpson seemed to be in danger. Would that help in resolving cases of this sort?

WELSH v. WISCONSIN

Certiorari to the Supreme Court of Wisconsin
466 U.S. 740 (1984)

MR. JUSTICE BRENNAN delivered the opinion of the Court.

Shortly before 9 o'clock on the rainy night of April 24, 1978, a lone witness, Randy Jablonic, observed a car being driven erratically. After changing speeds and veering from side to side, the car eventually swerved off the road and came to a stop in an open field. No damage to any person or property occurred. Concerned about the driver and fearing that the car would get back on the highway, Jablonic drove his truck up behind the car so as to block it from returning to the road. Another passerby also stopped at the scene, and Jablonic asked her to call the police. Before the police arrived, however, the driver of the car emerged from his vehicle, approached Jablonic's truck, and asked Jablonic for a ride home. Jablonic instead suggested that they wait for assistance in removing or repairing the car. Ignoring Jablonic's suggestion, the driver walked away from the scene.

A few minutes later, the police arrived and questioned Jablonic. He told one officer what he had seen, specifically noting that the driver was either very inebriated or very sick. The officer checked the motor vehicle registration of the abandoned car and learned that it was registered to the petitioner, Edward G. Welsh. In addition, the officer noted that the petitioner's residence was a short distance from the scene, and therefore easily within walking distance.

Without securing any type of warrant, the police proceeded to the petitioner's home, arriving about 9 p.m. When the petitioner's stepdaughter answered the door, the police gained entry into the house.[1] Proceeding upstairs to the petitioner's bedroom, they found him lying naked in bed. At this point, the petitioner was placed under arrest for driving or operating a motor vehicle while under the influence of an intoxicant. . . .

---

1. The state trial court never decided whether there was consent to the entry because it deemed decision of that issue unnecessary in light of its finding that exigent circumstances justified the warrantless arrest. . . . For purposes of this decision, . . . we assume that there was no valid consent to enter the petitioner's home.

It is axiomatic that the "physical entry of the home is the chief evil against which the wording of the Fourth Amendment is directed." And a principal protection against unnecessary intrusions into private dwellings is the warrant requirement imposed by the Fourth Amendment on agents of the government who seek to enter the home for purposes of search or arrest. It is not surprising, therefore, that the Court has recognized, as "a 'basic principle of Fourth Amendment law[,]' that searches and seizures inside a home without a warrant are presumptively unreasonable." Payton v. New York, 445 U.S. [573,] 586 [(1980)] ("a search or seizure carried out on a suspect's premises without a warrant is per se unreasonable, unless the police can show . . . the presence of 'exigent circumstances'").

Consistently with these long-recognized principles, the Court decided in Payton v. New York, supra, that warrantless felony arrests in the home are prohibited by the Fourth Amendment, absent probable cause and exigent circumstances. 445 U.S., at 583-590. At the same time, the Court declined to consider the scope of any exception for exigent circumstances that might justify warrantless home arrests, id., at 583, thereby leaving to the lower courts the initial application of the exigent-circumstances exception. Prior decisions of this Court, however, have emphasized that exceptions to the warrant requirement are "few in number and carefully delineated," and that the police bear a heavy burden when attempting to demonstrate an urgent need that might justify warrantless searches or arrests. . . .

Our hesitation in finding exigent circumstances, especially when warrantless arrests in the home are at issue, is particularly appropriate when the underlying offense for which there is probable cause to arrest is relatively minor. Before agents of the government may invade the sanctity of the home, the burden is on the government to demonstrate exigent circumstances that overcome the presumption of unreasonableness that attaches to all warrantless home entries. See Payton v. New York, supra, 445 U.S., at 586. When the government's interest is only to arrest for a minor offense, that presumption of unreasonableness is difficult to rebut, and the government usually should be allowed to make such arrests only with a warrant issued upon probable cause by a neutral and detached magistrate. . . .

Consistently with this approach, the lower courts have looked to the nature of the underlying offense as an important factor to be considered in the exigent-circumstances calculus. . . .

We . . . conclude that the common-sense approach utilized by most lower courts is required by the Fourth Amendment prohibition on "unreasonable searches and seizures," and hold that an important factor to be considered when determining whether any exigency exists is the gravity of the underlying offense for which the arrest is being made. Moreover, although no exigency is created simply because there is probable cause to believe that a serious crime has been committed, application of the exigent-circumstances exception in the context of a home entry should rarely be sanctioned when there is probable cause to believe that only a minor offense, such as the kind at issue in this case, has been committed.

Application of this principle to the facts of the present case is relatively straightforward. The petitioner was arrested in the privacy of his own bedroom for a noncriminal, traffic offense. The State attempts to justify the arrest by relying on the hot-pursuit doctrine, on the threat to public safety, and on the need to preserve evidence of the petitioner's blood-alcohol level. On the facts of this case, however, the claim of hot pursuit is unconvincing because there was no immediate or continuous pursuit of the petitioner from the scene of a crime. Moreover, because the petitioner had already arrived home, and had abandoned his car at the scene of the accident, there was little remaining threat to the public safety. Hence, the only potential emergency claimed by the State was the need to ascertain the petitioner's blood-alcohol level.

Even assuming, however, that the underlying facts would support a finding of this exigent circumstance, mere similarity to other cases involving the imminent destruction of evidence is not sufficient. The State of Wisconsin has chosen to classify the first offense for driving while intoxicated as a noncriminal, civil forfeiture offense for which no imprisonment is possible. This is the best indication of the State's interest in precipitating an arrest, and is one that can be easily identified both by the courts and by officers faced with a decision to arrest. Given this expression of the State's interest, a warrantless home arrest cannot be upheld simply because evidence of the petitioner's blood-alcohol level might have dissipated while the police obtained a warrant. To allow a warrantless home entry on these facts would be to approve unreasonable police behavior that the principles of the Fourth Amendment will not sanction.

The Supreme Court of Wisconsin let stand a warrantless, nighttime entry into the petitioner's home to arrest him for a civil traffic offense. Such an arrest, however, is clearly prohibited by the special protection afforded the individual in his home by the Fourth Amendment. The petitioner's arrest was therefore invalid, the judgment of the Supreme Court of Wisconsin is vacated, and the case is remanded for further proceedings not inconsistent with this opinion. . . .

THE CHIEF JUSTICE would dismiss the writ as having been improvidently granted and defer resolution of the question presented to a more appropriate case.

[Justice Blackmun's concurring opinion is omitted.]

JUSTICE WHITE, with whom JUSTICE REHNQUIST joins, dissenting. . . .

A test under which the existence of exigent circumstances turns on the perceived gravity of the crime would significantly hamper law enforcement and burden courts with pointless litigation concerning the nature and gradation of various crimes. . . . The decision to arrest without a warrant typically is made in the field under less-than-optimal circumstances; officers have neither the time nor the competence to determine whether a particular offense . . . is serious enough to justify a warrantless home entry to prevent the imminent destruction or removal of evidence. . . .

Even if the Court were correct in concluding that the gravity of the offense is an important factor to consider in determining whether a warrantless in-home arrest is justified by exigent circumstances, it has erred in assessing the seriousness of the civil-forfeiture offense for which the officers thought they were arresting Welsh. As the Court observes, the statutory scheme in force at the time of Welsh's arrest provided that the first offense for driving under the influence of alcohol involved no potential incarceration. Nevertheless, this Court has long recognized the compelling state interest in highway safety, the Supreme Court of Wisconsin identified a number of factors suggesting a substantial and growing governmental interest in apprehending and convicting intoxicated drivers and in deterring alcohol-related offenses, and recent actions of the Wisconsin Legislature evince its "belief that significant benefits, in the reduction of the costs attributable to drunk driving, may be achieved by the increased apprehension and conviction of even first time . . . offenders." Note, 1983 Wis. L. Rev. 1023, 1053. . . .

In short, the fact that Wisconsin has chosen to punish the first offense for driving under the influence with a fine rather than a prison term does not demand the conclusion that the State's interest in punishing first offenders is insufficiently substantial to justify warrantless in-home arrests under exigent circumstances. As the Supreme Court of Wisconsin observed, "[t]his is a model case demonstrating the urgency involved in arresting the suspect in order to preserve evidence of the statutory violation." We have previously recognized that "the percentage of alcohol in the blood begins to diminish shortly after drinking stops, as the body functions to eliminate it from the system." Schmerber v. California, 384 U.S. 757, 770 (1966). Moreover, a suspect could cast substantial doubt on the validity of a blood or breath test by consuming additional alcohol upon arriving at his home. In light of the promptness with which the officers reached Welsh's house, therefore, I would hold that the need to prevent the imminent and ongoing destruction of evidence of a serious violation of Wisconsin's traffic laws provided an exigent circumstance justifying the warrantless in-home arrest. . . .

NOTES AND QUESTIONS

1. Is *Welsh* a proper application of exigent circumstances analysis? It seems clear that the police had probable cause to believe Welsh guilty of driving while intoxicated. It seems equally clear that evidence of that crime would dissipate if the police waited to obtain a warrant before examining Welsh. Why, then, was the entry into Welsh's home improper?

2. The answer, apparently, is that the offense in question was not sufficiently serious to justify the intrusion. That may be a sensible principle — though its application to *Welsh* is surely contestable, given that drunk drivers kill thousands of Americans every year. If it *is* sensible to restrict police authority to enter private homes to enforce minor crimes, though, presumably it is also sensible to restrict other kinds of police authority to enforce minor crimes. Suppose, for example, the police had encountered Welsh before he entered his house. Could they arrest Welsh, take him back to the police station, "book" him, and put him in a holding cell? The answer is yes. See Atwater v. Lago Vista, 532 U.S. 318 (2001); *Atwater* is excerpted infra at page 518. Why should the police be allowed to make full-custody arrests in cases in which they would not be permitted to enter the defendant's home without a warrant?

3. Consider the way the *Welsh* Court weighed Wisconsin's interest in enforcement of its drunk driving law:

> [T]he Court [in *Welsh*] asserts without adequate argumentation or support that the "best indication" of the strength of a state's interest in the effective enforcement of a particular statute will be reflected in the penalties which the state attaches to its violation. But surely this is not necessarily so. A state might have a very strong interest in, for example, enforcing housing or health codes, and yet may impose fairly light penalties for their violation.

Silas J. Wasserstrom, The Court's Turn toward a General Reasonableness Interpretation of the Fourth Amendment, 27 Am. Crim. L. Rev. 119, 133 (1989).

Isn't this absolutely right? Indeed, if *Welsh*'s approach were applied more gener-ally, wouldn't this give legislatures an incentive to be overly punitive? But if the Court *doesn't* look to the penalty structure in assessing the state's interest in effec-tive enforcement, how exactly is this interest to be weighed? And the balancing problem doesn't go away, even conceding the relevance of the penalty structure to assessing the state interest in enforcement. Suppose drunk driving in Wisconsin carried a penalty of up to six months in prison:

> How is the "gravity" of this offense to be factored into what the Court calls "the exigent-circumstances calculus," a calculus which the Court refuses in *Welsh* to tell us anything about? And, even if courts can somehow make this "calculation" correctly, how is the officer in the field to determine whether a particular offense is serious enough to justify a warrantless home entry to prevent the imminent loss of evidence?

Id. at 133-134.

4. Is exigency really the issue in *Welsh*? The most likely effect of the Court's decision, after all, is that police in Wisconsin forget about gathering blood-alcohol evidence in cases where a suspect has returned home. In the time it takes to obtain a warrant, such evidence loses its value; police won't bother to seek it. The Court seems to be ruling, sub silentio, that the forcible entry into a home to obtain evidence of this type is simply unreasonable—with or without a warrant. Assume for the moment that the police in *Welsh* had immediate access to a magis-trate so that they might have obtained a warrant before the evidence lost its value. Should this magistrate take into account that under Wisconsin law drunk driving is only a "noncriminal civil forfeiture offense"? For an incisive argument that *Welsh* is best understood in such terms, see id. at 131-140.

5. What if the officers in *Welsh* had actually been in hot pursuit of the defendant? Should it make a difference to the exigent circumstances analysis if a suspect like Welsh flees from police before entering his house?

6. Consider United States v. Rohrig, 98 F.3d 1506 (6th Cir. 1996). In that case, two Canton, Ohio, police officers responded in the early morning hours to a complaint about loud music emanating from a private home. Police first heard the music from a block away. When they drove up, several pajama-clad neighbors came out to complain. The officers banged on the front door of the house from which the music was blaring, tapped on the first floor windows, and repeatedly shouted out their presence, but to no avail. So the police opened an unlocked screen door and went inside. They walked through the house, continuing loudly to call for an occupant, before locating the offending stereo and turning down the volume. In the same room, they found the defendant Rohrig asleep on the floor.

What were the police doing in *Rohrig*? Were they enforcing a law against making unreasonable noise? Or were they abating a nuisance? Either way, do you think police were justified in entering Rohrig's home without a warrant? If so, how do you square that result with *Welsh*, given that police were presumably enforcing a local noise ordinance? It may be worth noting that, while looking for Rohrig's stereo (and Rohrig), the officers stumbled upon "wall-to-wall" marijuana plants in a basement equipped with fans and running water—evidence that was subse-quently introduced against Rohrig in his trial on federal drug charges.

7. One era's trivial offense is another era's major crime. *Welsh* is an example: In many places, driving under the influence of alcohol was once treated like driving a

few miles an hour over the speed limit. Drivers paid a small fine and went on with their lives. Today, it is taken a lot more seriously. Does that change your view of the Court's analysis in *Welsh*? Are appellate courts likely to do a good job of assessing which crimes are serious and which ones aren't?

8. Suppose Welsh had used a different drug — say, marijuana. What result then? Consider the next case.

ILLINOIS v. McARTHUR

Certiorari to the Appellate Court of Illinois, Fourth District
531 U.S. 326 (2001)

JUSTICE BREYER delivered the opinion of the Court.

... On April 2, 1997, Tera McArthur asked two police officers to accompany her to the trailer where she lived with her husband, Charles, so that they could keep the peace while she removed her belongings. The two officers, Assistant Chief John Love and Officer Richard Skidis, arrived with Tera at the trailer at about 3:15 p.m. Tera went inside, where Charles was present. The officers remained outside.

When Tera emerged after collecting her possessions, she spoke to Chief Love, who was then on the porch. She suggested he check the trailer because "Chuck had dope in there." She added (in Love's words) that she had seen Chuck "slide some dope underneath the couch."

Love knocked on the trailer door, told Charles what Tera had said, and asked for permission to search the trailer, which Charles denied. Love then sent Officer Skidis with Tera to get a search warrant.

Love told Charles, who by this time was also on the porch, that he could not reenter the trailer unless a police officer accompanied him. Charles subsequently reentered the trailer two or three times (to get cigarettes and to make phone calls), and each time Love stood just inside the door to observe what Charles did.

Officer Skidis obtained the warrant by about 5 p.m. He returned to the trailer and, along with other officers, searched it. The officers found under the sofa a marijuana pipe, a box for marijuana (called a "one-hitter" box), and a small amount of marijuana. They then arrested Charles.

Illinois subsequently charged Charles McArthur with unlawfully possessing drug paraphernalia and marijuana (less than 2.5 grams), both misdemeanors. See Ill. Comp. Stat., ch. 720, §§550/4(a), 600/3.5(a) (1998). McArthur moved to suppress the pipe, box, and marijuana on the ground that they were the "fruit" of an unlawful police seizure, namely, the refusal to let him reenter the trailer unaccompanied, which would have permitted him, he said, to "have destroyed the marijuana."

The trial court granted McArthur's suppression motion. The Appellate Court of Illinois affirmed, 713 N.E.2d 93 (1999), and the Illinois Supreme Court denied the State's petition for leave to appeal, 720 N.E.2d 1101 (1999). We granted certiorari to determine whether the Fourth Amendment prohibits the kind of temporary seizure at issue here. . . .

In the circumstances of the case before us, we cannot say that the warrantless seizure was per se unreasonable. It involves a plausible claim of specially pressing or urgent law enforcement need, i.e., "exigent circumstances." Moreover, the restraint at issue was tailored to that need, being limited in time and scope, and avoiding significant intrusion into the home itself. Consequently, rather than employing a per se rule of unreasonableness, we balance the privacy-related and law enforcement-related concerns to determine if the intrusion was reasonable.

We conclude that the restriction at issue was reasonable, and hence lawful, in light of the following circumstances . . . . First, the police had probable cause to believe that McArthur's trailer home contained evidence of a crime and contraband, namely, unlawful drugs. The police had had an opportunity to speak with Tera McArthur and make at least a very rough assessment of her reliability. They knew she had had a firsthand opportunity to observe her husband's behavior, in particular with respect to the drugs at issue. . . .

Second, the police had good reason to fear that, unless restrained, McArthur would destroy the drugs before they could return with a warrant. They reasonably might have thought that McArthur realized that his wife knew about his marijuana stash; observed that she was angry or frightened enough to ask the police to accompany her; saw that after leaving the trailer she had spoken with the police; and noticed that she had walked off with one policeman while leaving the other outside to observe the trailer. They reasonably could have concluded that McArthur, consequently suspecting an imminent search, would, if given the chance, get rid of the drugs fast.

Third, the police made reasonable efforts to reconcile their law enforcement needs with the demands of personal privacy. They neither searched the trailer nor arrested McArthur before obtaining a warrant. Rather, they imposed a significantly less restrictive restraint, preventing McArthur only from entering the trailer unaccompanied. They left his home and his belongings intact—until a neutral Magistrate, finding probable cause, issued a warrant.

Fourth, the police imposed the restraint for a limited period of time, namely, two hours. As far as the record reveals, this time period was no longer than reasonably necessary for the police, acting with diligence, to obtain the warrant. Given the nature of the intrusion and the law enforcement interest at stake, this brief seizure of the premises was permissible. . . .

The Appellate Court of Illinois concluded that the police could not order McArthur to stay outside his home because McArthur's porch, where he stood at the time, was part of his home; hence the order "amounted to a constructive eviction" of McArthur from his residence. 713 N.E.2d at 98. This Court has held, however, that a person standing in the doorway of a house is "in a 'public' place," and hence subject to arrest without a warrant permitting entry of the home. United States v. Santana, 427 U.S. 38, 42 (1976). Regardless, we do not believe the difference to which the Appellate Court points—porch versus, e.g., front walk—could make a significant difference here as to the reasonableness of the police restraint; and that, from the Fourth Amendment's perspective, is what matters.

The Appellate Court also found negatively significant the fact that Chief Love, with McArthur's consent, stepped inside the trailer's doorway to observe McArthur when McArthur reentered the trailer on two or three occasions. 713 N.E.2d, at 98. McArthur, however, reentered simply for his own convenience, to make phone calls and to obtain cigarettes. Under these circumstances, the reasonableness of the greater restriction (preventing reentry) implies the reasonableness of the lesser (permitting reentry conditioned on observation).

Finally, McArthur points to a case (and we believe it is the only case) that he believes offers direct support, namely, Welsh v. Wisconsin, [466 U.S. 740 (1984)]. In *Welsh*, this Court held that police could not enter a home without a warrant in order to prevent the loss of evidence (namely, the defendant's blood alcohol level) of the "nonjailable traffic offense" of driving while intoxicated. 466 U.S. at 742, 754. McArthur notes that his two convictions are for misdemeanors, which, he says, are as minor, and he adds that the restraint, keeping him out of his home, was nearly as serious.

We nonetheless find significant distinctions. The evidence at issue here was of crimes that were "jailable," not "nonjailable." See Ill. Comp. Stat., ch. 720, §550/4(a) (1998); ch. 730, §5/5-8-3(3) (possession of less than 2.5 grams of marijuana punishable by up to 30 days in jail); ch. 720, §600/3.5; ch. 730, §5/5-8-3(1) (possession of drug paraphernalia punishable by up to one year in jail). In *Welsh*, we noted that, "[g]iven that the classification of state crimes differs widely among the States, the penalty that may attach to any particular offense seems to provide the clearest and most consistent indication of the State's interest in arresting individuals suspected of committing that offense." 466 U.S. at 754, n. 14. The same reasoning applies here, where class C misdemeanors include such widely diverse offenses as drag racing, drinking alcohol in a railroad car or on a railroad platform, bribery by a candidate for public office, and assault.

And the restriction at issue here is less serious. Temporarily keeping a person from entering his home, a consequence whenever police stop a person on the street, is considerably less intrusive than police entry into the home itself in order to make a warrantless arrest or conduct a search.

We have explained above why we believe that the need to preserve evidence of a "jailable" offense was sufficiently urgent or pressing to justify the restriction upon entry that the police imposed. We need not decide whether the circumstances before us would have justified a greater restriction for this type of offense or the same restriction were only a "nonjailable" offense at issue. . . .

The judgment of the Illinois Appellate Court is reversed, and the case is remanded for further proceedings not inconsistent with this opinion. . . .

JUSTICE SOUTER, concurring.

I join the Court's opinion subject to this afterword on two points: the constitutionality of a greater intrusion than the one here and the permissibility of choosing impoundment over immediate search. Respondent McArthur's location made the difference between the exigency that justified temporarily barring him from his own dwelling and circumstances that would have supported a greater interference with his privacy and property. As long as he was inside his trailer, the police had probable cause to believe that he had illegal drugs stashed . . . and that with any sense he would flush them down the drain before the police could get a warrant to enter and search. . . . That risk would have justified the police in entering McArthur's trailer promptly to make a lawful, warrantless search. Warden, Md. Penitentiary v. Hayden, 387 U.S. 294, 298-299 (1967). When McArthur stepped outside and left the trailer uninhabited, the risk abated and so did the reasonableness of entry by the police for as long as he was outside. . . .

Since, however, McArthur wished to go back in, why was it reasonable to keep him out when the police could perfectly well have let him do as he chose, and then enjoyed the ensuing opportunity to follow him and make a warrantless search justified by the renewed danger of destruction? The answer is not that the law officiously insists on safeguarding a suspect's privacy from search, in preference to respecting the suspect's liberty to enter his own dwelling. Instead, the legitimacy of the decision to impound the dwelling follows from the law's strong preference for warrants. . . . The law can hardly raise incentives to obtain a warrant without giving the police a fair chance to take their probable cause to a magistrate and get one.

JUSTICE STEVENS, dissenting.

The Illinois General Assembly has decided that the possession of less than 2.5 grams of marijuana is a class C misdemeanor. In so classifying the offense, the legislature made a concerted policy judgment that the possession of small amounts of marijuana for personal use does not constitute a particularly significant public policy concern. While it is true that this offense — like feeding livestock on a public highway or offering a movie for rent without clearly displaying its rating[1] — may warrant a jail sentence of up to 30 days, the detection and prosecution of possessors of small quantities of this substance is by no means a law enforcement priority in the State of Illinois. . . .

. . . As the majority explains, the essential inquiry in this case involves a balancing of the "privacy-related and law enforcement-related concerns to determine if the intrusion was reasonable." Under the specific facts of this case, I believe the majority gets the balance wrong. Each of the Illinois jurists who participated in the decision of this case placed a higher value on the sanctity of the ordinary citizen's home than on the prosecution of this petty offense. They correctly viewed that interest — whether the home be a humble cottage, a secondhand trailer, or a stately mansion — as one meriting the most serious constitutional protection. Following their analysis and the reasoning in our decision in Welsh v. Wisconsin, 466 U.S. 740 (1984) (holding that some offenses may be so minor as to make it unreasonable for police to undertake searches that would be constitutionally permissible if graver offenses were suspected), I would affirm.

NOTES AND QUESTIONS

1. *McArthur* is not a typical exigent circumstances case. In the typical case, police enter a home with probable cause but without a warrant, fearing that if they delay, evidence will be destroyed. In *McArthur* the police applied for and got a warrant, but in order to do so, they had to detain the suspect for two hours and on two occasions followed him into his home. The validity of the warrant was fairly clear. The only issues, then, were whether police could keep McArthur from using his home for two hours, and whether police could follow him when he went inside the house to get cigarettes and make some phone calls.

The Court answers the second of those issues by answering the first. Because the police are permitted to keep McArthur outside his home while they wait for a

---

1. See Ill. Comp. Stat., ch. 605, §5/9-124.1 (1998) (making feeding livestock on a public highway a class C misdemeanor); Ill. Comp. Stat., ch. 720, §§395/3-395/4 (1998) (making it a class C misdemeanor to sell or rent a video that does not display the official rating of the motion picture from which it is copied). Other examples of offenses classified as Class C misdemeanors in Illinois include camping on the side of a public highway, Ill. Comp. Stat., ch. 605, §5/9-124 (1998), interfering with the "lawful taking of wild animals," Ill. Comp. Stat., ch. 720, §125/2 (1998), and tattooing the body of a person under 21 years of age, Ill. Comp. Stat., ch. 720, §5/12-10 (1998).

warrant, they may take the lesser step of allowing him to go inside as long as a police officer accompanies him. This much seems fairly easy.

But how, precisely, does the Court answer the first question? Justice Breyer's opinion says that exigent circumstances justified temporarily seizing McArthur (i.e., keeping him outside his home). The exigency was straightforward (but see Note 3, below): If the police let McArthur go inside without a police officer watching, he would destroy evidence. But that would presumably justify searching McArthur's home as readily as it would justify seizing McArthur while seeking a search warrant. Thus, while *McArthur* isn't a typical exigency case, it appears to turn on a standard exigency issue: Could the police have searched McArthur's home without a warrant, based on their fear that he would destroy evidence? Oddly, the Court never resolves that issue. One is left to wonder whether Justice Souter's concurrence — which states explicitly that a warrantless search of the home would have been legal — states the law, or only Justice Souter's opinion.

2. Assume that Justice Souter accurately states the law in *McArthur*. Why are the police allowed to choose between a warrantless search and a temporary seizure while they seek a warrant? Why not let McArthur choose?

3. Notice the nature of the exigency in *McArthur*. Chief Love — isn't that a great name for a police chief? — feared that McArthur would destroy evidence once he realized that Love knew that McArthur had marijuana inside the house. That might seem like a fairly innocuous assumption in *McArthur*, but its implications are not so innocuous. Does the Court mean to say that anytime a defendant knows the police suspect him of crime, the defendant will destroy evidence? If so, the police can easily manufacture exigent circumstances: Just approach the suspect's home, identify themselves, and announce that they believe the suspect's home contains evidence of crime. Does *that* establish exigency? If not, how do you distinguish *McArthur*?

4. Welsh v. Wisconsin, supra page 470, creates an exception to the exigent circumstances exception to the warrant requirement (got that?) for minor crimes. The police had reason to believe McArthur was guilty of nothing more than possessing a small amount of marijuana. Should that qualify as a minor crime?

b.   Plain View

When he was stopped by New York City police officers, Benigno Class was driving over the speed limit in a car with a cracked windshield — both traffic violations under state law. After the car was stopped, Class got out and one of the officers opened the car door to look for the Vehicle Identification Number (VIN), which is found on the left doorjamb in older cars. When the officer did not find the VIN on the door jamb, he reached into the car to move some papers that obscured the area of the dashboard where the VIN is located on later-model automobiles. In so doing, the officer saw the handle of a gun protruding from underneath the driver's seat. The officer seized the gun. Class was later charged and convicted of a state-law weapons offense.

In New York v. Class, 475 U.S. 106 (1986), the Supreme Court determined that Class had no reasonable expectation of privacy in the VIN, which is required by federal law to be placed in the plain view of someone outside the automobile.

Because the officer could not see the VIN from outside the car and because the driver had exited the vehicle, it was constitutionally permissible for the officer to enter the car to the limited extent necessary to uncover the VIN. Of course, "[t]he evidence that [Class] sought to have suppressed was not the VIN, . . . but a gun, the handle of which the officer saw from the interior of the car while reaching for the papers that covered the VIN." Id. at 114. The officer was allowed to seize the gun, the Court found, because of the plain view doctrine, since the officer in *Class* saw the gun from a position he was authorized to be and from which he could legally gain physical control over it. Consider what "plain view" means as you read the following case — involving not a VIN, but the serial numbers on some stereo components.

ARIZONA v. HICKS

Certiorari to the Court of Appeals of Arizona
480 U.S. 321 (1987)

JUSTICE SCALIA delivered the opinion of the Court. . . .

On April 18, 1984, a bullet was fired through the floor of respondent's apartment, striking and injuring a man in the apartment below. Police officers arrived and entered respondent's apartment to search for the shooter, for other victims, and for weapons. They found and seized three weapons, including a sawed-off rifle, and in the course of their search also discovered a stocking-cap mask.

One of the policemen, Officer Nelson, noticed two sets of expensive stereo components, which seemed out of place in the squalid and otherwise ill-appointed four-room apartment. Suspecting that they were stolen, he read and recorded their serial numbers — moving some of the components, including a Bang and Olufsen turntable, in order to do so — which he then reported by phone to his headquarters. On being advised that the turntable had been taken in an armed robbery, he seized it immediately. It was later determined that some of the other serial numbers matched those on other stereo equipment taken in the same armed robbery, and a warrant was obtained and executed to seize that equipment as well. Respondent was subsequently indicted for the robbery. . . .

The state trial court granted respondent's motion to suppress. . . . The Court of Appeals of Arizona affirmed. . . . The Arizona Supreme Court denied review, and the State filed this petition.

As an initial matter, the State argues that Officer Nelson's actions constituted neither a "search" nor a "seizure" within the meaning of the Fourth Amendment. We agree that the mere recording of the serial numbers did not constitute a seizure. To be sure, that was the first step in a process by which respondent was eventually deprived of the stereo equipment. In and of itself, however, it did not "meaningfully interfere" with respondent's possessory interest in either the serial numbers or the equipment, and therefore did not amount to a seizure.

Officer Nelson's moving of the equipment, however, did constitute a "search" separate and apart from the search for the shooter, victims, and weapons that was the lawful objective of his entry into the apartment. Merely inspecting those parts of the turntable that came into view during the latter search would not have constituted an independent search, because it would have produced no additional invasion of respondent's privacy interest. But taking action, unrelated to the objectives of the authorized intrusion, which exposed to view concealed portions of the apartment or its contents, did produce a new invasion of respondent's privacy unjustified by the exigent circumstance that validated the entry. . . . It matters not that the search uncovered nothing of any great personal value to respondent — serial numbers rather than (what might conceivably have been hidden behind or under the equipment) letters or photographs. A search is a search, even if it happens to disclose nothing but the bottom of a turntable.

The remaining question is whether the search was "reasonable" under the Fourth Amendment. . . .

. . . "It is well established that under certain circumstances the police may *seize* evidence in plain view without a warrant," Coolidge v. New Hampshire, 403 U.S. [443], 465 [1971] (plurality opinion) (emphasis added). Those circumstances include situations "[w]here the initial intrusion that brings the police within plain view of such [evidence] is supported . . . by one of the recognized exceptions to the warrant requirement," ibid., such as the exigent-circumstances intrusion here. It would be absurd to say that an object could lawfully be seized and taken from the premises, but could not be moved for closer examination. It is clear, therefore, that the search here was valid if the "plain view" doctrine would have sustained a seizure of the equipment.

There is no doubt it would have done so if Officer Nelson had probable cause to believe that the equipment was stolen. The State has conceded, however, that he had only a "reasonable suspicion," by which it means something less than probable cause. We have not ruled on the question whether probable cause is required in order to invoke the "plain view" doctrine. . . .

We now hold that probable cause is required. To say otherwise would be to cut the "plain view" doctrine loose from its theoretical and practical moorings. The theory of that doctrine consists of extending to nonpublic places such as the home, where searches and seizures without a warrant are presumptively unreasonable, the police's longstanding authority to make warrantless seizures in public places of such objects as weapons and contraband. And the practical justification for that extension is the desirability of sparing police, whose viewing of the object in the course of a lawful search is as legitimate as it would have been in a public place, the inconvenience and the risk — to themselves or to preservation of the evidence — of going to obtain a warrant. Dispensing with the need for a warrant is worlds apart from permitting a lesser standard of *cause* for the seizure than a warrant would require, i.e., the standard of probable cause. No reason is apparent why an object should routinely be seizable on lesser grounds, during an unrelated search and seizure, than would have been needed to obtain a warrant for that same object if it had been known to be on the premises.

We do not say, of course, that a seizure can never be justified on less than probable cause. We have held that it can — where, for example, the seizure is minimally intrusive and operational necessities render it the only practicable means of detecting certain types of crime. See, e.g., United States v. Cortez, 449 U.S. 411 (1981) (investigative detention of vehicle suspected to be transporting illegal aliens); United States v. Place, 462 U.S. 696, 709, and n. 9 (1983) (dictum) (seizure of suspected drug dealer's luggage at airport to permit exposure to specially trained dog). No special operational necessities are relied on here, however — but rather the mere fact that the items in question came lawfully within the officer's plain view. That alone cannot supplant the requirement of probable cause.

The same considerations preclude us from holding that, even though probable cause would have been necessary for a *seizure*, the *search* of objects in plain view that occurred here could be sustained on lesser grounds. A dwelling-place search, no less than a dwelling-place seizure, requires probable cause, and there is no reason in theory or practicality why application of the "plain view" doctrine would supplant that requirement. . . .

JUSTICE O'CONNOR's dissent suggests that we uphold the action here on the ground that it was a "cursory inspection" rather than a "full-blown search," and could therefore be justified by reasonable suspicion instead of probable cause. As already noted, a truly cursory inspection — one that involves merely looking at what is already exposed to view, without disturbing it — is not a "search" for Fourth Amendment purposes, and therefore does not even require reasonable suspicion. We are unwilling to send police and judges into a new thicket of Fourth Amendment law, to seek a creature of uncertain description that is neither a "plain view" inspection nor yet a "full-blown search." . . .

JUSTICE POWELL's dissent reasonably asks what it is we would have had Officer Nelson do in these circumstances. The answer depends, of course, upon whether he had probable cause to conduct a search. . . . If he had, then he should have done precisely what he did. If not, then he should have followed up his suspicions, if possible, by means other than a search — just as he would have had to do if, while walking along the street, he had noticed the same suspicious stereo equipment sitting inside a house a few feet away from him, beneath an open window. It may well be that, in such circumstances, no effective means short of a search exist. But there is nothing new in the realization that the Constitution sometimes insulates the criminality of a few in order to protect the privacy of us all. . . .

For the reasons stated, the judgment of the Court of Appeals of Arizona is Affirmed.

[The concurring opinion of Justice White is omitted.]

JUSTICE POWELL, with whom THE CHIEF JUSTICE and JUSTICE O'CONNOR join, dissenting. . . .

It is fair to ask what Officer Nelson should have done in these circumstances. Accepting the State's concession that he lacked probable cause, he could not have obtained a warrant to seize the stereo components. Neither could he have remained on the premises and forcibly prevented their removal. . . .

The Court holds that there was an unlawful search of the turntable. It agrees that the "mere recording of the serial numbers did not constitute a seizure." Thus, if the computer had identified as stolen property a component with a visible serial number, the evidence would have been admissible. But the Court further holds that "Officer Nelson's moving of the equipment . . . did constitute a 'search . . .'" It perceives a constitutional distinction between reading a serial number on an object and moving or picking up an identical object to see its serial number. . . . With all respect, this distinction between "looking" at a suspicious object in plain view and "moving" it even a few inches trivializes the Fourth Amendment.

The Court's new rule will cause uncertainty, and could deter conscientious police officers from lawfully obtaining evidence necessary to convict guilty persons. . . . Accordingly, I dissent.

JUSTICE O'CONNOR, with whom THE CHIEF JUSTICE and JUSTICE POWELL join, dissenting.

The Court today gives the right answer to the wrong question. The Court asks whether the police must have probable cause before either seizing an object in plain view or conducting a full-blown search of that object, and concludes that they must. I agree. In my view, however, this case presents a different question: whether police must have probable cause before conducting a cursory inspection of an item in plain view. . . . I conclude that such an inspection is reasonable if the police are aware of facts or circumstances that justify a reasonable suspicion that the item is evidence of a crime. . . .

. . . If an officer could indiscriminately search every item in plain view, a search justified by a limited purpose — such as exigent circumstances — could be used to eviscerate the protections of the Fourth Amendment. In order to prevent such a general search, therefore, we require that the relevance of the item be "immediately apparent." . . .

Thus, I agree with the Court that even under the plain-view doctrine, probable cause is required before the police seize an item, or conduct a full-blown search of evidence in plain view. . . . This is not to say, however, that even a mere inspection of a suspicious item must be supported by probable cause. When a police officer makes a cursory inspection of a suspicious item in plain view in order to determine whether it is indeed evidence of a crime, there is no "exploratory rummaging." Only those items that the police officer "reasonably suspects" as evidence of a crime may be inspected, and perhaps more importantly, the scope of such an inspection is quite limited . . .

This distinction between searches based on their relative intrusiveness . . . is entirely consistent with our Fourth Amendment jurisprudence. We have long recognized that searches can vary in intrusiveness, and that some brief searches "may be so minimally intrusive of Fourth Amendment interests that strong countervailing governmental interests will justify a [search] based only on specific articulable facts" that the item in question is contraband or evidence of a crime. United States v. Place, 462 U.S. 696, 706 (1983). . . .

In my view, the balance of the governmental and privacy interests strongly supports a reasonable-suspicion standard for the cursory examination of items in plain view. The additional intrusion caused by an inspection of an item in plain view for its serial number is minuscule. . . .

Weighed against this minimal additional invasion of privacy are rather major gains in law enforcement. The use of identification numbers in tracing stolen property is a powerful law enforcement tool. Serial numbers are far more helpful and accurate in detecting stolen property than simple police recollection of the evidence. Cf. New York v. Class, 475 U.S. 106, 111 (1986) (observing importance of vehicle identification numbers). . . .

Unfortunately, in its desire to establish a "bright-line" test, the Court has taken a step that ignores a substantial body of precedent and that places serious roadblocks to reasonable law enforcement practices. . . . The theoretical advantages of the "search is a search" approach adopted by the Court today are simply too remote to justify the tangible and severe damage it inflicts on legitimate and effective law enforcement. . . .

NOTES ON "PLAIN VIEW" DOCTRINE

1. In many Fourth Amendment cases, the issue is whether the police were behaving legally when they first saw the evidence in question. It is important to understand that *that* question is not a matter of plain view doctrine at all. For example, suppose a police officer standing on a public street sees a drug transaction through an open window in a nearby house. Plain view doctrine does not justify entry into the house; indeed, plain view doctrine does not even come into play. The officer can enter the house if what he saw gives him both probable cause and exigent circumstances or if he obtains a valid warrant, but not otherwise. Plain view doctrine deals with a different sort of question: Assuming the officer was behaving legally when he *saw* the evidence in question, and also assuming that he is legally in a place where he can gain physical control over the evidence, can he *seize* it? *Hicks* says yes, if the officer has probable cause. But short of probable cause, even the most cursory "search" to confirm one's suspicions cannot be upheld.

2. Speaking of probable cause, was the state wise to concede that the police lacked probable cause to believe the stereos were stolen in *Hicks*? In Justice O'Connor's dissent, she expressed "little doubt" that this standard was satisfied. Had the concession not been made, how should the issue have been resolved?

3. Consider the following discussion of the majority's approach in *Hicks*:

> Having concluded that a search did occur, Justice Scalia asserts that the "remaining question" is whether the search was reasonable under the fourth amendment. However, not a single word of the Court's opinion is directed to this question. Instead, Justice Scalia focuses exclusively on the fact that the officer lacked probable cause to believe that the turntable was stolen and that, in the absence of probable cause, the doctrine authorizing warrantless searches and seizures of items in "plain view" was not applicable.
>
> The Court's treatment of the constitutional problem posed by *Hicks* is puzzling in two respects. First, there is a startling disjunction between the requirements imposed by the text of the fourth amendment and those imposed by the Court in the name of the text. . . . There was no claim in *Hicks* that the kind of warrant outlawed by the second clause of the amendment had been issued and . . . the opinion did not inquire into whether the police action was 'unreasonable.'
>
> These deficiencies might be understandable if the requirements the Court imposed were associated with the policy concerns that, according to the Court, lie behind the fourth amendment. But a second puzzling aspect of the opinion is how little of the Court's reasoning relates to these concerns. Although one can imagine other substantive goals, the Court seems to have settled on using the fourth amendment to balance personal privacy against effective law enforcement. . . . Even when measured against the Court's own goals, however, the analysis in *Hicks* fares poorly.
>
> Thus, the Court virtually concedes that the marginal privacy loss when Officer Nelson picked up the turntable was de minimis. The Court also appears to concede that the loss to law enforcement created by the rule it announces might be considerable. Yet despite these concessions, which to the uninitiated might appear to establish that the officer's conduct was "reasonable," the Court slavishly adheres to a series of rules relating to warrants and probable cause that have no basis in constitutional text.

Silas J. Wasserstrom and Louis Michael Seidman, The Fourth Amendment as Constitutional Theory, 77 Geo. L.J. 19, 23-25 (1988). Do you agree? Does *Hicks* represent a strong argument for less focus on probable cause and warrants and more focus on reasonableness as the touchstone of Fourth Amendment interpretation? Or is there more to the majority's approach?

4. Consider the relationship between *Hicks* and Mincey v. Arizona, page 463 supra. In *Mincey*, the police conducted "an exhaustive and intrusive search" of the defendant's apartment in the wake of a shooting; the police did not obtain a warrant for the search. The Court held that the search lasted longer than exigent circumstances would justify. In *Hicks* too, the police entered the defendant's apartment based on probable cause and exigent circumstances — and as in *Mincey*, the Court held that the police exceeded their legal authority once inside. Both exigent circumstances doctrine in *Mincey* and plain view doctrine in *Hicks* serve to limit police officers' ability to conduct wide-ranging searches of private dwellings in the absence of a warrant.

That sounds sensible. But plain view doctrine does not, by its terms, differ for warrant-based and warrantless searches — if the officers had been in Hicks' apartment pursuant to a warrant to search for weapons, the plain view issue should be analyzed precisely the same as in the actual case. Is *that* sensible?

5. Justice O'Connor suggests that the *Hicks* majority is fixated on establishing a bright-line test for plain view doctrine. Does the majority achieve this goal? How far does the concept of a "plain view search" go? Would the police in *Hicks* have been permitted to search the contents of a suitcase if they had probable cause to believe the suitcase contained drugs?

6. Notice that when *Hicks* was decided, at least some of the Justices were of the view that there were three requirements for a plain view search or seizure: (1) that the police must lawfully be in a position from which they can view particular items and gain physical custody over them; (2) that it must be "immediately apparent" to the police that the items they observe are subject to seizure; and (3) that these items are discovered "inadvertently" — that the police weren't looking for what they stumbled upon. *Hicks* elaborated on the second of these requirements. The next case focused on whether the third "requirement" is an aspect of plain view doctrine at all.

HORTON v. CALIFORNIA

Certiorari to the Court of Appeal of California, Sixth Appellate District
496 U.S. 128 (1990)

JUSTICE STEVENS delivered the opinion of the Court.

In this case we revisit . . . [the question whether] the warrantless seizure of evidence of crime in plain view is prohibited by the Fourth Amendment if the discovery of the evidence was not inadvertent. We conclude that even though inadvertence is a characteristic of most legitimate "plain-view" seizures, it is not a necessary condition.

Petitioner was convicted of the armed robbery of Erwin Wallaker, the treasurer of the San Jose Coin Club. When Wallaker returned to his home after the Club's annual show, he entered his garage and was accosted by two masked men, one armed with a machine gun and the other with an electrical shocking device, sometimes referred to as a "stun gun." The two men shocked Wallaker, bound and handcuffed him, and robbed him of jewelry and cash. During the encounter sufficient conversation took place to enable Wallaker subsequently to identify petitioner's distinctive voice. His identification was partially corroborated by a witness who saw the robbers leaving the scene, and by evidence that petitioner had attended the coin shows.

Sergeant LaRault ... investigated the crime and determined that there was probable cause to search petitioner's home for the proceeds of the robbery and for the weapons used by the robbers. His affidavit for a search warrant referred to police reports that described the weapons as well as the proceeds, but the warrant issued by the Magistrate only authorized a search for the proceeds, including three specifically described rings.

Pursuant to the warrant, LaRault searched petitioner's residence, but he did not find the stolen property. During the course of the search, however, he discovered the weapons in plain view and seized them. Specifically, he seized an Uzi machine gun, a.38 caliber revolver, two stun guns, a handcuff key, a San Jose Coin Club advertising brochure, and a few items of clothing identified by the victim. LaRault testified that while he was searching for the rings, he also was interested in finding other evidence connecting petitioner to the robbery. Thus, the seized evidence was not discovered "inadvertently."

The trial court refused to suppress the evidence found in petitioner's home and, after a jury trial, petitioner was found guilty and sentenced to prison. The California Court of Appeal affirmed[, rejecting] petitioner's argument that ... suppression of the seized evidence that had not been listed in the warrant [was required] because its discovery was not inadvertent. ...

... The "plain view" doctrine is often considered an exception to the general rule that warrantless searches are presumptively unreasonable, but this characterization overlooks the important difference between searches and seizures. If an article is already in plain view, neither its observation nor its seizure would involve any invasion of privacy. A seizure of the article, however, would obviously invade the owner's possessory interest. If "plain view" justifies an exception from an otherwise applicable warrant requirement, therefore, it must be an exception that is addressed to the concerns that are implicated by seizures rather than by searches.

The criteria that generally guide "plain view" seizures were set forth in Coolidge v. New Hampshire, 403 U.S. 443 (1971). The Court held that [the seizure of] two automobiles parked in plain view on the defendant's driveway in the course of arresting the defendant, violated the Fourth Amendment. Accordingly, particles of gunpowder that had been subsequently found in vacuum sweepings from one of the cars could not be introduced in evidence against the defendant. The State endeavored to justify the seizure of the automobiles, and their subsequent search at the police station, on four different grounds, including the "plain-view" doctrine. The scope of that doctrine as it had developed in earlier cases was fairly summarized in ... Justice Stewart's opinion. ... Justice Stewart ... described the two limitations on the doctrine that he found implicit in its rationale: First, "that plain view *alone* is never enough to justify the warrantless seizure of evidence," id., at 468; and second, "that the discovery of evidence in plain view must be inadvertent." Id., at 469.

Justice Stewart's analysis of the "plain view" doctrine did not command a majority[9] . . . .

It is, of course, an essential predicate to any valid warrantless seizure of incriminating evidence that the officer did not violate the Fourth Amendment in arriving at the place from which the evidence could be plainly viewed. There are, moreover, two additional conditions that must be satisfied to justify [a] warrantless seizure. First, not only must the item be in plain view, its incriminating character must also be "immediately apparent." Id., at 466; see also Arizona v. Hicks, 480 U.S., at 326-327. Thus, in *Coolidge*, the cars were obviously in plain view, but their probative value remained uncertain until after the interiors were swept and examined microscopically. Second, not only must the officer be lawfully located in a place from which the object can be plainly seen, but he or she must also have a lawful right of access to the object itself. . . . [I]n *Coolidge* . . . the seizure of the cars was accomplished by means of a warrantless trespass on the defendant's property . . . [W]e are satisfied that the absence of inadvertence was not essential to the Court's rejection of the State's "plain-view" argument in *Coolidge*.

Justice Stewart concluded that the inadvertence requirement was necessary to avoid a violation of the express constitutional requirement that a valid warrant must particularly describe the things to be seized. He explained:

> "The rationale of the exception to the warrant requirement, as just stated, is that a plain-view seizure will not turn an initially valid (and therefore limited) search into a 'general' one, while the inconvenience of procuring a warrant to cover an inadvertent discovery is great. But where the discovery is anticipated, where the police know in advance the location of the evidence and intend to seize it, the situation is altogether different. The requirement of a warrant to seize imposes no inconvenience whatever, or at least none which is constitutionally cognizable in a legal system that regards warrantless searches as 'per se unreasonable' in the absence of 'exigent circumstances.'
>
> "If the initial intrusion is bottomed upon a warrant that fails to mention a particular object, though the police know its location and intend to seize it, then there is a violation of the express constitutional requirement of 'Warrants . . . particularly describing . . . [the] things to be seized.'" 403 U.S., at 469-471.

We find two flaws in this reasoning. First, evenhanded law enforcement is best achieved by the application of objective standards of conduct, rather than standards that depend upon the subjective state of mind of the officer. The fact that an officer is interested in an item of evidence and fully expects to find it in the course of a search should not invalidate its seizure if the search is confined in area and duration by the terms of a warrant or a valid exception to the warrant requirement. If the officer has knowledge approaching certainty that the item will be found, we see no reason why he or she would deliberately omit a particular description of the item to be seized from the application for a search warrant. Specification of the additional item could only permit the officer to expand the scope of the search. On the other hand, if he or she has a valid warrant to search for one item and merely

---

9. The portion of Justice Stewart's opinion in *Coolidge* that discussed plain view was joined by Justices Douglas, Brennan, and Marshall. Justice Harlan was the fifth vote in *Coolidge*; his opinion did not mention plain view. — EDS.

a suspicion concerning the second, whether or not it amounts to probable cause, we fail to see why that suspicion should immunize the second item from seizure if it is found during a lawful search for the first. The hypothetical case put by JUSTICE WHITE in his concurring and dissenting opinion in *Coolidge* is instructive:

> "Let us suppose officers secure a warrant to search a house for a rifle. While staying well within the range of a rifle search, they discover two photographs of the murder victim, both in plain sight in the bedroom. Assume also that the discovery of the one photograph was inadvertent but finding the other was anticipated. The Court would permit the seizure of only one of the photographs. But in terms of the 'minor' peril to Fourth Amendment values there is surely no difference between these two photographs: the interference with possession is the same in each case and the officers' appraisal of the photograph they expected to see is no less reliable than their judgment about the other. And in both situations the actual inconvenience and danger to evidence remain identical if the officers must depart and secure a warrant." Id., at 516.

Second, the suggestion that the inadvertence requirement is necessary to prevent the police from conducting general searches, or from converting specific warrants into general warrants, is not persuasive because that interest is already served by the requirements that no warrant issue unless it "particularly describ[es] the place to be searched and the persons or things to be seized," see Maryland v. Garrison, 480 U.S. 79, 84 (1987), and that a warrantless search be circumscribed by the exigencies which justify its initiation. See, e.g., Mincey v. Arizona, 437 U.S. 385, 393 (1978). Scrupulous adherence to these requirements serves the interests in limiting the area and duration of the search that the inadvertence requirement inadequately protects. Once those commands have been satisfied and the officer has a lawful right of access, however, no additional Fourth Amendment interest is furthered by requiring that the discovery of evidence be inadvertent. . . .

In this case, the scope of the search was not enlarged in the slightest by the omission of any reference to the weapons in the warrant. Indeed, if the three rings and other items named in the warrant had been found at the outset — or petitioner had them in his possession and had responded to the warrant by producing them immediately — no search for weapons could have taken place. Again, JUSTICE WHITE's concurring and dissenting opinion in *Coolidge* is instructive:

> "Police with a warrant for a rifle may search only places where rifles might be and must terminate the search once the rifle is found; the inadvertence rule will in no way reduce the number of places into which they may lawfully look." 403 U.S., at 517. . . .

[T]he items seized from petitioner's home were discovered during a lawful search authorized by a valid warrant. When they were discovered, it was immediately apparent to the officer that they constituted incriminating evidence. He had probable cause, not only to obtain a warrant to search for the stolen property, but also to believe that the weapons and handguns had been used in the crime he was investigating. The search was authorized by the warrant; the seizure was authorized by the "plain view" doctrine. The judgment is affirmed. . . .

[The dissenting opinion of Justice Brennan, joined by Justice Marshall, is omitted.]

If *Horton* had come out the other way, what incentives would plain view doctrine create for police? Imagine two suspects, Smith and Jones. Smith is suspected of a series of robberies and rapes. Jones is suspected of being Smith's accomplice in one of the robberies; the police do not believe Jones is involved in any other crimes. The police have enough evidence to give them probable cause to search both suspects' homes for evidence of the one robbery; they lack probable cause with respect to the rest of Smith's possible crimes. It is easy for the police to search Jones's home, assuming they can get a warrant to do so. Smith is another matter. If the police submit their evidence on the one robbery to a magistrate, get a warrant, and then find evidence linking Smith to other crimes, they might effectively immunize Smith for those other crimes. That is what an inadvertence requirement would mean.

Of course, the police could always submit everything they had to the magistrate. But why should they have to do that? At the least, it would make the warrant process more costly, for magistrates and police officers alike. And notice where the extra cost arises — in investigations of suspects like Smith, who are suspected of committing not one crime but several. Surely it doesn't make sense to have an inadvertence requirement that would benefit primarily repeat criminals. Or does it?

c. Automobiles

As technology evolves and both shapes and changes American society, it tends to shape Fourth Amendment law as well. See, for instance, the law relating to the definition of a "search," which has been influenced substantially by such technological advances as eavesdropping microphones (*Katz*), radio transmitters (*White*), beepers (*Karo*), thermal imaging scans (*Kyllo*), and aerial surveillance technology (*Riley, Ciraolo,* and *Dow Chemical*).

Arguably the most important single technological advance of the twentieth century was the automobile. There are about 107 million households in the United States, and about 204 million private cars, trucks, and SUVs — an average of 1.9 per household.[10] This makes the motor vehicle one of the most commonly owned items in America — much more common, for example, than a privately owned residence, a computer, or a passport.[11]

As one might expect, the Fourth Amendment law relating to automobiles has evolved significantly in response to the automobile's increasing ubiquity. The starting point of this evolution was the Supreme Court's decision in Carroll v. United States, 267 U.S. 132 (1925). In *Carroll*, federal prohibition agents (together with a state police officer) encountered a car, on the highway between Detroit and

10. See "Americans' Love Affair With Cars, Trucks, and SUVs Continues," USA Today Online Edition, August 30, 2003, *www.usatoday.com/news/nation/2003-08-30-outnumbered-cars_x.html.*

11. About 68 percent of American households live in a privately owned home. See "Moving to America — Moving to Home Ownership: 1994-2002," U.S. Census Bureau, *www.census.gov/prod/2003pubs/h121-03-1.pdf.* About 56.5 percent own a computer. See "A Nation Online: How Americans are Expanding Their Use of the Internet," National Telecommunications and Information Administration, *www.ntia.doc.gov/ntiahome/dn/hhs/Charth1.html.* And, at most, about 64 million Americans hold valid passports (this figure is the sum of all U.S. passports issued within the past 10 years; for adults, 10 years is the duration of a passport's validity). See Passport Statistics, U.S. Department of State, *www.travel.state.gov/passport/other_stats.html.*

Grand Rapids, whose occupants they believed (based on "reasonably trustworthy information") to be bootleggers. The agents stopped the car and searched it without a warrant, and found 68 bottles of whiskey and gin stuffed inside the hollowed-out upholstery.[12] The Court upheld the search, concluding that the traditional Fourth Amendment warrant requirement was unsuited to the search of "a ship, motor boat, wagon or automobile, for contraband goods, where it is not practicable to secure a warrant because the vehicle can be quickly moved out of the locality or jurisdiction in which the warrant must be sought." This led the Court to recognize what came to be called the "automobile exception" to the warrant requirement: for searches and seizures of cars stopped along the road, if obtaining a warrant is not "reasonably practicable," then "[t]he measure of legality . . . is that the seizing officer shall have reasonable or probable cause for believing that the automobile which he stops and seizes has contraband liquor therein which is being illegally transported."

Even in its day, *Carroll* was a controversial decision. America was in the midst of its first war on drugs — the drug in question was alcohol, not heroin or cocaine — and as in later drug wars, many people worried that Fourth Amendment freedoms were giving way to the convenience of police seeking to enforce a criminal prohibition that was widely violated. Justices McReyonds and Sutherland captured that concern in their *Carroll* dissent when they noted that "[t]he damnable character of the 'bootlegger's' business should not close our eyes to the mischief which will surely follow any attempt to destroy it by unwarranted methods." Id. at 163 (McReynolds, J., dissenting). Later in the decade, the Court would respond differently to that concern; Fourth Amendment restrictions on federal agents enforcing Prohibition were ratcheted up in the late 1920s and early 1930s. See Kenneth M. Murchison, Prohibition and the Fourth Amendment: A New Look at Some Old Cases, 73 J. Crim. L. & Criminology 471 (1982). But in 1925, the law still favored the agents, not the bootleggers.

On this somewhat shaky foundation, the Supreme Court slowly built an elaborate body of law governing warrantless searches of automobiles and their contents. The scope of police authority under that body of law was expanded in Chambers v. Maroney, 399 U.S. 42 (1970). In *Chambers*, the police stopped a car based on probable cause that its occupants had just committed a late-night armed robbery. The police arrested the suspects and drove the car to the police station, where a thorough warrantless search of the car was conducted, producing two handguns and other evidence of the crime. The issue in *Chambers* was whether the "automobile exception" of *Carroll* applied to the search of a car in police custody, at the police station, rather than along the road. The Court noted that, under *Carroll*, the car could have been searched immediately upon being stopped. The car also could have been immobilized while the police awaited issuance of a search warrant, but the Court found "little to choose in terms of practical consequences" between that option and an immediate warrantless search. The decision to move the car to the police station before conducting the search was "not unreasonable," because it would have been potentially dangerous for the police (and perhaps inconvenient for the car's owner) to conduct the search on a dark street in the middle of the night. Because the police had probable cause to conduct the search, and because they behaved

12. The agents had to rip open the upholstery to find the liquor. See United States v. Ross, 456 U.S. 798, 817-818 (1982).

reasonably in dealing with the car's mobility, the search was valid under the Fourth Amendment.

After *Carroll* and *Chambers*, it was clear that, as a general matter, the search of a car could be based solely on probable cause to believe that the car contained evidence or contraband, and did not require a warrant. This included any and all "integral part[s] of the automobile," such as the glove compartment, South Dakota v. Opperman, 428 U.S. 364 (1978), or the trunk, Cady v. Dombrowski, 413 U.S. 433 (1973). The Court next turned its attention to the subsidiary — but hugely important, in practical terms — issue of the warrantless search of containers that happened to be located within cars. The first three such cases, United States v. Chadwick, 433 U.S. 1 (1977), Arkansas v. Sanders, 442 U.S. 753 (1979), and Robbins v. California, 435 U.S. 420 (1981) (plurality opinion), all were decided against the police.

In *Chadwick*, federal agents had probable cause to believe that a locked footlocker being transported by a train passenger contained marijuana. They waited until the suspect disembarked the train and placed the footlocker in the trunk of a car. Then — before the car's engine even was started — they arrested the suspect and his traveling companion, as well as the driver of the car. The car and footlocker were brought to a federal building, and subsequently searched without a warrant, revealing a "large quantity" of marijuana.[14] The Court rejected the government's argument that the rationale of the *Carroll-Chambers* "automobile exception" also should apply to luggage. According to the Court, the "automobile exception" is based only in part on the "inherent mobility" of automobiles; an additional, important basis for the exception is the "diminished expectation of privacy which surrounds the automobile." Cars are registered with, and heavily regulated by, the state, including (in many states) a periodic inspection requirement. None of these characteristics applies to a footlocker, which is "intended as a repository of personal effects," and in which "expectations of privacy . . . are substantially greater than in an automobile." Moreover, as compared to cars, smaller containers can be secured more easily while awaiting issuance of a warrant. The Court held that the police should have maintained custody of the footlocker until they could obtain a warrant to search it.

In *Sanders*, police had probable cause to believe that a green suitcase, being transported by an airline passenger, contained marijuana. They waited until the suspect put the suitcase in the trunk of a taxicab, and left the airport, before giving chase. The police stopped the taxicab a few blocks from the airport and immediately searched the suitcase, finding 9.3 pounds of marijuana. The Court found no basis for upholding the search in the fact that, unlike in *Chadwick*, the police waited to act until the car was moving; "the exigency of mobility must be assessed at the point immediately before the search — after the police have seized the object to be searched and have it securely within their control." Nor did the suitcase have a "diminished expectation of privacy" simply because it was seized from the trunk of a car. The "automobile exception" therefore did not apply to the suitcase.

In *Robbins*, police stopped a car for erratic driving, and noticed the odor of marijuana wafting from the car. They arrested the driver, and conducted

---

14. The court did not say exactly how much marijuana was inside, but the footlocker weighed 200 pounds, and it took three persons to lift it into the trunk of the car.

a warrantless search of the car. In a recessed luggage compartment, they found two "bricks" covered with green opaque plastic, which they unwrapped. The packages contained 30 pounds of marijuana. The Court concluded that this search, too, violated the Fourth Amendment, although there was no majority opinion. A four-Justice plurality based the result on the fact that the "bricks" were in a "closed, opaque container" that was indistinguishable from the foot-locker in *Chadwick* and the suitcase in *Sanders*. The fact that the kind of container in *Robbins* was not the kind normally used to transport "personal effects" did not matter; "[w]hat one person may put into a suitcase, another person may put into a paper bag."

Justice Powell, in concurrence, found that Robbins had manifested a "reason-able expectation of privacy" by carefully wrapping the "bricks," and thus was entitled to the protection of the warrant requirement, but he disagreed with the plurality's extension of the *Chadwick-Sanders* rule to other "insubstantial contain-ers" that did not reflect such an expectation. Powell noted in passing that, arguably, neither *Chadwick* nor *Sanders* really was an "automobile case" at all, because the probable cause in both cases attached to the respective containers "before either came near an automobile." But he declined to rely on that argument in *Robbins*, because the parties had not argued or briefed it.

Only a few years later, the Court shifted course and handed the police a major victory. In United States v. Ross, 456 U.S. 798 (1982), police had probable cause to believe that Ross was selling narcotics out of the trunk of his maroon Chevy Malibu. They found the car, but did not see Ross nearby, so they kept circling the neighborhood. A few minutes later, they saw Ross driving the Malibu, stopped the car, and arrested Ross. They conducted a warrantless search of the car, includ-ing the trunk, where they found a "closed brown paper bag." Inside the bag were "a number of glassine bags containing a white powder," which turned out to be heroin.

The Court upheld the search in *Ross*. Noting the importance of "striving for clarification in this area of the law," which affected "countless" police-citizen encounters every day, the Court reviewed the entire line of cases recounted above. The key aspect in *Ross*, according to the Court, was the same one that had been noted (but not relied upon) by Justice Powell in *Robbins* — that the police in *Ross*, as in *Robbins*, had probable cause that extended to the entire car, rather than being limited (as in *Chadwick* and *Sanders*) to a particular container that happened to be located in the car. "A lawful search of fixed premises generally extends to the entire area in which the object of the search may be found and is not limited by the possibility that separate acts of entry or opening may be required to complete the search. . . . When a legitimate search is underway, . . . nice distinc-tions . . . between glove compartments, upholstered seats, trunks, and wrapped packages . . . must give way to the interest in the prompt and efficient completion of the task at hand." Without such a rule, the "practical consequences" of *Carroll* would be "nullified." Nor would such a rule violate "reasonable expectations of privacy"; such expectations, with respect to "a vehicle and its contents[,] may not survive if probable cause is given to believe that the vehicle is transporting contra-band." The *Ross* Court agreed with the *Robbins* plurality that the same rule must apply equally to all containers, from a "paper bag" to a "locked attache case." The Court concluded: "The scope of a warrantless search of an automobile thus is not defined by the nature of the container in which the contraband is secreted. Rather, it is defined by the object of the search and the places in which there is probable cause to believe that it may be found."

After the decision in *Ross*, the legality of warrantless searches of containers in cars generally depended on whether the probable cause possessed by the police was "container-specific" (in which case the *Chadwick-Sanders* rule applied) or "car-general" (in which case the *Ross* rule applied). But *Ross* did not put an end to litigation about searches of containers in cars — still the subject of a great deal of Fourth Amendment litigation, as the following two cases demonstrate.

CALIFORNIA v. ACEVEDO

Certiorari to the Court of Appeal of California, Fourth Appellate District
500 U.S. 565 (1991)

JUSTICE BLACKMUN delivered the opinion of the Court.

This case requires us once again to consider the so-called "automobile exception" to the warrant requirement of the Fourth Amendment and its application to the search of a closed container in the trunk of a car.

On October 28, 1987, Officer Coleman of the Santa Ana, Cal., Police Department received a telephone call from a federal drug enforcement agent in Hawaii. The agent informed Coleman that he had seized a package containing marijuana which was to have been delivered to the Federal Express Office in Santa Ana and which was addressed to J. R. Daza at 805 West Stevens Avenue in that city. The agent arranged to send the package to Coleman instead. Coleman then was to take the package to the Federal Express office and arrest the person who arrived to claim it.

Coleman received the package on October 29, verified its contents, and took it to the Senior Operations Manager at the Federal Express office. At about 10:30 a.m. on October 30, a man, who identified himself as Jamie Daza, arrived to claim the package. He accepted it and drove to his apartment on West Stevens. He carried the package into the apartment.

At 11:45 a.m., officers observed Daza leave the apartment and drop the box and paper that had contained the marijuana into a trash bin. Coleman at that point left the scene to get a search warrant. About 12:05 p.m., the officers saw Richard St. George leave the apartment carrying a blue knapsack which appeared to be half full. The officers stopped him as he was driving off, searched the knapsack, and found 1½ pounds of marijuana.

At 12:30 p.m., respondent Charles Steven Acevedo arrived. He entered Daza's apartment, stayed for about 10 minutes, and reappeared carrying a brown paper bag that looked full. The officers noticed that the bag was the size of one of the wrapped marijuana packages sent from Hawaii. Acevedo walked to a silver Honda in the parking lot. He placed the bag in the trunk of the car and started to drive away. Fearing the loss of evidence, officers in a marked police car stopped him. They opened the trunk and the bag, and found marijuana.[1]

---

1. When Officer Coleman returned with a warrant, the apartment was searched and bags of marijuana were found there. We are here concerned, of course, only with what was discovered in the automobile.

Respondent was charged in state court with possession of marijuana for sale. . . . He moved to suppress the marijuana found in the car. The motion was denied. He then pleaded guilty but appealed the denial of the suppression motion.

The California Court of Appeal, Fourth District, concluded that the marijuana found in the paper bag in the car's trunk should have been suppressed. The court concluded that the officers had probable cause to believe that the paper bag contained drugs but lacked probable cause to suspect that Acevedo's car, itself, otherwise contained contraband. Because the officers' probable cause was directed specifically at the bag, the court held that the case was controlled by United States v. Chadwick, 433 U.S. 1 (1977), rather than by United States v. Ross, 456 U.S. 798 (1982). Although the court agreed that the officers could seize the paper bag, it held that, under *Chadwick*, they could not open the bag without first obtaining a warrant for that purpose. The court then recognized "the anomalous nature" of the dichotomy between the rule in *Chadwick* and the rule in *Ross*. That dichotomy dictates that if there is probable cause to search a car, then the entire car — including any closed container found therein — may be searched without a warrant, but if there is probable cause only as to a container in the car, the container may be held but not searched until a warrant is obtained.

The Supreme Court of California denied the State's petition for review. . . .

We granted certiorari to reexamine the law applicable to a closed container in an automobile, a subject that has troubled courts and law enforcement officers since it was first considered in *Chadwick*.

The Fourth Amendment protects the "right of the people to be secure in their persons, houses, papers, and effects, against unreasonable searches and seizures." Contemporaneously with the adoption of the Fourth Amendment, the First Congress, and, later, the Second and Fourth Congresses, distinguished between the need for a warrant to search for contraband concealed in "a dwelling house or similar place" and the need for a warrant to search for contraband concealed in a movable vessel. See Carroll v. United States, 267 U.S. 132, 151 (1925). See also Boyd v. United States, 116 U.S. 616, 623-624 (1886). In *Carroll*, this Court established an exception to the warrant requirement for moving vehicles, for it recognized

> a necessary difference between a search of a store, dwelling house or other structure in respect of which a proper official warrant readily may be obtained, and a search of a ship, motor boat, wagon or automobile, for contraband goods, where it is not practicable to secure a warrant because the vehicle can be quickly moved out of the locality or jurisdiction in which the warrant must be sought. 267 U.S., at 153.

It therefore held that a warrantless search of an automobile, based upon probable cause to believe that the vehicle contained evidence of crime in the light of an exigency arising out of the likely disappearance of the vehicle, did not contravene the Warrant Clause of the Fourth Amendment. See id., at 158-159.

The Court refined the exigency requirement in Chambers v. Maroney, 399 U.S. 42 (1970), when it held that the existence of exigent circumstances was to be determined at the time the automobile is seized. The car search at issue in *Chambers* took place at the police station, where the vehicle was immobilized, some time after the driver had been arrested. Given probable cause and exigent circumstances at the time the vehicle was first stopped, the Court held that the later warrantless search at the station passed constitutional muster. . . .

In United States v. Ross, 456 U.S. 798, decided in 1982, we held that a warrantless search of an automobile under the *Carroll* doctrine could include a search of a container or package found inside the car when such a search was supported by probable cause. The warrantless search of Ross' car occurred after an informant told the police that he had seen Ross complete a drug transaction using drugs stored in the trunk of his car. The police stopped the car, searched it, and discovered in the trunk a brown paper bag containing drugs. We decided that the search of Ross' car was not unreasonable under the Fourth Amendment: "The scope of a warrantless search based on probable cause is no narrower — and no broader — than the scope of a search authorized by a warrant supported by probable cause." Id., at 823. Thus, "[i]f probable cause justifies the search of a lawfully stopped vehicle, it justifies the search of every part of the vehicle and its contents that may conceal the object of the search." Id., at 825. In *Ross*, therefore, we clarified the scope of the *Carroll* doctrine as properly including a "probing search" of compartments and containers within the automobile so long as the search is supported by probable cause. Id., at 800.

In addition to this clarification, *Ross* distinguished the *Carroll* doctrine from the separate rule that governed the search of closed containers. See 456 U.S. at 817. The Court had announced this separate rule, unique to luggage and other closed packages, bags, and containers, in United States v. Chadwick, 433 U.S. 1 (1977). In *Chadwick*, federal narcotics agents had probable cause to believe that a 200-pound double-locked footlocker contained marijuana. The agents tracked the locker as the defendants removed it from a train and carried it through the station to a waiting car. As soon as the defendants lifted the locker into the trunk of the car, the agents arrested them, seized the locker, and searched it. In this Court, the United States did not contend that the locker's brief contact with the automobile's trunk sufficed to make the *Carroll* doctrine applicable. Rather, the United States urged that the search of movable luggage could be considered analogous to the search of an automobile. 433 U.S. at 11-12.

The Court rejected this argument because, it reasoned, a person expects more privacy in his luggage and personal effects than he does in his automobile. Id., at 13. Moreover, it concluded that as "may often not be the case when automobiles are seized," secure storage facilities are usually available when the police seize luggage. Id., at 13, n. 7.

In Arkansas v. Sanders, 442 U.S. 753 (1979), the Court extended *Chadwick*'s rule to apply to a suitcase actually being transported in the trunk of a car. In *Sanders*, the police had probable cause to believe a suitcase contained marijuana. They watched as the defendant placed the suitcase in the trunk of a taxi and was driven away. The police pursued the taxi for several blocks, stopped it, found the suitcase in the trunk, and searched it. Although the Court had applied the *Carroll* doctrine to searches of integral parts of the automobile itself, (indeed, in *Carroll*, contraband whiskey was in the upholstery of the seats, see 267 U.S. at 136), it did not extend the doctrine to the warrantless search of personal luggage "merely because it was located in an automobile lawfully stopped by the police." 442 U.S. at 765. Again, the *Sanders* majority stressed the heightened privacy expectation in personal luggage and concluded that the presence of luggage in an automobile did not diminish the owner's expectation of privacy in his personal items. Id., at 764-765.

In *Ross*, the Court endeavored to distinguish between *Carroll*, which governed the *Ross* automobile search, and *Chadwick*, which governed the *Sanders* automobile search. It held that the *Carroll* doctrine covered searches of automobiles when the police had probable cause to search an entire vehicle, but that the *Chadwick* doctrine governed searches of luggage when the officers had probable cause to search only a container within the vehicle. Thus, in a *Ross* situation, the police could conduct a reasonable search under the Fourth Amendment without obtaining a warrant, whereas in a *Sanders* situation, the police had to obtain a warrant before they searched. . . .

III

The facts in this case closely resemble the facts in *Ross*. In *Ross*, the police had probable cause to believe that drugs were stored in the trunk of a particular car. See 456 U.S., at 800. Here, the California Court of Appeal concluded that the police had probable cause to believe that respondent was carrying marijuana in a bag in his car's trunk. . . .

. . . We now must decide the question deferred in *Ross*: whether the Fourth Amendment requires the police to obtain a warrant to open the sack in a movable vehicle simply because they lack probable cause to search the entire car. We conclude that it does not.

IV

. . . [A] container found after a general search of the automobile and a container found in a car after a limited search for the container are equally easy for the police to store and for the suspect to hide or destroy. In fact, we see no principled distinction in terms of either the privacy expectation or the exigent circumstances between the paper bag found by the police in *Ross* and the paper bag found by the police here. Furthermore, by attempting to distinguish between a container for which the police are specifically searching and a container which they come across in a car, we have provided only minimal protection for privacy and have impeded effective law enforcement.

The line between probable cause to search a vehicle and probable cause to search a package in that vehicle is not always clear, and separate rules that govern the two objects to be searched may enable the police to broaden their power to make warrantless searches and disserve privacy interests. We noted this in *Ross* in the context of a search of an entire vehicle. Recognizing that under *Carroll*, the "entire vehicle itself . . . could be searched without a warrant," we concluded that "prohibiting police from opening immediately a container in which the object of the search is most likely to be found and instead forcing them first to comb the entire vehicle would actually exacerbate the intrusion on privacy interests." 456 U.S. at 821, n. 28. At the moment when officers stop an automobile, it may be less than clear whether they suspect with a high degree of certainty that the vehicle contains drugs in a bag or simply contains drugs. If the police know that they may open a bag only if they are actually searching the entire car, they may search more extensively than they otherwise would in order to establish the general probable cause required by *Ross*. . . .

To the extent that the *Chadwick-Sanders* rule protects privacy, its protection is minimal. Law enforcement officers may seize a container and hold it until they obtain a search warrant. *Chadwick*, 433 U.S. at 13. "Since the police, by hypothesis, have probable cause to seize the property, we can assume that a warrant will be routinely forthcoming in the overwhelming majority of cases." *Sanders*, 442 U.S. at 770 (dissenting opinion). . . .

Finally, the search of a paper bag intrudes far less on individual privacy than does the incursion sanctioned long ago in *Carroll*. In that case, prohibition agents slashed the upholstery of the automobile. This Court nonetheless found their search to be reasonable under the Fourth Amendment. If destroying the interior of an automobile is not unreasonable, we cannot conclude that looking inside a closed container is. In light of the minimal protection to privacy afforded by the *Chadwick-Sanders* rule, and our serious doubt whether that rule substantially serves privacy interests, we now hold that the Fourth Amendment does not compel separate treatment for an automobile search that extends only to a container within the vehicle.

V

The *Chadwick-Sanders* rule not only has failed to protect privacy but also has confused courts and police officers and impeded effective law enforcement. . . . One leading authority on the Fourth Amendment, after comparing *Chadwick* and *Sanders* with *Carroll* and its progeny, observed: "These two lines of authority cannot be completely reconciled, and thus how one comes out in the container-in-the-car situation depends upon which line of authority is used as a point of departure." 3 W. LaFave, Search and Seizure 53 (2d ed. 1987).

The discrepancy between the two rules has led to confusion for law enforcement officers. For example, when an officer, who has developed probable cause to believe that a vehicle contains drugs, begins to search the vehicle and immediately discovers a closed container, which rule applies? The defendant will argue that the fact that the officer first chose to search the container indicates that his probable cause extended only to the container and that *Chadwick* and *Sanders* therefore require a warrant. On the other hand, the fact that the officer first chose to search in the most obvious location should not restrict the propriety of the search. The *Chadwick* rule, as applied in *Sanders*, has devolved into an anomaly such that the more likely the police are to discover drugs in a container, the less authority they have to search it. We have noted the virtue of providing "clear and unequivocal guidelines to the law enforcement profession." Minnick v. Mississippi, 498 U.S. 146, 151 (1990). The *Chadwick-Sanders* rule is the antithesis of a "clear and unequivocal guideline." . . .

Although we have recognized firmly that the doctrine of stare decisis serves profoundly important purposes in our legal system, this Court has overruled a prior case on the comparatively rare occasion when it has bred confusion or been a derelict or led to anomalous results. *Sanders* was explicitly undermined in *Ross*, 456 U.S. at 824, and the existence of the dual regimes for automobile searches that uncover containers has proved as confusing as the *Chadwick* and *Sanders* dissenters predicted. We conclude that it is better to adopt one clear-cut rule to govern automobile searches and eliminate the warrant requirement for closed containers set forth in *Sanders*.

VI

The interpretation of the *Carroll* doctrine set forth in *Ross* now applies to all searches of containers found in an automobile. In other words, the police may search without a warrant if their search is supported by probable cause. The Court in *Ross* put it this way:

> The scope of a warrantless search of an automobile . . . is not defined by the nature of the container in which the contraband is secreted. Rather, it is defined by the object of the search and the places in which there is probable cause to believe that it may be found. 456 U.S. at 824.

It went on to note: "Probable cause to believe that a container placed in the trunk of a taxi contains contraband or evidence does not justify a search of the entire cab." Ibid. We reaffirm that principle. In the case before us, the police had probable cause to believe that the paper bag in the automobile's trunk contained marijuana. That probable cause now allows a warrantless search of the paper bag. The facts in the record reveal that the police did not have probable cause to believe that contraband was hidden in any other part of the automobile and a search of the entire vehicle would have been without probable cause and unreasonable under the Fourth Amendment.

Our holding today neither extends the *Carroll* doctrine nor broadens the scope of the permissible automobile search delineated in *Carroll, Chambers*, and *Ross*. It remains a "cardinal principle that 'searches conducted outside the judicial process, without prior approval by judge or magistrate, are per se unreasonable under the Fourth Amendment — subject only to a few specifically established and well-delineated exceptions.'" Mincey v. Arizona, 437 U.S. 385, 390 (1978), quoting Katz v. United States, 389 U.S. 347, 357 (1967). We held in *Ross*: "The exception recognized in *Carroll* is unquestionably one that is 'specifically established and well delineated.'" 456 U.S. at 825.

Until today, this Court has drawn a curious line between the search of an automobile that coincidentally turns up a container and the search of a container that coincidentally turns up in an automobile. The protections of the Fourth Amendment must not turn on such coincidences. We therefore interpret *Carroll* as providing one rule to govern all automobile searches. The police may search an automobile and the containers within it where they have probable cause to believe contraband or evidence is contained.

The judgment of the California Court of Appeal is reversed. . . .

JUSTICE SCALIA, concurring in the judgment.

I agree with the dissent that it is anomalous for a briefcase to be protected by the "general requirement" of a prior warrant when it is being carried along the street, but for that same briefcase to become unprotected as soon as it is carried into an automobile. On the other hand, I agree with the Court that it would be anomalous for a locked compartment in an automobile to be unprotected by the "general requirement" of a prior warrant, but for an unlocked briefcase within the automobile to be protected. I join in the judgment of the Court because I think its holding is more faithful to the text and tradition of the Fourth Amendment, and if these anomalies in our jurisprudence are ever to be eliminated that is the direction in which we should travel.

The Fourth Amendment does not by its terms require a prior warrant for searches and seizures; it merely prohibits searches and seizures that are "unreasonable."

What it explicitly states regarding warrants is by way of limitation upon their issuance rather than requirement of their use. For the warrant was a means of insulating officials from personal liability assessed by colonial juries. An officer who searched or seized without a warrant did so at his own risk; he would be liable for trespass, including exemplary damages, unless the jury found that his action was "reasonable." Amar, The Bill of Rights as a Constitution, 100 Yale L.J. 1131, 1178-1180 (1991); Huckle v. Money, 2 Wils. 205, 95 Eng. Rep. 768 (K.B. 1763). If, however, the officer acted pursuant to a proper warrant, he would be absolutely immune. See Bell v. Clapp, 10 Johns. 263 (N.Y. 1813); 4 W. Blackstone, Commentaries 288 (1769). By restricting the issuance of warrants, the Framers endeavored to preserve the jury's role in regulating searches and seizures. Amar, supra; Posner, Rethinking the Fourth Amendment, 1981 S. Ct. Rev. 49, 72-73; see also T. Taylor, Two Studies in Constitutional Interpretation 41 (1969).

Although the Fourth Amendment does not explicitly impose the requirement of a warrant, it is of course textually possible to consider that implicit within the requirement of reasonableness. For some years after the (still continuing) explosion in Fourth Amendment litigation that followed our announcement of the exclusionary rule in Weeks v. United States, 232 U.S. 383 (1914), our jurisprudence lurched back and forth between imposing a categorical warrant requirement and looking to reasonableness alone. (The opinions preferring a warrant involved searches of structures.) By the late 1960s, the preference for a warrant had won out, at least rhetorically. See Chimel [v. California, 395 U.S. 752 (1969)]; Coolidge v. New Hampshire, 403 U.S. 443 (1971).

The victory was illusory. Even before today's decision, the "warrant requirement" had become so riddled with exceptions that it was basically unrecognizable. In 1985, one commentator cataloged nearly 20 such exceptions, including "searches incident to arrest . . . automobile searches . . .border searches . . . administrative searches of regulated businesses . . . exigent circumstances . . . search[es] incident to nonarrest when there is probable cause to arrest . . . boat boarding for document checks . . . welfare searches . . . inventory searches . . . airport searches . . . school search[es]. . . . " Bradley, Two Models of the Fourth Amendment, 83 Mich. L. Rev. 1468, 1473-1474. Since then, we have added at least two more. California v. Carney, 471 U.S. 386 (1985) (searches of mobile homes); O'Connor v. Ortega, 480 U.S. 709 (1987) (searches of offices of government employees). Our intricate body of law regarding "reasonable expectation of privacy" has been developed largely as a means of creating these exceptions, enabling a search to be denominated not a Fourth Amendment "search" and therefore not subject to the general warrant requirement.

Unlike the dissent, therefore, I do not regard today's holding as some momentous departure, but rather as merely the continuation of an inconsistent jurisprudence that has been with us for years. Cases like United States v. Chadwick, 433 U.S. 1 (1977), and Arkansas v. Sanders, 442 U.S. 753 (1979), have taken the "preference for a warrant" seriously, while cases like United States v. Ross, 456 U.S. 798 (1982), and Carroll v. United States, 267 U.S. 132 (1925), have not. There can be no clarity in this area unless we make up our minds, and unless the principles we express comport with the actions we take.

In my view, the path out of this confusion should be sought by returning to the first principle that the "reasonableness" requirement of the Fourth Amendment affords the protection that the common law afforded. I have no difficulty with the proposition that that includes the requirement of a warrant, where the common law required a warrant; and it may even be that changes in the surrounding legal rules (for example, elimination of the common-law rule that reasonable, good-faith belief was no defense to absolute liability for trespass), may make a warrant indispensable to reasonableness where it once was not. But the supposed "general rule" that a warrant is always required does not appear to have any basis in the common law, and confuses rather than facilitates any attempt to develop rules of reasonableness in light of changed legal circumstances, as the anomaly eliminated and the anomaly created by today's holding both demonstrate.

And there are more anomalies still. Under our precedents (as at common law), a person may be arrested outside the home on the basis of probable cause, without an arrest warrant. United States v. Watson, 423 U.S. 411, 418-421 (1976). Upon arrest, the person, as well as the area within his grasp, may be searched for evidence related to the crime. Chimel v. California, supra, at 762-763. Under these principles, if a known drug dealer is carrying a briefcase reasonably believed to contain marijuana (the unauthorized possession of which is a crime), the police may arrest him and search his person on the basis of probable cause alone. And, under our precedents, upon arrival at the station house, the police may inventory his possessions, including the briefcase, even if there is no reason to suspect that they contain contraband. Illinois v. Lafayette, 462 U.S. 640 (1983). According to our current law, however, the police may not, on the basis of the same probable cause, take the less intrusive step of stopping the individual on the street and demanding to see the contents of his briefcase. That makes no sense a priori, and in the absence of any common-law tradition supporting such a distinction, I see no reason to continue it.

I would reverse the judgment in the present case, not because a closed container carried inside a car becomes subject to the "automobile" exception to the general warrant requirement, but because the search of a closed container, outside a privately owned building, with probable cause to believe that the container contains contraband, and when it in fact does contain contraband, is not one of those searches whose Fourth Amendment reasonableness depends upon a warrant. For that reason I concur in the judgment of the Court.

[Justice White's dissenting opinion is omitted.]

JUSTICE STEVENS, with whom JUSTICE MARSHALL joins, dissenting.

. . . The Fourth Amendment is a restraint on Executive power. The Amendment constitutes the Framers' direct constitutional response to the unreasonable law enforcement practices employed by agents of the British Crown. See Boyd v. United States, 116 U.S. 616, 624-625 (1886). Over the years—particularly in the period immediately after World War II and particularly in opinions authored by Justice Jackson after his service as a special prosecutor at the Nuremburg trials— the Court has recognized the importance of this restraint as a bulwark against police practices that prevail in totalitarian regimes. See, e.g., United States v. Di Re, 332 U.S. 581, 595 (1948); Johnson v. United States, 333 U.S. 10, 17 (1948).

This history is, however, only part of the explanation for the warrant requirement. The requirement also reflects the sound policy judgment that, absent exceptional circumstances, the decision to invade the privacy of an individual's personal effects should be made by a neutral magistrate rather than an agent of the Executive. . . .

The Court does not attempt to identify any exigent circumstances that would justify its refusal to apply the general rule against warrantless searches. Instead, it advances these three arguments: First, the rules identified in the foregoing cases are confusing and anomalous. Second, the rules do not protect any significant interest in privacy. And, third, the rules impede effective law enforcement. None of these arguments withstands scrutiny. . . .

The Court summarizes the alleged "anomaly" created by the coexistence of *Ross*, *Chadwick*, and *Sanders* with the statement that "the more likely the police are to discover drugs in a container, the less authority they have to search it." This juxtaposition is only anomalous, however, if one accepts the flawed premise that the degree to which the police are likely to discover contraband is correlated with their authority to search *without a warrant*. Yet, even proof beyond a reasonable doubt will not justify a warrantless search that is not supported by one of the exceptions to the warrant requirement. And, even when the police have a warrant or an exception applies, once the police possess probable cause, the extent to which they are more or less certain of the contents of a container has no bearing on their authority to search it.

To the extent there was any "anomaly" in our prior jurisprudence, the Court has "cured" it at the expense of creating a more serious paradox. For surely it is anomalous to prohibit a search of a briefcase while the owner is carrying it exposed on a public street yet to permit a search once the owner has placed the briefcase in the locked trunk of his car. One's privacy interest in one's luggage can certainly not be diminished by one's removing it from a public thoroughfare and placing it — out of sight — in a privately owned vehicle. Nor is the danger that evidence will escape increased if the luggage is in a car rather than on the street. In either location, if the police have probable cause, they are authorized to seize the luggage and to detain it until they obtain judicial approval for a search. Any line demarking an exception to the warrant requirement will appear blurred at the edges, but the Court has certainly erred if it believes that, by erasing one line and drawing another, it has drawn a clearer boundary.

The Court's statement that *Chadwick* and *Sanders* provide only "minimal protection to privacy" is also unpersuasive. Every citizen clearly has an interest in the privacy of the contents of his or her luggage, briefcase, handbag or any other container that conceals private papers and effects from public scrutiny. That privacy interest has been recognized repeatedly in cases spanning more than a century.

Under the Court's holding today, the privacy interest that protects the contents of a suitcase or a briefcase from a warrantless search when it is in public view simply vanishes when its owner climbs into a taxicab. Unquestionably the rejection of the *Sanders* line of cases by today's decision will result in a significant loss of individual privacy. . . .

The Court's suggestion that *Chadwick* and *Sanders* have created a significant burden on effective law enforcement is unsupported, inaccurate, and, in any event, an insufficient reason for creating a new exception to the warrant requirement.

Despite repeated claims that *Chadwick* and *Sanders* have "impeded effective law enforcement," the Court cites no authority for its contentions. Moreover, all evidence that does exist points to the contrary conclusion. In the years since *Ross* was decided, the Court has heard argument in 30 Fourth Amendment cases involving narcotics. In all but one, the government was the petitioner. All save two involved a search or seizure without a warrant or with a defective warrant. And, in all except three, the Court upheld the constitutionality of the search or seizure. . . .

Even if the warrant requirement does inconvenience the police to some extent, that fact does not distinguish this constitutional requirement from any other procedural protection secured by the Bill of Rights. It is merely a part of the price that our society must pay in order to preserve its freedom. . . .

NOTES AND QUESTIONS

1. In California v. Carney, 471 U.S. 386 (1985), the Court faced the question whether the automobile exception applies to a mobile home. It does. Chief Justice Burger's majority opinion justifies this conclusion by reference to "the lesser expectation of privacy resulting from its use as a readily mobile vehicle." Id. at 391. That lesser privacy expectation, in turn, "derive[s] . . . from the pervasive regulation of vehicles capable of traveling on the public highways." Id. at 392. What does that mean? How, precisely, does traffic regulation reduce one's privacy interest in the contents of one's car?

2. *Carney* raises a basic question about the automobile exception: What is its point? Is it exigency? Or is it reduced privacy expectations? Language in cases like *Carroll* suggests exigency is the problem—automobiles can move. But in *Chambers*, also discussed in *Acevedo*, the Court applied the automobile exception even though the police had already impounded the car when the search took place—the car was in police custody, and hence no longer mobile. And, of course, in *Acevedo* itself, it is clear, as Justice Stevens emphasizes in dissent, that the police could have seized and held the paper bag pending the outcome of a warrant application. Exigency seems absent.

3. Which leads to the rationale the Court used in *Carney*—reduced privacy expectations. The extent of the privacy interest in cars is surely contestable, but assume for the moment the Court is right to conclude that this interest is weaker than the privacy interest in, say, houses and apartments. What does that have to do with warrants? The question whether to require a warrant is a question about *process*; the same substantive standard—probable cause—applies either way. It seems easy to understand why one would want to vary the substantive standard based on the seriousness of the privacy interest at stake. But why vary the process?

Perhaps the answer is that process determines substance—that requiring warrants effectively means mandating a tougher probable cause standard. Judges decide suppression motions after the search has happened; such motions are filed only in cases in which incriminating evidence was found. It would be natural for judges to "tilt" toward finding probable cause in such cases. After all, the police officer's suspicion was justified—he found the evidence. By contrast, magistrates decide on warrant applications before the search has taken place; they are in a better position to evaluate the officer's suspicion neutrally. Maybe, then, we actually have two probable cause standards—"probable cause plus" in warrant cases, and "probable cause minus" in nonwarrant cases. For a detailed argument along these lines, see William J. Stuntz, Warrants and Fourth Amendment Remedies, 77 Va. L. Rev. 881 (1991).

If all of that is right, where do car searches belong—under the more protective standard, or the less protective one?

4. Imagine four searches. In the first, police search a house. In the second, police search a bag of the sort at issue in *Acevedo*, but on the street outside a car. In the third, police search the same bag, now inside a car. In the fourth, police search the glove compartment of a car.

Fourth Amendment law could, of course, treat all four searches the same, and apply the warrant requirement to each (with an exception for exigent circumstances). Or it could apply the warrant requirement to the searches that involve the more serious privacy intrusions, and exempt the police from having to get a warrant where the privacy interest is less serious. If the law chose the latter option, where would the line be drawn among these four searches?

The answer seems clear: Houses would get extra protection, and the other three searches would not. Yet that position does not win in *any* of the cases discussed here — indeed, the one time the government took that position, in *Chadwick*, the Supreme Court unanimously rejected it. And note — though the Court explicitly overrules *Sanders*, it does not overrule *Chadwick*: a warrant is still required to search Chadwick's footlocker.

5. One of the things the car search exception does is to lower the cost of searching cars. Police need not go through the hassles and incur the administrative costs of impounding containers or whole cars while waiting for a magistrate to rule on a warrant application. If they are confident of their probable cause judgment, they can search on the spot and take their chances that a judge in a suppression hearing will disagree. All of which will naturally lead police to do what they did in *Acevedo*: search the car. What would happen if the rule were otherwise — if there were no automobile exception to the warrant requirement? That would *raise* the cost of car searches, which would presumably lead police to search cars less frequently. It would also lower the relative cost of other searches — if the police have to wait for a warrant to search Acevedo's car, they might conclude that they may as well seek a warrant to search Acevedo's house or apartment. Fewer car searches would probably mean more house searches. In this sense, a more protective Fourth Amendment rule for cars might actually lead to greater privacy intrusions overall.

This is a particular instance of a general point. If the police are resource constrained, anything that lowers the cost of some police tactics (as *Acevedo* does for car searches) raises the relative cost of some others. *Acevedo*, together with other Court decisions that make searches outside homes easier to justify, may have the effect of limiting the number of searches of homes. That may actually make for *more* privacy protection.

WYOMING v. HOUGHTON

Certiorari to the Supreme Court of Wyoming
526 U.S. 295 (1999)

JUSTICE SCALIA delivered the opinion of the Court.

This case presents the question whether police officers violate the Fourth Amendment when they search a passenger's personal belongings inside an automobile that they have probable cause to believe contains contraband.

In the early morning hours of July 23, 1995, a Wyoming Highway Patrol officer stopped an automobile for speeding and driving with a faulty brake light. There were three passengers in the front seat of the car: David Young (the driver), his girlfriend, and respondent. While questioning Young, the officer noticed a hypodermic syringe in Young's shirt pocket. He left the occupants under the supervision of two backup officers as he went to get gloves from his patrol car. Upon his return, he instructed Young to step out of the car and place the syringe on the hood. The officer then asked Young why he had a syringe; with refreshing candor, Young replied that he used it to take drugs.

At this point, the backup officers ordered the two female passengers out of the car and asked them for identification. Respondent falsely identified herself as "Sandra James" and stated that she did not have any identification. Meanwhile, in light of Young's admission, the officer searched the passenger compartment of the car for contraband. On the back seat, he found a purse, which respondent claimed as hers. He removed from the purse a wallet containing respondent's driver's license, identifying her properly as Sandra K. Houghton. When the officer asked her why she had lied about her name, she replied: "In case things went bad."

Continuing his search of the purse, the officer found a brown pouch and a black wallet-type container. Respondent denied that the former was hers, and claimed ignorance of how it came to be there; it was found to contain drug paraphernalia and a syringe with 60 ccs of methamphetamine. Respondent admitted ownership of the black container, which was also found to contain drug paraphernalia, and a syringe (which respondent acknowledged was hers) with 10 ccs of methamphetamine — an amount insufficient to support the felony conviction at issue in this case. The officer also found fresh needle-track marks on respondent's arms. He placed her under arrest.

The State of Wyoming charged respondent with felony possession of methamphetamine in a liquid amount greater than three-tenths of a gram. After a hearing, the trial court denied her motion to suppress all evidence obtained from the purse as the fruit of a violation of the Fourth and Fourteenth Amendments. The court held that the officer had probable cause to search the car for contraband, and, by extension, any containers therein that could hold such contraband. A jury convicted respondent as charged.

The Wyoming Supreme Court, by divided vote, reversed the conviction and announced the following rule:

> Generally, once probable cause is established to search a vehicle, an officer is entitled to search all containers therein which may contain the object of the search. However, if the officer knows or should know that a container is the personal effect of a passenger who is not suspected of criminal activity, then the container is outside the scope of the search unless someone had the opportunity to conceal the contraband within the personal effect to avoid detection. 956 P.2d 363, 372 (1998).

The court held that the search of respondent's purse violated the Fourth and Fourteenth Amendments because the officer "knew or should have known that the purse did not belong to the driver, but to one of the passengers," and because "there was no probable cause to search the passengers' personal effects and no reason to believe that contraband had been placed within the purse." Ibid. . . .

The Fourth Amendment protects "[t]he right of the people to be secure in their persons, houses, papers, and effects, against unreasonable searches and seizures." In determining whether a particular governmental action violates this provision, we inquire first whether the action was regarded as an unlawful search or seizure under the common law when the Amendment was framed. See Wilson v. Arkansas, 514 U.S. 927, 931 (1995); California v. Hodari D., 499 U.S. 621, 624 (1991). Where that inquiry yields no answer, we must evaluate the search or seizure under traditional standards of reasonableness by assessing, on the one hand, the degree to which it intrudes upon an individual's privacy and, on the other, the degree to which it is needed for the promotion of legitimate governmental interests.

It is uncontested in the present case that the police officers had probable cause to believe there were illegal drugs in the car. Carroll v. United States, 267 U.S. 132 (1925), similarly involved the warrantless search of a car that law enforcement officials had probable cause to believe contained contraband—in that case, bootleg liquor. The Court concluded that the Framers would have regarded such a search as reasonable in light of legislation enacted by Congress from 1789 through 1799—as well as subsequent legislation from the founding era and beyond—that empowered customs officials to search any ship or vessel without a warrant if they had probable cause to believe that it contained goods subject to a duty. Id., at 150-153. Thus, the Court held that "contraband goods concealed and illegally transported in an automobile or other vehicle may be searched for without a warrant" where probable cause exists. Carroll, supra, at 153.

We have furthermore read the historical evidence to show that the Framers would have regarded as reasonable (if there was probable cause) the warrantless search of containers *within* an automobile. In [United States v. Ross, 456 U.S. 798 (1982)], we upheld as reasonable the warrantless search of a paper bag and leather pouch found in the trunk of the defendant's car by officers who had probable cause to believe that the trunk contained drugs. JUSTICE STEVENS, writing for the Court, observed:

> It is noteworthy that the early legislation on which the Court relied in *Carroll* concerned the enforcement of laws imposing duties on imported merchandise. . . . Presumably such merchandise was shipped then in containers of various kinds, just as it is today. Since Congress had authorized warrantless searches of vessels and beasts for imported merchandise, it is inconceivable that it intended a customs officer to obtain a warrant for every package discovered during the search; certainly Congress intended customs officers to open shipping containers when necessary and not merely to examine the exterior of cartons or boxes in which smuggled goods might be concealed. During virtually the entire history of our country—whether contraband was transported in a horse-drawn carriage, a 1921 roadster, or a modern automobile—it has been assumed that a lawful search of a vehicle would include a search of any container that might conceal the object of the search. Id., at 820, n. 26.

. . . To be sure, there was no passenger in *Ross*, and it was not claimed that the package in the trunk belonged to anyone other than the driver. Even so, if the rule of law that *Ross* announced were limited to contents belonging to the driver, or contents other than those belonging to passengers, one would have expected that substantial limitation to be expressed. And, more importantly, one would have expected that limitation to be apparent in the historical evidence that formed the basis for *Ross*'s holding. In fact, however, nothing in the statutes *Ross* relied upon, or in the practice under those statutes, would except from authorized warrantless search packages belonging to passengers on the suspect ship, horse-drawn carriage, or automobile.

Finally, we must observe that the analytical principle underlying the rule announced in *Ross* is fully consistent — as respondent's proposal is not — with the balance of our Fourth Amendment jurisprudence. *Ross* concluded from the historical evidence that the permissible scope of a warrantless car search "is defined by the object of the search and the places in which there is probable cause to believe that it may be found." 456 U.S. at 824. The same principle is reflected in an earlier case involving the constitutionality of a search warrant directed at premises belonging to one who is not suspected of any crime: "The critical element in a reasonable search is not that the owner of the property is suspected of crime but that there is reasonable cause to believe that the specific 'things' to be searched for and seized are located on the property to which entry is sought." Zurcher v. Stanford Daily, 436 U.S. 547, 556 (1978). This statement was illustrated by citation and description of *Carroll*, 267 U.S., at 158-159, 167.

In sum, neither *Ross* itself nor the historical evidence it relied upon admits of a distinction among packages or containers based on ownership. When there is probable cause to search for contraband in a car, it is reasonable for police officers — like customs officials in the founding era — to examine packages and containers without a showing of individualized probable cause for each one. A passenger's personal belongings, just like the driver's belongings or containers attached to the car like a glove compartment, are "in" the car, and the officer has probable cause to search for contraband *in* the car.

Even if the historical evidence . . . were thought to be equivocal, we would find that the balancing of the relative interests weighs decidedly in favor of allowing searches of a passenger's belongings. Passengers, no less than drivers, possess a reduced expectation of privacy with regard to the property that they transport in cars, which "trave[l] public thoroughfares," Cardwell v. Lewis, 417 U.S. 583, 590 (1974), "seldom serv[e] as . . . the repository of personal effects," ibid., are subjected to police stop and examination to enforce "pervasive" governmental controls "[a]s an everyday occurrence," South Dakota v. Opperman, 428 U.S. 364, 368 (1976), and, finally, are exposed to traffic accidents that may render all their contents open to public scrutiny.

In this regard — the degree of intrusiveness upon personal privacy and indeed even personal dignity — the two cases the Wyoming Supreme Court found dispositive differ substantially from the package search at issue here. United States v. Di Re, 332 U.S. 581 (1948), held that probable cause to search a car did not justify a body search of a passenger. And Ybarra v. Illinois, 444 U.S. 85 (1979), held that a search warrant for a tavern and its bartender did not permit body searches of all the bar's patrons. These cases turned on the unique, significantly heightened protection afforded against searches of one's person. "Even a limited search of the outer clothing . . . constitutes a severe, though brief, intrusion upon cherished personal security, and it must surely be an annoying, frightening, and perhaps humiliating experience." Terry v. Ohio, 392 U.S. 1, 24-25 (1968). Such traumatic consequences are not to be expected when the police examine an item of personal property found in a car.

Whereas the passenger's privacy expectations are, as we have described, considerably diminished, the governmental interests at stake are substantial. Effective law enforcement would be appreciably impaired without the ability to search a passenger's personal belongings when there is reason to believe contraband or evidence of criminal wrongdoing is hidden in the car. As in all car-search cases, the "ready mobility" of an automobile creates a risk that the evidence or contraband will be permanently lost while a warrant is obtained. California v. Carney, 471 U.S. 386, 390 (1985). In addition, a car passenger—unlike the unwitting tavern patron in *Ybarra*—will often be engaged in a common enterprise with the driver, and have the same interest in concealing the fruits or the evidence of their wrong-doing. A criminal might be able to hide contraband in a passenger's belongings as readily as in other containers in the car—perhaps even surreptitiously, without the passenger's knowledge or permission. (This last possibility provided the basis for respondent's defense at trial; she testified that most of the seized contraband must have been placed in her purse by her traveling companions at one or another of various times, including the time she was "half asleep" in the car.)

To be sure, these factors favoring a search will not always be present, but the balancing of interests must be conducted with an eye to the generality of cases. To require that the investigating officer have positive reason to believe that the pas-senger and driver were engaged in a common enterprise, or positive reason to believe that the driver had time and occasion to conceal the item in the passenger's belongings, surreptitiously or with friendly permission, is to impose requirements so seldom met that a "passenger's property" rule would dramatically reduce the ability to find and seize contraband and evidence of crime. Of course these require-ments would not attach (under the Wyoming Supreme Court's rule) until the police officer knows or has reason to know that the container belongs to a passenger. But once a "passenger's property" exception to car searches became widely known, one would expect passenger-confederates to claim everything as their own. And one would anticipate a bog of litigation—in the form of both civil lawsuits and motions to suppress in criminal trials—involving such questions as whether the officer should have believed a passenger's claim of ownership, whether he should have inferred ownership from various objective factors, whether he had probable cause to believe that the passenger was a confederate, or to believe that the driver might have introduced the contraband into the package with or without the passenger's knowledge. When balancing the competing interests, our determinations of "rea-sonableness" under the Fourth Amendment must take account of these practical realities. We think they militate in favor of the needs of law enforcement, and against a personal-privacy interest that is ordinarily weak. . . .

We hold that police officers with probable cause to search a car may inspect passengers' belongings found in the car that are capable of concealing the object of the search. The judgment of the Wyoming Supreme Court is reversed.

[Justice Breyer's concurring opinion is omitted.]

JUSTICE STEVENS, with whom JUSTICE SOUTER and JUSTICE GINSBURG join, dis-senting.

. . . In all of our prior cases applying the automobile exception to the Fourth Amendment's warrant requirement, either the defendant was the operator of the vehicle and in custody of the object of the search, or no question was raised as to the defendant's ownership or custody. In the only automobile case confronting the search of a passenger defendant—United States v. Di Re, 332 U.S. 581 (1948)—the Court held that the exception to the warrant requirement did not apply. Id. at 583-587 (addressing searches of the passenger's pockets and the space between his shirt and underwear, both of which uncovered counterfeit fuel rations). In *Di Re*, as here, the information prompting the search directly implicated the driver, not the passenger. . . . Moreover, unlike the Court, I think it quite plain that the search of a passenger's purse or briefcase involves an intrusion on privacy that may be just as serious as was the intrusion in *Di Re*. . . .

Nor am I persuaded that the mere spatial association between a passenger and a driver provides an acceptable basis for presuming that they are partners in crime or for ignoring privacy interests in a purse. Whether or not the Fourth Amendment required a warrant to search Houghton's purse, at the very least the trooper in this case had to have probable cause to believe that her purse contained contraband. The Wyoming Supreme Court concluded that he did not.

Finally, in my view, the State's legitimate interest in effective law enforcement does not outweigh the privacy concerns at issue.[3] I am as confident in a police officer's ability to apply a rule requiring a warrant or individualized probable cause to search belongings that are — as in this case — obviously owned by and in the custody of a passenger as is the Court in a "passenger-confederate[']s" ability to circumvent the rule. Certainly the ostensible clarity of the Court's rule is attractive. But that virtue is insufficient justification for its adoption. Moreover, a rule requiring a warrant or individualized probable cause to search passenger belongings is every bit as simple as the Court's rule; it simply protects more privacy. . . .

NOTES AND QUESTIONS

1. Before California v. Acevedo, car search cases often focused on containers — suitcases, paper bags, purses, and the like — and on whether a valid car search could include them. *Acevedo* seemed to promise an end to that debate: After *Acevedo*, authority to search an automobile includes authority to search containers found within the automobile, period.

That sounds simple enough. But what happens when *Acevedo* is applied to containers that are attached to people? Can an officer search your jacket pockets if you're a passenger in a car and the officer is entitled to search the car? Does the answer depend on whether you're wearing the jacket at the time the car is stopped? In United States v. Di Re, 332 U.S. 581 (1948), a case cited by both the *Houghton* majority and the *Houghton* dissent, the Court held that searches of a passenger's clothing were not included within a lawful car search. In *Houghton*, the Court holds that a search of a passenger's purse *is* included within a lawful car search. Apparently, the hypothetical jacket pocket search *does* turn on whether the passenger is wearing the jacket. If the purse is slung around the passenger's shoulder, does that change the result in *Houghton*? If a passenger is holding a paper bag in his lap, is the bag treated like an article of clothing (because it is attached to the passenger) or like a container?

2. Does the *Houghton* line, however that line is defined, make sense? Surely the privacy interest in purses or jacket pockets is the same whether or not those articles

3. To my knowledge, we have never restricted ourselves to a two-step Fourth Amendment approach wherein the privacy and governmental interests at stake must be considered only if 18th-century common law "yields no answer." . . . In a later discussion, the Court does attempt to address the contemporary privacy and governmental interests at issue in cases of this nature. Either the majority is unconvinced by its own recitation of the historical materials, or it has determined that considering additional factors is appropriate in any event. The Court does not admit the former; and of course the latter, standing alone, would not establish uncertainty in the common law as the prerequisite to looking beyond history in Fourth Amendment cases.

are being worn by passengers when they are searched. On the other hand, does any *other* line make sense? As the majority notes, it would be hard for the police to have to make judgments about what belonged to whom whenever a car with several passengers is searched.

3. The most important thing about *Houghton* may be the Court's methodology. Justice Scalia, speaking for a Court majority, states that Fourth Amendment analysis follows two steps: First, one asks "whether the action was regarded as an unlawful search or seizure under the common law when the Amendment was framed." Only if that inquiry yields no clear answer does one go to the second step, which consists of the familiar balance of individual privacy and law enforcement need. Does this sound like the analysis followed in other Fourth Amendment cases? Should a similar analysis apply to the question whether the Fourth Amendment should be enforced through an exclusionary rule—a remedy unknown to the common law in 1791? If not, why not?

Houghton is one more piece of evidence of a growing judicial interest in the original understanding as a guide to decision in search and seizure cases. What are the merits of that approach in this context?

d. Arrests

The central object of the Fourth Amendment is to protect the individual's "right to be let alone—the most comprehensive of rights and the right most valued by civilized men." Olmsted v. United States, 277 U.S. 438, 478 (1928) (Brandeis, J., dissenting). It would seem to follow that, of all the police behaviors that Fourth Amendment law regulates, arrests should be subject to the most stringent legal standards. "The invasion and disruption of a man's life and privacy which stem from his arrest are ordinarily far greater than the relatively minor intrusions attending a search of his premises." Chimel v. California, 395 U.S. 752, 776 (1969) (White, J., dissenting). The arrest is likely to be an "awesome and frightening" experience for the arrestee. See ALI Model Code of Pre-Arraignment Procedure, section 120.1, Commentary at 290-91 (1975). Professor Schroeder has described some of the reasons:

> Any arrest has a profound and long-lasting effect on the arrestee. Even if an arrest is for a minor offense, and charges against the arrestee are ultimately dropped or the arrestee is acquitted, the records of the arrest probably will be retained and disseminated. Moreover, widespread public feeling that "where there's smoke, there's fire" often leaves a cloud of suspicion hanging over an arrestee even if no conviction follows. The result will often be lost employment opportunities[13] and future law enforcement scrutiny.
>
> A custodial arrest is an especially "awesome and frightening" experience. The arrestee is abruptly constrained and usually searched, even if the arrest is for a minor offense. He is then forcibly taken to an unfamiliar place, booked, fingerprinted, photographed, searched more extensively, and held in jail, possibly under unsanitary and unsafe conditions, until, and unless, he can obtain his release. The

---

13. To give just one example, applicants for the bar generally must disclose all prior arrests, even if the charges eventually were dismissed. See Deborah L. Rhode, Moral Character as a Professional Credential, 94 Yale L.J. 491, 520-521 (1985).—Eds.

arrestee may suffer emotional distress and public humiliation, and may lose contact with family and friends. He may lose time from work and will probably be required to retain an attorney and spend money on bail. If the detention is at all prolonged, he may lose his job or suffer other adverse consequences. . . . Because the consequences of an arrest are so severe, substantial civil damages have been awarded to persons improperly arrested for minor offenses.

William A. Schroeder, Warrantless Misdemeanor Arrests and the Fourth Amendment, 58 Mo. L. Rev. 771 (1993).

The legal rules that govern arrests historically have been derived from three distinct but related sources: the common law, statutes, and the Constitution. A complete understanding of arrests thus requires an examination of all three sources. At common law, arrests for misdemeanors generally were prohibited without a warrant. The main exception was for breaches of the peace[14] committed in the arrestor's[15] presence,[16] as long as the arrest was made at the time of or shortly after the offense. For felonies, the common-law rule was broader: warrantless arrests were generally allowed, so long as the arrestor had "reasonable grounds" to believe that a felony had been committed and that the arrestee had committed it. "Reasonable grounds" meant something very much like the modern concept of "probable cause." See Draper v. United States, 358 U.S. 307, 310 n. 3 (1959).

Over time, statutes gradually expanded the common-law rules of arrest, at least as applied to arrests made by police officers.[17] For misdemeanors, most modern statutes authorize arrests without a warrant whenever the offense is committed within the officer's presence, or for certain offenses even when committed outside the officer's presence (such as domestic abuse or violations of protective orders), or for any misdemeanor offenses under certain factual circumstances (such as when the suspect is attempting to flee or to destroy evidence). This authority to arrest without a warrant for misdemeanors generally is not limited to breaches of the peace, although such arrests still must be made promptly after the offense. For felonies, most modern statutes generally reflect the common-law rule and authorize warrantless arrests based on "probable cause."

As far as the Constitution is concerned, the first and most important rule is that all custodial arrests must be based on "probable cause." See Henry v. United States, 361 U.S. 98 (1959); Dunaway v. New York, 442 U.S. 200 (1979). The constitutional rule with respect to warrants, however, is not so clear. In at least some situations, police officers may arrest without a warrant. The leading case is

14. But see Atwater v. Lago Vista, 532 U.S. 318 (2001), infra, in which the Court concludes that the common-law rule for misdemeanor arrests was not strictly limited to breaches of the peace.

15. Notice that the "arrestor" could be an ordinary citizen as well as a police officer. Indeed, these common-law rules of arrest developed at a time when police forces did not yet exist.

16. "In the arrestor's presence" generally meant that the arrestor must have learned of the offense through one or more of the senses. Some jurisdictions also allowed a police officer to rely on sensory knowledge acquired by another police officer.

17. See supra note 15. Today, many statutes continue to authorize arrests by private persons in at least some situations. Such authority often has been expanded beyond its common-law scope, although it is still generally less extensive than the authority granted to police officers. See, e.g., 725 Ill. Comp. Stat. Ann. §5/107-3 (Smith-Hurd 1993) ("Any person may arrest another when he has reasonable grounds to believe that an offense other than an ordinance violation is being committed."); Utah Code Ann. §77-7-3 (1990) ("A private person may arrest another: (1) For a public offense committed or attempted in his presence; or (2) When a felony has been committed and he has reasonable cause to believe the person arrested has committed it.").

United States v. Watson, 423 U.S. 411 (1976). Federal Postal Inspectors received a reliable tip that Watson was in possession of stolen credit cards. The inspectors persuaded the tipster (who had worked with Watson in the past to profit from such credit cards) to arrange a meeting with Watson at a restaurant. At the restaurant, the tipster signaled the inspectors that Watson did, indeed, possess stolen credit cards. The inspectors moved in and arrested Watson without a warrant (as they were authorized to do by the relevant statutes and regulations of the U.S. Postal Service), but they found no credit cards on Watson's person. They asked Watson if they could search his nearby car, and Watson replied, "Go ahead." Using keys provided by Watson, the inspectors searched the car, and found two stolen credit cards under the floor mat. Watson was convicted of two counts of possessing stolen mail, and subsequently challenged, under the Fourth Amendment, the admission into evidence of the credit cards.[18]

According to the Court in *Watson*:

> Contrary to the Court of Appeals' view, Watson's arrest was not invalid because executed without a warrant. Title 18 U.S.C. §3061(a)(3) expressly empowers the Board of Governors of the Postal Service to authorize Postal Service officers and employees "performing duties related to the inspection of postal matters" to "make arrests without warrant for felonies cognizable under the laws of the United States if they have reasonable grounds to believe that the person to be arrested has committed or is committing such a felony." By regulation, 39 CFR §232.5(a)(3) (1975), and in identical language, the Board of Governors has exercised that power and authorized warrantless arrests. Because there was probable cause in this case to believe that Watson had violated [the federal statute banning possession of stolen mail], the inspector and his subordinates, in arresting Watson, were acting strictly in accordance with the governing statute and regulations. . . .
>
> . . . Section 3061 represents a judgment by Congress that it is not unreasonable under the Fourth Amendment for postal inspectors to arrest without a warrant provided they have probable cause to do so. This was not an isolated or quixotic judgment of the legislative branch. Other federal law enforcement officers have been expressly authorized by statute for many years to make felony arrests on probable cause but without a warrant. This is true of United States marshals, 18 U.S.C. §3053, and of agents of the Federal Bureau of Investigation, 18 U.S.C. §3052; the Drug Enforcement Administration, 84 Stat. 1273, 21 U.S.C. §878; the Secret Service, 18 U.S.C. §3056(a); and the Customs Service, 26 U.S.C. §7607.
>
> Because there is a "strong presumption of constitutionality due to an Act of Congress, especially when it turns on what is 'reasonable,'" "[o]bviously the Court should be reluctant to decide that a search thus authorized by Congress was

---

18. The Court of Appeals' opinion in *Watson* did not state clearly whether the Fourth Amendment was implicated because the credit cards were the "fruits" of an illegal arrest, or because the illegal arrest tainted Watson's subsequent consent to the search of his car. The Supreme Court concluded that this ambiguity was immaterial, since the outcome of the case — under either theory — turned on the constitutionality of the arrest.

Incidentally, *Watson* represents the typical way that issues involving arrest warrants get litigated. Even if an arrest is improperly made without a warrant, the custody itself is not unlawful, and the resulting conviction therefore does not become invalid. See United States v. Crews, 445 U.S. 463 (1980); Gerstein v. Pugh, 420 U.S. 103 (1975). But a person who has been improperly arrested without a warrant may be able to challenge the admission of any evidence that was obtained as a result of the arrest.

unreasonable and that the Act was therefore unconstitutional." United States v. Di Re, 332 U.S. 581, 585 (1948). . . .

The cases construing the Fourth Amendment . . . reflect the ancient common-law rule that a peace officer was permitted to arrest without a warrant for a misdemeanor or felony committed in his presence as well as for a felony not committed in his presence if there was reasonable ground for making the arrest. 10 Halsbury's Laws of England 344-345 (3d ed. 1955); 4 W. Blackstone, Commentaries *292; 1 J. Stephen, A History of the Criminal Law of England 193 (1883); 2 M. Hale, Pleas of the Crown *72-74; Wilgus, Arrest Without a Warrant, 22 Mich. L. Rev. 541, 547-550, 686-688 (1924); Samuel v. Payne, 1 Doug. 359, 99 Eng. Rep. 230 (K.B. 1780); Beckwith v. Philby, 6 Barn. & Cress. 635, 108 Eng. Rep. 585 (K.B. 1827). This has also been the prevailing rule under state constitutions and statutes. . . .

The balance struck by the common law in generally authorizing felony arrests on probable cause, but without a warrant, has survived substantially intact. It appears in almost all of the States in the form of express statutory authorization. In 1963, the American Law Institute undertook the task of formulating a model statute governing police powers and practice in criminal law enforcement and related aspects of pretrial procedure. In 1975, after years of discussion, A Model Code of Pre-arraignment Procedure was proposed. Among its provisions was §120.1 which authorizes an officer to take a person into custody if the officer has reasonable cause to believe that the person to be arrested has committed a felony, or has committed a misdemeanor or petty misdemeanor in his presence. The commentary to this section said: "The Code thus adopts the traditional and almost universal standard for arrest without a warrant."

This is the rule Congress has long directed its principal law enforcement officers to follow. Congress has plainly decided against conditioning warrantless arrest power on proof of exigent circumstances. Law enforcement officers may find it wise to seek arrest warrants where practicable to do so, and their judgments about probable cause may be more readily accepted where backed by a warrant issued by a magistrate. But we decline to transform this judicial preference into a constitutional rule when the judgment of the Nation and Congress has for so long been to authorize warrantless public arrests on probable cause rather than to encumber criminal prosecutions with endless litigation with respect to the existence of exigent circumstances, whether it was practicable to get a warrant, whether the suspect was about to flee, and the like.

Watson's arrest did not violate the Fourth Amendment, and the Court of Appeals erred in holding to the contrary.

Because our judgment is that Watson's arrest comported with the Fourth Amendment, Watson's consent to the search of his car was not the product of an illegal arrest. To the extent that the issue of the voluntariness of Watson's consent was resolved on the premise that his arrest was illegal, the Court of Appeals was also in error. . . .

Justice Powell, in concurrence, noted the "anomaly" created by the Court's decision:

> Since the Fourth Amendment speaks equally to both searches and seizures, and since an arrest, the taking hold of one's person, is quintessentially a seizure, it would seem that the constitutional provision should impose the same limitations upon arrests that it does upon searches. Indeed, as an abstract matter an argument can be made that the restrictions upon arrest perhaps should be greater. A search may cause only annoyance and temporary inconvenience to the law-abiding citizen, assuming more serious dimension only when it turns up evidence of criminality. An arrest, however, is a serious personal intrusion regardless of whether the person seized is

guilty or innocent. Although an arrestee cannot be held for a significant period without some neutral determination that there are grounds to do so, see [Gerstein v. Pugh, 420 U.S. 103, 113 (1975)], no decision that he should go free can come quickly enough to erase the invasion of his privacy that already will have occurred. Logic therefore would seem to dictate that arrests be subject to the warrant requirement at least to the same extent as searches.

But logic sometimes must defer to history and experience. . . . There is no historical evidence that the Framers or proponents of the Fourth Amendment, outspokenly opposed to the infamous general warrants and writs of assistance, were at all concerned about warrantless arrests by local constables and other peace officers. . . .

Moreover, a constitutional rule permitting felony arrests only with a warrant or in exigent circumstances could severely hamper effective law enforcement. Good police practice often requires postponing an arrest, even after probable cause has been established, in order to place the suspect under surveillance or otherwise develop further evidence necessary to prove guilt to a jury. Under the holding of the Court of Appeals such additional investigative work could imperil the entire prosecution. Should the officers fail to obtain a warrant initially, and later be required by unforeseen circumstances to arrest immediately with no chance to procure a last-minute warrant, they would risk a court decision that the subsequent exigency did not excuse their failure to get a warrant in the interim since they first developed probable cause. If the officers attempted to meet such a contingency by procuring a warrant as soon as they had probable cause and then merely held it during their subsequent investigation, they would risk a court decision that the warrant had grown stale by the time it was used.[5] Law enforcement personnel caught in this squeeze could ensure validity of their arrests only by obtaining a warrant and arresting as soon as probable cause existed, thereby foreclosing the possibility of gathering vital additional evidence from the suspect's continued actions.

In sum, the historical and policy reasons sketched above fully justify the Court's sustaining of a warrantless arrest upon probable cause, despite the resulting divergence between the constitutional rule governing searches and that now held applicable to seizures of the person. . . .

Justice Marshall wrote the dissent:

The Court . . . relies on the English common-law rule of arrest and the many state and federal statutes following it. There are two serious flaws in this approach. First, as a matter of factual analysis, the substance of the ancient common-law rule provides no support for the far-reaching modern rule that the Court fashions on its model. Second, as a matter of doctrine, the longstanding existence of a Government practice does not immunize the practice from scrutiny under the mandate of our Constitution.

The common-law rule was indeed as the Court states it: "[A] peace officer was permitted to arrest without a warrant for a misdemeanor or felony committed in his presence as well as for a felony not committed in his presence if there was reasonable ground for making the arrest." To apply the rule blindly today, however, makes as much sense as attempting to interpret Hamlet's admonition to Ophelia, "Get thee to a nunnery, go," without understanding the meaning of Hamlet's words in the

---

5. The probable cause to support issuance of an arrest warrant normally would not grow stale as easily as that which supports a warrant to search a particular place for particular objects. This is true because once there is probable cause to believe that someone is a felon the passage of time often will bring new supporting evidence. But in some cases the original grounds supporting the warrant could be disproved by subsequent investigation that at the same time turns up wholly new evidence supporting probable cause on a different theory. In those cases the warrant could be stale because based upon discredited information.

context of their age.[3] For the fact is that a felony at common law and a felony today bear only slight resemblance, with the result that the relevance of the common-law rule of arrest to the modern interpretation of our Constitution is minimal.

. . . Only the most serious crimes were felonies at common law, and many crimes now classified as felonies under federal or state law were treated as misdemeanors. [NOTE — This includes, among many others, such crimes as assault with intent to murder or rape, escape from lawful arrest, kidnapping, mayhem, obstructing justice, and perjury. — EDS.] . . . To make an arrest for any of these crimes at common law, the police officer was required to obtain a warrant, unless the crime was committed in his presence. Since many of these same crimes are commonly classified as felonies today, however, under the Court's holding a warrant is no longer needed to make such arrests, a result in contravention of the common law.

Thus the lesson of the common law, and those courts in this country that have accepted its rule, is an ambiguous one. Applied in its original context, the common-law rule would allow the warrantless arrest of some, but not all, of those we call felons today. Accordingly, the Court is simply historically wrong when it tells us that "[t]he balance struck by the common law in generally authorizing felony arrests on probable cause, but without a warrant, has survived substantially intact." . . . Indeed, the only clear lesson of history is contrary to the one the Court draws: the common law considered the arrest warrant far more important than today's decision leaves it.

I do not mean by this that a modern warrant requirement should apply only to arrests precisely analogous to common-law misdemeanors, and be inapplicable to analogues of common-law felonies. Rather, the point is simply that the Court's unblinking literalism cannot replace analysis of the constitutional interests involved. While we can learn from the common law, the ancient rule does not provide a simple answer directly transferable to our system. . . .

My Brother Powell concludes: "Logic . . . would seem to dictate that arrests be subject to the warrant requirement at least to the same extent as searches." I agree. . . .

Surely there is no reason to place greater trust in the partisan assessment of a police officer that there is probable cause for an arrest than in his determination that probable cause exists for a search. . . .

We come then to the [question] whether a warrant requirement would unduly burden legitimate law enforcement interests. . . .

The Government's assertion that a warrant requirement would impose an intolerable burden stems, in large part, from the specious supposition that procurement of an arrest warrant would be necessary as soon as probable cause ripens. [But t]here is no requirement that a search warrant be obtained the moment police have probable cause to search. The rule is only that present probable cause be shown and a warrant obtained before a search is undertaken. The same rule should obtain for arrest warrants, where it may even make more sense. Certainly, there is less need for prompt procurement of a warrant in the arrest situation. Unlike probable cause to search, probable cause to arrest, once formed, will continue to exist for the indefinite future, at least if no intervening exculpatory facts come to light.

This sensible approach obviates most of the difficulties that have been suggested with an arrest warrant rule. Police would not have to cut their investigation short the moment they obtain probable cause to arrest, nor would undercover agents be forced suddenly to terminate their work and forfeit their covers. Moreover, if in the course of the continued police investigation exigent circumstances develop that demand an immediate arrest, the arrest may be made without fear of unconstitutionality, so

---

3. Nunnery was Elizabethan slang for house of prostitution. 7 Oxford English Dictionary 264 (1933).

long as the exigency was unanticipated and not used to avoid the arrest warrant requirement. Likewise, if in the course of the continued investigation police uncover evidence tying the suspect to another crime, they may immediately arrest him for that crime if exigency demands it, and still be in full conformity with the warrant rule. This is why the arrest in this case was not improper. Other than where police attempt to evade the warrant requirement, the rule would invalidate an arrest only in the obvious situation: where police, with probable cause but without exigent circumstances, set out to arrest a suspect. Such an arrest must be void, . . . otherwise the warrant requirement would be reduced to a toothless prescription. . . .

Thus, the practical reasons marshaled against an arrest warrant requirement are unimpressive. If anything, the virtual nonexistence of a staleness problem suggests that such a requirement would be less burdensome for police than the search warrant rule. And given the significant protection our citizens will gain from a warrant requirement, accepted Fourth Amendment analysis dictates that a warrant rule be imposed. . . . Thus, I believe the proper result is application of the warrant requirement, as it has developed in the search context, to all arrests. . . .

NOTES ON THE SCOPE OF THE ARREST POWER

1. In County of Riverside v. McLaughlin, 500 U.S. 44 (1991), the Court held that a defendant arrested without a warrant and held in custody must receive, within 48 hours, a judicial determination of whether his arrest met the probable cause standard. The Court added:

> This is not to say that the probable cause determination in a particular case passes constitutional muster simply because it is provided within 48 hours. Such a hearing may nonetheless violate [the Fourth Amendment] if the arrested individual can prove that his or her probable cause determination was delayed unreasonably. Examples of unreasonable delay are delays for the purpose of gathering additional evidence to justify the arrest, a delay motivated by ill will against the arrested individual, or delay for delay's sake. In evaluating whether the delay in a particular case is unreasonable, however, courts must allow a substantial degree of flexibility. Courts cannot ignore the often unavoidable delays in transporting arrested persons from one facility to another, handling late-night bookings where no magistrate is readily available, obtaining the presence of an arresting officer who may be busy processing other suspects or securing the premises of an arrest, and other practical realities.

Id. at 56-57. *Watson* potentially raises serious concerns about police arresting defendants without any judicial review. Does *McLaughlin* put those concerns to rest?

2. Justice Powell's concurrence and Justice Marshall's dissent debate the administrability of a warrant requirement for arrests. Who wins the debate? Staleness seems a non-issue: either the suspect committed the crime or he didn't; that fact will not change — unlike searches, for the location of evidence *can* change while police are waiting to search. As Justice Marshall notes, precisely because of this point a warrant requirement would seem *more* administrable in arrest cases than in search cases.

So why not require arrest warrants? Aren't arrests at least as important as, say, house searches? Perhaps *Watson* suggests that, in the eyes of the law, the answer is no. Certainly after *Watson* it seems fair to say that privacy interests receive more

Fourth Amendment protection than liberty interests. At the least, that hierarchy of protection is contestable. And it may have significant distributive implications:

> Privacy, in Fourth Amendment terms, is something that exists only in certain types of spaces; not surprisingly, the law protects it only where it exists. Rich people have more access to those spaces than poor people; they therefore enjoy more legal protection. That is not true of some other interests Fourth Amendment law protects. Thus, to the extent the law focuses on privacy rather than, say, the interest in avoiding police harassment or discrimination, it shifts something valuable — legal protection — from poorer suspects to wealthier ones.

William J. Stuntz, The Distribution of Fourth Amendment Privacy, 67 Geo. Wash. L. Rev. 1265, 1266-1267 (1999). Is this an argument for overturning *Watson*?

3. At one point in *Watson*, the Court suggests that a contrary rule would "encumber criminal prosecutions with endless litigation with respect to the existence of exigent circumstances, whether it was practicable to get a warrant, whether the suspect was about to flee, and the like." This may be a serious concern. Consider Justice Marshall's conclusion that, in *Watson* itself, exigent circumstances existed. If that conclusion holds true in *Watson*, it must hold true in a great many arrests outside the suspect's home. Still, if exigent circumstances were a condition of a valid warrantless arrest, there would presumably be a great deal of litigation about just what circumstances are exigent — much more than one now sees, if only because there are vastly more warrantless arrests than there are warrantless searches where the government relies on exigency. Courts might find themselves swamped — there are more than 13 million arrests each year, see Sourcebook of Criminal Justice Statistics — 2002, at 342 tbl. 4.1 (available online at *http://www.albany.edu/sourcebook/*), and the large majority of them happen outside homes.

4. *Watson* plainly allows warrantless arrests outside homes. What about arrests *inside* homes? In Payton v. New York, 445 U.S. 573 (1980), the Court struck down a New York statute that authorized warrantless entries into private homes for the purpose of making felony arrests. The Court concluded that, if warrants were necessary to look for property in a private home, warrants should be necessary to look for people as well:

> The simple language of the Amendment applies equally to seizures of persons and to seizures of property. Our analysis in this case may therefore properly commence with rules that have been well established in Fourth Amendment litigation involving tangible items. As the Court reiterated just a few years ago, the "physical entry of the home is the chief evil against which the wording of the Fourth Amendment is directed." United States v. United States District Court, 407 U.S. 297, 313. And we have long adhered to the view that the warrant procedure minimizes the danger of needless intrusions of that sort.

Id. at 585-586. Interestingly, the Court did *not* require the use of *search* warrants:

> . . . [W]e note the State's suggestion that only a search warrant based on probable cause to believe the suspect is at home at a given time can adequately protect the privacy interests at stake, and since such a warrant requirement is manifestly impractical, there need be no warrant of any kind. We find this ingenious argument unpersuasive. It is true that an arrest warrant requirement may afford less protection

than a search warrant requirement, but it will suffice to interpose the magistrate's determination of probable cause between the zealous officer and the citizen. If there is sufficient evidence of a citizen's participation in a felony to persuade a judicial officer that his arrest is justified, it is constitutionally reasonable to require him to open his doors to the officers of the law. Thus, for Fourth Amendment purposes, an arrest warrant founded on probable cause implicitly carries with it the limited authority to enter a dwelling in which the suspect lives when there is reason to believe the suspect is within.

Id. at 602-603. Note the last clause: Presumably police cannot get an arrest warrant, wait until the suspect has left home, and then break into and search the home, using the warrant as authority for the entry.

5. Steagald v. United States, 451 U.S. 204 (1981), involved a twist on *Payton*. In *Steagald*, officers had an arrest warrant for one Ricky Lyons; an informant's tip had reported that Lyons could be found at Steagald's house. Officers went to Steagald's house and searched it; they did not find Lyons but did find a substantial quantity of cocaine. The question was whether an arrest warrant justified the search of the home of someone other than the arrestee. The Court held that it did not:

> . . . [W]hether the arrest warrant issued in this case adequately safeguarded the interests protected by the Fourth Amendment depends upon what the warrant authorized the agents to do. To be sure, the warrant embodied a judicial finding that there was probable cause to believe that Ricky Lyons had committed a felony, and the warrant therefore authorized the officers to seize Lyons. However, the agents sought to do more than use the warrant to arrest Lyons in a public place or in his home; instead, they relied on the warrant as legal authority to enter the home of a third person based on their belief that Ricky Lyons might be a guest there. Regardless of how reasonable this belief might have been, it was never subjected to the detached scrutiny of a judicial officer. Thus, while the warrant in this case may have protected Lyons from an unreasonable seizure, it did absolutely nothing to protect petitioner's privacy interest in being free from an unreasonable invasion and search of his home. . . .
>
> In sum, two distinct interests were implicated by the search at issue here — Ricky Lyons' interest in being free from an unreasonable seizure and petitioner's interest in being free from an unreasonable search of his home. Because the arrest warrant for Lyons addressed only the former interest, the search of petitioner's home was no more reasonable from petitioner's perspective than it would have been if conducted in the absence of any warrant. Since warrantless searches of a home are impermissible absent consent or exigent circumstances, we conclude that the instant search violated the Fourth Amendment. . . .
>
> . . . Thus, in order to render the instant search reasonable under the Fourth Amendment, a search warrant was required.

Id. at 213-214, 216, 222.

Both *Payton* and *Steagald* contained long discussions of common-law history. In both cases, the Court concluded that the history was inconclusive. In both cases, dissenting opinions argued forcefully, and persuasively, that the weight of the historical evidence counseled against requiring a warrant, that warrantless felony arrests in the felon's home were both common and generally permissible at common law. See *Steagald*, 451 U.S. at 227-230 (Rehnquist, J., dissenting); *Payton*, 445 U.S. at 604-613 (White, J., dissenting). Was the Court's discussion of history in *Watson* a smokescreen? Or should the Court have stuck to its historical guns and permitted warrantless arrests in homes in *Payton* and *Steagald*? Only in *Payton*?

6. Two decades after *Steagald*, the Supreme Court again addressed the scope of the arrest power. This time, the warrant requirement was not at issue.

ATWATER v. LAGO VISTA

Certiorari to the United States Court of Appeals for the Fifth Circuit
532 U.S. 318 (2001)

JUSTICE SOUTER delivered the opinion of the Court.

The question is whether the Fourth Amendment forbids a warrantless arrest for a minor criminal offense, such as a misdemeanor seatbelt violation punishable only by a fine. We hold that it does not.

I

In Texas, if a car is equipped with safety belts, a front-seat passenger must wear one, Tex. Tran. Code Ann. §545.413(a) (1999), and the driver must secure any small child riding in front, §545.413(b). Violation of either provision is "a misdemeanor punishable by a fine not less than $25 or more than $50." §545.413(d). Texas law expressly authorizes "[a]ny peace officer [to] arrest without warrant a person found committing a violation" of these seatbelt laws, §543.001, although it permits police to issue citations in lieu of arrest, §§543.003-543.005.

In March 1997, Petitioner Gail Atwater was driving her pickup truck in Lago Vista, Texas, with her 3-year-old son and 5-year-old daughter in the front seat. None of them was wearing a seatbelt. Respondent Bart Turek, a Lago Vista police officer at the time, observed the seatbelt violations and pulled Atwater over. According to Atwater's complaint (the allegations of which we assume to be true for present purposes), Turek approached the truck and "yelled" something to the effect of "we've met before" and "you're going to jail."[1] He then called for backup and asked to see Atwater's driver's license and insurance documentation, which state law required her to carry. When Atwater told Turek that she did not have the papers because her purse had been stolen the day before, Turek said that he had "heard that story two-hundred times."

Atwater asked to take her "frightened, upset, and crying" children to a friend's house nearby, but Turek told her, "you're not going anywhere." As it turned out, Atwater's friend learned what was going on and soon arrived to take charge of the children. Turek then handcuffed Atwater, placed her in his squad car, and drove her to the local police station, where booking officers had her remove her shoes, jewelry, and eyeglasses, and empty her pockets. Officers took Atwater's "mug shot" and placed her, alone, in a jail cell for about one hour, after which she was taken before a magistrate and released on $310 bond.

Atwater was charged with driving without her seatbelt fastened, failing to secure her children in seatbelts, driving without a license, and failing to provide proof of

---

1. Turek had previously stopped Atwater for what he had thought was a seatbelt violation, but had realized that Atwater's son, although seated on the vehicle's armrest, was in fact belted in. Atwater acknowledged that her son's seating position was unsafe, and Turek issued a verbal warning.

insurance. She ultimately pleaded no contest to the misdemeanor seatbelt offenses and paid a $50 fine; the other charges were dismissed.

Atwater and her husband, petitioner Michael Haas, filed suit . . . under 42 U.S.C. §1983 against Turek and respondents City of Lago Vista and Chief of Police Frank Miller. So far as concerns us, petitioners (whom we will simply call Atwater) alleged that respondents (for simplicity, the City) had violated Atwater's Fourth Amendment "right to be free from unreasonable seizure," App. 23, and sought compensatory and punitive damages.

. . . Given Atwater's admission that she had "violated the law" and the absence of any allegation "that she was harmed or detained in any way inconsistent with the law," the District Court ruled the Fourth Amendment claim "meritless" and granted the City's summary judgment motion. A panel of the United States Court of Appeals for the Fifth Circuit reversed. 165 F.3d 380 (1999). It concluded that "an arrest for a first-time seat belt offense" was an unreasonable seizure within the meaning of the Fourth Amendment, id., at 387, and held that Turek was not entitled to qualified immunity, id., at 389.

Sitting en banc, the Court of Appeals vacated the panel's decision and affirmed the District Court's summary judgment for the City. 195 F.3d 242 (CA5 1999). . . . [T]he en banc court observed that, although the Fourth Amendment generally requires a balancing of individual and governmental interests, where "an arrest is based on probable cause then 'with rare exceptions . . . the result of that balancing is not in doubt.'" 195 F.3d, at 244 (quoting [Whren v. United States, 517 U.S. 806, 817 (1996)]). Because "neither party disputed that Officer Turek had probable cause to arrest Atwater," and because "there [was] no evidence in the record that Officer Turek conducted the arrest in an 'extraordinary manner, unusually harmful' to Atwater's privacy interests," the en banc court held that the arrest was not unreasonable for Fourth Amendment purposes. 195 F.3d at 245-246 (quoting *Whren*, supra, at 818). . . .

II

The Fourth Amendment safeguards "[t]he right of the people to be secure in their persons, houses, papers, and effects, against unreasonable searches and seizures." In reading the Amendment, we are guided by "the traditional protections against unreasonable searches and seizures afforded by the common law at the time of the framing," Wilson v. Arkansas, 514 U.S. 927, 931 (1995). . . . Thus, the first step here is to assess Atwater's claim that peace officers' authority to make warrantless arrests for misdemeanors was restricted at common law (whether "common law" is understood strictly as law judicially derived or, instead, as the whole body of law extant at the time of the framing). Atwater's specific contention is that "founding-era common-law rules" forbade peace officers to make warrantless misdemeanor arrests except in cases of "breach of the peace," a category she claims was then understood narrowly as covering only those nonfelony offenses "involving or tending toward violence." Brief for Petitioners 13. Although her historical argument is by no means insubstantial, it ultimately fails.

We begin with the state of pre-founding English common law and find that, even after making some allowance for variations in the common-law usage of the term "breach of the peace," the "founding-era common-law rules" were not nearly as clear as Atwater claims; on the contrary, the common-law commentators (as well as the sparsely reported cases) reached divergent conclusions with respect to officers' warrantless misdemeanor arrest power. Moreover, in the years leading up to American independence, Parliament repeatedly extended express warrantless arrest authority to cover misdemeanor-level offenses not amounting to or involving any violent breach of the peace. . . .

[JUSTICE SOUTER characterized English treatises and case law as inconclusive.]

A second, and equally serious, problem for Atwater's historical argument is posed by the "divers Statutes," M. Dalton, Country Justice ch. 170, §4, p. 582 (1727), enacted by Parliament well before this Republic's founding that authorized warrantless misdemeanor arrests without reference to violence or turmoil. . . . [T]he legal background of any conception of reasonableness the Fourth Amendment's Framers might have entertained would have included English statutes, some centuries old, authorizing peace officers (and even private persons) to make warrantless arrests for all sorts of relatively minor offenses unaccompanied by violence. The so-called "nightwalker" statutes are perhaps the most notable examples. From the enactment of the Statute of Winchester in 1285, through its various readoptions and until its repeal in 1827, night watchmen were authorized and charged "as . . . in Times past" to "watch the Town continually all Night, from the Sun-setting unto the Sun-rising" and were directed that "if any Stranger do pass by them, he shall be arrested until Morning. . . . " 13 Edw. I, ch. 4, §§5-6, 1 Statutes at Large 232-233. . . . [A]ccording to Blackstone, these watchmen had virtually limitless warrantless nighttime arrest power: "Watchmen, either those appointed by the statute of Winchester . . . or such as are merely assistants to the constable, may *virtute officii* arrest all offenders, and particularly nightwalkers, and commit them to custody till the morning." 4 Blackstone 289. . . .

Nor were the nightwalker statutes the only legislative sources of warrantless arrest authority absent real or threatened violence. . . . On the contrary, following the Edwardian legislation and throughout the period leading up to the framing, Parliament repeatedly extended warrantless arrest power to cover misdemeanor-level offenses not involving any breach of the peace. [Such statutes included a 16th-century statute authorizing warrantless arrests for persons playing "unlawful games," as well as those "haunting" the places where such games were played; a 17th-century act applicable to any "hawker, pedlar, petty chapman, or other trading person" found selling without a license; and 18th-century statutes authorizing warrantless arrests of "rogues, vagabonds, beggars, and other idle and disorderly persons"; "horrid" persons who "profanely swear or curse"; those who obstruct "publick streets, lanes or open passages" with "pipes, butts, barrels, casks or other vessels" or an "empty cart, car, dray or other carriage";] and, most significantly of all given the circumstances of the case before us, negligent carriage drivers, 27 Geo. II, ch. 16, §7, 21 Statutes at Large 188 (1754).

. . . [T]hese early English statutes . . . riddle Atwater's supposed common-law rule with enough exceptions to unsettle any contention that the law of the mother country would have left the Fourth Amendment's Framers of a view that it would necessarily have been unreasonable to arrest without warrant for a misdemeanor unaccompanied by real or threatened violence.

An examination of specifically American evidence is to the same effect. Neither the history of the framing era nor subsequent legal development indicates that the Fourth Amendment was originally understood, or has traditionally been read, to embrace Atwater's position.

To begin with, Atwater has cited no particular evidence that those who framed and ratified the Fourth Amendment sought to limit peace officers' warrantless misdemeanor arrest authority to instances of actual breach of the peace. . . . Nor have we found in any of the modern historical accounts of the Fourth Amendment's adoption any substantial indication that the Framers intended such a restriction. Indeed, to the extent these modern histories address the issue, their conclusions are to the contrary. See [J. Landynski, Search and Seizure and the Supreme Court 45 (1966)] (Fourth Amendment arrest rules are "based on common-law practice," which "dispensed with" a warrant requirement for misdemeanors "committed in the presence of the arresting officer").

The evidence of actual practice also counsels against Atwater's position. During the period leading up to and surrounding the framing of the Bill of Rights, colonial and state legislatures, like Parliament before them, regularly authorized local peace officers to make warrantless misdemeanor arrests without conditioning statutory authority on breach of the peace. [Here, JUSTICE SOUTER cited numerous state statutes from the late 1700s that authorized warrantless arrests of drunks, gamblers, vagrants, prostitutes, "night-walkers," fortune-tellers, profane swearers, Sabbath-breakers, and others. — EDS.]

. . . Given the early state practice, it is likewise troublesome for Atwater's view that just one year after the ratification of the Fourth Amendment, Congress vested federal marshals with "the same powers in executing the laws of the United States, as sheriffs and their deputies in the several states have by law, in executing the laws of their respective states." Act of May 2, 1792, ch. 28, §9, 1 Stat. 265. Thus, as we have said before in only slightly different circumstances, the Second Congress apparently "saw no inconsistency between the Fourth Amendment and legislation giving United States marshals the same power as local peace officers" to make warrantless arrests. United States v. Watson, 423 U.S. 411, 420 (1976).

The record thus supports Justice Powell's observation that "there is no historical evidence that the Framers or proponents of the Fourth Amendment, outspokenly opposed to the infamous general warrants and writs of assistance, were at all concerned about warrantless arrests by local constables and other peace officers." Id., at 429 (concurring opinion). We simply cannot conclude that the Fourth Amendment, as originally understood, forbade peace officers to arrest without a warrant for misdemeanors not amounting to or involving breach of the peace.

Nor does Atwater's argument from tradition pick up any steam from the historical record as it has unfolded since the framing. . . . The story, on the contrary, is of two centuries of uninterrupted (and largely unchallenged) state and federal practice permitting warrantless arrests for misdemeanors not amounting to or involving breach of the peace. . . .

[JUSTICE SOUTER's opinion proceeds to survey Supreme Court cases, state cases, and commentaries spanning the nineteenth and twentieth centuries.]

Small wonder, then, that today statutes in all 50 States and the District of Columbia permit warrantless misdemeanor arrests by at least some (if not all) peace officers without requiring any breach of the peace, as do a host of congressional enactments. The American Law Institute has long endorsed the validity of such legislation, see American Law Institute, Code of Criminal Procedure §21(a), p. 28 (1930); American Law Institute, Model Code of Pre-Arraignment Procedure §120.1(1)(c), p. 13 (1975), and the consensus, as stated in the current literature, is that statutes "remov[ing] the breach of the peace limitation and thereby permitt[ing] arrest without warrant for *any* misdemeanor committed in the arresting officer's presence" have "'never been successfully challenged and stand as the law of the land.'" 3 W. LaFave, Search and Seizure §5.1(b), pp. 13-14, and n. 76 (1996) (citation omitted). This, therefore, simply is not a case in which the claimant can point to "a clear answer [that] existed in 1791 and has been generally adhered to by the traditions of our society ever since." County of Riverside v. McLaughlin, 500 U.S. 44, 60 (1991) (SCALIA, J., dissenting).

III

. . . Atwater does not wager all on history. Instead, she asks us to mint a new rule of constitutional law on the understanding that when historical practice fails to speak conclusively to a claim grounded on the Fourth Amendment, courts are left to strike a current balance between individual and societal interests by subjecting particular contemporary circumstances to traditional standards of reasonableness. Atwater accordingly argues for a modern arrest rule, one not necessarily requiring violent breach of the peace, but nonetheless forbidding custodial arrest, even upon probable cause, when conviction could not ultimately carry any jail time and when the government shows no compelling need for immediate detention.[15]

If we were to derive a rule exclusively to address the uncontested facts of this case, Atwater might well prevail. She was a known and established resident of Lago Vista with no place to hide and no incentive to flee, and common sense says she would almost certainly have buckled up as a condition of driving off with a citation. In her case, the physical incidents of arrest were merely gratuitous humiliations imposed by a police officer who was (at best) exercising extremely poor judgment. Atwater's claim to live free of pointless indignity and confinement clearly outweighs anything the City can raise against it specific to her case.

But we have traditionally recognized that a responsible Fourth Amendment balance is not well served by standards requiring sensitive, case-by-case determinations of government need, lest every discretionary judgment in the field be converted into an occasion for constitutional review. Often enough, the Fourth Amendment has to be applied on the spur (and in the heat) of the moment, and the object in implementing its command of reasonableness is to draw standards sufficiently clear and simple to be applied with a fair prospect of surviving judicial second-guessing months and years after an arrest or search is made. Courts attempting to strike a reasonable Fourth Amendment balance thus credit the government's side with an essential interest in readily administrable rules.

At first glance, Atwater's argument may seem to respect the values of clarity and simplicity, so far as she claims that the Fourth Amendment generally forbids warrantless arrests for minor crimes not accompanied by violence or some demonstrable threat of it. . . . But the claim is not ultimately so simple, nor could it be, for complications arise the moment we begin to think about . . . the several criteria Atwater proposes for drawing a line between minor crimes with limited arrest authority and others not so restricted.

15. Although it is unclear from Atwater's briefs whether the rule she proposes would bar custodial arrests for fine-only offenses even when made pursuant to a warrant, at oral argument Atwater's counsel "conceded that if a warrant were obtained, this arrest . . . would . . . be reasonable." Tr. of Oral Arg. 5.

One line, she suggests, might be between "jailable" and "fine-only" offenses. . . . The trouble with this distinction, of course, is that an officer on the street might not be able to tell. It is not merely that we cannot expect every police officer to know the details of frequently complex penalty schemes, but that penalties for ostensibly identical conduct can vary on account of facts difficult (if not impossible) to know at the scene of an arrest. Is this the first offense or is the suspect a repeat offender? Is the weight of the marijuana a gram above or a gram below the fine-only line? Where conduct could implicate more than one criminal prohibition, which one will the district attorney ultimately decide to charge? And so on.

But Atwater's refinements would not end there. She represents that if the line were drawn at nonjailable traffic offenses, her proposed limitation should be qualified by a proviso authorizing warrantless arrests where "necessary for enforcement of the traffic laws or when [an] offense would otherwise continue and pose a danger to others on the road." Brief for Petitioners 46. (Were the line drawn at misdemeanors generally, a comparable qualification would presumably apply.) The proviso only compounds the difficulties. Would, for instance, either exception apply to speeding? At oral argument, Atwater's counsel said that "it would not be reasonable to arrest a driver for speeding unless the speeding rose to the level of reckless driving." Tr. of Oral Arg. 16. But is it not fair to expect that the chronic speeder will speed again despite a citation in his pocket, and should that not qualify as showing that the "offense would . . . continue" under Atwater's rule? And why, as a constitutional matter, should we assume that only reckless driving will "pose a danger to others on the road" while speeding will not?

There is no need for more examples to show that Atwater's general rule and limiting proviso promise very little in the way of administrability. It is no answer that the police routinely make judgments on grounds like risk of immediate repetition; they surely do and should. But there is a world of difference between making that judgment in choosing between the discretionary leniency of a summons in place of a clearly lawful arrest, and making the same judgment when the question is the lawfulness of the warrantless arrest itself. It is the difference between no basis for legal action challenging the discretionary judgment, on the one hand, and the prospect of evidentiary exclusion or (as here) personal §1983 liability for the misapplication of a constitutional standard, on the other. Atwater's rule therefore would not only place police in an almost impossible spot but would guarantee increased litigation over many of the arrests that would occur. For all these reasons, Atwater's various distinctions between permissible and impermissible arrests for minor crimes strike us as "very unsatisfactory line[s]" to require police officers to draw on a moment's notice. Carroll v. United States, [267 U.S. 132, 157 (1925)]. . . .

Just how easily the costs could outweigh the benefits may be shown by asking, as one Member of this Court did at oral argument, "how bad the problem is out there." Tr. of Oral Arg. 20. The very fact that the law has never jelled the way Atwater would have it leads one to wonder whether warrantless misdemeanor arrests need constitutional attention. . . . So far as such arrests might be thought to pose a threat to the probable-cause requirement, anyone arrested for a crime without formal process, whether for felony or misdemeanor, is entitled to a magistrate's review of probable cause within 48 hours, County of Riverside v. McLaughlin, 500 U.S. at 55-58, and there is no reason to think the procedure in this case atypical in giving the suspect a prompt opportunity to request release, see Tex. Tran. Code Ann. §543.002 (1999) (persons arrested for traffic offenses to be taken "immediately" before a magistrate). Many jurisdictions, moreover, have chosen to impose more restrictive safeguards through statutes limiting warrantless arrests for minor offenses. It is of course easier to devise a minor-offense limitation by statute than to derive one through the Constitution, simply because the statute can let the arrest power turn on any sort of practical consideration without having to subsume it under a broader principle. . . . Finally, and significantly, under current doctrine the preference for categorical treatment of Fourth Amendment claims gives way to individualized review when a defendant makes a colorable argument that an arrest, with or without a warrant, was "conducted in an extraordinary manner, unusually harmful to [his] privacy or even physical interests." Whren v. United States, 517 U.S. at 818; see also Graham v. Connor, 490 U.S. 386, 395-396 (1989) (excessive force actionable under §1983).

The upshot of all these influences, combined with the good sense (and, failing that, the political accountability) of most local lawmakers and law-enforcement officials, is a dearth of horribles demanding redress. Indeed, when Atwater's counsel was asked at oral argument for any indications of comparably foolish, warrantless misdemeanor arrests, he could offer only one.[23] We are sure that there are others,[24] but just as surely the country is not confronting anything like an epidemic of unnecessary minor-offense arrests. . . .

Accordingly, we confirm today what our prior cases have intimated: the standard of probable cause "applie[s] to all arrests, without the need to 'balance' the interests and circumstances involved in particular situations." Dunaway v. New York, 442 U.S. 200, 208 (1979). If an officer has probable cause to believe that an individual has committed even a very minor criminal offense in his presence, he may, without violating the Fourth Amendment, arrest the offender.

IV

Atwater's arrest satisfied constitutional requirements. There is no dispute that Officer Turek had probable cause to believe that Atwater had committed a crime in his presence. She admits that neither she nor her children were wearing seatbelts . . . Turek was accordingly authorized (not required, but authorized) to make a custodial arrest without balancing costs and benefits or determining whether or not Atwater's arrest was in some sense necessary.

Nor was the arrest made in an "extraordinary manner, unusually harmful to [her] privacy or . . . physical interests." Whren v. United States, 517 U.S. at 818. As our citations in *Whren* make clear, the question whether a search or seizure is "extraordinary" turns, above all else, on the manner in which the search or seizure is executed. See id., at 818 (citing Tennessee v. Garner, 471 U.S. 1 (1985) ("seizure

23. He referred to a newspaper account of a girl taken into custody for eating french fries in a Washington, D.C., subway station. Tr. of Oral Arg. 20-21; see also Washington Post, Nov. 16, 2000, p. A1 (describing incident). Not surprisingly, given the practical and political considerations discussed in text, the Washington Metro Transit Police recently revised their "zero-tolerance" policy to provide for citation in lieu of custodial arrest of subway snackers. Washington Post, Feb. 27, 2001, at B1.

24. One of Atwater's amici described a handful in its brief. Brief for American Civil Liberties Union et al. as Amici Curiae 7-8 (reporting arrests for littering, riding a bicycle without a bell or gong, operating a business without a license, and "walking as to create a hazard").

by means of deadly force"), Wilson v. Arkansas, 514 U.S. 927 (1995) ("unannounced entry into a home"), Welsh v. Wisconsin, 466 U.S. 740 (1984) ("entry into a home without a warrant"), and Winston v. Lee, 470 U.S. 753 (1985) ("physical penetration of the body")). Atwater's arrest was surely "humiliating," as she says in her brief, but it was no more "harmful to . . . privacy or . . . physical interests" than the normal custodial arrest. She was handcuffed, placed in a squad car, and taken to the local police station, where officers asked her to remove her shoes, jewelry, and glasses, and to empty her pockets. They then took her photograph and placed her in a cell, alone, for about an hour, after which she was taken before a magistrate, and released on $310 bond. The arrest and booking were inconvenient and embarrassing to Atwater, but not so extraordinary as to violate the Fourth Amendment. . . .

JUSTICE O'CONNOR, with whom JUSTICE STEVENS, JUSTICE GINSBURG, and JUSTICE BREYER join, dissenting.

. . . The majority . . . acknowledges that "Atwater's claim to live free of pointless indignity and confinement clearly outweighs anything the City can raise against it specific to her case." But instead of remedying this imbalance, the majority allows itself to be swayed by the worry that "every discretionary judgment in the field [will] be converted into an occasion for constitutional review." It therefore mints a new rule that "[i]f an officer has probable cause to believe that an individual has committed even a very minor criminal offense in his presence, he may, without violating the Fourth Amendment, arrest the offender." This rule . . . runs contrary to the principles that lie at the core of the Fourth Amendment. . . .

. . . [W]e have held that the existence of probable cause is a necessary condition for an arrest. And in the case of felonies punishable by a term of imprisonment, we have held that the existence of probable cause is also a sufficient condition for an arrest. See United States v. Watson, 423 U.S. 411, 416-417 (1976). In *Watson*, however, there was a clear and consistently applied common law rule permitting warrantless felony arrests. See id., at 417-422. Accordingly, our inquiry ended there and we had no need to assess the reasonableness of such arrests by weighing individual liberty interests against state interests.

Here, however, we have no such luxury. The Court's thorough exegesis makes it abundantly clear that warrantless misdemeanor arrests were not the subject of a clear and consistently applied rule at common law. We therefore must engage in the balancing test required by the Fourth Amendment. See Wyoming v. Houghton, [526 U.S. 295,] 299-300 [(1995)]. While probable cause is surely a necessary condition for warrantless arrests for fine-only offenses, any realistic assessment of the interests implicated by such arrests demonstrates that probable cause alone is not a sufficient condition. . . .

A custodial arrest exacts an obvious toll on an individual's liberty and privacy, even when the period of custody is relatively brief. The arrestee is subject to a full search of her person and confiscation of her possessions. United States v. Robinson, [414 U.S. 218 (1973)]. If the arrestee is the occupant of a car, the entire passenger compartment of the car, including packages therein, is subject to search as well. See New York v. Belton, 453 U.S. 454 (1981). The arrestee may be detained for up to 48 hours without having a magistrate determine whether there in fact was probable cause for the arrest. See County of Riverside v. McLaughlin, 500 U.S. 44 (1991). Because people arrested for all types of violent and nonviolent offenses may be housed together awaiting such review, this detention period is potentially dangerous. And once the period of custody is over, the fact of the arrest is a permanent part of the public record. . . .

. . . In light of the availability of citations to promote a State's interests when a fine-only offense has been committed, I cannot concur in a rule which deems a full custodial arrest to be reasonable in every circumstance. Giving police officers constitutional carte blanche to effect an arrest whenever there is probable cause to believe a fine-only misdemeanor has been committed is irreconcilable with the Fourth Amendment's command that seizures be reasonable. Instead, I would require that when there is probable cause to believe that a fine-only offense has been committed, the police officer should issue a citation unless the officer is "able to point to specific and articulable facts which, taken together with rational inferences from those facts, reasonably warrant [the additional] intrusion" of a full custodial arrest. Terry v. Ohio, [392 U.S. 1, 21 (1968)].

The majority insists that a bright-line rule focused on probable cause is necessary to vindicate the State's interest in easily administrable law enforcement rules. Probable cause itself, however, is not a model of precision. "The quantum of information which constitutes probable cause — evidence which would 'warrant a man of reasonable caution in the belief' that a [crime] has been committed — must be measured by the facts of the particular case." Wong Sun v. United States, 371 U.S. 471, 479 (1963). The rule I propose — which merely requires a legitimate reason for the decision to escalate the seizure into a full custodial arrest — thus does not undermine an otherwise "clear and simple" rule. . . .

The record in this case makes it abundantly clear that Ms. Atwater's arrest was constitutionally unreasonable. . . .

There is no question that Officer Turek's actions severely infringed Atwater's liberty and privacy. Turek was loud and accusatory from the moment he approached Atwater's car. Atwater's young children were terrified and hysterical. Yet when Atwater asked Turek to lower his voice because he was scaring the children, he responded by jabbing his finger in Atwater's face and saying, "You're going to jail." Record 382, 384. . . .

Atwater asked if she could at least take her children to a friend's house down the street before going to the police station. Record 384. But Turek — who had just castigated Atwater for not caring for her children — refused and said he would take the children into custody as well. Id., at 384, 427, 704-705. Only the intervention of neighborhood children who had witnessed the scene and summoned one of Atwater's friends saved the children from being hauled to jail with their mother. Id., at 382, 385-386.

With the children gone, Officer Turek handcuffed Ms. Atwater with her hands behind her back, placed her in the police car, and drove her to the police station. Id., at 386-387. Ironically, Turek did not secure Atwater in a seat belt for the drive. Id., at 386. At the station, Atwater was forced to remove her shoes, relinquish her possessions, and wait in a holding cell for about an hour. Id., at 387, 706. A judge finally informed Atwater of her rights and the charges against her, and released her when she posted bond. Id., at 387-388, 706. Atwater returned to the scene of the arrest, only to find that her car had been towed. Id., at 389.

Ms. Atwater ultimately pleaded no contest to violating the seatbelt law and was fined $50. Id., at 403. Even though that fine was the maximum penalty for her crime, Tex. Tran. Code Ann. §545.413(d) (1999), and even though Officer Turek has never articulated any justification for his actions, the city contends that arresting Atwater was constitutionally reasonable because it advanced two legitimate interests: "the enforcement of child safety laws and encouraging [Atwater] to appear for trial." Brief for Respondents 15.

It is difficult to see how arresting Atwater served either of these goals any more effectively than the issuance of a citation. With respect to the goal of law enforcement generally, Atwater did not pose a great danger to the community. She had been driving very slowly — approximately 15 miles per hour — in broad daylight on a residential street that had no other traffic. Record 380. Nor was she a repeat offender; until that day, she had received one traffic citation in her life — a ticket, more than 10 years earlier, for failure to signal a lane change. Id., at 378. Although Officer Turek had stopped Atwater approximately three months earlier because he thought that Atwater's son was not wearing a seatbelt, id., at 420, Turek had been mistaken, id., at 379, 703. Moreover, Atwater immediately accepted responsibility and apologized for her conduct. Id., at 381, 384, 420. Thus, there was every indication that Atwater would have buckled herself and her children in had she been cited and allowed to leave. . . .

Respondents also contend that the arrest was necessary to ensure Atwater's appearance in court. Atwater, however, was far from a flight risk. A 16-year resident of Lago Vista, population 2,486, Atwater was not likely to abscond. Although she was unable to produce her driver's license because it had been stolen, she gave Officer Turek her license number and address. In addition, Officer Turek knew from their previous encounter that Atwater was a local resident.

The city's justifications fall far short of rationalizing the extraordinary intrusion on Gail Atwater and her children. Measuring "the degree to which [Atwater's custodial arrest was] needed for the promotion of legitimate governmental interests," against "the degree to which it intrude[d] upon [her] privacy," Wyoming v. Houghton, 526 U.S. at 300, it can hardly be doubted that Turek's actions were disproportionate to Atwater's crime. The majority's assessment that "Atwater's claim to live free of pointless indignity and confinement clearly outweighs anything the City can raise against it specific to her case," is quite correct. In my view, the Fourth Amendment inquiry ends there.

The Court's error, however, does not merely affect the disposition of this case. The per se rule that the Court creates has potentially serious consequences for the everyday lives of Americans. A broad range of conduct falls into the category of fine-only misdemeanors. In Texas alone, for example, disobeying any sort of traffic warning sign is a misdemeanor punishable only by fine, see Tex. Tran. Code Ann. §472.022 (1999 and Supp. 2000-2001), as is failing to pay a highway toll, see §284.070, and driving with expired license plates, see §502.407. Nor are fine-only crimes limited to the traffic context. In several States, for example, littering is a criminal offense punishable only by fine. See, e.g., Cal. Penal Code Ann. §374.7 (West 1999); Ga. Code Ann. §16-7-43 (1996); Iowa Code §§321.369, 805.8(2)(af) (Supp. 2001). . . .

Such unbounded discretion carries with it grave potential for abuse. The majority takes comfort in the lack of evidence of "an epidemic of unnecessary minor-offense arrests." But the relatively small number of published cases dealing with such arrests proves little and should provide little solace. Indeed, as the recent debate over racial profiling demonstrates all too clearly, a relatively minor traffic infraction may often serve as an excuse for stopping and harassing an individual. . . .

The Court neglects the Fourth Amendment's express command in the name of administrative ease. In so doing, it cloaks the pointless indignity that Gail Atwater suffered with the mantle of reasonableness. I respectfully dissent.

NOTES AND QUESTIONS

1. In Whren v. United States, 517 U.S. 806 (1996), the Court held that a police officer's motive for making a traffic stop (and accompanying brief detention) does not affect the constitutionality of the stop, so long as there was probable cause to believe that the traffic violation had occurred. (*Whren* is excerpted infra, at page 597.) Along the way, the Court stated that probable cause is the sole constitutional requirement for arrests, save when the arrest is "conducted in an extraordinary manner, unusually harmful to an individual's privacy or . . . physical interests." Id. at 818. Justice Souter quoted this language in support of his position in *Atwater*. Was he right to do so? Was Atwater treated "in an extraordinary manner"? Not if "ordinary" is defined by the treatment of arrestees as a whole. But if only those persons stopped for seat belt violations are considered, Atwater's treatment surely *was* "extraordinary." Why should Atwater be treated like murderers and robbers rather than like other traffic offenders? Doesn't *that* seem "extraordinary"?

2. Justice Souter's extended discussion of pre-1791 cases and statutes may be another piece of evidence for the ascendancy of originalism in Fourth Amendment law. For an interesting and sometimes scathing discussion of what that ascendancy might mean, see David A. Sklansky, The Fourth Amendment and Common Law, 100 Colum. L. Rev. 1739 (2000). Sklansky maintains that neither the Fourth Amendment's text nor its history support the idea that the Fourth Amendment incorporates the eighteenth-century common law of search and seizure. He also argues that the common law as the Framers knew it was too vague and too varied to answer many of the questions the Court asks of it. (*Atwater* seems a nice example of this point, does it not?) But, he contends, the kind of originalism one sees in Fourth Amendment cases may have large consequences for the long-range shape of the law:

> . . . [T]he rhetoric of the new Fourth Amendment originalism legitimizes some outcomes more easily than others and is relatively uncongenial to certain broad uses to which the Fourth Amendment might otherwise be put. The problem is not so much the answers provided by eighteenth-century common law—those are rare—but rather the limited range of the questions it asked.
>
> To take perhaps the most obvious example, of late the Supreme Court has studiously avoided considerations of equality in assessing the reasonableness of searches and seizures. . . . [C]onsiderations of race, class, and gender equity . . . are difficult to read into the common law of 1791. Indeed, . . . eighteenth-century rules of search and seizure, far from reflecting a broad commitment to equality, systematically codified class privilege. . . .
>
> Other long-range implications, if less obvious, may be no less important. Dramatic improvements in the technology of data management and retrieval, for example, may increasingly make what government *does* with information as important as what information the government *gets*. Harold Krent has sensibly suggested that the reasonableness of a search should depend in part on how, and for what purposes,

the government disseminates what it learns.[214] But precisely because eighteenth-century record keeping was so rudimentary, the common law showed little interest in how information was shared. Accordingly, if use restrictions become part of the Fourth Amendment, it will be in spite of the new Fourth Amendment originalism. . . .

100 Colum. L. Rev. at 1772-1774. Are you persuaded? Should evidence of the sort discussed in part II of Justice Souter's opinion affect outcomes in cases like *Atwater*?

3. Consider Justice Souter's claim that the doctrine proposed by the dissent is not administrable. At first blush, the argument seems powerful. Substantive distinctions of the sort Souter mentions—whether a suspect is a first-time or repeat offender, whether the weight of the drugs the suspect possesses are over or under the jailable line, which crime or crimes the prosecutor's office will want to charge—would surely be difficult, perhaps impossible, to sort out at the time of arrest. Yet if the seriousness of the crime determines the scope of the arrest power, police would *have* to make such distinctions. But this administrability argument may not be as strong as it seems. The alternative to the Court's bright-line rule is (as is always the case with bright-line rules) a standard: Officers should behave reasonably, considering all the circumstances—including the circumstance that some circumstances are harder for the arresting officer to discern than others. Arrests are presumptively reasonable when the crime is serious; not so when the crime isn't. That seems to be, roughly, what Justice O'Connor's dissent argues for. Why, precisely, would that be unadministrable?

The answer comes down to a claim about the unique needs of the police. Regulated actors are often subject to vague standards like negligence; courts don't assume that such standards are unworkable elsewhere. If they are unworkable here, it must be because, as the Court seems to believe, police *uniquely* need clear rules to do their jobs. Perhaps they do: Certainly police officers must make many quick decisions based on limited information; they often lack the time to calculate their actions carefully. But perhaps they don't: Unlike most regulated actors, police officers receive fairly detailed legal training and are frequently in court, so they can see how the relevant standards are applied by local magistrates. As Justice O'Connor suggests, that is why the probable cause standard works reasonably well: Over time, police officers come to know what "probable cause" means to the magistrates in their jurisdictions. Perhaps the same would be true of a standard like "crime serious enough to justify a full custodial arrest."

4. The practical problem that underlies *Atwater* is nicely captured by its facts: Police arrested for a low-level crime when they could easily have given the offender a ticket instead. What do you make of the argument between the majority and the dissent over how serious a problem this is? The Court argues that cases like *Atwater* must be rare: Otherwise, there would be many more reported decisions in such cases. The dissent responds that "the relatively small number of published cases dealing with such arrests proves little and should provide little solace." Who is right? What should we infer from the absence of large numbers of cases like *Atwater* from published case reports?

214. See Harold J. Krent, Of Diaries and Data Banks: Use Restrictions Under the Fourth Amendment, 74 Tex. L. Rev. 49, 51 & n. 114 (1995).

5. Notice the reference in Justice O'Connor's dissent to racial profiling. If *Atwater* had come out the other way, would it have much effect on that practice? By "racial profiling," Justice O'Connor presumably means the practice of stopping a disproportionate number of black drivers for traffic offenses; these stops are often followed by requests for consent to search and, if drugs are found in the car, by arrests for drug offenses (not for the traffic violation). Even if Justice O'Connor had written the majority in *Atwater* and not the dissent, such stops would still comply with the Fourth Amendment. Or so it would seem: After all, both sides in *Atwater* took for granted that Officer Turek could stop Atwater and give her a ticket. Presumably he could also ask her for consent to search her truck. And, if she consented and if Turek found evidence of a more serious crime in the course of the search, he could presumably arrest her for that more serious crime. Is there anything about that chain of events to which the *Atwater* dissenters could object?

6. In some cases, the arrest power may apply even *without* probable cause to believe the arrestee has committed a crime. Consider United States v. Awadallah, 349 F.3d 42 (2d Cir. 2003). In that case, a Second Circuit panel rejected a Fourth Amendment challenge to a detention based on the federal material witness statute, 18 U.S.C. §3144, the current version of which reads:

> If it appears from an affidavit filed by a party that the testimony of a person is material in a criminal proceeding, and if it is shown that it may become impracticable to secure the presence of the person by subpoena, a judicial officer may order the arrest of the person. . . . No material witness may be detained because of inability to comply with any condition of release if the testimony of such witness can adequately be secured by deposition, and if further detention is not necessary to prevent a failure of justice. Release of a material witness may be delayed for a reasonable period of time until the deposition of the witness can be taken pursuant to the Federal Rules of Criminal Procedure.

Federal agents had evidence that the defendant, Osama Awadallah, had been in contact with two of the September 11 hijackers in the days immediately before the attacks on the Pentagon and the World Trade Center. Awadallah was taken into custody and interviewed extensively; three weeks after his arrest, he testified before a federal grand jury investigating the attacks. Awadallah was charged and convicted of false statements he made during that testimony. He claimed that those statements were the fruit of an unconstitutional arrest.

Judge Jacobs' opinion "conclude[d] that §3144 sufficiently limits [the] infringement [on individual liberty] and reasonably balances it against the government's countervailing interests." 349 F.3d at 49. The Court addressed the particular circumstances of Awadallah's detention as follows:

> . . . [W]e must ask whether Awadallah was properly detained when he was held for several weeks without being allowed to give his deposition and obtain release. Such a detention constitutes a significant intrusion on liberty, since a material witness can be arrested with little or no notice, transported across the country, and detained for several days or weeks. Under the circumstances of this case, however, we are satisfied that Awadallah's detention was not unreasonably prolonged.

Id. at 58. Is *Awadallah* correct as a matter of Fourth Amendment law? Should courts pay attention to the seriousness of the crime under investigation when evaluating material witness detentions? Would that approach be contrary to *Atwater*? If the government may arrest people for fine-only offenses as in *Atwater*, and for having information (as opposed to committing crimes) as in *Awadallah*, is there any serious limit to the arrest power?

e. Searches Incident to Arrest

When a person is validly arrested, should the arresting officer also be allowed to search the person of the arrestee without first obtaining a search warrant? Can the officer search the place where the arrest is made? These questions have long vexed the Supreme Court, with the pendulum of precedent swinging first one way and then the other for most of the past eighty years. And the Court's most recent decision in this area, Thornton v. United States, 124 S. Ct. 2127 (2004), suggests that the pendulum may once again be in motion.

The modern "search incident to arrest" doctrine has its origins in the following dictum, which appeared in Weeks v. United States, 232 U.S. 383, 392 (1914):

> What then is the present case? Before answering that inquiry specifically, it may be well by a process of exclusion to state what it is not. It is not an assertion of the right on the part of the Government, always recognized under English and American law, to search the person of the accused when legally arrested to discover and seize the fruits or evidences of crime. . . .

In Carroll v. United States, 267 U.S. 132 (1925), the first car-search case, the Court suggested that the rule alluded to in *Weeks* includes "whatever is found upon [the arrestee's] person or in his control which it is unlawful for him to have and which may be used to prove the offense." In Agnello v. United States, 269 U.S. 20 (1925), the Court went even further, stating that the rule also encompasses "the place where the arrest is made in order to find and seize things connected with the crime as its fruits or as the means by which it was committed, as well as weapons and other things to effect an escape from custody. . . . " And in Marron v. United States, 275 U.S. 192 (1927), the Court specifically relied upon *Weeks* to uphold a search that was conducted pursuant to a warrant, but that clearly exceeded the scope of the warrant; the Court explained that the search-incident authority "extended to all parts of the premises used for the unlawful purpose."

The next two search-incident cases, Go-Bart Importing Co. v. United States, 282 U.S. 344 (1931), and United States v. Lefkowitz, 285 U.S. 452 (1932), cut back on the developing doctrine. In *Go-Bart*, the Court held that the search of a desk, safe, and other parts of an office was unlawful, in part because the arresting police "had an abundance of information and time" to obtain a search warrant. And in *Lefkowitz*, the Court invalidated the warrantless search of desk drawers and a cabinet, despite the fact that the search was conducted in connection with a valid arrest.

In Harris v. United States, 331 U.S. 145 (1947), police arrested the defendant in the living room of his apartment, on a forgery charge, and proceeded to search the entire apartment for forged checks. Instead, they found (and seized) altered Selective Service documents. The Court upheld the search in *Harris* as "incident to arrest." Only one year later, however, in Trupiano v. United States, 334 U.S. 699 (1948), the Court found a Fourth Amendment violation when police officers arrested a bootlegger in the act of distilling illegal liquor, and proceeded to seize (without a warrant) the still. Finally, in United States v. Rabinowitz, 339 U.S. 56 (1950), federal agents obtained a warrant to arrest the defendant for forgery of stamps. The warrant was served at defendant's one-room business office. The agents then conducted a 90-minute search, including a desk, safe, and file cabinets, and seized 573 forged stamps. The Court upheld the search, citing *Harris*, and finding that the agents had "the right to search the place where the arrest is made in order to find and seize things connected with the crime."

As you can see, the Court's early search-incident-to-arrest decisions were marked by "shifting constitutional standards" and "remarkable instability." See Chimel v. California, 395 U.S. 752 (1969) (White, J., dissenting). And the beat goes on . . .

CHIMEL v. CALIFORNIA

Certiorari to the Supreme Court of California
395 U.S. 752 (1969)

JUSTICE STEWART delivered the opinion of the Court.

. . . Late in the afternoon of September 13, 1965, three police officers arrived at the Santa Ana, California, home of the petitioner with a warrant authorizing his arrest for the burglary of a coin shop. The officers knocked on the door, identified themselves to the petitioner's wife, and asked if they might come inside. She ushered them into the house, where they waited 10 or 15 minutes until the petitioner returned home from work. When the petitioner entered the house, one of the officers handed him the arrest warrant and asked for permission to "look around." The petitioner objected, but was advised that "on the basis of the lawful arrest," the officers would nonetheless conduct a search. No search warrant had been issued.

Accompanied by the petitioner's wife, the officers then looked through the entire three-bedroom house, including the attic, the garage, and a small workshop. In some rooms the search was relatively cursory. In the master bedroom and sewing room, however, the officers directed the petitioner's wife to open drawers and "to physically move contents of the drawers from side to side so that [they] might view any items that would have come from [the] burglary." After completing the search, they seized numerous items — primarily coins, but also several medals, tokens, and a few other objects. The entire search took between 45 minutes and an hour.

At the petitioner's subsequent state trial on two charges of burglary, the items taken from his house were admitted into evidence against him, over his objection that they had been unconstitutionally seized. He was convicted, and the judgments of conviction were affirmed by both the California Court of Appeal, 61 Cal. Rptr. 714, and the California Supreme Court, 68 Cal. 2d 436, 439 P. 2d 333. Both courts accepted the petitioner's contention that the arrest warrant was invalid because the supporting affidavit was set out in conclusory terms, but held that since the arresting officers had procured the warrant "in good faith," and since in any event they had had sufficient information to constitute probable cause for the petitioner's arrest, that arrest had been lawful. From this conclusion the appellate courts went on to hold that the search of the petitioner's home had been justified, despite the absence of a search warrant, on the ground that it had been incident to a valid arrest. We granted certiorari in order to consider the petitioner's substantial constitutional claims.

Without deciding the question, we proceed on the hypothesis that the California courts were correct in holding that the arrest of the petitioner was valid under the Constitution. This brings us directly to the question whether the warrantless search of the petitioner's entire house can be constitutionally justified as incident to that arrest. The decisions of this Court bearing upon that question have been far from consistent, as even the most cursory review makes evident.

[Here, JUSTICE STEWART reviewed the history of the search-incident-to-arrest doctrine as described above. — EDS.]

Rabinowitz has come to stand for the proposition, inter alia, that a warrantless search "incident to a lawful arrest" may generally extend to the area that is considered to be in the "possession" or under the "control" of the person arrested. And it was on the basis of that proposition that the California courts upheld the search of the petitioner's entire house in this case. That doctrine, however, at least in the broad sense in which it was applied by the California courts in this case, can withstand neither historical nor rational analysis.

Even limited to its own facts, the *Rabinowitz* decision was, as we have seen, hardly founded on an unimpeachable line of authority. As Mr. Justice Frankfurter commented in dissent in that case, the "hint" contained in *Weeks* was, without persuasive justification, "loosely turned into dictum and finally elevated to a decision." 339 U.S., at 75. And the approach taken in cases such as *Go-Bart, Lefkowitz,* and *Trupiano* was essentially disregarded by the *Rabinowitz* Court.

Nor is the rationale by which the State seeks here to sustain the search of the petitioner's house supported by a reasoned view of the background and purpose of the Fourth Amendment. Mr. Justice Frankfurter wisely pointed out in his *Rabinowitz* dissent that the Amendment's proscription of "unreasonable searches and seizures" must be read in light of "the history that gave rise to the words" — a history of "abuses so deeply felt by the Colonies as to be one of the potent causes of the Revolution. . . . " 339 U.S., at 69. The Amendment was in large part a reaction to the general warrants and warrantless searches that had so alienated the colonists and had helped speed the movement for independence.[5] In the scheme of the Amendment, therefore, the requirement that "no Warrants shall issue, but upon probable cause," plays a crucial part. As the Court put it in McDonald v. United States, 335 U.S. 451:

> "We are not dealing with formalities. The presence of a search warrant serves a high function. Absent some grave emergency, the Fourth Amendment has interposed a magistrate between the citizen and the police. This was done not to shield criminals nor to make the home a safe haven for illegal activities. It was done so that an objective mind might weigh the need to invade that privacy in order to enforce the law. The right of privacy was deemed too precious to entrust to the discretion of those whose job is the detection of crime and the arrest of criminals. . . . And so the Constitution requires a magistrate to pass on the desires of the police before they violate the privacy

5. See generally Boyd v. United States, 116 U.S. 616, 624-625. . . .

of the home. We cannot be true to that constitutional requirement and excuse the absence of a search warrant without a showing by those who seek exemption from the constitutional mandate that the exigencies of the situation made that course imperative." Id., at 455-456.

Even in the *Agnello* case the Court relied upon the rule that "belief, however well founded, that an article sought is concealed in a dwelling house furnishes no justification for a search of that place without a warrant. And such searches are held unlawful notwithstanding facts unquestionably showing probable cause." 269 U.S., at 33. Clearly, the general requirement that a search warrant be obtained is not lightly to be dispensed with, and "the burden is on those seeking [an] exemption [from the requirement] to show the need for it. . . ." United States v. Jeffers, 342 U.S. 48, 51. . . .

Only last Term in Terry v. Ohio, 392 U.S. 1, we emphasized that "the police must, whenever practicable, obtain advance judicial approval of searches and seizures through the warrant procedure," id., at 20, and that "the scope of [a] search must be 'strictly tied to and justified by' the circumstances which rendered its initiation permissible." Id., at 19. The search undertaken by the officer in that "stop and frisk" case was sustained under that test, because it was no more than a "protective . . . search for weapons." Id., at 29. . . .

A similar analysis underlies the "search incident to arrest" principle, and marks its proper extent. When an arrest is made, it is reasonable for the arresting officer to search the person arrested in order to remove any weapons that the latter might seek to use in order to resist arrest or effect his escape. Otherwise, the officer's safety might well be endangered, and the arrest itself frustrated. In addition, it is entirely reasonable for the arresting officer to search for and seize any evidence on the arrestee's person in order to prevent its concealment or destruction. And the area into which an arrestee might reach in order to grab a weapon or evidentiary items must, of course, be governed by a like rule. A gun on a table or in a drawer in front of one who is arrested can be as dangerous to the arresting officer as one concealed in the clothing of the person arrested. There is ample justification, therefore, for a search of the arrestee's person and the area "within his immediate control" — construing that phrase to mean the area from within which he might gain possession of a weapon or destructible evidence.

There is no comparable justification, however, for routinely searching any room other than that in which an arrest occurs — or, for that matter, for searching through all the desk drawers or other closed or concealed areas in that room itself. Such searches, in the absence of well-recognized exceptions, may be made only under the authority of a search warrant. The "adherence to judicial processes" mandated by the Fourth Amendment requires no less. . . .

It is argued in the present case that it is "reasonable" to search a man's house when he is arrested in it. But that argument is founded on little more than a subjective view regarding the acceptability of certain sorts of police conduct, and not on considerations relevant to Fourth Amendment interests. Under such an unconfined analysis, Fourth Amendment protection in this area would approach the evaporation point. It is not easy to explain why, for instance, it is less subjectively "reasonable" to search a man's house when he is arrested on his front lawn — nor just down the street — than it is when he happens to be in the house at the time of arrest. . . .

It would be possible, of course, to draw a line between *Rabinowitz* and *Harris* on the one hand, and this case on the other. For *Rabinowitz* involved a single room, and *Harris* a four-room apartment, while in the case before us an entire house was searched. But such a distinction would be highly artificial. The rationale that allowed the searches and seizures in *Rabinowitz* and *Harris* would allow the searches and seizures in this case. No consideration relevant to the Fourth Amendment suggests any point of rational limitation, once the search is allowed to go beyond the area from which the person arrested might obtain weapons or evidentiary items. The only reasoned distinction is one between a search of the person arrested and the area within his reach on the one hand, and more extensive searches on the other.[12]

The petitioner correctly points out that one result of decisions such as *Rabinowitz* and *Harris* is to give law enforcement officials the opportunity to engage in searches not justified by probable cause, by the simple expedient of arranging to arrest suspects at home rather than elsewhere. We do not suggest that the petitioner is necessarily correct in his assertion that such a strategy was utilized here,[13] but the fact remains that had he been arrested earlier in the day, at his place of employment rather than at home, no search of his house could have been made without a search warrant. In any event, even apart from the possibility of such police tactics, the general point so forcefully made by Judge Learned Hand in United States v. Kirschenblatt, 16 F.2d 202, remains:

> "After arresting a man in his house, to rummage at will among his papers in search of whatever will convict him, appears to us to be indistinguishable from what might be done under a general warrant; indeed, the warrant would give more protection, for presumably it must be issued by a magistrate. True, by hypothesis the power would not exist, if the supposed offender were not found on the premises; but it is small consolation to know that one's papers are safe only so long as one is not at home." Id., at 203.

Rabinowitz and *Harris* have been the subject of critical commentary for many years, and have been relied upon less and less in our own decisions. It is time, for the reasons we have stated, to hold that on their own facts, and insofar as the

12. It is argued in dissent that so long as there is probable cause to search the place where an arrest occurs, a search of that place should be permitted even though no search warrant has been obtained. This position seems to be based principally on two premises: first, that once an arrest has been made, the additional invasion of privacy stemming from the accompanying search is "relatively minor"; and second, that the victim of the search may "shortly thereafter" obtain a judicial determination of whether the search was justified by probable cause. With respect to the second premise, one may initially question whether all of the States in fact provide the speedy suppression procedures the dissent assumes. More fundamentally, however, we cannot accept the view that Fourth Amendment interests are vindicated so long as "the rights of the criminal" are "protect[ed] . . . against introduction of evidence seized without probable cause." The Amendment is designed to prevent, not simply to redress, unlawful police action. In any event, we cannot join in characterizing the invasion of privacy that results from a top-to-bottom search of a man's house as "minor." And we can see no reason why, simply because some interference with an individual's privacy and freedom of movement has lawfully taken place, further intrusions should automatically be allowed despite the absence of a warrant that the Fourth Amendment would otherwise require.

13. Although the warrant was issued at 10:39 a.m. and the arrest was not made until late in the afternoon, the State suggests that the delay is accounted for by normal police procedures and by the heavy workload of the officer in charge. In addition, that officer testified that he and his colleagues went to the petitioner's house "to keep from approaching him at his place of business to cause him any problem there."

principles they stand for are inconsistent with those that we have endorsed today, they are no longer to be followed.

Application of sound Fourth Amendment principles to the facts of this case produces a clear result. The search here went far beyond the petitioner's person and the area from within which he might have obtained either a weapon or something that could have been used as evidence against him. There was no constitutional justification, in the absence of a search warrant, for extending the search beyond that area. The scope of the search was, therefore, "unreasonable" under the Fourth and Fourteenth Amendments, and the petitioner's conviction cannot stand.

Reversed.

[The concurring opinion of Justice Harlan is omitted.]

JUSTICE WHITE, with whom JUSTICE BLACK joins, dissenting.

. . . The [Fourth] Amendment does not proscribe "warrantless searches" but instead it proscribes "unreasonable searches" and this Court has never held nor does the majority today assert that warrantless searches are necessarily unreasonable.

Applying this reasonableness test to the area of searches incident to arrests, one thing is clear at the outset. Search of an arrested man and of the items within his immediate reach must in almost every case be reasonable. There is always a danger that the suspect will try to escape, seizing concealed weapons with which to overpower and injure the arresting officers, and there is a danger that he may destroy evidence vital to the prosecution. Circumstances in which these justifications would not apply are sufficiently rare that inquiry is not made into searches of this scope, which have been considered reasonable throughout.

The justifications which make such a search reasonable obviously do not apply to the search of areas to which the accused does not have ready physical access. This is not enough, however, to prove such searches unconstitutional. The Court has always held, and does not today deny, that when there is probable cause to search and it is "impracticable" for one reason or another to get a search warrant, then a warrantless search may be reasonable. This is the case whether an arrest was made at the time of the search or not.[3]

This is not to say that a search can be reasonable without regard to the probable cause to believe that seizable items are on the premises. But when there are exigent circumstances, and probable cause, then the search may be made without a warrant, reasonably. An arrest itself may often create an emergency situation making it impracticable to obtain a warrant before embarking on a related search. Again assuming that there is probable cause to search premises at the spot where a suspect is arrested, it seems to me unreasonable to require the police to leave the scene in order to obtain a search warrant when they are already legally there to make a valid arrest, and when there must almost always be a strong possibility that confederates of the arrested man will in the meanwhile remove the items for which the police have probable cause to search. This must so often be the case that it seems to me as unreasonable to require a warrant for a search of the premises as to require a warrant for search of the person and his very immediate surroundings.

---

3. Even Mr. Justice Frankfurter, joined in dissent in *Rabinowitz* by Mr. Justice Jackson, admitted that there was an exception to the search-warrant requirement in cases of necessity, and noted that this applied, for example, to vehicles which could readily be moved. 339 U.S. 56, at 73.

This case provides a good illustration of my point that it is unreasonable to require police to leave the scene of an arrest in order to obtain a search warrant when they already have probable cause to search and there is a clear danger that the items for which they may reasonably search will be removed before they return with a warrant. Petitioner was arrested in his home after an arrest . . . which I will now assume was valid. There was doubtless probable cause not only to arrest petitioner, but also to search his house. He had obliquely admitted, both to a neighbor and to the owner of the burglarized store, that he had committed the burglary. In light of this, and the fact that the neighbor had seen other admittedly stolen property in petitioner's house, there was surely probable cause on which a warrant could have issued to search the house for the stolen coins. Moreover, had the police simply arrested petitioner, taken him off to the station house, and later returned with a warrant,[5] it seems very likely that petitioner's wife, who in view of petitioner's generally garrulous nature must have known of the robbery, would have removed the coins. For the police to search the house while the evidence they had probable cause to search out and seize was still there cannot be considered unreasonable. . . .

. . . [W]here as here the existence of probable cause is independently established and would justify a warrant for a broader search for evidence, I would follow past cases and permit such a search to be carried out without a warrant, since the fact of arrest supplies an exigent circumstance justifying police action before the evidence can be removed, and also alerts the suspect to the fact of the search so that he can immediately seek judicial determination of probable cause in an adversary proceeding, and appropriate redress.

This view, consistent with past cases, would not authorize the general search against which the Fourth Amendment was meant to guard, nor would it broaden or render uncertain in any way whatsoever the scope of searches permitted under the Fourth Amendment. The issue in this case is not the breadth of the search, since there was clearly probable cause for the search which was carried out. No broader search than if the officers had a warrant would be permitted. The only issue is whether a search warrant was required as a precondition to that search. It is agreed that such a warrant would be required absent exigent circumstances.[15] I would hold that the fact of arrest supplies such an exigent circumstance, since the police had lawfully gained entry to the premises to effect the arrest and since delaying the search to secure a warrant would have involved the risk of not recovering the fruits of the crime.

The majority today proscribes searches for which there is probable cause and which may prove fruitless unless carried out immediately. This rule will have no

---

5. There were three officers at the scene of the arrest, one from the city where the coin burglary had occurred, and two from the city where the arrest was made. Assuming that one policeman from each city would be needed to bring the petitioner in and obtain a search warrant, one policeman could have been left to guard the house. However, if he not only could have remained in the house against petitioner's wife's will, but followed her about to assure that no evidence was being tampered with, the invasion of her privacy would be almost as great as that accompanying an actual search. Moreover, had the wife summoned an accomplice, one officer could not have watched them both.

15. . . . There is . . . no question that a warrant to search petitioner's house would have been required had he not been arrested there. In such cases, the officers are not already lawfully on the premises, and there is not so often the same risk of the destruction of evidence nor the necessity to make an immediate search without the delay involved in securing a warrant.

added effect whatsoever in protecting the rights of the criminal accused at trial against introduction of evidence seized without probable cause. Such evidence could not be introduced under the old rule. Nor does the majority today give any added protection to the right of privacy of those whose houses there is probable cause to search. A warrant would still be sworn out for those houses, and the privacy of their owners invaded. The only possible justification for the majority's rule is that in some instances arresting officers may search when they have no probable cause to do so and that such unlawful searches might be prevented if the officers first sought a warrant from a magistrate. Against the possible protection of privacy in that class of cases, in which the privacy of the house has already been invaded by entry to make the arrest—an entry for which the majority does not assert that any warrant is necessary—must be weighed the risk of destruction of evidence for which there is probable cause to search, as a result of delays in obtaining a search warrant. Without more basis for radical change than the Court's opinion reveals, I would not upset the balance of these interests which has been struck by the former decisions of this Court. . . .

NOTES AND QUESTIONS

1. *Chimel* clarified the scope of a permissible search incident to arrest in the arrestee's home. What about the arrestee's person? In United States v. Robinson, 414 U.S. 218 (1973), a D.C. police officer stopped a 1965 Cadillac based on reliable information that the driver's operating license had been revoked. All three occupants exited the car, and the officer arrested the driver, Robinson. (For purposes of the Court's opinion, it was assumed that Robinson's full-custody arrest was valid.) The officer proceeded to search Robinson, and felt a package whose contents the officer could not immediately identify. Upon removing the package—a crumpled cigarette packet—and opening it, the officer discovered "14 gelatin capsules of white powder" that turned out to be heroin. In an opinion by then-Justice Rehnquist, the Court upheld the search:

> It is well settled that a search incident to a lawful arrest is a traditional exception to the warrant requirement of the Fourth Amendment. This general exception has historically been formulated into two distinct propositions. The first is that a search may be made of the *person* of the arrestee by virtue of the lawful arrest. The second is that a search may be made of the area within the control of the arrestee.
>
> Examination of this Court's decisions shows that these two propositions have been treated quite differently. The validity of the search of a person incident to a lawful arrest has been regarded as settled from its first enunciation, and has remained virtually unchallenged until the present case. The validity of the second proposition, while likewise conceded in principle, has been subject to differing interpretations as to the extent of the area which may be searched. . . .
>
> The Court of Appeals in effect determined that the *only* reason supporting the authority for a *full* search incident to lawful arrest was the possibility of discovery of evidence or fruits. . . .
>
> [But the] justification or reason for the authority to search incident to a lawful arrest rests quite as much on the need to disarm the suspect in order to take him into custody as it does on the need to preserve evidence on his person for later use at trial. The standards traditionally governing a search incident to

lawful arrest are not, therefore, [altered] . . . by the absence of probable fruits or further evidence of the particular crime for which the arrest is made.

Nor are we inclined, on the basis of what seems to us to be a rather speculative judgment, to qualify the breadth of the general authority to search incident to a lawful custodial arrest on an assumption that persons arrested for the offense of driving while their licenses have been revoked are less likely to possess dangerous weapons than are those arrested for other crimes.[5] It is scarcely open to doubt that the danger to an officer is far greater in the case of the extended exposure which follows the taking of a suspect into custody and transporting him to the police station than in the case of the relatively fleeting contact resulting from the typical [street] stop. This is an adequate basis for treating all custodial arrests alike for purposes of search justification.

But quite apart from these distinctions, our more fundamental disagreement with the Court of Appeals arises from its suggestion that there must be litigated in each case the issue of whether or not there was present one of the reasons supporting the authority for a search of the person incident to a lawful arrest. We do not think the long line of authorities of this Court . . . or what we can glean from the history of practice in this country and in England, requires such a case-by-case adjudication. A police officer's determination as to how and where to search the person of a suspect whom he has arrested is necessarily a quick ad hoc judgment which the Fourth Amendment does not require to be broken down in each instance into an analysis of each step in the search. The authority to search the person incident to a lawful custodial arrest, while based upon the need to disarm and to discover evidence, does not depend on what a court may later decide was the probability in a particular arrest situation that weapons or evidence would in fact be found upon the person of the suspect. A custodial arrest of a suspect based on probable cause is a reasonable intrusion under the Fourth Amendment; that intrusion being lawful, a search incident to the arrest requires no additional justification. It is the fact of the lawful arrest which establishes the authority to search, and we hold that in the case of a lawful custodial arrest a full search of the person is not only an exception to the warrant requirement of the Fourth Amendment, but is also a "reasonable" search under that Amendment.

The search of respondent's person conducted by Officer Jenks in this case and the seizure from him of the heroin, were permissible under established Fourth Amendment law. . . . Since it is the fact of custodial arrest which gives rise to the authority to search, it is of no moment that Jenks did not indicate any subjective fear of the respondent or that he did not himself suspect that respondent was armed. Having in the course of a lawful search come upon the crumpled package of cigarettes, he was entitled to inspect it; and when his inspection revealed the heroin capsules, he was entitled to seize them as "fruits, instrumentalities, or contraband" probative of criminal conduct. . . .

414 U.S. at 224, 233-236.

---

5. Such an assumption appears at least questionable in light of the available statistical data concerning assaults on police officers who are in the course of making arrests. The danger to the police officer flows from the fact of the arrest, and its attendant proximity, stress, and uncertainty, and not from the grounds for arrest. One study concludes that approximately 30% of the shootings of police officers occur when an officer stops a person in an automobile. Bristow, Police Officer Shootings — A Tactical Evaluation, 54 J. Crim. L.C. & P.S. 93 (1963). The Government in its brief notes that the Uniform Crime Reports, prepared by the Federal Bureau of Investigation, indicate that a significant percentage of murders of police officers occurs when the officers are making traffic stops. Those reports indicate that during January-March 1973, 35 police officers were murdered; 11 of those officers were killed while engaged in making traffic stops.

Justice Marshall wrote a sharp dissent joined by Justices Douglas and Brennan. Marshall argued that the majority's decision would facilitate pretextual arrests: police officers arresting suspects for minor traffic infractions in order to search those suspects for drugs. He also contended that, even if the rest of the search was permissible, opening the crumpled cigarette pack was another story: "[E]ven were we to assume, arguendo, that it was reasonable for Jenks to remove the object he felt in respondent's pocket, clearly there was no justification consistent with the Fourth Amendment which would authorize his opening the package and looking inside." Id. at 255-256 (Marshall, J., dissenting). He continued:

> One wonders if the result in this case would have been the same were respondent a businessman who was lawfully taken into custody for driving without a license and whose wallet was taken from him by the police. Would it be reasonable for the police officer, because of the possibility that a razor blade was hidden somewhere in the wallet, to open it, remove all the contents, and examine each item carefully? Or suppose a lawyer lawfully arrested for a traffic offense is found to have a sealed envelope on his person. Would it be permissible for the arresting officer to tear open the envelope in order to make sure that it did not contain a clandestine weapon — perhaps a pin or a razor blade?

Id. at 257.

2. Is *Robinson* consistent with *Chimel*? Notice that even the dissenters in *Chimel* assumed that searches incident to arrest would be justified by probable cause. Was there probable cause to believe Robinson's cigarette packet contained evidence of crime? Was it a source of danger to the police? How would you respond to the hypotheticals in Justice Marshall's dissent, where police searched a wallet or a sealed envelope rather than a crumpled cigarette packet? Are those searches legal under *Robinson*?

3. Which way does history cut in *Robinson*? The conventional—though contested—wisdom among historians is that there has long been broad authority for police officers to search incident to arrest. The leading discussion is Telford Taylor, Two Studies in Constitutional Interpretation 23-50 (1969). For the best and most detailed version of the contrary argument, see Thomas Y. Davies, Recovering the Original Fourth Amendment, 98 Mich. L. Rev. 547 (1999). But even if the conventional wisdom is correct, the historical search-incident-to-arrest doctrine also included a search of the arrestee's house, if the arrest occurred there. See Taylor, supra, at 29 ("Neither in the reported cases nor the legal literature is there any indication that search of the person of an arrestee, *or the premises in which he was taken*, was ever challenged in England until the end of the nineteenth century") (emphasis added). Recall that in *Chimel*, the Court expressly rejected *that* rule. Does it make sense for the Court to follow the historical practice in *Robinson* but not in *Chimel*?

4. In Maryland v. Buie, 494 U.S. 325 (1990), the Court addressed the question—closely related to *Chimel* and *Robinson*—whether police may conduct a "protective sweep" through a home when executing an arrest warrant there. The Court determined that officers may "as a precautionary matter and without probable cause or reasonable suspicion, look in closets and other spaces immediately adjoining the place of arrest from which an attack could be immediately launched." Id. at 334. Relying on Terry v. Ohio, 392 U.S. 1 (1968), the *Buie* majority also concluded that to look in additional areas not immediately adjoining

the scene, there must be articulable suspicion that the area swept harbors an individual posing a danger to those present. (*Terry* is excerpted infra at page 557.) The Court emphasized that "a protective sweep, aimed at protecting the arresting officers, . . . may extend only to a cursory inspection of those spaces where a person may be found." Id. at 335.

5. *Chimel, Robinson*, and *Buie* all involve a basic choice: whether to define the scope of police authority with a rule, or with a standard. Broadly speaking, *Chimel* and *Buie* opted for standards: police may search the areas from which the suspect might grab a weapon, or may look for accomplices in places from which an attack could be quickly launched. *Robinson* chose a rule: all suspects who may be arrested may be searched, along with items found on their persons at the time of arrest. Are these decisions consistent? Are they wise? For the leading argument in support of rules in this context, see Wayne R. LaFave, "Case-by-Case Adjudication" versus "Standardized Procedures": The *Robinson* Dilemma, 1974 Sup. Ct. Rev. 127, 141-143. For the leading argument in favor of standards, see Albert W. Alschuler, Bright Line Fever and the Fourth Amendment, 45 U. Pitt. L. Rev. 227 (1984).

6. The Court issued another rule-like decision in New York v. Belton, 453 U.S. 454 (1981). Belton was pulled over for speeding; when the officer saw a small quantity of marijuana on the floor of Belton's car, he arrested Belton for possession of marijuana. The officer then searched the passenger compartment of the car and, inside the pocket of a jacket on the back seat, found cocaine. The Court held that "when a policeman has made a lawful custodial arrest of the occupant of an automobile, he may, as a contemporaneous incident of that arrest, search the passenger compartment of that automobile," id. at 460 — including examining the contents of any containers found there.

Notice that, for many cases (including *Belton* itself), *Belton* does no more than replicate a portion of the authority police are given by California v. Acevedo, page 493 supra. *Acevedo* authorizes a search of the whole car, including the contents of containers, if the police have probable cause to believe evidence will be found there. *Belton* was decided a decade earlier than *Acevedo*; had it been decided later, the Court would probably have found the search permissible under the car search exception, and search-incident-to-arrest doctrine would have been unaffected.

Belton nevertheless matters a great deal in the many cases where the offense for which the defendant is arrested is not one for which evidence is likely to be found in the car. Suppose, for example, that the officer had arrested Belton not for marijuana possession but for speeding — a crime in some states, though only a civil violation in others. The search of the car would still be permissible, would it not? Doesn't that give the police an incentive to make traffic arrests in order to make drug searches — one of the problems Justice Marshall raised in his *Robinson* dissent?

THORNTON v. UNITED STATES

Certiorari to the United States Court of Appeals for the Fourth Circuit
124 S. Ct. 2127 (2004)

CHIEF JUSTICE REHNQUIST delivered the opinion of the Court except as to footnote 4.

In New York v. Belton, 453 U.S. 454 (1981), we held that when a police officer has made a lawful custodial arrest of an occupant of an automobile, the Fourth Amendment allows the officer to search the passenger compartment of that vehicle as a contemporaneous incident of arrest . . . We now . . . conclude that *Belton* governs even when an officer does not make contact until the person arrested has left the vehicle.

Officer Deion Nichols of the Norfolk, Virginia, Police Department, who was in uniform but driving an unmarked police car, first noticed petitioner Marcus Thornton when petitioner slowed down so as to avoid driving next to him. . . . His suspicions aroused, Nichols pulled off onto a side street and petitioner passed him. After petitioner passed him, Nichols ran a check on petitioner's license tags, which revealed that the tags had been issued to a 1982 Chevy two-door and not to a Lincoln Town Car, the model of car petitioner was driving. Before Nichols had an opportunity to pull him over, petitioner drove into a parking lot, parked, and got out of the vehicle. Nichols saw petitioner leave his vehicle as he pulled in behind him. He parked the patrol car, accosted petitioner, and asked him for his driver's license. He also told him that his license tags did not match the vehicle that he was driving.

Petitioner appeared nervous. He began rambling and licking his lips; he was sweating. Concerned for his safety, Nichols asked petitioner if he had any narcotics or weapons on him or in his vehicle. Petitioner said no. Nichols then asked petitioner if he could pat him down, to which petitioner agreed. Nichols felt a bulge in petitioner's left front pocket and again asked him if he had any illegal narcotics on him. This time petitioner stated that he did, and he reached into his pocket and pulled out two individual bags, one containing three bags of marijuana and the other containing a large amount of crack cocaine. Nichols handcuffed petitioner, informed him that he was under arrest, and placed him in the back seat of the patrol car. He then searched petitioner's vehicle and found a BryCo.9-millimeter handgun under the driver's seat.

A grand jury charged petitioner with possession with intent to distribute cocaine base, possession of a firearm after having been previously convicted of a crime punishable by a term of imprisonment exceeding one year, and possession of a firearm in furtherance of a drug trafficking crime. Petitioner sought to suppress, inter alia, the firearm as the fruit of an unconstitutional search. After a hearing, the District Court denied petitioner's motion to suppress, holding that the automobile search was valid under New York v. Belton, supra. . . . A jury convicted petitioner on all three counts; he was sentenced to 180 months' imprisonment and 8 years of supervised release.

Petitioner appealed, challenging only the District Court's denial of the suppression motion. He argued that *Belton* was limited to situations where the officer initiated contact with an arrestee while he was still an occupant of the car. The United States Court of Appeals for the Fourth Circuit affirmed. . . . We granted certiorari, and now affirm.

In *Belton*, an officer overtook a speeding vehicle on the New York Thruway and ordered its driver to pull over. Suspecting that the occupants possessed marijuana, the officer directed them to get out of the car and arrested them for unlawful possession. He searched them and then searched the passenger compartment of the car. [453 U.S. at 454-455.] We considered the constitutionally permissible scope of a search in these circumstances and sought to lay down a workable rule governing that situation.

We first referred to Chimel v. California, 395 U.S. 752 (1969), a case where the arrestee was arrested in his home, and we had described the scope of a search incident to a lawful arrest as the person of the arrestee and the area immediately surrounding him. 453 U.S., at 457 (citing *Chimel*, supra, 395 U.S. at 763). This rule was justified by the need to remove any weapon the arrestee might seek to use to resist arrest or to escape, and the need to prevent the concealment or destruction of evidence. Although easily stated, the *Chimel* principle had proved difficult to apply in specific cases. We pointed out that in United States v. Robinson, 414 U.S. 218 (1973), a case dealing with the scope of the search of the arrestee's person, we had rejected a suggestion that " 'there must be litigated in each case the issue of whether or not there was present one of the reasons supporting the authority' " to conduct such a search. 453 U.S., at 459 (quoting *Robinson*, 414 U.S. at 235). Similarly, because "courts had found no workable definition of the 'area within the immediate control of the arrestee' when that area arguably included the interior of an automobile and the arrestee was its recent occupant," 453 U.S., at 460, we sought to set forth a clear rule for police officers and citizens alike. We therefore held that "when a policeman has made a lawful custodial arrest of the occupant of an automobile, he may, as a contemporaneous incident of that arrest, search the passenger compartment of that automobile." Ibid.

In so holding, we placed no reliance on the fact that the officer in *Belton* ordered the occupants out of the vehicle, or initiated contact with them while they remained within it. Nor do we find such a factor persuasive in distinguishing the current situation, as it bears no logical relationship to *Belton*'s rationale. There is simply no basis to conclude that the span of the area generally within the arrestee's immediate control is determined by whether the arrestee exited the vehicle at the officer's direction, or whether the officer initiated contact with him while he remained in the car. . . .

In all relevant aspects, the arrest of a suspect who is next to a vehicle presents identical concerns regarding officer safety and the destruction of evidence as the arrest of one who is inside the vehicle. An officer may search a suspect's vehicle under *Belton* only if the suspect is arrested. A custodial arrest is fluid and "the danger to the police officer flows from *the fact of the arrest*, and its attendant proximity, stress, and uncertainty," *Robinson*, supra, 414 U.S. at 234-235, and n. 5 (emphasis added). . . . The stress is no less merely because the arrestee exited his car before the officer initiated contact, nor is an arrestee less likely to attempt to lunge for a weapon or to destroy evidence if he is outside of, but still in control of, the vehicle. In either case, the officer faces a highly volatile situation. It would make little sense to apply two different rules to what is, at bottom, the same situation.

In some circumstances it may be safer and more effective for officers to conceal their presence from a suspect until he has left his vehicle. Certainly that is a judgment officers should be free to make. But under the strictures of petitioner's proposed "contact initiation" rule, officers who do so would be unable to search the car's passenger compartment in the event of a custodial arrest, potentially compromising their safety and placing incriminating evidence at risk of concealment or destruction. The Fourth Amendment does not require such a gamble.

Petitioner argues, however, that *Belton* will fail to provide a "bright-line" rule if it applies to more than vehicle "occupants." Brief for Petitioner 29-34. But *Belton* allows police to search the passenger compartment of a vehicle incident to a lawful custodial arrest of both "occupants" and "recent occupants." 453 U.S., at 460. Indeed, the respondent in *Belton* was not inside the car at the time of the arrest and search; he was standing on the highway. In any event, while an arrestee's status as a "recent occupant" may turn on his temporal or spatial relationship to the car at the time of the arrest and search, it certainly does not turn on whether he was inside or outside the car at the moment that the officer first initiated contact with him.

To be sure, not all contraband in the passenger compartment is likely to be readily accessible to a "recent occupant." It is unlikely in this case that petitioner could have reached under the driver's seat for his gun once he was outside of his automobile. But the firearm and the passenger compartment in general were no more inaccessible than were the contraband and the passenger compartment in *Belton*. The need for a clear rule, readily understood by police officers and not depending on differing estimates of what items were or were not within reach of an arrestee at any particular moment, justifies the sort of generalization which *Belton* enunciated. Once an officer determines that there is probable cause to make an arrest, it is reasonable to allow officers to ensure their safety and to preserve evidence by searching the entire passenger compartment.

Rather than clarifying the constitutional limits of a *Belton* search, petitioner's "contact initiation" rule would obfuscate them. Under petitioner's proposed rule, an officer approaching a suspect who has just alighted from his vehicle would have to determine whether he actually confronted or signaled confrontation with the suspect while he remained in the car, or whether the suspect exited his vehicle unaware of, and for reasons unrelated to, the officer's presence. This determination would be inherently subjective and highly fact specific, and would require precisely the sort of ad hoc determinations on the part of officers in the field and reviewing courts that *Belton* sought to avoid. Experience has shown that such a rule is impracticable, and we refuse to adopt it. So long as an arrestee is the sort of "recent occupant" of a vehicle such as petitioner was here, officers may search that vehicle incident to the arrest.[4] . . .

JUSTICE O'CONNOR, concurring in part.

I join all but footnote 4 of the Court's opinion. Although the opinion is a logical extension of the holding of New York v. Belton, 453 U.S. 454 (1981), I write separately to express my dissatisfaction with the state of the law in this area. As JUSTICE SCALIA forcefully argues, lower court decisions seem now to treat the ability to search a vehicle incident to the arrest of a recent occupant as a police

---

4. Whatever the merits of JUSTICE SCALIA's opinion concurring in the judgment, this is the wrong case in which to address them. Petitioner has never argued that *Belton* should be limited "to cases where it is reasonable to believe evidence relevant to the crime of arrest might be found in the vehicle," nor did any court below consider JUSTICE SCALIA's reasoning. . . . The question presented—"whether the bright-line rule announced in New York v. Belton is confined to situations in which the police initiate contact with the occupant of a vehicle while that person is in the vehicle,"—does not fairly encompass JUSTICE SCALIA's analysis. . . . And the United States has never had an opportunity to respond to such an approach. Under these circumstances, it would be imprudent to overrule, for all intents and purposes, our established constitutional precedent, which governs police authority in a common occurrence such as automobile searches pursuant to arrest, and we decline to do so at this time.

entitlement rather than as an exception justified by the twin rationales of Chimel v. California, 395 U.S. 752 (1969). That erosion is a direct consequence of *Belton's* shaky foundation. While the approach JUSTICE SCALIA proposes appears to be built on firmer ground, I am reluctant to adopt it in the context of a case in which neither the Government nor the petitioner has had a chance to speak to its merit.

JUSTICE SCALIA, with whom JUSTICE GINSBURG joins, concurring in the judgment.

In Chimel v. California, 395 U.S. 752, 762-763 (1969), we held that a search incident to arrest was justified only as a means to find weapons the arrestee might use or evidence he might conceal or destroy. We accordingly limited such searches to the area within the suspect's "immediate control" — i.e., "the area into which an arrestee might reach in order to grab a weapon or evidentiary item." 395 U.S. at 763. In New York v. Belton, 453 U.S. 454, 460 (1981), we set forth a bright-line rule for arrests of automobile occupants, holding that, because the vehicle's entire passenger compartment is "in fact generally, even if not inevitably," within the arrestee's immediate control, a search of the whole compartment is justified in every case.

When petitioner's car was searched in this case, he was neither in, nor anywhere near, the passenger compartment of his vehicle. Rather, he was handcuffed and secured in the back of the officer's squad car. The risk that he would nevertheless "grab a weapon or evidentiary item" from his car was remote in the extreme. The Court's effort to apply our current doctrine to this search stretches it beyond its breaking point, and for that reason I cannot join the Court's opinion.

I see three reasons why the search in this case might have been justified to protect officer safety or prevent concealment or destruction of evidence. None ultimately persuades me.

The first is that, despite being handcuffed and secured in the back of a squad car, petitioner might have escaped and retrieved a weapon or evidence from his vehicle — a theory that calls to mind Judge Goldberg's reference to the mythical arrestee "possessed of the skill of Houdini and the strength of Hercules." United States v. Frick, 490 F.2d 666, 673 (CA5 1973) (opinion concurring in part and dissenting in part). The United States, endeavoring to ground this seemingly speculative fear in reality, points to a total of seven instances over the past 13 years in which state or federal officers were attacked with weapons by handcuffed or formerly handcuffed arrestees. Brief for United States 38-39, and n. 12. These instances do not, however, justify the search authority claimed. Three involved arrestees who retrieved weapons concealed *on their own person*. Three more involved arrestees who seized a weapon *from the arresting officer*. Authority to search the arrestee's own person is beyond question; and of course no search could prevent seizure of the officer's gun. Only one of the seven instances involved a handcuffed arrestee who escaped from a squad car to retrieve a weapon from somewhere else: In Plakas v. Drinski, 19 F.3d 1143, 1144-1146 (CA7 1994), the suspect jumped out of the squad car and ran through a forest to a house, where (still in handcuffs) he struck an officer on the wrist with a fireplace poker before ultimately being shot dead.

Of course, the Government need not document specific instances in order to justify measures that avoid obvious risks. But the risk here is far from obvious, and in a context as frequently recurring as roadside arrests, the Government's inability to come up with even a single example of a handcuffed arrestee's retrieval of arms or evidence from his vehicle undermines its claims. The risk that a suspect hand-cuffed in the back of a squad car might escape and recover a weapon from his vehicle is surely no greater than the risk that a suspect handcuffed in his residence might escape and recover a weapon from the next room—a danger we held insufficient to justify a search in *Chimel*, supra, 395 U.S. at 763.

The second defense of the search in this case is that, since the officer could have conducted the search at the time of arrest (when the suspect was still near the car), he should not be penalized for having taken the sensible precaution of securing the suspect in the squad car first. . . . The weakness of this argument is that it assumes that, one way or another, the search must take place. But conducting a *Chimel* search is not the Government's right; it is an exception—justified by neces-sity—to a rule that would otherwise render the search unlawful. If "sensible police procedures" require that suspects be handcuffed and put in squad cars, then police should handcuff suspects, put them in squad cars, and not conduct the search. Indeed, if an officer leaves a suspect unrestrained nearby just to manufacture authority to search, one could argue that the search is unreasonable *precisely because* the dangerous conditions justifying it existed only by virtue of the officer's failure to follow sensible procedures.

The third defense of the search is that, even though the arrestee posed no risk here, *Belton* searches in general are reasonable, and the benefits of a bright-line rule justify upholding that small minority of searches that, on their particular facts, are not reasonable. The validity of this argument rests on the accuracy of *Belton*'s claim that the passenger compartment is "in fact generally, even if not inevitably," within the suspect's immediate control. 453 U.S., at 460. By the United States' own admission, however, "the practice of restraining an arrestee on the scene before searching a car that he just occupied is so prevalent that holding that *Belton* does not apply in that setting would . . . largely render *Belton* a dead letter." Brief for United States 36-37. Reported cases involving this precise factual scenario—a motorist handcuffed and secured in the back of a squad car when the search takes place—are legion. . . . Some courts uphold such searches even when the squad car carrying the handcuffed arrestee has already left the scene. See, e.g., [United States v. McLaughlin, 170 F.3d 889, 890-891 (CA9 1999)] (upholding search because only five minutes had elapsed since squad car left).

The popularity of the practice is not hard to fathom. If *Belton entitles* an officer to search a vehicle upon arresting the driver despite having taken measures that eliminate any danger, what rational officer would not take those measures? Cf. Moskovitz, A Rule in Search of a Reason: An Empirical Reexamination of *Chimel* and *Belton*, 2002 Wis. L. Rev. 657, 665-666 (citing police training materials). If it was ever true that the passenger compartment is "in fact generally, even if not inevitably," within the arrestee's immediate control at the time of the search, it certainly is not true today. As one judge has put it: "In our search for clarity, we have now abandoned our constitutional moorings and floated to a place where the law approves of purely exploratory searches of vehicles during which officers with no definite objective or reason for the search are allowed to rummage around in a car to see what they might find." *McLaughlin*, supra, at 894 (Trott, J., concurring). I agree entirely with that assessment.

If *Belton* searches are justifiable, it is not because the arrestee might grab a weapon or evidentiary item from his car, but simply because the car might contain evidence relevant to the crime for which he was arrested. This more general sort of evidence-gathering search is not without antecedent. For example, in United States v. Rabinowitz, 339 U.S. 56 (1950), we upheld a search of the suspect's place of business after he was arrested there. We did not restrict the officers' search authority to "the area into which [the] arrestee might reach in order to grab a weapon or evidentiary item," *Chimel*, 395 U.S., at 763, and we did not justify the search as a means to prevent concealment or destruction of evidence. Rather, we relied on a more general interest in gathering evidence relevant to the crime for which the suspect had been arrested. See 339 U.S., at 60-64. . . .

. . . There is nothing irrational about broader police authority to search for evidence when and where the perpetrator of a crime is lawfully arrested. The fact of prior lawful arrest distinguishes the arrestee from society at large, and distinguishes a search for evidence of *his* crime from general rummaging. Moreover, it is not illogical to assume that evidence of a crime is most likely to be found where the suspect was apprehended. . . .

In short, both *Rabinowitz* and *Chimel* are plausible accounts of what the Constitution requires, and neither is so persuasive as to justify departing from settled law. But if we are going to continue to allow *Belton* searches on stare decisis grounds, we should at least be honest about why we are doing so. *Belton* cannot reasonably be explained as a mere application of *Chimel*. Rather, it is a return to the broader sort of search incident to arrest that we allowed before *Chimel* — limited, of course, to searches of motor vehicles, a category of "effects" which give rise to a reduced expectation of privacy and heightened law enforcement needs.

Recasting *Belton* in these terms would have at least one important practical consequence. In United States v. Robinson, 414 U.S. 218, 235 (1973), we held that authority to search an arrestee's person does not depend on the actual presence of one of *Chimel*'s two rationales in the particular case; rather, the fact of arrest alone justifies the search. That holding stands in contrast to *Rabinowitz*, where we did not treat the fact of arrest alone as sufficient, but upheld the search only after noting that it was "not general or exploratory for whatever might be turned up" but reflected a reasonable belief that evidence would be found. 339 U.S., at 62-63. . . . The two different rules make sense: When officer safety or imminent evidence concealment or destruction is at issue, officers should not have to make fine judgments in the heat of the moment. But in the context of a general evidence-gathering search, the state interests that might justify any overbreadth are far less compelling. A motorist may be arrested for a wide variety of offenses; in many cases, there is no reasonable basis to believe relevant evidence might be found in the car. See Atwater v. Lago Vista, 532 U.S. 318, 323-324 (2001). I would therefore limit *Belton* searches to cases where it is reasonable to believe evidence relevant to the crime of arrest might be found in the vehicle.

In this case, as in *Belton*, petitioner was lawfully arrested for a drug offense. It was reasonable for Officer Nichols to believe that further contraband or similar evidence relevant to the crime for which he had been arrested might be found in the vehicle from which he had just alighted and which was still within his vicinity at the time of arrest. I would affirm the decision below on that ground.

JUSTICE STEVENS, with whom JUSTICE SOUTER joins, dissenting.

. . . The Court in *Belton* noted that the lower courts had discovered *Chimel*'s reaching-distance principle difficult to apply in the context of automobile searches incident to arrest, and that "no straightforward rule had emerged from the litigated cases." 453 U.S., at 458-459. None of the cases cited by the Court to demonstrate the disarray in the lower courts involved a pedestrian who was in the vicinity, but outside the reaching distance, of his or her car. . . . Thus, *Belton* was demonstrably concerned only with the narrow but common circumstance of a search occasioned by the arrest of a suspect who was seated in or driving an automobile at the time the law enforcement official approached. Normally, after such an arrest has occurred, the officer's safety is no longer in jeopardy, but he must decide what, if any, search for incriminating evidence he should conduct. *Belton* provided previously unavailable and therefore necessary guidance for that category of cases.

The bright-line rule crafted in *Belton* is not needed for cases in which the arrestee is first accosted when he is a pedestrian, because *Chimel* itself provides all the guidance that is necessary. The only genuine justification for extending *Belton* to cover such circumstances is the interest in uncovering potentially valuable evidence. In my opinion, that goal must give way to the citizen's constitutionally protected interest in privacy when there is already in place a well-defined rule limiting the permissible scope of a search of an arrested pedestrian. The *Chimel* rule should provide the same protection to a "recent occupant" of a vehicle as to a recent occupant of a house. . . .

Unwilling to confine the *Belton* rule to the narrow class of cases it was designed to address, the Court extends *Belton*'s reach without supplying any guidance for the future application of its swollen rule. We are told that officers may search a vehicle incident to arrest "so long as [the] arrestee is the sort of 'recent occupant' of a vehicle such as petitioner was here." But we are not told how recent is recent, or how close is close, perhaps because in this case "the record is not clear." 325 F.3d 189, 196 (CA4 2003). . . . As the Court cautioned in *Belton* itself, "when a person cannot know how a court will apply a settled principle to a recurring factual situation, that person cannot know the scope of his constitutional protection, nor can a policeman know the scope of his authority." 453 U.S., at 459-460. Without some limiting principle, I fear that today's decision will contribute to "a massive broadening of the automobile exception," Robbins [v. California, 453 U.S. 420, 452 (1981) (Stevens, J., dissenting)], when officers have probable cause to arrest an individual but not to search his car. . . .

NOTES AND QUESTIONS

1. Does *Thornton* state a rule or does it define a standard? The Chief Justice states the Court's holding as follows: "So long as an arrestee is the sort of 'recent occupant' of a vehicle such as petitioner was here, officers may search that vehicle incident to the arrest." How recent? Must the arrestee be anywhere in the vicinity of the car at the time of the search? Recall *McLaughlin*, the Ninth Circuit decision cited and discussed in Justice Scalia's concurrence. In that case, the defendant's car was searched five minutes after the defendant had left the scene; relying on *Belton*, the court upheld the search. Is *McLaughlin* good law after *Thornton*?

2. Perhaps *Thornton* isn't good law after *Thornton*. Justice O'Connor's concurrence all but announced that she will take the same position as Justices Scalia and Ginsburg in future cases. And Justices Stevens and Souter would presumably prefer Justice Scalia's narrower authority to search incident to arrest (query whether it

really *is* narrower; see Note 3 below) to the broader authority the Chief Justice grants in his majority opinion. Counting noses, it appears there are five votes to limit searches incident to arrest to settings in which (i) the officer's safety is at issue, or (ii) the discovery of contraband or other evidence is reasonably likely — at least if the search extends beyond the arrestee's person.

If that is so, why should the rule be any different when the search is of the arrestee himself? The logic of Justice Scalia's argument would seem to apply as strongly to *Robinson*, where the police searched the defendant's jacket pocket, as to *Thornton*, where they searched the defendant's car. If a rule is unnecessary in the latter situation, perhaps it is unnecessary in the former as well. *Robinson* may soon be questionable authority. Or are the cases different?

3. It may seem fairly obvious that Justice Scalia's argument could restrict police authority to search cars, and perhaps persons as well. But the same argument might also *expand* police authority to search homes. Suppose, for example, Justice Scalia and his colleagues applied his *Thornton* argument to cases like *Chimel*. As long as the crime was one that made discovery of evidence reasonably likely, the police might have the power to search the arrestee's entire home. (The law allowed precisely that before *Chimel* limited such searches to the area within the arrestee's reach.) So Justice Scalia's position might mean narrower search authority with respect to cars and possibly persons, but broader search authority with respect to homes: *Chimel* might be questionable authority too.

4. *Chimel* held that the scope of the search incident to arrest (at least in the arrestee's home) — *what* could be searched — was governed by a standard, known by most police officers as "the grabbable area." *Robinson* held that the range of cases to which the doctrine applied — *who* could be searched — was governed by a rule: anyone who could be arrested could also be searched. *Belton* altered this pattern. *Belton* was a "what" case; the question was whether the passenger compartment of Belton's car could be searched incident to his arrest. But the Court decided it with a rule, not a standard: if the arrestee was in his car, the police could search the passenger compartment of the car incident to arrest. *Thornton* married that rule to a standard: for now, *Belton* applies to all cases where the defendant is a "recent occupant" of his car when he is arrested. So as the law stands now, the "who" issue is decided by a rule. The "what" issue is decided by a rule for persons, a quasi-rule for cars, and a standard for homes. Does that configuration make sense?

Is it obvious which issues are best decided with rules and which are best decided with standards? Justice Scalia suggests that rules are preferable where officer safety is a concern. But the question whether officers are in danger is itself a fact-bound question: one would have to apply a standard in order to decide whether to apply a rule. Is there any good way to resolve this question?

5. The defendant in Colorado v. Bertine, 479 U.S. 367 (1987), was arrested for driving under the influence of alcohol. Shortly before a tow truck arrived to take the defendant's van to the police impoundment lot, the police "inventoried" the contents of the van. The Court held this inventory search permissible, and summarized its rationale as follows: "[I]nventory procedures serve to protect an owner's property while it is in the custody of the police, to insure against claims of lost, stolen, or vandalized, property, and to guard the police from danger." Id. at 372. Note the use of the phrase "inventory procedures" — language in earlier inventory search cases had suggested that the police must follow regular procedures in order to take advantage of this particular doctrine. See Illinois v.

Lafayette, 462 U.S. 640 (1983); South Dakota v. Opperman, 428 U.S. 364 (1976). *Bertine* seemed less concerned with regular procedures:

> Bertine . . . argues that the inventory search of his van was unconstitutional because departmental regulations gave the police officers discretion to choose between impounding his van and parking and locking it in a public parking place. . . . [W]e reject [this argument]. Nothing in *Opperman* or *Lafayette* prohibits the exercise of police discretion so long as that discretion is exercised according to standard criteria and on the basis of something other than suspicion of evidence of criminal activity. Here, the discretion afforded the Boulder police was exercised in light of standardized criteria, related to the feasibility and appropriateness of parking and locking a vehicle rather than impounding it.

Id. at 375-376.

It seems fair to see inventory search doctrine as an adjunct to search-incident-to-arrest doctrine: Both are triggered by a decision to take the defendant into custody, and under both the police have something close to blanket authority to search anything the defendant has with him at the time of arrest. Consider how these doctrines change the meaning of arrests. Not only are arrests the means by which the police gain physical control over criminal defendants; not only are they a mechanism for triggering more formal criminal proceedings. Arrests are also a powerful means of gathering evidence. Which means that *both* liberty *and* privacy are at stake in arrests. Inventory search doctrine may also mean that cases like *Robinson*, *Belton*, and *Thornton* have small practical consequences: If the police may not search at the time of arrest, they may impound the car and inventory its contents, plus the contents of any items the defendant is carrying on his person, later at the police station. Given the breadth of inventory search authority, why restrict police authority to search incident to arrest?

KNOWLES v. IOWA

Certiorari to the Supreme Court of Iowa
525 U.S. 113 (1998)

CHIEF JUSTICE REHNQUIST delivered the opinion of the Court.

An Iowa police officer stopped petitioner Knowles for speeding, but issued him a citation rather than arresting him. The question presented is whether such a procedure authorizes the officer, consistently with the Fourth Amendment, to conduct a full search of the car. We answer this question "no."

Knowles was stopped in Newton, Iowa, after having been clocked driving 43 miles per hour on a road where the speed limit was 25 miles per hour. The police officer issued a citation to Knowles, although under Iowa law he might have arrested him. The officer then conducted a full search of the car, and under the driver's seat he found a bag of marijuana and a "pot pipe." Knowles was then arrested and charged with violation of state laws dealing with controlled substances.

Before trial, Knowles moved to suppress the evidence so obtained. He argued that the search could not be sustained under the "search incident to arrest" exception recognized in United States v. Robinson, 414 U.S. 218 (1973), because he had not been placed under arrest. At the hearing on the motion to suppress, the police officer conceded that he had neither Knowles' consent nor probable cause to conduct the search. He relied on Iowa law dealing with such searches.

Iowa Code Ann. §321.485(1)(a) (West 1997) provides that Iowa peace officers having cause to believe that a person has violated any traffic or motor vehicle equipment law may arrest the person and immediately take the person before a magistrate. Iowa law also authorizes the far more usual practice of issuing a citation in lieu of arrest or in lieu of continued custody after an initial arrest.[1] See Iowa Code Ann. §805.1(1) (West Supp. 1997). Section 805.1(4) provides that the issuance of a citation in lieu of an arrest "does not affect the officer's authority to conduct an otherwise lawful search." The Iowa Supreme Court has interpreted this provision as providing authority to officers to conduct a full-blown search of an automobile and driver in those cases where police elect not to make a custodial arrest and instead issue a citation — that is, a search incident to citation.

Based on this authority, the trial court denied the motion to suppress and found Knowles guilty. The Supreme Court of Iowa, sitting en banc, affirmed by a divided vote. Relying on its earlier opinion in State v. Doran, 563 N.W.2d 620 (1997), the Iowa Supreme Court upheld the constitutionality of the search under a bright-line "search incident to citation" exception to the Fourth Amendment's warrant requirement, reasoning that so long as the arresting officer had probable cause to make a custodial arrest, there need not in fact have been a custodial arrest. We granted certiorari, and we now reverse. . . .

In *Robinson*, supra, we noted the two historical rationales for the "search incident to arrest" exception: (1) the need to disarm the suspect in order to take him into custody, and (2) the need to preserve evidence for later use at trial. 414 U.S. at 234. But neither of these underlying rationales for the search incident to arrest exception is sufficient to justify the search in the present case.

We have recognized that the first rationale — officer safety — is "both legitimate and weighty," Maryland v. Wilson, 519 U.S. 408, 412 (1997). The threat to officer safety from issuing a traffic citation, however, is a good deal less than in the case of a custodial arrest. In *Robinson*, we stated that a custodial arrest involves "danger to an officer" because of "the extended exposure which follows the taking of a suspect into custody and transporting him to the police station." 414 U.S. at 234-235. We recognized that "the danger to the police officer flows from the fact of the arrest, and its attendant proximity, stress, and uncertainty, and not from the grounds for arrest." Id. at 234, n. 5. A routine traffic stop, on the other hand, is a relatively brief encounter. . . .

This is not to say that the concern for officer safety is absent in the case of a routine traffic stop. It plainly is not. But while the concern for officer safety in this context may justify the "minimal" additional intrusion of ordering a driver and passengers out of the car, it does not by itself justify the often considerably greater intrusion attending a full field-type search. . . .

---

1. Iowa law permits the issuance of a citation in lieu of arrest for most offenses for which an accused person would be "eligible for bail." See Iowa Code Ann. §805.1(1) (West Supp. 1997). In addition to traffic and motor vehicle equipment violations, this would permit the issuance of a citation in lieu of arrest for such serious felonies as second-degree burglary, §713.5 (West Supp. 1997), and first-degree theft, Iowa Code Ann. §714.2(1) (West 1993), both bailable offenses under Iowa law. See §811.1 (West Supp. 1997) (listing all nonbailable offenses). . . .

Nor has Iowa shown the second justification for the authority to search incident to arrest—the need to discover and preserve evidence. Once Knowles was stopped for speeding and issued a citation, all the evidence necessary to prosecute that offense had been obtained. No further evidence of excessive speed was going to be found either on the person of the offender or in the passenger compartment of the car.

Iowa nevertheless argues that a "search incident to citation" is justified because a suspect who is subject to a routine traffic stop may attempt to hide or destroy evidence related to his identity (e.g., a driver's license or vehicle registration), or destroy evidence of another, as yet undetected crime. As for the destruction of evidence relating to identity, if a police officer is not satisfied with the identification furnished by the driver, this may be a basis for arresting him rather than merely issuing a citation. As for destroying evidence of other crimes, the possibility that an officer would stumble onto evidence wholly unrelated to the speeding offense seems remote.

In *Robinson*, we held that the authority to conduct a full field search as incident to an arrest was a "bright-line rule," which was based on the concern for officer safety and destruction or loss of evidence, but which did not depend in every case upon the existence of either concern. Here we are asked to extend that "bright-line rule" to a situation where the concern for officer safety is not present to the same extent and the concern for destruction or loss of evidence is not present at all. We decline to do so. The judgment of the Supreme Court of Iowa is reversed, and the cause remanded for further proceedings not inconsistent with this opinion.

Suppose the officer who stopped Knowles had announced, "You're under arrest," as the officer was entitled to do under Iowa law. Could he then have searched Knowles's car incident to arrest? Apparently the answer is yes, under *Belton* and Atwater v. Lago Vista, supra at page 518. Now suppose that the search had uncovered no evidence of crime, so that the only offense involved was speeding. Could the officer have then said, "I've changed my mind. Here's a speeding ticket; you're free to go," and let Knowles go on his way? Presumably the answer is again yes: Police officers do not have to arrest in every case in which arrest is authorized, and there is no ban on an officer changing his mind.

Now consider what *Knowles* means. Isn't the officer free to do exactly what he did in *Knowles*, as long as he uses the right words? *Knowles* makes the officer's authority to search dependent on the fact of arrest, but the fact of arrest is in turn wholly within the discretion of the officer—*and* the officer is not bound by his initial announcement that the suspect is under arrest. So an officer can pull over a car, arrest the driver, search the car and, if he finds nothing, rescind the arrest. Is there any limit on the officer's ability to use his arrest power strategically in this way?

D. Reasonableness

The Fourth Amendment protects privacy broadly defined: the "right to be let alone" that Justice Brandeis celebrated in his dissent in Olmstead v. United

States, 277 U.S. 438, 478 (1928), the "privacies of life" that the Supreme Court praised in Boyd v. United States, 116 U.S. 616, 630 (1886). But how is that privacy right to be protected? *Boyd*'s protection was absolute: the invoices in that case were simply free from official inspection, whatever the means employed. Katz v. United States, 389 U.S. 347 (1967), by contrast, offered conditional privacy protection: given a warrant based on probable cause, the intrusion on the suspect's privacy is permissible. (Many of the cases in the preceding section add a qualification to *Katz*-style protection: given an appropriate exception to the warrant requirement, probable cause alone is enough to justify a Fourth Amendment intrusion.) There is a third way to approach privacy protection, and this third way is increasingly coming to dominate Fourth Amendment case law: Privacy is not protected absolutely, nor by the warrant and probable cause requirements. Instead, privacy protection is rooted in the constitutional command that searches and seizures be reasonable.

This section takes up cases in which the Supreme Court has employed an open-ended "reasonableness" standard to judge the propriety of Fourth Amendment intrusions. This approach has the virtue of permitting courts to consider factors not formally taken into account in the more traditional warrant-and-probable-cause formula. The seriousness of the crime under investigation, the importance of evidence sought by the government, and the extent of the government's privacy invasion, for instance, might be deemed relevant in determining whether a given search or seizure or category of searches and seizures should be permitted, and upon what showing. Notice that reasonableness need not mean less stringent limits on police searches and seizures. Fourth Amendment reasonableness could be *more* demanding—a point demonstrated by Winston v. Lee, 470 U.S. 753 (1985). In *Winston*, a shopkeeper was wounded during an attempted robbery but, being armed, also wounded his assailant in the left side as the assailant fled. The defendant, who was suffering from a gunshot wound to his left chest area, was found shortly after the crime about eight blocks away from the scene. The issue in *Winston* involved a proposed "search" for the shopkeeper's bullet. The Court determined that on the facts before it, searching for the evidence—even with probable cause and advance judicial authorization—would be unreasonable, given that the bullet was lodged in the suspect's body and could only be retrieved through surgery requiring general anesthesia.

Despite cases like *Winston*, however, many commentators have worried that any sliding scale, balancing, or "all circumstances considered" approach to Fourth Amendment interpretation inevitably means in practice that

> . . . appellate courts [will] defer to trial courts and trial courts . . . to the police. What other results should we expect? If there are no fairly clear rules telling the policeman what he may and may not do, courts are seldom going to say that what he did was unreasonable.

Anthony G. Amsterdam, Perspectives on the Fourth Amendment, 58 Minn. L. Rev. 349, 394 (1974). Carol Steiker has warned that "[j]udgments couched in terms of 'reasonableness' slide very easily into the familiar constitutional rubric of 'rational basis' review—a level of scrutiny that has proven to be effectively no scrutiny at all." Carol S. Steiker, Second Thoughts About First Principles, 107 Harv. L. Rev. 820, 855 (1994). And if reasonableness is decided case by case, with the propriety of each Fourth Amendment intrusion judged in light of its particular facts, it is worth wondering whether this approach can provide adequate guidance to police as they decide when to search or seize, and when not to.

Perhaps it can. Professor Alschuler has argued that the case for bright-line Fourth Amendment rules has been overstated, and that the desire for such rules has needlessly complicated the case law. He urges courts to reconsider the virtues of the case-by-case approach:

> [C]ourts sometimes can give law enforcement officers significant guidance within a framework of case-by-case adjudication by establishing subordinate, presumptive rules for the resolution of recurring fourth amendment issues. . . . In addition, every ruling in a system of case-by-case adjudication becomes part of a dialogue between judges and law enforcement officers. This dialogue can—and has in fact—established standards that may not be subject to precise verbalization. . . . [Nevertheless,] [o]ur traditional regime of case-by-case adjudication plainly does communicate.

Albert W. Alschuler, Bright Line Fever and the Fourth Amendment, 45 U. Pitt. L. Rev. 227, 256 (1984).

But there may be another objection to an open-ended reasonableness, interest-balancing approach to Fourth Amendment cases. The Court as an institution has an interest in providing a convincing rationale for its resolution of these cases. After all, they frequently present questions about the exercise of state power in their starkest and most compelling form. Consider the following:

> Ironically, the [balancing] methodology's most significant disadvantages are consequences of its advantages. Precisely because balancing surfaces the competing interests at stake, it calls out for a convincing explanation for the inevitable choice that must be made between those interests. Unfortunately, the Court lacks the tools for providing such an explanation.

Silas J. Wasserstrom & Louis Michael Seidman, The Fourth Amendment as Constitutional Theory, 77 Geo. L.J. 19, 49 (1988).

Whatever the merits of these arguments, consider-all-the-circumstances reasonableness has played an important role in Fourth Amendment doctrine—a role that has only increased in significance in recent years. Interestingly, the early cases using this approach fell outside the traditional concerns of criminal investigation. In Camara v. Municipal Court, 387 U.S. 523 (1967), and See v. City of Seattle, 387 U.S. 541 (1967), the Court took up the question of Fourth Amendment constraints on fire, health, and housing code inspection programs, overruling Franks v. Maryland, 359 U.S. 360 (1959), which had deemed such programs to be at the periphery of Fourth Amendment concerns. Suspicionless government inspections to enforce safety code regulations posed a problem for the then-prevailing approach to Fourth Amendment interpretation, with its emphasis on probable cause and search warrants. Consider Professor Sundby's account:

> . . . Because requiring a warrant based on probable cause would have precluded suspicionless government inspections, the Court did not extend the amendment's coverage very far beyond the context of criminal arrests and searches. When the

fourth amendment governed, therefore, it provided the full protections of the warrant clause—but the protections generally did not apply to government intrusions other than criminal investigations.

The Court's warrant clause emphasis and corresponding reluctance to expand fourth amendment protections beyond criminal investigations largely explain its holding in Frank v. Maryland. In *Frank* the Court addressed the issue whether the defendant's conviction for resisting a warrantless inspection of his house violated the fourth amendment. Upholding the conviction and fine, the *Frank* majority espoused the traditional view that if inspections like those at issue were subject to full fourth amendment protections, the search would have to satisfy the warrant requirement. Yet requiring a warrant based on probable cause for housing inspections would defeat the inspections' objective of maintaining community health . . . .

[T]he *Frank* majority . . . argued that because Frank's asserted privacy interest did not concern a criminal investigation, his claim, at most, touched "upon the periphery" of the important fourth amendment interests protected against invasion by government officials. Stressing that the housing inspection was not a search for criminal evidence, Justice Frankfurter argued that the Constitution's prohibition against official invasion arose almost entirely from the individual's fundamental right to be secure from evidentiary searches made in connection with criminal prosecutions. . . . Consequently, the majority concluded that any legitimate liberty interest Frank had was overwhelmed by the government's need for inspection and the desirability of not tampering with the fourth amendment's rigorous protections.

Scott E. Sundby, A Return to Fourth Amendment Basics: Undoing the Mischief of *Camara* and *Terry*, 72 Minn. L. Rev. 383, 388-391 (1988).

Camara and *See* rejected the *Frank* Court's conclusion that regulatory inspections lie at the periphery of Fourth Amendment concerns: "We may agree that a routine inspection of the physical condition of private property is a less hostile intrusion than the typical policeman's search for the fruits and instrumentalities of crime. But we cannot agree that the Fourth Amendment interests at stake in these inspections are merely 'peripheral.' It is surely anomalous to say that the individual and his private property are fully protected by the Fourth Amendment only when the individual is suspected of criminal behavior." *Camara*, 387 U.S. at 530. But the Court brought both the housing inspection at issue in *Camara* and the commercial warehouse inspection at stake in *See* into the core of Fourth Amendment concerns only by redefining the warrant procedure and the concept of probable cause:

> In cases in which the Fourth Amendment requires that a warrant to search be obtained, "probable cause" is the standard by which a particular decision to search is tested against the constitutional mandate of reasonableness. To apply this standard, it is obviously necessary first to focus upon the governmental interest which allegedly justifies official intrusion upon the constitutionally protected interests of the private citizen. . . .
>
> Unlike the search pursuant to a criminal investigation, the inspection programs at issue here are aimed at securing city-wide compliance with minimum physical standards for private property. The primary governmental interest at stake is to prevent even the unintentional development of conditions which are hazardous to public health and safety. . . . In determining whether a particular inspection is reasonable—and thus in determining whether there is probable cause to issue a warrant for that inspection—the need for the inspection must be weighed in terms of these reasonable goals of code enforcement. . . .

... [T]here can be no ready test for determining reasonableness other than by balancing the need to search against the invasion which the search entails. But we think that a number of persuasive factors combine to support the reasonableness of area code-enforcement inspections. First, such programs have a long history of judicial and public acceptance. Second, the public interest demands that all dangerous conditions be prevented or abated, yet it is doubtful that any other canvassing technique would achieve acceptable results. ... Finally, because the inspections arc neither personal in nature nor aimed at the discovery of evidence of crime, they involve a relatively limited invasion of the urban citizen's privacy. ...

Having concluded that the area inspection is a "reasonable" search of private property within the meaning of the Fourth Amendment, it is obvious that "probable cause" to issue a warrant to inspect must exist if reasonable legislative or administrative standards for conducting an area inspection are satisfied with respect to a particular dwelling. Such standards ... may be based upon the passage of time, the nature of the building ..., or the condition of the entire area, but they will not necessarily depend upon specific knowledge of the condition of the particular dwelling. ... The warrant procedure is designed to guarantee that a decision to search private property is justified by a reasonable governmental interest. But reasonableness is still the ultimate standard. ...

Id. at 534-539. The Court thus redefined the probable cause necessary for issuance of a warrant in terms of the reasonableness of the inspection program. As Professor Sundby has argued:

> Ironically, in redefining probable cause as a flexible concept, the Court's effort to satisfy the warrant clause gave reasonableness a foot in the door as an independent factor in fourth amendment analysis. Prior to *Camara* the warrant clause had dictated the meaning of the reasonableness clause. A search or arrest was reasonable only when a warrant based on probable cause issued. *Camara*, in contrast, reversed the roles of probable cause and reasonableness. Instead of probable cause defining a reasonable search, after *Camara*, reasonableness, in the form of a balancing test, defined probable cause. ... Reasonableness ... had finally gained entrance into fourth amendment analysis, albeit through the back door of the warrant clause. ...

Sundby, 72 Minn. L. Rev. at 393-394.

Within a year of the decisions in *Camara* and *See*, the Court had extended the balancing methodology they employed into a context very familiar to the criminal process—the street confrontation between a police officer and a citizen. Terry v. Ohio, 392 U.S. 1 (1968), the first case taken up in the materials that follow, arose in a turbulent political context. As one of Chief Justice Earl Warren's law clerks recalled some thirty years later, the period leading up to *Terry* was a time of rioting in urban ghettoes and protest over the Vietnam War: "It was the decade of the long, hot summers. ... [And] [o]nly two months before *Terry* was handed down, there was a major outbreak of rioting in many cities, including Washington, D.C., in the wake of the assassination of Dr. Martin Luther King, Jr." Earl C. Dudley, Jr., *Terry v. Ohio*, The Warren Court, and the Fourth Amendment: A Law Clerk's Perspective, 72 St. John's L. Rev. 891, 892 (1998). Crime was skyrocketing, and with spiraling crime came increased criticism of the Court:

> [T]he Supreme Court had come under heavy fire for its decisions enforcing the constitutional claims of those accused of crimes. In 1964 the Court's criminal procedure

decisions were for the first time a major target of the Republican presidential campaign, and similar attacks were to be expected in the upcoming 1968 election.

Id. Spiraling crime rates and urban rioting were coupled with heightened racial tension. In 1968 many urban police forces were nearly all-white, and charges of police racism were both common and credible. In that charged context, the Court took up the question whether probable cause was the right standard for street stops—or whether *Camara*-style reasonableness should rule.

1. Stops and Frisks

TERRY v. OHIO

Certiorari to the Supreme Court of Ohio
392 U.S. 1 (1968)

MR. CHIEF JUSTICE WARREN delivered the opinion of the Court. . . .

Petitioner Terry was convicted of carrying a concealed weapon and sentenced to the statutorily prescribed term of one to three years in the penitentiary. Following the denial of a pretrial motion to suppress, the prosecution introduced in evidence two revolvers and a number of bullets seized from Terry and a codefendant, Richard Chilton, by Cleveland Police Detective Martin McFadden. At the hearing on the motion to suppress this evidence, Officer McFadden testified that while he was patrolling in plain clothes in downtown Cleveland at approximately 2:30 in the afternoon of October 31, 1963, his attention was attracted by two men, Chilton and Terry, standing on the corner of Huron Road and Euclid Avenue. He had never seen the two men before, and he was unable to say precisely what first drew his eye to them. However, he testified that he had been a policeman for 39 years and a detective for 35 and that he had been assigned to patrol this vicinity of downtown Cleveland for shoplifters and pickpockets for 30 years. He explained that he had developed routine habits of observation over the years and that he would "stand and watch people or walk and watch people at many intervals of the day." He added "Now, in this case when I looked over they didn't look right to me at the time."

His interest aroused, Officer McFadden took up a post of observation in the entrance to a store 300 to 400 feet away from the two men. "I get more purpose to watch them when I seen their movements," he testified. He saw one of the men leave the other one and walk southwest on Huron Road, past some stores. The man paused for a moment and looked in a store window, then walked on a short distance, turned around and walked back toward the corner, pausing once again to look in the same store window. He rejoined his companion at the corner, and the two conferred briefly. Then the second man went through the same series of motions, strolling down Huron Road, looking in the same window, walking on a short distance, turning back, peering in the store window again, and returning to confer with the first man at the corner. The two men repeated this ritual alternately between five and six times apiece—in all, roughly a dozen trips. At one point, while the two were standing together on the corner, a third man approached them and engaged them briefly in conversation. This man then left the two others and walked west on Euclid Avenue. Chilton and Terry resumed their measured pacing, peering and conferring. After this had gone on for 10 to 12 minutes, the two men walked off together, heading west on Euclid Avenue, following the path taken earlier by the third man.

By this time Officer McFadden had become thoroughly suspicious. He testified that after observing their elaborately casual and oft-repeated reconnaissance of the store window on Huron Road, he suspected the two men of "casing a job, a stick-up," and that he considered it his duty as a police officer to investigate further. He added that he feared "they may have a gun." Thus, Officer McFadden followed Chilton and Terry and saw them stop in front of Zucker's store to talk to the same man who had conferred with them earlier on the street corner. Deciding that the situation was ripe for direct action, Officer McFadden approached the three men, identified himself as a police officer and asked for their names. At this point his knowledge was confined to what he had observed. He was not acquainted with any of the three men by name or by sight, and he had received no information concerning them from any other source. When the men "mumbled something" in response to his inquiries, Officer McFadden grabbed petitioner Terry, spun him around so that they were facing the other two, with Terry between McFadden and the others, and patted down the outside of his clothing. In the left breast pocket of Terry's overcoat Officer McFadden felt a pistol. He reached inside the overcoat pocket, but was unable to remove the gun. At this point, keeping Terry between himself and the others, the officer ordered all three men to enter Zucker's store. As they went in, he removed Terry's overcoat completely, removed a .38-caliber revolver from the pocket and ordered all three men to face the wall with their hands raised. Officer McFadden proceeded to pat down the outer clothing of Chilton and the third man, Katz. He discovered another revolver in the outer pocket of Chilton's overcoat, but no weapons were found on Katz. The officer testified that he only patted the men down to see whether they had weapons, and that he did not put his hands beneath the outer garments of either Terry or Chilton until he felt their guns. So far as appears from the record, he never placed his hands beneath Katz' outer garments. Officer McFadden seized Chilton's gun, asked the proprietor of the store to call a police wagon, and took all three men to the station, where Chilton and Terry were formally charged with carrying concealed weapons. . . .

I

. . . Unquestionably petitioner was entitled to the protection of the Fourth Amendment as he walked down the street in Cleveland. The question is whether in all the circumstances of this on-the-street encounter, his right to personal security was violated by an unreasonable search and seizure.

We would be less than candid if we did not acknowledge that this question thrusts to the fore difficult and troublesome issues regarding a sensitive area of police activity — issues which have never before been squarely presented to this Court. Reflective of the tensions involved are the practical and constitutional arguments pressed with great vigor on both sides of the public debate over the power of the police to "stop and frisk" — as it is sometimes euphemistically termed — suspicious persons.

On the one hand, it is frequently argued that in dealing with the rapidly unfolding and often dangerous situations on city streets the police are in need of an escalating set of flexible responses, graduated in relation to the amount of information they possess. For this purpose it is urged that distinctions should be made between a "stop" and an "arrest" (or a "seizure" of a person), and between a "frisk" and a "search." Thus, it is argued, the police should be allowed to "stop" a person and detain him briefly for questioning upon suspicion that he may be connected with criminal activity. Upon suspicion that the person may be armed, the police should have the power to "frisk" him for weapons. If the "stop" and the "frisk" give rise to probable cause to believe that the suspect has committed a crime, then the police should be empowered to make a formal "arrest" and a full incident "search" of the person. This scheme is justified in part upon the notion that a "stop" and a "frisk" amount to a mere "minor inconvenience and petty indignity," which can properly be imposed upon the citizen in the interest of effective law enforcement on the basis of a police officer's suspicion.

On the other side the argument is made that the authority of the police must be strictly circumscribed by the law of arrest and search as it has developed to date in the traditional jurisprudence of the Fourth Amendment. It is contended with some force that there is not — and cannot be — a variety of police activity which does not depend solely upon the voluntary cooperation of the citizen and yet which stops short of an arrest based upon probable cause to make such an arrest. The heart of the Fourth Amendment, the argument runs, is a severe requirement of specific justification for any intrusion upon protected personal security, coupled with a highly developed system of judicial controls to enforce upon the agents of the State the commands of the Constitution. Acquiescence by the courts in the compulsion inherent in the field interrogation practices at issue here, it is urged, would constitute an abdication of judicial control over, and indeed an encouragement of, substantial interference with liberty and personal security by police officers whose judgment is necessarily colored by their primary involvement in "the often competitive enterprise of ferreting out crime." This, it is argued, can only serve to exacerbate police-community tensions in the crowded centers of our Nation's cities.

In this context we approach the issues in this case mindful of the limitations of the judicial function in controlling the myriad daily situations in which policemen and citizens confront each other on the street. . . . Ever since its inception, the rule excluding evidence seized in violation of the Fourth Amendment has been recognized as a principal mode of discouraging lawless police conduct. . . . A ruling admitting evidence in a criminal trial, we recognize, has the necessary effect of legitimizing the conduct which produced the evidence, while an application of the exclusionary rule withholds the constitutional imprimatur.

The exclusionary rule has its limitations, however, as a tool of judicial control. It cannot properly be invoked to exclude the products of legitimate police investigative techniques on the ground that much conduct which is closely similar involves unwarranted intrusions upon constitutional protections. Moreover, in some contexts the rule is ineffective as a deterrent. Street encounters between citizens and police officers are incredibly rich in diversity. They range from wholly friendly exchanges of pleasantries or mutually useful information to hostile confrontations of armed men involving arrests, or injuries, or loss of life. Moreover, hostile confrontations are not all of a piece. Some of them begin in a friendly enough manner, only to take a different turn upon the injection of some unexpected element into the conversation. Encounters are initiated by the police for a wide variety of purposes, some of which are wholly unrelated to a desire to prosecute for crime.[9] Doubtless some police "field interrogation" conduct violates the Fourth Amendment. But a stern refusal by this Court to condone such activity does not necessarily render it responsive to the exclusionary rule. Regardless of how effective the rule may be where obtaining convictions is an important objective of the police, it is powerless to deter invasions of constitutionally guaranteed rights where the police either have no interest in prosecuting or are willing to forgo successful prosecution in the interest of serving some other goal.

Proper adjudication of cases in which the exclusionary rule is invoked demands a constant awareness of these limitations. The wholesale harassment by certain elements of the police community, of which minority groups, particularly Negroes, frequently complain,[11] will not be stopped by the exclusion of any evidence from any criminal trial. Yet a rigid and unthinking application of the exclusionary rule, in futile protest against practices which it can never be used effectively to control, may exact a high toll in human injury and frustration of efforts to prevent crime. No judicial opinion can comprehend the protean variety of the street encounter, and we can only judge the facts of the case before us. Nothing we say today is to be taken as indicating approval of police conduct outside the legitimate investigative sphere. Under our decision, courts still retain their traditional responsibility to guard against police conduct which is overbearing or harassing, or which trenches upon personal security without the objective evidentiary justification which the Constitution requires. When such conduct is identified, it must be condemned by the judiciary and its fruits must be excluded from evidence in criminal trials. And, of course, our approval of legitimate and restrained investigative conduct undertaken on the basis of ample factual justification should in no way discourage the employment of other remedies than the exclusionary rule to curtail abuses for which that sanction may prove inappropriate.

. . . [W]e turn our attention to the quite narrow question posed by the facts before us: whether it is always unreasonable for a policeman to seize a person and subject him to a limited search for weapons unless there is probable cause for an arrest. . . .

9. See L. Tiffany, D. McIntyre & D. Rotenberg, Detection of Crime: Stopping and Questioning, Search and Seizure, Encouragement and Entrapment 18-56 (1967). This sort of police conduct may, for example, be designed simply to help an intoxicated person find his way home, with no intention of arresting him unless he becomes obstreperous. Or the police may be seeking to mediate a domestic quarrel which threatens to erupt into violence. They may accost a woman in an area known for prostitution as part of a harassment campaign designed to drive prostitutes away without the considerable difficulty involved in prosecuting them. Or they may be conducting a dragnet search of all teenagers in a particular section of the city for weapons because they have heard rumors of an impending gang fight.

11. The President's Commission on Law Enforcement and Administration of Justice found that "[i]n many communities, field interrogations are a major source of friction between the police and minority groups." President's Commission on Law Enforcement and Administration of Justice, Task Force Report: The Police 183 (1967). It was reported that the friction caused by "[m]isuse of field interrogations" increases "as more police departments adopt 'aggressive patrol' in which officers are encouraged routinely to stop and question persons on the street who are unknown to them, who are suspicious, or whose purpose for being abroad is not readily evident." Id., at 184. While the frequency with which "frisking" forms a part of field interrogation practice varies tremendously with the locale, the objective of the interrogation, and the particular officer, see Tiffany, McIntyre & Rotenberg, supra, n. 9, at 47-48, it cannot help but be a severely exacerbating factor in police-community tensions. This is particularly true in situations where the "stop and frisk" of youths or minority group members is "motivated by the officers' perceived need to maintain the power image of the beat officer, an aim sometimes accomplished by humiliating anyone who attempts to undermine police control of the streets." Ibid.

II

... There is some suggestion in the use of such terms as "stop" and "frisk" that such police conduct is outside the purview of the Fourth Amendment because neither action rises to the level of a "search" or "seizure" within the meaning of the Constitution. We emphatically reject this notion. It is quite plain that the Fourth Amendment governs "seizures" of the person which do not eventuate in a trip to the station house and prosecution for crime — "arrests" in traditional terminology. It must be recognized that whenever a police officer accosts an individual and restrains his freedom to walk away, he has "seized" that person. And it is nothing less than sheer torture of the English language to suggest that a careful exploration of the outer surfaces of a person's clothing all over his or her body in an attempt to find weapons is not a "search." Moreover, it is simply fantastic to urge that such a procedure performed in public by a policeman while the citizen stands helpless, perhaps facing a wall with his hands raised, is a "petty indignity."[13] It is a serious intrusion upon the sanctity of the person, which may inflict great indignity and arouse strong resentment, and it is not to be undertaken lightly.

The danger in the logic which proceeds upon distinctions between a "stop" and an "arrest," or "seizure" of the person, and between a "frisk" and a "search" is twofold. It seeks to isolate from constitutional scrutiny the initial stages of the contact between the policeman and the citizen. And by suggesting a rigid all-or-nothing model of justification and regulation under the Amendment, it obscures the utility of limitations upon the scope, as well as the initiation, of police action as a means of constitutional regulation. ...

In this case there can be no question, then, that Officer McFadden "seized" petitioner and subjected him to a "search" when he took hold of him and patted down the outer surfaces of his clothing. We must decide whether at that point it was reasonable for Officer McFadden to have interfered with petitioner's personal security as he did.[16] And in determining whether the seizure and search were "unreasonable" our inquiry is a dual one—whether the officer's action was justified at its inception, and whether it was reasonably related in scope to the circumstances which justified the interference in the first place.

III

If this case involved police conduct subject to the Warrant Clause of the Fourth Amendment, we would have to ascertain whether "probable cause" existed to justify the search and seizure which took place. However, that is not the case. We do not retreat from our holdings that the police must, whenever practicable,

13. Consider the following apt description: "[T]he officer must feel with sensitive fingers every portion of the prisoner's body. A thorough search must be made of the prisoner's arms and armpits, waistline and back, the groin and area about the testicles, and entire surface of the legs down to the feet." Priar & Martin, Searching and Disarming Criminals, 45 J. Crim. L.C. & P.S. 481 (1954).

16. We thus decide nothing today concerning the constitutional propriety of an investigative "seizure" upon less than probable cause for purposes of "detention" and/or interrogation. Obviously, not all personal intercourse between policemen and citizens involves "seizures" of persons. Only when the officer, by means of physical force or show of authority, has in some way restrained the liberty of a citizen may we conclude that a "seizure" has occurred. We cannot tell with any certainty upon this record whether any such "seizure" took place here prior to Officer McFadden's initiation of physical contact for purposes of searching Terry for weapons, and we thus may assume that up to that point no intrusion upon constitutionally protected rights had occurred.

obtain advance judicial approval of searches and seizures through the warrant procedure, or that in most instances failure to comply with the warrant requirement can only be excused by exigent circumstances. But we deal here with an entire rubric of police conduct—necessarily swift action predicated upon the on-the-spot observations of the officer on the beat—which historically has not been, and as a practical matter could not be, subjected to the warrant procedure. Instead, the conduct involved in this case must be tested by the Fourth Amendment's general proscription against unreasonable searches and seizures.

Nonetheless, the notions which underlie both the warrant procedure and the requirement of probable cause remain fully relevant in this context. In order to assess the reasonableness of Officer McFadden's conduct as a general proposition, it is necessary "first to focus upon the governmental interest which allegedly justifies official intrusion upon the constitutionally protected interests of the private citizen," for there is "no ready test for determining reasonableness other than by balancing the need to search [or seize] against the invasion which the search [or seizure] entails." Camara v. Municipal Court, 387 U.S. 523, 534-535, 536-537 (1967). And in justifying the particular intrusion the police officer must be able to point to specific and articulable facts which, taken together with rational inferences from those facts, reasonably warrant that intrusion. The scheme of the Fourth Amendment becomes meaningful only when it is assured that at some point the conduct of those charged with enforcing the laws can be subjected to the more detached, neutral scrutiny of a judge who must evaluate the reasonableness of a particular search or seizure in light of the particular circumstances. And in making that assessment it is imperative that the facts be judged against an objective standard: would the facts available to the officer at the moment of the seizure or the search "warrant a man of reasonable caution in the belief" that the action taken was appropriate? Anything less would invite intrusions upon constitutionally guaranteed rights based on nothing more substantial than inarticulate hunches, a result this Court has consistently refused to sanction. . . .

Applying these principles to this case, we consider first the nature and extent of the governmental interests involved. One general interest is of course that of effective crime prevention and detection; it is this interest which underlies the recognition that a police officer may in appropriate circumstances and in an appropriate manner approach a person for purposes of investigating possibly criminal behavior even though there is no probable cause to make an arrest. It was this legitimate investigative function Officer McFadden was discharging when he decided to approach petitioner and his companions. He had observed Terry, Chilton, and Katz go through a series of acts, each of them perhaps innocent in itself, but which taken together warranted further investigation. There is nothing unusual in two men standing together on a street corner, perhaps waiting for someone. Nor is there anything suspicious about people in such circumstances strolling up and down the street, singly or in pairs. Store windows, moreover, are made to be looked in. But the story is quite different where, as here, two men hover about a street corner for an extended period of time, at the end of which it becomes apparent that they are not waiting for anyone or anything; where these men pace alternately along an identical route, pausing to stare in the same window roughly 24 times; where each completion of this route is followed immediately by a conference between the two men on the corner; where they are joined in one of these conferences by a third man who leaves swiftly; and where the two men finally follow the third and rejoin him a couple of blocks away. It would have been poor police work indeed for an officer of 30 years' experience in the detection of thievery from stores in this same neighborhood to have failed to investigate this behavior further.

The crux of this case, however, is not the propriety of Officer McFadden's taking steps to investigate petitioner's suspicious behavior, but rather, whether there was justification for McFadden's invasion of Terry's personal security by searching him for weapons in the course of that investigation. We are now concerned with more than the governmental interest in investigating crime; in addition, there is the more immediate interest of the police officer in taking steps to assure himself that the person with whom he is dealing is not armed with a weapon that could unexpectedly and fatally be used against him. Certainly it would be unreasonable to require that police officers take unnecessary risks in the performance of their duties. American criminals have a long tradition of armed violence, and every year in this country many law enforcement officers are killed in the line of duty, and thousands more are wounded. Virtually all of these deaths and a substantial portion of the injuries are inflicted with guns and knives.

In view of these facts, we cannot blind ourselves to the need for law enforcement officers to protect themselves and other prospective victims of violence in situations where they may lack probable cause for an arrest. When an officer is justified in believing that the individual whose suspicious behavior he is investigating at close range is armed and presently dangerous to the officer or to others, it would appear to be clearly unreasonable to deny the officer the power to take necessary measures to determine whether the person is in fact carrying a weapon and to neutralize the threat of physical harm.

We must still consider, however, the nature and quality of the intrusion on individual rights which must be accepted if police officers are to be conceded the right to search for weapons in situations where probable cause to arrest for crime is lacking. Even a limited search of the outer clothing for weapons constitutes a severe, though brief, intrusion upon cherished personal security, and it must surely be an annoying, frightening, and perhaps humiliating experience. Petitioner contends that such an intrusion is permissible only incident to a lawful arrest. . . .

There are two weaknesses in this line of reasoning, however. First, it . . . recognizes no distinction in purpose, character, and extent between a search incident to an arrest and a limited search for weapons. The former, although justified in part by the acknowledged necessity to protect the arresting officer from assault with a concealed weapon, is also justified on other grounds and can therefore involve a relatively extensive exploration of the person. A search for weapons in the absence of probable cause to arrest, however, must, like any other search, be strictly circumscribed by the exigencies which justify its initiation. Thus it must be limited to that which is necessary for the discovery of weapons which might be used to harm the officer or others nearby, and may realistically be characterized as something less than a "full" search, even though it remains a serious intrusion.

A second, and related, objection to petitioner's argument is that it assumes that the law of arrest has already worked out the balance between the particular interests involved here—the neutralization of danger to the policeman in the investigative circumstance and the sanctity of the individual. But this is not so.

An arrest is a wholly different kind of intrusion upon individual freedom from a limited search for weapons, and the interests each is designed to serve are likewise quite different. An arrest is the initial stage of a criminal prosecution. It is intended to vindicate society's interest in having its laws obeyed, and it is inevitably accompanied by future interference with the individual's freedom of movement, whether or not trial or conviction ultimately follows. The protective search for weapons, on the other hand, constitutes a brief, though far from inconsiderable, intrusion upon the sanctity of the person. . . .

Our evaluation of the proper balance that has to be struck in this type of case leads us to conclude that there must be a narrowly drawn authority to permit a reasonable search for weapons for the protection of the police officer, where he has reason to believe that he is dealing with an armed and dangerous individual, regardless of whether he has probable cause to arrest the individual for a crime. The officer need not be absolutely certain that the individual is armed; the issue is whether a reasonably prudent man in the circumstances would be warranted in the belief that his safety or that of others was in danger. And in determining whether the officer acted reasonably in such circumstances, due weight must be given, not to his inchoate and unparticularized suspicion or "hunch," but to the specific reasonable inferences which he is entitled to draw from the facts in light of his experience.

IV

We must now examine the conduct of Officer McFadden in this case to determine whether his search and seizure of petitioner were reasonable, both at their inception and as conducted. . . . We think on the facts and circumstances Officer McFadden detailed before the trial judge a reasonably prudent man would have been warranted in believing petitioner was armed and thus presented a threat to the officer's safety while he was investigating his suspicious behavior. The actions of Terry and Chilton were consistent with McFadden's hypothesis that these men were contemplating a daylight robbery—which, it is reasonable to assume, would be likely to involve the use of weapons—and nothing in their conduct from the time he first noticed them until the time he confronted them and identified himself as a police officer gave him sufficient reason to negate that hypothesis. . . .

We need not develop at length in this case . . . the limitations which the Fourth Amendment places upon a protective seizure and search for weapons. These limitations will have to be developed in the concrete factual circumstances of individual cases. Suffice it to note that such a search, unlike a search without a warrant incident to a lawful arrest, is not justified by any need to prevent the disappearance or destruction of evidence of crime. The sole justification of the search in the present situation is the protection of the police officer and others nearby, and it must therefore be confined in scope to an intrusion reasonably designed to discover guns, knives, clubs, or other hidden instruments for the assault of the police officer.

The scope of the search in this case presents no serious problem in light of these standards. . . . Officer McFadden confined his search strictly to what was minimally necessary to learn whether the men were armed and to disarm them once he discovered the weapons. He did not conduct a general exploratory search for whatever evidence of criminal activity he might find.

V

We conclude that the revolver seized from Terry was properly admitted in evidence against him. . . . Each case of this sort will, of course, have to be decided on its own facts. We merely hold today that where a police officer observes unusual conduct which leads him reasonably to conclude in light of his experience that criminal activity may be afoot and that the persons with whom he is dealing may be armed and presently dangerous, where in the course of investigating this behavior he identifies himself as a policeman and makes reasonable inquiries, and where nothing in the initial stages of the encounter serves to dispel his reasonable fear for his own or others' safety, he is entitled for the protection of himself and others in the area to conduct a carefully limited search of the outer clothing of such persons in an attempt to discover weapons which might be used to assault him. Such a search is a reasonable search under the Fourth Amendment, and any weapons seized may properly be introduced in evidence against the person from whom they were taken. Affirmed.

[The concurring opinion of MR. JUSTICE BLACK is omitted.]

MR. JUSTICE HARLAN, concurring.
While I unreservedly agree with the Court's ultimate holding in this case, I am constrained to fill in a few gaps. . . .
. . . [I]f the frisk is justified in order to protect the officer during an encounter with a citizen, the officer must first have constitutional grounds to insist on an encounter, to make a *forcible* stop. Any person, including a policeman, is at liberty to avoid a person he considers dangerous. If and when a policeman has a right instead to disarm such a person for his own protection, he must first have a right not to avoid him but to be in his presence. That right must be more than the liberty (again, possessed by every citizen) to address questions to other persons, for ordinarily the person addressed has an equal right to ignore his interrogator and walk away; he certainly need not submit to a frisk for the questioner's protection. . . .
Where such a stop is reasonable, however, the right to frisk must be immediate and automatic if the reason for the stop is, as here, an articulable suspicion of a crime of violence. Just as a full search incident to a lawful arrest requires no additional justification, a limited frisk incident to a lawful stop must often be rapid and routine. There is no reason why an officer, rightfully but forcibly confronting a person suspected of a serious crime, should have to ask one question and take the risk that the answer might be a bullet. . . .
I would affirm this conviction for what I believe to be the same reasons the Court relies on. I would, however, make explicit what I think is implicit in affirmance on the present facts. Officer McFadden's right to interrupt Terry's freedom of movement and invade his privacy arose only because circumstances warranted forcing an encounter with Terry in an effort to prevent or investigate a crime. Once that forced encounter was justified, however, the officer's right to take suitable measures for his own safely followed automatically.
Upon the foregoing premises, I join the opinion of the Court.

MR. JUSTICE WHITE, concurring. . . .
. . . I think an additional word is in order concerning the matter of interrogation during an investigative stop. There is nothing in the Constitution which prevents a policeman from addressing questions to anyone on the streets.

Absent special circumstances, the person approached may not be detained or frisked but may refuse to cooperate and go on his way. However, given the proper circumstances, such as those in this case, it seems to me the person may be briefly detained against his will while pertinent questions are directed to him. Of course, the person stopped is not obliged to answer, answers may not be compelled, and refusal to answer furnishes no basis for an arrest, although it may alert the officer to the need for continued observation. In my view, it is temporary detention, warranted by the circumstances, which chiefly justifies the protective frisk for weapons. Perhaps the frisk itself, where proper, will have beneficial results whether questions are asked or not. If weapons are found, an arrest will follow. If none are found, the frisk may nevertheless serve preventive ends because of its unmistakable message that suspicion has been aroused. But if the investigative stop is sustainable at all, constitutional rights are not necessarily violated if pertinent questions are asked and the person is restrained briefly in the process.

MR. JUSTICE DOUGLAS, dissenting. . . .

The opinion of the Court disclaims the existence of "probable cause." . . . Had a warrant been sought, a magistrate would, therefore, have been unauthorized to issue one, for he can act only if there is a showing of "probable cause." We hold today that the police have greater authority to make a "seizure" and conduct a "search" than a judge has to authorize such action. We have said precisely the opposite over and over again.

. . . The term "probable cause" rings a bell of certainty that is not sounded by phrases such as "reasonable suspicion." Moreover, the meaning of "probable cause" is deeply imbedded in our constitutional history. . . .

The infringement on personal liberty of any "seizure" of a person can only be "reasonable"' under the Fourth Amendment if we require the police to possess "probable cause" before they seize him. Only that line draws a meaningful distinction between an officer's mere inkling and the presence of facts within the officer's personal knowledge which would convince a reasonable man that the person seized has committed, is committing, or is about to commit a particular crime. . . .

To give the police greater power than a magistrate is to take a long step down the totalitarian path. Perhaps such a step is desirable to cope with modern forms of lawlessness. But if it is taken, it should be the deliberate choice of the people through a constitutional amendment. . . .

There have been powerful hydraulic pressures throughout our history that bear heavily on the Court to water down constitutional guarantees and give the police the upper hand. That hydraulic pressure has probably never been greater than it is today.

Yet if the individual is no longer to be sovereign, if the police can pick him up whenever they do not like the cut of his jib, if they can "seize" and "search" him in their discretion, we enter a new regime. The decision to enter it should be made only after a full debate by the people of this country.

NOTES AND QUESTIONS

1. What was Officer McFadden doing when he approached Terry and his companions? He certainly wasn't engaged in the retrospective investigation of an historical crime — what detectives do when citizens call them to a crime scene and police start looking for clues. McFadden's actions, instead, were proactive

and preventive in character. In many respects, McFadden did exactly what we want the police to do: He used his professional experience and good judgment to intervene and prevent a serious crime before it was ever committed. The traditional Fourth Amendment approach — with its heavy reliance on probable cause, subject to advance review by a neutral magistrate — may make sense in the context of investigating past crimes, but it seems completely ill-suited to the kind of proactive, preventive policing that was practiced in *Terry* by Officer McFadden.

The same might also be said of police investigations of so-called "victimless" crimes — most notably, in contemporary America, the investigation of drug crimes. The point here is that even after such crimes have already occurred, there's usually no victim who is willing to complain and provide information to the police about the crime or its perpetrator. This makes it extremely difficult for the police to satisfy traditional standards of probable cause, both with respect to whether a drug crime actually happened, and with respect to who committed it. Thus, from the viewpoint of the police, the investigation of drug crimes turns out to be much like the proactive prevention of crimes that have not yet happened. Perhaps it should not be surprising that most of the Court's "reasonableness" cases (like *Terry*) have involved either preventive policing or drug crimes. In both contexts, the traditional Fourth Amendment approach — which was developed mostly to regulate a very different kind of police activity — seems to impose unreasonable constraints on the police.

Notice some further implications of the differences between these two kinds of police activity. Whatever its benefits, proactive crime prevention by police, in which police select the targets of their attention and attempt to intervene to disrupt possible criminal activity, "presents heightened risks of discriminatory law enforcement and inappropriate police involvement in community life and private affairs" — at least as compared to a reactive style of policing in which police mobilize in response to serious crimes that have already taken place. Debra Livingston, Police Discretion and the Quality of Life in Public Places: Courts, Communities, and the New Policing, 97 Colum. L. Rev. 551, 578 (1997). This is certainly manifest in the area of stop and frisk:

> [O]ne of the problems with stop and frisk . . . is that any review of police-community relations finds that there is hostility between the police and minority communities. A lot of that has to do with stop and frisk. Field interrogations that are excessive, that are discourteous, and that push people around, generate friction.

Jerome H. Skolnick, *Terry* and Community Policing, 72 St. John's L. Rev. 1265, 1267 (1998). Do the risks associated with proactive, preventive strategies argue more generally in favor of reactive strategies in which police departments principally respond to citizen complaints? Perhaps not:

> The philosophical choice is deceptively simple, with reactive policing appearing to be far more democratic than proactive policing. What could be more egalitarian than to give all citizens an equal right to pick the targets of police crime control? Yet absent an equal willingness to use that right, reactive policing becomes anything but egalitarian.
>
> Enormous "selection bias" . . . afflicts every choice of police targets by citizens. Many crime victims never call the police . . . for reasons ranging from fear of retaliation to lack of homeowner's insurance. Other people falsely accuse enemies and relatives, using police as a tool for private disputes. Reactive policing is completely

vulnerable to racial, class, religious, sexual, and ethnic prejudices in citizen decisions to complain about other citizens.

Lawrence W. Sherman, Attacking Crime: Police and Crime Control, in Modern Policing: 15 Crime and Justice, 159, 173 (M. Tonry & N. Morris eds. 1992). Notice, too, that many crimes may go underenforced in a reactive regime. Think about the bribery of public officials, for instance, where there may be no readily identifiable victim to complain, or gang crime, where victims may be too intimidated to come forward. In practice, all police departments employ both proactive and reactive mobilization. And preventing crime is also a goal of all police organizations — albeit a goal pursued to varying degrees and in different ways.

Notice finally that at least with regard to terrorist activity, prevention has become the watchword for *federal* law enforcement post-9/11. In the words of one former Justice Department official: "We cannot afford to wait for them to execute their plans; the death toll is too high; the consequences too great. . . . The overriding goal is to prevent and disrupt terrorist activity by questioning, investigating, and arresting those who violate the law and threaten our national security." Viet D. Dinh, Freedom and Security After September 11, 25 Harv. J.L. &. Pub. Pol'y 399, 401 (2002). Today, terrorism prevention occupies a large fraction of the FBI's resources: agents that once investigated reports of federal crimes now focus their energy on preventing further attacks.

2. *Terry* contained all the seeds that eventually grew into modern stop-and-frisk doctrine. The results reached in *Terry* and its progeny have been often defended as practical, reasonable, and necessary. Consider Professor Saltzburg:

> The common sense of *Terry* is that law enforcement officers should not be required to wait to act until a crime is complete, whereby society suffers a criminal injury, if they have reasonable grounds to suspect that criminal activity is under way and the ability to establish quickly whether their suspicion is correct . . . As a result of *Terry*, officers are not compelled to make a Hobson's choice between waiting for suspicious activity to play out in terms of completed crimes, and prematurely intervening to arrest suspects who may be innocent. *Terry* permits an intermediate approach. . . .

Stephen A. Saltzburg, Terry v. Ohio, A Practially Perfect Doctrine, 72 St. John's L. Rev. 911, 952 (1998). But did that "intermediate approach" adequately address longstanding concerns with racial and ethnic discrimination? Proactive and preventive policing means that the police are choosing where to put officers, and when — and against whom — to intervene. That greater police discretion may give rise to discrimination. Consider the following:

> Terry v. Ohio . . . may be the Court's single most important Fourth Amendment case in terms of its role in constituting a legal environment broadly supportive of the street-level discretion of officers on patrol. . . . [D]etentions and frisks take place without prior judicial authorization. In the great majority of cases, moreover, there is no subsequent judicial review of the officer's judgment about the propriety of his actions.
>
> No one could deny that patrol officers employ significant street-level discretion in this context, nor that the proper exercise of this discretion is of tremendous importance both to communities and to police. Indiscriminate street stops and searches, after all, were blamed by the Kerner Commission for helping to foster the "deep

hostility between police and ghetto communities" that contributed to numerous tragic riots between 1964 and 1968. And even when properly employed, aggressive use of stop and frisk can alienate and estrange communities in ways that ultimately detract from, rather than contribute to, the maintenance of a vibrant civil order.

But these considerations have not led the Court to attempt more stringently to regulate the area of stop and frisk. The Court has found both street detentions and frisks based on reasonable suspicion to be consistent with Fourth Amendment principles despite its recognition that such encounters are not trivial, but are often "annoying," "frightening," and even "humiliating" to the persons involved. The Court has upheld the stop-and-frisk authority even though police departments vary widely in the degree to which they train and oversee officers so as to minimize its abuse. . . .

Debra Livingston, Gang Loitering, The Court, and Some Realism About Police Patrol, 1999 Supreme Court Review 141, 177-178 (2000). Given the broad discretion afforded to police by the *Terry* Court, was it incumbent on the Court to deal with the threat of discrimination more directly?

Actually, *Terry* is one of the very few of the Court's Fourth Amendment cases that explicitly discuss issues of race. But does the Court address these issues in a meaningful way? Professor Cole argues that though the stop-and-frisk rule "is in theory color-blind, [it] has in practice created a double standard. It does so principally by extending a wide degree of discretion to police officers in settings where race and class considerations frequently play a significant role." David Cole, No Equal Justice 43 (1999).

There is substantial evidence that aggressive use, and misuse, of the stop-and-frisk power continues to be a major source of tension between police and people of color. In a 1999 study on the New York City Police Department's stop-and-frisk practices, New York's Attorney General found that while blacks made up 26 percent of the City's population, they accounted for 51 percent of all persons stopped by police from January 1, 1998, to March 31, 1999 — a disparity that the study concluded could not be explained in terms of the differing crime rates among the City's racial and ethnic groups.[19] The report cited a consensus among leading law enforcement professionals, civil rights advocates, community and religious leaders, legal scholars, and others to the effect that the use of "stop and frisk" tactics in New York City during this period was "a particular flash point in the matrix of police-community relations," with serious consequences for the relationship between police and people of color: "In communities of color, 'stop & frisk' is cited by some as an example of a tactic that has been misused and overused." Id. at 8.

Do such observations suggest that the *Terry* Court's rather fleeting attention to racial issues was inadequate? In particular, did the Court too easily avoid such issues with its conclusion that police harassment of minorities "will not be stopped

19. The New York City Police Department's "Stop & Frisk" Practices: A Report to the People of the State of New York vii, ix-x (Office of the Attorney General, State of New York 1999). The study was based upon the Attorney General's analysis of data derived from approximately 175,000 "stop & frisk" forms completed by NYPD officers. It employed the terms "blacks," "Hispanics," and "whites" in its analysis of racial and ethnic disparities in stops because these were the terms used in the relevant census data. The study also found that for the covered period, though Hispanics constituted only 24 percent of the City's population, they accounted for 33 percent of stops. Whites were 43 percent of the City's population, but accounted for only 13 percent of stops. Id. at vi-vii.

by the exclusion of any evidence from any criminal trial"? It may be that the Court wisely put the responsibility for addressing these issues with the organs of government in a better position to make improvements. For an argument that the Court should have taken facts about racial impact more seriously in delineating the scope of the stop-and-frisk power, however, see Adina Schwartz, "Just Take Away Their Guns": The Hidden Racism of Terry v. Ohio, 23 Fordham Urb. L.J. 317 (1996).

3. Let's return to *Terry* and its impact on Fourth Amendment law. Professor Amar has argued that "in place of the misguided notions that every search or seizure always requires a warrant, and always requires probable cause," *Terry* properly insisted "that the Fourth Amendment means what it says and says what it means: All searches and seizures must be reasonable." Akhil Reed Amar, *Terry* and Fourth Amendment First Principles, 72 St. John's L. Rev. 1097, 1098 (1997). He goes on to contend that *Terry* accurately identified some of the basic components of Fourth Amendment reasonableness:

> Reasonable intrusions must be *proportionate* to legitimate governmental purposes — more intrusive government action requires more justification. Reasonableness must focus not only on privacy and secrecy but also on *bodily integrity* and *personal dignity:* Cops act unreasonably not just when they paw through my pockets without good reason, but also when they beat me up for fun or toy with me for sport. Reasonableness also implicates *race* — a complete Fourth Amendment analysis must be sensitive to the possibility of racial oppression and harassment.

Id. No doubt Amar correctly identifies aspects of what a reasonableness approach to Fourth Amendment interpretation should encompass. But what about the merits of adopting such an approach in the first place? *Terry* significantly changed existing law by employing a balancing test to hold that the police could subject individual criminal suspects to a Fourth Amendment intrusion without probable cause. Others have suggested that the case thus "unwittingly cracked the door for a decline in the role of traditional probable cause," thus jeopardizing "the foundation of Fourth Amendment safeguards." See Scott E. Sundby, An Ode to Probable Cause, 72 St. John's L. Rev. 1133, 1134 (1997). Under what circumstances should a particular police practice qualify for assessment under *Terry*'s balancing test?

4. The Court made clear that some types of police intrusion would *not* qualify for such consideration in Dunaway v. New York, 442 U.S. 200 (1979). In that case the defendant, a murder suspect, was taken into custody without probable cause, and "although he was not told he was under arrest, he would have been physically restrained if he had attempted to leave." He was questioned while in custody and made incriminating statements that were used against him at his murder trial. The Court, in an opinion by Justice Brennan, ruled that the statements were the fruits of an illegal seizure:

> Respondent State now urges the Court to apply a balancing test, rather than the general rule, to custodial interrogations, and to hold that "seizures" such as that in this case may be justified by mere "reasonable suspicion." *Terry* and its progeny clearly do not support such a result. The narrow intrusions involved in those cases were judged by a balancing test rather than by the general principle that Fourth Amendment seizures must be supported by the "long-prevailing standards" of probable cause only because these intrusions fell far short of the kind of intrusion associated with an arrest. . . .

. . . [T]he detention of petitioner was in important respects indistinguishable from a traditional arrest. Petitioner was not questioned briefly where he was found. Instead, he was taken from a neighbor's home to a police car, transported to a police station, and placed in an interrogation room. He was never informed that he was "free to go"; indeed, he would have been physically restrained if he had refused to accompany the officers or had tried to escape their custody. The application of the Fourth Amendment's requirement of probable cause does not depend on whether an intrusion of this magnitude is termed an "arrest" under state law. The mere facts that petitioner was not told he was under arrest, was not "booked," and would not have had an arrest record if the interrogation had proved fruitless, obviously do not make petitioner's seizure even roughly analogous to the narrowly defined intrusions involved in *Terry*, and its progeny. Indeed, any "exception" that could cover a seizure as intrusive as that in this case would threaten to swallow the general rule that Fourth Amendment seizures are "reasonable" only if based on probable cause.

Id. at 211-212.

5. *Dunaway* refused to extend *Terry*'s balancing test to cover all seizures falling short of a technical arrest. It's important to note, however, that by the time *Dunaway* was decided, the *Terry* "progeny" to which it referred had already considerably expanded *Terry*'s scope along the lines suggested in Justice Harlan's concurrence. Thus, although the *Terry* Court carefully refrained from lending a constitutional imprimatur to the investigative "stop" (meaning the temporary detention of an individual for investigative purposes), later decisions clearly upheld such detentions so long as police had some articulable basis for suspecting criminal activity.

These later cases also made clear that the suspected criminal activity legitimating an investigative stop need not involve a potential armed robbery, as in *Terry*. Indeed, by the 1990s, the more routine fact pattern to be found in *"Terry* stop" cases before the Court involved the detention of people passing through airports and suspected of being drug couriers. The Court addressed one such airport confrontation in Florida v. Royer, 460 U.S. 491 (1983):

On January 3, 1978, Royer was observed at Miami International Airport by two plainclothes detectives of the Dade County, Florida, Public Safety Department assigned to the county's Organized Crime Bureau, Narcotics Investigation Section. Detectives Johnson and Magdalena believed that Royer's appearance, mannerisms, luggage, and actions fit the so-called "drug courier profile." Royer, apparently unaware of the attention he had attracted, purchased a one-way ticket to New York City and checked his two suitcases, placing on each suitcase an identification tag bearing the name "Holt" and the destination, "LaGuardia." As Royer made his way to the concourse which led to the airline boarding area, the two detectives approached him, identified themselves as policemen working out of the sheriff's office, and asked if Royer had a "moment" to speak with them; Royer said "Yes."

Upon request, but without oral consent, Royer produced for the detectives his airline ticket and his driver's license. The airline ticket, like the baggage identification tags, bore the name "Holt," while the driver's license carried respondent's correct name, "Royer." When the detectives asked about the discrepancy, Royer explained that a friend had made the reservation in the name of "Holt." Royer became noticeably more nervous during this conversation, whereupon the detectives informed Royer that they were in fact narcotics investigators and that they had reason to suspect him of transporting narcotics.

Id. at 493-494.

Without returning his airline ticket or identification, the detectives asked Royer to accompany them to a room about 40 feet away. The detectives then retrieved Royer's suitcases, brought them to the room, and asked for Royer's permission to search them—a process that took about 15 minutes. The *Royer* plurality concluded that the drugs recovered in the resulting search should have been suppressed because at the time Royer produced a key to his luggage, his detention had already escalated from the type of stop authorized by the *Terry* line of cases into "a more serious intrusion . . . than is allowable on mere suspicion of criminal activity." Id. at 502. The plurality emphasized Royer's removal to a police interrogation room and also the conclusion that the officers' conduct was more intrusive than necessary—that police could have asked Royer for consent to search his bags on the concourse, or that they might have exposed the bags to a narcotics detection dog, confirming or dispelling their suspicions more expeditiously.

Royer raises a number of interesting questions about *Terry* stops. Can a person ever be moved to another location in the midst of a legitimate *Terry* detention? Would imposing what amounts to a "least intrusive alternative" requirement on the circumstances surrounding a stop and frisk be a good idea? Would it be defensible as a matter of Fourth Amendment interpretation? *Royer* is also noteworthy for what it illustrates about the development of *Terry* doctrine. None of the Justices questioned the authority of the officers to conduct a *Terry*-style detention to pursue their suspicions that Royer was carrying narcotics once officers had ascertained that he was traveling under an alias:

> We agree with the State that when the officers discovered that Royer was traveling under an assumed name, this fact, and the facts already known to the officers—paying cash for a one-way ticket, the mode of checking the two bags, and Royer's appearance and conduct in general—were adequate grounds for suspecting Royer of carrying drugs and for temporarily detaining him and his luggage while they attempted to verify or dispel their suspicions in a manner that did not exceed the limits of an investigative detention.[20]

Id. at 502.

If *Terry* is taken narrowly to be about the necessary authority that a patrol officer must have to react to observations giving him significant reason, but not probable cause, to fear that a violent crime may soon be committed by armed and dangerous men, cases like *Royer* are a far cry from *Terry*. They involve a well-financed federal "War on Drugs" being waged by scores of law enforcement agents who employ the *Terry* power proactively, not to prevent imminent violent crime, but to investigate drug transportation. Justice Marshall concluded only a few years after joining the majority opinion in *Terry* that "the delicate balance that *Terry* struck was simply too delicate" to withstand the "hydraulic pressures" to which Justice Douglas referred in his *Terry* dissent. Adams v. Williams, 407 U.S. 143, 162 (1972). Do such cases

20. None of the other Justices questioned the propriety of an investigative detention, assuming the existence of reasonable suspicion. Justice Brennan concurred in the result but dissented from the plurality's suggestion that the initial encounter with Royer, when officers asked him to produce his driver's license and ticket, was consensual. Four Justices dissented on the ground that even though Royer may have been seized, his seizure was supported by reasonable suspicion, and the police lawfully obtained Royer's consent to search his luggage.—EDS.

prove his point? Don't they at least suggest that the fact pattern in *Terry* may have been disarmingly simple?

6. *Terry*'s usefulness as a tool in the investigation of drug crimes was further extended when its reasoning was held to have application not only to the detention of persons, but also in at least some circumstances to property. Recall United States v. Place, 462 U.S. 695 (1983), first discussed supra at pages 366-367. Federal narcotics officers had articulable suspicion to believe that two suitcases in the possession of a deplaning passenger at LaGuardia Airport contained narcotics. Raymond Place, the passenger, refused to consent to a search. The officers thereafter seized the suitcases and took them to Kennedy Airport. When the suitcases were subjected to a "sniff test" by a narcotics detection dog approximately 90 minutes after their initial seizure, the dog reacted positively to one suitcase. The officers obtained a search warrant for the bag and discovered it to contain cocaine. Place was charged and eventually convicted of possession with intent to distribute.

The Supreme Court, in an opinion by Justice O'Connor, held that the cocaine found in Place's luggage should have been suppressed because the 90-minute retention of the suitcases without probable cause violated the Fourth Amendment. The Court recognized, however, that "when an officer's observations lead him reasonably to believe that a traveler is carrying luggage that contains narcotics, the principles of *Terry* and its progeny would permit the officer to detain the luggage briefly to investigate the circumstances that aroused his suspicion, provided that the investigative detention is properly limited in scope." Id. at 706.

In a concurring opinion Justice Blackmun agreed that the lengthy detention of the suitcases without probable cause violated the Fourth Amendment. He then went on to address the *Terry* issue:

> I am concerned . . . with what appears to me to be an emerging tendency on the part of the Court to convert the *Terry* decision into a general statement that the Fourth Amendment requires only that any seizure be reasonable. . . .
> Terry v. Ohio, however, teaches that in some circumstances a limited seizure that is less restrictive than a formal arrest may constitutionally occur upon mere reasonable suspicion, if "supported by a special law enforcement need for greater flexibility." Florida v. Royer, 460 U.S., at 514 (dissenting opinion) . . .
> Because I agree with the Court that there is a significant law enforcement interest in interdicting illegal drug traffic in the Nation's airports, . . . a limited intrusion caused by a temporary seizure of luggage for investigative purposes could fall within the *Terry* exception. The critical threshold issue is the intrusiveness of the seizure.

Id. at 721-722.

Do you agree that special law enforcement needs associated with the interdiction of drugs in airports are sufficient to invoke the *Terry* balancing test? Why wasn't the option of temporary seizure available in Arizona v. Hicks, 480 U.S. 321 (1987), at page 480 supra?

NOTES ON THE REFINEMENT OF "STOP AND FRISK"

1. Fourth Amendment "searches" are defined with a mix of rules and standards, as Katz v. United States, 389 U.S. 347 (1967), and its progeny show. Fourth Amendment "seizures" have been defined less precisely. The same is true of

the line that separates *Terry* "stops" from the more substantial seizures that require probable cause. Consider in this connection United States v. Sharpe, 470 U.S. 675 (1985). In *Sharpe*, a federal drug agent and a highway patrolman, in separate cars, attempted to stop a Pontiac and a blue pickup with an attached camper on suspicion that the vehicles, which were traveling in tandem, were transporting contraband. Highway Patrol Officer Thrasher pulled alongside the Pontiac, which was driven by the defendant Sharpe, and signaled for the driver to stop. As Sharpe pulled to the side of the road, the defendant Savage drove his pickup truck between Officer Thrasher and Sharpe, nearly hitting the trooper's car, and proceeded down the road. DEA Agent Cooke remained with Sharpe while Officer Thrasher pursued Savage's pickup and stopped it a half mile down the highway.

DEA Agent Cooke radioed the local police to assist him with Sharpe. After they arrived, he joined Officer Thrasher, who had removed Savage from the pickup and was waiting for Cooke's arrival. Upon detecting the odor of marijuana emanating from the camper attached to Savage's vehicle, Agent Cooke subjected the vehicle to a search and recovered a large quantity of marijuana.

Twenty minutes had elapsed between the initial stop of Savage and this search.[21] The government argued that the length of this detention did not exceed the permissible scope of a *Terry* seizure, that the odor of marijuana detected by Agent Cooke thereafter provided probable cause for the search, and that the automobile exception justified dispensing with the warrant requirement.

Chief Justice Burger, in an opinion for the Court, upheld the legality of the stop:

> Obviously, if an investigative stop continues indefinitely, at some point it can no longer be justified as an investigative stop. But our cases impose no rigid time limitation on *Terry* stops. While it is clear that "the brevity of the invasion of the individual's Fourth Amendment interests is an important factor in determining whether the seizure is so minimally intrusive as to be justifiable on reasonable suspicion," we have emphasized the need to consider the law enforcement purposes to be served by the stop as well as the time reasonably needed to effectuate those purposes. Much as a "bright line" rule would be desirable, in evaluating whether an investigative detention is unreasonable, common sense and ordinary human experience must govern over rigid criteria. . . .
>
> In assessing whether a detention is too long in duration to be justified as an investigative stop, we consider it appropriate to examine whether the police diligently pursued a means of investigation that was likely to confirm or dispel their suspicions quickly, during which time it was necessary to detain the defendant. A court making this assessment should take care to consider whether the police are acting in a swiftly developing situation, and in such cases the court should not indulge in unrealistic second-guessing. . . . The question is not simply whether some other alternative was available, but whether the police acted unreasonably in failing to recognize and pursue it.
>
> We readily conclude that, given the circumstances facing him, Agent Cooke pursued his investigation in a diligent and reasonable manner. . . .

Id. at 685-687.

---

21. Defendant Sharpe was obviously detained for a longer period, but as the Court noted, there was no causal connection between this detention and discovery of the contraband. 470 U.S. at 683.

In a separate opinion, Justice Marshall argued that "fidelity to the rationales that justify *Terry* stops requires that the intrusiveness of the stop be measured independently of law enforcement needs. A stop must first be found not unduly intrusive, particularly in its length, before it is proper to consider whether law enforcement aims warrant limited investigation." Id. at 696. He suggested that normally a 20-minute stop would be unduly intrusive, but he concurred with the majority on the ground that the delay in this case was primarily attributable to the evasive actions of Savage when Sharpe pulled off to the side of the highway.[22]

2. The Court has been more willing to adopt bright-line rules in the context of *Terry*-style intrusions when such rules are urged by law enforcement as necessary to officer safety. Consider Pennsylvania v. Mimms, 434 U.S. 105 (1977) (per curiam). There, the defendant was lawfully stopped for driving with an expired license plate and was ordered out of his car. As the defendant emerged from the automobile, the officer noticed a large bulge under his sports jacket. A frisk revealed the bulge to be a .38 caliber revolver. The issue arising from the defendant's trial on concealed weapons charges was whether the officer had acted properly under *Terry* in commanding the defendant to exit his vehicle:

> [W]e look first to that side of the balance which bears the officer's interest in taking the action that he did. The State freely concedes the officer had no reason to suspect foul play from the particular driver at the time of the stop, there having been nothing unusual or suspicious about his behavior. It was apparently his practice to order all drivers out of their vehicles as a matter of course whenever they had been stopped for a traffic violation. The State argues that this practice was adopted as a precautionary measure to afford a degree of protection to the officer and that it may be justified on that ground. Establishing a face-to-face confrontation diminishes the possibility, otherwise substantial, that the driver can make unobserved movements; this, in turn, reduces the likelihood that the officer will be the victim of an assault.
>
> We think it too plain for argument that the State's proffered justification — the safety of the officer — is both legitimate and weighty. . . .
>
> The hazard of accidental injury from passing traffic to an officer standing on the driver's side of the vehicle may also be appreciable in some situations. Rather than conversing while standing exposed to moving traffic, the officer prudently may prefer to ask the driver of the vehicle to step out of the car and off onto the shoulder of the road where the inquiry may be pursued with greater safety to both.
>
> Against this important interest we are asked to weigh the intrusion into the driver's personal liberty occasioned not by the initial stop of the vehicle, which was admittedly justified, but by the order to get out of the car. We think this additional intrusion can only be described as de minimis. . . .

Id. at 109-111.

In Maryland v. Wilson, 519 U.S. 408 (1997), the Court applied a similar analysis to passengers:

> On the personal liberty side of the balance, the case for the passengers is in one sense stronger than that for the driver. There is probable cause to believe that the driver has committed a minor vehicular offense, but there is no such reason to stop or detain the passengers. But as a practical matter, the passengers are already stopped by

virtue of the stop of the vehicle. The only change in their circumstances which will result from ordering them out of the car is that they will be outside of, rather than inside of, the stopped car. Outside the car, the passengers will be denied access to any possible weapon that might be concealed in the interior of the passenger compartment.

Id. at 413.

How persuasive is the Court's assessment of the relative interests at stake? The majority in *Mimms* cited a study to the effect that 30 percent of all shootings of police occur when a police officer approaches a suspect seated in an automobile. Even acknowledging serious officer safety concerns, however, routine traffic stops may not seem so routine when a car's occupants are ordered out of the car by a police officer shouting commands over a bullhorn and crouched behind the driver's side door of his patrol car with gun drawn. Do *Mimms* and *Wilson* support a bright-line rule giving officers the discretion to so order a car's occupants to exit a vehicle and to raise their hands above their heads while a traffic summons is issued? And if officers are left to choose whether to employ such methods in a routine traffic stop, in what circumstances are they likely to exercise this authority?

3. Michigan v. Long, 463 U.S. 1032 (1983), further attests to the Court's deference to law enforcement in the face of plausible claims that officer safety is at stake. The case involved the following facts:

> Deputies Howell and Lewis were on patrol in a rural area one evening when, shortly after midnight, they observed a car traveling erratically and at excessive speed. The officers observed the car turning down a side road, where it swerved off into a shallow ditch. The officers stopped to investigate. Long, the only occupant of the automobile, met the deputies at the rear of the car, which was protruding from the ditch onto the road. The door on the driver's side of the vehicle was left open.
>
> Deputy Howell requested Long to produce his operator's license, but he did not respond. After the request was repeated, Long produced his license. Long again failed to respond when Howell requested him to produce the vehicle registration. After another repeated request, Long, whom Howell thought "appeared to be under the influence of something," turned from the officers and began walking toward the open door of the vehicle. The officers followed Long and both observed a large hunting knife on the floorboard of the driver's side of the car. The officers then stopped Long's progress and subjected him to a *Terry* protective pat-down, which revealed no weapons.
>
> Long and Deputy Lewis then stood by the rear of the vehicle while Deputy Howell shined his flashlight into the interior of the vehicle, but did not actually enter it. The purpose of Howell's action was "to search for other weapons." The officer noticed that something was protruding from under the armrest on the front seat. He knelt in the vehicle and lifted the armrest. He saw an open pouch on the front seat, and upon flashing his light on the pouch, determined that it contained what appeared to be marijuana. After Deputy Howell showed the pouch and its contents to Deputy Lewis, Long was arrested for possession of marijuana.

Id. at 1035-1036.

In an opinion by Justice O'Connor, the Court noted that "investigative detentions involving suspects in vehicles are especially fraught with danger to police officers." Even though the suspect may be outside the car at the time it is searched, because a stop is a temporary intrusion, the suspect "will be permitted to reenter his automobile, and he will then have access to any weapons inside." The Court held that Deputy Howell's search of the passenger compartment of Long's vehicle was a permissible *Terry*-type search: "[T]he search of the passenger compartment of an automobile, limited to those areas in which a weapon may be placed or hidden, is permissible if the police . . . [have reasonable suspicion to believe] that the suspect is dangerous and . . . may gain immediate control of the weapons." Id. at 1049.

Justice Brennan argued in dissent that the officers could have pursued a less intrusive but equally effective means of ensuring their safety by continuing to detain Long outside his car, while asking him to tell them where his registration was and then retrieving the registration themselves. Do you agree that this approach would have been preferable? Would it have been more protective of Long's privacy? Equally effective at ensuring the officer's safety?

4. Officer safety concerns pervade the Court's opinion in *Terry*. But have such concerns taken the frisk authority too far? David Harris argues that lower courts have inappropriately made categorical judgments that frisks are permissible in certain situations — for instance, in stops involving drug offenses, even when only small-time street corner sales are involved, or in cases involving the companions of arrested people, whether or not there is any reason to believe these bystanders pose a threat. David A. Harris, Particularized Suspicion, Categorical Judgments: Supreme Court Rhetoric Versus Lower Court Reality under *Terry v. Ohio*, 72 St. John's L. Rev. 975, 1001-1012 (1998). Courts generally see cases challenging the propriety of a frisk, of course, when the frisk has resulted in the seizure of evidence — most commonly some weapon. Is it surprising given this context that judges have been generous in upholding police officers' judgments?

For that matter, is this an area where judicial rulings are likely to have all that much effect on officer behavior anyway? Consider Professor Skolnick's observation that a preoccupation with danger is a central element of the police officer's "working personality" and that the perception of danger "undermines the judicious use of authority." Jerome H. Skolnick, Justice Without Trial 43 (3d ed. 1994). Is it realistic to think that an officer making a nighttime stop in a poorly lit place and facing a suspect who is wearing clothing that could easily conceal a weapon will *not* frisk — regardless of any individualized suspicion? Indeed, isn't there an argument in favor of encouraging frisks in such circumstances — to protect the safety of the suspect as well as the officer? See Stephen A. Saltzburg, Terry v. Ohio: A Practically Perfect Doctrine, 72 St. John's L. Rev. at 970 (arguing that self-protective frisks of this type should be permitted).

5. Despite the consideration shown to law enforcement interests in cases like *Mimms*, *Wilson*, and *Long*, the Court has been considerably less willing to tolerate elaborations on the stop-and-frisk authority in the absence of officer safety concerns. This holds true even when such elaborations involve relatively minor additional intrusions on privacy. Thus, in Minnesota v. Dickerson, 508 U.S. 366 (1993), the Court considered what happens when an officer during a *Terry* frisk feels an item that he believes may be contraband. Just as there is a "plain view" exception to the warrant requirement, the Court said, there is a "plain feel" exception. But a plain feel seizure, like a plain view seizure, must be based on probable cause. Moreover, the "feel" that leads to probable cause is narrowly circumscribed. In *Dickerson*, the officer concluded that the object he felt in the defendant's pocket was not a weapon. The officer then squeezed and manipulated the object in an effort to ascertain its character. The squeezing and manipulating provided the

officer with probable cause to believe that the item was a lump of crack cocaine in a plastic bag, but because that activity exceeded the scope of a legitimate frisk for weapons, the Court held that the seizure was illegal. Is *Dickerson* an example of sensible line-drawing, or foolish hair-splitting?

One might expect that the issue in *Dickerson* would arise constantly, that officers would regularly be confronted with unidentified lumps in pockets that might be anything from drugs to a pair of eyeglasses. Judging from reported decisions, though, such cases are rare. Why would that be so? Perhaps officers do a very good job of identifying what they feel during the course of a *Terry* frisk, so doubtful cases like *Dickerson* simply don't occur. Or perhaps officers have learned, through decisions like *Dickerson*, to say they felt something that could have been a weapon. And perhaps courts, hearing such testimony, usually approve the frisk.

NOTE ON THE MEANING OF REASONABLE SUSPICION

Though the majority opinion in *Terry* never used the phrase, "reasonable suspicion" has come to define the legal standard applied to *Terry*-style encounters. Like the probable cause standard, the "reasonable" or "articulable suspicion" standard has never been given a precise definition. It is yet another of those "consider-all-the-circumstances" inquiries found throughout Fourth Amendment case law. The Court discussed the standard in the context of anonymous tips in Alabama v. White, 496 U.S. 325 (1990). The case involved a tip that one Vanessa White would be leaving 235-C Lynwood Terrace Apartments at a particular time in a brown Plymouth station wagon with the right taillight lens broken, that she would be going to Dobey's Motel, and that she would be in possession of about an ounce of cocaine inside a brown attache case. After observing a woman leave the 235 building at the proper time, enter a station wagon matching the tipster's description, and travel the route to the highway on which the motel was located, police stopped the vehicle. The Court noted that "[r]easonable suspicion is a less demanding standard than probable cause not only in the sense that reasonable suspicion can be established with information that is different in quantity or content than that required to establish probable cause, but also in the sense that reasonable suspicion can arise from information that is less reliable than that required to show probable cause." Id. at 330. While emphasizing that it was a close case, the Court held that "under the totality of the circumstances the anonymous tip, as corroborated, exhibited sufficient indicia of reliability to justify the investigatory stop of respondent's car." Id. at 332. The Court revisited *White* — and the meaning of reasonable suspicion — in the following case.

FLORIDA v. J.L.

Certiorari to the Supreme Court of Florida
529 U.S. 266 (2000)

JUSTICE GINSBURG delivered the opinion for a unanimous Court.

The question presented in this case is whether an anonymous tip that a person is carrying a gun is, without more, sufficient to justify a police officer's stop and frisk of that person. We hold that it is not.

On October 13, 1995, an anonymous caller reported to the Miami-Dade Police that a young black male standing at a particular bus stop and wearing a plaid shirt was carrying a gun. So far as the record reveals, there is no audio recording of the tip, and nothing is known about the informant. Sometime after the police received the tip—the record does not say how long—two officers were instructed to respond. They arrived at the bus stop about six minutes later and saw three black males "just hanging out [there]." One of the three, respondent J.L., was wearing a plaid shirt. Apart from the tip, the officers had no reason to suspect any of the three of illegal conduct. The officers did not see a firearm, and J.L. made no threatening or otherwise unusual movements. One of the officers approached J.L., told him to put his hands up on the bus stop, frisked him, and seized a gun from J.L.'s pocket. The second officer frisked the other two individuals, against whom no allegations had been made, and found nothing.

J.L., who was at the time of the frisk "10 days shy of his 16th birth[day]," was charged under state law with carrying a concealed firearm without a license and possessing a firearm while under the age of 18. He moved to suppress the gun as the fruit of an unlawful search. . . .

In the instant case, the officers' suspicion that J.L. was carrying a weapon arose not from any observations of their own but solely from a call made from an unknown location by an unknown caller. Unlike a tip from a known informant whose reputation can be assessed and who can be held responsible if her allegations turn out to be fabricated, "an anonymous tip alone seldom demonstrates the informant's basis of knowledge or veracity," Alabama v. White, 496 U.S. [325], 329 [1990]. As we have recognized, however, there are situations in which an anonymous tip, suitably corroborated, exhibits "sufficient indicia of reliability to provide reasonable suspicion to make the investigatory stop." Id., at 327. The question we here confront is whether the tip pointing to J.L. had those indicia of reliability.

In *White*, the police received an anonymous tip asserting that a woman was carrying cocaine and predicting that she would leave an apartment building at a specified time, get into a car matching a particular description, and drive to a named motel. Standing alone, the tip would not have justified a *Terry* stop. Only after police observation showed that the informant had accurately predicted the woman's movements . . . did it become reasonable to think the tipster had inside knowledge about the suspect and therefore to credit his assertion about the cocaine. Although the Court held that the suspicion in *White* became reasonable after police surveillance, we regarded the case as borderline. Knowledge about a person's future movements indicates some familiarity with that person's affairs, but having such knowledge does not necessarily imply that the informant knows, in particular, whether that person is carrying hidden contraband. We accordingly classified *White* as a "close case."

The tip in the instant case lacked the moderate indicia of reliability present in *White* and essential to the Court's decision in that case. The anonymous call concerning J.L. provided no predictive information and therefore left the police without means to test the informant's knowledge or credibility. . . . All the police had to go on in this case was the bare report of an unknown, unaccountable informant who neither explained how he knew about the gun nor supplied any basis for believing he had inside information about J.L. If *White* was a close case on the reliability of anonymous tips, this one surely falls on the other side of the line.

Florida contends that the tip was reliable because its description of the suspect's visible attributes proved accurate: There really was a young black male wearing a plaid shirt at the bus stop. The United States as amicus curiae makes a similar argument, proposing that a stop and frisk should be permitted "when (1) an anonymous tip provides a description of a particular person at a particular location illegally carrying a concealed firearm, (2) police promptly verify the pertinent details of the tip except the existence of the firearm, and (3) there are no factors that cast doubt on the reliability of the tip. . . . " These contentions misapprehend the reliability needed for a tip to justify a *Terry* stop.

An accurate description of a subject's readily observable location and appearance is of course reliable in this limited sense: It will help the police correctly identify the person whom the tipster means to accuse. Such a tip, however, does not show that the tipster has knowledge of concealed criminal activity. The reasonable suspicion here at issue requires that a tip be reliable in its assertion of illegality, not just in its tendency to identify a determinate person.

A second major argument advanced by Florida and the United States as amicus is, in essence, that the standard *Terry* analysis should be modified to license a "firearm exception." Under such an exception, a tip alleging an illegal gun would justify a stop and frisk even if the accusation would fail standard pre-search reliability testing. We decline to adopt this position.

Firearms are dangerous, and extraordinary dangers sometimes justify unusual precautions. Our decisions recognize the serious threat that armed criminals pose to public safety; *Terry*'s rule, which permits protective police searches on the basis of reasonable suspicion rather than demanding that officers meet the higher standard of probable cause, responds to this very concern. But an automatic firearm exception to our established reliability analysis would rove too far. Such an exception would enable any person seeking to harass another to set in motion an intrusive, embarrassing police search of the targeted person simply by placing an anonymous call falsely reporting the target's unlawful carriage of a gun. . . . [T]he Fourth Amendment is not so easily satisfied.

The facts of this case do not require us to speculate about the circumstances under which the danger alleged in an anonymous tip might be so great as to justify a search even without a showing of reliability. We do not say, for example, that a report of a person carrying a bomb need bear the indicia of reliability we demand for a report of a person carrying a firearm before the police can constitutionally conduct a frisk. Nor do we hold that public safety officials in quarters where the reasonable expectation of Fourth Amendment privacy is diminished, such as airports and schools, cannot conduct protective searches on the basis of information insufficient to justify searches elsewhere.

Finally, the requirement that an anonymous tip bear standard indicia of reliability in order to justify a stop in no way diminishes a police officer's prerogative, in accord with *Terry*, to conduct a protective search of a person who has already been legitimately stopped. We speak in today's decision only of cases in which the officer's authority to make the initial stop is at issue. . . .

The judgment of the Florida Supreme Court is affirmed.

[Justice Kennedy's concurring opinion, joined by Chief Justice Rehnquist, is omitted.]

NOTES AND QUESTIONS

1. Does the Court really address the issue here? After *J.L.*, what is a police officer to do when he receives an anonymous tip that a person of a given description is unlawfully carrying a weapon in a specified public place? Is he supposed to approach this person but not to seize him? If so, is it realistic to believe that an officer will engage in a face-to-face encounter with such a person *without* conduct-ing a frisk—and therefore seizing him? Is it reasonable for courts to instruct police to behave in this way? Perhaps the Justices are implicitly saying that an officer receiving such information should place the suspect under observation, but not approach. Such observation might add to the information from the tipster if the officer, for instance, observes a bulge or sees that the suspect's coat is weighted down in a way consistent with carrying a weapon. But what if the officer observes nothing to add to the information he has already received? Should he be on his way? Perhaps the Court too easily dismissed the case for a "firearms exception" to standard *Terry* analysis.

2. Even assuming that there is something to this analysis, however, could such an exception authorize the frisks of J.L.'s associates?

3. The unanimous Court in *J.L.* seems explicitly to affirm that reasonable suspicion does not refer to a fixed quantum of evidence. Indeed, the case sug-gests that reasonable suspicion is not a single standard—or at least that the evidence needed to satisfy it may differ, depending on whether the matter at issue is a report of a person carrying a bomb or a firearm. Commentators have long noted that both reasonable suspicion and probable cause vary in their practical meaning depending on the circumstances in which these standards are invoked. But do cases like *J.L.* and *Gates*, see pages 426-437 supra, both stressing the flexibility in their respective standards, go a step further? Do they in effect treat reasonable suspicion and probable cause as a general require-ment that officers behave reasonably in the circumstances? For an incisive argument to this effect, see Silas J. Wasserstrom, The Court's Turn toward a General Reasonableness Interpretation of the Fourth Amendment, 27 Am. Crim. L. Rev. 119, 129-130 (1989).

4. Professors Wasserstrom and Seidman have suggested that one problem with the general reasonableness approach is that courts cannot offer persuasive accounts of how they have "balanced" the various interests at stake to arrive at their outcomes. See page 554 supra. Does the opinion in *J.L.* illustrate the point? Who is to say, for instance, that the danger posed by the unlawful carrying of a concealed firearm at a crime-ridden urban bus stop is not enough to authorize a frisk based upon an anonymous tip, but that the very same frisk is permissible in an airport? Isn't this precisely what the Court suggests?

5. *J.L.* was decided before 9/11; in this regard, its allusion to anonymous tips about bombs and other great dangers sounds strangely prophetic. Now consider United States v. Arvizu, 534 U.S. 266 (2002), a post-9/11 case that likewise addresses the reasonable suspicion standard. A border patrol agent in southern Arizona stopped a minivan with two adults and three children; the agent suspected that the van might contain drugs. (The agent turned out to be right—once he was stopped, Arvizu consented to a search of the van, which yielded over a hundred pounds of marijuana.) A unanimous Supreme Court found the reasonable

suspicion standard satisfied based on the following facts: (1) the vehicle "was a minivan, a type of automobile that [the agent] knew smugglers used"; (2) the van was driving along a dirt road sometimes used by drug smugglers (though it was also sometimes used by vacationers); (3) the trip "coincided with the point when agents begin heading back to the checkpoint for a shift change, which leaves the area unpatrolled"; (4) when the van's driver saw the agent, the van slowed down considerably; (5) the driver of the van "appeared stiff and his posture very rigid"; (6) the children in the back of the van waved at the agent "in an abnormal pattern . . . as if the children were being instructed"; (7) the children's knees seemed to be propped up on something in the back of the van; (8) the van was registered to an address near the Mexican border, in an area "notorious for alien and narcotics smuggling."

Most of the facts relied on in *Arvizu* seem innocuous. If minivans with two adults and three kids are likely drug couriers, one wonders whether there is any type of automobile that *isn't* likely to be carrying drugs. Slowing down when one sees a police officer is common behavior, the obvious explanation for which is the driver's desire not to get a speeding ticket. So too with regard to the driver's nervous look: how many drivers look "stiff" or "rigid" once they've spotted a police car? The children's knees were likely to be propped up on luggage, not marijuana. And as for the children's abnormal waving, it isn't clear what *normal* waving by three children in the back of a minivan would look like. The Court of Appeals for the Ninth Circuit concluded that these facts were, as a matter of law, not suspicious, and that the other facts cited by the Government were not enough to establish reasonable suspicion. That seems like a reasonable application of the reasonable suspicion standard.

Or is it? The natural conclusion is that the Supreme Court got *Arvizu* wrong. But that conclusion might shortchange the agent who made the stop. The truth may be that *something* about the van looked suspicious to the agent. Perhaps it was something the agent couldn't quite put his finger on, or perhaps it was the combination of all the facts mentioned above—facts that might be innocent on their own but suspicious in combination. Either way, it might be important to remember that border patrol agents—and police officers generally—are not lawyers; they are likely to be better at spotting suspicious behavior than at analyzing the bases for their suspicion.

The Court's opinion does not mention 9/11. But *Arvizu* was argued in November 2001, two months after the terrorist attacks on the World Trade Center and the Pentagon. Terrorism was in no way at issue in the case, but Justice O'Connor made several thinly veiled references to the September 11 attacks during oral argument. Speaking to Arvizu's lawyer, Justice O'Connor noted that "we live in perhaps a more dangerous age today than we did when this event took place," confessed concern that "the Ninth Circuit opinion seemed to be a little more rigid than . . . common sense would dictate today," and noted that "it may become very important to us" to preserve the flexibility of the reasonable suspicion standard. Linda Greenhouse, Court Rules on Police Search of Motorists, N.Y. Times, Jan. 16, 2002, at A17. One wonders whether the Court might have viewed the stop with a more critical eye *before* September 11.

6. How should a suspect's flight on sight of the police be factored into the reasonable suspicion equation? Consider the following case.

ILLINOIS v. WARDLOW

Certiorari to the Supreme Court of Illinois
528 U.S. 119 (2000)

CHIEF JUSTICE REHNQUIST delivered the opinion of the Court.

. . . On September 9, 1995, Officers Nolan and Harvey were working as uniformed officers in the special operations section of the Chicago Police Department. The officers were driving the last car of a four car caravan converging on an area known for heavy narcotics trafficking in order to investigate drug transactions. . . .

As the caravan passed 4035 West Van Buren, Officer Nolan observed respondent Wardlow standing next to the building holding an opaque bag. Respondent looked in the direction of the officers and fled. Nolan and Harvey turned their car southbound, watched him as he ran through the gangway and an alley, and eventually cornered him on the street. Nolan then exited his car and stopped respondent. He immediately conducted a protective pat-down search for weapons because in his experience it was common for there to be weapons in the near vicinity of narcotics transactions. During the frisk, Officer Nolan squeezed the bag respondent was carrying and felt a heavy, hard object similar to the shape of a gun. The officer then opened the bag and discovered a .38-caliber handgun with five live rounds of ammunition. The officers arrested Wardlow. . . .

This case, involving a brief encounter between a citizen and a police officer on a public street, is governed by the analysis we first applied in *Terry*. In *Terry*, we held that an officer may, consistent with the Fourth Amendment, conduct a brief, investigatory stop when the officer has a reasonable, articulable suspicion that criminal activity is afoot. While "reasonable suspicion" is a less demanding standard than probable cause and requires a showing considerably less than preponderance of the evidence, the Fourth Amendment requires at least a minimal level of objective justification for making the stop. The officer must be able to articulate more than an "inchoate and unparticularized suspicion or 'hunch'" of criminal activity.

Nolan and Harvey were among eight officers in a four-car caravan that was converging on an area known for heavy narcotics trafficking, and the officers anticipated encountering a large number of people in the area, including drug customers and individuals serving as lookouts. It was in this context that Officer Nolan decided to investigate Wardlow after observing him flee. An individual's presence in an area of expected criminal activity, standing alone, is not enough to support a reasonable, particularized suspicion that the person is committing a crime. But officers are not required to ignore the relevant characteristics of a location in determining whether the circumstances are sufficiently suspicious to warrant further investigation. Accordingly, we have previously noted the fact that the stop occurred in a "high crime area" among the relevant contextual considerations in a *Terry* analysis. Adams v. Williams, 407 U.S. 143, 144, and 147-148 (1972).

In this case, moreover, it was not merely respondent's presence in an area of heavy narcotics trafficking that aroused the officers' suspicion but his unprovoked flight upon noticing the police. Our cases have also recognized that nervous, evasive behavior is a pertinent factor in determining reasonable suspicion. Headlong flight—wherever it occurs—is the consummate act of evasion: It is not necessarily indicative of wrongdoing, but it is certainly suggestive of such. In reviewing the propriety of an officer's conduct, courts do not have available empirical studies dealing with inferences drawn from suspicious behavior, and we cannot reasonably demand scientific certainty from judges or law enforcement officers where none exists. Thus, the determination of reasonable suspicion must be based on commonsense judgments and inferences about human behavior. We conclude Officer Nolan was justified in suspecting that Wardlow was involved in criminal activity, and, therefore, in investigating further.

Such a holding is entirely consistent with our decision in Florida v. Royer, 460 U.S. 491 (1983), where we held that when an officer, without reasonable suspicion or probable cause, approaches an individual, the individual has a right to ignore the police and go about his business. And any "refusal to cooperate, without more, does not furnish the minimal level of objective justification needed for a detention or seizure." Florida v. Bostick, 501 U.S. 429, 437 (1991). But unprovoked flight is simply not a mere refusal to cooperate. Flight, by its very nature, is not "going about one's business"; in fact, it is just the opposite. Allowing officers confronted with such flight to stop the fugitive and investigate further is quite consistent with the individual's right to go about his business or to stay put and remain silent in the face of police questioning.

Respondent and amici also argue that there are innocent reasons for flight from police and that, therefore, flight is not necessarily indicative of ongoing criminal activity. This fact is undoubtedly true, but does not establish a violation of the Fourth Amendment. Even in *Terry*, the conduct justifying the stop was ambiguous and susceptible of an innocent explanation. The officer observed two individuals pacing back and forth in front of a store, peering into the window and periodically conferring. All of this conduct was by itself lawful, but it also suggested that the individuals were casing the store for a planned robbery. *Terry* recognized that the officers could detain the individuals to resolve the ambiguity.

In allowing such detentions, *Terry* accepts the risk that officers may stop innocent people. Indeed, the Fourth Amendment accepts that risk in connection with more drastic police action; persons arrested and detained on probable cause to believe they have committed a crime may turn out to be innocent. The *Terry* stop is a far more minimal intrusion, simply allowing the officer to briefly investigate further. If the officer does not learn facts rising to the level of probable cause, the individual must be allowed to go on his way. . . .

JUSTICE STEVENS, with whom JUSTICE SOUTER, JUSTICE GINSBURG, and JUSTICE BREYER join, concurring in part and dissenting in part.

The State of Illinois asks this Court to announce a "bright-line rule" authorizing the temporary detention of anyone who flees at the mere sight of a police officer. Respondent counters by asking us to adopt the opposite per se rule — that the fact that a person flees upon seeing the police can never, by itself, be sufficient to justify a temporary investigative stop of the kind authorized by Terry v. Ohio, 392 U.S. 1 (1968). . . .

Although I agree with the Court's rejection of the per se rules proffered by the parties, unlike the Court, I am persuaded that in this case the brief testimony of the officer who seized respondent does not justify the conclusion that he had reasonable suspicion to make the stop. . . .

The question in this case concerns "the degree of suspicion that attaches to" a person's flight—or, more precisely, what "commonsense conclusions" can be drawn respecting the motives behind that flight. A pedestrian may break into a run for a variety of reasons—to catch up with a friend a block or two away, to seek shelter from an impending storm, to arrive at a bus stop before the bus leaves, to get home in time for dinner, to resume jogging after a pause for rest, to avoid contact with a bore or a bully, or simply to answer the call of nature—any of which might coincide with the arrival of an officer in the vicinity. A pedestrian might also run because he or she has just sighted one or more police officers. In the latter instance, the State properly points out "that the fleeing person may be, inter alia, (1) an escapee from jail; (2) wanted on a warrant; (3) in possession of contraband, (i.e. drugs, weapons, stolen goods, etc.); or (4) someone who has just committed another type of crime." In short, there are unquestionably circumstances in which a person's flight is suspicious, and undeniably instances in which a person runs for entirely innocent reasons.[3]

Given the diversity and frequency of possible motivations for flight, it would be profoundly unwise to endorse either per se rule. The inference we can reasonably draw about the motivation for a person's flight, rather, will depend on a number of different circumstances. Factors such as the time of day, the number of people in the area, the character of the neighborhood, whether the officer was in uniform, the way the runner was dressed, the direction and speed of the flight, and whether the person's behavior was otherwise unusual might be relevant in specific cases. This number of variables is surely sufficient to preclude either a bright-line rule that always justifies, or that never justifies, an investigative stop based on the sole fact that flight began after a police officer appeared nearby.

Still, Illinois presses for a per se rule regarding "unprovoked flight upon seeing a clearly identifiable police officer." The phrase "upon seeing," as used by Illinois, apparently assumes that the flight is motivated by the presence of the police officer. Illinois contends that unprovoked flight is "an extreme reaction," because innocent people simply do not "flee at the mere sight of the police." To be sure, Illinois concedes, an innocent person—even one distrustful of the police—might "avoid eye contact or even sneer at the sight of an officer," and that would not justify a *Terry* stop or any sort of per se inference. But, Illinois insists, unprovoked flight is altogether different. Such behavior is so "aberrant" and "abnormal" that a per se inference is justified.

Even assuming we know that a person runs because he sees the police, the inference to be drawn may still vary from case to case. Flight to escape police detection, we have said, may have an entirely innocent motivation:

> "[I]t is a matter of common knowledge that men who are entirely innocent do sometimes fly from the scene of a crime through fear of being apprehended as the guilty parties, or from an unwillingness to appear as witnesses. Nor is it true as an accepted axiom of criminal law that the 'wicked flee when no man pursueth, but the righteous are as bold as a lion.' Innocent men sometimes hesitate to confront a jury—not necessarily because they fear that the jury will not protect them, but because they do not wish their names to appear in connection with criminal acts, are humiliated

3. Compare, e.g., Proverbs 28:1 ("The wicked flee when no man pursueth: but the righteous are as bold as a lion") with Proverbs 22:3 ("A shrewd man sees trouble coming and lies low; the simple walk into it and pay the penalty"). . . .

at being obliged to incur the popular odium of an arrest and trial, or because they do not wish to be put to the annoyance or expense of defending themselves." Alberty v. United States, 162 U.S. 499, 511 (1896).

In addition to these concerns, a reasonable person may conclude that an officer's sudden appearance indicates nearby criminal activity. And where there is criminal activity there is also a substantial element of danger — either from the criminal or from a confrontation between the criminal and the police. These considerations can lead to an innocent and understandable desire to quit the vicinity with all speed.

Among some citizens, particularly minorities and those residing in high crime areas, there is also the possibility that the fleeing person is entirely innocent, but, with or without justification, believes that contact with the police can itself be dangerous, apart from any criminal activity associated with the officer's sudden presence.[7] For such a person, unprovoked flight is neither "aberrant" nor "abnormal."[8] Moreover, these concerns and fears are known to the police officers themselves,[9] and are validated by law enforcement investigations into their own practices.[10] Accordingly, the evidence supporting the reasonableness of these

7. See Johnson, Americans' Views on Crime and Law Enforcement: Survey Findings, National Institute of Justice Journal 13 (Sept. 1997) (reporting study by the Joint Center for Political and Economic Studies in April 1996, which found that 43% of African Americans consider "police brutality and harassment of African-Americans a serious problem" in their own community); President's Comm'n on Law Enforcement and Administration of Justice, Task Force Report: The Police 183-184 (1967) (documenting the belief, held by many minorities, that field interrogations are conducted "indiscriminately" and "in an abusive . . . manner," and labeling this phenomenon a "principal problem" causing "friction" between minorities and the police) (cited in *Terry*, 392 U.S., at 14, n. 11); see also Casimir, Minority Men: We Are Frisk Targets, N.Y. Daily News, Mar. 26, 1999, p. 34 (informal survey of 100 young black and Hispanic men living in New York City; 81 reported having been stopped and frisked by police at least once; none of the 81 stops resulted in arrests); Brief for NAACP Legal Defense & Educational Fund as Amicus Curiae 17-19 (reporting figures on disproportionate street stops of minority residents in Pittsburgh and Philadelphia, Pennsylvania, and St. Petersburg, Florida); U.S. Dept. of Justice, Bureau of Justice Statistics, S. Smith, Criminal Victimization and Perceptions of Community Safety in 12 Cities 25 (June 1998) (African-American residents in 12 cities are more than twice as likely to be dissatisfied with police practices than white residents in same community).

8. See, e.g., Kotlowitz, Hidden Casualties: Drug War's Emphasis on Law Enforcement Takes a Toll on Police, Wall Street Journal, Jan. 11, 1991, p. A2, col. 1 ("Black leaders complained that innocent people were picked up in the drug sweeps. . . . Some teen-agers were so scared of the task force they ran even if they weren't selling drugs"). . . .

9. The Chief of the Washington, D.C., Metropolitan Police Department, for example, confirmed that "sizeable percentages of Americans today — especially Americans of color — still view policing in the United States to be discriminatory, if not by policy and definition, certainly in its day-to-day application." P. Verniero, Attorney General of New Jersey, Interim Report of the State Police Review Team Regarding Allegations of Racial Profiling 46 (Apr. 20, 1999) (hereinafter Interim Report). And a recent survey of 650 Los Angeles Police Department officers found that 25% felt that "'racial bias (prejudice) on the part of officers toward minority citizens currently exists and contributes to a negative interaction between police and the community.'" Report of the Independent Comm'n on the Los Angeles Police Department 69 (1991); see also 5 United States Comm'n on Civil Rights, Racial and Ethnic Tensions in American Communities: Poverty, Inequality and Discrimination, The Los Angeles Report 26 (June 1999).

10. New Jersey's Attorney General, in a recent investigation into allegations of racial profiling on the New Jersey Turnpike, concluded that "minority motorists have been treated differently [by New Jersey State Troopers] than non-minority motorists during the course of traffic stops on the New Jersey Turnpike." "[T]he problem of disparate treatment is real—not imagined," declared the Attorney General. Not surprisingly, the report concluded that this disparate treatment "engender[s] feelings of fear, resentment, hostility, and mistrust by minority citizens." See Interim Report 4, 7. Recently, the United States Department of Justice, citing this very evidence, announced that it would appoint an outside monitor to oversee the actions of the New Jersey State Police and ensure that it enacts policy

beliefs is too pervasive to be dismissed as random or rare, and too persuasive to be disparaged as inconclusive or insufficient. In any event, just as we do not require "scientific certainty" for our commonsense conclusion that unprovoked flight can sometimes indicate suspicious motives, neither do we require scientific certainty to conclude that unprovoked flight can occur for other, innocent reasons.[12]

The probative force of the inferences to be drawn from flight is a function of the varied circumstances in which it occurs. Sometimes those inferences are entirely consistent with the presumption of innocence, sometimes they justify further investigation, and sometimes they justify an immediate stop and search for weapons. These considerations have led us to avoid categorical rules concerning a person's flight and the presumptions to be drawn therefrom. . . .

Guided by [the] totality-of-the-circumstances test, the Court concludes that Officer Nolan had reasonable suspicion to stop respondent. In this respect, my view differs from the Court's. The entire justification for the stop is articulated in the brief testimony of Officer Nolan. . . .

Respondent Wardlow was arrested a few minutes after noon on September 9, 1995. Nolan was part of an eight-officer, four-car caravan patrol team. The officers were headed for "one of the areas in the 11th District [of Chicago] that's high [in] narcotics traffic." The reason why four cars were in the caravan was that "[n]ormally in these different areas there's an enormous amount of people, sometimes lookouts, customers." Officer Nolan testified that he was in uniform on that day, but he did not recall whether he was driving a marked or an unmarked car.

Officer Nolan and his partner were in the last of the four patrol cars that "were all caravaning eastbound down Van Buren." Nolan first observed respondent "in front of 4035 West Van Buren." Wardlow "looked in our direction and began fleeing." Nolan then "began driving southbound down the street observing [respondent] running through the gangway and the alley southbound," and observed that Wardlow was carrying a white, opaque bag under his arm. After the car turned south and intercepted respondent as he "ran right towards us,"

---

changes advocated by the Interim Report, and keeps records on racial statistics and traffic stops. See Kocieniewski, U.S. Will Monitor New Jersey Police on Race Profiling, N.Y. Times, Dec. 23, 1999, p. A1, col. 6.

Likewise, the Massachusetts Attorney General investigated similar allegations of egregious police conduct toward minorities. The report stated:

"We conclude that Boston police officers engaged in improper, and unconstitutional, conduct in the 1989-90 period with respect to stops and searches of minority individuals. . . . Although we cannot say with precision how widespread this illegal conduct was, we believe that it was sufficiently common to justify changes in certain Department practices.

"Perhaps the most disturbing evidence was that the *scope* of a number of *Terry* searches went far beyond anything authorized by that case and indeed, beyond anything that we believe would be acceptable under the federal and state constitutions even where probable cause existed to conduct a full search incident to an arrest. Forcing young men to lower their trousers, or otherwise searching inside their underwear, on public streets or in public hallways, is so demeaning and invasive of fundamental precepts of privacy that it can only be condemned in the strongest terms. The fact that not only the young men themselves, but independent witnesses complained of strip searches, should be deeply alarming to all members of this community." J. Shannon, Attorney General of Massachusetts, Report of the Attorney General's Civil Rights Division on Boston Police Department Practices 60-61 (Dec. 18, 1990).

12. As a general matter, local courts often have a keener and more informed sense of local police practices and events that may heighten these concerns at particular times or locations. Thus, a reviewing court may accord substantial deference to a local court's determination that fear of the police is especially acute in a specific location or at a particular time.

Officer Nolan stopped him and conducted a "protective search," which revealed that the bag under respondent's arm contained a loaded handgun.

This terse testimony is most noticeable for what it fails to reveal. Though asked whether he was in a marked or unmarked car, Officer Nolan could not recall the answer. He was not asked whether any of the other three cars in the caravan were marked, or whether any of the other seven officers were in uniform. Though he explained that the size of the caravan was because "[n]ormally in these different areas there's an enormous amount of people, sometimes lookouts, customers," Officer Nolan did not testify as to whether *anyone* besides Wardlow was nearby 4035 West Van Buren. Nor is it clear that that address was the intended destination of the caravan. As the Appellate Court of Illinois interpreted the record, "it appears that the officers were simply driving by, on their way to some unidentified location, when they noticed defendant standing at 4035 West Van Buren." Officer Nolan's testimony also does not reveal how fast the officers were driving. It does not indicate whether he saw respondent notice the other patrol cars. And it does not say whether the caravan, or any part of it, had already passed Wardlow by before he began to run.

Indeed, the Appellate Court thought the record was even "too vague to support the inference that . . . defendant's flight was related to his expectation of police focus on him." Presumably, respondent did not react to the first three cars, and we cannot even be sure that he recognized the occupants of the fourth as police officers. The adverse inference is based entirely on the officer's statement: "He looked in our direction and began fleeing."[17]

No other factors sufficiently support a finding of reasonable suspicion. Though respondent was carrying a white, opaque bag under his arm, there is nothing at all suspicious about that. Certainly the time of day — shortly after noon — does not support Illinois' argument. Nor were the officers "responding to any call or report of suspicious activity in the area." Officer Nolan did testify that he expected to find "an enormous amount of people," including drug customers or lookouts, and the Court points out that "[i]t was in this context that Officer Nolan decided to investigate Wardlow after observing him flee." This observation, in my view, lends insufficient weight to the reasonable suspicion analysis; indeed, in light of the absence of testimony that anyone else was nearby when respondent began to run, this observation points in the opposite direction.

The State, along with the majority of the Court, relies as well on the assumption that this flight occurred in a high crime area. Even if that assumption is accurate, it is insufficient because even in a high crime neighborhood unprovoked flight does not invariably lead to reasonable suspicion. On the contrary, because many factors providing innocent motivations for unprovoked flight are concentrated in high crime areas, the character of the neighborhood arguably makes an inference of guilt less appropriate, rather than more so. Like unprovoked flight itself, presence in a high crime neighborhood is a fact too generic and susceptible to innocent explanation to satisfy the reasonable suspicion inquiry.

It is the State's burden to articulate facts sufficient to support reasonable suspicion. In my judgment, Illinois has failed to discharge that burden. I am not persuaded that the mere fact that someone standing on a sidewalk looked in

---

17. Officer Nolan also testified that respondent "was looking *at* us," (emphasis added), though this minor clarification hardly seems sufficient to support the adverse inference.

the direction of a passing car before starting to run is sufficient to justify a forcible stop and frisk. . . .

NOTES AND QUESTIONS

1. Is there a problem here that the Court ignores? Flight may give rise to reasonable suspicion that a suspect is involved in crime of some sort, at least in certain circumstances. But flight alone — or even flight in a high-crime area — does not provide reasonable suspicion that a suspect is engaged in any *particular* crime, does it? Yet in other Fourth Amendment settings — in arresting individuals, or in searching in specific places — we require a certain level of probability that a particular crime has been committed or that evidence of a particular crime will be found. No one would argue that police can arrest someone for "crime in general." How and why is the *Terry* context different?

2. Consider the following account of how young African American men viewed encounters with police in one urban neighborhood:

> On the streets late at night, the average young black man is suspicious of others he encounters, and he is particularly wary of the police. If he is dressed in the uniform of the "gangster," such as a black leather jacket, sneakers, and a "gangster cap," if he is carrying a radio or a suspicious bag (which may be confiscated), or if he is moving too fast or too slow, the police may stop him. As part of the routine, they search him and make him sit in the police car while they run a check to see whether there is a "detainer" on him. If there is nothing, he is allowed to go on his way. After this ordeal the youth is often left afraid, sometimes shaking, and uncertain about the area he had previously taken for granted. He is upset in part because he is painfully aware of how close he has come to being in "big trouble." He knows of other youths who have gotten into a "world of trouble" simply by being on the streets at the wrong time or when the police were pursuing a criminal. In these circumstances, particularly at night, it is relatively easy for one black man to be mistaken for another. . . .

Elijah Anderson, Streetwise: Race, Class, and Change in an Urban Community 195-196 (1990). Does this account explain why some suspects might run from police even if they have nothing to hide?

3. What type of evidence should courts consider in drawing the conclusion that a particular neighborhood lies within a "high-crime area"? Officers relying upon this claim to help justify a stop typically offer testimony about a given neighborhood's reputation in the precinct or in the community, or about their own experiences with crime in that neighborhood. Such testimony has probative value, but precisely what weight should be afforded to it? Professor Harris asserts that judges credit conclusory statements by police that a suspect was observed in a "high crime" or "high drug-trafficking" area. David A. Harris, Particularized Suspicion, Categorical Judgments: Supreme Court Rhetoric Versus Lower Court Reality under Terry v. Ohio, 72 St. John's L. Rev. 975, 998 (1998). Is there anything wrong with affording *some* weight to such statements?

4. Consider the following: "Those who live in high crime areas will likely be poor and members of minority groups, and these very same people may also have strong reasons to avoid the police, given their past experiences. Thus, if the law allows stops based on membership in just these two categories, it effectively allows

police nearly complete discretion to stop African Americans who live in crime-prone urban neighborhoods." Id. at 1000.

5. The New York Attorney General's report on NYPD stop-and-frisk practices, see page 569 supra, concluded that for the period from January 1, 1998, to March 31, 1999, police in New York stopped nine people for every *Terry* stop that yielded an arrest. Id. at 111. The report specifically noted that "the fact that a large number of 'stops' did not result in an arrest is *not* evidence of poor policing." Id. In a portion of his *Wardlow* opinion that is not excerpted here, Justice Stevens observed, in contrast, that the fact that many stops never lead to an arrest "exacerbates the perceptions of discrimination felt by racial minorities and people living in high crime areas" and also "indicate[s] that society as a whole is paying a significant cost in infringement on liberty" by virtue of such stops. 528 U.S. at 133, n. 8. Should a more nearly even ratio of stops to arrests be taken as evidence of good policing? How would one go about deciding what a good stop/arrest ratio is?

2. Police Discretion and Profiling

As we have seen, police officers enjoy considerable discretion. That is true even under the traditional Fourth Amendment approach, with its preference for warrants and probable cause. It is still more true under the "reasonableness" approach of *Terry* and its progeny. Officers every day decide to intervene or ignore suspicious circumstances, applying broad legal standards like probable cause or reasonable suspicion, often without prior or subsequent judicial supervision. They may arrest, or choose to treat an infraction in some other way. One of the principal questions in Fourth Amendment law is how strictly or loosely police discretion should be regulated. This broad question lurks behind a host of issues we have already addressed: the warrant requirement, for instance, and the propriety of departing from it; the meaning of "searches" and "seizures"; the boundaries of "stops" and "frisks."

One way police exercise their discretionary power is through the use of profiles: sets of characteristics that may (or may not) be correlated to particular kinds of criminal activity. Consider drug courier profiles. Such profiles list characteristics said to be commonly found among people engaged in drug trafficking. In United States v. Sokolow, 490 U.S. 1 (1989), DEA agents using a "drug courier profile" stopped the defendant at the Honolulu International Airport. The Supreme Court upheld the legality of this *Terry* stop, which was based on the following information:

(1) [The defendant] paid $2,100 for two airplane tickets from a roll of $20 bills;
(2) he traveled under a name that did not match the name under which his telephone number was listed;
(3) his original destination was Miami, a source city for illicit drugs;
(4) he stayed in Miami for only 48 hours, even though a round-trip flight from Honolulu to Miami takes 20 hours;
(5) he appeared nervous during his trip; and
(6) he checked none of his luggage.

Id. at 3. The Court did not rely on the drug courier profile in concluding that there was reasonable suspicion for the stop. But neither did it condemn the use of such profiles:

> A court sitting to determine the existence of reasonable suspicion must require the agent to articulate the factors leading to that conclusion, but the fact that these factors may be set forth in a "profile" does not somehow detract from their evidentiary significance as seen by a trained agent.

Id. at 10.

Justice Marshall, in a dissenting opinion joined by Justice Brennan, disagreed that the DEA agents' use of a drug courier profile to focus attention on suspects was benign:

> It is highly significant that the DEA agents stopped Sokolow because he matched one of the DEA's "profiles" of a paradigmatic drug courier. In my view, a law enforcement officer's mechanistic application of a formula of personal and behavioral traits in deciding whom to detain can only dull the officer's ability and determination to make sensitive and fact-specific inferences "in light of his experience," *Terry*, [392 U.S. at 27], particularly in ambiguous or borderline cases. Reflexive reliance on a profile of drug courier characteristics runs a far greater risk than does ordinary, case-by-case police work, of subjecting innocent individuals to unwarranted police harassment and detention.

490 U.S. at 13 (Marshall, J., dissenting).

When officers use race or ethnicity as an element of suspicion in the profiles they employ, the stakes are even higher — implicating not just Fourth Amendment, but equal protection concerns. But racial profiling, like profiling in general,

> . . . depends on police discretion in choosing suspects. At one end of the continuum, racial profiling is impossible once the police are looking for a particular person — the victim's partner, the woman in the surveillance video, Osama bin Laden — although it may be a factor at an earlier stage, in determining who to look for. At the other extreme, racial profiling can flourish in proactive investigations in which the police scan large numbers of people in search of culprits in crimes that have not been reported or have not yet occurred. Recently it has been a controversial topic in debates over the conduct of anti-terror investigations following the September 11, 2001 attacks on the World Trade Center and the Pentagon. Before that, racial profiling was primarily an issue in investigations of crimes of possession, usually of guns or drugs. It has received particular attention in the context of highway drug interdiction. . . .

Samuel R. Gross and Katherine Y. Barnes, Road Work: Racial Profiling and Drug Interdiction on the Highway, 101 Mich. L. Rev. 651, 655 (2002).

"Racial profiling" is a term that has no fixed legal meaning. It began appearing in published opinions only in the 1990s. Yet today it represents a central issue in law enforcement — and one that bears dramatically on the question of how closely Fourth Amendment law should regulate police discretion in choosing among suspects. We take up two cases in this section — Whren v. United States, 517 U.S. 806 (1996), a leading Fourth Amendment case, and Chicago v. Morales, 527 U.S. 41

(1999), a case addressing due process limits on the scope of substantive criminal law. The cases implicate different legal doctrines, but both involve a kind of regulatory strategy for addressing profiling. Before turning to these cases, however, consider the following analyses of the uses—and misuses—of profiles.

RANDALL L. KENNEDY, RACE, CRIME AND THE LAW 158-161 (1997)

When a Mexican-American motorist is selected for questioning in part on the basis of his perceived ancestry, he is undoubtedly being burdened more heavily at that moment on account of his race than his white Anglo counterpart. He is being made to pay a type of racial tax for the campaign against illegal immigration that whites, blacks, and Asians escape. Similarly, a young black man selected for questioning by police as he alights from an airplane or drives a car is being made to pay a type of racial tax for the war against drugs that whites and other groups escape. That tax is the cost of being subjected to greater scrutiny than others. But is that tax illegitimate?

One defense of it is that, under the circumstances, people of other races are simply not in a position to pay the tax effectively. In contrast to apparent Mexican ancestry, neither apparent white nor black nor Asian ancestry appreciably raises the risk that a person near the Mexican border is illegally resident in the United States. Similarly, the argument would run that in contrast to the young black man, the young white man is not as likely to be a courier of illicit drugs. The defense could go on to say that, in this context, race is *not* being used invidiously. It is not being used as a marker to identify people to harm through enslavement, or exclusion, or segregation. Rather, race is being used merely as a signal that facilitates efficient law enforcement. In this context, apparent Mexican ancestry or blackness is being used for unobjectionable ends in the same way that whiteness is used in the affirmative action context: as a marker that has the effect, though not the purpose, of burdening a given racial group. Whereas whites are made to pay a racial tax for the purpose of opening up opportunities for people of color in education and employment, Mexican-Americans and blacks are made to pay a racial tax for the purpose of more efficient law enforcement.

We need to pause here to consider the tremendous controversy that has surrounded affirmative action policies aimed at helping racial minorities. Many of the same arguments against race-based affirmative action are applicable as well in the context of race-based police stops. With affirmative action, many whites claim that they are victims of racial discrimination. With race-based police stops, many people of color complain that they are victims of racial discrimination. With affirmative action, many adversely affected whites claim that they are *innocent* victims of a policy that penalizes them for the misconduct of others who also happened to have been white. With race-based police stops, many adversely affected people of color maintain that they are *innocent* victims of a policy that penalizes them for the misconduct of others who also happen to be colored. . . .

Whatever one thinks of the conclusions drawn by the Court with respect to affirmative action, at least it begins at the correct starting point for analysis — that race-dependent decisions by officials call for more than ordinary justification. With respect to race-dependent policing, however, the Court, mirroring public opinion, has made the terrible error of permitting race-dependent decisionmaking to become a normal part of police practice.

Many of those who defend the current regime of race-dependent policing speak as if there existed no sensible alternative. But there is an alternative: spending more on other means of enforcement to make up for any diminution in crime control caused by the reform I seek: prohibiting officers (except in absolutely extraordinary circumstances) from using race as a proxy for increased risk of criminality. Instead of placing a racial tax on blacks, Mexican-Americans, and other colored people, governments should, if necessary, increase taxes across the board. More specifically, rather than authorizing police to count apparent Mexican ancestry or apparent blackness as negative proxies, states and the federal government should be forced either to hire more officers or to inconvenience everyone at checkpoints by subjecting all motorists and passengers to questioning (or to the same chance at random questioning). . . .

The law should authorize police to engage in racially discriminatory investigative conduct only on atypical, indeed extraordinary, occasions in which the social need is absolutely compelling: weighty, immediate, and incapable of being addressed sensibly by any other means. I have in mind a real emergency, a situation . . . in which there is clear reason to believe that a violent crime has been or is about to be committed and that the reported characteristics of the perpetrator are such that using racial criteria to narrow the pool of potential suspects clearly increases the ability of the police to apprehend the criminal quickly. This formulation is by no means foolproof. Recall *Korematsu*. Implemented properly, however, this proposal would prohibit officers from using racial criteria as a *routine* element of patrolling. . . .

SAMUEL R. GROSS AND DEBRA LIVINGSTON, RACIAL PROFILING UNDER ATTACK

102 Colum. L. Rev. 1413 (2002)

We had just reached a consensus on racial profiling. By September 10, 2001, virtually everyone, from Jesse Jackson to Al Gore to George W. Bush to John Ashcroft, agreed that racial profiling was very bad. We also knew what racial profiling was: Police officers would stop, question, and search African American and Hispanic citizens disproportionately, because of their race or ethnicity, in order to try to catch common criminals. All this has changed in the wake of the September 11 attacks on the World Trade Center and the Pentagon. Now racial profiling is more likely to mean security checks or federal investigations that target Muslim men from Middle Eastern countries, in order to try to catch terrorists. And now lots of people are for it. In the fall of 1999, 81% of respondents in a national poll said they disapproved of "racial profiling," which was defined as the practice by some police officers of stopping "motorists of certain racial or ethnic groups because the officers believe that these groups are more likely than others to commit certain types of crimes." Two years later, 58% said they favored "requiring Arabs, including those who are U.S. citizens, to undergo special, more intrusive security checks before boarding airplanes in the U.S." . . .

Needless to say, racial profiling has not become a national fad. Most newfound supporters are reluctant and ambivalent, and most public officials continue to say they oppose the practice. . . . But the nature of the debate has changed. Before September 11, the disputes appeared to be factual. Critics would argue that the police acted on the basis of race, and the police would deny it. Now the differences are more likely to be definitional or frankly normative: Does it constitute racial profiling to do what the Department of Justice says it is doing? And if so, are the Department's actions nevertheless justified? . . .

As we use the term, "racial profiling" occurs whenever a law enforcement officer questions, stops, arrests, searches, or otherwise investigates a person because the officer believes that members of that person's racial or ethnic group are more likely than the population at large to commit the sort of crime the officer is investigating. The essence of racial profiling is a global judgment that the targeted group — before September 11, usually African Americans or Hispanics — is more prone to commit crime in general, or to commit a particular type of crime, than other racial or ethnic groups. If the officer's conduct is based at least in part on such a general racial or ethnic judgment, it does not matter if she uses other criteria as well in deciding on her course of action. It is racial profiling to target young black men on the basis of a belief that they are more likely than others to commit crimes, even though black women and older black men are not directly affected.

It is not racial profiling for an officer to question, stop, search, arrest, or otherwise investigate a person because his race or ethnicity matches information about a perpetrator of a specific crime that the officer is investigating. That use of race — which usually occurs when there is a racially specific description of the criminal — does not entail a global judgment about a racial or ethnic group as a whole. . . .

. . . In November 2001, the Department of Justice began efforts to interview "more than 5,000 people nationwide — the majority Middle Eastern men ages eighteen to thirty-three who came here within the last two years on nonimmigrant visas — in search of information on terrorist organizations such as al Qaeda." . . . The Department said that these men [were] not suspected of crimes but "might, either wittingly or unwittingly, be in the same circles, communities, or social groups as those engaged in terrorist activities." . . .

Is the Justice Department's interview campaign an ethnic profiling program? Some civil libertarians, Arab American organizations, and local police departments say it is; the Department of Justice says it is not. Who is right? And would answering this question tell us whether the Justice Department's program is appropriate? . . .

. . . By our definition, [even assuming that ethnicity was a central factor in the selection of subjects], it is not ethnic profiling for officers to focus their attention on people of a given ethnicity because the police have information that the specific crime they are investigating was committed by someone of that ethnic group. There is plenty of information that Middle Eastern men, some of whom remain at large, engaged in a conspiracy to commit acts of mass terror in the United States on September 11, 2001. Granted, the concept of a "specific crime" grows somewhat hazy when the crime at issue is an ongoing conspiracy of indeterminate size — and one that potentially involves not just Middle Eastern men, but also others, from different racial or ethnic groups. Nevertheless, if the sole purpose for this interview program was to determine whether any of the thousands to be interviewed was involved in this conspiracy, or had information that might lead to those who were, this would not be ethnic profiling. (Which is not to say that such a broad brush investigation would be unproblematic; that's a different question, as we will see.) . . .

The range of things the government can do on the basis of racial or ethnic information is enormous. If mass imprisonment defines the high end (short of torture or execution), paying close attention may define the low end. After September 11, nobody could seriously complain about the FBI paying more attention to reports of suspicious behavior by Saudi men than to similar reports about Hungarian women — even though as a consequence many more Saudi men will set off false alarms. In between there are infinite gradations, as the government's conduct becomes increasingly intrusive, disruptive, frightening, and humiliating. There are, however, two important questions that cut across the terrain.

The first separates out a class of cases near the bottom of the slope: Did the investigators impinge on the suspect by confronting him, or by covertly invading his privacy? If not — if, in the clearest case, the authorities did no more than gather information at a distance, from public sources — the worst consequences will be minimal. . . .

The second question is more important because it affects the experience of people who do know what is being done to them: Is the subject treated as one of *us* or as one of *them*, as a law abiding person to be checked out or as a criminal to be caught and punished? Security checkpoints are democratic; everybody must go through them, so no stigma is attached to the process. Some people these days get angry if they are *not* checked carefully enough, but even those who are asked to open their bags or scanned by hand are treated essentially like ordinary members of the public. The operating assumption for any individual, Muslim or Presbyterian, is that she will clear security and rejoin the crowd. On the other hand, a passenger who is kicked off an airliner (for good reasons or bad) is treated as a presumptive terrorist. Not only are his plans disrupted, but he is singled out and humiliated in public. . . .

Those of us who have not been through this sort of experience probably underestimate its impact. To be treated as a criminal is a basic insult to a person's self image and to his position in society. It cannot easily be shrugged off. Of course, many victims of racial profiling are not surprised by this treatment. They know why they were stopped — which makes it worse. It's bad enough to have the accidental misfortune of being mistaken for a bad guy; it's worse to feel that you are assumed to be a criminal because of your race. Short of imprisonment, intimidation, or physical abuse, most of the pain of racial profiling is caused by treating law abiding people like criminals. . . .

To return to the Justice Department's program: Does the plan to interview thousands of Middle Eastern men who came here within the last two years on nonimmigrant visas constitute ethnic profiling? The answer turns out to be draw. It is ethnic profiling to the extent that the FBI is operating on a general assumption that Middle Eastern men are more likely than others to commit acts of terror; it is not to the extent that the agents are pursuing case-specific information about the September 11 attacks, albeit in a dragnet fashion. . . .

We also think that neither the question nor the answer is all-important. . . . The Justice Department's program may or may not fall within our definitional line. Its wisdom and morality, however, do not depend on the pigeonhole in which it is placed but on what the Justice Department in fact does. Are the interviews conducted respectfully, in a manner designed to seek out relevant information from those who are willing to give it? If so, the program is acceptable; it may even be an example of good investigative work. On the other hand, if the "voluntary" character of these interviews is merely a ruse — if men against whom there is no evidence are treated as suspects and demeaned — then the program is an intolerable form of ethnic discrimination. . . .

Is all this to suggest that racial and ethnic profiling is less troubling than we once thought? Not at all. It is certainly true that other race-based practices by Government can be as bad, or worse, in criminal investigations as elsewhere. Nonetheless we should be deeply suspicious of racial profiling, however mild the government's actions and however justified they may appear. Investigative choices that are made on the basis of global assumptions about the criminal propensities of racial or ethnic groups are stigmatizing. They reinforce the negative stereotypes on which they are based because investigators are more likely to detect criminal behavior in groups they target than in the groups they overlook. This is dangerous both because it may be misleading, and because it is humiliating to the targeted group. It is a substantial cost of the Justice Department's interview program — whether or not it is ethnic profiling — that many Arab Americans see it as a slap in the face of their entire ethnic group. . . .

U.S. DEPARTMENT OF JUSTICE, CIVIL RIGHTS DIVISION GUIDANCE REGARDING THE USE OF RACE BY FEDERAL LAW ENFORCEMENT AGENCIES

June 2003

In his February 27, 2001, Address to a Joint Session of Congress, President George W. Bush declared that racial profiling is "wrong and we will end it in America." He directed the Attorney General to review the use by Federal law enforcement authorities of race as a factor in conducting stops, searches and other law enforcement investigative procedures. The Attorney General, in turn, instructed the Civil Rights Division to develop guidance for Federal officials to ensure an end to racial profiling in law enforcement. . . .

The use of race as the basis for law enforcement decision-making clearly has a terrible cost, both to the individuals who suffer invidious discrimination and to the Nation, whose goal of "liberty and justice for all" recedes with every act of discrimination. For this reason, this guidance in many cases imposes more restrictions on the consideration of race and ethnicity in Federal law enforcement than the Constitution requires. . . .

I. TRADITIONAL LAW ENFORCEMENT ACTIVITIES.

Two standards in combination should guide use by Federal law enforcement authorities of race or ethnicity in law enforcement activities:

- In making routine or spontaneous law enforcement decisions, such as ordinary traffic stops, Federal law enforcement officers may not use race or ethnicity to any degree, except that officers may rely on race and ethnicity in a specific suspect description. . . .

* In conducting activities in connection with a specific investigation, Federal law enforcement officers may consider race and ethnicity only to the extent that there is trustworthy information, relevant to the locality or time frame, that links persons of a particular race or ethnicity to an identified criminal incident, scheme, or organization. . . .

II. NATIONAL SECURITY AND BORDER INTEGRITY.

The above standards do not affect current Federal policy with respect to law enforcement activities and other efforts to defend and safeguard against threats to national security or the integrity of the Nation's borders, to which the following applies:

* In investigating or preventing threats to national security or other catastrophic events (including the performance of duties related to air transportation security), or in enforcing laws protecting the integrity of the Nation's borders, Federal law enforcement officers may not consider race or ethnicity except to the extent permitted by the Constitution and laws of the United States.

Suppose an FBI agent receives credible information from several informants that a gang composed primarily of Asian males is engaged in narcotics trafficking in a given neighborhood. Does the Justice Department's Guideline permit this agent to consider race as a factor adding to the suspicion that a young Asian man standing on a street corner in the neighborhood is a member of the gang? What is the agent authorized to do, based on this suspicion? What does the Guideline say about taking race or ethnicity into account in connection with the prevention of terrorist incidents? Is it permissible to consider ethnicity in enforcing the traffic laws around a nuclear power plant? Consider this question again after you have looked at the following case.

WHREN v. UNITED STATES

Certiorari to the United States Court of Appeals for the District of Columbia Circuit
517 U.S. 806 (1996)

JUSTICE SCALIA delivered the opinion of the Court.

In this case we decide whether the temporary detention of a motorist who the police have probable cause to believe has committed a civil traffic violation is inconsistent with the Fourth Amendment's prohibition against unreasonable seizures unless a reasonable officer would have been motivated to stop the car by a desire to enforce the traffic laws.

On the evening of June 10, 1993, plainclothes vice-squad officers of the District of Columbia Metropolitan Police Department were patrolling a "high drug area" of the city in an unmarked car. Their suspicions were aroused when they passed a dark Pathfinder truck with temporary license plates and youthful occupants waiting at a stop sign, the driver looking down into the lap of the passenger at his right. The truck remained stopped at the intersection for what seemed an unusually long time — more than 20 seconds. When the police car executed a U-turn in order to head back toward the truck, the Pathfinder turned suddenly to its right, without signalling, and sped off at an "unreasonable" speed. The policemen followed, and in a short while overtook the Pathfinder when it stopped behind other traffic at a red light. They pulled up alongside, and Officer Ephraim Soto stepped out and approached the driver's door, identifying himself as a police officer and directing the driver, petitioner Brown, to put the vehicle in park. When Soto drew up to the driver's window, he immediately observed two large plastic bags of what appeared to be crack cocaine in petitioner Whren's hands. Petitioners were arrested, and quantities of several types of illegal drugs were retrieved from the vehicle.

Petitioners were charged in a four-count indictment with violating various federal drug laws. . . . At a pretrial suppression hearing, they challenged the legality of the stop and the resulting seizure of the drugs. They argued that the stop had not been justified by probable cause to believe, or even reasonable suspicion, that petitioners were engaged in illegal drug-dealing activity; and that Officer Soto's asserted ground for approaching the vehicle — to give the driver a warning concerning traffic violations — was pretextual. The District Court denied the suppression motion. . . .

Petitioners were convicted of the counts at issue here. The Court of Appeals affirmed the convictions, holding with respect to the suppression issue that, "regardless of whether a police officer subjectively believes that the occupants of an automobile may be engaging in some other illegal behavior, a traffic stop is permissible as long as a reasonable officer in the same circumstances *could have* stopped the car for the suspected traffic violation." We granted certiorari. . . .

Petitioners accept that Officer Soto had probable cause to believe that various provisions of the District of Columbia traffic code had been violated. See 18 D.C. Mun. Regs. §§2213.4 (1995) ("An operator shall . . . give full time and attention to the operation of the vehicle"); 2204.3 ("No person shall turn any vehicle . . . without giving an appropriate signal"); 2200.3 ("No person shall drive a vehicle . . . at a speed greater than is reasonable and prudent under the conditions"). They argue, however, that "in the unique context of civil traffic regulations" probable cause is not enough. Since, they contend, the use of automobiles is so heavily and minutely regulated that total compliance with traffic and safety rules is nearly impossible, a police officer will almost invariably be able to catch any given motorist in a technical violation. This creates the temptation to use traffic stops as a means of investigating other law violations, as to which no probable cause or even articulable suspicion exists. Petitioners, who are both black, further contend that police officers might decide which motorists to stop based on decidedly impermissible factors, such as the race of the car's occupants. To avoid this danger, they say, the Fourth Amendment test for traffic stops should be, not the normal one . . . of whether probable cause existed to justify the stop; but rather, whether a police officer, acting reasonably, would have made the stop for the reason given.

Petitioners contend that the standard they propose is consistent with our past cases' disapproval of police attempts to use valid bases of action against citizens as pretexts for pursuing other investigatory agendas. We are reminded . . . that in Colorado v. Bertine, 479 U.S. 367, 372 (1987), in approving an inventory search, we apparently thought it significant that there had been "no showing that the police, who were following standardized procedures, acted in bad faith or for the sole purpose of investigation"; and that in New York v. Burger, 482 U.S. 691, 716-717, n. 27 (1987), we observed, in upholding the constitutionality of a warrantless administrative inspection, that the search did not appear to be "a 'pretext' for obtaining evidence of . . . violation of . . . penal laws." But only an undiscerning reader would regard these cases as endorsing the principle that ulterior motives can invalidate police conduct that is justifiable on the basis of probable cause to believe that a violation of law has occurred. In each case we were addressing the validity of a search conducted in the *absence* of probable cause. Our quoted statements simply explain that the exemption from the need for probable cause (and warrant), which is accorded to searches made for the purpose of inventory or administrative regulation, is not accorded to searches that are *not* made for those purposes. . . .

. . . Petitioners' difficulty is not simply a lack of affirmative support for their position. Not only have we never held, outside the context of inventory search or administrative inspection (discussed above), that an officer's motive invalidates objectively justifiable behavior under the Fourth Amendment; but we have repeatedly held and asserted the contrary. In United States v. Villamonte-Marquez, 462 U.S. 579, 584, n. 3 (1983), we held that an otherwise valid warrantless boarding of a vessel by customs officials was not rendered invalid "because the customs officers were accompanied by a Louisiana state policeman, and were following an informant's tip that a vessel in the ship channel was thought to be carrying marihuana." We flatly dismissed the idea that an ulterior motive might serve to strip the agents of their legal justification. In United States v. Robinson, 414 U.S. 218 (1973), we held that a traffic-violation arrest (of the sort here) would not be rendered invalid by the fact that it was "a mere pretext for a narcotics search," id., at 221, n. 1; and that a lawful postarrest search of the person would not be rendered invalid by the fact that it was not motivated by the officer-safety concern that justifies such searches, see id., at 236. . . .

We think these cases foreclose any argument that the constitutional reasonableness of traffic stops depends on the actual motivations of the individual officers involved. We of course agree with petitioners that the Constitution prohibits selective enforcement of the law based on considerations such as race. But the constitutional basis for objecting to intentionally discriminatory application of laws is the Equal Protection Clause, not the Fourth Amendment. Subjective intentions play no role in ordinary, probable-cause Fourth Amendment analysis.

Recognizing that we have been unwilling to entertain Fourth Amendment challenges based on the actual motivations of individual officers, petitioners disavow any intention to make the individual officer's subjective good faith the touchstone of "reasonableness." They insist that the standard they have put forward — whether the officer's conduct deviated materially from usual police practices, so that a reasonable officer in the same circumstances would not have made the stop for the reasons given — is an "objective" one.

But although framed in empirical terms, this approach is plainly and indisputably driven by subjective considerations. Its whole purpose is to prevent the police from doing under the guise of enforcing the traffic code what they would like to do for different reasons. Petitioners' proposed standard may not use the word "pre-text," but it is designed to combat nothing other than the perceived "danger" of the pretextual stop, albeit only indirectly and over the run of cases. Instead of asking whether the individual officer had the proper state of mind, the petitioners would have us ask, in effect, whether (based on general police practices) it is plausible to believe that the officer had the proper state of mind.

Why one would frame a test designed to combat pretext in such fashion that the court cannot take into account *actual and admitted pretext* is a curiosity that can only be explained by the fact that our cases have foreclosed the more sensible option. If those cases were based only upon the evidentiary difficulty of establishing subjec-tive intent, petitioners' attempt to root out subjective vices through objective means might make sense. But they were not based only upon that, or indeed even principally upon that. Their principal basis—which applies equally to attempts to reach subjective intent through ostensibly objective means—is simply that the Fourth Amendment's concern with "reasonableness" allows certain actions to be taken in certain circumstances, *whatever* the subjective intent. See, e.g., *Robinson*, supra, at 236 ("Since it is the fact of custodial arrest which gives rise to the authority to search, it is of no moment that [the officer] did not indicate any subjective fear of the [arrestee] or that he did not himself suspect that [the arrestee] was armed") (footnotes omitted). But even if our concern had been only an evidentiary one, petitioners' proposal would by no means assuage it. Indeed, it seems to us somewhat easier to figure out the intent of an individual officer than to plumb the collective consciousness of law enforcement in order to determine whether a "reasonable officer" would have been moved to act upon the traffic violation. While police manuals and standard procedures may sometimes provide objective assistance, ordinarily one would be reduced to speculating about the hypothetical reaction of a hypothetical constable—an exercise that might be called virtual subjectivity.

Moreover, police enforcement practices, even if they could be practically assessed by a judge, vary from place to place and from time to time. We cannot accept that the search and seizure protections of the Fourth Amendment are so variable, and can be made to turn upon such trivialities. The difficulty is illustrated by petitioners' arguments in this case. Their claim that a reasonable officer would not have made this stop is based largely on District of Columbia police regulations which permit plainclothes officers in unmarked vehicles to enforce traffic laws "only in the case of a violation that is so grave as to pose an *immediate threat* to the safety of others." This basis of invalidation would not apply in jurisdictions that had a different practice. And it would not have applied even in the District of Columbia, if Officer Soto had been wearing a uniform or patrolling in a marked police cruiser. . . .

In what would appear to be an elaboration on the "reasonable officer" test, petitioners argue that the balancing inherent in any Fourth Amendment inquiry requires us to weigh the governmental and individual interests implicated in a traffic stop such as we have here. That balancing, petitioners claim, does not support investigation of minor traffic infractions by plainclothes police in unmarked vehicles. . . .

It is of course true that in principle, every Fourth Amendment case, since it turns upon a "reasonableness" determination, involves a balancing of all relev-ant factors. With rare exceptions not applicable here, however, the result of that balancing is not in doubt where the search or seizure is based upon probable cause. . . .

Petitioners urge as an extraordinary factor in this case that the "multitude of applicable traffic and equipment regulations" is so large and so difficult to obey perfectly that virtually everyone is guilty of violation, permitting the police to single out almost whomever they wish for a stop. But we are aware of no principle that would allow us to decide at what point a code of law becomes so expansive and so commonly violated that infraction itself can no longer be the ordinary measure of the lawfulness of enforcement. And even if we could identify such exorbitant codes, we do not know by what standard (or what right) we would decide, as petitioners would have us do, which particular provisions are sufficiently important to merit enforcement.

For the run-of-the-mine case, which this surely is, we think there is no realistic alternative to the traditional common-law rule that probable cause justifies a search and seizure. . . .

NOTES AND QUESTIONS

1. Racial profiling is a means of exercising police discretion. The broader the discretion, the greater the opportunity to profile. One obvious way to limit police discretion is to ban the use of pretexts: i.e., to require that, if the police target a suspect due to suspicion of drug crime, the police must have sufficient cause to believe evidence of *that same crime* is present before stopping or searching the suspect. *Whren* rejects that position as a matter of Fourth Amendment law. Why? Is the Court's reasoning persuasive?

2. On the surface, *Whren* looks like an easy case. The police made a U-turn, which plainly did not amount to a "search" or a "seizure." The defendants then turned and sped away, committing a traffic violation for which, naturally, they could be pulled over. What the police saw when they caught up with the defendants was in plain view, and hence was the fruit of a legal seizure. Underneath that simple fact pattern, though, lies a complex issue: the proper relationship between the Fourth Amendment and substantive criminal law. That relationship is, surprisingly, almost never discussed in the cases and rarely explored in the literature. It nevertheless is both important and a little unusual.

For most searches and seizures, the Fourth Amendment requires probable cause. That standard has no independent meaning; it necessarily incorporates the contents of the relevant jurisdiction's criminal law. Thus, if a court concludes that a police officer had probable cause to believe a suspect had just committed a burglary, the court has determined that (1) based on the information available at the time, there was a fair probability (2) that the suspect had engaged in the behavior defined by the state's criminal code as "burglary." The first of these two parts of Fourth Amendment standards — the part that refers to the level of probability — is constitutionally required. No state legislature or local police department could decide, for example, to authorize arrests based on something *less* than probable cause that the suspect had committed a crime. But the second part — the part that refers to the crime the suspect is thought to have committed — is completely within the control of the state.

This obviously creates an opportunity from the state's point of view. If the state defines driving 56 miles per hour or more as a crime, and if virtually every driver on the highway drives at least 56 miles per hour, then the police will have probable cause to arrest virtually every driver on the highway. In that event, Fourth Amendment law does not really do any work — by defining "crime" broadly, the state no longer needs to worry about probable cause, for it will always exist. *Whren* holds, unanimously, that this is not a problem — that the Fourth Amendment ordinarily has nothing to say about the content of criminal law, even though the content of criminal law determines what Fourth Amendment standards mean.

3. Does that holding make sense? If the point of the Fourth Amendment is to ensure that the police have a good reason before searching or seizing someone, shouldn't the Fourth Amendment place some limits on the state's ability to define innocuous conduct as a crime? How can the police have a good reason for, say, arresting someone if all they have is probable cause to believe something innocuous (but nominally criminal) happened? One response is that the only alternative to the position the Court took in *Whren* is to look to police officers' motivations. Justice Scalia suggests this when he says that the defendants' proposed objective standard is "plainly and indisputably driven by subjective considerations." But that raises a different question: What is so wrong with a standard "driven by subjective considerations"? A good deal of constitutional law, including a number of doctrines covered in this book, turns on the subjective motives of government officials. Why are police motives such a problematic basis for Fourth Amendment regulation?

4. Note that at one point Justice Scalia criticizes the defendants' argument on the ground that it would lead to Fourth Amendment standards that vary from place to place. Isn't that what Justice Scalia's standard leads to? After *Whren*, doesn't the Fourth Amendment provide less protection to citizens in states with very broad criminal codes than it does to citizens in states with narrower criminal codes? What is the solution to this problem — or is it a problem?

5. *Whren* reaffirms the proposition that there is no "pretext search" or "pretext seizure" doctrine in Fourth Amendment law — that the legality of a search or seizure does not depend on why the officer carried it out. The defense argued that this proposition creates an enormous potential for discrimination — that it leaves the police free to engage in racial profiling, stopping black motorists under circumstances where they would not stop whites. The Court responded, in effect, by saying that this is a problem for equal protection doctrine, not for the Fourth Amendment.

In evaluating this conclusion, you might consider what equal protection doctrine requires in this setting. In order to make out an equal protection claim, a defendant would have to show that the police intentionally discriminated against him based on a protected characteristic like race. How would the defendant go about making that showing? Successful equal protection claims against the police are extremely rare. Is that surprising?

6. For a rare example of a successful equal protection challenge to a police intervention — in a case that did not involve any allegations of race discrimination — see People v. Kail, 501 N.E.2d 969 (Ill. App. 1986). Kail was a suspected prostitute; she was arrested not for prostitution but for violating an obscure local ordinance requiring all bicycles to be equipped with bells. The arrest stemmed from a police-department policy requiring strict enforcement of all laws against

suspected prostitutes. (The arresting officer testified that she had seen hundreds if not thousands of bicycles without bells during her career, but had never arrested anyone before for that offense.) Kail eventually was convicted of a drug offense when a post-arrest inventory search turned up a small quantity of marijuana. The Illinois Court of Appeals reversed, finding — even under a "rational basis" approach (since suspected prostitutes are not a "suspect class") — that the arrest was a violation of equal protection:

> While the State has broad discretion to enforce its laws, that discretion may not be exercised on the basis of an arbitrary classification. . . . Where heightened scrutiny is inappropriate, the challenged State action is presumed to be valid and will be sustained where the classification is rationally related to a legitimate State interest. . . .
>
> While we recognize the State's right to legislate and enforce laws designed to combat prostitution, the law before us is of a different character. The purpose of the ordinance requiring a bell on a bicycle clearly does not envision the eradication of prostitution. There is no conceivable set of facts which would establish a rational relationship between the class of suspected prostitutes and the State's legitimate interest in enforcing the ordinance requiring bells on bicycles. . . . To suggest that the requirement of a bell on one's bicycle should be enforced only against suspected prostitutes because it helps combat prostitution is clearly so attenuated as to render the classification arbitrary or irrational.

The dissent in *Kail* argued that the majority's position would bar, for example, prosecuting Al Capone for tax evasion, since the government was primarily interested in other, unrelated offenses Capone had allegedly committed. Is that right? It bears noting that there is a long legal tradition of permitting pretextual prosecutions like the one in the Capone case — prosecutions for crimes other than the ones that attracted the government's interest. Should the standards for pretextual searches and seizures by police be the same?

7. It is often said that when police rely on race or ethnicity as part of a description provided by a victim or witness, profiling is not at issue and few questions arise about the propriety of police conduct. But consider the following discussion of Brown v. City of Oneonta, 221 F.3d 329 (2d Cir.), reh'g en banc denied, 235 F.3d 769 (2d Cir. 2000):

> Another controversial investigation with racial overtones began at 2 a.m. on September 4, 1992, in the small town of Oneonta, New York, when someone broke into the house of a seventy-seven year old woman, attacked her, and fled, all under cover of darkness. The victim described the assailant as a young black man with a knife, and told the police that he had cut his hand. Over the next several days the police located every black male student in the local college, questioned them, and inspected their hands for cuts. They then did the same for every other nonwhite man they could find, and at least one nonwhite woman — over 200 people in all. Their objective, according to the investigator in charge, was "to examine the hands of all the black people in the community."
>
> The Second Circuit held that those stopped and questioned in Oneonta had no cause of action under the Equal Protection Clause because the police were acting on the victim's racial description rather than their own racial stereotypes or preferences. For the same reasons, we would not classify this as a case of racial profiling. But the incident is disturbing all the same . . . : The police conducted an aggressive investigation, stopping and questioning hundreds of innocent people,

with some unpleasantness along the way; they did so on the basis of extremely limited information; they were responding to a serious crime, but not an emergency. The police were criticized for doing something they would never have done if the criminal had been white. . . . [A]nd it is hard to believe that the police would have considered treating the white residents of Oneonta in this humiliating manner in an attempt to solve a single burglary and assault, even if it were feasible. What is most striking from our point of view is that the problem with the Oneonta investigation was not its racial specificity but the number of innocent people affected, and the manner in which they were treated. If the police had stopped and questioned black men only but had confined themselves to those few who were in the vicinity near the time of the crime, or if they had asked the neighbors if they had seen any black men in the area, no one would have blinked.

Gross and Livingston, supra, at 1435-1436. In discussing the use of case-specific information about the race or ethnicity of a suspect, Gross and Livingston assert the following: "If reliable witnesses report that they saw a white man running from the scene of a murder and going into a bar in which there are only three white men, the police have enough information to detain all three — 'reasonable suspicion' — and they might have probable cause to arrest them as well." Id. at 1428. Do you agree? How is this hypothetical different from *Oneonta*?

8. Police discrimination in traffic stops has received a good deal of attention recently, with frequent claims that police are much more likely to stop black motorists than white ones. See, e.g., David A. Harris, The Stories, the Statistics, and the Law: Why "Driving While Black" Matters, 84 Minn. L. Rev. 265 (1999); Wesley MacNeil Oliver, With an Evil Eye and an Unequal Hand: Pretextual Stops and Doctrinal Remedies to Racial Profiling, 74 Tul. L. Rev. 1409 (2000). Those claims find support in work by John L. Lamberth, a psychology professor at Temple University. A government report summarizes Lamberth's findings as follows:

> An analysis . . . of motorists traveling along a segment of the New Jersey Turnpike found the following: (1) 14 percent of the cars traveling the roadway had an African American driver or other occupant; (2) 15 percent of cars exceeding the speed limit by at least 6 miles per hour had an African American driver or other occupant; (3) of stops where race was noted by police, 44 percent of the individuals in one section of the roadway and 35 percent of the individuals in this section and a larger section combined were African American. Lamberth also reported that 98 percent of all drivers violated the speed limit by at least 6 miles per hour. . . .
>
> In a similar analysis of motorists traveling along a segment of Interstate 95 in northeastern Maryland, Lamberth found the following: (1) 17 percent of the cars had an African American driver; (2) 18 percent of cars exceeding the speed limit by at least 1 mile per hour or violating another traffic law had an African American driver; (3) 29 percent of the motorists stopped by the Maryland State Police were African American. This study also found that 92 percent of all motorists were violating the speeding law, [and] 2 percent were violating another traffic law. . . .

United States General Accounting Office, Racial Profiling: Limited Data Available on Motorists Stops 8-9 (Mar. 2000) (footnotes omitted). As the GAO report noted, the data do not indicate the racial breakdown of drivers who violate the speed limit by a large margin. Id. at 1 & n. 1. Still, the percentages cited above do suggest discrimination by the New Jersey and Maryland state police, and it is widely believed that similar patterns exist in many other states.

Assume the suggestion is accurate. How might a different result in *Whren* affect that state of affairs? Could a court find that any stop of a motorist going only six miles per hour over the speed limit on the New Jersey Turnpike is constitutionally unreasonable, since 98 percent of the drivers go at least that fast? If so, presumably the court would have to determine what speed is fast enough to justify a stop. How would that determination be made? Is it feasible for courts to be in the business of defining traffic rules?

Another possible means of redressing the kind of discrimination suggested by Lamberth's work would involve the exclusionary rule. The Supreme Court has steadfastly avoided using Fourth Amendment exclusion prophylactically — excluding evidence even when the police behaved properly in order to give the police the right incentives. Might such an approach make sense in the *Whren* context? Suppose the law required suppression of any evidence of non-traffic offenses found during the course of a traffic stop. Would that requirement reduce the racial disparity in traffic stops? Would it be a wise use of the exclusionary rule?

9. Now consider the following argument:

> The strategic brilliance of the campaign against racial profiling is that it reduces complex issues of race, policing, and the drug war to the simple and arresting image of the irrational and racially discriminatory investigation of innocent, middle-class people. But the appeal of the means should not seduce us into mistaking it for the end.

R. Richard Banks, Beyond Profiling: Race, Policing, and the Drug War, 56 Stan. L. Rev. 571, 602 (2003). Professor Banks argues that "efforts to prove racial profiling will founder on empirical findings that invite contrary interpretations." He notes that the elimination of racial profiling might not solve many problems commonly associated with the practice: "Such problems may persist in the absence of racial profiling or be remedied without eliminating racial profiling." He also warns that remedial efforts may be "futile or counterproductive":

> [N]o simple prohibition of racial profiling will suffice. If racial profiling helps officers to apprehend drug traffickers, then officers will have a powerful incentive to use racial profiling, no matter what the rules say. . . . Indeed, recent findings from New Jersey and Maryland, jurisdictions that have sought to end racial profiling, are consistent with its continued use by state troopers.
>
> In any event, the absence of proof of racial profiling by individual officers or against individual citizens precludes individualized remedies. Remedies must take the form of broad prophylactic measures, such as monitoring, or the elimination of discretionary actions. . . . Although such reforms will narrow the opportunities for racial profiling, they may also prompt officers to conceal their racial profiling. Moreover, limitations on officer discretion might influence the behavior of other actors within the criminal justice system. Because the discretion that enables racial profiling is also integral to effective law enforcement, remedies that constrain discretion should be evaluated based on the full scope of their consequences, not simply whether they would diminish racial profiling.

Id. at 588-589. Banks argues that given these problems, "policymakers should abandon efforts to ferret out and eliminate racial profiling in drug interdiction," and should focus instead on race-related consequences of the drug war, regardless of whether these consequences flow from profiling:

> Analyses should fully assess the consequences of the drug war, prominent among them the astoundingly high level of incarceration of disadvantaged racial minorities. Analyses of policing practices more generally should confront law enforcement officers' mistreatment of racial minorities and minorities' distrust of the criminal justice system and their perception of injustice. Reform should aim to generate effective and practical solutions. . . .
>
> My primary purpose . . . [is] to counter the tendency to reduce questions of race, policing, and the drug war to questions of racial profiling. However politically appealing that approach, it may obscure rather than clarify potential remedies for problems that deserve immediate attention.

Id. at 602-603. Is Banks' analysis sound? Is it consistent with the Court's decision in *Whren*? Might the national debate about profiling be a distraction from more important criminal justice issues?

NOTES ON POLICE DISCRETION AND SUBSTANTIVE CRIMINAL LAW

1. *Whren* rules out regulating police use of profiles by banning police use of pretexts. And the practical obstacles of proving impermissible police motives rule out the Equal Protection Clause as a viable regulatory tool. The chief alternative is to limit the criminal prohibitions that give police officers their discretionary power.

That means limiting the range of "public order" offenses that provide a large portion of that discretionary power: loitering laws, curfews, anti-noise ordinances, anti-"cruising" ordinances, anti-gang laws, and the like. In the 1960s and 1970s, an older generation of such laws — chiefly loitering and vagrancy statutes — were widely held to be unconstitutionally vague; the leading case was Papachristou v. Jacksonville, 405 U.S. 156 (1972). But public order offenses made a comeback in the 1980s and 1990s, partly due to an argument by social scientists James Q. Wilson and George L. Kelling. See Broken Windows, Atlantic Monthly, Mar. 1982, at 29. Wilson and Kelling maintained that public disorder — they used broken windows that go unrepaired as an example; hence their article's title — signals law-abiding citizens to steer clear of the streets, which in turn promotes more disorder, signaling would-be criminals that the streets are safe for criminal enterprises. Police intervention to address disorder, they suggested, might be critically important to enhance citizens' quality of life in public places and to shore up the sense of security in neighborhoods under threat. For a more detailed exposition of the argument, see George L. Kelling & Catherine M. Coles, Fixing Broken Windows (1996).

The "broken windows" thesis was implemented, at least to some degree, in New York and in some other large cities. With some success: most famously, a crackdown on subway vandalism and turnstile jumping in the New York City subway system led to a sharp drop in other, more serious crime in the subways. That success has been disputed; some scholars have claimed that the data do not support the "broken windows" thesis. For the leading argument, see Bernard

Harcourt, Illusion of Order: The False Promise of Broken Windows Policing (2001). Nevertheless, a large fraction of police agencies have adopted the principle that enforcing *minor* crimes is a useful way to reduce the incidence of *major* crimes. And major crimes are down by more than 40 percent since 1991. See Federal Bureau of Investigation, U.S. Dep't of Justice, Uniform Crime Reports: Crime in the United States — 2002 (available at *http://www.fbi.gov/ucr*).

2. Even if the particulars of the "broken windows" thesis are wrong, it is possible that the courts, and the Court, went too far in the many *Papachristou*-era decisions striking down criminal statutes and ordinances designed to help the police keep order on the streets. For an argument along these lines, see Robert C. Ellickson, Controlling Chronic Misconduct in City Spaces: Of Panhandlers, Skid Rows, and Public-Space Zoning, 105 Yale L.J. 1165, 1247-1248 (1996):

> Unchecked street misconduct creates an ambience of unease, and for some, of menace. Pedestrians can sense that even minor disorder in public spaces tends to encourage more severe crime. City dwellers who perceive that their streets are out of control are apt to take defensive measures. They may use sidewalks and parks less, or favor architectural designs that discourage leisurely stays in public spaces. In particular, they may relocate to more inviting locales. . . .
>
> Since about 1965, federal constitutional decisions have limited the power of cities to control panhandling, bench squatting, public drunkenness, and other minor street nuisances. By allowing the denizens of Skid Rows to spend more time in the central business district, these decisions contributed to the demise of Skid Rows. These constitutional rulings, in combination with the attenuation of informal social controls and the increase in the size of the urban underclass, also made American downtowns much more disorderly. . . .

Elsewhere in his article, Ellickson argues that cities should be able to authorize their police to enforce different standards of street behavior in different parts of town — to keep downtown business districts free of panhandlers and bench squatters, while allowing freer rein to such behavior in "skid row"-type areas.

3. Partly out of a desire to expand police authority on the street, a number of legislatures have passed identification statutes. The Supreme Court addressed the constitutionality of one such statute in Hiibel v. Sixth Judicial District Court of Nevada, 124 S. Ct. 2451 (2004). The sheriff's department in Humboldt County, Nevada received a telephone call in which the caller reported seeing a man assault a woman in a red and silver GMC truck on Grass Valley Road. A deputy sheriff arrived to find the truck parked on the side of the road with a man standing next to it and a young woman sitting inside. The officer observed skid marks in the gravel behind the vehicle, leading him to believe the truck had come to a sudden stop.

The officer approached the man, who appeared to be intoxicated, and asked him if he had any identification. The man refused to identify himself and became agitated. After repeated requests for identification and repeated refusals, the man began to taunt the officer by putting his hands behind his back and daring the officer to arrest him. After a final warning that he would be arrested if he continued to refuse to comply, the officer placed the man, subsequently identified as Hiibel, under arrest. Hiibel was charged with obstructing the officer in discharging his duties by refusing to comply with Nevada's "stop and identify" statute. Hiibel argued that arresting someone for refusing to give his name violated the Fourth Amendment. The Court disagreed:

> [T]he Fourth Amendment does not impose obligations on the citizen but instead provides rights against the government. As a result, the Fourth Amendment itself cannot require a suspect to answer questions. This case concerns a different issue, however. Here, the source of the legal obligation arises from Nevada state law, not the Fourth Amendment. . . .
>
> The principles of *Terry* permit a State to require a suspect to disclose his name in the course of a *Terry* stop. The reasonableness of a seizure under the Fourth Amendment is determined "by balancing its intrusion on the individual's Fourth Amendment interests against its promotion of legitimate government interests." Delaware v. Prouse, 440 U.S. 648, 654 (1979). The Nevada statute satisfies that standard. The request for identity has an immediate relation to the purpose, rationale, and practical demands of a *Terry* stop. . . . [T]he Nevada statute does not alter the nature of the stop itself: it does not change its duration, or its location. A state law requiring a suspect to disclose his name in the course of a valid *Terry* stop is consistent with Fourth Amendment prohibitions against unreasonable searches and seizures.
>
> Petitioner argues that the Nevada statute circumvents the probable cause requirement, in effect allowing an officer to arrest a person for being suspicious. According to petitioner, this creates a risk of arbitrary police conduct that the Fourth Amendment does not permit. . . . Petitioner's concerns are met by the requirement that a *Terry* stop must be justified at its inception and "reasonably related in scope to the circumstances which justified" the initial stop. 392 U.S., at 20. . . . It is clear in this case that the request for identification was "reasonably related in scope to the circumstances which justified" the stop. The officer's request was a commonsense inquiry, not an effort to obtain an arrest for failure to identify after a *Terry* stop yielded insufficient evidence. . . .

Id. at 2459-2460. Notice that the deputy sheriff clearly had reasonable suspicion to stop Hiibel in connection with the reported assault. The statutory obligation to identify himself did not arise until Hiibel was already suspected of criminal activity.

That is the primary difference between *Hiibel* and the Court's previous stop-and-identify cases: in those earlier decisions, the legality of the stop rested on the identification requirement. So, in Brown v. Texas, 443 U.S. 47 (1979), the Court invalidated a conviction for violating a Texas stop and identify statute on Fourth Amendment grounds—ruling that the initial stop was not based on reasonable suspicion and that absent that factual basis for detaining the defendant, the risk of arbitrary and abusive police practices was too great. (In *Brown*, one of the arresting officers explained the stop by saying that "we had never seen that subject in that area before.") Kolender v. Lawson, 461 U.S. 352 (1983), was a civil suit brought by Edward Lawson, an African American man who liked to take late-night walks in San Diego neighborhoods and who was arrested some 15 times, evidently because he looked out of place to the local police. The Court held that the California law requiring a suspect to give an officer "credible and reliable" identification when asked to identify himself was void for vagueness. In light of *Brown* and *Kolender*, *Hiibel* appears to be no more than a modest extension, perhaps even a straightforward application, of *Terry*.

4. Or perhaps *Hiibel* is about the change in climate that the terrorist attacks of September 11 produced. Since those attacks, there has been an ongoing public debate about the merits of a mandatory national identification card, which all Americans would be required to carry when in public. Would such a requirement,

coupled with a requirement that the card be produced whenever a police officer had reasonable suspicion to justify a stop, violate the Fourth Amendment? Presumably not, after *Hiibel*. Now imagine a federal statute requiring that individuals produce their identity cards whenever a federal agent (but only a federal agent) requests. Would that statute violate the Fourth Amendment? Would your answer change if the federal government defended the statute as a necessary tool in the war on terrorism?

5. As "public order" offenses have proliferated, legislatures have sought to cure the constitutional defects that caused courts to strike down loitering laws in earlier decades. And police departments have sought to use these newer, more targeted loitering laws to attack urban gangs. The next case involves the intersection of these two trends.

CHICAGO v. MORALES

Certiorari to the Supreme Court of Illinois
527 U.S. 41 (1999)

JUSTICE STEVENS announced the judgment of the Court and delivered the opinion of the Court with respect to Parts I, II, and V, and an opinion with respect to Parts III, IV, and VI, in which JUSTICE SOUTER and JUSTICE GINSBURG join.

In 1992, the Chicago City Council enacted the Gang Congregation Ordinance, which prohibits "criminal street gang members" from "loitering" with one another or with other persons in any public place. The question presented is whether the Supreme Court of Illinois correctly held that the ordinance violates the Due Process Clause of the Fourteenth Amendment to the Federal Constitution.

I

... The ordinance creates a criminal offense punishable by a fine of up to $500, imprisonment for not more than six months, and a requirement to perform up to 120 hours of community service. Commission of the offense involves four predicates. First, the police officer must reasonably believe that at least one of the two or more persons present in a "public place" is a "criminal street gang member." Second, the persons must be "loitering," which the ordinance defines as "remaining in any one place with no apparent purpose." Third, the officer must then order "all" of the persons to disperse and remove themselves "from the area." Fourth, a person must disobey the officer's order. If any person, whether a gang member or not, disobeys the officer's order, that person is guilty of violating the ordinance.[2]

---

2. The ordinance states in pertinent part:

"(a) Whenever a police officer observes a person whom he reasonably believes to be a criminal street gang member loitering in any public place with one or more other persons, he shall order all such persons to disperse and remove themselves from the area. Any person who does not promptly obey such an order is in violation of this section.

"(b) It shall be an affirmative defense to an alleged violation of this section that no person who was observed loitering was in fact a member of a criminal street gang.

"(c) As used in this Section:

"(1) 'Loiter' means to remain in any one place with no apparent purpose.

"(2) 'Criminal street gang' means any ongoing organization, association in fact or group of three or more persons, whether formal or informal, having as one of its substantial activities the commission of one or more of the criminal acts enumerated in paragraph (3), and whose

Two months after the ordinance was adopted, the Chicago Police Department promulgated General Order 92-4 to provide guidelines to govern its enforcement. That order purported to establish limitations on the enforcement discretion of police officers "to ensure that the anti-gang loitering ordinance is not enforced in an arbitrary or discriminatory way." Chicago Police Department, General Order 92-4. The limitations confine the authority to arrest gang members who violate the ordinance to sworn "members of the Gang Crime Section" and certain other designated officers, and establish detailed criteria for defining street gangs and membership in such gangs. In addition, the order directs district commanders to "designate areas in which the presence of gang members has a demonstrable effect on the activities of law abiding persons in the surrounding community," and provides that the ordinance "will be enforced only within the designated areas." The city, however, does not release the locations of these "designated areas" to the public.

II

During the three years of its enforcement, the police issued over 89,000 dispersal orders and arrested over 42,000 people for violating the ordinance. In the ensuing enforcement proceedings, 2 trial judges upheld the constitutionality of the ordinance, but 11 others ruled that it was invalid. In respondent Youkhana's case, the trial judge held that the "ordinance fails to notify individuals what conduct is prohibited, and it encourages arbitrary and capricious enforcement by police."

The Illinois Appellate Court affirmed the trial court's ruling in the *Youkhana* case, consolidated and affirmed other pending appeals in accordance with *Youkhana*, and reversed the convictions of respondents Gutierrez, Morales, and others. . . .

The Illinois Supreme Court affirmed. . . .

We granted certiorari, and now affirm. Like the Illinois Supreme Court, we conclude that the ordinance enacted by the city of Chicago is unconstitutionally vague.

III

The basic factual predicate for the city's ordinance is not in dispute. As the city argues in its brief, "the very presence of a large collection of obviously brazen, insistent, and lawless gang members and hangers-on on the public ways intimidates residents, who become afraid even to leave their homes and go about their business. That, in turn, imperils community residents' sense of safety and security, detracts from property values, and can ultimately destabilize entire neighborhoods." The findings in the ordinance explain that it was motivated by these

---

members individually or collectively engage in or have engaged in a pattern of criminal gang activity. . . .

"(5) 'Public place' means the public way and any other location open to the public, whether publicly or privately owned. . . .

"(e) Any person who violates this Section is subject to a fine of not less than $100 and not more than $500 for each offense, or imprisonment for not more than six months, or both.

"In addition to or instead of the above penalties, any person who violates this section may be required to perform up to 120 hours of community service pursuant to section 1-4-120 of this Code." Chicago Municipal Code §8-4-015 (added June 17, 1992).

concerns. We have no doubt that a law that directly prohibited such intimidating conduct would be constitutional,[17] but this ordinance broadly covers a significant amount of additional activity. Uncertainty about the scope of that additional coverage provides the basis for respondents' claim that the ordinance is too vague. . . .

. . . [T]he freedom to loiter for innocent purposes is part of the "liberty" protected by the Due Process Clause of the Fourteenth Amendment. We have expressly identified this "right to remove from one place to another according to inclination" as "an attribute of personal liberty" protected by the Constitution. Williams v. Fears, 179 U.S. 270, 274 (1900); see also Papachristou v. Jacksonville, 405 U.S. 156, 164 (1972). Indeed, it is apparent that an individual's decision to remain in a public place of his choice is as much a part of his liberty as the freedom of movement inside frontiers that is "a part of our heritage," Kent v. Dulles, 357 U.S. 116, 126 (1958), or the right to move "to whatsoever place one's own inclination may direct" identified in Blackstone's Commentaries. 1 W. Blackstone, Commentaries on the Laws of England 130 (1765).

There is no need, however, to decide whether the impact of the Chicago ordinance on constitutionally protected liberty alone would suffice to support a facial challenge under the overbreadth doctrine. For it is clear that the vagueness of this enactment makes a facial challenge appropriate. This is not an ordinance that "simply regulates business behavior and contains a scienter requirement." See Hoffman Estates v. Flipside, Hoffman Estates, Inc., 455 U.S. 489, 499 (1982). It is a criminal law that contains no mens rea requirement, and infringes on constitutionally protected rights. When vagueness permeates the text of such a law, it is subject to facial attack.

Vagueness may invalidate a criminal law for either of two independent reasons. First, it may fail to provide the kind of notice that will enable ordinary people to understand what conduct it prohibits; second, it may authorize and even encourage arbitrary and discriminatory enforcement. Accordingly, we first consider whether the ordinance provides fair notice to the citizen and then discuss its potential for arbitrary enforcement.

IV

. . . The Illinois Supreme Court recognized that the term "loiter" may have a common and accepted meaning, but the definition of that term in this ordinance — "to remain in any one place with no apparent purpose" — does not. It is difficult to imagine how any citizen of the city of Chicago standing in a public place with a group of people would know if he or she had an "apparent purpose." If she were talking to another person, would she have an apparent purpose? If she were frequently checking her watch and looking expectantly down the street, would she have an apparent purpose?

Since the city cannot conceivably have meant to criminalize each instance a citizen stands in public with a gang member, the vagueness that dooms this ordinance is not the product of uncertainty about the normal meaning of "loitering," but rather about what loitering is covered by the ordinance and what is not. . . .

17. In fact the city already has several laws that serve this purpose. See, e.g., Ill. Comp. Stat. ch. 720 §§5/12-6 (1998) (intimidation); 570/405.2 (streetgang criminal drug conspiracy); 147/1 et seq. (Illinois Streetgang Terrorism Omnibus Prevention Act); 5/25-1 (mob action). . . .

The city's principal response to this concern about adequate notice is that loiterers are not subject to sanction until after they have failed to comply with an officer's order to disperse. . . . We find this response unpersuasive for at least two reasons.

First, . . . [a]lthough it is true that a loiterer is not subject to criminal sanctions unless he or she disobeys a dispersal order, the loitering is the conduct that the ordinance is designed to prohibit. If the loitering is in fact harmless and innocent, the dispersal order itself is an unjustified impairment of liberty. . . . Because an officer may issue an order only after prohibited conduct has already occurred, it cannot provide the kind of advance notice that will protect the putative loiterer from being ordered to disperse. Such an order cannot retroactively give adequate warning of the boundary between the permissible and the impermissible applications of the law.

Second, the terms of the dispersal order compound the inadequacy of the notice afforded by the ordinance. It provides that the officer "shall order all such persons to disperse and remove themselves from the area." This vague phrasing raises a host of questions. After such an order issues, how long must the loiterers remain apart? How far must they move? If each loiterer walks around the block and they meet again at the same location, are they subject to arrest or merely to being ordered to disperse again? . . .

V

The broad sweep of the ordinance also violates "the requirement that a legislature establish minimal guidelines to govern law enforcement." Kolender v. Lawson, 461 U.S. at 358. There are no such guidelines in the ordinance. In any public place in the city of Chicago, persons who stand or sit in the company of a gang member may be ordered to disperse unless their purpose is apparent. . . . It matters not whether the reason that a gang member and his father, for example, might loiter near Wrigley Field is to rob an unsuspecting fan or just to get a glimpse of Sammy Sosa leaving the ballpark; in either event, if their purpose is not apparent to a nearby police officer, she may — indeed, she "shall" — order them to disperse.

Recognizing that the ordinance does reach a substantial amount of innocent conduct, we turn, then, to its language to determine if it "necessarily entrusts lawmaking to the moment-to-moment judgment of the policeman on his beat." Kolender v. Lawson, 461 U.S., at 359 (internal quotation marks omitted). As we discussed in the context of fair notice, the principal source of the vast discretion conferred on the police in this case is the definition of loitering as "to remain in any one place with no apparent purpose."

As the Illinois Supreme Court interprets that definition, it "provides absolute discretion to police officers to determine what activities constitute loitering." 177 Ill. 2d, at 457. We have no authority to construe the language of a state statute more narrowly than the construction given by that State's highest court. . . .

It is true, as the city argues, that the requirement that the officer reasonably believe that a group of loiterers contains a gang member does place a limit on the authority to order dispersal. That limitation would no doubt be sufficient if the ordinance only applied to loitering that had an apparently harmful purpose or effect, or possibly if it only applied to loitering by persons reasonably believed to be criminal gang members. But this ordinance . . . requires no harmful purpose and applies to non-gang members as well as suspected gang members. . . . Friends, relatives, teachers, counselors, or even total strangers might unwittingly engage in forbidden loitering if they happen to engage in idle conversation with a gang member . . .

Finally, in its opinion striking down the ordinance, the Illinois Supreme Court refused to accept the general order issued by the police department as a sufficient limitation on the "vast amount of discretion" granted to the police in its enforcement. We agree. That the police have adopted internal rules limiting their enforcement to certain designated areas in the city would not provide a defense to a loiterer who might be arrested elsewhere. Nor could a person who knowingly loitered with a well-known gang member anywhere in the city safely assume that they would not be ordered to disperse no matter how innocent and harmless their loitering might be.

VI

In our judgment, the Illinois Supreme Court correctly concluded that the ordinance does not provide sufficiently specific limits on the enforcement discretion of the police "to meet constitutional standards for definiteness and clarity." 177 Ill. 2d, at 459. . . .

JUSTICE O'CONNOR, with whom JUSTICE BREYER joins, concurring in part and concurring in the judgment. . . .

As it has been construed by the [Illinois Supreme Court], Chicago's gang loitering ordinance is unconstitutionally vague because it lacks sufficient minimal standards to guide law enforcement officers. In particular, it fails to provide police with any standard by which they can judge whether an individual has an "*apparent* purpose." Indeed, because any person standing on the street has a general "purpose" — even if it is simply to stand — the ordinance permits police officers to choose which purposes are *permissible*. . . .

This vagueness consideration alone provides a sufficient ground for affirming the Illinois court's decision, and I agree with Part V of the Court's opinion, which discusses this consideration. . . . Accordingly, there is no need to consider the other issues briefed by the parties and addressed by the plurality. I express no opinion about them.

It is important to courts and legislatures alike that we characterize more clearly the narrow scope of today's holding. . . . [T]here remain open to Chicago reasonable alternatives to combat the very real threat posed by gang intimidation and violence. For example, the Court properly and expressly distinguishes the ordinance from laws that require loiterers to have a "harmful purpose," from laws that target only gang members, and from laws that incorporate limits on the area and manner in which the laws may be enforced. . . .

In my view, the gang loitering ordinance could have been construed more narrowly. The term "loiter" might possibly be construed in a more limited fashion to mean "to remain in any one place with no apparent purpose other than to establish control over identifiable areas, to intimidate others from entering those areas, or to conceal illegal activities." Such a definition would be consistent with the Chicago City Council's findings and would avoid the vagueness problems of the ordinance as construed by the Illinois Supreme Court. . . .

The Illinois Supreme Court did not choose to give a limiting construction to Chicago's ordinance. . . . Accordingly, I join Parts I, II, and V of the Court's opinion and concur in the judgment.

JUSTICE KENNEDY, concurring in part and concurring in the judgment.

I join Parts I, II, and V of the Court's opinion and concur in the judgment.

I also share many of the concerns JUSTICE STEVENS expressed in Part IV. . . . As interpreted by the Illinois Supreme Court, the Chicago ordinance would reach a broad range of innocent conduct. For this reason it is not necessarily saved by the requirement that the citizen must disobey a police order to disperse before there is a violation.

We have not often examined these types of orders. It can be assumed, however, that some police commands will subject a citizen to prosecution for disobeying whether or not the citizen knows why the order is given. Illustrative examples include when the police tell a pedestrian not to enter a building and the reason is to avoid impeding a rescue team, or to protect a crime scene, or to secure an area for the protection of a public official. It does not follow, however, that any unexplained police order must be obeyed without notice of the lawfulness of the order. The predicate of an order to disperse is not, in my view, sufficient to eliminate doubts regarding the adequacy of notice under this ordinance. A citizen, while engaging in a wide array of innocent conduct, is not likely to know when he may be subject to a dispersal order based on the officer's own knowledge of the identity or affiliations of other persons with whom the citizen is congregating; nor may the citizen be able to assess what an officer might conceive to be the citizen's lack of an apparent purpose.

JUSTICE BREYER, concurring in part and concurring in the judgment.

. . . The law authorizes a police officer to order any person to remove himself from any "location open to the public, whether publicly or privately owned," Chicago Municipal Code §8-4-015(c)(5) (1992), i.e., any sidewalk, front stoop, public park, public square, lakeside promenade, hotel, restaurant, bowling alley, bar, barbershop, sports arena, shopping mall, etc., but with two, and only two, limitations: First, that person must be accompanied by (or must himself be) someone police reasonably believe is a gang member. Second, that person must have remained in that public place "with no apparent purpose." §8-4-015(c)(1).

The first limitation cannot save the ordinance. Though it limits the number of persons subject to the law, it leaves many individuals, gang members and nongang members alike, subject to its strictures. Nor does it limit in any way the range of conduct that police may prohibit. The second limitation is . . . not a limitation at all. Since one always has some apparent purpose, the so-called limitation invites, in fact requires, the policeman to interpret the words "no apparent purpose" as meaning "no apparent purpose except for. . . . " And it is in the ordinance's delegation to the policeman of open-ended discretion to fill in that blank that the problem lies. . . .

Nor does it violate "our rules governing facial challenges," (SCALIA, J., dissenting), to forbid the city to apply the unconstitutional ordinance in this case. The reason *why* the ordinance is invalid explains how that is so. As I have said,

I believe the ordinance violates the Constitution because it delegates too much discretion to a police officer to decide whom to order to move on, and in what circumstances. . . . The ordinance is unconstitutional, not because a policeman applied this discretion wisely or poorly in a particular case, but rather because the policeman enjoys too much discretion in *every* case. . . . The city of Chicago may be able validly to apply some *other* law to the defendants in light of their conduct. But the city of Chicago may no more apply *this* law to the defendants, no matter how they behaved, than it could apply an (imaginary) statute that said, "It is a crime to do wrong," even to the worst of murderers. . . .

JUSTICE SCALIA, dissenting.

The citizens of Chicago were once free to drive about the city at whatever speed they wished. At some point Chicagoans (or perhaps Illinoisans) decided this would not do, and imposed prophylactic speed limits designed to assure safe operation by the average (or perhaps even subaverage) driver with the average (or perhaps even subaverage) vehicle. This infringed upon the "freedom" of all citizens, but was not unconstitutional.

Similarly, the citizens of Chicago were once free to stand around and gawk at the scene of an accident. At some point Chicagoans discovered that this obstructed traffic and caused more accidents. They did not make the practice unlawful, but they did authorize police officers to order the crowd to disperse, and imposed penalties for refusal to obey such an order. Again, this prophylactic measure infringed upon the "freedom" of all citizens, but was not unconstitutional.

Until the ordinance that is before us today was adopted, the citizens of Chicago were free to stand about in public places with no apparent purpose — to engage, that is, in conduct that appeared to be loitering. In recent years, however, the city has been afflicted with criminal street gangs. . . . Many residents of the inner city felt that they were prisoners in their own homes. Once again, Chicagoans decided that to eliminate the problem it was worth restricting some of the freedom that they once enjoyed. The means they took was similar to the second, and more mild, example given above rather than the first: Loitering was not made unlawful, but when a group of people occupied a public place without an apparent purpose and in the company of a known gang member, police officers were authorized to order them to disperse, and the failure to obey such an order was made unlawful. The minor limitation upon the free state of nature that this prophylactic arrangement imposed upon all Chicagoans seemed to them (and it seems to me) a small price to pay for liberation of their streets. . . .

Respondents' consolidated appeal presents a facial challenge to the Chicago ordinance on vagueness grounds. When a facial challenge is successful, the law in question is declared to be unenforceable in *all* its applications, and not just in its particular application to the party in suit. . . .

. . . When our normal criteria for facial challenges are applied, it is clear that the Justices in the majority have transposed the burden of proof. Instead of requiring the respondents, who are challenging the ordinance, to show that it is invalid in all its applications, they have required the petitioner to show that it is valid in all its applications. . . .

The plurality's explanation for its departure from the usual rule governing facial challenges is seemingly contained in the following statement: "[This] is a criminal law that . . . infringes on constitutionally protected rights . . . When vagueness permeates the text of *such* a law, it is subject to facial attack." (emphasis added) . . .

. . . I turn first to the support for the proposition that there is a constitutionally protected right to loiter — or, as the plurality more favorably describes it, for a person to "remain in a public place of his choice." The plurality thinks much of this Fundamental Freedom to Loiter, which it contrasts with such lesser, constitutionally *un*protected, activities as doing (ugh!) *business*: "This is not an ordinance that simply regulates business behavior and contains a scienter requirement. . . . It is a criminal law that contains no mens rea requirement . . . and infringes on constitutionally protected rights." Ante, at 55 (internal quotation marks omitted). . . .

Of course every activity, even scratching one's head, can be called a "constitutional right" if one means by that term nothing more than the fact that the activity is covered (as all are) by the Equal Protection Clause, so that those who engage in it cannot be singled out without "rational basis." But using the term in that sense utterly impoverishes our constitutional discourse. We would then need a new term for those activities — such as political speech or religious worship — that cannot be forbidden even *with* rational basis.

The plurality tosses around the term "constitutional right" in this renegade sense, because there is not the slightest evidence for the existence of a genuine constitutional right to loiter. JUSTICE THOMAS recounts the vast historical tradition of criminalizing the activity. It is simply not maintainable that the right to loiter would have been regarded as an essential attribute of liberty at the time of the framing or at the time of adoption of the Fourteenth Amendment. . . .

It would be unfair, however, to criticize the plurality's failed attempt to establish that loitering is a constitutionally protected right while saying nothing of the concurrences. The plurality at least makes an attempt. The concurrences, on the other hand, make no pretense at attaching their broad "vagueness invalidates" rule to a liberty interest. As far as appears from JUSTICE O'CONNOR's and JUSTICE BREYER's opinions, *no* police officer may issue *any* order, affecting *any* insignificant sort of citizen conduct (except, perhaps, an order addressed to the unprotected class of "gang members") unless the standards for the issuance of that order are precise. No modern urban society — and probably none since London got big enough to have sewers — could function under such a rule. There are innumerable reasons why it may be important for a constable to tell a pedestrian to "move on" — and even if it were possible to list in an ordinance all of the reasons that are known, many are simply unpredictable. Hence the (entirely reasonable) Rule of the City of New York which reads: "No person shall fail, neglect or refuse to comply with the lawful direction or command of any Police Officer, Urban Park Ranger, Parks Enforcement Patrol Officer or other [Parks and Recreation] Department employee, indicated verbally, by gesture or otherwise." 56 RCNY §1-03(c)(1) (1996). . . . [T]o say that such a general ordinance permitting "lawful orders" is void *in all its applications* demands more than a safe and orderly society can reasonably deliver. . . .

Finally, I address the . . . proposition that the ordinance is vague. It is not. . . . A law is unconstitutionally vague if its lack of definitive standards either (1) fails to apprise persons of ordinary intelligence of the prohibited conduct, or (2) encourages arbitrary and discriminatory enforcement.

The plurality relies primarily upon the first of these aspects. Since, it reasons, "the loitering is the conduct that the ordinance is designed to prohibit," and "an officer may issue an order only after prohibited conduct has already occurred," the order to disperse cannot itself serve "to apprise persons of ordinary intelligence of the prohibited conduct." What counts for purposes of vagueness analysis, however, is not what the ordinance is "designed to prohibit," but what it actually subjects to criminal penalty. [T]hat consists of nothing but the refusal to obey a dispersal order, as to which there is no doubt of adequate notice of the prohibited conduct. The plurality's suggestion that even the dispersal order *itself* is unconstitutionally vague, because it does not specify *how far to disperse (!)*, scarcely requires a response. . . .

For its determination of unconstitutional vagueness, the Court relies secondarily — and JUSTICE O'CONNOR's and JUSTICE BREYER's concurrences exclusively — upon the second aspect of that doctrine, which requires sufficient specificity to prevent arbitrary and discriminatory law enforcement. . . .

The criteria for issuance of a dispersal order under the Chicago ordinance could hardly be clearer. First, the law requires police officers to "reasonably believe" that one of the group to which the order is issued is a "criminal street gang member." This resembles a probable-cause standard, and the Chicago Police Department's General Order 92-4 (1992) — promulgated to govern enforcement of the ordinance — makes the probable cause requirement explicit. Under the Order, officers must have probable cause to believe that an individual is a member of a criminal street gang, to be substantiated by the officer's "experience and knowledge of the alleged offenders" and by "specific, documented and reliable information" such as reliable witness testimony or an individual's admission of gang membership or display of distinctive colors, tattoos, signs, or other markings worn by members of particular criminal street gangs.

Second, the ordinance requires that the group be "remaining in one place with no apparent purpose." JUSTICE O'CONNOR's assertion that this applies to "any person standing in a public place," is a distortion. The ordinance does not apply to "standing," but to "remain[ing]" — a term which in this context obviously means "[to] endure or persist," see American Heritage Dictionary 1525 (1992). There may be some ambiguity at the margin, but "remain[ing] in one place" requires more than a temporary stop, and is clear in most of its applications, including all of those represented by the facts surrounding the respondents' arrests. . . .

As for the phrase "with no apparent purpose": JUSTICE O'CONNOR again distorts this adjectival phrase, by separating it from the word that it modifies. "Any person standing on the street," her concurrence says, "has a general 'purpose' — even if it is simply to stand," and thus "the ordinance permits police officers to choose which purposes are *permissible*." But Chicago police officers enforcing the ordinance are not looking for people with no apparent purpose (who are regrettably in oversupply); they are looking for people who "remain in any one place with no apparent purpose" — that is, who remain there without any apparent reason *for remaining there*. That is not difficult to perceive. . . .

The plurality points out that Chicago already has several laws that reach the intimidating and unlawful gang-related conduct the ordinance was directed at. The problem, of course, well recognized by Chicago's city council, is that the gang members cease their intimidating and unlawful behavior under the watchful eye of police officers, but return to it as soon as the police drive away. The only solution, the council concluded, was to clear the streets of congregations of gangs, their drug customers, and their associates. . . .

. . . The citizens of Chicago have decided that depriving themselves of the freedom to "hang out" with a gang member is necessary to eliminate pervasive gang crime and intimidation — and that the elimination of the one is worth the deprivation of the other. This Court has no business second-guessing either the degree of necessity or the fairness of the trade. . . .

JUSTICE THOMAS, with whom THE CHIEF JUSTICE and JUSTICE SCALIA join, dissenting. . . .

The human costs exacted by criminal street gangs are inestimable. In many of our Nation's cities, gangs have "[v]irtually overtak[en] certain neighborhoods, contributing to the economic and social decline of these areas and causing fear and lifestyle changes among law-abiding residents." U.S. Dept. of Justice, Office of Justice Programs, Bureau of Justice Assistance, Monograph: Urban Street Gang Enforcement 3 (1997). . . .

The city of Chicago has suffered the devastation wrought by this national tragedy. Last year, in an effort to curb plummeting attendance, the Chicago Public Schools hired dozens of adults to escort children to school. The youngsters had become too terrified of gang violence to leave their homes alone. Martinez, Parents Paid to Walk Line Between Gangs and School, Chicago Tribune, Jan. 21, 1998, p. 1. The children's fears were not unfounded. In 1996, the Chicago Police Department estimated that there were 132 criminal street gangs in the city. Illinois Criminal Justice Information Authority, Research Bulletin: Street Gangs and Crime 4 (Sept. 1996). Between 1987 and 1994, these gangs were involved in 63,141 criminal incidents, including 21,689 nonlethal violent crimes and 894 homicides. Id. at 4-5. Many of these criminal incidents and homicides result from gang "turf battles," which take place on the public streets and place innocent residents in grave danger.

Before enacting its ordinance, the Chicago City Council held extensive hearings on the problems of gang loitering. Concerned citizens appeared to testify poignantly as to how gangs disrupt their daily lives. Ordinary citizens like Ms. D'Ivory Gordon explained that she struggled just to walk to work:

> "When I walk out my door, these guys are out there. . . .
> "They watch you. . . . They know where you live. They know what time you leave, what time you come home. I am afraid of them. I have even come to the point now that I carry a meat cleaver to work with me . . .
> " . . . I don't want to hurt anyone, and I don't want to be hurt. We need to clean these corners up. Clean these communities up and take it back from them." Transcript of Proceedings before the City Council of Chicago, Committee on Police and Fire 66-67 (May 15, 1992).

Eighty-eight-year-old Susan Mary Jackson echoed her sentiments, testifying, "We used to have a nice neighborhood. We don't have it anymore. . . . I am scared to go out in the daytime. . . . You can't pass because they are standing. I am afraid to go to the store. I don't go to the store because I am afraid. . . . " Id., at 93-95. . . .

Following these hearings, the council found that "criminal street gangs establish control over identifiable areas . . . by loitering in those areas and intimidating others from entering those areas." App. to Pet. for Cert. 60a-61a. It further found that the mere presence of gang members "intimidate[s] many law abiding citizens" and "creates a justifiable fear for the safety of persons and property in the arca." It is the product of this democratic process—the council's attempt to address these social ills—that we are asked to pass judgment upon today.

. . . The [Chicago] ordinance does nothing more than confirm the well-established principle that the police have the duty and the power to maintain the public peace, and, when necessary, to disperse groups of individuals who threaten it. The plurality, however, concludes that the city's commonsense effort to combat gang loitering fails constitutional scrutiny for two separate reasons— because it infringes upon gang members' constitutional right to "loiter for innocent purposes," and because it is vague on its face. A majority of the Court endorses the latter conclusion. I respectfully disagree. . . .

The plurality's sweeping conclusion that this ordinance infringes upon a liberty interest protected by the Fourteenth Amendment's Due Process Clause withers when exposed to the relevant history: Laws prohibiting loitering and vagrancy have been a fixture of Anglo-American law at least since the time of the Norman Conquest. See generally C. Ribton-Turner, A History of Vagrants and Vagrancy and Beggars and Begging (reprint 1972) (discussing history of English vagrancy laws); see also Papachristou v. Jacksonville, 405 U.S. 156, 161-162 (1972) (recounting history of vagrancy laws). The American colonists enacted laws modeled upon the English vagrancy laws, and at the time of the founding, state and local governments customarily criminalized loitering and other forms of vagrancy. Vagrancy laws were common in the decades preceding the ratification of the Fourteenth Amendment, and remained on the books long after. . . .

The Court concludes that the ordinance is also unconstitutionally vague because it fails to provide adequate standards to guide police discretion and because, in the plurality's view, it does not give residents adequate notice of how to conform their conduct to the confines of the law. I disagree on both counts.

. . . Far from according officers too much discretion, the ordinance merely enables police officers to fulfill one of their traditional functions. Police officers are not, and have never been, simply enforcers of the criminal law. They wear other hats—importantly, they have long been vested with the responsibility for preserving the public peace. . . .

In their role as peace officers, the police long have had the authority and the duty to order groups of individuals who threaten the public peace to disperse. . . . The authority to issue dispersal orders continues to play a commonplace and crucial role in police operations, particularly in urban areas. . . .

In order to perform their peace-keeping responsibilities satisfactorily, the police inevitably must exercise discretion. . . . That is not to say that the law should not provide objective guidelines for the police, but simply that it cannot rigidly constrain their every action. By directing a police officer not to issue a dispersal order unless he "observes a person whom he reasonably believes to be a criminal street gang member loitering in any public place," Chicago's ordinance strikes an appropriate balance between those two extremes. Just as we trust officers to rely on their experience and expertise in order to make spur-of-the-moment determinations about amorphous legal standards such as "probable cause" and "reasonable suspicion," so we must trust them to determine whether a group of loiterers contains individuals (in this case members of criminal street gangs) whom the city has determined threaten the public peace. . . .

Today, the Court focuses extensively on the "rights" of gang members and their companions. It can safely do so — the people who will have to live with the consequences of today's opinion do not live in our neighborhoods. Rather, the people who will suffer from our lofty pronouncements are people like Ms. Susan Mary Jackson; people who have seen their neighborhoods literally destroyed by gangs and violence and drugs. They are good, decent people who must struggle to overcome their desperate situation, against all odds, in order to raise their families, earn a living, and remain good citizens. As one resident described, "There is only about maybe one or two percent of the people in the city causing these problems maybe, but it's keeping 98 percent of us in our houses and off the streets and afraid to shop." By focusing exclusively on the imagined "rights" of the two percent, the Court today has denied our most vulnerable citizens the very thing that JUSTICE STEVENS elevates above all else — the "freedom of movement." And that is a shame. I respectfully dissent.

NOTES AND QUESTIONS

1. *Morales* was litigated and decided as a due process case, not a Fourth Amendment case. But it raises issues that go to the heart of Fourth Amendment law: How much discretion should police have when dealing with suspects on the street? What is a proper basis for police intervention? Does the answer change if the intervention takes the form of an "order to disperse"?

2. Maybe it does, for reasons that build on Justice Thomas's dissent. Police, Justice Thomas notes, are not simply enforcers of criminal law; they also are keepers of public order. It follows that police must be able, in some settings, to search or seize people — to intrude on places in which people have a reasonable expectation of privacy, or to command people to leave places they are otherwise permitted to be — even when there is no suspicion of crime. We have already seen in our discussion of the "community caretaking" cases, see pages 468-470 supra, that police sometimes enter homes or other private places not expecting to find evidence of crime, but instead responding to illness, missing person reports, and the like. Justice Scalia offers us the example of a traffic accident with a crowd of onlookers. Surely, he says, the officer can order the onlookers to leave. Or, take Justice Kennedy's example of a police officer telling pedestrians not to enter a public building where a crime scene is being investigated. Such police commands are common, and it is commonly assumed that the commands are legitimate and must be obeyed.

These examples might suggest that police authority to "search" or "seize" does not always depend on suspicion of crime. Or, perhaps in hypotheticals like Justice Scalia's and Justice Kennedy's, no "seizure" has taken place: recall the discussion of "seizure" doctrine and public demonstrations at pages 408-409 supra. Do examples like these mean that *Morales* was wrongly decided?

3. The void-for-vagueness doctrine that was the basis for the majority's holding in *Morales* is designed, in large part, to address the potential for arbitrary and discriminatory enforcement by police. It thus constitutes one strategy for dealing with problems like racial profiling. In practice, though, the doctrine's scope is

rather narrow. For instance, it does not reach the *Whren*-type opportunity for arbitrariness in police enforcement—where police may employ commonly violated but relatively clear laws to pick and choose among the violators they will stop. See pages 597-603 supra. It also has limited application to broad but clear laws, such as juvenile curfews. As of 1995, 77 percent of American cities with populations of 200,000 or more had some form of juvenile curfew. See William Ruefle & Kenneth Mike Reynolds, Curfews and Delinquency in Major American Cities, 41 Crime & Delinq. 347, 353 (1995). These laws, however unambiguous, undoubtedly create at least the opportunity for police arbitrariness. Consider that the existence of a juvenile curfew in a locality in effect authorizes police during the hours of its operation to stop any person who looks young enough to fit within its prohibitions. That is a very large pool of potential targets of police attention.

The facial vagueness doctrine *does* apply to laws deemed to encourage arbitrary police conduct by virtue of their vagueness. But docs thc invalidation of vague laws really contribute to the reasonable use of discretion by local police? At least on its face, the General Order promulgated by the Chicago Police Department to regulate administration of the gang loitering law had several provisions that might be thought helpful to the restraint of police arbitrariness. Only specially trained officers who were knowledgeable about the gang problems in local neighborhoods were to enforce the law. The ordinance was only to be enforced in designated areas where gangs were prevalent. Officers were required to prepare written reports after each arrest describing, among other things, the circumstances giving rise to probable cause to arrest. Should the Court have taken account of administrative measures like these in considering the potential for arbitrariness in the enforcement of Chicago's gang loitering law? Particularly since alternatives to this law (for instance, a juvenile curfew) present many of the same problems of constraining police? For an argument to this effect, see Debra Livingston, Gang Loitering, the Court, and Some Realism about Police Patrol, 1999 Sup. Ct. Rev. 141.

4. Is facial invalidation the right way to deal with the potential for racial discrimination in the enforcement of laws like Chicago's gang loitering ordinance? Professors Meares and Kahan argue that the vagueness cases from the era of Papachristou v. Jacksonville, 405 U.S. 156 (1972), were "decided against the background of institutionalized racism," in a context in which law enforcement was a key instrument of racial repression. Tracey L. Meares & Dan M. Kahan, The Wages of Antiquated Procedural Thinking: A Critique of *Chicago v. Morales*, [1998] U. Chi. Legal F. 197, 205. They urge that the distrust of community-based policing and the skepticism about even guided police discretion reflected in these cases, while appropriate to the 1960s and 1970s, do not map well onto the contemporary scene, in which members of minority communities in the inner city have sometimes been in the forefront of the push for the enactment of laws like Chicago's gang loitering ordinance:

> The anti-community and anti-discretion principles that animate *Papachristou* address problems that no longer characterize American political life. Given the emergence of African American political power in the inner cities, it is no longer plausible to presume that all law enforcement policies adopted by local institutions are designed to oppress minority citizens. These new conditions require a new conception of rights—one that assures that the individuals who have the most at stake make the difficult choices anti-loitering provisions and the like present.

Id. at 209. It is true that Chicago's gang loitering ordinance received significant support among the city's black and Latino aldermen — though the proposed ordinance "drew both support and opposition from Chicago citizens of all backgrounds." Brief of Chicago Alliance for Neighborhood Safety, et al., as Amici Curiae in Support of Respondents, p. 1. Alderman Ed Smith, an African American representing a heavily minority district with severe crime problems, was particularly outspoken in the ordinance's defense: "This doesn't allow the police to go hog wild. But we're tired of seeing the rights of gangbangers get protected when . . . a mother can't send her children outside for fear of them getting shot to death in a drive-by shooting." John Kass, Old Tactic Sought in Crime War, Chi. Trib., at A1 (May 15, 1992).

But is all this relevant to the constitutional issues at stake in *Morales*? Professor Roberts argues that contemporary loitering laws, like those of the 1960s and 1970s, involve "expansive and ambiguous allocations of police discretion [that] are likely to unjustly burden members of unpopular or minority groups." Dorothy E. Roberts, Foreword: Race, Vagueness, and the Social Meaning of Order-Maintenance Policing, 89 J. Crim. L. & Criminology 775, 783 (1999). She responds to Meares and Kahan as follows:

> Kahan and Meares . . . correctly observe that racial politics are more complicated today than at the time liberal criminal procedure doctrines were instituted. But the increase in Black political participation and shift from de jure discrimination to other forms of institutional inequality does not erase the need for these constitutional protections. To the contrary, the changed conditions of American social and political life require a constitutional jurisprudence that recognizes how seemingly color blind laws continue to produce glaring racial inequities in the criminal justice system. . . .
>
> Even if it could be proven that a majority of Black inner-city residents endorse [Chicago's] loitering law, what relevance would that support have to the law's constitutionality? . . .
>
> . . . The gang loitering ordinance was passed by the predominantly white Chicago City Council, not an inner-city political body. Elected officials of white districts enacted the ordinance while minority communities were disproportionately subjected to the violations of liberty it imposed. . . . Although Black citizens certainly influence politics in cities like Chicago, they do not (yet) determine, design, or implement the law enforcement policies that govern their communities.

Id. at 821, 827-828. Should the Court in *Morales* have confronted these issues more directly? Do you think the majority's holding is important one way or the other to the issue of racial discrimination in law enforcement? To addressing the often strained relationship between police and minority communities?

5. In February 2000, the Chicago City Council enacted a new gang loitering ordinance designed to address the Court's constitutional concerns. The drafters of this new law attempted to use Justice O'Connor's opinion as a roadmap. The new ordinance reads as follows:

> §8-4-015 Gang Loitering.
>
> (a) Whenever a police officer observes a member of a criminal street gang engaged in gang loitering with one or more other persons in any public place designated for the enforcement of this section under subsection (b), the police officer shall,

subject to all applicable procedures promulgated by the superintendent of police:

(i) inform all such persons that they are engaged in gang loitering within an area in which loitering by groups containing criminal street gang members is prohibited;

(ii) order all such persons to disperse and remove themselves from within sight and hearing of the place at which the order was issued; and

(iii) inform those persons that they will be subject to arrest if they fail to obey the order promptly or engage in further gang loitering within sight or hearing of the place at which the order was issued during the next three hours.

(b) The superintendent of police shall by written directive designate areas of the City in which the superintendent has determined that enforcement of this section is necessary because gang loitering has enabled criminal street gangs to establish control over identifiable areas, to intimidate others from entering those areas, or to conceal illegal activities. Prior to making a determination under this subsection, the superintendent shall consult as he or she deems appropriate with persons who are knowledgeable about the effects of gang activity in areas in which the ordinance may be enforced. Such persons may include, but need not be limited to, members of the department of police with special training or experience related to criminal street gangs; other personnel of the department with particular knowledge of gang activities in the proposed designated area; elected and appointed officials of the area; community-based organizations; and participants in the Chicago Alternative Policing Strategy who are familiar with the area. The superintendent shall develop and implement procedures for the periodic review and update of designations made under this subsection.

(c) The superintendent shall by written directive promulgate procedures to prevent the enforcement of this section against persons who are engaged in collective advocacy activities that are protected by the Constitution of the United States or the State of Illinois.

(d) As used in this section:

(1) "Gang loitering" means remaining in any one place under circumstances that would warrant a reasonable person to believe that the purpose or effect of that behavior is to enable a criminal street gang to establish control over identifiable areas, to intimidate others from entering those areas, or to conceal illegal activities.

(2) "Criminal street gang" means any ongoing organization, association in fact or group of three or more persons, whether formal or informal, having as one of its substantial activities the commission of one or more of the criminal acts enumerated in paragraph (3), and whose members individually or collectively engage in or have engaged in a pattern of criminal gang activity.

(3) "Criminal gang activity" means the commission, attempted commission, or solicitation of the following offenses, provided that the offenses are committed by two or more persons, or by an individual at the direction of, or in association with, any criminal street gang, with the specific intent to promote, further or assist in any criminal conduct by gang members. . . . [There follows a long list of violent crimes, drug crimes, weapons violations, criminal coercion, and theft offenses.]

(4) "Pattern of criminal gang activity" means two or more acts of criminal gang activity of which at least two such acts were committed within five years of each other.

(5) "Public place" means the public way and any other location open to the public, whether publicly or privately owned.

(e) Any person who fails to obey promptly an order issued under subsection (a), or who engages in further gang loitering within sight or hearing of the place at which such an order was issued during the three hour period following the time the order was issued, is subject to a fine of not less than $100 and not more than $500 for each offense, or imprisonment for not more than six months for each offense, or both. . . .

Does this law sufficiently constrain the discretion of Chicago police?

3. "Special Needs"

The Court often has used an interest-balancing approach, similar to the one in *Terry*, to uphold administrative inspections, regulatory searches, and other kinds of governmental action involving "special needs" beyond those to be found in the typical law enforcement context. The basic methodology was outlined in Brown v. Texas, 443 U.S. 47 (1979):

> The reasonableness of seizures that are less intrusive than a traditional arrest, see Dunaway v. New York, 442 U.S. 200, 209-210 (1979); Terry v. Ohio, 392 U.S. 1, 20 (1968), depends "on a balance between the public interest and the individual's right to personal security free from arbitrary interference by law officers." Pennsylvania v. Mimms, 434 U.S. 106, 109 (1977). Consideration of the constitutionality of such seizures involves a weighing of the gravity of the public concerns served by the seizure, the degree to which the seizure advances the public interest, and the severity of the interference with individual liberty.

Id. at 50.

The first case to refer to "special needs" in so many words was New Jersey v. T.L.O., 469 U.S. 325 (1985), where the Court considered the Fourth Amendment's application to the search of a student's purse by an assistant vice principal enforcing anti-smoking rules. The Court determined that neither the warrant nor probable cause requirements were suitable to "maintenance of the swift and informal disciplinary procedures needed in the school." Id. at 340. Instead, the Court concluded that "the legality of a search of a student should depend simply on [its] reasonableness, under all the circumstances." Id. at 341. In his concurrence, Justice Blackmun noted that "exceptional circumstances" may at times arise "in which special needs, beyond the normal need for law enforcement, make the warrant and probable-cause requirement impracticable." Id. at 351.

Since *T.L.O.*, the Court has invoked the "special needs" rationale repeatedly. In Griffin v. Wisconsin, 483 U.S. 868 (1987), for instance, the Court concluded that a Wisconsin regulation permitting probation officers to engage in warrantless searches of their probationers' homes on "reasonable grounds" (meaning, less than probable cause) to believe contraband was present satisfied the Fourth Amendment's reasonableness requirement. The warrant and probable cause requirements would, among other things, prevent probation officers from responding quickly to evidence of misconduct and interfere with officers' judgment about how close the supervision of a probationer should be. They were thus deemed inconsistent with the state's "special need" in this context to supervise the probationer. Similarly, O'Connor v. Ortega, 480 U.S. 709 (1987), involved a doctor employed by a government hospital who was suspected by hospital administrators of mismanaging a psychiatric residency program. Citing the "special needs" associated with the proper operation of the workplace, a plurality concluded that the test for whether a public employer's work-related search of its employee's office, desk, or file cabinet comports with the Fourth Amendment should be simply the "reasonableness" of the search, under all the circumstances.

How can such results be explained? After all, the privacy interest in a student's purse, a probationer's home, and an employee's desk certainly do not vary depending on whether a school principal, a probation officer, a boss, or a police officer is performing the search. Indeed, why shouldn't the "special need" to solve or prevent violent crimes justify searches outside the warrant and probable cause framework? Isn't the need to stop criminal violence as important as the need to enforce a no-smoking rule in a junior high school? Why should the less important interest receive more Fourth Amendment deference?

Keep these questions in mind as you read the materials that follow. Below, we examine two kinds of "special needs" cases. The first deals with vehicle road-blocks, which the government often tries to justify under the Brown v. Texas interest-balancing approach. The second deals with searches conducted by persons other than police officers, such as regulatory agency officials or public-school administrators.

a. Roadblocks

Terry is generally seen as a major doctrinal innovation. In one respect, however, *Terry* was quite traditional: the Court required individualized suspicion of criminal activity to justify an intrusion on Fourth Amendment interests. Roadblocks raise the question whether the police may seize a group of drivers and passengers — all those who pass a particular point on a particular roadway during the time when the roadblock is in place — without any reason to believe that any one driver or passenger is violating the law. As you read the cases that follow, consider these questions. What could be the justification for this police tactic? Why dispense with probable cause and reasonable suspicion? Is it because of the strength of the government's interest? The weakness of the individuals' privacy and autonomy interests? The presence of alternative constraints on police abuse? Something else?

A few years after *Terry*, the Court approved the suspicionless stopping of vehicles at a permanent checkpoint on a highway leading away from the Mexican border. See United States v. Martinez-Fuerte, 428 U.S. 543 (1976). The theory of *Martinez-Fuerte* was interest balancing: "the need to make routine checkpoint stops is great, [and] the consequent intrusion on Fourth Amendment rights is quite limited." Id. at 557. In Delaware v. Prouse, 440 U.S. 648 (1979), the Court declined to permit random, suspicionless police stops of automobiles to check drivers' licenses and registrations. But the *Prouse* Court noted that it was not preventing states "from developing methods for spot checks that involve less intrusion or that do not involve the unconstrained exercise of discretion." The Court expanded on that idea in Michigan Department of State Police v. Sitz, 496 U.S. 444 (1990), where it faced a challenge to roadblocks used to check for drunk drivers. As in *Martinez-Fuerte* and *Prouse*, the police had no reason to suspect any of the drivers stopped in *Sitz* before the stop itself. Nevertheless, the Court held — relying on both *Martinez-Fuerte* and the above-quoted language from Brown v. Texas — that these suspicionless roadblock stops were permissible, due to the "magnitude of the drunken driving problem [and] the States' interest in eradicating it," as well as the fact that, unlike the random stops in *Prouse*, *all* cars were stopped at the roadblocks in *Sitz*.

These cases raised the possibility that, at least within the narrow sphere of vehicle stops, the police might be able to stop *anyone* as long as they stopped *everyone* — that seizures of many motorists were permissible absent suspicion of any of them. The next case cast serious doubt on that possibility.

INDIANAPOLIS v. EDMOND

Certiorari to the United States Court of Appeals for the Seventh Circuit
531 U.S. 32 (2000)

JUSTICE O'CONNOR delivered the opinion of the Court.

... In August 1998, the city of Indianapolis began to operate vehicle checkpoints on Indianapolis roads in an effort to interdict unlawful drugs. The city conducted six such roadblocks between August and November that year, stopping 1,161 vehicles and arresting 104 motorists. Fifty-five arrests were for drug-related crimes, while 49 were for offenses unrelated to drugs. The overall "hit rate" of the program was thus approximately nine percent. The parties stipulated to the facts concerning the operation of the checkpoints.

... At each checkpoint location, the police stop a predetermined number of vehicles. Approximately 30 officers are stationed at the checkpoint. Pursuant to written directives issued by the chief of police, at least one officer approaches the vehicle, advises the driver that he or she is being stopped briefly at a drug checkpoint, and asks the driver to produce a license and registration. The officer also looks for signs of impairment and conducts an open-view examination of the vehicle from the outside. A narcotics-detection dog walks around the outside of each stopped vehicle.

The directives instruct the officers that they may conduct a search only by consent or based on the appropriate quantum of particularized suspicion. The officers must conduct each stop in the same manner until particularized suspicion develops, and the officers have no discretion to stop any vehicle out of sequence. The city agreed in the stipulation to operate the checkpoints in such a way as to ensure that the total duration of each stop, absent reasonable suspicion or probable cause, would be five minutes or less.

The affidavit of Indianapolis Police Sergeant Marshall DePew, although it is technically outside the parties' stipulation, provides further insight concerning the operation of the checkpoints. According to Sergeant DePew, checkpoint locations are selected weeks in advance based on such considerations as area crime statistics and traffic flow. The checkpoints are generally operated during daylight hours and are identified with lighted signs reading, "NARCOTICS CHECKPOINT____MILE AHEAD, NARCOTICS K-9 IN USE, BE PREPARED TO STOP." Once a group of cars has been stopped, other traffic proceeds without interruption until all the stopped cars have been processed or diverted for further processing. Sergeant DePew also stated that the average stop for a vehicle not subject to further processing lasts two to three minutes or less.

Respondents James Edmond and Joell Palmer were each stopped at a narcotics checkpoint in late September 1998. Respondents then filed a lawsuit on behalf of themselves and the class of all motorists who had been stopped or were subject to being stopped in the future at the Indianapolis drug checkpoints. Respondents claimed that the roadblocks violated the Fourth Amendment of the United States Constitution and the search and seizure provision of the Indiana Constitution. Respondents requested declaratory and injunctive relief for the class, as well as damages and attorney's fees for themselves.

Respondents then moved for a preliminary injunction. ... The United States District Court for the Southern District of Indiana ... denied the motion for a preliminary injunction, holding that the checkpoint program did not violate the Fourth Amendment. Edmond v. Goldsmith, 38 F. Supp. 2d 1016 (1998). A divided panel of the United States Court of Appeals for the Seventh Circuit reversed, holding that the checkpoints contravened the Fourth Amendment. 183 F.3d 659 (1999). . . . We granted certiorari, and now affirm.

The Fourth Amendment requires that searches and seizures be reasonable. A search or seizure is ordinarily unreasonable in the absence of individualized suspicion of wrongdoing. While such suspicion is not an "irreducible" component of reasonableness, [United States v. Martinez-Fuerte, 428 U.S. 543, 561 (1976)], we have recognized only limited circumstances in which the usual rule does not apply. . . .

We have . . . upheld brief, suspicionless seizures of motorists at a fixed Border Patrol checkpoint designed to intercept illegal aliens, *Martinez-Fuerte*, supra, and at a sobriety checkpoint aimed at removing drunk drivers from the road, Michigan Dept. of State Police v. Sitz, 496 U.S. 444 (1990). In addition, in Delaware v. Prouse, 440 U.S. 648 (1979), we suggested that a similar type of roadblock with the purpose of verifying drivers' licenses and vehicle registrations would be permissible. In none of these cases, however, did we indicate approval of a checkpoint program whose primary purpose was to detect evidence of ordinary criminal wrongdoing.

In *Martinez-Fuerte*, we entertained Fourth Amendment challenges to stops at two permanent immigration checkpoints located on major United States highways less than 100 miles from the Mexican border. We noted at the outset the particular context in which the constitutional question arose, describing in some detail the "formidable law enforcement problems" posed by the northbound tide of illegal entrants into the United States. 428 U.S. at 551-554. . . . [W]e found that the balance tipped in favor of the Government's interests in policing the Nation's borders. 428 U.S. at 561-564. In so finding, we emphasized the difficulty of effectively containing illegal immigration at the border itself. 428 U.S. at 556. We also stressed the impracticality of the particularized study of a given car to discern whether it was transporting illegal aliens, as well as the relatively modest degree of intrusion entailed by the stops. 428 U.S. at 556-564. . . .

In *Sitz*, we evaluated the constitutionality of a Michigan highway sobriety checkpoint program. The *Sitz* checkpoint involved brief, suspicionless stops of motorists so that police officers could detect signs of intoxication and remove impaired drivers from the road. 496 U.S. at 447-448. Motorists who exhibited signs of intoxication were diverted for a license and registration check and, if warranted, further sobriety tests. 496 U.S. at 447. This checkpoint program was clearly aimed at reducing the immediate hazard posed by the presence of drunk drivers on the highways, and there was an obvious connection between the imperative of highway safety and the law enforcement practice at issue. The gravity of the drunk driving problem and the magnitude of the State's interest in getting drunk drivers off the road weighed heavily in our determination that the program was constitutional. See 496 U.S. at 451.

In *Prouse*, we invalidated a discretionary, suspicionless stop for a spot check of a motorist's driver's license and vehicle registration. The officer's conduct in that case was unconstitutional primarily on account of his exercise of "standardless and unconstrained discretion." 440 U.S. at 661. We nonetheless acknowledged the States' "vital interest in ensuring that only those qualified to do so are permitted to operate motor vehicles, that these vehicles are fit for safe operation, and hence that licensing, registration, and vehicle inspection requirements are being observed." 440 U.S. at 658. Accordingly, we suggested that "questioning of all oncoming traffic at roadblock-type stops" would be a lawful means of serving this interest in highway safety. 440 U.S. at 663. . . .

. . . [W]hat principally distinguishes [the Indianapolis] checkpoints from those we have previously approved is their primary purpose.

As petitioners concede, the Indianapolis checkpoint program unquestionably has the primary purpose of interdicting illegal narcotics. In their stipulation of facts, the parties repeatedly refer to the checkpoints as "drug checkpoints" and describe them as "being operated by the City of Indianapolis in an effort to interdict unlawful drugs in Indianapolis." App. to Pet. for Cert. 51a-52a. In addition, the first document attached to the parties' stipulation is entitled "DRUG CHECKPOINT CONTACT OFFICER DIRECTIVES BY ORDER OF THE CHIEF OF POLICE." Id. at 53a. These directives instruct officers to "advise the citizen that they are being stopped briefly at a drug checkpoint." Ibid. . . .

We have never approved a checkpoint program whose primary purpose was to detect evidence of ordinary criminal wrongdoing. Rather, our checkpoint cases have recognized only limited exceptions to the general rule that a seizure must be accompanied by some measure of individualized suspicion. We suggested in *Prouse* that we would not credit the "general interest in crime control" as justification for a regime of suspicionless stops. 440 U.S. at 659, n. 18. Consistent with this suggestion, each of the checkpoint programs that we have approved was designed primarily to serve purposes closely related to the problems of policing the border or the necessity of ensuring roadway safety. Because the primary purpose of the Indianapolis narcotics checkpoint program is to uncover evidence of ordinary criminal wrongdoing, the program contravenes the Fourth Amendment.

Petitioners propose several ways in which the narcotics-detection purpose of the instant checkpoint program may instead resemble the primary purposes of the checkpoints in *Sitz* and *Martinez-Fuerte*. Petitioners state that the checkpoints in those cases had the same ultimate purpose of arresting those suspected of committing crimes. Securing the border and apprehending drunk drivers are, of course, law enforcement activities, and law enforcement officers employ arrests and criminal prosecutions in pursuit of these goals. If we were to rest the case at this high level of generality, there would be little check on the ability of the authorities to construct roadblocks for almost any conceivable law enforcement purpose. Without drawing the line at roadblocks designed primarily to serve the general interest in crime control, the Fourth Amendment would do little to prevent such intrusions from becoming a routine part of American life.

Petitioners also emphasize the severe and intractable nature of the drug problem as justification for the checkpoint program. There is no doubt that traffic in illegal narcotics creates social harms of the first magnitude. The law enforcement problems that the drug trade creates likewise remain daunting and complex, particularly in light of the myriad forms of spin-off crime that it spawns. The same can be said of various other illegal activities, if only to a lesser degree. But the gravity of the threat alone cannot be dispositive of questions concerning what means law enforcement officers may employ to pursue a given purpose. Rather, in determining whether individualized suspicion is required, we must consider the nature of the interests threatened and their connection to the particular law enforcement practices at issue. We are particularly reluctant to recognize exceptions to the general rule of individualized suspicion where governmental authorities primarily pursue their general crime control ends.

Nor can the narcotics-interdiction purpose of the checkpoints be rationalized in terms of a highway safety concern similar to that present in *Sitz*. The detection and punishment of almost any criminal offense serves broadly the safety of the community, and our streets would no doubt be safer but for the scourge of illegal drugs. Only with respect to a smaller class of offenses, however, is society confronted with the type of immediate, vehicle-bound threat to life and limb that the sobriety checkpoint in *Sitz* was designed to eliminate.

Petitioners also liken the anticontraband agenda of the Indianapolis checkpoints to the antismuggling purpose of the checkpoints in *Martinez-Fuerte*. Petitioners cite this Court's conclusion in *Martinez-Fuerte* that the flow of traffic was too heavy to permit "particularized study of a given car that would enable it to be identified as a possible carrier of illegal aliens," 428 U.S. at 557, and claim that this logic has even more force here. The problem with this argument is that the same logic prevails any time a vehicle is employed to conceal contraband or other evidence of a crime. . . . [T]he Indianapolis checkpoints are far removed from the border context that was crucial in *Martinez-Fuerte*. While the difficulty of examining each passing car was an important factor in validating the law enforcement technique employed in *Martinez-Fuerte*, this factor alone cannot justify a regime of suspicionless searches or seizures. Rather, we must look more closely at the nature of the public interests that such a regime is designed principally to serve.

The primary purpose of the Indianapolis narcotics checkpoints is in the end to advance "the general interest in crime control," *Prouse*, 440 U.S. at 659, n. 18. We decline to suspend the usual requirement of individualized suspicion where the police seek to employ a checkpoint primarily for the ordinary enterprise of investigating crimes. We cannot sanction stops justified only by the generalized and ever-present possibility that interrogation and inspection may reveal that any given motorist has committed some crime.

Of course, there are circumstances that may justify a law enforcement checkpoint where the primary purpose would otherwise, but for some emergency, relate to ordinary crime control. For example, . . . the Fourth Amendment would almost certainly permit an appropriately tailored roadblock set up to thwart an imminent terrorist attack or to catch a dangerous criminal who is likely to flee by way of a particular route. The exigencies created by these scenarios are far removed from the circumstances under which authorities might simply stop cars as a matter of course to see if there just happens to be a felon leaving the jurisdiction. While we do not limit the purposes that may justify a checkpoint program to any rigid set of categories, we decline to approve a program whose primary purpose is ultimately indistinguishable from the general interest in crime control.[1]

Petitioners argue that our prior cases preclude an inquiry into the purposes of the checkpoint program. For example, they cite Whren v. United States, 517 U.S.

---

1. THE CHIEF JUSTICE's dissent erroneously characterizes our opinion as resting on the application of a "non-law-enforcement primary purpose test." Post, at 6. Our opinion nowhere describes the purposes of the *Sitz* and *Martinez-Fuerte* checkpoints as being "not primarily related to criminal law enforcement." Post, at 3. Rather, our judgment turns on the fact that the primary purpose of the Indianapolis checkpoints is to advance the general interest in crime control. . . .

806 (1996) . . . to support the proposition that "where the government articulates and pursues a legitimate interest for a suspicionless stop, courts should not look behind that interest to determine whether the government's 'primary purpose' is valid." Brief for Petitioners 34. [That case], however, [does] not control the instant situation.

In *Whren*, we held that an individual officer's subjective intentions are irrelevant to the Fourth Amendment validity of a traffic stop that is justified objectively by probable cause to believe that a traffic violation has occurred. . . . In so holding, we expressly distinguished cases where we had addressed the validity of searches conducted in the absence of probable cause. See 517 U.S. at 811-812 (distinguishing Florida v. Wells, 495 U.S. 1, 4 (1990) (stating that "an inventory search must not be a ruse for a general rummaging in order to discover incriminating evidence") [and] Colorado v. Bertine, 479 U.S. 367, 372 (1987) (suggesting that the absence of bad faith and the lack of a purely investigative purpose were relevant to the validity of an inventory search)).

Whren therefore reinforces the principle that, while "subjective intentions play no role in ordinary, probable-cause Fourth Amendment analysis," 517 U.S. at 813, programmatic purposes may be relevant to the validity of Fourth Amendment intrusions undertaken pursuant to a general scheme without individualized suspicion. . . .

Petitioners argue that the Indianapolis checkpoint program is justified by its lawful secondary purposes of keeping impaired motorists off the road and verifying licenses and registrations. If this were the case, however, law enforcement authorities would be able to establish checkpoints for virtually any purpose so long as they also included a license or sobriety check. For this reason, we examine the available evidence to determine the primary purpose of the checkpoint program. While we recognize the challenges inherent in a purpose inquiry, courts routinely engage in this enterprise in many areas of constitutional jurisprudence as a means of sifting abusive governmental conduct from that which is lawful. As a result, a program driven by an impermissible purpose may be proscribed while a program impelled by licit purposes is permitted, even though the challenged conduct may be outwardly similar. . . .[2]

It goes without saying that our holding today does nothing to alter the constitutional status of the sobriety and border checkpoints that we approved in *Sitz* and *Martinez-Fuerte*, or of the type of traffic checkpoint that we suggested would be lawful in *Prouse*. The constitutionality of such checkpoint programs still depends on a balancing of the competing interests at stake and the effectiveness of the program. See *Sitz*, 496 U.S. at 450-455; *Martinez-Fuerte*, 428 U.S. at 556-564. When law enforcement authorities pursue primarily general crime control purposes at checkpoints such as here, however, stops can only be justified by some quantum of individualized suspicion.

Our holding also does not affect the validity of border searches or searches at places like airports and government buildings, where the need for such measures

---

2. Because petitioners concede that the primary purpose of the Indianapolis checkpoints is narcotics detection, we need not decide whether the State may establish a checkpoint program with the primary purpose of checking licenses or driver sobriety and a secondary purpose of interdicting narcotics. Specifically, we express no view on the question whether police may expand the scope of a license or sobriety checkpoint seizure in order to detect the presence of drugs in a stopped car.

to ensure public safety can be particularly acute. Nor does our opinion speak to other intrusions aimed primarily at purposes beyond the general interest in crime control. . . .

CHIEF JUSTICE REHNQUIST, with whom [JUSTICE SCALIA and] JUSTICE THOMAS join[], . . . dissenting.

. . . As it is nowhere to be found in the Court's opinion, I begin with blackletter roadblock seizure law. "The principal protection of Fourth Amendment rights at checkpoints lies in appropriate limitations on the scope of the stop." United States v. Martinez-Fuerte, 428 U.S. 543, 566-567 (1976). Roadblock seizures are consistent with the Fourth Amendment if they are "carried out pursuant to a plan embodying explicit, neutral limitations on the conduct of individual officers." Brown v. Texas, 443 U.S. 47, 51 (1979). Specifically, the constitutionality of a seizure turns upon "a weighing of the gravity of the public concerns served by the seizure, the degree to which the seizure advances the public interest, and the severity of the interference with individual liberty." 443 U.S. at 50-51.

We first applied these principles in *Martinez-Fuerte*, supra, which approved highway checkpoints for detecting illegal aliens. In *Martinez-Fuerte*, we balanced the United States' formidable interest in checking the flow of illegal immigrants against the limited "objective" and "subjective" intrusion on the motorists. The objective intrusion—the stop itself, the brief questioning of the occupants, and the visual inspection of the car—was considered "limited" because "neither the vehicle nor its occupants [were] searched." 428 U.S. at 558. Likewise, the subjective intrusion, or the fear and surprise engendered in law-abiding motorists by the nature of the stop, was found to be minimal because the "regularized manner in which [the] established checkpoints [were] operated [was] visible evidence, reassuring to law-abiding motorists, that the stops [were] duly authorized and believed to serve the public interest." 428 U.S. at 559. . . . And although the decision in *Martinez-Fuerte* did not turn on the checkpoints' effectiveness, the record in one of the consolidated cases demonstrated that illegal aliens were found in 0.12 percent of the stopped vehicles. See 428 U.S. at 554.

In Michigan Dept. of State Police v. Sitz, 496 U.S. 444 (1990), we upheld the State's use of a highway sobriety checkpoint. . . . There, we recognized the gravity of the State's interest in curbing drunken driving and found the objective intrusion of the approximately 25-second seizure to be "slight." 496 U.S. at 451. Turning to the subjective intrusion, we noted that the checkpoint was selected pursuant to guidelines and was operated by uniformed officers. See 496 U.S. at 453. Finally, we concluded that the program effectively furthered the State's interest because the checkpoint resulted in the arrest of two drunk drivers, or 1.6 percent of the 126 drivers stopped. See 496 U.S. at 455-456.

This case follows naturally from *Martinez-Fuerte* and *Sitz*. Petitioners acknowledge that the "primary purpose" of these roadblocks is to interdict illegal drugs, but this fact should not be controlling. . . . The District Court found that another "purpose of the checkpoints is to check driver's licenses and vehicle registrations," App. to Pet. for Cert. 44a, and the written directives state that the police officers are to "look for signs of impairment." Id. at 53a. The use of roadblocks to look for signs of impairment was validated by *Sitz*, and the use of roadblocks to check for driver's licenses and vehicle registrations was expressly recognized in Delaware v. Prouse, 440 U.S. 648, 663 (1979). That the roadblocks serve these legitimate state interests cannot be seriously disputed, as the 49 people arrested for offenses unrelated to drugs can attest. Edmond v. Goldsmith, 183 F.3d 659, 661 (CA7 1999). And it would be speculative to conclude—given the District Court's findings, the written directives, and the actual arrests—that petitioners would not have operated these roadblocks but for the State's interest in interdicting drugs. . . .

JUSTICE THOMAS, dissenting.

Taken together, our decisions in Michigan Dept. of State Police v. Sitz, 496 U.S. 444 (1990), and United States v. Martinez-Fuerte, 428 U.S. 543 (1976), stand for the proposition that suspicionless roadblock seizures are constitutionally permissible if conducted according to a plan that limits the discretion of the officers conducting the stops. I am not convinced that Sitz and Martinez-Fuerte were correctly decided. Indeed, I rather doubt that the Framers of the Fourth Amendment would have considered "reasonable" a program of indiscriminate stops of individuals not suspected of wrongdoing.

Respondents did not, however, advocate the overruling of Sitz and Martinez-Fuerte, and I am reluctant to consider such a step without the benefit of briefing and argument. For the reasons given by THE CHIEF JUSTICE, I believe that those cases compel upholding the program at issue here. I, therefore, join his opinion.

NOTES AND QUESTIONS

1. Why does the "primary purpose" of the Indianapolis checkpoints matter? Would the drivers' liberty have been any less invaded had the purpose been to check for drunk drivers? For illegal aliens? For licenses and registrations? Would the state's interest have been stronger in those cases?

2. The answer to the last question is probably "no." The state's interest in stopping motorists—or, to be more precise, the law enforcement gain from stopping motorists—is a function of two things: the importance of the violations the police are detecting or deterring, and the number of violations detected or deterred. Consider these factors one at a time.

It is not obvious how to rank order drunk driving (the harm in Sitz), evading immigration law (the harm in Martinez-Fuerte), unlicensed driving (the harm the Court thought sufficient in dicta in Prouse), and illegal drug possession. Still, the last category of violations on that list, detection of which was the goal of the roadblocks in Edmond, is surely not the least important. And it seems plausible to imagine that catching and deterring drug violations is the most important item on that list—at least some jurisdictions might legitimately think so. Besides, couldn't Indianapolis plausibly claim that its roadblocks had multiple purposes, that while the chief goal may have been to catch drug violations, subsidiary goals included catching unlicensed or intoxicated drivers? The fact that 49 non-drug arrests were made, some of them for those other crimes, suggests that those other purposes were in fact advanced by the roadblocks. Does that mean Indianapolis is being punished for the 55 drug arrests? Why?

With regard to the other factor in the law enforcement side of the balance in Edmond—the number of violations caught or deterred—consider the success rates in the roadblocks in Martinez-Fuerte (0.12 percent), Sitz (1.6 percent), and

Edmond (4.7 percent for drug violations alone, 9.0 percent counting all arrests). Isn't it odd that the Court approved the two less successful roadblock programs, and disapproved the most successful one?

3. Consider the other side of the balance: the individual privacy and liberty interests at stake in roadblocks. Here the *state*'s argument is a little odd: stopping a lot of people is less of an intrusion than stopping a few. Justice Rehnquist, dissenting in Delaware v. Prouse, 440 U.S. 648 (1979), noted the irony:

> The Court holds, in successive sentences, that absent an articulable, reasonable suspicion of unlawful conduct, a motorist may not be subjected to a random license check, but that the States are free to develop "methods for spot checks that . . . do not involve the unconstrained exercise of discretion," such as "[q]uestioning . . . all oncoming traffic at roadblock-type stops. . . ." Because motorists, apparently like sheep, are much less likely to be "frightened" or "annoyed" when stopped en masse, a highway patrolman needs neither probable cause nor articulable suspicion to stop *all* motorists on a particular thoroughfare, but he cannot without articulable suspicion stop *less* than all motorists. The Court thus elevates the adage "misery loves company" to a novel role in Fourth Amendment jurisprudence. The rule becomes "curiouser and curiouser" as one attempts to follow the Court's explanation for it. . . .

Id. at 664. Does he have a point? Or do constraints (or the lack thereof) on police discretion really change the nature of the harm individuals suffer from searches and seizures? Perhaps an isolated seizure is stigmatizing, even humiliating, in a way that a group seizure is not. For an argument along these lines, see Sherry F. Colb, Innocence, Privacy, and Targeting in Fourth Amendment Jurisprudence, 96 Colum. L. Rev. 1456 (1996). Colb maintains that individuals suffer a cognizable Fourth Amendment injury she calls "targeting harm" when they are "singled out from others through an exercise of official discretion that is not based on an adequate evidentiary foundation." Id. at 1487. If that is right, it would seem to follow that "[w]hen the police stop fifty people, they do not cause fifty times the injury inflicted when they stop one. On the contrary, they are likely to cause a small fraction of the injury inflicted by stopping the same fifty people one by one." William J. Stuntz, Local Policing After the Terror, 111 Yale L.J. 2137, 2166 (2002). Perhaps cases like *Martinez-Fuerte* and *Sitz* rest on the idea not that misery loves company, but that group seizures inflict less misery than individual ones.

4. Suppose there really is a reduced harm suffered when a group of people are seized together; suppose further that that reduced harm is part of the justification for approving the roadblocks designed to catch drunk drivers in *Sitz*. Is the harm any different in *Edmond*? Is being stopped at a drug checkpoint a qualitatively different experience from being stopped at a drunk driving checkpoint? Perhaps so. But the most obvious difference between the stops in *Sitz* and the stops in *Edmond* has to do with the use of drug-sniffing dogs in *Edmond*—a difference the Court expressly stated does not affect its result.

5. Note that the roadblock program in *Edmond*—whatever else might be its pros and cons—at least minimized the aforementioned problem of police discretion, with all of the concomitant opportunities for abuse. At least as long as the roadblocks are not situated in a discriminatory manner, one big advantage of a roadblock program is that it affects all motorists—no matter what their race, ethnicity, or socioeconomic class—equally. All motorists are in the same boat

(so to speak), which means that all motorists have the same motivation to invoke the political process to regulate or even eliminate such roadblocks, should they become overly intrusive. Because the political process might be expected to work pretty well to regulate roadblocks, perhaps the courts need not worry so much about regulating them.

The *Edmond* Court nevertheless struck down the City of Indianapolis's non-discriminatory approach to proactive policing. At the same time, the Court consistently has approved the alternative, discretionary approach to proactive policing typified by *Terry* and, even worse, *Whren* (in which the Court upheld a concededly pretextual automobile stop) — despite the fact that such a discretionary approach seems tailor-made for discriminatory application.

Do these results seem backward? Think about the following argument:

> Consider why constitutional regulation of searches and seizures is necessary in the first place. Police are in the business of imposing costs on suspects. Stops, frisks, arrests, detentions, questioning — these things are generally unpleasant and can be seriously harmful. The benefits of this sort of activity are diffused among the local population. The costs, at least the nonmonetary sort (which are more severe than the monetary costs), are concentrated; they are felt primarily by those whom the police target. Anytime the government does something that has concentrated costs but diffused benefits, there is a danger that it will do too much — harming one voter to please ten is generally thought to be a good deal from the point of view of politically accountable decisionmakers. That is the theory behind the Takings Clause, which requires compensation as a condition of seizing one person's property for the benefit of the larger public. Law enforcement presents what looks like a recurring takings problem. . . . That is the strongest case for constitutional regulation of law enforcement. Some kind of regulation is needed, and political checks will not do the job, given politicians' natural tendency to worry too little about those who bear the nonmonetary cost of police work.
>
> Notice that the argument concerns police searches and seizures of *individuals*. When the police stop large groups of people, the story is quite different. Law enforcement's costs are spread more broadly; the effect is to convert searches and seizures from takings, burdening only isolated individuals, into taxes, burdening classes of people. And when groups are searched or seized, the burdens are more visible — a larger slice of the population can see and hear them. These differences mean that political checks are much more likely to function. If the police treat individual arrestees badly, there may be no pressure brought to bear to treat them well, but if they treat groups of citizens badly, the bad treatment is likely to have political costs. To put it another way, spreading the cost of policing through a larger slice of the population (which is what things like roadblocks and security checkpoints do) reduces the odds of voters demanding harsh and intrusive police tactics secure in the knowledge that those tactics will be applied only to others.
>
> The point is not that searching and seizing groups is always better than the alternatives. Usually, it isn't. Police work generally involves differentiating people, not lumping them together, and the law neither can nor should change that. Rather, the point is that with across-the-board search procedures — police work that taxes instead of takes — those who enforce the law tend to take account of both the benefits and the costs of their tactics. With individual searches, the costs tend to be externalized. It follows that when police officers *want* to deal with suspects wholesale rather than retail, the law should encourage them to do so. In terms of regulatory strategy, group searches and seizures are an opportunity, not a problem.

Stuntz, Local Policing After the Terror, 111 Yale L.J. at 2164-2166. This argument might apply to more than roadblocks:

> ... Suppose the police officers investigating drug trafficking in a poor African-American neighborhood have to choose between two tactics—street sweeps, with everyone in the vicinity of a supposed drug market stopped and questioned, or targeted individual stops. Both tactics may involve a species of discrimination, since in white neighborhoods the tactics may be different, and the number and severity of the stops smaller. But the sweeps have a large advantage: transparency. The more people who see a police raid and feel its effects, the more people who are in a position to complain if police tactics are needlessly harsh, and in a position to counter false police testimony if the need arises. (How likely is it that Rodney King would have become a cause célèbre without the famous videotape? How likely is it that Officer Koon and his friends would have behaved so brutally had they been dealing with a dozen citizens instead of three?) Discriminatory street sweeps and discriminatory street stops are both discriminatory, but the first kind of discrimination is more likely to occasion public complaint, and hence less likely to involve the kind of behavior that prompts complaint, than the second. The idea is much the same as the one behind requiring public trials: Visibility is a powerful regulatory tool. The ban on group seizures gets that idea backward.

Id. at 2167. Is *Edmond* right? Is *Sitz*? When, if ever, should the police be able to target groups rather than individuals?

6. What about roadblocks that are designed to elicit information, not about a crime that is still in progress (as in *Martinez-Fuerte*, *Sitz*, and *Edmond*), but about one that occurred in the past? The next case addresses this question.

ILLINOIS v. LIDSTER

Certiorari to the Supreme Court of Illinois
540 U.S. 419 (2004)

JUSTICE BREYER delivered the opinion of the Court.

This Fourth Amendment case focuses upon a highway checkpoint where police stopped motorists to ask them for information about a recent hit-and-run accident. We hold that the police stops were reasonable, hence, constitutional.

I

The relevant background is as follows: On Saturday, August 23, 1997, just after midnight, an unknown motorist traveling eastbound on a highway in Lombard, Illinois, struck and killed a 70-year-old bicyclist. The motorist drove off without identifying himself. About one week later at about the same time of night and at about the same place, local police set up a highway checkpoint designed to obtain more information about the accident from the motoring public.

Police cars with flashing lights partially blocked the eastbound lanes of the highway. The blockage forced traffic to slow down, leading to lines of up to 15 cars in each lane. As each vehicle drew up to the checkpoint, an officer would stop it for 10 to 15 seconds, ask the occupants whether they had seen anything happen there the previous weekend, and hand each driver a flyer. The flyer said "ALERT . . . FATAL HIT & RUN ACCIDENT" and requested "assistance in identifying the vehicle and driver in this accident which killed a 70 year old bicyclist." App. 9.

Robert Lidster, the respondent, drove a minivan toward the checkpoint. As he approached the checkpoint, his van swerved, nearly hitting one of the officers. The officer smelled alcohol on Lidster's breath. He directed Lidster to a side street where another officer administered a sobriety test and then arrested Lidster. Lidster was tried and convicted in Illinois state court of driving under the influence of alcohol.

Lidster challenged the lawfulness of his arrest and conviction on the ground that the government had obtained much of the relevant evidence through use of a checkpoint stop that violated the Fourth Amendment. The trial court rejected that challenge. But an Illinois appellate court reached the opposite conclusion. 319 Ill. App. 3d 825, 747 N.E.2d 419, 254 Ill. Dec. 379 (2001). The Illinois Supreme Court agreed with the appellate court. It held (by a vote of 4 to 3) that our decision in *Indianapolis* v. *Edmond*, 531 U.S. 32 (2000), required it to find the stop unconstitutional. 202 Ill. 2d 1, 779 N.E.2d 855, 269 Ill. Dec. 1 (2002). . . . We now reverse the Illinois Supreme Court's determination.

II

The Illinois Supreme Court basically held that our decision in *Edmond* governs the outcome of this case. We do not agree. *Edmond* involved a checkpoint at which police stopped vehicles to look for evidence of drug crimes committed by occupants of those vehicles. After stopping a vehicle at the checkpoint, police would examine (from outside the vehicle) the vehicle's interior; they would walk a drug-sniffing dog around the exterior; and, if they found sufficient evidence of drug (or other) crimes, they would arrest the vehicle's occupants. 531 U.S., at 35. We found that police had set up this checkpoint primarily for general "crime control" purposes, i.e., "to detect evidence of ordinary criminal wrongdoing." Id., at 41. We noted that the stop was made without individualized suspicion. And we held that the Fourth Amendment forbids such a stop, in the absence of special circumstances. Id., at 44.

The checkpoint stop here differs significantly from that in *Edmond*. The stop's primary law enforcement purpose was *not* to determine whether a vehicle's occupants were committing a crime, but to ask vehicle occupants, as members of the public, for their help in providing information about a crime in all likelihood committed by others. The police expected the information elicited to help them apprehend, not the vehicle's occupants, but other individuals.

Edmond's language, as well as its context, makes clear that the constitutionality of this latter, information-seeking kind of stop was not then before the Court. *Edmond* refers to the subject matter of its holding as "stops justified only by the generalized and ever-present possibility that interrogation and inspection may reveal that *any given motorist has committed some crime*." Ibid. (emphasis added). We concede that *Edmond* describes the law enforcement objective there in question as a "general interest in crime control," but it specifies that the phrase "general interest in crime control" does not refer to every "law enforcement" objective. Id., at 44, n. 1. We must read this and related general language in *Edmond* as we often read general language in judicial opinions—as referring in context to circumstances similar to the circumstances then before the Court and not referring to quite different circumstances that the Court was not then considering.

Neither do we believe, *Edmond* aside, that the Fourth Amendment would have us apply an *Edmond*-type rule of automatic unconstitutionality to brief, information-seeking highway stops of the kind now before us. For one thing, the fact that such stops normally lack individualized suspicion cannot by itself determine the constitutional outcome. As in *Edmond*, the stop here at issue involves a motorist. The Fourth Amendment does not treat a motorist's car as his castle. See, e.g., New York v. Class, 475 U.S. 106, 112-113 (1986); United States v. Martinez-Fuerte, 428 U.S. 543, 561 (1976). And special law enforcement concerns will sometimes justify highway stops without individualized suspicion. See Michigan Dept. of State Police v. Sitz, 496 U.S. 444 (1990) (sobriety checkpoint); *Martinez-Fuerte*, supra (Border Patrol checkpoint). Moreover, unlike *Edmond*, the context here (seeking information from the public) is one in which, by definition, the concept of individualized suspicion has little role to play. Like certain other forms of police activity, say, crowd control or public safety, an information-seeking stop is not the kind of event that involves suspicion, or lack of suspicion, of the relevant individual.

For another thing, information-seeking highway stops are less likely to provoke anxiety or to prove intrusive. The stops are likely brief. The police are not likely to ask questions designed to elicit self-incriminating information. And citizens will often react positively when police simply ask for their help as "responsible citizen[s]" to "give whatever information they may have to aid in law enforcement." Miranda v. Arizona, 384 U.S. 436, 477-478 (1966).

Further, the law ordinarily permits police to seek the voluntary cooperation of members of the public in the investigation of a crime. "[L]aw enforcement officers do not violate the Fourth Amendment by merely approaching an individual on the street or in another public place, by asking him if he is willing to answer some questions, [or] by putting questions to him if the person is willing to listen." Florida v. Royer, 460 U.S. 491, 497 (1983). See also ALI, Model Code of Pre-Arraignment Procedure §110.1(1) (1975) ("[L]aw enforcement officer may . . . request any person to furnish information or otherwise cooperate in the investigation or prevention of crime"). That, in part, is because voluntary requests play a vital role in police investigatory work. See, e.g., Haynes v. Washington, 373 U.S. 503, 515 (1963) ("[I]nterrogation of witnesses . . . is undoubtedly an essential tool in effective law enforcement"); U.S. Dept. of Justice, Eyewitness Evidence: A Guide for Law Enforcement 14-15 (1999) (instructing law enforcement to gather information from witnesses near the scene).

The importance of soliciting the public's assistance is offset to some degree by the need to stop a motorist to obtain that help — a need less likely present where a pedestrian, not a motorist, is involved. The difference is significant in light of our determinations that such an involuntary stop amounts to a "seizure" in Fourth Amendment terms. E.g., *Edmond*, 531 U.S., at 40. That difference, however, is not important enough to justify an *Edmond*-type rule here. After all, as we have said, the motorist stop will likely be brief. Any accompanying traffic delay should prove no more onerous than many that typically accompany normal traffic congestion. And the resulting voluntary questioning of a motorist is as likely to prove important for police investigation as is the questioning of a pedestrian. Given these considerations, it would seem anomalous were the law (1) ordinarily to allow police freely to seek the voluntary cooperation of pedestrians but (2) ordinarily to forbid police to seek similar voluntary cooperation from motorists.

Finally, we do not believe that an *Edmond*-type rule is needed to prevent an unreasonable proliferation of police checkpoints. . . . Practical considerations — namely, limited police resources and community hostility to related traffic tie-ups — seem likely to inhibit any such proliferation. See Fell, Ferguson, Williams, & Fields, Why Aren't Sobriety Checkpoints Widely Adopted as an Enforcement Strategy in the United States?, 35 Accident Analysis & Prevention 897 (Nov. 2003) (finding that sobriety checkpoints are not more widely used due to the lack of police resources and the lack of community support). And, of course, the Fourth Amendment's normal insistence that the stop be reasonable in context will still provide an important legal limitation on police use of this kind of information-seeking checkpoint.

These considerations, taken together, convince us that an *Edmond*-type presumptive rule of unconstitutionality does not apply here. That does not mean the stop is automatically, or even presumptively, constitutional. It simply means that we must judge its reasonableness, hence, its constitutionality, on the basis of the individual circumstances. And as this Court said in Brown v. Texas, 443 U.S. 47, 51 (1979), in judging reasonableness, we look to "the gravity of the public concerns served by the seizure, the degree to which the seizure advances the public interest, and the severity of the interference with individual liberty." . . .

III

We now consider the reasonableness of the checkpoint stop before us in light of the factors just mentioned. . . . We hold that the stop was constitutional.

The relevant public concern was grave. Police were investigating a crime that had resulted in a human death. No one denies the police's need to obtain more information at that time. And the stop's objective was to help find the perpetrator of a specific and known crime, not of unknown crimes of a general sort. Cf. *Edmond*, supra, at 44.

The stop advanced this grave public concern to a significant degree. The police appropriately tailored their checkpoint stops to fit important criminal investigatory needs. The stops took place about one week after the hit-and-run accident, on the same highway near the location of the accident, and at about the same time of night. And police used the stops to obtain information from drivers, some of whom might well have been in the vicinity of the crime at the time it occurred. See App. 28-29 (describing police belief that motorists routinely leaving work after night shifts at nearby industrial complexes might have seen something relevant).

Most importantly, the stops interfered only minimally with liberty of the sort the Fourth Amendment seeks to protect. Viewed objectively, each stop required only a brief wait in line — a very few minutes at most. Contact with the police lasted only a few seconds. Cf. *Martinez-Fuerte*, 428 U.S., at 547 (upholding stops of three-to-five minutes); *Sitz*, 496 U.S., at 448 (upholding delays of 25 seconds). Police contact consisted simply of a request for information and the distribution of a flyer. Cf. *Martinez-Fuerte*, supra, at 546 (upholding inquiry as to motorists' citizenship and immigration status); *Sitz*, supra, at 447 (upholding examination of all drivers for signs of intoxication). Viewed subjectively, the contact provided little reason for anxiety or alarm. The police stopped all vehicles systematically. And there is no allegation here that the police acted in a discriminatory or otherwise unlawful manner while questioning motorists during stops.

For these reasons we conclude that the checkpoint stop was constitutional.

The judgment of the Illinois Supreme Court is reversed.

JUSTICE STEVENS, with whom JUSTICE SOUTER and JUSTICE GINSBURG join, concurring in part and dissenting in part.

There is a valid and important distinction between seizing a person to determine whether she has committed a crime and seizing a person to ask whether she has any information about an unknown person who committed a crime a week earlier. I therefore join Parts I and II of the Court's opinion explaining why our decision in Indianapolis v. Edmond, 531 U.S. 32 (2000), is not controlling in this case. However, I find the issue discussed in Part III of the opinion closer than the Court does and believe it would be wise to remand the case to the Illinois state courts to address that issue in the first instance.

In contrast to pedestrians, who are free to keep walking when they encounter police officers handing out flyers or seeking information, motorists who confront a roadblock are required to stop, and to remain stopped for as long as the officers choose to detain them. Such a seizure may seem relatively innocuous to some, but annoying to others who are forced to wait for several minutes when the line of cars is lengthened — for example, by a surge of vehicles leaving a factory at the end of a shift. Still other drivers may find an unpublicized roadblock at midnight on a Saturday somewhat alarming.

On the other side of the equation, the likelihood that questioning a random sample of drivers will yield useful information about a hit-and-run accident that occurred a week earlier is speculative at best. To be sure, the sample in this case was not entirely random: The record reveals that the police knew that the victim had finished work at the Post Office shortly before the fatal accident, and hoped that other employees of the Post Office or the nearby industrial park might work on similar schedules and, thus, have been driving the same route at the same time the previous week. That is a plausible theory, but there is no evidence in the record that the police did anything to confirm that the nearby businesses in fact had shift changes at or near midnight on Saturdays, or that they had reason to believe that a roadblock would be more effective than, say, placing flyers on the employees' cars.

In short, the outcome of the multifactor test prescribed in Brown v. Texas, 443 U.S. 47 (1979), is by no means clear on the facts of this case. Because the Illinois Appellate Court and the State Supreme Court held that the Lombard roadblock was per se unconstitutional under Indianapolis v. Edmond, neither court attempted to apply the *Brown* test. . . . We should be especially reluctant to abandon our role as a court of review in a case in which the constitutional inquiry requires analysis of local conditions and practices more familiar to judges closer to the scene. I would therefore remand the case to the Illinois courts to undertake the initial analysis of the issue that the Court resolves in Part III of its opinion. To that extent, I respectfully dissent.

NOTES AND QUESTIONS

1. In *Edmond*, the Court rejects Indianapolis's use of roadblocks to deal with the difficult problem of drug crimes — precisely the kind of proactive policing to

which *Terry*-style reasonableness analysis often applies. In *Lidster*, on the other hand, the Court upholds the use of a roadblock to investigate a known past crime—precisely the kind of situation to which traditional Fourth Amendment analysis (with its reliance on probable cause and warrants) usually applies. Do these results seem backward? Is there a reasonable explanation for them?

2. What happened to the idea, expressed so forcefully in *Edmond*, that exceptions to the requirement of individualized suspicion should not be approved "where the police seek to employ a checkpoint primarily for the ordinary enterprise of investigating crimes"? Isn't that exactly what the police were doing in *Lidster*? In *Edmond*, the Court seemed to be saying that the Brown v. Texas interest-balancing approach applies only when the government's "primary purpose" lies outside of traditional crime control, i.e., when it is a so-called "special need." Why, then, did the *Lidster* Court—unanimously, on this issue—decide to use the interest-balancing approach? Is crime control now a "special need"?

3. Notice the Court's emphasis on the fact that the police in *Lidster* were chiefly looking for witnesses, not suspects. Why should that fact matter? If the Indianapolis police had printed up a flyer asking for citizens' cooperation in gathering information about local drug distribution networks, would *Edmond* have been decided differently?

4. The legal status of most roadblocks may be uncertain after *Edmond* and *Lidster*. But *Martinez-Fuerte* seems to be on stable ground. Courts have traditionally regarded certain types of searches and seizures at an international border (or its functional equivalent) as reasonable, and have required neither reasonable suspicion nor constraints on officer discretion to justify them. Routine luggage inspections upon entering the country are the most common example. Detention of travelers beyond the scope of a routine customs search requires more in the way of justification, but the government is still afforded broad authority in this context. Consider United States v. Montoya de Hernandez, 473 U.S. 531 (1985). There, customs officials had reasonable suspicion to believe that the defendant, who had traveled from Colombia, was smuggling contraband in her alimentary canal. After she refused to submit to an X ray, Montoya de Hernandez remained in detention for 16 hours before customs officials obtained a court order for a medical examination that ultimately revealed narcotics. The Supreme Court held that though the length of her detention exceeded any other it had approved on reasonable suspicion, it was nonetheless acceptable, noting that the defendant herself had contributed to this time period by attempting to avoid a bowel movement. The Fourth Amendment balance of interests, the Court said, "leans heavily to the Government" at an international border:

> At the border, customs officials have more than merely an investigative law enforcement role. They are also charged, along with immigration officials, with protecting this Nation from entrants who bring anything harmful into this country, whether that be communicable diseases, narcotics, or explosives. In this regard, the detention of a suspected alimentary canal smuggler at the border is analogous to the detention of a suspected tuberculosis carrier at the border; both are detained until their bodily processes dispel the suspicion that they will introduce a harmful agent into this country.

Id. at 543-544.

The Court reaffirmed the Government's broad authority to conduct border searches in United States v. Flores-Montano, 124 S. Ct. 1582 (2004). The gas tank of Flores-Montano's 1987 Ford Taurus station wagon was removed, disassembled and searched when Flores-Montano attempted to enter the United States at the Otay Mesa Port of Entry in southern California. Customs officials seized 37 kilograms of marijuana from the tank. The Ninth Circuit, relying on language from *Montoya de Hernandez* to the effect that *routine* searches of persons and effects at the border are not subject to any requirement of reasonable suspicion, probable cause, or warrant, had earlier determined that the search of a vehicle's gas tank is not a routine border search and must be supported by reasonable suspicion. The Supreme Court disagreed:

> The Court of Appeals took the term "routine," fashioned a new balancing test, and extended it to searches of vehicles. But the reasons that might support a requirement of some level of suspicion in the case of highly intrusive searches of the person — dignity and privacy interests of the person being searched — simply do not carry over to vehicles. Complex balancing tests to determine what is a "routine" search of a vehicle, as opposed to a more "intrusive" search of a person, have no place in border searches of vehicles.

Id. at 1585. The Court noted that it was hard to conceive how the search of a gas tank, "which should be solely a repository for fuel, could be more of an invasion of privacy than the search of an automobile's passenger compartment" — a search commonly performed in the context of border inspections. The Justices unanimously concluded that while it might be true that some searches of property at the border are so destructive as to require more in the way of justification, the Government's general authority to conduct suspicionless border inspections "includes the authority to remove, disassemble, and reassemble a vehicle's fuel tank." Id. at 1587.

b. Non-Police Searches

Many "special needs" cases involve actions that would require probable cause and a warrant if they were undertaken by police officers, in the course of traditional law enforcement, but that may require far less — such as reasonable suspicion, or even no individualized suspicion at all — if the relevant actors are not police officers. For example, the aforementioned case in which the term "special needs" was first used, New Jersey v. T.L.O., 469 U.S. 325 (1985), involved the search of a student's purse by the assistant vice principal of a public school. The Court approved the search based on a test of "reasonableness, under all the circumstances," which generally means that school officials must have "reasonable grounds for suspecting" that the student to be searched is violating (or has violated) the law or the rules of the school, and must also limit the scope of the search so that it is not "excessively intrusive." Id., at 341-342.

In Vernonia School District v. Acton, 515 U.S. 646 (1995), the Court relied on *T.L.O.*'s recognition of the "special needs" of public-school teachers and adminstrators to uphold a program of random, suspicionless drug-testing of school athletes:

> As the text of the Fourth Amendment indicates, the ultimate measure of the constitutionality of a governmental search is "reasonableness." . . . A search unsupported by probable cause can be constitutional, we have said, "when special needs, beyond the normal need for law enforcement, make the warrant and probable-cause requirement impracticable." Griffin v. Wisconsin, 483 U.S. 868 (1987).
>
> We have found such "special needs" to exist in the public school context. . . . The school search we approved in *T.L.O.* . . . *was* based on individualized *suspicion* of wrongdoing. As we explicitly acknowledged, however, " 'the Fourth Amendment imposes no irreducible requirement of such suspicion,' " id., at 342, n. 8 (quoting United States v. Martinez-Fuerte, 428 U.S. 543, 560-561 (1976)). . . .
>
> Taking into account all the factors . . . — the decreased expectation of privacy, the relative unobtrusiveness of the search, and the severity of the need met by the search — we conclude Vernonia's Policy is reasonable and hence constitutional.
>
> We caution against the assumption that suspicionless drug testing will readily pass constitutional muster in other contexts. The most significant element in this case is the first we discussed: that the Policy was undertaken in furtherance of the government's responsibilities, under a public school system, as guardian and tutor of children entrusted to its care. Just as when the government conducts a search in its capacity as employer (a warrantless search of an absent employee's desk to obtain an urgently needed file, for example), the relevant question is whether that intrusion upon privacy is one that a reasonable employer might engage in, see O'Connor v. Ortega, 480 U.S. 709 (1987); so also when the government acts as guardian and tutor the relevant question is whether the search is one that a reasonable guardian and tutor might undertake. . . . [W]e conclude that in the present case it is.

Acton is but one of several "special needs" cases in which the Court has sustained suspicionless drug-testing programs as reasonable under the Fourth Amendment. See Treasury Employees v. Von Raab, 489 U.S. 656 (1989) (drug tests for United States Customs Service employees who seek transfer or promotion to positions directly involving drug interdiction or requiring the employee to carry a firearm); Skinner v. Railway Labor Executives' Assn., 489 U.S. 602 (1989) (drug and alcohol tests for railway employees involved in train accidents or violating particular safety rules).

In Chandler v. Miller, 520 U.S. 305 (1997), however, the Court made good on its caution in *Acton* that suspicionless drug testing will not always pass constitutional muster. *Chandler* involved a Georgia law requiring that candidates for designated state offices pass a drug test. The procedures at issue were relatively unintrusive, compared to the earlier cases: a candidate was permitted to provide a urine specimen in the office of a personal physician and the test results were first given to the candidate, who controlled their further dissemination. The Court nevertheless found the law invalid, noting that "the proffered special need for drug testing must be substantial — important enough to override the individual's acknowledged privacy interest, sufficiently vital to suppress the Fourth Amendment's normal requirement of individualized suspicion." Id. at 318. The majority observed that nothing in the record suggested that there was a real problem with drug use among Georgia's office holders and noted that, at any rate, the challenged drug testing scheme, permitting candidates to schedule their own test dates, could hardly be defended as a credible means of deterring drug use or ferreting it out. The Court concluded that the need served by Georgia's drug testing scheme was "symbolic, not 'special,' as that term draws meaning from our case law." Id. at 322.

The fact patterns in all of these cases seem fairly far removed from criminal law enforcement. Some "special needs" cases, however, do involve situations where law enforcement officials may foreseeably obtain evidence of criminal wrongdoing as a result of a non-police search and, indeed, may even participate in it. What difference should this make to the "special needs" analysis? The Court considered the problem of "entanglement" with law enforcement in the following case:

FERGUSON v. CHARLESTON

Certiorari to the United States Court of Appeals for the Fourth Circuit
532 U.S. 67 (2001)

JUSTICE STEVENS delivered the opinion of the Court.

I

In the fall of 1988, staff members at the public hospital operated in the city of Charleston by the Medical University of South Carolina (MUSC) became concerned about an apparent increase in the use of cocaine by patients who were receiving prenatal treatment. In response to this perceived increase, as of April 1989, MUSC began to order drug screens to be performed on urine samples from maternity patients who were suspected of using cocaine. If a patient tested positive, she was then referred by MUSC staff to the county substance abuse commission for counseling and treatment. However, despite the referrals, the incidence of cocaine use among the patients at MUSC did not appear to change.

Some four months later, Nurse Shirley Brown, the case manager for the MUSC obstetrics department, heard a news broadcast reporting that the police in Greenville, South Carolina, were arresting pregnant users of cocaine on the theory that such use harmed the fetus and was therefore child abuse. Nurse Brown discussed the story with MUSC's general counsel, Joseph C. Good, Jr., who then contacted Charleston Solicitor Charles Condon in order to offer MUSC's cooperation in prosecuting mothers whose children tested positive for drugs at birth.[3]

After receiving Good's letter, Solicitor Condon took the first steps in developing the policy at issue in this case. He organized the initial meetings, decided who would participate, and issued the invitations, in which he described his plan to prosecute women who tested positive for cocaine while pregnant. The task force that Condon formed included representatives of MUSC, the police, the County Substance Abuse Commission and the Department of Social Services. Their deliberations led to MUSC's adoption of a 12-page document entitled "POLICY M-7," dealing with the subject of "Management of Drug Abuse During Pregnancy." App. to Pet. for Cert. A-53.

---

3. In his letter dated August 23, 1989, Good wrote: "Please advise us if your office is anticipating future criminal action and what if anything our Medical Center needs to do to assist you in this matter." App. to Pet. for Cert. A-67.

The first three pages of Policy M-7 set forth the procedure to be followed by the hospital staff to "identify/assist pregnant patients suspected of drug abuse." Id., at A-53 to A-56. The first section, entitled the "Identification of Drug Abusers," provided that a patient should be tested for cocaine through a urine drug screen if she met one or more of nine criteria.[4] . . . The policy also provided for education and referral to a substance abuse clinic for patients who tested positive. Most important, it added the threat of law enforcement intervention that "provided the necessary 'leverage' to make the [p]olicy effective." Brief for Respondents 8. . . .

The threat of law enforcement involvement was set forth in two protocols, the first dealing with the identification of drug use during pregnancy, and the second with identification of drug use after labor. Under the latter protocol, the police were to be notified without delay and the patient promptly arrested. Under the former, after the initial positive drug test, the police were to be notified (and the patient arrested) only if the patient tested positive for cocaine a second time or if she missed an appointment with a substance abuse counselor.[5] In 1990, however, the policy was modified at the behest of the solicitor's office to give the patient who tested positive during labor, like the patient who tested positive during a prenatal care visit, an opportunity to avoid arrest by consenting to substance abuse treatment.

The last six pages of the policy contained forms for the patients to sign, as well as procedures for the police to follow when a patient was arrested. The policy also prescribed in detail the precise offenses with which a woman could be charged, depending on the stage of her pregnancy. If the pregnancy was 27 weeks or less, the patient was to be charged with simple possession. If it was 28 weeks or more, she was to be charged with possession and distribution to a person under the age of 18—in this case, the fetus. If she delivered "while testing positive for illegal drugs," she was also to be charged with unlawful neglect of a child. App. to Pet. for Cert. A-62. Under the policy, the police were instructed to interrogate the arrestee in order "to ascertain the identity of the subject who provided illegal drugs to the suspect." Id., at A-63. Other than the provisions describing the substance abuse treatment to be offered to women who tested positive, the policy made no mention of any change in the prenatal care of such patients, nor did it prescribe any special treatment for the newborns.

II

Petitioners are 10 women who received obstetrical care at MUSC and who were arrested after testing positive for cocaine. Four of them were arrested during the

---

4. Those criteria were as follows:

"1. No prenatal care
"2. Late prenatal care after 24 weeks gestation
"3. Incomplete prenatal care
"4. Abruptio placentae
"5. Intrauterine fetal death
"6. Preterm labor 'of no obvious cause'
"7. IUGR [intrauterine growth retardation] 'of no obvious cause'
"8. Previously known drug or alcohol abuse
"9. Unexplained congenital anomalies." Id., at A-53 to A-54.

5. Despite the conditional description of the first category, when the policy was in its initial stages, a positive test was immediately reported to the police, who then promptly arrested the patient.

initial implementation of the policy; they were not offered the opportunity to receive drug treatment as an alternative to arrest. The others were arrested after the policy was modified in 1990; they either failed to comply with the terms of the drug treatment program or tested positive for a second time. . . .

Petitioners' complaint challenged the validity of the policy under various theories, including the claim that warrantless and nonconsensual drug tests conducted for criminal investigatory purposes were unconstitutional searches. Respondents advanced two principal defenses to the constitutional claim: (1) that, as a matter of fact, petitioners had consented to the searches; and (2) that, as a matter of law, the searches were reasonable, even absent consent, because they were justified by special non-law-enforcement purposes. The District Court rejected the second defense because the searches in question "were not done by the medical university for independent purposes. [Instead,] the police came in and there was an agreement reached that the positive screens would be shared with the police." App. 1248-1249. Accordingly, the District Court submitted the factual defense to the jury with instructions that required a verdict in favor of petitioners unless the jury found consent.[6] The jury found for respondents.

Petitioners appealed, arguing that the evidence was not sufficient to support the jury's consent finding. The Court of Appeals for the Fourth Circuit affirmed, but without reaching the question of consent. Disagreeing with the District Court, the majority of the appellate panel held that the searches were reasonable as a matter of law under our line of cases recognizing that "special needs" may, in certain exceptional circumstances, justify a search policy designed to serve non-law-enforcement ends. On the understanding "that MUSC personnel conducted the urine drug screens for medical purposes wholly independent of an intent to aid law enforcement efforts," the majority applied the balancing test used in Treasury Employees v. Von Raab, 489 U.S. 656 (1989), and Vernonia School Dist. 47J v. Acton, 515 U.S. 646 (1995), and concluded that the interest in curtailing the pregnancy complications and medical costs associated with maternal cocaine use outweighed what the majority termed a minimal intrusion on the privacy of the patients. . . .

We granted certiorari to review the appellate court's holding on the "special needs" issue. Because we do not reach the question of the sufficiency of the evidence with respect to consent, we necessarily assume for purposes of our decision — as did the Court of Appeals — that the searches were conducted without the informed consent of the patients. We conclude that the judgment should be reversed and the case remanded for a decision on the consent issue.

III

Because MUSC is a state hospital, the members of its staff are government actors, subject to the strictures of the Fourth Amendment. Moreover, the urine tests conducted by those staff members were indisputably searches within the meaning

---

6. . . . Under the judge's instructions, in order to find that the plaintiffs had consented to the searches, it was necessary for the jury to find that they had consented to the taking of the samples, to the testing for evidence of cocaine, and to the possible disclosure of the test results to the police. Respondents have not argued, as JUSTICE SCALIA does, that it is permissible for members of the staff of a public hospital to use diagnostic tests "deceivingly" to obtain incriminating evidence from their patients.

of the Fourth Amendment. Skinner v. Railway Labor Executives' Assn., 489 U.S. 602, 617 (1989). Neither the District Court nor the Court of Appeals concluded that any of the nine criteria used to identify the women to be searched provided either probable cause to believe that they were using cocaine, or even the basis for a reasonable suspicion of such use. Rather, the District Court and the Court of Appeals viewed the case as one involving MUSC's right to conduct searches without warrants or probable cause. Furthermore, given the posture in which the case comes to us, we must assume for purposes of our decision that the tests were performed without the informed consent of the parties.

Because the hospital seeks to justify its authority to conduct drug tests and to turn the results over to law enforcement agents without the knowledge or consent of the patients, this case differs from the four previous cases in which we have considered whether comparable drug tests "fit within the closely guarded category of constitutionally permissible suspicionless searches." Chandler v. Miller, 520 U.S. 305, 309 (1997). In three of those cases, we sustained drug tests for railway employees involved in train accidents, Skinner v. Railway Labor Executives' Assn., 489 U.S. 602 (1989), for United States Customs Service employees seeking promotion to certain sensitive positions, Treasury Employees v. Von Raab, 489 U.S. 656 (1989), and for high school students participating in interscholastic sports, Vernonia School Dist. 47J v. Acton, 515 U.S. 646. In the fourth case, we struck down such testing for candidates for designated state offices as unreasonable. Chandler v. Miller, 520 U.S. 305 (1997).

In each of those cases, we employed a balancing test that weighed the intrusion on the individual's interest in privacy against the "special needs" that supported the program. As an initial matter, we note that the invasion of privacy in this case is far more substantial than in those cases. In the previous four cases, there was no misunderstanding about the purpose of the test or the potential use of the test results, and there were protections against the dissemination of the results to third parties. The use of an adverse test result to disqualify one from eligibility for a particular benefit, such as a promotion or an opportunity to participate in an extracurricular activity, involves a less serious intrusion on privacy than the unauthorized dissemination of such results to third parties. The reasonable expectation of privacy enjoyed by the typical patient undergoing diagnostic tests in a hospital is that the results of those tests will not be shared with nonmedical personnel without her consent. In none of our prior cases was there any intrusion upon that kind of expectation.[14]

The critical difference between those four drug-testing cases and this one, however, lies in the nature of the "special need" asserted as justification for the warrantless searches. In each of those earlier cases, the "special need" that was advanced as a justification for the absence of a warrant or individualized suspicion was one divorced from the State's general interest in law enforcement.[15] . . . In this case, however, the central and indispensable feature of the policy from its

14. In fact, we have previously recognized that an intrusion on that expectation may have adverse consequences because it may deter patients from receiving needed medical care. Whalen v. Roe, 429 U.S. 589, 599-600 (1977).

15. . . . In other special needs cases, we have tolerated suspension of the Fourth Amendment's warrant or probable-cause requirement in part because there was no law enforcement purpose behind the searches in those cases, and there was little, if any, entanglement with law enforcement. . . .

inception was the use of law enforcement to coerce the patients into substance abuse treatment. This fact distinguishes this case from circumstances in which physicians or psychologists, in the course of ordinary medical procedures aimed at helping the patient herself, come across information that under rules of law or ethics is subject to reporting requirements, which no one has challenged here. See, e.g., Council on Ethical and Judicial Affairs, American Medical Association, PolicyFinder, Current Opinions E-5.05 (2000) (requiring reporting where "a patient threatens to inflict serious bodily harm to another person or to him or herself and there is a reasonable probability that the patient may carry out the threat"); Ark. Code Ann. §12-12-602 (1999) (requiring reporting of intentionally inflicted knife or gunshot wounds); Ariz. Rev. Stat. Ann. §13-3620 (Supp. 2000) (requiring "any . . . person having responsibility for the care or treatment of children" to report suspected abuse or neglect to a peace officer or child protection agency).

Respondents argue in essence that their ultimate purpose — namely, protecting the health of both mother and child — is a beneficent one. . . . [A] review of the M-7 policy plainly reveals that the purpose actually served by the MUSC searches "is ultimately indistinguishable from the general interest in crime control." Indianapolis v. Edmond, 531 U.S. 32, 44 (2000).

In looking to the programmatic purpose, we consider all the available evidence in order to determine the relevant primary purpose. See, e.g., id., at 45-47. In this case, as Judge Blake put it in her dissent below, "it . . . is clear from the record that an initial and continuing focus of the policy was on the arrest and prosecution of drug-abusing mothers. . . . " Tellingly, the document codifying the policy incorporates the police's operational guidelines. It devotes its attention to the chain of custody, the range of possible criminal charges, and the logistics of police notification and arrests. Nowhere, however, does the document discuss different courses of medical treatment for either mother or infant, aside from treatment for the mother's addiction.

Moreover, throughout the development and application of the policy, the Charleston prosecutors and police were extensively involved in the day-to-day administration of the policy. Police and prosecutors decided who would receive the reports of positive drug screens and what information would be included with those reports. Law enforcement officials also helped determine the procedures to be followed when performing the screens. In the course of the policy's administration, they had access to Nurse Brown's medical files on the women who tested positive, routinely attended the substance abuse team's meetings, and regularly received copies of team documents discussing the women's progress. Police took pains to coordinate the timing and circumstances of the arrests with MUSC staff, and, in particular, Nurse Brown.

While the ultimate goal of the program may well have been to get the women in question into substance abuse treatment and off of drugs, the immediate objective of the searches was to generate evidence *for law enforcement purposes* in order to reach that goal. The threat of law enforcement may ultimately have been intended as a means to an end, but the direct and primary purpose of MUSC's policy was to ensure the use of those means. In our opinion, this distinction is critical. Because law enforcement involvement always serves some broader social purpose or objective, under respondents' view, virtually any nonconsensual suspicionless search could be immunized under the special needs doctrine by defining the search solely in terms of its ultimate, rather than immediate, purpose. Such an approach is inconsistent with the Fourth Amendment. Given the primary purpose of the Charleston program, which was to use the threat of arrest and prosecution in order to force women into treatment, and given the extensive involvement of law enforcement officials at every stage of the policy, this case simply does not fit within the closely guarded category of "special needs."

The fact that positive test results were turned over to the police does not merely provide a basis for distinguishing our prior cases applying the "special needs" balancing approach to the determination of drug use. It also provides an affirmative reason for enforcing the strictures of the Fourth Amendment. While state hospital employees, like other citizens, may have a duty to provide the police with evidence of criminal conduct that they inadvertently acquire in the course of routine treatment, when they undertake to obtain such evidence from their patients *for the specific purpose of incriminating those patients*, they have a special obligation to make sure that the patients are fully informed about their constitutional rights, as standards of knowing waiver require.[24] Cf. Miranda v. Arizona, 384 U.S. 436 (1966).

As respondents have repeatedly insisted, their motive was benign rather than punitive. Such a motive, however, cannot justify a departure from Fourth Amendment protections, given the pervasive involvement of law enforcement with the development and application of the MUSC policy. The stark and unique fact that characterizes this case is that Policy M-7 was designed to obtain evidence of criminal conduct by the tested patients that would be turned over to the police and that could be admissible in subsequent criminal prosecutions. While respondents are correct that drug abuse both was and is a serious problem, "the gravity of the threat alone cannot be dispositive of questions concerning what means law enforcement officers may employ to pursue a given purpose." Indianapolis v. Edmond, 531 U.S., at 42-43. The Fourth Amendment's general prohibition against nonconsensual, warrantless, and suspicionless searches necessarily applies to such a policy.

Accordingly, the judgment of the Court of Appeals is reversed, and the case is remanded for further proceedings consistent with this opinion.

JUSTICE KENNEDY, concurring in the judgment.

I agree that the search procedure in issue cannot be sustained under the Fourth Amendment. My reasons for this conclusion differ somewhat from those set forth by the Court, however, leading to this separate opinion.

The Court does not dispute that the search policy at some level serves special needs, beyond those of ordinary law enforcement, such as the need to protect the health of mother and child when a pregnant mother uses cocaine. Instead, the majority characterizes these special needs as the "ultimate goal[s]" of the policy, as distinguished from the policy's "immediate purpose," the collection of evidence of

24. ... The dissent ... mischaracterizes our opinion as holding that "material which a person voluntarily entrusts to someone else cannot be given by that person to the police, and used for whatever evidence it may contain." But, as we have noted elsewhere, given the posture of the case, we must assume for purposes of decision that the patients did *not* consent to the searches, and we leave the question of consent for the Court of Appeals to determine. ...

drug use, which, the Court reasons, is the appropriate inquiry for the special needs analysis.

The majority views its distinction between the ultimate goal and immediate purpose of the policy as critical to its analysis. The distinction the Court makes, however, lacks foundation in our special needs cases. All of our special needs cases have turned upon what the majority terms the policy's ultimate goal. For example, in Skinner v. Railway Labor Executives' Assn., 489 U.S. 602 (1989), had we employed the majority's distinction, we would have identified as the relevant need the collection of evidence of drug and alcohol use by railway employees. Instead, we identified the relevant need as "[t]he Government's interest in regulating the conduct of railroad employees to ensure [railroad] safety." Id., at 620. In Treasury Employees v. Von Raab, 489 U.S. 656 (1989), the majority's distinction should have compelled us to isolate the relevant need as the gathering of evidence of drug abuse by would-be drug interdiction officers. Instead, the special needs the Court identified were the necessities "to deter drug use among those eligible for promotion to sensitive positions within the [United States Customs] Service and to prevent the promotion of drug users to those positions." Id., at 666. In Vernonia School Dist. 47J v. Acton, 515 U.S. 646 (1995), the majority's distinction would have required us to identify the immediate purpose of gathering evidence of drug use by student-athletes as the relevant "need" for purposes of the special needs analysis. Instead, we sustained the policy as furthering what today's majority would have termed the policy's ultimate goal: "[d]eterring drug use by our Nation's schoolchildren," and particularly by student-athletes, because "the risk of immediate physical harm to the drug user or those with whom he is playing his sport is particularly high." Id., at 661-662.

It is unsurprising that in our prior cases we have concentrated on what the majority terms a policy's ultimate goal, rather than its proximate purpose. By very definition, in almost every case the immediate purpose of a search policy will be to obtain evidence. The circumstance that a particular search, like all searches, is designed to collect evidence of some sort reveals nothing about the need it serves. Put a different way, although procuring evidence is the immediate result of a successful search, until today that procurement has not been identified as the special need which justifies the search.

While the majority's reasoning seems incorrect in the respects just discussed, I agree with the Court that the search policy cannot be sustained. As the majority demonstrates and well explains, there was substantial law enforcement involvement in the policy from its inception. None of our special needs precedents has sanctioned the routine inclusion of law enforcement, both in the design of the policy and in using arrests, either threatened or real, to implement the system designed for the special needs objectives. . . . The traditional warrant and probable-cause requirements are waived in our previous cases on the explicit assumption that the evidence obtained in the search is not intended to be used for law enforcement purposes. Most of those tested for drug use under the policy at issue here were not brought into direct contact with law enforcement. This does not change the fact, however, that, as a systemic matter, law enforcement was a part of the implementation of the search policy in each of its applications. Every individual who tested positive was given a letter explaining the policy not from the hospital but from the solicitor's office. Everyone who tested positive was told a second positive test or failure to undergo substance abuse treatment would result in arrest and prosecution. As the Court holds, the hospital acted, in some respects, as an institutional arm of law enforcement for purposes of the policy. . . .

In my view, it is necessary and prudent to be explicit in explaining the limitations of today's decision. The beginning point ought to be to acknowledge the legitimacy of the State's interest in fetal life and of the grave risk to the life and health of the fetus, and later the child, caused by cocaine ingestion. . . . There should be no doubt that South Carolina can impose punishment upon an expectant mother who has so little regard for her own unborn that she risks causing him or her lifelong damage and suffering. The State, by taking special measures to give rehabilitation and training to expectant mothers with this tragic addiction or weakness, acts well within its powers and its civic obligations.

The holding of the Court, furthermore, does not call into question the validity of mandatory reporting laws such as child abuse laws which require teachers to report evidence of child abuse to the proper authorities, even if arrest and prosecution is the likely result. That in turn highlights the real difficulty. As this case comes to us, and as reputable sources confirm, see K. Farkas, Training Health Care and Human Services Personnel in Perinatal Substance Abuse, in Drug & Alcohol Abuse Reviews, Substance Abuse During Pregnancy and Childhood, 13, 27-28 (R. Watson ed. 1995); U.S. Dept. of Health and Human Services, Substance Abuse and Mental Health Services Administration, Pregnant, Substance-Using Women 48 (1993), we must accept the premise that the medical profession can adopt acceptable criteria for testing expectant mothers for cocaine use in order to provide prompt and effective counseling to the mother and to take proper medical steps to protect the child. If prosecuting authorities then adopt legitimate procedures to discover this information and prosecution follows, that ought not to invalidate the testing. One of the ironies of the case, then, may be that the program now under review, which gives the cocaine user a second and third chance, might be replaced by some more rigorous system. . . .

An essential, distinguishing feature of the special needs cases is that the person searched has consented, though the usual voluntariness analysis is altered because adverse consequences, (e.g., dismissal from employment or disqualification from playing on a high school sports team), will follow from refusal. The person searched has given consent, as defined to take into account that the consent was not voluntary in the full sense of the word. The consent, and the circumstances in which it was given, bear upon the reasonableness of the whole special needs program.

Here, on the other hand, the question of consent, even with the special connotation used in the special needs cases, has yet to be decided. Indeed, the Court finds it necessary to take the unreal step of assuming there was no voluntary consent at all. Thus, we have erected a strange world for deciding the case.

My discussion has endeavored to address the permissibility of a law enforcement purpose in this artificial context. The role played by consent might have affected our assessment of the issues. . . . Had we the prerogative to discuss the role played by consent, the case might have been quite a different one. All are in agreement, of course, that the Court of Appeals will address these issues in further proceedings on remand.

With these remarks, I concur in the judgment.

JUSTICE SCALIA, with whom THE CHIEF JUSTICE and JUSTICE THOMAS join as to Part II, dissenting. . . .

I

The first step in Fourth Amendment analysis is to identify the search or seizure at issue. What petitioners, the Court, and to a lesser extent the concurrence really object to is not the urine testing, but the hospital's reporting of positive drug-test results to police. But the latter is obviously not a search. . . . There is only one act that could conceivably be regarded as a search of petitioners in the present case: the *taking* of the urine sample. I suppose the *testing* of that urine for traces of unlawful drugs could be considered a search of sorts, but the Fourth Amendment protects only against searches of citizens' "persons, houses, papers, and effects"; and it is entirely unrealistic to regard urine as one of the "effects" (i.e., part of the property) of the person who has passed and abandoned it. Cf. California v. Greenwood, 486 U.S. 35 (1988) (garbage left at curb is not property protected by the Fourth Amendment). Some would argue, I suppose, that testing of the urine is prohibited by some generalized privacy right "emanating" from the "penumbras" of the Constitution (a question that is not before us); but it is not even arguable that the testing of urine that has been lawfully obtained is a Fourth Amendment search. (I may add that, even if it were, the factors legitimizing the taking of the sample, which I discuss below, would likewise legitimize the testing of it.)

It is rudimentary Fourth Amendment law that a search which has been consented to is not unreasonable. There is no contention in the present case that the urine samples were extracted forcibly. The only conceivable bases for saying that they were obtained without consent are the contentions (1) that the consent was coerced by the patients' need for medical treatment, (2) that the consent was uninformed because the patients were not told that the tests would include testing for drugs, and (3) that the consent was uninformed because the patients were not told that the results of the tests would be provided to the police. . . .

Under our established Fourth Amendment law, the last two contentions would not suffice, even without reference to the special-needs doctrine. The Court's analogizing of this case to Miranda v. Arizona, 384 U.S. 436 (1966), and its claim that "standards of knowing waiver" apply, are flatly contradicted by our jurisprudence, which shows that using lawfully (but deceivingly) obtained material for purposes other than those represented, and giving that material or information derived from it to the police, is not unconstitutional. In Hoffa v. United States, 385 U.S. 293 (1966), "[t]he argument [was] that [the informant's] failure to disclose his role as a government informant vitiated the consent that the petitioner gave" for the agent's access to evidence of criminal wrongdoing, id., at 300. We rejected that argument, because "the Fourth Amendment [does not protect] a wrongdoer's misplaced belief that a person to whom he voluntarily confides his wrongdoing will not reveal it." Id., at 302. Because the defendant had voluntarily provided access to the evidence, there was no reasonable expectation of privacy to invade. . . .

Until today, we have *never* held—or even suggested—that material which a person voluntarily entrusts to someone else cannot be given by that person to the police, and used for whatever evidence it may contain. Without so much as discussing the point, the Court today opens a hole in our Fourth Amendment jurisprudence, the size and shape of which is entirely indeterminate. Today's holding would be remarkable enough if the confidential relationship violated by the police conduct were at least one protected by state law. It would be surprising to learn, for example, that in a State which recognizes a spousal evidentiary privilege the police cannot use evidence obtained from a cooperating husband or wife. But today's holding goes even beyond that, since there does not exist any physician-patient privilege in South Carolina. See, e.g., Peagler v. Atlantic Coast R.R. Co., 232 S.C. 274 (1958). Since the Court declines even to discuss the issue, it leaves law enforcement officials entirely in the dark as to when they can use incriminating evidence obtained from "trusted" sources. Presumably the lines will be drawn in the case-by-case development of a whole new branch of Fourth Amendment jurisprudence, taking yet another social judgment (which confidential relationships ought not be invaded by the police) out of democratic control, and confiding it to the uncontrolled judgment of this Court—uncontrolled because there is no common-law precedent to guide it. I would adhere to our established law, which says that information obtained through violation of a relationship of trust is obtained consensually, and is hence not a search.[4]

There remains to be considered the first possible basis for invalidating this search, which is that the patients were coerced to produce their urine samples by their necessitous circumstances, to-wit, their need for medical treatment of their pregnancy. If that was coercion, it was not coercion applied by the government—and if such nongovernmental coercion sufficed, the police would never be permitted to use the ballistic evidence obtained from treatment of a patient with a bullet wound. And the Fourth Amendment would invalidate those many state laws that require physicians to report gunshot wounds, evidence of spousal abuse, and (like the South Carolina law relevant here, see S.C. Code Ann. §20-7-510 (2000)) evidence of child abuse.

II

I think it clear, therefore, that there is no basis for saying that obtaining of the urine sample was unconstitutional. The special-needs doctrine is thus quite irrelevant, since it operates only to validate searches and seizures that are otherwise unlawful. In the ensuing discussion, however, I shall assume (contrary to legal precedent) that the taking of the urine sample was (either because of the patients'

---

4. The Court contends that I am "mischaracteriz[ing]" its opinion, since the Court is merely "assum[-ing] for purposes of decision that the patients did *not* consent to the searches, and [leaves] the question of consent for the Court of Appeals to determine." That is not responsive. The "question of consent" that the Court leaves open is whether the patients consented, not merely to the taking of the urine samples, but to the drug testing in particular, and to the provision of the results to the police. Consent to the taking of the samples alone—or even to the taking of the samples *plus* the drug testing—does not suffice. The Court's contention that the question of the sufficiency of that more limited consent is not before us because respondents did not raise it is simply mistaken. Part II of respondents' brief, entitled "The Petitioners consented to the searches," argues that "Petitioners . . . freely and voluntarily . . . -provided the urine samples"; that "each of the Petitioners signed a consent to treatment form which authorized the MUSC medical staff to conduct all necessary tests of those urine samples—including drug tests"; and that "[t]here is no precedent in this Court's Fourth Amendment search and seizure jurisprudence which imposes any . . . requirement that the searching agency inform the consenting party that the results of the search will be turned over to law enforcement." Brief for Respondent 38-39. . . .

In sum, I think it clear that the Court's disposition requires the holding that violation of a relationship of trust constitutes a search. . . .

necessitous circumstances, or because of failure to disclose that the urine would be tested for drugs, or because of failure to disclose that the results of the test would be given to the police) coerced. Indeed, I shall even assume (contrary to common sense) that the testing of the urine constituted an unconsented search of the patients' effects. On those assumptions, the special-needs doctrine *would* become relevant; and, properly applied, would validate what was done here.

The conclusion of the Court that the special-needs doctrine is inapplicable rests upon its contention that respondents "undert[ook] to obtain [drug] evidence from their patients" not for any medical purpose, but "*for the specific purpose of incriminating those patients.*" Ante, at 85 (emphasis in original). In other words, the purported medical rationale was merely a pretext; there was no special need. This contention contradicts the District Court's finding of fact that the goal of the testing policy "was not to arrest patients but to facilitate their treatment and protect both the mother and unborn child." This finding is binding upon us unless clearly erroneous, see Fed. Rule Civ. Proc. 52(a). Not only do I find it supportable; I think any other finding would have to be overturned.

The cocaine tests started in April 1989, *neither at police suggestion nor with police involvement.* Expectant mothers who tested positive were referred by hospital staff for substance-abuse treatment—an obvious health benefit to both mother and child. See App. 43 (testimony that a single use of cocaine can cause fetal damage). And, since "[i]nfants whose mothers abuse cocaine during pregnancy are born with a wide variety of physical and neurological abnormalities," ante, at 89 (KENNEDY, J., concurring in judgment), which require medical attention, see Brief in Opposition A76-A77, the tests were of additional medical benefit in predicting needed postnatal treatment for the child. Thus, in their origin—before the police were in any way involved—the tests had an immediate, not merely an "ultimate," purpose of improving maternal and infant health. Several months after the testing had been initiated, a nurse discovered that local police were arresting pregnant users of cocaine for child abuse, the hospital's general counsel wrote the county solicitor to ask "what, if anything, our Medical Center needs to do to assist you in this matter," App. 499 (South Carolina law requires child abuse to be reported, see S.C. Code Ann. §20-7-510), the police suggested ways to avoid tainting evidence, and the hospital and police in conjunction used the testing program as a means of securing what the Court calls the "ultimate" health benefit of coercing drug-abusing mothers into drug treatment. Why would there be any reason to believe that, once this policy of using the drug tests for their "ultimate" health benefits had been adopted, use of them for their original, *immediate*, benefits somehow disappeared, and testing somehow became in its entirety nothing more than a "pretext" for obtaining grounds for arrest? On the face of it, this is incredible. The only evidence of the exclusively arrest-related purpose of the testing adduced by the Court is that the police-cooperation policy *itself* does not describe how to care for cocaine-exposed infants. But *of course* it does not, since that policy, adopted months after the cocaine testing was initiated, had as its only health object the "ultimate" goal of inducing drug treatment through threat of arrest. Does the Court really believe (or even *hope*) that, once invalidation of the program challenged here has been decreed, drug testing will cease?

In sum, there can be no basis for the Court's purported ability to "distinguis[h] this case from circumstances in which physicians or psychologists, in the course of ordinary medical procedures aimed at helping the patient herself, come across information that . . . is subject to reporting requirements," ante, at 80-81, unless it is this: That the *addition* of a law-enforcement-related purpose *to* a legitimate medical purpose destroys applicability of the "special-needs" doctrine. But that is quite impossible, since the special-needs doctrine was developed, and is ordinarily employed, precisely to enable searches *by law enforcement officials* who, of course, ordinarily have a law enforcement objective. Thus, in Griffin v. Wisconsin, 483 U.S. 868 (1987), a probation officer received a tip from a detective that petitioner, a felon on parole, possessed a firearm. Accompanied by police, he conducted a warrantless search of petitioner's home. The weapon was found and used as evidence in the probationer's trial for unlawful possession of a firearm. Affirming denial of a motion to suppress, we concluded that the "special need" of assuring compliance with terms of release justified a warrantless search of petitioner's home. Notably, we observed that a probation officer is not

> "the police officer who normally conducts searches against the ordinary citizen. He is an employee of the State Department of Health and Social Services who, while assuredly charged with protecting the public interest, is also supposed to have in mind the welfare of the probationer. . . . In such a setting, we think it reasonable to dispense with the warrant requirement." Id., at 876-877.

Like the probation officer, the doctors here do not "ordinarily conduc[t] searches against the ordinary citizen," and they are "supposed to have in mind the welfare of the [mother and child]." That they have in mind in addition the provision of evidence to the police should make no difference. The Court suggests that if police involvement in this case was in some way incidental and after-the-fact, that would make a difference in the outcome. But in *Griffin*, even more than here, police were involved in the search from the very beginning; indeed, the initial tip about the gun came from a detective. Under the factors relied upon by the Court, the use of evidence approved in *Griffin* would have been permitted only if the parole officer had been untrained in chain-of-custody procedures, had not known of the possibility a gun was present, and had been unaccompanied by police when he simply happened upon the weapon. Why any or all of these is constitutionally significant is baffling.

Petitioners seek to distinguish *Griffin* by observing that probationers enjoy a lesser expectation of privacy than does the general public. That is irrelevant to the point I make here, which is that the presence of a law enforcement purpose does not render the special-needs doctrine inapplicable. In any event, I doubt whether Griffin's reasonable expectation of privacy in his home was any less than petitioners' reasonable expectation of privacy in their urine taken, or in the urine tests performed, in a hospital — especially in a State such as South Carolina, which recognizes no physician-patient testimonial privilege and requires the physician's duty of confidentiality to yield to public policy, see McCormick v. England, 328 S.C. 627, 633, 640-642 (Ct. App. 1997); and which requires medical conditions that indicate a violation of the law to be reported to authorities, see, e.g., S.C. Code Ann. §20-7-510 (2000) (child abuse).

The concurrence makes essentially the same basic error as the Court, though it puts the point somewhat differently: "The special needs cases we have decided," it says, "do not sustain the active use of law enforcement . . . as an integral part of a program which seeks to achieve legitimate, civil objectives." Ante, at 88. *Griffin* shows that is not true. . . . The concurrence concedes that if the testing is conducted for medical reasons, the fact that "prosecuting authorities *then* adopt legitimate procedures to discover this information and prosecution follows . . . ought not to invalidate the testing." Ante, at 90 (emphasis added). But here the police involvement in each case did *take place after* the testing was conducted for independent reasons. Surely the concurrence cannot mean that no police-suggested procedures (such as preserving the chain of custody of the urine sample) can be applied until *after* the testing; or that the police-suggested procedures must have been *designed* after the testing. The facts in *Griffin* (and common sense) show that this cannot be so. It seems to me that the only real distinction between what the concurrence must reasonably be thought to be approving, and what we have here, is that here the police took the lesser step of initially *threatening* prosecution rather than bringing it.

[I]t is not the function of this Court—at least not in Fourth Amendment cases—to weigh petitioners' privacy interest against the State's interest in meeting the crisis of "crack babies" that developed in the late 1980s. I cannot refrain from observing, however, that the outcome of a wise weighing of those interests is by no means clear. The initial goal of the doctors and nurses who conducted cocaine-testing in this case was to refer pregnant drug addicts to treatment centers, and to prepare for necessary treatment of their possibly affected children. When the doctors and nurses agreed to the program providing test results to the police, they did so because (in addition to the fact that child abuse was required by law to be reported) they wanted to use the sanction of arrest as a strong incentive for their addicted patients to undertake drug-addiction treatment. And the police themselves used it for that benign purpose, as is shown by the fact that only 30 of 253 women testing positive for cocaine were ever arrested, and only 2 of those prosecuted. It would not be unreasonable to conclude that today's judgment, authorizing the assessment of damages against the county solicitor and individual doctors and nurses who participated in the program, proves once again that no good deed goes unpunished. . . .

NOTES AND QUESTIONS

1. What is *Ferguson*'s import? Suppose a state hospital designed a urine testing policy for its obstetrics patients without consulting with police in any way. Pursuant to this policy, patients testing positive for cocaine were to be encouraged to seek substance abuse counseling. The postnatal regime was also to be modified, to at least partly address the risk of substance abuse. In addition, positive test results were to be reported to law enforcement officials. (Urine samples would only be obtained with the consent of the patients, who would be informed that the samples would be tested for cocaine. Patients, however, were not to be advised that test results could be provided to police.) Would such a policy be constitutional after *Ferguson*?

2. What if the hospital's policy did not require positive test results to be provided to police, but these results were subpoenaed by a grand jury. Would such a subpoena raise any Fourth Amendment concerns?

3. Does *Ferguson* reprise certain problems in the analysis the Court employed in Indianapolis v. Edmond, supra, at page 626? Recall that in that case, the Court

held that a checkpoint program violated the Fourth Amendment because the "primary purpose" of the roadblocks was to uncover evidence of crime — there, narcotics violations. The Court distinguished earlier checkpoint cases, including the sobriety checkpoint it had approved in Michigan Dept. of State Police v. Sitz, 496 U.S. 444 (1990), on the ground that in those cases, the primary purpose served was not the detection of evidence of criminal violations. (The Court distinguished Sitz on the ground that, though the sobriety checkpoint program was used by police to identify drunk drivers, the principal aim of the program was highway safety rather than criminal investigation.)

In Ferguson, the Court tries to draw a similar line between medical procedures that may incidentally produce evidence of crime (like the examination of a battered child that reveals abuse that must then be reported) and procedures whose aim is to produce such evidence (supposedly the case in Ferguson). But how does the Court discern the "primary purpose" behind programs like the ones at issue in these cases? As Justice Scalia suggests in dissent, excessive "entanglement" with law enforcement cannot be the test — for surely the probation officer who received a tip from police before conducting a search of a probationer's home in Griffin was acting closely in concert with law enforcement authorities. And think for a moment about Ferguson. If gathering evidence of criminal wrongdoing was the primary purpose of the program there, it's not apparent that using such evidence to prosecute drug offenders was a paramount goal: as the dissent points out, only two of the 253 women who tested positive for cocaine were ever prosecuted. In either the checkpoint or special needs cases, is a test premised on purpose likely to prove workable in practice? Will such a test adequately safeguard privacy interests?

4. What about Justice Scalia's argument that this case involves no Fourth Amendment event at all — a proposition for which he is the single vote? What distinguishes this case from Hoffa, White, and the other "misplaced confidence" cases discussed beginning on page 367?

5. Various administrative inspections of closely regulated businesses have been upheld as "reasonable" for Fourth Amendment purposes — without requiring probable cause or warrants. See, e.g., Donovan v. Dewey, 452 U.S. 594 (1981) (warrantless inspections of mines and stone quarries to ensure compliance with health and safety standards); United States v. Biswell, 406 U.S. 311 (1972) (warrantless inspection of pawnshop licensed to sell sporting weapons for compliance with gun control laws). Of these cases, New York v. Burger, 482 U.S. 691 (1987), most clearly illustrates the degree to which the Court sometimes is willing to recognize "special needs" in settings where law enforcement interests clearly are also present. Burger involved a New York statute that required the owners of automobile junkyards and related businesses to maintain records of cars and major parts in their possession and to make these records, as well as the automobiles and components listed in them, available for warrantless inspection by police during regular business hours. These inspections were for the purpose of deterring motor vehicle theft. (The police in Burger had inspected a junkyard pursuant to the statute, found evidence of stolen vehicles, and arrested the owner.)

The Court observed that the warrantless inspection of premises in a "closely regulated" industry is reasonable when three criteria are met. First, there must be a "substantial" government interest informing the regulatory scheme pursuant to which the inspection is made. Second, warrantless inspections must be necessary to further the regulatory scheme. And third, the inspection program must provide a "constitutionally adequate substitute" for a warrant (by informing proprietors that regular inspections of a defined type take place pursuant to law in this industry and by placing appropriate limits on the time, place, and scope of inspections). The Court found the New York statute met these criteria. The fact that the regulatory goals in *Burger* — separating legitimate dealers in used auto parts from "chop shops" that "fenced" parts from stolen cars, and ensuring that stolen cars and parts could be traced — overlapped with purposes in the penal laws did not render the regulatory scheme invalid. "Nor do we think," the Court continued, "that this administrative scheme is unconstitutional simply because, in the course of enforcing it, an inspecting officer may discover evidence of crimes, besides violations of the scheme itself." Id. at 716.

6. Is there any justification for the relaxed Fourth Amendment standards to be found in all of these "special needs" cases? Consider how the government might behave if its authority to search were more limited: if, say, the probable cause and warrant requirements applied. The state might pass regulations extensive enough that probable cause to search regulated businesses would be easily established, or enact intrusive record-keeping and reporting requirements and gather information that way. School principals told they cannot search students' purses for cigarettes might simply impose punishments on the best available information, or create a system of hall passes and monitors that leaves students with less privacy than they would otherwise have. Government employers barred from searching their employees' file cabinets might remove the cabinets, and put all files in public areas. And if probation officers could not easily search probationers, those probationers might serve longer prison terms. In all these settings, the power to search is just one aspect of the government's regulatory power — and limiting search authority risks pushing the government to exercise its power in other ways. Search targets might be better off with broad search authority. For elaboration, see William J. Stuntz, Implicit Bargains, Government Power, and the Fourth Amendment, 44 Stan. L. Rev. 553 (1992).

Is that rationale sound? Is it consistent with the "special needs" cases? With the way Fourth Amendment law regulates ordinary police investigation of crime?

7. The forebear of the "special needs" cases was a Warren Court decision that aimed at extending, not relaxing, Fourth Amendment protections. In Camara v. Municipal Court of San Francisco, 387 U.S. 523 (1967) (also discussed supra at page 554), the Court overturned an earlier decision, Frank v. Maryland, 359 U.S. 360 (1959), which permitted a municipal health inspector to perform a home inspection without a warrant. The *Camara* Court held that a warrant was necessary for such inspections. Noting that the routine periodic inspection of all structures was the only way to achieve universal compliance with health and safety codes, however, the Court redefined the probable cause needed for such an "administrative warrant." It concluded that in the housing inspection context, probable cause exists to issue a warrant to inspect if reasonable legislative or administrative standards for conducting area inspections are satisfied — even though these standards do not require specific knowledge that code violations exist in a particular dwelling.

Does requiring an "administrative warrant" in the absence of traditional probable cause protect Fourth Amendment values? Should the Court require such warrants more frequently in its special needs cases? Or does the crafting of a new kind of warrant instead endanger the integrity of the probable-cause-and-warrant framework?

4. Reasonableness and Police Use of Force

TENNESSEE v. GARNER

Certiorari to the United States Court of Appeals for the Sixth Circuit
471 U.S. 1 (1985)

JUSTICE WHITE delivered the opinion of the Court.

This case requires us to determine the constitutionality of the use of deadly force to prevent the escape of an apparently unarmed suspected felon. We conclude that such force may not be used unless it is necessary to prevent the escape and the officer has probable cause to believe that the suspect poses a significant threat of death or serious physical injury to the officer or others.

I

At about 10:45 p.m. on October 3, 1974, Memphis Police Officers Elton Hymon and Leslie Wright were dispatched to answer a "prowler inside call." Upon arriving at the scene they saw a woman standing on her porch and gesturing toward the adjacent house. She told them she had heard glass breaking and that "they" or "someone" was breaking in next door. While Wright radioed the dispatcher to say that they were on the scene, Hymon went behind the house. He heard a door slam and saw someone run across the backyard. The fleeing suspect, who was appellee-respondent's decedent, Edward Garner, stopped at a 6-feet-high chain link fence at the edge of the yard. With the aid of a flashlight, Hymon was able to see Garner's face and hands. He saw no sign of a weapon, and, though not certain, was "reasonably sure" and "figured" that Garner was unarmed. He thought Garner was 17 or 18 years old and about 5' 5" or 5' 7" tall.[2] While Garner was crouched at the base of the fence, Hymon called out "police, halt" and took a few steps toward him. Garner then began to climb over the fence. Convinced that if Garner made it over the fence he would elude capture, Hymon shot him. The bullet hit Garner in the back of the head. Garner was taken by ambulance to a hospital, where he died on the operating table. Ten dollars and a purse taken from the house were found on his body.

In using deadly force to prevent the escape, Hymon was acting under the authority of a Tennessee statute and pursuant to Police Department policy . . .

Garner's father . . . brought this action . . . seeking damages under 42 U.S.C. §1983 for asserted violations of Garner's constitutional rights. . . . After a 3-day bench trial, the District Court entered judgment for all defendants. . . .

The Court of Appeals reversed and remanded. . . .

II

. . . [T]here can be no question that apprehension by the use of deadly force is a seizure subject to the reasonableness requirement of the Fourth Amendment.

A police officer may arrest a person if he has probable cause to believe that person committed a crime. Petitioners and appellant argue that if this requirement is satisfied the Fourth Amendment has nothing to say about *how* that seizure

---

2. In fact, Garner, an eighth-grader, was 15. He was 5' 4" tall and weighed somewhere around 100 or 110 pounds.

is made. This submission ignores the many cases in which this Court, by balancing the extent of the intrusion against the need for it, has examined the reasonableness of the manner in which a search or seizure is conducted. . . . Because one of the factors is the extent of the intrusion, it is plain that reasonableness depends on not only when a seizure is made, but also how it is carried out. . . .

. . . [N]otwithstanding probable cause to seize a suspect, an officer may not always do so by killing him. The intrusiveness of a seizure by means of deadly force is unmatched. The suspect's fundamental interest in his own life need not be elaborated upon. The use of deadly force also frustrates the interest of the individual, and of society, in judicial determination of guilt and punishment. Against these interests are ranged governmental interests in effective law enforcement. It is argued that overall violence will be reduced by encouraging the peaceful submission of suspects who know that they may be shot if they flee. Effectiveness in making arrests requires the resort to deadly force, or at least the meaningful threat thereof. "Being able to arrest such individuals is a condition precedent to the state's entire system of law enforcement." Brief for Petitioners 14.

Without in any way disparaging the importance of these goals, we are not convinced that the use of deadly force is a sufficiently productive means of accomplishing them to justify the killing of nonviolent suspects. . . . [W]hile the meaningful threat of deadly force might be thought to lead to the arrest of more live suspects by discouraging escape attempts, the presently available evidence does not support this thesis. The fact is that a majority of police departments in this country have forbidden the use of deadly force against nonviolent suspects. If those charged with the enforcement of the criminal law have abjured the use of deadly force in arresting nondangerous felons, there is a substantial basis for doubting that the use of such force is an essential attribute of the arrest power in all felony cases. Petitioners and appellant have not persuaded us that shooting nondangerous fleeing suspects is so vital as to outweigh the suspect's interest in his own life.

The use of deadly force to prevent the escape of all felony suspects, whatever the circumstances, is constitutionally unreasonable. It is not better that all felony suspects die than that they escape. Where the suspect poses no immediate threat to the officer and no threat to others, the harm resulting from failing to apprehend him does not justify the use of deadly force to do so. It is no doubt unfortunate when a suspect who is in sight escapes, but the fact that the police arrive a little late or are a little slower afoot does not always justify killing the suspect. A police officer may not seize an unarmed, nondangerous suspect by shooting him dead. . . .

. . . Where the officer has probable cause to believe that the suspect poses a threat of serious physical harm, either to the officer or to others, it is not constitutionally unreasonable to prevent escape by using deadly force. Thus, if the suspect threatens the officer with a weapon or there is probable cause to believe that he has committed a crime involving the infliction or threatened infliction of serious physical harm, deadly force may be used if necessary to prevent escape, and if, where feasible, some warning has been given. . . .

III

It is insisted that the Fourth Amendment must be construed in light of the common-law rule, which allowed the use of whatever force was necessary to effect the arrest of a fleeing felon, though not a misdemeanant. . . .

The State and city argue that because this was the prevailing rule at the time of the adoption of the Fourth Amendment and for some time thereafter, and is still in force in some States, use of deadly force against a fleeing felon must be "reasonable." It is true that this Court has often looked to the common law in evaluating the reasonableness, for Fourth Amendment purposes, of police activity. On the other hand, it "has not simply frozen into constitutional law those law enforcement practices that existed at the time of the Fourth Amendment's passage." Because of sweeping change in the legal and technological context, reliance on the common-law rule in this case would be a mistaken literalism that ignores the purposes of a historical inquiry.

It has been pointed out many times that the common-law rule is best understood in light of the fact that it arose at a time when virtually all felonies were punishable by death. . . . Courts have also justified the common-law rule by emphasizing the relative dangerousness of felons.

Neither of these justifications makes sense today. Almost all crimes formerly punishable by death no longer are or can be. . . . Many crimes classified as misdemeanors, or nonexistent, at common law are now felonies. . . . [N]umerous misdemeanors involve conduct more dangerous than many felonies.

There is an additional reason why the common-law rule cannot be directly translated to the present day. The common-law rule developed at a time when weapons were rudimentary. Deadly force could be inflicted almost solely in a hand-to-hand struggle during which, necessarily, the safety of the arresting officer was at risk. Handguns were not carried by police officers until the latter half of the last century. Only then did it become possible to use deadly force from a distance as a means of apprehension. As a practical matter, the use of deadly force under the standard articulation of the common-law rule has an altogether different meaning — and harsher consequences — now than in past centuries. . . .

In evaluating the reasonableness of police procedures under the Fourth Amendment, we have also looked to prevailing rules in individual jurisdictions. [Of the states in which the rule is relatively clear, 21 follow the fleeing felon rule, and 23 limit the right to use deadly force to apprehend a fleeing felon.] . . .

It cannot be said that there is a constant or overwhelming trend away from the common-law rule. In recent years, some States have reviewed their laws and expressly rejected abandonment of the common-law rule. Nonetheless, the long-term movement has been away from the rule that deadly force may be used against any fleeing felon, and that remains the rule in less than half the States.

This trend is more evident and impressive when viewed in light of the policies adopted by the police departments themselves. Overwhelmingly, these are more restrictive than the common-law rule. The Federal Bureau of Investigation and the New York City Police Department, for example, both forbid the use of firearms except when necessary to prevent death or grievous bodily harm. For accreditation by the Commission on Accreditation for Law Enforcement Agencies, a department must restrict the use of deadly force to situations where "the officer reasonably believes that the action is in defense of human life . . . or in defense of any person in immediate danger of serious physical injury." . . . Overall, only 7.5% of departmental and municipal policies explicitly permit the use of deadly force against any felon; 86.8% explicitly do not. . . .

Actual departmental policies are important for an additional reason. We would hesitate to declare a police practice of long standing "unreasonable" if doing so would severely hamper effective law enforcement. But the indications are to the contrary. There has been no suggestion that crime has worsened in any way in jurisdictions that have adopted, by legislation or departmental policy, rules similar to that announced today. . . .

Nor do we agree with petitioners and appellant that the rule we have adopted requires the police to make impossible, split-second evaluations of unknowable facts. We do not deny the practical difficulties of attempting to assess the suspect's dangerousness. However, similarly difficult judgments must be made by the police in equally uncertain circumstances. See, e.g., Terry v. Ohio, 392 U.S., at 20, 27. Nor is there any indication that in States that allow the use of deadly force only against dangerous suspects, the standard has been difficult to apply or has led to a rash of litigation involving inappropriate second-guessing of police officers' split-second decisions. . . .

IV

The District Court concluded that . . . Garner appeared to be unarmed, though Hymon could not be certain that was the case. Restated in Fourth Amendment terms, this means Hymon had no articulable basis to think Garner was armed.

. . . [T]he fact that Garner was a suspected burglar could not, without regard to the other circumstances, automatically justify the use of deadly force. Hymon did not have probable cause to believe that Garner, whom he correctly believed to be unarmed, posed any physical danger to himself or others.

The dissent argues that the shooting was justified by the fact that Officer Hymon had probable cause to believe that Garner had committed a nighttime burglary. While we agree that burglary is a serious crime, we cannot agree that it is so dangerous as automatically to justify the use of deadly force. The FBI classifies burglary as a "property" rather than a "violent" crime. Although the armed burglar would present a different situation, the fact that an unarmed suspect has broken into a dwelling at night does not automatically mean he is physically dangerous. This case demonstrates as much. In fact, the available statistics demonstrate that burglaries only rarely involve physical violence. During the 10-year period from 1973-1982, only 3.8% of all burglaries involved violent crime. Bureau of Justice Statistics, Household Burglary 4 (1985).[23]

V

. . . We hold that the [Tennessee] statute is invalid insofar as it purported to give Hymon the authority to act as he did. . . .

---

23. The dissent points out that three-fifths of all rapes in the home, three-fifths of all home robberies, and about a third of home assaults are committed by burglars. These figures mean only that if one knows that a suspect committed a rape in the home, there is a good chance that the suspect is also a burglar. That has nothing to do with the question here, which is whether the fact that someone has committed a burglary indicates that he has committed, or might commit, a violent crime.

The dissent also points out that this 3.8% adds up to 2.8 million violent crimes over a 10-year period, as if to imply that today's holding will let loose 2.8 million violent burglars. The relevant universe is, of course, far smaller. At issue is only that tiny fraction of cases where violence has taken place and an officer who has no other means of apprehending the suspect is unaware of its occurrence.

The judgment of the Court of Appeals is affirmed, and the case is remanded for further proceedings consistent with this opinion. . . .

[The dissenting opinion of Justice O'Connor, joined by Chief Justice Burger and Justice Rehnquist, is omitted.]

NOTES AND QUESTIONS

1. *Garner* is yet another "reasonableness" case in which the Court employs a free-wheeling balancing methodology to arrive at its result. But *Garner* is different from the other cases in this section. Usually, reasonableness and interest balancing mean less Fourth Amendment protection: the sliding scale slides only in one direction. In *Garner*, the Court crafts a test for police use of deadly force that is *more* stringent than the ordinary probable cause requirement.

Perhaps this should be unsurprising. There is nothing about interest balancing that automatically yields results favorable to the police. Yet the pattern of the Court's cases is striking. The largest category of "reasonableness" cases involve street stops and frisks, where the standard is explicitly lower than probable cause, and where warrants are never required. Why should the balance tilt so consistently in the government's favor? As is often the case, the circumstances of the question tend to determine the answer. The Court turned to the Fourth Amendment's reasonableness clause, and to consider-all-the-circumstances balancing, in cases where the probable cause and warrant requirements seemed too stringent. A brief street stop is less intrusive than an arrest; a pat-down of the suspect's outer clothing invades privacy less than a top-to-bottom house search. Naturally, interest-balancing would tend to produce a less stringent standard for such cases — which is how we ended up with *Terry* doctrine. Similar stories might be told about the "special needs" cases or drunk driving checkpoints. Meanwhile, cases where the probable cause standard seems too *low*, where the intrusiveness of the relevant police conduct is higher than in house searches or full-custody arrests — cases like *Garner* — are rare. The methodology is neutral; it neither favors the police nor criminal suspects. But the cases to which the methodology is applied tend to cluster at one end of the spectrum. That is why the government wins so often where "reasonableness" is the test.

Are you persuaded? Is the balance struck appropriately in *Garner*?

2. As the Court's opinion points out, many police departments, particularly big-city departments, had moved to deadly force policies more restrictive than the fleeing felon rule long before the decision in *Garner*. The results of efforts by police departments to define more narrowly the circumstances in which the use of deadly force is permitted have been positive:

> In sum, the empirical research suggests with remarkable unanimity . . . that restrictive policies seem to have worked well where they have been tried. Their adoption usually is followed by marked decreases in shootings by police, increases in the proportion of the shootings that are responses to serious criminal activity, greater or unchanged officer safety, and no resultant adverse impact on crime levels or arrest aggressiveness.

William A. Geller & Michael S. Scott, Deadly Force: What We Know, in Carl B. Klockars & Stephen D. Mastrofski, Thinking About Police 446, 465 (2d ed. 1991).

This is particularly true in places that have combined restrictive shooting policies with the institution of administrative review of shooting incidents within the police department. (In New York City, for instance, a Firearms Discharge Review Board was created in 1972 to review each and every incident in which a shot is fired by an NYPD officer; shootings by police were reduced significantly.) Some researchers have concluded that "continuing administrative pressure [of this type] is an essential supplement to a restrictive written policy." Id. at 466. If this is true, should municipal liability for Fourth Amendment violations involving police shootings turn in part on whether the relevant police department had adequate procedures in place for administrative review of shooting incidents? Consider in this connection Canton v. Harris, 489 U.S. 378, 388 (1989), which held that municipalities may be liable for inadequately training police pursuant to §1983 "only where the failure to train amounts to deliberate indifference to the rights of persons with whom the police come into contact."

3. A few police departments forbid the use of firearms except strictly in the defense of life. Others impose a requirement that officers reasonably believe that a suspect poses an *imminent* threat to the officer or to others. Does *Garner* do either of these things? Precisely what is the *Garner* standard?

GRAHAM v. CONNOR

Certiorari to the United States Court of Appeals for the Fourth Circuit
490 U.S. 386 (1989)

CHIEF JUSTICE REHNQUIST delivered the opinion of the Court.

This case requires us to decide what constitutional standard governs a free citizen's claim that law enforcement officials used excessive force in the course of making an arrest, investigatory stop, or other "seizure" of his person. . . .

In this action under 42 U.S.C. §1983, petitioner Dethorne Graham seeks to recover damages for injuries allegedly sustained when law enforcement officers used physical force against him during the course of an investigatory stop. Because the case comes to us from a decision of the Court of Appeals affirming the entry of a directed verdict for respondents, we take the evidence hereafter noted in the light most favorable to petitioner. On November 12, 1984, Graham, a diabetic, felt the onset of an insulin reaction. He asked a friend, William Berry, to drive him to a nearby convenience store so he could purchase some orange juice to counteract the reaction. Berry agreed, but when Graham entered the store, he saw a number of people ahead of him in the checkout line. Concerned about the delay, he hurried out of the store and asked Berry to drive him to a friend's house instead.

Respondent Connor, an officer of the Charlotte, North Carolina, Police Department, saw Graham hastily enter and leave the store. The officer became suspicious that something was amiss and followed Berry's car. About one-half mile from the store, he made an investigative stop. Although Berry told Connor that Graham was simply suffering from a "sugar reaction," the officer ordered Berry and Graham to wait while he found out what, if anything, had happened at the convenience store. When Officer Connor returned to his patrol car to call for backup assistance, Graham got out of the car, ran around it twice, and finally sat down on the curb, where he passed out briefly.

In the ensuing confusion, a number of other Charlotte police officers arrived on the scene in response to Officer Connor's request for backup. One of the officers rolled Graham over on the sidewalk and cuffed his hands tightly behind his back, ignoring Berry's pleas to get him some sugar. Another officer said: "I've seen a lot of people with sugar diabetes that never acted like this. Ain't nothing wrong with the M.F. but drunk. Lock the S.B. up." Several officers then lifted Graham up from behind, carried him over to Berry's car, and placed him face down on its hood. Regaining consciousness, Graham asked the officers to check in his wallet for a diabetic decal that he carried. In response, one of the officers told him to "shut up" and shoved his face down against the hood of the car. Four officers grabbed Graham and threw him headfirst into the police car. A friend of Graham's brought some orange juice to the car, but the officers refused to let him have it. Finally, Officer Connor received a report that Graham had done nothing wrong at the convenience store, and the officers drove him home and released him.

At some point during his encounter with the police, Graham sustained a broken foot, cuts on his wrists, a bruised forehead, and an injured shoulder; he also claims to have developed a loud ringing in his right ear that continues to this day. He commenced this action under 42 U.S.C. §1983 against the individual officers involved in the incident . . . alleging that they had used excessive force in making the investigatory stop, in violation of "rights secured to him under the Fourteenth Amendment to the United States Constitution and 42 U.S.C. §1983." The case was tried before a jury. At the close of petitioner's evidence, respondents moved for a directed verdict. In ruling on that motion, the District Court considered the following four factors, which it identified as "[t]he factors to be considered in determining when the excessive use of force gives rise to a cause of action under §1983": (1) the need for the application of force; (2) the relationship between that need and the amount of force that was used; (3) the extent of the injury inflicted; and (4) "[w]hether the force was applied in a good faith effort to maintain and restore discipline or maliciously and sadistically for the very purpose of causing harm." Finding that the amount of force used by the officers was "appropriate under the circumstances," that "[t]here was no discernable injury inflicted," and that the force used "was not applied maliciously or sadistically for the very purpose of causing harm," but in "a good faith effort to maintain or restore order in the face of a potentially explosive situation," the District Court granted respondents' motion for a directed verdict.

A divided panel of the Court of Appeals for the Fourth Circuit affirmed. . . . We granted certiorari, and now reverse.

Fifteen years ago, in Johnson v. Glick, 481 F.2d 1028 (1973), the Court of Appeals for the Second Circuit addressed a §1983 damages claim filed by a pretrial detainee who claimed that a guard had assaulted him without justification. In evaluating the detainee's claim, Judge Friendly applied neither the Fourth Amendment nor the Eighth, the two most textually obvious sources of constitutional protection against physically abusive governmental conduct. Instead, he looked to "substantive due process," holding that "quite apart from any 'specific' provisions of the Bill of Rights, application of undue force by law enforcement officers deprives a suspect of liberty without due process of law." 481 F.2d, at 1032. As support for this proposition, he relied upon our decision in Rochin v. California, 342 U.S. 165 (1952), which used the Due Process Clause to void a state criminal conviction based on evidence obtained by pumping the defendant's stomach. If a police officer's use of force which "shocks the conscience" could justify setting aside a criminal conviction, Judge Friendly reasoned, a correctional officer's use of similarly excessive force must give rise to a due process violation actionable under §1983. Judge Friendly went on to set forth four factors to guide courts in determining "whether the constitutional line has been crossed" by a particular use of force — the same four factors relied upon by the courts below in this case. . . .

We reject this notion that all excessive force claims brought under §1983 are governed by a single generic standard. . . . In addressing an excessive force claim brought under §1983, analysis begins by identifying the specific constitutional right allegedly infringed by the challenged application of force. . . .

Where, as here, the excessive force claim arises in the context of an arrest or investigatory stop of a free citizen, it is most properly characterized as one invoking the protections of the Fourth Amendment, which guarantees citizens the right "to be secure in their persons . . . against unreasonable . . . seizures" of the person. This much is clear from our decision in Tennessee v. Garner[, 471 U.S. 1 (1985)]. In *Garner*, we addressed a claim that the use of deadly force to apprehend a fleeing suspect who did not appear to be armed or otherwise dangerous violated the suspect's constitutional rights, notwithstanding the existence of probable cause to arrest. Though the complaint alleged violations of both the Fourth Amendment and the Due Process Clause, we analyzed the constitutionality of the challenged application of force solely by reference to the Fourth Amendment's prohibition against unreasonable seizures of the person, holding that the "reasonableness" of a particular seizure depends not only on *when* it is made, but also on *how* it is carried out. Today we make explicit what was implicit in *Garner*'s analysis, and hold that *all* claims that law enforcement officers have used excessive force — deadly or not — in the course of an arrest, investigatory stop, or other "seizure" of a free citizen should be analyzed under the Fourth Amendment and its "reasonableness" standard, rather than under a "substantive due process" approach. Because the Fourth Amendment provides an explicit textual source of constitutional protection against this sort of physically intrusive governmental conduct, that Amendment, not the more generalized notion of "substantive due process," must be the guide for analyzing these claims.

Determining whether the force used to effect a particular seizure is "reasonable" under the Fourth Amendment requires a careful balancing of " 'the nature and quality of the intrusion on the individual's Fourth Amendment interests' " against the countervailing governmental interests at stake. [471 U.S.] at 8, quoting United States v. Place, 462 U.S. 696, 703 (1983). Our Fourth Amendment jurisprudence has long recognized that the right to make an arrest or investigatory stop necessarily carries with it the right to use some degree of physical coercion or threat thereof to effect it. See Terry v. Ohio, 392 U.S., at 22-27. Because "[t]he test of reasonableness under the Fourth Amendment is not capable of precise definition or mechanical application," Bell v. Wolfish, 441 U.S. 520, 559 (1979), however, its proper application requires careful attention to the facts and circumstances of each particular case, including the severity of the crime at issue, whether the suspect poses an immediate threat to the safety of the officers or others, and whether he is actively resisting arrest or attempting to evade arrest by flight. See Tennessee v. Garner, 471 U.S., at 8-9 (the question is "whether the totality of the circumstances justifie[s] a particular sort of . . . seizure").

The "reasonableness" of a particular use of force must be judged from the perspective of a reasonable officer on the scene, rather than with the 20/20 vision of hindsight. The Fourth Amendment is not violated by an arrest based on probable cause, even though the wrong person is arrested, nor by the mistaken execution of a valid search warrant on the wrong premises. With respect to a claim of excessive force, the same standard of reasonableness at the moment applies: "Not every push or shove, even if it may later seem unnecessary in the peace of a judge's chambers," Johnson v. Glick, 481 F.2d, at 1033, violates the Fourth Amendment. The calculus of reasonableness must embody allowance for the fact that police officers are often forced to make split-second judgments—in circumstances that are tense, uncertain, and rapidly evolving—about the amount of force that is necessary in a particular situation.

As in other Fourth Amendment contexts, however, the "reasonableness" inquiry in an excessive force case is an objective one: the question is whether the officers' actions are "objectively reasonable" in light of the facts and circumstances confronting them, without regard to their underlying intent or motivation. An officer's evil intentions will not make a Fourth Amendment violation out of an objectively reasonable use of force; nor will an officer's good intentions make an objectively unreasonable use of force constitutional.

Because petitioner's excessive force claim is one arising under the Fourth Amendment, the Court of Appeals erred in analyzing it under the four-part Johnson v. Glick test. That test, which requires consideration of whether the individual officers acted in "good faith" or "maliciously and sadistically for the very purpose of causing harm," is incompatible with a proper Fourth Amendment analysis. We do not agree with the Court of Appeals' suggestion, that the "malicious and sadistic" inquiry is merely another way of describing conduct that is objectively unreasonable under the circumstances. Whatever the empirical correlations between "malicious and sadistic" behavior and objective unreasonableness may be, the fact remains that the "malicious and sadistic" factor puts in issue the subjective motivations of the individual officers, which our prior cases make clear has no bearing on whether a particular seizure is "unreasonable" under the Fourth Amendment. . . . The Fourth Amendment inquiry is one of "objective reasonableness" under the circumstances, and subjective concepts like "malice" and "sadism" have no proper place in that inquiry.

Because the Court of Appeals reviewed the District Court's ruling on the motion for directed verdict under an erroneous view of the governing substantive law, its judgment must be vacated and the case remanded to that court for reconsideration of that issue under the proper Fourth Amendment standard. . . .

[Justice Blackmun's opinion, joined by Justice Brennan and Justice Marshall, concurring in part and concurring in the judgment, is omitted.]

NOTES AND QUESTIONS

1. *Graham* squarely rejects using officers' subjective intent as part of Fourth Amendment analysis in excessive force cases. Is that sensible? What difference, if any, does it make?

2. Compare the legal standard *Graham* establishes with the standards the Court has established in many other Fourth Amendment areas. *Graham*'s standard seems

unusually vague and open-ended, does it not? Why would that be? How would one go about constructing a more definite rule structure, something that would give police officers greater guidance when it comes to the police use of force? If more definite rules are not possible, what does that say about the ability of courts to regulate police violence effectively?

3. In the one passage of its opinion that seems designed to give some content to its reasonableness standard for excessive force claims, the Court says attention must be paid to "the severity of the crime at issue, whether the suspect poses an immediate threat to the safety of the officers or others, and whether he is actively resisting arrest or attempting to evade arrest by flight." What if these factors cut in different directions? Suppose, for example, a defendant is suspected of a minor and nonviolent crime but is "attempting to evade arrest by flight." Can the police use (nondeadly) force to apprehend him?

4. The *Graham* Court cautions that Fourth Amendment reasonableness in the context of use of force "must embody allowance for the fact that police officers are often forced to make split-second judgments — in circumstances that are tense, uncertain, and rapidly evolving — about the amount of force that is necessary in a particular situation." But consider what one use-of-force expert has to say about what he terms the "split-second syndrome":

> [S]hould police receive a report of an armed robbery in a crowded supermarket, [the split-second syndrome holds that] they should be granted great leeway in their manner of response, because no two armed-robbery calls are precisely alike. If, in the course of responding, they decide that, to prevent the robber from escaping, the best course of action is to confront him immediately in the midst of a crowd of shoppers, they should not be told they should have acted otherwise. When they do challenge the alleged robber and he suddenly reacts to their calls from behind by turning on them with a shiny object in his hand, the only issue to be decided by those who subsequently review police actions is whether, at that instant, the suspect's actions were sufficiently provocative to justify their shooting him. That is so regardless of how the prior actions of the police may have contributed to their peril; regardless of how predictable it was that the suspect would be alarmed and would turn toward the police when they shouted to him; regardless of how many innocent bystanders were hit by bullets; and regardless of whether the reported armed robber was in fact an unhappy customer who, with pen in hand to complete a check for his purchase, had been engaged in a loud argument with a clerk. . . .

James J. Fyfe, The Split-Second Syndrome and Other Determinants of Police Violence, in Violent Transactions 207, 218 (Anne Campbell & John Gibbs eds. 1986). Professor Fyfe urges that this approach to the analysis of use of force condones unnecessary violence and encourages an operating style among police "that eschews advance diagnosis, planning and training." Was the Court in *Graham* too lenient?

5. Does *Graham* alter the standard for deadly force claims? If so, how? Suppose a murder suspect is fleeing but does not pose an immediate danger to anyone (though he might pose some danger to others if he gets away)? Is the use of deadly force justified under *Garner* and *Graham*?

This last series of questions was at issue in the Senate hearings over the now-famous Ruby Ridge incident. In August 1992, federal marshals went to the Idaho home of Randy Weaver to arrest him for selling two illegally sawed-off shotguns to an undercover agent. (Weaver was later acquitted of the firearms charge, apparently on the ground that he was entrapped.) The agents encountered Weaver, his son, and a friend — Kevin Harris — and shots were fired. (Each side claimed the other fired first.) Weaver's son and one of the marshals were killed in the exchange. Weaver, his wife, their three other children, and Harris were holed up in a cabin on Weaver's property, and FBI agents moved into the surrounding area. The next day, Weaver and Harris were outside the cabin, armed, and according to the agents Weaver appeared to be preparing to take a shot at an FBI helicopter circling overhead. One of the agents on the ground, Lon Horiuchi, then fired at Weaver. Immediately after that first shot, Weaver and Harris ran back toward the cabin, still armed but not aiming at anyone. Horiuchi fired a second shot at Harris, mistakenly believing him to be the person who had been trying to get a shot off at the helicopter. Horiuchi's second shot missed Harris and struck and killed Vicki Weaver, Randy Weaver's wife, who was standing near the doorway of the cabin at the time. No warnings were issued before either of the two shots.

In Idaho v. Horiuchi, 215 F.3d 896 (9th Cir. 1999), a panel of the Ninth Circuit Court of Appeals concluded, over a strong dissent by Judge Kozinski, that both of Agent Horiuchi's shots were "objectively reasonable" under *Garner*. When the Ninth Circuit Court of Appeals, sitting en banc, reconsidered the Ruby Ridge incident, Judge Kozinski ended up writing the opinion for the majority, concluding that material questions of disputed fact had to be resolved before it could be determined whether Agent Horiuchi's shots were objectively reasonable. 253 F.3d 359 (9th Cir. 2001). Which conclusion seems correct?

E. Consent Searches

SCHNECKLOTH v. BUSTAMONTE

Certiorari to the United States Court of Appeals for the Ninth Circuit
412 U.S. 218 (1973)

JUSTICE STEWART delivered the opinion of the Court.

. . . [O]ne of the specifically established exceptions to the requirements of both a warrant and probable cause is a search that is conducted pursuant to consent. The constitutional question in the present case concerns the definition of "consent" in this Fourth and Fourteenth Amendment context.

The respondent was brought to trial in a California court upon a charge of possessing a check with intent to defraud. He moved to suppress the introduction of certain material as evidence against him on the ground that the material had been acquired through an unconstitutional search and seizure. . . .

While on routine patrol in Sunnyvale, California, at approximately 2:40 in the morning, Police Officer James Rand stopped an automobile when he observed that one headlight and its license plate light were burned out. Six men were in the vehicle. Joe Alcala and the respondent, Robert Bustamonte, were in the front seat with Joe Gonzales, the driver. Three older men were seated in the rear. When, in response to the policeman's question, Gonzales could not produce a driver's license, Officer Rand asked if any of the other five had any evidence of identification. Only Alcala produced a license, and he explained that the car was his brother's. After the six occupants had stepped out of the car at the officer's request and after two additional policemen had arrived, Officer Rand asked Alcala if he could search the car. Alcala replied, "Sure, go ahead." Prior to the search no one was threatened with arrest and, according to Officer Rand's uncontradicted testimony, it "was all very congenial at this time." Gonzales testified that Alcala actually helped in the search of the car, by opening the trunk and glove compartment. In Gonzales' words: "[T]he police officer asked Joe [Alcala], he goes, 'Does the trunk open?' And Joe said, 'Yes.' He went to the car and got the keys and opened up the trunk." Wadded up under the left rear seat, the police officers found three checks that had previously been stolen from a car wash.

The trial judge denied the motion to suppress, and the checks in question were admitted in evidence at Bustamonte's trial. On the basis of this and other evidence he was convicted, and the California Court of Appeal for the First Appellate District affirmed the conviction. . . .

Thereafter, the respondent sought a writ of habeas corpus in a federal district court. It was denied. On appeal, the Court of Appeals for the Ninth Circuit . . . set aside the District Court's order. . . .

. . . [T]he State concedes that "[w]hen a prosecutor seeks to rely upon consent to justify the lawfulness of a search, he has the burden of proving that the consent was, in fact, freely and voluntarily given."

The precise question in this case, then, is what must the prosecution prove to demonstrate that a consent was "voluntarily" given. . . . The Court of Appeals for the Ninth Circuit concluded that it is an essential part of the State's initial burden to prove that a person knows he has a right to refuse consent. The California courts have followed the rule that voluntariness is a question of fact to be determined from the totality of all the circumstances, and that the state of a defendant's knowledge is only one factor to be taken into account in assessing the voluntariness of a consent.

The most extensive judicial exposition of the meaning of "voluntariness" has been developed in those cases in which the Court has had to determine the "voluntariness" of a defendant's confession for purposes of the Fourteenth Amendment. . . .

Those cases yield no talismanic definition of "voluntariness," mechanically applicable to the host of situations where the question has arisen. "The notion of 'voluntariness,'" Mr. Justice Frankfurter once wrote, "is itself an amphibian." Culombe v. Connecticut, 367 U.S. 568, 604-605. It cannot be taken literally to mean a "knowing" choice. "Except where a person is unconscious or drugged or otherwise lacks capacity for conscious choice, all incriminating statements — even those made under brutal treatment — are 'voluntary' in the sense of representing a choice of alternatives. On the other hand, if 'voluntariness' incorporates notions of 'but-for' cause, the question should be whether the statement would have been made even absent inquiry or other official action. Under such a test, virtually no statement would be voluntary because very few people give incriminating statements in the absence of official action of some kind."[7] It is thus evident that

7. Bator & Vorenberg, Arrest, Detention, Interrogation and the Right to Counsel: Basic Problems and Possible Legislative Solutions, 66 Col. L. Rev. 62, 72-73. . . .

neither linguistics nor epistemology will provide a ready definition of the meaning of "voluntariness."

Rather, "voluntariness" has reflected an accommodation of the complex of values implicated in police questioning of a suspect. . . .

" . . . Is the confession the product of an essentially free and unconstrained choice by its maker? If it is, if he has willed to confess, it may be used against him. If it is not, if his will has been overborne and his capacity for self-determination critically impaired, the use of his confession offends due process." [Culombe v. Connecticut, 367 U.S. 568, 602 (1961).]

In determining whether a defendant's will was overborne in a particular case, the Court has assessed the totality of all the surrounding circumstances — both the characteristics of the accused and the details of the interrogation. . . .

[None of this Court's voluntary confession cases] . . . turned on the presence or absence of a single controlling criterion. . . .

Similar considerations lead us to agree with the courts of California that the question whether a consent to a search was in fact "voluntary" or was the product of duress or coercion, express or implied, is a question of fact to be determined from the totality of all the circumstances. While knowledge of the right to refuse consent is one factor to be taken into account, the government need not establish such knowledge as the sine qua non of an effective consent. As with police questioning, two competing concerns must be accommodated in determining the meaning of a "voluntary" consent — the legitimate need for such searches and the equally important requirement of assuring the absence of coercion.

In situations where the police have some evidence of illicit activity, but lack probable cause to arrest or search, a search authorized by a valid consent may be the only means of obtaining important and reliable evidence. . . . And in those cases where there is probable cause to arrest or search, but where the police lack a warrant, a consent search may still be valuable. If the search is conducted and proves fruitless, that in itself may convince the police that an arrest with its possible stigma and embarrassment is unnecessary, or that a far more extensive search pursuant to a warrant is not justified. In short, a search pursuant to consent may result in considerably less inconvenience for the subject of the search, and, properly conducted, is a constitutionally permissible and wholly legitimate aspect of effective police activity.

But the Fourth and Fourteenth Amendments require that a consent not be coerced, by explicit or implicit means, by implied threat or covert force. For, no matter how subtly the coercion was applied, the resulting "consent" would be no more than a pretext for the unjustified police intrusion against which the Fourth Amendment is directed. . . .

The problem of reconciling the recognized legitimacy of consent searches with the requirement that they be free from any aspect of official coercion cannot be resolved by any infallible touchstone. . . . In examining all the surrounding circumstances to determine if in fact the consent to search was coerced, account must be taken of subtly coercive police questions, as well as the possibly vulnerable subjective state of the person who consents. . . .

. . . [The Court of Appeals'] ruling, that the State must affirmatively prove that the subject of the search knew that he had a right to refuse consent, would, in practice, create serious doubt whether consent searches could continue to be conducted. There might be rare cases where it could be proved from the record that a person in fact affirmatively knew of his right to refuse. . . . But more commonly where there was no evidence of any coercion, explicit or implicit, the prosecution would nevertheless be unable to demonstrate that the subject of the search in fact had known of his right to refuse consent. . . .

One alternative that would go far toward proving that the subject of a search did know he had a right to refuse consent would be to advise him of that right before eliciting his consent. That, however, is a suggestion that has been almost universally repudiated by both federal and state courts, and, we think, rightly so. For it would be thoroughly impractical to impose on the normal consent search the detailed requirements of an effective warning. Consent searches are part of the standard investigatory techniques of law enforcement agencies. They normally occur on the highway, or in a person's home or office, and under informal and unstructured conditions. The circumstances that prompt the initial request to search may develop quickly or be a logical extension of investigative police questioning. The police may seek to investigate further suspicious circumstances or to follow up leads developed in questioning persons at the scene of a crime. These situations are a far cry from the structured atmosphere of a trial where, assisted by counsel if he chooses, a defendant is informed of his trial rights. And, while surely a closer question, these situations are still immeasurably far removed from "custodial interrogation" where, in Miranda v. Arizona, [384 U.S. 436 (1966)], we found that the Constitution required certain now familiar warnings as a prerequisite to police interrogation. . . .

It is said, however, that a "consent" is a "waiver" of a person's rights under the Fourth and Fourteenth Amendments. The argument is that by allowing the police to conduct a search, a person "waives" whatever right he had to prevent the police from searching. It is argued that under the doctrine of Johnson v. Zerbst, 304 U.S. 458, 464 [(1938)], to establish such a "waiver" the State must demonstrate "an intentional relinquishment or abandonment of a known right or privilege."

But these standards were enunciated in *Johnson* in the context of the safeguards of a fair criminal trial. Our cases do not reflect an uncritical demand for a knowing and intelligent waiver in every situation where a person has failed to invoke a constitutional protection. . . .

Almost without exception, the requirement of a knowing and intelligent waiver has been applied only to those rights which the Constitution guarantees to a criminal defendant in order to preserve a fair trial. Hence, . . . the standard of a knowing and intelligent waiver has most often been applied to test the validity of a waiver of counsel, either at trial, or upon a guilty plea. And the Court has also applied the *Johnson* criteria to assess the effectiveness of a waiver of other trial rights such as the right to confrontation, to a jury trial, and to a speedy trial, and the right to be free from twice being placed in jeopardy. Guilty pleas have been carefully scrutinized to determine whether the accused knew and understood all the rights to which he would be entitled at trial, and that he had intentionally chosen to forgo them. . . .

The guarantees afforded a criminal defendant at trial also protect him at certain stages before the actual trial, and any alleged waiver must meet the strict standard of an intentional relinquishment of a "known" right. But the "trial" guarantees that have been applied to the "pretrial" stage of the criminal process are similarly designed to protect the fairness of the trial itself. . . .

There is a vast difference between those rights that protect a fair criminal trial and the rights guaranteed under the Fourth Amendment. . . .

The protections of the Fourth Amendment . . . have nothing whatever to do with promoting the fair ascertainment of truth at a criminal trial. Rather, as Justice Frankfurter's opinion for the Court put it in Wolf v. Colorado, 338 U.S. 25, 27, the Fourth Amendment protects the "security of one's privacy against arbitrary intrusion by the police." . . .

Nor can it even be said that a search, as opposed to an eventual trial, is somehow "unfair" if a person consents to a search. While the Fourth and Fourteenth Amendments limit the circumstances under which the police can conduct a search, there is nothing constitutionally suspect in a person's voluntarily allowing a search. . . . Rather, the community has a real interest in encouraging consent, for the resulting search may yield necessary evidence for the solution and prosecution of crime, evidence that may insure that a wholly innocent person is not wrongly charged with a criminal offense.

. . . It would be unrealistic to expect that in the informal, unstructured context of a consent search, a policeman, upon pain of tainting the evidence obtained, could make the detailed type of examination demanded by *Johnson*. And, if for this reason a diluted form of "waiver" were found acceptable, that would itself be ample recognition of the fact that there is no universal standard that must be applied in every situation where a person forgoes a constitutional right.

Similarly, a "waiver" approach to consent searches would be thoroughly inconsistent with our decisions that have approved "third party consents." . . . Frazier v. Cupp, 394 U.S. 731, 740, held that evidence seized from the defendant's duffel bag in a search authorized by his cousin's consent was admissible at trial. We found that the defendant had assumed the risk that his cousin, with whom he shared the bag, would allow the police to search it. . . .

Much of what has already been said disposes of the argument that the Court's decision in the *Miranda* case requires the conclusion that knowledge of a right to refuse is an indispensable element of a valid consent. The considerations that informed the Court's holding in *Miranda* are simply inapplicable in the present case. In *Miranda* the Court found that the techniques of police questioning and the nature of custodial surroundings produce an inherently coercive situation. The Court concluded that "[u]nless adequate protective devices are employed to dispel the compulsion inherent in custodial surroundings, no statement obtained from the defendant can truly be the product of his free choice." And at another point the Court noted that "without proper safeguards the process of in-custody interrogation of persons suspected or accused of crime contains inherently compelling pressures which work to undermine the individual's will to resist and to compel him to speak where he would not otherwise do so freely."

In this case, there is no evidence of any inherently coercive tactics — either from the nature of the police questioning or the environment in which it took place. Indeed, since consent searches will normally occur on a person's own familiar territory, the specter of incommunicado police interrogation in some remote station house is simply inapposite.[36] . . .

---

36. [T]he present case does not require a determination of what effect custodial conditions might have on a search authorized solely by an alleged consent.

It is also argued that the failure to require the Government to establish knowledge as a prerequisite to a valid consent, will relegate the Fourth Amendment to the special province of "the sophisticated, the knowledgeable and the privileged." We cannot agree. The traditional definition of voluntariness we accept today has always taken into account evidence of minimal schooling, low intelligence, and the lack of any effective warnings to a person of his rights; and the voluntariness of any statement taken under those conditions has been carefully scrutinized to determine whether it was in fact voluntarily given.

Our decision today is a narrow one. We hold only that when the subject of a search is not in custody and the State attempts to justify a search on the basis of his consent, the Fourth and Fourteenth Amendments require that it demonstrate that the consent was in fact voluntarily given, and not the result of duress or coercion, express or implied. Voluntariness is a question of fact to be determined from all the circumstances, and while the subject's knowledge of a right to refuse is a factor to be taken into account, the prosecution is not required to demonstrate such knowledge as a prerequisite to establishing a voluntary consent. Because the California court followed these principles in affirming the respondent's conviction, and because the Court of Appeals for the Ninth Circuit in remanding for an evidentiary hearing required more, its judgment must be reversed.

It is so ordered.

[The concurring opinions of Justice Blackmun and Justice Powell and the dissenting opinions of Justice Douglas and Justice Brennan are omitted.]

JUSTICE MARSHALL, dissenting. . . .

If consent to search means that a person has chosen to forgo his right to exclude the police from the place they seek to search, it follows that his consent cannot be considered a meaningful choice unless he knew that he could in fact exclude the police. The Court appears, however, to reject even the modest proposition that, if the subject of a search convinces the trier of fact that he did not know of his right to refuse assent to a police request for permission to search, the search must be held unconstitutional. For it says only that "knowledge of the right to refuse consent is one factor to be taken into account." I find this incomprehensible. I can think of no other situation in which we would say that a person agreed to some course of action if he convinced us that he did not know that there was some other course he might have pursued. I would therefore hold, at a minimum, that the prosecution may not rely on a purported consent to search if the subject of the search did not know that he could refuse to give consent. . . .

If one accepts this view, the question then is a simple one: must the Government show that the subject knew of his rights, or must the subject show that he lacked such knowledge?

I think that any fair allocation of the burden would require that it be placed on the prosecution. On this question, the Court indulges in what might be called the "straw man" method of adjudication. The Court responds to this suggestion by overinflating the burden. And, when it is suggested that the *prosecution*'s burden of proof could be easily satisfied if the police informed the subject of his rights, the Court responds by refusing to require the *police* to make a "detailed" inquiry. If the Court candidly faced the real question of allocating the burden of proof, neither of these maneuvers would be available to it.

If the burden is placed on the defendant, all the subject can do is to testify that he did not know of his rights. And I doubt that many trial judges will find for the defendant simply on the basis of that testimony. Precisely because the evidence is very hard to come by, courts have traditionally been reluctant to require a party to prove negatives such as the lack of knowledge.

In contrast, there are several ways by which the subject's knowledge of his rights may be shown. The subject may affirmatively demonstrate such knowledge by his responses at the time the search took place. . . . Denials of knowledge may be disproved by establishing that the subject had, in the recent past, demonstrated his knowledge of his rights, for example, by refusing entry when it was requested by the police. The prior experience or training of the subject might in some cases support an inference that he knew of his right to exclude the police.

The burden on the prosecutor would disappear, of course, if the police, at the time they requested consent to search, also told the subject that he had a right to refuse consent and that his decision to refuse would be respected. The Court's assertions to the contrary notwithstanding, there is nothing impractical about this method of satisfying the prosecution's burden of proof. . . .

The Court contends that if an officer paused to inform the subject of his rights, the informality of the exchange would be destroyed. I doubt that a simple statement by an officer of an individual's right to refuse consent would do much to alter the informality of the exchange, except to alert the subject to a fact that he surely is entitled to know. It is not without significance that for many years the agents of the Federal Bureau of Investigation have routinely informed subjects of their right to refuse consent, when they request consent to search. . . .

The proper resolution of this case turns, I believe, on a realistic assessment of the nature of the interchange between citizens and the police, and of the practical import of allocating the burden of proof in one way rather than another. The Court seeks to escape such assessments by escalating its rhetoric to unwarranted heights, but no matter how forceful the adjectives the Court uses, it cannot avoid being judged by how well its image of these interchanges accords with reality. . . .

NOTES AND QUESTIONS

1. *Schneckloth* is a strange decision, is it not? If the search target does not know he may refuse consent, it would seem to follow that any "consent" was fictive, since the target believed he had no choice. Yet the Court holds that knowledge of the right to refuse is only one of many factors that goes into an analysis of voluntary consent. What does "voluntary" mean in this context? More generally, why would a suspect ever voluntarily consent to a search that the suspect knows will reveal incriminating evidence? If you were a judge deciding a suppression motion, would you assume such consent was probably voluntary, or would you assume the opposite?

2. Both the majority and the dissent in *Schneckloth* seem to think that warnings would have a large effect on suspects' behavior. The truth may be otherwise. Professor Nadler has examined the Court's consent doctrine in light of evidence about the psychology of compliance and consent. She points out that "empirical studies over the last several decades on the social psychology of compliance, conformity, social influence, and politeness have all converged on a single

conclusion: the extent to which people feel free to refuse to comply is extremely limited under situationally induced pressures" of the sort common to many police-citizen encounters. Janice Nadler, No Need to Shout: Bus Sweeps and the Psychology of Coercion, 2002 Sup. Ct. Rev. 153, 155. Consider the following:

> . . . [T]he majority in *Schneckloth* appears to have assumed that if warnings were required, virtually all citizens would refuse to consent to a search.
>
> That assumption turns out to be mistaken, at least in instances where it has been explicitly examined. A study of all Ohio highway stops conducted between 1995 and 1997 found no decrease in consent rates after police were required to advise motorists of their right to refuse to cooperate with a request for consent to search. In fact, the same number of citizens consent with the warnings as without the warnings. Apparently, people are unaffected by the warnings because they do not believe them — they feel that they will be searched regardless of whether or not they consent. Why would people who are told by police that they have a right to refuse to consent to search persist in believing that they have no choice and will be searched anyway? Many . . . factors . . . come into play here: we comply with the police not because we make a deliberate conscious choice to respond in a particular way, but rather because we mindlessly respond in a manner consistent with social roles; just as we do not hear "May I see your license and registration please?" as a genuine question, we do not hear "You have the right to refuse to consent" as a genuine option; under time pressure we respond to requests of authorities in the same way we usually do, by automatically complying. In this way, the experimental research suggests generally what the survey of motorists finds explicitly: people who are targeted for a search by police and informed that they have a right to refuse nonetheless feel intense pressure to comply and feel that refusal is not a genuine option.
>
> [T]here is no reason to think that police advising citizens that they have a right not to cooperate with their request for consent to search will significantly reduce coercion experienced by citizens in this situation. In this sense the issue of police warnings in consensual search situations . . . is something of a red herring and should be put aside. This issue simply diverts attention away from the real question — whether citizens who are approached and searched in these situations have consented freely or perceived themselves as having no choice.

Id. at 204-206.

3. Note that despite the Court's assurance that the voluntariness of consent to search is "carefully scrutinized" by courts in light of subjective factors that would draw it into question, there is scant evidence that such searching inquiries commonly take place. Professor Cole cites one study based on a review of all cases involving consent searches decided by the United States Court of Appeals for the District of Columbia Circuit from January 1, 1989, to April 15, 1995. In each case in which the validity of consent was challenged, the court found the consent voluntary. "In most of the cases, the courts did not even discuss the subjective factors that the Supreme Court . . . said would be relevant in determining voluntariness." David Cole, No Equal Justice 32 (1999). Professor Cole goes on to charge that the voluntariness doctrine enunciated in *Schneckloth* in practice creates a race-and class-based double standard:

> Because a consent search requires no objective individualized suspicion, it is more likely to be directed at poor young black men than wealthy white elderly women. In addition, those who are white and wealthy are more likely to know their rights and to feel secure in asserting them.

Id. at 31. Professor Thomas has argued, further, that "[t]he consent search doctrine is the handmaiden of racial profiling. . . . If police are routinely rewarded with consent, they have little incentive to develop individualized probable cause. . . . " George C. Thomas III, Terrorism, Race and a New Approach to Consent Searches, 73 Miss. L.J. 525, 542 (2003). Does this argue for rethinking the Court's approach?

4. Speaking of this approach, just why is a warrantless and suspicionless consent search consistent with the Fourth Amendment — even assuming that consent is "voluntary"? Granted, constitutional rights can generally be waived. But as the Court points out in *Schneckloth*, the waiver approach cannot explain "third-party consent" doctrine. This doctrine permits police to search based on the consent of someone other than the suspect, provided that this third person has common authority over the area searched. In *Schneckloth*, the Court treated the third-party cases as "assumption of risk" cases in which the defendant against whom evidence is proffered had assumed the risk that police would be permitted to search areas in which he had granted joint access and control to another. See also United States v. Matlock, 415 U.S. 164 (1974) (where people mutually use property and have joint access or control for most purposes, "it is reasonable to recognize that any of the co-inhabitants has the right to permit the inspection in his own right and that the others have assumed the risk that one of their number might permit the common area to be searched"). In Illinois v. Rodriguez, 497 U.S. 177 (1990), however, the Court further extended the doctrine — to intrusions based on the consent of a third party whom the police *reasonably believed* to possess common authority over the premises, even when no such authority existed.

Justice Scalia, writing for the *Rodriguez* majority, addressed both the third-party consent doctrine and the underlying rationale for consent searches:

> On July 26, 1985, police were summoned to the residence of Dorothy Jackson on South Wolcott in Chicago. They were met by Ms. Jackson's daughter, Gail Fischer, who showed signs of a severe beating. She told the officers that she had been assaulted by respondent Edward Rodriguez earlier that day in an apartment on South California Avenue. Fischer stated that Rodriguez was then asleep in the apartment, and she consented to travel there with the police in order to unlock the door with her key so that officers could enter and arrest him. During this conversation, Fischer several times referred to the apartment on South California as "our" apartment, and said that she had clothes and furniture there. It is unclear whether she indicated that she currently lived at the apartment, or only that she used to live there. . . .
>
> [When the officers and Fischer arrived at the apartment, she unlocked the door and gave the officers permission to enter. Police arrested Rodriguez and also seized narcotics in plain view. The state courts held that the narcotics were not admissible against Rodriguez because Fisher, who in fact was not currently residing in the apartment, did not have authority to consent to the search. They also ruled as a matter of law that the officers' reasonable belief in Fisher's authority would not validate the search.]
>
> . . . What [the defendant] is assured by the Fourth Amendment . . . is not that no government search of his house will occur unless he consents; but that no such search will occur that is "unreasonable." There are various elements, of course, that can make a search of a person's house "reasonable" — one of which is the consent of the person or his cotenant. The essence of respondent's argument is that we should impose upon this element a requirement that we have not imposed upon other elements that regularly compel government officers to exercise judgment regarding the facts: namely, the requirement that their judgment be not only responsible but correct.

The fundamental objective that alone validates all unconsented government searches is, of course, the seizure of persons who have committed or are about to commit crimes, or of evidence related to crimes. But "reasonableness," with respect to this necessary element, does not demand that the government be factually correct in its assessment that that is what a search will produce. Warrants need only be supported by "probable cause". . . . If a magistrate, based upon seemingly reliable but factually inaccurate information, issues a warrant for the search of a house in which the sought-after felon is not present, has never been present, and was never likely to have been present, the owner of that house suffers one of the inconveniences we all expose ourselves to as the cost of living in a safe society; he does not suffer a violation of the Fourth Amendment. . . .

[I]n order to satisfy the "reasonableness" requirement of the Fourth Amendment, what is generally demanded of the many factual determinations that must regularly be made by agents of the government—whether the magistrate issuing a warrant, the police officer executing a warrant, or the police officer conducting a search or seizure under one of the exceptions to the warrant requirement—is not that they always be correct, but that they always be reasonable. . . .

We see no reason to depart from this general rule with respect to facts bearing upon the authority to consent to a search. . . .

497 U.S. at 179-186.

5. Do you find Justice Scalia's perspective on third-party consents persuasive? Consider the view of Justice Marshall, joined by Justices Brennan and Stevens, in the *Rodriguez* dissent:

. . . The majority's . . . position rests on a misconception of the basis for third-party consent searches. That such searches do not give rise to claims of constitutional violations rests not on the premise that they are "reasonable" under the Fourth Amendment, but on the premise that a person may voluntarily limit his expectation of privacy by allowing others to exercise authority over his possessions. Cf. Katz v. United States, 389 U.S. 347, 351 (1967) ("What a person knowingly exposes to the public, even in his home or office, is not a subject of Fourth Amendment protection."). Thus, an individual's decision to permit another "joint access [to] or control [over the property] for most purposes" limits that individual's reasonable expectation of privacy and to that extent limits his Fourth Amendment protections. If an individual has not so limited his expectation of privacy, the police may not dispense with the safeguards established by the Fourth Amendment.

The baseline for the reasonableness of a search or seizure in the home is the presence of a warrant. Indeed, "searches and seizures inside a home without a warrant are presumptively unreasonable." Exceptions to the warrant requirement must therefore serve "compelling" law enforcement goals. Because the sole law enforcement purpose underlying third-party consent searches is avoiding the inconvenience of securing a warrant, a departure from the warrant requirement is not justified simply because an officer reasonably believes a third party has consented to a search of the defendant's home. In holding otherwise, the majority ignores our long-standing view that "the informed and deliberate determination of magistrates . . . as to what searches and seizures are permissible under the Constitution are to be preferred over the hurried action of officers and others who may happen to make arrests."

Id. at 189-191 (Marshall, J., dissenting). Consider also the majority's response:

To describe a consented search as a noninvasion of privacy and thus a nonsearch is strange in the extreme. And while it must be admitted that this ingenious device can explain why consented searches are lawful, it cannot explain why seemingly consented searches are "unreasonable," which is all that the Constitution forbids. The only basis for contending that the constitutional standard could not possibly have been met here is the argument that reasonableness must be judged by the facts as they were, rather than by the facts as they were known. As we have discussed . . . , that argument has long since been rejected.

Id. at 186-187.

6. Florida v. Jimeno, 500 U.S. 248 (1991), involved the permissible scope of a consent search. In that case, Officer Frank Trujillo overheard a telephone conversation in which Jimeno appeared to be arranging a drug transaction. Suspecting that Jimeno was in possession of narcotics, he began to follow Jimeno's car. When Jimeno failed to stop at a red light, Officer Trujillo pulled him over and obtained his consent to search the car. The officer discovered cocaine in a folded brown paper bag located on the floorboard. The Florida Supreme Court held that the cocaine was properly suppressed on the ground that the consent did not extend to the search of the paper bag. The Supreme Court, in an opinion by Chief Justice Rehnquist, disagreed:

> . . . The Fourth Amendment is satisfied when, under the circumstances, it is objectively reasonable for the officer to believe that the scope of the suspect's consent permitted him to open a particular container within the automobile. . . .
>
> . . . The standard for measuring the scope of a suspect's consent under the Fourth Amendment is that of "objective" reasonableness — what would the typical reasonable person have understood by the exchange between the officer and the suspect? The question before us, then, is whether it is reasonable for an officer to consider a suspect's general consent to a search of his car to include consent to examine a paper bag lying on the floor of the car. We think that it is.
>
> . . . Trujillo had informed Jimeno that he believed Jimeno was carrying narcotics, and that he would be looking for narcotics in the car. We think that it was objectively reasonable for the police to conclude that the general consent to search respondent's car included consent to search containers within the car which might bear drugs. . . .
>
> The facts of this case are . . . different from those in State v. Wells, [539 So. 2d 464 (Fla. 1989)], on which the Supreme Court of Florida relied in affirming the suppression order in this case. There the Supreme Court of Florida held that consent to search the trunk of a car did not include authorization to pry open a locked briefcase found inside the trunk. It is very likely unreasonable to think that a suspect, by consenting to the search of his trunk, has agreed to the breaking open of a locked briefcase within the trunk, but it is otherwise with respect to a closed paper bag.
>
> Respondent argues . . . that if the police wish to search closed containers within a car they must separately request permission to search each container. But we see no basis for adding this sort of superstructure to the Fourth Amendment's basic test of objective reasonableness. A suspect may of course delimit as he chooses the scope of the search to which he consents. But if his consent would reasonably be understood to extend to a particular container, the Fourth Amendment provides no grounds for requiring a more explicit authorization.

500 U.S. at 249, 251-252. Isn't *Jimeno* something of a reprise on the container search issue that *Acevedo*, see page 493 supra, supposedly put to rest — at least for containers in automobiles? The *Jimeno* Court might have considered a bright-line

rule for the consent search of an automobile similar to the one it adopted in *Acevedo* — authority to search an automobile includes the authority to search containers. To the extent that the Court in *Jimeno* declined to offer police such a rule, is it more appropriate in this context to leave them to act at their peril?

OHIO v. ROBINETTE

Certiorari to the Ohio Supreme Court
519 U.S. 33 (1996)

CHIEF JUSTICE REHNQUIST delivered the opinion of the Court.

We are here presented with the question whether the Fourth Amendment requires that a lawfully seized defendant must be advised that he is "free to go" before his consent to search will be recognized as voluntary. We hold that it does not.

This case arose on a stretch of Interstate 70 north of Dayton, Ohio, where the posted speed limit was 45 miles per hour because of construction. Respondent Robert D. Robinette was clocked at 69 miles per hour as he drove his car along this stretch of road, and was stopped by Deputy Roger Newsome of the Montgomery County Sheriff's Office. Newsome asked for and was handed Robinette's driver's license, and he ran a computer check which indicated that Robinette had no previous violations. Newsome then asked Robinette to step out of his car, turned on his mounted video camera, issued a verbal warning to Robinette, and returned his license.

At this point, Newsome asked, "One question before you get gone: [A]re you carrying any illegal contraband in your car? Any weapons of any kind, drugs, anything like that?" Robinette answered "no" to these questions, after which Deputy Newsome asked if he could search the car. Robinette consented. In the car, Deputy Newsome discovered a small amount of marijuana and, in a film container, a pill which was later determined to be methylenedioxymethamphetamine (MDMA). Robinette was then arrested and charged with knowing possession of a controlled substance. . . .

Before trial, Robinette unsuccessfully sought to suppress this evidence. He then pleaded "no contest," and was found guilty. On appeal, the Ohio Court of Appeals reversed, ruling that the search resulted from an unlawful detention. The Supreme Court of Ohio, by a divided vote, affirmed. In its opinion, that court established a bright-line prerequisite for consensual interrogation under these circumstances:

> "The right, guaranteed by the federal and Ohio Constitutions, to be secure in one's person and property requires that citizens stopped for traffic offenses be clearly informed by the detaining officer when they are free to go after a valid detention, before an officer attempts to engage in a consensual interrogation. Any attempt at consensual interrogation must be preceded by the phrase 'At this time you legally are free to go' or by words of similar import."

We granted certiorari to review this per se rule, and we now reverse. . . .

. . . We have long held that the "touchstone of the Fourth Amendment is reasonableness." Florida v. Jimeno, 500 U.S. 248, 250 (1991). Reasonableness, in turn, is measured in objective terms by examining the totality of the circumstances.

In applying this test we have consistently eschewed bright-line rules, instead emphasizing the fact-specific nature of the reasonableness inquiry. Thus, in Florida v. Royer, 460 U.S. 491 (1983), we expressly disavowed any "litmus-paper test" or single "sentence or . . . paragraph . . . rule," in recognition of the "endless variations in the facts and circumstances" implicating the Fourth Amendment. Id. at 506. . . . And again, in Florida v. Bostick, 501 U.S. 429 (1991), when the Florida Supreme Court adopted a per se rule that questioning aboard a bus always constitutes a seizure, we reversed, reiterating that the proper inquiry necessitates a consideration of "all the circumstances surrounding the encounter." Id. at 439.

We have previously rejected a per se rule very similar to that adopted by the Supreme Court of Ohio in determining the validity of a consent to search. In Schneckloth v. Bustamonte, 412 U.S. 218 (1973), it was argued that such a consent could not be valid unless the defendant knew that he had a right to refuse the request. We rejected this argument: "While knowledge of the right to refuse consent is one factor to be taken into account, the government need not establish such knowledge as the sine qua non of an effective consent." Id., at 227. And just as it "would be thoroughly impractical to impose on the normal consent search the detailed requirements of an effective warning," id., at 231, so too would it be unrealistic to require police officers to always inform detainees that they are free to go before a consent to search may be deemed voluntary.

The Fourth Amendment test for a valid consent to search is that the consent be voluntary, and "[v]oluntariness is a question of fact to be determined from all the circumstances," id., at 248-249. The Supreme Court of Ohio having held otherwise, its judgment is reversed, and the case is remanded for further proceedings not inconsistent with this opinion. . . .

[Justice Ginsburg's opinion concurring in the judgment and Justice Stevens' dissenting opinion are omitted.]

NOTES AND QUESTIONS

1. Why would it be "unrealistic" to require police to inform detainees that they are free to go before obtaining consent to search?

2. One question lurking underneath the surface in *Robinette* involves the relationship between the definition of "consent" and the definition of "seizure." In *Schneckloth*, the Court determined that a consensual search is one that is voluntary under all the circumstances. In Florida v. Bostick, 501 U.S. 429 (1991), the Court said that a suspect is "seized" if a reasonable person in his circumstances would not feel free to leave or otherwise to disregard the police request. (*Bostick* is excerpted supra at page 394.) One obvious possibility is that these definitions might merge — that the same facts that would lead a reasonable person to feel detained (hence "seized" under the *Bostick* standard) would also lead the defendant to feel he had to give permission to search (thereby making consent "involuntary" under *Schneckloth*). The natural upshot of this line of argument would be a rule like the one adopted by the Ohio Supreme Court — that coercion rather than consent is presumed where the suspect is seized, so the officer must do something to dispel the coercion. Hence the requirement of a warning.

Robinette rejects this line of argument. But perhaps not completely. The Court's brief discussion emphasizes the importance of avoiding bright-line rules; perhaps a more nuanced requirement might survive. What would such a requirement look like? More broadly, should a court treat consent by a detained suspect differently from consent by a person (or suspect) who has not been seized? It seems commonsensical to say yes, since a detained suspect by definition is subject to police control and hence not a fully free agent. And nothing in *Robinette* bars that conclusion. But the most obvious way to take account of the fact that a suspect subject to police control may be in a different position is to require a warning of some sort, and *Robinette does* bar that approach. What is a court to do in such a case?

3. *Robinette* was decided the same Term as *Whren*, excerpted at page 597 supra. Together, those two decisions suggest a real reluctance on the Court's part to use the Fourth Amendment to address pretext in the enforcement of commonly violated traffic offenses. Note that in *Robinette*, the initial seizure was justified by a traffic offense, but the search was for drugs. And in testimony given in another case, Officer Newsome, who pulled Robinette over, stated that he sought consent to search in 786 traffic stops in 1992, the year Robinette was stopped. 519 U.S. at 40. As Justice Ginsburg noted in her opinion concurring in the judgment:

> [O]hio's courts observed that traffic stops in the State were regularly giving way to contraband searches, characterized as consensual, even when officers had no reason to suspect illegal activity. One Ohio appellate court noted: "[H]undreds, and perhaps thousands of Ohio citizens are being routinely delayed in their travels and asked to relinquish to uniformed police officers their right to privacy in their automobiles and luggage, sometimes for no better reason than to provide an officer the opportunity to 'practice' his drug interdiction technique." [State v. Retherford, 93 Ohio App. 3d 586, 594, dism'd, 69 Ohio St. 3d 1488 (1994)].

Id. at 40-41. What are the potential costs of aggressive use of the broad discretion that police have in the context of traffic enforcement? Illya Lichtenberg randomly sampled people who had been asked for consent to search their cars after being stopped for traffic violations on Ohio interstates between 1995 and 1997 and interviewed them about their experiences. As recounted in Professor Nadler's survey of the empirical evidence:

> . . . The Lichtenberg survey provides strong evidence that a substantial portion of citizens whose consent was requested . . . felt negatively affected by the police encounter. . . .
>
> After the search happened to them, most respondents (60%) reported that they thought about it often — about once a day. When asked about how they felt about the experience, a small proportion of respondents (26%) made positive or neutral comments, such as the following:
>
>> I wish they would do it more.
>> I'm just glad I had nothing to hide.
>> I guess they were just doing their job.
>
> A large majority (74%), however, had decidedly negative feelings about the experience:
>
>> I don't know if you ever had your house broken into or ripped off . . . [it's] an empty feeling, like you're nothing. . . .

> I feel really violated. I felt like my rights had been infringed upon. I feel really
>   bitter about the whole thing.
> I don't trust [police] anymore. I've lost all trust in them.

Janice Nadler, No Need to Shout: Bus Sweeps and the Psychology of Coercion,
2002 Sup. Ct. Rev. 153, 211-212. Nadler concludes that "consent search encounters with police often have a substantial impact on people — they do not forget
about the experience quickly, and most people, in this sample at least, had lasting
negative attitudes toward the incident (and sometimes toward the police) as a
result." Id. at 212-213.

4. One final wrinkle on consent searches. How should courts deal with consent
given in advance of the need to search? In 1994, Attorney General Janet Reno and
Secretary of Housing and Urban Development Henry Cisneros proposed, as
part of a comprehensive program for combating violence in public housing,
that leases for public housing apartments include "consent clauses" giving the
police permission to inspect apartments for firearms. Would such clauses be binding on anyone? On a tenant who wished to revoke consent at the time of the
search? On a tenant who did not wish to sign, but did so only because it was a
necessary condition for receiving public housing? Consider a portion of the discussion in the proposal:

> A search is lawful if it is conducted pursuant to an uncoerced consent. Leases in
> housing projects, as elsewhere, typically include a standard consent clause permitting
> the housing authority to conduct routine maintenance inspections and to enter the
> tenant's apartment in case of emergency. Where crime conditions in the housing
> development make unit-by-unit inspections essential, similar lease consent clauses
> could be employed to authorize periodic administrative inspections of tenants'
> units for unlicensed or unauthorized firearms.
>
> As in the case of maintenance inspections, such firearms inspections should be
> conducted on a routine basis, during daylight hours, and should be no more intrusive
> than absolutely necessary to determine whether weapons are present in the tenant's
> unit.
>
> If the agency gives advance notice of the fact that an inspection will be conducted
> and the general period within which it will take place the intrusiveness of the inspec-
> tion will be lessened and any constitutional objection to the inspection thereby
> reduced.
>
> In appropriate circumstances, tenant associations should be encouraged to
> endorse the use of building entrance security devices and the inclusion of consent
> clauses in lease agreements. A resolution by a tenant association would demonstrate
> widespread tenant support for such measures, which is an important factor in deter-
> mining whether to include such a clause in the lease. In addition, a showing of
> widespread tenant support would be helpful in responding to challenges by particular
> tenants to the constitutionality of restrictions on entry and consent clauses in leases.

Letter from Janet Reno and Henry Cisneros to President Clinton, reprinted in 140
Cong. Rec. S4660 (daily ed. Apr. 21, 1994). What do you think is meant by the last
sentence in the passage quoted above? Surely the views of a majority of tenants,
even a large majority, could not constitute consent for *all* tenants. Or could they? Is
there any other argument available to the government that could make use of
"widespread tenant support"?

F.   Remedies

Rights depend on remedies. If no adverse consequences flow from the violation of a constitutional right, government officials will violate the right as often as they wish. And if no relief flows to the victim of a constitutional violation, victims will not press their claims in court; the right will go unenforced.

These truths apply to the Fourth Amendment as they apply to other constitutional protections. For most of our history, Fourth Amendment rights were enforced chiefly through civil suits for damages. Such lawsuits were extremely rare. As a practical matter, before Mapp v. Ohio, 367 U.S. 643 (1961), the Fourth Amendment was not enforced at all — at least not against local police, who perform the vast majority of searches and seizures in the United States. (*Mapp* is excerpted supra, at page 336.) *Mapp* changed that state of affairs by applying the exclusionary rule, previously limited to federal criminal cases, in state criminal cases. Ever since, exclusion of illegally seized evidence has been the primary remedy for Fourth Amendment violations.

But it is not the only remedy for Fourth Amendment violations. Civil damages are available — along with attorneys' fees for successful plaintiffs, a change that has led to a great deal more Fourth Amendment damages litigation than in the years before *Mapp*. Injunctions against offending police officers or (more importantly) their departments are also available, though much more rarely. Officers who purposely violate the Fourth Amendment may be criminally prosecuted. Last but not least, administrative sanctions and political checks constrain police behavior.

In this section, we take up each of these remedies in turn. We begin by exploring the limits of the exclusionary rule. We then turn to damages, injunctions, criminal prosecutions, and administrative and political remedies. The remedies other than evidentiary exclusion are explored in less detail because they are used less often. But that may not always be the case; the existing system of enforcing the Fourth Amendment may not continue indefinitely. Consider, as you read this material, what the best mix of remedies might be. What form of relief best compensates victims of illegal searches and arrests? What remedy best deters violations? And, importantly, what remedy or remedies pose the least danger of stifling *good* police work?

1.   Limits on the Exclusionary Remedy

a.   The "Good Faith" Exception

UNITED STATES v. LEON

Certiorari to the United States Court of Appeals for the Ninth Circuit
468 U.S. 897 (1984)

JUSTICE WHITE delivered the opinion of the Court.

This case presents the question whether the Fourth Amendment exclusionary rule should be modified so as not to bar the use in the prosecution's case in chief of evidence obtained by officers acting in reasonable reliance on a search warrant. . . .

In August 1981, a confidential informant of unproven reliability informed an officer of the Burbank Police Department that two persons known to him as "Armando" and "Patsy" were selling large quantities of cocaine and methaqualone from their residence at 620 Price Drive in Burbank, Cal. The informant also indicated that he had witnessed a sale of methaqualone by "Patsy" at the residence approximately five months earlier and had observed at that time a shoebox containing a large amount of cash that belonged to "Patsy." He further declared that "Armando" and "Patsy" generally kept only small quantities of drugs at their residence and stored the remainder at another location in Burbank.

On the basis of this information, the Burbank police initiated an extensive investigation. . . . Cars parked at the Price Drive residence were determined to belong to respondents Armando Sanchez, who had previously been arrested for possession of marihuana, and Patsy Stewart, who had no criminal record. During the course of the investigation, officers observed an automobile belonging to respondent Ricardo Del Castillo, who had previously been arrested for possession of 50 pounds of marihuana, arrive at the Price Drive residence. The driver of that car entered the house, exited shortly thereafter carrying a small paper sack, and drove away. A check of Del Castillo's probation records led the officers to respondent Alberto Leon, whose telephone number Del Castillo had listed as his employer's. Leon had been arrested in 1980 on drug charges, and a companion had informed the police at that time that Leon was heavily involved in the importation of drugs into this country. Before the current investigation began, the Burbank officers had learned that an informant had told a Glendale police officer that Leon stored a large quantity of methaqualone at his residence in Glendale. During the course of this investigation, the Burbank officers learned that Leon was living at 716 South Sunset Canyon in Burbank.

Subsequently, the officers observed several persons, at least one of whom had prior drug involvement, arriving at the Price Drive residence and leaving with small packages [and] observed a variety of other material activity at the two residences. . . . Based on these and other observations summarized in the affidavit, Officer Cyril Rombach of the Burbank Police Department, an experienced and well-trained narcotics investigator, prepared an application for a warrant to search 620 Price Drive [and] 716 South Sunset Canyon, . . . and automobiles registered to each of the respondents for an extensive list of items believed to be related to respondents' drug-trafficking activities. Officer Rombach's extensive application was reviewed by several Deputy District Attorneys.

A facially valid search warrant was issued in September 1981 by a State Superior Court Judge. The ensuing searches produced large quantities of drugs at the . . . Sunset Canyon [address] and a small quantity at the Price Drive residence. Other evidence was discovered at each of the residences and in Stewart's and Del Castillo's automobiles. Respondents were indicted by a grand jury in the District Court for the Central District of California and charged with conspiracy to possess and distribute cocaine and a variety of substantive counts.

The respondents then filed motions to suppress the evidence seized pursuant to the warrant. The District Court held an evidentiary hearing and, while recognizing that the case was a close one, granted the motions to suppress in part. It concluded that the affidavit was insufficient to establish probable cause, but did not suppress all of the evidence as to all of the respondents because none of the respondents had standing to challenge all of the searches. In response to a request from the Government, the court made clear that Officer Rombach had acted in good faith. . . .

[A] divided panel of the Court of Appeals for the Ninth Circuit affirmed. . . .

The Government's petition for certiorari expressly declined to seek review of the lower courts' determinations that the search warrant was unsupported by probable cause and presented only the question "[whether] the Fourth Amendment exclusionary rule should be modified so as not to bar the admission of evidence seized in reasonable, good-faith reliance on a search warrant that is subsequently held to be defective." We granted certiorari to consider the propriety of such a modification. Although it undoubtedly is within our power to consider the question whether probable cause existed under the "totality of the circumstances" test announced last Term in Illinois v. Gates, 462 U.S. 213 (1983), that question has not been briefed or argued; and it is also within our authority, which we choose to exercise, to take the case as it comes to us, accepting the Court of Appeals' conclusion that probable cause was lacking under the prevailing legal standards.

We have concluded that . . . the exclusionary rule can be modified somewhat without jeopardizing its ability to perform its intended functions. Accordingly, we reverse the judgment of the Court of Appeals. . . .

The Fourth Amendment contains no provision expressly precluding the use of evidence obtained in violation of its commands, and an examination of its origin and purposes makes clear that the use of fruits of a past unlawful search or seizure "[works] no new Fourth Amendment wrong." United States v. Calandra, 414 U.S. 338, 354 (1974). The wrong condemned by the Amendment is "fully accomplished" by the unlawful search or seizure itself, ibid., and the exclusionary rule is neither intended nor able to "cure the invasion of the defendant's rights which he has already suffered." Stone v. Powell, [428 U.S. 465,] 540 [(1976)] (WHITE, J., dissenting). The rule thus operates as "a judicially created remedy designed to safeguard Fourth Amendment rights generally through its deterrent effect, rather than a personal constitutional right of the party aggrieved." United States v. Calandra, supra, at 348.

Whether the exclusionary sanction is appropriately imposed in a particular case, our decisions make clear, is "an issue separate from the question whether the Fourth Amendment rights of the party seeking to invoke the rule were violated by police conduct." Illinois v. Gates, supra, at 223. Only the former question is currently before us, and it must be resolved by weighing the costs and benefits of preventing the use in the prosecution's case in chief of inherently trustworthy tangible evidence obtained in reliance on a search warrant issued by a detached and neutral magistrate that ultimately is found to be defective.

The substantial social costs exacted by the exclusionary rule for the vindication of Fourth Amendment rights have long been a source of concern. "Our cases have consistently recognized that unbending application of the exclusionary sanction to enforce ideals of governmental rectitude would impede unacceptably the truth-finding functions of judge and jury." United States v. Payner, 447 U.S. 727, 734 (1980). An objectionable collateral consequence of this interference with the criminal justice system's truth-finding function is that some guilty defendants may go free or receive reduced sentences as a result of favorable plea bargains.[6]

---

6. Researchers have only recently begun to study extensively the effects of the exclusionary rule on the disposition of felony arrests. One study suggests that the rule results in the nonprosecution or nonconviction of between 0.6% and 2.35% of individuals arrested for felonies. Davies, A Hard Look

Particularly when law enforcement officers have acted in objective good faith or their transgressions have been minor, the magnitude of the benefit conferred on such guilty defendants offends basic concepts of the criminal justice system . . . Accordingly, "[as] with any remedial device, the application of the rule has been restricted to those areas where its remedial objectives are thought most efficaciously served." United States v. Calandra, supra, at 348.

Close attention to those remedial objectives has characterized our recent decisions concerning the scope of the Fourth Amendment exclusionary rule. . . . [There follows a discussion of contexts in which the Court has declined to apply the exclusionary rule, including grand jury proceedings, see *Calandra*, supra; habeas corpus litigation, see Stone v. Powell, supra; and civil tax proceedings, see United States v. Janis, 428 U.S. 433 (1976). The opinion then goes on to note the significant limits imposed on the exclusionary rule by standing doctrine and by fruit-of-the-poisonous-tree doctrine.]

As yet, we have not recognized any form of good-faith exception to the Fourth Amendment exclusionary rule. But the balancing approach that has evolved during the years of experience with the rule provides strong support for the modification currently urged upon us. . . .

. . . Reasonable minds frequently may differ on the question whether a particular affidavit establishes probable cause, and we have thus concluded that the preference for warrants is most appropriately effectuated by according "great deference" to a magistrate's determination. Spinelli v. United States, 393 U.S., at 419. See Illinois v. Gates, 462 U.S., at 236. Deference to the magistrate, however, is not boundless. It is clear, first, that the deference accorded to a magistrate's finding of probable cause does not preclude inquiry into the knowing or reckless falsity of the affidavit on which that determination was based. Franks v. Delaware, 438 U.S. 154 (1978). Second, . . . [a] magistrate failing to "manifest that neutrality and detachment demanded of a judicial officer when presented with a warrant application" and who acts instead as "an adjunct law enforcement officer" cannot provide valid authorization for an otherwise unconstitutional search. Lo-Ji Sales, Inc. v. New York, 442 U.S. 319, 326-327 (1979).

Third, reviewing courts will not defer to a warrant based on an affidavit that does not "provide the magistrate with a substantial basis for determining the

---

at What We Know (and Still Need to Learn) About the "Costs" of the Exclusionary Rule: The NIJ Study and Other Studies of "Lost" Arrests, 1983 A.B.F. Res. J. 611, 621. The estimates are higher for particular crimes the prosecution of which depends heavily on physical evidence. Thus, the cumulative loss due to nonprosecution or nonconviction of individuals arrested on felony drug charges is probably in the range of 2.8% to 7.1%. Id., at 680. Davies' analysis of California data suggests that screening by police and prosecutors results in the release because of illegal searches or seizures of as many as 1.4% of all felony arrestees, id., at 650, that 0.9% of felony arrestees are released, because of illegal searches or seizures, at the preliminary hearing or after trial, id., at 653, and that roughly 0.05% of all felony arrestees benefit from reversals on appeal because of illegal searches. Id., at 654. See also National Institute of Justice, The Effects of the Exclusionary Rule: A Study in California 1-2 (1982); Nardulli, The Societal Cost of the Exclusionary Rule: An Empirical Assessment, 1983 A.B.F. Res. J. 585, 600. . . .

Many of these researchers have concluded that the impact of the exclusionary rule is insubstantial, but the small percentages with which they deal mask a large absolute number of felons who are released because the cases against them were based in part on illegal searches or seizures. "[Any] rule of evidence that denies the jury access to clearly probative and reliable evidence must bear a heavy burden of justification, and must be carefully limited to the circumstances in which it will pay its way by deterring official unlawlessness." Illinois v. Gates, 462 U.S., at 257-258 (WHITE, J., concurring in judgment). Because we find that the rule can have no substantial deterrent effect in the sorts of situations under consideration in this case, we conclude that it cannot pay its way in those situations.

existence of probable cause." Illinois v. Gates, 462 U.S., at 239.... Even if the warrant application was supported by more than a "bare bones" affidavit, a reviewing court may properly conclude that, notwithstanding the deference that magistrates deserve, the warrant was invalid because the magistrate's prob-able-cause determination reflected an improper analysis of the totality of the circumstances. . . .

Only in the first of these three situations, however, has the Court set forth a rationale for suppressing evidence obtained pursuant to a search warrant; in the other areas, it has simply excluded such evidence without considering whether Fourth Amendment interests will be advanced. To the extent that proponents of exclusion rely on its behavioral effects on judges and magistrates in these areas, their reliance is misplaced. First, the exclusionary rule is designed to deter police misconduct rather than to punish the errors of judges and magistrates. Second, there exists no evidence suggesting that judges and magistrates are inclined to ignore or subvert the Fourth Amendment or that lawlessness among these actors requires application of the extreme sanction of exclusion.

Third, and most important, we discern no basis, and are offered none, for believing that exclusion of evidence seized pursuant to a warrant will have a sig-nificant deterrent effect on the issuing judge or magistrate . . . Judges and magistrates are not adjuncts to the law enforcement team; as neutral judicial offi-cers, they have no stake in the outcome of particular criminal prosecutions. The threat of exclusion thus cannot be expected significantly to deter them. . . .

If exclusion of evidence obtained pursuant to a subsequently invalidated war-rant is to have any deterrent effect, therefore, it must alter the behavior of individual law enforcement officers or the policies of their departments. One could argue that applying the exclusionary rule in cases where the police failed to demonstrate probable cause in the warrant application deters future inadequate presentations or "magistrate shopping" and thus promotes the ends of the Fourth Amendment. Suppressing evidence obtained pursuant to a technically defective warrant supported by probable cause also might encourage officers to scruti-nize more closely the form of the warrant and to point out suspected judicial errors. We find such arguments speculative and conclude that suppression of evidence obtained pursuant to a warrant should be ordered only on a case-by-case basis and only in those unusual cases in which exclusion will further the purposes of the exclusionary rule.

We have frequently questioned whether the exclusionary rule can have any deterrent effect when the offending officers acted in the objectively reasonable belief that their conduct did not violate the Fourth Amendment. "No empirical researcher, proponent or opponent of the rule, has yet been able to establish with any assurance whether the rule has a deterrent effect. . . ." United States v. Janis, 428 U.S., at 452, n. 22. But even assuming that the rule effectively deters some police misconduct and provides incentives for the law enforcement profession as a whole to conduct itself in accord with the Fourth Amendment, it cannot be expected, and should not be applied, to deter objectively reasonable law enforce-ment activity. . . .

This is particularly true, we believe, when an officer acting with objective good faith has obtained a search warrant from a judge or magistrate and acted within its scope. In most such cases, there is no police illegality and thus nothing to deter. It is the magistrate's responsibility to determine whether the officer's allegations establish probable cause and, if so, to issue a warrant comporting in form with the requirements of the Fourth Amendment. In the ordinary case, an officer cannot be expected to question the magistrate's probable-cause determination or his judgment that the form of the warrant is technically sufficient . . . Penalizing the officer for the magistrate's error, rather than his own, cannot logically contribute to the deterrence of Fourth Amendment violations.

We conclude that the marginal or nonexistent benefits produced by suppressing evidence obtained in objectively reasonable reliance on a subsequently invalidated search warrant cannot justify the substantial costs of exclusion. We do not suggest, however, that exclusion is always inappropriate in cases where an officer has obtained a warrant and abided by its terms. . . . [T]he officer's reliance on the magistrate's probable-cause determination and on the technical sufficiency of the warrant he issues must be objectively reasonable, and it is clear that in some circumstances the officer will have no reasonable grounds for believing that the warrant was properly issued.

Suppression therefore remains an appropriate remedy if the magistrate or judge in issuing a warrant was misled by information in an affidavit that the affiant knew was false or would have known was false except for his reckless disregard of the truth. Franks v. Delaware, 438 U.S. 154 (1978). The exception we recognize today will also not apply in cases where the issuing magistrate wholly abandoned his judicial role in the manner condemned in Lo-Ji Sales, Inc. v. New York, 442 U.S. 319 (1979); in such circumstances, no reasonably well trained officer should rely on the warrant. Nor would an officer manifest objective good faith in relying on a warrant based on an affidavit "so lacking in indicia of probable cause as to render official belief in its existence entirely unreasonable." Brown v. Illinois, 422 U.S., at 610-611 (POWELL, J., concurring in part). Finally, depending on the circumstances of the particular case, a warrant may be so facially deficient — i.e., in failing to particularize the place to be searched or the things to be seized — that the executing officers cannot reasonably presume it to be valid.

In so limiting the suppression remedy, we leave untouched the probable-cause standard and the various requirements for a valid warrant. Other objections to the modification of the Fourth Amendment exclusionary rule we consider to be insubstantial. The good-faith exception for searches conducted pursuant to warrants is not intended to signal our unwillingness strictly to enforce the requirements of the Fourth Amendment, and we do not believe that it will have this effect. . . .

Nor are we persuaded that application of a good-faith exception to searches conducted pursuant to warrants will preclude review of the constitutionality of the search or seizure, deny needed guidance from the courts, or freeze Fourth Amendment law in its present state. There is no need for courts to adopt the inflexible practice of always deciding whether the officers' conduct manifested objective good faith before turning to the question whether the Fourth Amendment has been violated. . . .

If the resolution of a particular Fourth Amendment question is necessary to guide future action by law enforcement officers and magistrates, nothing will prevent reviewing courts from deciding that question before turning to the good-faith issue. Indeed, it frequently will be difficult to determine whether the officers acted reasonably without resolving the Fourth Amendment issue. . . .

When the principles we have enunciated today are applied to the facts of this case, it is apparent that the judgment of the Court of Appeals cannot stand. . . . Officer Rombach's application for a warrant clearly was supported by much more than a "bare bones" affidavit. The affidavit related the results of an extensive investigation and, as the opinions of the divided panel of the Court of Appeals make clear, provided evidence sufficient to create disagreement among thoughtful and competent judges as to the existence of probable cause. Under these circumstances, the officers' reliance on the magistrate's determination of probable cause was objectively reasonable, and application of the extreme sanction of exclusion is inappropriate. . . .

JUSTICE BLACKMUN, concurring.

. . . As the Court's opinion in this case makes clear, the Court has narrowed the scope of the exclusionary rule because of an empirical judgment that the rule has little appreciable effect in cases where officers act in objectively reasonable reliance on search warrants. Because I share the view that the exclusionary rule is not a constitutionally compelled corollary of the Fourth Amendment itself, I see no way to avoid making an empirical judgment of this sort, and I am satisfied that the Court has made the correct one on the information before it. . . .

What must be stressed, however, is that any empirical judgment about the effect of the exclusionary rule in a particular class of cases necessarily is a provisional one. By their very nature, the assumptions on which we proceed today cannot be cast in stone. To the contrary, they now will be tested in the real world of state and federal law enforcement, and this Court will attend to the results. If it should emerge from experience that, contrary to our expectations, the good-faith exception to the exclusionary rule results in a material change in police compliance with the Fourth Amendment, we shall have to reconsider what we have undertaken here. . . .

JUSTICE BRENNAN, with whom JUSTICE MARSHALL joins, dissenting.

. . . At bottom, the Court's decision turns on the proposition that the exclusionary rule is merely a "judicially created remedy designed to safeguard Fourth Amendment rights generally through its deterrent effect, rather than a personal constitutional right." This reading of the Amendment implies that its proscriptions are directed solely at those government agents who may actually invade an individual's constitutionally protected privacy. The courts are not subject to any direct constitutional duty to exclude illegally obtained evidence, because the question of the admissibility of such evidence is not addressed by the Amendment. This view of the scope of the Amendment relegates the judiciary to the periphery. Because the only constitutionally cognizable injury has already been "fully accomplished" by the police by the time a case comes before the courts, the Constitution is not itself violated if the judge decides to admit the tainted evidence. Indeed, the most the judge can do is wring his hands and hope that perhaps by excluding such evidence he can deter future transgressions by the police.

Such a reading appears plausible, because, as critics of the exclusionary rule never tire of repeating, the Fourth Amendment makes no express provision for the exclusion of evidence secured in violation of its commands. A short answer to this claim, of course, is that many of the Constitution's most vital imperatives are stated in general terms and the task of giving meaning to these precepts is therefore left to subsequent judicial decisionmaking in the context of concrete cases. The nature of our Constitution, as Chief Justice Marshall long ago explained, "requires that only its great outlines should be marked, its important objects designated, and the minor ingredients which compose those objects be deduced from the nature of the objects themselves." McCulloch v. Maryland, 4 Wheat. 316, 407 (1819).

A more direct answer may be supplied by recognizing that the Amendment, like other provisions of the Bill of Rights, restrains the power of the government as a whole; it does not specify only a particular agency and exempt all others. The judiciary is responsible, no less than the executive, for ensuring that constitutional rights are respected.

When that fact is kept in mind, the role of the courts and their possible involvement in the concerns of the Fourth Amendment comes into sharper focus. Because seizures are executed principally to secure evidence, and because such evidence generally has utility in our legal system only in the context of a trial supervised by a judge, it is apparent that the admission of illegally obtained evidence implicates the same constitutional concerns as the initial seizure of that evidence. Indeed, by admitting unlawfully seized evidence, the judiciary becomes a part of what is in fact a single governmental action prohibited by the terms of the Amendment. Once that connection between the evidence-gathering role of the police and the evidence-admitting function of the courts is acknowledged, the plausibility of the Court's interpretation becomes more suspect. . . . The Amendment therefore must be read to condemn not only the initial unconstitutional invasion of privacy — which is done, after all, for the purpose of securing evidence — but also the subsequent use of any evidence so obtained. . . .

. . . For my part, "[the] right of the people to be secure in their persons, houses, papers, and effects, against unreasonable searches and seizures" comprises a personal right to exclude all evidence secured by means of unreasonable searches and seizures. The right to be free from the initial invasion of privacy and the right of exclusion are coordinate components of the central embracing right to be free from unreasonable searches and seizures. . . .

By remaining within its redoubt of empiricism and by basing the [exclusionary] rule solely on the deterrence rationale, the Court has robbed the rule of legitimacy. A doctrine that is explained as if it were an empirical proposition but for which there is only limited empirical support is both inherently unstable and an easy mark for critics. The extent of this Court's fidelity to Fourth Amendment requirements, however, should not turn on such statistical uncertainties. . . .

Even if I were to accept the Court's general approach to the exclusionary rule, I could not agree with today's result. There is no question that in the hands of the present Court the deterrence rationale has proved to be a powerful tool for confining the scope of the rule. In *Calandra*, for example, the Court concluded that the "speculative and undoubtedly minimal advance in the deterrence of police misconduct," was insufficient to outweigh the "expense of substantially impeding the role of the grand jury." 414 U.S., at 351-352. In Stone v. Powell, the Court found that "the additional contribution, if any, of the consideration of search-and-seizure claims of state prisoners on collateral review is small in relation to the costs." 428 U.S., at 493. In United States v. Janis, 428 U.S. 433 (1976), the Court concluded that "exclusion from federal civil proceedings of evidence unlawfully seized by a state criminal enforcement officer has not been shown to have a sufficient likelihood of deterring the conduct of the state police so that it outweighs the societal costs imposed by the exclusion." Id., at 454. And in an opinion handed down today, the Court finds that the "balance between costs and benefits comes out against applying the exclusionary rule in civil deportation hearings held by the [Immigration and Naturalization Service]." INS v. Lopez-Mendoza, [468 U.S.], at 1050.

Thus, in this bit of judicial stagecraft, while the sets sometimes change, the actors always have the same lines. Given this well-rehearsed pattern, one might have predicted with some assurance how the present case would unfold. First there is the ritual incantation of the "substantial social costs" exacted by the exclusionary rule, followed by the virtually foreordained conclusion that, given the marginal benefits, application of the rule in the circumstances of these cases is not warranted. Upon analysis, however, such a result cannot be justified even on the Court's own terms. . . .

. . . [A]s the Court acknowledges, see ante, at n. 6, recent studies have demonstrated that the "costs" of the exclusionary rule—calculated in terms of dropped prosecutions and lost convictions—are quite low. Contrary to the claims of the rule's critics that exclusion leads to "the release of countless guilty criminals," Bivens v. Six Unknown Federal Narcotics Agents, 403 U.S. 388, 416 (1971) (Burger, C.J., dissenting), these studies have demonstrated that federal and state prosecutors very rarely drop cases because of potential search and seizure problems. For example, a 1979 study prepared at the request of Congress by the General Accounting Office reported that only 0.4% of all cases actually declined for prosecution by federal prosecutors were declined primarily because of illegal search problems. Report of the Comptroller General of the United States, Impact of the Exclusionary Rule on Federal Criminal Prosecutions 14 (1979). If the GAO data are restated as a percentage of all arrests, the study shows that only 0.2% of all felony arrests are declined for prosecution because of potential exclusionary rule problems. See Davies, A Hard Look at What We Know (and Still Need to Learn) About the "Costs" of the Exclusionary Rule: The NIJ Study and Other Studies of "Lost" Arrests, 1983 A.B.F. Res. J. 611, 635.[11] Of course, these data describe only the costs attributable to the exclusion of evidence in all cases; the costs due to the

11. In a series of recent studies, researchers have attempted to quantify the actual costs of the rule. A recent National Institute of Justice study based on data for the 4-year period 1976-1979 gathered by the California Bureau of Criminal Statistics showed that 4.8% of all cases that were declined for prosecution by California prosecutors were rejected because of illegally seized evidence. National Institute of Justice, Criminal Justice Research Report—The Effects of the Exclusionary Rule: A Study in California 1 (1982). However, if these data are calculated as a percentage of all arrests, they show that only 0.8% of all arrests were rejected for prosecution because of illegally seized evidence. See Davies, 1983 A.B.F. Res. J., at 619.

In another measure of the rule's impact—the number of prosecutions that are dismissed or result in acquittals in cases where evidence has been excluded—the available data again show that the Court's past assessment of the rule's costs has generally been exaggerated. For example, a study based on data from nine midsized counties in Illinois, Michigan, and Pennsylvania reveals that motions to suppress physical evidence were filed in approximately 5% of the 7,500 cases studied, but that such motions were successful in only 0.7% of all these cases. Nardulli, The Societal Cost of the Exclusionary Rule: An Empirical Assessment, 1983 A.B.F. Res. J. 585, 596. The study also shows that only 0.6% of all cases resulted in acquittals because evidence had been excluded. Id., at 600. In the GAO study, suppression motions were filed in 10.5% of all federal criminal cases surveyed, but of the motions filed, approximately 80-90% were denied. GAO Report, at 8, 10. Evidence was actually excluded in only 1.3% of the cases studied, and only 0.7% of all cases resulted in acquittals or dismissals after evidence was excluded. Id., at 9-11. See Davies, supra, at 660. And in another study based on data from cases during 1978 and 1979 in San Diego and Jacksonville, it was shown that only 1% of all cases resulting in nonconviction were caused by illegal searches. F. Feeney, F. Dill, & A. Weir, Arrests Without Conviction: How Often They Occur and Why (National Institute of Justice 1983).

exclusion of evidence in the narrower category of cases where police have made objectively reasonable mistakes must necessarily be even smaller. . . .

When the public, as it quite properly has done in the past as well as in the present, demands that those in government increase their efforts to combat crime, it is all too easy for those government officials to seek expedient solutions. In contrast to such costly and difficult measures as building more prisons, improving law enforcement methods, or hiring more prosecutors and judges to relieve the overburdened court systems in the country's metropolitan areas, the relaxation of Fourth Amendment standards seems a tempting, costless means of meeting the public's demand for better law enforcement. In the long run, however, we as a society pay a heavy price for such expediency, because . . . [o]nce lost, such rights are difficult to recover. There is hope, however, that in time this or some later Court will restore these precious freedoms to their rightful place as a primary protection for our citizens against overreaching officialdom. . . .

[Justice Stevens's dissenting opinion is omitted.]

NOTES AND QUESTIONS

1. Reread the facts in *Leon*. Did the police have probable cause?

2. The majority and dissenting opinions in *Leon* disagree strongly over the constitutional status of the exclusionary rule. Who has the better of the argument? What would Justice Brennan have said of the constitutional status of damages remedies in cases of illegal searches or seizures in which no incriminating evidence was found? See Bivens v. Six Unknown Named Agents of Federal Bureau of Narcotics, 403 U.S. 388 (1971), where the Court appeared to hold that some kind of damages remedy *is* constitutionally required. (At any rate, the Court found such a remedy in the absence of any statute — 42 U.S.C. §1983, which creates a cause of action for deprivation of constitutional rights, applies only to state and local officials.) Does it make sense to conclude that *both* damages *and* exclusion are constitutionally required? It may be that, as John Marshall famously suggested in Marbury v. Madison, 5 U.S. 137 (1803), every right requires a remedy. But does every right require two?

3. The *Leon* holding seems to have had little effect — there is no body of evidence suggesting that warrants are either more or less common now than before *Leon*, or that magistrates are either more or less careful in deciding on warrant applications. Perhaps the reason is that *Leon*'s holding is little more than a convoluted way of restating the standard of review established by Illinois v. Gates, 462 U.S. 213 (1983). Recall that *Gates* stated that a magistrate's decision to issue a warrant is to receive substantial deference in later litigation. (Recall too that Ornelas v. United States, page 437 supra, states that trial judges' decisions on suppression motions are not to receive such deference.) *Leon* holds that the magistrate's probable cause determination is binding in a later suppression hearing unless it was unreasonable for the police to rely on that determination.

When will it be unreasonable for the police to rely on a warrant? Presumably when the magistrate's decision to issue it was obviously wrong. Merely "wrong" is not enough; magistrates must get the benefit of close calls. When will a magistrate's decision to issue a warrant be overturned on appeal, given the deference due to such decisions? Again, presumably when the decision was obviously wrong. *Leon*'s "good faith" exception does not extend to obviously wrong warrants, just as obviously wrong warrants do not benefit from the deference required by *Gates*. Close calls *do* fall within the good-faith exception, just as they fall within *Gates* deference. Are there any cases where *Leon* matters?

4. At the time it was decided, *Leon* was thought to matter a lot—for warrant*less* search cases. Imagine, for example, a case in which the permissible scope of a search incident to arrest was at issue. The government argues that, even if the search was not constitutional, it was at least close enough that a reasonable officer could have *believed* it was constitutional. The Court's argument in *Leon* would seem to apply fairly readily to such a case. The result would be a vast expansion in the scope of warrantless searches, as each of the many exceptions to the warrant requirement would be expanded to include close calls. It might not be much of an exaggeration to say that the warrant requirement might disappear altogether.

That is what *Leon*'s critics thought the case would mean. More than twenty years later, it hasn't happened: the good faith exception has remained fairly cabined. Why might that be so? Is it a sign that the Court has re-thought its position in *Leon*? Or is it a sign that the good-faith exception has less merit for warrantless searches than for searches pursuant to warrants?

5. There have been some legislative proposals to broaden the good-faith exception. As part of the Contract With America, in 1995 the House of Representatives passed a measure that purported to eliminate the exclusionary rule in federal courts for all searches conducted in good faith, whether with or without a warrant. (The measure died in the Senate.) See Exclusionary Rule Reform Act of 1995, H.R. 666 (Feb. 8, 1995). Are such proposals constitutional?

The answer turns on what, precisely, the exclusionary rule's constitutional status is. On the one hand, the Court states clearly that the rule is not constitutionally compelled. On the other hand, the Court regularly overturns state-court convictions based on the rule—that is, if a state court fails to suppress evidence that ought to be suppressed under the exclusionary rule, the Supreme Court will reverse the state-court decision. Needless to say, the Supreme Court has no authority to reverse state-court decisions unless those decisions violate federal law. There is no federal *statute* that requires state courts to have an exclusionary rule, and the exclusionary rule would not seem to be part of some binding general federal common law. So its only possible source is the federal constitution—which the Court says doesn't require it. Where does that leave things?

Perhaps the answer is that the exclusionary rule is a species of "constitutional common law." For the classic discussion of this much-contested category, see Henry Monaghan, The Supreme Court, 1974 Term—Foreword: Constitutional Common Law, 89 Harv. L. Rev. 1 (1975). Assuming it is, there would seem to be two possibilities. First, it may be that legislatures could simply overturn the exclusionary rule if they wished. On this theory, the exclusionary rule is a kind of constitutional law that is subject to legislative definition; courts have no interpretive primacy in this sphere. Second, legislatures may not have the power simply to do away with the exclusionary rule, but they may have the power to replace it with another, equally effective remedy. If the first possibility is correct, the House Republican proposal was constitutional; if the second possibility is correct, it wasn't.

Dickerson v. United States, 530 U.S. 428 (2000), may cast some light on this question. In *Dickerson*, the Court considered a federal statute that purported to, basically, overrule Miranda v. Arizona, 384 U.S. 436 (1966), and reinstate the pre-*Miranda* standard for the admissibility of confessions in federal court. See 18 U.S.C. §3501. The argument in *Dickerson* was quite similar to some of the arguments raised in connection with the exclusionary rule. And with respect to both *Miranda* and the exclusionary rule, the Court has been (to say the least) unclear about the constitutional status of its decisions. So there was some thought that the Court might hold that *Miranda* could be overturned by legislation. It did not do so. Instead, in a 7-2 decision and in an opinion by Chief Justice Rehnquist, the Court declared that "*Miranda* is a constitutional decision," and that it remains binding on legislatures. Perhaps the Court would say the same thing about the exclusionary rule, notwithstanding the language it used in *Leon*.

6. *Leon* has yet to be extended to warrantless searches generally, but it *has* been extended in some other respects. In Illinois v. Krull, 480 U.S. 340 (1987), the Court applied the good-faith exception to a search pursuant to an unconstitutional state statute. The defendants operated a junkyard that housed old automobiles and automobile parts. An Illinois statute authorized police inspection of records and vehicles at such places at the discretion of the police, without the need for probable cause or reasonable suspicion. During the course of such an inspection, police discovered several stolen vehicles. In separate litigation, the Illinois statute was declared unconstitutional, on the ground that it vested police with too much discretionary power. (Note: In New York v. Burger, 482 U.S. 691 (1987), a similar state statute was upheld, on the ground that there were "special needs" for the regulatory authority the government was exercising.) The Supreme Court nevertheless declined to suppress the stolen cars:

> The approach used in *Leon* is equally applicable to the present case. The application of the exclusionary rule to suppress evidence obtained by an officer acting in objectively reasonable reliance on a statute would have as little deterrent effect on the officer's actions as would the exclusion of evidence when an officer acts in objectively reasonable reliance on a warrant. Unless a statute is clearly unconstitutional, an officer cannot be expected to question the judgment of the legislature that passed the law. If the statute is subsequently declared unconstitutional, excluding evidence obtained pursuant to it prior to such a judicial declaration will not deter future Fourth Amendment violations by an officer who has simply fulfilled his responsibility to enforce the statute as written. To paraphrase the Court's comment in *Leon*: "Penalizing the officer for the [legislature's] error, rather than his own, cannot logically contribute to the deterrence of Fourth Amendment violations."

Krull, 480 U.S. at 349-350.

The police in Arizona v. Evans, 514 U.S. 1 (1995), made a traffic stop, entered the defendant's name into a computer terminal in the police car, and learned that there was an outstanding warrant for the defendant's arrest. The officers proceeded to arrest the defendant, and during the course of a search incident to arrest found drugs.

As it turned out, there was no outstanding arrest warrant; the information in the police computer was the result of an error in the court clerk's office. In an opinion by Chief Justice Rehnquist, the Court nevertheless held that the drugs found during the search incident to this mistaken arrest were admissible:

> . . . If court employees were responsible for the erroneous computer record, the exclusion of evidence at trial would not sufficiently deter future errors so as to warrant such a severe sanction. First, as we noted in *Leon*, the exclusionary rule was historically designed as a means of deterring police misconduct, not mistakes by court employees. Second, respondent offers no evidence that court employees are inclined to ignore or subvert the Fourth Amendment or that lawlessness among these actors requires application of the extreme sanction of exclusion. . . .
>
> Finally, and most important, there is no basis for believing that application of the exclusionary rule in these circumstances will have a significant effect on court employees. . . . Because court clerks are not adjuncts to the law enforcement team engaged in the often competitive enterprise of ferreting out crime, they have no stake in the outcome of particular criminal prosecutions. The threat of exclusion of evidence could not be expected to deter such individuals. . . .
>
> If it were indeed a court clerk who was responsible for the erroneous entry on the police computer, application of the exclusionary rule also could not be expected to alter the behavior of the arresting officer. As the trial court in this case stated: "I think the police officer [was] bound to arrest. I think he would [have been] derelict in his duty if he failed to arrest." . . . There is no indication that the arresting officer was not acting objectively reasonably when he relied upon the police computer record.

Id. at 14-16. The Chief Justice emphasized that it was a court clerk who made the error in *Evans*. Why does that matter? Couldn't one make the same argument if one police officer supplied another with bad information? What would be the response?

7. Apparently, errors by police officers themselves *are* different. Groh v. Ramirez, 124 S. Ct. 1284 (2004), was a civil case; the plaintiff's home was searched based on a warrant that contained no description of "the persons or things to be seized" (to use the constitutional language). The omission was the result of an error on the part of the police officer who prepared the warrant application — the application and the accompanying affidavit contained a list of items, but the warrant itself did not. The issue before the Court was whether, in such a case, police officers had "qualified immunity" under 42 U.S.C. §1983; the standard for qualified immunity is the same as *Leon*'s "good faith" standard.

Justice Stevens, writing for a five-vote majority, concluded that the officer's behavior was *not* objectively reasonable:

> Given that the particularity requirement is set forth in the text of the Constitution, no reasonable officer could believe that a warrant that plainly did not comply with that requirement was valid. . . . Moreover, because the [police officer] himself prepared the invalid warrant, he may not argue that he reasonably relied on the Magistrate's assurance that the warrant contained an adequate description of the things to be seized and was therefore valid. . . . [E]ven a cursory reading of the warrant in this case — perhaps just a simple glance — would have revealed a glaring deficiency that any reasonable police officer would have known was constitutionally fatal. . . .

Notice that the error in *Groh* did not harm the search target at all: if the officer had behaved properly, the warrant would still have issued and the search would still have taken place. The error in *Evans*, by contrast, led to a search that should never have happened. Why, then, was the police behavior in *Evans* reasonable, while the behavior in *Groh* was *un*reasonable?

NOTE ON STATE CONSTITUTIONAL LAW

Although *Leon*'s "good-faith" exception is settled Fourth Amendment law, it is not applied everywhere. A number of state courts, construing their own state constitutions, have adhered to the position that officers' good faith is irrelevant when reviewing a magistrate's finding of probable cause.

That position is perfectly consistent with the Fourth Amendment. All state constitutions have search and seizure provisions; frequently the wording of those provisions is similar, even identical, to the federal Fourth Amendment. Obviously, states cannot really use their constitutions to nullify the Fourth Amendment—no state supreme court could say, in our jurisdiction even *bad*-faith reliance on a warrant is protected. But state courts are free to conclude that their constitutions require *more* than the Fourth Amendment—for example, that good-faith reliance on a warrant is not enough, that the decision to issue the warrant must actually have been correct or the evidence found thereby must be suppressed. In other words, Fourth Amendment law represents a constitutional floor below which no state court may go. But each state—meaning, in practice, each state's highest court—can decide for itself how high to set the ceiling.

Some state courts exercise this power on a regular basis. Consider the following discussion of New Jersey constitutional law, written by a sitting judge in that state:

> The Fourth Amendment to the United States Constitution and Article 1, Paragraph 7 of the New Jersey Constitution both address the right of citizens to be free from unreasonable searches and seizures by the government. The language of the two provisions is virtually identical. [The only differences are that "warrant" is singular in the New Jersey Constitution, the word "except" is used instead of "but," and instead of the phrase "particularly describing . . . the persons or things to be seized," the New Jersey Constitution says "particularly describing . . . the papers and things to be seized."—EDS.] . . .
>
> Despite the identical language, the New Jersey Supreme Court has interpreted Article 1, Paragraph 7, . . . so as to provide greater protection to criminal defendants than they would have under the Fourth Amendment.
>
> The areas in which the New Jersey Supreme Court deviates from federal [Fourth Amendment doctrine] are: (1) consent to search; (2) standing to challenge seized evidence; (3) good faith exception to the warrant requirement; (4) search of garbage left out on the curb for pick-up; (5) what constitutes a seizure in the context of a citizen who flees from the police; (6) search of toll billing records; (7) the [scope of the] automobile exception to the warrant requirement; and (8) a warrantless automobile search [incident to arrest].

Dennis Braithwaite, An Analysis of the "Divergence Factors": A Misguided Approach to Search and Seizure Jurisprudence Under the New Jersey Constitution, 33 Rutgers L.J. 1, 1-2 (2001). As the title of Judge Braithwaite's article suggests, the New Jersey Supreme Court has developed a list of "divergence factors" that, the court says, counsel in favor of replacing the governing Fourth Amendment standard with a different, more protective standard. These "divergence factors" are, taken together, quite broad: They include "state traditions" and "public attitudes" as well as (undefined) "structural differences" between the state and federal constitutions, and "matters of particular state interest or local concern." Predictably, the New Jersey Supreme Court has been able to find one or more "divergence factors" in a wide range of cases — as the above-quoted list of state-law rules demonstrates.

Judge Braithwaite argues that this search for special justifications for deviating from the Fourth Amendment is a mistake, that the New Jersey Supreme Court (and, by extension, courts in the other forty-nine states) should feel free to construe its own constitution as it thinks best. Is he right? Aren't there substantial benefits from having a uniform law of search and seizure that crosses state boundaries? On the other hand, aren't there also benefits from having state-by-state experimentation, as long as all states give criminal suspects at least as much protection as the Fourth Amendment requires?

Whatever the right answers to these questions are, a number of state courts behave similarly to the New Jersey Supreme Court. But even in those jurisdictions whose search and seizure law varies most from Fourth Amendment law, the United States Supreme Court continues to set the agenda. In each of the New Jersey cases Judge Braithwaite cited, the New Jersey Supreme Court took issue with some U.S. Supreme Court majority opinion; in almost all of them, the New Jersey Court adopted the position of some U.S. Supreme Court dissent. That is a common pattern: State search and seizure law generally consists of scattered exceptions to Fourth Amendment doctrine, with the exceptions in turn consisting of a few Supreme Court dissents that the relevant state court has adopted as state law. In this way, the Supreme Court has managed to dominate not only the federal law of search and seizure but also the law of the 50 states. For a criticism of this pattern, in the context of a more general criticism of the poverty of state constitutional argument, see James A. Gardner, The Failed Discourse of State Constitutionalism, 90 Mich. L. Rev. 761 (1991). For a defense of state-court behavior like that in New Jersey, see Ronald K. L. Collins, Foreword: The Once "New Judicial Federalism" & Its Critics, 64 Wash. L. Rev. 5 (1989).

Return to the issue in *Leon*. What should state courts do when faced with questions like the relevance of good-faith reliance on search warrants? Recapitulate the Supreme Court's debate, but maybe come out the other way? Adhere to whatever the Supreme Court decided? Something else?

b. Standing

One of the most basic questions about the exclusionary rule is who gets to invoke it. One possible answer is simple: anyone, meaning that any defendant could seek to exclude all illegally obtained evidence, regardless of where the evidence was found. The Court offered a different answer in Jones v. United States, 362 U.S. 257, 261 (1960): In order to have standing to challenge an illegal search or seizure, "one must have been a victim of [the] search or seizure, one against whom the search was directed, as distinguished from one who claims prejudice only through the use of evidence gathered as a consequence of a search or seizure directed at someone else." *Jones* seemed to adopt a "target theory" of standing. Later, in Alderman v. United States, 394 U.S. 165, 174 (1969), the Court appeared to reject that theory, stating that "Fourth Amendment rights are personal rights which, like some other constitutional rights, may not be vicariously asserted." *Jones* and *Alderman* left Fourth Amendment standing doctrine in a state of chaos.

In Rakas v. Illinois, 439 U.S. 128 (1978), the Court imposed a measure of order on the chaos. The facts in *Rakas* were as follows:

> A police officer on a routine patrol received a radio call notifying him of a robbery of a [nearby] clothing store . . . and describing the getaway car. Shortly thereafter, the officer spotted an automobile which he thought might be the getaway car. After following the car for some time and after the arrival of assistance, he and several other officers stopped the vehicle. The occupants of the automobile, petitioners and two female companions, were ordered out of the car and, after the occupants had left the car, two officers searched the interior of the vehicle. They discovered a box of rifle shells in the glove compartment, which had been locked, and a sawed-off rifle under the front passenger seat. After discovering the rifle and the shells, the officers took petitioners to the station and placed them under arrest.

Id. at 130. Rakas and his codefendant conceded that they did not own the car. Nor, apparently, did they own the shells or the rifle.

In an opinion by then-Justice Rehnquist, the Court concluded that Rakas lacked standing to complain about the car search. Rehnquist began by dismissing the target theory, on the ground that it empowers defendants to seek relief for searches that did not infringe any protected privacy interest of theirs:

> A person who is aggrieved by an illegal search and seizure only through the introduction of damaging evidence secured by a search of a third person's premises or property has not had any of his Fourth Amendment rights infringed. And since the exclusionary rule is an attempt to effectuate the guarantees of the Fourth Amendment, it is proper to permit only defendants whose Fourth Amendment rights have been violated to benefit from the rule's protections.

Id. at 134. In addition, Rehnquist argued that the target theory imposed serious administrative burdens on courts, for it required findings about police officers' motivations when searching. Instead, he (and the Court) concluded, standing "is more properly subsumed under substantive Fourth Amendment doctrine." Id. at 139. Rehnquist stated the rule as follows: "[T]he question is whether the challenged search and seizure violated the Fourth Amendment rights of a criminal defendant who seeks to exclude the evidence obtained during it." Id. at 140.

In short, a defendant may seek to exclude evidence based on an illegal search only if the search infringed *his own* reasonable expectation of privacy, not someone else's. What that rule means in practice, and especially what it means for searches of dwellings, is the subject of the next case.

MINNESOTA v. CARTER

Certiorari to the Supreme Court of Minnesota
525 U.S. 83 (1998)

CHIEF JUSTICE REHNQUIST delivered the opinion of the Court.

Respondents and the lessee of an apartment were sitting in one of its rooms, bagging cocaine. While so engaged they were observed by a police officer, who looked through a drawn window blind. The Supreme Court of Minnesota held that the officer's viewing was a search which violated respondents' Fourth Amendment rights. We hold that no such violation occurred.

James Thielen, a police officer in the Twin Cities' suburb of Eagan, Minnesota, went to an apartment building to investigate a tip from a confidential informant. The informant said that he had walked by the window of a ground-floor apartment and had seen people putting a white powder into bags. The officer looked in the same window through a gap in the closed blind and observed the bagging operation for several minutes. He then notified headquarters, which began preparing affidavits for a search warrant while he returned to the apartment building. When two men left the building in a previously identified Cadillac, the police stopped the car. Inside were respondents Carter and Johns. As the police opened the door of the car to let Johns out, they observed a black zippered pouch and a handgun, later determined to be loaded, on the vehicle's floor. Carter and Johns were arrested, and a later police search of the vehicle the next day discovered pagers, a scale, and 47 grams of cocaine in plastic sandwich bags.

After seizing the car, the police returned to Apartment 103 and arrested the occupant, Kimberly Thompson, who is not a party to this appeal. A search of the apartment pursuant to a warrant revealed cocaine residue on the kitchen table and plastic baggies similar to those found in the Cadillac. Thielen identified Carter, Johns, and Thompson as the three people he had observed placing the powder into baggies. The police later learned that while Thompson was the lessee of the apartment, Carter and Johns lived in Chicago and had come to the apartment for the sole purpose of packaging the cocaine. Carter and Johns had never been to the apartment before and were only in the apartment for approximately 2 hours. In return for the use of the apartment, Carter and Johns had given Thompson one-eighth of an ounce of the cocaine.

Carter and Johns . . . moved to suppress all evidence obtained from the apartment and the Cadillac, as well as to suppress several post-arrest incriminating statements they had made. They argued that Thielen's initial observation of their drug packaging activities was an unreasonable search in violation of the Fourth Amendment and that all evidence obtained as a result of this unreasonable search was inadmissible as fruit of the poisonous tree. The Minnesota trial court held that since, unlike the defendant in Minnesota v. Olson, 495 U.S. 91 (1990), Carter and Johns were not overnight social guests but temporary out-of-state visitors, they were not entitled to claim the protection of the Fourth Amendment against the government intrusion into the apartment. . . .

A divided Minnesota Supreme Court reversed, holding that respondents had "standing" to claim the protection of the Fourth Amendment because they had "a legitimate expectation of privacy in the invaded place." The court noted that even though "society does not recognize as valuable the task of bagging cocaine, we conclude that society does recognize as valuable the right of property owners or leaseholders to invite persons into the privacy of their homes to conduct a common task, be it legal or illegal activity." . . . We granted certiorari, and now reverse.

The Minnesota courts analyzed whether respondents had a legitimate expectation of privacy under the rubric of "standing" doctrine, an analysis which this Court expressly rejected 20 years ago in [Rakas v. Illinois, 439 U.S. 128 (1978)]. In that case, we held that automobile passengers could not assert the protection of the Fourth Amendment against the seizure of incriminating evidence from a vehicle where they owned neither the vehicle nor the evidence. Ibid. Central to our analysis was the idea that in determining whether a defendant is able to show the violation of his (and not someone else's) Fourth Amendment rights, the "definition of those rights is more properly placed within the purview of substantive Fourth Amendment law than within that of standing." 439 U.S. at 140. Thus, we held that in order to claim the protection of the Fourth Amendment, a defendant must demonstrate that he personally has an expectation of privacy in the place searched, and that his expectation is reasonable. . . .

The Fourth Amendment . . . protects persons against unreasonable searches of "their persons [and] houses" and thus indicates that the Fourth Amendment is a personal right that must be invoked by an individual. See Katz v. United States, 389 U.S. 347, 351 (1967) ("The Fourth Amendment protects people, not places"). But the extent to which the Fourth Amendment protects people may depend upon where those people are. We have held that "capacity to claim the protection of the Fourth Amendment depends . . . upon whether the person who claims the protection of the Amendment has a legitimate expectation of privacy in the invaded place." Rakas, supra, at 143.

The text of the Amendment suggests that its protections extend only to people in "their" houses. But we have held that in some circumstances a person may have a legitimate expectation of privacy in the house of someone else. In Minnesota v. Olson, 495 U.S. 91 (1990), for example, we decided that an overnight guest in a house had the sort of expectation of privacy that the Fourth Amendment protects. We said:

> To hold that an overnight guest has a legitimate expectation of privacy in his host's home merely recognizes the every day expectations of privacy that we all share. Staying overnight in another's home is a long-standing social custom that serves functions recognized as valuable by society. We stay in others' homes when we travel to a strange city for business or pleasure, we visit our parents, children, or more distant relatives out of town, when we are in between jobs, or homes, or when we house-sit for a friend. . . .
>
> From the overnight guest's perspective, he seeks shelter in another's home precisely because it provides him with privacy, a place where he and his possessions will not be disturbed by anyone but his host and those his host allows inside. We are at our most vulnerable when we are asleep because we cannot monitor our own safety or the security of our belongings. It is for this reason that, although we may spend all day in public places, when we cannot sleep in our own home we seek out another private place to sleep, whether it be a hotel room, or the home of a friend. 495 U.S. at 98-99.

In Jones v. United States, 362 U.S. 257, 259 (1960), the defendant seeking to exclude evidence resulting from a search of an apartment had been given the use of the apartment by a friend. He had clothing in the apartment, had slept there "maybe a night," and at the time was the sole occupant of the apartment. But while the holding of Jones — that a search of the apartment violated the defendant's Fourth Amendment rights — is still valid, its statement that "anyone legitimately on the premises where a search occurs may challenge its legality," id. at 267, was expressly repudiated in Rakas v. Illinois, 439 U.S. 128 (1978). Thus an overnight guest in a home may claim the protection of the Fourth Amendment, but one who is merely present with the consent of the householder may not.

Respondents here were obviously not overnight guests, but were essentially present for a business transaction and were only in the home a matter of hours. There is no suggestion that they had a previous relationship with Thompson, or that there was any other purpose to their visit. Nor was there anything similar to the overnight guest relationship in *Olson* to suggest a degree of acceptance into the household. While the apartment was a dwelling place for Thompson, it was for these respondents simply a place to do business. . . .

If we regard the overnight guest in Minnesota v. Olson as typifying those who may claim the protection of the Fourth Amendment in the home of another, and one merely "legitimately on the premises" as typifying those who may not do so, the present case is obviously somewhere in between. But the purely commercial nature of the transaction engaged in here, the relatively short period of time on the premises, and the lack of any previous connection between respondents and the householder, all lead us to conclude that respondents' situation is closer to that of one simply permitted on the premises. We therefore hold that any search which may have occurred did not violate their Fourth Amendment rights.

Because we conclude that respondents had no legitimate expectation of privacy in the apartment, we need not decide whether the police officer's observation constituted a "search." The judgment of the Supreme Court of Minnesota is accordingly reversed, and the cause is remanded for proceedings not inconsistent with this opinion.

JUSTICE SCALIA, with whom JUSTICE THOMAS joins, concurring.

I join the opinion of the Court because I believe it accurately applies our recent case law, including Minnesota v. Olson, 495 U.S. 91 (1990). I write separately to express my view that that case law — like the submissions of the parties in this case — gives short shrift to the text of the Fourth Amendment, and to the well and long understood meaning of that text. Specifically, it leaps to apply the fuzzy standard of "legitimate expectation of privacy" — a consideration that is often relevant to whether a search or seizure covered by the Fourth Amendment is "unreasonable" — to the threshold question whether a search or seizure covered by the Fourth Amendment has occurred. If that latter question is addressed first and analyzed under the text of the Constitution as traditionally understood, the present case is not remotely difficult.

The Fourth Amendment protects "the right of the people to be secure in their persons, houses, papers, and effects, against unreasonable searches and seizures. . . ." U.S. Const., Amdt. 4. It must be acknowledged that the phrase "their . . . houses" in this provision is, in isolation, ambiguous. It could mean "their respective houses," so that the protection extends to each person only in his own house. But it could also mean "their respective and each other's houses," so that each person would be protected even when visiting the house of someone else. As today's opinion for the Court suggests, however, it is not linguistically possible to give the provision the latter, expansive interpretation with respect to "houses" without giving it the same interpretation with respect to the nouns that are parallel to "houses" — "persons, . . . papers, and effects" — which would give me a constitutional right not to have your person unreasonably searched. This is so absurd that it has to my knowledge never been contemplated. The obvious meaning of the provision is that each person has the right to be secure against unreasonable searches and seizures in his own person, house, papers, and effects.

The Founding-era materials that I have examined confirm that this was the understood meaning. (Strangely, these materials went unmentioned by the State and its amici — unmentioned even in the State's reply brief, even though respondents had thrown down the gauntlet: "In briefs totaling over 100 pages, the State of Minnesota, the amici 26 attorneys general, and the Solicitor General of the United States of America have not mentioned one word about the history and purposes of the Fourth Amendment or the intent of the framers of that amendment." Brief for Respondents 12, n. 4.) Like most of the provisions of the Bill of Rights, the Fourth Amendment was derived from provisions already existing in state constitutions. Of the four of those provisions that contained language similar to that of the Fourth Amendment, two used the same ambiguous "their" terminology. See Pa. Const., Art. X (1776) ("That the people have a right to hold themselves, their houses, papers, and possessions free from search and seizure . . ."); Vt. Const., ch. I, §XI (1777) ("That the people have a right to hold themselves, their houses, papers, and possessions free from search or seizure . . ."). The other two, however, avoided the ambiguity by using the singular instead of the plural. See Mass. Const., pt. I, Art. XIV (1780) ("Every subject has a right to be secure from all unreasonable searches, and seizures of his person, his houses, his papers, and all his possessions"); N.H. Const. §XIX (1784) ("Every subject hath a right to be secure from all unreasonable searches and seizures of his person, his houses, his papers, and all his possessions"). The New York Convention that ratified the Constitution proposed an amendment that would have given every freeman "a right to be secure from all unreasonable searches and seizures of his person, his papers or his property," 4 B. Schwartz, The Roots of the Bill of Rights 913 (1980) (reproducing New York proposed amendments, 1778), and the Declaration of Rights that the North Carolina Convention demanded prior to its ratification contained a similar provision protecting a freeman's right against "unreasonable searches and seizures of his person, his papers and property," id. at 968 (reproducing North Carolina proposed Declaration of Rights, 1778). There is no indication anyone believed that the Massachusetts, New Hampshire, New York, and North Carolina texts, by using the word "his" rather than "their," narrowed the protections contained in the Pennsylvania and Vermont Constitutions.

That "their . . . houses" was understood to mean "their respective houses" would have been clear to anyone who knew the English and early American law of arrest and trespass that underlay the Fourth Amendment. The people's protection against unreasonable search and seizure in their "houses" was drawn from the English common-law maxim, "A man's home is his castle." As far back as Semayne's Case of 1604, the leading English case for that proposition . . . the King's Bench proclaimed that "the house of any one is not a castle or privilege but for himself, and shall not extend to protect any person who flies to his house." Semayne v. Gresham, 5 Co. Rep. 91a, 93a, 77 Eng. Rep. 194, 198 (K.B. 1604). . . .

Of course this is not to say that the Fourth Amendment protects only the Lord of the Manor who holds his estate in fee simple. People call a house "their" home when legal title is in the bank, when they rent it, and even when they merely occupy it rent-free — so long as they actually live there. That this is the criterion of the people's protection against government intrusion into "their" houses is established by the leading American case of Oystead v. Shed, 13 Mass. 520 (1816), which held it a trespass for the sheriff to break into a dwelling to capture a boarder who lived there. The court reasoned that the "inviolability of dwelling houses" . . . extends to "the occupier or any of his family . . . who have their domicile or ordinary residence there," including "a boarder or a servant" "who have made the house their home." Id. at 523. But, it added, "the house shall not be made a sanctuary" for one such as "a stranger, or perhaps a visitor," who "upon a pursuit, takes refuge in the house of another," for "the house is not his castle; and the officer may break open the doors or windows in order to execute his process." Ibid.

Thus, in deciding the question presented today we write upon a slate that is far from clean. The text of the Fourth Amendment, the common-law background against which it was adopted, and the understandings consistently displayed after its adoption make the answer clear. We were right to hold in Chapman v. United States, 365 U.S. 610 (1961), that the Fourth Amendment protects an apartment tenant against an unreasonable search of his dwelling, even though he is only a leaseholder. And we were right to hold in Bumper v. North Carolina, 391 U.S. 543 (1968), that an unreasonable search of a grandmother's house violated her resident grandson's Fourth Amendment rights because the area searched "was his home," id. at 548, n. 11. We went to the absolute limit of what text and tradition permit in Minnesota v. Olson, 495 U.S. 91 (1990), when we protected a mere overnight guest against an unreasonable search of his hosts' apartment. But whereas it is plausible to regard a person's overnight lodging as at least his "temporary" residence, it is entirely impossible to give that characterization to an apartment that he uses to package cocaine. Respondents here were not searched in "their . . . house" under any interpretation of the phrase that bears the remotest relationship to the well understood meaning of the Fourth Amendment. . . .

The dissent may be correct that a person invited into someone else's house to engage in a common business (even common monkey-business, so to speak) ought to be protected against government searches of the room in which that business is conducted; and that persons invited in to deliver milk or pizza (whom the dissent dismisses as "classroom hypotheticals," as opposed, presumably, to flesh-and-blood hypotheticals) ought not to be protected against government searches of the rooms that they occupy. I am not sure of the answer to those policy questions. But I am sure that the answer is not remotely contained in the Constitution, which means that it is left — as many, indeed most, important questions are left — to the judgment of state and federal legislators. We go beyond our proper role as judges in a democratic society when we restrict the people's power to govern themselves over the full range of policy choices that the Constitution has left available to them.

JUSTICE KENNEDY, concurring.

I join the Court's opinion, for its reasoning is consistent with my view that almost all social guests have a legitimate expectation of privacy, and hence protection against unreasonable searches, in their host's home. . . .

. . . I would expect that most, if not all, social guests legitimately expect that, in accordance with social custom, the homeowner will exercise her discretion to include or exclude others for the guests' benefit. As we recognized in Minnesota v. Olson, 495 U.S. 91 (1990), where these social expectations exist — as in the case of an overnight guest — they are sufficient to create a legitimate expectation of privacy, even in the absence of any property right to exclude others. In this respect, the dissent must be correct that reasonable expectations of the owner are shared, to some extent, by the guest. This analysis suggests that, as a general rule, social guests will have an expectation of privacy in their host's home. That is not the case before us, however.

In this case respondents have established nothing more than a fleeting and insubstantial connection with Thompson's home. For all that appears in the record, respondents used Thompson's house simply as a convenient processing station, their purpose involving nothing more than the mechanical act of chopping and packing a substance for distribution. There is no suggestion that respondents engaged in confidential communications with Thompson about their transaction. Respondents had not been to Thompson's apartment before, and they left it even before their arrest. The Minnesota Supreme Court, which overturned respondents' convictions, acknowledged that respondents could not be fairly characterized as Thompson's "guests."

If respondents here had been visiting twenty homes, each for a minute or two, to drop off a bag of cocaine and were apprehended by a policeman wrongfully present in the nineteenth home; or if they had left the goods at a home where they were not staying and the police had seized the goods in their absence, we would have said that *Rakas* compels rejection of any privacy interest respondents might assert. So it does here, given that respondents have established no meaningful tie or connection to the owner, the owner's home, or the owner's expectation of privacy. . . .

JUSTICE BREYER, concurring in the judgment.

I agree with JUSTICE GINSBURG that respondents can claim the Fourth Amendment's protection. Petitioner, however, raises a second question, whether under the circumstances Officer Thielen's observation made "from a public area outside the curtilage of the residence" violated respondents' Fourth Amendment rights. See Pet. for Cert. i. In my view, it did not.

I would answer the question on the basis of the following factual assumptions, derived from the evidentiary record presented here: (1) On the evening of May 15, 1994, an anonymous individual approached Officer Thielen, telling him that he had just walked by a nearby apartment window through which he had seen some people bagging drugs; (2) the apartment in question was a garden apartment that was partly below ground level; (3) families frequently used the grassy area just outside the apartment's window for walking or for playing; (4) members of the public also used the area just outside the apartment's window to store bicycles; (5) in an effort to verify the tipster's information, Officer Thielen walked to a position about 1 to $1\frac{1}{2}$ feet in front of the window; (6) Officer Thielen stood there for about 15 minutes looking down through a set of Venetian blinds; (7) what he saw, namely, people putting white powder in bags, verified the account he had heard; and (8) he then used that information to help obtain a search warrant. [Following is a long series of citations to the record.]

The trial court concluded that persons then within Ms. Thompson's kitchen "did not have an expectation of privacy from the location where Officer Thielen made his observations . . . ," because Officer Thielen stood outside the apartment's "curtilage" when he made his observations. And the Minnesota Supreme Court, while finding that Officer Thielen had violated the Fourth Amendment, did not challenge the trial court's curtilage determination; indeed, it assumed that

Officer Thielen stood outside the apartment's curtilage. 569 N.W.2d 169, 177, and n. 10 (1987) (stating "it is plausible that Thielen's presence just outside the apartment window was legitimate").

Officer Thielen, then, stood at a place used by the public and from which one could see through the window into the kitchen. The precautions that the apartment's dwellers took to maintain their privacy would have failed in respect to an ordinary passerby standing in that place. Given this Court's well-established case law, I cannot say that the officer engaged in what the Constitution forbids, namely, an "unreasonable search." See, e.g., Florida v. Riley, 488 U.S. 445, 448 (1989) (finding observation of greenhouse from helicopters in public airspace permissible, even though owners had enclosed greenhouse on two sides, relied on bushes blocking ground-level observations through remaining two sides, and covered 90% of roof); California v. Ciraolo, 476 U.S. 207, 209 (1986) (finding observation of backyard from plane in public airspace permissible despite 6-foot outer fence and 10-foot inner fence around backyard).

The Minnesota Supreme Court reached a different conclusion in part because it believed that Officer Thielen had engaged in unusual activity, that he "climbed over some bushes, crouched down and placed his face 12 to 18 inches from the window," and in part because he saw into the apartment through "a small gap" in blinds that were drawn. 569 N.W.2d at 177-178. But I would not here determine whether the crouching and climbing or "placing his face" makes a constitutional difference because the record before us does not contain support for those factual conclusions. That record indicates that Officer Thielen would not have needed to, and did not, climb over bushes or crouch. [Following are citations to Officer Thielen's testimony and to a photograph of the apartment complex.] And even though the primary evidence consists of Officer Thielen's own testimony, who else could have known? Given the importance of factual nuance in this area of constitutional law, I would not determine the constitutional significance of factual assertions that the record denies.

Neither can the matter turn upon "gaps" in drawn blinds. Whether there were holes in the blinds or they were simply pulled the "wrong way" makes no difference. One who lives in a basement apartment that fronts a publicly traveled street, or similar space, ordinarily understands the need for care lest a member of the public simply direct his gaze downward.

Putting the specific facts of this case aside, there is a benefit to an officer's decision to confirm an informant's tip by observing the allegedly illegal activity from a public vantage point. Indeed, there are reasons why Officer Thielen stood in a public place and looked through the apartment window. He had already received information that a crime was taking place in the apartment. He intended to apply for a warrant. He needed to verify the tipster's credibility. He might have done so in other ways, say, by seeking general information about the tipster's reputation and then obtaining a warrant and searching the apartment. But his chosen method — observing the apartment from a public vantage point — would more likely have saved an innocent apartment dweller from a physically intrusive, though warrant-based, search if the constitutionally permissible observation revealed no illegal activity.

For these reasons, while agreeing with JUSTICE GINSBURG, I also concur in the Court's judgment reversing the Minnesota Supreme Court.

JUSTICE GINSBURG, with whom JUSTICE STEVENS and JUSTICE SOUTER join, dissenting.

The Court's decision undermines not only the security of short-term guests, but also the security of the home resident herself. In my view, when a homeowner or lessor personally invites a guest into her home to share in a common endeavor, whether it be for conversation, to engage in leisure activities, or for business purposes licit or illicit, that guest should share his host's shelter against unreasonable searches and seizures. . . .

. . . [E]ven within the home itself, the position to which I would adhere would not permit "a casual visitor who has never seen, or been permitted to visit, the basement of another's house to object to a search of the basement if the visitor happened to be in the kitchen of the house at the time of the search." *Rakas*, 439 U.S. at 142. Further, I would here decide only the case of the homeowner who chooses to share the privacy of her home and her company with a guest, and would not reach classroom hypotheticals like the milkman or pizza deliverer.

My concern centers on an individual's choice to share her home and her associations there with persons she selects. Our decisions indicate that people have a reasonable expectation of privacy in their homes in part because they have the prerogative to exclude others. See id. at 149 (legitimate expectation of privacy turns in large part on ability to exclude others from place searched). The power to exclude implies the power to include. . . .

Through the host's invitation, the guest gains a reasonable expectation of privacy in the home. Minnesota v. Olson, 495 U.S. 91 (1990), so held with respect to an overnight guest. The logic of that decision extends to shorter term guests as well. . . . Visiting the home of a friend, relative, or business associate, whatever the time of day, "serves functions recognized as valuable by society." *Olson*, 495 U.S. at 98. One need not remain overnight to anticipate privacy in another's home, "a place where [the guest] and his possessions will not be disturbed by anyone but his host and those his host allows inside." Id. at 99. In sum, when a homeowner chooses to share the privacy of her home and her company with a short-term guest, the twofold requirement "emerging from prior decisions" has been satisfied: Both host and guest "have exhibited an actual (subjective) expectation of privacy"; that "expectation [is] one [our] society is prepared to recognize as 'reasonable.'" Katz v. United States, 389 U.S. 347, 361 (1967) (Harlan, J., concurring).[2]

. . . [T]he illegality of the host-guest conduct, the fact that they were partners in crime, would not alter the analysis. In *Olson*, for example, the guest whose security this Court's decision shielded stayed overnight while the police searched for him. 495 U.S. at 93-94. The Court held that the guest had Fourth Amendment protection against a warrantless arrest in his host's home despite the guest's involvement in grave crimes (first-degree murder, armed robbery, and assault). . . .

2. In his concurring opinion, JUSTICE KENNEDY maintains that respondents here lacked "an expectation of privacy that society recognizes as reasonable," because they "established nothing more than a fleeting and insubstantial connection" with the host's home. As the Minnesota Supreme Court reported, however, the stipulated facts showed that respondents were inside the apartment with the host's permission, remained inside for at least 2 hours, and, during that time, engaged in concert with the host in a collaborative venture. These stipulated facts . . . securely demonstrate that the host intended to share her privacy with respondents. . . . I think it noteworthy that five Members of the Court would place under the Fourth Amendment's shield, at least, "almost all social guests." (KENNEDY, J., concurring).

Indeed, it must be this way. If the illegality of the activity made constitutional an otherwise unconstitutional search, such Fourth Amendment protection, reserved for the innocent only, would have little force in regulating police behavior toward either the innocent or the guilty. . . .

NOTES AND QUESTIONS

1. Is Justice Breyer right? Regardless of the identity of the persons Officer Thielen saw through the apartment window, was anyone "searched" within the meaning of the Fourth Amendment?

2. When evaluating the privacy interests of houseguests, consider the following possibility. A houseguest is likely to have no significant privacy interest in things that can be found in his host's home: They are, after all, his host's things. On the other hand, a guest may have a considerable — and quite reasonable, in the ordinary sense of that word — expectation of privacy in the guest's own *activities*, in what the guest is *doing* while in the host's home. Should this distinction matter for purposes of Fourth Amendment doctrine? Does it?

3. Under Minnesota v. Olson, 495 U.S. 91 (1990), overnight houseguests *do* have a reasonable expectation of privacy in the home in which they are staying. Carter and Johns, on the other hand, don't. Where is the line that separates Olson from Carter and Johns?

In this connection, reread the last sentence of footnote 2 in Justice Ginsburg's dissent, where she claims that five Justices support the proposition that virtually all social guests have a reasonable expectation of privacy in their hosts' homes. Her head count is accurate. Justices Ginsburg, Stevens, and Souter take the position that *all* guests have a reasonable expectation of privacy. Justice Breyer, who concurs in the judgment on other grounds (see Note 1), states that he agrees with Justice Ginsburg's dissent. And Justice Kennedy says "almost all social guests" are protected. Why, then, aren't Carter and Johns protected? Justice Kennedy says it is because their connection with Thompson's apartment was "fleeting and insubstantial," and their activities there "mechanical." What does this mean?

Some of the language in Chief Justice Rehnquist's opinion suggests the problem with Carter's and Johns's claim is that they were engaged in illegal activity in Thompson's apartment — packaging cocaine — and they can have no legitimate expectation of privacy in such behavior. It is hard to take this language seriously. After all, if Carter has no claim because he was packaging cocaine when Officer Thielen saw him, then Carter would have no claim even if he had been packaging cocaine *in his own apartment*. Virtually every motion to suppress drugs would fail, because no one can have a legitimate expectation of privacy in illegal drug possession.

Of course, the Court does not carry the point nearly so far. But this suggests a problem with the analysis in *Carter*, and in *Rakas*. Both of those cases emphasize that a defendant can base his Fourth Amendment claim only on the violation of *his own* privacy interests. But in a system with an exclusionary rule, the Fourth Amendment claims of defendants like Carter and Johns protect the privacy interests of law-abiding citizens — by making it harder to search apartments for drugs, the Fourth Amendment makes it harder to search apartments where no drugs will be found. One might say that all exclusionary rule litigation involves a form of third-party standing, where the claimant is permitted to raise his claim in order to protect other parties not before the court. The theory underlying *Rakas* and *Carter* seems inconsistent with the primary remedy the Court uses to enforce the Fourth Amendment.

4. Recall the facts of Wyoming v. Houghton, page 503 supra. There the defendant was a passenger in someone else's car; the police stopped and searched the car, including the defendant's purse, which was found sitting on the back seat. The Court assumed that the defendant had standing to challenge the search of her purse. In Rakas v. Illinois, 439 U.S. 128 (1978), the defendant was likewise a passenger in someone else's car. There, the Court held that the defendant lacked standing to challenge the search of the car's glove compartment. Is the line between *Rakas* and *Houghton* obvious? Is it right?

5. The defendant in United States v. Payner, 447 U.S. 727 (1980), was charged with falsifying his income tax return; among other things, the government claimed that the defendant had a foreign bank account that he denied having. In the course of the government's investigation, federal agents lured a bank officer to dinner, while other agents entered the bank officer's hotel room, removed his briefcase, and photographed documents found there. Those documents were in turn used against the defendant. The Court found that the defendant lacked standing, because the hotel room, briefcase, and documents had belonged to the bank officer, not to him.

There is some reason to believe the search in *Payner* was strategic. As Carol Steiker reports,

> In testimony before the Distrct Court in [*Payner*], it came to light that a Mr. Hyatt, an attorney with the Department of Justice, explicitly had instructed the I.R.S. agents in the case that the bank officer whose briefcase was stolen to obtain information against the defendant would be the only individual to have standing to object to the blatantly illegal search and that he was not a target of the investigation.

Carol S. Steiker, Counter-Revolution in Constitutional Criminal Procedure? Two Audiences, Two Answers, 94 Mich. L. Rev. 2466, 2536 (1996). Steiker argues that this sort of behavior is natural given the state of standing doctrine. The problem, she suggests, is this: Standing rules are "decision rules" whose proper audience is the courts. Ideally, the police should be unaware of them. The rules the police should pay attention to are the Fourth Amendment's many "conduct rules," the doctrines that define what searches and seizures the police may or may not undertake. But decision rules like standing doctrine cannot be kept from the police, and the police cannot be expected to ignore such rules once they know about them. As Steiker puts it,

> As for the police, [what] ought to concern us is the likelihood that . . . decision rules will, in effect, become conduct rules. Where the police "hear" the Court's decision rules and thus are able to predict the likely legal consequences of their unconstitutional behavior, they may see little reason to continue to obey conduct rules that are consistently unenforced. . . . [C]hanges in decision rules will necessarily change compliance with conduct rules.

Id. at 2543. What does Steiker's argument imply for standing doctrine? Should the Court grant everyone standing, to avoid the kind of strategic behavior that appears in *Payner*? Or should standing simply be made less predictable, so that police would find it harder to anticipate who would and who wouldn't be able to object to any given illegal search? Might standing be one area of Fourth Amendment doctrine where standards rather than rules are appropriate?

6. Consider Justice Scalia's textual argument in *Carter*. According to Justice Scalia, the *Rakas* principle — one can only assert one's own Fourth Amendment interests — is compelled by the Fourth Amendment's text. But the only privacy interest likely to be asserted in suppression hearings is the interest in keeping private one's criminal activities: Once again, people like Carter and Johns are permitted to raise Fourth Amendment claims in order to vindicate the privacy interests of people like you. Does it follow that Justice Scalia's argument is really an argument that the Fourth Amendment's text bars the exclusionary rule?

As long as Fourth Amendment law has important features like the exclusionary rule, features that do not derive from either text or history, is it sensible to place much weight on text and history when deciding issues like the meaning of Fourth Amendment standing? Might we be better off being wholly faithless to text and history than being only partly faithful?

c. "Fruit of the Poisonous Tree" Doctrine

WONG SUN v. UNITED STATES

Certiorari to the United States Court of Appeals for the Ninth Circuit
371 U.S. 471 (1963)

MR. JUSTICE BRENNAN delivered the opinion of the Court.

The petitioners were tried without a jury in the District Court for the Northern District of California under a two-count indictment for violation of the Federal Narcotics Laws. They were acquitted under the first count which charged a conspiracy, but convicted under the second count which charged the substantive offense of fraudulent and knowing transportation and concealment of illegally imported heroin. The Court of Appeals for the Ninth Circuit, one judge dissenting, affirmed the convictions. 288 F.2d 366. We granted certiorari. . . .

About 2 a.m. on the morning of June 4, 1959, federal narcotics agents in San Francisco, after having had one Hom Way under surveillance for six weeks, arrested him and found heroin in his possession. Hom Way, who had not before been an informant, stated after his arrest that he had bought an ounce of heroin the night before from one known to him only as "Blackie Toy," proprietor of a laundry on Leavenworth Street.

About 6 a.m. that morning six or seven federal agents went to a laundry at 1733 Leavenworth Street. The sign above the door of this establishment said "Oye's Laundry." It was operated by the petitioner James Wah Toy. There is, however, nothing in the record which identifies James Wah Toy and "Blackie Toy" as the same person. The other federal officers remained nearby out of sight while Agent Alton Wong, who was of Chinese ancestry, rang the bell. When petitioner Toy appeared and opened the door, Agent Wong told him that he was calling for laundry and dry cleaning. Toy replied that he didn't open until 8 o'clock and told the agent to come back at that time. Toy started to close the door. Agent Wong thereupon took his badge from his pocket and said, "I am a federal narcotics agent." Toy immediately "slammed the door and started running" down the hallway through the laundry to his living quarters at the back where his wife and child were sleeping in a bedroom. Agent Wong and the other federal officers broke open the door and followed Toy down the hallway to the living quarters and into the bedroom. Toy reached into a nightstand drawer. Agent Wong thereupon drew his pistol, pulled Toy's hand out of the drawer, placed him under arrest and handcuffed him. There was nothing in the drawer and a search of the premises uncovered no narcotics.

One of the agents said to Toy ". . . [Hom Way] says he got narcotics from you." Toy responded, "No, I haven't been selling any narcotics at all. However, I do know somebody who has." When asked who that was, Toy said, "I only know him as Johnny. I don't know his last name." . . . Toy described a house on Eleventh Avenue where he said Johnny lived; he also described a bedroom in the house where he said "Johnny kept about a piece"[2] of heroin, and where he and Johnny had smoked some of the drug the night before. The agents left immediately for Eleventh Avenue and located the house. They entered and found one Johnny Yee in the bedroom. After a discussion with the agents, Yee took from a bureau drawer several tubes containing in all just less than one ounce of heroin, and surrendered them. Within the hour Yee and Toy were taken to the Office of the Bureau of Narcotics. Yee there stated that the heroin had been brought to him some four days earlier by petitioner Toy and another Chinese known to him only as "Sea Dog."

Toy was questioned as to the identity of "Sea Dog" and said that "Sea Dog" was Wong Sun. Some agents, including Agent Alton Wong, took Toy to Wong Sun's neighborhood where Toy pointed out a multifamily dwelling where he said Wong Sun lived. Agent Wong rang a downstairs door bell and a buzzer sounded, opening the door. The officer identified himself as a narcotics agent to a woman on the landing and asked "for Mr. Wong." The woman was the wife of petitioner Wong Sun. She said that Wong Sun was "in the back room sleeping." Alton Wong and some six other officers climbed the stairs and entered the apartment. One of the officers went into the back room and brought petitioner Wong Sun from the bedroom in handcuffs. A thorough search of the apartment followed, but no narcotics were discovered.

Petitioner Toy and Johnny Yee were arraigned . . . on June 4 on a complaint charging [narcotics violations]. Later that day, each was released on his own recognizance. Petitioner Wong Sun was arraigned on a similar complaint filed the next day and was also released on his own recognizance. Within a few days, both petitioners and Yee were interrogated at the office of the Narcotics Bureau by Agent William Wong, also of Chinese ancestry. The agent advised each of the three of his right to withhold information which might be used against him, and stated to each that he was entitled to the advice of counsel, though it does not appear that any attorney was present during the questioning of any of the three. The officer also explained to each that no promises or offers of immunity or leniency were being or could be made.

The agent interrogated each of the three separately. After each had been interrogated the agent prepared a statement in English from rough notes. The agent read petitioner Toy's statement to him in English and interpreted certain portions

2. A "piece" is approximately one ounce.

of it for him in Chinese. Toy also read the statement in English aloud to the agent, said there were corrections to be made, and made the corrections in his own hand. Toy would not sign the statement, however. . . . Wong Sun had considerable difficulty understanding the statement in English and the agent restated its substance in Chinese. Wong Sun refused to sign the statement although he admitted the accuracy of its contents. . . .

. . . The Government's evidence tending to prove the petitioners' possession (the petitioners offered no exculpatory testimony) consisted of four items which the trial court admitted over timely objections that they were inadmissible as "fruits" of unlawful arrests or of attendant searches: (1) the statements made orally by petitioner Toy in his bedroom at the time of his arrest; (2) the heroin surrendered to the agents by Johnny Yee; (3) petitioner Toy's pretrial unsigned statement; and (4) petitioner Wong Sun's similar statement. The dispute below and here has centered around the correctness of the rulings of the trial judge allowing these items in evidence.

The Court of Appeals held that the arrests of both petitioners were illegal because not based on "'probable cause' within the meaning of the Fourth Amendment." . . . The Court of Appeals nevertheless held that the four items of proof were not the "fruits" of the illegal arrests and that they were therefore properly admitted in evidence.

The Court of Appeals rejected two additional contentions of the petitioners. The first was that there was insufficient evidence to corroborate the petitioners' unsigned admissions of possession of narcotics. The court held that the narcotics in evidence surrendered by Johnny Yee, together with Toy's statements in his bedroom at the time of arrest corroborated petitioners' admissions. The second contention was that the confessions were inadmissible because they were not signed. The Court of Appeals held on this point that the petitioners were not prejudiced, since the agent might properly have testified to the substance of the conversations which produced the statements.

We believe that significant differences between the cases of the two petitioners require separate discussion of each. We shall first consider the case of petitioner Toy.

I

The Court of Appeals found there was neither reasonable grounds nor probable cause for Toy's arrest. Giving due weight to that finding, we think it is amply justified by the facts clearly shown on this record. . . . The quantum of information which constitutes probable cause — evidence which would "warrant a man of reasonable caution in the belief" that a felony has been committed, Carroll v. United States, 267 U.S. 132, 162 — must be measured by the facts of the particular case. The history of the use, and not infrequent abuse, of the power to arrest cautions that a relaxation of the fundamental requirements of probable cause would "leave law-abiding citizens at the mercy of the officers' whim or caprice." Brinegar v. United States, 338 U.S. 160, 176.

Whether or not the requirements of reliability and particularity of the information on which an officer may act are more stringent where an arrest warrant is absent, they surely cannot be less stringent than where an arrest warrant is obtained. . . . The threshold question in this case, therefore, is whether the officers could, on the information which impelled them to act, have procured a warrant for the arrest of Toy. We think that no warrant would have issued on evidence then available.

The narcotics agents had no basis in experience for confidence in the reliability of Hom Way's information; he had never before given information. And yet they acted upon his imprecise suggestion that a person described only as "Blackie Toy," the proprietor of a laundry somewhere on Leavenworth Street, had sold one ounce of heroin. We have held that identification of the suspect by a reliable informant may constitute probable cause for arrest where the information given is sufficiently accurate to lead the officers directly to the suspect. Draper v. United States, 358 U.S. 307. That rule does not, however, fit this case. For aught that the record discloses, Hom Way's accusation merely invited the officers to roam the length of Leavenworth Street (some 30 blocks) in search of one "Blackie Toy's" laundry — and whether by chance or other means (the record does not say) they came upon petitioner Toy's laundry, which bore not his name over the door, but the unrevealing label "Oye's." Not the slightest intimation appears on the record . . . to suggest that the agents had information giving them reason to equate "Blackie" Toy and James Wah Toy. . . .

The Government contends, however, that any defects in the information which somehow took the officers to petitioner Toy's laundry were remedied by events which occurred after they arrived. Specifically, it is urged that Toy's flight down the hall when the supposed customer at the door revealed that he was a narcotics agent adequately corroborates the suspicion generated by Hom Way's accusation. . . . [I]n Miller v. United States, 357 U.S. 301, . . . [w]e held that when an officer insufficiently or unclearly identifies his office or his mission, the occupant's flight from the door must be regarded as ambiguous conduct. . . . Agent Wong did eventually disclose that he was a narcotics officer. However, he affirmatively misrepresented his mission at the outset, by stating that he had come for laundry and dry cleaning. And before Toy fled, the officer never adequately dispelled the misimpression engendered by his own ruse.

. . . Toy's refusal to admit the officers and his flight down the hallway thus signified a guilty knowledge no more clearly than it did a natural desire to repel an apparently unauthorized intrusion. . . .

A contrary holding here would mean that a vague suspicion could be transformed into probable cause for arrest by reason of ambiguous conduct which the arresting officers themselves have provoked. That result would have the same essential vice as a proposition we have consistently rejected — that a search unlawful at its inception may be validated by what it turns up. Byars v. United States, 273 U.S. 28; United States v. Di Re, 332 U.S. 581, 595. Thus we conclude that the Court of Appeals' finding that the officers' uninvited entry into Toy's living quarters was unlawful and that the bedroom arrest which followed was likewise unlawful, was fully justified on the evidence. It remains to be seen what consequences flow from this conclusion.

II

It is conceded that Toy's declarations in his bedroom are to be excluded if they are held to be "fruits" of the agents' unlawful action.

In order to make effective the fundamental constitutional guarantees of sanctity of the home and inviolability of the person, Boyd v. United States, 116 U.S. 616, this Court held nearly half a century ago that evidence seized during an unlawful search could not constitute proof against the victim of the search. Weeks v. United States, 232 U.S. 383. The exclusionary prohibition extends as well to the indirect as the direct products of such invasions. Silverthorne Lumber Co. v. United States, 251 U.S. 385. Mr. Justice Holmes, speaking for the Court in that case, in holding that the Government might not make use of information obtained during an unlawful search to subpoena from the victims the very documents illegally viewed, expressed succinctly the policy of the broad exclusionary rule:

> "The essence of a provision forbidding the acquisition of evidence in a certain way is that not merely evidence so acquired shall not be used before the Court but that it shall not be used at all. Of course this does not mean that the facts thus obtained become sacred and inaccessible. If knowledge of them is gained from an independent source they may be proved like any others, but the knowledge gained by the Government's own wrong cannot be used by it in the way proposed." 251 U.S., at 392.

The exclusionary rule has traditionally barred from trial physical, tangible materials obtained either during or as a direct result of an unlawful invasion. It follows from our holding in Silverman v. United States, 365 U.S. 505, that the Fourth Amendment may protect against the overhearing of verbal statements as well as against the more traditional seizure of "papers and effects." Similarly, testimony as to matters observed during an unlawful invasion has been excluded in order to enforce the basic constitutional policies. Thus, verbal evidence which derives so immediately from an unlawful entry and an unauthorized arrest as the officers' action in the present case is no less the "fruit" of official illegality than the more common tangible fruits of the unwarranted intrusion. Nor do the policies underlying the exclusionary rule invite any logical distinction between physical and verbal evidence. Either in terms of deterring lawless conduct by federal officers, or of closing the doors of the federal courts to any use of evidence unconstitutionally obtained, the danger in relaxing the exclusionary rules in the case of verbal evidence would seem too great to warrant introducing such a distinction.

The Government argues that Toy's statements to the officers in his bedroom, although closely consequent upon the invasion which we hold unlawful, were nevertheless admissible because they resulted from "an intervening independent act of a free will." This contention, however, takes insufficient account of the circumstances. Six or seven officers had broken the door and followed on Toy's heels into the bedroom where his wife and child were sleeping. He had been almost immediately handcuffed and arrested. Under such circumstances it is unreasonable to infer that Toy's response was sufficiently an act of free will to purge the primary taint of the unlawful invasion. . . .

III

We now consider whether the exclusion of Toy's declarations requires also the exclusion of the narcotics taken from Yee, to which those declarations led the police. The prosecutor candidly told the trial court that "we wouldn't have found those drugs except that Mr. Toy helped us to." Hence this is not the case envisioned by this Court where the exclusionary rule has no application because the Government learned of the evidence "from an independent source," Silverthorne Lumber Co. v. United States, 251 U.S. 385, 392; nor is this a case in which the connection between the lawless conduct of the police and the discovery of the challenged evidence has "become so attenuated as to dissipate the taint." Nardone v. United States, 308 U.S. 338, 341. We need not hold that all evidence is "fruit of the poisonous tree" simply because it would not have come to light but for the illegal actions of the police. Rather, the more apt question in such a case is "whether, granting establishment of the primary illegality, the evidence to which instant objection is made has been come at by exploitation of that illegality or instead by means sufficiently distinguishable to be purged of the primary taint." Maguire, Evidence of Guilt, 221 (1959). We think it clear that the narcotics were "come at by the exploitation of that illegality" and hence that they may not be used against Toy.

IV

It remains only to consider Toy's unsigned statement. We need not decide whether, in light of the fact that Toy was free on his own recognizance when he made the statement, that statement was a fruit of the illegal arrest. Since we have concluded that his declarations in the bedroom and the narcotics surrendered by Yee should not have been admitted in evidence against him, the only proofs remaining to sustain his conviction are his and Wong Sun's unsigned statements. Without scrutinizing the contents of Toy's ambiguous recitals, we conclude that no reference to Toy in Wong Sun's statement constitutes admissible evidence corroborating any admission by Toy. We arrive at this conclusion upon two clear lines of decisions which converge to require it. One line of our decisions establishes that criminal confessions and admissions of guilt require extrinsic corroboration; the other line of precedents holds that an out-of-court declaration made after arrest may not be used at trial against one of the declarant's partners in crime.

It is a settled principle of the administration of criminal justice in the federal courts that a conviction must rest upon firmer ground than the uncorroborated admission or confession of the accused. . . .

. . . The second governing principle, likewise well settled in our decisions, is that an out-of-court declaration made after arrest may not be used at trial against one of the declarant's partners in crime. . . . We have never ruled squarely on the question presented here, whether a codefendant's statement might serve to corroborate even where it will not suffice to convict. We see no warrant for a different result so long as the rule which regulates the use of out-of-court statements is one of admissibility, rather than simply of weight, of the evidence. The import of our previous holdings is that a co-conspirator's hearsay statements may be admitted against the accused for no purpose whatever, unless made during and in furtherance of the conspiracy. Thus as to Toy the only possible source of corroboration is removed and his conviction must be set aside for lack of competent evidence to support it.

V

We turn now to the case of the other petitioner, Wong Sun. We have no occasion to disagree with the finding of the Court of Appeals that his arrest, also, was without probable cause or reasonable grounds. At all events no evidentiary consequences turn upon that question. For Wong Sun's unsigned confession was not the fruit of that arrest, and was therefore properly admitted at trial. On the evidence that Wong Sun had been released on his own recognizance after a lawful arraignment, and had returned voluntarily several days later to make the statement, we hold that the connection between the arrest and the statement had "become so attenuated as to dissipate the taint." Nardone v. United States, 308 U.S. 338, 341. The fact that the statement was unsigned, whatever bearing this may have upon its weight and credibility, does not render it inadmissible; Wong Sun understood and adopted its substance, though he could not comprehend the English words. The petitioner has never suggested any impropriety in the interrogation itself which would require the exclusion of this statement.

We must then consider the admissibility of the narcotics surrendered by Yee. Our holding that this ounce of heroin was inadmissible against Toy does not compel a like result with respect to Wong Sun. The exclusion of the narcotics as to Toy was required solely by their tainted relationship to information unlawfully obtained from Toy, and not by any official impropriety connected with their surrender by Yee. The seizure of this heroin invaded no right of privacy of person or premises which would entitle Wong Sun to object to its use at his trial.

However, for the reasons that Wong Sun's statement was incompetent to corroborate Toy's admissions contained in Toy's own statement, any references to Wong Sun in Toy's statement were incompetent to corroborate Wong Sun's admissions. Thus, the only competent source of corroboration for Wong Sun's statement was the heroin itself. We cannot be certain, however, on this state of the record, that the trial judge may not also have considered the contents of Toy's statement as a source of corroboration. . . .

We intimate no view one way or the other as to whether the trial judge might have found in the narcotics alone sufficient evidence to corroborate Wong Sun's admissions that he delivered heroin to Yee and smoked heroin at Yee's house around the date in question. But because he might, as the factfinder, have found insufficient corroboration from the narcotics alone, we cannot be sure that the scales were not tipped in favor of conviction by reliance upon the inadmissible Toy statement. . . .

. . . We therefore hold that petitioner Wong Sun is also entitled to a new trial. . . .

[The concurring opinion of Justice Douglas, and the dissenting opinion of Justice Clark, joined by Justices Harlan, Stewart, and White, are omitted.]

NOTES ON *WONG SUN*

1. It is important to follow the chain of events in *Wong Sun*. Federal agents first got a tip from Hom Way, then proceeded to Toy's laundry. Toy answered the door and then fled; agents followed him inside and arrested him in his bedroom. Toy made various incriminating statements at the scene of his arrest, which led the police to Johnny Yee's home. The police found heroin in Yee's bedroom; shortly

afterward, Yee made statements that incriminated Wong Sun. Later, some time after Toy and Wong Sun had both been arraigned, agents interrogated both men; both made various incriminating statements during the course of those interrogations.

2. As that description suggests, the chief potential "poisonous tree" in *Wong Sun* is Toy's arrest. If Toy's arrest were legal, then Toy's contemporaneous statements and the heroin found in Yee's bedroom would both be admissible against him. Why *wasn't* the arrest legal? The Court explains that Hom Way's identification was not detailed enough to amount to probable cause by itself, which sounds right. But Toy's flight upon hearing Agent Wong identify himself suggested that Hom Way's tip was correct — that Toy was indeed "Blackie Toy" and that he was involved in heroin trafficking. The Court concludes otherwise, on the ground that Toy's flight was "ambiguous," because Agent Wong never "adequately disspelled the misimpression" he created when he said, initially, that he was there to pick up some laundry. Does *that* sound right? It's hard to believe that Toy ran because he thought Wong was an angry customer; it is much easier to believe that he ran because he thought Wong was there to arrest him. In short, the "fruit of the poisonous tree" analysis in *Wong Sun* depends on the probable cause analysis — and the probable cause analysis looks seriously flawed.

3. There is also a standing issue in *Wong Sun*. On that score, Justice Brennan's analysis is more conventional. Notice that the drugs taken from Yee could not be used against Toy, since the search of Yee's bedroom was the fruit of Toy's illegal arrest. But those same drugs *could* be used against Wong Sun, because Wong Sun had no standing to complain of Toy's illegal arrest. (And, of course, neither Toy nor Wong Sun had any standing to complain about any aspect of Yee's arrest.) All of those conclusions would hold true under standing doctrine today, as they did in 1963.

4. Which leads to the "fruit of the poisonous tree" aspect of *Wong Sun*. Justice Brennan's opinion for the Court offers three key "fruits" holdings. First, Toy's statements at the scene of his own arrest were the fruit of that arrest. Second, the drugs found in Yee's bedroom were also the fruit of Toy's arrest. And third, Wong Sun's statement, given several days after his arraignment, was *not* the fruit of Wong Sun's illegal arrest. Do those holdings make sense? Is *Wong Sun* a wise application of the exclusionary rule?

NOTES ON "FRUIT OF THE POISONOUS TREE" DOCTRINE

1. To answer those questions, it helps to step back from the factual tangles in *Wong Sun* and consider the basic issue underlying "fruit of the poisonous tree" doctrine. The exclusionary rule obviously requires the suppression of illegally seized evidence — when the police illegally search a suspect's home and find heroin, the heroin must be suppressed (at least in any trial of that suspect — remember standing doctrine). That obvious principle resolves most cases; suppression motions typically involve claims that a given piece of physical evidence was itself obtained in violation of the Fourth Amendment. But the principle does not resolve all cases. Sometimes, criminal defendants claim that a given piece of evidence is inadmissible not because it was illegally seized, but because it was the "fruit" of — i.e., its discovery was caused by — an illegal search or seizure.

Why are such claims taken seriously? Why not suppress *only* illegally seized evidence? One possible answer is that the government should not benefit from its own wrongdoing. (That is the basic point behind Justice Holmes' language in *Silverthorne Lumber*, quoted in *Wong Sun*.) In order to avoid that illegitimate benefit, the government must forgo use of all evidence obtained because of police illegality, not just evidence obtained at the scene of the illegal search. Another, more conventional answer would be that if the police know they can still use the fruits of illegal searches, they will have an incentive to search illegally. In order to eliminate the incentive to violate the Fourth Amendment, the exclusionary rule must make sure that police gain nothing from violations, and the only way to do that is, again, to suppress all evidence obtained *because of* the violations.

The response to these arguments goes roughly as follows: Suppressing reliable evidence is a bad thing, because it takes criminal trials further from the truth. The law should therefore suppress evidence only when it must do so to ensure an acceptable level of compliance with the Fourth Amendment. And suppressing fruits of illegal searches is not necessary to ensure compliance with the Fourth Amendment. It is hard enough for police to know what evidence they will find when they search. Surely it is much harder still for police to anticipate evidence that they will find sometime down the road *because of* the search. When the police in *Wong Sun* arrested Hom Way or followed James Wah Toy into his bedroom, they had no idea what other evidence (and which other suspects) they might uncover as a result. On this account, the incentive problem is simply not worth worrying about; it is enough to tell the police that they cannot use any evidence found in the course of—not because of—an illegal search.

Which side is right depends, at least in part, on some empirical judgments. How often do police search in order to find evidence other than the evidence at the scene of the search? How well do police anticipate later discoveries when making earlier ones? Reliable answers to those questions do not exist; courts must make educated guesses.

Perhaps that explains why the law has basically split the difference. Along with many other cases, *Wong Sun* holds that when evidence is obtained because of an illegal search, it must be suppressed (unless the "taint" of the illegal search has somehow "dissipated"). On the other hand, Minnesota v. Carter, page 698 supra, holds that no defendant can complain of an illegal search of someone else— meaning (to use the facts of *Wong Sun*) that if the police search Toy's bedroom illegally, Yee cannot complain of *that* illegality when the police later wind up in Yee's bedroom. The upshot of these two rules is that some fruits of illegal searches are suppressed, and some are not. Standing doctrine and fruit-of-the-poisonous-tree doctrine deal with the same problem—a given illegal search produces other evidence, or leads to other suspects—but they resolve that problem very differently. The other evidence might be suppressed, but not against the other suspects. Does this strike you as a sensible compromise? An unprincipled conflict?

2. The basic concept underlying "fruit of the poisonous tree" doctrine is causation. Whenever the law deals with causation, the inquiry divides into two questions: But for this event, would that event have happened? And if not, was this event *responsible* for that one? In tort law, the first question is dealt with under the doctrinal heading of "cause in fact," sometimes called "but-for cause." The second question is the subject of "proximate cause" doctrine.

Fruit of the poisonous tree doctrine uses the same division and the same concepts, but different labels. As in torts, one must ask whether, but for the illegal search, the evidence in question would have been found. In Fourth Amendment law, that question turns into two other questions: Was the evidence at issue obtained through an "independent source"? If so, it is not suppressible, because the illegal search did not cause the police to find it. Would the evidence inevitably have been discovered? Again, if so, it is not suppressible; again, the reason is that the illegal search did not cause the police to discover it. Only if the evidence was neither obtained through an independent source nor inevitably discovered can it be suppressed.

This means that "cause in fact" or "but-for cause" is, in Fourth Amendment law, dealt with through two doctrines — independent source and inevitable discovery — and those doctrines define the cases where cause in fact is not satisfied. We will take up those doctrines in the next main case.

3. What about proximate cause? There, the Fourth Amendment analogue is the concept of attenuation. Notice that the Court in *Wong Sun* referred to whether the "taint" of the illegal search had "dissipated." The idea is the same as in proximate cause cases: Sometimes, the chain of causation is sufficiently long or complicated that one can say that a particular earlier link should not be deemed responsible for a later one.

Like proximate cause, attenuation is hard to define. In *Wong Sun*, the Court says it is "clear" that the drugs taken from Yee were not too attenuated a result of the illegal search of Toy's bedroom. On the other hand, the Court holds, with little explanation, that Wong Sun's statement several days after his arrest *was* too attenuated a result of his arrest. Are these conclusions right? Can they be justified, or is the Court's conclusory treatment unavoidable?

The Court tried, not entirely successfully, to define the concept of attenuation a little more fully in United States v. Ceccolini, 435 U.S. 268 (1978). The illegal search in *Ceccolini* took place in the defendant's flower shop; Officer Biro, who was involved in an ongoing investigation of various gambling activities, opened an envelope behind the cash register and saw policy slips. Biro returned the envelope before the search was noticed, and he told his superiors what he had found. Four months later, relying in part on Biro's report, another officer interviewed one Lois Hennessey, a clerk at the same flower shop. Hennessey in turn supplied critical testimony at the defendant's later perjury trial, and the defendant was convicted. The defendant argued that Hennessey's testimony was the fruit of the illegal search of the envelope. The Court disagreed:

> . . . [T]he question of causal connection in this setting, as in so many other questions with which the law concerns itself, is not to be determined solely through the sort of analysis which would be applicable in the physical sciences. The issue cannot be decided on the basis of causation in the logical sense alone, but necessarily includes other elements as well. . . .
>
> [We] reject the Government's suggestion that we adopt what would in practice amount to a per se rule that the testimony of a live witness should not be excluded at trial no matter how close and proximate the connection between it and a violation of the Fourth Amendment. We also reaffirm the holding of *Wong Sun* that "verbal evidence which derives so immediately from an unlawful entry and an unauthorized arrest as the officers' action in the present case is no less the 'fruit' of official illegality than the more common tangible fruits of the unwarranted intrusion." We are of the

view, however, that cases decided since *Wong Sun* significantly qualify its further observation that "the policies underlying the exclusionary rule [do not] invite any logical distinction between physical and verbal evidence." . . .

The greater the willingness of the witness to freely testify, the greater the likelihood that he or she will be discovered by legal means and, concomitantly, the smaller the incentive to conduct an illegal search to discover the witness. Witnesses are not like guns or documents which remain hidden from view until one turns over a sofa, or opens a filing cabinet. Witnesses can, and often do, come forward and offer evidence entirely of their own volition. And evaluated properly, the degree of free will necessary to dissipate the taint will very likely be found more often in the case of live-witness testimony than other kinds of evidence. . . .

Viewing this case in the light of the principles just discussed, we hold that . . . the degree of attenuation was . . . sufficient to dissipate the connection between the illegality and the testimony. The evidence indicates overwhelmingly that the testimony given by the witness was an act of her own free will in no way coerced or even induced by official authority as a result of Biro's discovery of the policy slips. Nor were the slips themselves used in questioning Hennessey. Substantial periods of time elapsed between the time of the illegal search and the initial contact with the witness, on the one hand, and between the latter and the testimony at trial on the other. . . .

There is, in addition, not the slightest evidence to suggest that Biro . . . entered the shop and searched [the envelope] with the intent of finding a willing and knowledgeable witness to testify against respondent. Application of the exclusionary rule in this situation could not have the slightest deterrent effect on the behavior of an officer such as Biro. . . .

Obviously no mathematical weight can be assigned to any of the factors which we have discussed, but just as obviously they all point to the conclusion that the exclusionary rule should be invoked with much greater reluctance where the claim is based on a causal relationship between a constitutional violation and the discovery of a live witness than when a similar claim is advanced to support suppression of an inanimate object.

Id. at 274-280. Is the definition clear now?

MURRAY v. UNITED STATES

Certiorari to the United States Court of Appeals for the First Circuit
487 U.S. 533 (1988)

Justice Scalia delivered the opinion of the Court.

. . . Based on information received from informants, federal law enforcement agents had been surveilling petitioner Murray and several of his co-conspirators. At about 1:45 p.m. on April 6, 1983, they observed Murray drive a truck and Carter drive a green camper, into a warehouse in South Boston. When the petitioners drove the vehicles out about 20 minutes later, the surveilling agents saw within the warehouse two individuals and a tractor-trailer rig bearing a long, dark container. Murray and Carter later turned over the truck and camper to other drivers, who were in turn followed and ultimately arrested, and the vehicles lawfully seized. Both vehicles were found to contain marijuana.

After receiving this information, several of the agents converged on the South Boston warehouse and forced entry. They found the warehouse unoccupied, but observed in plain view numerous burlap-wrapped bales that were later found to contain marijuana. They left without disturbing the bales, kept the warehouse under surveillance, and did not reenter it until they had a search warrant. In applying for the warrant, the agents did not mention the prior entry, and did not rely on any observations made during that entry. When the warrant was issued — at 10:10 p.m., approximately eight hours after the initial entry — the agents immediately reentered the warehouse and seized 270 bales of marijuana and notebooks listing customers for whom the bales were destined.

Before trial, petitioners moved to suppress the evidence found in the warehouse. The District Court denied the motion, rejecting petitioners' arguments that the warrant was invalid because the agents did not inform the Magistrate about their prior warrantless entry, and that the warrant was tainted by that entry. The First Circuit affirmed. . . .

The exclusionary rule prohibits introduction into evidence of tangible materials seized during an unlawful search, and of testimony concerning knowledge acquired during an unlawful search. Beyond that, the exclusionary rule also prohibits the introduction of derivative evidence, both tangible and testimonial, that is the product of the primary evidence, or that is otherwise acquired as an indirect result of the unlawful search, up to the point at which the connection with the unlawful search becomes "so attenuated as to dissipate the taint," Nardone v. United States, 308 U.S. 338, 341 (1939). See Wong Sun v. United States, 371 U.S. 471, 484-485 (1963). Almost simultaneously with our development of the exclusionary rule, in the first quarter of this century, we also announced what has come to be known as the "independent source" doctrine. See Silverthorne Lumber Co. v. United States, 251 U.S. 385, 392 (1920). That doctrine, which has been applied to evidence acquired not only through Fourth Amendment violations but also through Fifth and Sixth Amendment violations, has recently been described as follows:

> [T]he interest of society in deterring unlawful police conduct and the public interest in having juries receive all probative evidence of a crime are properly balanced by putting the police in the same, not a worse, position that they would have been in if no police error or misconduct had occurred. . . . When the challenged evidence has an independent source, exclusion of such evidence would put the police in a worse position than they would have been in absent any error or violation. Nix v. Williams, 467 U.S. 431, 443 (1984).

The dispute here is over the scope of this doctrine. Petitioners contend that it applies only to evidence obtained for the first time during an independent lawful search. The Government argues that it applies also to evidence initially discovered during, or as a consequence of, an unlawful search, but later obtained independently from activities untainted by the initial illegality. We think the Government's view has better support in both precedent and policy. Our cases have used the concept of "independent source" in a more general and a more specific sense. The more general sense identifies all evidence acquired in a fashion untainted by the illegal evidence-gathering activity. Thus, where an unlawful entry has given investigators knowledge of facts x and y, but fact z has been learned by other means, fact z can be said to be admissible because derived from an "independent source." This is how we used the term in Segura v. United States, 468 U.S. 796 (1984). In that case, agents unlawfully entered the defendant's apartment and remained there until a search warrant was obtained. The admissibility of what they discovered while waiting in the apartment was not before us, id., at 802-803, n. 4, but we held that the evidence found for the first time during the execution of the valid and untainted search warrant was admissible because it was discovered pursuant to an "independent source," id., at 813-814.

The original use of the term, however, and its more important use for purposes of these cases, was more specific. It was originally applied in the exclusionary rule context, by Justice Holmes, with reference to that particular category of evidence acquired by an untainted search which is identical to the evidence unlawfully acquired — that is, in the example just given, to knowledge of facts x and y derived from an independent source:

> The essence of a provision forbidding the acquisition of evidence in a certain way is that not merely evidence so acquired shall not be used before the Court but that it shall not be used at all. Of course this does not mean that the facts thus obtained become sacred and inaccessible. If knowledge of them is gained from an independent source they may be proved like any others. Silverthorne Lumber, supra, at 392.

. . . We recently assumed this application of the independent source doctrine (in the Sixth Amendment context) in Nix v. Williams, supra. There incriminating statements obtained in violation of the defendant's right to counsel had led the police to the victim's body. The body had not in fact been found through an independent source as well, and so the independent source doctrine was not itself applicable. We held, however, that evidence concerning the body was nonetheless admissible because a search had been under way which would have discovered the body, had it not been called off because of the discovery produced by the unlawfully obtained statements. This "inevitable discovery" doctrine obviously assumes the validity of the independent source doctrine as applied to evidence initially acquired unlawfully. It would make no sense to admit the evidence because the independent search, had it not been aborted, would have found the body, but to exclude the evidence if the search had continued and had in fact found the body. The inevitable discovery doctrine, with its distinct requirements, is in reality an extrapolation from the independent source doctrine: Since the tainted evidence would be admissible if in fact discovered through an independent source, it should be admissible if it inevitably would have been discovered. Petitioners' asserted policy basis for excluding evidence which is initially discovered during an illegal search, but is subsequently acquired through an independent and lawful source, is that a contrary rule will remove all deterrence to, and indeed positively encourage, unlawful police searches. As petitioners see the incentives, law enforcement officers will routinely enter without a warrant to make sure that what they expect to be on the premises is in fact there. If it is not, they will have spared themselves the time and trouble of getting a warrant; if it is, they can get the warrant and use the evidence despite the unlawful entry. We see the incentives differently. An officer with probable cause sufficient to obtain a search warrant would be foolish to enter the premises first in an unlawful manner. By doing so, he would risk suppression of all evidence on the premises, both seen and unseen, since his action would add to the normal burden of convincing a magistrate that there is probable cause the much more onerous burden of convincing a trial court that no information gained from the illegal entry affected either the law enforcement officers' decision to seek a warrant or the magistrate's decision to grant it. Nor would the officer without sufficient probable cause to obtain a search warrant have any added incentive to conduct an unlawful entry, since whatever he finds cannot be used to establish probable cause before a magistrate. . . .

To apply what we have said to the present cases: Knowledge that the marijuana was in the warehouse was assuredly acquired at the time of the unlawful entry. But it was also acquired at the time of entry pursuant to the warrant, and if that later acquisition was not the result of the earlier entry there is no reason why the independent source doctrine should not apply. Invoking the exclusionary rule would put the police (and society) not in the same position they would have occupied if no violation occurred, but in a worse one. See Nix v. Williams, 467 U.S., at 443. . . .

The ultimate question, therefore, is whether the search pursuant to warrant was in fact a genuinely independent source of the information and tangible evidence at issue here. This would not have been the case if the agents' decision to seek the warrant was prompted by what they had seen during the initial entry, or if information obtained during that entry was presented to the Magistrate and affected his decision to issue the warrant. . . .

. . . The District Court found that the agents did not reveal their warrantless entry to the Magistrate, and that they did not include in their application for a warrant any recitation of their observations in the warehouse. It did not, however, explicitly find that the agents would have sought a warrant if they had not earlier entered the warehouse. . . . Accordingly, we vacate the judgment and remand these cases to the Court of Appeals with instructions that it remand to the District Court for determination whether the warrant-authorized search of the warehouse was an independent source of the challenged evidence in the sense we have described.

[The dissenting opinion of Justice Marshall, joined by Justice Stevens and Justice O'Connor, is omitted.]

NOTES ON THE "INDEPENDENT SOURCE" AND "INEVITABLE DISCOVERY" DOCTRINES

1. No one argues that the exclusionary rule should extend to *more than* evidence obtained because of the illegal search or seizure. It would seem to follow that evidence obtained through some independent legal source should be admissible, as should evidence that would have been discovered, "inevitably" or otherwise, even if the illegal search had never taken place. Both independent source doctrine and inevitable discovery doctrine seem not only right, but obvious.

2. But if the doctrines are easy in principle, they may be very hard indeed in application, as Craig Bradley's discussion of *Murray* illustrates:

> Consider the position of the rational police officer. Assume that it is true, as the Court avers, that if he has ample probable cause and ample time, he will go ahead and get a warrant in order to avoid the additional explanations that a warrantless search will entail. But suppose, as is frequently the case, that his probable cause is shaky or nonexistent. *Murray* positively encourages him to proceed with an illegal search. If he

finds nothing, he simply shrugs his shoulders and walks away. If he finds evidence, he leaves his partner to watch over it, repairs to the magistrate, and reports that "an anonymous reliable informant who has given information on three occasions in the past that has led to convictions called to tell me that he had just seen bales of marijuana stored at a warehouse at 123 Elm Street." The warrant issues and the marijuana is seized. Before trial (assuming that the defense has found out about the illegal search), the officer admits it, chalks it up to a fear that the evidence would be lost if the warehouse were not immediately secured, apologizes for being wrong in this assessment, and introduces the warrant affidavit to demonstrate an independent source. . . .

Of course, it has always been the case that the police could make up the existence of "Old Reliable," the informant, and use his fictitious "tip" as the basis for a search warrant. The problem with this tactic is that, if the police are wrong and no evidence is found, they are forced to return to the magistrate empty-handed. This is embarrassing to the police department and would only have to happen a few times before the magistrates and defense attorneys would realize that the police were liars. After *Murray*, there is no such fear, because the fictitious "Old Reliable" will always be right! His "tip" will always lead to evidence because the police will have found it in advance.

Craig M. Bradley, Murray v. United States: The Bell Tolls for the Warrant Requirement, 64 Ind. L.J. 907, 917-918 (1989).

Bradley's point is that figuring out what sources are truly "independent" may be impossible; given *Murray*, it will often be easy for officers to turn a run-of-the-mill illegal search into a plausible "independent source" search. Of course, this assumes that police officers will be willing to lie. Should the law so assume? Is police perjury any more of a problem here than in an ordinary warrantless search case in which a dishonest officer could concoct a set of facts that made the search legal?

3. Causation in "independent source" cases like *Murray* may be hard because of concerns about the trustworthiness of police testimony. Causation in inevitable discovery cases is hard, period. The defendant in Nix v. Williams, 467 U.S. 431 (1984) (discussed in *Murray*) was subjected to police questioning that violated his Sixth Amendment right to counsel. In response to the questioning, the defendant led the police to the body of a 10-year-old girl; the defendant was later charged with the girl's murder. The defendant sought to suppress evidence obtained from the girl's body, on the ground that all such evidence constituted fruits of the illegal questioning. The state responded that the body would inevitably have been found without the illegal questioning.

The body was found "in a ditch beside a gravel road." Id. at 436. At the time it was found multiple police search teams were looking for the missing girl; the closest search team was two-and-one-half miles away. Id. The trial court concluded, and the Supreme Court agreed, that the search teams probably would have found the girl's body fairly soon had the search not been called off once the defendant showed police to the right spot.

How accurate do you think such conclusions are? In some cases the issue is easy: Suppose, for example, the search team had only been a hundred yards away when the body was found. But in cases like *Nix* itself, the inquiry involves an enormous amount of speculation. How long would the search have gone on? What directions would it have moved? How far? The questions are, if anything, even harder when the case involves a less sensational crime. When a young girl is murdered and her body is missing, the police will invest a great deal in finding the body and catching the killer. For an investigation of a convenience store robbery, on the other hand, the police may much more quickly conclude that the investigation is going nowhere, and drop it. Thus, the "inevitable discovery" question turns into this: Had the police not illegally discovered the evidence in question, would they have kept investigating long enough to find it legally? Again, how accurately can courts answer that question?

4. Note that *Nix* is a Sixth Amendment case, not a Fourth Amendment case. Nevertheless, as *Murray*'s discussion of *Nix* shows, the independent source and inevitable discovery doctrines arise in both settings. You should be aware, however, that *Nix* is not a *Miranda* case; for *Miranda* doctrine, conventional fruit-of-the-poisonous-tree analysis does not apply. See Missouri v. Seibert and United States v. Patane, pages 906 and 915 infra.

5. Can inevitable discovery doctrine apply to warrant cases? Suppose, in *Murray*, the officers seize the marijuana when they first enter the warehouse illegally. The defendant moves to suppress, on the ground that the police failed to get a warrant and lack exigent circumstances. The government concedes that the search was illegal but argues that the marijuana would inevitably have been discovered. The reasoning goes as follows: The police had probable cause and so could have gotten a warrant had they tried to do so. Had they not searched illegally, they would have applied for a warrant, gotten one, searched, and found the marijuana. All of which adds up to inevitable discovery.

This argument seems entirely natural, does it not? Yet if it works, the police never need to get a warrant again—and they also do not need to lie to a magistrate in order to prevail; see Note 2. It would seem to follow that a special rule must apply in warrant cases, that inevitable discovery doctrine simply cannot apply there. Is that consistent with *Murray*?

d. Impeachment

UNITED STATES v. HAVENS

Certiorari to the United States Court of Appeals for the Fifth Circuit
446 U.S. 620 (1980)

MR. JUSTICE WHITE delivered the opinion of the Court.

The petition for certiorari filed by the United States in this criminal case presented a single question: whether evidence suppressed as the fruit of an unlawful search and seizure may nevertheless be used to impeach a defendant's false trial testimony, given in response to proper cross-examination, where the evidence does not squarely contradict the defendant's testimony on direct examination. . . .

Respondent was convicted of importing, conspiring to import, and intentionally possessing a controlled substance, cocaine. According to the evidence at his trial, Havens and John McLeroth, both attorneys from Ft. Wayne, Ind., boarded a flight from Lima, Peru, to Miami, Fla. In Miami, a customs officer searched McLeroth and found cocaine sewed into makeshift pockets in a T-shirt he was wearing under his outer clothing. McLeroth implicated respondent, who had previously cleared customs and who was then arrested. His luggage was seized and searched without a warrant. The officers found no drugs but seized a T-shirt from which pieces had been cut that matched the pieces that had been sewn to McLeroth's T-shirt. The T-shirt and other evidence seized in the course of the search were suppressed on motion prior to trial.

Both men were charged in a three-count indictment, but McLeroth pleaded guilty to one count and testified against Havens. Among other things, he asserted that Havens had supplied him with the altered T-shirt and had sewed the makeshift pockets shut. Havens took the stand in his own defense and denied involvement in smuggling cocaine. His direct testimony included the following:

> Q. And you heard Mr. McLeroth testify earlier as to something to the effect that this material was taped or draped around his body and so on, you heard that testimony?
> A. Yes, I did.
> Q. Did you ever engage in that kind of activity with Mr. McLeroth and Augusto or Mr. McLeroth and anyone else on that fourth visit to Lima, Peru?
> A. I did not.

On cross-examination, Havens testified as follows:

> Q. Now, on direct examination, sir, you testified that on the fourth trip you had absolutely nothing to do with the wrapping of any bandages or tee shirts or anything involving Mr. McLeroth; is that correct?
> A. I don't — I said I had nothing to do with any wrapping or bandages or anything, yes. I had nothing to do with anything with McLeroth in connection with this cocaine matter. . . .
> Q. And your testimony is that you had nothing to do with the sewing of the cotton swatches to make pockets on that tee shirt?
> A. Absolutely not. . . .
> Q. On that day, sir, did you have in your luggage a Size 38-40 medium man's tee shirt with swatches of clothing missing from the tail of that tee shirt?
> A. Not to my knowledge.
> Q. Mr. Havens, I'm going to hand you what is Government's Exhibit 9 for identification and ask you if this tee shirt was in your luggage on October 2nd, 1975 [*sic*]?
> A. Not to my knowledge. No. [Id., at 46.]

Respondent Havens also denied having told a Government agent that the T-shirts found in his luggage belonged to McLeroth.

On rebuttal, a Government agent testified that Exhibit 9 had been found in respondent's suitcase and that Havens claimed the T-shirts found in his bag, including Exhibit 9, belonged to McLeroth. Over objection, the T-shirt was then admitted into evidence, the jury being instructed that the rebuttal evidence should be considered only for impeaching Havens' credibility. . . .

In Walder v. United States, [437 U.S. 62 (1954)], the use of evidence obtained in an illegal search and inadmissible in the Government's case in chief was admitted to impeach the direct testimony of the defendant. This Court approved, saying that it would pervert the [federal exclusionary rule] to hold otherwise. Similarly, in Harris v. New York, 401 U.S. 222 (1971), and Oregon v. Hass, 420 U.S. 714 (1975), statements taken in violation of Miranda v. Arizona, 384 U.S. 436 (1966), and unusable by the prosecution as part of its own case, were held admissible to impeach statements made by the defendant in the course of his direct testimony. . . .

These cases were understood by the Court of Appeals to hold that tainted evidence, inadmissible when offered as part of the Government's main case, may not be used as rebuttal evidence to impeach a defendant's credibility unless the evidence is offered to contradict a particular statement made by a defendant during his direct examination; a statement made for the first time on cross-examination may not be so impeached. This approach required the exclusion of the T-shirt taken from Havens' luggage because, as the Court of Appeals read the record, Havens was asked nothing on his direct testimony about the incriminating T-shirt or about the contents of his luggage; the testimony about the T-shirt, which the Government desired to impeach first appeared on cross-examination, not on direct. . . .

There is no gainsaying that arriving at the truth is a fundamental goal of our legal system. We have repeatedly insisted that when defendants testify, they must testify truthfully or suffer the consequences. . . . It is essential, therefore, to the proper functioning of the adversary system that when a defendant takes the stand, the government be permitted proper and effective cross-examination in an attempt to elicit the truth. The defendant's obligation to testify truthfully is fully binding on him when he is cross-examined. His privilege against self-incrimination does not shield him from proper questioning. He would unquestionably be subject to a perjury prosecution if he knowingly lies on cross-examination. In terms of impeaching a defendant's seemingly false statements with his prior inconsistent utterances or with other reliable evidence available to the government, we see no difference of constitutional magnitude between the defendant's statements on direct examination and his answers to questions put to him on cross-examination that are plainly within the scope of the defendant's direct examination. Without this opportunity, the normal function of cross-examination would be severely impeded.

We also think that the policies of the exclusionary rule no more bar impeachment here than they did in *Walder, Harris*, and *Hass*. In those cases, the ends of the exclusionary rules were thought adequately implemented by denying the government the use of the challenged evidence to make out its case in chief. The incremental furthering of those ends by forbidding impeachment of the defendant who testifies was deemed insufficient to permit or require that false testimony go unchallenged, with the resulting impairment of the integrity of the factfinding goals of the criminal trial. We reaffirm this assessment of the competing interests, and hold that a defendant's statements made in response to proper cross-examination reasonably suggested by the defendant's direct examination are subject to otherwise proper impeachment by the government, albeit by evidence that has been illegally obtained and that is inadmissible on the government's direct case, or otherwise, as substantive evidence of guilt. . . .

[The dissenting opinion of Justice Brennan, joined by Justice Stewart, Justice Marshall, and Justice Stevens, is omitted.]

NOTES AND QUESTIONS

1. One strong piece of conventional wisdom is that juries tend to believe defendants guilty if they don't testify. Knowing that a piece of damning evidence will come out on cross-examination is presumably a strong disincentive to testify. This

is likely the biggest effect of *Havens*: It decreases the likelihood, perhaps substantially, that defendants who were the victims of illegal searches will take the witness stand. Doesn't that seriously undermine the exclusionary rule?

2. On the other hand, if *Havens* came out the other way, that would create large opportunities for defendant perjury. Can the legal system, or the public, be expected to tolerate that? Is there any way out of this box?

3. In Illinois v. James, 493 U.S. 307 (1990), the Court faced the question whether *Havens* applies not just to defendants but to all defense witnesses. Defendant James was a teenager suspected of involvement in a shooting. At the time of his arrest, James had curly black hair. Shortly afterward, James told the police that he had changed his hair color and style — that at the time of the shooting, James admitted, his hair was reddish-brown, straight, and combed back. The trial judge suppressed James' post-arrest statements to the police on the ground that those statements were the fruit of an illegal arrest. At trial, James put on a witness who claimed that he had had curly black hair at the time of the shooting. The prosecution introduced James's statements to the police in order to impeach that defense witness.

Speaking for a five-vote majority (himself plus Justices White, Marshall, Blackmun, and Stevens), Justice Brennan concluded that the statements should not have been admitted into evidence, that *Havens* applies only to defendants:

> The previously recognized [impeachment] exception penalizes defendants for committing perjury by allowing the prosecution to expose their perjury through impeachment using illegally obtained evidence. . . . But the exception leaves defendants free to testify truthfully on their own behalf; they can offer probative and exculpatory evidence to the jury without opening the door to impeachment by carefully avoiding any statements that directly contradict the suppressed evidence. The exception thus generally discourages perjured testimony without discouraging truthful testimony.
>
> . . . [E]xpanding the impeachment exception to encompass the testimony of all defense witnesses would not have the same beneficial effects. First, the mere threat of a subsequent criminal prosecution for perjury is far more likely to deter a witness from intentionally lying on a defendant's behalf than to deter a defendant, already facing conviction for the underlying offense, from lying on his own behalf. . . .
>
> More significantly, expanding the impeachment exception to encompass the testimony of all defense witnesses likely would chill some defendants from presenting their best defense — and sometimes any defense at all — through the testimony of others. Whenever police obtained evidence illegally, defendants would have to assess prior to trial the likelihood that the evidence would be admitted to impeach the otherwise favorable testimony of any witness they call. Defendants might reasonably fear that one or more of their witnesses, in a position to offer truthful and favorable testimony, would also make some statement in sufficient tension with the tainted evidence to allow the prosecutor to introduce that evidence for impeachment. . . . As a result, an expanded impeachment exception likely would chill some defendants from calling witnesses who would otherwise offer probative evidence. . . .

Id. at 314-317. Are you persuaded?

4. Are *James* and *Havens* consistent? Most of the Justices didn't think so. Six Justices — Brennan, White, Marshall, Blackmun, Rehnquist, and Stevens — voted in both cases. Five of those six supported the same result in both cases. Justices Brennan, Marshall, Blackmun, and Stevens all thought that the Fourth

Amendment's exclusionary rule barred use of illegally obtained evidence to impeach *either* defendants *or* other defense witnesses. Justice, later Chief Justice Rehnquist thought the exclusionary rule should permit the use of illegally obtained evidence to impeach *all* defense witnesses. Only Justice White thought some line should be drawn between defendants and other witnesses.

What is the proper result in such a case? One might argue that an appropriate respect for precedent should have required the *Havens* dissenters (Justices Brennan, Marshall, Blackmun, and Stevens) to support whatever result in *James* was most consistent with *Havens*. Had they done so, it seems likely that the result in *James* would be different. What should a Justice do in such situations? Vote his conscience, and precedent be damned? Honor precedent that he thinks foolish? Something else?

5. The impeachment issue in *Havens* and *James* is a variant on the question posed by the standing and fruit-of-the-poisonous-tree doctrines. In all three settings, the police conduct an illegal search; in all three settings the illegal search produces some collateral benefit — it leads the police to evidence against other suspects (standing), it leads them to further evidence against the same suspect (fruit of the poisonous tree), or it keeps the suspect or some other defense witness from taking the witness stand at a later criminal trial (impeachment). And in all three settings, there is a common set of arguments. Defendants argue that the police will search illegally in order to obtain the collateral benefit — that unless the law takes away all gains from illegal searches, too many illegal searches will happen. The government argues that the collateral benefit is not foreseeable — that, for example, officers were not thinking about Havens taking the witness stand when they searched his luggage — and that police will not conduct illegal searches in order to get such unforeseeable benefits. As you have seen, the argument is basically resolved in the government's favor in standing doctrine, mostly resolved in defendants' favor in fruit-of-the-poisonous-tree doctrine, while impeachment doctrine splits the difference.

Does that set of results make sense? Is the benefit the government obtained in *Havens* or *James* more foreseeable, less foreseeable, or no different than the benefit obtained in *Carter* (page 698 supra) or in *Wong Sun* (page 709 supra)?

2. Damages

There are a number of damages actions that are at least potentially available to people whose Fourth Amendment rights have been violated. Unconstitutional searches and seizures may give rise to state tort claims such as false arrest or trespass, or to claims under state constitutions. In addition, 42 U.S.C. §1983 gives plaintiffs a cause of action in federal or state court when their federal constitutional rights have been violated by persons acting under color of state law.[23]

---

23. Section 1983 provides as follows:

Every person who, under color of any statute, ordinance, regulation, custom, or usage of any State or Territory, subjects, or causes to be subjected, any citizen of the United States or any other person within the jurisdiction thereof to the deprivation of any rights, privileges, or immunities secured by the Constitution and laws, shall be liable to the party injured in an action at law, suit in equity, or other proper proceeding for redress.

In Bivens v. Six Unknown Named Agents of Federal Bureau of Narcotics, 403 U.S. 388 (1971), the Supreme Court recognized a parallel federal common law claim against federal officials. Finally, the Federal Tort Claims Act makes the federal government liable for specified torts of its law enforcement officers; some of those torts may involve violations of the Fourth Amendment.

Federal civil rights claims present some distinct advantages for plaintiffs, including the possibility of class actions and the recovery of attorneys' fees for prevailing litigants. There are, however, substantial obstacles to such claims. The typical Fourth Amendment case — say, a gratuitous frisk or car search — does not involve the kind of physical injury or property damage that would translate into significant money damages, even assuming liability can be established. Particularly if the plaintiffs are unsympathetic (as many criminal suspects are), juries may be unwilling to impose liability or to award more than nominal amounts in such cases, making lawsuits seem not worth the trouble. Even a cursory survey of reported §1983 cases bears out this intuition. Very few involve the automobile, briefcase, or pocket searches common in exclusionary rule litigation. Claims of illegal arrest and police brutality are more common.

Another major obstacle is doctrinal: the courts have created a variety of immunity doctrines that limit government damages liability. Liability against a state or local government for state-law torts may only be obtained when sovereign immunity has been waived. States often limit the circumstances in which suit may be brought against a government agency, while various forms of official immunity may shield its officers. Under the Eleventh Amendment and §1983, meanwhile, states and state agencies are absolutely immune from damages liability for constitutional violations. That immunity does not extend to local governments — or to local police departments — but another one does: Local governments are liable under §1983 only if the relevant constitutional violation was caused by an official policy or custom. Monell v. Department of Social Services, 436 U.S. 658, 694 (1978).

That leaves the question of damages liability for individual police officers. The key doctrine here is qualified immunity — a constitutional fault standard that applies whenever government officials are sued for damages under either §1983 or Bivens. The next case explores that doctrine.

ANDERSON v. CREIGHTON

Certiorari to the United States Court of Appeals for the Eighth Circuit
483 U.S. 635 (1987)

JUSTICE SCALIA delivered the opinion of the Court. . . .

Petitioner Russell Anderson is an agent of the Federal Bureau of Investigation. On November 11, 1983, Anderson and other state and federal law enforcement officers conducted a warrantless search of the home of respondents, the Creighton family. The search was conducted because Anderson believed that Vadaain Dixon, a man suspected of a bank robbery committed earlier that day, might be found there. He was not.

The Creightons later filed suit against Anderson in a Minnesota state court, asserting among other things a claim for money damages under the Fourth Amendment, see Bivens v. Six Unknown Fed. Narcotics Agents, 403 U.S. 388

(1971). After removing the suit to Federal District Court, Anderson filed a motion . . . for summary judgment, arguing that the *Bivens* claim was barred by Anderson's qualified immunity from civil damages liability. See Harlow v. Fitzgerald, 457 U.S. 800 (1982). Before any discovery took place, the District Court granted summary judgment on the ground that the search was lawful, holding that the undisputed facts revealed that Anderson had had probable cause to search the Creighton's home and that his failure to obtain a warrant was justified by the presence of exigent circumstances.

The Creightons appealed to the Court of Appeals for the Eighth Circuit, which reversed. The Court of Appeals held that the issue of the lawfulness of the search could not properly be decided on summary judgment, because unresolved factual disputes made it impossible to determine as a matter of law that the warrantless search had been supported by probable cause and exigent circumstances. The Court of Appeals also held that Anderson was not entitled to summary judgment on qualified immunity grounds, since the right Anderson was alleged to have violated — the right of persons to be protected from warrantless searches of their home unless the searching officers have probable cause and there are exigent circumstances — was clearly established. . . .

When government officials abuse their offices, "action[s] for damages may offer the only realistic avenue for vindication of constitutional guarantees." Harlow v. Fitzgerald, 457 U.S., at 814. On the other hand, permitting damages suits against government officials can entail substantial social costs, including the risk that fear of personal monetary liability and harassing litigation will unduly inhibit officials in the discharge of their duties. Our cases have accommodated these conflicting concerns by generally providing government officials performing discretionary functions with a qualified immunity, shielding them from civil damages liability as long as their actions could reasonably have been thought consistent with the rights they are alleged to have violated. Somewhat more concretely, whether an official protected by qualified immunity may be held personally liable for an allegedly unlawful official action generally turns on the "objective legal reasonableness" of the action, *Harlow*, 457 U.S., at 819, assessed in light of the legal rules that were "clearly established" at the time it was taken, id., at 818.

The operation of this standard, however, depends substantially upon the level of generality at which the relevant "legal rule" is to be identified. For example, the right to due process of law is quite clearly established by the Due Process Clause, and thus there is a sense in which any action that violates that Clause (no matter how unclear it may be that the particular action is a violation) violates a clearly established right. Much the same could be said of any other constitutional or statutory violation. But if the test of "clearly established law" were to be applied at this level of generality, it would bear no relationship to the "objective legal reasonableness" that is the touchstone of *Harlow*. Plaintiffs would be able to convert the rule of qualified immunity that our cases plainly establish into a rule of virtually unqualified liability simply by alleging violation of extremely abstract rights. *Harlow* would be transformed from a guarantee of immunity into a rule of pleading. . . . It should not be surprising, therefore, that our cases establish that the right the official is alleged to have violated must have been "clearly established" in a more particularized, and hence more relevant, sense: The contours of the right must be sufficiently clear that a reasonable official would understand that what he is doing violates that right. This is not to say that an official action is protected by qualified immunity unless the very action in question has previously been held unlawful, but it is to say that in the light of pre-existing law the unlawfulness must be apparent.

Anderson contends that the Court of Appeals misapplied these principles. We agree. The Court of Appeals' brief discussion of qualified immunity consisted of little more than an assertion that a general right Anderson was alleged to have violated — the right to be free from warrantless searches of one's home unless the searching officers have probable cause and there are exigent circumstances — was clearly established. The Court of Appeals specifically refused to consider the argument that it was not clearly established that the circumstances with which Anderson was confronted did not constitute probable cause and exigent circumstances. The previous discussion should make clear that this refusal was erroneous. . . .

We have recognized that it is inevitable that law enforcement officials will in some cases reasonably but mistakenly conclude that probable cause is present, and we have indicated that in such cases those officials . . . should not be held personally liable. The same is true of their conclusions regarding exigent circumstances.

It follows from what we have said that the determination whether it was objectively legally reasonable to conclude that a given search was supported by probable cause or exigent circumstances will often require examination of the information possessed by the searching officials. But contrary to the Creighton's assertion, this does not reintroduce into qualified immunity analysis the inquiry into officials' subjective intent that *Harlow* sought to minimize. See *Harlow*, supra, 457 U.S., at 815-820. The relevant question in this case, for example, is the objective (albeit fact-specific) question whether a reasonable officer could have believed Anderson's warrantless search to be lawful, in light of clearly established law and the information the searching officers possessed. Anderson's subjective beliefs about the search are irrelevant. . . .

. . . [T]he Creightons argue that it is inappropriate to give officials alleged to have violated the Fourth Amendment — and thus necessarily to have unreasonably searched or seized — the protection of a qualified immunity intended only to protect reasonable official action. It is not possible, that is, to say that one "reasonably" acted unreasonably. The short answer to this argument is that it is foreclosed by the fact that we have previously extended qualified immunity to officials who were alleged to have violated the Fourth Amendment. Even if that were not so, however, we would still find the argument unpersuasive. Its surface appeal is attributable to the circumstance that the Fourth Amendment's guarantees have been expressed in terms of "unreasonable" searches and seizures. Had an equally serviceable term, such as "undue" searches and seizures been employed, what might be termed the "reasonably unreasonable" argument against application of *Harlow* to the Fourth Amendment would not be available — just as it would be available against application of *Harlow* to the Fifth Amendment if the term "reasonable process of law" had been employed there. The fact is that, regardless of the terminology used, the precise content of most of the Constitution's civil-liberties guarantees rests upon an assessment of what accommodation between governmental need and individual freedom is reasonable, so that the Creightons' objection, if it has any substance, applies to the application of *Harlow* generally. We have frequently observed, and our many cases on the point amply demonstrate, the difficulty of determining whether particular searches or seizures comport with the Fourth Amendment. Law enforcement officers whose judgments in making these difficult determinations are objectively legally reasonable should no more be held personally liable in damages than should officials making analogous determinations in other areas of law. . . .

For the reasons stated, we vacate the judgment of the Court of Appeals and remand the case for further proceedings consistent with this opinion.

JUSTICE STEVENS, with whom JUSTICE BRENNAN and JUSTICE MARSHALL join, dissenting. . . .

[T]his Court has decided to apply a double standard of reasonableness in damages actions against federal agents who are alleged to have violated an innocent citizen's Fourth Amendment rights. By double standard I mean a standard that affords a law enforcement official two layers of insulation from liability. . . . Having already adopted such a double standard in applying the exclusionary rule to searches authorized by an invalid warrant, United States v. Leon, 468 U.S. 897 (1984), the Court seems prepared and even anxious in this case to remove any requirement that the officer must obey the Fourth Amendment when entering a private home. I remain convinced that in a suit for damages as well as in a hearing on a motion to suppress evidence, "an official search and seizure cannot be both 'unreasonable' and 'reasonable' at the same time." Id., at 960 (STEVENS, J., dissenting).

A "federal official may not with impunity ignore the limitations which the controlling law has placed on his powers." Butz v. Economou, 438 U.S. 478, 489 (1978). The effect of the Court's (literally unwarranted) extension of qualified immunity, I fear, is that it allows federal agents to ignore the limitations of the probable-cause and warrant requirements with impunity. The Court does so in the name of avoiding interference with legitimate law enforcement activities even though the probable-cause requirement, which limits the police's exercise of coercive authority, is itself a form of immunity that frees them to exercise that power without fear of strict liability. . . .

. . . [U]ntil now the Court has not found intolerable the use of a probable-cause standard to protect the police officer from exposure to liability simply because his reasonable conduct is subsequently shown to have been mistaken. Today, however, the Court counts the law enforcement interest twice and the individual's privacy interest only once.

The Court's double-counting approach reflects understandable sympathy for the plight of the officer and an overriding interest in unfettered law enforcement. It ascribes a far lesser importance to the privacy interest of innocent citizens than did the Framers of the Fourth Amendment. The importance of that interest and the possible magnitude of its invasion are both illustrated by the facts of this case. The home of an innocent family was invaded by several officers without a warrant, without the owner's consent, with a substantial show of force, and with blunt expressions of disrespect for the law and for the rights of the family members. As the case comes to us, we must assume that the intrusion violated the Fourth Amendment. Proceeding on that assumption, I see no reason why the family's interest in the security of its own home should be accorded a lesser weight than the Government's interest in carrying out an invasion that was unlawful. Arguably, if the Government considers it important not to discourage such conduct, it should provide indemnity to its officers. Preferably, however, it should furnish the kind of training for its law enforcement agents that would entirely eliminate the necessity for the Court to distinguish between the conduct that a competent officer considers reasonable and the conduct that the Constitution deems reasonable. . . . [S]urely an innocent family should not bear the entire risk that a trial court, with the benefit of hindsight, will find that a federal agent reasonably believed that he could break into their home equipped with force and arms but without probable cause or a warrant.

NOTES AND QUESTIONS

1. What was the claimed Fourth Amendment violation in Anderson v. Creighton? The Court says the issue is whether "the warrantless search had been supported by probable cause and exigent circumstances." Did the Creightons have any *other* potential Fourth Amendment claims? Consider the statement of facts in the Court of Appeals:

> Because this case was dismissed on Anderson's motion for summary judgment, we set out the facts in the light most favorable to the Creightons and draw all inferences from the underlying facts in their favor. On the night of November 11, 1983, Sarisse and Robert Creighton and their three young daughters were spending a quiet evening at their home when a spotlight suddenly flashed through their front window. Mr. Creighton opened the door and was confronted by several uniformed and plain clothes officers, many of them brandishing shotguns. All of the officers were white; the Creightons are black. Mr. Creighton claims that none of the officers responded when he asked what they wanted. Instead, by his account (as verified by a St. Paul police report), one of the officers told him to "keep his hands in sight" while the other officers rushed through the door. When Mr. Creighton asked if they had a search warrant, one of the officers told him, "We don't have a search warrant [and] don't need [one]; you watch too much TV."
>
> Mr. Creighton asked the officers to put their guns away because his children were frightened, but the officers refused. Mrs. Creighton awoke to the shrieking of her children, and was confronted by an officer who pointed a shotgun at her. She allegedly observed the officers yelling at her three daughters to "sit their damn asses down and stop screaming." She asked the officer, "What the hell is going on?" The officer allegedly did not explain the situation and simply said to her, "Why don't you make your damn kids sit on the couch and make them shut up."
>
> One of the officers asked Mr. Creighton if he had a red and silver car. As Mr. Creighton led the officers downstairs to his garage, where his maroon Oldsmobile was parked, one of the officers punched him in the face, knocking him to the ground, and causing him to bleed from the mouth and forehead. Mr. Creighton alleges that he was attempting to move past the officer to open the garage door when the officer panicked and hit him. The officer claims that Mr. Creighton attempted to grab his shotgun, even though Mr. Creighton was not a suspect in any crime and had no contraband in his home or on his person. Shaunda, the Creightons' ten-year-old daughter, witnessed the assault and screamed for her mother to come help. She claims that one of the officers then hit her.
>
> Mrs. Creighton phoned her mother, but an officer allegedly kicked [her] and grabbed the phone and told her to "hang up that damn phone." She told her children to run to their neighbor's house for safety. The children ran out and a plain clothes officer chased them. The Creightons' neighbor allegedly told Mrs. Creighton that the officer ran into her house and grabbed Shaunda by the shoulders and shook her. The neighbor allegedly told the officer, "Can't you see she's in shock; leave her alone and

get out of my house." Mrs. Creighton's mother later brought Shaunda to the emergency room at Children's Hospital for an arm injury caused by the officer's rough handling.

During the melee, family members and friends began arriving at the Creightons' home. Mrs. Creighton claims that she was embarrassed in front of her family and friends by the invasion of their home and their rough treatment as if they were suspects in a major crime. At this time, she again asked Anderson for a search warrant. He allegedly replied, "I don't need a damn search warrant when I'm looking for a fugitive." The officers did not discover the allegedly unspecified "fugitive" at the Creightons' home or any evidence whatsoever that he had been there or that the Creightons were involved in any type of criminal activity. Nonetheless, the officers then arrested and handcuffed Mr. Creighton for obstruction of justice and brought him to the police station where he was jailed overnight, then released without being charged.

The Creightons claim that it was not until during or shortly after the melee that they learned the officers were looking for Vadaain Dixon, Mrs. Creighton's brother, who, unbeknownst to the Creightons, was a suspect in an armed robbery committed several hours earlier that afternoon. They learned that the officers, before arriving at the Creightons' home, had made warrantless searches of the home of Iris Dixon, the mother of Vadaain Dixon and Mrs. Creighton, and the home of Minnie Dixon, the grandmother of Vadaain Dixon and Mrs. Creighton. Anderson claims that he had probable cause to search the homes of Vadaain Dixon's relatives, that it would have been too difficult to get a search warrant because it was nighttime on Veteran's Day, and that he believed the exigent circumstances justified the searches without a search warrant.

Creighton v. St. Paul, 766 F.2d 1269, 1270-1271 (8th Cir. 1985). To be sure, the Creightons may have a claim on these facts that the entry into their home was improper, either because the officers lacked probable cause or because exigent circumstances were absent. But they surely also have a claim that the search was *performed* unreasonably — that, even if it was legal to enter their home forcibly, the officers conducted the search with needless violence and cruelty. Isn't that a violation of the Fourth Amendment? Recall that in Wilson v. Layne, 526 U.S. 603 (1999), the Court held that an otherwise permissible search might be unconstitutional if it were conducted with members of the media present throughout. (*Wilson* is excerpted supra, at page 458.) It follows that the manner in which searches are conducted bears on their constitutionality. Recall too that the police may use only that amount of physical force that is reasonable under all the circumstances. See Graham v. Connor, 490 U.S. 386 (1989). (*Graham* is excerpted supra, at page 663.)

On that statement of facts, it seems that the Creightons' strongest claim is not the absence of probable cause or exigency, but rather the unreasonably violent manner in which the search was conducted. That claim dropped out of the litigation in Anderson v. Creighton; it is ignored in the Eighth Circuit opinion and again in the Supreme Court. Does it affect your view about the appropriate qualified immunity analysis? Could a reasonable police officer have believed that a search conducted in the manner described above was *not* unreasonably violent?

2. The plaintiff in Saucier v. Katz, 533 U.S. 194 (2001), was an animal-rights protester who was attending a speech by then-Vice President Al Gore. When Katz began to unfurl a cloth banner he was carrying, two officers grabbed him and led him away; one of the officers shoved Katz into a waiting police van. Katz sued, claiming that the shove constituted excessive use of force in violation of the Fourth

Amendment. Graham v. Connor, 490 U.S. 386 (1990), governed Katz's claim; under *Graham*, officers may use only that level of force which is reasonable under all the circumstances. Katz made Creighton's argument: he contended that qualified immunity must mean the same thing as the underlying Fourth Amendment doctrine, since two layers of "reasonableness" would make no sense. Citing Anderson v. Creighton, the Court rejected the argument:

> Officers can have reasonable, but mistaken, beliefs as to the facts establishing the existence of probable cause or exigent circumstances, . . . and in those situations courts will not hold that they have violated the Constitution. Yet, even if a court were to hold that the officer violated the Fourth Amendment by conducting an unreasonable, warrantless search, *Anderson* still operates to grant officers immunity for reasonable mistakes as to the legality of their actions. The same analysis is applicable in excessive force cases, where in addition to the deference officers receive on the underlying constitutional claim, qualified immunity can apply in the event the mistaken belief was reasonable.

533 U.S. at 206. The Court made another, equally important point in *Saucier*. Justice Kennedy's majority opinion instructed district courts in §1983 cases to consider *first* whether there was a constitutional violation, and only if the answer is yes, whether the defendant is entitled to qualified immunity.

3. The vast majority of Fourth Amendment damages claims involve either an allegedly unlawful arrest or allegations of excessive police violence. Why would that be so? What does that fact say about the feasibility of using damages actions to enforce compliance with the Fourth Amendment?

4. Anderson v. Creighton says that damages are available against a police officer who has violated the Fourth Amendment only when he has behaved with something akin to gross negligence — when the governing law and its application to the circumstances facing the officer are clear, and he has nevertheless disregarded them. Why limit recovery in this way? After all, a large number of people whose Fourth Amendment rights admittedly have been violated will receive no compensation under this regime, thus depriving the damages remedy of one of its chief virtues over exclusion — namely, that it will compensate the *innocent* victim.

5. Perhaps the limits placed on compensating victims in *Anderson* speak to a larger problem with the damages remedy — specifically, that in furthering the goal of compensating individual victims, the remedy may have the effect of deterring socially desirable (and constitutional) enforcement activity. Consider the following:

> Property damage aside, the injury [from a typical Fourth Amendment violation] consists of the victim's humiliation and loss of privacy, and the more diffuse harm to society's sense of security. Harms such as these cannot be priced by the legal system with any accuracy. Yet, accurate pricing is essential to a well-functioning damages system. The actors (police officers) receive no tangible reward for the marginal legal search or arrest, and are usually free to avoid acting altogether — that is, to avoid performing the search or making the arrest — without suffering substantial sanctions. Under these circumstances, if damages are imposed for illegal action (and if, as is probably the case in all legal systems, the standards that determine what is legal are somewhat vague), there is the serious danger that society will not

only get fewer illegal searches and seizures, but will also get many fewer legal ones. This activity-level effect is exacerbated if the relevant damages are overestimated — and the risk of such overestimates is likely to be high, given that the harms in question are both socially sensitive and irreducibly subjective.

Saul Levmore & William J. Stuntz, Remedies and Incentives in Private and Public Law: A Comparative Essay, [1990] Wis. L. Rev. 483, 490. Do the difficulties in "pricing" Fourth Amendment damages justify denying compensation to people whose rights have been violated?

6. At the same time that damages awards may chill appropriate governmental functions, it's worth considering whether they may also fail effectively to deter constitutional violations. Professors Skolnick and Fyfe have argued that Monell v. New York City Department of Social Services, 436 U.S. 658 (1978), which first assigned liability to local governments under Section 1983 for those constitutional violations by officers that occurred as a result of official policy or custom, probably "has had, and will continue to have, as broad an effect on police operations as any criminal case decided by the liberal Warren Court." Jerome H. Skolnick & James J. Fyfe, Above the Law 205 (1993). But others have suggested that while increased exposure to money damages has prompted smaller municipalities to improve policies and training in their police departments (since the effect of a single judgment on municipal coffers could be monumental), there is less evidence of positive effects in big-city departments. Consider the following:

> The damages the city governments of New York and Los Angeles have paid would seem to have been large enough to make them sit up and take notice. . . . [T]he City of Los Angeles paid out more than $20 million for police excessive-force suits in the five years 1986-90, averaging more than $1,300 per officer in 1990. The City of New York . . . paid out more than $50 million for "police misconduct" for the six years 1987-92, averaging about $400 per officer for a much larger department. It is likely that the actual trials of such cases, in which officers testify and may be found liable, make some difference in the way individual officers think about their work. . . .
>
> But trials are relatively rare; most civil cases are settled. The officers almost never pay the damages themselves, even when they are technically held personally liable. And the total damages are very small in relation to the police budgets, more than $1 billion dollars a year in New York and more than $400 million in Los Angeles; the damages, moreover, are not even paid out of police budgets but out of general city funds, of which they are but the tiniest fraction. The cities are self-insured; they have no out-side insurance company telling them their rates will rise unless they change their practices.

Paul Chevigny, Edge of the Knife 101-102 (1995). Professor Chevigny concludes that the effects of civil tort damages on police operations in these cities has been small — though he goes on to suggest that things may be changing as a result of large damages awards in the 1990s. He suggests that "the cities, which usually have detailed knowledge about the cases at the time they dispose of them by trial or settlement, ought to make much more active use of them." Id. at 105.

7. The qualified immunity doctrine is most often defended as being necessary to avoid depressing legitimate government functions. But is it possible to

offer a defense of the curtailment of money damages that speaks to *constitutional* concerns? Consider the following:

> On the one hand, strict liability would reduce the incidence of constitutional violations. On the other hand, it would risk the ossification of constitutional law by raising the cost of innovation. The current regime of fault-based liability for constitutional violations has the opposite vices and virtues. Qualified immunity reduces government's incentives to avoid constitutional violations. At the same time, it allows courts to embrace innovation without the potentially paralyzing cost of full remediation for past practice.

John C. Jeffries, Jr., The Right-Remedy Gap in Constitutional Law, 109 Yale L.J. 87, 99-100 (1999). This concern may be less important in the context of those Fourth Amendment claims rarely seen in civil cases anyway—claims involving things like car searches, where damages awards may be relatively small. But Fourth Amendment cases involving excessive force, unlawful arrest, or even the night-time entry into a home, as in *Creighton*, can involve substantial damages. Does Dean Jeffries have a point with regard to such cases?

Note that the second half of Jeffries's point—the idea that limiting damages will promote constitutional innovation—depends on there being *some* remedy available for constitutional violations; otherwise, courts will have no cases in which to innovate. One might say this is an argument for the exclusionary rule, which carries lower costs to police officers than damages. But one might also say it is an argument for broader use of injunctive relief against police officers. Would it be better if cases such as *Creighton* led to the issuance of injunctions against police officers or their departments? What, precisely, would courts enjoin?

NOTE ON PRIVATE POLICE

The Fourth Amendment regulates government action—meaning, usually, the police. But policing is not always performed by public police officers. Indeed, there are more private security guards in the United States today than there are government-employed law enforcement personnel. Those private-sector police are regulated not by the Fourth Amendment but by a combination of tort law and, in extreme cases, criminal prosecution. Damages are thus the chief remedy for private police misconduct.

Is that wise? To answer that question, it helps to think about the scope of private policing. Here is Professor Sklansky's account:

> Uniformed private officers guard and patrol office buildings, factories, warehouses, schools, sports facilities, concert halls, train stations, airports, shipyards, shopping centers, parks, government facilities—and, increasingly, residential neighborhoods. On any given day, many Americans are already far more likely to encounter a security guard than a police officer; in the words of one industry executive, "[t]he plain truth is that today much of the protection of our people, their property and their businesses, has been turned over to private security."
>
> Nor is private policing limited to uniformed security guards. America has over 70,000 private investigators and over 26,000 store detectives; together these individuals outnumber FBI agents by almost ten to one. The ranks of private investigators, in particular, have swelled in recent years, growing by nearly 50% during the 1980s.

Private detectives increasingly are hired not only to watch for shoplifters, but also to investigate, and not infrequently to spy on, everyone from insurance claimants and litigation opponents to employees, business partners, and even prospective neighbors.

David A. Sklansky, The Private Police, 46 UCLA L. Rev. 1165, 1175-1176 (1999).

The searches and seizures of these "private police" generally fall outside the coverage of the Fourth Amendment. ("The main legal limitations on the private police today are tort and criminal doctrines of assault, trespass, and false imprisonment. . . ." Id. at 1183.) But this is not to suggest that the authority of such police to search and seize is insubstantial. Like private citizens generally, private police may typically arrest for misdemeanors committed in their presence, and for felonies they have probable cause to believe the arrestee has committed, so long as the felony has in fact been committed by someone. Most states have also codified a "merchant's privilege" that allows store investigators to conduct brief investigatory detentions not unlike *Terry* stops. See id. at 1184.

The growth of private policing is of particular interest today because large numbers of private police "appear chiefly engaged in what is, in essence, patrol work—work once understood as the principal function of public law enforcement." Id. at 1180. And this proliferation of private patrol has more than a little to do with the disappearance of the "cop on the beat." Private police "tend at least in broad out-line to do the kinds of things that public police departments are faulted for *not* doing: patrol visibly and intensively, consult frequently with the people they are charged with protecting, and—most basically—view themselves as service providers." Id. at 1222. Professor Sklansky points out that "[t]he past few years, in fact, have seen increasing calls for a revival of traditional beat policing—calls, in other words, for police officers to act more like security guards." Id. at 1180.

The private security industry thus casts light on public policing:

Private policing would not have ballooned the way it has in recent decades if customers were unwilling to pay for it, and today's private guard companies . . . provide an indication of the kinds of police services for which the government has left demand unmet.

Obviously, not all demands *should* be met, particularly not by government. . . . Today, some part of the demand for private security services is a demand for keeping certain kinds of people—typically poor or members of racial minorities—out of the business districts, amusement parks, and residential areas that private guards are hired to patrol. Not only is this a demand that government has no business helping to meet; it is one that most people today believe that government should help suppress.

But private security firms also serve more benign interests, interests that a wide spectrum of Americans believe the government itself should pursue more aggressively. Chief among these are protecting people against serious crime—and protecting them against the *fear* of serious crime, in part by preserving public order. These are of course among the principal goals of current efforts at police reform. Among the simplest lessons that police privatization offers to students of public law enforcement are not to dismiss these efforts, and not to underestimate the breadth and the depth of the dissatisfaction to which they respond.

Id. at 1224-1225.

Is the explosive growth of private police "benign"? Is it distributively just? Public police are likely to be allocated according to crime levels — the more street crime in a particular neighborhood, the more officers assigned to work that neighborhood. Private police go not where the crimes are, but where the money is. Should police services be allocated by the economic market, or by the political market?

Fourth Amendment law has played an indirect role in the growth of private policing. Consider the following discussion of the ways constitutional reforms of the 1960s and 1970s tended to reinforce more distant, reactive police strategies by public police — which may in turn contribute to the demand for private substitutes:

> . . . Before the 1960s, the police could seize just about anyone on the street: vagrancy and loitering laws applied to almost any public behavior, so the police always had probable cause to arrest. When those laws were invalidated in the late 1960s and early 1970s, street seizures immediately became a legal problem. In the absence of blanket authority to arrest, the police needed more specific grounds to justify ad hoc seizures on the street. But in many cases those grounds did not exist — the whole point of informal, preventive police work was to anticipate trouble, not to react to it. The gains to the police from these interventions were and are small, meaning that even a small risk of legal sanction could generate a large amount of deterrence. So the police reacted to greater regulation by distancing themselves. The movement from foot patrols to cars, from preventive to reactive policing, accelerated. The law [thus] created an incentive to wait until crimes happened, after which reasonable suspicion and probable cause would be easier to establish, rather than intervening to stop them.

William J. Stuntz, Privacy's Problem and the Law of Criminal Procedure, 93 Mich. L. Rev. 1016, 1075-1076 (1995).

Something similar may be happening today. When courts invalidate, usually on vagueness grounds, contemporary statutes that authorize police to maintain order in public places, they may contribute to the demand for private police:

> With the law of trespass on their side, security guards ensure a high degree of safety in policed areas by intervening early in the face of threatening conditions and even expelling from the areas for which they are responsible those people defined as risks. The historical evidence demonstrates compellingly that return to a legal regime in which public police had "order maintaining" authority rivaling that of private security patrols would be a serious mistake: when granted such authority in the past, police . . . exercised it indiscriminately, to the detriment of the poor and, especially, racial minorities. On the other hand, the absence of narrower public police authority to address minor problems of street disorder could contribute to some degree to individuals' reliance on private police to perform order maintenance in the publicly accessible areas that these individuals control. This expansion in private security (and the resulting decline in support for the public police that many scholars have assumed may attend it) poses potential difficulties of its own: "a more unequal distribution of security; less respect for the rights of defendants; less professional competence overall to be drawn on in times of trouble."

Debra Livingston, Police Discretion and the Quality of Life in Public Places: Courts, Communities, and the New Policing, 97 Colum. L. Rev. 551, 632-633

(1997). Do you agree? Could it be that the careful regulation of low-level seizures is inconsistent with a style of police work that many people support and, indeed, seek out in the private sector? Is the private-sector policing that results a problem? Is it cause for concern that the public share of policing is steeply declining? Or is this a healthy kind of privatization, where the market provides services that the government rightly shies away from?

3.   Injunctions

LOS ANGELES v. LYONS

Certiorari to the United States Court of Appeals for the Ninth Circuit
461 U.S. 95 (1983)

JUSTICE WHITE delivered the opinion of the Court.

This case began on February 7, 1977, when respondent, Adolph Lyons, filed a complaint for damages, injunction, and declaratory relief in the United States District Court for the Central District of California. The defendants were the City of Los Angeles and four of its police officers. The complaint alleged that on October 6, 1976, at 2 a.m., Lyons was stopped by the defendant officers for a traffic or vehicle code violation and that although Lyons offered no resistance or threat whatsoever, the officers, without provocation or justification, seized Lyons and applied a "chokehold" . . . rendering him unconscious and causing damage to his larynx. Counts I through IV of the complaint sought damages against the officers and the City. Count V, with which we are principally concerned here, sought a preliminary and permanent injunction against the City barring the use of the control holds. . . .

It goes without saying that those who seek to invoke the jurisdiction of the federal courts must satisfy the threshhold requirement imposed by Article III of the Constitution by alleging an actual case or controversy. . . .

[A] relevant decision for present purposes is Rizzo v. Goode, 423 U.S. 362 (1976), a case in which plaintiffs alleged widespread illegal and unconstitutional police conduct aimed at minority citizens and against City residents in general. The Court [noted] . . . that past wrongs do not in themselves amount to that real and immediate threat of injury necessary to make out a case or controversy. The claim of injury rested upon "what one or a small, unnamed minority of policemen might do to them in the future because of that unknown policeman's perception" of departmental procedures. 423 U.S., at 372. . . . The Court also held that plaintiffs' showing at trial of a relatively few instances of violations by individual police officers, without any showing of a deliberate policy on behalf of the named defendants, did not provide a basis for equitable relief.

No extension of . . . Rizzo is necessary to hold that respondent Lyons has failed to demonstrate a case or controversy with the City that would justify the equitable relief sought. Lyons' standing to seek the injunction requested depended on whether he was likely to suffer future injury from the use of the chokeholds by police officers. Count V of the complaint alleged the traffic stop and choking incident five months before. That Lyons may have been illegally choked by the police on October 6, 1976, while presumably affording Lyons standing to claim damages against the individual officers and perhaps against the City, does nothing to establish a real and immediate threat that he would again be stopped for a traffic violation, or for any other offense, by an officer or officers who would illegally choke him into unconsciousness without any provocation or resistance on his part. The additional allegation in the complaint that the police in Los Angeles routinely apply chokeholds in situations where they are not threatened by the use of deadly force falls far short of the allegations that would be necessary to establish a case or controversy between these parties.

In order to establish an actual controversy in this case, Lyons would have had not only to allege that he would have another encounter with the police but also to make the incredible assertion either, (1) that all police officers in Los Angeles always choke any citizen with whom they happen to have an encounter, whether for the purpose of arrest, issuing a citation or for questioning or, (2) that the City ordered or authorized police officers to act in such manner. Although Count V alleged that the City authorized the use of the control holds in situations where deadly force was not threatened, it did not indicate why Lyons might be realistically threatened by police officers who acted within the strictures of the City's policy. If, for example, chokeholds were authorized to be used only to counter resistance to an arrest by a suspect, or to thwart an effort to escape, any future threat to Lyons from the City's policy or from the conduct of police officers would be no more real than the possibility that he would again have an encounter with the police and that either he would illegally resist arrest or detention or the officers would disobey their instructions and again render him unconscious without any provocation. . . .

[T]he Court of Appeals thought that Lyons was more immediately threatened . . . since, according to the Court of Appeals, Lyons need only be stopped for a minor traffic violation to be subject to the strangleholds. But even assuming that Lyons would again be stopped for a traffic or other violation in the reasonably near future, it is untenable to assert, and the complaint made no such allegation, that strangleholds are applied by the Los Angeles police to every citizen who is stopped or arrested regardless of the conduct of the person stopped. We cannot agree that the "odds," 615 F.2d, at 1247, that Lyons would not only again be stopped for a traffic violation but would also be subjected to a chokehold without any provocation whatsoever are sufficient to make out a federal case for equitable relief. We note that five months elapsed between October 6, 1976, and the filing of the complaint, yet there was no allegation of further unfortunate encounters between Lyons and the police.

Of course, it may be that among the countless encounters between the police and the citizens of a great city such as Los Angeles, there will be certain instances in which strangleholds will be illegally applied and injury and death unconstitutionally inflicted on the victim. As we have said, however, it is no more than conjecture to suggest that in every instance of a traffic stop, arrest, or other encounter between the police and a citizen, the police will act unconstitutionally and inflict injury without provocation or legal excuse. And it is surely no more than speculation to assert either that Lyons himself will again be involved in one of those unfortunate instances . . .

Lyons fares no better if it be assumed that his pending damages suit affords him Article III standing to seek an injunction as a remedy for the claims arising out of the October 1976 events. The equitable remedy is unavailable absent a showing of irreparable injury, a requirement that cannot be met where there is no showing of any real or immediate threat that the plaintiff will be wronged again. . . .

. . . If Lyons has suffered an injury barred by the Federal Constitution, he has a remedy for damages under §1983. Furthermore, those who deliberately deprive a citizen of his constitutional rights risk conviction under the federal criminal laws.

Beyond these considerations the state courts need not impose the same standing or remedial requirements that govern federal court proceedings. The individual states may permit their courts to use injunctions to oversee the conduct of law enforcement authorities on a continuing basis. But this is not the role of a federal court absent far more justification than Lyons has proffered in this case. . . .

[Justice Marshall's dissenting opinion, joined by Justice Brennan, Justice Blackmun, and Justice Stevens, is omitted.]

NOTES AND QUESTIONS

1. During the five years preceding Lyons's encounter with the Los Angeles police, "sixteen people had died after LAPD officers applied [chokeholds] to them, twice as many chokehold-related deaths as the combined total of the other twenty largest U.S. police departments." Jerome Skolnick & James J. Fyfe, Above the Law 42 (1993). As pointed out in Justice Marshall's dissent, 12 of the 16 were black males. 461 U.S. at 116. The LAPD was virtually alone among big-city departments at this time in instructing officers that chokeholds were pain compliance techniques, rather than a form of deadly force.[26] Assume that following this instruction and using the chokehold in the course of an ordinary police encounter would violate the Fourth Amendment's prohibition on unreasonable seizures. In light of Lyons, would any plaintiff have standing to bring an action for injunctive relief against the LAPD?

2. Cases like Lyons and Rizzo have not prevented plaintiffs from successfully seeking federal injunctions against police in some cases. But the effect of such decisions, "if not their overt strategy, is to push claimants toward damages actions and away from systematic relief against cities and police departments." Paul Chevigny, Edge of the Knife 110 (1995). Given that damages awards do not always prompt timely reform in police operations—partly because the damages rarely come out of police budgets—is this result wise? Do principles of federalism support it? Justice Marshall argued in his Lyons dissent that while district courts should be mindful that federal court intervention into the daily operations of a large city's police department is undesirable and to be avoided whenever possible, the injunctive relief at issue in Lyons—involving simply a prohibition on the use of chokeholds absent the threat of deadly force—"does not implicate the federalism concerns" that arise when a federal court undertakes to supervise the running of a police department. 461 U.S. at 133-134. Do you agree?

3. Partly because of Lyons, current doctrine encourages damages claims relative to claims for injunctive relief, and also encourages claims against individual police officers to relative to claims against police departments. An interesting article by

---

26. The LAPD reclassified the carotid control hold as a type of deadly force during the Lyons litigation. See Skolnick and Fyfe, supra at 42.

Professor Armacost argues that those preferences are backward — that police misconduct often, maybe usually flows from the culture of the relevant police department, and that diseased departmental cultures can only be remedied by institutional injunctions imposed on the departments themselves. See Barbara E. Armacost, Organizational Culture and Police Misconduct, 72 Geo. Wash. L. Rev. 453 (2004).

4. In 1994, Congress enacted 42 U.S.C. §14141, which prohibits governmental authorities or those acting on their behalf from engaging in "a pattern or practice of conduct by law enforcement officials" that deprives persons of "rights, privileges, or immunities secured or protected by the Constitution or laws of the United States." Whenever the Attorney General has reasonable cause to believe that a violation has occurred, the Justice Department is authorized to sue for equitable and declaratory relief "to eliminate the pattern or practice." The Justice Department's Civil Rights Division has investigated a number of police agencies to determine whether to bring §14141 litigation; it has instituted suit against several others.

In the fall of 2000, Los Angeles reached an agreement with the federal government to settle a §14141 investigation. The federal investigation and resulting consent decree came in the wake of revelations of widespread corruption among anti-gang unit officers in the LAPD's Rampart Division. (The corrupt activity included planting evidence, lying under oath, and falsifying reports to secure convictions, and resulted in more than 100 criminal convictions being overturned.) The Police Department agreed to abide by the terms of a consent decree that contains more than 180 paragraphs and specifies dozens of discrete reforms relating both to the Rampart corruption and other alleged patterns of police misconduct. Consider one paragraph relating to pedestrian stops:

> 105. By November 1, 2001, the Department shall require LAPD officers to complete a written or electronic report each time an officer conducts a pedestrian stop.
>> a. The report shall include the following:
>>> (i) the officer's serial number;
>>> (ii) date and approximate time of the stop;
>>> (iii) reporting district where the stop occurred;
>>> (iv) person's apparent race, ethnicity, or national origin;
>>> (v) person's gender and apparent age;
>>> (vi) reason for the stop, to include check boxes for: (1) suspected violation of the Penal Code; (2) suspected violation of the Health and Safety Code; (3) suspected violation of the Municipal Code; (4) suspected violation of the Vehicle Code; (5) Departmental briefing (including crime broadcast/crime bulletin/roll call briefing); (6) suspect flight; (7) consensual (which need only be checked if there is a citation, arrest, completion of a field interview card, search or seizure (other than searches or seizures incident to arrest) or pat-down/frisk); (8) call for service; or (9) other (with brief text field);
>>> (vii) whether a pat-down/frisk was conducted;
>>> (viii) action taken, to include check boxes for (1) warning; (2) citation; (3) arrest; and (4) completion of a field interview card, with appropriate identification number for the citation or arrest report; and
>>> (ix) whether the person was asked to submit to a consensual search of their person or belongings, and whether permission was granted or denied.

b. If a warrantless search is conducted, the report shall include check boxes for the following:

(i) search authority, to include: (1) consent; (2) incident to arrest; (3) parole/probation; (4) visible contraband; (5) odor of contraband; (6) incident to a pat-down/frisk; and (7) other (with a brief text field);

(ii) what was searched, to include: (1) vehicle; (2) person; and (3) container; and

(iii) what was discovered/seized, to include: (1) weapons, (2) drugs; (3) alcohol; (4) money; (5) other contraband; (6) other evidence of a crime; and (7) nothing.

c. In preparing the form of the reports required by paragraph[] . . . 105, the Department may use "check off" type boxes to facilitate completion of such reports. In documenting . . . pedestrian stops as required by [this] paragraph[], the Department may create new forms or modify existing forms.

United States v. City of Los Angeles, Civil No. 00-11769 GAF, Consent Decree Agreement. Paragraph 104 of the consent decree requires similar information to be recorded for motor vehicle stops.

One purpose in collecting such information is to identify problem officers through the use of a computerized "early warning system." The LAPD has agreed to develop and maintain a database containing information such as: all uses of deadly force by an officer, all uses of non-deadly force by an officer, all injuries caused by an officer, all automobile chases, all claims filed against an officer, and so forth. Does the "early warning" concept seem helpful in addressing patterns of Fourth Amendment violations? What are the pros and cons of the approach suggested by the Los Angeles consent decree?

5. For a positive assessment of the approach to police reform reflected in these decrees, see Samuel Walker, The New Paradigm of Police Accountability: The U.S. Justice Department "Pattern or Practice" Suits in Context, 22 St. Louis U. Pub. L. Rev. 3 (2003). Professor Walker argues that §14141 consent decrees like the one entered in Los Angeles are evidence of significant progress, nationwide, in promoting police accountability. The specific organizational reforms mandated in these consent decrees, he notes, "were not developed by the Justice Department itself but were drawn from recognized 'best practices' related to accountability already in place in other more progressive police departments." Id. at 6. These "best practices" include: "(a) a comprehensive use-of-force reporting system, (b) an open and accessible citizen complaint system, (c) an early intervention (or warning) system to identify potential 'problem' officers, and (d) the collection of data on traffic stops for the purpose of curbing racial profiling." Id. at 6-7.

Walker suggests that the consent decrees reflect a new paradigm with regard to police accountability, one that "focus[es] on organizational change rather than individual officers or discrete police problems (e.g., use of deadly force)." Id. at 51. And this new paradigm might, Walker argues, "achieve a life of its own, independent of future §14141 litigation by the Justice Department," as different police departments pursue the "best practices" approach on their own. Id.

6. Three years before the Los Angeles consent decree, the Justice Department entered into a consent decree with Pittsburgh, Pennsylvania, its Bureau of Police, and its Department of Public Safety in connection with another §14141 complaint. The complaint alleged a litany of Fourth Amendment abuses: that Pittsburgh police had used excessive force in making arrests and detaining people suspected

of criminal activity; that they had improperly searched homes and businesses and unlawfully seized arrestees' property; that Pittsburgh police had engaged in a pattern of improper stops and unlawful car searches. The Justice Department charged that the defendants had tolerated or caused and condoned the unlawful conduct through their failure to supervise, train, investigate, and discipline police officers adequately. The Pittsburgh consent decree mandated broad changes in the operations of the Pittsburgh Bureau of Police and contained numerous provisions that specified dozens of reforms. Compliance with its terms was made subject to monitoring by an independent auditor.

For a fuller account of the Pittsburgh consent decree and its provisions, see Debra Livingston, Police Reform and the Department of Justice: An Essay on Accountability, 2 Buff. Crim. L. Rev. 815 (1999). To date, there have not been many §14141 cases; these suits can only be brought by the government and the Justice Department has limited staff available for them. Is that an argument for letting private parties bring such suits? Or is centralized control of this kind of litigation a useful way to limit the power of the injunctive remedy?

4. Criminal Prosecution

Some violations of the Fourth Amendment lead to criminal prosecution. 18 U.S.C. §242 makes it a crime willfully to deprive citizens of their constitutional rights. Prosecutions under §242 are rare — a few dozen per year, nationwide. But a large fraction of those prosecutions are against police officers charged with excessive use of physical force against suspects.

Consider the prosecutions of Sergeant Stacey Koon and LAPD officers Laurence Powell, Timothy Wind, and Ted Briseno in connection with the beating of Rodney King on March 2, 1991. Justice Kennedy recounted the relevant facts in Koon v. United States, 518 U.S. 81, 85-87 (1996):

> On the evening of March 2, 1991, Rodney King and two of his friends sat in King's wife's car in Altadena, California, a city in Los Angeles County, and drank malt liquor for a number of hours. Then, with King driving, they left Altadena via a major freeway. King was intoxicated.
>
> California Highway Patrol officers observed King's car traveling at a speed they estimated to be in excess of 100 m.p.h. The officers followed King with red lights and sirens activated and ordered him by loudspeaker to pull over, but he continued to drive. The Highway Patrol officers called on the radio for help. Units of the Los Angeles Police Department joined in the pursuit, one of them manned by petitioner Laurence Powell and his trainee, Timothy Wind.
>
> King left the freeway, and after a chase of about eight miles, stopped at an entrance to a recreation area. The officers ordered King and his two passengers to exit the car and to assume a felony prone position — that is, to lie on their stomachs with legs spread and arms behind their backs. King's two friends complied. King, too, got out of the car but did not lie down. Petitioner Stacey Koon arrived, at once followed by Ted Briseno and Roland Solano. All were officers of the Los Angeles Police Department, and as sergeant, Koon took charge. The officers again ordered King to assume the felony prone position. King got on his hands and knees but did not lie down. Officers Powell, Wind, Briseno and Solano tried to force King down, but King resisted and became combative, so the officers retreated. Koon then fired taser darts (designed to stun a combative suspect) into King.

The events that occurred next were captured on videotape by a bystander. As the videotape begins, it shows that King rose from the ground and charged toward Officer Powell. Powell took a step and used his baton to strike King on the side of his head. King fell to the ground. From the 18th to the 30th second on the videotape, King attempted to rise, but Powell and Wind each struck him with their batons to prevent him from doing so. From the 35th to the 51st second, Powell administered repeated blows to King's lower extremities; one of the blows fractured King's leg. At the 55th second, Powell struck King on the chest, and King rolled over and lay prone. At that point, the officers stepped back and observed King for about 10 seconds. Powell began to reach for his handcuffs. . . .

At one-minute-five-seconds (1:05) on the videotape, Briseno, in the District Court's words, "stomped" on King's upper back or neck. King's body writhed in response. At 1:07, Powell and Wind again began to strike King with a series of baton blows, and Wind kicked him in the upper thoracic or cervical area six times until 1:26. At about 1:29, King put his hands behind his back and was handcuffed. . . .

Powell radioed for an ambulance. He sent two messages over a communications network to the other officers that said "'ooops'" and "'I havent [sic] beaten anyone this bad in a long time.'" Koon sent a message to the police station that said: "'U[nit] just had a big time use of force. . . . Tased and beat the suspect of CHP pursuit big time.'"

King was taken to a hospital where he was treated for a fractured leg, multiple facial fractures, and numerous bruises and contusions. Learning that King worked at Dodger Stadium, Powell said to King: "'We played a little ball tonight, didn't we Rodney? . . . You know, we played a little ball, we played a little hardball tonight, we hit quite a few home runs. . . . Yes, we played a little ball and you lost and we won.'"

Koon, Powell, Briseno and Wind were tried in state court on charges of assault with a deadly weapon and excessive use of force by a police officer. The trial resulted in acquittals on all charges, with the exception of one assault charge against Powell on which the jury hung. The verdicts sparked one of the largest civil disorders in American history. More than 40 people were killed in the rioting, more than 2,000 were injured, and nearly $1 billion in property was destroyed.

A federal grand jury subsequently indicted the four officers under 18 U.S.C. §242, charging them with violating King's constitutional rights under color of law. The second jury convicted Koon and Powell but acquitted Wind and Briseno.

The history of Koon v. United States may illustrate the importance of vindicating constitutional rights through the mechanism of criminal prosecution in appropriate cases. But doesn't it also speak to the range of factors that have led many scholars to conclude that "[c]riminal law is . . . not a system of 'discipline' for police misconduct. . . ."? Paul Chevigny, Edge of the Knife 101 (1995). Consider Professor Chevigny's analysis of the reasons why criminal prosecution cannot be expected to be a major vehicle for reform in the area of excessive force:

> Criminal prosecution is the most cumbersome tool for the accountability of officials. As an instrument for policy, it presents the difficulties with disciplinary proceedings writ large: the charges are made after the fact; it is a matter of hazard which cases can be proved and which cannot; and because the burden of proof is extremely high, the likelihood of success is small. Prosecutions are brought in the few cases where the evidence happens to be available, and the results thus create a patchy deterrent; they may have no effect on police policy at all if police executives do not agree with the decision to prosecute. Furthermore, the standards of the criminal

law usually cannot delineate what is good police work that will minimize the unnecessary use of force — that must be shaped by police regulations, training, and practice. Police standards for the use of firearms, for example, are commonly more restrictive than the criminal law of justification, because a shooting may be "wrong" in the sense that there was a better way to handle the situation, without being "wrong" in the sense of a flagrantly offensive act that ought to be punished as a crime. The state prosecution in California for the Rodney King beating presents a rather complex example of the problems. The police who beat King were first prosecuted in state court for felony assault and were acquitted; one of their defenses was that they believed King was a threat to them and that they responded as they claimed they had been taught to respond. Thus, within limits, poor police practices throughout a department can aid the defense of a criminal case by suggesting that there is not criminal intent on the part of a police defendant.

Id. at 98-99. Despite this analysis, Professor Chevigny emphasizes that "[i]t is very important . . . to prosecute acts that are clearly criminal, whether deliberate or reckless," and that with regard to the use of force, such prosecutions "do have a broad deterrent effect, making officers aware that the lawful use of force is always at the border of actions that may be criminal." Id. at 99. In what sort of circumstances do you think criminal prosecution may play an important role in remedying Fourth Amendment harms?

5. Administrative and Political Remedies

Police regulation and discipline are generally directed at deterring police misconduct rather than compensating victims. Similarly, police training aims at avoiding Fourth Amendment violations before they occur. These internal administrative functions, however, should not be overlooked in any discussion of minimizing Fourth Amendment harms:

> Given the decentralized and dispersed nature of police organizations, it is utterly hopeless to attempt to control police conduct other than by making the administrative system work. No court or specially constituted civilian body, based outside the police agency, can possibly provide the kind of day-to-day direction that is essential if the behavior of police officers at the operating level is to be effectively controlled. This means that even in the most acute situations, when administrators and supervisors are either unwilling or incapable of asserting themselves, there is simply no way to work around them. They must be replaced or forced to function properly.

Herman Goldstein, Policing a Free Society 174 (1977). At the same time, "there is widespread recognition that police departments have failed to develop adequate methods of accountability. In particular, there has been a failure both to identify and punish chronic misconduct and to reward good conduct." Samuel Walker, The Police in America 289 (2d ed. 1992). This may be particularly true in the context of illegal searches and seizures, where misconduct can occur in the normal course of law enforcement and may be condoned by police managers and tolerated by prosecutors.

There are external influences on these internal controls, of course, and these should also be considered in the context of controlling Fourth Amendment abuses. Consider the role of local politics on police operations:

> . . . In those communities where top police officials are still popularly elected, political control [of the police function] is direct. And even when police chiefs or police commissioners are appointed, they are today accountable to elected officials in all major American cities. "At the municipal level a police chief who is by legislation required to function under the direction of an elected mayor and who is appointed by the mayor, is obviously considered responsible to the mayor for all aspects of police operations." Police departments are also at least theoretically accountable to local legislative bodies, since these bodies perform an oversight function that . . . might be enhanced: "[A]ccountability might be increased by regular reporting and discussion in city council meetings or council committee meetings of the kinds of problems police are dealing with in the community and how they are handling them. . . .
>
> There is reason, however, to be less than sanguine about the role that both formal and informal mechanisms of political control can play in holding police managers and their departments accountable. . . . The historical effort to wrest control of policing from local ward politicians resulted in broad dissemination of the ideas associated with reform era policing. . . . These ideas, like faith in police professionalism and in neutral law enforcement in lieu of potentially corrupting political controls, have sometimes been interpreted to condemn as corrupt *any* political oversight of the police. . . . "[I]t is not uncommon for mayors running for reelection to brag about the degree of independence they allowed their police departments." Politicians also have their own reasons for disclaiming much of their responsibility for monitoring police operations. Policing is a risky business, and distance between politicians and the police helps the former avoid blame when the latter become ensnared in controversy. Police "are not autonomous; the sensitive function they perform in our society requires that they be accountable, through the political process, to the community." Achieving this accountability, however, is no small feat.

Debra Livingston, Police Discretion and the Quality of Life in Public Places: Courts, Communities, and the New Policing, 97 Colum. L. Rev. 551, 654, 656-657 (1997) (footnotes omitted).

Local political agitation in many cities has resulted in the creation of various forms of "citizen review" boards to monitor police. Indeed, the establishment of citizen complaint review procedures has been a primary political objective of many civil rights and civil liberties advocates in recent years. In cities that have adopted one or another version of "citizen review," citizens share responsibility with police for the review of complaints brought against individual police officers. In some places, agencies independent of the police department investigate and review such complaints, thereafter making recommendations about the discipline of officers found to have engaged in misconduct. A majority of big cities currently have at least a hybrid complaint system in which police may investigate complaints, but civilians sit on the board that recommends discipline. See Paul Chevigny, Edge of the Knife 88 (1995). These boards could come to play an important role in monitoring police departments for Fourth Amendment violations. But they have not as yet emerged as a principal form of redress for such violations, nor as a significant vehicle for police reform: "To date, most such boards have focused narrowly on the performance of individual police officers rather than on broader questions about the quality of police services or the overall acceptability of particular policing practices within local neighborhoods." Livingston, supra, at 665.

There is good reason to believe that close attention to the information in complaints could improve policing services — including police compliance with Fourth Amendment constraints. But citizen review agencies may need to transcend the limitations of their narrow focus on holding individual officers to account:

> . . . Given the dispersed nature of patrol work and the relatively limited opportunities for intensive on-scene observation by supervisors, complaints are a particularly valuable source of management information in policing. We know this already with regard to problem officers. A relatively small percentage of officers in many departments amass a disproportionate share of citizen complaints, as well as use-of-force reports, and other indicia of adversarial citizen encounters. Good police supervisors use information of this type to determine whether there is a need for retraining, counseling, or reassignment in a given case — and often well before any complaint is ever substantiated, or discipline is imposed. . . .
>
> But the information in citizen complaints has uses that go well beyond even the important task of identifying at-risk officers and intervening with them before serious problems develop. Indeed, the close examination of complaints can shed light on a broad range of matters: like oversights in training that are producing cases in which force is unnecessarily, but not maliciously, used; recurrent supervisory lapses of the sort that set the stage for serious problems down the line; or even simple inattention to duty by officers on patrol.
>
> Consider an example. In 2001, New York's [Citizen Complaint Review Board] did a study of complaints involving street stops. The report found, among other things, that in over half of the hundreds of fully investigated complaints involving the street stop of an individual that formed the principal data for the study's findings, the officer or officers involved failed to fill out a form required by the Police Department for such encounters. Now, the CCRB's jurisdiction does not extend to the failure to fill out internal NYPD forms, and this finding emerged only as a result of the study. But this example demonstrates how analysis of the information in complaints can shed light on broader police management issues: in this instance, widespread noncompliance with an organizational policy facilitating managerial control over the stop-and-frisk practices of police.
>
> There is something of an irony here. The citizen review movement began in the perception that internal police complaint review procedures (such as they were) were too often properly faulted "for lax and incomplete investigations, for a low rate of substantiation of complaints, and for failure to inform the public of the reasons for the results of complaints." These problems were real, and have been ameliorated in many places by the institution of citizen review. . . . The move to independent, all-civilian review agencies . . . , however, may make it harder, not easier for the *management* information in complaints to be effectively employed. Complaints are investigated outside the day-to-day operations of the [police department] by personnel who may be more objective and dispassionate when it comes to holding individual officers to account, but who are also almost certainly less expert in recognizing and evaluating police management issues.

Debra Livingston, The Unfulfilled Promise of Citizen Review, 1 Ohio St. J. of Crim. L. 653, 658-659 (2004).

Given these observations, is there a way that administrative and political controls over police might be strengthened so as to increase their effectiveness in addressing Fourth Amendment harms? More generally, might these regulatory mechanisms, if given broader scope, serve as a substitute for *judicial* regulation of police misconduct? Plainly, political checks and institutional controls have important weaknesses. Yet the same is true of Supreme Court-driven constitutional regulation. Based on the cases and materials in this chapter, does Fourth Amendment law work? Would a different system of regulation — one focused more on well-functioning administrative review mechanisms and political checks — work better?

Chapter 6
The Fifth Amendment

The Fifth Amendment privilege against self-incrimination is a doctrine in search of a theory. With respect to most constitutional rights, there is broad agreement about the right's basic purpose. Freedom of speech protects some combination of artistic expression and political argument. The right to equal protection of the laws protects against official discrimination. Fourth Amendment law protects individual privacy. There are of course complications and exceptions, but the basic vision behind these rights is widely and well understood.

The privilege is not like that. There is no agreement on the privilege's purpose; indeed, some writers challenge the idea that it should exist at all. Our legal system (for that matter, any legal system) regularly compels witnesses to turn over documents and give testimony when they would prefer not to do those things. Why make an exception for one whose testimony would incriminate him? As Judge Henry Friendly famously argued:

> No parent would teach such a doctrine to his children; the lesson parents preach is that while a misdeed, even a serious one, will generally be forgiven, a failure to make a clean breast of it will not be. Every hour of the day people are being asked to explain their conduct to parents, employers and teachers. Those who are questioned consider themselves to be morally bound to respond, and the questioners believe it proper to take action if they do not.

Henry J. Friendly, The Fifth Amendment Tomorrow: The Case for Constitutional Change, 37 U. Cin. L. Rev. 671, 680 (1968). And the privilege is puzzling in another respect. In general, the law of criminal procedure seems designed to grant broader legal protection to innocent citizens than to criminals. For example, Fourth Amendment law holds that the police may search private spaces only if they have good reason (probable cause or reasonable suspicion) to believe the search will uncover evidence of crime. The greater the risk of incrimination, the smaller the legal protection—and the broader the authority granted to police. The privilege against self-incrimination tilts in the opposite direction. If the government asks a witness a question and the answer cannot possibly provide evidence that the witness is guilty of a crime, the witness must answer—even if the question intrudes grievously on the witness's privacy. The greater the risk of incrimination, the *broader* the legal protection—and the narrower the authority that is granted to the government. Why do we have this odd right?

Text and History

Begin with the text. The Fifth Amendment contains several different constitutional protections: the ban on double jeopardy, the requirement of a grand jury in federal cases, the right to due process of law (again, in federal cases — the due process requirement in state cases comes from the Fourteenth Amendment), and of course the privilege. The privilege's text is spare: "No person . . . shall be compelled in any criminal case to be a witness against himself." From this text come the privilege's three basic elements: compulsion, incrimination, and testimony. But what are those elements designed to protect?

Like most provisions of the Bill of Rights, the privilege against self-incrimination was picked up from English common law, where it arose out of two sorts of cases: heresy and sedition. The English High Commission of the late sixteenth and early seventeenth centuries forced suspected heretics to swear an oath to answer questions honestly before being informed of the nature of any charges against them; questioning usually went to the content of the witnesses' religious beliefs and the identities of their fellow believers. Some of these alleged heretics claimed that the questioning was unlawful on the ground that no one should be forced to give testimony against himself; to do so would be to "put the conscience upon the racke." Leonard W. Levy, Origins of the Fifth Amendment 177 (1968) (quoting a statement made around 1591 by Thomas Cartwright and eight Puritan colleagues). Political dissidents made a similar argument. John Lilburne, a popular English pamphleteer and political gadfly of the mid-seventeenth century, was charged with authoring various items critical of those in power. When asked about his authorship, Lilburne refused to answer. He was acquitted, and the privilege against self-incrimination was born.

Its incorporation into the Fifth Amendment was not the subject of much debate, either in the Congress that wrote the Bill of Rights or in the states' ratification processes. Criminal defendants in the eighteenth century had no right to testify — parties in civil and criminal cases alike were forbidden to testify under oath — so a right *not* to testify seemed unimportant. Besides, defense lawyers were rare in eighteenth-century American criminal trials, and without counsel, defendants were forced to speak (albeit not under oath) on their own behalf. That state of affairs changed gradually during the course of the nineteenth century. The rise of professional prosecutors and the increasingly common use of defense counsel made criminal litigation into something like the lawyers' battle that we know today. And the common law soon adopted the notion that litigants, including criminal defendants, could testify under oath if they wished, giving new meaning to a legal right to avoid giving testimony. The privilege slowly became a staple of the criminal trial process.

When the Supreme Court decided Boyd v. United States, 116 U.S. 616 (1886), the privilege became something else as well: a constitutional guarantee of individual privacy. Boyd was a glass importer. Suspecting customs fraud, the government initiated a civil forfeiture action against some shipments of glass; in the course of that proceeding, a subpoena was issued ordering Boyd to produce the invoices for those shipments. He challenged the subpoena, claiming that it was both an unreasonable search in violation of the Fourth Amendment and compelled self-incrimination in violation of the Fifth. The Supreme Court agreed, holding that that the two prohibitions covered "any forcible and compulsory extortion of a man's own testimony or of his private papers to be used as evidence to convict him of crime or to forfeit his goods." The Court added: "In this regard the Fourth and Fifth Amendments run almost into each other." *Boyd* is excerpted and discussed in Chapter 4, at page 278.

This privacy-based privilege has had its ups and downs, as the balance of this chapter will show. Other, competing theories have risen to the fore. And sometimes, the Supreme Court has restricted the privilege's scope not because of any theory, but as a pragmatic accommodation to the government's need to gather evidence and information in order to govern. This last point is particularly important. If the government can never obtain incriminating evidence from suspects, the criminal justice system may be unable to do its job. On the other hand, if the government can obtain whatever information it likes whenever it likes, the privacy and autonomy values underlying the privilege might become a practical nullity. This may be one area of constitutional law where the conflict between individual rights and government needs is especially stark.

The balance of this chapter deals with the ways in which Fifth Amendment law manages that conflict. In Section A, we explore the underlying purposes of the privilege, using the history of Fifth Amendment immunity as a vehicle. Section B turns to the privilege's basic doctrinal structure, which is built around three portions of constitutional text: compulsion ("No person . . . shall be compelled"), incrimination ("in any criminal case"), and testimony ("to be a witness against himself"). Section C deals with the ways in which the Supreme Court has limited the privilege's scope in deference to the government's interest in regulation. Section D then turns to police interrogation, where the "right to remain silent" has acquired a special meaning, and a large and intricate body of law supports and surrounds (some would say undermines) it. As you read these materials, it is wise to keep two questions in mind. First, what theory of the privilege best explains the cases? And second, how do courts—and how does the Supreme Court—negotiate the tension between the individual's right to keep silent and the government's interest in gathering evidence?

A. The Fifth Amendment Privilege Against Self-Incrimination and Its Justifications

The earliest interpretation of the Fifth Amendment by a sitting Supreme Court Justice gave the privilege very broad scope. The case was the trial of Aaron Burr in 1807, and the justice was Chief Justice John Marshall. A witness was called before the grand jury considering the Burr case; the witness was asked whether, on Burr's orders, he had copied a particular document. The witness refused to answer, on the ground that his answer might be incriminating. The Chief Justice heard argument on the question whether the witness's assertion of the privilege was proper. Using (typically, for Marshall) sweeping language, he upheld the witness's claim:

> When a question is propounded, it belongs to the court to consider and to decide whether any direct answer to it can implicate the witness. If this be decided in the negative, then he may answer it without violating the privilege which is secured to him by law. If a direct answer to it *may* criminate himself, then he must be the sole judge

what his answer would be. The court cannot participate with him in this judgment; because they cannot decide on the effect of his answer without knowing what it would be; and a disclosure of that fact to the judges would strip him of the privileges which the law allows, and which he claims. It follows, necessarily, then, from this state of things, that if the question be of such a description that an answer to it may or may not criminate the witness, according to the purport of that answer, it must rest with himself, who alone can tell what it would be, to answer the question or not. If, in such a case, he say, upon his oath, that his answer would criminate himself, the court can demand no other testimony of the fact. If the declaration be untrue, it is in conscience and in law as much a perjury as if he had declared any other untruth upon his oath; as it is one of those cases in which the rule of law must be abandoned, or the oath of the witness be received. The counsel for the United States have also laid down this rule, according to their understanding of it, but they appear to the court to have made it as much too narrow as the counsel for the witness have made it too broad. According to their statement, a witness can never refuse to answer any question, unless that answer, unconnected with other testimony, would be sufficient to convict him of a crime. This would be rendering the rule almost perfectly worthless. Many links frequently compose that chain of testimony which is necessary to convict any individual of a crime. It appears to the court to be the true sense of the rule that no witness is compellable to furnish any one of them against himself. It is certainly not only a possible, but a probable, case, that a witness, by disclosing a single fact, may complete the testimony against himself, and to every effectual purpose accuse himself as entirely as he would by stating every circumstance which would be required for his conviction. That fact of itself might be unavailing; but all other facts without it might be insufficient. While that remains concealed within his own bosom he is safe; but draw it from thence, and he is exposed to a prosecution. The rule which declares that no man is compelled to accuse himself, would most obviously be infringed by compelling a witness to disclose a fact of this description. What testimony may be possessed, or is attainable, against any individual, the court can never know. It would seem, then, that the court ought never to compel a witness to give an answer which discloses a fact that might form a necessary and essential part of a crime, which is punishable by the laws. . . . In such a case, the witness must himself judge what his answer will be; and if he say, on oath, that he cannot answer without accusing himself, he cannot be compelled to answer.

1 Burr's Trial, 244, 245, quoted in Brown v. Walker, 161 U.S. 591, 612-615 (1896) (Shiras, J., dissenting).

Predictably, the government found Marshall's literal interpretation of the Fifth Amendment too confining, and in the century following Aaron Burr's trial, state and federal governments alike passed statutes providing witnesses with various types of immunity from prosecution in order to compel testimony over an otherwise legitimate invocation of the privilege. These statutes were premised on the view that a witness could hardly be seen as incriminating himself if he was given immunity from prosecution with respect to the acts testified to or, alternatively, if the state was not allowed to use the compelled testimony against the witness. When the Court first reviewed the constitutionality of one of these statues, it relied heavily on Chief Justice Marshall's opinion in the Burr trial, and on the then recent case of Boyd v. United States, 116 U.S. 616 (1886), in striking down the statute.

COUNSELMAN v. HITCHCOCK, 142 U.S. 547, 560-561, 562-564, 585-586 (1892):[The federal statute in question in *Counselman* provided:] ". . . No pleading of a party, nor any discovery or evidence obtained from a party or witness by means of a judicial proceeding in this or any foreign country, shall be given in evidence, or in any manner used against him or his property or estate, in any court of the United States, in any criminal proceeding, or for the enforcement of any penalty or forfeiture: *Provided*, That this section shall not exempt any party or witness from prosecution and punishment for perjury committed in discovering or testifying as aforesaid. . . ."

[In finding it unconstitutional, the Court first held that the Fifth Amendment is not limited to testimony given at the trial of a criminal case:]

It is broadly contended on the part of the appellee that a witness is not entitled to plead the privilege of silence, except in a criminal case against himself; but such is not the language of the Constitution. Its provision is that no person shall be compelled in *any* criminal case to be a witness against himself. This provision must have a broad construction in favor of the right which it was intended to secure. The matter under investigation by the grand jury in this case was a criminal matter, to inquire whether there had been a criminal violation of the Interstate Commerce Act. If Counselman had been guilty of the matters inquired of in the questions which he refused to answer, he himself was liable to criminal prosecution under the act. The case before the grand jury was, therefore, a criminal case. The reason given by Counselman for his refusal to answer the questions was that his answers might tend to criminate him, and showed that his apprehension was that, if he answered the questions truly and fully (as he was bound to do if he should answer them at all), the answers might show that he had committed a crime against the Interstate Commerce Act, for which he might be prosecuted. His answers, therefore, would be testimony against himself, and he would be compelled to give them in a criminal case.

It is impossible that the meaning of the constitutional provision can only be, that a person shall not be compelled to be a witness against himself in a criminal prosecution against himself. It would doubtless cover such cases; but it is not limited to them. The object was to insure that a person should not be compelled, when acting as a witness in any investigation, to give testimony which might tend to show that he himself had committed a crime. The privilege is limited to criminal matters, but it is as broad as the mischief against which it seeks to guard.

It is argued for the appellee that the investigation before the grand jury was not a criminal case, but was solely for the purpose of finding out whether a crime had been committed, or whether any one should be accused of an offence, there being no accuser and no parties plaintiff or defendant, and that a case could arise only when an indictment should be returned. In support of this view reference is made to article 6 of the amendments to the Constitution of the United States, which provides that in all criminal prosecutions the accused shall enjoy the right to a speedy and public trial by an impartial jury, to be confronted with the witnesses against him, to have compulsory process for witnesses, and the assistance of counsel for his defence.

But this provision distinctly means a criminal prosecution against a person who is accused and who is to be tried by a petit jury. A criminal prosecution under article 6 of the amendments, is much narrower than a "criminal case," under article 5 of the amendments. It is entirely consistent with the language of article 5, that the privilege of not being a witness against himself is to be exercised in a proceeding before a grand jury. . . .

It is an ancient principle of the law of evidence, that a witness shall not be compelled, in any proceeding, to make disclosures or to give testimony which will tend to criminate him or subject him to fines, penalties or forfeitures. . . .

The relations of Counselman to the subject of inquiry before the grand jury, as shown by the questions put to him, in connection with the provisions of the Interstate Commerce Act, entitled him to invoke the protection of the Constitution. . . .

[The Court then proceeded to determine whether the immunity provided in the statute was sufficient to protect Counselman's rights:]

It remains to consider whether §860 of the Revised Statutes removes the protection of the constitutional privilege of Counselman. That section must be construed as declaring that no evidence obtained from a witness by means of a judicial proceeding shall be given in evidence, or in any manner used against him or his property or estate, in any court of the United States, in any criminal proceeding, or for the enforcement of any penalty or forfeiture. It follows, that any evidence which might have been obtained from Counselman by means of his examination before the grand jury could not be given in evidence or used against him or his property in any court of the United States, in any criminal proceeding, or for the enforcement of any penalty or forfeiture. This, of course, protected him against the use of his testimony against him or his property in any prosecution against him or his property, in any criminal proceeding, in a court of the United States. But it had only that effect. It could not, and would not, prevent the use of his testimony to search out other testimony to be used in evidence against him or his property, in a criminal proceeding in such court. It could not prevent the obtaining and the use of witnesses and evidence which should be attributable directly to the testimony he might give under compulsion, and on which he might be convicted, when otherwise, and if he had refused to answer, he could not possibly have been convicted. . . .

We are clearly of opinion that no statute which leaves the party or witness subject to prosecution after he answers the criminating question put to him, can have the effect of supplanting the privilege conferred by the Constitution of the United States. Section 860 of the Revised Statutes does not supply a complete protection from all the perils against which the constitutional prohibition was designed to guard, and is not a full substitute for that prohibition. In view of the constitutional provision, a statutory enactment, to be valid, must afford absolute immunity against future prosecution for the offence to which the question relates. In this respect, . . . we consider that the ruling of this court in Boyd v. United States . . . supports the view we take. Section 860, moreover, affords no protection against that use of compelled testimony which consists in gaining therefrom a knowledge of the details of a crime, and of sources of information which may supply other means of convicting the witness or party. . . .

From a consideration of the language of the constitutional provision, and of all the authorities referred to, we are clearly of opinion that the appellant was entitled to refuse, as he did, to answer. The judgment of the Circuit Court must, therefore, be

Reversed, and the case remanded to that court, with a direction to discharge the appellant from custody, on the writ of habeas corpus.

Congress responded to the Court's decision in *Counselman* by enacting a broader immunity statute. The new law stated that "no person shall be excused from attending and testifying or from producing books, papers, tariffs, contracts, agreements and documents before the Interstate Commerce Commission, or in obedience to the subpoena of the Commission, . . . on the ground or for the reason that the testimony or evidence, documentary or otherwise, required of him, may tend to criminate him or subject him to a penalty or forfeiture. But no person shall be prosecuted or subjected to any penalty or forfeiture for or on account of any transaction, matter or thing, concerning which he may testify, or produce evidence, documentary or otherwise, before said Commission, or in obedience to its subpoena, or the subpoena of either of them, or in any such case or proceeding."

In Brown v. Walker, 161 U.S. 591 (1896), the Court upheld this new, transactional immunity statute:

The clause of the Constitution in question is obviously susceptible of two interpretations. If it be construed literally, as authorizing the witness to refuse to disclose any fact which might tend to incriminate, disgrace or expose him to unfavorable comments, then as he must necessarily to a large extent determine upon his own conscience and responsibility whether his answer to the proposed question will have that tendency, . . . the practical result would be, that no one could be compelled to testify to a material fact in a criminal case, unless he chose to do so. . . . If, upon the other hand, the object of the provision be to secure the witness against a criminal prosecution, which might be aided directly or indirectly by his disclosure, then, if no such prosecution be possible — in other words, if his testimony operate as a complete pardon for the offence to which it relates — a statute absolutely securing to him such immunity from prosecution would satisfy the demands of the clause in question. . . .

The maxim nemo tenetur seipsum accusare had its origin in a protest against the inquisitorial and manifestly unjust methods of interrogating accused persons, which has long obtained in the continental system, and, until the expulsion of the Stuarts from the British throne in 1688, and the erection of additional barriers for the protection of the people against the exercise of arbitrary power, was not uncommon even in England. While the admissions or confessions of the prisoner, when voluntarily and freely made, have always ranked high in the scale of incriminating evidence, if an accused person be asked to explain his apparent connection with a crime under investigation, the ease with which the questions put to him may assume an inquisitorial character, the temptation to press the witness unduly, to browbeat him if he be timid or reluctant, to push him into a corner, and to entrap him into fatal contradictions, which is so painfully evident in many of the earlier state trials, notably in those of Sir Nicholas Throckmorton, and Udal, the Puritan minister, made the system so odious as to give rise to a demand for its total abolition. The change in the English criminal procedure in that particular seems to be founded upon no statute and no judicial opinion, but upon a general and silent acquiescence of the courts in a popular demand. But, however adopted, it has become firmly embedded in English, as well as in American jurisprudence. So deeply did the iniquities of the ancient system impress themselves upon the minds of the American colonists that the States, with one accord, made a denial of the right to question an accused person a part of their fundamental law, so that a maxim, which in England was a mere rule of evidence, became clothed in this country with the impregnability of a constitutional enactment.

Stringent as the general rule is, however, certain classes of cases have always been treated as not falling within the reason of the rule. . . . When examined, these cases will all be found to be based upon the idea that, if the testimony sought cannot possibly be used as a basis for, or in aid of, a criminal prosecution against the witness, the rule ceases to apply. . . .

1. Thus, if the witness himself elects to waive his privilege, as he may doubtless do, since the privilege is for his protection and not for that of other parties, and

discloses his criminal connections, he is not permitted to stop, but must go on and make a full disclosure. . . . So, under modern statutes permitting accused persons to take the stand in their own behalf, they may be subjected to cross-examination upon their statements. . . .

2.   For the same reason if a prosecution for a crime, concerning which the witness is interrogated, is barred by the statute of limitations, he is compellable to answer. . . .

3.   If the answer of the witness may have a tendency to disgrace him or bring him into disrepute [but not to incriminate him], and the proposed evidence be material to the issue on trial, the great weight of authority is that he may be compelled to answer. . . . The extent to which the witness is compelled to answer such questions as do not fix upon him a criminal culpability is within the control of the legislature. . . .

4.   . . . [I]f the witness has already received a pardon, he cannot longer set up his privilege, since he stands with respect to such offence as if it had never been committed. . . .

The danger of extending the principle announced in Counselman v. Hitchcock is that the privilege may be put forward for a sentimental reason, or for a purely fanciful protection of the witness against an imaginary danger, and for the real purpose of securing immunity to some third person, who is interested in concealing the facts to which he would testify. Every good citizen is bound to aid in the enforcement of the law, and has no right to permit himself, under the pretext of shielding his own good name, to be made the tool of others, who are desirous of seeking shelter behind his privilege. . . .

It is entirely true that the statute does not purport . . . to shield the witness from the personal disgrace or opprobrium attaching to the exposure of his crime; but . . . the authorities are numerous and very nearly uniform to the effect that, if the proposed testimony is material to the issue on trial, the fact that the testimony may tend to degrade the witness in public estimation does not exempt him from the duty of disclosure. A person who commits a criminal act is bound to contemplate the consequences of exposure to his good name and reputation, and ought not to call upon the courts to protect that which he has himself esteemed to be of such little value. The safety and welfare of an entire community should not be put into the scale against the reputation of a self-confessed criminal, who ought not, either in justice or in good morals, to refuse to disclose that which may be of great public utility, in order that his neighbors may think well of him. The design of the constitutional privilege is not to aid the witness in vindicating his character, but to protect him against being compelled to furnish evidence to convict him of a criminal charge. If he secure legal immunity from prosecution, the possible impairment of his good name is a penalty which it is reasonable he should be compelled to pay for the common good. . . .

If, as was justly observed in the opinion of the court below, witnesses standing in Brown's position were at liberty to set up an immunity from testifying, the enforcement of the Interstate Commerce law or other analogous acts, wherein it is for the interest of both parties to conceal their misdoings, would become impossible, since it is only from the mouths of those having knowledge of the inhibited contracts that the facts can be ascertained. While the constitutional provision in question is justly regarded as one of the most valuable prerogatives of the citizen, its object is fully accomplished by the statutory immunity, and we are, therefore, of opinion that the witness was compellable to answer, and that the judgment of the court below must be affirmed.

161 U.S. at 595-606, 610. In dicta, the Court expressed the view that the statutory immunity would extend to state criminal prosecutions — that immunized witnesses

could not be criminally punished by any American jurisdiction for any of the conduct about which they testified. Notwithstanding the breadth of this immunity, four Justices (Field, Shiras, Gray, and White) took the position that it was not broad enough to overcome the privilege. The following excerpts from Justice Field's dissent capture their argument:

> The [Fifth Amendment] . . . protects [the witness] from all compulsory testimony which would expose him to infamy and disgrace, though the facts disclosed might not lead to a criminal prosecution. It is contended, indeed, that it was not the object of the constitutional safeguard to protect the witness against infamy and disgrace. It is urged that its sole purpose was to protect him against incriminating testimony with reference to the offence under prosecution. But I do not agree that such limited protection was all that was secured. As stated by counsel of the appellant,
>
>> it is entirely possible, and certainly not impossible, that the framers of the Constitution reasoned that in bestowing upon witnesses in criminal cases the privilege of silence when in danger of self-incrimination, they would at the same time save him *in all such cases* from the shame and infamy of confessing disgraceful crimes and thus preserve to him some measure of self-respect. . . .
>
> It is true, as counsel observes, that
>
>> both the safeguard of the Constitution and the common law rule spring alike from that sentiment of *personal self-respect, liberty, independence and dignity* which has inhabited the breasts of English speaking peoples for centuries, and to save which they have always been ready to sacrifice many governmental facilities and conveniences. In scarcely anything has that sentiment been more manifest than in the abhorrence felt at the legal compulsion upon witnesses to make concessions which must cover the witness with lasting shame and leave him degraded both in his own eyes and those of others. What can be more abhorrent . . . than to compel a man who has fought his way from obscurity to dignity and honor to reveal crimes of which he had repented and of which the world was ignorant? . . .
>
> The essential and inherent cruelty of compelling a man to expose his own guilt is obvious to every one, and needs no illustration. It is plain to every person who gives the subject a moment's thought. . . .

Id. at 631-632, 637. Interestingly, Justice Field also noted in passing that "[t]he Fourth Amendment . . . is equally encroached upon by the act in question." Id. at 636.

As Counselman v. Hitchcock and Brown v. Walker indicate, the analytic foundation of Fifth Amendment law rests on three dependent variables: (1) the policies that inform the privilege; (2) the appropriate scope of the privilege in light of those policies; and (3) the extent of immunity necessary to satisfy those policies. As you think about *Counselman, Brown*, and the cases that follow, try to assess each variable separately and then in relation to the other two.

Consider the possibility that, depending on what the relevant policies are, the privilege might apply differently to different crimes. Both *Counselman* and *Brown* involved the enforcement of the Interstate Commerce Act, which regulated railroad shipping practices. Does that affect your view of the proper construction of the Fifth Amendment in those cases? How? Recall the *Brown* Court's statement that such regulatory legislation would be unenforceable in the absence of some provision for compelled, immunized testimony. And notice that Justice Field, whose dissent in *Brown* advanced a broad theory of the privilege, was famous for his opinions invalidating state and federal legislation regulating business and economic affairs. The privacy-autonomy right that Field defends so strongly was, in practice, closely tied to a particular vision of *property* rights — a vision that is, to say the least, not widely accepted today.

Whatever the merits of Justice Field's position, at least since *Brown* the privilege has been unavailable unless the witness's testimony could lead to some kind of punishment. Why should the threat of punishment obviate the need to testify truthfully?

As Professor Dolinko notes, our society forces people to testify in a number of other circumstances where testifying would be painful: Witnesses must testify notwithstanding threats of reprisal; they can also be forced to testify against close friends or (for the most part) family members. See David Dolinko, Is There a Rationale for the Privilege against Self-Incrimination?, 33 UCLA L. Rev. 1063, 1093-1095 (1986). Is there any way to square these practices with the privilege? This question arose again in Ullmann v. United States, 350 U.S. 422 (1956). The petitioner in *Ullmann* was given a grant of immunity and called to testify before a grand jury about "attempts to endanger the national security by espionage and conspiracy to commit espionage." The petitioner refused to testify, notwithstanding the immunity grant, and was held in contempt. The Court reaffirmed Brown v. Walker, including the congressional power to extend immunity to state offenses, and rejected the petitioner's attempt to distinguish it:

> Petitioner . . . argues that this case is different from Brown v. Walker because the impact of the disabilities imposed by federal and state authorities and the public in general — such as loss of job, expulsion from labor unions, state registration and investigation statutes, passport eligibility, and general public opprobrium — is so oppressive that the statute does not give him true immunity. This, he alleges, is significantly different from the impact of testifying on the auditor in Brown v. Walker, who could the next day resume his job with reputation unaffected. But, as this Court has often held, the immunity granted need only remove those sanctions which generate the fear justifying invocation of the privilege: "The interdiction of the Fifth Amendment operates only where a witness is asked to incriminate himself — in other words, to give testimony which may possibly expose him to a criminal charge. But if the criminality has already been taken away, the Amendment ceases to apply." Hale v. Henkel, 201 U.S. 43, 67. Here, since the Immunity Act protects a witness who is compelled to answer to the extent of his constitutional immunity, he has of course, when a particular sanction is sought to be imposed against him, the right to claim that it is criminal in nature. . . .

Id. at 430-431. Justices Douglas and Black dissented, in an opinion that struck many of the same notes as Justice Field's dissent in Brown v. Walker:

> The "mischief" to be prevented [by the Fifth Amendment] falls under at least three heads.
> (1) One "mischief" is not only the risk of conviction but the risk of prosecution. . . .
> [T]he statute protects the accused only on account of the "transaction, matter, or thing" concerning which he is compelled to testify and bars the use as evidence of the "testimony so compelled." The forced disclosure may open up vast new vistas for the prosecutor. . . . What related offenses may be disclosed by leads furnished by the confession? How remote need the offense be before the immunity ceases to protect it? . . .
> It is, for example, a crime for a person who is a member of a Communist organization registered under the Subversive Activities Control Act, 64 Stat. 987, 50 U.S.C. §781, to be employed by the United States, to be employed in any defense facility, to

hold office or employment with any labor organization, §5(a)(1), or to apply for a passport or to use a passport. §6(a). The crime under that Act is the application for a passport, the use of a passport, or employment by one of the named agencies, as the case may be. Are those crimes included within the "transaction, matter, or thing" protected by the Immunity Act? . . .

(2) The guarantee against self-incrimination contained in the Fifth Amendment is not only a protection against conviction and prosecution but a safeguard of conscience and human dignity and freedom of expression as well. My view is that the Framers put it beyond the power of Congress to *compel* anyone to confess his crimes. The evil to be guarded against was partly self-accusation under legal compulsion. But that was only a part of the evil. The conscience and dignity of man were also involved. So too was his right to freedom of expression guaranteed by the First Amendment. The Framers, therefore, created the federally protected right of silence and decreed that the law could not be used to pry open one's lips and make him a witness against himself.

A long history and a deep sentiment lay behind this decision. Some of those who came to these shores were Puritans who had known the hated oath ex officio used both by the Star Chamber and the High Commission. See Mary Hume Maguire, Attack of the Common Lawyers on the Oath Ex Officio as Administered in the Ecclesiastical Courts in England, Essays in History and Political Theory (1936), c. VII. They had known the great rebellion of Lilburn, Cartwright and others against those instruments of oppression. . . .

(3) . . . The Fifth Amendment was designed to protect the accused against infamy as well as against prosecution. . . . The history of infamy as a punishment was notorious. Luther had inveighed against excommunication. The Massachusetts Body of Liberties of 1641 had provided in Article 60: "No church censure shall degrade or depose any man from any Civill dignitie, office, or Authoritie he shall have in the Commonwealth." Loss of office, loss of dignity, loss of face were feudal forms of punishment. Infamy was historically considered to be punishment as effective as fine and imprisonment.

The Beccarian attitude toward infamy was a part of the background of the Fifth Amendment. The concept of infamy was explicitly written into it. We need not guess as to that. For the first Clause of the Fifth Amendment contains the concept in haec verba: "No person shall be held to answer for a capital, or otherwise *infamous* crime, unless on a presentment or indictment of a Grand Jury. . . . " (Italics added.) And the third Clause, the one we are concerned with here — "No person . . . shall be compelled in any criminal case to be a witness against himself . . . " — also reflects the revulsion of society at infamy imposed by the State. . . .

. . . The critical point is that the Constitution places the right of silence *beyond the reach of government*. The Fifth Amendment stands between the citizen and his government. When public opinion casts a person into the outer darkness, as happens today when a person is exposed as a Communist, the government brings infamy on the head of the witness when it compels disclosure. That is precisely what the Fifth Amendment prohibits.

Id. at 443-454 (Douglas, J., dissenting).

Justice Douglas suggests that the privilege should be available whenever the witness would be subject to "infamy." What does that mean? If his position were adopted, would courts need to develop a body of doctrine defining what sorts of questioning might produce infamous answers, or would witnesses simply be able to claim the privilege whenever they were asked questions they preferred not to answer? Recall Chief Justice Marshall's ruling in the *Burr* case, quoted at page 753 supra.

Notice the way Justice Douglas' opinion links the Fifth Amendment privilege with First Amendment values. That link has a long history. The Puritans who were forced to testify before the English High Commission were being persecuted for their faith, just as John Lilburne was being persecuted for his politics. Indeed, the preconstitutional history of the privilege against self-incrimination reads like a catalogue of religious and political persecution. See Leonard W. Levy, The Origins of the Fifth Amendment (2d ed. 1986). *Ullmann* arguably falls in the same tradition. Is this the right role for the privilege? Should rules for ordinary criminal cases be made with an eye toward protecting against McCarthyite harassment of political dissidents? For an argument in the affirmative, see Erwin Griswold, The Fifth Amendment Today (1955). For a thorough review of the history of the self-incrimination clause, see Richard H. Helmholz et al., The Privilege against Self-Incrimination (1997).

Today the privilege is rarely invoked in cases with free speech overtones, which may be why the dissenters' argument in *Ullmann* seems to have fallen out of favor. The next case has more to do with criminal conduct than with free speech—though the subject matter was politically charged: the defendants refused to answer questions concerning fraudulent medical deferments in a grand jury investigation of Vietnam War-era violations of the selective service laws.

KASTIGAR v. UNITED STATES

Certiorari to the United States Court of Appeals for the Ninth Circuit
406 U.S. 441 (1972)

MR. JUSTICE POWELL delivered the opinion of the Court.

This case presents the question whether the United States Government may compel testimony from an unwilling witness, who invokes the Fifth Amendment privilege against compulsory self-incrimination, by conferring on the witness immunity from use of the compelled testimony in subsequent criminal proceedings, as well as immunity from use of evidence derived from the testimony.

Petitioners were subpoenaed to appear before a United States grand jury in the Central District of California on February 4, 1971. . . .

Petitioners appeared but refused to answer questions, asserting their privilege against compulsory self-incrimination. They were brought before the District Court, and each persisted in his refusal to answer the grand jury's questions, notwithstanding the grant of immunity. The court found both in contempt, and committed them to the custody of the Attorney General until either they answered the grand jury's questions or the term of the grand jury expired. The Court of Appeals for the Ninth Circuit affirmed. Stewart v. United States, 440 F.2d 954 (C.A.9 1971). This Court granted certiorari to resolve the important question whether testimony may be compelled by granting immunity from the use of compelled testimony and evidence derived therefrom ("use and derivative use" immunity), or whether it is necessary to grant immunity from prosecution for offenses to which compelled testimony relates ("transactional" immunity). . . .

III

Petitioners' . . . contention is that the scope of immunity provided by the federal witness immunity statute, 18 U.S.C. §6002, is not coextensive with the scope of the Fifth Amendment privilege against compulsory self-incrimination, and therefore is not sufficient to supplant the privilege and compel testimony over a claim of the privilege. The statute provides that when a witness is compelled by district court order to testify over a claim of the privilege:

> the witness may not refuse to comply with the order on the basis of his privilege against self-incrimination; but no testimony or other information compelled under the order (or any information directly or indirectly derived from such testimony or other information) may be used against the witness in any criminal case, except a prosecution for perjury, giving a false statement, or otherwise failing to comply with the order.

The constitutional inquiry, rooted in logic and history, as well as in the decisions of this Court, is whether the immunity granted under this statute is coextensive with the scope of the privilege. . . .

Petitioners draw a distinction between statutes that provide transactional immunity and those that provide, as does the statute before us, immunity from use and derivative use. They contend that a statute must at a minimum grant full transactional immunity in order to be coextensive with the scope of the privilege. . . .

The statute's explicit proscription of the use in any criminal case of "testimony or other information compelled under the order (or any information directly or indirectly derived from such testimony or other information)" is consonant with Fifth Amendment standards. We hold that such immunity from use and derivative use is coextensive with the scope of the privilege against self-incrimination, and therefore is sufficient to compel testimony over a claim of the privilege. While a grant of immunity must afford protection commensurate with that afforded by the privilege, it need not be broader. Transactional immunity, which accords full immunity from prosecution for the offense to which the compelled testimony relates, affords the witness considerably broader protection than does the Fifth Amendment privilege. The privilege has never been construed to mean that one who invokes it cannot subsequently be prosecuted. Its sole concern is to afford protection against being "forced to give testimony leading to the infliction of 'penalties affixed to . . . criminal acts.' "[38] Immunity from the use of compelled testimony, as well as evidence derived directly and indirectly therefrom, affords this protection. It prohibits the prosecutorial authorities from using the compelled testimony in *any* respect, and it therefore insures that the testimony cannot lead to the infliction of criminal penalties on the witness. . . .

In Murphy v. Waterfront Commn., 378 U.S. 52 (1964), the Court carefully considered immunity from use of compelled testimony and evidence derived therefrom. The *Murphy* petitioners were subpoenaed to testify at a hearing conducted by the Waterfront Commission of New York Harbor. After refusing to answer certain questions on the ground that the answers might tend to incriminate them, petitioners were granted immunity from prosecution under the laws of New Jersey and New York. They continued to refuse to testify, however, on the ground

---

38. Ullmann v. United States, 350 U.S., at 438-439, quoting Boyd v. United States, 116 U.S., at 634.

that their answers might tend to incriminate them under federal law, to which the immunity did not purport to extend. They were adjudged in civil contempt, and that judgment was affirmed by the New Jersey Supreme Court.

The issue before the Court in *Murphy* was whether New Jersey and New York could compel the witnesses, whom these States had immunized from prosecution under their laws, to give testimony that might then be used to convict them of a federal crime. Since New Jersey and New York had not purported to confer immunity from federal prosecution, the Court was faced with the question what limitations the Fifth Amendment privilege imposed on the prosecutorial powers of the Federal Government, a nonimmunizing sovereign. After undertaking an examination of the policies and purposes of the privilege, the Court overturned the rule that one jurisdiction within our federal structure may compel a witness to give testimony which could be used to convict him of a crime in another jurisdiction.[42] The Court held that the privilege protects state witnesses against incrimination under federal as well as state law, and federal witnesses against incrimination under state as well as federal law. Applying this principle to the state immunity legislation before it, the Court held the constitutional rule to be that:

> [A] state witness may not be compelled to give testimony which may be incriminating under federal law unless the compelled testimony and its fruits cannot be used in any manner by federal officials in connection with a criminal prosecution against him. We conclude, moreover, that in order to implement this constitutional rule and accommodate the interests of the State and Federal Governments in investigating and prosecuting crime, the Federal Government must be prohibited from making any such use of compelled testimony and its fruits.

The Court emphasized that this rule left the state witness and the Federal Government, against which the witness had immunity only from the *use* of the compelled testimony and evidence derived therefrom, "in substantially the same position as if the witness had claimed his privilege in the absence of a state grant of immunity." Ibid. . . .

IV

. . . Petitioners argue that use and derivative-use immunity will not adequately protect a witness from various possible incriminating uses of the compelled testimony: for example, the prosecutor or other law enforcement officials may obtain leads, names of witnesses, or other information not otherwise available that might result in a prosecution. It will be difficult and perhaps impossible, the argument goes, to identify . . . the subtle ways in which the compelled testimony may disadvantage a witness. . . .

This argument presupposes that the statute's prohibition will prove impossible to enforce. The statute provides a sweeping proscription of any use, direct or indirect, of the compelled testimony and any information derived therefrom: "[N]o

42. Reconsideration of the rule that the Fifth Amendment privilege does not protect a witness in one jurisdiction against being compelled to give testimony that could be used to convict him in another jurisdiction was made necessary by the decision in Malloy v. Hogan, 378 U.S. 1 (1964), in which the Court held the Fifth Amendment privilege applicable to the States through the Fourteenth Amendment. Murphy v. Waterfront Commn, 378 U.S., at 57.

testimony or other information compelled under the order (or any information directly or indirectly derived from such testimony or other information) may be used against the witness in any criminal case." This total prohibition on use provides a comprehensive safeguard, barring the use of compelled testimony as an "investigatory lead,"[50] and also barring the use of any evidence obtained by focusing investigation on a witness as a result of his compelled disclosures.

A person accorded this immunity under 18 U.S.C. §6002, and subsequently prosecuted, is not dependent for the preservation of his rights upon the integrity and good faith of the prosecuting authorities. As stated in *Murphy:* "Once a defendant demonstrates that he has testified, under a state grant of immunity, to matters related to the federal prosecution, the federal authorities have the burden of showing that their evidence is not tainted by establishing that they had an independent, legitimate source for the disputed evidence." 378 U.S., at 79 n. 18. This burden of proof, which we reaffirm as appropriate, is not limited to a negation of taint; rather, it imposes on the prosecution the affirmative duty to prove that the evidence it proposes to use is derived from a legitimate source wholly independent of the compelled testimony. . . .

The statutory [immunity] is analogous to the Fifth Amendment requirement in cases of coerced confessions. A coerced confession, as revealing of leads as testimony given in exchange for immunity, is inadmissible in a criminal trial, but it does not bar prosecution. . . .

There can be no justification in reason or policy for holding that the Constitution requires an amnesty grant where, acting pursuant to statute and accompanying safeguards, testimony is compelled in exchange for immunity from use and derivative use when no such amnesty is required where the government, acting without colorable right, coerces a defendant into incriminating himself.

We conclude that the immunity provided by 18 U.S.C. §6002 leaves the witness and the prosecutorial authorities in substantially the same position as if the witness had claimed the Fifth Amendment privilege. The immunity therefore is coextensive with the privilege and suffices to supplant it. The judgment of the Court of Appeals for the Ninth Circuit accordingly is affirmed.

MR. JUSTICE BRENNAN and MR. JUSTICE REHNQUIST took no part in the consideration or decision of this case.

MR. JUSTICE MARSHALL, dissenting.

Today the Court holds that the United States may compel a witness to give incriminating testimony, and subsequently prosecute him for crimes to which that testimony relates. I cannot believe the Fifth Amendment permits that result.

The Fifth Amendment gives a witness an absolute right to resist interrogation, if the testimony sought would tend to incriminate him. A grant of immunity may strip the witness of the right to refuse to testify, but only if it is broad enough to eliminate all possibility that the testimony will in fact operate to incriminate him. It must put him in precisely the same position, vis-a-vis the government that has compelled his testimony, as he would have been in had he remained silent in reliance on the privilege. . . .

The Court recognizes that an immunity statute must be tested by that standard. . . . I assume, moreover, that in theory that test would be met by

---

50. See, e.g., Albertson v. Subversive Activities Control Board, 382 U.S., at 80.

a complete ban on the use of the compelled testimony, including all derivative use, however remote and indirect. But I cannot agree that a ban on use will in practice be total, if it remains open for the government to convict the witness on the basis of evidence derived from a legitimate independent source. The Court asserts that the witness is adequately protected by a rule imposing on the government a heavy burden of proof if it would establish the independent character of evidence to be used against the witness. But in light of the inevitable uncertainties of the factfinding process, a greater margin of protection is required. . . . That margin can be provided only by immunity from prosecution for the offenses to which the testimony relates, i.e., transactional immunity.

I do not see how it can suffice merely to put the burden of proof on the government. . . . A witness who suspects that his compelled testimony was used to develop a lead will be hard pressed indeed to ferret out the evidence necessary to prove it. And of course it is no answer to say he need not prove it, for though the Court puts the burden of proof on the government, the government will have no difficulty in meeting its burden by mere assertion if the witness produces no contrary evidence. The good faith of the prosecuting authorities is thus the sole safeguard of the witness' rights. . . . [And] even their good faith is not a sufficient safeguard. For the paths of information through the investigative bureaucracy may well be long and winding, and even a prosecutor acting in the best of faith cannot be certain that somewhere in the depths of his investigative apparatus, often including hundreds of employees, there was not some prohibited use of the compelled testimony. The Court today sets out a loose net to trap tainted evidence and prevent its use against the witness, but it accepts an intolerably great risk that tainted evidence will in fact slip through that net. . . .

[The dissenting opinion of Justice Douglas is omitted.]

NOTES AND QUESTIONS

1. The Court consistently asserts that for an immunity grant to displace the privilege, it must be "co-extensive" with the privilege. What does that mean? Consider the arguments raised by Justice Field's dissent in *Brown* (page 759 supra) and Justice Douglas' dissent in *Ullmann* (page 760 supra) as well as Justice Marshall's dissent in *Kastigar*.

2. Justice Marshall argued that, in practice, the kind of immunity the *Kastigar* Court approved would leave defendants in a worse position than before their immunized testimony: the government would use the immunized testimony to generate new leads and to identify new witnesses, and courts would be unable to separate what *was* the fruit of immunized testimony from what was *not*.

Two Court of Appeals cases from the early 1990s raise the question whether Justice Marshall's prediction has proved accurate. The first is United States v. North, 910 F.2d 843, *modified*, 920 F.2d 940 (D.C. Cir. 1990). Defendant Oliver North gave immunized testimony on the Iran-contra affair before a congressional committee on national television. North's prosecutor made no direct use of the testimony; indeed, the prosecution took elaborate steps to ensure that his staff avoided all exposure to the immunized testimony. At trial, the independent counsel relied on witnesses who had testified before the grand jury prior to North's immunized congressional testimony. But because the trial witnesses were found to have been exposed to North's immunized testimony, the court of appeals remanded to the district court with instructions to analyze the government's case "line by line" to ensure that neither its content nor the source of the testimony was derived from North's testimony. That being an impossible task, the charges were ultimately dismissed.

The second is United States v. Helmsley, 941 F.2d 71 (2d Cir. 1991). In *Helmsley*, a newspaper article covering the defendant's immunized state testimony prompted a reporter to investigate the possibility that Helmsley had misappropriated corporate funds for her own use. The resulting article contributed to a subsequent federal prosecution for tax fraud. The court of appeals found the relationship between the immunized testimony and the subsequent prosecution to be too attenuated to violate the Fifth Amendment.

Are *North* and *Helmsley* consistent? If not, which approach do you prefer?

3. Notice how thoroughly Justice Douglas's position in *Ullmann* has been rejected. Both the *Kastigar* majority and Justice Marshall's dissent seem to agree that all the privilege requires is to keep the government from forcing people to testify and then somehow using that testimony to help convict them of crime. Compelling people to talk about the crimes they've committed is perfectly permissible as long as their statements do not advantage the government in any subsequent criminal prosecution of the witness. What does this say about the values that the privilege now serves? One common argument for the privilege is that it is wrong for the state to force an individual to pass judgment on himself. See Robert S. Gerstein, The Demise of *Boyd:* Self-Incrimination and Private Papers in the Burger Court, 27 UCLA L. Rev. 343 (1979); R. Kent Greenawalt, Silence as a Moral and Constitutional Right, 23 Wm. & Mary L. Rev. 15 (1981). Isn't a defendant passing judgment on himself anytime he confesses to crime, whether or not the confession is immunized?

4. In Murphy v. Waterfront Commission of New York Harbor, 378 U.S. 52 (1964), discussed in *Kastigar,* Justice Goldberg's opinion for the Court addressed the policies then perceived to underlie the privilege:

> The privilege against self-incrimination "registers an important advance in the development of our liberty — 'one of the great landmarks in man's struggle to make himself civilized.'" Ullmann v. United States, 350 U.S. 422, 426.[4] It reflects many of our fundamental values and most noble aspirations: our unwillingness to subject those suspected of crime to the cruel trilemma of self-accusation, perjury or contempt; our preference for an accusatorial rather than an inquisitorial system of criminal justice; our fear that self-incriminating statements will be elicited by inhumane treatment and abuses; our sense of fair play which dictates "a fair state-individual balance by requiring the government to leave the individual alone until good cause is shown for disturbing him and by requiring the government in its contest with the individual to shoulder the entire load," 8 Wigmore, Evidence (McNaughton rev., 1961), 317; our respect for the inviolability of the human personality and of the right of each individual "to a private enclave where he may lead a private life," United States v. Grunewald, 233 F.2d 556, 581-582 (Frank, J., dissenting), *rev'd* 353 U.S. 391; our distrust of self-deprecatory statements; and our realization that the privilege, while sometimes "a shelter to the guilty," is often "a protection to the innocent." Quinn v. United States, 349 U.S. 155, 162.

---

4. The quotation is from Erwin N. Griswold, The Fifth Amendment Today 7 (1955).

Consider Professor Arenella's analysis of Justice Goldberg's effort to articulate the policies of the privilege:

> An examination of Justice Goldberg's fundamental values reveals three obvious points. First, some of them seem to overlap with each other (e.g., numbers two and four; or numbers one, three, and six). Second, many of these values are stated so abstractly that they can be used to justify almost any result. For example, what does it mean to speak of "our preference for an accusatorial rather than an inquisitorial system" (number two)? What criteria should a court use to determine whether state practices have upset a fair state-individual balance (number four)? Finally, this list of fundamental values suggests that the privilege against self-incrimination protects both *substantive values* (e.g., privacy, human dignity, and moral autonomy) and *accusatorial process norms* (e.g., a fair state-individual balance of advantage and adversarial determination of guilt) whose applicability may vary with the procedural context involved and whose significance may depend on the countervailing state interests at stake. Thus, when the Court confronts procedural contexts and state objectives not envisioned by the Constitution's framers, it must first identify which fifth amendment values are implicated and what state interests are at stake that might justify some impairment of these values. In other words, the Court must inevitably engage in a balancing analysis of these competing interests before it can interpret fifth amendment concepts like "compulsion" or "to be a witness against himself."

Peter Arenella, *Schmerber* and the Privilege against Self-Incrimination: A Reappraisal, 20 Am. Crim. L. Rev. 31, 37 (1982).

5. The Court recently addressed *Murphy*'s list of policies underlying the privilege. United States v. Balsys, 542 U.S. 666 (1998), held that the Fifth Amendment does not extend to the risk of prosecution by a foreign nation. In the course of his opinion for the Court, Justice Souter wrote:

> The *Murphy* majority opens its discussion with a catalog of "Policies of the Privilege." . . . Some of the policies listed would seem to point no further than domestic arrangements and so raise no basis for any privilege looking beyond fear of domestic prosecution. Others however, might suggest a concern broad enough to encompass foreign prosecutions and accordingly to support a more expansive theory of the privilege. . . .
>
> . . . The most general of *Murphy*'s policy items ostensibly suggesting protection as comprehensive as that sought by Balsys is listed in the opinion as "the inviolability of the human personality and . . . the right of each individual to a private enclave where he may lead a private life." . . . If in fact these values were reliable guides to the actual scope of protection under the Clause, they would be seen to demand a very high degree of protection indeed: "inviolability" is, after all, an uncompromising term, and we know as well from Fourth Amendment law as from a layman's common sense that breaches of privacy are complete at the moment of illicit intrusion, whatever use may or may not later be made of their fruits.
>
> The Fifth Amendment tradition, however, offers no such degree of protection. If the Government is ready to provide the requisite use and derivative use immunity, the protection goes no further: no violation of personality is recognized and no claim of privilege will avail. One might reply that the choice of the word "inviolability" was just unfortunate; while testimonial integrity may not be inviolable, it is sufficiently served by requiring the Government to pay a price in the form of use (and derivative use) immunity before a refusal to testify will be overruled. But that answer overlooks the

fact that when a witness's response will raise no fear of criminal penalty, there is no protection for testimonial privacy at all.

Thus, what we find in practice is not the protection of personal testimonial inviolability, but a conditional protection of testimonial privacy subject to basic limits recognized before the framing and refined through immunity doctrine in the intervening years. Since the Judiciary could not recognize fear of foreign prosecution and at the same time preserve the Government's existing rights to seek testimony in exchange for immunity (because domestic courts could not enforce the immunity abroad), it follows that extending protection as Balsys requests would change the balance of private and governmental interests that has seemingly been accepted for as long as there has been Fifth Amendment doctrine. . . .

For a discussion of self-incrimination in the international context, see Diane Marie Amann, A Whipsaw Cuts Both Ways: The Privilege against Self-Incrimination in an International Court, 45 UCLA L. Rev. 1201 (1998).

6. Perhaps because the Court has not plainly specified what value or values it is trying to advance in its Fifth Amendment cases, a large and constantly growing literature seeks to explain why we have a privilege against self-incrimination. For a sampling, see Robert S. Gerstein, Privacy and Self-Incrimination, 80 Ethics 87 (1970) (privilege protects individual privacy and autonomy); R. Kent Greenawalt, Silence as a Moral and Constitutional Right, 23 Wm. & Mary L. Rev. 15 (1981) (privilege protects against forced self-judgment); Stephen J. Schulhofer, Some Kind Words for the Privilege against Self-Incrimination, 26 Val. U. L. Rev. 311 (1991) (privilege protects innocent defendants); Louis Michael Seidman, Rubashov's Question: Self-Incrimination and the Problem of Coerced Preferences, 2 Yale J.L. & Human. 149 (1990) (privilege prevents government from coercing "consent" to punishment); William J. Stuntz, Self-Incrimination and Excuse, 88 Colum. L. Rev. 1227 (1988) (privilege bars compelled testimony where ordinary person would likely lie); George C. Thomas III & Marshall D. Bilder, Aristotle's Paradox and the Self-Incrimination Puzzle, 82 J. Crim. L. & Criminology 243 (1991) (privilege protects free choice). See also David Dolinko, Is There a Rationale for the Privilege against Self-Incrimination?, 33 UCLA L. Rev. 1063 (1986) (criticizing all major theories of the privilege); Donald A. Dripps, Self-Incrimination and Self-Preservation: A Skeptical View, 1991 U. Ill. L. Rev. 329 (criticizing theories of the privilege based on self-preservation); Ronald J. Allen, The Simpson Affair, Reform of the Criminal Justice Process, and Magic Bullets, 67 U. Colo. L. Rev. 989 (1996).

B.   *The Contours of the Privilege Against Self-Incrimination*

In order to make out a claim that the privilege against self-incrimination was violated, a claimant must satisfy the privilege's three elements, which track its three clauses: compulsion ("no person . . . shall be compelled"), incrimination ("in any criminal case"), and testimony ("to be a witness against himself"). The claimant must also explicitly claim the privilege — save only for three exceptions: police interrogation, considered in Section D infra; a peculiar and rarely used exception that excuses statutory reporting requirements for "inherently suspect classes," considered in Section C infra; and cases in which exercising one's rights would be penalized. See, e.g., Garrity v. New Jersey, 385 U.S. 493 (1967). Apart from these exceptions, a witness must invoke the Fifth Amendment on being questioned, and a failure to do so is deemed a waiver. Moreover, once a witness answers a question, the witness cannot refuse to be examined further concerning the general area of the answer — "Disclosure of a fact waives the privilege as to details." Rogers v. United States, 340 U.S. 367, 373 (1951). As to each subsequent question asked, the issue is whether the answer might subject the witness to a "real danger of further crimination," id. at 379, beyond that contained in the original answer. The *Rogers* test is not easy to apply, however, as the trial judge must make very refined appraisals of the effect of any admission as well as the potential effect of any subsequent statements. The lower courts have also required subsequent disclosure where an answer to a question would result in a distortion of truth. For a discussion, see Note, Testimonial Waiver of the Privilege against Self Incrimination, 92 Harv. L. Rev. 1752 (1979).

1. "No Person ... Shall Be Compelled": The Meaning of Compulsion

The paradigmatic case of Fifth Amendment compulsion is sworn testimony under threat of legal penalty. A person called as a witness at a trial is required to testify by a state actor — the judge — and will be held in contempt if he or she refuses to answer questions. The same analysis applies to the many administrative or legislative settings in which witnesses are ordered to respond to questions or face legal sanctions.

Fifth Amendment compulsion extends beyond these obvious cases. As we will see in Section D below, the Supreme Court has found that jailhouse interrogation is sufficiently coercive to amount to compulsion, even though the police have no formal authority to require a suspect to speak. And in Lefkowitz v. Turley, 414 U.S. 70 (1973), the Court struck down a New York statute that conditioned all state contracts on contractors' willingness to waive their Fifth Amendment rights if asked to testify about the subject matter of their contracts. According to the Court, the rule in *Lefkowitz* constituted Fifth Amendment compulsion. So did a state statute decreeing that government employees should lose their jobs if they invoked their Fifth Amendment rights in response to questions within the scope of their employment. See Garrity v. New Jersey, 385 U.S. 493 (1967). And so did the threat of disbarment for a lawyer. See Spevack v. Klein, 385 U.S. 511 (1967).

Perhaps unsurprisingly, compulsion receives its broadest construction when the witness in question is the defendant at a criminal trial. In Griffin v. California, 380 U.S. 609 (1965), the Court forbade the prosecutor from commenting to the jury on the defendant's failure to take the stand. Such comment had been common in a number of jurisdictions for as long as criminal defendants had been permitted to testify under oath. Nevertheless, the Court held that prosecutorial comment on the defendant's silence impermissibly penalizes the defendant's exercise of his Fifth Amendment rights — and the threat of such comments puts pressure on the defendant to testify, hence to waive those rights. In Carter v. Kentucky, 450 U.S. 288 (1981), the Court concluded that defendants who choose not to testify also have the right to have their juries instructed *not* to draw inferences from their silence. It is not clear how much difference the rules in *Griffin* and *Carter* make. If the prosecution has put on a reasonably strong case, everyone in the courtroom, jurors included, knows who is in the best position to rebut it. A reasonably strong case that goes unanswered by the defendant almost always leads to a conviction, no matter how often or how strongly the jury is admonished not to infer guilt from silence. Perhaps the chief effect of the cautionary instructions *Griffin* and *Carter* require is to undermine jurors' faith in judges' instructions.

Outside of defendants in criminal trials, the person who wishes to claim the privilege may be examined, and the privilege must be invoked in response to the relevant questions. Adverse inferences from the refusal to testify are permissible. See, e.g., Baxter v. Palmigiano, 425 U.S. 308 (1976) (prison authorities are entitled to draw adverse inferences from silence in prison disciplinary proceedings). Such proceedings do not "compel" testimony, under the Court's cases. In Ohio Adult Parole Authority v. Woodward, 523 U.S. 272 (1998), the Court considered whether Ohio's clemency proceedings for inmates under sentence of death violated the Fifth Amendment:

> Respondent . . . presses on us the Court of Appeals' conclusion that the provision of a voluntary inmate interview, without the benefit of counsel or a grant of immunity . . . , implicates the inmate's Fifth and Fourteenth Amendment right not to incriminate himself. . . . In our opinion, the procedures of the Authority do not under any view violate the Fifth Amendment privilege. . . .
>
> Assuming . . . that the Authority will draw adverse inferences from respondent's refusal to answer questions—which it may do in a civil proceeding without offending the Fifth Amendment—we do not think that respondent's testimony at a clemency interview would be "compelled" within the meaning of the Fifth Amendment. It is difficult to see how a voluntary interview could "compel" respondent to speak. He merely faces a choice quite similar to the sorts of choices that a criminal defendant must make in the course of criminal proceedings, none of which has ever been held to violate the Fifth Amendment.
>
> Long ago we held that a defendant who took the stand in his own defense could not claim the privilege against self-incrimination when the prosecution sought to cross-examine. . . .
>
> A defendant whose motion for acquittal at the close of the Government's case is denied must then elect whether to stand on his motion or to put on a defense, with the accompanying risk that in doing so he will augment the Government's case against him. In each of these situations, there are undoubted pressures—generated by the strength of the Government's case against him—pushing the criminal defendant to testify. But it has never been suggested that such pressures constitute "compulsion" for Fifth Amendment purposes.

Id. at 285-287. The Court went on to discuss its holding in Williams v. Florida, 399 U.S. 78 (1970). Florida law required defendants to give notice prior to trial that they planned to raise an alibi defense; the defendant in *Williams* claimed such mandatory notice amounted to compelled self-incrimination. The Court disagreed, reasoning that the pressure involved was no different than the kind of pressure that defendants often bear in a criminal trial process due to the strength of the government's evidence and arguments. The pressure to testify in the clemency proceeding in *Woodard*, the Court concluded, was similar.

With *Woodard* and *Williams*, compare McKune v. Lile, 536 U.S. 24 (2002). The facts in *McKune* were as follows:

> In 1982, respondent lured a high school student into his car as she was returning home from school. At gunpoint, respondent forced the victim to perform oral sodomy

on him and then drove to a field where he raped her. After the sexual assault, the victim went to her school, where, crying and upset, she reported the crime. The police arrested respondent and recovered on his person the weapon he used to facilitate the crime. Although respondent maintained that the sexual intercourse was consensual, a jury convicted him of rape, aggravated sodomy, and aggravated kidnaping. . . .

In 1994, a few years before respondent was scheduled to be released, prison officials ordered him to participate in a Sexual Abuse Treatment Program (SATP). As part of the program, participating inmates are required to complete and sign an "Admission of Responsibility" form, in which they discuss and accept responsibility for the crime for which they have been sentenced. Participating inmates also are required to complete a sexual history form, which details all prior sexual activities, regardless of whether such activities constitute uncharged criminal offenses. A polygraph examination is used to verify the accuracy and completeness of the offender's sexual history.

While information obtained from participants advances the SATP's rehabilitative goals, the information is not privileged. Kansas leaves open the possibility that new evidence might be used against sex offenders in future criminal proceedings. In addition, Kansas law requires the SATP staff to report any uncharged sexual offenses involving minors to law enforcement authorities. Although there is no evidence that incriminating information has ever been disclosed under the SATP, the release of information is a possibility.

Department officials informed respondent that if he refused to participate in the SATP, his privilege status would be reduced from Level III to Level I. As part of this reduction, respondent's visitation rights, earnings, work opportunities, ability to send money to family, canteen expenditures, access to a personal television, and other privileges automatically would be curtailed. In addition, respondent would be transferred to a maximum-security unit, where his movement would be more limited, he would be moved from a two-person to a four-person cell, and he would be in a potentially more dangerous environment.

Id. at 29-30. By a 5–4 vote, the Supreme Court held that these facts did not constitute Fifth Amendment compulsion. Justice Kennedy, speaking for himself, the Chief Justice, and Justices Scalia and Thomas, stressed the large degree of control prison officials have over prisoners:

The SATP does not compel prisoners to incriminate themselves in violation of the Constitution. . . . The consequences in question here — a transfer to another prison where television sets are not placed in each inmate's cell, where exercise facilities are not readily available, and where work and wage opportunities are more limited — are not ones that compel a prisoner to speak about his past crimes despite a desire to remain silent. The fact that these consequences are imposed on prisoners, rather than ordinary citizens, moreover, is important in weighing respondent's constitutional claim. . . .

In the present case, respondent's decision not to participate in the Kansas SATP did not extend his term of incarceration. Nor did his decision affect his eligibility for good-time credits or parole. Respondent instead complains that if he remains silent about his past crimes, he will be transferred from the medium-security unit — where the program is conducted — to a less desirable maximum-security unit.

No one contends, however, that the transfer is intended to punish prisoners for exercising their Fifth Amendment rights. Rather, the limitation on these rights is incidental to Kansas' legitimate penological reason for the transfer: Due to limited space, inmates who do not participate in their respective programs will be moved out of the facility where the programs are held to make room for other inmates. As the Secretary of Corrections has explained, "it makes no sense to have someone who's not participating in a program taking up a bed in a setting where someone else who may be willing to participate in a program could occupy that bed and participate in a program." App. 99.

Respondent also complains that he will be demoted from Level III to Level I status as a result of his decision not to participate. This demotion means the loss of his personal television; less access to prison organizations and the gym area; a reduction in certain pay opportunities and canteen privileges; and restricted visitation rights. An essential tool of prison administration, however, is the authority to offer inmates various incentives to behave. The Constitution accords prison officials wide latitude to bestow or revoke these perquisites as they see fit. . . . [B]y virtue of their convictions, inmates must expect significant restrictions, inherent in prison life, on rights and privileges free citizens take for granted.

. . . [R]elying on the so-called penalty cases, respondent treats the fact of his incarceration as if it were irrelevant. See, e.g., Garrity v. New Jersey, 385 U.S. 493 (1967); Spevack v. Klein, 385 U.S. 511 (1967). Those cases, however, involved free citizens given the choice between invoking the Fifth Amendment privilege and sustaining their economic livelihood. See, e.g., id., at 516 ("Threat of disbarment and the loss of professional standing, professional reputation, and of livelihood are powerful forms of compulsion"). Those principles are not easily extended to the prison context, where inmates surrender upon incarceration their rights to pursue a livelihood and to contract freely with the State, as well as many other basic freedoms. The persons who asserted rights in *Garrity* and *Spevack* had not been convicted of a crime. It would come as a surprise if *Spevack* stands for the proposition that when a lawyer has been disbarred by reason of a final criminal conviction, the court or agency considering reinstatement of the right to practice law could not consider that the disbarred attorney has admitted his guilt and expressed contrition. Indeed, this consideration is often given dispositive weight by this Court itself on routine motions for reinstatement. The current case is more complex, of course, in that respondent is also required to discuss other criminal acts for which he might still be liable for prosecution. On this point, however, there is still a critical distinction between the instant case and *Garrity* or *Spevack*. Unlike those cases, respondent here is asked to discuss other past crimes as part of a legitimate rehabilitative program conducted within prison walls.

To reject out of hand these considerations would be to ignore the State's interests in offering rehabilitation programs and providing for the efficient administration of its prisons. There is no indication that the SATP is an elaborate attempt to avoid the protections offered by the privilege against compelled self-incrimination. Rather, the program serves an important social purpose. It would be bitter medicine to treat as irrelevant the State's legitimate interests and to invalidate the SATP on the ground that it incidentally burdens an inmate's right to remain silent. . . .

Id. at 35-41 (plurality opinion).

Justice O'Connor provided the fifth vote for the result in *McKune*. She concluded that Fifth Amendment compulsion was broader than Justice Kennedy's opinion would have it—but not broad enough to encompass the situation in *McKune*.

. . . Our precedents establish that certain types of penalties are capable of coercing incriminating testimony: termination of employment, Uniformed Sanitation Men Assn., Inc. v. Commissioner of Sanitation of City of New York, 392 U.S. 280 (1968), the loss of a professional license, Spevack v. Klein, 385 U.S. 511 (1967), ineligibility to receive government contracts, Lefkowitz v. Turley, 414 U.S. 70

(1973), and the loss of the right to participate in political associations and to hold public office, Lefkowitz v. Cunningham, 431 U.S. 801 (1977). All of these penalties, however, are far more significant than those facing respondent here.

The first three of these so-called "penalty cases" involved the potential loss of one's livelihood, either through the loss of employment, loss of a professional license essential to employment, or loss of business through government contracts. In *Lefkowitz* we held that the loss of government contracts was constitutionally equivalent to the loss of a profession because "[a government contractor] lives off his contracting fees just as surely as a state employee lives off his salary." 414 U.S. at 83. To support oneself in one's chosen profession is one of the most important abilities a person can have. A choice between incriminating oneself and being deprived of one's livelihood is the very sort of choice that is likely to compel someone to be a witness against himself. The choice presented in the last case, *Cunningham*, implicated not only political influence and prestige, but also the First Amendment right to run for office and to participate in political associations. 431 U.S. at 807-808. In holding that the penalties in that case constituted compulsion for Fifth Amendment purposes, we properly referred to those consequences as "grave." Id., at 807.

I do not believe the consequences facing respondent in this case are serious enough to compel him to be a witness against himself. These consequences involve a reduction in incentive level, and a corresponding transfer from a medium-security to a maximum-security part of the prison. In practical terms, these changes involve restrictions on the personal property respondent can keep in his cell, a reduction in his visitation privileges, a reduction in the amount of money he can spend in the canteen, and a reduction in the wage he can earn through prison employment. These changes in living conditions seem to me minor. Because the prison is responsible for caring for respondent's basic needs, his ability to support himself is not implicated by the reduction in wages he would suffer as a result. While his visitation is reduced as a result of his failure to incriminate himself, he still retains the ability to see his attorney, his family, and members of the clergy. The limitation on the possession of personal items, as well as the amount that respondent is allowed to spend at the canteen, may make his prison experience more unpleasant, but seems very unlikely to actually compel him to incriminate himself.

Id. at 49-51 (O'Connor, J., concurring in the judgment).

Both the plurality and concurring opinions in *McKune* emphasize the fact that people in the claimant's position — prison inmates — regularly face burdens similar to those imposed for failure to participate in the prison's rehabilitation program for sexual offenders. But does that fact really distinguish *McKune* from the so-called "penalty cases" Justices Kennedy and O'Connor cite? After all, employees regularly face the risk of losing their jobs, in settings that have nothing to do with the privilege against self-incrimination. Why isn't that risk the same as the risk of being assigned to a maximum security prison?

There is an argument that the Court's cases have it backward — that the threat of losing one's government job should *not* amount to Fifth Amendment compulsion, but the threat of assignment to a more unpleasant prison *should*. Consider: The Fifth Amendment claimants in Garrity v. New Jersey were police officers; they were asked to testify about taking bribes in the course of an investigation of police corruption. State law required that they testify in such circumstances or else lose their jobs. That threat amounted to compulsion, in the Court's view. But suppose the *Garrity* claimants had been private security guards and the corruption investigation was being run by their employer, a private corporation. Plainly, the private-sector employer could fire any security guards who refused to answer the employer's questions. Equally plainly, the security guards would have no valid Fifth Amendment claim on these facts. Why should government employees be treated differently? Shouldn't a police department have as much right to weed out corrupt or brutal officers as a private security company? Notice that no such argument can be made in *McKune*. There is no private-sector analogue to the penalties imposed on the prisoner in *McKune*, because private actors are not allowed to incarcerate people: the state has a monopoly on criminal punishment. It has no such monopoly on employment. Why doesn't Fifth Amendment compulsion treat disabilities only the state can impose more seriously than disabilities that private employers can (and do) impose?

2. "In Any Criminal Case": The Meaning of Incrimination

The Fifth Amendment states that no one "shall be compelled *in any criminal case* to be a witness against himself" (emphasis added). The phrase "in any criminal case" is most naturally read to refer to the procedural setting in which the testimony takes place. Historically, that is not how the phrase has been construed. Rather, "in any criminal case" refers not to the timing or context of the question but to the consequences of a truthful answer. If the witness's answer poses a sufficiently serious risk of criminal punishment (and if the other two elements — compulsion and testimony — are satisfied), the privilege applies. If not, it doesn't. That is the basic meaning of "incrimination" in Fifth Amendment law.

That definition gives rise to two basic questions: What counts as criminal punishment? And how serious must the risk of criminal punishment be in order to trigger the privilege? On the first question, the courts have been less than consistent. On the one hand, there is a long doctrinal tradition, going back to Boyd v. United States, 116 U.S. 616 (1886), holding that various sorts of civil forfeiture proceedings should be deemed criminal for purposes of Fifth Amendment law. In more recent cases, however, the Court has emphasized the primary importance of legislative intent when classifying penalties as civil or criminal under the Fifth Amendment. United States v. Ward, 448 U.S. 242 (1980), involved a statute requiring any ship or facility that spilled oil into navigable waters to report to the relevant federal authorities. The statute gave the reported information "use immunity" from criminal prosecution, but a different subsection allowed the imposition of a "civil" monetary fine for the relevant conduct. Coincidentally, an 1899 statute made the same conduct a crime. The Court rejected Ward's contention that the statute's reporting requirements violated the Fifth Amendment if used to support the civil penalty.

UNITED STATES v. WARD, 448 U.S. 242, 248-256 (1980): This Court has often stated that the question whether a particular statutorily-defined penalty is civil or criminal is a matter of statutory construction. See, e.g., One Lot Emerald Cut Stones v. United States, 409 U.S. 232, 237 (1972). . . . Our inquiry in this regard has traditionally proceeded on two levels. First, we have set out to determine whether Congress, in establishing the penalizing mechanism, indicated either expressly or impliedly a preference for one label or the other. See [id.], at 236-237. Second, where Congress has indicated an intention to establish a civil penalty, we have inquired further whether the statutory scheme was so punitive either in purpose or effect as to negate that intention. See Flemming v. Nestor, 363 U.S. 603, 617-621 (1960). In regard to this latter inquiry, we have noted that "only the clearest proof could suffice to establish the unconstitutionality of a statute on such a ground." Id., at 617. See also Rex Trailer Co. v. United States, 350 U.S. 148, 154 (1956).

As for our first inquiry in the present case, we believe it quite clear that Congress intended to impose a civil penalty upon persons in Ward's position. Initially, and importantly, Congress labeled the sanction authorized in §311(b)(6) a "civil penalty," a label that takes on added significance given its juxtaposition with the criminal penalties set forth in the immediately preceding subparagraph, §311(b)(5). Thus, we have no doubt that Congress intended to allow imposition of penalties under §311(b)(6) without regard to the procedural protections and restrictions available in criminal prosecutions.

We turn then to consider whether Congress, despite its manifest intention to establish a civil, remedial mechanism, nevertheless provided for sanctions so punitive as to "transfor[m] what was clearly intended as a civil remedy into a criminal penalty." Rex Trailer Co. v. United States, supra, at 154. In making this determination, both the District Court and the Court of Appeals found it useful to refer to the seven considerations listed in Kennedy v. Mendoza-Martinez, [372 U.S. 144,] at 168-169. This list of considerations, while certainly neither exhaustive nor dispositive, . . . provides some guidance in the present case.[7]

Without setting forth here our assessment of each of the seven *Mendoza-Martinez* factors, we think only one, the fifth, aids respondent. That is a consideration of whether "the behavior to which [the penalty] applies is already a crime." 372 U.S., at 168-169. In this regard, respondent contends that §13 of the Rivers and Harbors Appropriation Act of 1899, 33 U.S.C. §407, makes criminal the precise conduct penalized in the present case. Moreover, respondent points out that at least one federal court has held that §13 of the Rivers and Harbors Appropriation Act defines a "strict liability crime," for which the Government need prove no scienter. See United States v. White Fuel Corp., 498 F.2d 619 (1st Cir. 1974). According to respondent, this confirms the lower court's conclusion that this fifth factor "falls clearly in favor of a finding that [§311(b)(6)] is criminal in nature." 598 F.2d, at 1193.

While we agree that this consideration seems to point toward a finding that §311(b)(6) is criminal in nature, that indication is not as strong as it seems at first blush. We have noted on a number of occasions that "Congress may impose both a criminal and a civil sanction in respect to the same act or omission." . . . One Lot Emerald Cut Stones v. United States, supra, at 235. Moreover, in Helvering [v. Mitchell, 303 U.S. 391 (1938)] where we held a 50% penalty for tax fraud to be civil, we found it quite significant that "the Revenue Act of 1928 contains two separate and distinct provisions imposing sanctions," and that "these appear in different parts of the statute. . . ." 303 U.S., at 404. See also One Lot Emerald Cut Stones v. United States, supra, at 236-237. To the extent that we found significant the separation of civil and criminal penalties within the same statute, we believe

---

7. The standards set forth were "[w]hether the sanction involves an affirmative disability or restraint, whether it has historically been regarded as a punishment, whether it comes into play only on a finding of *scienter*, whether its operation will promote the traditional aims of punishment—retribution and deterrence, whether the behavior to which it applies is already a crime, whether an alternative purpose to which it may rationally be connected is assignable for it, and whether it appears excessive in relation to the alternative purpose assigned. . . ." 372 U.S., at 168-169 (footnotes omitted).

that the placement of criminal penalties in one statute and the placement of civil penalties in another statute enacted 70 years later tends to dilute the force of the fifth *Mendoza-Martinez* criterion in this case.

In sum, we believe that the factors set forth in *Mendoza-Martinez*, while neither exhaustive nor conclusive on the issue, are in no way sufficient to render unconstitutional the congressional classification of the penalty established in §311(b)(6) as civil. Nor are we persuaded by any of respondent's other arguments that he has offered the "clearest proof" that the penalty here in question is punitive in either purpose or effect. . . .

Our conclusion that §311(b)(6) does not trigger all the protections afforded by the Constitution to a criminal defendant does not completely dispose of this case. Respondent asserts that, even if the penalty imposed upon him was not sufficiently criminal in nature to trigger other guarantees, it was "quasi-criminal," and therefore sufficient to implicate the Fifth Amendment's protection against compulsory self-incrimination. He relies primarily in this regard upon Boyd v. United States, 116 U.S. 616 (1886), and later cases quoting its language.

In *Boyd*, [the] . . . Court found the Fifth Amendment applicable, even though the action in question was one contesting the forfeiture of certain goods. According to the Court: "We are . . . clearly of opinion that proceedings instituted for the purpose of declaring the forfeiture of a man's property by reason of offences committed by him, though they may be civil in form, are in their nature criminal." Id., at 633-634. While at this point in its opinion, the Court seemed to limit its holding to proceedings involving the forfeiture of property, shortly after the quoted passage it broadened its reasoning in a manner that might seem to apply to the present case:

> As, therefore, suits for *penalties and forfeitures* incurred by the commission of offences against the law, are of this quasi-criminal nature, we think that they are within the reason of criminal proceedings for all the purposes of the Fourth Amendment of the Constitution, and of that portion of the Fifth Amendment which declares that no person shall be compelled in any criminal case to be a witness against himself. . . .

Id., at 634 (emphasis added).

. . . Read broadly, *Boyd* might control the present case. This Court has declined, however, to give full scope to the reasoning and dicta in *Boyd*, noting on at least one occasion that "[s]everal of *Boyd*'s express or implicit declarations have not stood the test of time." Fisher v. United States, 425 U.S. 391, 407 (1976). . . .

The question before us, then, is whether the penalty imposed in this case, although clearly not "criminal" enough to trigger the protections of the Sixth Amendment, the Double Jeopardy Clause of the Fifth Amendment, or the other procedural guarantees normally associated with criminal prosecutions, is nevertheless "so far criminal in [its] nature" as to trigger the Self-Incrimination Clause of the Fifth Amendment. Initially, we note that the penalty and proceeding considered in *Boyd* were quite different from those considered in this case. *Boyd* dealt with forfeiture of property, a penalty that had absolutely no correlation to any damages sustained by society or to the cost of enforcing the law. . . . Here the penalty is much more analogous to traditional civil damages. Moreover, the statute under scrutiny in *Boyd* listed forfeiture along with fine and imprisonment as one possible punishment for customs fraud, a fact of some significance to the *Boyd*

Court. See 116 U.S., at 634. Here, as previously stated, the civil remedy and the criminal remedy are contained in separate statutes enacted 70 years apart. The proceedings in *Boyd* also posed a danger that the appellants would prejudice themselves in respect to later criminal proceedings. Here, respondent is protected by §311(b)(5), which expressly provides that "[n]otification received pursuant to this paragraph or information obtained by the exploitation of such notification shall not be used against any such person in any criminal case, except [for] prosecution for perjury or for giving a false statement." 33 U.S.C. §1321(b)(5).

More importantly, however, we believe that in the light of what we have found to be overwhelming evidence that Congress intended to create a penalty civil in all respects and quite weak evidence of any countervailing punitive purpose or effect it would be quite anomalous to hold that §311(b)(6) created a criminal penalty for the purposes of the Self-Incrimination Clause but a civil penalty for all other purposes. We do not read *Boyd* as requiring a contrary conclusion. . . .

NOTES ON THE MEANING OF INCRIMINATION

1. What does the phrase "civil penalty" mean?
2. In Allen v. Illinois, 478 U.S. 364 (1986), the Court held that the Illinois Sexually Dangerous Persons Act was civil rather than criminal in nature and thus that the Fifth Amendment does not apply to it. The Court based its conclusion on the state's assertion of its civil nature and the statute's "benign purpose" of providing treatment rather than punishment. As the dissent pointed out, however, the statute could be triggered only by a related criminal proceeding, could be initiated only by the state, required proof beyond reasonable doubt as well as the establishment of a criminal offense, and resulted in incarceration in the state's penal system.

Cases like *Ward* and *Allen* seem to leave the definition of "incrimination" in the hands of state legislatures and Congress. Is that appropriate? Should legislatures have the power to opt out of the Fifth Amendment by declaring that a given penalty is civil rather than criminal? Is this consistent with the Court's definition of Fifth Amendment compulsion?

3. *Ward* and *Allen* address the question whether the threat of a given penalty qualifies as incriminating for purposes of the privilege. A separate question is how great must the risk be in order for a witness to invoke the privilege. There too, the Court has spoken inconsistently. In Brown v. Walker, 161 U.S. 591 (1896), the Court stated that Fifth Amendment claimants must show

> reasonable ground to apprehend danger to the witness from his being compelled to answer. . . . The danger to be apprehended must be real and appreciable, with reference to the ordinary operation of law in the ordinary course of things — not a danger of an imaginary and unsubstantial character, having reference to some extraordinary and barely possible contingency, so improbable that no reasonable man would suffer it to influence his conduct.

Id. at 599-600. Hoffman v. United States, 341 U.S. 479, 487 (1951), describes the relevant standard more leniently:

> The privilege afforded not only extends to answers that would in themselves support a conviction under a federal criminal statute but likewise embraces those which would

furnish a link in the chain of evidence needed to prosecute the claimant for a federal crime. . . . To sustain the privilege, it need only be evident from the implications of the question, in the setting in which it is asked, that a responsive answer to the question or an explanation of why it cannot be answered might be dangerous because injurious disclosure could result."

In Hiibel v. Sixth Judicial District Court of Nevada, 124 S. Ct. 2451 (2004), the Court repeatedly quoted *Hoffman*'s "link in the chain of evidence" language — but did not quote the portion of the above passage stating that "it need only be evident . . . that a responsive answer . . . *might* be dangerous because injurious disclosure *could* result" (emphasis added). Instead, Justice Kennedy's opinion for the Court in *Hiibel* contained the quoted passage from Brown v. Walker, emphasizing that Fifth Amendment incrimination did not include "imaginary and unsubstantial" risks that "no reasonable man" would credit. If adjectives in Supreme Court opinions matter, *Hiibel* may signal a change in the meaning of incrimination.

Whether or not adjectives matter, context certainly does. *Hiibel* arose out of a police stop. The police had received a phone call reporting an assault, and describing the truck the perpetrator was driving. The officer stopped Hiibel because his truck fit the description. At the scene, the officer asked Hiibel for identification, which he refused to provide. At no time did he expressly invoke his Fifth Amendment privilege. Hiibel was arrested and charged with "willfully resisting, delaying, or obstructing a public officer in discharging or attempting to discharge any legal duty of his office" in violation of Nevada law. According to the charging documents, the "legal duty" that Hiibel obstructed was defined by Nev. Rev. Stat. §171.123, which provides that:

> "1. Any peace officer may detain any person whom the officer encounters under circumstances which reasonably indicate that the person has committed, is committing or is about to commit a crime. . . .
>
> "3. The officer may detain the person pursuant to this section only to ascertain his identity and the suspicious circumstances surrounding his presence abroad. Any person so detained shall identify himself, but may not be compelled to answer any other inquiry of any peace officer."

Hiibel claimed that this stop-and-identify statute violated the Fifth Amendment. The Court rejected the claim out of hand, while reserving the question whether disclosing one's identity might sometimes be sufficiently incriminating to trigger the privilege:

> In this case petitioner's refusal to disclose his name was not based on any articulated real and appreciable fear that his name would be used to incriminate him. . . . As best we can tell, petitioner refused to identify himself only because he thought his name was none of the officer's business. Even today, petitioner does not explain how the disclosure of his name could have been used against him in a criminal case. While we recognize petitioner's strong belief that he should not have to disclose his identity, the Fifth Amendment does not override the Nevada Legislature's judgment to the contrary absent a reasonable belief that the disclosure would tend to incriminate him.
>
> The narrow scope of the disclosure requirement is also important. One's identity is, by definition, unique; yet it is, in another sense, a universal characteristic.

Answering a request to disclose a name is likely to be so insignificant in the scheme of things as to be incriminating only in unusual circumstances. . . . In every criminal case, it is known and must be known who has been arrested and who is being tried. Even witnesses who plan to invoke the Fifth Amendment privilege answer when their names are called to take the stand. Still, a case may arise where there is a substantial allegation that furnishing identity at the time of a stop would have given the police a link in the chain of evidence needed to convict the individual of a separate offense. In that case, the court can then consider whether the privilege applies, and, if the Fifth Amendment has been violated, what remedy must follow. We need not resolve those questions here. . . .

124 S. Ct. at 2461. The second of the two paragraphs just quoted suggests that claims like Hiibel's are not likely to succeed, even on more favorable facts — notice the reference to witnesses in court answering when their names are called. Is that the right answer? Surely one's name may sometimes provide a link in an incriminating chain of evidence. Indeed, that must be true in a large fraction of criminal prosecutions. Why should identity be treated differently than other potentially incriminating information?

4. The doctrine that has the greatest practical effect on the meaning of incrimination deals with immunity. See Kastigar v. United States, supra, at page 762. Under *Kastigar*, the government may compel testimony if it immunizes the witness; in any subsequent criminal prosecution of that witness, the government bears the burden of proving that neither the immunized testimony nor its fruits were used against the defendant. Section A, supra, discusses the evolution of Fifth Amendment immunity and its implications for the privilege's rationale.

5. Return to the relevant constitutional language: "no person . . . shall be compelled in any criminal case to be a witness against himself." The preceding cases all treat the phrase "in any criminal case" as referring to the consequences of answering the relevant questions. In Chavez v. Martinez, 538 U.S. 760 (2003), four Justices asserted that that phrase also refers to the setting in which the compelled testimony is used. *Chavez* was a civil damages action brought by Oliverio Martinez, who claimed that Officer Chavez had interrogated him while he was in extreme physical pain, in violation of both due process and Miranda v. Arizona, 384 U.S. 436 (1966). A fractured Court concluded that section 1983 does not establish a cause of action for damages for *Miranda* violations, and remanded to the Court of Appeals for the Ninth Circuit to determine whether Martinez had a valid cause of action under the Fourteenth Amendment's due process clause. Justice Thomas, speaking for himself, the Chief Justice, and Justices O'Connor and Scalia, concluded that Martinez's Fifth Amendment rights were not violated by Chavez's questioning — no matter how coercive that questioning was — because Martinez's statements were never used against him in a criminal trial. Only when testimony is introduced "in [a] criminal case" is the Fifth Amendment violated.

The other five Justices declined to adopt Justice Thomas's position. Had they done so, the meaning of incrimination — and the application of the privilege to a host of out-of-court conversations between state officials and criminal suspects — would be quite different than it has been in the past. *Chavez*'s implications for police interrogation doctrine are addressed below, at page 920.

3. "To Be a Witness Against Himself": The Meaning of Testimony

In order to make out a valid Fifth Amendment claim, the claimant must show that he was compelled to "be a witness"—in other words, to give testimony. In most cases, this requirement is easy, because most Fifth Amendment claims involve spoken questions that call for spoken answers, as with testimony given by witnesses in court. Problems arise when the evidence in question consists of something other than oral statements. Recall that in Schmerber v. California, 384 U.S. 757 (1966), the Supreme Court held that blood taken from a defendant (for the purpose of testing the defendant's blood alcohol content—breathalyzers did not yet exist) was not "testimonial," and hence did not trigger Fifth Amendment protection. *Schmerber* appears in Chapter 4 at page 291; you may wish to reread it now.

Schmerber suggests that physical evidence is not covered by the privilege, on the ground that it is not communicative in the way that oral testimony is. The same logic has been applied to requirements that a defendant stand in a lineup while wearing particular clothing, that he furnish a voice sample, or that he furnish a handwriting sample—even when the "sample" is used to authorize production of clearly incriminating evidence. For example, the defendant in Doe v. United States, 487 U.S. 201 (1988), was ordered to sign a form authorizing foreign banks to turn over his account records; the defendant was not asked either to identify any accounts or to verify their existence but only to sign the form. Relying on *Schmerber*, the Court held that this process did not compel Fifth Amendment testimony:

> . . . [I]n order to be testimonial, an accused's communication must itself, explicitly or implicitly, relate a factual assertion or disclose information.[9] Only then is a person compelled to be a "witness" against himself.
>
> This understanding is perhaps most clearly revealed in those cases in which the Court has held that certain acts, though incriminating, are not within the privilege. Thus, a suspect may be compelled to furnish a blood sample, *Schmerber;* to provide a handwriting exemplar, Gilbert [v. California, 388 U.S. 263 (1967)], or a voice exemplar, United States v. Dionisio, 410 U.S. 1, 7 (1973); to stand in a lineup, [United States v. Wade, 388 U.S. 218 (1967)]; and to wear particular clothing, Holt v. United States, 218 U.S. 245, 252-253 (1910). These decisions are grounded on the proposition that "the privilege protects an accused only from being compelled to testify against himself, or otherwise provide the State with evidence of a testimonial or communicative nature." *Schmerber*, 384 U.S., at 761. The Court accordingly held that the privilege was not implicated in each of those cases, because the suspect was not required "to disclose any knowledge he might have," or "to speak his guilt," *Wade,* 388 U.S., at 222-223. It is the "extortion of information from the accused," Couch v. United States, 409 U.S., at 328, the attempt to force him "to disclose the contents of his own mind," Curcio v. United States, 354 U.S. 118, 128

---

9. We do not disagree with the dissent that "[t]he expression of the contents of an individual's mind" is testimonial communication for purposes of the Fifth Amendment. We simply disagree with the dissent's conclusion that the execution of the consent directive at issue here forced petitioner to express the contents of his mind. In our view, such compulsion is more like [in the words of the dissent] "be[ing] forced to surrender a key to a strong box containing incriminating documents," than it is like "be[ing] compelled to reveal the combination to [petitioner's] wall safe."

(1957), that implicates the Self-Incrimination Clause.[10] It is consistent with the history of and the policies underlying the Self-Incrimination Clause to hold that the privilege may be asserted only to resist compelled explicit or implicit disclosures of incriminating information. . . . These policies are served when the privilege is asserted to spare the accused from having to reveal, directly or indirectly, his knowledge of facts relating him to the offense or from having to share his thoughts and beliefs with the Government.[11]

487 U.S. at 210-213.

Justice Stevens' dissent in *Doe* sought to distinguish *Schmerber*.

A defendant can be compelled to produce material evidence that is incriminating. Fingerprints, blood samples, voice exemplars, handwriting specimens or other items of physical evidence may be extracted from a defendant against his will. But can he be compelled to use his mind to assist the prosecution in convicting him of a crime? I think not. He may in some cases be forced to surrender a key to a strong box containing incriminating documents, but I do not believe he can be compelled to reveal the combination to his wall safe — by word or deed.

The document the Government seeks to extract from John Doe purports to order third parties to take action that will lead to the discovery of incriminating evidence. The directive itself may not betray any knowledge petitioner may have about the circumstances of the offenses being investigated by the Grand Jury, but it nevertheless purports to evidence a reasoned decision by Doe to authorize action by others. The forced execution of this document differs from the forced production of physical evidence just as human beings differ from other animals.[1]

Id. at 219 (Stevens, J., dissenting).

10. Petitioner's reliance on a statement in this Court's decision in *Schmerber* for the proposition that all verbal statements sought for their content are testimonial is misplaced. In *Schmerber*, the Court stated that the privilege extends to "an accused's communications, whatever form they might take," but it did so in the context of clarifying that the privilege may apply not only to verbal communications, as was once thought, but also to physical communications. Contrary to petitioner's urging, the *Schmerber* line of cases does not draw a distinction between unprotected evidence sought for its physical characteristics and protected evidence sought for its content. Rather, the Court distinguished between the suspect's being compelled himself to serve as evidence and the suspect's being compelled to disclose or communicate information or facts that might serve as or lead to incriminating evidence. . . . In order to be privileged, it is not enough that the compelled communication is sought for its content. The content itself must have testimonial significance.

11. Petitioner argues that at least some of these policies would be undermined unless the Government is required to obtain evidence against an accused from sources other than his compelled statements, whether or not the statements make a factual assertion or convey information. Petitioner accordingly maintains that the policy of striking an appropriate balance between the power of the Government and the sovereignty of the individual precludes the Government from compelling an individual to utter or write words that lead to incriminating evidence. Even if some of the policies underlying the privilege might support petitioner's interpretation of the privilege, "it is clear that the scope of the privilege does not coincide with the complex of values it helps to protect. Despite the impact upon the inviolability of the human personality, and upon our belief in an adversary system of criminal justice in which the Government must produce the evidence against an accused through its own independent labors, the prosecution is allowed to obtain and use . . . evidence which although compelled is generally speaking not 'testimonial,' Schmerber v. California, 384 U.S. 757, 761." Grosso v. United States, 390 U.S. 62, 72-73 (1968) (Brennan, J., concurring). If the societal interests in privacy, fairness, and restraint of governmental power are not unconstitutionally offended by compelling the accused to have his body serve as evidence that leads to the development of highly incriminating testimony, as *Schmerber* and its progeny make clear, it is difficult to understand how compelling a suspect to make a nonfactual statement that facilitates the production of evidence by someone else offends the privilege.

1. The forced production of physical evidence, which we have condoned involves no intrusion upon the contents of the mind of the accused. See *Schmerber*, 384 U.S., at 765 (forced blood test permissible

The disagreement between the Court and Justice Stevens in *Doe* is a disagreement about the applicable theory of the Fifth Amendment. Both sides agree that the Fifth Amendment applies to compelled, self-incriminating testimony. Both agree that physical evidence, like the blood sample in *Schmerber*, falls outside the definition of "testimony." But the two sides use different definitions. Justice Stevens believes that the no one may be "compelled to use his mind to assist the prosecution in convicting him of a crime." Doe, in his view, was forced to use his mind when he signed his name; that mental exercise plainly "assist[ed] the prosecution in convicting him of a crime," since it led to the production of incriminating bank records.

The Court, by contrast, holds that "the accused's communication must itself, explicitly or implicitly, relate a factual assertion or disclose information" in order to qualify as Fifth Amendment testimony. The reason for this definition is not entirely clear in *Doe*, but it does appear in some other Supreme Court opinions. Consider the choice the defendant faced *Schmerber*. When the government told Schmerber to extend his arm so blood could be drawn, he had no choice to make as long as the privilege did not apply. Schmerber could not by an act of will change the alcohol content of his blood, and if he refused to comply, the government could presumably strap him down and take the blood test anyway. That makes *Schmerber* quite different from the paradigmatic case where the privilege *does* apply: the guilty defendant ordered to take the witness stand and say whether he committed the crime. The defendant on the witness stand has a choice to confess, to lie, or to remain silent and face contempt sanctions. Perhaps the nature of that choice is the key to what is (and what isn't) testimonial.

That is the implication of the many references in Fifth Amendment cases to the "cruel trilemma": the three-pronged choice a guilty witness would face if forced to answer questions about his crime; such a witness could confess crime and send himself to prison, he could lie and risk a perjury prosecution, or he could keep

---

because it does not involve "even a shadow of testimonial compulsion upon or enforced communication by the accused"). The forced execution of a document that purports to convey the signer's authority, however, does invade the dignity of the human mind; it purports to communicate a deliberate command. The intrusion on the dignity of the individual is not diminished by the fact that the document does not reflect the true state of the signer's mind. Indeed, that the assertions petitioner is forced to utter by executing the document are false causes an even greater violation of human dignity. For the same reason a person cannot be forced to sign a document purporting to authorize the entry of judgment against himself, cf. Brady v. United States, 397 U.S. 742, 748 (1970), I do not believe he can be forced to sign a document purporting to authorize the disclosure of incriminating evidence. In both cases the accused is being compelled "to be a witness against himself"; indeed, here he is being compelled to bear false witness against himself.

The expression of the contents of an individual's mind falls squarely within the protection of the Fifth Amendment. Justice Holmes' observation that "the prohibition of compelling a man in a criminal court to be witness against himself is a prohibition of the use of physical or moral compulsion to extort communications from him," Holt v. United States, 218 U.S., at 252-253, manifests a recognition that virtually any communication reveals the contents of the mind of the speaker. Thus the Fifth Amendment privilege is fulfilled only when the person is guaranteed the right " 'to remain silent unless he chooses to speak in the unfettered exercise of his own will.' " Miranda v. Arizona, 384 U.S. 436, 460 (1966) (quoting Malloy v. Hogan, 378 U.S. 1, 8 (1964)). The deviation from this principle can only lead to mischievous abuse of the dignity the Fifth Amendment commands the Government afford its citizens. The instant case is illustrative. In allowing the Government to compel petitioner to execute the directive, the Court permits the Government to compel petitioner to speak against his will in answer to the question "Do you consent to the release of these documents?" Beyond this affront, however, the Government is being permitted also to demand that the answer be "yes."

quiet and be held in contempt. Whatever else the privilege bars, it plainly bars the government from putting witnesses to that choice. On the prevailing view, the concept of "testimony" is really a stand-in for the presence or absence of that choice. Justice Brennan (author of the Court's opinion in *Schmerber*) articulated this position most clearly:

> . . . Whatever else it may include, . . . the definition of "testimonial" evidence articulated in *Doe* must encompass all responses to questions that, if asked of a sworn suspect during a criminal trial, could place the suspect in the "cruel trilemma." This conclusion is consistent with our recognition in *Doe* that "the vast majority of verbal statements thus will be testimonial" because "there are very few instances in which a verbal statement, either oral or written, will not convey information or assert facts." 487 U.S., at 213. Whenever a suspect is asked for a response requiring him to communicate an express or implied assertion of fact or belief, the suspect confronts the "trilemma" of truth, falsity, or silence and hence the response . . . contains a testimonial component.
>
> This approach accords with each of our post-*Schmerber* cases finding that a particular oral or written response to express or implied questioning was nontestimonial; the questions presented in these cases did not confront the suspects with this trilemma. As we noted in *Doe*, 487 U.S., at 210-211, the cases upholding compelled writing and voice exemplars did not involve situations in which suspects were asked to communicate any personal beliefs or knowledge of facts, and therefore the suspects were not forced to choose between truthfully or falsely revealing their thoughts. We carefully noted in Gilbert v. California, 388 U.S. 263 (1967), for example, that a "mere handwriting exemplar, in contrast to the content of what is written, like the voice or body itself, is an identifying physical characteristic outside [the privilege's] protection." Id., at 266-267. . . . And in *Doe*, the suspect was asked merely to sign a consent form waiving a privacy interest in foreign bank records. Because the consent form spoke in the hypothetical and did not identify any particular banks, accounts, or private records, the form neither "communicated any factual assertions, implicit or explicit, nor conveyed any information to the Government." 487 U.S., at 215. . . .

Pennsylvania v. Muniz, 496 U.S. 582, 596-598 (1990) (plurality opinion).

On that theory, did *Doe* reach the right result? It may well be that Doe's signature communicated nothing more than the fact that he could sign his name, which the government presumably knew and which he would presumably concede. Still, he could have refused to sign — he could have forced federal agents to wrap his hand around the pen and move it along the page. Or, he could have lied: perhaps by signing some other name, or signing in a way that did not match the signature on file with the bank. Was his choice really so different from the paradigmatic "cruel trilemma"? For a discussion concluding that the choice theory does not very well explain the Fifth Amendment cases, Ronald J. Allen & Kristin Mace, The Fifth Amendment Explained and Its Future Predicted, 94 J. Crim. L. & Crim. 243 (2004). Allen & Mace demonstrate that the cases cannot be reconciled by whether the use of "mind" is somehow compelled, either. Instead, the cases are consistent with forbidding the government to use the substantive results of cognition created by government action (such as asking questions, giving orders, serving subpoenas). One plainly employs one's "mind" in putting on a shirt, signing a document, or turning over an object, but will is different from cognition, which is the critical distinction Justice Stevens neglected. Allen & Mace do not claim that the Court has ever explicitly adopted this theory, but do claim that it is the best explanation of the actual results in the cases.

The Justices in *Muniz* (the case just quoted) referred liberally to the cruel trilemma theory, though they disagreed about how to apply the theory to the facts. The police picked up Muniz for drunk driving and brought him back to the police station. There, in the course of filling out some forms, an officer asked Muniz eight questions: his name, address, height, weight, eye color, date of birth, current age, and the date of his sixth birthday. Both questions and answers were videotaped. Muniz's answers were obviously slurred, and he responded to what the Court referred to as "the sixth birthday question" by saying that he did not remember.

Justice Marshall concluded that all aspects of Muniz's answers were testimonial and hence protected by the privilege. Justice Brennan, joined by Justices O'Connor, Scalia, and Kennedy, concluded that the slurred speech was not "testimonial," because it communicated only physical characteristics (indeed, the same physical characteristic that Schmerber's blood communicated). On the other hand, Justice Brennan and his colleagues decided that the nonresponse to the sixth birthday question *was* testimonial:

> In contrast, the sixth birthday question in this case required a testimonial response. When Officer Hosterman asked Muniz if he knew the date of his sixth birthday and Muniz . . . could not remember or calculate that date, he was confronted with the trilemma. By hypothesis, the inherently coercive environment created by the custodial interrogation precluded the option of remaining silent. Muniz was left with the choice of incriminating himself by admitting that he did not then know the date of his sixth birthday, or answering untruthfully by reporting a date that he did not then believe to be accurate (an incorrect guess would be incriminating as well as untruthful). The content of his truthful answer supported an inference that his mental faculties were impaired, because his assertion (he did not know the date of his sixth birthday) was different from the assertion . . . that the trier of fact might reasonably have expected a lucid person to provide. Hence, the incriminating inference of impaired mental faculties stemmed, not just from the fact that Muniz slurred his response, but also from a testimonial aspect of that response.

496 U.S. at 598-599. Chief Justice Rehnquist, joined by Justices White, Blackmun, and Stevens — *Muniz* produced an odd lineup of Justices — accepted the premise but disputed the conclusion:

> The sixth birthday question here was an effort on the part of the police to check how well Muniz was able to do a simple mathematical exercise. . . . Muniz may be required to perform a "horizontal gaze nystagmus" test, the "walk and turn" test, and the "one leg stand" test, all of which are designed to test a suspect's physical coordination. If the police may require Muniz to use his body in order to demonstrate the level of his physical coordination, there is no reason why they should not be able to require him to speak or write in order to determine his mental coordination. That was all that was sought here. Since it was permissible for the police to extract and examine a sample of Schmerber's blood to determine how much that part of his system had been affected by alcohol, I see no reason why they may not examine the functioning of Muniz' mental processes for the same purpose.
>
> Surely if it were relevant, a suspect might be asked to take an eye examination in the course of which he might have to admit that he could not read the letters on the

third line of the chart. At worst, he might utter a mistaken guess. Muniz likewise might have attempted to guess the correct response to the sixth birthday question instead of attempting to calculate the date or answer "I don't know." But the potential for giving a bad guess does not subject the suspect to the truth-falsity-silence predicament that renders a response testimonial and, therefore, within the scope of the Fifth Amendment privilege.

Id. at 607-608 (Rehnquist, C.J., concurring in part and dissenting in part).

Which side was right in *Muniz*? In *Doe*? In *Schmerber*? Is the so-called "cruel trilemma" a helpful way to think about these questions, or a distraction? After all, the "trilemma" is "cruel" only because the defendant's past conduct makes honesty a painful option; it is not clear why this is a form of "cruelty" that deserves sympathy, much less constitutional protection. Besides, honesty is often painful for reasons that have nothing to do with criminal liability. On a regular basis, our legal system requires witnesses to testify truthfully when they would rather not. Is that cruel? If not, is there a better way to think about what is and isn't testimonial? One possible answer is that the Fifth Amendment is an adjunct to the Fourth: where the latter protects privacy interests in physical items and spaces, the former protects "mental privacy," the privacy of one's mind. For an extended argument along these lines, written partly as a defense of *Schmerber*, see Peter Arenella, *Schmerber* and the Privilege against Self-Incrimination: A Reappraisal, 20 Am. Crim. L. Rev. 31 (1982). Of course, if privacy is the reigning theory of the privilege, it is hard to explain the "incrimination" requirement: Testimony about even the most private matters can be compelled if the witness is immunized.

C. Limiting the Privilege?

In most Fifth Amendment cases, courts apply the standard compulsion-incrimination-testimony model outlined in Section B. Sometimes, though, that model yields very substantial restrictions on the government's ability to gather information — which, in turn, substantially restricts the government's ability to regulate a wide range of behavior. When that happens — when standard application of the privilege against self-incrimination appears to pose some danger to the regulatory state's ability to regulate — the Supreme Court often limits the privilege. As you read the cases and notes below, consider the question whether the limits conform to any coherent rationale, aside from a desire not to have a privilege against self-incrimination that costs the government too much.

One way to limit the privilege's cost is to limit the conduct the privilege can be used to shield. The most common limit has to do with misrepresentation. Virtually all immunity statutes contain an exception that permits the use of immunized testimony in prosecutions for perjury or false statements. The Court cast some doubt on the constitutionality of those exceptions in New Jersey v. Portash, 440 U.S. 450 (1979). Portash gave immunized testimony to a grand jury; he was subsequently charged with extortion. The government asked for and received permission to use Portash's immunized testimony to impeach him if he testified at his criminal trial, and if his trial testimony was inconsistent with his statements to the grand jury. The threatened use of his immunized testimony kept Portash from taking the stand, and he was convicted. The Supreme Court held that the Fifth Amendment barred this procedure:

> Testimony given in response to a grant of legislative immunity is the essence of coerced testimony. In such cases there is no question whether physical or psychological pressures overrode the defendant's will; the witness is told to talk or face the government's coercive sanctions, notably, a conviction for contempt. The information given in response to a grant of immunity may well be more reliable than information beaten from a helpless defendant, but it is no less compelled. The Fifth and Fourteenth Amendments provide a privilege against *compelled* self-incrimination, not merely against unreliable self-incrimination. . . . Here . . . we deal with the constitutional privilege against compulsory self-incrimination in its most pristine form.
>
> . . . [A] person's testimony before a grand jury under a grant of immunity cannot constitutionally be used to impeach him when he is a defendant in a later criminal trial.

Id. at 459-460.

The form of the privilege seemed a bit less pristine in United States v. Apfelbaum, 445 U.S. 115 (1980). The federal immunity statute, 18 U.S.C. §6002, provides that when a witness is compelled to testify over his claim of a Fifth Amendment privilege, "no testimony or other information compelled under the order (or any information directly or indirectly derived from such testimony or other information) may be used against the witness in any criminal case, except a prosecution for perjury, giving a false statement, or otherwise failing to comply with the order." The question before the Court was whether the statute was constitutional, given that it "makes no distinction between truthful and untruthful statements made during the course of the immunized testimony. Rather, it creates a blanket exemption from the bar against the use of immunized testimony in cases in which the witness is subsequently prosecuted for making false statements." The Court found that there is "no doctrine of 'anticipatory perjury'" and thus upheld the statute.

In Brogan v. United States, 522 U.S. 398 (1998), the Court addressed the question whether a defendant can be held criminally liable when, instead of claiming his right to remain silent, he falsely denies some form of misconduct; the denial is known as an "exculpatory no." The Court concluded that an "exculpatory no" can be criminally punished, just like any other misrepresentation:

> The second line of defense that petitioner invokes for the "exculpatory no" doctrine is inspired by the Fifth Amendment. He argues that a literal reading of [18 U.S.C. §1001, criminalizing false statements to federal investigators] violates the "spirit" of the Fifth Amendment because it places a "cornered suspect" in the "cruel trilemma" of admitting guilt, remaining silent, or falsely denying guilt. This "trilemma" is wholly of the guilty suspect's own making, of course. An innocent person will not find himself in a similar quandary (as one commentator has put it, the innocent person lacks even a "lemma," Allen, The Simpson Affair, Reform of the Criminal Justice Process, and Magic Bullets, 67 U. Colo. L. Rev. 989, 1016 (1996)). And even the honest and contrite guilty person will not regard the third prong of the "trilemma" (the blatant lie) as an available option. . . . In order to validate the "exculpatory no," the elements of this "cruel trilemma" have now been altered — ratcheted up, as it were, so that the right to remain silent, which was the liberation from the original trilemma, is now itself a cruelty. We are not disposed to write into our law this species of compassion inflation.

Whether or not the predicament of the wrongdoer run to ground tugs at the heart strings, neither the text nor the spirit of the Fifth Amendment confers a privilege to lie. "[P]roper invocation of the Fifth Amendment privilege against compulsory self-incrimination allows a witness to remain silent, but not to swear falsely." United States v. Apfelbaum, 445 U.S. 115, 117 (1980). Petitioner contends that silence is an "illusory" option because a suspect may fear that his silence will be used against him later, or may not even know that silence is an available option. As to the former: It is well established that the fact that a person's silence can be used against him — either as substantive evidence of guilt or to impeach him if he takes the stand — does not exert a form of pressure that exonerates an otherwise unlawful lie. And as for the possibility that the person under investigation may be unaware of his right to remain silent: In the modern age of frequently dramatized "Miranda" warnings, that is implausible. . . .

522 U.S. at 404-405.

Apfelbaum and *Brogan* suggest that the privilege does not protect lies. (Except, *Portash* suggests, when it does.) A second means of limiting the privilege's coverage is to limit the parties who can invoke it. At the beginning of the twentieth century, it was widely believed that the privilege against self-incrimination could be claimed by corporations — just as corporations had been deemed "persons" for purposes of the Fourteenth Amendment's due process clause. See Santa Clara County v. Southern Pacific R.R., 118 U.S. 394 (1886). Nevertheless, in Hale v. Henkel, 201 U.S. 43 (1906), the Court held that only natural persons could assert the privilege; corporations have no Fifth Amendment rights. The rationale for this rule was simple government necessity: "Of what use would it be for the legislature to declare these combinations unlawful [the reference is to antitrust conspiracies; *Hale* arose out of a Sherman Act investigation] if the judicial power may close the door of access to every available source of information upon the subject?" Id. at 70.

Limiting the privilege to natural persons was essential to extensive government regulation of economic affairs. So was a more obscure exception to the privilege's coverage known as the "required records" doctrine. The key case is Shapiro v. United States, 335 U.S. 1 (1948). Shapiro was a fruit wholesaler. In the course of an investigation of violations of federal price controls, he was asked to turn over various invoices and other business records. He claimed the privilege. The Court denied Shapiro's claim, both because the law required him to keep the records in question, and because the records were used not merely for criminal law enforcement but in service of a civil regulatory regime:

> It may be assumed at the outset that there are limits which the Government cannot constitutionally exceed in requiring the keeping of records which may be inspected by an administrative agency and may be used in prosecuting statutory violations committed by the recordkeeper himself. But no serious misgiving that those bounds have been overstepped would appear to be evoked when there is a sufficient relation between the activity sought to be regulated and the public concern so that the Government can constitutionally regulate or forbid the basic activity concerned, and can constitutionally require the keeping of particular records. . . .

Id. at 32.

Shapiro seemed to give the government broad authority to require any disclosures it wished, but the authority turned out to be less broad than first appeared. The defendant in Marchetti v. United States, 390 U.S. 39 (1968), was a professional gambler. A federal statute required gamblers to register and pay an occupational tax — notwithstanding that their "profession" was a crime. That took the "required records" concept too far, in the Court's view. It distinguished *Shapiro* as follows:

> Each of the three principal elements of the doctrine, as it is described in *Shapiro*, is absent from this situation. *First*, petitioner Marchetti was not, by the provisions now at issue, obliged to keep and preserve records "of the same kind as he has customarily kept"; he was required simply to provide information, unrelated to any records which he may have maintained, about his wagering activities. This requirement is not significantly different from a demand that he provide oral testimony. *Second*, whatever "public aspects" there were to the records at issue in *Shapiro*, there are none to the information demanded from Marchetti. The Government's anxiety to obtain information known to a private individual does not without more render that information public; if it did, no room would remain for the application of the constitutional privilege. Nor does it stamp information with a public character that the Government has formalized its demands in the attire of a statute; if this alone were sufficient, the constitutional privilege could be entirely abrogated by any Act of Congress. *Third*, the requirements at issue in *Shapiro* were imposed in "an essentially non-criminal and regulatory area of inquiry" while those here are directed to a "selective group inherently suspect of criminal activities." Cf. Albertson v. Subversive Activities Control Board, 382 U.S. 70, 79. The United States' principal interest is evidently the collection of revenue, and not the punishment of gamblers; but the characteristics of the activities about which information is sought, and the composition of the groups to which inquiries are made, readily distinguish this situation from that in *Shapiro*. There is no need to explore further the elements and limitations of *Shapiro* and the cases involving public papers; these points of difference in combination preclude any appropriate application of those cases to the present one.

390 U.S. at 56-57. Notice that Marchetti did not have to assert his privilege; the Court concluded that any such assertion would have been incriminating under the circumstances.

Yet another way to limit the privilege's scope is to require some balancing of interests in Fifth Amendment cases, with the autonomy and privacy interests the privilege protects weighed against the government's interest in regulating the relevant conduct. As should be clear by now, ordinary Fifth Amendment analysis does not involve that kind of balancing. *Fourth* Amendment law does: probable cause and reasonable suspicion, the two leading standards for Fourth Amendment "searches," are both ways of establishing the government's need to conduct the search. Fifth Amendment law works differently: regardless of how great is the government's suspicion or need for the defendant's testimony, if that testimony would be incriminating, the government cannot force the defendant to provide it.

Except sometimes. California v. Byers, 402 U.S. 424 (1971), raised the question whether California's hit-and-run statute — every state has one; such statutes require those involved in traffic accidents to remain at the scene of the accident and to identify themselves when the police arrive — violated the Fifth Amendment. A four-Justice plurality held that the compelled conduct, staying at the scene and identifying oneself, was neither testimonial nor incriminating.

See id. at 425-434 (opinion of Burger, C.J.). Four Justices dissented, arguing that such conduct was as testimonial and as incriminating as the compelled registration in *Marchetti*. See id. at 459-464 (Black, J., dissenting); id. at 464-478 (Brennan, J., dissenting). Justice Harlan's was the deciding vote. In Harlan's view, remaining at the scene of an accident and identifying oneself communicated vital information in cases where the accident involved criminal conduct, and the information was plainly incriminating. Thus, ordinary Fifth Amendment analysis would suggest that the hit-and-run statutes were unconstitutional. But Harlan refused to extend the privilege that far, because of the cost to the government's interest in civil regulation of traffic accidents:

> . . . [T]he public regulation of driving behavior through a pattern of laws which includes compelled self-reporting to ensure financial responsibility for accidents and criminal sanctions to deter dangerous driving entails genuine risks of self-incrimination from the driver's point of view. The conclusion that the Fifth Amendment extends to this regulatory scheme will impair the capacity of the State to pursue these objectives simultaneously. For compelled self-reporting is a necessary part of an effective scheme of assuring personal financial responsibility for automobile accidents. Undoubtedly, it can be argued that self-reporting is at least as necessary to an effective scheme of criminal law enforcement in this area. The fair response to that latter contention may be that the purpose of the Fifth Amendment is to compel the State to opt for the less efficient methods of an "accusatorial" system. . . . But it would not follow that the constitutional values protected by the "accusatorial" system . . . are of such overriding significance that they compel substantial sacrifices in the efficient pursuit of other governmental objectives in all situations where the pursuit of those objectives requires the disclosure of information which will undoubtedly significantly aid in criminal law enforcement. . . .
>
> These values are implicated by government compulsion to disclose information about driving behavior as part of a regulatory scheme including criminal sanctions. . . . It is also true that, unlike the ordinary civil lawsuit context, special governmental interests in addition to the deterrence of antisocial behavior by use of criminal sanctions are affected by extension of the privilege to this regulatory context. If the privilege is extended to the circumstances of this case, it must, I think, be potentially available in every instance where the government relies on self-reporting. And the considerable risks to efficient government of a self-executing claim of privilege will require acceptance of, at the very least, a use restriction of unspecified dimensions. Technological progress creates an ever-expanding need for governmental information about individuals. If the individual's ability in any particular case to perceive a genuine risk of self-incrimination is to be a sufficient condition for imposition of use restrictions on the government in all self-reporting contexts, then the privilege threatens the capacity of the government to respond to societal needs with a realistic mixture of criminal sanctions and other regulatory devices. To the extent that [*Marchetti*] appears to suggest that the presence of perceivable risks of incrimination in and of itself justifies imposition of a use restriction on the information gained by the Government through compelled self-reporting, I think that [case] should be explicitly limited by this Court.

Id. at 448-452 (Harlan, J., concurring in the judgment).

Is this sort of open-ended interest balancing an appropriate way to define the boundaries of the privilege? See whether your answer is affected by the next case.

BALTIMORE CITY DEPARTMENT OF SOCIAL SERVICES v. BOUKNIGHT

Certiorari to Maryland Court of Appeals
493 U.S. 549 (1990)

JUSTICE O'CONNOR delivered the opinion of the Court.

In this action, we must decide whether a mother, the custodian of a child pursuant to a court order, may invoke the Fifth Amendment privilege against self-incrimination to resist an order of the Juvenile Court to produce the child. We hold that she may not.

I

Petitioner Maurice M. is an abused child. When he was three months old, he was hospitalized with a fractured left femur, and examination revealed several partially healed bone fractures and other indications of severe physical abuse. In the hospital, respondent Bouknight, Maurice's mother, was observed shaking Maurice, dropping him in his crib despite his spica cast, and otherwise handling him in a manner inconsistent with his recovery and continued health. Hospital personnel notified Baltimore City Department of Social Services (BCDSS) of suspected child abuse. In February 1987, BCDSS secured a court order removing Maurice from Bouknight's control and placing him in shelter care. Several months later, the shelter care order was inexplicably modified to return Maurice to Bouknight's custody temporarily. Following a hearing held shortly thereafter, the Juvenile Court declared Maurice to be a "child in need of assistance," thus asserting jurisdiction over Maurice and placing him under BCDSS's continuing oversight. BCDSS agreed that Bouknight could continue as custodian of the child, but only pursuant to extensive conditions set forth in a court-approved protective supervision order. The order required Bouknight to "co-operate with BCDSS," "continue in therapy," participate in parental aid and training programs, and "refrain from physically punishing [Maurice]." The order's terms were "all subject to the further Order of the Court." Bouknight's attorney signed the order, and Bouknight in a separate form set forth her agreement to each term.

Eight months later, fearing for Maurice's safety, BCDSS returned to Juvenile Court. BCDSS caseworkers related that Bouknight would not cooperate with them and had in nearly every respect violated the terms of the protective order. BCDSS states that Maurice's father had recently died in a shooting incident and that Bouknight, in light of the results of a psychological examination and her history of drug use, could not provide adequate care for the child. On April 20, 1988, the Court granted BCDSS's petition to remove Maurice from Bouknight's control for placement in foster care. BCDSS officials also petitioned for judicial relief from Bouknight's failure to produce Maurice or reveal where he could be found. The petition recounted that on two recent visits by BCDSS officials to Bouknight's home, she had refused to reveal the location of the child or had indicated that the child was with an aunt whom she would not identify. The petition further asserted that inquiries of Bouknight's known relatives had revealed that none of them had recently seen Maurice and that BCDSS had prompted the police to issue a missing persons report and referred the case for investigation by the police homicide division. Also on April 20, the Juvenile Court, upon a hearing on the petition, cited Bouknight for violating the protective custody order and for failing to appear at the hearing. Bouknight had indicated to her attorney that she would appear with the child, but also expressed fear that if she appeared the State would "snatch the child." The court issued an order to show cause why Bouknight should not be held in civil contempt for failure to produce the child.

Expressing concern that Maurice was endangered or perhaps dead, the court issued a bench warrant for Bouknight's appearance.

Maurice was not produced at subsequent hearings. At a hearing one week later, Bouknight claimed that Maurice was with a relative in Dallas. Investigation revealed that the relative had not seen Maurice. The next day, following another hearing at which Bouknight again declined to produce Maurice, the Juvenile Court found Bouknight in contempt for failure to produce the child as ordered. There was and has been no indication that she was unable to comply with the order. The court directed that Bouknight be imprisoned until she "purge[d] herself of contempt by either producing [Maurice] before the court or revealing to the court his exact whereabouts."

The Juvenile Court rejected Bouknight's subsequent claim that the contempt order violated the Fifth Amendment's guarantee against self-incrimination. The court stated that the production of Maurice would purge the contempt and that "[t]he contempt is issued not because she refuse[d] to testify in any proceeding . . . [but] because she had failed to abide by the Order of this Court mainly [for] the production of Maurice M." While that decision was being appealed, Bouknight was convicted of theft and sentenced to 18 months' imprisonment in separate proceedings. The Court of Appeals of Maryland vacated the Juvenile Court's judgment upholding the contempt order. The Court of Appeals found that the contempt order unconstitutionally compelled Bouknight to admit through the act of production "a measure of continuing control and dominion over Maurice's person" in circumstances in which "Bouknight has a reasonable apprehension that she will be prosecuted." We granted certiorari, and we now reverse.

II

. . . The courts below concluded that Bouknight could comply with the order through the unadorned act of producing the child, and we thus address that aspect of the order. When the government demands that an item be produced, "the only thing compelled is the act of producing the [item]." Fisher [v. United States, 425 U.S. 391, 410 n. 11 (1976)]. The Fifth Amendment's protection may nonetheless be implicated because the act of complying with the government's demand testifies to the existence, possession, or authenticity of the things produced. But a person may not claim the Amendment's protection based upon the incrimination that may result from the contents or nature of the thing demanded. Bouknight therefore cannot claim the privilege based upon anything that examination of Maurice might reveal, nor can she assert the privilege upon the theory that compliance would assert that the child produced is in fact Maurice (a fact the State could readily establish, rendering any testimony regarding existence of authenticity insufficiently incriminating). Rather, Bouknight claims the benefit of the privilege because the act of production would amount to testimony regarding her control over and possession of Maurice. Although the State could readily introduce evidence of Bouknight's continuing control over the child—e.g., the custody order, testimony of relatives, and Bouknight's own statements to Maryland officials before invoking the privilege—her implicit communication of control over Maurice at the moment of production might aid the State in prosecuting Bouknight.

The possibility that a production order will compel testimonial assertions that may prove incriminating does not, in all contexts, justify invoking the privilege to resist production. Even assuming that this limited testimonial assertion is sufficiently incriminating and "sufficiently testimonial for purposes of the privilege," *Fisher*, supra, at 411, Bouknight may not invoke the privilege to resist the production order because she has assumed custodial duties related to production and because production is required as part of a noncriminal regulatory regime.

The Court has on several occasions recognized that the Fifth Amendment privilege may not be invoked to resist compliance with a regulatory regime constructed to effect the State's public purposes unrelated to the enforcement of its criminal laws. In Shapiro v. United States, 335 U.S. 1 (1948), the Court considered an application of the Emergency Price Control Act and a regulation issued thereunder which required licensed businesses to maintain records and make them available for inspection by administrators. The Court indicated that no Fifth Amendment protection attached to production of the "required records," which the "'defendant was required to keep, not for his private uses, but for the benefit of the public, and for public inspection.'" Id., at 17-18 (quoting Wilson v. United States, 221 U.S. 361, 381 (1911)). . . .

The Court has since [defined] limits to the government's authority to gain access to items or information vested with this public character. The Court has noted that "the requirements at issue in *Shapiro* were imposed in "an essentially non-criminal and regulatory area of inquiry," and that *Shapiro's* reach is limited where requirements "are directed to a 'selective group inherently suspect of criminal activities,'" Marchetti v. United States, 390 U.S. 39, 57 (1968) (quoting Albertson v. Subversive Activities Control Board, 382 U.S. 70, 79 (1965)). . . .

California v. Byers confirms that the ability to invoke the privilege may be greatly diminished when invocation would interfere with the effective operation of a generally applicable, civil regulatory requirement. . . .

When a person assumes control over items that are the legitimate object of the government's non-criminal regulatory powers, the ability to invoke the privilege is reduced. . . . In *Shapiro*, the Court interpreted this principle as extending well beyond the corporate context, and emphasized that Shapiro had assumed and retained control over documents in which the government had a direct and particular regulatory interest. Indeed, it was in part Shapiro's custody over items having this public nature that allowed the Court in *Marchetti* . . . to distinguish the measures considered in those cases from the regulatory requirement at issue in *Shapiro*. These principles readily apply to this case. Once Maurice was adjudicated a child in need of assistance, his care and safety became the particular object of the State's regulatory interests. . . . Maryland first placed Maurice in shelter care, authorized placement in foster care, and then entrusted responsibility for Maurice's care to Bouknight. By accepting care of Maurice subject to the custodial order's conditions (including requirements that she cooperate with BCDSS, follow a prescribed training regime, and be subject to further court orders), Bouknight submitted to the routine operation of the regulatory system and agreed to hold Maurice in a manner consonant with the State's regulatory interests and subject to inspection by BCDSS. In assuming the obligations attending custody, Bouknight "has accepted the incident obligation to permit inspection." *Wilson*, 221 U.S., at 382. The State imposes and enforces that obligation as part of a broadly directed, noncriminal regulatory regime governing children cared for pursuant to custodial orders.

Persons who care for children pursuant to a custody order, and who may be subject to a request for access to the child, are hardly a "selective group inherently suspect of criminal activities." The Juvenile Court may place a child within its jurisdiction with social service officials or "under supervision in his own home or in the custody or under the guardianship of a relative or other fit person, upon terms the court deems appropriate." Md. Cts. & Jud. Proc. Code Ann. §3-820(c)(1)(i) (Supp. 1989). Children may be placed, for example, in foster care, in homes of relatives, or in the care of state officials. Even when the court allows a parent to retain control of a child within the court's jurisdiction, that parent is not one singled out for criminal conduct, but rather has been deemed to be, without the State's assistance, simply "unable or unwilling to give proper care and attention to the child and his problems." Md. Cts. & Jud. Proc. Code Ann. §3-801(e) (Supp. 1989).

Similarly, BCDSS's efforts to gain access to children, as well as judicial efforts to the same effect, do not "focu[s] almost exclusively on conduct which was criminal." *Byers*, 402 U.S., at 454 (Harlan, J., concurring in judgment). Many orders will arise in circumstances entirely devoid of criminal conduct. Even when criminal conduct may exist, the court may properly request production and return of the child, and enforce that request through exercise of the contempt power, for reasons related entirely to the child's well-being and through measures unrelated to criminal law enforcement or investigation. This case provides an illustration: concern for the child's safety underlay the efforts to gain access to and then compel production of Maurice. Finally, production in the vast majority of cases will embody no incriminating testimony, even if in particular cases the act of production may incriminate the custodian through an assertion of possession, the existence, or the identity of the child. These orders to produce children cannot be characterized as efforts to gain some testimonial component of the act of production. The government demands production of the very public charge entrusted to a custodian, and makes the demand for compelling reasons unrelated to criminal law enforcement and as part of a broadly applied regulatory regime. In these circumstances, Bouknight cannot invoke the privilege to resist the order to produce Maurice.

We are not called upon to define the precise limitations that may exist upon the State's ability to use the testimonial aspects of Bouknight's act of production in subsequent criminal proceedings. But we note that imposition of such limitations is not foreclosed. The same custodial role that limited the ability to resist the production order may give rise to corresponding limitations upon the direct and indirect use of that testimony. See *Braswell*, 487 U.S., at 118, and n. 11. The State's regulatory requirement in the usual case may neither compel incriminating testimony nor aid a criminal prosecution, but the Fifth Amendment protections are not thereby necessarily unavailable to the person who complies with the regulatory requirement after invoking the privilege and subsequently faces prosecution. See *Marchetti*, 390 U.S., at 58-59 (the "attractive and apparently practical" course of subsequent use restriction not appropriate where a significant element of the regulatory requirement is to aid law enforcement). In a broad range of contexts, the Fifth Amendment limits prosecutors' ability to use testimony that has been compelled. . . .

III

The judgment of the Court of Appeals of Maryland is reversed, and the cases are remanded to that court for further proceedings not inconsistent with this opinion.

JUSTICE MARSHALL, with whom JUSTICE BRENNAN joins, dissenting.

Although the Court assumes that respondent's act of producing her child would be testimonial and could be incriminating, it nonetheless concludes that she cannot invoke her privilege against self-incrimination and refuse to reveal her son's current location. Neither of the reasons the Court articulates to support its refusal to permit respondent to invoke her constitutional privilege justifies its decision. I therefore dissent.

The Court correctly assumes that Bouknight's production of her son to the Maryland court would be testimonial because it would amount to an admission of Bouknight's physical control over her son. The Court also assumes that Bouknight's act of production would be self-incriminating. I would not hesitate to hold explicitly that Bouknight's admission of possession or control presents a "real and appreciable" threat of self-incrimination. Marchetti v. United States, 390 U.S. 39, 48 (1968). Bouknight's ability to produce the child would conclusively establish her actual and present physical control over him, and thus might "prove a significant 'link in a chain' of evidence tending to establish [her] guilt."

Indeed, the stakes for Bouknight are much greater than the Court suggests. Not only could she face criminal abuse and neglect charges for her alleged mistreatment of Maurice, but she could also be charged with causing his death. The State acknowledges that it suspects that Maurice is dead, and the police are investigating his case as a possible homicide. In these circumstances, the potentially incriminating aspects to Bouknight's act of production are undoubtedly significant.

Notwithstanding the real threat of self-incrimination, the Court holds that "Bouknight may not invoke the privilege to resist the production order because she has assumed custodial duties related to production and because production is required as part of a noncriminal regulatory regime." In characterizing Bouknight as Maurice's "custodian," and in describing the relevant Maryland juvenile statutes as part of a noncriminal regulatory regime, the Court relies on two distinct lines of Fifth Amendment precedent, neither of which applies to this case.

The Court's first line of reasoning turns on its view that Bouknight has agreed to exercise on behalf of the State certain custodial obligations with respect to her son, obligations that the Court analogizes to those of a custodian of the records of a collective entity. This characterization is baffling. . . .

. . . [T]he rationale for denying a corporate custodian Fifth Amendment protection for acts done in her representative capacity . . . rests on the well-established principle that a collective entity, unlike a natural person, has no Fifth Amendment privilege against self-incrimination. Because an artificial entity can act only through its agents, a custodian of such an entity's documents may not invoke her personal privilege to resist producing documents. . . . Jacqueline Bouknight is not the agent for an artificial entity that possesses no Fifth

Amendment privilege. Her role as Maurice's parent is very different from the role of a corporate custodian who is merely the instrumentality through whom the corporation acts. I am unwilling to extend the collective entity doctrine into a context where it denies individuals, acting in their personal rather than representative capacities, their constitutional privilege against self-incrimination.

The Court's decision rests as well on cases holding that "the ability to invoke the privilege may be greatly diminished when invocation would interfere with the effective operation of a generally applicable, civil regulatory requirement." The cases the Court cites have two common features: they concern civil regulatory systems not primarily intended to facilitate criminal investigations, and they target the general public. See California v. Byers, 402 U.S. 424, 430-431 (1971) (determining that a "hit and run" statute that required a driver involved in an accident to stop and give certain information was primarily civil). In contrast, regulatory regimes that are directed at a " 'selective group inherently suspect of criminal activities,' " Marchetti, 390 U.S., at 57 (quoting Albertson v. Subversive Activities Control Board, 382 U.S. 70, 79 (1965)), do not result in a similar diminution of the Fifth Amendment privilege.

. . . In contrast to Marchetti, the Court here disregards the practical implications of the civil scheme and holds that the juvenile protection system does not " 'focu[s] almost exclusively on conduct which was criminal' " (quoting Byers, supra, at 454 (Harlan, J., concurring in judgment)). I cannot agree. . . . The State's goal of protecting children from abusive environments through its juvenile welfare system cannot be separated from criminal provisions that serve the same goal. When the conduct at which a civil statute aims — here, child abuse and neglect — is frequently the same conduct subject to criminal sanction, it strikes me as deeply problematic to dismiss the Fifth Amendment concerns by characterizing the civil scheme as "unrelated to criminal law enforcement investigation." A civil scheme that *inevitably* intersects with criminal sanctions may not be used to coerce, on pain of contempt, a potential criminal defendant to furnish evidence crucial to the success of her own prosecution.

The Court's approach includes a second element; it holds that a civil regulatory scheme cannot override Fifth Amendment protection unless it is targeted at the general public. . . . Maryland's juvenile welfare scheme clearly is *not* generally applicable. A child is considered in need of assistance because "[h]e is mentally handicapped or is not receiving ordinary and proper care and attention, and . . . [h]is parents . . . are unable or unwilling to give proper care and attention to the child and his problems." The juvenile court has jurisdiction only over children who are alleged to be in need of assistance, not over all children in the State. . . . In other words, the regulatory scheme that the Court describes as "broadly directed," is actually narrowly targeted at parents who through abuse or neglect deny their children the minimal reasonable level of care and attention. Not all such abuse or neglect rises to the level of criminal child abuse, but parents of children who have been so seriously neglected or abused as to warrant allegations that the children are in need of state assistance are clearly "a selective group inherently suspect of criminal activities." . . .

Although I am disturbed by the Court's willingness to apply inapposite precedent to deny Bouknight her constitutional right against self-incrimination, especially in light of the serious allegations of homicide that accompany this civil proceeding, I take some comfort in the Court's recognition that the State may be prohibited from using any testimony given by Bouknight in subsequent criminal proceedings.[2] Because I am not content to deny Bouknight the constitutional protection required by the Fifth Amendment now in the hope that she will not be convicted later on the basis of her own testimony, I dissent.

NOTES AND QUESTIONS

1. Bouknight remained in prison until 1995, refusing to disclose Maurice's location. After she was released, there were further proceedings in the case but they were closed to the public. For a procedural history, see Baltimore Sun Company v. Maryland, 340 Md. 437, 667 A.2d 166 (1995).

2. It was reasonable to suspect that Bouknight had either murdered or seriously injured Maurice, and was refusing to report on his whereabouts because doing so would lead to criminal liability. That sounds like a straightforward claim of the privilege, does it not? If a murder suspect were ordered to take the police to the victim's dead body and the suspect refused, invoking his Fifth Amendment privilege, any court would hold that the privilege applied and the state's investigators would have to find the body on their own. Why should the conclusion be different in *Bouknight*?

3. Justice O'Connor's answer is: There are civil regulatory interests at stake — the same answer that Justice Harlan gave (in response to the same argument) in California v. Byers. Think about that argument in the context of *Bouknight*. If the state were certain that Maurice was dead, the civil regulatory interests would disappear; the state's only goal would be to prosecute and convict Maurice's killer. In that event, Bouknight would be able to assert the privilege and keep quiet. But because Maurice might be alive, the story is different — Bouknight must talk, or else face an indeterminate prison sentence for contempt (she ended up sitting in prison for seven years). Does this seem odd? Bouknight has more of a privilege if she is a murderer than if she is "merely" guilty of child abuse and aggravated assault. Is that a sensible application of the principles underlying the privilege? Does it seem sensible to weigh the government's interest in regulating child custody more heavily than its interest in prosecuting people who murder children?

4. One might defend the Court's approach by noting that if Maurice were alive, the state would have a serious interest in protecting him *in the future* — not just an interest in punishing past crimes against him. That argument suggests that the privilege should yield to important interests in protecting public safety. Today, the government is regularly seeking information about terrorist plans to kill Americans, which sounds like an important public safety interest. Should the privilege yield to *that* interest? Should the government be able to compel suspected

---

2. I note, with both exasperation and skepticism about the bona fide nature of the State's intentions, that the State may be able to grant Bouknight use immunity under a recently enacted immunity statute, even though it has thus far failed to do so. See 1989 Md. Laws, Ch. 288 (amending §9-123). Although the statute applies only to testimony "in a criminal prosecution or a proceeding before a grand jury of the State," Md. Cts. & Jud. Proc. Code Ann. §9-123(b)(1) (Supp. 1989), the State represented to this Court that "[a]s a matter of law, [granting limited use immunity for the testimonial aspects of Bouknight's compliance with the production order] would now be possible," Tr. of Oral Arg. 10. If such a grant of immunity has been possible since July 1989 and the State has refused to invoke it so that it can litigate Bouknight's claim of privilege, I have difficulty believing that the State is sincere in its protestations of concern for Maurice's well-being.

terrorists to answer questions about their activities and their associates? Does your answer change if the suspected terrorists are American citizens on American soil? If so, why?

5. What is the significance of the last paragraph of Justice O'Connor's opinion? After a long and elaborate argument for the proposition that the privilege does not protect Bouknight, Justice O'Connor reminds us that "[i]n a broad range of contexts, the Fifth Amendment limits prosecutors' ability to use testimony that has been compelled"—and hints that such limits may apply even in cases like *Bouknight*. (Notice the last paragraph of Justice Marshall's dissent, where he refers to this passage.) What is the purpose of the hint?

Here is one possible answer: Like the other cases discussed in this section, *Bouknight* arises at the borders of the Fifth Amendment privilege. Bouknight's claim is plausible, even powerful in conventional Fifth Amendment terms, but granting that claim would impose serious and difficult-to-calibrate costs on the government. One response to that phenomenon is to split the difference: to grant Bouknight's claim while hinting that similar claims may be denied in future cases, or to deny Bouknight's claim while hinting that similar claims may be granted in the future. In *Marchetti*, the Court chose the former option; in *Byers* Justice Harlan chose the latter, and in *Bouknight* Justice O'Connor followed Justice Harlan's lead. Bouknight herself lost, but Justice O'Connor's opinion gives room to some future Court majority to award victory to some future Bouknight-like claimant, perhaps at a time when the social costs of the privilege seem less substantial than they did in 1990.

How should such a case be resolved today? On the one hand, the years since 1990 have seen serious non-drug crime fall by more than 40 percent. That fact suggests that the government's interest in gathering information is perhaps less urgent than it was when *Bouknight* was decided. On the other hand, the rise of terrorism means that the situation in *Bouknight*—a suspect has information that might save innocent lives—probably arises more frequently today than it did in 1990. If interest balancing is the proper way to resolve these cases, which way does the balance tilt now?

6. In part, *Bouknight* is an application of the cases discussed in Chapter 4, governing the Fifth Amendment law on subpoenas. Those cases are, to say the least, complex. And they squarely raise the question that animates *Bouknight, Byers*, and *Marchetti*: When application of ordinary Fifth Amendment analysis would make government regulation difficult, what should yield—the government regulation, or the Fifth Amendment?

NOTES ON SUBPOENAS AND THE PRIVILEGE AGAINST SELF-INCRIMINATION

1. If you have not done so already, you may wish to read pages 308-314 and 322-330 in Chapter 4, dealing with Fisher v. United States, 425 U.S. 391 (1976); and United States v. Hubbell, 530 U.S. 27 (2000).

2. Subpoenas are orders to testify or to produce some piece of evidence. In *Bouknight*, the "evidence" was a child—or, the police feared, the child's body. Most

subpoenas are more mundane; they order the production of documents, usually financial records and related correspondence. Document production is a small matter in most criminal cases. Murders and drug deals do not usually leave paper trails. Physical evidence and live witnesses tend to be the keys to solving those crimes, and police tend to gather that evidence through searches and sei-zures and interrogation of witnesses and suspects. White-collar criminal investigations are different. The police cannot feasibly search through hundreds of file cabinets looking for a single piece of paper. And pieces of paper are critical to the proof of crime in white-collar cases. So the government requires suspects (or witnesses, or custodians of relevant corporate documents) to do the work of search-ing through the file cabinets and assembling the relevant pieces of paper.

Under Boyd v. United States, 116 U.S. 616 (1886), that process was usually unconstitutional—the papers in question were private property (in two senses of the word "private"), and so were protected by both the Fourth and Fifth Amendments. The Court cut back substantially on that rule in Hale v. Henkel, 201 U.S. 43 (1906), when it decided that corporations have no privilege against self-incrimination—and that corporate officers must produce corporate docu-ments, whether or not those documents incriminate the corporation or even the officers themselves. After *Hale*, it was easy to subpoena corporate documents, but still very hard to obtain documents from individual white-collar suspects, unless the suspects consented.

3. Then came Fisher v. United States, 425 U.S. 391 (1976). *Fisher* involved a subpoena for documents related to the defendant's income taxes. The documents in question had been prepared by the defendant's accountant and were in the defendant's possession until he gave them to his lawyer for safekeeping. The question before the Court was whether the lawyer had to hand over the documents. The Court held that, if the defendant would have had a valid Fifth Amendment objection to turning over the documents himself, the lawyer could raise that objec-tion on his client's behalf. So, in a roundabout way, *Fisher* raised the question whether the Fifth Amendment allowed a defendant to refuse to hand over incri-minating documents that he owned and possessed: the same issue the Court had decided in defendants' favor 90 years earlier in *Boyd*.

In *Fisher*, the Court went the other way. The Court held that, since the govern-ment had not compelled the defendant to produce the documents, the documents themselves were not covered by the privilege. Rather, the privilege covered only that which the government compelled: the act of production. And since the pri-vilege protects testimonial communications, only the "testimonial aspects" of the defendant's act of production are protected. According to Justice White's majority opinion, when a subpoena target hands over incriminating documents, the target potentially "testifies" to three things. First, he testifies that the documents exist. Second, he testifies to the documents' authenticity—in effect, he says "these are the documents described in the subpoena." Third, he testifies to his possession of the documents. (If they were not in his control, he could not hand them over.) So under *Fisher*, this "testimony" concerning existence, authenticity, and possession of the subpoenaed documents is protected by the Fifth Amendment, at least if it is incriminating. The documents themselves are *not* protected.

As if this formula were not complicated enough, two more concepts are neces-sary to unpack *Fisher*. The first is a concept the *Fisher* Court itself introduced. Though the Court noted that every subpoena target "testifies" that the documents he hands over exist, are authentic, and were in his possession, the Court went on to say that in some cases, one or more of those issues is a "foregone conclusion": i.e., the government already knows and can prove that the documents exist, that they are what they purport to be, and that they were in the defendant's possession when the subpoena was issued. Where that is so, the Court said in *Fisher*, the Fifth Amendment "testimony" involved in handing over the documents is too insubstantial to merit protection. How broadly the concept of "foregone conclusions" might apply was left unclear in *Fisher*.

The second concept is one you have already encountered: immunity. The law has long established that the government may compel a witness to answer incriminating questions if the witness's testimony is immunized. The consequences of immunity are likewise clear: The government may not use the immunized testimony or its fruits against the defendant in any future criminal prosecution. See Kastigar v. United States, 406 U.S. 441 (1972). (*Kastigar* is excerpted supra, at page 762.) Notice the question this formula raises after *Fisher*. If the government immunizes the subpoena target's act of production, may the government then introduce the documents in a future criminal prosecution, as long as no mention is made of how the government obtained them? That would seem logical in light of the *Fisher* Court's decision to protect the act of production but not the documents themselves. But if that logical conclusion holds, *Fisher* protects very little in practice. Prosecutors in white-collar cases rarely need to tell juries that the defendant handed over incriminating documents. Prosecutors can authenticate documents through experts, possession of the documents usually doesn't matter, and the documents prove their own existence. What matters to the prosecutor is usually the *documents themselves* — what they say, not where they came from. If, even after a grant of immunity, the documents themselves may be introduced into evidence, the privilege means little. If not, it means a great deal. As with "foregone conclusions," the scope of Fifth Amendment immunity in subpoena cases after *Fisher* was left unclear.

4. Depending on how these two concepts — "foregone conclusion" and the scope of immunity in the subpoena context — were fleshed out, *Fisher*'s protection might be nearly as broad as *Boyd*'s. Or, *Fisher*'s Fifth Amendment protection might be a sham; it might never apply. To put it another way, *Fisher* could be read to protect everything, or nothing.

The "everything" reading of *Fisher* goes roughly as follows. If federal agents (white-collar cases are almost always prosecuted in federal court) knew that a given document existed, knew what the document said, and knew where to find it, presumably the agents would obtain a search warrant and go seize the document. The only reason to use a subpoena instead of a police search is precisely because the prosecutors and agents *don't* know those things. In that event, the defendant's act of producing the document, compelled by court order (compliance with subpoenas is mandatory), communicates important incriminating information to the government. The document itself is the fruit of that incriminating, testimonial communication. Using the document against the defendant would thus be a clear violation of the privilege. If this reading of *Fisher* were adopted, the "foregone conclusion" concept would almost never apply, and immunizing the act of production would almost always mean immunizing the documents themselves.

The "nothing" reading of *Fisher* goes like this. Documents are not protected; only the act of producing them is. As long as the government avoids introducing into evidence the fact that the defendant handed the documents over, the government is not using the defendant's act of production against him. All *Fisher* requires is that, in any criminal trial of a subpoena target, the government must treat subpoenaed documents as though they came in "over the transom"—as though the documents magically fell into the government's lap. In almost all white-collar cases, that is easy to do: Once again, expert witnesses can authenticate documents; the documents can prove their own existence; and possession is generally unimportant—what counts is what the documents say, not where they came from. *Fisher* thus imposes only the lightest of burdens on the government.

5. A number of commentators suggested that, in the wake of *Fisher*, the Court might hold that custodians of corporate documents can assert the privilege when asked to turn those documents over, as long as the act of production would incriminate the custodian personally. In Braswell v. United States, 487 U.S. 99 (1988), a five-vote Court majority held otherwise. In the Court's view, "the custodian's act of production is not . . . a personal act, but rather an act of the corporation. Any claim of Fifth Amendment privilege asserted by [the custodian] would be tantamount to a claim of privilege by the corporation—which of course posesses no such privilege." Id. at 110. Justice Kennedy's opinion for the Court closed with an odd paragraph suggesting that the government could not use the fact that the custodian turned over the documents against the custodian personally—but it *could* tell the jury that the corporation produced the documents. See id. at 117-118 and n. 11. In practice, that suits the government just fine, for reasons explored in the preceding notes. *Braswell* seemed to suggest that the "nothing" version of *Fisher* might well be the law.

6. Hubbell v. United States, 530 U.S. 27 (2000), suggests otherwise. Defendant Webster Hubbell had been an Arkansas lawyer and judge and later served in Bill Clinton's Justice Department. The wide-ranging independent counsel investigation of Whitewater—the same investigation that uncovered Monica Lewinsky's famous blue dress—led to a prosecution of Hubbell for mail fraud and tax evasion. In the course of investigating Hubbell, the government subpoenaed a host of documents related to Hubbell's taxes and finances over a period of several years. Hubbell took the Fifth. The prosecution granted him immunity, whereupon Hubbell complied with the subpoena, producing over 13,000 pages of documents. Hubbell was then indicted; the government conceded that its charges were based on information provided by the documents Hubbell turned over, together with other information to which those documents led. Hubbell moved to dismiss the charges, on the ground that the government violated his immunity by using the fruits of his act of producing the documents against him.

The Supreme Court bought Hubbell's argument:

> The Government correctly emphasizes that the testimonial aspect of a response to a subpoena duces tecum does nothing more than establish the existence, authenticity, and custody of items that are produced. We assume that the Government is also entirely correct in its submission that it would not have to advert to respondent's act of production in order to prove the existence, authenticity, or custody of any documents that it might offer in evidence at a criminal trial; indeed, the Government disclaims any need to introduce any of the documents produced by respondent into evidence in order to prove the charges against him. It follows, according to the Government, that it has no intention of making improper "use" of respondent's compelled testimony.

The question, however, is not whether the response to the subpoena may be introduced into evidence at his criminal trial. That would surely be a prohibited "use" of the immunized act of production. But the fact that the Government intends no such use of the act of production leaves open the separate question whether it has already made "derivative use" of the testimonial aspect of that act in obtaining the indictment against respondent and in preparing its case for trial. It clearly has.

It is apparent from the text of the subpoena itself that the prosecutor needed respondent's assistance both to identify potential sources of information and to produce those sources. Given the breadth of the description of the 11 categories of documents called for by the subpoena, the collection and production of the materials demanded was tantamount to answering a series of interrogatories asking a witness to disclose the existence and location of particular documents fitting certain broad descriptions. . . . Entirely apart from the contents of the 13,120 pages of materials that respondent produced in this case, it is undeniable that providing a catalog of existing documents fitting within any of the 11 broadly worded subpoena categories could provide a prosecutor with a "lead to incriminating evidence," or "a link in the chain of evidence needed to prosecute."

Indeed, the record makes it clear that that is what happened in this case. . . . It is abundantly clear that the testimonial aspect of respondent's act of producing subpoenaed documents was the first step in a chain of evidence that led to this prosecution. The documents did not magically appear in the prosecutor's office like "manna from heaven." They arrived there only after respondent asserted his constitutional privilege, received a grant of immunity, and—under the compulsion of the District Court's order—took the mental and physical steps necessary to provide the prosecutor with an accurate inventory of the many sources of potentially incriminating evidence sought by the subpoena. It was only through respondent's truthful reply to the subpoena that the Government received the incriminating documents of which it made "substantial use . . . in the investigation that led to the indictment." Brief for United States 3.

For these reasons, we cannot accept the Government's submission that respondent's immunity did not preclude its derivative use of the produced documents because its "possession of the documents [was] the fruit only of a simple physical act—the act of producing the documents." Id. at 29. It was unquestionably necessary for respondent to make extensive use of "the contents of his own mind" in identifying the hundreds of documents responsive to the requests in the subpoena. See Curcio v. United States, 354 U.S. 118, 128 (1957). The assembly of those documents was like telling an inquisitor the combination to a wall safe, not like being forced to surrender the key to a strongbox. The Government's anemic view of respondent's act of production as a mere physical act that is principally non-testimonial in character and can be entirely divorced from its "implicit" testimonial aspect so as to constitute a "legitimate, wholly independent source" (as required by Kastigar [v. United States, 406 U.S. 441 (1972)]) for the documents produced simply fails to account for these realities.

. . . [T]he Government has argued that the communicative aspect of respondent's act of producing ordinary business records is insufficiently "testimonial" to support a claim of privilege because the existence and possession of such records by any businessman is a "foregone conclusion" under our decision in Fisher v. United States, 425 U.S. [391, 411 (1976)]. This argument . . . misreads Fisher. . . .

. . . Fisher involved summonses seeking production of working papers prepared by the taxpayers' accountants that the IRS knew were in the possession of the taxpayers' attorneys. In rejecting the taxpayers's claim that these documents were protected by the Fifth Amendment privilege, we stated:

> "It is doubtful that implicitly admitting the existence and possession of the papers rises to the level of testimony within the protection of the Fifth Amendment. The papers belong to

> the *accountant*, were prepared by him, and are the kind usually prepared by an accountant working on the tax returns of his client. Surely the Government is in no way relying on the 'truthtelling' of the *taxpayer* to prove the existence of or his access to the documents. . . . The existence and location of the papers are a foregone conclusion and the taxpayer adds little or nothing to the sum total of the Government's information by conceding that he in fact has the papers." 425 U.S. at 411 (emphases added).

Whatever the scope of this "foregone conclusion" rationale, the facts of this case plainly fall outside of it. While in *Fisher* the Government already knew that the documents were in the attorneys' possession and could independently confirm their existence and authenticity through the accountants who created them, here the Government has not shown that it had any prior knowledge of either the existence or the whereabouts of the 13,120 pages of documents ultimately produced by respondent. The Government cannot cure this deficiency through the overbroad argument that a businessman such as respondent will always possess general business and tax records that fall within the broad categories described in this subpoena. . . .

. . . [It follows that] respondent could not be compelled to produce those documents without first receiving a grant of immunity. . . . [S]uch immunity is co-extensive with the constitutional privilege. *Kastigar* requires that respondent's motion to dismiss the indictment on immunity grounds be granted unless the Government proves that the evidence it used in obtaining the indictment and proposed to use at trial was derived from legitimate sources "wholly independent" of the testimonial aspect of respondent's immunized conduct in assembling and producing the documents described in the subpoena. The Government, however, does not claim that it could make such a showing. Rather, it contends that its prosecution of respondent must be considered proper unless someone — presumably respondent — shows that "there is some substantial relation between the compelled testimonial communications implicit in the act of production (as opposed to the act of production standing alone) and some aspect of the information used in the investigation or the evidence presented at trial." Brief for United States 9. We could not accept this submission without repudiating the basis for our conclusion in *Kastigar* that the statutory guarantee of use and derivative-use immunity is as broad as the constitutional privilege itself. This we are not prepared to do. . . .

530 U.S. at 41-46.

7. How far does the privilege extend after *Hubbell*? Notice that *Fisher*'s "foregone conclusion" concept seems quite narrow after *Hubbell*. And the scope of immunity in subpoena cases seems quite broad. *Hubbell* plainly rejects the "nothing" interpretation of *Fisher*. Does it embrace the "everything" interpretation?

A straightforward reading of the Court's opinion would suggest that the answer is yes. Reread the following language:

> The documents did not magically appear in the prosecutor's office like "manna from heaven." They arrived there only after respondent asserted his constitutional privilege, received a grant of immunity, and — under the compulsion of the District Court's order — took the mental and physical steps necessary to provide the prosecutor with an accurate inventory of the many sources of potentially incriminating evidence sought by the subpoena. It was only through respondent's truthful reply to the subpoena that the Government received the incriminating documents . . .

Save for a couple of adjectives, one could say these things in virtually any white-collar investigation in which a subpoena target becomes a defendant. If the "mental and physical steps necessary" to comply with a subpoena are enough to trigger the privilege, and if the privilege extends as far as this passage implies, then a great many subpoena targets will have valid Fifth Amendment claims, and a great many white-collar crime investigations will never get off the ground. *Hubbell* could take Fifth Amendment law almost back to *Boyd*.

It could, but it probably won't. Consider another phrase in Justice Stevens' opinion for the Court in *Hubbell*: "It was unquestionably necessary for respondent to make *extensive use* of the contents of his own mind in identifying the hundreds of documents responsive to the requests in the subpoena" (emphasis added, internal quotation marks and citation omitted). Now imagine a case in which, instead of 13,000 pages of documents, the target must produce 5,000—or 500. Or, imagine a case in which the number of pages is even higher than in *Hubbell*, but in which the relevant files are all stored neatly in one place, so that compliance with the subpoena is not terribly burdensome. Might the Court decide that *that* defendant did not have to "make *extensive* use of the contents of his own mind" in order to comply with the subpoena? What does "extensive use" mean anyway?

The answer is, it could mean anything. Like *Marchetti*, *Byers*, and *Bouknight*, *Hubbell* is cast in broad terms that could have enormous implications for the privilege's scope. But the one constant in recent Fifth Amendment history is that the broadest implications of the Court's decisions—either in the government's favor, or in favor of the criminal defendants who claim the privilege—don't pan out. We seem to live in an era of a split-the-difference privilege, a privilege that must be protected even at some cost to the government—but not if the cost is too high. Periodically, the Court pushes lower courts toward a little broader protection (*Marchetti*, *Hubbell*) or a little narrower protection (*Byers*, *Bouknight*). The operative words are "a little." When the pendulum swings too far in the view of a centrist Supreme Court, the Justices swing in the other direction.

This is not terribly satisfying for those who like intellectual consistency, or for those who believe Fifth Amendment law should conform neatly to some overarching theory. Yet it may be wise institutional management. Crime in the United States fell by about half between the mid-1930s and the mid-1950s. The Supreme Court of the 1960s responded with a broad agenda of expanded constitutional rights for criminal defendants. Crime rose sharply in the 1960s and early 1970s; after a brief plateau, it rose sharply again in the late 1980s. Beginning around 1968, the Court responded with 30 years of tough-on-crime decisions, in Fifth Amendment law and elsewhere. Since 1991, crime has again fallen sharply, and the current Court has responded with more expansion of criminal defendants' rights—again, in Fifth Amendment law and elsewhere. (An obvious recent example is the growth of the rights to jury trial and to proof beyond a reasonable doubt under Apprendi v. New Jersey, 530 U.S. 466 (2000), and Blakely v. Washington, 124 S. Ct. 2531 (2004). See Chapter 13 for details.) The current expansion in defendants' rights is not comparable to the expansion of the 1960s. But then the Court of the 1960s did not have to worry about a government-sponsored war on terrorism. For all its inconsistencies and theoretical wrong turns, Fifth Amendment law in particular and the law of criminal procedure more generally may be healthier than is commonly supposed.

D. Police Interrogation

1. Police Interrogation and the *Miranda* Revolution

Since earliest recorded times, officialdom has interrogated individuals suspected of or charged with criminality. In more barbaric times, the questioning was often accompanied by physical abuse or torture, and a confession resulting from such methods, no matter the extent of the physical coercion applied to the suspect, could form part of the basis of a conviction. Nonetheless, the factual accuracy of statements made under extreme duress is obviously problematic where the only means of halting an interrogation is to assent to the views of the interrogator. Thus, there developed the view that a person ought not to face coercive interrogation designed to yield self-incriminating responses.

The opposition to coercive interrogation gained support from the opposition to the practices of the High Commission and the Court of Star Chamber in England — in particular, the use of the oath ex officio, which required those called before the court to swear to answer truthfully all questions, on pain of perjury, without being informed of the subject matter of the inquiry and prior to any official allegation of criminality. The resistance to the practices of the High Commission and the Star Chamber, while initially resting on the common law principle that a person could not be compelled to answer questions under oath regarding charges that had not been formally made, came to rest on the moral ground that it was unfair for the state to attempt to coerce an individual to contribute to his or her own conviction. These interrelated concerns about trustworthiness, the developing view of the requirements of fairness, and the demands for privacy and autonomy, discussed in Section A supra at page 753 and in Chapter 4 supra at page 277, together seem to have formed the basis of the Fifth Amendment privilege.[1]

Nonetheless, the applicability of the Fifth Amendment to pretrial interrogation was not generally accepted at an early date in this country. Notwithstanding the periodic recognition of the abuses of pretrial interrogation similar to those that gave rise in part to the Fifth Amendment,[2] confessions were excluded only if they were untrustworthy, see, e.g., Hopt v. Utah, 110 U.S. 574 (1884), although one important determinant of trustworthiness was the nature of the interrogation process that led to the incriminating statements. In 1897, however, the Supreme Court, in a remarkable opinion, appeared to bring pretrial interrogation within the scope of the Fifth Amendment in a fashion that unified the Court's treatment of the various issues underlying the Fourth and Fifth Amendments.

---

1. For discussions of these developments, see Leonard W. Levy, The Origins of the Fifth Amendment (1968); Richard H. Helmholz et al., The Privilege against Self-Incrimination (1997). The constitutional debates over the Fifth Amendment are peculiarly unenlightening — thus, the word "seem" in the text. Recent scholarship has called into question the conventional understanding of the origins of the right to be free from compelled self-incrimination. In a very interesting article, John Langbein argues that the origins of the privilege lie in the latter part of the eighteenth century — in particular, the introduction of defense counsel. John Langbein, The Historical Origins of the Privilege against Self-Incrimination at Common Law, 92 Mich. L. Rev. 1047 (1994).

2. See, e.g., National Commission on Law Observance and Enforcement, Report on Lawlessness in Law Enforcement (1931) (often referred to as the Wickersham Commission).

The case was Bram v. United States, 168 U.S. 532 (1897). Bram was first officer on a ship bound from Boston to South America; he and a shipmate were charged with killing the ship's master.

> On reaching port, these two suspected persons were delivered to the custody of the police authorities of Halifax and were there held in confinement awaiting the action of the United States consul, which was to determine whether the suspicions which had caused the arrest justified the sending of one or both of the prisoners into the United States for formal charge and trial. Before this examination had taken place the police detective caused Bram to be brought from jail to his private office, and when there alone with the detective *he was stripped of his clothing*, and either whilst the detective was in the act of so stripping him, or after he was denuded, the conversation offered as a confession took place. The detective repeats what he said to the prisoner, whom he had thus stripped, as follows:
>
>> When Mr. Bram came into my office I said to him: "Bram, we are trying to unravel this horrible mystery." I said: "Your position is rather an awkward one. I have had Brown in this office, and he made a statement that he saw you do the murder." He said: "He could not have seen me. Where was he?" I said: "He states he was at the wheel." "Well," he said, "he could not see me from there."

Id. at 561-562. On these facts, the Court concluded that

> the situation of the accused, and the nature of the communication made to him by the detective, necessarily overthrows any possible implication that his reply to the detective could have been the result of a purely voluntary mental action; that is to say, when all the surrounding circumstances are considered in their true relations, not only is the claim that the statement was voluntary overthrown, but the impression is irresistibly produced that it must necessarily have been the result of either hope or fear, or both, operating on the mind.

Id. at 562. "Either hope or fear, or both" failed the constitutional standard, which the Court defined in expansive terms:

> In criminal trials, in the courts of the United States, wherever a question arises whether a confession is incompetent because not voluntary, the issue is controlled by that portion of the Fifth Amendment to the Constitution of the United States, commanding that no person "shall be compelled in any criminal case to be a witness against himself." The legal principle by which the admissibility of the confession of an accused person is to be determined is expressed in the textbooks.
>
>> In 3 Russell on Crimes, (6th ed.) 478, it is stated as follows:
>>
>>> But a confession, in order to be admissible, must be free and voluntary: that is, must not be extracted by any sort of threats or violence, nor obtained by any direct or implied promises, however slight, nor by the exertion of any improper influence. . . . A confession can never be received in evidence where the prisoner has been influenced by any threat or promise; for the law cannot measure the force of the influence used, or decide upon its effect upon the mind of the prisoner, and therefore excludes the declaration if any degree of influence has been exerted. . . .

Id. at 542. On that standard, *Bram* was an easy case: "A plainer violation as well of the letter as of the spirit and purpose of the constitutional immunity could scarcely be conceived of." Id. at 564. The Court's opinion continued:

> Moreover, aside from the natural result arising from the situation of the accused and the communication made to him by the detective, the conversation conveyed an express intimation rendering the confession involuntary within the rule laid down by the authorities. What further was said by the detective? "Now, look here, Bram, I am satisfied that you killed the captain from all I have heard from Mr. Brown. But, 'I said', some of us here think you could not have done all that crime alone. If you had an accomplice, you should say so, and not have the blame of this horrible crime on your own shoulders." But how could the weight of the whole crime be removed from the shoulders of the prisoner as a consequence of his speaking, unless benefit as to the crime and its punishment was to arise from his speaking? Conceding that, closely analyzed, the hope of benefit which the conversation suggested was that of the removal from the conscience of the prisoner of the merely moral weight resulting from concealment, and therefore would not be an inducement, we are to consider the import of the conversation, not from a mere abstract point of view, but by the light of the impression that it was calculated to produce on the mind of the accused, situated as he was at the time the conversation took place. Thus viewed, the weight to be removed by speaking naturally imported a suggestion of some benefit as to the crime and its punishment as arising from making a statement. . . .

Id. at 564-565.

The *Bram* decision proved remarkably prescient; 70 years later, the Court and commentators would debate police interrogation in terms that coincide almost exactly with the Court's opinion. Yet, just as remarkably, *Bram* had little immediate impact. Two facts contributed to its unimportance. First, it was not until 1964 that the Supreme Court ruled that the Fifth Amendment privilege was applicable to the states. Malloy v. Hogan, 378 U.S. 1 (1964). Thus, *Bram* was limited to federal cases — and the vast majority of prosecutions for ordinary street crime, hence the vast majority of police interrogation sessions, are litigated in state courts. Second, although *Bram* invoked the Fifth Amendment, the standard the Court actually employed was the common law's voluntariness standard.

Roughly 40 years after *Bram* was decided, the Supreme Court held that a constitutional voluntariness requirement applied to state courts as well as federal courts. But that voluntariness standard rested on due process, not on the Fifth Amendment. And it was a good deal less rigorous, as the notes below illustrate.

NOTES ON THE DUE PROCESS VOLUNTARINESS TEST

1. The case that inaugurated the voluntariness requirement for state cases was Brown v. Mississippi, 297 U.S. 278 (1936). Chief Justice Hughes drew his chilling statement of facts from a dissenting opinion in the state court below:

> ". . . On Sunday night, . . . the same deputy, accompanied by a number of white men, one of whom was also an officer, and by the jailer, came to the jail, and [defendants Ed Brown and Henry Shields] were made to strip and they were laid over chairs and their backs were cut to pieces with a leather strap with buckles on it, and they were likewise

made by the said deputy definitely to understand that the whipping would be continued unless and until they confessed, and not only confessed, but confessed in every
matter of detail as demanded by those present; and in this manner the defendants
confessed the crime, and as the whippings progressed and were repeated, they
changed or adjusted their confession in all particulars of detail so as to conform to
the demands of their torturers. When the confessions had been obtained in the exact
form and contents as desired by the mob, they left with the parting admonition and
warning that, if the defendants changed their story at any time in any respect from
that last stated, the perpetrators of the outrage would administer the same or equally
effective treatment. . . ."

Id. at 282 (citation omitted). The state argued that the admission of these confessions into evidence violated no federal right, citing Twining v. New Jersey, 211
U.S. 78 (1908), which had held that the Fifth Amendment's privilege against self-
incrimination did not bind state courts. Hughes responded:

. . . [T]he question of the right of the State to withdraw the privilege against self-
incrimination is not here involved. The compulsion to which the quoted statements
[in *Twining*] refer is that of the processes of justice by which the accused may be called
as a witness and required to testify. Compulsion by torture to extort a confession is a
different matter.

The State is free to regulate the procedure of its courts in accordance with its own
conceptions of policy, unless in so doing it "offends some principle of justice so rooted
in the traditions and conscience of our people as to be ranked as fundamental."
Snyder v. Massachusetts, [291 U.S. 97 (1933)]. The State may abolish trial by jury.
It may dispense with indictment by a grand jury and substitute complaint or information. But the freedom of the State in establishing its policy is the freedom of
constitutional government and is limited by the requirement of due process of law.
Because a State may dispense with a jury trial, it does not follow that it may substitute
trial by ordeal. The rack and torture chamber may not be substituted for the witness
stand. . . . It would be difficult to conceive of methods more revolting to the sense of
justice than those taken to procure the confessions of these petitioners, and the use of
the confessions thus obtained as the basis for conviction and sentence was a clear
denial of due process.

297 U.S. at 285-286.

The torture in *Brown* was not hidden; the police officers and their accomplices
did not fear any court declaration that the confessions were involuntary and hence
inadmissible, because no such federal doctrine existed. After *Brown*, voluntariness
cases were more complicated. Some aspects of compelled questioning, such as the
timing of the relevant events, were uncontested; as to other facts, the parties rarely
agreed. Defendants often claimed physical brutality. The police generally denied
it. Whether or not the Justices believed the denial was often critical to the Court's
decisions — though opinions rarely said so.

2. The facts in Ashcraft v. Tennessee, 322 U.S. 143 (1944), were typical:

. . . It appears that the officers placed Ashcraft at a table in this room on the fifth floor of
the county jail with a light over his head and began to quiz him. They questioned him in
relays until the following Monday morning, June 16, 1941, around nine-thirty or ten
o'clock. It appears that Ashcraft from Saturday evening at seven o'clock until Monday
morning at approximately nine-thirty never left this homicide room on the fifth floor.

Testimony of the officers shows that the reason they questioned Ashcraft "in relays" was that they became so tired they were compelled to rest. But from 7:00 Saturday evening until 9:30 Monday morning Ashcraft had no rest. . . .

As to what happened in the fifth-floor jail room during this thirty-six hour secret examination the testimony follows the usual pattern and is in hopeless conflict. Ashcraft swears that . . . during the course of the examination he was threatened and abused in various ways; and that as the hours passed his eyes became blinded by a powerful electric light, his body became weary, and the strain on his nerves became unbearable. The officers, on the other hand, swear that throughout the questioning they were kind and considerate. . . . [T]he officers declare that . . . Ashcraft was "cool," "calm," "collected," "normal"; that his vision was unimpaired and his eyes not bloodshot; and that he showed no outward signs of being tired or sleepy.

Id. at 149-151. Ashcraft claimed that he never confessed; the police contended that he did. The Court concluded that

if Ashcraft made a confession it was not voluntary but compelled. We reach this conclusion from facts which are not in dispute at all. . . . We think a situation such as that here shown by uncontradicted evidence is so inherently coercive that its very existence is irreconcilable with the possession of mental freedom by a lone suspect against whom its full coercive force is brought to bear. It is inconceivable that any court of justice in the land, conducted as our courts are, open to the public, would permit prosecutors serving in relays to keep a defendant witness under continuous cross-examination for thirty-six hours without rest or sleep in an effort to extract a "voluntary" confession. Nor can we, consistently with Constitutional due process of law, hold voluntary a confession where prosecutors do the same thing away from the restraining influences of a public trial in an open court room.

Id. at 153-154. Justices Jackson, Roberts, and Frankfurter dissented, arguing that the Court was overturning state court findings of fact without good cause. Jackson added: "[D]oes the Constitution prohibit use of all confessions made after arrest because questioning, while one is deprived of freedom, is 'inherently coercive'? The Court does not quite say so, but it is moving far and fast in that direction." Id. at 161 (Jackson, J., dissenting).

3. In Watts v. Indiana, 338 U.S. 49 (1949),

. . . [The police] took [petitioner] from the county jail to State Police Headquarters, where he was questioned by officers in relays from about 11:30 that night [the date was November 12] until sometime between 2:30 and 3 o'clock the following morning. The same procedure of persistent interrogation from about 5:30 in the afternoon until about 3 o'clock the following morning, by a relay of six to eight officers, was pursued on Thursday the 13th, Friday the 14th, Saturday the 15th, Monday the 17th. Sunday was a day of rest from interrogation. About 3 o'clock on Tuesday morning, November 18, the petitioner made an incriminating statement after continuous questioning since 6 o'clock of the preceding evening. . . .

Until his inculpatory statements were secured, the petitioner was a prisoner in the exclusive control of the prosecuting authorities. He was kept for the first two days in solitary confinement in a cell aptly enough called "the hole" in view of its physical conditions as described by the State's witnesses. . . . Although the law of Indiana required that petitioner be given a prompt preliminary hearing before a magistrate, . . . the petitioner was not only given no hearing during the entire period of interrogation but was without friendly or professional aid and without advice as to his constitutional rights. Disregard of rudimentary needs of life — opportunities for sleep and a decent allowance of food — are also relevant, not as aggravating elements of petitioner's treatment, but as part of the total situation out of which his confessions came and which stamped their character.

Id. at 52-53. Justice Frankfurter wrote for the Court:

. . . A statement to be voluntary of course need not be volunteered. But if it is the product of sustained pressure by the police it does not issue from a free choice. . . . We would have to shut our minds to the plain significance of what here transpired to deny that this was a calculated endeavor to secure a confession through the pressure of unrelenting interrogation. The very relentlessness of such interrogation implies that it is better for the prisoner to answer than to persist in the refusal of disclosure which is his constitutional right. To turn the detention of an accused into a process of wrenching from him evidence which could not be extorted in open court with all its safeguards, is so grave an abuse of the power of arrest as to offend the procedural standards of due process.

Id. at 53-54.

Justice Jackson again dissented in *Watts* — two companion cases were decided the same day; Jackson dissented in one and concurred in the other — and offered the following criticism of the Court's path:

These three cases, from widely separated states, present essentially the same problem. Its recurrence suggests that it has roots in some condition fundamental and general to our criminal system.

In each case police were confronted with one or more brutal murders which the authorities were under the highest duty to solve. Each of these murders was unwitnessed, and the only positive knowledge on which a solution could be based was possessed by the killer. In each there was reasonable ground to *suspect* an individual but not enough legal evidence to *charge* him with guilt. In each the police attempted to meet the situation by taking the suspect into custody and interrogating him. This extended over varying periods. In each, confessions were made and received in evidence at the trial. Checked with external evidence, they are inherently believable, and were not shaken as to truth by anything that occurred at the trial. Each confessor was convicted by a jury and state courts affirmed. This Court sets all three convictions aside.

The seriousness of the Court's judgment is that no one suggests that any course held promise of solution of these murders other than to take the suspect into custody for questioning. The alternative was to close the books on the crime and forget it, with the suspect at large. This is a grave choice for a society in which two-thirds of the murders already are closed out as insoluble. . . .

Others would strike down these confessions because of conditions which they say make them "involuntary." In this, on only a printed record, they pit their judgment against that of the trial judge and the jury. Both, with the great advantage of hearing and seeing the confessor and also the officers whose conduct and bearing toward him is in question, have found that the confessions were voluntary. In addition, the majority overrule in each case one or more state appellate courts, which have the same limited opportunity to know the truth that we do.

Amid much that is irrelevant or trivial, one serious situation seems to me to stand out in these cases. The suspect neither had nor was advised of his right to get counsel. This presents a real dilemma in a free society. To subject one without counsel to questioning which may and is intended to convict him, is a real peril to individual freedom. To bring in a lawyer means a real peril to solution of the crime, because, under our adversary system, he deems that his sole duty is to protect his client — guilty or innocent — and that in such a capacity he owes no duty whatever to help society solve its crime problem. Under this conception of criminal procedure, any lawyer worth his salt will tell the suspect in no uncertain terms to make no statement to police under any circumstances.

If the State may arrest on suspicion and interrogate without counsel, there is no denying the fact that it largely negates the benefits of the constitutional guaranty of the right to assistance of counsel. Any lawyer who has ever been called into a case after his client has "told all" and turned any evidence he has over to the Government, knows how helpless he is to protect his client against the facts thus disclosed.

I suppose the view one takes will turn on what one thinks should be the right of an accused person against the State. Is it his right to have the judgment on the facts? Or is it his right to have a judgment based on only such evidence as he cannot conceal from the authorities, who cannot compel him to testify in court and also cannot question him before? Our system comes close to the latter by any interpretation, for the defendant is shielded by such safeguards as no system of law except the Anglo-American concedes to him.

Of course, no confession that has been obtained by any form of physical violence to the person is reliable and hence no conviction should rest upon one obtained in that manner. Such treatment not only breaks the will to conceal or lie, but may even break the will to stand by the truth. Nor is it questioned that the same result can sometimes be achieved by threats, promises, or inducements, which torture the mind but put no scar on the body. If the opinion of Mr. Justice Frankfurter in the *Watts* case were based solely on the State's admissions as to the treatment of Watts, I should not disagree. But if ultimate quest in a criminal trial is the truth and if the circumstances indicate no violence or threats of it, should society be deprived of the suspect's help in solving a crime merely because he was confined and questioned when uncounseled?

We must not overlook that, in these as in some previous cases, once a confession is obtained it supplies ways of verifying its trustworthiness. In these cases before us the verification is sufficient to leave me in no doubt that the admissions of guilt were genuine and truthful. Such corroboration consists in one case of finding a weapon where the accused has said he hid it, and in others that conditions which could only have been known to one who was implicated correspond with his story. It is possible, but it is rare, that a confession, if repudiated on the trial, standing alone will convict unless there is external proof of its verity.

In all such cases, along with other conditions criticized, the continuity and duration of the questioning is invoked and it is called an "inquiry," "inquest" or "inquisition," depending mainly on the emotional state of the writer. But as in some of the cases here, if interrogation is permissible at all, there are sound reasons for prolonging it — which the opinions here ignore. The suspect at first perhaps makes an effort to exculpate himself by alibis or other statements. These are verified, found false, and he is then confronted with his falsehood. Sometimes (though such cases do not reach us) verification proves them true or credible and the suspect is released. Sometimes, as here, more than one crime is involved. The duration of an interrogation may well depend on the temperament, shrewdness and cunning of the accused and the competence of the examiner. But, assuming a right to examine at all, the right must include what is made reasonably necessary by the facts of the particular case.

If the right of interrogation be admitted, then it seems to me that we must leave it to trial judges and juries and state appellate courts to decide individual cases, unless they show some want of proper standards of decision. I find nothing to indicate that any of the courts below in these cases did not have a correct understanding of the

Fourteenth Amendment, unless this Court thinks it means absolute prohibition of interrogation while in custody before arraignment.

I suppose no one would doubt that our Constitution and Bill of Rights, grounded in revolt against the arbitrary measures of George III and in the philosophy of the French Revolution, represent the maximum restrictions upon the power of organized society over the individual that are compatible with the maintenance of organized society itself. They were so intended and should be so interpreted. It cannot be denied that, even if construed as these provisions traditionally have been, they contain an aggregate of restrictions which seriously limit the power of society to solve such crimes as confront us in these cases. Those restrictions we should not for that reason cast aside, but that is good reason for indulging in no unnecessary expansion of them.

I doubt very much if they require us to hold that the State may not take into custody and question one suspected reasonably of an unwitnessed murder. If it does, the people of this country must discipline themselves to seeing their police stand by helplessly while those suspected of murder prowl about unmolested. Is it a necessary price to pay for the fairness which we know as "due process of law"? And if not a necessary one, should it be demanded by this Court? I do not know the ultimate answer to these questions; but, for the present, I should not increase the handicap on society.

338 U.S. at 57-62 (Jackson, J., dissenting).

4. The debate in *Watts* continued for another 15 years. Judging from case results, Justice Jackson's position did poorly: The Court reversed convictions based on involuntary confessions with growing frequency in the 1950s and early 1960s. The fact patterns of the cases began to change; allegations of physical brutality were replaced with the kind of psychological brutality found in Payne v. Arkansas, 356 U.S. 560 (1958), where an African American defendant with a fifth-grade education was told that a white mob would be waiting for him unless he confessed. The Court's focus began to change as well; the opinions devoted less space to the question whether the suspect's will was "overborne" (what do you suppose that means?) and more to the question whether the police conduct was unacceptable in a free society. Usually, the Court concluded that it was.

Another trend in the cases is harder to document but clear to everyone who followed the law's development in this area: More and more, the Justices distrusted state-court factfinding processes. Plainly, if the state courts could not be counted on to do a conscientious job of applying constitutional mandates, a fact-bound test like voluntariness would not do. A court not wishing to apply the test could simply manipulate its factual findings to reach whatever result it desired. For excellent discussions of this phenomenon and the Court's response to it, see Anthony G. Amsterdam, The Supreme Court and the Rights of Suspects in Criminal Cases, 45 N.Y.U. L. Rev. 785 (1970); Geoffrey R. Stone, The *Miranda* Doctrine in the Burger Court, [1977] Sup. Ct. Rev. 99. This skepticism on the Court's part made it even harder for lower courts — or the police — to tell what the governing legal standard for confessions was; by the early 1960s, it was not clear to anyone what it would take to render a confession voluntary.

Increasing dissatisfaction with the voluntariness approach, growing distrust of state factfinding procedures, the Court's practical inability to act as an effective court of error over the state criminal process, and the fact that the implications of habeas corpus had not yet been fully recognized — all these forces drove the

Justices to seek out alternatives to the voluntariness test. They found one in the right to counsel, as is indicated in the next case.[3]

MASSIAH v. UNITED STATES

Certiorari to the United States Court of Appeals for the Second Circuit
377 U.S. 201 (1964)

MR. JUSTICE STEWART delivered the opinion of the Court.

The petitioner was indicted for violating the federal narcotics laws. He retained a lawyer, pleaded not guilty, and was released on bail. While he was free on bail a federal agent succeeded by surreptitious means in listening to incriminating statements made by him. Evidence of these statements was introduced against the petitioner at his trial over his objection. He was convicted, and the Court of Appeals affirmed. We granted certiorari to consider whether, under the circumstances here presented, the prosecution's use at the trial of evidence of the petitioner's own incriminating statements deprived him of any right secured to him under the Federal Constitution. . . .

The petitioner, a merchant seaman, was in 1958 a member of the crew of the S.S. Santa Maria. In April of that year federal customs officials in New York received information that he was going to transport a quantity of narcotics aboard that ship from South America to the United States. As a result of this and other information, the agents searched the Santa Maria upon its arrival in New York and found in the afterpeak of the vessel five packages containing about three and a half pounds of cocaine. They also learned of circumstances, not here relevant, tending to connect the petitioner with the cocaine. He was arrested, promptly arraigned, and subsequently indicted for possession of narcotics aboard a United States vessel. In July a superseding indictment was returned, charging the petitioner and a man named Colson with the same substantive offense, and in separate counts charging the petitioner, Colson, and others with having conspired to possess narcotics aboard a United States vessel, and to import, conceal, and facilitate the sale of narcotics. The petitioner, who had retained a lawyer, pleaded not guilty and was released on bail, along with Colson.

A few days later, and quite without the petitioner's knowledge, Colson decided to cooperate with the government agents in their continuing investigation of the narcotics activities in which the petitioner, Colson, and others had allegedly been engaged. Colson permitted an agent named Murphy to install a Schmidt radio transmitter under the front seat of Colson's automobile, by means of which Murphy, equipped with an appropriate receiving device, could overhear from some distance away conversations carried on in Colson's car.

On the evening of November 19, 1959, Colson and the petitioner held a lengthy conversation while sitting in Colson's automobile, parked on a

---

3. The Court toyed with another alternative in two federal cases, McNabb v. United States, 318 U.S. 332 (1943), and Mallory v. United States, 354 U.S. 449 (1957). Together, the cases structured what has come to be known as the McNabb-Mallory Rule, which excludes confessions obtained in violation of Fed. R. Crim. P. 5(a)'s requirement that an arrested person be taken without unnecessary delay to the nearest community officer. The Court invoked its supervisory power over the federal courts as the basis for the rule, and it never applied the rule to the states through the Fourteenth Amendment.

New York street. By prearrangement with Colson, and totally unbeknown to the petitioner, the agent Murphy sat in a car parked out of sight down the street and listened over the radio to the entire conversation. The petitioner made several incriminating statements during the course of this conversation. At the petitioner's trial these incriminating statements were brought before the jury through Murphy's testimony, despite the insistent objection of defense counsel. The jury convicted the petitioner of several related narcotics offenses, and the convictions were affirmed by the Court of Appeals.

The petitioner argues that it was an error of constitutional dimensions to permit the agent Murphy at the trial to testify to the petitioner's incriminating statements which Murphy had overheard under the circumstances disclosed by this record. This argument is based upon two distinct and independent grounds. First, we are told that Murphy's use of the radio equipment violated the petitioner's rights under the Fourth Amendment, and, consequently, that all evidence which Murphy thereby obtained was, under the rule Weeks v. United States, 232 U.S. 383, inadmissible against the petitioner at the trial. Secondly, it is said that the petitioner's Fifth and Sixth Amendment rights were violated by the use in evidence against him of incriminating statements which government agents had deliberately elicited from him after he had been indicted and in the absence of his retained counsel. Because of the way we dispose of the case, we do not reach the Fourth Amendment issue.

In Spano v. New York, 360 U.S. 315, this Court reversed a state criminal conviction because a confession had been wrongly admitted into evidence against the defendant at his trial. In that case the defendant had already been indicted for first-degree murder at the time he confessed. The Court held that the defendant's conviction could not stand under the Fourteenth Amendment. While the Court's opinion relied upon the totality of the circumstances under which the confession had been obtained, four concurring justices pointed out that the Constitution required reversal of the conviction upon the sole and specific ground that the confession had been deliberately elicited by the police after the defendant had been indicted, and therefore at a time when he was clearly entitled to a lawyer's help. It was pointed out that under our system of justice the most elemental concepts of due process of law contemplate that an indictment be followed by a trial, "in an orderly courtroom, presided over by a judge, open to the public, and protected by all the procedural safeguards of the law." 360 U.S., at 327 (Stewart, J., concurring). It was said that a Constitution which guarantees a defendant the aid of counsel at such a trial could surely vouchsafe no less to an indicted defendant under interrogation by the police in a completely extrajudicial proceeding. Anything less, it was said, might deny a defendant "effective representation by counsel at the only stage when legal aid and advice would help him." 360 U.S., at 326 (Douglas, J., concurring). . . .

This view no more than reflects a constitutional principle established as long ago as Powell v. Alabama, 287 U.S. 45, where the Court noted that ". . . during perhaps the most critical period of the proceedings . . . that is to say, from the time of their arraignment until the beginning of their trial, when consultation, thoroughgoing investigation and preparation [are] vitally important, the defendants . . . [are] as much entitled to such aid [of counsel] during that period as at the trial itself." Id., at 57. And since the *Spano* decision the same basic constitutional principle has been broadly reaffirmed by this Court. Hamilton v. Alabama, 368

U.S. 52; White v. Maryland, 373 U.S. 59. See Gideon v. Wainwright, 372 U.S. 335. Here we deal not with a state court conviction, but with a federal case, where the specific guarantee of the Sixth Amendment directly applies. Johnson v. Zerbst, 304 U.S. 458. We hold that the petitioner was denied the basic protections of that guarantee when there was used against him at his trial evidence of his own incriminating words, which federal agents had deliberately elicited from him after he had been indicted and in the absence of his counsel. It is true that in the *Spano* case the defendant was interrogated in a police station, while here the damaging testimony was elicited from the defendant without his knowledge while he was free on bail. But, as Judge Hays pointed out in his dissent in the Court of Appeals, "if such a rule is to have any efficacy it must apply to indirect and surreptitious interrogations as well as those conducted in the jailhouse. In this case, Massiah was more seriously imposed upon . . . because he did not even know that he was under interrogation by a government agent." 307 F.2d, at 72-73.

The Solicitor General, in his brief and oral argument, has strenuously contended that the federal law enforcement agents had the right, if not indeed the duty, to continue their investigation of the petitioner and his alleged criminal associates even though the petitioner had been indicted. He points out that the Government was continuing its investigation in order to uncover not only the source of narcotics found on the S.S. Santa Maria, but also their intended buyer. He says that the quantity of narcotics involved was such as to suggest that the petitioner was part of a large and well-organized ring, and indeed that the continuing investigation confirmed this suspicion, since it resulted in criminal charges against many defendants. Under these circumstances the Solicitor General concludes that the government agents were completely "justified in making use of Colson's cooperation by having Colson continue his normal associations and by surveilling them."

We may accept and, at least for present purposes, completely approve all that this argument implies, Fourth Amendment problems to one side. We do not question that in this case, as in many cases, it was entirely proper to continue an investigation of the suspected criminal activities of the defendant and his alleged confederates, even though the defendant had already been indicted. All that we hold is that the defendant's own incriminating statements, obtained by federal agents under the circumstances here disclosed, could not constitutionally be used by the prosecution as evidence against *him* at his trial. Reversed.

MR. JUSTICE WHITE, with whom MR. JUSTICE CLARK and MR. JUSTICE HARLAN join, dissenting. . . .

It is . . . a rather portentous occasion when a constitutional rule is established barring the use of evidence which is relevant, reliable and highly probative of the issue which the trial court has before it—whether the accused committed the act with which he is charged. Without the evidence, the quest for truth may be seriously impeded and in many cases the trial court, although aware of proof showing defendant's guilt, must nevertheless release him because the crucial evidence is deemed inadmissible. This result is entirely justified in some circumstances because exclusion serves other policies of overriding importance, as where evidence seized in an illegal search is excluded, not because of the quality of the proof, but to secure meaningful enforcement of the Fourth Amendment. Weeks v. United States, 232 U.S. 383; Mapp v. Ohio, 367 U.S. 643. But this only emphasizes that the soundest of reasons is necessary to warrant the exclusion of evidence otherwise admissible and the creation of another area of privileged testimony. With all due deference, I am not at all convinced that the additional barriers to the pursuit of truth which the Court today erects rest on anything like the solid foundations which decisions of this gravity should require.

The importance of the matter should not be underestimated, for today's rule promises to have wide application well beyond the facts of this case. The reason given for the result here—the admissions were obtained in the absence of counsel—would seem equally pertinent to statements obtained at any time after the right to counsel attaches, whether there has been an indictment or not; to admissions made prior to arraignment, at least where the defendant has counsel or asks for it; to the fruits of admissions improperly obtained under the new rule; to criminal proceedings in state courts; and to defendants long since convicted upon evidence including such admissions. The new rule will immediately do service in a great many cases.

Whatever the content or scope of the rule may prove to be, I am unable to see how this case presents an unconstitutional interference with Massiah's right to counsel. Massiah was not prevented from consulting with counsel as often as he wished. No meetings with counsel were disturbed or spied upon. Preparation for trial was in no way obstructed. It is only a sterile syllogism—an unsound one, besides—to say that because Massiah had a right to counsel's aid before and during the trial, his out-of-court conversations and admissions must be excluded if obtained without counsel's consent or presence. The right to counsel has never meant as much before, . . . and its extension in this case requires some further explanation, so far unarticulated by the Court.

Since the new rule would exclude all admissions made to the police, no matter how voluntary and reliable, the requirement of counsel's presence or approval would seem to rest upon the probability that counsel would foreclose any admissions at all. This is nothing more than a thinly disguised constitutional policy of minimizing or entirely prohibiting the use in evidence of voluntary out-of-court admissions and confessions made by the accused. Carried as far as blind logic may compel some to go, the notion that statements from the mouth of the defendant should not be used in evidence would have a severe and unfortunate impact upon the great bulk of criminal cases. . . .

Applying the new exclusionary rule is peculiarly inappropriate in this case. At the time of the conversation in question, petitioner was not in custody but free on bail. He was not questioned in what anyone could call an atmosphere of official coercion. What he said was said to his partner in crime who had also been indicted. There was no suggestion or any possibility of coercion. What petitioner did not know was that Colson had decided to report the conversation to the police. Had there been no prior arrangements between Colson and the police, had Colson simply gone to the police after the conversation had occurred, his testimony relating Massiah's statements would be readily admissible at the trial, as would a recording which he might have made of the conversation. In such event, it would simply be said that Massiah risked talking to a friend who decided to disclose what he knew of Massiah's criminal activities. But if, as occurred here, Colson had been cooperating with the police prior to his meeting with Massiah, both his evidence and the recorded conversation are somehow transformed into inadmissible evidence despite the fact that the hazard to Massiah remains precisely the same—the defection of a confederate in crime.

Reporting criminal behavior is expected or even demanded of the ordinary citizen. Friends may be subpoenaed to testify about friends, relatives about relatives and partners about partners. I therefore question the soundness of insulating Massiah from the apostasy of his partner in crime and of furnishing constitutional sanctions for the strict secrecy and discipline of criminal organizations. Neither the ordinary citizen nor the confessed criminal should be discouraged from reporting what he knows to the authorities and from lending his aid to secure evidence of crime. Certainly after this case the Colsons will be few and far between; and the Massiahs can breathe much more easily, secure in the knowledge that the Constitution furnishes an important measure of protection against faithless compatriots and guarantees sporting treatment for sporting peddlers of narcotics. . . .

Undoubtedly, the evidence excluded in this case would not have been available but for the conduct of Colson in cooperation with Agent Murphy, but is it this kind of conduct which should be forbidden to those charged with law enforcement? It is one thing to establish safeguards against procedures fraught with the potentiality of coercion and to outlaw "easy but self-defeating ways in which brutality is substituted for brains as an instrument of crime detection." McNabb v. United States, 318 U.S. 332, 344. But here there was no substitution of brutality for brains, no inherent danger of police coercion justifying the prophylactic effect of another exclusionary rule. Massiah was not being interrogated in a police station, was not surrounded by numerous officers or questioned in relays, and was not forbidden access to others. Law enforcement may have the elements of a contest about it, but it is not a game. McGuire v. United States, 273 U.S. 95, 99. Massiah and those like him receive ample protection from the long line of precedents in this Court holding that confessions may not be introduced unless they are voluntary. In making these determinations the courts must consider the absence of counsel as one of several factors by which voluntariness is to be judged.

. . . This is a wiser rule than the automatic rule announced by the Court, which requires courts and juries to disregard voluntary admissions which they might well find to be the best possible evidence in discharging their responsibility for ascertaining truth. . . .

The meaning of *Massiah* was not altogether clear, however. For example, did it matter whether the defendant had been indicted? Been arraigned? Obtained counsel? The Court returned to these matters a year later in Escobedo v. Illinois. In *Escobedo*, the defendant had been arrested but not charged and had invoked his right to counsel (presuming he had one), his lawyer was present at the station house but not allowed to see his client, and the defendant was subject to interrogation during which incriminating statements were made. Over a sharp dissent, the Court, in a schizoid opinion marked by an uneasy relationship between sweeping assertion and narrow holding, held that the defendant's constitutional rights had been violated. The curious progression of the opinion can be seen in the following excerpt.

ESCOBEDO v. ILLINOIS, 378 U.S. 478, 488-491 (1964): It is argued that if the right to counsel is afforded prior to indictment, the number of confessions obtained by the police will diminish significantly, because most confessions are obtained during the period between arrest and indictment, and "any lawyer worth his salt will tell the suspect in no uncertain terms to make no statement to police under any circumstances." Watts v. Indiana, 338 U.S. 49, 59 (Jackson, J., concurring in part and dissenting in part). This argument, of course, cuts two ways. The fact that many confessions are obtained during this period points up its critical nature as a "stage when legal aid and advice" are surely needed. . . . The right to counsel would indeed be hollow if it began at a period when few confessions were obtained. There is necessarily a direct relationship between the importance of a stage to the police in their quest for a confession and the criticalness of that stage to the accused in his need for legal advice. Our Constitution, unlike some others, strikes the balance in favor of the right of the accused to be advised by his lawyer of his privilege against self-incrimination. . . .

We have learned the lesson of history, ancient and modern, that a system of criminal law enforcement which comes to depend on the "confession" will, in the long run, be less reliable and more subject to abuses than a system which depends on extrinsic evidence independently secured through skillful investigation. As Dean Wigmore so wisely said:

> "[A]ny system of administration which permits the prosecution to trust habitually to compulsory self-disclosure as a source of proof must itself suffer morally thereby. The inclination develops to rely mainly upon such evidence, and to be satisfied with an incomplete investigation of the other sources. The exercise of the power to extract answers begets a forgetfulness of the just limitations of that power. The simple and peaceful process of questioning breeds a readiness to resort to bullying and to physical force and torture. If there is a right to an answer, there soon seems to be a right to the expected answer, — that is, to a confession of guilt. Thus the legitimate use grows into the unjust abuse; ultimately, the innocent are jeopardized by the encroachments of a bad system. Such seems to have been the course of experience in those legal systems where the privilege was not recognized." 8 Wigmore, Evidence (3d ed. 1940), 309. (Emphasis in original.)

This Court also has recognized that "history amply shows that confessions have often been extorted to save law enforcement officials the trouble and effort of obtaining valid and independent evidence. . . ." Haynes v. Washington, 373 U.S. 503, 519.

We have also learned the companion lesson of history that no system of criminal justice can, or should, survive if it comes to depend for its continued effectiveness on the citizens' abdication through unawareness of their constitutional rights. No system worth preserving should have to *fear* that if an accused is permitted to consult with a lawyer, he will become aware of, and exercise, these rights.[13] If

---

13. Cf. Report of Attorney General's Committee on Poverty and the Administration of Federal Criminal Justice (1963), 10-11:

> The survival of our system of criminal justice and the values which it advances depends upon a constant, searching, and creative questioning of official decisions and assertions of authority at all stages of the process. . . . Persons [denied access to counsel] are incapable of providing the challenges that are indispensable to satisfactory operation of the system. The loss to the interests of accused individuals, occasioned by these failures, are great and apparent. It is also clear that a situation in which persons are required to contest a serious accusation but are denied access to the tools of contest is offensive to fairness and equity. Beyond these considerations, however, is the fact that [this situation is] detrimental to the proper functioning of the system of justice and that the loss in vitality of the adversary system, thereby occasioned, significantly endangers the basic interests of a free community.

the exercise of constitutional rights will thwart the effectiveness of a system of law enforcement then there is something very wrong with that system.

We hold, therefore, that where, as here, the investigation is no longer a general inquiry into an unsolved crime but has begun to focus on a particular suspect, the suspect has been taken into police custody, the police carry out a process of interrogations that lends itself to eliciting incriminating statements, the suspect has requested and been denied an opportunity to consult with his lawyer, and the police have not effectively warned him of his absolute constitutional right to remain silent, the accused has been denied "the Assistance of Counsel" in violation of the Sixth Amendment to the Constitution as "made obligatory upon the States by the Fourteenth Amendment," Gideon v. Wainwright, 372 U.S., at 342, and that no statement elicited by the police during the interrogation may be used against him at a criminal trial. . . .

Was *Escobedo* a simple application of *Massiah*? Was it a harbinger of the complete elimination of confessions, or at least of police interrogation as then conceived? Or was it an example of a Court realizing that it was breaking new ground, but not altogether sure of the way to proceed or of the implications of its actions? Some of these questions were answered two years later in the *Miranda* case.

MIRANDA v. ARIZONA

Certiorari to the Supreme Court of Arizona
384 U.S. 436 (1966)

MR. CHIEF JUSTICE WARREN delivered the opinion of the Court.

The cases before us raise questions which go to the roots of our concepts of American criminal jurisprudence: the restraints society must observe consistent with the Federal Constitution in prosecuting individuals for crime. More specifically, we deal with the admissibility of statements obtained from an individual who is subjected to custodial police interrogation and the necessity for procedures which assure that the individual is accorded his privilege under the Fifth Amendment to the Constitution not to be compelled to incriminate himself. We dealt with certain phases of this problem recently in Escobedo v. Illinois, 378 U.S. 478 (1964). . . .

Our holding will be spelled out with some specificity in the pages which follow but briefly stated it is this: the prosecution may not use statements, whether exculpatory or inculpatory, stemming from custodial interrogation of the defendant unless it demonstrates the use of procedural safeguards effective to secure the privilege against self-incrimination. By custodial interrogation, we mean questioning initiated by law enforcement officers after a person has been taken into custody or otherwise deprived of his freedom of action in any significant way.[4] As for the procedural safeguards to be employed, unless other fully effective means are devised to inform accused persons of their right of silence and to assure a

---

4. This is what we meant in *Escobedo* when we spoke of an investigation which had focused on an accused.

continuous opportunity to exercise it, the following measures are required. Prior to any questioning, the person must be warned that he has a right to remain silent, that any statement he does make may be used as evidence against him, and that he has a right to the presence of an attorney, either retained or appointed. The defendant may waive effectuation of these rights, provided the waiver is made voluntarily, knowingly and intelligently. If, however, he indicates in any manner and at any stage of the process that he wishes to consult with an attorney before speaking there can be no questioning. Likewise, if the individual is alone and indicates in any manner that he does not wish to be interrogated, the police may not question him. The mere fact that he may have answered some questions or volunteered some statements on his own does not deprive him of the right to refrain from answering any further inquiries until he has consulted with an attorney and thereafter consents to be questioned.

I

. . . An understanding of the nature and setting of this in-custody interrogation is essential to our decisions today. The difficulty in depicting what transpires at such interrogations stems from the fact that in this country they have largely taken place incommunicado. From extensive factual studies undertaken in the early 1930s, including the famous Wickersham Report to Congress by a Presidential Commission, it is clear that police violence and the "third degree" flourished at that time.[5] In a series of cases decided by this Court long after these studies, the police resorted to physical brutality—beating, hanging, whipping—and to sustained and protracted questioning incommunicado in order to extort confessions. . . . The use of physical brutality and violence is not, unfortunately, relegated to the past or to any part of the country. Only recently in Kings County, New York, the police brutally beat, kicked and placed lighted cigarette butts on the back of a potential witness under interrogation for the purpose of securing a statement incriminating a third party. People v. Portelli, 15 N.Y. 2d 235, 205 N.E.2d 857 (1965).[7]

The examples given above are undoubtedly the exception now, but they are sufficiently widespread to be the object of concern. Unless a proper limitation upon custodial interrogation is achieved—such as these decisions will advance—there can be no assurance that practices of this nature will be eradicated in the foreseeable future. . . .

. . . [T]he modern practice of in-custody interrogation is psychologically rather than physically oriented. . . . Interrogation still takes place in privacy. Privacy results in secrecy and this in turn results in a gap in our knowledge as to what in fact goes on in the interrogation rooms. A valuable source of information about present police practices, however, may be found in various police manuals and texts which document procedures employed with success in the past, and which

5. See, for example, IV National Commission on Law Observance and Enforcement, Report on Lawlessness in Law Enforcement (1931) [Wickersham Report]. . . .

7. In addition, see People v. Wakat, 415 Ill. 610, 114 N.E.2d 706 (1953); Wakat v. Harlib, 253 F.2d 59 (C.A. 7th Cir. 1958) (defendant suffering from broken bones, multiple bruises and injuries sufficiently serious to require eight months' medical treatment after being manhandled by five policemen). . . .

recommend various other effective tactics.[8] These texts are used by law enforcement agencies themselves as guides. It should be noted that these texts professedly present the most enlightened and effective means presently used to obtain statements through custodial interrogation. By considering these texts and other data, it is possible to describe procedures observed and noted around the country.

The officers are told by the manuals that the "principal psychological factor contributing to a successful interrogation is *privacy* — being alone with the person under interrogation."[10] The efficacy of this tactic has been explained as follows:

> If at all practicable, the interrogation should take place in the investigator's office or at least in a room of his own choice. The subject should be deprived of every psychological advantage. In his own home he may be confident, indignant, or recalcitrant. He is more keenly aware of his rights and more reluctant to tell of his indiscretions or criminal behavior within the walls of his home. Moreover his family and other friends are nearby, their presence lending moral support. In his own office, the investigator possesses all the advantages. The atmosphere suggests the invincibility of the forces of the law.[11]

To highlight the isolation and unfamiliar surroundings, the manuals instruct the police to display an air of confidence in the suspect's guilt and from outward appearance to maintain only an interest in confirming certain details. The guilt of the subject is to be posited as a fact. The interrogator should direct his comments toward the reasons why the subject committed the act, rather than court failure by asking the subject whether he did it. Like other men, perhaps the subject has had a bad family life, had an unhappy childhood, had too much to drink, had an unrequited desire for women. The officers are instructed to minimize the moral seriousness of the offense,[12] to cast blame on the victim or on society.[13] These tactics are designed to put the subject in a psychological state where his story is but an elaboration of what the police purport to know already — that he is guilty. Explanations to the contrary are dismissed and discouraged.

The texts thus stress that the major qualities an interrogator should possess are patience and perseverance. One writer describes the efficacy of these characteristics in this manner:

> In the preceding paragraphs emphasis has been placed on kindness and stratagems. The investigator will, however, encounter many situations where the sheer weight of his personality will be the deciding factor. Where emotional appeals and tricks

8. The manuals quoted in the text following are the most recent and representative of the texts currently available. Material of the same nature appears in Kidd, Police Interrogation (1940); Mulbar, Interrogation (1951); Dienstein, Technics for the Crime Investigator 97-115 (1952). Studies concerning the observed practices of the police appear in LaFave, Arrest: The Decision to Take a Suspect into Custody 244-437, 490-521 (1965); LaFave, Detention for Investigation by the Police: An Analysis of Current Practices, 1962 Wash. U. L.Q. 331; Barrett, Police Practices and the Law — From Arrest to Release or Charge, 50 Calif. L. Rev. 11 (1962); Sterling, supra, n. 7, at 47-65.

10. Inbau & Reid, Criminal Interrogation and Confessions (1962), at 1.

11. O'Hara, [Fundamentals of Criminal Investigation (1956),] at 99.

12. Inbau & Reid, supra, at 34-43, 87. For example, in Leyra v. Denno, 347 U.S. 556 (1954), the interrogator-psychiatrist told the accused, "We do sometimes things that are not right, but in a fit of temper or anger we sometimes do things we aren't really responsible for," id., at 562, and again, "We know that morally you were just in anger. Morally, you are not to be condemned," id., at 582.

13. Inbau & Reid, supra, at 43-55.

are employed to no avail, he must rely on an oppressive atmosphere of dogged persistence. He must interrogate steadily and without relent, leaving the subject no prospect of surcease. He must dominate his subject and overwhelm him with his inexorable will to obtain the truth. He should interrogate for a spell of several hours pausing only for the subject's necessities in acknowledgment of the need to avoid a charge of duress that can be technically substantiated. In a serious case, the interrogation may continue for days, with the required intervals for food and sleep, but with no respite from the atmosphere of domination. It is possible in this way to induce the subject to talk without resorting to duress or coercion. The method should be used only when the guilt of the subject appears highly probable.[14]

The manuals suggest that the suspect be offered legal excuses for his actions in order to obtain an initial admission of guilt. Where there is a suspected revenge-killing, for example, the interrogator may say:

Joe, you probably didn't go out looking for this fellow with the purpose of shooting him. My guess is, however, that you expected something from him and that's why you carried a gun — for your own protection. You knew him for what he was, no good. Then when you met him he probably started using foul, abusive language and he gave some indication that he was about to pull a gun on you, and that's when you had to act to save your own life. That's about it, isn't it Joe?[15]

Having then obtained the admission of shooting, the interrogator is advised to refer to circumstantial evidence which negates the self-defense explanation. This should enable him to secure the entire story. One text notes that "Even if he fails to do so, the inconsistency between the subject's original denial of the shooting and his present admission of at least doing the shooting will serve to deprive him of a self-defense 'out' at the time of trial."[16]

When the techniques described above prove unavailing, the texts recommend they be alternated with a show of some hostility. One ploy often used has been termed the "friendly-unfriendly" or the "Mutt and Jeff" act:

. . . In this technique, two agents are employed. Mutt, the relentless investigator, who knows the subject is guilty and is not going to waste any time. He's sent a dozen men away for this crime and he's going to send the subject away for the full term. Jeff, on the other hand, is obviously a kindhearted man. He has a family himself. He has a brother who was involved in a little scrape like this. He disapproves of Mutt and his tactics and will arrange to get him off the case if the subject will cooperate. He can't hold Mutt off for very long. The subject would be wise to make a quick decision. The technique is applied by having both investigators present while Mutt acts out his role. Jeff may stand by quietly and demur at some of Mutt's tactics. When Jeff makes his plea for cooperation, Mutt is not present in the room.[17]

14. O'Hara, supra, at 112.
15. Inbau & Reid, supra, at 40.
16. Ibid.
17. O'Hara, supra, at 104, Inbau & Reid, supra, at 58-59. See Spano v. New York, 360 U.S. 315 (1959). A variant on the technique of creating hostility is one of engendering fear. This is perhaps best described by the prosecuting attorney in Malinski v. New York, 324 U.S. 401, 407 (1945): "Why this talk about being undressed? Of course, they had a right to undress him to look for bullet scars, and keep the clothes off him. That was quite proper police procedure. That is some more psychology — let him sit around with a blanket on him, humiliate him there for a while; let him sit in the corner, let him think he is going to get a shellacking."

The interrogators sometimes are instructed to induce a confession out of trickery. The technique here is quite effective in crimes which require identification or which run in series. In the identification situation, the interrogator may take a break in his questioning to place the subject among a group of men in a line-up. "The witness or complainant (previously coached, if necessary) studies the line-up and confidently points out the subject as the guilty party."[18] Then the questioning resumes "as though there were now no doubt about the guilt of the subject." A variation on this technique is called the "reverse line-up":

> The accused is placed in a line-up, but this time he is identified by several fictitious witnesses or victims who associated him with different offenses. It is expected that the subject will become desperate and confess to the offense under investigation in order to escape from the false accusations.[19]

The manuals also contain instructions for police on how to handle the individual who refuses to discuss the matter entirely, or who asks for an attorney or relatives. The examiner is to concede him the right to remain silent. "This usually has a very undermining effect. First of all, he is disappointed in his expectation of an unfavorable reaction on the part of the interrogator. Secondly, a concession of this right to remain silent impresses the subject with the apparent fairness of his interrogator."[20] After this psychological conditioning, however, the officer is told to point out the incriminating significance of the suspect's refusal to talk:

> Joe, you have a right to remain silent. That's your privilege and I'm the last person in the world who'll try to take it away from you. If that's the way you want to leave this, O.K. But let me ask you this. Suppose you were in my shoes and I were in yours and you called me in to ask me about this and I told you, "I don't want to answer any of your questions." You'd think I had something to hide, and you'd probably be right in thinking that. That's exactly what I'll have to think about you, and so will everybody else. So let's sit here and talk this whole thing over.[21]

Few will persist in their initial refusal to talk, it is said, if this monologue is employed correctly.

In the event that the subject wishes to speak to a relative or an attorney, the following advice is tendered:

> [T]he interrogator should respond by suggesting that the subject first tell the truth to the interrogator himself rather than get anyone else involved in the matter. If the request is for an attorney, the interrogator may suggest that the subject save himself or his family the expense of any such professional service, particularly if he is innocent of the offense under investigation. The interrogator may also add, "Joe, I'm only looking for the truth, and if you're telling the truth, that's it. You can handle this by yourself."[22] . . .

18. O'Hara, supra, at 105-106.
19. Id., at 106.
20. Inbau & Reid, supra, at 111.
21. Ibid.
22. Inbau & Reid, supra, at 112.

Even without employing brutality, the "third degree" or the specific stratagems described above, the very fact of custodial interrogation exacts a heavy toll on individual liberty and trades on the weakness of individuals. This fact may be illustrated simply by referring to three confession cases decided by this Court in the Term immediately preceding our *Escobedo* decision. In Townsend v. Sain, 372 U.S. 293 (1963), the defendant was a 19-year-old heroin addict, described as a "near mental defective," id., at 307-310. The defendant in Lynumn v. Illinois, 372 U.S. 528 (1963), was a woman who confessed to the arresting officer after being importuned to "cooperate" in order to prevent her children from being taken by relief authorities. This Court as in those cases reversed the conviction of a defendant in Haynes v. Washington, 373 U.S. 503 (1963), whose persistent request during his interrogation was to phone his wife or attorney. In other settings, these individuals might have exercised their constitutional rights. In the incommunicado police-dominated atmosphere, they succumbed.

In the cases before us today, . . . we might not find the defendant's statements to have been involuntary in traditional terms. Our concern for adequate safeguards to protect precious Fifth Amendment rights is, of course, not lessened in the slightest. In each of the cases, the defendant was thrust into an unfamiliar atmosphere and run through menacing police interrogation procedures. The potentiality for compulsion is forcefully apparent, for example, in *Miranda*, where the indigent Mexican defendant was a seriously disturbed individual with pronounced sexual fantasies, and in *Stewart*, in which the defendant was an indigent Los Angeles Negro who had dropped out of school in the sixth grade. To be sure, the records do not evince overt physical coercion or patent psychological ploys. The fact remains that in none of these cases did the officers undertake to afford appropriate safeguards at the outset of the interrogation to insure that the statements were truly the product of free choice.

It is obvious that such an interrogation environment is created for no purpose other than to subjugate the individual to the will of his examiner. This atmosphere carries its own badge of intimidation. To be sure, this is not physical intimidation, but it is equally destructive of human dignity.[26] The current practice of incommunicado interrogation is at odds with one of our Nation's most cherished principles — that the individual may not be compelled to incriminate himself. Unless adequate protective devices are employed to dispel the compulsion inherent in custodial surroundings, no statement obtained from the defendant can truly be the product of his free choice.

From the foregoing, we can readily perceive an intimate connection between the privilege against self-incrimination and police custodial questioning. It is

---

26. The absurdity of denying that a confession obtained under these circumstances is compelled is aptly portrayed by an example in Professor Sutherland's recent article, Crime and Confession, 79 Harv. L. Rev. 21, 37 (1965):

Suppose a well-to-do testatrix says she intends to will her property to Elizabeth. John and James want her to bequeath it to them instead. They capture the testatrix, put her in a carefully designed room, out of touch with everyone but themselves and their convenient "witness," keep her secluded there for hours while they make insistent demands, weary her with contradictions of her assertions that she wants to leave her money to Elizabeth, and finally induce her to execute the will in their favor. Assume that John and James are deeply and correctly convinced that Elizabeth is unworthy and will make base use of the property if she gets her hands on it, whereas John and James have the noblest and most righteous intentions. Would any judge of probate accept the will so procured as the "voluntary" act of the testatrix?

fitting to turn to history and precedent underlying the Self-Incrimination Clause to determine its applicability in this situation.

II

. . . The question in these cases is whether the privilege is fully applicable during a period of custodial interrogation. In this Court, the privilege has consistently been accorded a liberal construction. . . . We are satisfied that all the principles embodied in the privilege apply to informal compulsion exerted by law enforcement officers during in-custody questioning. An individual swept from familiar surroundings into police custody, surrounded by antagonistic forces, and subjected to the techniques of persuasion described above cannot be otherwise than under compulsion to speak. As a practical matter, the compulsion to speak in the isolated setting of the police station may well be greater than in courts or other official investigations, where there are often impartial observers to guard against intimidation or trickery.

This question, in fact, could have been taken as settled in federal courts almost 70 years ago, when, in Bram v. United States, 168 U.S. 532, 542 (1897), this Court held:

> In criminal trials, in the courts of the United States, wherever a question arises whether a confession is incompetent because not voluntary, the issue is controlled by that portion of the Fifth Amendment . . . commanding that no person "shall be compelled in any criminal case to be a witness against himself." . . .

In addition to the expansive historical development of the privilege and the sound policies which have nurtured its evolution, judicial precedent thus clearly establishes its application to incommunicado interrogation. . . .

III

Today, then, there can be no doubt that the Fifth Amendment privilege is available outside of criminal court proceedings and serves to protect persons in all settings in which their freedom of action is curtailed in any significant way from being compelled to incriminate themselves. We have concluded that without proper safeguards the process of in-custody interrogation of persons suspected or accused of crime contains inherently compelling pressures which work to undermine the individual's will to resist and to compel him to speak where he would not otherwise do so freely. In order to combat these pressures and to permit a full opportunity to exercise the privilege against self-incrimination, the accused must be adequately and effectively apprised of his rights and the exercise of those rights must be fully honored.

It is impossible for us to foresee the potential alternatives for protecting the privilege which might be devised by Congress or the States in the exercise of their creative rule-making capacities. Therefore we cannot say that the Constitution necessarily requires adherence to any particular solution for the inherent compulsions of the interrogation process as it is presently conducted. Our decision in no way creates a constitutional straitjacket which will handicap sound efforts at reform, nor is it intended to have this effect. We encourage Congress and the States to continue their laudable search for increasingly effective ways of protecting the rights of the individual while promoting efficient enforcement of our criminal laws. However, unless we are shown other procedures which are at least as effective in apprising accused persons of their right of silence and in assuring a continuous opportunity to exercise it, the following safeguards must be observed.

At the outset, if a person in custody is to be subjected to interrogation, he must first be informed in clear and unequivocal terms that he has the right to remain silent. For those unaware of the privilege, the warning is needed simply to make them aware of it — the threshold requirement for an intelligent decision as to its exercise. More important, such a warning is an absolute prerequisite in overcoming the inherent pressures of the interrogation atmosphere. It is not just the subnormal or woefully ignorant who succumb to an interrogator's imprecations, whether implied or expressly stated, that the interrogation will continue until a confession is obtained or that silence in the face of accusation is itself damning and will bode ill when presented to a jury. Further, the warning will show the individual that his interrogators are prepared to recognize his privilege should he choose to exercise it.

The Fifth Amendment privilege is so fundamental to our system of constitutional rule and the expedient of giving an adequate warning as to the availability of the privilege so simple, we will not pause to inquire in individual cases whether the defendant was aware of his rights without a warning being given. Assessments of the knowledge the defendant possessed, based on information as to his age, education, intelligence, or prior contact with authorities, can never be more than speculation; a warning is a clearcut fact. More important, whatever the background of the person interrogated, a warning at the time of the interrogation is indispensable to overcome its pressures and to insure that the individual knows he is free to exercise the privilege at that point in time.

The warning of the right to remain silent must be accompanied by the explanation that anything said can and will be used against the individual in court. This warning is needed in order to make him aware not only of the privilege, but also of the consequences of forgoing it. It is only through an awareness of these consequences that there can be any assurance of real understanding and intelligent exercise of the privilege. Moreover, this warning may serve to make the individual more acutely aware that he is faced with a phase of the adversary system — that he is not in the presence of persons acting solely in his interest.

The circumstances surrounding in-custody interrogation can operate very quickly to overbear the will of one merely made aware of his privilege by his interrogators. Therefore, the right to have counsel present at the interrogation is indispensable to the protection of the Fifth Amendment privilege under the system we delineate today. Our aim is to assure that the individual's right to choose between silence and speech remains unfettered throughout the interrogation process. A once-stated warning, delivered by those who will conduct the interrogation, cannot itself suffice to that end among those who most require knowledge of their rights. A mere warning given by the interrogators is not alone sufficient to accomplish that end. . . . Even preliminary advice given to the accused by his own attorney can be swiftly overcome by the secret interrogation process. . . . Thus, the need for counsel to protect the Fifth Amendment privilege comprehends not merely a right to consult with counsel prior to questioning, but also to have counsel present during any questioning if the defendant so desires. . . .

Accordingly we hold that an individual held for interrogation must be clearly informed that he has the right to consult with a lawyer and to have the lawyer with him during interrogation under the system for protecting the privilege we delineate today. As with the warnings of the right to remain silent and that anything stated can be used in evidence against him, this warning is an absolute prerequisite to interrogation. No amount of circumstantial evidence that the person may have been aware of this right will suffice to stand in its stead. Only through such a warning is there ascertainable assurance that the accused was aware of this right. . . .

In order fully to apprise a person interrogated of the extent of his rights under this system . . . , it is necessary to warn him not only that he has the right to consult with an attorney, but also that if he is indigent a lawyer will be appointed to represent him. Without this additional warning, the admonition of the right to consult with counsel would often be understood as meaning only that he can consult with a lawyer if he has one or has the funds to obtain one. The warning of a right to counsel would be hollow if not couched in terms that would convey to the indigent—the person most often subjected to interrogation—the knowledge that he too has a right to have counsel present. As with the warnings of the right to remain silent and of the general right to counsel, only by effective and express explanation to the indigent of this right can there be assurance that he was truly in a position to exercise it.

Once warnings have been given, the subsequent procedure is clear. If the individual indicates in any manner, at any time prior to or during questioning, that he wishes to remain silent, the interrogation must cease. At this point he has shown that he intends to exercise his Fifth Amendment privilege; any statement taken after the person invokes his privilege cannot be other than the product of compulsion, subtle or otherwise. Without the right to cut off questioning, the setting of in-custody interrogation operates on the individual to overcome free choice in producing a statement after the privilege has been once invoked. If the individual states that he wants an attorney, the interrogation must cease until an attorney is present. At that time, the individual must have an opportunity to confer with the attorney and to have him present during any subsequent questioning. If the individual cannot obtain an attorney and he indicates that he wants one before speaking to police, they must respect his decision to remain silent. This does not mean, as some have suggested, that each police station must have a "station house lawyer" present at all times to advise prisoners. It does mean, however, that if police propose to interrogate a person they must make known to him that he is entitled to a lawyer and that if he cannot afford one, a lawyer will be provided for him prior to any interrogation. If authorities conclude that they will not provide counsel during a reasonable period of time in which investigation in the field is carried out, they may refrain from doing so without violating the person's Fifth Amendment privilege so long as they do not question him during that time.

If the interrogation continues without the presence of an attorney and a statement is taken, a heavy burden rests on the government to demonstrate that the defendant knowingly and intelligently waived his privilege against self-incrimination and his right to retained or appointed counsel. Escobedo v. Illinois, 378 U.S. 478, 490, n.14. This Court has always set high standards of proof for the waiver of constitutional rights, Johnson v. Zerbst, 304 U.S. 458 (1938), and we re-assert these standards as applied to in-custody interrogation. Since the State is responsible for establishing the isolated circumstances under which the interrogation takes place and has the only means of making available corroborated evidence of warnings given during incommunicado interrogation, the burden is rightly on its shoulders.

An express statement that the individual is willing to make a statement and does not want an attorney followed closely by a statement could constitute a waiver. But a valid waiver will not be presumed simply from the silence of the accused after warnings are given or simply from the fact that a confession was in fact eventually obtained. . . . Moreover, where in-custody interrogation is involved, there is no room for the contention that the privilege is waived if the individual answers some questions or gives some information on his own prior to invoking his right to remain silent when interrogated.

Whatever the testimony of the authorities as to waiver of rights by an accused, the fact of lengthy interrogation or incommunicado incarceration before a statement is made is strong evidence that the accused did not validly waive his rights. In these circumstances the fact that the individual eventually made a statement is consistent with the conclusion that the compelling influence of the interrogation finally forced him to do so. It is inconsistent with any notion of a voluntary relinquishment of the privilege. Moreover, any evidence that the accused was threatened, tricked, or cajoled into a waiver will, of course, show that the defendant did not voluntarily waive his privilege. The requirement of warnings and waiver of rights is a fundamental with respect to the Fifth Amendment privilege and not simply a preliminary ritual to existing methods of interrogation.

The warnings required and the waiver necessary in accordance with our opinion today are, in the absence of a fully effective equivalent, prerequisites to the admissibility of any statement made by a defendant. No distinction can be drawn between statements which are direct confessions and statements which amount to "admissions" of part or all of an offense. The privilege against self-incrimination protects the individual from being compelled to incriminate himself in any manner; it does not distinguish degrees of incrimination. . . .

The principles announced today deal with the protection which must be given to the privilege against self-incrimination when the individual is first subjected to police interrogation while in custody at the station or otherwise deprived of his freedom of action in any significant way. It is at this point that our adversary system of criminal proceedings commences, distinguishing itself at the outset from the inquisitorial system recognized in some countries. Under the system of warnings we delineate today or under any other system which may be devised and found effective, the safeguards to be erected about the privilege must come into play at this point.

Our decision is not intended to hamper the traditional function of police officers in investigating crime. . . . When an individual is in custody on probable cause, the police may, of course, seek out evidence in the field to be used at trial against him. Such investigation may include inquiry of persons not under restraint. General on-the-scene questioning as to facts surrounding a crime or other general questioning of citizens in the fact-finding process is not affected by our holding. It is an act of responsible citizenship for individuals to give whatever information they may have to aid in law enforcement. In such situations the compelling atmosphere inherent in the process of in-custody interrogation is not necessarily present.

In dealing with statements obtained through interrogation, we do not purport to find all confessions inadmissible. Confessions remain a proper element in law enforcement. Any statement given freely and voluntarily without any compelling influences is, of course, admissible in evidence. The fundamental import of the privilege while an individual is in custody is not whether he is allowed to talk to the police without the benefit of warnings and counsel, but whether he can be interrogated. There is no requirement that police stop a person who enters a police station and states that he wishes to confess to a crime, or a person who calls the police to offer a confession or any other statement he desires to make. Volunteered statements of any kind are not barred by the Fifth Amendment and their admissibility is not affected by our holding today. . . .

IV

A recurrent argument made in these cases is that society's need for interrogation outweighs the privilege. . . .

Over the years the Federal Bureau of Investigation has compiled an exemplary record of effective law enforcement while advising any suspect or arrested person, at the outset of an interview, that he is not required to make a statement, that any statement may be used against him in court, that the individual may obtain the services of an attorney of his own choice and, more recently, that he has a right to free counsel if he is unable to pay. . . .

The practice of the FBI can readily be emulated by state and local enforcement agencies. The argument that the FBI deals with different crimes than are dealt with by state authorities does not mitigate the significance of the FBI experience. . . .

V

Because of the nature of the problem and because of its recurrent significance in numerous cases, we have to this point discussed the relationship of the Fifth Amendment privilege to police interrogation without specific concentration on the facts of the cases before us. We turn now to these facts to consider the application to these cases of the constitutional principles discussed above. In each instance, we have concluded that statements were obtained from the defendant under circumstances that did not meet constitutional standards for protection of the privilege.

NO. 759. MIRANDA V. ARIZONA

On March 13, 1963, petitioner, Ernesto Miranda, was arrested at his home and taken in custody to a Phoenix police station. He was there identified by the complaining witness. The police then took him to "Interrogation Room No. 2" of the detective bureau. There he was questioned by two police officers. The officers admitted at trial that Miranda was not advised that he had a right to have an attorney present. Two hours later, the officers emerged from the interrogation room with a written confession signed by Miranda. At the top of the statement was a typed paragraph stating that the confession was made voluntarily, without threats or promises of immunity and "with full knowledge of my legal rights, understanding any statement I make may be used against me."[67]

At his trial before a jury, the written confession was admitted into evidence over the objection of defense counsel, and the officers testified to the prior oral confession made by Miranda during the interrogation. Miranda was found guilty of kidnapping and rape. . . .

We reverse. From the testimony of the officers and by the admission of respondent, it is clear that Miranda was not in any way apprised of his right to consult with an attorney and to have one present during the interrogation, nor was his right not to be compelled to incriminate himself effectively protected in any other manner. Without these warnings the statements were inadmissible. The mere fact that he signed a statement which contained a typed-in clause stating that he had "full knowledge" of his "legal rights" does not approach the knowing and intelligent waiver required to relinquish constitutional rights.

NO. 760. VIGNERA V. NEW YORK

Petitioner, Michael Vignera, was picked up by New York police on October 14, 1960, in connection with the robbery three days earlier of a Brooklyn dress shop. . . . [A] detective questioned Vignera with respect to the robbery. Vignera orally admitted the robbery. . . . The detective was asked on cross-examination at trial by defense counsel whether Vignera was warned of his right to counsel before being interrogated. The prosecution objected to the question and the trial judge sustained the objection. Thus, the defense was precluded from making any showing that warnings had not been given. . . . [Several hours later,] Vignera was questioned by an assistant district attorney in the presence of a hearing reporter who transcribed the questions and Vignera's answers. This verbatim account of these proceedings contains no statement of any warnings given by the assistant district attorney. At Vignera's trial on a charge of first degree robbery, the detective testified as to the oral confession. The transcription of the statement taken was also introduced in evidence. . . .

Vignera was found guilty of first degree robbery. We reverse. The foregoing indicates that Vignera was not warned of any of his rights before the questioning by the detective and by the assistant district attorney. No other steps were taken to protect these rights. . . .

NO. 761. WESTOVER V. UNITED STATES

At approximately 9:45 p.m. on March 20, 1963, petitioner, Carl Calvin Westover, was arrested by local police in Kansas City as a suspect in two Kansas City robberies. A report was also received from the FBI that he was wanted on a felony charge in California. . . . Kansas City police interrogated Westover on the night of his arrest. He denied any knowledge of criminal activities. The next day local officers interrogated him again throughout the morning. Shortly before noon they informed the FBI that they were through interrogating Westover and that the FBI could proceed to interrogate him. There is nothing in the record to

---

67. One of the officers testified that he read this paragraph to Miranda. Apparently, however, he did not do so until after Miranda had confessed orally.

indicate that Westover was ever given any warning as to his rights by local police. At noon, three special agents of the FBI continued the interrogation in a private interview room of the Kansas City Police Department, this time with respect to the robbery of a savings and loan association and a bank in Sacramento, California. After two or two and one-half hours, Westover signed separate confessions to each of these two robberies which had been prepared by one of the agents during the interrogation. At trial one of the agents testified, and a paragraph on each of the statements states, that the agents advised Westover that he did not have to make a statement, that any statement he made could be used against him, and that he had the right to see an attorney.

Westover was tried by a jury in federal court and convicted of the California robberies. His statements were introduced at trial. He was sentenced to 15 years' imprisonment on each count, the sentences to run consecutively. On appeal, the conviction was affirmed by the Court of Appeals for the Ninth Circuit. 342 F.2d 684.

We reverse. On the facts of this case we cannot find that Westover knowingly and intelligently waived his right to remain silent and his right to consult with counsel prior to the time he made the statement. At the time the FBI agents began questioning Westover, he had been in custody for over 14 hours and had been interrogated at length during that period. The FBI interrogation began immediately upon the conclusion of the interrogation by Kansas City police and was conducted in local police headquarters. Although the two law enforcement authorities are legally distinct and the crimes for which they interrogated Westover were different, the impact on him was that of a continuous period of questioning. There is no evidence of any warning given prior to the FBI interrogation nor is there any evidence of an articulated waiver of rights after the FBI commenced its interrogation. . . . Despite the fact that the FBI agents gave warnings at the outset of their interview, from Westover's point of view the warnings came at the end of the interrogation process. In these circumstances an intelligent waiver of constitutional rights cannot be assumed. . . .

NO. 584. CALIFORNIA V. STEWART

In the course of investigating a series of purse-snatch robberies in which one of the victims had died of injuries inflicted by her assailant, respondent, Roy Allen Stewart, was pointed out to Los Angeles police as the endorser of dividend checks taken in one of the robberies. At about 7:15 p.m., January 31, 1963, police officers went to Stewart's house and arrested him. One of the officers asked Stewart if they could search the house, to which he replied, "Go ahead." The search turned up various items taken from the five robbery victims. . . . Stewart was taken to the University Station of the Los Angeles Police Department where he was placed in a cell. During the next five days, police interrogated Stewart on nine different occasions. Except during the first interrogation session, when he was confronted with an accusing witness, Stewart was isolated with his interrogators.

During the ninth interrogation session, Stewart admitted that he had robbed the deceased and stated that he had not meant to hurt her. Police then brought Stewart before a magistrate for the first time. . . .

Nothing in the record specifically indicates whether Stewart was or was not advised of his right to remain silent or his right to counsel. In a number of instances, however, the interrogating officers were asked to recount everything that was said during the interrogations. None indicated that Stewart was ever advised of his rights.

Stewart was charged with kidnapping to commit robbery, rape, and murder. At his trial, transcripts of the first interrogation and the confession at the last interrogation were introduced in evidence. The jury found Stewart guilty of robbery and first degree murder and fixed the penalty as death. On appeal, the Supreme Court of California reversed. 62 Cal. 2d 571, 400 P.2d 97, 43 Cal. Rptr. 201. It held that under this Court's decision in *Escobedo*, Stewart should have been advised of his right to remain silent and of his right to counsel and that it would not presume in the face of a silent record that the police advised Stewart of his rights.

We affirm. In dealing with custodial interrogation, we will not presume that a defendant has been effectively apprised of his rights and that his privilege against self-incrimination has been adequately safeguarded on a record that does not show that any warnings have been given or that any effective alternative has been employed. Nor can a knowing and intelligent waiver of these rights be assumed on a silent record. . . .

MR. JUSTICE CLARK's opinion, dissenting in Nos. 759, 760, and 761, and concurring in the result in No. 584, is omitted.

MR. JUSTICE HARLAN, whom MR. JUSTICE STEWART and MR. JUSTICE WHITE join, dissenting.

. . . The Court's opening contention, that the Fifth Amendment governs police station confessions, is perhaps not an impermissible extension of the law but it has little to commend itself in the present circumstances. Historically, the privilege against self-incrimination did not bear at all on the use of extra-legal confessions, for which distinct standards evolved; indeed, "the *history* of the two principles is wide apart, differing by one hundred years in origin, and derived through separate lines of precedents. . . . " 8 Wigmore, Evidence §2266, at 401 (McNaughton rev. 1961). Practice under the two doctrines has also differed in a number of important respects.[6] Even those who would readily enlarge the privilege must concede some linguistic difficulties since the Fifth Amendment in terms proscribes only compelling any person "in any criminal case to be a witness against himself."

. . . Certainly the privilege does represent a protective concern for the accused and an emphasis upon accusatorial rather than inquisitorial values in law enforcement. . . . Accusatorial values, however, have openly been absorbed into the due process standard governing confessions; this indeed is why at present "the kinship of the two rules [governing confessions and self-incrimination] is too apparent for denial." McCormick, Evidence 155 (1954). Since extension of the general principle has already occurred, to insist that the privilege applies as such serves only to carry over inapposite historical details and engaging rhetoric and to obscure the policy choices to be made in regulating confessions.

---

6. Among the examples given in 8 Wigmore, Evidence §2266, at 401 (McNaughton rev. 1961), are these: the privilege applies to any witness, civil or criminal, but the confession rule protects only criminal defendants; the privilege deals only with compulsion, while the confession rule may exclude statements obtained by trick or promise; and where the privilege has been nullified — as by the English Bankruptcy Act — the confession rule may still operate.

Having decided that the Fifth Amendment privilege does apply in the police station, the Court reveals that the privilege imposes more exacting restrictions than does the Fourteenth Amendment's voluntariness test. It then emerges ... that the Fifth Amendment requires for an admissible confession that it be given by one distinctly aware of his right not to speak and shielded from "the compelling atmosphere" of interrogation. ... From these key premises, the Court finally develops the safeguards of warning, counsel, and so forth. I do not believe these premises are sustained by precedents under the Fifth Amendment.

The more important premise is that pressure on the suspect must be eliminated though it be only the subtle influence of the atmosphere and surroundings. The Fifth Amendment, however, has never been thought to forbid *all* pressure to incriminate one's self in the situations covered by it. On the contrary, it has been held that failure to incriminate one's self can result in denial of removal of one's case from state to federal court, Maryland v. Soper, 270 U.S. 9; in refusal of a military commission, Orloff v. Willoughby, 345 U.S. 83; in denial of a discharge in bankruptcy, Kaufman v. Hurwitz, 176 F.2d 210; and in numerous other adverse consequences. See 8 Wigmore, Evidence §2272, at 441-444, n. 18 (McNaughton rev. 1961); Maguire, Evidence of Guilt §2.062 (1959). This is not to say that short of jail or torture any sanction is permissible in any case; policy and history alike may impose sharp limits. See, e.g., Griffin v. California, 380 U.S. 609. However, the Court's unspoken assumption that *any* pressure violates the privilege is not supported by the precedents and it has failed to show why the Fifth Amendment prohibits that relatively mild pressure the Due Process Clause permits.

The Court appears similarly wrong in thinking that precise knowledge of one's rights is a settled prerequisite under the Fifth Amendment to the loss of its protections. ... No Fifth Amendment precedent is cited for the Court's contrary view. ...

A closing word must be said about the Assistance of Counsel Clause of the Sixth Amendment, which is never expressly relied on by the Court but whose judicial precedents turn out to be linchpins of the confession rules announced today. ... While the Court finds no pertinent difference between judicial proceedings and police interrogation, I believe the differences are so vast as to disqualify wholly the Sixth Amendment precedents as suitable analogies in the present cases.

The only attempt in this Court to carry the right to counsel into the station house occurred in *Escobedo*, the Court repeating several times that that stage was no less "critical" than trial itself. See 378 U.S., 485-488. This is hardly persuasive when we consider that a grand jury inquiry, the filing of a certiorari petition, and certainly the purchase of narcotics by an undercover agent from a prospective defendant may all be equally "critical" yet provision of counsel and advice on that score have never been thought compelled by the Constitution in such cases. The sound reason why this right is so freely extended for a criminal trial is the severe injustice risked by confronting an untrained defendant with a range of technical points of law, evidence, and tactics familiar to the prosecutor but not to himself. This danger shrinks markedly in the police station where indeed the lawyer in fulfilling his professional responsibilities of necessity may become an obstacle to truthfinding. ...

Examined as an expression of public policy, the Court's new regime proves so dubious that there can be no due compensation for its weakness in constitutional law. . . .

Without at all subscribing to the generally black picture of police conduct painted by the Court, I think it must be frankly recognized at the outset that police questioning allowable under due process precedents may inherently entail some pressure on the suspect and may seek advantage in his ignorance or weaknesses. The atmosphere and questioning techniques, proper and fair though they be, can in themselves exert a tug on the suspect to confess, and in this light "[t]o speak of any confessions of crime made after arrest as being 'voluntary' or 'uncoerced' is somewhat inaccurate, although traditional. A confession is wholly and incontestably voluntary only if a guilty person gives himself up to the law and becomes his own accuser." Ashcraft v. Tennessee, 322 U.S. 143, 161 (Jackson, J., dissenting). Until today, the role of the Constitution has been only to sift out *undue* pressure, not to assure spontaneous confessions. . . .

What the Court largely ignores is that its rules impair, if they will not eventually serve wholly to frustrate, an instrument of law enforcement that has long and quite reasonably been thought worth the price paid for it. There can be little doubt that the Court's new code would markedly decrease the number of confessions. To warn the suspect that he may remain silent and remind him that his confession may be used in court are minor obstructions. To require also an express waiver by the suspect and an end to questioning whenever he demurs must heavily handicap questioning. And to suggest or provide counsel for the suspect simply invites the end of the interrogation. . . .

While passing over the costs and risks of its experiment, the Court portrays the evils of normal police questioning in terms which I think are exaggerated. . . . [I]nterrogation is no doubt often inconvenient and unpleasant for the suspect. However, it is no less so for a man to be arrested and jailed, to have his house searched, or to stand trial in court, yet all this may properly happen to the most innocent given probable cause, a warrant, or an indictment. Society has always paid a stiff price for law and order, and peaceful interrogation is not one of the dark moments of the law.

This brief statement of the competing considerations seems to me ample proof that the Court's preference is highly debatable at best and therefore not to be read into the Constitution. However, it may make the analysis more graphic to consider the actual facts of one of the four cases reversed by the Court. Miranda v. Arizona serves best, being neither the hardest nor easiest of the four under the Court's standards.

On March 3, 1963, an 18-year-old girl was kidnapped and forcibly raped near Phoenix, Arizona. Ten days later, on the morning of March 13, petitioner Miranda was arrested and taken to the police station. At this time Miranda was 23 years old, indigent, and educated to the extent of completing half the ninth grade. He had "an emotional illness" of the schizophrenic type, according to the doctor who eventually examined him; the doctor's report also stated that Miranda was "alert and oriented as to time, place, and person," intelligent within normal limits, competent to stand trial, and sane within the legal definition. At the police station, the victim picked Miranda out of a lineup, and two officers then took him into a separate room to interrogate him, starting about 11:30 a.m. Though at first denying his guilt, within a short time Miranda gave a detailed oral confession and then wrote out in his own hand and signed a brief statement admitting and describing the crime. All this was accomplished in two hours or less without any force, threats or promises and — I will assume this though the record is uncertain . . . —without any effective warnings at all.

Miranda's oral and written confessions are now held inadmissible under the Court's new rules. One is entitled to feel astonished that the Constitution can be read to produce this result. These confessions were obtained during brief, daytime questioning conducted by two officers and unmarked by any of the traditional indicia of coercion. They assured a conviction for a brutal and unsettling crime. . . . There was, in sum, a legitimate purpose, no perceptible unfairness, and certainly little risk of injustice in the interrogation. Yet the resulting confessions, and the responsible course of police practice they represent, are to be sacrificed to the Court's own finespun conception of fairness. . . .

MR. JUSTICE WHITE, with whom MR. JUSTICE HARLAN and MR. JUSTICE STEWART join, dissenting. . . .

. . . To reach the result announced on the grounds it does, the Court must stay within the confines of the Fifth Amendment, which forbids self-incrimination only if *compelled*. Hence the core of the Court's opinion is that because of the "compulsion inherent in custodial surroundings, no statement obtained from [a] defendant [in custody] can truly be the product of his free choice," . . . absent the use of adequate protective devices as described by the Court. However, the Court does not point to any sudden inrush of new knowledge requiring the rejection of 70 years' experience. Nor does it assert that its novel conclusion reflects a changing consensus among state courts, see Mapp v. Ohio, 367 U.S. 643, or that a succession of cases had steadily eroded the old rule and proved it unworkable, see Gideon v. Wainwright, 372 U.S. 335. Rather than asserting new knowledge, the Court concedes that it cannot truly know what occurs during custodial questioning, because of the innate secrecy of such proceedings. It extrapolates a picture of what it conceives to be the norm from police investigatorial manuals, published in 1959 and 1962 or earlier, without any attempt to allow for adjustments in police practices that may have occurred in the wake of more recent decisions of state appellate tribunals or this Court. But even if the relentless application of the described procedures could lead to involuntary confessions, it most assuredly does not follow that each and every case will disclose this kind of interrogation or this kind of consequence.[2] Insofar as appears from the Court's opinion, it has not examined a single transcript of any police interrogation, let alone the interrogation that took place in any one of these cases which it decides today. Judged by any of the standards for empirical investigation utilized in the social sciences the factual basis for the Court's premise is patently inadequate.

Although in the Court's view in-custody interrogation is inherently coercive, the Court says that the spontaneous product of the coercion of arrest and detention is

2. In fact, the type of sustained interrogation described by the Court appears to be the exception rather than the rule. A survey of 399 cases in one city found that in almost half of the cases the interrogation lasted less than 30 minutes. Barrett, Police Practices and the Law — From Arrest to Release or Charge, 50 Calif. L. Rev. 11, 41-45 (1962). Questioning tends to be confused and sporadic and is usually concentrated on confrontations with witnesses or new items of evidence, as these are obtained by officers conducting the investigation. See generally LaFave, Arrest: The Decision to Take a Suspect into Custody 386 (1965); ALI, A Model Code of Pre-Arraignment Procedure, Commentary §5.01, at 17, n. 4 (Tent. Draft No. 1, 1966).

still to be deemed voluntary. An accused, arrested on probable cause, may blurt out a confession which will be admissible despite the fact that he is alone and in custody, without any showing that he had any notion of his right to remain silent or of the consequences of his admission. Yet, under the Court's rule, if the police ask him a single question such as "Do you have anything to say?" or "Did you kill your wife?" his response, if there is one, has somehow been compelled, even if the accused has been clearly warned of his right to remain silent. Common sense informs us to the contrary. . . .

Today's result would not follow even if it were agreed that to some extent custodial interrogation is inherently coercive. . . . The test has been whether the totality of circumstances deprived the defendant of a "free choice to admit, to deny, or to refuse to answer," Lisenba v. California, 314 U.S. 219, 241, and whether physical or psychological coercion was of such a degree that "the defendant's will was overborne at the time he confessed," Haynes v. Washington, 373 U.S. 503, 513; Lynumn v. Illinois, 372 U.S. 528, 534. The duration and nature of incommunicado custody, the presence or absence of advice concerning the defendant's constitutional rights, and the granting or refusal of requests to communicate with lawyers, relatives or friends have all been rightly regarded as important data bearing on the basic inquiry. . . . But it has never been suggested, until today, that such questioning was so coercive and accused persons so lacking in hardihood that the very first response to the very first question following the commencement of custody must be conclusively presumed to be the product of an overborne will. . . .

On the other hand, even if one assumed that there was an adequate factual basis for the conclusion that all confessions obtained during in-custody interrogation are the product of compulsion, the rule propounded by the Court would still be irrational, for, apparently, it is only if the accused is also warned of his right to counsel and waives both that right and the right against self-incrimination that the inherent compulsiveness of interrogation disappears. But if the defendant may not answer without a warning a question such as "Where were you last night?" without having his answer be a compelled one, how can the Court ever accept his negative answer to the question of whether he wants to consult his retained counsel or counsel whom the court will appoint? And why if counsel is present and the accused nevertheless confesses, or counsel tells the accused to tell the truth, and that is what the accused does, is the situation any less coercive insofar as the accused is concerned? The Court apparently realizes its dilemma of foreclosing questioning without the necessary warnings but at the same time permitting the accused, sitting in the same chair in front of the same policemen, to waive his right to consult an attorney. It expects, however, that the accused will not often waive the right; and if it is claimed that he has, the State faces a severe, if not impossible burden of proof. . . .

In sum, for all the Court's expounding on the menacing atmosphere of police interrogation procedures, it has failed to supply any foundation for the conclusions it draws or the measures it adopts.

. . . The obvious underpinning of the Court's decision is a deep-seated distrust of all confessions. As the Court declares that the accused may not be interrogated without counsel present, absent a waiver of the right to counsel, and as the Court all but admonishes the lawyer to advise the accused to remain silent, the result adds up to a judicial judgment that evidence from the accused should not be used against him in any way, whether compelled or not. This is the not so subtle overtone of the opinion—that it is inherently wrong for the police to gather evidence from the accused himself. . . . I see nothing wrong or immoral, and certainly nothing unconstitutional, in the police's asking a suspect whom they have reasonable cause to arrest whether or not he killed his wife or in confronting him with the evidence on which the arrest was based, at least where he has been plainly advised that he may remain completely silent. . . .

Much of the trouble with the Court's new rule is that it will operate indiscriminately in all criminal cases, regardless of the severity of the crime or the circumstances involved. It applies to every defendant, whether the professional criminal or one committing a crime of momentary passion who is not part and parcel of organized crime. It will slow down the investigation and the apprehension of confederates in those cases where time is of the essence, . . . and some of those involving organized crime. In the latter context the lawyer who arrives may also be the lawyer for the defendant's colleagues and can be relied upon to insure that no breach of the organization's security takes place even though the accused may feel that the best thing he can do is to cooperate. . . .

Applying the traditional standards to the cases before the Court, I would hold these confessions voluntary.

NOTES AND QUESTIONS

1. Compare *Bram* and *Miranda*. Which, in your view, is "better" and why? Which is more realistic? Which better relates the remedy provided to the wrong done? Which provides more serious protections for the accused? In this regard, consider the contemporary role of plea bargaining, in which the accused and the state negotiate a plea where the accused "trades" his procedural protections for sentencing or charging concessions by the state. The normal outcome is a plea of guilty that is generally tantamount to a legally binding confession. The Supreme Court has legitimized this practice, Brady v. United States, 397 U.S. 742 (1970), but how would it have fared under *Bram*? How *should* it fare today?

2. Chief Justice Warren begins his argument in *Miranda* with a discussion of the ongoing problem of physical brutality in police interrogation. Does that problem justify the Court's holding? It would seem more natural to conclude that physical force and psychological ploys are substitutes for one another—the more the police rely on one, the less they are likely to rely on the other. Physical force was already illegal before *Miranda*; Warren's opinion seems designed to make psychological ploys illegal as well. Is that likely to diminish police brutality, or to increase its frequency?

3. If *Miranda* is sound policy for domestic police interrogation, is it also sound policy for military interrogation of suspected terrorists? Terrorists are different from most criminal suspects: smarter than the average street criminal, and vastly more committed to their enterprise. If *Miranda*'s rules are applied to them, the Jose Padillas of the world will ask for a lawyer sometime soon after questioning begins—whereupon questioning will cease, if *Miranda*'s rules are followed. That may make men like Padilla (an American citizen accused of conspiring with fellow Al Qaeda members to set off a "dirty bomb" in an American city) unconvictable. Worse, it may make their crimes unpreventable. And by holding the government to that standard, we risk encouraging precisely the kind of game-playing we saw in

Padilla's case — shortly after his arrest, he was reclassified as an enemy combatant in order to evade various domestic criminal procedure doctrines. Finally, interrogators facing such suspects, if barred from using fraud and deceit to get what they want, may be tempted to use force.

Are these claims simply rationalizations for an "anything goes" policy — the sort of policy that produced the interrogation abuses at Abu Ghraib prison in Iraq? Or are these sound arguments for restricting *Miranda*? Might these arguments apply to some categories of domestic criminals? Note Justice White's complaint that the Court's formula takes no account of differences among crimes, or differences among criminals. Should police interrogation rules be different for murder suspects than for securities fraud suspects? Which group should receive more legal protection?

4. The Court in *Miranda* relies heavily on various interrogation manuals that the Court apparently thought were of great relevance to the cases before it. Review the facts in the four cases before the Court. Were any of the "abuses" of the interrogation process that the Court used the manuals to document present in these cases? If not, what is the relevance of the manuals? On the other hand, is it clear what tactics police officers *did* use in these cases? One of the motivating factors in *Miranda* appears to have been the Court's concern that police interrogation practices were something of a mystery. Assuming the concern was valid, what was the proper response? Why not require video- and/or audiotaping of interrogation sessions rather than the Court's warnings and waiver restrictions? See, e.g., Paul G. Cassell, *Miranda*'s Social Cost: An Empirical Assessment, 90 Nw. U. L. Rev. 387, 486 (1996) (making this proposal). Indeed, if trial judges were unable to uncover the truth about police interrogation before *Miranda*, why should one assume that they could uncover the truth about *Miranda* waivers afterward?

Alaska and Minnesota have required the taping of interrogations by court decision. Stephen v. State, 711 P.2d 1156 (Alaska 1985); State v. Scales, 518 N.W.2d 587 (Minn. 1994). Illinois requires it by statute for certain crimes (mostly homicide). Ill. Comp. Stat. Ann. §5/103-2.1. And a number of police agencies tape interrogations on their own. Estimates of the number of agencies taping interrogations ran as high as one-sixth a dozen years ago. William A. Geller, Police Videotaping of Suspect Interrogations and Confessions: A Preliminary Examination of Issues and Practices 54, 107-149 (NIJ 1993). According to Cassell, most officers with experience with videotaping approve of the practice, and England apparently has had success with videotaping.

5. Speaking of *Miranda* waivers, consider Justice White's argument: All the same factors that make police interrogation "inherently coercive" must apply equally to the suspect who waives his *Miranda* rights. Does it follow that *Miranda* waivers should be almost impossible to show? In practice, that has not been the case: Something in the vicinity of 80 percent of suspects routinely waive their *Miranda* rights and talk to the police. See Richard A. Leo, The Impact of *Miranda* Revisited, 86 J. Crim. L. & Criminology 621, 653 (1996). Is that statistic evidence for the proposition that *Miranda* has not proved very costly, or does it suggest that courts do not rigorously enforce *Miranda*'s requirements?

6. The Court suggests that the standards it is imposing on the states are not that burdensome, as proven by the fact that the FBI has labored successfully under similar restrictions for years. As Justice Harlan pointed out, in a portion of his

dissent not excerpted above, the Court was not quite right about the analogy: The FBI's pre-*Miranda* practice was not to require waivers, and when suspects invoked their rights, agents were free to try to persuade them to change their minds. Putting these differences to one side, how cogent is the Court's analogy? The FBI does not deal with routine street crimes; that is the job of local police departments. Meanwhile, the FBI *does* deal with organized crime and white-collar crime, areas in which suspects are likely to be more sophisticated than those whom local police must interrogate. How do these differences play out when it comes to a proper analysis of police interrogation?

7. Though *Miranda* displaced the due process voluntariness test as the primary constitutional limit on police interrogation, voluntariness still matters in two distinct ways. Waivers of the *Miranda* right must be, among other things, voluntary. (*Miranda* waivers are discussed below, at pages 858-887.) And the due process requirement of voluntariness continues to apply to confessions — in addition to *Miranda*, and in addition to the Sixth Amendment right granted by Massiah v. United States, 377 U.S. 201 (1964). (*Massiah* is excerpted supra, at page 813.)

In the wake of *Miranda*, some wondered whether the due process voluntariness requirement might extend more broadly than *Miranda*'s elaborate rule structure, in the following respect: Plainly, *Miranda* was limited to police conduct; its rules do not apply to questioning by private parties. That conclusion is not as obvious with respect to voluntariness. If the key to the voluntariness requirement is ensuring that admissible confessions are not the product of "overborne" wills, one might imagine that the requirement would apply regardless of the source of the pressure that overpowered the defendant. The Supreme Court faced this question in Colorado v. Connelly, 479 U.S. 157 (1986). The defendant in *Connelly* approached a Denver, Colorado police officer and confessed to a murder. The officer to whom this confession was made immediately gave the defendant his *Miranda* warnings, whereupon he confessed again. The confession was thoroughly corroborated; there was no doubt as to its accuracy. The day after he delivered this confession, the defendant "stated that 'voices' had told him to come to Denver and that he had followed the directions of these voices in confessing." Id. at 161. Later, the defendant described what he heard as "the voice of God." He was examined by a psychiatrist and diagnosed as a schizophrenic.

The defendant claimed that these voices rendered his confession involuntary. The Supreme Court held otherwise:

> . . . [T]he cases considered by this Court over the 50 years since Brown v. Mississippi [, 297 U.S. 278 (1936),] have focused upon the crucial element of police overreaching. While each confession case has turned on its own set of factors justifying the conclusion that police conduct was oppressive, all have contained a substantial element of coercive police conduct. Absent police conduct causally related to the confession, there is simply no basis for concluding that any state actor has deprived a criminal defendant of due process of law. Respondent correctly notes that as interrogators have turned to more subtle forms of psychological persuasion, courts have found the mental condition of the defendant a more significant factor in the "voluntariness" calculus. But this fact does not justify a conclusion that a defendant's mental condition, by itself and apart from its relation to official coercion, should ever dispose of the inquiry into constitutional "voluntariness."

479 U.S. at 163-164.

8. Is there a middle ground between the dictates of *Miranda* and the awkwardness of the voluntariness test to judge the admissibility of confessions obtained through pretrial interrogation? Note that in *Miranda* the Court said that equally effective procedures to ensure the Fifth Amendment's protections could supplement the Court's requirements. Yet before "equally effective" procedures can be provided, one must know the answer to this question: "Equally effective" as to what? Consider once again the fact that the answer to that question cannot be to protect the unfettered exercise of the suspect's "free will." Every time a person provides incriminating statements, there is a reason for giving the statement acting on the "will." To be sure, some distinctions can be made. There are, for example, a number of reasons why we do not countenance the use of serious physical abuse to induce statements, but does it follow from that proposition that no incentive to speak should be brought to bear on the suspect by the state? If you think it does not follow, again you must construct what does. In that regard, consider the following short excerpt from a remarkable article written over seventy years ago by Professor Kauper. Bear in mind that Professor Kauper was writing prior to the "procedural revolution" and also that his focus was a means to eliminate brutal police practices. Nonetheless, consider whether his proposal has any relevance to contemporary society.

KAUPER, JUDICIAL EXAMINATION OF THE ACCUSED — A REMEDY FOR THE THIRD DEGREE, 30 MICH. L. REV. 1224, 1239-1241 (1932): The remedy proposed consists of two essentials:

(1)   That the accused be promptly produced before a magistrate for interrogation; and,

(2)   That the interrogation be supported by the threat that refusal to answer questions of the magistrate will be used against the accused at the trial.

It is submitted that the two features of the proposed plan must be linked together. The magistrate must have power to interrogate the prisoner. The present system which allows the accused an opportunity to make a statement but denies the magistrate power to ask questions is not effective for the purpose of securing information. And the power to interrogate must be supported by some compulsion to answer questions; otherwise it will be rendered impotent. Neither is the compulsion afforded by the right to comment on *failure to testify at the trial* sufficient. The comment must be upon the prisoner's *refusal to answer questions at the interrogation*. It is true that some writers have asserted that the problem of the police third degree would be solved if the judge and prosecutor were given the right to comment on the prisoner's failure to testify at his trial. But analysis of that proposition makes the conclusion appear to be a non sequitur. The possibility that at the trial an inference of guilt may be drawn from the accused's silence is hardly equivalent in the eyes of the police to a confession or other valuable information obtained shortly after arrest. In other words, making criminal procedure at the trial more effective against the accused does not satisfy police motives that demand interrogation immediately upon arrest. . . .

The plan proposed of requiring prompt interrogation by a magistrate supported by the threat of comment on failure to answer carries considerable promise. The plan necessarily involves prompt production of the accused before a magistrate. This is a sine qua non in the mitigation of third degree abuses, for so long as prisoners are in the control of officers there is a temptation to resort to third degree practices.

The plan provides an *immediate* opportunity for questioning the accused while the pursuit is still hot and the clues are yet fresh. By warning the accused that the whole record of the interrogation will go to the trial court, so that his silence in refusing to answer questions or make explanations will be used with telling effect against him before the jury, a strong psychic pressure will induce him to break his silence. Nor should it be forgotten that the larger number of those who are arrested are willing to speak and answer questions.[82] Even the fact of a false statement made by a prisoner after arrest in order to cover his guilt can be used against him at the trial often with as much effectiveness as a truthful incriminating statement. Questioned immediately upon arrest, the accused does not have time to work out a coherent fabricated story or defense alibi. From the viewpoint of police psychology it appears that inauguration of a scheme of magisterial interrogation will greatly weaken the police motive for private interrogation since that motive will find vicarious expression in a substituted device. Viewing the problem historically, Dean Pound ascribes the extra-legal development of the "unhappy system of police examination" in the United States to the sloughing off by justices of the peace of their police powers, including examination of the accused, thereby leaving "a gap which in practice had to be filled outside of the law."[83] The proposed plan would fill the gap which resulted from the differentiation in function between magistrate and police with the effect of forcing the police to adopt the system of extra-legal interrogation. It would vest the power of interrogation in officers who are better qualified to exercise the power of interrogation fairly and effectively. . . .

2. The Scope of *Miranda*

a. *What Is "Custody"?*

Miranda has consistently been interpreted to be applicable only to custodial interrogation, but "custody" has been given a functional definition. For example, in Orozco v. Texas, 394 U.S. 324 (1969), the Court applied *Miranda* to the questioning of a suspect in his bedroom at 4:00 a.m. by four police. The Court also applied *Miranda* to the testimony of a psychiatrist at the penalty stage of a capital case based on his psychiatric examination of the defendant where the defendant was not given the *Miranda* warnings prior to the examination. Estelle v. Smith, 451 U.S. 454 (1981). In contrast, the Court found no violation of *Miranda* in Oregon v.

82. "In Washtenaw County, Michigan, of the 312 judgments of the county court in criminal cases in one year, 305 were on pleas of guilty. The prosecuting attorney's explanation of his success in obtaining so many confessions of guilt was his practice of himself interviewing every person arrested on a felony charge immediately after the arrest while he was still excited and before he had opportunity to consult with a lawyer. In that way, the prosecutor said, he got the truth. None of the confessions were repudiated in court nor did any of the 305 defendants make allegations of mistreatment. If all be as it appears, that prompt interrogation produced justice." John Barker Waite, 30 Mich. L. Rev. 54 at 59 (1931).

83. Criminal Justice in America 88 (1930). See also Wickersham Comm. Rep. No. 8, pp. 9, 10 (1930).

Mathiason, 429 U.S. 492 (1977), and California v. Beheler, 463 U.S. 1121 (1983), where the defendants voluntarily went to the station houses, were not under arrest, and gave confessions there. Nor has it been applied to grand jury witnesses. United States v. Mandujano, 425 U.S. 564 (1976). Nor is *Miranda* applicable when an investigation has focused on a suspect but the police have not made an arrest. Beckwith v. United States, 425 U.S. 341 (1976).

These cases left the meaning of "custody" uncertain. Berkemer v. McCarty, 468 U.S. 420 (1984), offered some clarification. The facts in *Berkemer* were as follows:

> . . . On the evening of March 31, 1980, Trooper Williams of the Ohio State Highway Patrol observed respondent's car weaving in and out of a lane on Interstate Highway 270. After following the car for two miles, Williams forced respondent to stop and asked him to get out of the vehicle. When respondent complied, Williams noticed that he was having difficulty standing. At that point, "Williams concluded that [respondent] would be charged with a traffic offense and, therefore, his freedom to leave the scene was terminated." However, respondent was not told that he would be taken into custody. Williams then asked respondent to perform a field sobriety test, commonly known as a "balancing test." Respondent could not do so without falling.
>
> While still at the scene of the traffic stop, Williams asked respondent whether he had been using intoxicants. Respondent replied that "he had consumed two beers and had smoked several joints of marijuana a short time before." Respondent's speech was slurred, and Williams had difficulty understanding him. Williams thereupon formally placed respondent under arrest and transported him in the patrol car to the Franklin County Jail.

468 U.S. at 423. By an 8–1 vote (Justice Stevens did not reach the issue), the Court concluded that these facts do not amount to "custody" for purposes of *Miranda*:

> Two features of an ordinary traffic stop mitigate the danger that a person questioned will be induced "to speak where he would not otherwise do so freely," Miranda v. Arizona, 384 U.S., at 467. First, detention of a motorist pursuant to a traffic stop is presumptively temporary and brief. The vast majority of roadside detentions last only a few minutes. A motorist's expectations, when he sees a policeman's light flashing behind him, are that he will be obliged to spend a short period of time answering questions and waiting while the officer checks his license and registration, that he may then be given a citation, but that in the end he most likely will be allowed to continue on his way. In this respect, questioning incident to an ordinary traffic stop is quite different from stationhouse interrogation, which frequently is prolonged, and in which the detainee often is aware that questioning will continue until he provides his interrogators the answers they seek. See id., at 451.
>
> Second, circumstances associated with the typical traffic stop are not such that the motorist feels completely at the mercy of the police. To be sure, the aura of authority surrounding an armed, uniformed officer and the knowledge that the officer has some discretion in deciding whether to issue a citation, in combination, exert some pressure on the detainee to respond to questions. But other aspects of the situation substantially offset these forces. Perhaps most importantly, the typical traffic stop is public, at least to some degree. Passersby, on foot or in other cars witness the interaction of officer and motorist. This exposure to public view both reduces the ability of an unscrupulous policeman to use illegitimate means to elicit self-incriminating statements and diminishes the motorist's fear that, if he does not cooperate, he will be subjected to abuse. The fact that the detained motorist typically is confronted by only one or at most two policemen further mutes his sense of vulnerability. In short, the

atmosphere surrounding an ordinary traffic stop is substantially less "police dominated" than that surrounding the kinds of interrogation at issue in *Miranda* itself, see 384 U.S., at 445, 491-498. . . .

In both of these respects, the usual traffic stop is more analogous to a so-called "*Terry* stop," see Terry v. Ohio, 392 U.S. 1 (1968), than to a formal arrest. Under the Fourth Amendment, we have held, a policeman who lacks probable cause but whose "observations lead him reasonably to suspect" that a particular person has committed, is committing, or is about to commit a crime, may detain that person briefly in order to "investigate the circumstances that provoke suspicion." United States v. Brignoni-Ponce, 422 U.S. 873, 881 (1975). "[The] stop and inquiry must be 'reasonably related in scope to the justification for their initiation.'" Ibid. (quoting Terry v. Ohio, supra, at 29.) Typically, this means that the officer may ask the detainee a moderate number of questions to determine his identity and to try to obtain information confirming or dispelling the officer's suspicions. But the detainee is not obliged to respond. And, unless the detainee's answers provide the officer with probable cause to arrest him, he must then be released. The comparatively nonthreatening character of detentions of this sort explains the absence of any suggestion in our opinions that *Terry* stops are subject to the dictates of *Miranda*. The similarly noncoercive aspect of ordinary traffic stops prompts us to hold that persons temporarily detained pursuant to such stops are not "in custody" for the purposes of *Miranda*.

468 U.S. at 437-440. Elsewhere in his opinion for the Court in *Berkemer*, Justice Marshall made clear that once the suspect is arrested, *Miranda*'s restrictions apply — no matter how minor the crime that prompts the arrest.

After *Berkemer*, *Terry* stops do not implicate *Miranda*, while arrests presumably do. Note the practical importance of this line: A great many encounters between police officers and citizens begin with a *Terry* stop and "ripen" into an arrest as the officer obtains incriminating information, often through conversation with the suspect. If *Miranda* applied whenever a suspect was "seized" under the Fourth Amendment, those encounters might look very different: The officer would have to precede any conversation (and presumably any request for consent to search) with the *Miranda* warnings. *Berkemer* means that these street encounters will continue to be governed solely by a fairly flexible body of Fourth Amendment law, without any interference from Fifth Amendment doctrine.

Is this the right answer? Are brief street stops really "comparatively nonthreatening"? What does this test mean in other contexts? Consider Minnesota v. Murphy, 465 U.S. 420 (1984):

In 1974, Marshall Murphy was twice questioned by Minneapolis Police concerning the rape and murder of a teenage girl. No charges were then brought. In 1980, in connection with a prosecution for criminal sexual conduct arising out of an unrelated incident, Murphy pleaded guilty to a reduced charge of false imprisonment. He was sentenced to a prison term of 16 months, which was suspended, and three years' probation. The terms of Murphy's probation required, among other things, that he participate in a treatment program for sexual offenders at Alpha House, report to his probation officer as directed, and be truthful with the probation officer "in all matters." Failure to comply with these conditions, Murphy was informed, could result in his return to the sentencing court for a probation revocation hearing.

Murphy met with his probation officer at her office approximately once a month, and his probation continued without incident until July 1981, when the officer learned that he had abandoned the treatment program. The probation officer then wrote to

Murphy and informed him that failure to set up a meeting would "result in an immediate request for a warrant." . . . At a meeting in late July, the officer agreed not to seek revocation of probation for nonparticipation in the treatment program since Murphy was employed and doing well in other areas.

In September 1981, an Alpha House counselor informed the probation officer that, during the course of treatment, Murphy had admitted to a rape and murder in 1974. After discussions with her superior, the officer determined that the police should have this information. She then wrote to Murphy and asked him to contact her to discuss a treatment plan for the remainder of his probationary period. Although she did not contact the police before the meeting, the probation officer knew in advance that she would report any incriminating statements.

Upon receipt of the letter, Murphy arranged to meet with his probation officer in her office on September 28, 1981. The officer opened the meeting by telling Murphy about the information she had received from the Alpha House counselor and expressing her belief that this information evinced his continued need for treatment. Murphy became angry about what he considered to be a breach of his confidences and stated that he "felt like calling a lawyer." The probation officer replied that Murphy would have to deal with that problem outside the office; for the moment, their primary concern was the relationship between the crimes that Murphy had admitted to the Alpha House counselor and the incident that led to his conviction for false imprisonment.

During the course of the meeting, Murphy denied the false imprisonment charge, admitted that he had committed the rape and murder, and attempted to persuade the probation officer that further treatment was unnecessary because several extenuating circumstances explained the prior crimes. At the conclusion of the meeting, the officer told Murphy that she had a duty to relay the information to the authorities and encouraged him to turn himself in. Murphy then left the office. Two days later, Murphy called his probation officer and told her that he had been advised by counsel not to surrender himself to the police. The officer then procured the issuance of an arrest and detention order from the judge who had sentenced Murphy on the false imprisonment charge. On October 29, 1981, a State grand jury returned an indictment charging Murphy with first-degree murder.

465 U.S. at 422-425. The Court found *Miranda* inapplicable:

> . . . [I]t is clear that Murphy was not "in custody" for purposes of receiving *Miranda* protection since there was no " 'formal arrest or restraint on freedom of movement' of the degree associated with a formal arrest." California v. Beheler, 463 U.S. 1121, 1125 (1983) (per curiam) (quoting Oregon v. Mathiason, 429 U.S., at 495). . . .
>
> Even a cursory comparison of custodial interrogation and probation interviews reveals the inaptness of the . . . analogy to *Miranda*. Custodial arrest is said to convey to the suspect a message that he has no choice but to submit to the officers' will and to confess. Miranda v. Arizona, 384 U.S., at 456-457. It is unlikely that a probation interview, arranged by appointment at a mutually convenient time, would give rise to a similar impression. Moreover, custodial arrest thrusts an individual into "an unfamiliar atmosphere" or "an interrogation environment . . . created for no purpose other than to subjugate the individual to the will of his examiner." Id., at 457. Many of the psychological ploys discussed in *Miranda* capitalize on the suspect's unfamiliarity with the officers and the environment. Murphy's regular meetings with his probation officer should have served to familiarize him with her and her office and to insulate him from psychological intimidation that might overbear his desire to claim the privilege. Finally, the coercion inherent in custodial interrogation derives in large measure from an interrogator's insinuations that the interrogation will continue until

a confession is obtained. Id., at 468. Since Murphy was not physically restrained and could have left the office, any compulsion he might have felt from the possibility that terminating the meeting would have led to revocation of probation was not comparable to the pressure on a suspect who is painfully aware that he literally cannot escape a persistent custodial interrogator.

We conclude, therefore, that Murphy cannot claim the benefit of the [*Miranda*] exception to the general rule that the Fifth Amendment privilege is not self-executing. . . .

465 U.S. at 430-434.

Does the presence or absence of "custody" depend, at least in part, on the intent of the police? A unanimous Supreme Court said no in Stansbury v. California, 511 U.S. 318 (1994). In *Stansbury*, police officers investigating a homicide went to the defendant's home late at night and when the defendant answered the door, the officers "told him [they] were investigating a homicide to which Stansbury was a possible witness and asked if he would accompany them to the police station to answer some questions." Id. at 320. After he got to the police station, Stansbury made several incriminating statements. Only then did the police give him *Miranda* warnings and tell him he was under arrest. The California Supreme Court had concluded that Stansbury was not in custody at the time he made the statements because the officers investigating the case had not considered him their prime suspect. The Court reversed, stating that the officers' intent was irrelevant, and remanded for a new "custody" determination.

b. What Is "Interrogation"?

RHODE ISLAND v. INNIS

Certiorari to the Rhode Island Supreme Court
446 U.S. 291 (1980)

MR. JUSTICE STEWART delivered the opinion of the Court. . . .

I

On the night of January 12, 1975, John Mulvaney, a Providence, R.I., taxicab driver, disappeared after being dispatched to pick up a customer. His body was discovered four days later buried in a shallow grave in Coventry, R.I. He had died from a shotgun blast aimed at the back of his head.

On January 17, 1975, shortly after midnight, the Providence police received a telephone call from Gerald Aubin, also a taxicab driver, who reported that he had just been robbed by a man wielding a sawed-off shotgun. Aubin further reported that he had dropped off his assailant near Rhode Island College in a section of Providence known as Mount Pleasant. While at the Providence police station waiting to give a statement, Aubin noticed a picture of his assailant on a bulletin board. Aubin so informed one of the police officers present. The officer prepared a photo array, and again Aubin identified a picture of the same person. That person was the respondent. Shortly thereafter, the Providence police began a search of the Mount Pleasant area.

At approximately 4:30 a.m. on the same date, Patrolman Lovell, while cruising the streets of Mount Pleasant in a patrol car, spotted the respondent standing in the street facing him. When Patrolman Lovell stopped his car, the respondent walked towards it. Patrolman Lovell then arrested the respondent, who was unarmed, and advised him of his so-called *Miranda* rights. While the two men waited in the patrol car for other police officers to arrive, Patrolman Lovell did not converse with the respondent other than to respond to the latter's request for a cigarette.

Within minutes, Sergeant Sears arrived at the scene of the arrest, and he also gave the respondent the *Miranda* warnings. Immediately thereafter, Captain Leyden and other police officers arrived. Captain Leyden advised the respondent of his *Miranda* rights. The respondent stated that he understood those rights and wanted to speak with a lawyer. Captain Leyden then directed that the respondent be placed in a "caged wagon," a four-door police car with a wire screen mesh between the front and rear seats, and be driven to the central police station. Three officers, Patrolmen Gleckman, Williams, and McKenna, were assigned to accompany the respondent to the central station. They placed the respondent in the vehicle and shut the doors. Captain Leyden then instructed the officers not to question the respondent or intimidate or coerce him in any way. The three officers then entered the vehicle, and it departed.

While en route to the central station, Patrolman Gleckman initiated a conversation with Patrolman McKenna concerning the missing shotgun.[1] As Patrolman Gleckman later testified:

> *A.* At this point, I was talking back and forth with Patrolman McKenna stating that I frequent this area while on patrol and [that because a school for handicapped children is located nearby,] there's a lot of handicapped children running around in this area, and God forbid one of them might find a weapon with shells and they might hurt themselves.

Patrolman McKenna apparently shared his fellow officer's concern:

> *A.* I more or less concurred with him [Gleckman] that it was a safety factor and that we should, you know, continue to search for the weapon and try to find it.

While Patrolman Williams said nothing, he overheard the conversation between the two officers:

> *A.* He [Gleckman] said it would be too bad if the little—I believe he said a girl—would pick up the gun, maybe kill herself.

The respondent then interrupted the conversation, stating that the officers should turn the car around so he could show them where the gun was located. At this point, Patrolman McKenna radioed back to Captain Leyden that they were returning to the scene of the arrest, and that the respondent would inform them of the location of the gun. At the time the respondent indicated that the officers should turn back, they had traveled no more than a mile, a trip encompassing only a few minutes.

---

1. Although there was conflicting testimony about the exact seating arrangements, it is clear that everyone in the vehicle heard the conversation.

The police vehicle then returned to the scene of the arrest where a search for the shotgun was in progress. There, Captain Leyden again advised the respondent of his *Miranda* rights. The respondent replied that he understood those rights but that he "wanted to get the gun out of the way because of the kids in the area in the school." The respondent then led the police to a nearby field, where he pointed out the shotgun under some rocks by the side of the road. . . .

We granted certiorari to address for the first time the meaning of "interrogation" under Miranda v. Arizona.

II . . .

A

The starting point for defining "interrogation" in this context is, of course, the Court's *Miranda* opinion. There the Court observed that "[b]y custodial interrogation, we mean *questioning* initiated by law enforcement officers after a person has been taken into custody or otherwise deprived of his freedom of action in any significant way." Id., at 444 (emphasis added). This passage and other references throughout the opinion to "questioning" might suggest that the *Miranda* rules were to apply only to those police interrogation practices that involve express questioning of a defendant while in custody.

We do not, however, construe the *Miranda* opinion so narrowly. The concern of the Court in *Miranda* was that the "interrogation environment" created by the interplay of interrogation and custody would "subjugate the individual to the will of his examiner" and thereby undermine the privilege against compulsory self-incrimination. Id., at 457-458. The police practices that evoked this concern included several that did not involve express questioning. For example, one of the practices discussed in *Miranda* was the use of lineups in which a coached witness would pick the defendant as the perpetrator. This was designed to establish that the defendant was in fact guilty as a predicate for further interrogation. Id., at 453. A variation on this theme discussed in *Miranda* was the so-called "reverse line-up" in which a defendant would be identified by coached witnesses as the perpetrator of a fictitious crime, with the object of inducing him to confess to the actual crime of which he was suspected in order to escape the false prosecution. Ibid. The Court in *Miranda* also included in its survey of interrogation practices the use of psychological ploys, such as to "posi[t]" "the guilt of the subject," to "minimize the moral seriousness of the offense," and "to cast blame on the victim or on society." Id., at 450. It is clear that these techniques of persuasion, no less than express questioning, were thought, in a custodial setting, to amount to interrogation.[3]

This is not to say, however, that all statements obtained by the police after a person has been taken into custody are to be considered the product of interrogation. . . . [T]he special procedural safeguards outlined in *Miranda* are required not where a suspect is simply taken into custody, but rather where a suspect in custody is subjected to interrogation. "Interrogation," as conceptualized in the *Miranda* opinion, must reflect a measure of compulsion above and beyond that inherent in custody itself.

---

3. To limit the ambit of *Miranda* to express questioning would "place a premium on the ingenuity of the police to devise methods of indirect interrogation, rather than to implement the plain mandate of *Miranda*." Commonwealth v. Hamilton, 445 Pa. 292, 297, 285 A.2d 172, 175.

We conclude that the *Miranda* safeguards come into play whenever a person in custody is subjected to either express questioning or its functional equivalent. That is to say, the term "interrogation" under *Miranda* refers not only to express questioning, but also to any words or actions on the part of the police (other than those normally attendant to arrest and custody) that the police should know are reasonably likely to elicit an incriminating response from the suspect.[6] The latter portion of this definition focuses primarily upon the perceptions of the suspect, rather than the intent of the police. This focus reflects the fact that the *Miranda* safeguards were designed to vest a suspect in custody with an added measure of protection against coercive police practices, without regard to objective proof of the underlying intent of the police. A practice that the police should know is reasonably likely to evoke an incriminating response from a suspect thus amounts to interrogation.[7] But, since the police surely cannot be held accountable for the unforeseeable results of their words or actions, the definition of interrogation can extend only to words or actions on the part of police officers that they *should have known* were reasonably likely to elicit an incriminating response.[8]

B

Turning to the facts of the present case, we conclude that the respondent was not "interrogated" within the meaning of *Miranda*. It is undisputed that the first prong of the definition of "interrogation" was not satisfied, for the conversation between Patrolmen Gleckman and McKenna included no express questioning of the respondent. Rather, that conversation was, at least in form, nothing more than a dialogue between the two officers to which no response from the respondent was invited.

Moreover, it cannot be fairly concluded that the respondent was subjected to the "functional equivalent" of questioning. It cannot be said, in short, that Patrolmen Gleckman and McKenna should have known that their conversation was reasonably likely to elicit an incriminating response from the respondent. There is nothing in the record to suggest that the officers were aware that the respondent was peculiarly susceptible to an appeal to his conscience concerning the safety of handicapped children. Nor is there anything in the record to suggest that the police knew that the respondent was unusually disoriented or upset at the time of his arrest.[9]

The case thus boils down to whether, in the context of a brief conversation, the officers should have known that the respondent would suddenly be moved to make

6. One of the dissenting opinions seems totally to misapprehend this definition in suggesting that it "will almost certainly exclude every statement [of the police] that is not punctuated with a question mark." . . .

7. This is not to say that the intent of the police is irrelevant, for it may well have a bearing on whether the police should have known that their words or actions were reasonably likely to evoke an incriminating response. In particular, where a police practice is designed to elicit an incriminating response from the accused, it is unlikely that the practice will not also be one which the police should have known was reasonably likely to have that effect.

8. Any knowledge the police may have had concerning the unusual susceptibility of a defendant to a particular form of persuasion might be an important factor in determining whether the police should have known that their words or actions were reasonably likely to elicit an incriminating response from the suspect.

9. The record in no way suggests that the officers' remarks were *designed* to elicit a response. See n. 7, supra. It is significant that the trial judge, after hearing the officers' testimony, concluded that it was "entirely understandable that [the officers] would voice their concern [for the safety of the handicapped children] to each other."

a self-incriminating response. Given the fact that the entire conversation appears to have consisted of no more than a few offhand remarks, we cannot say that the officers should have known that it was reasonably likely that Innis would so respond. This is not a case where the police carried on a lengthy harangue in the presence of the suspect. Nor does the record support the respondent's contention that, under the circumstances, the officers' comments were particularly "evocative." It is our view, therefore, that the respondent was not subjected by the police to words or actions that the police should have known were reasonably likely to elicit an incriminating response from him.

The Rhode Island Supreme Court erred, in short, in equating "subtle compulsion" with interrogation. That the officers' comments struck a responsive chord is readily apparent. Thus, it may be said, as the Rhode Island Supreme Court did say, that the respondent was subjected to "subtle compulsion." But that is not the end of the inquiry. It must also be established that a suspect's incriminating response was the product of words or actions on the part of the police that they should have known were reasonably likely to elicit an incriminating response.[10] This was not established in the present case.

For the reasons stated, the judgment of the Supreme Court of Rhode Island is vacated, and the case is remanded to that court for further proceedings not inconsistent with this opinion.

It is so ordered.

JUSTICE STEVENS, dissenting.

[I]n order to give full protection to a suspect's right to be free from any interrogation at all, the definition of "interrogation" must include any police statement or conduct that has the same purpose or effect as a direct question. Statements that appear to call for a response from the suspect, as well as those that are designed to do so, should be considered interrogation. By prohibiting only those relatively few statements or actions that a police officer should know are likely to elicit an incriminating response, the Court today accords a suspect considerably less protection. Indeed, since I suppose most suspects are unlikely to incriminate themselves even when questioned directly, this new definition will almost certainly exclude every statement that is not punctuated with a question mark from the concept of "interrogation."

The difference between the approach required by a faithful adherence to *Miranda* and the stinted test applied by the Court today can be illustrated by comparing three different ways in which Officer Gleckman could have communicated his fears about the possible dangers posed by the shotgun to handicapped children. He could have:

(1) directly asked Innis:
Will you please tell me where the shotgun is so we can protect handicapped schoolchildren from danger?

10. By way of example, if the police had done no more than to drive past the site of the concealed weapon while taking the most direct route to the police station, and if the respondent, upon noticing for the first time the proximity of the school for handicapped children, had blurted out that he would show the officers where the gun was located, it could not seriously be argued that this "subtle compulsion" would have constituted "interrogation" within the meaning of the *Miranda* opinion.

(2)   announced to the other officers in the wagon:

If the man sitting in the back seat with me should decide to tell us where the gun is, we can protect handicapped children from danger.

or

(3)   stated to the other officers:

It would be too bad if a little handicapped girl would pick up the gun that this man left in the area and maybe kill herself.

In my opinion, all three of these statements should be considered interrogation because all three appear to be designed to elicit a response from anyone who in fact knew where the gun was located.[12] Under the Court's test, on the other hand, the form of the statements would be critical. The third statement would not be interrogation because in the Court's view there was no reason for Officer Gleckman to believe that Innis was susceptible to this type of an implied appeal, ... therefore, the statement would not be reasonably likely to elicit an incriminating response. Assuming that this is true, ... then it seems to me that the first two statements, which would be just as unlikely to elicit such a response, should also not be considered interrogation. But, because the first statement is clearly an express question, it *would* be considered interrogation under the Court's test. The second statement, although just as clearly a deliberate appeal to Innis to reveal the location of the gun, would presumably not be interrogation because (a) it was not in form a direct question and (b) it does not fit within the "reasonably likely to elicit an incriminating response" category that applies to indirect interrogation.

As this example illustrates, the Court's test creates an incentive for police to ignore a suspect's invocation of his rights in order to make continued attempts to extract information from him. If a suspect does not appear to be susceptible to a particular type of psychological pressure, the police are apparently free to exert that pressure on him despite his request for counsel, so long as they are careful not to punctuate their statements with question marks. And if, contrary to all reasonable expectations, the suspect makes an incriminating statement, that statement can be used against him at trial. The Court thus turns *Miranda*'s unequivocal rule against any interrogation at all into a trap in which unwary suspects may be caught by police deception. ...

CHIEF JUSTICE BURGER's and JUSTICE WHITE's concurring opinions are omitted, as is JUSTICE MARSHALL's dissent, in which JUSTICE BRENNAN joined.

NOTES AND QUESTIONS

1. Would *Innis* have come out differently if the officer's remarks had been directed at Innis? If they had been directed at him in the form of a question? If so, what is the point of imposing a "reasonable likelihood of success" limitation on

---

12. See Welsh S. White, Rhode Island v. Innis: The Significance of a Suspect's Assertion of His Right to Counsel, 17 Am. Crim. L. Rev. 53, 68 (1979), where the author proposes the same test and applies it to the facts of this case, stating: "Under the proposed objective standard, the result is obvious. Since the conversation indicates a strong desire to know the location of the shotgun, any person with knowledge of

what actually occurred? Is it because possibly the *Miranda* rules already go too far and an arbitrary limitation is better than extending them further still?

2. Suppose an individual is arrested for murder and invokes his *Miranda* rights. Suppose further that his wife is also being interrogated and insists on seeing her husband. The police attempt to dissuade her from talking with her husband, but she insists. The police accede to her demand, but inform the couple that a police officer will be present during the meeting and their conversation will be tape-recorded. During the meeting of husband and wife, a conversation occurs that is subsequently admitted at the husband's trial to demonstrate that he was not insane at the time of the alleged event. Assuming that the police knew that there was a substantial risk that incriminating statements would be made, does the husband have a legitimate claim that his Fifth Amendment rights have been violated?

No, according to the Court in a 5-to-4 decision in Arizona v. Mauro, 481 U.S. 421 (1987). Although the police knew that there was a substantial likelihood that incriminating material would be obtained, the police attempted to discourage the wife from seeing her husband. Thus, this was not a "psychological ploy that properly could be treated as the functional equivalent of interrogation," a conclusion bolstered in the Court's view by the fact that there was "no evidence that the officers sent Mrs. Mauro in to see her husband for the purpose of eliciting incriminating statements."

What do you think of the wisdom of incorporating the subjective state of mind of the police into the definition of "interrogation"? How could a suspect's will possibly be overborne merely because the police consciously constructed a ruse analogous to the facts of *Mauro*, but not overborne in the actual case? From Mauro's point of view, what is the significance of whether the police (1) had no idea what would occur during the meeting, (2) hoped an incriminating conversation would occur, (3) intended for it to occur, or (4) urged the wife to bring about such a conversation? If these four possibilities cannot be distinguished in terms of their effect on Mauro, should they all be allowed or all disallowed? *Innis* suggests the first two are acceptable and the last two are violations of *Miranda*. Is the problem in *Innis* or in *Miranda*?

Three years after *Mauro*, the Court returned to the question whether police officers' intent determines whether "interrogation" has taken place.

ILLINOIS v. PERKINS

Certiorari to the Appellate Court of Illinois
496 U.S. 292 (1990)

JUSTICE KENNEDY delivered the opinion of the Court.

An undercover government agent was placed in the cell of respondent Perkins, who was incarcerated on charges unrelated to the subject of the agent's investigation. Respondent made statements that implicated him in the crime that the agent

---

the weapon's location would be likely to believe that the officers wanted him to disclose its location. Thus, a reasonable person in Innis's position would believe that the officers were seeking to solicit precisely the type of response that was given."

sought to solve. Respondent claims that the statements should be inadmissible because he had not been given *Miranda* warnings by the agent. We hold that the statements are admissible. *Miranda* warnings are not required when the suspect is unaware that he is speaking to a law enforcement officer and gives a voluntary statement.

I

In November 1984, Richard Stephenson was murdered in a suburb of East St. Louis, Illinois. The murder remained unsolved until March 1986, when one Donald Charlton told police that he had learned about a homicide from a fellow inmate at the Graham Correctional Facility, where Charlton had been serving a sentence for burglary. The fellow inmate was Lloyd Perkins, who is the respondent here. Charlton told police that, while at Graham, he had befriended respondent, who told him in detail about a murder that respondent had committed in East St. Louis. On hearing Charlton's account, the police recognized details of the Stephenson murder that were not well known, and so they treated Charlton's story as a credible one.

By the time the police heard Charlton's account, respondent had been released from Graham, but police traced him to a jail in Montgomery County, Illinois, where he was being held pending trial on a charge of aggravated battery, unrelated to the Stephenson murder. The police wanted to investigate further respondent's connection to the Stephenson murder, but feared that the use of an eavesdropping device would prove impracticable and unsafe. They decided instead to place an undercover agent in the cellblock with respondent and Charlton. The plan was for Charlton and undercover agent John Parisi to pose as escapees from a work release program who had been arrested in the course of a burglary. Parisi and Charlton were instructed to engage respondent in casual conversation and report anything he said about the Stephenson murder.

Parisi, using the alias "Vito Bianco," and Charlton, both clothed in jail garb, were placed in the cellblock with respondent at the Montgomery County jail. The cellblock consisted of 12 separate cells that opened onto a common room. Respondent greeted Charlton who, after a brief conversation with respondent, introduced Parisi by his alias. Parisi told respondent that he "wasn't going to do any more time," and suggested that the three of them escape. Respondent replied that the Montgomery County jail was "rinky-dink" and that they could "break out." The trio met in respondent's cell later that evening, after the other inmates were asleep, to refine their plan. Respondent said that his girlfriend could smuggle in a pistol. Charlton said: "Hey, I'm not a murderer, I'm a burglar. That's your guys' profession." After telling Charlton that he would be responsible for any murder that occurred, Parisi asked respondent if he had ever "done" anybody. Respondent said that he had, and proceeded to describe at length the events of the Stephenson murder. Parisi and respondent then engaged in some casual conversation before respondent went to sleep. Parisi did not give respondent *Miranda* warnings before the conversations.

Respondent was charged with the Stephenson murder. Before trial, he moved to suppress the statements made to Parisi in the jail. The trial court granted the motion to suppress, and the State appealed. The Appellate Court of Illinois affirmed, holding that Miranda v. Arizona prohibits all undercover contacts with incarcerated suspects which are reasonably likely to elicit an incriminating response.

We granted certiorari to decide whether an undercover law enforcement officer must give *Miranda* warnings to an incarcerated suspect before asking him questions that may elicit an incriminating response. We now reverse.

II

In Miranda v. Arizona, the Court held that the Fifth Amendment privilege against self-incrimination prohibits admitting statements given by a suspect during "custodial interrogation" without a prior warning. Custodial interrogation means "questioning initiated by law enforcement officers after a person has been taken into custody. . . ." The warning mandated by *Miranda* was meant to preserve the privilege during "incommunicado interrogation of individuals in a police-dominated atmosphere." That atmosphere is said to generate "inherently compelling pressures which work to undermine the individual's will to resist and to compel him to speak where he would not otherwise do so freely." "Fidelity to the doctrine announced in *Miranda* requires that it be enforced strictly, but only in those types of situations in which the concerns that powered the decision are implicated." Berkemer v. McCarty, 468 U.S. 420, 437 (1984).

Conversations between suspects and undercover agents do not implicate the concerns underlying *Miranda*. The essential ingredients of a "police-dominated atmosphere" and compulsion are not present when an incarcerated person speaks freely to someone that he believes to be a fellow inmate. Coercion is determined from the perspective of the suspect. When a suspect considers himself in the company of cellmates and not officers, the coercive atmosphere is lacking. There is no empirical basis for the assumption that a suspect speaking to those whom he assumes are not officers will feel compelled to speak by the fear of reprisal for remaining silent or in the hope of more lenient treatment should he confess.

It is the premise of *Miranda* that the danger of coercion results from the interaction of custody and official interrogation. We reject the argument that *Miranda* warnings are required whenever a suspect is in custody in a technical sense and converses with someone who happens to be a government agent. Questioning by captors, who appear to control the suspect's fate, may create mutually reinforcing pressures that the Court has assumed will weaken the suspect's will, but where a suspect does not know that he is conversing with a government agent, these pressures do not exist. The State Court here mistakenly assumed that because the suspect was in custody, no undercover questioning could take place. When the suspect has no reason to think that the listeners have official power over him, it should not be assumed that his words are motivated by the reaction he expects from his listeners. "[W]hen the agent carries neither badge nor gun and wears not 'police blue,' but the same prison gray" as the suspect, there is no "interplay between police interrogation and police custody." Yale Kamisar, Brewer v. Williams, *Massiah* and *Miranda:* What Is "Interrogation"? When Does It Matter?, 67 Geo. L.J. 1, 67, 63 (1978).

Miranda forbids coercion, not mere strategic deception by taking advantage of a suspect's misplaced trust in one he supposes to be a fellow prisoner. As we recognized in *Miranda*, "[c]onfessions remain a proper element in law enforcement. Any statement given freely and voluntarily without any compelling influences is, of course, admissible in evidence." 384 U.S., at 478. Ploys to mislead a suspect or lull him into a false sense of security that do not rise to the level of compulsion or coercion to speak are not within *Miranda's* concerns.

Miranda was not meant to protect suspects from boasting about their criminal activities in front of persons whom they believe to be their cellmates. This case is illustrative. Respondent had no reason to feel that undercover agent Parisi had any legal authority to force him to answer questions or that Parisi could affect respondent's future treatment. Respondent viewed the cellmate-agent as an equal and showed no hint of being intimidated by the atmosphere of the jail. In recounting the details of the Stephenson murder, respondent was motivated solely by the desire to impress his fellow inmates. He spoke at his own peril. . . .

We hold that an undercover law enforcement officer posing as a fellow inmate need not give *Miranda* warnings to an incarcerated suspect before asking questions that may elicit an incriminating response. The statements at issue in this case were voluntary, and there is no federal obstacle to their admissibility at trial. We now reverse and remand for proceedings not inconsistent with our opinion.

JUSTICE BRENNAN, concurring in the judgment.

The Court holds that Miranda v. Arizona does not require suppression of a statement made by an incarcerated suspect to an undercover agent. Although I do not subscribe to the majority's characterization of *Miranda* in its entirety, I do agree that when a suspect does not know that his questioner is a police agent, such questioning does not amount to "interrogation" in an "inherently coercive" environment so as to require application of *Miranda*. Since the only issue raised at this stage of the litigation is the applicability of *Miranda*, I concur in the judgment of the Court.

This is not to say that I believe the Constitution condones the method by which the police extracted the confession in this case. To the contrary, the deception and manipulation practiced on respondent raise a substantial claim that the confession was obtained in violation of the Due Process Clause. . . .

The method used to elicit the confession in this case deserves close scrutiny. The police devised a ruse to lure respondent into incriminating himself when he was in jail on an unrelated charge. A police agent, posing as a fellow inmate and proposing a sham escape plot, tricked respondent into confessing that he had once committed a murder, as a way of proving that he would be willing to do so again should the need arise during the escape. The testimony of the undercover officer and a police informant at the suppression hearing reveal the deliberate manner in which the two elicited incriminating statements from respondent. We have recognized that "the mere fact of custody imposes pressures on the accused; confinement may bring into play subtle influences that will make him particularly susceptible to the ploys of undercover Government agents." United States v. Henry, 447 U.S. 264, 274 (1980). As Justice Marshall points out [in dissent], the pressures of custody make a suspect more likely to confide in others and to engage in "jailhouse bravado." The State is in a unique position to exploit this vulnerability because it has virtually complete control over the suspect's environment. Thus, the State can ensure that a suspect is barraged with questions from an undercover agent until the suspect confesses. The testimony in this case suggests the State did just that.

The deliberate use of deception and manipulation by the police appears to be incompatible "with a system that presumes innocence and assures that a conviction will not be secured by inquisitorial means," Miller [v. Fenton, 474 U.S. 104, 116 (1985)], and raises serious concerns that respondent's will was overborne. It is open to the lower court on remand to determine whether, under the totality of the circumstances, respondent's confession was elicited in a manner that violated the Due Process Clause. That the confession was not elicited through means of physical torture, or overt psychological pressure, does not end the inquiry. "[A]s law enforcement officers become more responsible, and the methods used to extract confessions more sophisticated, [a court's] duty to enforce federal constitutional protections does not cease. It only becomes more difficult because of the more delicate judgments to be made." Spano [v. New York, 360 U.S. 315, 321 (1959)].

JUSTICE MARSHALL, dissenting.

... The Court does not dispute that the police officer here conducted a custodial interrogation of a criminal suspect. Perkins was incarcerated in county jail during the questioning at issue here; under these circumstances, he was in custody as that term is defined in *Miranda*. The Solicitor General argues that Perkins was not in custody for purpose of *Miranda* because he was familiar with the custodial environment as a result of being in jail for two days and previously spending time in prison. Perkins' familiarity with confinement, however, does not transform his incarceration into some sort of noncustodial arrangement. Cf. Orozco v. Texas, 394 U.S. 324 (1969) (holding that suspect who had been arrested in his home and then questioned in his bedroom was in custody, notwithstanding his familiarity with the surroundings).

While Perkins was confined, an undercover police officer, with the help of a police informant, questioned him about a serious crime. ...

Because Perkins was interrogated by police while he was in custody, *Miranda* required that the officer inform him of his rights. In rejecting that conclusion, the Court finds that "conversations" between undercover agents and suspects are devoid of the coercion inherent in stationhouse interrogations conducted by law enforcement officials who openly represent the State. *Miranda* was not, however, concerned solely with police coercion. It dealt with any police tactics that may operate to compel a suspect in custody to make incriminating statements without full awareness of his constitutional rights. See *Miranda*, supra, at 468 (referring to "inherent pressures of the interrogation atmosphere"); Estelle v. Smith, 451 U.S. 454, 467 (1981) ("The purpose of [the *Miranda*] admonitions is to combat what the Court saw as 'inherently compelling pressures' at work on the person and to provide him with an awareness of the Fifth Amendment privilege and the consequences of forgoing it") (quoting *Miranda*, 384 U.S., at 467). Thus, when a law enforcement agent structures a custodial interrogation so that a suspect feels compelled to reveal incriminating information, he must inform the suspect of his constitutional rights and give him an opportunity to decide whether or not to talk.

The compulsion proscribed by *Miranda* includes deception by the police. See *Miranda*, supra, at 453 (indicting police tactics "to induce a confession out of trickery," such as using fictitious witnesses or false accusations); Berkemer v. McCarty, 468 U.S. 420, 433 (1984) ("The purposes of the safeguards prescribed by *Miranda* are to ensure that the police do not coerce or trick captive suspects into confessing"). Cf. Moran v. Burbine, 475 U.S. 412, 421 (1986) [reproduced at page 874 infra] ("[T]he relinquishment of the right [protected by the *Miranda* warnings] must have been voluntary in the sense that it was the product of a free and deliberate choice rather than intimidation, coercion, or deception"). Although the Court did not find trickery by itself sufficient to constitute compulsion in Hoffa v. United States, the defendant in that case was not in custody. Perkins, however, was interrogated while incarcerated. As the Court has acknowledged in the Sixth Amendment context: "[T]he mere fact of custody imposes pressures on the accused; confinement may bring into play subtle influences that will make him particularly susceptible to the ploys of undercover Government agents." United States v. Henry, 447 U.S. 264, 274 (1980). . . .

Custody works to the State's advantage in obtaining incriminating information. The psychological pressures inherent in confinement increase the suspect's anxiety, making him likely to seek relief by talking with others. . . . The inmate is thus more susceptible to efforts by undercover agents to elicit information from him. Similarly, where the suspect is incarcerated, the constant threat of physical danger peculiar to the prison environment may make him demonstrate his toughness to other inmates by recounting or inventing past violent acts. "Because the suspect's ability to select people with whom he can confide is completely within their control, the police have a unique opportunity to exploit the suspect's vulnerability. In short, the police can insure that if the pressures of confinement lead the suspect to confide in anyone, it will be a police agent." Welsh S. White, Police Trickery in Inducing Confessions, 127 U. Pa. L. Rev. 581, 605 (1979). In this case, the police deceptively took advantage of Perkins' psychological vulnerability by including him in a sham escape plot, a situation in which he would feel compelled to demonstrate his willingness to shoot a prison guard by revealing his past involvement in a murder. . . .

Thus, the pressures unique to custody allow the police to use deceptive interrogation tactics to compel a suspect to make an incriminating statement. The compulsion is not eliminated by the suspect's ignorance of his interrogator's true identity. The Court therefore need not inquire past the bare facts of custody and interrogation to determine whether *Miranda* warnings are required. . . .

I dissent.

NOTES AND QUESTIONS

1. Perkins was unquestionably in custody at the time of the conversations with his cellmate. And the government unquestionably intended to use the cellmate/undercover agent to get information out of Perkins. Why doesn't that add up to custodial interrogation under *Innis*? Does *Perkins* mean that police officers' intent doesn't matter after all?

2. One hidden problem in *Perkins* is the relationship between Fifth Amendment doctrine and Fourth Amendment doctrine. The use of undercover agents is largely unregulated by Fourth Amendment law; under United States v. White, 401 U.S. 745 (1971), conversations with undercover agents, even agents wearing wires, are not "searches." Thus, if *Perkins* had come out differently, undercover agents would be almost totally unregulated before arrest, but forbidden after arrest. (If undercover agents had to give *Miranda* warnings, they obviously couldn't be undercover agents; treating what happened in *Perkins* as custodial interrogation is therefore the same as abolishing the use of police agents as cellmates.) Is there any reason to

draw such a line? Does the law's tolerance of police deception *before* arrest logically require the same posture *after?*

3. Note that the use of undercover agents to get information from defendants in custody can still run into constitutional problems. Under certain circumstances, the practice violates the Sixth Amendment. See United States v. Henry, 447 U.S. 264 (1980). It can also violate the due process clause. In Arizona v. Fulminante, 499 U.S. 279 (1991), the defendant, while incarcerated, made friends with an FBI informer masquerading as an organized crime figure. The defendant was apparently subjected to threats of assault from other inmates; the informant offered to protect him if he would tell the informant what happened in a rumored murder. The defendant confessed to the murder, and the informant passed the confession along to the police. The Court held that the confession was involuntary and hence inadmissible. For an argument suggesting that *Fulminante* leaves too much room for the use of prison informants, see Welsh S. White, Regulating Prison Informers under the Due Process Clause, [1991] Sup. Ct. Rev. 4. Professor White suggests that prison informants raise especially great concerns with reliability and that a focus on voluntariness does not sufficiently address those concerns.

4. *Perkins* seems a clear signal that trickery is an appropriate means of obtaining incriminating statements from criminal suspects. Is that the right signal to send to police? Is it the signal Earl Warren tried to send in his majority opinion in *Miranda?* For a vigorous argument that the answer to those last two questions is "no," see Welsh S. White, Police Trickery in Inducing Confessions, 127 U. Pa. L. Rev. 581 (1979). Notice that the permissibility (or not) of police trickery arises in two settings. The first is *Perkins*: Police use deceptive tactics to avoid *Miranda's* restrictions. Second, the police may mislead the suspect in an effort to induce him to waive his *Miranda* rights. Deception and *Miranda* waivers are discussed below, at pages 882-887.

5. The same year the Court decided *Perkins*, it also decided Pennsylvania v. Muniz, 496 U.S. 582 (1990). The defendant in *Muniz* was arrested for drunk driving; he was taken back to the police station, where he was asked a series of questions by a police officer who was doing the paperwork incident to the defendant's arrest. The state argued that these administrative questions — about the defendant's name, address, height, weight, eye color, date of birth, and current age — did not constitute "interrogation" within the meaning of *Miranda*. A four-Justice plurality disagreed, but found the questions fell within a "routine booking exception" to *Miranda*:

> We disagree with the Commonwealth's contention that Officer Hosterman's first seven questions regarding Muniz' name, address, height, weight, eye color, date of birth, and current age do not qualify as custodial interrogation as we defined the term in *Innis*, merely because the questions were not intended to elicit information for investigatory purposes. As explained above, the *Innis* test focuses primarily upon the perspective of the suspect. We agree with amicus United States, however, that Muniz' answers to these first seven questions are nonetheless admissible because the questions fall within a "routine booking question" exception which exempts from *Miranda's* coverage questions to secure the "biographical data necessary to complete booking or pretrial services." Brief for the United States as Amicus Curiae 12. The state court found that the first seven questions were "requested for record-keeping purposes only," and therefore the questions appear reasonably related to the police's

administrative concerns.[14] In this context, therefore, the first seven questions asked at the Booking Center fall outside the protections of *Miranda* and the answers thereto need not be suppressed.

496 U.S. at 601-602. Another four Justices concluded that the defendant's responses to the "booking" questions were not testimonial, and hence that the Fifth Amendment did not apply to the case. Id. at 608 (Rehnquist, C.J., concurring in part and dissenting in part). The "testimony" issue in *Muniz* is discussed supra, at pages 784-786.

c. What Constitutes a Valid Miranda Waiver?

Miranda held that incriminating statements made in response to custodial interrogation were presumptively "compelled" for purposes of the Fifth Amendment privilege, and hence inadmissible. But the compulsion is only presumptive, not automatic — plainly, Chief Justice Warren's majority opinion contemplated that some suspects would waive their *Miranda* rights.

Some, but not many. The language in Warren's opinion suggested that valid *Miranda* waivers would be rare. Consider:

> "The warnings required and the waiver necessary in accordance with our opinion today are, in the absence of a fully effective equivalent, prerequisites to the admissibility of any statement made by a defendant."

Miranda v. Arizona, 384 U.S. 436, 476 (1966).

> "In dealing with custodial interrogation, we will not presume that a defendant has been effectively apprised of his rights and that his privilege against self-incrimination has been adequately safeguarded on a record that does not show that any warnings have been given or that any effective alternative has been employed. Nor can a knowing and intelligent waiver of these rights be assumed on a silent record."

Id. at 498.

> "Once warnings have been given, the subsequent procedure is clear. If the individual indicates in any manner, at any time prior to or during questioning, that he wishes to remain silent, the interrogation must cease. At this point he has shown that he intends to exercise his Fifth Amendment privilege; any statement taken after the person invokes his privilege cannot be other than the product of compulsion."

Id. at 473-474.

> "If the individual states that he wants an attorney, the interrogation must cease until an attorney is present. At that time, the individual must have an opportunity to confer with the attorney and to have him present during any subsequent questioning."

Id. at 474.

14. As amicus United States explains, "[r]ecognizing a 'booking exception' to *Miranda* does not mean, of course, that any question asked during the booking process falls within that exception. Without obtaining a waiver of the suspect's *Miranda* rights, the police may not ask questions, even during booking, that are designed to elicit incriminatory admissions." Brief for United States as Amicus Curiae 13.

"If the interrogation continues without the presence of an attorney and a statement is taken, a heavy burden rests on the government to demonstrate that the defendant knowingly and intelligently waived his privilege against self-incrimination and his right to retained or appointed counsel."

Id. at 475.

"An express statement that the individual is willing to make a statement and does not want an attorney followed closely by a statement could constitute a waiver. But a valid waiver will not be presumed simply from the silence of the accused after warnings are given or simply from the fact that a confession was in fact eventually obtained."

Id.

"[T]he fact of lengthy interrogation or incommunicado incarceration before a statement is made is strong evidence that the accused did not validly waive his rights. . . . Moreover, any evidence that the accused was threatened, tricked, or cajoled into a waiver will, of course, show that the defendant did not voluntarily waive his privilege."

Id. at 476.

Given this language, it seemed natural to assume that waivers (and consequently, police station confessions) would not be common. But they *are* common. The best study to date appears in Richard A. Leo, The Impact of *Miranda* Revisited, 86 J. Crim. L. & Criminology 621 (1996). Of 182 interrogations observed in three California jurisdictions, only 38 suspects — 21 percent — invoked their *Miranda* rights; the rest waived their rights and agreed to talk to the police. (Interestingly, only two of the 38 invocations came after questioning had begun. The rest occurred immediately after the suspect received his *Miranda* warnings.) See id. at 653. Other studies have generated similar numbers. See, e.g., Paul G. Cassell & Bret S. Hayman, Police Interrogation in the 1990s: An Empirical Study of the Effects of *Miranda*, 43 UCLA L. Rev. 839 (1996). As you read the material that follows, ask yourself what those numbers mean. Is *Miranda* working as it should? Is it a sham? Whom does it protect? Who is left unprotected?

Warnings

If the required warnings have not been given, *Miranda* waiver is impossible; the presumption of police coercion is irrebuttable. That aspect of *Miranda* remains good law. Which means that police must know what the required warnings are. The Court listed four: "Prior to any questioning, the person must be warned that he has a right to remain silent, that any statement he does make may be used as evidence against him, and that he has a right to the presence of an attorney, either retained or appointed." 384 U.S. at 479. But as to precise language, the Court has been flexible. In California v. Prysock, 453 U.S. 355 (1981), the Court upheld a conviction where the warnings given the defendant did not expressly state that an attorney would be made available prior to interrogation, and in Duckworth v. Eagan,

492 U.S. 195 (1989), the Court held that the following statement of rights satisfied *Miranda:*

> Before we ask you any questions, you must understand your rights. You have the right to remain silent. Anything you say can be used against you in court. You have a right to talk to a lawyer for advice before we ask you any questions, and to have him with you during questioning. You have this right to the advice and the presence of a lawyer even if you cannot afford to hire one. We have no way of giving you a lawyer, but one will be appointed for you, if you wish, if and when you go to court. If you wish to answer questions now without a lawyer present, you have the right to stop answering questions at any time. You also have the right to stop answering at any time until you've talked to a lawyer.

The majority concluded that the "if and when" language accurately described Indiana procedure and anticipated a suspect's natural question concerning when counsel might be appointed. The Court also reiterated the language of *Miranda* to the effect that states are not required to have station house lawyers present at all times. The dissent argued that a suspect might construe the warnings as providing a right to counsel before questioning only to those who can afford to pay for it. In the dissent's view, "It poses no great burden on law enforcement officers to eradicate confusion stemming from the 'if and when' caveat." Does it impose any great burden on suspects who do not understand what they are told to inquire about the matter? And, of course, there is no evidence that Eagan did not understand. What, then, would justify reversing his conviction? Is it that the "compelling atmosphere of the jailhouse" will be presumed to make suspects incompetent in virtually every sense? Does carrying *Miranda* to such metaphysical heights obscure its real message?

If the warnings the police gave in *Duckworth* were confusing, the confusion is due to *Miranda*, not to the police. *Miranda* required that the police tell the suspect he could have a lawyer if he wished; the clear implication is that the government would get the suspect a lawyer *immediately* — i.e., at the police station. But *Miranda* does *not* require that suspects be given lawyers immediately. It requires only that, if suspects invoke their right to counsel, the police must stop questioning them. (See below.) The police do not have to get lawyers for suspects; those suspects who want appointed counsel will obtain counsel when they go to court — just as the police in *Duckworth* said.

Invocations

The *Miranda* Court placed special emphasis on protecting suspects who, having heard their rights, invoked them:

> "If, however, he indicates in any manner and at any stage of the process that he wishes to consult with an attorney before speaking there can be no questioning. Likewise, if the individual is alone and indicates in any manner that he does not wish to be interrogated, the police may not question him."

384 U.S. at 444-445. Those words have occasioned more litigation than any other passage of the Court's opinion.

An early example of such litigation involved a theft and homicide defendant named Richard Mosley. Mosley was arrested in connection with certain robberies, was briefly interrogated, and then invoked his right to remain silent (but not his right to counsel), at which point the interrogation ceased. Some time later a different police officer interrogated Mosley about a homicide. The second officer advised Mosley of his rights, obtained a waiver, and secured incriminating information. The Court found no violation of Mosley's rights:

MICHIGAN v. MOSLEY, 423 U.S. 96, 101-107 (1975): [*Miranda*] could be literally read to mean that a person who has invoked his "right to silence" can never again be subjected to custodial interrogation by any police officer at any time or place on any subject. Another possible construction of the passage would characterize "any statement taken after the person invokes his privilege" as "the product of compulsion" and would therefore mandate its exclusion from evidence, even if it were volunteered by the person in custody without any further interrogation whatever. Or the passage could be interpreted to require only the immediate cessation of questioning and to permit a resumption of interrogation after a momentary respite.

It is evident that any of these possible literal interpretations would lead to absurd and unintended results. To permit the continuation of custodial interrogation after a momentary cessation would clearly frustrate the purposes of *Miranda* by allowing repeated rounds of questioning to undermine the will of the person being questioned. At the other extreme, a blanket prohibition against the taking of voluntary statements or a permanent immunity from further interrogation, regardless of the circumstances, would transform the *Miranda* safeguards into wholly irrational obstacles to legitimate police investigative activity, and deprive suspects of an opportunity to make informed and intelligent assessments of their interests. Clearly, therefore, . . . the *Miranda* opinion can[not] sensibly be read to create a per se proscription of indefinite duration upon any further questioning by any police officer on any subject, once the person in custody has indicated a desire to remain silent.

A reasonable and faithful interpretation of the *Miranda* opinion must rest on the intention of the Court in that case to adopt "fully effective means . . . to notify the person of his right of silence and to assure that the exercise of the right will be scrupulously honored. . . . " 384 U.S., at 479. The critical safeguard identified in the passage at issue is a person's "right to cut off questioning." Id., at 474. Through the exercise of his option to terminate questioning he can control the time at which questioning occurs, the subjects discussed and the duration of the interrogation. The requirement that law enforcement authorities must respect a person's exercise of that option counteracts the coercive pressures of the custodial setting. We therefore conclude that the admissibility of statements obtained after the person in custody has decided to remain silent depends under *Miranda* on whether his "right to cut off questioning" was "scrupulously honored."

A review of the circumstances leading to Mosley's confession reveals that his "right to cut off questioning" was fully respected in this case. Before his initial interrogation, Mosley was carefully advised that he was under no obligation to answer any questions and could remain silent if he wished. He orally acknowledged that he understood the *Miranda* warnings and then signed a printed notification of rights form. When Mosley stated that he did not want to discuss the robberies, Detective Cowie immediately ceased the interrogation and did not

try either to resume the questioning or in any way to persuade Mosley to reconsider his position. After an interval of more than two hours, Mosley was questioned
by another police officer at another location about an unrelated holdup murder.
He was given full and complete *Miranda* warnings at the outset of the second
interrogation. He was thus reminded again that he could remain silent and
could consult with a lawyer, and was carefully given a full and fair opportunity
to exercise these options. The subsequent questioning did not undercut Mosley's
previous decision not to answer Detective Cowie's inquiries. Detective Hill did not
resume the interrogation about the White Tower Restaurant robbery or inquire
about the Blue Goose Bar robbery, but instead focused exclusively on the Leroy
Williams homicide, a crime different in nature and in time and place of occurrence
from the robberies for which Mosley had been arrested and interrogated by
Detective Cowie. Although it is not clear from the record how much Detective
Hill knew about the earlier interrogation, his questioning of Mosley about an
unrelated homicide was quite consistent with a reasonable interpretation of
Mosley's earlier refusal to answer any questions about the robberies.

This is not a case, therefore, where the police failed to honor a decision of a
person in custody to cut off questioning, either by refusing to discontinue the
interrogation upon request or by persisting in repeated efforts to wear down
his resistance and make him change his mind. In contrast to such practices, the
police here immediately ceased the interrogation, resumed questioning only after
the passage of a significant period of time and the provision of a fresh set of
warnings, and restricted the second interrogation to a crime that had not been
a subject of the earlier interrogation.

The Michigan Court of Appeals viewed this case as factually similar to Westover v.
United States, 384 U.S. 436, a companion case to *Miranda*. But the controlling
facts of the two cases are strikingly different.

In *Westover*, the petitioner was arrested by the Kansas City police at 9:45 p.m.
and taken to the police station. Without giving any advisory warnings of any kind
to Westover, the police questioned him that night and throughout the next morning about various local robberies. At noon, three FBI agents took over, gave
advisory warnings to Westover, and proceeded to question him about two
California bank robberies. After two hours of questioning, the petitioner confessed
to the California crimes. The Court held that the confession obtained by the FBI
was inadmissible because the interrogation leading to the petitioner's statement
followed on the heels of prolonged questioning that was commenced and continued by the Kansas City police without preliminary warnings to Westover of any
kind. The Court found that "the federal authorities were the beneficiaries of the
pressure applied by the local in-custody interrogation" and that the belated warnings given by the federal officers were "not sufficient to protect" Westover because
from his point of view "the warnings came at the end of the interrogation process."
384 U.S., at 496-497.

Here, by contrast, the police gave full "*Miranda* warnings" to Mosley at the very
outset of each interrogation, subjected him to only a brief period of initial questioning, and suspended questioning entirely for a significant period before
beginning the interrogation that led to his incriminating statement. The cardinal
fact of *Westover* — the failure of the police officers to give any warnings whatever to
the person in their custody before embarking on an intense and prolonged interrogation of him — was simply not present in this case. The Michigan Court of

Appeals was mistaken, therefore, in believing that Detective Hill's questioning of Mosley was "not permitted" by the *Westover* decision. 51 Mich. 105, 108, 214 N.W.2d 564, 566.

Are you convinced by the Court's treatment of *Westover?* Compare *Mosley* and *Westover* to the next case.

EDWARDS v. ARIZONA, 451 U.S. 477, 478-487 (1981): On January 19, 1976, a sworn complaint was filed against Edwards in Arizona state court charging him with robbery, burglary, and first-degree murder. . . . Edwards was arrested at his home later that same day. At the police station, he was informed of his rights as required by Miranda v. Arizona, 384 U.S. 436 (1966). Petitioner stated that he understood his rights, and was willing to submit to questioning. After being told that another suspect already in custody had implicated him in the crime, Edwards denied involvement and gave a taped statement presenting an alibi defense. He then sought to "make a deal." The interrogating officer told him that he wanted a statement, but that he did not have the authority to negotiate a deal. The officer provided Edwards with the number of a county attorney. Petitioner made the call, but hung up after a few moments. Edwards then said, "I want an attorney before making a deal." At that point, questioning ceased and Edwards was taken to county jail.

At 9:15 the next morning, two detectives, colleagues of the officer who had interrogated Edwards the previous night, came to the jail and asked to see Edwards. When the detention officer informed Edwards that the detectives wished to speak with him, he replied that he did not want to talk to anyone. The guard told him that "he had" to talk and then took him to meet with the detectives. The officers identified themselves, stated they wanted to talk to him and informed him of his *Miranda* rights. Edwards was willing to talk, but he first wanted to hear the taped statement of the alleged accomplice who had implicated him. After listening to the tape for several minutes, petitioner said that he would make a statement so long as it was not tape recorded. The detectives informed him that the recording was irrelevant since they could testify in court concerning whatever he said. Edwards replied: "I'll tell you anything you want to know, but I don't want it on tape." He thereupon implicated himself in the crime. . . .

Miranda . . . declared that an accused has a Fifth and Fourteenth Amendment right to have counsel present during custodial interrogation. Here, the critical facts . . . are that Edwards asserted his right to counsel and his right to remain silent on January 19, but that the police, without furnishing him counsel, returned the next morning to confront him and as a result of the meeting secured incriminating oral admissions. . . . Edwards insists that having exercised his right on the 19th to have counsel present during interrogation, he did not validly waive that right on the 20th. For the following reasons, we agree.

First, the Arizona Supreme Court applied an erroneous standard for determining waiver where the accused has specifically invoked his right to counsel. It is reasonably clear under our cases that waivers of counsel must not only be voluntary, but constitute a knowing and intelligent relinquishment or abandonment of a known right or privilege, a matter which depends in each case "upon the particular facts and circumstances surrounding that case, including the background, experience and conduct of the accused." Johnson v. Zerbst, 304 U.S. 458, 464 (1938). . . .

Considering the proceedings in the state courts in the light of this standard, we note that in denying petitioner's motion to suppress, the trial court found the admission to have been "voluntary" . . . without separately focusing on whether Edwards had knowingly and intelligently relinquished his right to counsel. The Arizona Supreme Court, in a section of its opinion entitled "Voluntariness of Waiver," stated that in Arizona, confessions are prima facie involuntary and that the State had the burden of showing by a preponderance of the evidence that the confession was freely and voluntarily made. The court stated that the issue of voluntariness should be determined based on the totality of the circumstances as it related to whether an accused's action was "knowing and intelligent and whether his will was overborne." Once the trial court determines that "the confession is voluntary, the finding will not be upset on appeal absent clear and manifest error."

. . . The court then upheld the trial court's finding that the "waiver and confession were voluntarily and knowingly made." . . .

In referring to the necessity to find Edwards' confession knowing and intelligent, the State Supreme Court cited Schneckloth v. Bustamonte, 412 U.S. 218, 226 (1973). Yet, it is clear that *Schneckloth* does not control the issue presented in this case. The issue in *Schneckloth* was under what conditions an individual could be found to have consented to a search and thereby waived his Fourth Amendment rights. The Court declined to impose the "intentional relinquishment or abandonment of a known right or privilege" standard and required only that the consent be voluntary under the totality of the circumstances. The Court specifically noted that the right to counsel was a prime example of those rights requiring the special protection of the knowing and intelligent waiver standard, id., at 241, but held that "[t]he considerations that informed the Court's holding in *Miranda* are simply inapplicable in the present case." 412 U.S., at 246. *Schneckloth* itself thus emphasized that the voluntariness of a consent or an admission on the one hand, and a knowing and intelligent waiver on the other, are discrete inquiries. Here, however sound the conclusion of the state courts as to the voluntariness of Edwards' admission may be, neither the trial court nor the Arizona Supreme Court undertook to focus on whether Edwards understood his right to counsel and intelligently and knowingly relinquished it. It is thus apparent that the decision below misunderstood the requirement for finding a valid waiver of the right to counsel, once invoked.

Second, although we have held that after initially being advised of his *Miranda* rights, the accused may himself validly waive his rights and respond to interrogation, see North Carolina v. Butler, 441 U.S., at 372-376, the Court has strongly indicated that additional safeguards are necessary when the accused asks for counsel; and we now hold that when an accused has invoked his right to have counsel present during custodial interrogation, a valid waiver of that right cannot be established by showing only that he responded to further police-initiated custodial interrogation even if he has been advised of his rights. We further hold that an accused, such as Edwards, having expressed his desire to deal with the police only through counsel, is not subject to further interrogation by the authorities until counsel has been made available to him, unless the accused himself initiates further communication, exchanges or conversations with the police.

Miranda itself indicated that the assertion of the right to counsel was a significant event and that once exercised by the accused, "interrogation must cease until an attorney is present." 384 U.S., at 474. Our later cases have not abandoned that view. In Michigan v. Mosley, 423 U.S. 96 (1975), the Court noted that *Miranda* had distinguished between the procedural safeguards triggered by a request to remain silent and a request for an attorney and had required that interrogation cease until an attorney was present only if the individual stated that he wanted counsel. In Fare v. Michael C., 442 U.S., at 719, the Court referred to *Miranda*'s "rigid rule that an accused's request for an attorney is per se an invocation of his Fifth Amendment rights, requiring that all interrogation cease." And just last Term, in a case where a suspect in custody had invoked his *Miranda* right to counsel, the Court again referred to the "undisputed right" under *Miranda* to remain silent and to be free of interrogation "until he had consulted with a lawyer." Rhode Island v. Innis, 446 U.S. 291, 298 (1980). We reconfirm these views and to lend them substance, emphasize that it is inconsistent with *Miranda* and its progeny for the authorities, at their instance, to reinterrogate an accused in custody if he has clearly asserted his right to counsel.

In concluding that the fruits of the interrogation initiated by the police on January 20 could not be used against Edwards, we do not hold or imply that Edwards was powerless to countermand his election or that the authorities could in no event use any incriminating statements made by Edwards prior to his having access to counsel. Had Edwards initiated the meeting on January 20, nothing in the Fifth and Fourteenth Amendments would prohibit the police from merely listening to his voluntary, volunteered statements and using them against him at the trial. The Fifth Amendment right identified in *Miranda* is the right to have counsel present at any custodial interrogation. Absent such interrogation, there would have been no infringement of the right that Edwards invoked and there would be no occasion to determine whether there had been a valid waiver. Rhode Island v. Innis, supra, makes this sufficiently clear. 446 U.S., at 298, n. 2.[9]

But this is not what the facts of this case show. Here, the officers conducting the interrogation on the evening of January 19, ceased interrogation when Edwards requested counsel as he had been advised he had the right to do. The Arizona Supreme Court was of the opinion that this was a sufficient invocation of his *Miranda* rights, and we are in accord. It is also clear that without making counsel available to Edwards, the police returned to him the next day. This was not at his suggestion or request. Indeed, Edwards informed the detention officer that he did not want to talk to anyone. At the meeting, the detectives told Edwards that they wanted to talk to him and again advised him of his *Miranda* rights. Edwards stated that he would talk, but what prompted this action does not appear. He listened at his own request to part of the taped statement made by one of his alleged accomplices and then made an incriminating statement, which was used against him at his trial. We think it is clear that Edwards was subjected to custodial interrogation on January 20 within the meaning of Rhode Island v. Innis, supra, and that this occurred at the instance of the authorities. His

9. If, as frequently would occur in the course of a meeting initiated by the accused, the conversation is not wholly one-sided, it is likely that the officers will say or do something that clearly would be "interrogation." In that event, the question would be whether a valid waiver of the right to counsel and the right to silence had occurred, that is, whether the purported waiver was knowing and intelligent and found to be so under the totality of the circumstances, including the necessary fact that the accused, not the police, reopened the dialogue with the authorities. . . .

statement made without having had access to counsel, did not amount to a valid waiver and hence was inadmissible.

Accordingly, the holding of the Arizona Supreme Court that Edwards had waived his right to counsel was infirm and the judgment of that court is reversed. . . .

NOTES ON *MIRANDA* INVOCATIONS

1. Can *Mosley* and *Edwards* be reconciled? Remember that the whole point of this exercise is supposed to be protection of the accused's right to remain silent. The *Miranda* right to counsel is given in order to help protect that right. Yet after *Edwards* and *Mosley*, invocation of the right to counsel gets greater protection than invocation of the right to remain silent. What's going on here?

2. *Edwards* holds that when a suspect in custody invokes his *Miranda* right to counsel, the police cannot initiate further questioning. The Court addressed the meaning and consequences of "initiating" questioning in Oregon v. Bradshaw, 462 U.S. 1039 (1983), in a badly splintered decision:

> [R]espondent was placed under arrest for furnishing liquor to Reynolds, a minor, and again advised of his *Miranda* rights. A police officer then told respondent the officer's theory of how the traffic accident that killed Reynolds occurred; a theory which placed respondent behind the wheel of the vehicle. Respondent again denied his involvement, and said "I do want an attorney before it goes very much further." . . . The officer immediately terminated the conversation.
>
> Sometime later respondent was transferred from the Rockaway Police Station to the Tillamook County jail, a distance of some ten or fifteen miles. Either just before, or during, his trip from Rockaway to Tillamook, respondent inquired of a police officer, "Well, what is going to happen to me now?" The officer answered by saying: "You do not have to talk to me. You have requested an attorney and I don't want you talking to me unless you so desire because anything you say — because — since you have requested an attorney, you know, it has to be at your own free will." App. 16. . . . Respondent said he understood. There followed a discussion between respondent and the officer concerning where respondent was being taken and the offense with which he would be charged. The officer suggested that respondent might help himself by taking a polygraph examination. Respondent agreed to take such an examination, saying that he was willing to do whatever he could to clear up the matter.
>
> The next day, following another reading to respondent of his *Miranda* rights, and respondent's signing a written waiver of those rights, the polygraph was administered. At its conclusion, the examiner told respondent that he did not believe respondent was telling the truth. Respondent then recanted his earlier story, admitting that he had been at the wheel of the vehicle in which Reynolds was killed, that he had consumed a considerable amount of alcohol, and that he had passed out at the wheel before the vehicle left the roadway and came to rest in the creek.

462 U.S. at 1041-1042 (opinion of Rehnquist, J.). On these facts, was *Edwards* violated? The plurality — Justice Rehnquist was joined by Chief Justice Burger and Justices White and O'Connor — thought not:

> There can be no doubt in this case that in asking, "Well, what is going to happen to me now?," respondent "initiated" further conversation in the ordinary dictionary sense of that word. While we doubt that it would be desirable to build a superstructure of legal

refinements around the word "initiate" in this context, there are undoubtedly situations where a bare inquiry by either a defendant or by a police officer should not be held to "initiate" any conversation or dialogue. There are some inquiries, such as a request for a drink of water or a request to use a telephone that are so routine that they cannot be fairly said to represent a desire on the part of an accused to open up a more generalized discussion relating directly or indirectly to the investigation. Such inquiries or statements, by either an accused or a police officer, relating to routine incidents of the custodial relationship, will not generally "initiate" a conversation in the sense in which that word was used in *Edwards*.

Although ambiguous, the respondent's question in this case as to what was going to happen to him evinced a willingness and a desire for a generalized discussion about the investigation; it was not merely a necessary inquiry arising out of the incidents of the custodial relationship. It could reasonably have been interpreted by the officer as relating generally to the investigation. That the police officer so understood it is apparent from the fact that he immediately reminded the accused that "you do not have to talk to me," and only after the accused told him that he "understood" did they have a generalized conversation. On these facts we believe that there was not a violation of the *Edwards* rule.

Justice Powell provided the fifth vote for the state in *Bradshaw*; he declined to apply the strict rule of *Edwards*, finding only that Bradshaw's waiver was valid on these facts. Id. at 1047-1051 (Powell, J., concurring in the judgment). Justice Marshall, joined by Justices Brennan, Blackmun, and Stevens, believed that *Edwards* barred the conversation in *Bradshaw*:

I agree with the plurality that, in order to constitute "initiation" under *Edwards*, an accused's inquiry must demonstrate a desire to discuss the subject matter of the criminal investigation. . . . I am baffled, however, at the plurality's application of that standard to the facts of this case. The plurality asserts that respondent's question, "What is going to happen to me now?," evinced both "a willingness and a desire for a generalized discussion about the investigation." . . . If respondent's question had been posed by Jean-Paul Sartre before a class of philosophy students, it might well have evinced a desire for a "generalized" discussion. But under the circumstances of this case, it is plain that respondent's only "desire" was to find out where the police were going to take him. As the Oregon Court of Appeals stated, respondent's query came only minutes after his invocation of the right to counsel and was simply "a normal reaction to being taken from the police station and placed in a police car, obviously for transport to some destination." 54 Or. App., at 949, 636 P.2d, at 1013.[3] On these facts, I fail to see how respondent's question can be considered "initiation" of a conversation about the subject matter of the criminal investigation.

To hold that respondent's question in this case opened a dialogue with the authorities flies in the face of the basic purpose of the *Miranda* safeguards. When someone in custody asks, "What is going to happen to me now?," he is surely responding to his

---

3. The plurality seems to place some reliance on the police officer's reaction to respondent's question. The officer described his response as follows. "I says, 'You do not have to talk to me. You have requested an attorney and I don't want you talking to me unless you so desire because anything you say—because—since you have requested an attorney, you know, it has to be at your own free will.' I says, 'I can't prevent you from talking, but you understand where your place—you know, where your standing is here?' and he agreed. He says 'I understand.'"

As the officer's testimony indicates, respondent's statement was at best ambiguous. In any event, as the Oregon Court of Appeals noted, the officer clearly took advantage of respondent's inquiry to commence once again his questioning—a practice squarely at odds with *Edwards*. See 54 Or. App., at 953, 636 P.2d, at 1013.

custodial surroundings. The very essence of custody is the loss of control over one's freedom of movement. The authorities exercise virtually unfettered control over the accused. To allow the authorities to recommence an interrogation based on such a question is to permit them to capitalize on the custodial setting. Yet *Miranda*'s procedural protections were adopted precisely in order "to dispel the compulsion inherent in custodial surrounding." 384 U.S., at 458.

462 U.S. at 1055-1056 (Marshall, J., dissenting).

3. As *Bradshaw* illustrates, the requirement that, after invoking his *Miranda* right to counsel, the suspect must initiate any further questioning puts a great deal of pressure on the definition of "initiate." It also makes the definition of "invocation" extremely important: once the suspect "invokes," the police may have no more chances to talk to him. In Davis v. United States, 512 U.S. 452 (1994), the Court addressed "how law enforcement officers should respond when a suspect makes a reference to counsel that is insufficiently clear to invoke the *Edwards* prohibition on further questioning":

> [I]f a suspect makes a reference to an attorney that is ambiguous or equivocal in that a reasonable officer in light of the circumstances would have understood only that the suspect might be invoking the right to counsel, our precedents do not require the cessation of questioning. . . . Rather, the suspect must unambiguously request counsel. Although a suspect need not "speak with the discrimination of an Oxford don," he must articulate his desire to have counsel present sufficiently clearly that a reasonable police officer in the circumstances would understand the statement to be a request for an attorney. If the statement fails to meet the requisite level of clarity, *Edwards* does not require that the officers stop questioning the suspect. . . . We decline petitioner's invitation to extend *Edwards* and require law enforcement officers to cease questioning immediately upon the making of an ambiguous or equivocal reference to an attorney. The rationale underlying *Edwards* is that the police must respect a suspect's wishes regarding his right to have an attorney present during custodial interrogation. But when the officers conducting the questioning reasonably do not know whether or not the suspect wants a lawyer, a rule requiring the immediate cessation of questioning "would transform the *Miranda* safeguards into wholly irrational obstacles to legitimate police investigative activity," Michigan v. Mosley, 423 U.S. 96, 102 (1975), because it would needlessly prevent the police from questioning a suspect in the absence of counsel even if the suspect did not wish to have a lawyer present. Nothing in *Edwards* requires the provision of counsel to a suspect who consents to answer questions without the assistance of a lawyer.

In evaluating *Davis*, it is helpful to consider the facts of some of the Court's earlier invocation cases. In Smith v. Illinois, 469 U.S. 91 (1984) (per curiam), the Court held (over a sharp dissent) that the following facts and "interrogation" violated *Miranda* and *Edwards*:

> Shortly after his arrest, 18-year-old Steven Smith was taken to an interrogation room at the Logan County Safety Complex for questioning by two police detectives. The session began as follows:
>
> *Q.* Steve, I want to talk with you in reference to the armed robbery that took place at McDonald's restaurant on the morning of the 19th. Are you familiar with this?
>
> *A.* Yeah. My cousin Greg was.

Q. Okay. But before I do that I must advise you of your rights. Okay? You have a right to remain silent. You do not have to talk to me unless you want to do so. Do you understand that?

A. Uh. She told me to get my lawyer. She said you guys would railroad me.

Q. Do you understand that as I gave it to you, Steve?

A. Yeah.

Q. If you do want to talk to me I must advise you that whatever you say can and will be used against you in court. Do you understand that?

A. Yeah.

Q. You have a right to consult with a lawyer and to have a lawyer present with you when you're being questioned. Do you understand that?

A. Uh, yeah, I'd like to do that.

Q. Okay.

Instead of terminating the questioning at this point, the interrogating officers proceeded to finish reading Smith his *Miranda* rights and then pressed him again to answer their questions:

Q. . . . If you want a lawyer and you're unable to pay for one a lawyer will be appointed to represent you free of cost, do you understand that?

A. Okay.

Q. Do you wish to talk to me at this time without a lawyer being present?

A. Yeah and no, uh, I don't know what's what really.

Q. Well. You either have to talk to me this time without a lawyer being present and if you do agree to talk with me without a lawyer being present you can stop at any time you want to.

A. All right. I'll talk to you then.

Smith then told the detectives that he knew in advance about the planned robbery, but contended that he had not been a participant. After considerable probing by the detectives, Smith confessed that "I committed it," but he then returned to his earlier story that he had only known about the planned crime. Upon further questioning, Smith again insisted that "I wanta get a lawyer." This time the detectives honored the request and terminated the interrogation.

In a curious linguistic exercise, the Court held "only that, under the logical force of settled precedent, an accused's responses to further interrogation after his request for counsel may not be used to cast retrospective doubt on the clarity of the initial request itself. Such subsequent statements are relevant only to the distinct question of waiver." Id. at 495. As the dissent pointed out, it is not clear why informing a suspect of the remainder of his rights amounts to "interrogation," nor is it clear why subsequent events that may shed light on prior ones should be ignored in attempting to determine the exact nature of those prior events.

4. Another case extensively cited in *Davis* is Connecticut v. Barrett, 479 U.S. 523 (1987). In *Barrett*, the defendant agreed to talk to the police, but he refused to make a written statement without counsel present. According to the Court, this did not amount to a generalized assertion of counsel sufficient to invoke the implications of *Edwards*. In *Edwards* itself, the defendant said, "I want an attorney before making a deal." Is there any way to explain why the Court found that Edwards had invoked his right to counsel but Barrett had not? How would these cases be decided under the standard announced in *Davis*?

5. In his opinion concurring in the judgment in *Davis* (the opinion is not excerpted above), Justice Souter argued that some defendants may respond hesitantly to the police, so that the only invocation they will give is conditional or tentative. If such responses do not trigger the *Edwards* rule, as a practical matter those defendants may be effectively forced to talk to the police — the very outcome *Edwards* is designed to prevent. For an argument that this is precisely the problem faced by criminal suspects generally and by female suspects in particular, see Janet E. Ainsworth, In a Different Register: The Pragmatics of Powerlessness in Police Interrogation, 103 Yale L.J. 259 (1993).

In light of Justice Souter's and Professor Ainsworth's argument, consider one final invocation case. In Fare v. Michael C., 442 U.S. 707 (1979), a juvenile was interrogated about a murder. After being given his rights, he asked, "Can I have my probation officer here?" The police officer said that he was not going to call the probation officer and "If you want to talk to us without an attorney present, you can. If you don't want to, you don't have to." The juvenile agreed to talk and made incriminating statements. The Court found the statements admissible, on the grounds that *Miranda* had not adequately been invoked and that attorneys play a unique role in the criminal justice system. Note that *Fare* was decided after Michigan v. Mosley but before *Edwards*.

6. *Davis*, *Smith*, *Barrett*, and *Fare* all have to do with what counts as an invocation. There has also been a great deal of litigation concerning the *consequences* of an invocation of the suspect's *Miranda* right to counsel. In Arizona v. Roberson, 486 U.S. 675 (1988), the defendant was arrested for burglary and given *Miranda* warnings, and he said that he "wanted a lawyer before answering any questions." Three days later a different police officer questioned Roberson about a different burglary; Roberson was again advised of his rights and this time agreed to talk. The Supreme Court held that Roberson's statements were inadmissible under *Edwards*. Michigan v. Mosley was distinguished on the ground that it involved an invocation of the right to remain silent, not of the right to counsel.

In Minnick v. Mississippi, 498 U.S. 146 (1990), the Court considered whether *Edwards* is satisfied when a suspect invokes his right to counsel, is then allowed to consult with counsel, and is subsequently interrogated. The Court held that this violates *Edwards*:

> In our view, a fair reading of *Edwards* and subsequent cases demonstrates that we have interpreted the rule to bar police-initiated interrogation unless the accused has counsel with him at the time of questioning. Whatever the ambiguities of our earlier cases on this point, we now hold that when counsel is requested, interrogation must cease, and officials may not reinitiate interrogation without counsel present, whether or not the accused has consulted with his attorney.
>
> We consider our ruling to be an appropriate and necessary application of the *Edwards* rule. A single consultation with an attorney does not remove the suspect from persistent attempts by officials to persuade him to waive his rights, or from the coercive pressures that accompany custody and that may increase as custody is prolonged. The case before us well-illustrates the pressures, and abuses, that may be concomitants of custody. Petitioner testified that though he resisted, he was required to submit to both the F.B.I. and the Denham interviews. In the latter instance, the compulsion to submit to interrogation followed petitioner's unequivocal request during the F.B.I. interview that questioning cease until counsel was present. The case illustrates also that consultation is not always effective in instructing the suspect of his

rights. One plausible interpretation of the record is that petitioner thought he could keep his admissions out of evidence by refusing to sign a formal waiver of rights. If the authorities had complied with Minnick's request to have counsel present during interrogation, the attorney could have corrected Minnick's misunderstanding or indeed counseled him that he need not make a statement at all. We decline to remove protection from police-initiated questioning based on isolated consultation with counsel who is absent when the interrogation resumes.

Justice Scalia, joined by Chief Justice Rehnquist, dissented:

Today's extension of the *Edwards* prohibition is the latest stage of prophylaxis built upon prophylaxis, producing a veritable fairyland castle of imagined Constitutional restrictions upon law enforcement. This newest tower, according to the court, is needed to avoid inconsistency with the purpose of *Edward*'s prophylactic rule, which was needed to protect *Miranda*'s prophylactic right to have counsel present, which was needed to protect the right against *compelled self-incrimination* found (at last!) in the Constitution.

It seems obvious to me that, even in *Edwards* itself but surely in today's decision, we have gone far beyond any genuine concern about suspects who do not *know* their right to remain silent, or who have been *coerced* to abandon it. Both holdings are explicable, in my view, only as an effort to protect suspects against what is regarded as their own folly. The sharp-witted criminal would know better than to confess; why should the dull-witted suffer for his lack of mental endowment? Providing him with an attorney at every stage where he might be induced or persuaded (though not coerced) to incriminate himself will even the odds. Apart from the fact that this protective enterprise is beyond our authority under the Fifth Amendment or any other provision of the Constitution, it is unwise. The procedural protections of the Constitution protect the guilty as well as the innocent. But it is not their objective to set the guilty free. That some clever criminals may employ those protections to their advantage is poor reason to allow criminals who have not done so to escape justice.

Thus, even if I were to concede that an honest confession is a foolish mistake, I would welcome rather than reject it; a rule that foolish mistakes do not count would leave most offenders not only unconvicted but undetected. More fundamentally, however, it is wrong, and subtly corrosive of our criminal justice system, to regard an honest confession as a "mistake." While every person is entitled to stand silent, it is more virtuous for the wrongdoer to admit his offense and accept the punishment he deserves. . . . To design our laws on premises contrary to these is to abandon belief in either personal responsibility or the moral claim of just government to obedience. Today's decision is misguided, it seems to me, in so readily exchanging, for marginal, super-*Zerbst* protection against genuinely compelled testimony, investigators' ability to urge, or even ask, a person in custody to do what is right.

7. Think about the combined effect of *Minnick* and *Roberson*. Suppose a suspect is arrested, is given his *Miranda* warnings, and invokes his right to counsel. The suspect remains in custody pending trial, and he is subsequently tried and convicted. Six months after his conviction, government agents approach him, while in prison, to talk about a different crime. Does *Edwards* bar the conversation? Under *Roberson*, it makes no difference that the subject of the questioning is a different crime; under *Minnick*, it makes no difference that the defendant has seen a lawyer in between his invocation and the questioning. Does that mean the postarrest invocation is "good" until the suspect is released from prison years later? If he

is serving a life sentence, does his invocation bar questioning for the rest of his life? If not, how should a court decide whether the invocation has lapsed? In United States v. Green, 592 A.2d 985 (D.C. App. 1991), *cert. granted*, 504 U.S. 908, *vacated and cert. dismissed*, 507 U.S. 545 (1993), on facts similar to those hypothesized in this note, the court held that *Edwards* does bar the subsequent interrogation absent initiation by the suspect. What if Green had been released because his sentence had been served? Or on parole or probation? What if an individual invokes his right to counsel but no charges are filed, or if filed, they are later dismissed? Is such a person also questionproof? See Laurie Magid, Questioning the Question-Proof Inmate: Defining *Miranda* Custody for Incarcerated Suspects, 58 Ohio St. L.J. 883 (1997).

8. The absolute nature of the *Edwards* rule, together with its broad scope after *Roberson* and *Minnick*, give police officers a strong incentive to avoid invocations — meaning, they have an incentive to avoid the kinds of questioning that will lead suspects to invoke their *Miranda* rights. Presumably coercive questioning, inter- rogation tactics that ratchet up the pressure on suspects, are more likely to lead to invocations than more polite (and perhaps more deceptive) questioning. So the *Edwards* rule pushes police toward less coercion.

But that happy conclusion holds only if suspects do, in fact, invoke their *Miranda* rights in response to coercive questioning. They may not. Recall Professor Leo's data on *Miranda* waivers and invocations: While 21 percent of suspects invoke their rights, only 1 percent invoke their rights after questioning has begun. The other 20 percent invoke right away, when the warnings are given — for them, *Miranda* is not a right to be free of coercive questioning; it is a right to opt out of police questioning altogether. If Leo's data are representative, *Edwards* may have little or no effect on police interrogation tactics: Police need not fear ratcheting up the pressure, because so few suspects invoke their rights in response to that pressure. If that conclusion holds true, the waiver rule that mat- ters is the one that governs the 79 percent of interrogations where there *is* no invocation.

Waivers Without Invocations

The *Miranda* majority indicated that the state would have to meet a "heavy burden" to demonstrate waiver, but subsequent Supreme Court decisions have lightened the load considerably. North Carolina v. Butler, 441 U.S. 369 (1979), played a prominent role in that process. Here are the facts in *Butler*:

> . . . Agent Martinez testified that at the time of the arrest he fully advised the respon- dent of the rights delineated in the *Miranda* case. According to the uncontroverted testimony of Martinez, the agents then took the respondent to the FBI office in nearby New Rochelle, N.Y. There, after the agents determined that the respondent had an 11th grade education and was literate, he was given the Bureau's "Advice of Rights" form which he read. When asked if he understood his rights, he replied that he did. The respondent refused to sign the waiver at the bottom of the form. He was told that he need neither speak nor sign the form, but that the agents would like him to talk to them. The respondent replied: "I will talk to you but I am not signing any form." He then made inculpatory statements. Agent Martinez testified that the respondent said nothing when advised of his right to the assistance of a lawyer. At

no time did the respondent request counsel or attempt to terminate the agents' questioning.

Id. at 370-371. The Court found a valid *Miranda* waiver:

> An express written or oral statement of waiver of the right to remain silent or of the right to counsel is usually strong proof of the validity of that waiver, but is not inevitably either necessary or sufficient to establish waiver. . . . The courts must presume that a defendant did not waive his rights; . . . but in at least some cases waiver can be clearly inferred from the actions and words of the person interrogated.

Id. at 373. The most natural inference to draw from Butler's behavior is that he believed oral statements would not be damaging to him, that only a written waiver or confession could harm him in later litigation. If that is what Butler believed, his belief was mistaken. The Court's decision seems to stand for the proposition that such mistakes should not stand in the way of finding *Miranda* waivers.

It is natural to think about the issue in *Butler* in terms of protecting the defendant's *Miranda* rights. But what about the defendant's right to waive *Miranda*? Shouldn't that right be protected as well? How much protection does it need? Compare this issue to Faretta v. California, page 215 supra, where the Court granted defendants the right to represent themselves in criminal litigation — i.e., the right to forgo the right to counsel. As you think about the question of *Miranda* waivers, should it matter matter whether the suspect is already represented by counsel? In New York it does. The New York Court of Appeals has rendered a series of decisions that do not permit the police to approach the suspect after the police are aware that the suspect is represented by counsel. See, e.g., People v. Arthur, 22 N.Y.2d 325, 239 N.E.2d 537 (1968); People v. Rogers, 48 N.Y.2d 167, 397 N.E.2d 709 (1979). The New York rule presumably gives an advantage to suspects who already have lawyers when they are arrested — presumably a more sophisticated category than unrepresented suspects. Is that fair?

Should oral *Miranda* waivers be permitted? Indeed, should the entire interrogation process be observed by a disinterested third party or taped in some fashion? In this regard, consider Stephan v. State, 711 P.2d 1156 (Alaska 1985), where the Alaska Supreme Court held that the failure to tape-record an interrogation occurring in a place of detention violates the state constitution.

In Colorado v. Spring, 479 U.S. 564 (1987), the Supreme Court held a *Miranda* waiver valid even though the defendant was not apprised of every alleged crime with respect to which the police intended to interrogate him. Even if the police deliberately failed to inform Spring that they intended to interrogate him about another crime, the Court "has never held that mere silence by law enforcement officials as to the subject matter of an interrogation is 'trickery' sufficient to invalidate a suspect's waiver of *Miranda* rights, and we expressly decline so to hold today. Once *Miranda* warnings are given, it is difficult to see how official silence could cause a suspect to misunderstand the nature of his constitutional right . . . to refuse to answer any question which might incriminate him. . . . Here, the additional information could affect only the wisdom of a . . . waiver, not its essential voluntary and knowing nature." The dissent, by contrast, again accused the majority of letting the state "take unfair advantage of the suspect's psychological state, as the unexpected questions cause the compulsive pressures [of custodial interrogation] suddenly to reappear."

What if the police inform a suspect of the scope of the investigation, but fail to mention that a lawyer is trying to contact the suspect? That was the question in the following case.

MORAN v. BURBINE

Certiorari to the United States Court of Appeals for the First Circuit
475 U.S. 412 (1986)

JUSTICE O'CONNOR delivered the opinion of the Court.

After being informed of his rights pursuant to Miranda v. Arizona, and after executing a series of written waivers, respondent confessed to the murder of a young woman. At no point during the course of the interrogation, which occurred prior to arraignment, did he request an attorney. While he was in police custody, his sister attempted to retain a lawyer to represent him. The attorney telephoned the police station and received assurances that respondent would not be questioned further until the next day. In fact, the interrogation session that yielded the inculpatory statements began later that evening. The question presented is whether either the conduct of the police or respondent's ignorance of the attorney's efforts to reach him taints the validity of the waivers and therefore requires exclusion of the confessions.

I

On the morning of March 3, 1977, Mary Jo Hickey was found unconscious in a factory parking lot in Providence, Rhode Island. Suffering from injuries to her skull apparently inflicted by a metal pipe found at the scene, she was rushed to a nearby hospital. Three weeks later she died from her wounds.

Several months after her death, the Cranston, Rhode Island, police arrested respondent and two others in connection with a local burglary. Shortly before the arrest, Detective Ferranti of the Cranston police force had learned from a confidential informant that the man responsible for Ms. Hickey's death lived at a certain address and went by the name of "Butch." Upon discovering that respondent lived at that address and was known by that name, Detective Ferranti informed respondent of his *Miranda* rights. When respondent refused to execute a written waiver, Detective Ferranti spoke separately with the two other suspects arrested on the breaking and entering charge and obtained statements further implicating respondent in Ms. Hickey's murder. At approximately 6 p.m., Detective Ferranti telephoned the police in Providence to convey the information he had uncovered. An hour later, three officers from that department arrived at the Cranston headquarters for the purpose of questioning respondent about the murder.

That same evening, at about 7:45 p.m., respondent's sister telephoned the Public Defender's Office to obtain legal assistance for her brother. Her sole concern was the breaking and entering charge, as she was unaware that respondent was then under suspicion for murder. She asked for Richard Casparian, who had been scheduled to meet with respondent earlier that afternoon to discuss another charge unrelated to either the break-in or the murder. As soon as the conversation ended, the attorney who took the call attempted to reach Mr. Casparian. When those efforts were unsuccessful, she telephoned Allegra Munson, another Assistant Public Defender, and told her about respondent's arrest and his sister's subsequent request that the office represent him.

At 8:15 p.m., Ms. Munson telephoned the Cranston police station and asked that her call be transferred to the detective division. In the words of the Supreme Court of Rhode Island . . . the conversation proceeded as follows:

> A male voice responded with the word "Detectives." Ms. Munson identified herself and asked if Brian Burbine was being held; the person responded affirmatively. Ms. Munson explained to the person that Burbine was represented by attorney Casparian who was not available; she further stated that she would act as Burbine's legal counsel in the event that the police intended to place him in a lineup or question him. The unidentified person told Ms. Munson that the police would not be questioning Burbine or putting him in a lineup and that they were through with him for the night. Ms. Munson was not informed that the Providence Police were at the Cranston police station or that Burbine was a suspect in Mary's murder.

At all relevant times, respondent was unaware of his sister's efforts to retain counsel and of the fact and contents of Ms. Munson's telephone conversation.

Less than an hour later, the police brought respondent to an interrogation room and conducted the first of a series of interviews concerning the murder. Prior to each session, respondent was informed of his *Miranda* rights, and on three separate occasions he signed a written form acknowledging that he understood his right to the presence of an attorney and explicitly indicating that he "[did] not want an attorney called or appointed for [him]" before he gave a statement. Uncontradicted evidence at the suppression hearing indicated that at least twice during the course of the evening, respondent was left in a room where he had access to a telephone, which he apparently declined to use. Eventually, respondent signed three written statements fully admitting to the murder.

Prior to trial, respondent moved to suppress the statements. The court denied the motion, finding that respondent had received the *Miranda* warnings and had "knowingly, intelligently, and voluntarily waived his privilege against self-incrimination [and] his right to counsel." . . . The jury found respondent guilty of murder in the first degree, and he appealed to the Supreme Court of Rhode Island. A divided court rejected his contention that the Fifth and Fourteenth Amendments to the Constitution required the suppression of the inculpatory statements and affirmed the conviction. . . . After unsuccessfully petitioning the United States District Court for the District of Rhode Island for a writ of habeas corpus, respondent appealed to the Court of Appeals for the First Circuit. That court reversed.

We granted certiorari to decide whether a prearraignment confession preceded by an otherwise valid waiver must be suppressed either because the police misinformed an inquiring attorney about their plans concerning the suspect or because they failed to inform the suspect of the attorney's efforts to reach him. We now reverse.

II

. . . Respondent does not dispute that the Providence police followed [the *Miranda*] procedures with precision. . . . Nor does respondent contest the Rhode Island courts' determination that he at no point requested the presence of a lawyer. He contends instead that the confessions must be suppressed because the police's failure to inform him of the attorney's telephone call deprived him of information essential to his ability to knowingly waive his Fifth Amendment rights. In the alternative, he suggests that to fully protect the Fifth Amendment values served by *Miranda*, we should extend that decision to condemn the conduct of the Providence police. We address each contention in turn.

A

Echoing the standard first articulated in Johnson v. Zerbst, 304 U.S. 458, 464 (1938), *Miranda* holds that "[t]he defendant may waive effectuation" of the rights conveyed in the warnings "provided the waiver is made voluntarily, knowingly and intelligently." The inquiry has two distinct dimensions. First, the relinquishment of the right must have been voluntary in the sense that it was the product of a free and deliberate choice rather than intimidation, coercion, or deception. Second, the waiver must have been made with a full awareness of both the nature of the right being abandoned and the consequences of the decision to abandon it. Only if the "totality of the circumstances surrounding the interrogation" reveals both an uncoerced choice and the requisite level of comprehension may a court properly conclude that the *Miranda* rights have been waived.

Under this standard, we have no doubt that respondent validly waived his right to remain silent and to the presence of counsel. The voluntariness of the waiver is not at issue. As the Court of Appeals correctly acknowledged, the record is devoid of any suggestion that police resorted to physical or psychological pressure to elicit the statements. Indeed it appears that it was respondent, and not the police, who spontaneously initiated the conversation that led to the first and most damaging confession. Nor is there any question about respondent's comprehension of the full panoply of rights set out in the *Miranda* warnings and of the potential consequences of a decision to relinquish them. Nonetheless, the Court of Appeals believed that the "[d]eliberate or reckless" conduct of the police, in particular their failure to inform respondent of the telephone call, fatally undermined the validity of the otherwise proper waiver. We find this conclusion untenable as a matter of both logic and precedent.

Events occurring outside of the presence of the suspect and entirely unknown to him surely can have no bearing on the capacity to comprehend and knowingly relinquish a constitutional right. Under the analysis of the Court of Appeals, the same defendant, armed with the same information and confronted with precisely the same police conduct, would have knowingly waived his *Miranda* rights had a lawyer not telephoned the police station to inquire about his status. Nothing in any of our waiver decisions or in our understanding of the essential components of a valid waiver requires so incongruous a result. No doubt the additional information would have been useful to respondent; perhaps even it might have affected his decision to confess. But we have never read the Constitution to require that the police supply a suspect with a flow of information to help him calibrate his self-interest in deciding whether to speak or stand by his rights. Once it is determined that a suspect's decision not to rely on his rights was uncoerced, that he at all times knew he could stand mute and request a lawyer, and that he was aware of the State's intention to use his statements to secure a conviction, the analysis is complete and the waiver is valid as a matter of law. The Court of Appeals' conclusion to the contrary was in error.

Nor do we believe that the level of the police's culpability in failing to inform respondent of the telephone call has any bearing on the validity of the waivers. In light of the state-court findings that there was no "conspiracy or collusion" on the part of the police, we have serious doubts about whether the Court of Appeals was free to conclude that their conduct constituted "deliberate or reckless irresponsibility." 753 F.2d, at 185. But whether intentional or inadvertent, the state of mind of the police is irrelevant to the question of the intelligence and voluntariness of respondent's election to abandon his rights. Although highly inappropriate, even deliberate deception of an attorney could not possibly affect a suspect's decision to waive his *Miranda* rights unless he were at least aware of the incident. Compare Escobedo v. Illinois (excluding confession where police incorrectly told the suspect that his lawyer " 'didn't want to see' him"). Nor was the failure to inform respondent of the telephone call the kind of "trick[ery]" that can vitiate the validity of a waiver. *Miranda*, 384 U.S., at 476. Granting that the "deliberate or reckless" withholding of information is objectionable as a matter of ethics, such conduct is only relevant to the constitutional validity of a waiver if it deprives a defendant of knowledge essential to his ability to understand the nature of his rights and the consequences of abandoning them. Because respondent's voluntary decision to speak was made with full awareness and comprehension of all the information *Miranda* requires the police to convey, the waivers were valid.

B

At oral argument respondent acknowledged that a constitutional rule requiring the police to inform a suspect of an attorney's efforts to reach him would represent a significant extension of our precedents. He contends, however, that the conduct of the Providence police was so inimical to the Fifth Amendment values *Miranda* seeks to protect that we should read that decision to condemn their behavior. Regardless of any issue of waiver, he urges, the Fifth Amendment requires the reversal of a conviction if the police are less than forthright in their dealings with an attorney or if they fail to tell a suspect of a lawyer's unilateral efforts to contact him. Because the proposed modification ignores the underlying purposes of the *Miranda* rules and because we think that the decision as written strikes the proper balance . . . , we decline the invitation to further extend *Miranda*'s reach.

At the outset, while we share respondent's distaste for the deliberate misleading of an officer of the court, reading *Miranda* to forbid police deception of an attorney would cut [the decision] completely loose from its own explicitly stated rationale. As is now well established, "[t]he . . . *Miranda* warnings are 'not themselves rights protected by the Constitution but [are] instead measures to insure that the [suspect's] right against compulsory self-incrimination [is] protected.' " New York v. Quarles, 467 U.S. 649, 654 (1984), quoting Michigan v. Tucker, 417 U.S. 433, 444 (1974). Their objective is not to mold police conduct for its own sake. Nothing in the Constitution vests in us the authority to mandate a code of behavior for state officials wholly unconnected to any federal right or privilege. The purpose of the *Miranda* warnings instead is to dissipate the compulsion inherent in custodial interrogation and, in so doing, guard against abridgment of the suspect's Fifth Amendment rights. Clearly, a rule that focuses on how the police treat an attorney — conduct that has no relevance at all to the degree of compulsion experienced by the defendant during interrogation — would ignore both *Miranda*'s mission and its only source of legitimacy. . . . [The Court also expressed concerns about adding unnecessary complexity to the *Miranda* rules.]

Moreover, problems of clarity to one side, reading *Miranda* to require the police in each instance to inform a suspect of an attorney's efforts to reach him would work a substantial and, we think, inappropriate shift in the subtle balance struck in that decision. Custodial interrogations implicate two competing concerns. On the one hand, the need for police questioning as a tool for effective enforcement of criminal laws cannot be doubted. Admissions of guilt are more than merely "desirable"; they are essential to society's compelling interest in finding, convicting, and punishing those who violate the law. On the other hand, the Court has recognized that the interrogation process is "inherently coercive" and that, as a consequence, there exists a substantial risk that the police will inadvertently traverse the fine line between legitimate efforts to elicit admissions and constitutionally impermissible compulsion. *Miranda* attempted to reconcile these opposing concerns by giving the defendant the power to exert some control over the course of the interrogation. Declining to adopt the more extreme position that the actual presence of a lawyer was necessary to dispel the coercion inherent in custodial interrogation, the Court found that the suspect's Fifth Amendment rights could be adequately protected by less intrusive means. Police questioning, often an essential part of the investigatory process, could continue in its traditional form, the Court held, but only if the suspect clearly understood that, at any time, he could bring the proceeding to a halt or, short of that, call in an attorney to give advice and monitor the conduct of his interrogators.

The position urged by respondent would upset this carefully drawn approach in a manner that is both unnecessary for the protection of the Fifth Amendment privilege and injurious to legitimate law enforcement. Because, as *Miranda* holds, full comprehension of the rights to remain silent and request an attorney are sufficient to dispel whatever coercion is inherent in the interrogation process, a rule requiring the police to inform the suspect of an attorney's efforts to contact him would contribute to the protection of the Fifth Amendment privilege only incidentally, if at all. This minimal benefit, however, would come at a substantial cost to society's legitimate and substantial interest in securing admissions of guilt. Indeed, the very premise of the Court of Appeals was not that awareness of Ms. Munson's phone call would have dissipated the coercion of the interrogation room, but that it might have convinced respondent not to speak at all. Because neither the letter nor purposes of *Miranda* require this additional handicap on otherwise permissible investigatory efforts, we are unwilling to expand the *Miranda* rules to require the police to keep the suspect abreast of the status of his legal representation.

III

[The Court rejected the argument that the Sixth Amendment applies in these circumstances. This part of the Court's opinion is reproduced at pages 942-944 infra.]

IV

Finally, respondent contends that the conduct of the police was so offensive as to deprive him of the fundamental fairness guaranteed by the Due Process Clause of the Fourteenth Amendment. Focusing primarily on the impropriety of conveying false information to an attorney, he invites us to declare that such behavior should be condemned as violative of canons fundamental to the "traditions and conscience of our people." We do not question that on facts more egregious than those presented here police deception might rise to a level of a due process violation. Accordingly, Justice Stevens' apocalyptic suggestion that we have approved any and all forms of police misconduct is demonstrably incorrect. We hold only that, on these facts, the challenged conduct falls short of the kind of misbehavior that so shocks the sensibilities of civilized society as to warrant a federal intrusion into the criminal processes of the States.

We hold therefore that the Court of Appeals erred in finding that the Federal Constitution required the exclusion of the three inculpatory statements. Accordingly, we reverse and remand for proceedings consistent with this opinion.

JUSTICE STEVENS, with whom JUSTICE BRENNAN and JUSTICE MARSHALL join, dissenting.

This case poses fundamental questions about our system of justice. As this Court has long recognized, and reaffirmed only weeks ago, "ours is an accusatorial and not an inquisitorial system." Miller v. Fenton, 474 U.S. 104, 110 (1985). The Court's opinion today represents a startling departure from that basic insight.

The Court concludes that the police may deceive an attorney by giving her false information about whether her client will be questioned, and that the police may deceive a suspect by failing to inform him of his attorney's communications and efforts to represent him. For the majority, this conclusion, though "distaste[ful]," is not even debatable. The deception of the attorney is irrelevant because the attorney has no right to information, accuracy, honesty, or fairness in the police response to her questions about her client. The deception of the client is acceptable, because, although the information would affect the client's assertion of his rights, the client's actions in ignorance of the availability of his attorney are voluntary, knowing, and intelligent; additionally, society's interest in apprehending, prosecuting, and punishing criminals outweighs the suspect's interest in information regarding his attorney's efforts to communicate with him. Finally, even mendacious police interference in the communications between a suspect and his lawyer does not violate any notion of fundamental fairness because it does not shock the conscience of the majority. . . .

II

Well-settled principles of law lead inexorably to the conclusion that the failure to inform Burbine of the call from his attorney makes the subsequent waiver of his constitutional rights invalid. Analysis should begin with an acknowledgment that the burden of proving the validity of a waiver of constitutional rights is always on the government. When such a waiver occurs in a custodial setting, that burden is an especially heavy one because custodial interrogation is inherently coercive, because disinterested witnesses are seldom available to describe what actually happened, and because history has taught us that the danger of overreaching during incommunicado interrogation is so real. . . .

In this case it would be perfectly clear that Burbine's waiver was invalid if, for example, Detective Ferranti had "threatened, tricked, or cajoled" Burbine in their private pre-confession meeting—perhaps by misdescribing the statements obtained from DiOrio and Sparks—even though, under the Court's truncated analysis of the issue, Burbine fully understood his rights. For *Miranda* clearly condemns threats or trickery that cause a suspect to make an unwise waiver of his rights even though he fully understands those rights. In my opinion there can be no constitutional distinction—as the Court appears to draw—between a deceptive misstatement and the concealment by the police of the critical fact that an attorney retained by the accused or his family has offered assistance, either by telephone or in person.

Thus, the Court's truncated analysis, which relies in part on a distinction between deception accomplished by means of an omission of a critically important fact and deception by means of a misleading statement, is simply untenable. If, as the Court asserts, "the analysis is at an end" as soon as the suspect is provided with enough information to have the capacity to understand and exercise his rights, I see no reason why the police should not be permitted to make the same kind of misstatements to the suspect that they are apparently allowed to make to his lawyer. *Miranda*, however, clearly establishes that both kinds of deception vitiate the suspect's waiver of his right to counsel. . . .

III

The Court makes the alternative argument that requiring police to inform a suspect of his attorney's communications to and about him is not required because it would upset the careful "balance" of *Miranda*. . . .

The Court's balancing approach is profoundly misguided. The cost of suppressing evidence of guilt will always make the value of a procedural safeguard appear "minimal," "marginal," or "incremental." Indeed, the value of any trial at all seems like a "procedural technicality" when balanced against the interest in administering prompt justice to a murderer or a rapist caught red-handed. The individual interest in procedural safeguards that minimize the risk of error is easily discounted when the fact of guilt appears certain beyond doubt.

What is the cost of requiring the police to inform a suspect of his attorney's call? It would decrease the likelihood that custodial interrogation will enable the police to obtain a confession. This is certainly a real cost, but it is the same cost that this Court has repeatedly found necessary to preserve the character of our free society and our rejection of an inquisitorial system. . . .

If the Court's cost-benefit analysis were sound, it would justify a repudiation of the right to a warning about counsel itself. There is only a difference in degree between a presumption that advice about the immediate availability of a lawyer would not affect the voluntariness of a decision to confess, and a presumption that every citizen knows that he has a right to remain silent and therefore no warnings of any kind are needed. In either case, the withholding of information serves precisely the same law enforcement interests. And in both cases, the cost can be described as nothing more than an incremental increase in the risk that an individual will make an unintelligent waiver of his rights.

In cases like *Escobedo* [and] *Miranda*, the Court has viewed the balance from a much broader perspective. In these cases — indeed, whenever the distinction between an inquisitorial and an accusatorial system of justice is implicated — the law enforcement interest served by incommunicado interrogation has been weighed against the interest in individual liberty that is threatened by such practices. The balance has never been struck by an evaluation of empirical data of the kind submitted to legislative decisionmakers — indeed, the Court relies on no such data today. Rather, the Court has evaluated the quality of the conflicting rights and interests. In the past, that kind of balancing process has led to the conclusion that the police have no right to compel an individual to respond to custodial interrogation, and that the interest in liberty that is threatened by incommunicado interrogation is so precious that special procedures must be followed to protect it. The Court's contrary conclusion today can only be explained by its failure to appreciate the value of the liberty that an accusatorial system seeks to protect. . . .

V

At the time attorney Munson made her call to the Cranston police station, she was acting as Burbine's attorney. Under ordinary principles of agency law the deliberate deception of Munson was tantamount to deliberate deception of her client. If an attorney makes a mistake in the course of her representation of her client, the client must accept the consequences of that mistake. It is equally clear that when an attorney makes an inquiry on behalf of her client, the client is entitled to a truthful answer. Surely the client must have the same remedy for a false representation to his lawyer that he would have if he were acting pro se and had propounded the question himself. The majority brushes aside the police deception involved in the misinformation of attorney Munson. It is irrelevant to the Fifth Amendment analysis, concludes the majority, because that right is personal.

In my view, as a matter of law, the police deception of Munson was tantamount to deception of Burbine himself. It constituted a violation of Burbine's right to have an attorney present during the questioning that began shortly thereafter. The existence of that right is undisputed. Whether the source of that right is the Sixth Amendment, the Fifth Amendment, or a combination of the two is of no special importance, for I do not understand the Court to deny the existence of the right.

The pertinent question is whether police deception of the attorney is utterly irrelevant to that right. In my judgment, it blinks at reality to suggest that misinformation which prevented the presence of an attorney has no bearing on the protection and effectuation of the right to counsel in custodial interrogation. . . .

The possible reach of the Court's opinion is stunning. For the majority seems to suggest that police may deny counsel all access to a client who is being held. At least since Escobedo v. Illinois, it has been widely accepted that police may not simply deny attorneys access to their clients who are in custody. This view has survived the recasting of *Escobedo* from a Sixth Amendment to a Fifth Amendment case that the majority finds so critically important. That this prevailing view is shared by the police can be seen in the state-court opinions detailing various forms of police deception of attorneys. For, if there were no obligation to give attorneys access, there would be no need to take elaborate steps to avoid access, such as shuttling the suspect to a different location, or taking the lawyer to different locations; police could simply refuse to allow the attorneys to see the suspects. But the law enforcement profession has apparently believed, quite rightly in my view, that denying lawyers access to their clients is impermissible. The Court today seems to assume that this view was error — that, from the federal constitutional perspective, the lawyer's access is, as a question from the Court put it in oral argument, merely "a matter of prosecutorial grace." Certainly, nothing in the Court's . . . analysis acknowledges that there is any federal constitutional bar to an absolute denial of lawyer access to a suspect who is in police custody. . . .

VI

The Court devotes precisely five sentences to its conclusion that the police interference in the attorney's representation of Burbine did not violate the Due Process Clause. In the majority's view, the due process analysis is a simple "shock the conscience" test. Finding its conscience troubled, but not shocked, the majority rejects the due process challenge. . . .

In my judgment, police interference in the attorney-client relationship is the type of governmental misconduct on a matter of central importance to the administration of justice that the Due Process Clause prohibits. Just as the police cannot impliedly promise a suspect that his silence will not be used against him and then proceed to break that promise, so too police cannot tell a suspect's attorney that they will not question the suspect and then proceed to question him. Just as the government cannot conceal from a suspect material and exculpatory evidence, so too the government cannot conceal from a suspect the material fact of his attorney's communication.

Police interference with communications between an attorney and his client violates the due process requirement of fundamental fairness. Burbine's attorney was given completely false information about the lack of questioning; moreover, she was not told that her client would be questioned regarding a murder charge about which she was unaware. Burbine, in turn, was not told that his attorney had phoned and that she had been informed that he would not be questioned. . . .

The majority does not "question that on facts more egregious than those presented here police deception might rise to a level of a due process violation." In my view, the police deception disclosed by this record plainly does rise to that level.

VII

This case turns on a proper appraisal of the role of the lawyer in our society. If a lawyer is seen as a nettlesome obstacle to the pursuit of wrongdoers — as in an inquisitorial society — then the Court's decision today makes a good deal of sense. If a lawyer is seen as an aid to the understanding and protection of constitutional rights — as in an accusatorial society — then today's decision makes no sense at all. . . .

NOTES AND QUESTIONS

1. Justice O'Connor's opinion for the Court and Justice Stevens' dissent in Moran v. Burbine read a good deal like the opinions in *Miranda* itself. But the

roles are reversed. It is Justice O'Connor's majority opinion that reminds us of law enforcement need and the important role station house confessions play in solving crimes, just as Justices Harlan and White reminded us of those factors in their *Miranda* dissents. And it is Justice Stevens' dissent that stresses the importance of rational, informed decisionmaking by suspects, and that emphasizes the role defense lawyers play in protecting that interest — just as Earl Warren did in his opinion for the Court. What explains this role reversal? What does it mean for *Miranda* waivers? If the *Moran* majority accepted the principles of the *Miranda* dissenters, why did it leave *Miranda* in place?

2. The burden of establishing a valid waiver depends on two factors: the waiver standard itself, and the burden of persuasion. Moran v. Burbine discusses the first factor. Concerning the second: in Colorado v. Connelly, 479 U.S. 157 (1986), the Court held that the state need only prove waiver by a preponderance of the evidence. Is the combination of *Moran* and *Connelly* appropriate?

3. The *Moran* Court assumed, for purposes of its decision, that the officers lied to Burbine's lawyer. Does Illinois v. Perkins, 496 U.S. 292 (1990), apply here? (*Perkins* is excerpted supra at pages 851-856.) Recall that in *Perkins*, the police put an undercover agent in the defendant's jail cell; the Court found no *Miranda* "interrogation." Justice Stevens' dissent in *Moran* seems to assume that lying to the suspect himself would be impermissible — yet *Perkins* plainly permitted lying to the suspect. Is lying to the suspect's lawyer worse than lying to the suspect himself? Is it worse when a police officer, acting as a police officer, lies than when an undercover police agent does so?

4. The relationship between police deception and *Miranda* waivers is complex. Consider Miller v. Fenton, 796 F.2d 598 (3d Cir. 1986), in which a divided Court of Appeals panel found a valid *Miranda* waiver on these facts:

> At the outset of our analysis, it is essential that we review the salient features of the interrogation. Because the state police taped the interrogation, we have had an opportunity actually to hear Detective Boyce's questions and Miller's responses. A significant portion of the questioning was in the typical police interrogation mode, developing chronologically Miller's whereabouts on the day in question, confronting him with the identification of his car, asking him point-blank whether he committed the crime, challenging his answers, and attempting to discover the details of the crime. This element of the interrogation is unexceptionable and unchallenged. We shall therefore focus primarily on the features of the interrogation that are at issue.
>
> It is clear that Boyce made no threats and engaged in no physical coercion of Miller. To the contrary, throughout the interview, Detective Boyce assumed a friendly, understanding manner and spoke in a soft tone of voice. He repeatedly assured Miller that he was sympathetic to him and wanted to help him unburden his mind. As the following excerpts demonstrate, the Detective's statements of sympathy at times approached the maudlin:
>
> > *Boyce:* Now listen to me, Frank. This hurts me more than it hurts you, because I love people. . . .
> >
> > *Boyce:* Let it come out, Frank. I'm here, I'm here with you now. I'm on your side, I'm on your side, Frank. I'm your brother, you and I are brothers, Frank. We are brothers, and I want to help my brother. . . .
> >
> > *Boyce:* We have, we have a relationship, don't we? Have I been sincere with you, Frank?

Boyce also gave Miller certain factual information, some of which was untrue. At the beginning of the interrogation, for example, Boyce informed Miller that the victim was still alive; this was false. During the interview, Boyce told Miller that Ms. Margolin had just died, although in fact she had been found dead several hours earlier.

Detective Boyce's major theme throughout the interrogation was that whoever had committed such a heinous crime had mental problems and was desperately in need of psychological treatment. From early in the interview, Detective Boyce led Miller to understand that he believed that Miller had committed the crime and that Miller now needed a friend to whom he could unburden himself. The Detective stated several times that Miller was not a criminal who should be punished, but a sick individual who should receive help. He assured Miller that he (Detective Boyce) was sincerely understanding and that he wished to help him with his problem. The following excerpts from the transcript of the interrogation provide examples of the statements about Miller's having psychological problems, as well as of the assurances of help:

> *Boyce:*   [L]et's forget this incident, [l]et's talk about your problem. This is what, this is what I'm concerned with, Frank, your problem.
> *Miller:*   Right.
> *Boyce:*   If I had a problem like your problem, I would want you to help me with my problem.
> *Miller:*   Uh, huh.
> *Boyce:*   Now, you know what I'm talking about.
> *Miller:*   Yeah.
> *Boyce:*   And I know, and I think that, uh, a lot of other people know. You know what I'm talking about. I don't think you're a criminal, Frank.
> *Miller:*   No, but you're trying to make me one.
> *Boyce:*   No I'm not, no I'm not, but I want you to talk to me so we can get this thing worked out. . . .
> *Boyce:*   I want you to talk to me. I want you to tell me what you think. I want you to tell me how you think about this, what you think about this.
> *Miller:*   What I think about it?
> *Boyce:*   Yeah.
> *Miller:*   I think whoever did it really needs help.
> *Boyce:*   And that's what I think and that's what I know. They don't, they don't need punishment, right? Like you said, they need help.
> *Miller:*   Right.
> *Boyce:*   They don't need punishment. They need help, good medical help.
> *Miller:*   That's right.
> *Boyce:*   [T]o rectify their problem. Putting them in, in a prison isn't going to solve it, is it?
> *Miller:*   No, sir. I know, I was in there for three and a half years. . . .
> *Boyce:*   You can see it Frank, you can feel it, you can feel it but you are not responsible. This is what I'm trying to tell you, but you've got to come forward and tell me. Don't, don't, don't let it eat you up, don't, don't fight it. You've got to rectify it, Frank. We've got to get together on this thing, or I, I mean really, you need help, you need proper help, and you know it, my God, you know, in God's name, you, you, you know it. You are not a criminal, you are not a criminal.

Boyce also appealed to Miller's conscience and described the importance of Miller's purging himself of the memories that must be haunting him. This aspect of the interrogation is exemplified in the preceding passage — "Don't, don't, don't let it eat you up, don't, don't fight it. You've got to rectify it, Frank." The following excerpts are representative of Boyce's arguments along this line:

> *Boyce:* Frank, listen to me, honest to God, I'm, I'm telling you, Frank, (inaudible). I know, it's going to bother you, Frank, it's going to bother you. It's there, it's not going to go away, it's there. It's right in front of you, Frank. Am I right or wrong?
>
> *Miller:* Yeah. . . .
>
> *Boyce:* Honest, Frank. It's got to come out. You can't leave it in. It's hard for you, I realize that, how hard it is, how difficult it is, I realize that, but you've got to help yourself before anybody else can help you. . . .
>
> *Boyce:* First thing we have to do is let it all come out. Don't fight it because it's worse, Frank, it's worse. It's hurting me because I feel it. I feel it wanting to come out, but it's hurting me, Frank. . . .
>
> *Boyce:* No, listen to me, Frank, please listen to me. The issue now is what happened. The issue now is truth. Truth is the issue now. You've got to believe this, and the truth prevails in the end, Frank. You have to believe that and I'm sincere when I'm saying it to you. You've got to be truthful with yourself. . . .
>
> *Boyce:* That's the most important thing, not, not what has happened, Frank. The fact that you were truthful, you came forward and you said, look I have a problem. I didn't mean to do what I did. I have a problem, this is what's important, Frank. This is very important, I got, I, I got to get closer to you, Frank, I got to make you believe this and I'm, and I'm sincere when I tell you this. You got to tell me exactly what happened, Frank. That's very important. I know how you feel inside, Frank, it's eating you up, am I right? It's eating you up, Frank. You've got to come forward. You've got to do it for yourself, for your family, for your father, this is what's important, the truth, Frank.

When Miller at last confessed, he collapsed in a state of shock. He slid off his chair and onto the floor with a blank stare on his face. The police officers sent for a first aid squad that took him to the hospital.

796 F.2d at 601-603. Are some kinds of deception more coercive than others? Was the deception in Miller v. Fenton coercive? Is your conclusion affected by the last three sentences quoted above? If so, why?

5. The status of police trickery issue depends in part on the meaning of the words "knowing" and "intelligent." The Moran Court found that Burbine's waiver was made "knowingly and intelligently." Is that finding correct? If Burbine had fully understood the practical implications of talking to the police as opposed to waiting to see a lawyer, do you think he would have talked? One might fairly argue that virtually no police station confessions are "knowing" or "intelligent" in the ordinary sense of those words because a well-informed suspect who is thinking would almost certainly keep quiet. So what do "knowing" and "intelligent" mean in this context?

6. How does *Moran* differ from *Escobedo*? Would the case have come out differently if the lawyer had been at the station house? If Burbine had asked if "anybody" had tried to contact him? If his lawyer had done so? Would it make any difference whether the police were truthful or dishonest in responding to such questions? In People v. McCauley, 645 N.E.2d 923 (Ill. 1994), the Supreme Court of Illinois concluded that "[r]egardless of the United States Supreme Court's current views on waiver of the right to counsel under the Federal Constitution, the law in Illinois remains that when police, prior to or during custodial interrogation, refuse an

attorney appointed or retained to assist a suspect access to the suspect, there can be no knowing waiver of the right to counsel if the suspect has not been informed that the attorney was present and seeking to consult with him." Some other state supreme courts agree. See State v. Stoddard, 537 A.2d 446 (Conn. 1988); Haliburton v. State, 514 So. 2d 1088 (Fla. 1987).

7. Is the dissenters' position coherent? How would the dissenters decide whether a suspect had waived his rights under *Miranda*? For an argument that the dissenters do not go far enough, see Charles J. Ogletree, Are Confessions Really Good for the Soul?: A Proposal to Mirandize *Miranda*, 100 Harv. L. Rev. 1826 (1987). Professor Ogletree argues that suspects should be given a non-waivable right to consult with counsel before any questioning takes place, since this is the only way to prevent waivers based on ignorance, lack of information, or police deception. Is that what *Miranda* is about? The *Moran* dissenters' disagreement with Professor Ogletree may be solely a disagreement about means, not about ends. Is that true of the *Moran* majority?

8. You may recall that, after a suspect invokes his *Miranda* right to counsel, the police may question him only if the suspect re-initiates conversation with the police. What waiver standard applies in such cases? The answer appears to be: the same standard as in *Moran*. Consider: In Wyrick v. Fields, 459 U.S. 42 (1982) (per curiam), the defendant invoked his *Miranda* right to counsel and later "initiated" a polygraph examination. Before beginning the polygraph, the defendant was given *Miranda* warnings. At the conclusion of the polygraph, the examiner told the defendant that his answers had not been true and asked the defendant "if he could explain why his answers were bothering him." The defendant proceeded to make several incriminating statements. The Court of Appeals for the Eighth Circuit concluded that the examiner should have given the defendant another set of *Miranda* warnings at the close of the polygraph before asking any further questions. In the court of appeals' view, the defendant had initiated the polygraph but not anything else, so the *Edwards* rule was violated — at least in the absence of further warnings. Fields v. Wyrick, 682 F.2d 154 (8th Cir. 1982). The Supreme Court reversed:

> In reaching [its] result, the Court of Appeals did not consider the "totality of the circumstances," as *Edwards* requires. Fields did not merely initiate a "meeting." By requesting a polygraph examination, he initiated interrogation. That is, Fields waived not only his right to be free of contact with the authorities in the absence of an attorney, but also his right to be free of interrogation about the crime of which he was suspected. Fields validly waived his right to have counsel present at "post-test" questioning, unless the circumstances changed so seriously that his answers no longer were voluntary, or unless he no longer was making a "knowing and intelligent relinquishment or abandonment" of his rights.

459 U.S. at 47.

9. Wyrick v. Fields states a relatively relaxed waiver standard, similar to the standard applied in Moran v. Burbine or North Carolina v. Butler, 441 U.S. 369 (1979). Under those cases, waiver is easily justified: it is permissible for the police to take advantage of suspects' ignorance and mistake; even outright deceptions seems to be allowed. Recall that under Edwards v. Arizona, 451 U.S. 477 (1981), and its progeny, the waiver standard is quite different when a suspect has invoked his *Miranda* rights: indeed, waiver is impossible in such cases. So too if the

police question the suspect without giving him his *Miranda* warnings—there too, waiver is impossible; there is an irrebuttable presumption that any incriminating statement is compelled.

It seems that there are two *Miranda* waiver standards, and which one applies depends on which triggering events have transpired. Think about *Miranda* waiver doctrine in light of the following time line:

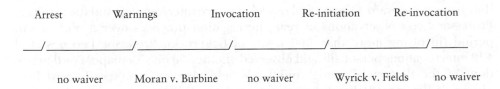

Arrest	Warnings	Invocation	Re-initiation	Re-invocation
no waiver	Moran v. Burbine	no waiver	Wyrick v. Fields	no waiver

What waiver rule applies depends on where on the time line the police interrogation takes place. If the questioning occurs after arrest (before arrest, *Miranda* does not apply—there is no "custody"; see Berkemer v. McCarty, 468 U.S. 420 (1984)) but before the *Miranda* warnings have been given, there can be no waiver. *Edwards* holds that the same is true if the questioning occurs after an invocation—at least if the invocation is of the *Miranda* right to counsel; recall that the right to remain silent receives somewhat less protection under Michigan v. Mosley, 423 U.S. 96 (1975). Presumably the same would be true if a suspect invokes under *Edwards*, then re-initiates questioning, and then re-invokes his *Miranda* right to counsel. But if the most recent triggering event is either the administration of the *Miranda* warnings or a re-initiation by the suspect, the waiver standard is a great deal more police-friendly. So the law oscillates between two standards—one where waiver is impermissible, the other where waivers are easily obtained. And remember: Most suspects fall under the easy waiver standard; *Moran* applies to many more cases than *Edwards*.

Is this a sensible way to apply *Miranda*? What values does it protect?

NOTE ON *MIRANDA*'S EFFECTS

How should a case like *Miranda* be appraised? By its aspirational content? By its symbolism? By its practical effects? And if its practical effects, which count? Its real effects on criminal justice, such as on police practices, the ability of interrogated suspects to exercise their right to remain silent, the conditions of interrogated suspects more generally, the number (absolute or relative) of inculpatory statements made, the rate at which police solve crimes (the "clearance" rate), the conviction rate? All the above? And what about the effect of *Miranda* on innocent people wrongly charged with an offense? Might the restrictions on interrogation actually result in wrongful convictions if the police cannot learn through interrogating one person that someone else has been wrongly accused? These issues, and many more, have been the subject of an astonishingly rich literature. For representative samples, see Joseph D. Grano, Confessions, Truth and the Law (1993); Richard Leo & George C. Thomas III, The *Miranda* Debate: Law Justice, and Policing (1998) (containing excerpts from numerous articles debating the merits of *Miranda*); Akhil Reed Amar & Renee Lettow, Fifth Amendment First Principles: The Self-Incrimination Clause, 93 Mich. L. Rev. 857 (1995); Dialogue on *Miranda* (with a debate between, on the one hand, George C. Thomas III and, on the other, Paul G. Cassell and Bret S. Hayman), 43 UCLA L. Rev. 821 (1996). The Grano book and the Amar and Lettow article have in turn generated a cottage industry of critique and response.

Most of the published material is analytical or rhetorical. There have been two recent efforts to investigate empirically various aspects of the *Miranda* regime. The first is by two sociologists, Richard Leo and Richard Ofshe. In a series of articles, they have put forward a theoretical model of police interrogation and the results of Professor Leo's observations of real interrogation practices over a nine-month period (involving more than 500 hours of fieldwork). Professor Leo observed 122 interrogations personally and observed another 60 on videotape. For descriptions of the theoretical model and Leo's field observations, see Richard Leo, *Miranda*'s Revenge: Police Interrogation as a Confidence Game, 30 Law & Soc. Rev. 259 (1996); Richard Leo, Inside the Interrogation Room, 86 J. Crim. & Criminology 266 (1996); Richard Leo, The Impact of *Miranda* Revisited, 86 J. Crim. L. & Criminology 621 (1996); Richard Ofshe & Richard Leo, The Social Psychology of Police Interrogation: The Theory and Classification of True and False Confessions, 16 Stud. L., Pol. & Soc. 189 (1997). Leo's findings are quite remarkable. Using a broad definition of "coercion," he found that in only 4 of the 182 cases examined was there anything that rose to the level of "coercion"; and in those 4 cases, none involved physical coercion. Moreover, only about a quarter of warned suspects invoked their rights after being warned, and approximately 65 percent of those interrogated following warnings and waivers made incriminating statements. Why do so many people act so self-destructively? Was this just what *Miranda* was supposed to stop, or was it only supposed to stop physical and psychological terrorism? Whatever it was supposed to stop, it seems to have affected only the latter. According to Leo, "[P]olice have successfully adapted their practices to the legal requirements of *Miranda* by using conditioning, deemphasizing [guilt], and persuasive strategies to orchestrate consent to custodial questioning in most cases. In addition, in response to *Miranda*, police have developed increasingly specialized, sophisticated, and effective interrogation techniques with which to elicit statements from suspects during interrogation." 86 J. Crim. L. & Criminology at 675. Moreover:

> These new methods appear to be just as effective as the earlier ones that they have replaced. That contemporary American police interrogation resembles the structure and sequence of a classic confidence game helps us understand not only why custodial suspects waive their *Miranda* rights and admit to wrongdoing in such high numbers but also how police power is exercised in the interrogation room. As we have seen, contemporary interrogation strategies are based fundamentally on the manipulation and betrayal of trust. Like confidence men, police interrogators attempt to induce compliance from their suspects by offering them the hope of a better situation in exchange for incriminating information. The interrogator exercises power through his ability to frame the suspect's definition of the situation, exploiting the suspect's ignorance to create the illusion of a relationship that is symbiotic rather than adversarial. In the exercise of his power, the interrogator relies on a series of appeals that mystify both the true nature of the detective's relationship to the suspect and the true extent of his influence with other actors in the criminal justice system. . . .
>
> *Miranda*'s revenge . . . has been to transform police power inside the interrogation room without undermining its effectiveness. Not only have *Miranda* warnings

exercised little or no effect on confession rates, but police have also embraced *Miranda* as a legitimating symbol of their professionalism. *Miranda* warnings symbolically declare that police take individual rights seriously. At the same time, *Miranda* inspired police to create more sophisticated interrogation strategies, effectively giving them the license to act as confidence men and develop their skills in human manipulation and deception. In ways not captured by doctrinal analysis, *Miranda* has changed profoundly both the psychological context and the moral ordering of the police interrogation. Driven by careful strategic considerations, police interrogators exercise power by manipulating custodial suspects' definition of the situation and of their role; by creating the appearance of a symbiotic rather than an adversarial relationship; by appealing to their insider knowledge and expertise; and by exploiting the suspects' ignorance, fear and trust. . . . That contemporary police interrogation resembles both the method and substance of a classic confidence game — and thus has become manipulative and deceptive to its very core — may be *Miranda*'s most enduring legacy.

30 Law & Socy. Rev. 259 (1996). Professor Leo and Professor White added to this literature with an extended discussion of the ways in which police turn *Miranda* to their advantage. See Richard Leo & Welsh S. White, Adapting to *Miranda:* Modern Interrogators' Strategies for Dealing with the Obstacles Posed by *Miranda*, 84 Minn. L. Rev. 397 (1999). A journalistic account of a reporter following a shift of detectives for a year throughout their responsibilities, including observing interrogations, which paints a harsher picture of the police/*Miranda* relationship, is contained in David Simon, Homicide: A Year on the Killing Streets (1991).

What is objectionable about exploiting a "suspect's ignorance, fear and trust" when there is very good reason to believe he has committed a heinous crime? Is it carrying appeals to sentiment a bit too far to look only at the police/suspect interaction and not at the events that give rise to such interactions — serious criminality? One answer obviously is that not all suspects are guilty and that the tactics of police may pry false confessions out of innocent suspects. For just such an argument, see Richard Leo & Richard Ofshe, The Consequences of False Confessions: Deprivations of Liberty and Miscarriages of Justice in the Age of Psychological Interrogation, 88 Nw. U. L. Rev. 429 (1998). The authors also demonstrate that individuals who made incriminating statements are systematically worse off throughout the criminal justice process. Although Leo and Ofshe do identify some cases of clearly, and more cases of apparently, false confessions, the total number is minuscule, according to Paul G. Cassell, Protecting the Innocent from False Confessions and Lost Confessions — and from *Miranda*, 88 Nw. U. L. Rev. 497 (1988). Moreover, according to Cassell, the decision whether to eliminate this risk by eliminating or reducing the effectiveness of interrogation must also take into account the total cost of proposed changes, such as the loss of true confessions as well.

In a second empirical development, Professor Cassell has taken head-on the assertion of Leo, Ofshe, and others, such as Professor Schulhofer, that *Miranda* has not had a dramatic impact on clearance and conviction rates. He has engaged in a running debate, involving data collection and analysis and reanalysis of previous studies, over the impact of *Miranda* on the rate of confessions and the resultant effect on clearance and conviction rates. In addition to the articles cited above, the main contributions to this debate have been Paul G. Cassell, *Miranda*'s Social Costs: An Empirical Assessment, 90 Nw. U. L. Rev. 387 (1996); Stephen J.

Schulhofer, *Miranda*'s Practical Effect: Substantial Benefits and Vanishingly Small Social Costs, id. at 500; Paul G. Cassell, All Benefits, No Costs: The Grand Illusion of *Miranda*'s Defenders, id. at 1084; Stephen J. Schulhofer, *Miranda* and Clearance Rates, 91 Nw. U. L. Rev. 278 (1996); Paul G. Cassell, *Miranda*'s "Negligible" Effect on Law Enforcement: Some Skeptical Observations, 20 Harv. J.L. & Pub. Poly. 327 (1997); Paul G. Cassell & Richard Fowles, Handcuffing the Cops? A Thirty-Year Perspective on *Miranda*'s Harmful Effects on Law Enforcement, 50 Stan. L. Rev. 1055 (1998); John Donohue III, Did *Miranda* Diminish Police Effectiveness?, id. at 1147; Paul G. Cassell and Richard Fowles, Falling Clearance Rates after *Miranda*: Coincidence or Consequence?, id. at 1181. According to Professor Cassell, the data show that *Miranda* has had a noticeable effect on all the FBI index crimes except murder and rape. His efforts have been systematically attacked by the supporters of the decision, such as Professor Schulhofer. And, indeed, the task that Cassell has undertaken is decidedly difficult. He is attempting to sort out one variable — the *Miranda* decision — from all the other variables that affected social change from the mid-'60s to the present, and doing so in the absence of the ability to run any controlled tests of the relevant phenomenon. Still, a number of the critiques of Cassell's efforts have an other-worldly quality about them. They appear to be defending *Miranda* in part on the basis of the argument that it has had little effect on crime enforcement. To the extent this is true, and to the extent that Professor Leo's description of actual interrogation practices is both accurate and troubling, is it time to replace *Miranda* with some alternative? Like what? And to solve exactly what problem? It should be noted that the most dispassionate of the responses to Cassell, the analysis of Professor John Donohue, concludes that a drop in some clearance rates following *Miranda* occurred that is not easy to explain, and thus possibly attributable to *Miranda*. Professor Donohue does not think the magnitude of this drop is as large as Cassell and Fowles suggest, but he reaches that conclusion through a reanalysis of the data involving certain adjustments that Cassell and Fowles plausibly argue should not be adopted. When those adjustments are not made, Donohue's analysis comes out quite similarly to Cassell's and Fowles's, although the question whether to attribute the results to *Miranda* or some other unspecified cause is not easily answerable.

Professor Schulhofer recognizes the "otherworldliness" of some of the criticisms of Cassell, including some of his own, or as he puts it: "Underlying my analysis is a paradox that will trouble many readers, whether they are inclined to support *Miranda* or oppose it. If *Miranda* really has so little impact on confessions and conviction rates, why bother defending it? Isn't *Miranda* simply a hollow promise for civil libertarians and an inconvenient nuisance for law enforcement?" No, says Professor Schulhofer, for a number of reasons. First, the symbolic purpose is not irrelevant; second, it is a great leap forward to substitute psychological ploys for physical abuse; and third, were *Miranda* overruled, the road back to physical abuse is cleared of its major hurdle. 90 Nw. U.L. Rev. at 561-562.

3. Miranda's *Constitutional Status*

At the time of the Court's decision, the common understanding was that *Miranda* was a piece of conventional constitutional law, a set of requirements that flowed from the Fifth Amendment, imposed on the states through the due process clause of the Fourteenth Amendment. That conventional wisdom did not hold for long.

The defendant in Michigan v. Tucker, 417 U.S. 433 (1974), was questioned before *Miranda* was decided. The police obeyed the law as it existed at the time of the questioning — they even gave Tucker some of what later became the *Miranda* warnings — but they did not tell Tucker that he had a right to state-appointed counsel. The Court ruled against Tucker, and had some interesting things to say about *Miranda*'s relationship with the Fifth Amendment:

> The [*Miranda*] Court recognized that these procedural safeguards were not themselves rights protected by the Constitution but were instead measures to insure that the right against compulsory self-incrimination was protected. As the Court remarked: "We cannot say that the Constitution necessarily requires adherence to any particular solution for the inherent compulsions of the interrogation process as it is presently conducted." [Miranda v. Arizona, 382 U.S. 436, 467 (1966)]. The suggested safeguards were not intended to "create a constitutional straitjacket," ibid., but rather to provide practical reinforcement for the right against compulsory self-incrimination.
>
> A comparison of the facts in this case with the historical circumstances underlying the privilege against compulsory self-incrimination strongly indicates that the police conduct here did not deprive respondent of his privilege against compulsory self-incrimination as such, but rather failed to make available to him the full measure of procedural safeguards associated with that right since *Miranda*.

417 U.S. at 444.

The defendant in New York v. Quarles, 467 U.S. 649 (1984), was arrested in a supermarket after a police pursuit. When he was arrested, the defendant was wearing an empty shoulder holster. The arresting officer asked the defendant where the gun was, and the defendant told him. Only then was the defendant given his *Miranda* warnings. The defendant was charged and convicted of a gun offense; the question before the Court was whether the gun itself was admissible. The Court held that it was, pursuant to a "public safety exception" to *Miranda*:

> The police in this case, in the very act of apprehending a suspect, were confronted with the immediate necessity of ascertaining the whereabouts of a gun which they had every reason to believe the suspect had just removed from his empty holster and discarded in the supermarket. So long as the gun was concealed somewhere in the supermarket, with its actual whereabouts unknown, it obviously posed more than one danger to the public safety: an accomplice might make use of it, a customer or employee might later come upon it.
>
> In such a situation, if the police are required to recite the familiar *Miranda* warnings before asking the whereabouts of the gun, suspects in Quarles' position might well be deterred from responding. Procedural safeguards which deter a suspect from responding were deemed acceptable in *Miranda* in order to protect the Fifth Amendment privilege; when the primary social cost of those added protections is the possibility of fewer convictions, the *Miranda* majority was willing to bear that cost. Here, had *Miranda* warnings deterred Quarles from responding to Officer Kraft's question about the whereabouts of the gun, the cost would have been something more than merely the failure to obtain evidence useful in convicting Quarles. Officer Kraft needed an answer to his question not simply to make his case against

Quarles but to insure that further danger to the public did not result from the concealment of the gun in a public area.

. . . [T]he need for answers to questions in a situation posing a threat to the public safety outweighs the need for the prophylactic rule protecting the Fifth Amendment's privilege against self-incrimination.

467 U.S. at 657. Notice that the Court's decision in *Quarles* obviated the need to decide on the admissibility of the fruits of *Miranda* violations. That issue is taken up below, at pages 906-920.

Notice, too, the Court's characterization of *Miranda* as a "prophylactic rule protecting the Fifth Amendment's privilege against self-incrimination." Then-Justice Rehnquist wrote the Court opinions in both *Tucker* and *Quarles*, and in both cases he went out of his way to describe *Miranda* as something other than, and presumably less than, a piece of conventional constitutional law. See, for example, the following passage from *Quarles*:

> The *Miranda* Court . . . presumed that interrogation in certain custodial circumstances is inherently coercive and held that statements made under those circumstances are inadmissible unless the suspect is specifically informed of his *Miranda* rights and freely decides to forgo those rights. The prophylactic *Miranda* warnings therefore are "not themselves rights protected by the Constitution but [are] instead measures to insure that the right against compulsory self-incrimination [is] protected." Michigan v. Tucker, 417 U.S. 433, 444 (1974). Requiring *Miranda* warnings before custodial interrogation provides "practical reinforcement" for the Fifth Amendment right. [Id.]

467 U.S. at 654. The Court made the same point even more explicitly in Oregon v. Elstad, 470 U.S. 298, 306-307 (1985):

> The *Miranda* exclusionary rule . . . serves the Fifth Amendment and sweeps more broadly than the Fifth Amendment itself. It may be triggered even in the absence of a Fifth Amendment violation. The Fifth Amendment prohibits use by the prosecution in its case in chief only of *compelled* testimony. Failure to administer *Miranda* warnings creates a presumption of compulsion. Consequently, unwarned statements that are otherwise voluntary within the meaning of the Fifth Amendment must nevertheless be excluded from evidence under *Miranda*. Thus, in the individual case, *Miranda*'s preventive medicine provides a remedy even to the defendant who has suffered no identifiable constitutional harm.

What is the justification for the Supreme Court making rules of this sort if the Constitution does not require it? For an argument that this position makes *Miranda* an illegitimate exercise of judicial power, see Joseph Grano, *Miranda*'s Constitutional Difficulties: A Reply to Professor Schulhofer, 55 U. Chi. L. Rev. 174 (1988). For a response, suggesting that *Miranda* is one of many prophylactic rules that have their grounding in the Constitution but may not themselves be constitutionally required, see David Strauss, The Ubiquity of Prophylactic Rules, 54 U. Chi. L. Rev. 190 (1988).

Miranda's awkward constitutional status raised an important question about the status of a piece of *non*constitutional federal law. In 1968, as part of the Omnibus Crime Control and Safe Streets Act, Congress purported to overrule *Miranda*, at least in federal cases. "In any criminal prosecution brought by the United States or by the District of Columbia, a confession . . . shall be admissible in evidence if it is voluntarily given." 18 U.S.C. §3501(a). In determining voluntariness, courts were directed to take account of all the circumstances, and they were specifically directed *not* to regard the giving or withholding of warnings as dispositive. 18 U.S.C. §3501(b). Surprisingly, this provision was almost completely ignored by the federal judiciary for the next 30 years. The government never raised arguments that relied on §3501, and federal courts consequently paid no attention to it. Given the Court's language in *Tucker, Quarles*, and *Elstad*, however, there was some reason to believe that §3501 would be deemed constitutional if ever the federal courts considered the issue. In 2000, the Supreme Court ruled on the status of §3501 — and on *Miranda*'s status as well.

DICKERSON v. UNITED STATES

Certiorari to the United States Court of Appeals for the Fourth Circuit
530 U.S. 428 (2000)

CHIEF JUSTICE REHNQUIST delivered the opinion of the Court.

In Miranda v. Arizona, 384 U.S. 436 (1966), we held that certain warnings must be given before a suspect's statement made during custodial interrogation could be admitted in evidence. In the wake of that decision, Congress enacted 18 U.S.C. §3501, which in essence laid down a rule that the admissibility of such statements should turn only on whether or not they were voluntarily made. We hold that *Miranda*, being a constitutional decision of this Court, may not be in effect overruled by an Act of Congress, and we decline to overrule *Miranda* ourselves. We therefore hold that *Miranda* and its progeny in this Court govern the admissibility of statements made during custodial interrogation in both state and federal courts. . . .

Given §3501's express designation of voluntariness as the touchstone of admissibility, its omission of any warning requirement, and the instruction for trial courts to consider a nonexclusive list of factors relevant to the circumstances of a confession, we agree with the Court of Appeals that Congress intended by its enactment to overrule *Miranda*. Because of the obvious conflict between our decision in *Miranda* and §3501, we must address whether Congress has constitutional authority to thus supersede *Miranda*. If Congress has such authority, §3501's totality-of-the-circumstances approach must prevail over *Miranda*'s requirement of warnings; if not, that section must yield to *Miranda*'s more specific requirements.

The law in this area is clear. This Court has supervisory authority over the federal courts, and we may use that authority to prescribe rules of evidence and procedure that are binding in those tribunals. However, the power to judicially create and enforce nonconstitutional rules of procedure and evidence for the federal courts exists only in the absence of a relevant Act of Congress. Congress retains the ultimate authority to modify or set aside any judicially created rules of evidence and procedure that are not required by the Constitution.

But Congress may not legislatively supersede our decisions interpreting and applying the Constitution. This case therefore turns on whether the *Miranda* Court announced a constitutional rule or merely exercised its supervisory authority to regulate evidence in the absence of congressional direction. Recognizing this point, the Court of Appeals surveyed *Miranda* and its progeny to determine the constitutional status of the *Miranda* decision. Relying on the fact that we have created several exceptions to *Miranda*'s warnings requirement and that we have repeatedly referred to the *Miranda* warnings as "prophylactic," and "not themselves rights protected by the Constitution," the Court of Appeals concluded that the protections announced in *Miranda* are not constitutionally required.

We disagree with the Court of Appeals' conclusion, although we concede that there is language in some of our opinions that supports the view taken by that court. But first and foremost of the factors on the other side—that *Miranda* is a constitutional decision—is that both *Miranda* and two of its companion cases applied the rule to proceedings in state courts—to wit, Arizona, California, and New York. Since that time, we have consistently applied *Miranda*'s rule to prosecutions arising in state courts. It is beyond dispute that we do not hold a supervisory power over the courts of the several States. Smith v. Phillips, 455 U.S. 209, 221 (1982) ("Federal courts hold no supervisory authority over state judicial proceedings and may intervene only to correct wrongs of constitutional dimension"); Cicenia v. Lagay, 357 U.S. 504, 508-509 (1958). With respect to proceedings in state courts, our "authority is limited to enforcing the commands of the United States Constitution." Mu'Min v. Virginia, 500 U.S. 415, 422 (1991).

The *Miranda* opinion itself begins by stating that the Court granted certiorari "to explore some facets of the problems of applying the privilege against self-incrimination to in-custody interrogation, and to give concrete constitutional guidelines for law enforcement agencies and courts to follow." In fact, the majority opinion is replete with statements indicating that the majority thought it was announcing a constitutional rule. Indeed, the Court's ultimate conclusion was that the unwarned confessions obtained in the four cases before the Court in *Miranda* "were obtained from the defendant under circumstances that did not meet constitutional standards for protection of the privilege."

Additional support for our conclusion that *Miranda* is constitutionally based is found in the *Miranda* Court's invitation for legislative action to protect the constitutional right against coerced self-incrimination. After discussing the "compelling pressures" inherent in custodial police interrogation, the *Miranda* Court concluded that, "[i]n order to combat these pressures and to permit a full opportunity to exercise the privilege against self-incrimination, the accused must be adequately and effectively apprised of his rights and the exercise of those rights must be fully honored." However, the Court emphasized that it could not foresee "the potential alternatives for protecting the privilege which might be devised by Congress or the States," and it accordingly opined that the Constitution would not preclude legislative solutions that differed from the prescribed *Miranda* warnings but which were "at least as effective in apprising accused persons of their right of silence and in assuring a continuous opportunity to exercise it."

The Court of Appeals also relied on the fact that we have, after our *Miranda* decision, made exceptions from its rule in cases such as New York v. Quarles, 467 U.S. 649 (1984), and Harris v. New York, 401 U.S. 222 (1971). But we have also broadened the application of the *Miranda* doctrine in cases such as Doyle v. Ohio, 426 U.S. 610 (1976), and Arizona v. Roberson, 486 U.S. 675 (1988). These decisions illustrate the principle—not that *Miranda* is not a constitutional rule—but that no constitutional rule is immutable. No court laying down a general rule can possibly foresee the various circumstances in which counsel will seek to apply it, and the sort of modifications represented by these cases are as much a normal part of constitutional law as the original decision.

The Court of Appeals also noted that in Oregon v. Elstad, 470 U.S. 298 (1985), we stated that " '[t]he *Miranda* exclusionary rule serves the Fifth Amendment and sweeps more broadly than the Fifth Amendment itself.' " Our decision in that case — refusing to apply the traditional "fruits" doctrine developed in Fourth Amendment cases — does not prove that *Miranda* is a nonconstitutional decision, but simply recognizes the fact that unreasonable searches under the Fourth Amendment are different from unwarned interrogation under the Fifth Amendment.

As an alternative argument for sustaining the Court of Appeals' decision, the court-invited amicus curiae contends that the section complies with the requirement that a legislative alternative to *Miranda* be equally as effective in preventing coerced confessions. See Brief for Paul G. Cassell as Amicus Curiae 28-39. We agree with the amicus' contention that there are more remedies available for abusive police conduct than there were at the time *Miranda* was decided. But we do not agree that these additional measures supplement §3501's protections sufficiently to meet the constitutional minimum. *Miranda* requires procedures that will warn a suspect in custody of his right to remain silent and which will assure the suspect that the exercise of that right will be honored. As discussed above, §3501 explicitly eschews a requirement of pre-interrogation warnings in favor of an approach that looks to the administration of such warnings as only one factor in determining the voluntariness of a suspect's confession. The additional remedies cited by amicus do not, in our view, render them, together with §3501 an adequate substitute for the warnings required by *Miranda*.

The dissent argues that it is judicial overreaching for this Court to hold §3501 unconstitutional unless we hold that the *Miranda* warnings are required by the Constitution, in the sense that nothing else will suffice to satisfy constitutional requirements. But we need not go farther than *Miranda* to decide this case. In *Miranda*, the Court noted that reliance on the traditional totality-of-the-circumstances test raised a risk of overlooking an involuntary custodial confession, a risk that the Court found unacceptably great when the confession is offered in the case in chief to prove guilt. The Court therefore concluded that something more than the totality test was necessary. As discussed above, §3501 reinstates the totality test as sufficient. Section 3501 therefore cannot be sustained if *Miranda* is to remain the law.

Whether or not we would agree with *Miranda*'s reasoning and its resulting rule, were we addressing the issue in the first instance, the principles of stare decisis weigh heavily against overruling it now. While " 'stare decisis is not an inexorable command,' " particularly when we are interpreting the Constitution, "even in constitutional cases, the doctrine carries such persuasive force that we have always required a departure from precedent to be supported by some 'special justification.' " United States v. International Business Machines Corp., 517 U.S. 843, 856 (1996).

We do not think there is such justification for overruling *Miranda*. *Miranda* has become embedded in routine police practice to the point where the warnings have become part of our national culture. While we have overruled our precedents when subsequent cases have undermined their doctrinal underpinnings, we do not believe that this has happened to the *Miranda* decision. If anything, our subsequent cases have reduced the impact of the *Miranda* rule on legitimate law enforcement while reaffirming the decision's core ruling that unwarned statements may not be used as evidence in the prosecution's case in chief.

The disadvantage of the *Miranda* rule is that statements which may be by no means involuntary, made by a defendant who is aware of his "rights," may nonetheless be excluded and a guilty defendant go free as a result. But experience suggests that the totality-of-the-circumstances test which §3501 seeks to revive is more difficult than *Miranda* for law enforcement officers to conform to, and for courts to apply in a consistent manner. The requirement that *Miranda* warnings be given does not, of course, dispense with the voluntariness inquiry. But as we said in Berkemer v. McCarty, 468 U.S. 420 (1984), "[c]ases in which a defendant can make a colorable argument that a self-incriminating statement was 'compelled' despite the fact that the law enforcement authorities adhered to the dictates of *Miranda* are rare."

In sum, we conclude that *Miranda* announced a constitutional rule that Congress may not supersede legislatively. Following the rule of stare decisis, we decline to overrule *Miranda* ourselves. The judgment of the Court of Appeals is therefore Reversed.

JUSTICE SCALIA, with whom JUSTICE THOMAS joins, dissenting.

Those to whom judicial decisions are an unconnected series of judgments that produce either favored or disfavored results will doubtless greet today's decision as a paragon of moderation, since it declines to overrule Miranda v. Arizona. Those who understand the judicial process will appreciate that today's decision is not a reaffirmation of *Miranda*, but a radical revision of the most significant element of *Miranda* (as of all cases): the rationale that gives it a permanent place in our jurisprudence.

Marbury v. Madison, 1 Cranch 137 (1803), held that an Act of Congress will not be enforced by the courts if what it prescribes violates the Constitution of the United States. That was the basis on which *Miranda* was decided. One will search today's opinion in vain, however, for a statement (surely simple enough to make) that what 18 U.S.C. §3501 prescribes—the use at trial of a voluntary confession, even when a *Miranda* warning or its equivalent has failed to be given—violates the Constitution. The reason the statement does not appear is not only (and perhaps not so much) that it would be absurd, inasmuch as §3501 excludes from trial precisely what the Constitution excludes from trial, viz., compelled confessions; but also that Justices whose votes are needed to compose today's majority are on record as believing that a violation of *Miranda* is not a violation of the Constitution. See Davis v. United States, 512 U.S. 452, 457-458 (1994) (opinion of the Court, in which Kennedy, J., joined); Duckworth v. Eagan, 492 U.S. 195, 203 (1989) (opinion of the Court, in which Kennedy, J., joined); Oregon v. Elstad, 470 U.S. 298 (1985) (opinion of the Court by O'Connor, J.); New York v. Quarles, 467 U.S. 649 (1984) (opinion of the Court by Rehnquist, J.). And so, to justify today's agreed-upon result, the Court must adopt a significant new, if not entirely comprehensible, principle of constitutional law. As the Court chooses to describe that principle, statutes of Congress can be disregarded, not only when what they prescribe violates the Constitution, but when what they prescribe contradicts a decision of this Court that "announced a constitutional rule." As I shall discuss in some detail, the only thing that can possibly mean in the context of this case is that this Court has the power, not merely to apply the Constitution but to expand it, imposing what it regards as useful "prophylactic" restrictions upon Congress and the States. That is an immense and frightening antidemocratic power, and it does not exist.

It takes only a small step to bring today's opinion out of the realm of power-judging and into the mainstream of legal reasoning: The Court need only go beyond its carefully couched iterations that "*Miranda* is a constitutional decision," that "*Miranda* is constitutionally based," that *Miranda* has "constitutional underpinnings," and come out and say quite clearly: "We reaffirm today that custodial interrogation that is not preceded by *Miranda* warnings or their equivalent violates the Constitution of the United States." It cannot say that, because a majority of the Court does not believe it. The Court therefore acts in plain violation of the Constitution when it denies effect to this Act of Congress.

I

Early in this Nation's history, this Court established the sound proposition that constitutional government in a system of separated powers requires judges to regard as inoperative any legislative act, even of Congress itself, that is "repugnant to the Constitution."

> So if a law be in opposition to the constitution; if both the law and the constitution apply to a particular case, so that the court must either decide that case conformably to the law, disregarding the constitution; or conformably to the constitution, disregarding the law; the court must determine which of these conflicting rules governs the case. *Marbury*, supra, at 178.

The power we recognized in *Marbury* will thus permit us, indeed require us, to "disregar[d]" §3501, a duly enacted statute governing the admissibility of evidence in the federal courts, only if it "be in opposition to the constitution" — here, assertedly, the dictates of the Fifth Amendment.

It was once possible to characterize the so-called *Miranda* rule as resting (however implausibly) upon the proposition that what the statute here before us permits — the admission at trial of un-Mirandized confessions — violates the Constitution. That is the fairest reading of the *Miranda* case itself. The Court began by announcing that the Fifth Amendment privilege against self-incrimination applied in the context of extrajudicial custodial interrogation, see 384 U.S., at 460-467 — itself a doubtful proposition as a matter both of history and precedent, see id., at 510-511 (Harlan, J., dissenting) (characterizing the Court's conclusion that the Fifth Amendment privilege, rather than the Due Process Clause, governed stationhouse confessions as a "trompe l'oeil"). Having extended the privilege into the confines of the station house, the Court liberally sprinkled throughout its sprawling 60-page opinion suggestions that, because of the compulsion inherent in custodial interrogation, the privilege was violated by any statement thus obtained that did not conform to the rules set forth in *Miranda*, or some functional equivalent.

So understood, *Miranda* was objectionable for innumerable reasons, not least the fact that cases spanning more than 70 years had rejected its core premise that, absent the warnings and an effective waiver of the right to remain silent and of the (thitherto unknown) right to have an attorney present, a statement obtained pursuant to custodial interrogation was necessarily the product of compulsion. See Crooker v. California, 357 U.S. 433 (1958) (confession not involuntary despite denial of access to counsel); Cicenia v. Lagay, 357 U.S. 504 (1958) (same); Powers v. United States, 223 U.S. 303 (1912) (lack of warnings and counsel did not render statement before United States Commisioner involuntary); Wilson v. United States, 162 U.S. 613 (1896) (same). Moreover, history and precedent aside, the decision in *Miranda*, if read as an explication of what the Constitution requires, is preposterous. There is, for example, simply no basis in reason for concluding that a response to the very first question asked, by a suspect who already knows all of the rights described in the *Miranda* warning, is anything other than a volitional act. And even if one assumes that the elimination of compulsion absolutely requires informing even the most knowledgeable suspect of his right to remain silent, it cannot conceivably require the right to have counsel present. There is a world of difference, which the Court recognized under the traditional voluntariness test but ignored in *Miranda*, between compelling a suspect to incriminate himself and preventing him from foolishly doing so of his own accord. Only the latter (which is not required by the Constitution) could explain the Court's inclusion of a right to counsel and the requirement that it, too, be knowingly and intelligently waived. Counsel's presence is not required to tell the suspect that he need not speak; the interrogators can do that. The only good reason for having counsel there is that he can be counted on to advise the suspect that he should not speak.

Preventing foolish (rather than compelled) confessions is likewise the only conceivable basis for the rules (suggested in *Miranda*, see 384 U.S., at 444-445, 473-474), that courts must exclude any confession elicited by questioning conducted, without interruption, after the suspect has indicated a desire to stand on his right to remain silent, see Michigan v. Mosley, 423 U.S. 96, 105-106 (1975), or initiated by police after the suspect has expressed a desire to have counsel present, see Edwards v. Arizona, 451 U.S. 477, 484-485 (1981). Nonthreatening attempts to persuade the suspect to reconsider that initial decision are not, without more, enough to render a change of heart the product of anything other than the suspect's free will. Thus, what is most remarkable about the *Miranda* decision — and what made it unacceptable as a matter of straightforward constitutional interpretation in the *Marbury* tradition — is its palpable hostility toward the act of confession per se, rather than toward what the Constitution abhors, compelled confession. The Constitution is not, unlike the *Miranda* majority, offended by a criminal's commendable qualm of conscience or fortunate fit of stupidity.

For these reasons, and others more than adequately developed in the *Miranda* dissents and in the subsequent works of the decision's many critics, any conclusion that a violation of the *Miranda* rules necessarily amounts to a violation of the privilege against compelled self-incrimination can claim no support in history, precedent, or common sense, and as a result would at least presumptively be worth reconsidering even at this late date. But that is unnecessary, since the Court has (thankfully) long since abandoned the notion that failure to comply with *Miranda*'s rules is itself a violation of the Constitution.

II

As the Court today acknowledges, since *Miranda* we have explicitly, and repeatedly, interpreted that decision as having announced, not the circumstances in which custodial interrogation runs afoul of the Fifth or Fourteenth Amendment, but rather only "prophylactic" rules that go beyond the right against compelled self-incrimination. Of course the seeds of this "prophylactic" interpretation of *Miranda* were present in the decision itself. In subsequent cases, the seeds have sprouted and borne fruit: The Court has squarely concluded that it is possible — indeed not uncommon — for the police to violate *Miranda* without also violating the Constitution.

The Court seeks to avoid this conclusion in two ways: First, by misdescribing these post-*Miranda* cases as mere dicta. The Court concedes only "that there is language in some of our opinions that supports the view" that *Miranda*'s protections are not "constitutionally required." It is not a matter of language; it is a matter of holdings. The proposition that failure to comply with *Miranda*'s rules does not establish a constitutional violation was central to the holdings of *Tucker, Hass, Quarles, and Elstad*.

The second way the Court seeks to avoid the impact of these cases is simply to disclaim responsibility for reasoned decisionmaking. It says:

> These decisions illustrate the principle — not that *Miranda* is not a constitutional rule — but that no constitutional rule is immutable. No court laying down a general rule can possibly foresee the various circumstances in which counsel will seek to apply it, and the sort of modifications represented by these cases are as much a normal part of constitutional law as the original decision.

The issue, however, is not whether court rules are "mutable"; they assuredly are. It is not whether, in the light of "various circumstances," they can be "modifi[ed]"; they assuredly can. The issue is whether, as mutated and modified, they must make sense. The requirement that they do so is the only thing that prevents this Court from being some sort of nine-headed Caesar, giving thumbs-up or thumbs-down to whatever outcome, case by case, suits or offends its collective fancy. And if confessions procured in violation of *Miranda* are confessions "compelled" in violation of the Constitution, the post-*Miranda* decisions I have discussed do not make sense. The only reasoned basis for their outcome was that a violation of *Miranda* is not a violation of the Constitution. If, for example, as the Court acknowledges was the holding of *Elstad*, "the traditional 'fruits' doctrine developed in Fourth Amendment cases" (that the fruits of evidence obtained unconstitutionally must be excluded from trial) does not apply to the fruits of *Miranda* violations, and if the reason for the difference is not that *Miranda* violations are not constitutional violations (which is plainly and flatly what *Elstad* said); then the Court must come up with some other explanation for the difference. (That will take quite a bit of doing, by the way, since it is not clear on the face of the Fourth Amendment that evidence obtained in violation of that guarantee must be excluded from trial, whereas it is clear on the face of the Fifth Amendment that unconstitutionally compelled confessions cannot be used.) To say simply that "unreasonable searches under the Fourth Amendment are different from unwarned interrogation under the Fifth Amendment," is true but supremely unhelpful.

Finally, the Court asserts that *Miranda* must be a "constitutional decision" announcing a "constitutional rule," and thus immune to congressional modification, because we have since its inception applied it to the States. If this argument is meant as an invocation of stare decisis, it fails because, though it is true that our cases applying *Miranda* against the States must be reconsidered if *Miranda* is not required by the Constitution, it is likewise true that our cases based on the principle that *Miranda* is not required by the Constitution will have to be reconsidered if it is. So the stare decisis argument is a wash. If, on the other hand, the argument is meant as an appeal to logic rather than stare decisis, it is a classic example of begging the question: Congress's attempt to set aside *Miranda*, since it represents an assertion that violation of *Miranda* is not a violation of the Constitution, also represents an assertion that the Court has no power to impose *Miranda* on the States. To answer this assertion — not by showing why violation of *Miranda* is a violation of the Constitution — but by asserting that *Miranda* does apply against the States, is to assume precisely the point at issue. In my view, our continued application of the *Miranda* code to the States despite our consistent statements that running afoul of its dictates does not necessarily — or even usually — result in an actual constitutional violation, represents not the source of *Miranda*'s salvation but rather evidence of its ultimate illegitimacy. As Justice Stevens has elsewhere explained, "[t]his Court's power to require state courts to exclude probative self-incriminatory statements rests entirely on the premise that the use of such evidence violates the Federal Constitution. If the Court does not accept that premise, it must regard the holding in the *Miranda* case itself, as well as all of the federal jurisprudence that has evolved from that decision, as nothing more than an illegitimate exercise of raw judicial power." *Elstad*, 470 U.S., at 370 (dissenting opinion). Quite so.

III

There was available to the Court a means of reconciling the established proposition that a violation of *Miranda* does not itself offend the Fifth Amendment with the Court's assertion of a right to ignore the present statute. That means of reconciliation was argued strenuously by both petitioner and the United States, who were evidently more concerned than the Court is with maintaining the coherence of our jurisprudence. It is not mentioned in the Court's opinion because, I assume, a majority of the Justices intent on reversing believes that incoherence is the lesser evil. They may be right.

Petitioner and the United States contend that there is nothing at all exceptional, much less unconstitutional, about the Court's adopting prophylactic rules to buttress constitutional rights, and enforcing them against Congress and the States. Indeed, the United States argues that "[p]rophylactic rules are now and have been for many years a feature of this Court's constitutional adjudication." That statement is not wholly inaccurate, if by "many years" one means since the mid-1960s. However, in their zeal to validate what is in my view a lawless practice, the United States and petitioner greatly overstate the frequency with which we have engaged in it. For instance, petitioner cites several cases in which the Court quite simply exercised its traditional judicial power to define the scope of constitutional protections and, relatedly, the circumstances in which they are violated.

Similarly unsupportive of the supposed practice is Bruton v. United States, 391 U.S. 123 (1968), where we concluded that the Confrontation Clause of the Sixth Amendment forbids the admission of a nontestifying co-defendant's facially incriminating confession in a joint trial, even where the jury has been given a limiting instruction. That decision was based, not upon the theory that this was desirable protection "beyond" what the Confrontation Clause technically required; but rather upon the self-evident proposition that the inability to cross-examine an available witness whose damaging out-of-court testimony is introduced violates the Confrontation Clause, combined with the conclusion that in these circumstances a mere jury instruction can never be relied upon to prevent the testimony from being damaging, see Richardson v. Marsh, 481 U.S. 200, 207-208 (1987). . . .

Petitioner and the United States are right on target, however, in characterizing the Court's actions in a case decided within a few years of *Miranda*, North Carolina v. Pearce, 395 U.S. 711 (1969). There, the Court concluded that due process would be offended were a judge vindictively to resentence with added severity a defendant who had successfully appealed his original conviction. Rather than simply announce that vindictive sentencing violates the Due Process Clause, the Court went on to hold that "[i]n order to assure the absence of such a [vindictive] motivation, . . . the reasons for [imposing the increased sentence] must affirmatively appear" and must "be based upon objective information concerning identifiable conduct on the part of the defendant occurring after the time of the original sentencing proceeding." The Court later explicitly acknowledged *Pearce*'s prophylactic character, see Michigan v. Payne, 412 U.S. 47, 53 (1973). It is true, therefore, that the case exhibits the same fundamental flaw as does *Miranda* when deprived (as it has been) of its original (implausible) pretension to announcement of what the Constitution itself required. That is, although the Due Process Clause may well prohibit punishment based on judicial vindictiveness, the Constitution by no means vests in the courts "any general power to prescribe particular devices 'in order to assure the absence of such a motivation,'" 395 U.S., at 741 (Black, J., dissenting). Justice Black surely had the right idea when he derided the Court's requirement as "pure legislation if there ever was legislation," ibid., although in truth *Pearce*'s rule pales as a legislative achievement when compared to the detailed code promulgated in *Miranda*.

The foregoing demonstrates that, petitioner's and the United States' suggestions to the contrary notwithstanding, what the Court did in *Miranda* (assuming, as later cases hold, that *Miranda* went beyond what the Constitution actually requires) is in fact extraordinary. That the Court has, on rare and recent occasion, repeated the mistake does not transform error into truth, but illustrates the potential for future mischief that the error entails. Where the Constitution has wished to lodge in one of the branches of the Federal Government some limited power to supplement its guarantees, it has said so. See Amdt. 14, §5 ("The Congress shall have power to enforce, by appropriate legislation, the provisions of this article"). The power with which the Court would endow itself under a "prophylactic" justification for *Miranda* goes far beyond what it has permitted Congress to do under authority of that text. Whereas we have insisted that congressional action under §5 of the Fourteenth Amendment must be "congruent" with, and "proportional" to, a constitutional violation, see City of Boerne v. Flores, 521 U.S. 507, 520 (1997), the *Miranda* nontextual power to embellish confers authority to prescribe preventive measures against not only constitutionally prohibited compelled confessions, but also (as discussed earlier) foolhardy ones.

I applaud, therefore, the refusal of the Justices in the majority to enunciate this boundless doctrine of judicial empowerment as a means of rendering today's decision rational. In nonetheless joining the Court's judgment, however, they overlook two truisms: that actions speak louder than silence, and that (in judge-made law at least) logic will out. Since there is in fact no other principle that can reconcile today's judgment with the post-*Miranda* cases that the Court refuses to abandon, what today's decision will stand for, whether the Justices can bring themselves to say it or not, is the power of the Supreme Court to write a prophylactic, extraconstitutional Constitution, binding on Congress and the States.

IV

Thus, while I agree with the Court that §3501 cannot be upheld without also concluding that *Miranda* represents an illegitimate exercise of our authority to review state-court judgments, I do not share the Court's hesitation in reaching that conclusion. For while the Court is also correct that the doctrine of stare decisis demands some "special justification" for a departure from longstanding precedent — even precedent of the constitutional variety — that criterion is more than met here. To repeat Justice Stevens' cogent observation, it is "[o]bviou[s]" that "the Court's power to reverse Miranda's conviction rested *entirely* on the determination that a violation of the Federal Constitution had occurred." *Elstad*, 470 U.S., at 367, n. 9 (dissenting opinion) (emphasis added). Despite the Court's Orwellian assertion to the contrary, it is undeniable that later cases (discussed above) have "undermined [*Miranda*'s] doctrinal underpinnings," denying constitutional violation and thus stripping the holding of its only constitutionally legitimate support. *Miranda*'s critics and supporters alike have long made this point. . . .

Neither am I persuaded by the argument for retaining *Miranda* that touts its supposed workability as compared with the totality-of-the-circumstances test it purported to replace. *Miranda*'s proponents cite ad nauseam the fact that the Court was called upon to make difficult and subtle distinctions in applying the "voluntariness" test in some 30-odd due process "coerced confessions" cases in the 30 years between Brown v. Mississippi, 297 U.S. 278 (1936), and *Miranda*. It is not immediately apparent, however, that the judicial burden has been eased by the "bright-line" rules adopted in *Miranda*. In fact, in the 34 years since *Miranda* was decided, this Court has been called upon to decide nearly 60 cases involving a host of *Miranda* issues, most of them predicted with remarkable prescience by Justice White in his *Miranda* dissent.

Moreover, it is not clear why the Court thinks that the "totality-of-the-circumstances test is more difficult than *Miranda* for law enforcement officers to conform to, and for courts to apply in a consistent manner."

But even were I to agree that the old totality-of-the-circumstances test was more cumbersome, it is simply not true that *Miranda* has banished it from the law and replaced it with a new test. Under the current regime, which the Court today retains in its entirety, courts are frequently called upon to undertake both inquiries. That is because, as explained earlier, voluntariness remains the constitutional standard, and as such continues to govern the admissibility for impeachment purposes of statements taken in violation of *Miranda*, the admissibility of the "fruits" of such statements, and the admissibility of statements challenged as unconstitutionally obtained despite the interrogator's compliance with *Miranda*.

Finally, I am not convinced by petitioner's argument that *Miranda* should be preserved because the decision occupies a special place in the "public's consciousness." Brief for Petitioner 44. As far as I am aware, the public is not under the illusion that we are infallible. I see little harm in admitting that we made a mistake in taking away from the people the ability to decide for themselves what protections (beyond those required by the Constitution) are reasonably affordable in the criminal investigatory process. And I see much to be gained by reaffirming for the people the wonderful reality that they govern themselves—which means that "[t]he powers not delegated to the United States by the Constitution" that the people adopted, "nor prohibited . . . to the States" by that Constitution, "are reserved to the States respectively, or to the people," U.S. Const., Amdt. 10. . . .

Today's judgment converts *Miranda* from a milestone of judicial overreaching into the very Cheops' Pyramid (or perhaps the Sphinx would be a better analogue) of judicial arrogance. In imposing its Court-made code upon the States, the original opinion at least asserted that it was demanded by the Constitution. Today's decision does not pretend that it is—and yet still asserts the right to impose it against the will of the people's representatives in Congress. Far from believing that stare decisis compels this result, I believe we cannot allow to remain on the books even a celebrated decision—especially a celebrated decision—that has come to stand for the proposition that the Supreme Court has power to impose extraconstitutional constraints upon Congress and the States. This is not the system that was established by the Framers, or that would be established by any sane supporter of government by the people.

I dissent from today's decision, and, until §3501 is repealed, will continue to apply it in all cases where there has been a sustainable finding that the defendant's confession was voluntary.

NOTES AND QUESTIONS

1. Did Chief Justice Rehnquist change his mind between the time he wrote the majority opinions in *Tucker* and *Quarles* and the time he wrote the majority opinion in *Dickerson*? Is there any way to square those decisions?

2. Reread the last sentence of Justice Scalia's dissent. Is it proper for a Supreme Court Justice to announce that he will not follow binding precedent?

3. Justice Scalia argues that, because *Miranda* cannot be justified by the Fifth Amendment privilege against self-incrimination, it amounts to "a prophylactic, extraconstitutional Constitution, binding on Congress and the States." Might *Miranda* instead be justified as an application of the Fourteenth Amendment's due process clause? Recall that, for 30 years prior to *Miranda*, the Court had struggled to draw lines between voluntary and involuntary confessions; the failure of that enterprise was the key factor precipitating the Court's decision in *Miranda*. Perhaps the real problem with *Miranda* was that the Court relied on the wrong piece of constitutional language. After all, if voluntariness is a constitutional requirement (a proposition that the Court and Justice Scalia both accept) and if voluntariness is difficult to determine after the fact (which seems hard to deny), courts presumably have the authority to craft legal rules that will ensure that only voluntary confessions are admitted into evidence. Might *Miranda*'s rules

fit that description? Most suspects continue to talk to the police, but they do so after being informed that they may remain silent, as Justice Scalia would agree they may.

And current *Miranda* doctrine clearly aims at preventing coercive police interrogation tactics — the same aim that motivates voluntariness doctrine. Illinois v. Perkins, 496 U.S. 292 (1990), holds that if a police officer pretends to be something other than a police officer and thereby induces a suspect to talk, the conversation falls outside of *Miranda*. Moran v. Burbine, 475 U.S. 412 (1986), seems to permit *Miranda* waivers in the face of deceptive police questioning. Whatever the *Miranda* Court intended, *Miranda* doctrine today serves as a kind of indirect voluntariness doctrine.

4. On the other hand, if *Miranda* guards against involuntary confessions, the current warnings and the current invocation rules are hard to justify, are they not? A due process-based *Miranda* rule might better justify warnings like these: "You have the right to remain silent. I have the right to ask you questions. If you do not wish to answer, you do not have to. And if you want questioning to stop, it will stop — for awhile." Would that be a better regime?

5. Assuming that some piece of constitutional text justifies *Miranda*, is it a wise piece of constitutional decision making? Supreme Court Justices do not know much about police interrogation. Historically, very few Justices have had any experience in criminal litigation before they became judges. And very few Justices serve as trial judges before they join the Court. What they know about police questioning depends on what they read — chiefly, briefs and judicial opinions. Is that an adequate grounding in the subject for the men and women who design the regulation of police interrogation?

One might respond that there is no alternative: The police will not respect suspects' interests on their own, and elected officials will not force them to do so. That pair of assumptions was reasonable at the time *Miranda* was decided, and at the time §3501 was enacted. Is it reasonable today? Even after the terrorist attacks of September 11, 2001, there is broad political support for civil liberties in the United States — broader in most respects than in the 1960s. And recent scandals involving military interrogation of prisoners in Iraq would seem to indicate that the public generally supports protections against the abuse of suspects and defendants. Should police interrogation be left to Congress and state legislatures?

6. Is *Dickerson* consistent with Harris v. New York, 401 U.S. 222 (1971)? *Harris* held that voluntary statements obtained in violation of *Miranda* may be used to impeach a defendant's trial testimony:

> . . . Petitioner's testimony in his own behalf concerning the events of January 7 contrasted sharply with what he told the police shortly after his arrest. The impeachment process here undoubtedly provided valuable aid to the jury in assessing petitioner's credibility, and the benefits of this process should not be lost, in our view, because of the speculative possibility that impermissible police conduct will be encouraged thereby. Assuming that the exclusionary rule has a deterrent effect on proscribed police conduct, sufficient deterrence flows when the evidence in question is made unavailable to the prosecution in its case in chief.
>
> Every criminal defendant is privileged to testify in his own defense, or to refuse to do so. But that privilege cannot be construed to include the right to commit perjury. Having voluntarily taken the stand, petitioner was under an obligation to

speak truthfully and accurately, and the prosecution here did no more than utilize the traditional truth-testing devices of the adversary process. . . .

The shield provided by *Miranda* cannot be perverted into a license to use perjury by way of a defense, free from the risk of confrontation with prior inconsistent utterances. We hold, therefore, that petitioner's credibility was appropriately impeached by use of his earlier conflicting statements.

If all *Miranda* violations are Fifth Amendment violations, how can it be appropriate to admit such statements for *any* purpose?

7. In Doyle v. Ohio, 426 U.S. 610 (1976), two defendants charged with sale of marijuana testified at trial that they had been framed by the government informant who had allegedly made the purchase. On cross-examination, each defendant was questioned about why he didn't give his exculpatory story to the police at the time of arrest. Before the Supreme Court, the state attempted to justify this line of questioning on the theory that the defendants' postarrest silence was inconsistent with their trial testimony and thus admissible to impeach their credibility. The Supreme Court disagreed and held that the impeachment use of the defendants' postarrest silence following *Miranda* warnings violated their right to due process:

> Silence in the wake of these warnings may be nothing more than an arrestee's exercise of these *Miranda* rights. Thus, every post-arrest silence is insolubly ambiguous because of what the State is required to advise the person arrested. Moreover, while it is true that the *Miranda* warnings contain no express assurance that silence will carry no penalty, such assurance is implicit to any person who receives the warnings. In such circumstances, it would be fundamentally unfair . . . to allow the arrested person's silence to be used to impeach an explanation subsequently offered at trial.

Id. at 617-618. In Jenkins v. Anderson, 447 U.S. 231 (1980), where a murder defendant testified at trial that the killing was in self-defense, the Court found no constitutional barrier to questions on cross-examination about why the defendant had remained silent and not reported the matter to the police during the two weeks between the killing and the time that he turned himself in to the authorities. According to the Court, "In this case, no governmental action induced petitioner to remain silent before arrest. The failure to speak occurred before the petitioner was taken into custody and given *Miranda* warnings. Consequently, the fundamental unfairness present in *Doyle* is not present in this case." Id. at 240.

Are *Doyle* and *Jenkins* consistent with *Harris*? Do these decisions comport with *Miranda*'s constitutional status as described in *Dickerson*?

8. Oregon v. Elstad, 470 U.S. 298 (1985) — one of the decisions in which the Court expressly declared that *Miranda* was something other than a constitutional mandate — raised the question whether the fruits of *Miranda* violations were admissible. The defendant in *Elstad* made incriminating statements to the police prior to receiving *Miranda* warnings; subsequently, he was warned and gave the police a written confession. Reasoning that "a careful and thorough administration of *Miranda* warnings serves to cure the condition that rendered the unwarned statement inadmissible," id. at 310-311, the Court found Elstad's confession admissible. Four years after *Dickerson*, the Court again considered the status of the fruits of *Miranda* violations.

MISSOURI v. SEIBERT

Certiorari to the Supreme Court of Missouri
124 S. Ct. 2601 (2004)

JUSTICE SOUTER announced the judgment of the Court and delivered an opinion, in which JUSTICE STEVENS, JUSTICE GINSBURG, and JUSTICE BREYER join.

This case tests a police protocol for custodial interrogation that calls for giving no warnings of the rights to silence and counsel until interrogation has produced a confession. . . .

Respondent Patrice Seibert's 12-year-old son Jonathan had cerebral palsy, and when he died in his sleep she feared charges of neglect because of bedsores on his body. In her presence, two of her teenage sons and two of their friends devised a plan to conceal the facts surrounding Jonathan's death by incinerating his body in the course of burning the family's mobile home, in which they planned to leave Donald Rector, a mentally ill teenager living with the family, to avoid any appearance that Jonathan had been unattended. Seibert's son Darian and a friend set the fire, and Donald died.

Five days later, the police awakened Seibert at 3 a.m. at a hospital where Darian was being treated for burns. In arresting her, Officer Kevin Clinton followed instructions from Rolla, Missouri, officer Richard Hanrahan that he refrain from giving *Miranda* warnings. After Seibert had been taken to the police station and left alone in an interview room for 15 to 20 minutes, Hanrahan questioned her without *Miranda* warnings for 30 to 40 minutes, squeezing her arm and repeating "Donald was also to die in his sleep." After Seibert finally admitted she knew Donald was meant to die in the fire, she was given a 20-minute coffee and cigarette break. Officer Hanrahan then turned on a tape recorder, gave Seibert the *Miranda* warnings, and obtained a signed waiver of rights from her. He resumed the questioning with "Ok, 'Ttrice, we've been talking for a little while about what happened on Wednesday the twelfth, haven't we?," and confronted her with her prewarning statements:

> *Hanrahan:* "Now, in discussion you told us, you told us that there was an understanding about Donald."
> *Seibert:* "Yes."
> *Hanrahan:* "Did that take place earlier that morning?"
> *Seibert:* "Yes."
> *Hanrahan:* "And what was the understanding about Donald?"
> *Seibert:* "If they could get him out of the trailer, to take him out of the trailer."
> *Hanrahan:* "And if they couldn't?"
> *Seibert:* "I, I never even thought about it. I just figured they would."
> *Hanrahan:* " 'Trice, didn't you tell me that he was supposed to die in his sleep?"
> *Seibert:* "If that would happen, 'cause he was on that new medicine, you know. . . . "
> *Hanrahan:* "The Prozac? And it makes him sleepy. So he was supposed to die in his sleep?"
> *Seibert:* "Yes."

After being charged with first-degree murder for her role in Donald's death, Seibert sought to exclude both her prewarning and postwarning statements. At the suppression hearing, Officer Hanrahan testified that he made a "conscious decision" to withhold *Miranda* warnings, thus resorting to an interrogation technique he had been taught: question first, then give the warnings, and then repeat the question "until I get the answer that she's already provided once." He acknowledged that Seibert's ultimate statement was "largely a repeat of information . . . obtained" prior to the warning.

The trial court suppressed the prewarning statement but admitted the responses given after the *Miranda* recitation. A jury convicted Seibert of second-degree murder. On appeal, the Missouri Court of Appeals affirmed, treating this case as indistinguishable from Oregon v. Elstad, 470 U.S. 298 (1985).

The Supreme Court of Missouri reversed, holding that "in the circumstances here, where the interrogation was nearly continuous, . . . the second statement, clearly the product of the invalid first statement, should have been suppressed." 93 S.W.3d 700, 701 (2002). . . .

We granted certiorari . . . We now affirm.

. . . "[T]o reduce the risk of a coerced confession and to implement the Self-Incrimination Clause," Chavez v. Martinez, 538 U.S. 760, 790 (2003) (KENNEDY, J., concurring in part and dissenting in part), this Court in *Miranda* concluded that "the accused must be adequately and effectively apprised of his rights and the exercise of those rights must be fully honored," 384 U.S., at 467. *Miranda* conditioned the admissibility at trial of any custodial confession on warning a suspect of his rights: failure to give the prescribed warnings and obtain a waiver of rights before custodial questioning generally requires exclusion of any statements obtained. Conversely, giving the warnings and getting a waiver has generally produced a virtual ticket of admissibility; maintaining that a statement is involuntary even though given after warnings and voluntary waiver of rights requires unusual stamina, and litigation over voluntariness tends to end with the finding of a valid waiver. See Berkemer v. McCarty, 468 U.S. 420, 433, n. 20 (1984) ("Cases in which a defendant can make a colorable argument that a self-incriminating statement was 'compelled' despite the fact that the law enforcement authorities adhered to the dictates of *Miranda* are rare"). . . . [T]his common consequence would not be common at all were it not that *Miranda* warnings are customarily given under circumstances allowing for a real choice between talking and remaining silent.

There are those, of course, who preferred the old way of doing things, giving no warnings and litigating the voluntariness of any statement in nearly every instance. In the aftermath of *Miranda*, Congress even passed a statute seeking to restore that old regime, 18 U.S.C. §3501, although the Act lay dormant for years until finally invoked and challenged in Dickerson v. United States, [530 U.S. 428 (2000)]. *Dickerson* reaffirmed *Miranda* and held that its constitutional character prevailed against the statute.

The technique of interrogating in successive, unwarned and warned phases raises a new challenge to *Miranda*. Although we have no statistics on the frequency of this practice, it is not confined to Rolla, Missouri. An officer of that police department testified that the strategy of withholding *Miranda* warnings until after interrogating and drawing out a confession was promoted not only by his own department, but by a national police training organization and other departments in which he had worked. Consistently with the officer's testimony, the Police Law Institute, for example, instructs that "officers may conduct a two-stage interrogation. . . . At any point during the pre-*Miranda* interrogation, usually after arrestees have confessed, officers may then read the *Miranda* warnings and ask for a waiver. If the arrestees waive their *Miranda* rights, officers will be able to repeat any *subsequent* incriminating statements later in court." Police Law Institute, Illinois Police Law Manual 83 (Jan. 2001-Dec. 2003).[2] The upshot of all this advice is a question-first practice of some popularity. . . .

. . . *Miranda* addressed "interrogation practices . . . likely . . . to disable [an individual] from making a free and rational choice" about speaking, 384 U.S., at 464-465, and held that a suspect must be "adequately and effectively" advised of the choice the Constitution guarantees, id., at 467. The object of question-first is to render *Miranda* warnings ineffective by waiting for a particularly opportune time to give them, after the suspect has already confessed.

Just as "no talismanic incantation [is] required to satisfy [*Miranda*'s] strictures," California v. Prysock, 453 U.S. 355, 359 (1981) (per curiam), it would be absurd to think that mere recitation of the litany suffices to satisfy *Miranda* in every conceivable circumstance. "The inquiry is simply whether the warnings reasonably 'convey to [a suspect] his rights as required by *Miranda*.'" Duckworth v. Eagan, 492 U.S. 195, 203 (1989) (quoting *Prysock*, supra, at 361). The threshold issue when interrogators question first and warn later is thus whether it would be reasonable to find that in these circumstances the warnings could function "effectively" as *Miranda* requires. Could the warnings effectively advise the suspect that he had a real choice about giving an admissible statement at that juncture? Could they reasonably convey that he could choose to stop talking even if he had talked earlier? For unless the warnings could place a suspect who has just been interrogated in a position to make such an informed choice, there is no practical justification for accepting the formal warnings as compliance with *Miranda*, or for treating the second stage of interrogation as distinct from the first, unwarned and inadmissible segment.[4]

There is no doubt about the answer that proponents of question-first give to this

2. Emphasizing the impeachment exception to the *Miranda* rule approved by this Court, Harris v. New York, 401 U.S. 222 (1971), some training programs advise officers to omit *Miranda* warnings altogether or to continue questioning after the suspect invokes his rights. See, e.g., Police Law Manual 83 ("There is no need to give a *Miranda* warning before asking questions if . . . the answers given . . . will not be required by the prosecutor during the prosecution's case-in-chief"); California Commission on Peace Officer Standards and Training, Video Training Programs for California Law Enforcement, *Miranda*: Post-Invocation Questioning (broadcast July 11, 1996) ("We . . . have been encouraging you to continue to question a suspect after they've invoked their *Miranda* rights"); D. Zulawski & D. Wicklander, Practical Aspects of Interview and Interrogation 50-51 (2d ed. 2002) (describing the practice of "beachheading" as useful for impeachment purpose (emphasis deleted)); see also Weisselberg, Saving *Miranda*, 84 Cornell L. Rev. 109, 110, 132-139 (1998) (collecting California training materials encouraging questioning "outside *Miranda*"). This training is reflected in the reported cases involving deliberate questioning after invocation of *Miranda* rights. See, e.g., California Attorneys for Criminal Justice v. Butts, 195 F.3d 1039, 1042-1044 (CA9 2000); People v. Neal, 31 Cal. 4th 63, 68, 72 P.3d 280, 282 (2003). Scholars have noted the growing trend of such practices. See, e.g., Leo, Questioning the Relevance of *Miranda* in the Twenty-First Century, 99 Mich. L. Rev. 1000, 1010 (2001); Weisselberg, In the Stationhouse After *Dickerson*, 99 Mich. L. Rev. 1121, 1123-1154 (2001). . . .

4. Respondent Seibert argues that her second confession should be excluded from evidence under the doctrine known by the metaphor of the "fruit of the poisonous tree," developed in the Fourth Amendment context in Wong Sun v. United States, 371 U.S. 471 (1963): evidence otherwise admissible but discovered as a result of an earlier violation is excluded as tainted, lest the law encourage future violations. But the Court in *Elstad* rejected the *Wong Sun* fruits doctrine for analyzing the admissibility of a subsequent warned confession following "an initial failure . . . to administer the warnings required by *Miranda*." *Elstad*, 470 U.S., at 300 . . . *Elstad* held that "a suspect who has once responded to unwarned yet uncoercive questioning is not thereby disabled from waiving his rights and confessing after he has been given the requisite *Miranda* warnings." Id., at 318. In a sequential confession case, clarity is served if the later confession is approached by asking whether in the circumstances the *Miranda* warnings given

question about the effectiveness of warnings given only after successful interrogation, and we think their answer is correct. By any objective measure, applied to circumstances exemplified here, it is likely that if the interrogators employ the technique of withholding warnings until after interrogation succeeds in eliciting a confession, the warnings will be ineffective in preparing the suspect for successive interrogation, close in time and similar in content. After all, the reason that question-first is catching on is as obvious as its manifest purpose, which is to get a confession the suspect would not make if he understood his rights at the outset; the sensible underlying assumption is that with one confession in hand before the warnings, the interrogator can count on getting its duplicate, with trifling additional trouble. Upon hearing warnings only in the aftermath of interrogation and just after making a confession, a suspect would hardly think he had a genuine right to remain silent, let alone persist in so believing once the police began to lead him over the same ground again. A more likely reaction on a suspect's part would be perplexity about the reason for discussing rights at that point, bewilderment being an unpromising frame of mind for knowledgeable decision. . . . By the same token, it would ordinarily be unrealistic to treat two spates of integrated and proximately conducted questioning as independent interrogations subject to independent evaluation simply because *Miranda* warnings formally punctuate them in the middle.

Missouri argues that a confession repeated at the end of an interrogation sequence envisioned in a question-first strategy is admissible on the authority of *Oregon v. Elstad*, 470 U.S. 298 (1985), but the argument disfigures that case. In *Elstad*, the police went to the young suspect's house to take him into custody on a charge of burglary. Before the arrest, one officer spoke with the suspect's mother, while the other one joined the suspect in a "brief stop in the living room," id., at 315, where the officer said he "felt" the young man was involved in a burglary, id., at 301. The suspect acknowledged he had been at the scene. This Court noted that the pause in the living room "was not to interrogate the suspect but to notify his mother of the reason for his arrest," id., at 315, and described the incident as having "none of the earmarks of coercion," id., at 316. The Court, indeed, took care to mention that the officer's initial failure to warn was an "oversight" that "may have been the result of confusion as to whether the brief exchange qualified as 'custodial interrogation' or . . . may simply have reflected . . . reluctance to initiate an alarming police procedure before [an officer] had spoken with respondent's mother." Id., at 315-316. At the outset of a later and systematic station house interrogation going well beyond the scope of the laconic prior admission, the suspect was given *Miranda* warnings and made a full confession. *Elstad*, supra, at 301, 314-315. In holding the second statement admissible and voluntary, *Elstad* rejected the "cat out of the bag" theory that any short, earlier admission, obtained in arguably innocent neglect of *Miranda*, determined the character of the later, warned confession, *Elstad*, 470 U.S., at 311-314; on the facts of that case, the Court thought any causal connection between the first and second responses to the police was "speculative and attenuated," id., at 313. Although the *Elstad* Court expressed

---

could reasonably be found effective. If yes, a court can take up the standard issues of voluntary waiver and voluntary statement; if no, the subsequent statement is inadmissible for want of adequate *Miranda* warnings, because the earlier and later statements are realistically seen as parts of a single, unwarned sequence of questioning.

no explicit conclusion about either officer's state of mind, it is fair to read *Elstad* as treating the living room conversation as a good-faith *Miranda* mistake, not only open to correction by careful warnings before systematic questioning in that particular case, but posing no threat to warn-first practice generally. . . .

The contrast between *Elstad* and this case reveals a series of relevant facts that bear on whether *Miranda* warnings delivered midstream could be effective enough to accomplish their object: the completeness and detail of the questions and answers in the first round of interrogation, the overlapping content of the two statements, the timing and setting of the first and the second, the continuity of police personnel, and the degree to which the interrogator's questions treated the second round as continuous with the first. In *Elstad*, it was not unreasonable to see the occasion for questioning at the station house as presenting a markedly different experience from the short conversation at home; since a reasonable person in the suspect's shoes could have seen the station house questioning as a new and distinct experience, the *Miranda* warnings could have made sense as presenting a genuine choice whether to follow up on the earlier admission.

At the opposite extreme are the facts here, which by any objective measure reveal a police strategy adapted to undermine the *Miranda* warnings. The unwarned interrogation was conducted in the station house, and the questioning was systematic, exhaustive, and managed with psychological skill. When the police were finished there was little, if anything, of incriminating potential left unsaid. The warned phase of questioning proceeded after a pause of only 15 to 20 minutes, in the same place as the unwarned segment. . . . [T]he same officer who had conducted the first phase recited the *Miranda* warnings . . . [T]he police did not advise that her prior statement could not be used.[7] . . . [A]ny uncertainty on her part about a right to stop talking about matters previously discussed would only have been aggravated by the way Officer Hanrahan set the scene by saying "we've been talking for a little while about what happened on Wednesday the twelfth, haven't we?" The impression that the further questioning was a mere continuation of the earlier questions and responses was fostered by references back to the confession already given. It would have been reasonable to regard the two sessions as parts of a continuum, in which it would have been unnatural to refuse to repeat at the second stage what had been said before. These circumstances must be seen as challenging the comprehensibility and efficacy of the *Miranda* warnings to the point that a reasonable person in the suspect's shoes would not have understood them to convey a message that she retained a choice about continuing to talk.[8]

Strategists dedicated to draining the substance out of *Miranda* cannot accomplish by training instructions what *Dickerson* held Congress could not do by statute. Because the question-first tactic effectively threatens to thwart *Miranda*'s purpose of reducing the risk that a coerced confession would be admitted, and because the facts here do not reasonably support a conclusion that the warnings given could have served their purpose, Seibert's postwarning statements are inadmissible. . . .

7. We do not hold that a formal addendum warning that a previous statement could not be used would be sufficient to change the character of the question-first procedure to the point of rendering an ensuing statement admissible, but its absence is clearly a factor that blunts the efficacy of the warnings and points to a continuing, not a new, interrogation.

8. Because we find that the warnings were inadequate, there is no need to assess the actual voluntariness of the statement.

JUSTICE BREYER, concurring.

In my view, the following simple rule should apply to the two-stage interrogation technique: Courts should exclude the "fruits" of the initial unwarned questioning unless the failure to warn was in good faith. Cf. Oregon v. Elstad, 470 U.S. 298, 309, 318, n. 5 (1985); United States v. Leon, 468 U.S. 897 (1984). I believe this is a sound and workable approach to the problem this case presents. Prosecutors and judges have long understood how to apply the "fruits" approach, which they use in other areas of law. See Wong Sun v. United States, 371 U.S. 471 (1963). And in the workaday world of criminal law enforcement the administrative simplicity of the familiar has significant advantages over a more complex exclusionary rule.

I believe the plurality's approach in practice will function as a "fruits" test. The truly "effective" *Miranda* warnings on which the plurality insists will occur only when certain circumstances — a lapse in time, a change in location or interrogating officer, or a shift in the focus of the questioning — intervene between the unwarned questioning and any postwarning statement. . . .

I consequently join the plurality's opinion in full. I also agree with JUSTICE KENNEDY's opinion insofar as it is consistent with this approach and makes clear that a good-faith exception applies.

JUSTICE KENNEDY, concurring in the judgment.

. . . The *Miranda* rule has become an important and accepted element of the criminal justice system. At the same time, not every violation of the rule requires suppression of the evidence obtained. Evidence is admissible when the central concerns of *Miranda* are not likely to be implicated and when other objectives of the criminal justice system are best served by its introduction. Thus, we have held that statements obtained in violation of the rule can be used for impeachment, so that the truth finding function of the trial is not distorted by the defense, see Harris v. New York, 401 U.S. 222 (1971); that there is an exception to protect countervailing concerns of public safety, see New York v. Quarles, 467 U.S. 649 (1984); and that physical evidence obtained in reliance on statements taken in violation of the rule is admissible, see United States v. Patane, [124 S. Ct. 2620 (2004)]. These cases, in my view, are correct. They recognize that admission of evidence is proper when it would further important objectives without compromising *Miranda*'s central concerns. Under these precedents, the scope of the *Miranda* suppression remedy depends on a consideration of those legitimate interests and on whether admission of the evidence under the circumstances would frustrate *Miranda*'s central concerns and objectives.

Oregon v. Elstad, 470 U.S. 298 (1985), reflects this approach. In *Elstad*, a suspect made an initial incriminating statement at his home. The suspect had not received a *Miranda* warning before making the statement, apparently because it was not clear whether the suspect was in custody at the time. The suspect was taken to the station house, where he received a proper warning, waived his *Miranda* rights, and made a second statement. He later argued that the postwarning statement should be suppressed because it was related to the unwarned first statement, and likely induced or caused by it. The Court held that, although a *Miranda* violation made the first statement inadmissible, the postwarning statements could be introduced against the accused because "neither the general goal of deterring improper police conduct nor the Fifth Amendment goal of assuring trustworthy evidence would be served by suppression" given the facts of that case. *Elstad*, supra, at 308.

In my view, *Elstad* was correct in its reasoning and its result. *Elstad* reflects a balanced and pragmatic approach to enforcement of the *Miranda* warning. An officer may not realize that a suspect is in custody and warnings are required. The officer may not plan to question the suspect or may be waiting for a more appropriate time. Skilled investigators often interview suspects multiple times, and good police work may involve referring to prior statements to test their veracity or to refresh recollection. In light of these realities it would be extravagant to treat the presence of one statement that cannot be admitted under *Miranda* as sufficient reason to prohibit subsequent statements preceded by a proper warning. . . . That approach would serve "neither the general goal of deterring improper police conduct nor the Fifth Amendment goal of assuring trustworthy evidence would be served by suppression of the . . . testimony." Id., at 308.

This case presents different considerations. The police used a two-step questioning technique based on a deliberate violation of *Miranda*. The *Miranda* warning was withheld to obscure both the practical and legal significance of the admonition when finally given. As JUSTICE SOUTER points out, the two-step technique permits the accused to conclude that the right not to respond did not exist when the earlier incriminating statements were made. The strategy is based on the assumption that *Miranda* warnings will tend to mean less when recited midinterrogation, after inculpatory statements have already been obtained. This tactic relies on an intentional misrepresentation of the protection that *Miranda* offers and does not serve any legitimate objectives that might otherwise justify its use.

Further, the interrogating officer here relied on the defendant's prewarning statement to obtain the postwarning statement used against her at trial. The postwarning interview resembled a cross-examination. The officer confronted the defendant with her inadmissible prewarning statements and pushed her to acknowledge them. See App. 70 ("Trice, didn't you tell me that he was supposed to die in his sleep?"). This shows the temptations for abuse inherent in the two-step technique. Reference to the prewarning statement was an implicit suggestion that the mere repetition of the earlier statement was not independently incriminating. The implicit suggestion was false.

. . . The *Miranda* rule would be frustrated were we to allow police to undermine its meaning and effect. The technique simply creates too high a risk that postwarning statements will be obtained when a suspect was deprived of "knowledge essential to his ability to understand the nature of his rights and the consequences of abandoning them." Moran v. Burbine, 475 U.S. 412, 423-424 (1986). When an interrogator uses this deliberate, two-step strategy, predicated upon violating *Miranda* during an extended interview, postwarning statements that are related to the substance of prewarning statements must be excluded absent specific, curative steps.

The plurality concludes that whenever a two-stage interview occurs, admissibility of the postwarning statement should depend on "whether the *Miranda* warnings delivered midstream could have been effective enough to accomplish their object" given the specific facts of the case. This test envisions an objective inquiry from the perspective of the suspect, and applies in the case of both intentional and unintentional two-stage interrogations. In my view, this test cuts too broadly. *Miranda*'s clarity is one of its strengths, and a multifactor test that applies to every two-stage interrogation may serve to undermine that clarity. I would apply a narrower test applicable only in the infrequent case, such as we have here, in which the two-step interrogation technique was used in a calculated way to undermine the *Miranda* warning.

The admissibility of postwarning statements should continue to be governed by the principles of *Elstad* unless the deliberate two-step strategy was employed. If the deliberate two-step strategy has been used, postwarning statements that are related to the substance of prewarning statements must be excluded unless curative measures are taken before the postwarning statement is made. Curative measures should be designed to ensure that a reasonable person in the suspect's situation would understand the import and effect of the *Miranda* warning and of the *Miranda* waiver. For example, a substantial break in time and circumstances between the prewarning statement and the *Miranda* warning may suffice in most circumstances, as it allows the accused to distinguish the two contexts and appreciate that the interrogation has taken a new turn. Alternatively, an additional warning that explains the likely inadmissibility of the prewarning custodial statement may be sufficient. No curative steps were taken in this case, however, so the postwarning statements are inadmissible and the conviction cannot stand. . . .

JUSTICE O'CONNOR, with whom THE CHIEF JUSTICE, JUSTICE SCALIA, and JUSTICE THOMAS join, dissenting.

. . . On two preliminary questions I am in full agreement with the plurality. First, the plurality appropriately follows [Oregon v. Elstad, 470 U.S. 298 (1985)] in concluding that Seibert's statement cannot be held inadmissible under a "fruit of the poisonous tree" theory. Ante, at [Note 4]. Second, the plurality correctly declines to focus its analysis on the subjective intent of the interrogating officer. . . .

Although the analysis the plurality ultimately espouses examines the same facts and circumstances that a "fruits" analysis would consider (such as the lapse of time between the two interrogations and change of questioner or location), it does so for entirely different reasons. The fruits analysis would examine those factors because they are relevant to the balance of deterrence value versus the "drastic and socially costly course" of excluding reliable evidence. Nix v. Williams, 467 U.S. 431, 442-443 (1984). The plurality, by contrast, looks to those factors to inform the psychological judgment regarding whether the suspect has been informed effectively of her right to remain silent. The analytical underpinnings of the two approaches are thus entirely distinct, and they should not be conflated just because they function similarly in practice.

The plurality's rejection of an intent-based test is also, in my view, correct. Freedom from compulsion lies at the heart of the Fifth Amendment, and requires us to assess whether a suspect's decision to speak truly was voluntary. Because voluntariness is a matter of the suspect's state of mind, we focus our analysis on the way in which suspects experience interrogation. . . .

Thoughts kept inside a police officer's head cannot affect that experience. See Moran v. Burbine, 475 U.S. 412, 422 (1986). In *Moran*, an attorney hired by the suspect's sister had been trying to contact the suspect and was told by the police, falsely, that they would not begin an interrogation that night. Id., at 416-418. The suspect was not aware that an attorney had been hired for him. Id., at 417. We rejected an analysis under which a different result would obtain for "the same defendant, armed with the same information and confronted with precisely the same police conduct" if something not known to the defendant—such as the fact that an attorney was attempting to contact him—had been different. Id., at 422.

The same principle applies here. A suspect who experienced the exact same interrogation as Seibert, save for a difference in the undivulged, subjective intent of the
interrogating officer when he failed to give *Miranda* warnings, would not experience the interrogation any differently. . . .

Because the isolated fact of Officer Hanrahan's intent could not have had any
bearing on Seibert's "capacity to comprehend and knowingly relinquish" her right
to remain silent, [ibid.], it could not by itself affect the voluntariness of her confession. Moreover, recognizing an exception to *Elstad* for intentional violations
would require focusing constitutional analysis on a police officer's subjective
intent, an unattractive proposition that we all but uniformly avoid. . . .

For these reasons, I believe that the approach espoused by JUSTICE KENNEDY is
ill advised.

JUSTICE KENNEDY would extend *Miranda*'s exclusionary rule to any case in
which the use of the "two-step interrogation technique" was "deliberate" or
"calculated." This approach untethers the analysis from facts knowable to,
and therefore having any potential directly to affect, the suspect. Far from
promoting "clarity," the approach will add a third step to the suppression
inquiry. In virtually every two-stage interrogation case, in addition to addressing the standard *Miranda* and voluntariness questions, courts will be forced
to conduct the kind of difficult, state-of-mind inquiry that we normally take
pains to avoid.

The plurality's adherence to *Elstad*, and mine to the plurality, end there. Our
decision in *Elstad* rejected two lines of argument advanced in favor of suppression.
The first was based on the "fruit of the poisonous tree" doctrine, discussed above.
The second was the argument that the "lingering compulsion" inherent in a defendant's having let the "cat out of the bag" required suppression. 470 U.S., at 311.
The Court of Appeals of Oregon, in accepting the latter argument, had endorsed a
theory indistinguishable from the one today's plurality adopts: "The coercive
impact of the unconstitutionally obtained statement remains, because in a defendant's mind it has sealed his fate. It is this impact that must be dissipated in order
to make a subsequent confession admissible." 61 Ore. App. 673, 677, 658 P.2d
552, 554 (1983).

We rejected this theory outright. We did so not because we refused to recognize
the "psychological impact of the suspect's conviction that he has let the cat out of
the bag," but because we refused to "endow" those "psychological effects" with
"constitutional implications." 470 U.S., at 311. . . . The plurality might very well
think that we struck the balance between Fifth Amendment rights and law enforcement interests incorrectly in *Elstad*; but that is not normally a sufficient reason
for ignoring the dictates of stare decisis.

I would analyze the two-step interrogation procedure under the voluntariness
standards central to the Fifth Amendment and reiterated in *Elstad*. *Elstad* commands that if Seibert's first statement is shown to have been involuntary, the court
must examine whether the taint dissipated through the passing of time or a
change in circumstances: "When a prior statement is actually coerced, the time
that passes between confessions, the change in place of interrogations, and the
change in identity of the interrogators all bear on whether that coercion has
carried over into the second confession." [Id.], at 310. In addition, Seibert's second
statement should be suppressed if she showed that it was involuntary despite the
Miranda warnings. Although I would leave this analysis for the Missouri courts to

conduct on remand, I note that, unlike the officers in *Elstad*, Officer Hanrahan referred to Seibert's unwarned statement during the second part of the interrogation when she made a statement at odds with her unwarned confession. App. 70 ("'Trice, didn't you tell me that he was supposed to die in his sleep?'"); cf. *Elstad*, supra, at 316 (officers did not "exploit the unwarned admission to pressure respondent into waiving his right to remain silent"). Such a tactic may bear on the voluntariness inquiry. . . .

Because I believe that the plurality gives insufficient deference to *Elstad* and that JUSTICE KENNEDY places improper weight on subjective intent, I respectfully dissent.

UNITED STATES v. PATANE

Certiorari to the United States Court of Appeals for the Tenth Circuit
124 S. Ct. 2620 (2004)

JUSTICE THOMAS announced the judgment of the Court and delivered an opinion, in which THE CHIEF JUSTICE and JUSTICE SCALIA join.

. . . In June 2001, respondent, Samuel Francis Patane, was arrested for harassing his ex-girlfriend, Linda O'Donnell. He was released on bond, subject to a temporary restraining order that prohibited him from contacting O'Donnell. Respondent apparently violated the restraining order by attempting to telephone O'Donnell. On June 6, 2001, Officer Tracy Fox of the Colorado Springs Police Department began to investigate the matter. On the same day, a county probation officer informed an agent of the Bureau of Alcohol, Tobacco, and Firearms (ATF), that respondent, a convicted felon, illegally possessed a .40 Glock pistol. The ATF relayed this information to Detective Josh Benner, who worked closely with the ATF. Together, Detective Benner and Officer Fox proceeded to respondent's residence.

After reaching the residence . . . Officer Fox arrested respondent for violating the restraining order. Detective Benner attempted to advise respondent of his *Miranda* rights but got no further than the right to remain silent. At that point, respondent interrupted, asserting that he knew his rights, and neither officer attempted to complete the warning.

Detective Benner then asked respondent about the Glock. Respondent was initially reluctant to discuss the matter, stating: "I am not sure I should tell you anything about the Glock because I don't want you to take it away from me." Detective Benner persisted, and respondent told him that the pistol was in his bedroom. Respondent then gave Detective Benner permission to retrieve the pistol. Detective Benner found the pistol and seized it.

A grand jury indicted respondent for possession of a firearm by a convicted felon, in violation of 18 U.S.C. §922(g)(1). The District Court granted respondent's motion to suppress the firearm, reasoning that the officers lacked probable cause to arrest respondent for violating the restraining order. It therefore declined to rule on respondent's alternative argument that the gun should be suppressed as the fruit of an unwarned statement.

The Court of Appeals reversed the District Court's ruling with respect to probable cause but affirmed the suppression order on respondent's alternative theory. . . .

As we explain below, the *Miranda* rule is a prophylactic employed to protect against violations of the Self-Incrimination Clause. The Self-Incrimination Clause, however, is not implicated by the admission into evidence of the physical fruit of a voluntary statement. Accordingly, there is no justification for extending the *Miranda* rule to this context. And just as the Self-Incrimination Clause primarily focuses on the criminal trial, so too does the *Miranda* rule. The *Miranda* rule is not a code of police conduct, and police do not violate the Constitution (or even the *Miranda* rule, for that matter) by mere failures to warn. For this reason, the exclusionary rule articulated in cases such as Wong Sun [v. United States, 371 U.S. 471 (1963)] does not apply. . . .

The Self-Incrimination Clause provides: "No person . . . shall be compelled in any criminal case to be a witness against himself." U.S. Const., Amdt. 5. We need not decide here the precise boundaries of the Clause's protection. For present purposes, it suffices to note that the core protection afforded by the Self-Incrimination Clause is a prohibition on compelling a criminal defendant to testify against himself at trial. See, e.g., Chavez v. Martinez, 538 U.S. 760, 764-768 (2003) (plurality opinion); id., at 777-779 (SOUTER, J., concurring in judgment). The Clause cannot be violated by the introduction of nontestimonial evidence obtained as a result of voluntary statements. . . .

To be sure, the Court has recognized and applied several prophylactic rules designed to protect the core privilege against self-incrimination. For example, although the text of the Self-Incrimination Clause at least suggests that "its coverage [is limited to] compelled testimony that is used against the defendant in the trial itself," [United States v. Hubbell, 530 U.S. 27, 37 (2000)], potential suspects may, at times, assert the privilege in proceedings in which answers might be used to incriminate them in a subsequent criminal case. We have explained that "the natural concern which underlies [these] decisions is that an inability to protect the right at one stage of a proceeding may make its invocation useless at a later stage." [Michigan v. Tucker, 417 U.S. 433, 440-441 (1974)].

Similarly, in *Miranda*, the Court concluded that the possibility of coercion inherent in custodial interrogations unacceptably raises the risk that a suspect's privilege against self-incrimination might be violated. 384 U.S., at 467. To protect against this danger, the *Miranda* rule creates a presumption of coercion, in the absence of specific warnings, that is generally irrebuttable for purposes of the prosecution's case in chief.

But because these prophylactic rules (including the *Miranda* rule) necessarily sweep beyond the actual protections of the Self-Incrimination Clause, any further extension of these rules must be justified by its necessity for the protection of the actual right against compelled self-incrimination. . . .

It is for these reasons that statements taken without *Miranda* warnings (though not actually compelled) can be used to impeach a defendant's testimony at trial, see Harris v. New York, 401 U.S. 222 (1971), though the fruits of actually compelled testimony cannot, see New Jersey v. Portash, 440 U.S. 450, 458-459 (1979). More generally, the *Miranda* rule "does not require that the statements [taken without complying with the rule] and their fruits be discarded as inherently tainted," [Oregon v. Elstad, 470 U.S. 298, 307 (1985)]. Such a blanket suppression rule could not be justified by reference to the "Fifth Amendment goal of assuring trustworthy evidence" or by any deterrence rationale, id., at 308, and would therefore fail our close-fit requirement.

Furthermore, the Self-Incrimination Clause contains its own exclusionary rule. It provides that "no person . . . shall be compelled in any criminal case to be a witness against himself." Unlike the Fourth Amendment's bar on unreasonable searches, the Self-Incrimination Clause is self-executing. We have repeatedly explained "that those subjected to coercive police interrogations have an automatic protection from the use of their involuntary statements (or evidence derived from their statements) in any subsequent criminal trial." *Chavez*, 538 U.S., at 769 (plurality opinion). This explicit textual protection supports a strong presumption against expanding the *Miranda* rule any further.

Finally, nothing in Dickerson [v. United States, 530 U.S. 428 (2000)], including its characterization of *Miranda* as announcing a constitutional rule, 530 U.S., at 444, changes any of these observations. Indeed, in *Dickerson*, the Court specifically noted that the Court's "subsequent cases have reduced the impact of the *Miranda* rule on legitimate law enforcement while reaffirming [*Miranda*]'s core ruling that unwarned statements may not be used as evidence in the prosecution's case in chief." Id., at 443-444. This description of *Miranda*, especially the emphasis on the use of "unwarned statements . . . in the prosecution's case in chief," makes clear our continued focus on the protections of the Self-Incrimination Clause. . . .

Our cases also make clear the related point that a mere failure to give *Miranda* warnings does not, by itself, violate a suspect's constitutional rights or even the *Miranda* rule. So much was evident in many of our pre-*Dickerson* cases, and we have adhered to this view since *Dickerson*. See *Chavez*, supra, at 772-773 (plurality opinion) (holding that a failure to read *Miranda* warnings did not violate the respondent's constitutional rights); 538 U.S., at 789 (KENNEDY, J., concurring in part and dissenting in part) (agreeing "that failure to give a *Miranda* warning does not, without more, establish a completed violation when the unwarned interrogation ensues"). . . .

It follows that police do not violate a suspect's constitutional rights (or the *Miranda* rule) by negligent or even deliberate failures to provide the suspect with the full panoply of warnings prescribed by *Miranda*. Potential violations occur, if at all, only upon the admission of unwarned statements into evidence at trial. And, at that point, "the exclusion of unwarned statements . . . is a complete and sufficient remedy" for any perceived *Miranda* violation. *Chavez*, supra, at 790.

Thus, unlike unreasonable searches under the Fourth Amendment or actual violations of the Due Process Clause or the Self-Incrimination Clause, there is, with respect to mere failures to warn, nothing to deter. There is therefore no reason to apply the "fruit of the poisonous tree" doctrine of *Wong Sun*, 371 U.S., at 488. It is not for this Court to impose its preferred police practices on either federal law enforcement officials or their state counterparts.

In the present case, the Court of Appeals, relying on *Dickerson*, wholly adopted the position that the taking of unwarned statements violates a suspect's constitutional rights. 304 F.3d at 1028-1029. And, of course, if this were so, a strong deterrence-based argument could be made for suppression of the fruits.

But *Dickerson*'s characterization of *Miranda* as a constitutional rule does not lessen the need to maintain the closest possible fit between the Self-Incrimination Clause and any judge-made rule designed to protect it. And there is no such fit here. Introduction of the nontestimonial fruit of a voluntary statement, such as respondent's Glock, does not implicate the Self-Incrimination Clause. The admission of such fruit presents no risk that a defendant's coerced statements (however defined) will be used against him at a criminal trial. . . . There is simply no need to extend (and therefore no justification for extending) the prophylactic rule of *Miranda* to this context. . . .

. . . And although it is true that the Court requires the exclusion of the physical fruit of actually coerced statements, it must be remembered that statements taken without sufficient *Miranda* warnings are presumed to have been coerced only for certain purposes and then only when necessary to protect the privilege against self-incrimination. For the reasons discussed above, we decline to extend that presumption further. . . .

JUSTICE KENNEDY, with whom JUSTICE O'CONNOR joins, concurring in the judgment.

In Oregon v. Elstad, 470 U.S. 298 (1985), New York v. Quarles, 467 U.S. 649 (1984), and Harris v. New York, 401 U.S. 222 (1971), evidence obtained following an unwarned interrogation was held admissible. This result was based in large part on our recognition that the concerns underlying the Miranda v. Arizona, 384 U.S. 436 (1966), rule must be accommodated to other objectives of the criminal justice system. I agree with the plurality that Dickerson v. United States, 530 U.S. 428 (2000), did not undermine these precedents and, in fact, cited them in support. Here, it is sufficient to note that the Government presents an even stronger case for admitting the evidence obtained as the result of Patane's unwarned statement. Admission of nontestimonial physical fruits (the Glock in this case), even more so than the postwarning statements to the police in *Elstad* and Michigan v. Tucker, 417 U.S. 433 (1974), does not run the risk of admitting into trial an accused's coerced incriminating statements against himself. In light of the important probative value of reliable physical evidence, it is doubtful that exclusion can be justified by a deterrence rationale sensitive to both law enforcement interests and a suspect's rights during an in-custody interrogation. Unlike the plurality, however, I find it unnecessary to decide whether the detective's failure to give Patane the full *Miranda* warnings should be characterized as a violation of the *Miranda* rule itself, or whether there is "anything to deter" so long as the unwarned statements are not later introduced at trial.

With these observations, I concur in the judgment of the Court.

JUSTICE SOUTER, with whom JUSTICE STEVENS and JUSTICE GINSBURG join, dissenting.

The majority repeatedly says that the Fifth Amendment does not address the admissibility of nontestimonial evidence, an overstatement that is beside the point. The issue actually presented today is whether courts should apply the fruit of the poisonous tree doctrine lest we create an incentive for the police to omit *Miranda* warnings before custodial interrogation. In closing their eyes to the consequences of giving an evidentiary advantage to those who ignore *Miranda*, the majority adds an important inducement for interrogators to ignore the rule in that case.

Miranda rested on insight into the inherently coercive character of custodial interrogation and the inherently difficult exercise of assessing the voluntariness of any confession resulting from it. Unless the police give the prescribed warnings meant to counter the coercive atmosphere, a custodial confession is inadmissible, there being no need for the previous time-consuming and difficult enquiry into voluntariness. That inducement to forestall involuntary statements and troublesome issues of fact can only atrophy if we turn around and recognize an evidentiary benefit when an unwarned statement leads investigators to tangible evidence. There is, of course, a price for excluding evidence, but the Fifth Amendment is worth a price, and in the absence of a very good reason, the logic of *Miranda* should be followed: a *Miranda* violation raises a presumption of coercion, Oregon v. Elstad, 470 U.S. 298, 306-307 (1985), and the Fifth Amendment privilege against compelled self-incrimination extends to the exclusion of derivative evidence, see United States v. Hubbell, 530 U.S. 27, 37-38 (2000) (recognizing "the Fifth Amendment's protection against the prosecutor's use of incriminating information derived directly or indirectly from . . . [actually] compelled testimony"). That should be the end of this case.

The fact that the books contain some exceptions to the *Miranda* exclusionary rule carries no weight here. In Harris v. New York, 401 U.S. 222 (1971), it was respect for the integrity of the judicial process that justified the admission of unwarned statements as impeachment evidence. But Patane's suppression motion can hardly be described as seeking to "pervert" *Miranda* "into a license to use perjury" or otherwise handicap the "traditional truth-testing devices of the adversary process." 401 U.S., at 225-226. Nor is there any suggestion that the officers' failure to warn Patane was justified or mitigated by a public emergency or other exigent circumstance, as in New York v. Quarles, 467 U.S. 649 (1984). And of course the premise of Oregon v. Elstad, supra, is not on point; although a failure to give *Miranda* warnings before one individual statement does not necessarily bar the admission of a subsequent statement given after adequate warnings, cf. Missouri v. Seibert, [124 S. Ct. 2601 (2004)] (plurality opinion), that rule obviously does not apply to physical evidence seized once and for all.

There is no way to read this case except as an unjustifiable invitation to law enforcement officers to flout *Miranda* when there may be physical evidence to be gained. The incentive is an odd one, coming from the Court on the same day it decides Missouri v. Seibert. I respectfully dissent.

JUSTICE BREYER, dissenting.

For reasons similar to those set forth in JUSTICE SOUTER's dissent and in my concurring opinion in Missouri v. Seibert, I would extend to this context the "fruit of the poisonous tree" approach, which I believe the Court has come close to adopting in *Seibert*. Under that approach, courts would exclude physical evidence derived from unwarned questioning unless the failure to provide *Miranda* warnings was in good faith. Because the courts below made no explicit finding as to good or bad faith, I would remand for such a determination.

NOTES ON *SEIBERT* AND *PATANE*

1. What rule can one infer from *Seibert* and *Patane*? In both cases, Justice Kennedy's opinion seems decisive. In *Seibert*, Justice Kennedy finds the defendant's statements inadmissible because the *Miranda* violation was intentional and the police took no steps to cure it. Kennedy's position in *Patane* is harder to understand. He seems to adopt the plurality's rule — no exclusion of physical fruits of a voluntary statement — but without the plurality's rationale. What is Justice Kennedy's rationale? Why treat physical fruits differently than testimonial fruits?

2. Why not instead draw a line between intentional violations of *Miranda* and unintentional ones? Doesn't Justice Breyer's position — exclude the fruits

of intentional *Miranda* violations, but not the fruits of good-faith violations — have a good deal of common sense to it?

3. Suppose a case like *Seibert* — an intentional violation of *Miranda* — where the violation leads the police to discover physical evidence: say, a gun. Is the gun admissible? How will Justice Kennedy vote in such a case? His *Seibert* opinion emphasizes the intentional nature of the *Miranda* violation. His *Patane* opinion emphasizes the lesser protection that (in his view) should be afforded to physical evidence, as opposed to testimony. What happens when those concerns cut in opposite directions?

4. Is it clear that there *was* a violation in *Patane*? Reread the statement of facts in Justice Thomas's opinion in the case. Should a suspect have the right *not* to hear the *Miranda* warnings if that is his preference? At the least, any violation in *Patane* seems likely to have been in good faith — something that cannot be said of the police conduct at issue in *Seibert*.

5. What do you think of the *Patane* plurality's theory? Your answer may depend on your view of another recent Supreme Court decision: Chavez v. Martinez, 538 U.S. 760 (2003). *Chavez* was a civil case arising under 42 U.S.C. §1983; plaintiff Martinez had been questioned by police officers in the emergency room of a local hospital. The interrogating officer never delivered the *Miranda* warnings. Martinez sued, seeking damages for this alleged violation of his Fifth Amendment rights. A divided Supreme Court found for the defendant. The plurality opinion by Justice Thomas (joined by Chief Justice Rehnquist and Justices O'Connor and Scalia) maintained that there could be no Fifth Amendment violation in *Chavez*, because Martinez's statements were never used against him in any criminal case. Justices Souter and Breyer did not go quite so far. They concluded that the constitutional violation in this case was "outside the Fifth Amendment's core," id. at 778 (Souter, J., concurring in the judgment), and so did not justify providing the protection of civil liability.

Is *Chavez* right? Is *Patane*?

4. The Right to Counsel Reconsidered

Miranda is not the only constitutional limit on police interrogation. The voluntariness requirement of the Due Process Clause still matters. And what about the Sixth Amendment? *Massiah* and *Escobedo* suggested the right to counsel would play a large role in regulating police questioning. Were those cases superseded by *Miranda*? Or do they carry independent weight? Consider the next case.

BREWER v. WILLIAMS

Certiorari to the Eighth Circuit Court of Appeals
430 U.S. 387 (1977)

MR. JUSTICE STEWART delivered the opinion of the Court.

An Iowa trial jury found the respondent, Robert Williams, guilty of murder. The judgment of conviction was affirmed in the Iowa Supreme Court by a closely divided vote. In a subsequent habeas corpus proceeding a Federal District Court ruled that under the United States Constitution Williams is entitled to a new trial, and a divided Court of Appeals for the Eighth Circuit agreed. The question before us is whether the District Court and the Court of Appeals were wrong.

I

On the afternoon of December 24, 1968, a 10-year-old girl named Pamela Powers went with her family to the YMCA in Des Moines, Iowa, to watch a wrestling tournament in which her brother was participating. When she failed to return from a trip to the washroom, a search for her began. The search was unsuccessful.

Robert Williams, who had recently escaped from a mental hospital, was a resident of the YMCA. Soon after the girl's disappearance Williams was seen in the YMCA lobby carrying some clothing and a large bundle wrapped in a blanket. He obtained help from a 14-year-old boy in opening the street door of the YMCA and the door to his automobile parked outside. When Williams placed the bundle in the front seat of his car the boy "saw two legs in it and they were skinny and white." Before anyone could see what was in the bundle Williams drove away. His abandoned car was found the following day in Davenport, Iowa, roughly 160 miles east of Des Moines. A warrant was then issued in Des Moines for his arrest on a charge of abduction.

On the morning of December 26, a Des Moines lawyer named Henry McKnight went to the Des Moines police station and informed the officers present that he had just received a long-distance call from Williams, and that he had advised Williams to turn himself in to the Davenport police. Williams did surrender that morning to the police in Davenport, and they booked him on the charge specified in the arrest warrant and gave him the warnings required by Miranda v. Arizona, 384 U.S. 436. The Davenport police then telephoned their counterparts in Des Moines to inform them that Williams had surrendered. McKnight, the lawyer, was still at the Des Moines police headquarters, and Williams conversed with McKnight on the telephone. In the presence of the Des Moines chief of police and a police detective named Leaming, McKnight advised Williams that Des Moines police officers would be driving to Davenport to pick him up, that the officers would not interrogate him or mistreat him, and that Williams was not to talk to the officers about Pamela Powers until after consulting with McKnight upon his return to Des Moines. As a result of these conversations, it was agreed between McKnight and the Des Moines police officials that Detective Leaming and a fellow officer would drive to Davenport to pick up Williams, that they would bring him directly back to Des Moines, and that they would not question him during the trip.

In the meantime Williams was arraigned before a judge in Davenport on the outstanding arrest warrant. The judge advised him of his Miranda rights and committed him to jail. Before leaving the courtroom, Williams conferred with a lawyer named Kelly, who advised him not to make any statements until consulting with McKnight back in Des Moines.

Detective Leaming and his fellow officer arrived in Davenport about noon to pick up Williams and return him to Des Moines. Soon after their arrival they met with Williams and Kelly, who, they understood, was acting as Williams' lawyer. Detective Leaming repeated the Miranda warnings, and told Williams: "[W]e both know that you're being represented here by Mr. Kelly and you're being represented by Mr. McKnight in Des Moines, and . . . I want you to remember this because we'll be visiting between here and Des Moines." Williams then conferred again with Kelly alone, and after this conference Kelly reiterated to Detective Leaming that Williams was not to be questioned about the disappearance of Pamela Powers until after he had consulted with McKnight back in Des Moines. When Leaming expressed some reservations, Kelly firmly stated that the agreement with McKnight was to be carried out—that there was to be no interrogation of Williams during the automobile journey to Des Moines. Kelly was denied permission to ride in the police car back to Des Moines with Williams and two officers.

The two detectives, with Williams in their charge, then set out on the 160-mile drive. At no time during the trip did Williams express a willingness to be interrogated in the absence of an attorney. Instead, he stated several times that "[w]hen I get to Des Moines and see Mr. McKnight, I am going to tell you the whole story." Detective Leaming knew that Williams was a former mental patient, and knew also that he was deeply religious.

The detective and his prisoner soon embarked on a wide-ranging conversation covering a variety of topics, including the subject of religion. Then, not long after leaving Davenport and reaching the interstate highway, Detective Leaming delivered what has been referred to in the briefs and oral arguments as the "Christian burial speech." Addressing Williams as "Reverend," the detective said:

> I want to give you something to think about while we're traveling down the road. . . . Number one, I want you to observe the weather conditions, it's raining, it's sleeting, it's freezing, driving is very treacherous, visibility is poor, it's going to be dark early this evening. They are predicting several inches of snow for tonight, and I feel that you yourself are the only person that knows where this little girl's body is, that you yourself have only been there once, and if you get a snow on top of it you yourself may be unable to find it. And, since we will be going right past the area on the way into Des Moines, I feel that we could stop and locate the body, that the parents of this little girl should be entitled to a Christian burial for the little girl who was snatched away from them on Christmas [E]ve and murdered. And I feel we should stop and locate it on the way in rather than waiting until morning and trying to come back out after a snow storm and possibly not being able to find it at all.

Williams asked Detective Leaming why he thought their route to Des Moines would be taking them past the girl's body, and Leaming responded that he knew the body was in the area of Mitchellville—a town they would be passing on the way to Des Moines.[1] Leaming then stated: "I do not want you to answer me. I don't want to discuss it any further. Just think about it as we're riding down the road."

As the car approached Grinnell, a town approximately 100 miles west of Davenport, Williams asked whether the police had found the victim's shoes. When Detective Leaming replied that he was unsure, Williams directed the officers to a service station where he said he had left the shoes; a search for them proved unsuccessful. As they continued towards Des Moines, Williams asked whether the police had found the blanket, and directed the officers to a rest area where he said he had disposed of the blanket. Nothing was found. The car continued towards

---

1. The fact of the matter, of course, was that Detective Leaming possessed no such knowledge.

Des Moines, and as it approached Mitchellville, Williams said that he would show the officers where the body was. He then directed the police to the body of Pamela Powers.

Williams was indicted for first-degree murder. Before trial, his counsel moved to suppress all evidence relating to or resulting from any statements Williams had made during the automobile ride from Davenport to Des Moines. After an evidentiary hearing the trial judge denied the motion. He found that "an agreement was made between defense counsel and the police officials to the effect that the Defendant was not to be questioned on the return trip to Des Moines," and that the evidence in question had been elicited from Williams during "a critical stage in the proceedings requiring the presence of counsel on his request." The judge ruled, however, that Williams had "waived his right to have an attorney present during the giving of such information."

II . . .

B

[T]he District Court based its judgment in this case on three independent grounds. The Court of Appeals appears to have affirmed the judgment on two of those grounds. We have concluded that only one of them need be considered here.

Specifically, there is no need to review in this case the doctrine of Miranda v. Arizona, a doctrine designed to secure the constitutional privilege against compulsory self-incrimination, Michigan v. Tucker, 417 U.S. 433, 438-439. It is equally unnecessary to evaluate the ruling of the District Court that Williams' self-incriminating statements were, indeed, involuntarily made. Cf. Spano v. New York, 360 U.S. 315. For it is clear that the judgment before us must in any event be affirmed upon the ground that Williams was deprived of a different constitutional right — the right to the assistance of counsel. . . .

There can be no doubt in the present case that judicial proceedings had been initiated against Williams before the start of the automobile ride from Davenport to Des Moines. A warrant had been issued for his arrest, he had been arraigned on that warrant before a judge in a Davenport courtroom, and he had been committed by the court to confinement in jail. The State does not contend otherwise.

There can be no serious doubt, either, that Detective Leaming deliberately and designedly set out to elicit information from Williams just as surely as — and perhaps more effectively than — if he had formally interrogated him. Detective Leaming was fully aware before departing for Des Moines that Williams was being represented in Davenport by Kelly and in Des Moines by McKnight. Yet he purposely sought during Williams' isolation from his lawyers to obtain as much incriminating information as possible. Indeed, Detective Leaming conceded as much when he testified at Williams' trial:

Q: In fact, Captain, whether he was a mental patient or not, you were trying to get all the information you could before he got to his lawyer, weren't you?
A: I was sure hoping to find out where that little girl was, yes sir. . . .

Q: Well, I'll put it this way: You was [*sic*] hoping to get all the information you could before Williams got back to McKnight, weren't you?
A: Yes, sir.[6]

The state courts clearly proceeded upon the hypothesis that Detective Leaming's "Christian burial speech" had been tantamount to interrogation. Both courts recognized that Williams had been entitled to the assistance of counsel at the time he made the incriminating statements. Yet no such constitutional protection would have come into play if there had been no interrogation.

The circumstances of this case are thus constitutionally indistinguishable from those presented in Massiah v. United States, supra. . . .

That the incriminating statements were elicited surreptitiously in the *Massiah* case, and otherwise here, is constitutionally irrelevant. . . . Rather, the clear rule of *Massiah* is that once adversary proceedings have commenced against an individual, he has a right to legal representation when the government interrogates him.[8] It thus requires no wooden or technical application of the *Massiah* doctrine to conclude that Williams was entitled to the assistance of counsel guaranteed to him by the Sixth and Fourteenth Amendments.

III

The Iowa courts recognized that Williams had been denied the constitutional right to the assistance of counsel. They held, however, that he had waived that right during the course of the automobile trip from Davenport to Des Moines. . . .

In the federal habeas corpus proceeding the District Court, believing that the issue of waiver was not one of fact but of federal law, held that the Iowa courts had "applied the wrong constitutional standards" in ruling that Williams had waived the protections that were his under the Constitution. 375 F. Supp., at 182. The court held "that it is the *government* which bears a heavy burden . . . but that is the burden which explicitly was placed on [Williams] by the state courts." Ibid. (emphasis in original). . . .

The Court of Appeals approved the reasoning of the District Court. . . .

The District Court and the Court of Appeals were correct in the view that the question of waiver was not a question of historical fact, but one which, in the words of Mr. Justice Frankfurter, requires "application of constitutional principles to the facts as found. . . ." Brown v. Allen, 344 U.S. 443, 507 (separate opinion). . . .

---

6. Counsel for petitioner, in the course of oral argument in this Court, acknowledged that the "Christian burial speech" was tantamount to interrogation:

> *Q:* But isn't the point, really, Mr. Attorney General, what you indicated earlier, and that is that the officer wanted to elicit information from Williams—
> *A:* Yes, sir.
> *Q:* —by whatever techniques he used, I would suppose a lawyer would consider that he were pursuing interrogation.
> *A:* It is, but it was very brief. [Tr. of Oral Arg. 17.]

8. The only other significant factual difference between the present case and *Massiah* is that here the police had *agreed* that they would not interrogate Williams in the absence of his counsel. This circumstance plainly provides petitioner with no argument for distinguishing away the protection afforded by *Massiah*.

It is argued that this agreement may not have been an enforceable one. But we do not deal here with notions of offer, acceptance, consideration, or other concepts of the law of contracts. We deal with constitutional law. And every court that has looked at this case has found an "agreement" in the sense of a commitment made by the Des Moines police officers that Williams would not be questioned about Pamela Powers in the absence of his counsel.

The District Court and the Court of Appeals were also correct in their understanding of the proper standard to be applied in determining the question of waiver as a matter of federal constitutional law — that it was incumbent upon the State to prove "an intentional relinquishment or abandonment of a known right or privilege." Johnson v. Zerbst, 304 U.S., at 464. . . .

We conclude . . . that the Court of Appeals was correct in holding that, judged by these standards, the record in this case falls far short of sustaining petitioner's burden. It is true that Williams had been informed of and appeared to understand his right to counsel. But waiver requires not merely comprehension but relinquishment, and Williams' consistent reliance upon the advice of counsel in dealing with the authorities refutes any suggestion that he waived that right. He consulted McKnight by long-distance telephone before turning himself in. He spoke with McKnight by telephone again shortly after being booked. After he was arraigned, Williams sought out and obtained legal advice from Kelly. Williams again consulted with Kelly after Detective Leaming and his fellow officer arrived in Davenport. Throughout, Williams was advised not to make any statements before seeing McKnight in Des Moines, and was assured that the police had agreed not to question him. His statements while in the car that he would tell the whole story after seeing McKnight in Des Moines were the clearest expressions by Williams himself that he desired the presence of an attorney before any interrogation took place. But even before making these statements, Williams had effectively asserted his right to counsel by having secured attorneys at both ends of the automobile trip, both of whom, acting as his agents, had made clear to the police that no interrogation was to occur during the journey. Williams knew of that agreement and, particularly in view of his consistent reliance on counsel, there is no basis for concluding that he disavowed it.

Despite Williams' express and implicit assertions of his right to counsel, Detective Leaming proceeded to elicit incriminating statements from Williams. Leaming did not preface this effort by telling Williams that he had a right to the presence of a lawyer, and made no effort at all to ascertain whether Williams wished to relinquish that right. The circumstances of record in this case thus provide no reasonable basis for finding that Williams waived his right to the assistance of counsel.

The Court of Appeals did not hold, nor do we, that under the circumstances of this case Williams *could not*, without notice to counsel, have waived his rights under the Sixth and Fourteenth Amendments. It only held, as do we, that he did not.

IV

The crime of which Williams was convicted was senseless and brutal, calling for swift and energetic action by the police to apprehend the perpetrator and gather evidence with which he could be convicted. No mission of law enforcement officials is more important. Yet "[d]isinterested zeal for the public good does not assure either wisdom or right in the methods it pursues." Haley v. Ohio, 332 U.S. 596, 605 (Frankfurter, J., concurring in judgment). Although we do not lightly affirm the issuance of a writ of habeas corpus in this case, so clear a violation of the Sixth and Fourteenth Amendments as here occurred cannot be condoned. The pressures on state executive and judicial officers charged with the administration of the criminal law are great, especially when the crime is murder and the victim a small child. But it is precisely the predictability of those pressures that makes imperative a resolute loyalty to the guarantees that the Constitution extends to us all.

The judgment of the Court of Appeals is affirmed.[12]

It is so ordered.

[Justice Marshall's, Justice Powell's, and Justice Stevens's concurring opinions are omitted.]

MR. CHIEF JUSTICE BURGER, dissenting.

The result in this case ought to be intolerable in any society which purports to call itself an organized society. It continues the Court — by the narrowest margin — on the much-criticized course of punishing the public for the mistakes and misdeeds of law enforcement officers, instead of punishing the officer directly, if in fact he is guilty of wrongdoing. It mechanically and blindly keeps reliable evidence from juries whether the claimed constitutional violation involves gross police misconduct or honest human error.

Williams is guilty of the savage murder of a small child; no member of the Court contends he is not. While in custody, and after no fewer than *five* warnings of his rights to silence and to counsel, he led police to the concealed body of his victim. The Court concedes Williams was not threatened or coerced and that he spoke and acted voluntarily and with full awareness of his constitutional rights. In the face of all this, the Court now holds that because Williams was prompted by the detective's statement — not interrogation but a statement — the jury must not be told how the police found the body.

Today's holding fulfills Judge (later Mr. Justice) Cardozo's grim prophecy that someday some court might carry the exclusionary rule to the absurd extent that its operative effect would exclude evidence relating to the body of a murder victim because of the means by which it was found.[1] In so ruling the Court regresses to playing a grisly game of "hide and seek," once more exalting the sporting theory of criminal justice which has been experiencing a decline in our jurisprudence. With Justices White, Blackmun, and Rehnquist, I categorically reject the remarkable notion that the police in this case were guilty of unconstitutional misconduct, or any conduct justifying the bizarre result reached by the Court. Apart from a brief comment on the merits, however, I wish to focus on the irrationality of applying the increasingly discredited exclusionary rule to this case.

---

12. The District Court stated that its decision "does not touch upon the issue of what evidence, if any, beyond the incriminating statements themselves must be excluded as 'fruit of the poisonous tree.'" 375 F. Supp. 170, 185. We, too, have no occasion to address this issue, and in the present posture of the case there is no basis for the view of our dissenting Brethren . . . that any attempt to retry the respondent would probably be futile. While neither Williams' incriminating statements themselves nor any testimony describing his having led the police to the victim's body can constitutionally be admitted into evidence, evidence of where the body was found and of its condition might well be admissible on the theory that the body would have been discovered in any event, even had incriminating statements not been elicited from Williams. Cf. Killough v. United States, 336 F.2d 929. In the event that a retrial is instituted, it will be for the state courts in the first instance to determine whether particular items of evidence may be admitted.

1. "The criminal is to go free because the constable has blundered. . . . A room is searched against the law, and the body of a murdered man is found. . . . The privacy of the home has been infringed, and the murderer goes free." People v. Defore, 242 N.Y. 13, 21, 23-24, 150 N.E. 585, 587, 588 (1926). . . .

(1) THE COURT CONCEDES WILLIAMS' DISCLOSURES WERE VOLUNTARY

Under well-settled precedents which the court freely acknowledges, it is very clear that Williams had made a valid waiver of his Fifth Amendment right to silence and his Sixth Amendment right to counsel when he led police to the child's body. Indeed, even under the Court's analysis I do not understand how a contrary conclusion is possible.

The Court purports to apply as the appropriate constitutional waiver standard the familiar "intentional relinquishment or abandonment of a known right or privilege" test of Johnson v. Zerbst, 304 U.S. 458, 464 (1938). . . . The Court assumes, without deciding, that Williams' conduct and statements were voluntary. It concedes, as it must, . . . that Williams had been informed of and fully understood his constitutional rights and the consequences of their waiver. Then, having either assumed or found every element necessary to make out a valid waiver under its own test, the Court reaches the astonishing conclusion that no valid waiver has been demonstrated. . . .

The evidence is uncontradicted that Williams had abundant knowledge of his right to have counsel present and of his right to silence. Since the Court does not question his mental competence, it boggles the mind to suggest that Williams could not understand that leading police to the child's body would have other than the most serious consequences. All of the elements necessary to make out a valid waiver are shown by the record and acknowledged by the Court; we thus are left to guess how the Court reached its holding. . . .

In any case, the Court assures us . . . that a valid waiver was *possible* in these circumstances, but was not quite made. Here, of course, Williams did not confess to the murder in so many words; it was his conduct in guiding police to the body, not his words, which incriminated him. And the record is replete with evidence that Williams knew precisely what he was doing when he guided police to the body. The human urge to confess wrongdoing is, of course, normal in all save hardened, professional criminals, as psychiatrists and analysts have demonstrated. T. Reik, The Compulsion to Confess (1972).

(2) THE EXCLUSIONARY RULE SHOULD NOT BE APPLIED TO NON-EGREGIOUS POLICE CONDUCT

. . . [I]t is striking that the Court fails even to consider whether the benefits secured by application of the exclusionary rule in this case outweigh its obvious social costs. Perhaps the failure is due to the fact that this case arises not under the Fourth Amendment, but under Miranda v. Arizona and the Sixth Amendment right to counsel. The Court apparently perceives the function of the exclusionary rule to be so different in these varying contexts that it must be mechanically and uncritically applied in all cases arising outside the Fourth Amendment.[5]

5. Indeed, if this were a Fourth Amendment case our course would be clear; only last Term, in Stone v. Powell, [428 U.S. 465 (1976)] we held that application of the exclusionary rule in federal habeas corpus has such a minimal deterrent effect on law enforcement officials that habeas relief should not be granted on the ground that unconstitutionally seized evidence was introduced at trial. Since the quantum of deterrence provided by federal habeas does not vary with the constitutional provision at issue, it appears that the Court sees fundamental, though unarticulated, differences in the exclusionary sanction when it is applied in other contexts.

But this is demonstrably not the case where police conduct collides with *Miranda*'s procedural safeguards rather than with the Fifth Amendment privilege against compulsory self-incrimination. Involuntary and coerced admissions are suppressed because of the inherent unreliability of a confession wrung from an unwilling suspect by threats, brutality, or other coercion. . . . We can all agree on " '[t]he abhorrence of society to the use of involuntary confessions,' " Linkletter v. Walker, [381 U.S.] at 638, and the need to preserve the integrity of the human personality and individual free will. . . .

But use of Williams' disclosures and their fruits carries no risk whatever of unreliability, for the body was found where he said it would be found. Moreover, since the Court makes no issue of voluntariness, no dangers are posed to individual dignity or free will. *Miranda*'s safeguards are premised on presumed unreliability long associated with confessions extorted by brutality or threats; they are not personal constitutional rights, but are simply judicially created prophylactic measures. Michigan v. Tucker, 417 U.S. 433 (1974). . . .

Thus, in cases where incriminating disclosures are voluntarily made without coercion, and hence not violative of the Fifth Amendment, but are obtained in violation of one of the *Miranda* prophylaxes, suppression is no longer automatic. Rather, we weigh the deterrent effect on unlawful police conduct, together with the normative Fifth Amendment justifications for suppression, against "the strong interest under any system of justice of making available to the trier of fact all concededly relevant and trustworthy evidence which either party seeks to adduce. . . . We also 'must consider society's interest in the effective prosecution of criminals. . . . ' " Michigan v. Tucker, supra, at 450.[6] This individualized consideration or balancing process with respect to the exclusionary sanction is possible in this case, as in others, because Williams' incriminating disclosures are not infected with any element of compulsion the Fifth Amendment forbids; nor, as noted earlier, does this evidence pose any danger of unreliability to the factfinding process. In short, there is no reason to exclude this evidence.

Similarly, the exclusionary rule is not uniformly implicated in the Sixth Amendment, particularly its pretrial aspects. We have held that "the core purpose of the counsel guarantee was to assure 'Assistance' at trial, when the accused was confronted with both the intricacies of the law and the advocacy of the public prosecutor." United States v. Ash, 413 U.S. 300, 309 (1973). Thus, the right to counsel is fundamentally a "trial" right necessitated by the legal complexities of a criminal prosecution and the need to offset, to the trier of fact, the power of the State as prosecutor. See Schneckloth v. Bustamonte, supra, at 241. . . .

In any event, the fundamental purpose of the Sixth Amendment is to safeguard the fairness of the trial and the integrity of the factfinding process.[7] In this case, where the evidence of how the child's body was found is of unquestioned reliability, and since the Court accepts Williams' disclosures as voluntary and uncoerced, there

---

6. Statements obtained in violation of *Miranda* have long been used for impeachment purposes. Oregon v. Hass, 420 U.S. 714 (1975); Harris v. New York, 401 U.S. 222 (1971). See also Walder v. United States, 347 U.S. 62 (1954).

7. Indeed, we determine whether pretrial proceedings are "critical" by asking whether counsel is there needed to protect the fairness of the trial. See United States v. Ash, 413 U.S. 300, 322 (1973) (Stewart, J., concurring); Schneckloth v. Bustamonte, 412 U.S. 218, 239 (1973). It is also clear that the danger of actual error was the moving force behind the counsel guarantee in such cases as United States v. Wade, 388 U.S. 218 (1967) (post-indictment lineups).

is no issue either of fairness or evidentiary reliability to justify suppression of truth. It appears suppression is mandated here for no other reason than the Court's general impression that it may have a beneficial effect on future police conduct; indeed, the Court fails to say even that much in defense of its holding.

Thus, whether considered under *Miranda* or the Sixth Amendment, there is no more reason to exclude the evidence in this case than there was in Stone v. Powell [428 U.S. 465 (1976)];[8] that holding was premised on the utter reliability of evidence sought to be suppressed, the irrelevancy of the constitutional claim to the criminal defendant's factual guilt or innocence, and the minimal deterrent effect of habeas corpus on police misconduct. . . . Relevant factors in this case are thus indistinguishable from those in *Stone*, and from those in other Fourth Amendment cases suggesting a balancing approach toward utilization of the exclusionary sanction. Rather than adopting a formalistic analysis varying with the constitutional provision invoked, we should apply the exclusionary rule on the basis of its benefits and costs, at least in those cases where the police conduct at issue is far from being outrageous or egregious. . . .

[Justice White's dissenting opinion, joined by Justices Blackmun and Rehnquist, is omitted.]

[Justice Blackmun's dissenting opinion, joined by Justices White and Rehnquist, is omitted.]

NOTES AND QUESTIONS

1. Brewer v. Williams, as well as virtually the entire law of confessions, is thoroughly reviewed in two exhaustive articles by Professor Yale Kamisar: Foreword: Brewer v. Williams — A Hard Look at a Discomfiting Record, 66 Geo. L.J. 209 (1977); *Brewer v. Williams, Massiah,* and *Miranda:* What Is "Interrogation"? When Does It Matter?, 67 Geo. L.J. 1 (1978).

2. *Williams* was retried on remand. The body was admitted at trial on the theory that it would have been inevitably discovered, and the Supreme Court ultimately approved of its admission. Nix v. Williams, 467 U.S. 431 (1984).

3. Although *Massiah* and *Miranda* apparently are premised on differing policies, the concerns of the cases are strikingly similar. Both elaborate when state may elicit information from a person suspected of criminality. Still, the conditions precedent for the application of each case do differ. The adversarial process must be initiated before the Sixth Amendment rights discussed in *Massiah* come into play, and custody is not directly relevant to the analysis. The Fifth Amendment rights discussed in *Miranda*, by contrast, are relevant only at the point of custodial interrogation, and the initiation of formal proceedings is irrelevant.

The significance of these distinctions was demonstrated by United States v. Henry, 447 U.S. 264 (1980). In *Henry*, an informant was planted in a cell with

---

8. This is a far cry from Massiah v. United States, 377 U.S. 201 (1964). Massiah's statements had no independent indicia of reliability as do respondent's. Moreover, Massiah was unaware that he was being interrogated by ruse and had not been advised of his right to counsel.

Here, as Mr. Justice Blackmun has noted, there was no interrogation of Williams in the sense that term was used in *Massiah*, Escobedo v. Illinois, 378 U.S. 478 (1964), or *Miranda*. That the detective's statement appealed to Williams' conscience is not a sufficient reason to equate it to a police station grilling. It could well be that merely driving on the road and passing the intersection where he had turned off to bury the body might have produced the same result without any suggestive comments.

Henry, who had previously been indicted. The informant apparently initiated conversations with Henry, who made incriminating comments later used against him. The Court held that this violated Henry's Sixth Amendment rights. Once formal proceedings have begun, the government may not "deliberately elicit" information from a suspect without first obtaining a waiver of rights. *Henry* was important for two reasons. First, it revived *Massiah*, indicating that *Massiah* had avoided *Escobedo*'s fate. Second, it suggested that merely planting an informant, even if the informant remained passive and did not initiate any conversations, would violate the Sixth Amendment: By "intentionally creating a situation likely to induce Henry to make incriminating statements without the assistance of counsel, the government violated the Sixth Amendment right to counsel." The broad implications of this language did not long survive, however. In Kuhlmann v. Wilson, 477 U.S. 436 (1986), the defendant had been placed in a cell with a police informant named Lee:

> [T]he trial court found that [Lee's superior] had instructed Lee "to ask no questions of [the defendant] about the crime but merely to listen as to what [he] might say in his presence." The court determined that Lee obeyed these instructions, that he "at no time asked any questions with respect to the crime," and that he "only listened to [respondent] and made notes regarding what [respondent] had to say." The trial court also found that respondent's statements to Lee were "spontaneous" and "unsolicited." Under state precedent, a defendant's volunteered statements to a police agent were admissible in evidence because the police were not required to prevent talkative defendants from making incriminating statements. The trial court accordingly denied the suppression motion. . . .
>
> . . . In United States v. Henry, the Court applied the *Massiah* test to incriminating statements made to a jailhouse informant. The Court of Appeals in that case found a violation of *Massiah* because the informant had engaged the defendant in conversations and "had developed a relationship of trust and confidence with [the defendant] such that [the defendant] revealed incriminating information." This Court affirmed, holding that the Court of Appeals reasonably concluded that the Government informant "deliberately used his position to secure incriminating information from [the defendant] when counsel was not present." Although the informant had not questioned the defendant, the informant had "stimulated" conversations with the defendant in order to "elicit" incriminating information. The Court emphasized that those facts, like the facts of *Massiah*, amounted to " 'indirect and surreptitious interrogatio[n]' " of the defendant.
>
> [T]he primary concern of the *Massiah* line of decisions is secret interrogation by investigatory techniques that are the equivalent of direct police interrogation. Since "the Sixth Amendment is not violated whenever — by luck or happenstance — the State obtains incriminating statements from the accused after the right to counsel has attached," a defendant does not make out a violation of that right simply by showing that an informant, either through prior arrangement or voluntarily, reported his incriminating statements to the police. Rather, the defendant must demonstrate that the police and their informant took some action, beyond merely listening, that was designed deliberately to elicit incriminating remarks. . . .

Justice Brennan, joined by Justice Marshall, dissented:

> In the instant case, as in *Henry*, the accused was incarcerated and therefore was "susceptible to the ploys of undercover Government agents." Like Nichols [the informant

in *Henry*], Lee was a secret informant, usually received consideration for the services he rendered the police, and therefore had an incentive to produce the information which he knew the police hoped to obtain. Just as Nichols had done, Lee obeyed instructions not to question respondent and to report to the police any statements made by the respondent in Lee's presence about the crime in question. And, like Nichols, Lee encouraged respondent to talk about his crime by conversing with him on the subject over the course of several days and by telling respondent that his exculpatory story would not convince anyone without more work. However, unlike the situation in *Henry*, a disturbing visit from respondent's brother, rather than a conversation with the informant, seems to have been the immediate catalyst for respondent's confession to Lee. While it might appear from this sequence of events that Lee's comment regarding respondent's story and his general willingness to converse with respondent about the crime were not the immediate causes of respondent's admission, I think that the deliberate-elicitation standard requires consideration of the entire course of government behavior.

The State intentionally created a situation in which it was forseeable that respondent would make incriminating statements without the assistance of counsel—it assigned respondent to a cell overlooking the scene of the crime and designated a secret informant to be respondent's cellmate. The informant, while avoiding direct questions, nonetheless developed a relationship of cellmate camaraderie with respondent and encouraged him to talk about his crime. While the coup de grace was delivered by respondent's brother, the groundwork for respondent's confession was laid by the State. Clearly the State's actions had a sufficient nexus with respondent's admission of guilt to constitute deliberate elicitation within the meaning of *Henry*. I would affirm the judgment of the Court of Appeals.

4. Why the differences between *Innis* on the one hand and *Henry* and *Kuhlmann* on the other? For a discussion, see Welsh S. White, Interrogation without Questions: Rhode Island v. Innis and United States v. Henry, 78 Mich. L. Rev. 1209 (1980).

5. Should it matter if the state takes advantage, postindictment, of a codefendant's offer to assist the state's investigation? In other words, does "deliberate elicitation" extend to obtaining information as a result of a meeting between codefendants that was initiated by the noncooperating defendant? In addition, does it matter whether the reason prompting the state authorities to accept the codefendant's offer of assistance was the ongoing investigation of other crimes for which no indictments had yet been returned? In Maine v. Moulton, 474 U.S. 159 (1985), the Court held that *Massiah* controls in such a case but that any information obtained may be used in the prosecution of those offenses for which an indictment had not been returned at the time the incriminating statements were made. What values are served by excluding such statements from the trial of the offense for which the defendant had previously been indicted? Compare *Moulton* to Arizona v. Roberson, 486 U.S. 675 (1988), in which the Court held that *Edwards* was violated where the police interrogate a suspect with respect to one crime if the suspect has already invoked his *Miranda* right to counsel with respect to some other crime. Why is it that the invocation of the *Miranda* right to counsel of a person in custody protects a suspect from any further state efforts to elicit information, but initiation of the Sixth Amendment right to counsel is limited to the particular charge with respect to which formal proceedings have begun?

Perhaps the answer is that the Fifth Amendment and Sixth Amendment are concerned with different matters, even if their concerns overlap in the confession area. If distinctions are going to be drawn, is there a value in respecting them? Does the majority opinion in the following case impress you more with its creativity or its lack of discipline?

MICHIGAN v. JACKSON

Certiorari to the Supreme Court of Michigan
475 U.S. 625 (1986)

JUSTICE STEVENS delivered the opinion of the Court.

In Edwards v. Arizona, 451 U.S. 477 (1981), we held that an accused person in custody who has "expressed his desire to deal with the police only through counsel, is not subject to further interrogation by the authorities until counsel has been made available to him, unless the accused himself initiates further communication, exchanges, or conversations with the police." In Solem v. Stumes, 465 U.S. 638 (1984), we reiterated that "*Edwards* established a bright-line rule to safeguard preexisting rights"[;] "once a suspect has invoked the right to counsel, any subsequent conversation must be initiated by him."

The question presented by these two cases is whether the same rule applies to a defendant who has been formally charged with a crime and who has requested appointment of counsel at his arraignment. In both cases, the Michigan Supreme Court held that postarraignment confessions were improperly obtained — and the Sixth Amendment violated — because the defendants had "requested counsel during their arraignments, but were not afforded an opportunity to consult with counsel before the police initiated further interrogations." We agree with that holding. . . .

II

The question is not whether respondents had a right to counsel at their postarraignment, custodial interrogations. The existence of that right is clear. It has two sources. The Fifth Amendment protection against compelled self-incrimination provides the right to counsel at custodial interrogations. The Sixth Amendment guarantee of the assistance of counsel also provides the right to counsel at postarraignment interrogations. The arraignment signals "the initiation of adversary judicial proceedings" and thus the attachment of the Sixth Amendment; thereafter, government efforts to elicit information from the accused, including interrogation, represent "critical stages" at which the Sixth Amendment applies. The question in these cases is whether respondents validly waived their right to counsel at the postarraignment custodial interrogations.

In *Edwards*, the request for counsel was made to the police during custodial interrogation, and the basis for the Court's holding was the Fifth Amendment privilege against compelled self-incrimination. The Court noted the relevance of various Sixth Amendment precedents, but found it unnecessary to rely on the possible applicability of the Sixth Amendment. In these cases, the request for counsel was made to a judge during arraignment, and the basis for the Michigan Supreme Court opinion was the Sixth Amendment's guarantee of the assistance of counsel. The State argues that the *Edwards* rule should not apply to these circumstances because there are legal differences in the basis for the claims;

because there are factual differences in the contexts of the claims; and because respondents signed valid waivers of their right to counsel at the postarraignment custodial interrogations. We consider these contentions in turn.

The State contends that differences in the legal principles underlying the Fifth and Sixth Amendments compel the conclusion that the *Edwards* rule should not apply to a Sixth Amendment claim. *Edwards* flows from the Fifth Amendment's right to counsel at custodial interrogations, the State argues; its relevance to the Sixth Amendment's provision of the assistance of counsel is far less clear, and thus the *Edwards* principle for assessing waivers is unnecessary and inappropriate.

In our opinion, however, the reasons for prohibiting the interrogation of an uncounseled prisoner who has asked for the help of a lawyer are even stronger after he has been formally charged with an offense than before. The State's argument misapprehends the nature of the pretrial protections afforded by the Sixth Amendment. In United States v. Gouveia [467 U.S. 180 (1984)], we explained the significance of the formal accusation, and the corresponding attachment of the Sixth Amendment right to counsel:

> [G]iven the plain language of the Amendment and its purpose of protecting the unaided layman at critical confrontations with his adversary, our conclusion that the right to counsel attaches at the initiation of adversary judicial criminal proceedings "is far from a mere formalism." Kirby v. Illinois, 460 U.S., at 689. It is only at that time "that the government has committed itself to prosecute, and only then that the adverse positions of government and defendant have solidified. It is then that a defendant finds himself faced with the prosecutorial forces of organized society, and immersed in the intricacies of substantive and procedural criminal law." [467 U.S., at 189.]

As a result, the "Sixth Amendment guarantees the accused, at least after the initiation of formal charges, the right to rely on counsel as a 'medium' between him and the State." Maine v. Moulton, 474 U.S., at 176. Thus, the Sixth Amendment right to counsel at a postarraignment interrogation requires at least as much protection as the Fifth Amendment right to counsel at any custodial interrogation.

Indeed, after a formal accusation has been made — and a person who had previously been just a "suspect" has become an "accused" within the meaning of the Sixth Amendment — the constitutional right to the assistance of counsel is of such importance that the police may no longer employ techniques for eliciting information from an uncounseled defendant that might have been entirely proper at an earlier stage of their investigation. Thus, the surreptitious employment of a cellmate may violate the defendant's Sixth Amendment right to counsel even though the same methods of investigation might have been permissible before arraignment or indictment. Far from undermining the *Edwards* rule, the difference between the legal basis for the rule applied in *Edwards* and the Sixth Amendment claim asserted in these cases actually provides additional support for the application of the rule in these circumstances.

The State also relies on the factual differences between a request for counsel during custodial interrogation and a request for counsel at an arraignment. The State maintains that respondents may not have actually intended their request for counsel to encompass representation during any further questioning by the police. This argument, however, must be considered against the backdrop of our standard for assessing waivers of constitutional rights. Almost a half century ago, in Johnson v. Zerbst, 304 U.S. 458 (1938), a case involving an alleged waiver of a defendant's

Sixth Amendment right to counsel, the Court explained that we should "indulge every reasonable presumption against waiver of fundamental constitutional rights." For that reason, it is the State that has the burden of establishing a valid waiver. Doubts must be resolved in favor of protecting the constitutional claim. This settled approach to questions of waiver requires us to give a broad, rather than a narrow, interpretation to a defendant's request for counsel — we presume that the defendant requests the lawyer's services at every critical stage of the prosecution.[6] We thus reject the State's suggestion that respondents' requests for the appointment of counsel should be construed to apply only to representation in formal legal proceedings.[7]

The State points to another factual difference: the police may not know of the defendant's request for attorney at the arraignment. That claimed distinction is similarly unavailing. In the cases at bar, in which the officers in charge of the investigations of respondents were present at the arraignments, the argument is particularly unconvincing. More generally, however, Sixth Amendment principles require that we impute the State's knowledge from one state actor to another. For the Sixth Amendment concerns the confrontation between the State and the individual. One set of state actors (the police) may not claim ignorance of defendants' unequivocal request for counsel to another state actor (the court).

The State also argues that, because of these factual differences, the application of *Edwards* in a Sixth Amendment context will generate confusion. However, we have frequently emphasized that one of the characteristics of *Edwards* is its clear, "bright line" quality. We do not agree that applying the rule when the accused requests counsel at an arraignment, rather than in the police station, somehow diminishes that clarity. To the extent that there may have been any doubts about interpreting a request for counsel at an arraignment, or about the police responsibility to know of and respond to such a request, our opinion today resolves them.

Finally, the State maintains that each of the respondents made a valid waiver of his Sixth Amendment rights by signing a postarraignment confession after again being advised of his constitutional rights. In *Edwards*, however, we rejected the notion that, after a suspect's request for counsel, advice of rights and acquiescence in police-initiated questioning could establish a valid waiver. We find no warrant for a different view under a Sixth Amendment analysis. Indeed, our rejection of the comparable argument in *Edwards* was based, in part, on our review of earlier Sixth Amendment cases. Just as written waivers are insufficient to justify police-

---

6. In construing respondents' request for counsel, we do not, of course, suggest that the right to counsel turns on such a request. See Brewer v. Williams, 430 U.S., at 404 ("the right to counsel does not depend upon a request by the defendant"); Carnley v. Cochran, 369 U.S. 506, 513 (1962) ("it is settled that where the assistance of counsel is a constitutional requisite, the right to be furnished counsel does not depend on a request"). Rather, we construe the defendant's request for counsel as an extremely important fact in considering the validity of a subsequent waiver in response to police-initiated interrogation.

7. We also agree with the comments of the Michigan Supreme Court about the nature of an accused's request for counsel:

Although judges and lawyers may understand and appreciate the subtle distinctions between the Fifth and Sixth Amendment rights to counsel, the average person does not. When an accused requests an attorney, either before a police officer or a magistrate, he does not know which constitutional right he is invoking; he therefore should not be expected to articulate exactly why or for what purposes he is seeking counsel. It makes little sense to afford relief from further interrogation to a defendant who asks a police officer for an attorney, but permit further interrogation to a defendant who makes an identical request to a judge. The simple fact that defendant has requested an attorney indicates that he does not believe that he is sufficiently capable of dealing with his adversaries single-handedly. 421 Mich., at 63-64, 365 N.W.2d, at 67.

initiated interrogations after the request for counsel in a Fifth Amendment analysis, so too they are insufficient to justify police-initiated interrogations after the
request for counsel in a Sixth Amendment analysis.

III

Edwards is grounded in the understanding that "the assertion of the right to counsel
[is] a significant event," and that "additional safeguards are necessary when the
accused asks for counsel." We conclude that the assertion is no less significant, and
the need for additional safeguards no less clear, when the request for counsel is
made at an arraignment and when the basis for the claim is the Sixth Amendment.
We thus hold that, if police initiate interrogation after a defendant's assertion, at an
arraignment or similar proceeding, of his right to counsel, any waiver of the defendant's right to counsel for that police-initiated interrogation is invalid.

Although the *Edwards* decision itself rested on the Fifth Amendment and concerned a request for counsel made during custodial interrogation, the Michigan
Supreme Court correctly perceived that the reasoning of that case applies with
even greater force to these cases. The judgments are accordingly affirmed.
It is so ordered.

JUSTICE REHNQUIST, with whom JUSTICE POWELL and JUSTICE O'CONNOR join,
dissenting.

The Court's decision today rests on the following deceptively simple line of
reasoning: Edwards v. Arizona created a bright-line rule to protect a defendant's
Fifth Amendment rights; Sixth Amendment rights are even more important than
Fifth Amendment rights; therefore, we must also apply the *Edwards* rule to the
Sixth Amendment. The Court prefers this neat syllogism to an effort to discuss or
answer the only relevant question: Does the *Edwards* rule make sense in the context
of the Sixth Amendment? I think it does not, and I therefore dissent from the
Court's unjustified extension of the *Edwards* rule to the Sixth Amendment.

My disagreement with the Court stems from our differing understandings of
Edwards. In *Edwards*, this Court held that once a defendant has invoked his right
under Miranda v. Arizona to have counsel present during custodial interrogation,
"a valid waiver of that right cannot be established by showing only that he
responded to further police-initiated custodial interrogation even if he has
been advised of his rights." 451 U.S., at 484. This "prophylactic rule" was deemed
necessary to prevent the police from effectively "overriding a defendant's assertion
of his *Miranda* rights" by "badgering" him into waiving those rights. In short, as we
explained in later cases "*Edwards* did not confer a substantive constitutional right
that had not existed before; it 'created a protective umbrella serving to enhance a
constitutional guarantee.'" Solem v. Stumes, 465 U.S. at 644 n. 4.

What the Court today either forgets or chooses to ignore is that the "constitutional guarantee" referred to in Solem v. Stumes is the Fifth Amendment's
prohibition on compelled self-incrimination. This prohibition, of course, is also
the constitutional underpinning for the set of prophylactic rules announced in
Miranda itself.[2] *Edwards*, like *Miranda*, imposes on the police a bright-line standard

---

2. The Court suggests, in dictum, that the Fifth Amendment also provides defendants with a "right
to counsel." But our cases make clear that the Fifth Amendment itself provides no such "right." See
Moran v. Burbine, 475 U.S., at 423, n. 1, Oregon v. Elstad, 470 U.S., at 304-305. Instead, *Miranda*

of conduct intended to help ensure that confessions obtained through custodial interrogation will not be "coerced" or "involuntary." Seen in this proper light, *Edwards* provides nothing more than a second layer of protection, in addition to those rights conferred by *Miranda*, for a defendant who might otherwise be compelled by the police to incriminate himself in violation of the Fifth Amendment.

The dispositive question in the instant case, and the question the Court should address in its opinion, is whether the same kind of prophylactic rule is needed to protect a defendant's right to counsel under the Sixth Amendment. The answer to this question, it seems to me, is clearly "no." The Court does not even suggest that the police commonly deny defendants their Sixth Amendment right to counsel. Nor, I suspect, would such a claim likely be borne out by empirical evidence. Thus, the justification for the prophylactic rules this Court created in *Miranda* and *Edwards*, namely, the perceived widespread problem that the police were violating, and would probably continue to violate, the Fifth Amendment rights of defendants during the course of custodial interrogations, is conspicuously absent in the Sixth Amendment context. To put it simply, the prophylactic rule set forth in *Edwards* makes no sense at all except when linked to the Fifth Amendment's prohibition against compelled self-incrimination.

Not only does the Court today cut the *Edwards* rule loose from its analytical moorings, it does so in a manner that graphically reveals the illogic of the Court's position. The Court phrases the question presented in this case as whether the *Edwards* rule applies "to a defendant who has been formally charged with a crime *and who has requested appointment of counsel at his arraignment*" (emphasis added). And the Court ultimately limits its holding to those situations where the police "initiate interrogation *after a defendant's assertion, at an arraignment or similar proceeding, of his right to counsel*" (emphasis added).

In other words, the Court most assuredly does *not* hold that the *Edwards* per se rule prohibiting all police-initiated interrogations applies from the moment the defendant's Sixth Amendment right to counsel attaches, with or without a request for counsel by the defendant. Such a holding would represent, after all, a shockingly dramatic restructuring of the balance this Court has traditionally struck between the rights of the defendant and those of the larger society. Applying the *Edwards* rule to situations in which a defendant has not made an explicit request for counsel would also render completely nugatory the extensive discussion of "waiver" in such prior Sixth Amendment cases as Brewer v. Williams.[4]

---

confers upon a defendant a "right to counsel," *but only when such counsel is requested during custodial interrogations*. Even under *Miranda*, the "right to counsel" exists solely as a means of protecting the defendant's Fifth Amendment right not to be compelled to incriminate himself.

4. See also Moran v. Burbine, 475 U.S., at 428. ("It is clear, of course, that, *absent a valid waiver*, the defendant has the right to the presence of an attorney during any interrogation occurring after the first formal charging proceeding, the point at which the Sixth Amendment right to counsel initially attaches"). Several of our Sixth Amendment cases have indeed erected virtually per se barriers against certain kinds of police conduct. See, e.g., Maine v. Moulton, 474 U.S. 159 (1985); United States v. Henry, 447 U.S. 264 (1980); Massiah v. United States, 377 U.S. 201 (1964). These cases, however, all share one fundamental characteristic that separates them from the instant case; in each case, the nature of the police conduct was such that it would have been impossible to find a valid waiver of the defendant's Sixth Amendment right to counsel. See Maine v. Moulton, supra, at 176-174 (undisclosed electronic surveillance of conversations with a third party); United States v. Henry, supra, 447 U.S., at 265, 273 (use of undisclosed police informant); Massiah v. United States, supra, 377 U.S., at 202 (undisclosed electronic surveillance). Here, on the other hand, the conduct of the police was totally open and above-board, and could not be said to prevent the defendant from executing a valid Sixth Amendment waiver under the standards set forth in Johnson v. Zerbst, 304 U.S. 458 (1938).

This leaves the Court, however, in an analytical straitjacket. The problem with the limitation the Court places on the Sixth Amendment version of the *Edwards* rule is that, unlike a defendant's "right to counsel" under *Miranda*, which does not arise until affirmatively invoked by the defendant during custodial interrogation, a defendant's Sixth Amendment right to counsel does not depend at all on whether the defendant has requested counsel. The Court acknowledges as much in footnote six of its opinion, where it stresses that "we do not, of course, suggest that the right to counsel turns on . . . a request [for counsel]."

The Court provides no satisfactory explanation for its decision to extend the *Edwards* rule to the Sixth Amendment, yet limit that rule to those defendants foresighted enough, or just plain lucky enough, to have made an explicit request for counsel which we have always understood to be completely unnecessary for Sixth Amendment purposes. The Court attempts to justify its emphasis on the otherwise legally insignificant request for counsel by stating that "we construe the defendant's request for counsel as an extremely important fact in considering the validity of a subsequent waiver in response to police-initiated interrogation." This statement sounds reasonable, but it is flatly inconsistent with the remainder of the Court's opinion, in which the Court holds that there can be no waiver of the Sixth Amendment right to counsel after a request for counsel has been made. It is obvious that, for the Court, the defendant's request for counsel is not merely an "extremely important fact"; rather, it is the *only* fact that counts.

The truth is that there is no satisfactory explanation for the position the Court adopts in this case. The glaring inconsistencies in the Court's opinion arise precisely because the Court lacks a coherent, analytically sound basis for its decision. The prophylactic rule of *Edwards*, designed from its inception to protect a defendant's right under the Fifth Amendment not to be compelled to incriminate himself, simply does not meaningfully apply to the Sixth Amendment. I would hold that *Edwards* has no application outside the context of the Fifth Amendment, and would therefore reverse the judgment of the court below.

Continuing the development begun in Michigan v. Jackson of ignoring the differences between the Fifth and Sixth Amendment "right to counsel," the Court in Patterson v. Illinois, 478 U.S. 285 (1988), held that *Miranda* warnings sufficed to warn an indicted suspect of his Sixth Amendment right to counsel and that a waiver following such warnings was a knowing and intelligent waiver of the Sixth Amendment right to counsel as well. The Court noted that it rejected the suggestion that the Sixth Amendment right to counsel is somehow "superior" to Fifth Amendment rights. In a somewhat curious passage, however, the Court stated that such a waiver would not be valid in the Sixth Amendment context, although it would in the Fifth Amendment context, if a suspect is not informed that his lawyer is trying to reach him. The Court cited Moran v. Burbine, 475 U.S. 424 (1986), in support of its view, although the proposition is not easily extracted from that case. When the Court returned to the interaction of and distinctions between the Sixth and Fifth Amendment rights to counsel, the outcome seemed less an obvious application of the preceding precedent and more an expression of frustration with that precedent. In McNeil v. Wisconsin 501 U.S. 171 (1991), the Court considered "whether an accused's invocation of his Sixth Amendment right to counsel during a judicial proceeding constitutes an invocation of his *Miranda* right to counsel." The answer was "no":

> The Sixth Amendment provides that "in all criminal prosecutions, the accused shall enjoy the right . . . to have the Assistance of Counsel for his defence." In Michigan v. Jackson, we held that once this right to counsel has attached and has been invoked, any subsequent waiver during a police-initiated custodial interview is ineffective. It is undisputed, and we accept for purposes of the present case, that at the time petitioner provided the incriminating statements at issue, his Sixth Amendment right had attached and had been invoked with respect to the West Allis armed robbery, for which he had been formally charged.
>
> The Sixth Amendment right, however, is offense-specific. It cannot be invoked once for all future prosecutions, for it does not attach until a prosecution is commenced, that is, " 'at or after the initiation of adversary judicial criminal proceedings—whether by way of formal charge, preliminary hearing, indictment, information, or arraignment,' " United States v. Gouveia, 467 U.S. 180, 188 (1984) (quoting Kirby v. Illinois, 406 U.S. 682, 689 (1972) (plurality opinion)). And just as the right is offense-specific, so also its Michigan v. Jackson effect of invalidating subsequent waivers in police-initiated interviews is offense-specific. "The police have an interest . . . in investigating new or additional crimes [after an individual is formally charged with one crime.] . . . To exclude evidence pertaining to charges as to which the Sixth Amendment right to counsel had not attached at the time the evidence was obtained, simply because other charges were pending at that time, would unnecessarily frustrate the public's interest in the investigation of criminal activities. . . . " Maine v. Moulton, 474 U.S. 159, 179-180 (1985). "Incriminating statements pertaining to other crimes, as to which the Sixth Amendment right has not yet attached, are, of course, admissible at a trial of those offenses." Id., at 180, n. 16. Because petitioner provided the statements at issue here before his Sixth Amendment right to counsel with respect to the Caledonia offenses had been (or even could have been) invoked, that right poses no bar to the admission of the statements in this case.
>
> Petitioner relies, however, upon a different "right to counsel," found not in the text of the Sixth Amendment, but in this Court's jurisprudence relating to the Fifth Amendment guarantee that "no person . . . shall be compelled in any criminal case to be a witness against himself." In Miranda v. Arizona, we established a number of prophylactic rights designed to counteract the "inherently compelling pressures" of custodial interrogation, including the right to have counsel present. *Miranda* did not hold, however, that those rights could not be waived. On the contrary, the opinion recognized that statements elicited during custodial interrogation would be admissible if the prosecution could establish that the suspect "knowingly and intelligently waived his privilege against self-incrimination and his right to retained or appointed counsel." Id., at 475.
>
> In Edwards v. Arizona, we established a second layer of prophylaxis for the *Miranda* right to counsel: once a suspect asserts the right, not only must the current interrogation cease, but he may not be approached for further interrogation "until counsel has been made available to him," 451 U.S., at 484-485—which means, we have most recently held, that counsel must be present, Minnick v. Mississippi, 498 U.S. 146 (1990). If the police do subsequently initiate an encounter in the absence of counsel (assuming there has been no break in custody), the suspect's statements are presumed involuntary and therefore inadmissible as substantive evidence at trial, even where the suspect executes a waiver and his statements would be considered voluntary under traditional standards. This is "designed to prevent police from badgering a defendant into waiving his previously asserted *Miranda* rights," Michigan v. Harvey, 494 U.S. 344, 350 (1990). The *Edwards* rule, moreover, is not offense-specific: once a suspect

invokes the *Miranda* right to counsel for interrogation regarding one offense, he may not be reapproached regarding any offense unless counsel is present. Arizona v. Roberson, 486 U.S. 675 (1988).

Having described the nature and effects of both the Sixth Amendment right to counsel and the *Miranda-Edwards* "Fifth Amendment" right to counsel, we come at last to the issue here: Petitioner seeks to prevail by combining the two of them. He contends that, although he expressly waived his *Miranda* right to counsel on every occasion he was interrogated, those waivers were the invalid product of impermissible approaches, because his prior invocation of the offense-specific Sixth Amendment right with regard to the West Allis burglary was also an invocation of the non-offense-specific *Miranda-Edwards* right. We think that is false as a matter of fact and inadvisable (if even permissible) as a contrary-to-fact presumption of policy.

As to the former: The purpose of the Sixth Amendment counsel guarantee — and hence the purpose of invoking it — is to "protect the unaided layman at critical confrontations" with his "expert adversary," the government, after "the adverse positions of government and defendant have solidified" with respect to a particular alleged crime. *Gouveia*, 467 U.S., at 189. The purpose of the *Miranda-Edwards* guarantee, on the other hand — and hence the purpose of invoking it — is to protect a quite different interest: the suspect's "desire to deal with the police only though counsel," *Edwards*, 451 U.S., at 484. This is in one respect narrower than the interest protected by the Sixth Amendment guarantee (because it relates only to custodial interrogation) and in another respect broader (because it relates to interrogation regarding any suspected crime and attaches whether or not the "adversarial relationship" produced by a pending prosecution has yet arisen). To invoke the Sixth Amendment interest is, as a matter of fact, not to invoke the *Miranda-Edwards* interest. One might be quite willing to speak to the police without counsel present concerning many matters, but not the matter under prosecution. It can be said, perhaps, that it is likely that one who has asked for counsel's assistance in defending against a prosecution would want counsel present for all custodial interrogation, even interrogation unrelated to the charge. That is not necessarily true, since suspects often believe that they can avoid the laying of charges by demonstrating an assurance of innocence through frank and unassisted answers to questions. But even if it were true, the likelihood that a suspect would wish counsel to be present is not the test for applicability of *Edwards*. The rule of that case applies only when the suspect "has expressed" his wish for the particular sort of lawyerly assistance that is the subject of *Miranda*. *Edwards*, supra, at 484. It requires, at a minimum, some statement that can reasonably be construed to be expression of a desire for the assistance of an attorney in dealing with custodial interrogation by the police. Requesting the assistance of an attorney at a bail hearing does not bear that construction. "To find that [the defendant] invoked his Fifth Amendment right to counsel on the present charges merely by requesting the appointment of counsel at his arraignment on the unrelated charge is to disregard the ordinary meaning of the request." State v. Stewart, 780 P.2d 844, 849 (1989).

Our holding in Michigan v. Jackson does not, as petitioner asserts, contradict the foregoing distinction; to the contrary, it rests upon it. That case, it will be recalled, held that after the Sixth Amendment right to counsel attaches and is invoked, any statements obtained from the accused during subsequent police-initiated custodial questioning regarding the charge at issue (even if the accused purports to waive his rights) are inadmissible. The State in *Jackson* opposed that outcome on the ground that assertion of the Sixth Amendment right to counsel did not realistically constitute the expression (as *Edwards* required) of a wish to have counsel present during custodial interrogation. See 475 U.S., at 632-633. Our response to that contention was not that it did constitute such an expression, but that it did not have to, since the relevant question was not whether the *Miranda* "Fifth Amendment" right had been asserted, but whether the Sixth Amendment right to counsel had been waived. We said that since our "settled approach to questions of waiver requires us to give a broad, rather than a narrow, interpretation to a defendant's request for counsel, . . . we presume that the defendant requests the lawyer's services at every critical stage of the prosecution." 475 U.S., at 633. The holding of *Jackson* implicitly rejects any equivalence in fact between invocation of the Sixth Amendment right to counsel and the expression necessary to trigger *Edwards*. If such invocation constituted a real (as opposed to merely a legally presumed) request for the assistance of counsel in custodial interrogation, it would have been quite unnecessary for *Jackson* to go on to establish, as it did, a new Sixth Amendment rule of no police-initiated interrogation; we could simply have cited and relied upon *Edwards*.[1]

There remains to be considered the possibility that, even though the assertion of the Sixth Amendment right to counsel does not in fact imply an assertion of the *Miranda* "Fifth Amendment" right, we should declare it to be such as matter of sound policy. Assuming we have such an expansive power under the Constitution, it would not wisely be exercised. Petitioner's proposed rule has only insignificant advantages. If a suspect does not wish to communicate with the police except through an attorney, he can simply tell them that when they give him the *Miranda* warnings. There is not the remotest chance that he will feel "badgered" by their asking to talk to him without counsel present, since the subject will not be the charge on which he has already requested counsel's assistance (for in that event *Jackson* would preclude initiation of the interview) and he will not have rejected uncounseled interrogation on any subject before (for in that event *Edwards* would preclude initiation of the interview). The proposed rule would, however, seriously impede effective law enforcement. The Sixth Amendment right to counsel attaches at the first formal proceeding against an accused, and in most States, at least with respect to serious offenses, free counsel is made available at that time and ordinarily requested. Thus, if we were to adopt petitioner's rule, most persons in pretrial custody for serious offenses would be unapproachable by police officers suspecting them of involvement in other crimes, even though they have never expressed any unwillingness to be questioned. Since the ready ability to obtain uncoerced confessions is not an evil but an unmitigated good, society would be the loser. Admissions of guilt resulting from valid *Miranda* waivers "are more than merely 'desirable'; they are essential to society's compelling interest in finding, convicting, and punishing those who violate the law." *Moran*, 475 U.S., at 462.

Petitioner urges upon us the desirability of providing a "clear and unequivocal" guideline for the police: no police-initiated questioning of any person in custody who has requested counsel to assist him in defense or in interrogation. But the police do not need our assistance to establish such a guideline; they are free, if they wish, to adopt it on their own. Of course it is our task to establish guidelines for judicial review. We like them to be "clear and unequivocal," but only when they guide sensibly, and in a direction we are authorized to go. Petitioner's proposal would in our view do much more harm than good, and is not contained within, or even in furtherance of, the

---

1. A footnote in *Jackson*, 475 U.S., at 633, n. 7, quoted with approval statements by the Michigan Supreme Court to the effect that the average person does not " 'understand and appreciate the subtle distinctions between the Fifth and Sixth Amendment rights to counsel,' " that it " 'makes little sense to afford relief from further interrogation to a defendant who asks a police officer for an attorney, but permit further interrogation to a defendant who makes an identical request to a judge,' " and that " 'the simple fact that defendant has requested an attorney indicates that he does not believe that he is sufficiently capable of dealing with his adversaries single-handedly.' " Michigan v. Bladel, 365 N.W.2d 56, 67 (1984). Those observations were perhaps true in the context of deciding whether a request for the assistance of counsel in defending against a particular charge implied a desire to have that counsel serve as an "intermediary" for all further interrogation on that charge. They are assuredly not true in the quite different context of deciding whether such a request implies a desire never to undergo custodial interrogation, about anything, without counsel present.

Sixth Amendment's right to counsel or the Fifth Amendment's right against compelled self-incrimination.

"This Court is forever adding new stories to the temples of constitutional law, and the temples have a way of collapsing when one story too many is added." Douglas v. Jeannette, 319 U.S. 157, 181 (1943) (opinion of Jackson, J.). We decline to add yet another story to *Miranda*. The judgment of the Wisconsin Supreme Court is affirmed.

NOTES AND QUESTIONS

1. Are things getting a bit ridiculous? How does one know whether to read the Fifth and Sixth Amendments as dealing with highly analogous problems, as in *Jackson*, or with quite distinct problems, as in *McNeil*? Should *McNeil* be criticized for its obvious disregard of the implications of *Jackson*, or should *Jackson* be criticized for its obvious disregard of the differences between the Fifth and Sixth Amendments? Should virtually all the justices be criticized for their rather curious commitment to a robust theory of precedent?

2. Consider Texas v. Cobb, 532 U.S. 162 (2001):

The Texas Court of Criminal Appeals held that a criminal defendant's Sixth Amendment right to counsel attaches not only to the offense with which he is charged, but to other offenses "closely related factually" to the charged offense. We hold that our decision in McNeil v. Wisconsin, 501 U.S. 171 (1991), meant what it said, and that the Sixth Amendment right is "offense specific."

As for the meaning of the word *offense*,

[A]lthough it is clear that the Sixth Amendment right to counsel attaches only to charged offenses, we have recognized in other contexts that the definition of an "offense" is not necessarily limited to the four corners of a charging instrument. In Blockburger v. United States, 284 U.S. 299 (1932), we explained that "where the same act or transaction constitutes a violation of two distinct statutory provisions, the test to be applied to determine whether there are two offenses or only one, is whether each provision requires proof of a fact which the other does not." Id., at 304. We have since applied the *Blockburger* test to delineate the scope of the Fifth Amendment's Double Jeopardy Clause, which prevents multiple or successive prosecutions for the "same offence." See, e.g., Brown v. Ohio, 432 U.S. 161, 164-166 (1977). We see no constitutional difference between the meaning of the term "offense" in the contexts of double jeopardy and of the right to counsel. Accordingly, we hold that when the Sixth Amendment right to counsel attaches, it does encompass offenses that, even if not formally charged, would be considered the same offense under the *Blockburger* test.

The dissenters worried that

[T]he majority's rule permits law enforcement officials to question those charged with a crime without first approaching counsel, through the simple device of asking questions about any other related crime not actually charged in the indictment. Thus, the police could ask the individual charged with robbery about, say, the assault of the cashier not yet charged, or about any other uncharged offense (unless under *Blockburger*'s definition it counts as the "same crime"), all *without notifying counsel*. Indeed, the majority's rule would permit law enforcement officials to question anyone charged with any crime in any one of the examples just given about his or her conduct on the single relevant occasion without notifying counsel unless the prosecutor has charged every possible crime arising out of that same brief course of conduct. What Sixth Amendment sense — what common sense — does such a rule make? What is left of the "communicate through counsel" rule? The majority's approach is inconsistent with any common understanding of the scope of counsel's representation. It will undermine the lawyer's role as " 'medium' " between the defendant and the government. Maine v. Moulton, supra, at 176. And it will, on a random basis, remove a significant portion of the protection that this Court has found inherent in the Sixth Amendment.

According to the dissenters,

[T]here is, of course, an alternative. We can, and should, define "offense" in terms of the conduct that constitutes the crime that the offender committed on a particular occasion, including criminal acts that are "closely related to" or "inextricably intertwined with" the particular crime set forth in the charging instrument. This alternative is not perfect. The language used lacks the precision for which police officers may hope; and it requires lower courts to specify its meaning further as they apply it in individual cases. Yet virtually every lower court in the United States to consider the issue has defined "offense" in the Sixth Amendment context to encompass such closely related acts.

3. Should the fact of representation alone matter for either Sixth or Fifth Amendment purposes? Consider one last aspect of Moran v. Burbine, 475 U.S. 412 (1986) (other aspects of which are discussed at page 874 supra):

Respondent also contends that the Sixth Amendment requires exclusion of his three confessions. It is clear, of course, that, absent a valid waiver, the defendant has the right to the presence of an attorney during any interrogation occurring after the first formal charging proceeding, the point at which the Sixth Amendment right to counsel initially attaches. And we readily agree that once the right has attached, it follows that the police may not interfere with the efforts of a defendant's attorney to act as a " 'medium' between [the suspect] and the State" during the interrogation. Maine v. Moulton, 474 U.S. 159, 176 (1985). The difficulty for respondent is that the interrogation sessions that yielded the inculpatory statements took place before the initiation of "adversary judicial proceedings." He contends, however, that this circumstance is not fatal to his Sixth Amendment claim. At least in some situations, he argues, the Sixth Amendment protects the integrity of the attorney-client relationship regardless of whether the prosecution has in fact commenced "by way of formal charge, preliminary hearing, indictment, information or arraignment." Placing principal reliance on a footnote in Miranda, and on Escobedo v. Illinois, he maintains that Gouveia, Kirby, and our other "critical stage" cases, concern only the narrow question of when the right to counsel — that is, to the appointment or presence of counsel — attaches. The right to noninterference with an attorney's dealings with a criminal suspect, he asserts, arises the moment that the relationship is formed, or, at the very least, once the defendant is placed in custodial interrogation.

We are not persuaded. At the outset, subsequent decisions foreclose any reliance on Escobedo and Miranda for the proposition that the Sixth Amendment right, in any of its manifestations, applies prior to the initiation of adversary judicial proceedings. Although Escobedo was originally decided as a Sixth Amendment case, "the Court in retrospect perceived that the 'prime purpose' of Escobedo was not to vindicate the constitutional right to counsel as such, but, like Miranda, 'to guarantee full effectuation of the privilege against self-incrimination. . . . '" Kirby v. Illinois, at 689, quoting Johnson v. New Jersey, 384 U.S. 719, 729 (1966). Clearly then, *Escobedo* provides no support for respondent's argument. Nor, of course, does *Miranda*, the holding of which rested exclusively on the Fifth Amendment. Thus, the decision's brief observation about the reach of *Escobedo*'s Sixth Amendment analysis is not only dictum, but reflects an understanding of the case that the Court has expressly disavowed.

Questions of precedent to one side, we find respondent's understanding of the Sixth Amendment both practically and theoretically unsound. As a practical matter, it makes little sense to say that the Sixth Amendment right to counsel attaches at different times depending on the fortuity of whether the suspect or his family happens to have retained counsel prior to interrogation. More importantly, the suggestion that the existence of an attorney-client relationship itself triggers the protections of the Sixth Amendment misconceives the underlying purposes of the right to counsel. The Sixth Amendment's intended function is not to wrap a protective cloak around the attorney-client relationship for its own sake any more than it is to protect a suspect from the consequences of his own candor. Its purpose, rather, is to assure that in any "criminal prosecutio[n]," U.S. Const., Amdt. 6, the accused shall not be left to his own devices in facing the "prosecutorial forces of organized society." Maine v. Moulton, at 170 (quoting Kirby v. Illinois, 406 U.S., at 689). By its very terms, it becomes applicable only when the government's role shifts from investigation to accusation. For it is only then that the assistance of one versed in the "intricacies . . . of law," is needed to assure that the prosecution's case encounters "the crucible of meaningful adversarial testing." United States v. Cronic, 466 U.S. 648, 656 (1984).

Indeed, in Maine v. Moulton, decided this Term, the Court again confirmed that looking to the initiation of adversary judicial proceedings, far from being mere formalism, is fundamental to the proper application of the Sixth Amendment right to counsel. There, we considered the constitutional implications of a surreptitious investigation that yielded evidence pertaining to two crimes. For one, the defendant had been indicted; for the other, he had not. Concerning the former, the Court reaffirmed that after the first charging proceeding the government may not deliberately elicit incriminating statements from an accused out of the presence of counsel. The Court made clear, however, that the evidence concerning the crime for which the defendant had not been indicted—evidence obtained in precisely the same manner from the identical suspect—would be admissible at a trial limited to those charges. The clear implication of the holding . . . is that the Sixth Amendment right to counsel does not attach until after the initiation of formal charges. Moreover, because Moulton already had legal representation, the decision all but forecloses respondent's argument that the attorney-client relationship itself triggers the Sixth Amendment right.

Respondent contends, however, that custodial interrogations require a different rule. Because confessions elicited during the course of police questioning often seal a suspect's fate, he argues, the need for an advocate—and the concomitant right to noninterference with the attorney-client relationship—is at its zenith, regardless of whether the State has initiated the first adversary judicial proceeding. We do not doubt that a lawyer's presence could be of value to the suspect; and we readily agree that if a suspect confesses, his attorney's case at trial will be that much more difficult. But these concerns are no more decisive in this context than they were for the equally damaging preindictment lineup at issue in *Kirby*, or the statements pertaining to the unindicted crime elicited from the defendant in Maine v. Moulton. For an interrogation, no more or less than for any other "critical" pretrial event, the possibility that the encounter may have important consequences at trial, standing alone, is insufficient to trigger the Sixth Amendment right to counsel. As *Gouveia* made clear, until such time as the "'government has committed itself to prosecute, and . . . the adverse positions of government and defendant have solidified'" the Sixth

Amendment right to counsel does not attach. 467 U.S., at 189 (quoting Kirby v. Illinois, supra, at 689).

Because, as respondent acknowledges, the events that led to the inculpatory statements preceded the formal initiation of adversary judicial proceedings, we reject the contention that the conduct of the police violated his rights under the Sixth Amendment.

What does the Court's discussion in *Moran* say about the role of defense lawyers in criminal litigation? In civil litigation, the strong norm is not to talk to represented parties except with their attorneys present. See Model Code of Professional Responsibility DR 7-104(A)(1) (1980) (essentially barring uncounseled contact with represented parties by attorneys or their agents on any matter within the scope of the representation). Why doesn't the same norm exist in criminal investigation? For an explanation and defense of both the civil and the criminal practices, see William J. Stuntz, Lawyers, Deception, and Evidence Gathering, 79 Va. L. Rev. 1903 (1993).

In recent years, defendants have tried to get around *Moran* — at least in cases where a prosecutor was involved at some level in the interrogation of the defendant — by arguing that contact with represented defendants violates legal ethics, see DR 7-104(A), and that any resulting incriminating statements should be suppressed (in addition to any potential ethical sanctions imposed on the offending prosecutor). In United States v. Hammad, 858 F.2d 834 (2d Cir. 1988), *cert. denied*, 498 U.S. 871 (1990), the court seemed to adopt this argument in principle, though it declined to enforce the ethical prohibition with an exclusionary rule. *Hammad* has engendered a great deal of litigation, and a great deal of uncertainty among prosecutors concerning what sorts of contact with represented suspects are allowed. See generally Roger C. Cramton & Lisa K. Udell, State Ethics Rules and Federal Prosecutors: The Controversies over the Anti-contact and Subpoena Rules, 53 U. Pitt. L. Rev. 291 (1992). See also United States v. Lopez, 4 F.3d 1455 (9th Cir. 1993) (adopting *Hammad* for postindictment contacts but overturning the dismissal of an indictment due to *Hammad* violation). In 1998, Congress ended the immediate controversy surrounding the applicability of state ethical rules to federal prosecutors through the enactment of 28 U.S.C.A. §530B(a): "An attorney for the Government shall be subject to State laws and rules, and local Federal court rules, governing attorneys in each State where such attorney engages in that attorney's duties, to the same extent and in the same manner as other attorneys in that State." For discussions, see Frank O. Bowman III, A Bludgeon by Any Other Name: The Misuse of "Ethical Rules" against Prosecutors to Control the Law of the State, 9 Geo. J. Legal Ethics 665 (1996); Carolyn Heck, Knowing the Dancer from the Dance: When the Prosecutor Is Punished for the Government's Conduct, 24 Stetson L. Rev. 68 (1999); Robert Weisberg, Foreword: A New Agenda for Criminal Procedure, 2 Buff. Crim. L. Rev. 367 (1999).

Chapter 7
Investigating Complex Crimes

Much of the law governing criminal investigations that we have looked at thus far has involved the investigation of street crimes — meaning offenses like homicide, robbery, and relatively low-level drug transactions. Most of the cases have grown out of simple investigations conducted for the most part by police. In many of these cases, the criminal investigation has been "reactive." It has begun in the aftermath of a particular crime, in response to a citizen's complaint, and has been directed at identifying and obtaining evidence to prosecute the perpetrator of the crime for the commission of that very offense. Many of the cases have also involved one or another form of "overt" investigation in which law enforcement agents *who are identified as such* have undertaken investigative steps that have included, among other things, conducting interviews, performing searches, and interrogating suspects. Not all of the cases we have addressed have had these characteristics. But neither have they tended to involve overly complicated crimes or, for that matter, sophisticated criminal investigations.

A significant number of criminal investigations, and particularly federal criminal investigations, deal with different types of crime — like securities fraud, public corruption, high-level drug distribution, and various forms of racketeering carried out by ongoing criminal associations. The investigation of such crimes is frequently long term and requires the commitment of substantial state resources. In such cases, law enforcement agents may select the targets of their investigation (or the subject matter) proactively, based on intelligence or leads from reliable sources rather than on complaints from identifiable victims or reports from contemporaneous witnesses. In some of these cases, potential targets may know they are under investigation long before charges are filed and may well be represented by counsel during the investigative phase. Prosecutors and grand juries may play a larger role in the conduct of the investigation. Other complex cases may focus on targets who remain unaware they are under scrutiny. Certain of these cases, however, are also substantially different from more routine criminal cases because they involve sophisticated covert investigative techniques used relatively less frequently in the context of simpler crimes.

Add to all this the added complexities of the post-9/11 environment. Terrorism investigations constituted a major species of complex criminal investigation long before 2001. But the events of September 11 have in many ways transformed the role of law enforcement in counterterrorism efforts. Thus, the imperative of preventing catastrophic terrorist events has placed a new premium on monitoring and surveillance. The relationship between the law enforcement and intelligence communities has changed. The role of preventive detention in our legal system has expanded. The military plays a central role. But the reality is not war or law enforcement, but war *and* law enforcement, intelligence *and* criminal prosecution. This reality is creating an extraordinary range of difficult legal questions at the boundaries, where the concerns of national security overlap or shade into something that, for want of better words, we might term "normal" law enforcement. Indeed, a central question for the study of criminal procedure today may be how the war on terror is transforming "normal" law enforcement or, at a minimum, drawing into question some of its basic assumptions.

The legal issues raised in this chapter usually (though not invariably) arise in the context of more complicated crimes and investigations — including those involving terrorism and the national security. In general, these legal issues have been resolved in favor of law enforcement. Indeed, one theme of the materials that follow may be the relative flexibility, from the government's point of view, of criminal investigation in these kinds of cases. The chapter begins by examining the law regulating the use of electronic surveillance and the search of electronic records. We then turn to the subjects of undercover and grand jury investigations. We conclude with a consideration of the special challenges posed by counterterrorism. Consider as you peruse the following materials why it might be that law enforcement has been afforded the powers it enjoys in the investigation of complex crimes. Also consider whether these powers are justifiable.

A. Electronic Surveillance and the Search of Electronic Data

The electronic surveillance of communications and the search of computer and other electronic files is essential to the investigation of some complex crimes. In organized crime investigations, for example, witnesses and victims may be too intimidated to offer testimony, while it may be nearly impossible for undercover agents to infiltrate the criminal organization so as to obtain evidence sufficient to prosecute its principals. In such cases, the covert electronic surveillance of conversations among the members of criminal associations has proven to be an important investigative technique. Similarly, as people have increasingly turned to computers and the Internet to communicate, transfer information, and engage in commerce, computer crime and the use of computers in criminal activity have also expanded. The evidence of such crimes has frequently come to rest in computer files of one sort or another; the successful investigation of these crimes has often required the government to obtain access to data stored in electronic form on a single computer, on a network, or at a remote location.

The materials considered in this section raise many Fourth Amendment questions but are unlike the search and seizure materials you have already considered in an important way — namely, in this area, legislation has played a central role in setting out the procedures by which law enforcement may investigate crime. There are reasons to applaud legislative involvement of this type. Indeed, Professor Amsterdam argued over 25 years ago that, in general, the "great American vacuum" of such "subconstitutional" controls on police practices constitutes a significant barrier to the effective constraint of arbitrary police conduct. See Anthony G. Amsterdam, Perspectives on the Fourth Amendment, 58 Minn. L. Rev. 349, 380 (1974). At the same time, there may be a downside to legislatures playing a substantial role in the articulation of the rules that will regulate criminal investigations involving computers and electronic records. Consider the following general observation about the protection of constitutional values in cyberspace:

> My fear about cyberspace is that . . . the institutions most responsible for articulating constitutional values will simply stand back while issues of constitutional import are legislatively determined. The institutions most responsible for articulating constitutional values today are the courts. My sense is that they will step back because they feel . . . that these are new questions that cyberspace has raised. Their newness will make them feel political, and when a question feels political, courts step away from resolving it.
>
> I fear this not because I fear legislatures, but because in our day constitutional discourse at the level of the legislature is a very thin sort of discourse. The philosopher Bernard Williams has argued that because the Supreme Court has taken so central a role in the articulation of constitutional values, legislatures no longer do. Whether Williams is correct or not, this much is clear: The constitutional discourse of our present Congress is far below the level it must be at to address the questions about constitutional values that will be raised by cyberspace.

Lawrence Lessig, Code and Other Laws of Cyberspace 120 (1999).

We begin our examination of this subject by stepping back from the new issues involving criminal investigations in cyberspace to consider a decades-old legislative articulation of the procedures that police must employ in the conduct of traditional electronic surveillance. As you may recall from Chapter 5, see supra at page 373, Title III of the Omnibus Crime Control and Safe Streets Act of 1968 was enacted in the wake of the Supreme Court's decisions in Katz v. United States, 389 U.S. 347 (1967), and Berger v. New York, 388 U.S. 41 (1967), to address the constitutional concerns with electronic surveillance raised by those cases. The statute regulates the "nonconsensual" interception through use of any electronic, mechanical, or other device of the contents of any wire, oral, or electronic communications.[1] (An interception for law enforcement purposes is "consensual," and thus falls outside Title III, when any party to the communication consents to being overheard.) The statute sets forth circumstances in which federal law enforcement agencies may obtain court orders from federal judges authorizing interceptions; further, it empowers states to enact statutes permitting state law enforcement agencies to seek similar orders from state judges in keeping with Title III's provisions. Most states have enacted statutes pursuant to this authorization.

We start with Title III and its provisions for the interception of communications. In the next section, we turn to the search and seizure of stored electronic records, using this discussion to take up some broader Fourth Amendment questions associated with the advent of the Information Age. As you read the materials below, consider both the benefits and the potential problems associated with comprehensive legislative approaches to articulating the scope of police powers, and

---

1. Electronic communications, which include facsimile transmissions and electronic mail, were added to Title III's coverage only in 1986, with passage of the Electronic Communications Privacy Act. (Title III's definition of "wire communications" is limited to communications containing the human voice, so that without the 1986 amendment Title III would not apply to communications via wire that transfer only electronic data.) Electronic communications are in some respects treated differently from wire and oral communications in the amended Title III. Significant differences are noted in this discussion.

particularly in investigations involving computers, electronic communications and records, and future technologies.

1. Wiretapping and Related Electronic Surveillance

As Professor Fishman has explained:

> Congress enacted Title III with at least four specific goals in mind. First, in permitting investigators to obtain court authorization to wiretap or eavesdrop, it sought to provide law enforcement officials with a much-needed weapon in their fight against crime, particularly organized crime. Second, it sought to safeguard the privacy of . . . communications. Third, Congress endeavored to satisfy the procedural and substantive requirements previously enunciated by the . . . Supreme Court in Berger v. New York and Katz v. United States as constitutional prerequisites to lawful court-authorized interception of private communications. Finally, it attempted to "define on a uniform basis the circumstances and conditions under which the interception of . . . communications may be authorized."

Clifford S. Fishman, Interception of Communications in Exigent Circumstances: The Fourth Amendment, Federal Legislation, and the United States Department of Justice, 22 Ga. L. Rev. 1, 5-7 (1987). Title III is a detailed legislative scheme. In it, Congress sought to satisfy constitutional prerequisites to electronic surveillance, but also to do more: "The statute does [not] merely parallel the Fourth Amendment and Supreme Court decisions. Congress included within the statute several procedural and substantive safeguards that are not constitutionally mandated, many of which are not applicable to conventional search warrants." Id. at 25.

Title III requires law enforcement agents in most circumstances to obtain a judicial warrant before resorting to the nonconsensual electronic surveillance of wire, oral, or electronic communications. (As noted previously, consensual intercepts — where one party to the communication gives consent to its interception — are generally not covered by Title III.) Federal applications for the interception of wire or oral communications (though not for electronic communications) must also be authorized by specially designated high-ranking Justice Department officials; state applications similarly require the approval of the district attorney or an analogous high-ranking state officer. Applications for surveillance orders, moreover, may be made to seek evidence of only certain statutorily enumerated offenses. (The list of such offenses is very broad as it applies to federal criminal investigations. Indeed, it includes any felony whatsoever when the application is to intercept electronic communications like e-mail or faxes, as opposed to voice communications. The list of offenses that may be investigated using electronic surveillance is considerably narrower, however, in some state statutes.)

Applications for interception orders must be in writing and under oath. They must include details regarding the particular offense under investigation; the type of communication sought to be intercepted; the identity of the person or persons, if known, committing the offense and whose communications are to be intercepted; and the facilities from which or the place where the communication is to be intercepted (unless the circumstances merit the issuance of a "roving" intercept order based on a showing that specification of a surveillance site is not practical with regard to oral communications or that the subject's actions could thwart interception from a specified facility in the case of wire or electronic communications). Applications must also include a "full and complete statement" as to whether or not other investigative techniques have been tried and failed or as to why they reasonably appear to be either unlikely to succeed or too dangerous to attempt. They must describe any previous applications for surveillance of the same persons or places.

An application must include a statement of the period of time for which the interception is required, not to exceed 30 days. When the nature of the investigation requires that the interception not automatically terminate when the described type of communication has been first obtained (for example, when the first drug-related conversation occurs in the investigation of a narcotics organization), the application must also include "a particular description of facts establishing probable cause to believe that additional communications of the same type will occur thereafter. . . ." Extensions of wiretap orders are available, but only on a new showing of probable cause and compliance with the same procedures used in obtaining the initial order. Extension applications must also include a statement setting forth the results obtained from the prior interception or a reasonable explanation of the failure to obtain such results.

Interception orders are premised on multiple probable cause determinations: that a person is about to commit, is committing, or has committed an offense falling within Title III's coverage, that the proposed surveillance will result in the interception of particular communications concerning that offense, and (outside the context of roving intercept orders) that the particular facilities or place where communications are to be intercepted is being or is about to be used in connection with the offense (or is listed in the name of, leased to, or otherwise commonly used by the person or persons under suspicion). The order must contain "a particular description of the type of communication sought to be intercepted." The court must make a finding that other investigative techniques will be inadequate. As the Supreme Court said in United States v. Kahn, 415 U.S. 143, 153 n. 12 (1974), electronic surveillance pursuant to Title III should not be permitted if "traditional investigative techniques would suffice to expose the crime."

The statute also provides that within a reasonable period, but no later than 90 days after the denial of an interception application or the termination of a period of authorized surveillance, the judge who reviewed the Title III application must serve an "inventory" on the people named in the order or application and on such other parties to intercepted communications as the judge may determine is in the interest of justice. (The service of the inventory may be postponed for good cause.) The inventory notifies the parties served of the fact of an interception order or application; the dates of the application, the order, and the period of interception; and the information whether or not communications were obtained.

Intercept orders may require periodic reports to be made to the issuing judge showing what progress has been made toward intercepting the sought-after communications and explaining the need for continued interception. In addition, agents executing a surveillance order are required where possible to record on tape or other comparable device all the communications they intercept. Title III requires that immediately upon the termination of an interception order, recordings must be made available to the judge who issued the interception order and sealed under his direction.

Title III provides for both criminal and civil remedies against those who willfully intercept, use, or disclose information in violation of the statute. Violations of Title III are also enforced by a statutory exclusionary rule that applies to the interception of wire and oral (but not electronic) communications in violation of its terms. This rule, however, does not require suppression of evidence whenever there is a failure to comply with the statute's provisions. In United States v. Giordano, 416 U.S. 505, 528 (1974), the Supreme Court concluded that the law's exclusionary remedy extends to violations of those statutory provisions that play "a central role in the statutory scheme."

Finally, Title III contains a "minimization" requirement. This requirement addresses the reality that law enforcement agents executing an intercept order frequently gain access to communications unrelated to the crimes under investigation. Title III requires that surveillance "be conducted in such a way as to minimize the interception of communications not otherwise subject to interception under this chapter. . . ." 18 U.S.C. §2518(5). The primary way that officers intercepting conversations have satisfied this requirement is by listening to the conversations as they take place and stopping their interception (and listening) when they determine that a particular conversation is not pertinent to the investigation. The Supreme Court addressed the question of what consequences flow from the deliberate disregard of this provision in the following case.

SCOTT v. UNITED STATES

Certiorari to the United States Court of Appeals for the D.C. Circuit
436 U.S. 128 (1978)

MR. JUSTICE REHNQUIST delivered the opinion of the Court.

In 1968, Congress enacted Title III of the Omnibus Crime Control and Safe Streets Act of 1968, which deals with wiretapping and other forms of electronic surveillance. In this Act Congress, after this Court's decisions in Berger v. New York, 388 U.S. 41 (1967), and Katz v. United States, 389 U.S. 347 (1967), set out to provide law enforcement officials with some of the tools thought necessary to combat crime without unnecessarily infringing upon the right of individual privacy. . . . This case requires us to construe the statutory requirement that wiretapping or electronic surveillance "be conducted in such a way as to minimize the interception of communications not otherwise subject to interception under this chapter. . . ." 18 U.S.C. §2518(5) (1976 ed.).

Pursuant to judicial authorization which required such minimization, Government agents intercepted all the phone conversations over a particular phone for a period of one month. The District Court for the District of Columbia suppressed all intercepted conversations and evidence derived therefrom in essence because the "admitted knowing and purposeful failure by the monitoring agents to comply with the minimization order was unreasonable . . . even if every intercepted call were narcotic-related." The Court of Appeals for the District of Columbia Circuit reversed, concluding that an assessment of the reasonableness of the efforts at minimization first requires an evaluation of the reasonableness of the actual interceptions in light of the purpose of the wiretap and the totality of the circumstances before any inquiry is made into the subjective intent of the agents conducting the surveillance. We granted certiorari to consider this important question and, finding ourselves in basic agreement with the Court of Appeals, affirm.

I

In January 1970, Government officials applied, pursuant to Title III, for authorization to wiretap a telephone registered to Geneva Jenkins. The supporting affidavits alleged that there was probable cause to believe nine individuals, all named, were participating in a conspiracy to import and distribute narcotics in the Washington, D.C., area and that Geneva Jenkins' telephone had been used in furtherance of the conspiracy, particularly by petitioner Thurmon, who was then living with Jenkins. The District Court granted the application on January 24, 1970. . . . Interception began that same day and continued, pursuant to a judicially authorized extension, until February 24, 1970, with the agents making the periodic reports to the judge as required. Upon cessation of the interceptions, search and arrest warrants were executed which led to the arrest of 22 persons and the indictment of 14.

Before trial the defendants . . . moved to suppress all the intercepted conversations on a variety of grounds. After comprehensive discovery and an extensive series of hearings, the District Court held that the agents had failed to comply with the minimization requirement contained in the wiretap order and ordered suppression of the intercepted conversations and all derivative evidence. The court relied in large part on the fact that virtually all the conversations were intercepted while only 40% of them were shown to be narcotics related . . .

The Court of Appeals for the District of Columbia Circuit reversed and remanded. . . .

Upon remand, the District Court again ordered suppression, this time relying largely on the fact that the agents were aware of the minimization requirement, "but made no attempt to comply therewith."[7] . . .

The Court of Appeals again reversed, holding that the District Court had yet to apply the correct standard. . . .

On the remand from the Court of Appeals, following a nonjury trial on stipulated evidence which consisted primarily of petitioners' intercepted conversations, Scott was found guilty of selling and purchasing narcotics not in the original

---

7. This conclusion was based on the fact that virtually all calls were intercepted and on the testimony of Special Agent Glennon Cooper, the agent in charge of the investigation, who testified that the only steps taken which actually resulted in the nonreception of a conversation were those taken when the agents discovered the wiretap had inadvertently been connected to an improper line. The Court laid particular stress on the following exchange:

"BY THE COURT:
"Q. The question I wish to ask you is this, whether at any time during the course of the wiretap — of the intercept, what if any steps were taken by you or any agent under you to minimize the listening?
"A. Well, as I believe I mentioned before, I would have to say that the only effective steps taken by us to curtail the reception of conversations was in that instance where the line was connected to — misconnected from the correct line and connected to an improper line. We discontinued at that time.
"Q. Do I understand from you then that the only time that you considered minimization was when you found that you had been connected with a wrong number?
"A. That is correct, Your Honor."

stamped package and Thurmon of conspiracy to sell narcotics. The Court of Appeals affirmed the convictions, and we granted certiorari.

II

Petitioners' principal contention is that the failure to make good-faith efforts to comply with the minimization requirement is itself a violation of §2518(5). ... Thus, argue petitioners, Agent Cooper's testimony, which is basically a concession that the Government made no efforts which resulted in the noninterception of any call, is dispositive of the matter. ...

The Government responds that petitioners' argument fails to properly distinguish between what is necessary to establish a statutory or constitutional violation and what is necessary to support a suppression remedy once a violation has been established. In view of the deterrent purposes of the exclusionary rule, consideration of official motives may play some part in determining whether application of the exclusionary rule is appropriate *after* a statutory or constitutional violation has been established. But the existence *vel non* of such a violation turns on an objective assessment of the officer's actions in light of the facts and circumstances confronting him at the time. Subjective intent alone, the Government contends, does not make otherwise lawful conduct illegal or unconstitutional.[11]

We think the Government's position ... embodies the proper approach for evaluating compliance with the minimization requirement. Although we have not examined this exact question at great length in any of our prior opinions, almost without exception in evaluating alleged violations of the Fourth Amendment the Court has first undertaken an objective assessment of an officer's actions in light of the facts and circumstances then known to him. The language of the Amendment itself proscribes only "unreasonable" searches and seizures. ...

We have ... held that the fact that the officer does not have the state of mind which is hypothecated by the reasons which provide the legal justification for the officer's action does not invalidate the action taken as long as the circumstances, viewed objectively, justify that action. In United States v. Robinson, 414 U.S. 218 (1973), a suspect was searched incident to a lawful arrest. He challenged the search on the ground that the motivation for the search did not coincide with the legal justification for the search-incident-to-arrest exception. We rejected this argument: "Since it is the fact of custodial arrest which gives rise to the authority to search, it is of no moment that [the officer] did not indicate any subjective fear of the respondent or that he did not himself suspect that respondent was armed." Id., at 236. ...

Petitioners do not appear, however, to rest their argument entirely on Fourth Amendment principles. Rather, they argue in effect that regardless of the search-and-seizure analysis conducted under the Fourth Amendment, the statute regulating wiretaps requires the agents to make good-faith efforts at minimization, and the failure to make such efforts is itself a violation of the statute which requires suppression.

This argument fails for more than one reason. In the first place, in the very section in which it directs minimization Congress, by its use of the word

11. The Government also adds that even if subjective intent were the standard, the record does not support the District Court's conclusion that the agents subjectively intended to violate the statute or the Constitution. It contends that the failure to stop intercepting calls, the interception of which was entirely reasonable, does not support a finding that the agents would have intercepted calls that should not have been intercepted had they been confronted with that situation. We express no view on this matter.

"conducted," made it clear that the focus was to be on the agents' actions not their motives. Any lingering doubt is dispelled by the legislative history which, as we have recognized before in another context, declares that §2515 was not intended "generally to press the scope of the suppression role beyond present search and seizure law." S. Rep. No. 1097, 90th Cong., 2d Sess., 96 (1968).

III

We turn now to the Court of Appeals' analysis of the reasonableness of the agents' conduct in intercepting all of the calls in this particular wiretap. Because of the necessarily ad hoc nature of any determination of reasonableness, there can be no inflexible rule of law which will decide every case. The statute does not forbid the interception of all nonrelevant conversations, but rather instructs the agents to conduct the surveillance in such a manner as to "minimize" the interception of such conversations. Whether the agents have in fact conducted the wiretap in such a manner will depend on the facts and circumstances of each case.

We agree with the Court of Appeals that blind reliance on the percentage of nonpertinent calls intercepted is not a sure guide to the correct answer. Such percentages may provide assistance, but there are surely cases, such as the one at bar, where the percentage of nonpertinent calls is relatively high and yet their interception was still reasonable. The reasons for this may be many. Many of the nonpertinent calls may have been very short. Others may have been one-time only calls. Still other calls may have been ambiguous in nature or apparently involved guarded or coded language. In all these circumstances agents can hardly be expected to know that the calls are not pertinent prior to their termination.

In determining whether the agents properly minimized, it is also important to consider the circumstances of the wiretap. For example, when the investigation is focusing on what is thought to be a widespread conspiracy more extensive sur-veillance may be justified in an attempt to determine the precise scope of the enterprise. And it is possible that many more of the conversations will be permis-sibly interceptible because they will involve one or more of the co-conspirators. The type of use to which the telephone is normally put may also have some bearing on the extent of minimization required. . . .

Other factors may also play a significant part in a particular case. For example, it may be important to determine at exactly what point during the authorized period the interception was made. During the early stages of surveillance the agents may be forced to intercept all calls to establish categories of nonpertinent calls which will not be intercepted thereafter. Interception of those same types of calls might be unreasonable later on. . . .

After consideration of the minimization claim in this case in the light of these observations, we find nothing to persuade us that the Court of Appeals was wrong in its rejection of that claim. Forty percent of the calls were clearly narcotics related and the propriety of their interception is, of course, not in dispute. Many of the remaining calls were very short, such as wrong-number calls, calls to persons who were not available to come to the phone, and calls to the telephone company to hear the recorded weather message which lasts less than 90 seconds. In a case such as this, involving a wide-ranging conspiracy with a large number of participants, even a seasoned listener would have been hard pressed to determine with any precision the relevancy of many of the calls before they were completed. A large number were ambiguous in nature. . . . And some of the nonpertinent conversations were one-time conversations. . . .

We are thus left with the seven calls between Jenkins and her mother. The first four calls were intercepted over a three-day period at the very beginning of the surveillance. They were of relatively short length and at least two of them indicated that the mother may have known of the conspiracy. The next two calls, which occurred about a week later, both contained statements from the mother to the effect that she had something to tell Jenkins regarding the "business" but did not want to do so over the phone. The final call was substantially longer and likewise contained a statement which could have been interpreted as having some bearing on the conspiracy, i.e., that one "Reds," a suspect in the conspiracy, had called to ask for a telephone number. Although none of these conversations turned out to be material . . . we cannot say that the Court of Appeals was incorrect in concluding that the agents did not act unreasonably at the time they made these interceptions. Its judgment is accordingly
   Affirmed.

MR. JUSTICE BRENNAN, with whom MR. JUSTICE MARSHALL joins, dissenting.

In 1968, Congress departed from the longstanding national policy forbidding surreptitious interception of wire communications, by enactment of Title III of the Omnibus Crime Control and Safe Streets Act of 1968, 18 U.S.C. §§2510-2520 (1976 ed.). That Act, for the first time authorizing law enforcement personnel to monitor private telephone conversations, provided strict guidelines and limitations on the use of wiretaps as a barrier to Government infringement of individual privacy. One of the protections thought essential by Congress as a bulwark against unconstitutional governmental intrusion on private conversations is the "minimization requirement" of §2518(5). The Court today eviscerates this congressionally mandated protection of individual privacy. . . .

. . . The District Court found a "knowing and purposeful failure" to comply with the minimization requirements. [This] finding, made on remand after reexamination, reiterated the District Court's initial finding that "[the agents] did not even attempt 'lip service compliance' with the provision of the order and statutory mandate but rather completely disregarded it." . . . [T]he Court holds that no violation of §2518(5) occurred. The basis for that conclusion is a *post hoc* reconstruction offered by the Government of what would have been reasonable assumptions on the part of the agents had they attempted to comply with the statute. Since, on the basis of this reconstruction of reality, it would have been reasonable for the agents to assume that each of the calls dialed and received was likely to be in connection with the criminal enterprise, there was no violation, notwithstanding the fact that the agents intercepted every call with no effort to minimize interception of the noninterceptable calls. That reasoning is thrice flawed.

First, and perhaps most significant, it totally disregards the explicit congressional command that the wiretap be *conducted* so as to minimize interception of communications not subject to interception. Second, it blinks reality by accepting, as a substitute for the good-faith exercise of judgment as to which calls should not be intercepted by the agent most familiar with the investigation, the *post hoc* conjectures of the Government as to how the agent would have acted had he exercised his judgment. Because it is difficult to know with any degree of certainty whether a given communication is subject to interception prior to its interception, there necessarily must be a margin of error permitted. But we do not enforce the basic premise of the Act that intrusions of privacy must be kept to the minimum by excusing the failure of the agent to make the good-faith effort to minimize which Congress mandated. . . . Finally, the Court's holding permits Government agents deliberately to flout the duty imposed upon them by Congress. In a linguistic *tour de force* the Court converts the mandatory language that the interception "shall be conducted" to a precatory suggestion. . . .

[T]he Court manifests a disconcerting willingness to unravel individual threads of statutory protection without regard to their interdependence and to whether the cumulative effect is to rend the fabric of Title III's "congressionally designed bulwark against conduct of authorized electronic surveillance in a manner that violates the constitutional guidelines announced in Berger v. New York, 388 U.S. 41 (1967), and Katz v. United States, 389 U.S. 347 (1967)," Bynum v. United States, 423 U.S. 952 (1975) (BRENNAN, J., dissenting from denial of certiorari). This process of myopic, incremental denigration of Title III's safeguards raises the specter that, as judicially "enforced," Title III may be vulnerable to constitutional attack for violation of Fourth Amendment standards, thus defeating the careful effort Congress made to avert that result.

NOTES AND QUESTIONS

1. Consider the *Scott* majority's Fourth Amendment analysis. The Court is correct, isn't it, that an objective standard of reasonableness is often employed in judging the propriety of searches and seizures? But even assuming this to be the case, should the same analysis necessarily be applicable in the context of the surreptitious electronic surveillance of private conversations? Clifford Fishman argues that "in complex investigations, where the government, with superficial plausibility can retroactively defend total interception, it is unlikely that any minimization will be achieved unless a good-faith effort is made to do so." Clifford Fishman, The "Minimization" Requirement in Electronic Surveillance: Title III, the Fourth Amendment and the Dred Scott Decision, 28 Am. U. L. Rev. 315, 354-355 (1979). Does this suggest the need for a different approach to Fourth Amendment questions here? What is the basis for the Court's reluctance to consider the subjective intent of the officers conducting electronic surveillance?

2. What about the Court's statutory analysis? Title III is not the only statute regulating law enforcement activities that implicate privacy concerns. By way of example, the Supreme Court's holdings in both United States v. Miller, 424 U.S. 435 (1976) (that a bank depositor has no Fourth Amendment interest in the bank's records of his financial transactions), and Smith v. Maryland, 442 U.S. 735 (1979) (that the installation of a pen register to record the numbers dialed on an individual's telephone raises no Fourth Amendment concern), first examined in Chapter 5 at page 378 supra, have been at least partially superseded by federal laws that provide limited statutory protections to privacy interests not found to raise Fourth Amendment concerns.[2]

---

2. In the context of financial records, Congress has generally prohibited the government from securing such records without obtaining a subpoena or a search warrant. 12 U.S.C. §3402. Federal law presently requires that a court order be obtained prior to the installation or use of a pen register. Such orders issue based on a certification by law enforcement authorities that the information likely to be obtained through use of such a device is relevant to an ongoing criminal investigation. 18 U.S.C. §3123.

At the same time, Title III is noteworthy in that it establishes standards for the conduct of law enforcement in a sensitive area implicating core Fourth Amendment interests. Note that the existence of a statute regulating police intrusions into areas protected by the Fourth Amendment may offer courts the opportunity to avoid constitutional decisions through statutory interpretation. Does this suggest that a court should approach Title III's interpretation any differently than in the normal statutory case?

3. Recall that the Court in *Berger* had numerous objections to New York's wiretapping statute: that it did not require specification that any particular offense had been or was being committed, or any particularization of the conversations sought; that it authorized continuous eavesdropping for a two-month period on a single showing of probable cause, and then permitted extensions "on a mere showing" that they were in the public interest; that it placed no termination date on the eavesdrop once the conversation sought was seized; that it did not require notice to parties whose conversations had been overheard or at least some showing of special facts as to why notice could not be given; and, finally, that it did not require a return on the warrant, "thereby leaving full discretion in the officer as to the use of seized conversations of innocent as well as guilty parties." See supra at page 304. Does Title III adequately deal with these concerns?

Note in particular that the *Berger* Court emphasized that permitting 60 days of eavesdropping pursuant to a wiretap order amounted to "the equivalent of a series of intrusions, searches, and seizures" on a single showing of probable cause in which "the conversations of any and all persons coming into the area covered by the device will be seized indiscriminately and without regard to their connection with the crime under investigation." Does shortening the maximum period of surveillance pursuant to an initial court order to no more than 30 days and requiring probable cause to believe pertinent interceptions will occur throughout that period sufficiently address this concern? Doesn't the *Berger* Court's analysis at least suggest that substantial efforts must be made to minimize the interception of communications unrelated to the investigation? Is *Scott* consistent with *Berger* in this regard?

4. Consider the following discussion:

> Given the difficulties of sorting out, in real time, the pertinent telephone calls from nonpertinent ones, the executing officers necessarily enjoy[] broad discretion in intercepting communications whose significance [is] ambiguous. As a result, it sometimes . . . is . . . difficult to enforce meaningfully the requirement that the intercepting officers minimize the interception of nonpertinent communications. But however difficult aural communications may be to minimize in real time, for electronic communications real time minimization is impossible. Electronic communications, such as e-mails and faxes, arrive at their destination more or less all at once. Even if transmission takes as long as several minutes, by the time it is intercepted, it usually must be intercepted in its entirety—without the ability to first determine who the sender or receiver is, where it's being sent from, or what the subject or even one part of the communication is. Such communications must be minimized, if at all, only after they are intercepted.

Martin Marcus and Christopher Slobogin, ABA Sets Standards for Electronic and Physical Surveillance, 18 Crim. Just. 5, 10-11 (2003). When the technological means by which a suspect is communicating do not permit officers to minimize the *interception* of nonpertinent communications, what (if anything) should the law require by way of minimization after the fact? Indeed, what should minimization mean in this context? Deletion of the nonpertinent e-mails? Retention, but with tight restrictions on dissemination? Something else? Note that Title III already provides that "[i]n the event the intercepted communication is in a code or foreign language, and an expert in that foreign language or code is not reasonably available during the interception period, minimization may be accomplished as soon as practicable after such interception." 18 U.S.C. §2518(5). Does this mean that nonpertinent communications are simply not to be translated or decoded?

5. Technological change since Title III was enacted has affected not only the ability to "minimize" in compliance with the law's terms, but also the way in which communications are intercepted in the first place. Consider the interception of e-mail and the controversy surrounding the FBI's ill-named "Carnivore" program:

> [T]he Internet is a packet-switched network. All Internet communications are broken down into discrete packets and sent over the network, and then reassembled into the original communications when they reach their final destination. As a result, a great deal of prospective Internet surveillance is packet surveillance. To conduct prospective surveillance, a tool must "tap" a particular line of Internet traffic at a particular physical location to look for the communication sought. . . . Any device or software programmed to do this on the Internet is generally known as a "packet sniffer," as it "sniffs" Internet packets flowing through the particular point in the network.
>
> One implication of this technology is that Internet packet surveillance must always involve examining all of the packet traffic streaming by a particular point on the network . . .
>
> [T]he Internet reverses the common associations about the relationship between technology and privacy. In the physical world, advanced technology provides a powerful way to invade privacy. A single police officer can search a single room . . . but cannot search an entire neighborhood, or a large city. To search an entire city, advanced technology would be required. At an intuitive level, a bigger and more invasive search requires a more powerful tool.
>
> In the case of Internet surveillance . . . the way that the technology works mandates that the default will be the most invasive search possible, and that advanced technology is needed to minimize the invasion of privacy. . . . [A] system administrator (or a twelve-year-old computer hacker) can easily monitor all information flowing through a particular point in a network by writing a simple program. The program simply instructs the computer to record all of the traffic flowing through that computer: It creates a packet sniffer and sets it to sniff all of the traffic. The system administrator (or hacker) can later convert the recorded digits into text and look through the entire world of traffic that flowed over the network. The real technological challenge is devising a tool that acts as an effective filter, and isolates and records only the exact packets that a court order allows, rather than a tool that collects everything and requires subsequent review by a human being. . . .
>
> In the mid- to late-1990s, the FBI . . . began designing surveillance tools that could filter and analyze Internet communications more effectively. The core difficulty lay in the private sector's inability to develop such a tool absent market demand. . . . The FBI needed a surveillance tool that protected the privacy of Internet users more than the surveillance tools routinely used by system administrators. . . .

The FBI therefore designed Carnivore — and its progeny, such as the third-generation tool given the more innocuous label "DCS-1000" — to ensure compliance with court orders while minimizing the invasion of privacy. . . . Carnivore is essentially an everyday Internet tool with a few extra features designed to ensure compliance with court orders. . . .

Unfortunately, both commentators and the press have portrayed Carnivore as a frightening and mysterious beast that invades privacy willy-nilly. The menacing name itself probably accounts for much of this criticism, and a misunderstanding of how the Internet inverts the traditional relationship between privacy and technology accounts for much of the rest. . . .

Orin S. Kerr, Internet Surveillance Law after the USA PATRIOT Act: The Big Brother that Isn't, 97 Nw. U. L. Rev. 607, 649-54 (2003). Assume that Professor Kerr is right about the need for filtering technology to protect privacy in Internet surveillance. (He probably is.) How can law enforcement overcome public concern about the use of technology that effectively scans all passing traffic, even if it is capable of retrieving for human eyes only the relevant communications of a suspect? Consider in this connection Professor Etzioni's description of the results of an outside review of Carnivore completed in 2000:

A review of Carnivore conducted by the Illinois Institute of Technology concluded that although it does not completely eliminate the risk of capturing unauthorized information, Carnivore is better than any existing alternatives because it can be configured to comply with the limitations of a court order. However, the report also determined that failure to include audit trails makes the FBI's internal review process deficient. Specifically, the operator implementing a Carnivore search selects either pen [obtaining addressing information] or full [obtaining e-mail contents] mode by clicking a box on a computer screen, and the program does not keep track of what kind of search has been run. Therefore, it is difficult, if not impossible, to determine if an operator has used the program only as specified in the court order. Furthermore, it is impossible to trace actions to specific individuals because everyone uses the same user ID. The head of the review panel commented, "Even if you conclude that the software is flawless and it will do what you set it to do and nothing more, you still have to make sure that the legal, human, and organizational controls are adequate." . . .

Amitai Etzioni, Implications of Select New Technologies for Individual Rights and Public Safety, 15 Harv. J. L. & Tech. 257, 278 (2002). Who is best positioned to provide such "legal, human, and organizational" controls: courts, legislatures, or the police organization itself?

6. Note that Title III restricts the ability of criminal investigators to disseminate intercepted communications. (Setting aside disclosure in court or legitimate use in the course of performing her official duties, a law enforcement officer is authorized to disclose the contents of taps only "to another investigative or law enforcement officer to the extent that such disclosure is appropriate to the proper performance of the official duties of the officer making or receiving the disclosure." 18 U.S.C. §2517(1).) This statutory restriction contrasts with the Fourth Amendment law we have examined. In Fourth Amendment law, there are relatively few cases that touch upon the reasonable *use* of private information lawfully obtained by police: Thus, we have many cases about whether police can look inside

a glove compartment, but very few implicating the question whether they can display the contents on the evening news. But there is a strong rationale for limitations on use:

> [A] limit [on the dissemination of evidence] serves to ensure that problematic search tactics will not be abused. If the police can disclose what they find, innocent but embarrassing discoveries can be the basis of a kind of blackmail. [If] there is no obvious law enforcement need for disclosure, this limit seems like a rare example of a nearly costless protection. Also one that nicely mirrors the solution our society has embraced for a whole host of necessary-but-potentially-problematic privacy intrusions: The IRS can find out a good deal of private information about my finances, but agents cannot leak that information to the local press or turn it over to just any government actor who asks for it. The consequence is that my privacy is reasonably well-protected, even while the government gets the information it needs to assess my tax liability.

William J. Stuntz, Local Policing After the Terror, 111 Yale L.J. 2137, 2185 (2002).

Note, however, that in the wake of the terrorist attacks of September 11, the USA PATRIOT Act (Uniting and Strengthening America by Providing Appropriate Tools Required to Intercept and Obstruct Terrorism Act) of 2001, Pub. L. No. 107-156, 115 Stat. 272, loosened Title III's restrictions on dissemination in the context of information related to foreign intelligence and terrorism, providing that:

> Any investigative or law enforcement officer, or attorney for the Government, who by any means authorized by [Title III], has obtained knowledge of the contents of any wire, oral, or electronic communications . . . may disclose such contents to any other Federal law enforcement, intelligence, protective, immigration, national defense, or national security official to the extent that such contents include foreign intelligence or counterintelligence . . . information . . . , to assist the official who is to receive that information in the performance of his official duties. Any Federal official who receives information pursuant to this provision may use that information only as necessary in the conduct of that person's official duties subject to any limitations on the unauthorized disclosure of such information.

18 U.S.C. §2517(6). The Act provides that disclosure may also be made to "any appropriate Federal, State, local, or foreign government official" to the extent that the contents of Title III surveillance reveal: (1) a threat of actual or potential attack or other grave hostile acts by foreign powers or their agents; (2) domestic or international sabotage; (3) domestic or international terrorism; or (4) certain clandestine intelligence gathering activities, for the purpose of preventing or responding to such threats. These provisions were drafted to sunset on December 31, 2005. What are the benefits of attaching a sunset provision to measures of this type?

7. What, precisely, is a roving wiretap? As Professor Fishman has explained:

> The [roving intercept provision in Title III] creates an express exception in certain circumstances to the requirement that an application and order specify the telephone to be tapped or the location to be bugged. . . .
>
> To obtain a roving intercept order, investigators must satisfy the standard Title III requirements and, in addition, must identify the intended interceptee, make a special

showing of need to justify waiving the particular location or facilities requirement, and "particularly describe" the sought-after conversations in ways that differ from a standard intercept order. Moreover, fewer Justice Department officials are empowered to authorize a roving intercept application than are empowered to authorize a standard intercept order application. . . .

In essence, in the roving intercept provision, Congress has substituted particularity of the interceptee's identity for particularity of the facilities or location of the intercept. A standard Title III application and order must include "the identity of the person, if known, committing the offense and whose communications are to be intercepted." . . . By contrast, under the roving intercept provision, an oral, wire, or electronic intercept application is sufficient only if it "identifies the person . . . committing the offense and whose communications are to be intercepted. . . ."

. . . This more demanding identification requirement precludes investigators from using a roving intercept order as authority to intercept communications between two "unknowns."

Clifford S. Fishman, Interception of Communications in Exigent Circumstances: The Fourth Amendment, Federal Legislation, and the United States Department of Justice, 22 Ga. L. Rev. 1, 48-51 (1987). Professor Maclin has more succinctly characterized the roving wiretap provision as authorizing "a wiretap that follows a person instead of a phone." Tracey Maclin, Amending the Fourth: Another Grave Threat to Liberty, National L. J. Nov. 12, 2001. Does such a provision square with the Fourth Amendment's requirement that "no Warrants shall issue, but upon probable cause . . . particularly describing the place to be searched, and the persons or things to be seized"? Note that Title III's roving wiretap provision, 18 U.S.C. §2518(11), was added to the statute in 1986. The Supreme Court has not ruled on the constitutionality of roving wiretaps, but a number of lower federal courts have found such taps to be consistent with the Fourth Amendment. See, e.g., United States v. Petti, 973 F.2d 1441, 1445 (9th Cir. 1992), *cert. denied*, 507 U.S. 1035 (1993) (concluding that "[t]he conditions imposed on 'roving' wiretap surveillance . . . satisfy the purposes of the particularity requirement").

8. Finally, let's return to Title III's minimization requirement. At least in the context of aural communications, this requirement often means that, in practice, officers must continuously monitor a tap to detect incriminating material, while minimizing the interception of unrelated communications. To the extent that the minimization requirement may in some cases impose an obligation on law enforcement to commit officers round-the-clock, does this administrative feature of the statute itself serve a civil liberties function? Might it at least help confine Title III's use to cases justifying a significant commitment of state resources?

9. Along similar lines, consider the following. According to the Sourcebook of Criminal Justice Statistics, there were 578 court-authorized orders for the interception of wire, oral, or electronic communications in 2003 in federal court and 864 such orders emanating from state courts. Narcotics investigations accounted for the bulk of these intercept orders (1,104 out of the 1,442), with racketeering coming in a distant second (96 orders). Given that some 70,092 criminal cases were filed by federal prosecutors alone in 2003, these figures would seem to suggest that Title III's use is confined to a relatively small percentage of criminal investigations. Why might this be so?

2. The Search of Electronic Files

Title III's core provisions apply only to the interception of wire, oral, and electronic communications as they are being made or transmitted, and not to the search and seizure of electronic communications that have reached a destination and are held in electronic storage—for instance, the e-mail that has traveled to an Internet service provider and sits there until its addressee logs on and downloads it. Government access to some communications of this type (like the copy of a friend's e-mail that you download from your online account to your personal home computer) are not governed by statute, but solely by the Fourth Amendment. Certain provisions of the Electronic Communications Privacy Act ("ECPA"), 18 U.S.C. §§2701-2712, however, regulate government access to communications held by the providers of electronic communication or remote computing services to the public.

Consider that when using the Internet, individuals typically have accounts consisting of a block of computer storage that is owned by an Internet service provider like America Online. Such Internet service providers

> . . . temporarily store e-mail communications. For example, suppose Doe sends an e-mail to Roe. The e-mail travels to Roe's ISP and sits there until Roe logs on and downloads her e-mail. Under certain circumstances, a copy of that e-mail may even be kept by Roe's ISP after it is downloaded. With many ISPs, users can also keep copies of previously read e-mail on the ISP's server. Maintaining copies of previously read e-mail with an ISP can be particularly useful, since this enables a person to access the e-mail from remote locations via the Internet. . . . Additionally, ISPs often maintain an outbox folder that contains copies of all the e-mail that a person has sent out.

Daniel J. Solove, Digital Dossiers and the Dissipation of Fourth Amendment Privacy, 75 S. Cal. L. Rev. 1083, 1141 (2002). The ECPA regulates government access to the contents of electronic communications stored by "electronic communications service" providers—Internet service providers, telephone companies, or any others that provide to users the ability to send or receive wire or electronic communications. The Act also provides statutory protection to communications held by providers of "remote computing services" (for example, Internet companies that offer remote backup storage to businesses, or Internet payroll processing services to which small businesses send their employee data for computer processing).

An Internet service provider like America Online can and often does provide both electronic communications service and remote computing service: In the example above, for instance, the ISP that received an e-mail for Roe provided electronic communications service while the e-mail sat in temporary storage until Roe downloaded it. If after reading the message Roe elects to store the e-mail with the ISP rather than delete it, however, the ISP will be providing remote computing services to Roe for the purposes of the ECPA.

The relevant provisions of the ECPA apply to communications in electronic storage—meaning, with regard to electronic communications services, any *temporary*, intermediate storage of the communication incidental to its electronic transmission to its final recipient or any associated backup of this communication by the server. (In the case of remote computing services, the law protects data received by electronic transmission and maintained on the remote computing service provider's system.) The statute does not apply to stored communications such as an individual's word processing files or downloaded e-mails residing on an enduser's hard drive, even when these files were once transmitted via e-mail. Nor does the law generally apply to data maintained on internal corporate computer networks. The Computer Crime and Intellectual Property Section of the Justice Department's Criminal Division has opined that the ECPA's drafters:

> . . . believed that computing services available to the public required more strict regulation than services not available to the public. (Perhaps this judgment reflects the view that providers available to the public are not likely to have close relationships with their customers, and therefore might have less incentive to protect their customers' privacy).

Searching and Seizing Computers and Obtaining Electronic Evidence in Criminal Investigations 83 (DOJ, July 2002).

The ECPA generally prohibits providers who serve the public from disclosing the contents of stored communications. It then articulates procedures by which the government may nevertheless obtain access to them. With regard to communications in temporary storage and awaiting retrival by their addressee, the government can obtain access to the contents during the first 180 days of electronic storage only by securing a search warrant based on probable cause. For unretrieved communications in storage for more than 180 days, as well as opened e-mail or other files left in remote storage, the government may obtain them without probable cause via subpoena. In the latter case, however, the customer or subscriber must receive prior notice of the disclosure, at least absent compliance with statutory provisions for delaying notice when, inter alia, such notice would seriously jeopardize the investigation. The ECPA permits notice to be delayed for 90 days upon the written certification of a supervisory official that notification of the subpoena may have such an effect. The government may extend the delay of notice for additional 90-day periods on application to a court.

If the government seeks noncontent information about an account such as the subscriber's name, address, and the method the customer uses to pay for the account (including any credit card or bank account number), a subpoena will suffice. For most other transactional records, such as the e-mail addresses of individuals with whom the account holder has corresponded, the government must generally apply for a court order based on a showing of reasonable grounds to believe that the information sought is relevant and material to an ongoing criminal investigation. No notice to the subscriber is necessary in either case.

The statute provides for a civil damages remedy for persons aggrieved by its violation and for disciplinary action against federal government employees who intentionally violate its terms. The law contains no exclusionary remedy, however, and provides specifically that its specified remedies and sanctions "are the only judicial remedies and sanctions for nonconstitutional violations of this chapter." 18 U.S.C. §2708.

NOTES AND QUESTIONS

1. Why treat e-mail in transmission (covered by Title III) and e-mail in electronic storage with a provider (covered by the ECPA) differently? To obtain e-mail

while it is being transmitted, investigators must satisfy Title III's multiple probable cause requirements, including the requirement of showing that other investigative techniques will not suffice. For e-mail in storage at a service provider, however, a standard search warrant or, after some time, even a subpoena will do. Note, too, that e-mail in storage may be obtained without contemporaneous notice, just as with Title III, provided that investigators make the appropriate showings. Consider the following:

> There is no logical reason to provide greater protection against covert police surveillance for an email in transmission than for the same email after it has reached the recipient's mailbox at his Internet Service Provider. In this regard, the statutory scheme lacks a coherent framework.
>
> It seems that the drafters of the [ECPA] were unable to anticipate a basic difference between telephone conversations and email messages. A telephone conversation can only be monitored while it is taking place since there is no permanent record left after the conversation ends. Similarly, an email message can be intercepted in transmission as it travels from sender to recipient. But the message can also be accessed while it is stored in the recipient's mailbox. In this respect, an email message shares some characteristics of a paper letter in that they both constitute a more permanent record than a phone call. . . .
>
> *Berger* did not explain why the Supreme Court assumed that telephone conversations deserved greater protections against police wiretapping than are afforded to letters in the mail. Maybe the court assumed that the real-time nature of the interception of a telephone call was somehow more intrusive than [even] covert interception of letters in the mail. But the intrusive nature of the wiretap does not come from the fact that it is contemporaneous with the communication. Rather, the highly intrusive aspect of the telephone wiretap derives from the fact that the police surreptitiously intercept private communications. . . .
>
> If so, then the constitutional protections for wire communications set out in *Berger* as codified and expanded by [Title III] should be equally applicable to the mail and [stored] electronic communications as well. It follows that the same safeguards against covert police surveillance should govern all media of communication. . . .

Robert A. Pikowsky, The Need for Revisions to the Law of Wiretapping and Interception of Email, 10 Mich. Telecomm. & Tech. L. Rev. 1, 49-51 (2003). Do you agree? Or is there something missing from this analysis?

2. The Justice Department has proffered an explanation for ECPA's provision allowing for access to opened e-mail using only a subpoena combined with prior notice to the subscriber:

> [This provision] appears to derive from Supreme Court case law interpreting the Fourth and Fifth Amendments. When an individual gives paper documents to a third party such as an accountant, the government may subpoena the paper documents from the third party without running afoul of either the Fourth or Fifth Amendment. In allowing the government to subpoena opened e-mail, Congress seems to have concluded that by renting computer storage space with a remote computing service, a customer places himself in the same situation as one who gives business records to an accountant or attorney.

Searching and Seizing Computers and Obtaining Electronic Evidence in Criminal Investigations 94 (DOJ, July 2002) (citations omitted). But does this analogy make sense? After all, when we give documents to our accountant, we expect him to look at them. We are sharing private information with him and, in standard Fourth Amendment terms, may have thus reduced any reasonable expectation of privacy we might have that this information will not be shared with others. But what are our expectations with regard to e-mail stored with an Internet provider? Are we sharing private information with the service provider in this sense? Or is this more like renting a hotel room and leaving a briefcase with personal papers in the closet? And what about the e-mail that is not opened, but left with a service provider for over 180 days? Why does it lose the protections of a warrant based on probable cause?

3. On the other hand, exactly what protection would the Fourth Amendment give to e-mail stored with a service provider, absent the ECPA? Consider the Justice Department's view:

> In a broad sense, ECPA fills in the gaps left by the uncertain application of Fourth Amendment protections in cyberspace. . . .
>
> Although the Fourth Amendment generally requires the government to obtain a warrant to search a home, it does not require the government to obtain a warrant to obtain the stored contents of a network account. Instead, the Fourth Amendment generally permits the government to issue a subpoena to a network provider ordering the provider to divulge the contents of an account. ECPA addressed this imbalance by offering network account holders a range of statutory privacy rights against access to stored account information held by network service providers.

Id. at 82-82. The Justice Department's analysis notes that network account holders may not possess a reasonable expectation of privacy in information sent to providers, citing United States v. Miller, 425 U.S. 435 (1976) (holding that bank records are not subject to Fourth Amendment protection), and Smith v. Maryland, 442 U.S. 735 (1979) (finding no reasonable expectation of privacy in dialed telephone numbers). Even apart from this point, the Justice Department notes, the Fourth Amendment generally permits the use of a subpoena to compel the disclosure of material, either directly from suspects or from third parties in possession of the suspect's property. Is there anything wrong with this analysis?

4. Perhaps the problem is not the analysis, but the fact that changes in technology and in our modes of communication have outdistanced our existing legal frameworks. Consider the following:

> Electronic mail is text-based message stored in digital form. It is like a transcribed telephone call. When sent from one person to another, e-mail is copied and transmitted from machine to machine; it sits on these different machines until removed either by routines — decisions by machines — or by people.
>
> The content of many e-mail messages is like the content of an ordinary telephone call — unplanned, unthinking, the ordinary chatter of friends. But unlike a telephone call, this content is saved, and once saved, it is monitorable, archivable, and searchable. . . .
>
> To be sure, in principle, such monitoring and searching are possible with telephone calls or letters. But in practice, they are not. To monitor telephones or regular mail requires time and money — that is, human intervention. . . . [T]he costs of control yield a certain kind of freedom.
>
> This freedom is reduced as the costs of searching fall. . . .

Lawrence Lessig, Code and Other Laws of Cyberspace 144-145 (1999).

5. New technologies also raise the possibility of new types of searches, never before considered. How should law (constitutional or statutory) adapt? Consider United States v. Scarfo, 180 F. Supp. 2d 572 (D. N.J. 2001). In *Scarfo*, FBI agents armed with search warrants entered Scarfo's Belleville, New Jersey business office to search for evidence of illegal gambling and loansharking. Inside, they came across a personal computer and attempted to access various files. They were unable to gain entry to an encrypted file named "Factors." As recounted by the court:

> Suspecting the "Factors" file contained evidence of an illegal gambling and loan-sharking operation, the F.B.I. returned to the location and, pursuant to two search warrants, installed what is known as a "Key Logger System" ("KLS") on the computer and/or computer keyboard in order to decipher the passphrase to the encrypted file, thereby gaining entry to the file. The KLS records the keystrokes an individual enters on a personal computer's keyboard. The government utilized the KLS in order to "catch" Scarfo's passphrases to the encrypted file while he was entering them onto his keyboard. . . . The F.B.I. obtained the passphrase to the "Factors" file and retrieved what is alleged to be incriminating evidence.

180 F. Supp. at 574.

The first search warrant authorized the FBI, for a period of 30 days, to "install and leave behind software, firmware, and/or hardware equipment which will monitor the inputted data entered on . . . Scarfo's computer . . . so that the F.B.I. can capture the password necessary to decrypt computer files by recording the key related information as they are entered." It also authorized the FBI to search for and seize "business records in whatever form they are kept (e.g., written, mechanically or computer maintained and any necessary computer hardware . . . as necessary to access such information, as well as, seizing the mirror hard drive to preserve configuration files, public keys, private keys, and other information that may be of assistance in interpreting the password). . . ." The second warrant contained identical language and "served to extend the period of the search for another 30 days."

Scarfo first argued that the warrants were written and executed as general warrants that violated the Fourth Amendment. Responding to his motion to suppress, the court disagreed, determining that it was of no consequence "[t]hat the KLS certainly recorded keystrokes typed into Scarfo's keyboard *other* than the searched-for passphrase." In the court's words:

> . . . This does not, as Scarfo argues, convert the limited search for the passphrase into a general exploratory search. During many lawful searches, police officers may not know the exact nature of the incriminating evidence sought until they stumble upon it. Just like searches for incriminating documents in a closet or filing cabinet, it is true that during a search for a passphrase "some innocuous [items] will be at least cursorily perused in order to determine whether they are among those [items] to be seized."
>
> . . . Where proof of wrongdoing depends upon . . . computer passphrases whose precise nature cannot be known in advance, law enforcement officers must be afforded the leeway to wade through a potential morass of information in the target location to find the particular evidence which is properly specified in the warrant . . .

Id. at 578 (citations omitted).

Because his computer featured a modem for communication over telephone lines so that Scarfo could access his America Online account, the defendant also argued that the KLS had no doubt intercepted wire communications in violation of Title III. The district court ordered the United States to file a report explaining fully how the KLS device functions. The government invoked the Classified Information Procedures Act, 18 U.S.C. app. III §§1-16 (1988) ("CIPA"), which sets forth procedures for the handling of classified information in criminal cases, and ultimately made an in camera, ex parte presentation to the judge:

> Pursuant to CIPA's regulations, the United States presented the Court with detailed and top-secret, classified information regarding the KLS, including how it operates in connection with a modem. The government also demonstrated to the Court how the KLS affects national security.

Id. at 575. Over defense objection, the court decided that the government's unclassified summary of information related to the KLS would be sufficient for the defense effectively to argue its motion to suppress. The court also concluded that the KLS used by the FBI had been designed to prohibit the capture of keyboard strokes whenever the modem operated — to avoid intercepting electronic communications typed on the keyboard and simultaneously transmitted in real time via the modem. The court therefore denied the motion to suppress for violation of Title III.

What do you think of the court's analysis? Is capturing keystrokes entered into a computer to obtain a password (albeit with probable cause to believe an encrypted file on that computer contains evidence of crime) like searching through a file cabinet? Note that the former search is of necessity covert and may extend over many days or weeks. Does this make a difference to your consideration of what constitutional or statutory protections may be necessary? (Is a simple search warrant enough?) Relatedly, what about the role of CIPA in this case? Can defense counsel adequately challenge the behavior of police if not given full access to information about how a search agent works?

Note that since *Scarfo* was decided, the FBI has reportedly developed another KLS called Magic Lantern. As described by Professor Adams:

> . . . Magic Lantern does not require physical entry into the premises or the target computer. Again, the government has not disclosed the exact nature of Magic Lantern, but it appears to be a virus-like program that can be e-mailed to a suspect, similar to the delivery of most other viruses. Magic Lantern may also be delivered by inducing the suspect to click on a Web link or through a breach in an operating system. Once the KLS burrows into the computer system, the program transmits the identification of keystrokes as they occur.

James Adams, Suppressing Evidence Gained by Government Surveillance of Computers, 19 Crim. Just. 46, 48-49 (2004).

Assume that Magic Lantern is configured so as only to record keystrokes as they occur (not searching data stored on the hard drive) and so as to prevent any recording of keystrokes that implicate Title III. Assume also that it is possible for Magic Lantern to filter the information it records, so that law enforcement agents ultimately see *only* the password for an encryption program, and nothing else. What should the law require before such a device may be used? Before use of a device providing *all* keystrokes to police?

6. Sometimes (believe it or not) real life imitates what law professors have already imagined. Consider the following:

> A "worm" is a bit of computer code that is spit out on the Net and works its way into the systems of vulnerable computers. It is not a "virus" because it doesn't attach itself to other programs and interfere with their operation. It is just a bit of extra code that does what the code writer says. The code could be harmless, simply sitting on someone's machine. Or it could be harmful, corrupting files or doing other damage that its author commands.
>
> Imagine a worm designed to do good (at least in the minds of some). Imagine that the code writer is the FBI and that the FBI is looking for a particular document belonging to the National Security Agency (NSA). Suppose that this document is classified and illegal to possess without the proper clearance. Imagine that the worm propagates itself on the Net, finding its way onto hard disks wherever it can; once on a computer's hard disk, it scans the entire disk. If it finds the NSA document, it sends a message back to the FBI saying as much. If it doesn't, it erases itself. Finally, assume that it can do all this without "interfering" with the operation of the machine. No one would know it was there; it would report back nothing except that the NSA document was on the hard disk.

Lawrence Lessig, Code and Other Laws of Cyberspace 17 (1999). Does the Fourth Amendment apply to the activities of Professor Lessig's worm? Here's his analysis:

> Is the worm . . . constitutional? That depends on your conception of what the Fourth Amendment protects. On one view, the amendment protects against suspicionless governmental invasion, whether those invasions are burdensome or not. On a second view, the amendment protects against invasions that are burdensome, allowing only those for which there is adequate suspicion that guilt will be uncovered. . . .
>
> . . . [W]e are describing a regime that allows the government to collect data about us in a highly efficient manner, that is, inexpensively for both the government and the innocent. This efficiency is made possible by technology, which permits searches that before would have been far too burdensome and far too invasive. . . . [T]he question comes to this: When the ability to search without burden increases, does the government's power to search increase as well? Or more darkly, as James Boyle puts it: "Is freedom inversely related to the efficiency of the available means of surveillance? If so, we have much to fear."
>
> . . . [O]ne of the defining features of modern life is the emergence of technologies that make data collection and processing extraordinarily efficient. Most of what we do — hence, most of what we are — is recorded. . . . When you make telephone calls, data are recorded about whom you called, when, how long you spoke, and how frequently you made such calls. When you use your credit cards, data are recorded about when, where, and from whom you made purchases. When you take a flight, your itinerary is recorded . . . and profiled by the government to determine whether you are likely to be a terrorist. No doubt Hollywood's image — of a world where one person sitting behind a terminal tracks the life of another — is wrong. But not terribly wrong. It's not that systems so easily track a single individual. But it is easy to imagine an agency sorting through all the data the system collects to identify those individuals most likely to be committing crimes. The intrusiveness is slight, and the payoff great.

Id. at 18-19.

7. Since 9/11, there has been even more focus on using information technology for terrorist screening. Some have argued that airline travel, for instance, is safer when passenger reservations are checked against commercial data banks for the purpose of authenticating identity, and also against law enforcement and intelligence data. As Paul Rosenzweig has argued, such screening

> . . . is not necessarily a decrease in privacy. Rather, it requires trade-offs in different kinds of privacy. It substitutes one privacy intrusion (into electronic data) for another privacy intrusion (the physical intrusiveness of body searches at airports). And it may have the salutary effect of reducing the need for random searches and eliminate the temptation for screeners to use objectionable characteristics of race, religion, or national origin as a proxy for threat indicators. For many Americans, the price of a little less electronic privacy might not be too great if it resulted in a little more physical privacy, fewer random searches, and a reduction in invidious racial profiling.

Paul Rosenzweig, Civil Liberty and the Response to Terrorism, 42 Duq. L. Rev. 663, 715 (2004).

Consider the following hypothetical based on the case of the 9/11 hijackers:

> *Hypothesis*: Each person buying an airplane ticket is checked against lists of possible terrorists. If there is a "hit," that person's available information is checked to identify possible associates.

> — Software already exists that can check names and addresses against multiple databases. It is capable of accounting for errors and variations in the way names are spelled, and can perform these functions on very large databases in seconds.

> *The Application*:

> — In late August 2001 Nawaq Alhamzi and Khalid Al-Midhar bought tickets to fly on American Airlines Flight 77 (which was flown into the Pentagon). They bought the tickets using their real names. Both names were then on a State Department/INS watch list called TIPOFF. Both men were sought by the FBI and CIA as suspected terrorists, in part because they had been observed at a terrorist meeting in Malaysia.
> — These two passenger names would have been exact matches when checked against the TIPOFF list. But that would only have been the first step. Further data checks could then have begun.
> — Checking for common addresses (address information is widely available, including on the Internet), analysts would have discovered that Salem Al-Hazmi (who also bought a seat on American 77) used the same address as Nawaq Alhazmi. More importantly, they could have discovered that Mohamed Atta (American 11, North Tower of the World Trade Center) and Marwan Al-Shehhi (United 175, South Tower of the World Trade Center) used the same address as Khalid Al-Midhar.
> — Checking for identical frequent flier numbers, analysts would have discovered that Majed Moqed (American 77) used the same number as Al-Midhar.
> — With Mohamed Atta now also identified as a possible associate of the wanted terrorist, Al-Midhar, analysts could have added Atta's phone numbers (also

publicly available information) to their checklist. By doing so they would have identified five other hijackers (Fayez Ahmed, Mohand Alshehri, Wail Alshehri, Waleed Alshehri, and Abdulaziz Alomari).

— With days still remaining before the scheduled flights, additional investigations could have turned up information about attendance at flight schools (information that the U.S. government then did not have in a digitally searchable form) or on puzzling foreign links (like common financial links to Hamburg, information that the government was not able to access in real time).

— Closer to September 11, a further check of passenger lists against a more innocuous INS watch list (for expired visas) would have identified Ahmed Alghamdi. Through him, the same sort of relatively simple correlations could have led to identifying the remaining hijackers, who boarded United 93 (which crashed in Pennsylvania).

Markle Foundation Task Force on National Security in the Information Age, Protecting America's Freedom in the Information Age 28 (October 2002).

According to the Markle Foundation, analysts could thus have used simple datamining techniques to determine that two suspected terrorists and a large number of associated people were boarding flights on the same day. Markle argues, moreover, that efforts to conceal identity need not frustrate screening such as this:

> In this hypothetical illustration . . . two of the 9/11 hijackers were wanted as suspected terrorists and bought airplane tickets using their real names. Let us assume, then, that future terrorists use false names or otherwise attempt to conceal their identity. The individuals can still be identified, not by a name but instead with a biometric algorithm derived from a photograph of the face or the digital measurement of the fingerprints.

Id. at 29. Does this example support the Markle Foundation's claim that data mining "can be a useful tool," that the events of 9/11 have demonstrated a need "to make more effective use of the mountains of data that are already in government hands or publicly available," and that data mining "like any other government data analysis, should occur where there is a focused and demonstrable need to know, balanced against the danger to civil liberties"? Id. at 27. How might controls and oversight be structured to guard against the dangers identified with various forms of data mining — dangers that Professor Sullivan has recently described:

> At the extreme [datamining] could be a vehicle for politically motivated spying and intimidation reminiscent of the worst features of the J. Edgar Hoover era. It might also permit more ordinary risks such as unauthorized snooping, leaking of information, blackmailing by employees, bureaucratic error, and hacking and identity theft by enterprising high school students or criminals. And it could create a broader if more subtle chilling effect from knowledge that government computers may be watching you and that something you read or someplace you go might form a fragment of a partial terrorist profile.

Kathleen M. Sullivan, Under a Watchful Eye: Incursions on Personal Privacy, in Richard C. Leone and Greg Anrig, Jr., eds., The War on Our Freedoms 128, 132 (2003).

B. Undercover Agents and Entrapment

In his study of undercover police practices in the United States, sociologist Gary Marx has observed that this country "once shared with England the fear of a centralized, permanently organized police force" that engaged in covert investigative tactics associated with despotism. Gary T. Marx, Undercover 22 (1988). Early police forces in nineteenth-century America, patterned after the London police, were organized on the theory that a visible police presence able to respond to citizen calls for assistance would deter would-be criminals and disorderly persons. Police, however, were not expected to act more proactively to discover law violations. And they were certainly not supposed to "'employ spies, resort to entrapment, or otherwise let their determination to stamp out crime carry them beyond the point at which decent and honorable men must stop.'" Id. at 23 (quoting an early Boston city councilman).

Marx identifies a number of reasons that this aversion to covert police practices gradually gave way — permitting the emergence of undercover policing as a principal tool of criminal investigation in this country today:

The United States has moved far in a short period of time with respect to the acceptance of secret police practices. What once occurred infrequently and was viewed with disdain as a characteristic of continental despotism is now routine administrative practice. This is related to broad changes in social organization, the nature of crime, and the relation of police to the law. In its gradual embrace of covert practices over the past century, the U.S. has broken sharply with its earlier attitudes. There has been a move away from the early British notion of a clearly identifiable citizen- or community-based police, where control agents do not have significant power beyond that of the ordinary citizen, toward the idea that police agents have much greater power than citizens and that policing is a function of the state, not of the citizen. . . .

Cultural images of social control have changed. Fear of crime has largely replaced fear of a militaristic police. . . . The secret agent, whether enshrined in film and television, literature, or song, has become something of a cultural hero. . . .

Broad processes of social transformation involving urbanization and industrialization created a context in which both crimes of deception and undercover means would increase. As the informal social controls associated with the small community and traditional family weakened and changed, formal control institutions grew in power. Large urban areas, rapid transportation, geographical and social mobility, and increased interaction with strangers, or interactions carried out electronically (by telegraph and later by telephone, teletypes, and computers) make deception easier. The impersonal relationships and anonymity associated with these conditions provide fertile ground for the projection of false selves, whether against or on behalf of the law.

The local bumbling gangs, street criminals, drunks, and relatively unorganized rioters who shocked upright citizens in the first half of the nineteenth century were supplemented in the last half of that century by skilled and inventive professionals using the latest technology and knowing how to manipulate the enforcement system.

. . . New forms of criminality appeared, and greater enforcement priority was given to types of crime for which evidence is not easily gathered by overt means, for example, counterfeiting and other monetary violations, fraud, and narcotics. The planned and conspiratorial nature of these lend themselves to secret means of discovery. . . .

The broad increase in covert means over the past century is part of a gradual shift in the United States from a largely rural, unpoliced society to an industrial, policed society. It is rooted in the rise of national and local police institutions. The significant increase in the number and power of the police is part of a broad trend involving the growth of the modern bureaucratic state.

Id. at 33-35. Marx also argues that changes in the relationship of police to law contributed to the expansion in covert practices:

At the turn of the [nineteenth] century, police, while formally engaged in law enforcement, were not oriented toward legal norms. As the twentieth century developed, law became increasingly important to the functioning of the criminal justice system, and legal norms have come to play a more prominent role in structuring and limiting police behavior. In the face of restrictions on traditional practices, undercover techniques have become more important as a means of gaining admissible evidence.

Id. at 35. Indeed, Marx contends that constitutional restrictions on overt search and seizure and interrogation tactics had the unintended consequence of promoting covert techniques: "[R]estrict police use of coercion, and the use of deception increases. Restrict investigative behavior after an offense, and increased attention will be paid to anticipating an offense." Id. at 47.

It is undeniable that undercover agents and informants operating in an undercover capacity play an important role in the investigation of crime in the United States today. Some "undercover" investigations are quite simple. (Consider the traditional "buy-and-bust" case, for example, in which an undercover police officer purchases a small quantity of narcotics from an individual selling on the street and this individual is arrested immediately after the transaction by the undercover's backup.) Other undercover investigations are extremely complex. They can require complicated ruses or protracted role-playing by an undercover agent. (Indeed, undercover agents sometimes operate over many months or even years to infiltrate a criminal organization or to close on negotiations with a suspect about a proposed criminal transaction.)

In the great majority of cases, neither kind of undercover investigation implicates the Fourth Amendment. Recall United States v. White, 401 U.S. 745 (1971), and the plurality's observation there that "one contemplating illegal activities must realize and risk that his companions may be reporting to the police." See supra at page 368. In fact, the defense of entrapment, rather than any constitutional prohibition, represents the principal legal restriction on the way in which undercover investigations are conducted. The Supreme Court first recognized the defense in Sorrells v. United States, 287 U.S. 425 (1932), a case in which a government agent posing as a tourist befriended the defendant and with repeated requests persuaded him to supply the agent with liquor in violation of the National Prohibition Act. The Court adopted the defense as a matter of statutory construction, concluding that Congress could not have intended in enacting the criminal prohibition at issue to permit law enforcement officers to instigate criminal acts by otherwise innocent people and then to punish them for such acts.

There are two principal versions of the entrapment defense—the subjective and the objective. The majority of courts, including federal courts, employ the subjective defense. It focuses on the defendant's "predisposition" to commit crimes by affording a defense to an individual who commits a crime pursuant to government inducement and who cannot be shown to be otherwise predisposed in that direction.

The objective defense looks instead to the conduct of police. It asks whether police have offered inducements to commit the crime that are of a sort to which even normally law abiding citizens would respond. If so, the defendant who committed a crime in response to these inducements cannot be convicted.

The entrapment defense is a difficult one and is unlikely to be successful in most cases involving the use of undercover agents or informants. Indeed, the defense is rarely successful at all. To the extent it does set limits on the conduct of undercover investigations, however, it generally plays a larger role in the second, more complex type of covert case. Consider why this might be so as you read the following case.

JACOBSON v. UNITED STATES

Certiorari to the United States Court of Appeals for the Eighth Circuit
503 U.S. 540 (1992)

JUSTICE WHITE delivered the opinion of the Court.

On September 24, 1987, petitioner Keith Jacobson was indicted for violating a provision of the Child Protection Act of 1984, which criminalizes the knowing receipt through the mails of a "visual depiction [that] involves the use of a minor engaging in sexually explicit conduct. . . ." Petitioner defended on the ground that the Government entrapped him into committing the crime through a series of communications from undercover agents that spanned the 26 months preceding his arrest. Petitioner was found guilty after a jury trial. The Court of Appeals affirmed his conviction, holding that the Government had carried its burden of proving beyond reasonable doubt that petitioner was predisposed to break the law and hence was not entrapped.

Because the Government overstepped the line between setting a trap for the "unwary innocent" and the "unwary criminal," Sherman v. United States, 356 U.S. 369, 372 (1958), and as a matter of law failed to establish that petitioner was independently predisposed to commit the crime for which he was arrested, we reverse the Court of Appeals' judgment affirming his conviction.

I

In February 1984, petitioner, a 56-year-old veteran-turned-farmer who supported his elderly father in Nebraska, ordered two magazines and a brochure from a California adult bookstore. The magazines, entitled Bare Boys I and Bare Boys II, contained photographs of nude preteen and teenage boys. The contents of the magazines startled petitioner, who testified that he had expected to receive photographs of "young men 18 years or older." On cross-examination, he explained his response to the magazines:

"[PROSECUTOR]:   [Y]ou were shocked and surprised that there were pictures of
    very young boys without clothes on, is that correct?
"[JACOBSON]:   Yes, I was.
"[PROSECUTOR]:   Were you offended?

> "[JACOBSON]: I was not offended because I thought these were a nudist type publication. Many of the pictures were out in a rural or outdoor setting. There was — I didn't draw any sexual connotation or connection with that."

The young men depicted in the magazines were not engaged in sexual activity, and petitioner's receipt of the magazines was legal under both federal and Nebraska law. Within three months, the law with respect to child pornography changed; Congress passed the Act illegalizing the receipt through the mails of sexually explicit depictions of children. In the very month that the new provision became law, postal inspectors found petitioner's name on the mailing list of the California bookstore that had mailed him Bare Boys I and II. There followed over the next 2½ years repeated efforts by two Government agencies, through five fictitious organizations and a bogus pen pal, to explore petitioner's willingness to break the new law by ordering sexually explicit photographs of children through the mail.

The Government began its efforts in January 1985 when a postal inspector sent petitioner a letter supposedly from the American Hedonist Society, which in fact was a fictitious organization. The letter included a membership application and stated the Society's doctrine: that members had the "right to read what we desire, the right to discuss similar interests with those who share our philosophy, and finally that we have the right to seek pleasure without restrictions being placed on us by outdated puritan morality." Petitioner enrolled in the organization and returned a sexual attitude questionnaire that asked him to rank on a scale of one to four his enjoyment of various sexual materials, with one being "really enjoy," two being "enjoy," three being "somewhat enjoy," and four being "do not enjoy." Petitioner ranked the entry "[p]re-teen sex" as a two, but indicated that he was opposed to pedophilia.

For a time, the Government left petitioner alone. But then a new "prohibited mailing specialist" in the Postal Service found petitioner's name in a file, and in May 1986, petitioner received a solicitation from a second fictitious consumer research company, "Midlands Data Research," seeking a response from those who "believe in the joys of sex and the complete awareness of those lusty and youthful lads and lasses of the neophite [*sic*] age." The letter never explained whether "neophite" referred to minors or young adults. Petitioner responded: "Please feel free to send me more information, I am interested in teenage sexuality. Please keep my name confidential."

Petitioner then heard from yet another Government creation, "Heartland Institute for a New Tomorrow" (HINT), which proclaimed that it was "an organization founded to protect and promote sexual freedom and freedom of choice. We believe that arbitrarily imposed legislative sanctions restricting *your* sexual freedom should be rescinded through the legislative process." The letter also enclosed a second survey. Petitioner indicated that his interest in "[p]reteen sex-homosexual" material was above average, but not high. In response to another question, petitioner wrote: "Not only sexual expression but freedom of the press is under attack. We must be ever vigilant to counter attack right wing fundamentalists who are determined to curtail our freedoms."

HINT replied, portraying itself as a lobbying organization seeking to repeal "all statutes which regulate sexual activities, except those laws which deal with violent behavior, such as rape. HINT is also lobbying to eliminate any legal definition of 'the age of consent.'" These lobbying efforts were to be funded by sales from a catalog to be published in the future "offering the sale of various items which we believe you will find to be both interesting and stimulating." HINT also provided computer matching of group members with similar survey responses; and, although petitioner was supplied with a list of potential "pen pals," he did not initiate any correspondence.

Nevertheless, the Government's "prohibited mailing specialist" began writing to petitioner, using the pseudonym "Carl Long." The letters employed a tactic known as "mirroring," which the inspector described as "reflect[ing] whatever the interests are of the person we are writing to." Petitioner responded at first, indicating that his interest was primarily in "male-male items." Inspector "Long" wrote back:

> "My interests too are primarily male-male items. Are you satisfied with the type of VCR tapes available? Personally, I like the amateur stuff better if its [sic] well produced as it can get more kinky and also seems more real. I think the actors enjoy it more."

Petitioner responded:

> "As far as my likes are concerned, I like good looking young guys (in their late teens and early 20's) doing their thing together."

Petitioner's letters to "Long" made no reference to child pornography. After writing two letters, petitioner discontinued the correspondence.

By March 1987, 34 months had passed since the Government obtained petitioner's name from the mailing list of the California bookstore, and 26 months had passed since the Postal Service had commenced its mailings to petitioner. Although petitioner had responded to surveys and letters, the Government had no evidence that petitioner had ever intentionally possessed or been exposed to child pornography. The Postal Service had not checked petitioner's mail to determine whether he was receiving questionable mailings from persons — other than the Government — involved in the child pornography industry.

At this point, a second Government agency, the Customs Service, included petitioner in its own child pornography sting, "Operation Borderline," after receiving his name on lists submitted by the Postal Service. Using the name of a fictitious Canadian company called "Produit Outaouais," the Customs Service mailed petitioner a brochure advertising photographs of young boys engaging in sex. Petitioner placed an order that was never filled.

The Postal Service also continued its efforts in the Jacobson case, writing to petitioner as the "Far Eastern Trading Company Ltd." The letter began:

> "As many of you know, much hysterical nonsense has appeared in the American media concerning 'pornography' and what must be done to stop it from coming across your borders. This brief letter does not allow us to give much comments; however, why is your government spending millions of dollars to exercise international censorship while tons of drugs, which makes yours the world's most crime ridden country are passed through easily."

The letter went on to say:

> "[W]e have devised a method of getting these to you without prying eyes of U.S. Customs seizing your mail. . . . After consultations with American solicitors, we

have been advised that once we have posted our material through your system, it cannot be opened for any inspection without authorization of a judge."

The letter invited petitioner to send for more information. It also asked petitioner to sign an affirmation that he was "not a law enforcement officer or agent of the U.S. Government acting in an undercover capacity for the purpose of entrapping Far Eastern Trading Company, its agents or customers." Petitioner responded. A catalog was sent, and petitioner ordered Boys Who Love Boys, a pornographic magazine depicting young boys engaged in various sexual activities. Petitioner was arrested after a controlled delivery of a photocopy of the magazine.

When petitioner was asked at trial why he placed such an order, he explained that the Government had succeeded in piquing his curiosity:

> "Well, the statement was made of all the trouble and the hysteria over pornography and I wanted to see what the material was. It didn't describe the — I didn't know for sure what kind of sexual action they were referring to in the Canadian letter."

In petitioner's home, the Government found the Bare Boys magazines and materials that the Government had sent to him in the course of its protracted investigation, but no other materials that would indicate that petitioner collected, or was actively interested in, child pornography. . . .

II

There can be no dispute about the evils of child pornography or the difficulties that laws and law enforcement have encountered in eliminating it. Likewise, there can be no dispute that the Government may use undercover agents to enforce the law. . . .

In their zeal to enforce the law, however, Government agents may not originate a criminal design, implant in an innocent person's mind the disposition to commit a criminal act, and then induce commission of the crime so that the Government may prosecute. Where the Government has induced an individual to break the law and the defense of entrapment is at issue, as it was in this case, the prosecution must prove beyond reasonable doubt that the defendant was disposed to commit the criminal act prior to first being approached by Government agents.

Thus, an agent deployed to stop the traffic in illegal drugs may offer the opportunity to buy or sell drugs and, if the offer is accepted, make an arrest on the spot or later. In such a typical case, or in a more elaborate "sting" operation involving government-sponsored fencing where the defendant is simply provided with the opportunity to commit a crime, the entrapment defense is of little use because the ready commission of the criminal act amply demonstrates the defendant's pre-disposition. Had the agents in this case simply offered petitioner the opportunity to order child pornography through the mails, and petitioner — who must be presumed to know the law — had promptly availed himself of this criminal opportunity, it is unlikely that his entrapment defense would have warranted a jury instruction.

But that is not what happened here. By the time petitioner finally placed his order, he had already been the target of 26 months of repeated mailings and communications from Government agents and fictitious organizations. Therefore, although he had become predisposed to break the law by May 1987, it is our view that the Government did not prove that this predisposition was independent and not the product of the attention that the Government had directed at petitioner since January 1985.

The prosecution's evidence of predisposition falls into two categories: evidence developed prior to the Postal Service's mail campaign, and that developed during the course of the investigation. The sole piece of preinvestigation evidence is petitioner's 1984 order and receipt of the Bare Boys magazines. But this is scant if any proof of petitioner's predisposition to commit an illegal act, the criminal character of which a defendant is presumed to know. It may indicate a predisposition to view sexually oriented photographs that are responsive to his sexual tastes; but evidence that merely indicates a generic inclination to act within a broad range, not all of which is criminal, is of little probative value in establishing predisposition.

Furthermore, petitioner was acting within the law at the time he received these magazines. . . . Evidence of predisposition to do what once was lawful is not, by itself, sufficient to show predisposition to do what is now illegal, for there is a common understanding that most people obey the law even when they disapprove of it. . . . Hence, the fact that petitioner legally ordered and received the Bare Boys magazines does little to further the Government's burden of proving that petitioner was predisposed to commit a criminal act. This is particularly true given petitioner's unchallenged testimony that he did not know until they arrived that the magazines would depict minors.

The prosecution's evidence gathered during the investigation also fails to carry the Government's burden. Petitioner's responses to the many communications prior to the ultimate criminal act were at most indicative of certain personal inclinations, including a predisposition to view photographs of preteen sex and a willingness to promote a given agenda by supporting lobbying organizations. Even so, petitioner's responses hardly support an inference that he would commit the crime of receiving child pornography through the mails.[3] . . .

On the other hand, the strong arguable inference is that, by waving the banner of individual rights and disparaging the legitimacy and constitutionality of efforts to restrict the availability of sexually explicit materials, the Government not only excited petitioner's interest in sexually explicit materials banned by law but also exerted substantial pressure on petitioner to obtain and read such material as part of a fight against censorship and the infringement of individual rights. . . .

Petitioner's ready response to these solicitations cannot be enough to establish beyond reasonable doubt that he was predisposed, prior to the Government acts intended to create predisposition, to commit the crime of receiving child pornography through the mails. The evidence that petitioner was ready and willing to commit the offense came only after the Government had devoted 2½ years to convincing him that he had or should have the right to engage in the very behavior proscribed by law. Rational jurors could not say beyond a reasonable doubt

3. We do not hold, as the dissent suggests, that the Government was required to prove that petitioner knowingly violated the law. We simply conclude that proof that petitioner engaged in legal conduct and possessed certain generalized personal inclinations is not sufficient evidence to prove beyond a reasonable doubt that he would have been predisposed to commit the crime charged independent of the Government's coaxing.

that petitioner possessed the requisite predisposition prior to the Government's investigation and that it existed independent of the Government's many and varied approaches to petitioner. As was explained in *Sherman*, where entrapment was found as a matter of law, "the Government [may not] pla[y] on the weaknesses of an innocent party and beguil[e] him into committing crimes which he otherwise would not have attempted." [356 U.S.] at 376.

Law enforcement officials go too far when they "implant in the mind of an innocent person the *disposition* to commit the alleged offense and induce its commission in order that they may prosecute." Sorrells [v. U.S., 287 U.S. 435, 442 (1932)] (emphasis added). Like the *Sorrells* Court, we are "unable to conclude that it was the intention of the Congress in enacting this statute that its processes of detection and enforcement should be abused by the instigation by government officials of an act on the part of persons otherwise innocent in order to lure them to its commission and to punish them." Id., at 448. When the Government's quest for convictions leads to the apprehension of an otherwise law-abiding citizen who, if left to his own devices, likely would have never run afoul of the law, the courts should intervene.

Because we conclude that this is such a case and that the prosecution failed, as a matter of law, to adduce evidence to support the jury verdict that petitioner was predisposed, independent of the Government's acts and beyond a reasonable doubt, to violate the law by receiving child pornography through the mails, we reverse the Court of Appeals' judgment. . . .

JUSTICE O'CONNOR, with whom THE CHIEF JUSTICE and JUSTICE KENNEDY join, and with whom JUSTICE SCALIA joins except as to Part II, dissenting.

Keith Jacobson was offered only two opportunities to buy child pornography through the mail. Both times, he ordered. Both times, he asked for opportunities to buy more. He needed no Government agent to coax, threaten, or persuade him; no one played on his sympathies, friendship, or suggested that his committing the crime would further a greater good. In fact, no Government agent even contacted him face to face. The Government contends that from the enthusiasm with which Mr. Jacobson responded to the chance to commit a crime, a reasonable jury could permissibly infer beyond a reasonable doubt that he was predisposed to commit the crime. I agree.

The first time the Government sent Mr. Jacobson a catalog of illegal materials, he ordered a set of photographs advertised as picturing "young boys in sex action fun." He enclosed the following note with his order: "I received your brochure and decided to place an order. If I like your product, I will order more later." For reasons undisclosed in the record, Mr. Jacobson's order was never delivered.

The second time the Government sent a catalog of illegal materials, Mr. Jacobson ordered a magazine called "Boys Who Love Boys," described as: "11 year old and 14 year old boys get it on in every way possible. Oral, anal sex and heavy masturbation. If you love boys, you will be delighted with this." Along with his order, Mr. Jacobson sent the following note: "Will order other items later. I want to be discreet in order to protect you and me."

Government agents admittedly did not offer Mr. Jacobson the chance to buy child pornography right away. Instead, they first sent questionnaires in order to make sure that he was generally interested in the subject matter. Indeed, a "cold call" in such a business would not only risk rebuff and suspicion, but might also shock and offend the uninitiated, or expose minors to suggestive materials. Mr. Jacobson's responses to the questionnaires gave the investigators reason to think he would be interested in photographs depicting preteen sex. . . .

I

This Court has held previously that a defendant's predisposition is to be assessed as of the time the Government agent first suggested the crime, not when the Government agent first became involved. Sherman v. United States, 356 U.S. 369, 372-376 (1958). Until the Government actually makes a suggestion of criminal conduct, it could not be said to have "implant[ed] in the mind of an innocent person the disposition to commit the alleged offense and induce its commission. . . ." Sorrells v. United States, 287 U.S. 435, 442 (1932). Even in Sherman v. United States, supra, in which the Court held that the defendant had been entrapped as a matter of law, the Government agent had repeatedly and unsuccessfully coaxed the defendant to buy drugs, ultimately succeeding only by playing on the defendant's sympathy. The Court found lack of predisposition based on the Government's numerous unsuccessful attempts to induce the crime, not on the basis of preliminary contacts with the defendant.

Today, the Court holds that Government conduct may be considered to create a predisposition to commit a crime, even before any Government action to induce the commission of the crime. In my view, this holding changes entrapment doctrine. Generally, the inquiry is whether a suspect is predisposed before the Government induces the commission of the crime, not before the Government makes initial contact with him. There is no dispute here that the Government's questionnaires and letters were not sufficient to establish inducement; they did not even suggest that Mr. Jacobson should engage in any illegal activity. If all the Government had done was to send these materials, Mr. Jacobson's entrapment defense would fail. Yet the Court holds that the Government must prove not only that a suspect was predisposed to commit the crime before the opportunity to commit it arose, but also before the Government came on the scene.

The rule that preliminary Government contact can create a predisposition has the potential to be misread by lower courts as well as criminal investigators as requiring that the Government must have sufficient evidence of a defendant's predisposition *before it ever seeks to contact him*. Surely the Court cannot intend to impose such a requirement, for it would mean that the Government must have a reasonable suspicion of criminal activity before it begins an investigation, a condition that we have never before imposed. The Court denies that its new rule will affect run-of-the-mill sting operations, and one hopes that it means what it says. Nonetheless, after this case, every defendant will claim that something the Government agent did before soliciting the crime "created" a predisposition that was not there before. For example, a bribetaker will claim that the description of the amount of money available was so enticing that it implanted a disposition to accept the bribe later offered. A drug buyer will claim that the description of the drug's purity and effects was so tempting that it created the urge to try it for the first time. In short, the Court's opinion could be read to prohibit the Government from advertising the seductions of criminal activity as part of its sting operation, for fear of creating a predisposition in its suspects. That limitation would be especially likely to hamper sting operations such as this one, which mimic the advertising done by genuine purveyors of pornography. No doubt the Court would protest that its opinion does not stand for so broad a proposition, but the apparent lack of a principled basis for distinguishing these scenarios exposes a flaw in the more limited rule the Court today adopts.

The Court's rule is all the more troubling because it does not distinguish between Government conduct that merely highlights the temptation of the crime itself, and Government conduct that threatens, coerces, or leads a suspect to commit a crime in order to fulfill some other obligation. For example, in *Sorrells*, the Government agent repeatedly asked for illegal liquor, coaxing the defendant to accede on the ground that "'one former war buddy would get liquor for another.'" 287 U.S., at 440. In *Sherman*, the Government agent played on the defendant's sympathies, pretending to be going through drug withdrawal and begging the defendant to relieve his distress by helping him buy drugs. 356 U.S., at 371.

The Government conduct in this case is not comparable. While the Court states that the Government "exerted substantial pressure on petitioner to obtain and read such material as part of a fight against censorship and the infringement of individual rights," one looks at the record in vain for evidence of such "substantial pressure." The most one finds are letters advocating legislative action to liberalize obscenity laws, letters which could easily be ignored or thrown away. Much later, the Government sent separate mailings of catalogs of illegal materials. Nowhere did the Government suggest that the proceeds of the sale of the illegal materials would be used to support legislative reforms. While one of the HINT letters suggested that lobbying efforts would be funded by sales from a catalog, the catalogs actually sent, nearly a year later, were from different fictitious entities . . . and gave no suggestion that money would be used for any political purposes. Nor did the Government claim to be organizing a civil disobedience movement, which would protest the pornography laws by breaking them. Contrary to the gloss given the evidence by the Court, the Government's suggestions of illegality may also have made buyers beware, and increased the mystique of the materials offered: "For those of you who have enjoyed youthful material . . . we have devised a method of getting these to you without prying eyes of U.S. Customs seizing your mail." Mr. Jacobson's curiosity to see what "'all the trouble and the hysteria'" was about, is certainly susceptible of more than one interpretation. And it is the jury that is charged with the obligation of interpreting it. In sum, the Court fails to construe the evidence in the light most favorable to the Government, and fails to draw all reasonable inferences in the Government's favor. It was surely reasonable for the jury to infer that Mr. Jacobson was predisposed beyond a reasonable doubt, even if other inferences from the evidence were also possible.

II

The second puzzling thing about the Court's opinion is its redefinition of predisposition. The Court acknowledges that "[p]etitioner's responses to the many communications prior to the ultimate criminal act were . . . indicative of certain personal inclinations, including a predisposition to view photographs of preteen sex. . . ." If true, this should have settled the matter; Mr. Jacobson was predisposed to engage in the illegal conduct. Yet, the Court concludes, "petitioner's responses hardly support an inference that he would commit the crime of receiving child pornography through the mails."

The Court seems to add something new to the burden of proving predisposition. Not only must the Government show that a defendant was predisposed to engage in the illegal conduct, here, receiving photographs of minors engaged in sex, but also that the defendant was predisposed to break the law knowingly in order to do so. The statute violated here, however, does not require proof of specific intent to break the law; it requires only knowing receipt of visual depictions produced by using minors engaged in sexually explicit conduct. Under the Court's analysis, however, the Government must prove *more* to show predisposition than it need prove in order to convict.

. . . The elements of predisposition should track the elements of the crime. The predisposition requirement is meant to eliminate the entrapment defense for those defendants who would have committed the crime anyway, even absent Government inducement. Because a defendant might very well be convicted of the crime here absent Government inducement even though he did not know his conduct was illegal, a specific intent requirement does little to distinguish between those who would commit the crime without the inducement and those who would not. In sum, although the fact that Mr. Jacobson's purchases of Bare Boys I and Bare Boys II were legal at the time may have some relevance to the question of predisposition, it is not, as the Court suggests, dispositive.

The crux of the Court's concern in this case is that the Government went too far and "abused" the "processes of detection and enforcement" by luring an innocent person to violate the law. Consequently, the Court holds that the Government failed to prove beyond a reasonable doubt that Mr. Jacobson was predisposed to commit the crime. It was, however, the jury's task, as the conscience of the community, to decide whether Mr. Jacobson was a willing participant in the criminal activity here or an innocent dupe. . . . Because I believe there was sufficient evidence to uphold the jury's verdict, I respectfully dissent.

NOTES AND QUESTIONS

1. The subjective version of entrapment supposedly being applied in *Jacobson* holds that once a defendant has raised an entrapment defense by showing some government inducement to commit the crime, the government must demonstrate that the defendant was predisposed. But was this really the test employed by the *Jacobson* majority? After all, the sole issue in this case was whether there was sufficient evidence to support the jury verdict. Can it really be maintained that reasonable jurors could not have concluded that Jacobson was predisposed to commit the crime? Does *Jacobson* mean that in complex cases where the government may have substantial contact with an individual before any crime occurs, the government must come forward with a strong showing of predisposition predating such contact in order to survive a motion for acquittal?

2. Of course, the preceding discussion assumes that we can define what it is we mean by predisposition. A standard federal jury instruction asks whether the defendant " 'was ready and willing to commit crimes such as are charged in the indictment, whenever opportunity was afforded, and that government officers or their agents did no more than offer the opportunity.' " Louis Michael Seidman, The Supreme Court, Entrapment, and Our Criminal Justice Dilemma, 1981 Sup. Ct. Rev. 111 (quoting I Edward J. Devitt & Charles B. Blackmar, Federal Jury

Practice and Instructions §13.09, at 364 (3d ed. 1977)). But as Professor Seidman has pointed out,

> [W]hether a person is "ready and willing" to break the law depends on what the person expects to get in return — that is, on the level of inducement. Like the rest of us, criminals do not generally work for free. . . .
>
> Consequently, so long as one equates "predisposition" with a readiness to commit crime, no definition of "predisposition" can be complete without an articulation of the level of inducement to which a "predisposed" defendant would respond. Furthermore, the "predisposed" cannot be distinguished from the "nondisposed" without focusing on the propriety of the government's conduct — the very factor that the subjective approach professes to ignore.

Id. at 118-119. Does this suggest that the distinction between the subjective and objective approaches to entrapment is less clear than might at first seem to be the case?

3. Some have suggested that *Jacobson* is an objective entrapment case posing as a subjective one — that the result in *Jacobson* is best understood as a reaction to what the Court may have seen as overbearing governmental tactics. Though most courts have adopted the subjective entrapment test, some 10 to 15 states have opted for the objective version, through either statutes or judicial rulings. The Model Penal Code also recommends an objective test — stating that police inducements should be deemed improper if they "create a substantial risk that an offense will be committed by persons other than those who are ready to commit it." See American Law Institute, Model Penal Code §2.13 (Official Draft 1962). Giving content to this test, however, may be as difficult as giving content to the subjective approach. Who are these people who would normally not be ready to commit a crime, but who can at least occasionally be induced to do so? Defining the "reasonable person" standard in tort may seem child's play when compared to defining the concept of the "sometimes criminal."

4. Ronald Allen, Melissa Luttrell, and Anne Kreeger have addressed these conundrums and have concluded as follows:

> There is a deeper difficulty with the controversy over the two tests for entrapment. The controversy is premised on the existence of a real something — state of mind, character, whatever — that is referred to as "predisposition." This assumption is false. We assume that there are a few people who would not commit any criminal acts no matter what the provocation or enticement. . . . Everyone else, we assume, has a price. That price may be quite high, for example because a person puts a high value on her good name, but it exists. If this assumption is true, then everyone except saints is predisposed to commit crimes. But, that in turn means that "predisposition" cannot usefully distinguish anyone from anyone else. . . .
>
> The discussion in the cases of whether the defendant was a willing participant, and whether the government implanted the criminal design in the defendant or created the crime verges on the silly. The defendant is always "willing" (otherwise there would be no need to rely on entrapment — duress would do) and to our knowledge, the government has never physically opened the brain of a defendant and "implanted" anything. Perhaps the government implants criminal designs psychologically, but again, if so, it is always so for the government always plays a causal role in the act. In all cases of police involvement, and thus of potential entrapment, the act would not

have occurred as it did but for the involvement of the police — a tautology if ever there were one. Nor does the objective test avoid this point, just because it pragmatically operates upon the [same] assumption of the existence of predisposition as a real thing. Without predisposition as a sorting mechanism, the objective test is rootless.

Ronald J. Allen, Melissa Luttrell, and Anne Kreeger, Clarifying Entrapment, 89 J. Crim. L. & Criminology 407, 413-414 (1999). The authors argue that a more fruitful criterion for sorting out "those who have a plausible claim for exoneration" is whether the "inducements [offered to these individuals] exceeded real world market rates, which includes both financial and emotional markets." Id. at 415. They justify this conclusion in part with reference to the aims of the criminal law:

> We assume, without regard to philosophical niceties, that the primary relevant objectives of the criminal law are to deter (general and specific), to incapacitate, and to rehabilitate (it is pointless to discuss retribution in this context). None of these objectives is likely to be accomplished by the punishment of an individual who accepted an extra-market inducement to act. The concern of deterrence surely is to reduce the occurrence of criminal acts in the world we actually inhabit, not some hypothetically different one. That a person responds to extra-market prices is uninformative of how he will respond to market prices, and thus is uninformative on the justification for incapacitation. A person who accepts extra-market prices provides evidence that indeed virtually everybody has a price, but not that this person is in need of rehabilitation, given the world we actually inhabit. The point generalized is that criminal acts occur in the real world, not an artificial one, and behavior in an artificial world is largely uninformative of behavior in this one.

Id. at 415-416. How would this approach to entrapment work in a case like *Jacobson*? Note that while they have not necessarily adopted a "market rate" limitation on permissible inducements, some courts in the wake of *Jacobson* have read that case to impose a requirement that the government's evidence demonstrate that a defendant would have responded affirmatively to an "ordinary" opportunity to commit the crime. See, e.g., United States v. Gendron, 18 F.3d 955, 962 (1st Cir. 1994).

5. In practice, procedural and evidentiary differences between the subjective and objective approaches to entrapment may be more important than substantive differences between the two defenses. Three principal differences of this type are worth mentioning. First, where the subjective test prevails, entrapment is generally a question for the jury. Under the objective test, the defense is more likely to be a question of law for the judge. Second, by raising an entrapment defense in a subjective jurisdiction, the criminal defendant will generally open the door for the government to introduce evidence regarding the defendant's reputation, character, prior convictions, and prior bad acts — to show his predisposition to commit the crime. The objective defense does not usually involve this consequence. Finally, the allocations of burdens of proof may well be different in jurisdictions adopting one or the other version of the defense. In subjective jurisdictions, the prosecution normally has the burden of proving predisposition beyond a reasonable doubt. On the other hand, the burden of persuading a factfinder that a normally law-abiding person would likely have succumbed to the government's inducements may well rest with the defendant in jurisdictions employing the objective test.

Note that these procedural and evidentiary features may not be necessary con-
comitants of the entrapment test normally associated with them. Would either of the
entrapment defenses be improved by changing one or another of these features?

6. In United States v. Russell, 411 U.S. 423, 431-432 (1973), the Court noted, in
dicta, that "we may some day be presented with a situation in which the conduct of
law enforcement agents is so outrageous that due process principles would absolutely bar the government from invoking judicial processes to obtain a conviction."
The "outrageous government conduct" doctrine could, in theory, provide additional judicial regulation of undercover investigations, beyond that afforded by
the entrapment defense. The Court, however, has never reversed a conviction for
"outrageous government conduct." Only three years after the decision in *Russell*,
moreover, the vitality of this due process doctrine as a basis for prohibiting the
conviction of even predisposed defendants was drawn into some question in
Hampton v. United States, 425 U.S. 484 (1976).

In *Hampton*, the defendant was convicted of selling heroin to two government
agents. The prosecution contended that the defendant had suggested the sale to
a friend, Hutton, who happened to be a police informant and who thereafter
arranged it. The defendant contended that Hutton had told him that he had a
pharmacist friend who could produce a nonnarcotic counterfeit drug that simulated
the effects of heroin; Hutton proposed selling this drug to gullible acquaintances
as heroin. Id. at 486-487. The trial court refused to instruct the jury that it should
acquit "[i]f you find that the defendant's sales of narcotics were sales of narcotics
supplied to him by an informer in the employ of or acting on behalf of the government." The principal issue before the Court was whether the defendant's
version of events, if true, constituted a due process violation. In an opinion joined
by Chief Justice Burger and Justice White, Justice Rehnquist, the author of the
Court's opinion in *Russell*, concluded:

> The remedy of the criminal defendant with respect to the acts of Government agents,
> which, far from being resisted, are encouraged by him, lies solely in the defense of
> entrapment. But . . . petitioner's conceded predisposition rendered this defense una-
> vailable to him.
>
> To sustain petitioner's contention here would run directly contrary to our statement
> in *Russell* that the defense of entrapment is not intended "to give the federal judiciary
> a 'chancellor's foot' veto over law enforcement practices of which it did not approve.
> The execution of the federal laws under our Constitution is confided primarily to
> the Executive Branch of the Government, subject to applicable constitutional and
> statutory limitations and to judicially fashioned rules to enforce those limitations."
>
> The limitations of the Due Process Clause of the Fifth Amendment come into play
> only when the Government activity in question violates some protected right of the
> *defendant*. Here, as we have noted, the police, the Government informant, and the
> defendant acted in concert with one another. If the result of the governmental activity
> is to "implant in the mind of an innocent person the disposition to commit the alleged
> offense and induce its commission . . ." Sorrell [v. United States, 287 U.S. 435], 442
> [(1932)], the defendant is protected by the defense of entrapment. If the police engage
> in illegal activity in concert with a defendant beyond the scope of their duties the remedy
> lies, not in freeing the equally culpable defendant, but in prosecuting the police under
> the applicable provisions of state or federal law.

Id. at 490.

In a separate opinion joined by Justice Blackmun, Justice Powell agreed that Hampton had not made out a due process violation but was "unwilling to join the plurality in concluding that, no matter what the circumstances, neither due process principles nor [the Court's] supervisory power could support a bar to conviction in any case where the Government is able to prove predisposition." Id. at 495. Justice Brennan, in an opinion joined by Justices Stewart and Marshall, dissented, noting that "[w]here the Government's agent deliberately sets up the accused by supplying him with contraband and then bringing him to another agent as a potential purchaser, the Government's role has passed the point of toleration." Id. at 498.

Many courts recognize a constitutional defense to criminal prosecution based on outrageous conduct during the investigation — at least in theory. But some courts don't. See, e.g., United States v. Boyd, 55 F.3d 239, 241 (7th Cir. 1995); United States v. Tucker, 28 F.3d 1420, 1427 (6th Cir. 1994). Moreover, the defense almost never succeeds even where recognized. In these circumstances, is the "outrageous governmental misconduct" doctrine an important supplement to the entrapment defense? Is it worth the candle? Consider Judge Easterbrook's complaint:

> "Outrageousness" as a defense does more than stretch the bounds of due process. It also creates serious problems of consistency. The circuits that recognize a "due process defense" can't agree on what it means. How much is "too much"? The nature of the question exposes it as (a) unanswerable, and (b) political. . . . Any line we draw would be unprincipled and therefore not judicial in nature. More likely there would be no line; judges would vote their lower intestines. Such a meandering, personal approach is the antithesis of justice under law, and we ought not indulge it. Inability to describe in general terms just what makes tactics too outrageous to tolerate suggests that there is no definition — and "I know it when I see it" is not a rule of any kind, let alone a command of the Due Process Clause.

United States v. Miller, 891 F.2d 1265, 1272-1273 (7th Cir. 1989) (Easterbrook, J., concurring). Do you agree? For a defense of the doctrine, see Paul Marcus, The Due Process Defense in Entrapment Cases: The Journey Back, 27 Am. Crim. L. Rev. 457 (1990).

7. The Justice Department has issued guidelines on FBI undercover operations that go beyond the judicial controls we have thus far considered. These guidelines require that certain sensitive undercover investigations be authorized only after review by an Undercover Review Committee consisting of FBI personnel designated by the Director and Justice Department attorneys named by the Assistant Attorney General in charge of the Department's Criminal Division. These sensitive investigations include operations involving possible criminal conduct by elected officials, political or religious organizations, or foreign governments. Also those involving a reasonable expectation that an undercover agent will be involved in a serious crime, be arrested, or supply falsely sworn testimony. Attorney General's Guidelines on FBI Undercover Operations, ¶IV.C (2002). In addition, supervisory personnel at FBI headquarters must authorize all undercover operations expected to involve expenditures over $50,000 (or $100,000 in narcotics cases), or to last more than one year. Id. Other, more routine investigations may be authorized by the Special Agent in Charge of an FBI field office.

Undercover employees are specifically prohibited from participating in acts of violence, except in self-defense, or in conduct constituting unlawful investigative techniques — for example, illegal wiretapping, breaking and entering, or trespassing amounting to an illegal search. Id. at ¶IV.H.

With regard to entrapment, the guidelines provide that the supervisory officials authorizing undercover activity involving inducements must be satisfied that: (a) the illegal nature of the activity is reasonably clear to potential subjects; (b) the nature of the inducement is justifiable "in view of the character of the illegal transaction in which the individual is invited to engage"; (c) there is a reasonable expectation that offering the inducement will reveal illegal activities; and (d) there is some reasonable indication that the subject is engaging, has engaged, or is likely to engage in the proposed illegal activity or in similar illegal conduct or, alternatively, that the inducement has been structured so that there is reason to believe that any persons drawn by it are predisposed to engage in the contemplated illegal conduct. Id. at ¶V.

Do these and other internal guidelines offer real checks on law enforcement — and particularly in the context of covert investigations? Professor Richman has argued that federal prosecutors and law enforcement agents, drawn as they are from two relatively distinct cultures, can operate as mutual monitors, promoting "more thoughtful decisionmaking, even in the absence of legislative or judicial oversight." Daniel Richman, Prosecutors and Their Agents, Agents and Their Prosecutors, 103 Col. L. Rev. 749, 810 (2003). Internal guidelines such as the ones regulating undercover operations can help promote this "mutual monitoring." Consider his analysis:

> . . . Any FBI field office seeking to engage in an "undercover operation" involving any sensitive circumstance" must first apply to FBI headquarters for approval. The application must contain a "letter from the appropriate Federal prosecutor indicating that he or she has reviewed the proposed operation, including the sensitive circumstances reasonably expected to occur, agrees with the proposal and its legality, and will prosecute any meritorious case that has developed." If favorably recommended by FBI headquarters, the proposal then goes to an "Undercover Review Committee," comprised of FBI personnel . . . and prosecutors. . . . Prosecutors from the relevant U.S. Attorney's Office and FBI agents from the field can attend the committee's meeting and, in practice, line assistants are "encouraged" to discuss the proposal with committee members before the meeting. Decisions within this committee are to be by consensus. If one of the prosecutors declines to join a favorable recommendation "because of legal, ethical, prosecutive, or departmental policy considerations," the Assistant Attorney General is consulted, and absent his approval or the approval of either the department's top two officials — the Deputy Attorney General or Attorney General — the operation will not proceed.
>
> The most salient operational feature of this administrative regime is the number of checkpoints it creates both at the local level and in Washington to ensure that as broad a variety of perspectives as the enforcement bureaucracy has to offer . . . are brought to bear on those operations most likely to spark allegations of government overreaching and targeting. An important by-product . . . is the colloboration it promotes at the field level, as prosecutors and agents become co-presenters of a joint proposal that each must sell up through his respective Washington hierarchy.

Id. at 815-816. Do these guidelines promote "mutual monitoring" by ensuring that both prosecutors and agents are part of the decision-making process — at least with regard to sensitive cases?

8. Finally, note that the war on terror has produced some pertinent changes to the Attorney General's Guidelines on General Crimes, Racketeering Enterprise and Terrorism Enterprise Investigations, the guidelines governing the circumstances in which FBI criminal investigations may be begun, as well as the permissible scope, duration, subject matter, and objectives of these investigations. According to the Justice Department in a May 13, 2003 letter to the House Judiciary Committee:

> The old Guidelines did not clearly authorize agents to gather information for counter-terrorism or other law enforcement purposes — for example, by visiting public places, or researching publicly available information — unless they were looking into particular crimes or criminal enterprises. In effect, agents had to wait for . . . some lead or evidence to come from others, before they could begin gathering information. The revised Guidelines were designed to enable law enforcement to proactively gather intelligence that could be useful to detecting and preventing terrorist attacks, by attending public events or collecting publicly available information.

First Amendment attorney Floyd Abrams has commented on the background of these guidelines and on the changes made after 9/11:

> [Should] FBI agents . . . be permitted to attend public meetings of a political or religious nature for the purpose of reporting upon what is said there[?] When [they] did so in the 1950s and 1960s, some of the worst abuses of the regime of J. Edgar Hoover occurred. The "chill" on speech was real; Hoover intended just that and achieved just that. It was a civil liberties disaster. After Hoover died, new guidelines, drafted by former Attorneys General Edward Levi and William French Smith, were adopted, effectively barring FBI agents from doing so in most circumstances. Those limits were hailed by civil libertarians — and they should have been.
>
> A quarter of a century has now passed, however, and we face new risks. Shall we now permit, as Attorney General Ashcroft has determined, FBI surveillance of such events? If the Bureau believes that public statements made in a particular mosque, say, may be of assistance in preventing future acts of terrorism, but it is short of proof sufficient to demonstrate the likelihood of criminal behavior, should surveillance of the event be permitted? I think so. Yet when we make that trade-off, we obviously risk the very governmental overreaching and misconduct that tends to accompany any broadening of governmental powers.

Floyd Abrams, The First Amendment and the War Against Terrorism, 5 U. Pa. J. Const. L. 1, 6 (2002). The revised guidelines provide that "[f]or the purpose of detecting or preventing terrorist activities, the FBI is authorized to visit any place and attend any event that is open to the public, on the same terms and conditions as members of the public generally." The FBI may do so even in the absence of any pre-existing lead or specific predication. The guidelines provide, however, that "[n]o information obtained from such visits shall be retained unless it relates to potential criminal or terrorist activity." They also prohibit the FBI from "maintaining files on individuals solely for the purpose of monitoring activities protected by the First Amendment. . . ."

In its May 2003 letter (and in response to a specific query from the Judiciary Committee), the Justice Department indicated that the FBI's Office of the General Counsel had conducted an informal survey of 45 FBI field offices. The Justice

Department reported that fewer than 10 of the 45 surveyed offices had conducted investigative activities at mosques in the aftermath of September 11. All but one of these cases related to open preliminary inquiries or full investigations for which some level of predication is required: "In the one reported instance where a visit was conducted pursuant to the Guidelines provision authorizing agents to visit public places and attend public events, no information relating to potential terrorism or criminal activity was found and, therefore, no substantive information from the visit was retained in FBI records."

Do these recent revisions to FBI guidelines threaten a return to abuses of the past? In closing, consider Professor Schulhofer's analysis:

> At least where terrorism investigations are concerned, old limits on agents' investigative discretion certainly should be open to reconsideration. The potential gains from easing those limits are obvious. But are there significant dangers in dropping objective prerequisites for an investigation, relaxing time limits on how long it can be pursued, and conferring broad discretion on investigating agents in the field? The parts of the new guidelines that Attorney General Ashcroft [has] spotlighted — those granting field agents the authority to read the newspaper, surf the Internet, or attend meetings open to any member of the public — sound innocuous enough. But the safeguards he dismantled have a history that remains pertinent, in fact especially pertinent, in the context of the aggressively proactive intelligence work he seeks to encourage. . . .
>
> It is therefore essential to recall the results of actual experience with broad investigatory discretion similar to that just restored at the FBI. Agents zealously pursuing leads and hunches saw nothing wrong in showing their badge and "just asking" employers and teachers whether an individual had been seen with communists, had expressed hatred of America, or had shown a desire to commit violent acts against the government. Agents spent years infiltrating and monitoring political groups of all stripes, from the Socialist Workers Party on the left to the Conservative American Christian Action Council and the John Birch Society on the right. Attending rallies and meetings open to the public, they monitored and maintained extensive files on student groups on college campuses, civil rights organizations including the National Association for the Advancement of Colored People (NAACP) and the Southern Christian Leadership Conference, national leaders such as the Rev. Martin Luther King, Jr., anti-war groups, and meetings they identified with the "Women's Liberation Movement."

Stephen J. Schulhofer, The Enemy Within 60 (2002). Do you agree with Professor Schulhofer that more attention should be paid to the scope of law enforcement's post-9/11 authority? Consider the following:

> September 11 was an extraordinary crisis, warranting emergency measures of extraordinary scope. But there is, unfortunately, no reason to believe that the threat of terrorism will recede any time soon. More likely, the "emergency" will be with us through several future presidential administrations. Thus, the enhanced size and prerogatives of the federal law enforcement establishment may not be reversed in our lifetimes. Along with concern for our safety and security, we must devote our utmost attention to the power of the government under which we will live over that very long term.

Id. at 68.

C.   Grand Jury Investigations

The grand jury's English origins are commonly traced to the twelfth century. It began as an accusatory body of citizens drawn from local communities that lent assistance to the Crown in the institution of criminal cases by identifying those in the locality who should be charged with crime. By the end of the seventeenth century, however, the grand jury had come to be viewed not as a convenient device for the lodging of criminal charges but as a buffer between the state and the citizen, protecting the latter against oppressive and unwarranted accusation. It was this view of the institution that was transplanted to colonial America, where it took firm root — particularly in the years leading up to the Revolutionary War, when "[g]rowing tension between the Crown and the colonies often surfaced in disagreements over enforcement of the criminal laws." Andrew D. Leipold, Why Grand Juries Do Not (and Cannot) Protect the Accused, 80 Cornell L. Rev. 260, 284-285 (1995). Indeed, the refusal of colonial grand juries to issue indictments requested by Crown officials (in the celebrated prosecution of John Peter Zenger for seditious libel, but also in more mundane cases involving the Crown's efforts to enforce unpopular tax laws) contributed to the popularity of grand juries and paved the way for the ultimate inclusion of the grand jury guarantee in the Fifth Amendment.

Given this history, it is somewhat ironic that the modern grand jury is more often viewed as an investigative tool for the state, particularly in complex criminal cases, than as a bulwark against the lodging of unfounded (or unpopular) criminal charges. This is not to claim that contemporary grand juries offer *no* protection against oppressive prosecution. The nature of that protection, such as it might be, and the role of the grand jury in screening criminal charges are explored in Chapter 8. It is beyond doubt, however, that the modern grand jury's most prominent role is investigatory. Federal grand juries, in particular, are extremely important to the unraveling of complex crimes that may be impervious to investigation and prosecution by means of traditional police investigative techniques.

There is more than a little irony in the preceding observation, as well. Grand jury investigations are cumbersome, time consuming, and expensive. It's easy to see why. Convening 16 to 23 citizens to hear what may turn out to be months of testimony and to review sometimes voluminous physical and documentary evidence in a federal grand jury proceeding is no small logistical feat. Nor would it seem a promising way to begin the investigation of a complex case. And yet it often is. You may want to consider just why grand juries are so important in the investigation of a range of complex criminal cases as you read the following materials.

1.   The Subpoena Power

UNITED STATES v. DIONISIO

Certiorari to the United States Court of Appeals for the Seventh Circuit
410 U.S. 1 (1973)

Mr. Justice Stewart delivered the opinion of the Court.

A special grand jury was convened in the Northern District of Illinois in February 1971, to investigate possible violations of federal criminal statutes relating to gambling. In the course of its investigation, the grand jury received in evidence certain voice recordings that had been obtained pursuant to court orders.

The grand jury subpoenaed approximately 20 persons, including the respondent Dionisio, seeking to obtain from them voice exemplars for comparison with the recorded conversations that had been received in evidence. . . . Dionisio and other witnesses refused to furnish the voice exemplars, asserting that these disclosures would violate their rights under the Fourth and Fifth Amendments. . . .

Following a hearing, the District Judge rejected the witnesses' constitutional arguments and ordered them to comply with the grand jury's request . . . When Dionisio persisted in his refusal to respond to the grand jury's directive, the District Court adjudged him in civil contempt and ordered him committed to custody until he obeyed the court order, or until the expiration of 18 months.

The Court of Appeals for the Seventh Circuit reversed. . . .

The Court of Appeals held that the Fourth Amendment required a preliminary showing of reasonableness before a grand jury witness could be compelled to furnish a voice exemplar, and that in this case the proposed "seizures" of the voice exemplars would be unreasonable because of the large number of witnesses summoned by the grand jury and directed to produce such exemplars. We disagree. . . .

[T]he obtaining of physical evidence from a person involves a potential Fourth Amendment violation at two different levels—the "seizure" of the "person" necessary to bring him into contact with government agents, and the subsequent search for and seizure of the evidence. . . . The constitutionality of the compulsory production of exemplars from a grand jury witness necessarily turns on [a] dual inquiry—whether either the initial compulsion of the person to appear before the grand jury, or the subsequent directive to make a voice recording is an unreasonable "seizure" within the meaning of the Fourth Amendment.

It is clear that a subpoena to appear before a grand jury is not a "seizure" in the Fourth Amendment sense, even though that summons may be inconvenient or burdensome. Last Term we again acknowledged what has long been recognized, that "[c]itizens generally are not constitutionally immune from grand jury subpoenas. . . ." Branzburg v. Hayes, 408 U.S. 665, 682. We concluded that:

> "Although the powers of the grand jury are not unlimited and are subject to the supervision of a judge, the longstanding principle that 'the public . . . has a right to every man's evidence,' except for those persons protected by a constitutional, common law, or statutory privilege, is particularly applicable to grand jury proceedings."

Id., at 688.

These are recent reaffirmations of the historically grounded obligation of every person to appear and give his evidence before the grand jury. "The personal sacrifice involved is a part of the necessary contribution of the individual to the welfare of the public." Blair v. United States, 250 U.S. 273, 281. . . .

The compulsion exerted by a grand jury subpoena differs from the seizure effected by an arrest or even an investigative "stop" in more than civic obligation. For, as Judge Friendly wrote for the Court of Appeals for the Second Circuit:

> "The latter is abrupt, is effected with force or the threat of it and often in demeaning circumstances, and, in the case of arrest, results in a record involving social stigma. A subpoena is served in the same manner as other legal process; it involves no stigma whatever; if the time for appearance is inconvenient, this can generally be altered; and

it remains at all times under the control and supervision of a court." United States v. Doe (Schwartz) 457 F.2d, [895, 898].

Thus the Court of Appeals for the Seventh Circuit correctly recognized in a case subsequent to the one now before us, that a "grand jury subpoena to testify is not that kind of governmental intrusion on privacy against which the Fourth Amendment affords protection once the Fifth Amendment is satisfied." Fraser v. United States, 452 F.2d 616, 620.

This case is thus quite different from Davis v. Mississippi, supra, on which the Court of Appeals primarily relied.[3] For in *Davis* it was the initial seizure — the lawless dragnet detention — that violated the Fourth and Fourteenth Amendments, not the taking of the fingerprints. We noted that "[i]nvestigatory seizures would subject unlimited numbers of innocent persons to the harassment and ignominy incident to involuntary detention," 394 U.S., at 726, and we left open the question whether, consistently with the Fourth and Fourteenth Amendments, narrowly circumscribed procedures might be developed for obtaining fingerprints from people when there was no probable cause to arrest them. Id., at 728. *Davis* is plainly inapposite to a case where the initial restraint does not itself infringe the Fourth Amendment.

This is not to say that a grand jury subpoena is some talisman that dissolves all constitutional protections. The grand jury cannot require a witness to testify against himself. It cannot require the production by a person of private books and records that would incriminate him. See Boyd v. United States, 116 U.S. 616, 633-635. The Fourth Amendment provides protection against a grand jury subpoena *duces tecum* too sweeping in its terms "to be regarded as reasonable." Hale v. Henkel, 201 U.S. 43, 76. . . .

But we are here faced with no such constitutional infirmities in the subpoena to appear before the grand jury or in the order to make the voice recordings. . . .

The Court of Appeals found critical significance in the fact that the grand jury had summoned approximately 20 witnesses to furnish voice exemplars. We think that fact is basically irrelevant to the constitutional issues here. The grand jury may have been attempting to identify a number of voices on the tapes in evidence, or it might have summoned the 20 witnesses in an effort to identify one voice. But whatever the case, "[a] grand jury's investigation is not fully carried out until every available clue has been run down and all witnesses examined in every proper way to find if a crime has been committed. . . ." United States v. Stone, 429 F.2d 138, 140. . . . The grand jury may well find it desirable to call numerous witnesses in the course of an investigation. It does not follow that each witness may resist a subpoena on the ground that too many witnesses have been called. Neither the order to Dionisio to appear nor the order to make a voice recording was rendered unreasonable by the fact that many others were subjected to the same compulsion.

3. In Davis v. Mississippi, 394 U.S. 721 (1969), the Court held that it was error to admit the defendant's fingerprints into evidence at his trial for rape because they had been obtained in violation of the Fourth Amendment. The defendant was one of 25 young black men rounded up and detained for fingerprinting in connection with the crime. These detentions were done without the authorization of a warrant and in the absence of any probable cause. The Court held that the fingerprints were the fruit of an unlawful seizure of the defendant's person. — EDS.

But the conclusion that Dionisio's compulsory appearance before the grand jury was not an unreasonable "seizure" is the answer to only the first part of the Fourth Amendment inquiry here. Dionisio argues that the grand jury's subsequent directive to make the voice recording was itself an infringement of his rights under the Fourth Amendment. We cannot accept that argument.

In Katz v. United States, we said that the Fourth Amendment provides no protection for what "a person knowingly exposes to the public, even in his own home or office. . . ." 389 U.S. [347,] 351. The physical characteristics of a person's voice, its tone and manner, as opposed to the content of a specific conversation, are constantly exposed to the public. Like a man's facial characteristics, or handwriting, his voice is repeatedly produced for others to hear. No person can have a reasonable expectation that others will not know the sound of his voice, any more than he can reasonably expect that his face will be a mystery to the world. . . .

Since neither the summons to appear before the grand jury nor its directive to make a voice recording infringed upon any interest protected by the Fourth Amendment, there was no justification for requiring the grand jury to satisfy even the minimal requirement of "reasonableness" imposed by the Court of Appeals. A grand jury has broad investigative powers to determine whether a crime has been committed and who has committed it. The jurors may act on tips, rumors, evidence offered by the prosecutor, or their own personal knowledge. No grand jury witness is "entitled to set limits to the investigation that the grand jury may conduct." Blair v. United States, 250 U.S., at 282. . . . Since Dionisio raised no valid Fourth Amendment claim, there is no more reason to require a preliminary showing of reasonableness here than there would be in the case of any witness who, despite the lack of any constitutional or statutory privilege, declined to answer a question or comply with a grand jury request. Neither the Constitution nor our prior cases justify any such interference with grand jury proceedings.

The Fifth Amendment guarantees that no civilian may be brought to trial for an infamous crime "unless on a presentment or indictment of a Grand Jury." This constitutional guarantee presupposes an investigative body "acting independently of either prosecuting attorney or judge," Stirone v. United States, 361 U.S. 212, 218, whose mission is to clear the innocent, no less than to bring to trial those who may be guilty. Any holding that would saddle a grand jury with minitrials and preliminary showings would assuredly impede its investigation and frustrate the public's interest in the fair and expeditious administration of the criminal laws. The grand jury may not always serve its historic role as a protective bulwark standing solidly between the ordinary citizen and an overzealous prosecutor, but if it is even to approach the proper performance of its constitutional mission, it must be free to pursue its investigations unhindered by external influence or supervision so long as it does not trench upon the legitimate rights of any witness called before it.

Since the Court of Appeals found an unreasonable search and seizure where none existed, and imposed a preliminary showing of reasonableness where none was required, its judgment is reversed and this case is remanded to that court for further proceedings consistent with this opinion.

It is so ordered.

[The opinion of Justice Brennan, concurring in part and dissenting in part, and the dissenting opinion of Justice Douglas are omitted.]

MR. JUSTICE MARSHALL, dissenting. . . .

There can be no question that investigatory seizures effected by the police are subject to the constraints of the Fourth and Fourteenth Amendments. In Davis v. Mississippi, 394 U.S. 721, 727 (1969), the Court observed that only the Term before, in Terry v. Ohio, 392 U.S. 1, 19 (1968), it had rejected "the notions that the Fourth Amendment does not come into play at all as a limitation upon police conduct if the officers stop short of something called a 'technical arrest' or a 'full-blown search.'" . . . Certainly, the peculiarly offensive exercise of investigatory powers in *Davis* heightened the Court's sensitivity to the dangers inherent in Mississippi's argument that the Fourth Amendment was not applicable to investigatory seizures. But the presence of a dragnet was not the constitutional determinant there; rather, it was police interference with the petitioner's own liberty that brought the Fourth and Fourteenth Amendments into play, as should be evident from the Court's substantial reliance on *Terry*, which involved no dragnet.

Like *Davis*, the present case[ ] involve[s] official investigatory seizures that interfere with personal liberty. The Court considers dispositive, however, the fact that the seizures were effected by the grand jury, rather than the police. I cannot agree.

First, in Hale v. Henkel, 201 U.S. 43, 76 (1906), the Court held that a subpoena *duces tecum* ordering "the production of books and papers [before a grand jury] may constitute an unreasonable search and seizure within the Fourth Amendment," and on the particular facts of the case, it concluded that the subpoena was "far too sweeping in its terms to be regarded as reasonable." Considered alone, *Hale* would certainly seem to carry a strong implication that a subpoena compelling an individual's personal appearance before a grand jury, like a subpoena ordering the production of private papers, is subject to the Fourth Amendment standard of reasonableness. The protection of the Fourth Amendment is not, after all, limited to personal "papers," but extends also to "persons," "houses," and "effects." It would seem a strange hierarchy of constitutional values that would afford papers more protection from arbitrary governmental interference than people.

The Court, however, offers two interrelated justifications for excepting grand jury subpoenas directed at "persons," rather than "papers," from the constraints of the Fourth Amendment. These are a "historically grounded obligation of every person to appear and give his evidence before the grand jury," and the relative unintrusiveness of the grand jury subpoena on an individual's liberty.

In my view, the Court makes more of history than is justified. The Court treats the "historically grounded obligation" which it now discerns as extending to all "evidence," whatever its character. Yet, so far as I am aware, the obligation "to appear and give evidence" has heretofore been applied by this Court only in the context of testimonial evidence, either oral or documentary. . . .

The Court seems to reason that the exception to the Fourth Amendment for grand jury subpoenas directed at persons is justified by the relative unintrusiveness of the grand jury process on an individual's liberty. The Court . . . suggests that arrests or even investigatory "stops" are inimical to personal liberty because they may involve the use of force; they may be carried out in demeaning circumstances; and at least an arrest may yield the social stigma of a record. By contrast, we are told, a grand jury subpoena is a simple legal process that is served in an unoffensive manner; it results in no stigma; and a convenient time for appearance may always be arranged. The Court would have us believe, in short, that, unlike an arrest or an investigatory "stop," a grand jury subpoena entails little more inconvenience than a visit to an old friend. Common sense and practical experience indicate otherwise.

It may be that service of a grand jury subpoena does not involve the same potential for momentary embarrassment as does an arrest or investigatory "stop." But this difference seems inconsequential in comparison to the substantial stigma that — contrary to the Court's assertion — may result from a grand jury appearance as well as from an arrest or investigatory seizure. Public knowledge that a man has been summoned by a federal grand jury investigating, for instance, organized criminal activity can mean loss of friends, irreparable injury to business, and tremendous pressures on one's family life. Whatever nice legal distinctions may be drawn between police and prosecutor, on the one hand, and the grand jury, on the other, the public often treats an appearance before a grand jury as tantamount to a visit to the station house. Indeed, the former is frequently more damaging than the latter, for a grand jury appearance has an air of far greater gravity than a brief visit "downtown" for a "talk." The Fourth Amendment was placed in our Bill of Rights to protect the individual citizen from such potentially disruptive governmental intrusion into his private life. . . .

Nor do I believe that the constitutional problems inherent in such governmental interference with an individual's person are substantially alleviated because one may seek to appear at a "convenient time." . . . No matter how considerate a grand jury may be in arranging for an individual's appearance, the basic fact remains that his liberty has been officially restrained for some period of time. . . .

Of course, the Fourth Amendment does not bar all official seizures of the person, but only those that are unreasonable and are without sufficient cause. With this in mind, it is possible, at least, to explain, if not justify, the failure to apply the protection of the Fourth Amendment to grand jury subpoenas requiring individuals to appear and *testify*. . . .

Certainly the most celebrated function of the grand jury is to stand between the Government and the citizen and thus to protect the latter from harassment and unfounded prosecution. The grand jury does not shed those characteristics that give it insulating qualities when it acts in its investigative capacity. Properly functioning, the grand jury is to be the servant of neither the Government nor the courts, but of the people. As such, we assume that it comes to its task without bias or self-interest. Unlike the prosecutor or policeman, it has no election to win or executive appointment to keep. The anticipated neutrality of the grand jury, even when acting in its investigative capacity, may perhaps be relied upon to prevent unwarranted interference with the lives of private citizens and to ensure that the grand jury's subpoena powers over the person are exercised in only a reasonable fashion. Under such circumstances, it may be justifiable to give the grand jury broad personal subpoena powers that are outside the purview of the Fourth Amendment for — in contrast to the police — it is not likely that it will abuse those powers.

Whatever the present day validity of the historical assumption of neutrality which underlies the grand jury process, it must at least be recognized that if a grand jury is deprived of the independence essential to the assumption of neutrality — if it effectively surrenders that independence to a prosecutor — the dangers of excessive and unreasonable official interference with personal liberty are exactly those which the Fourth Amendment was intended to prevent. So long as the grand jury carries on its investigatory activities only through the mechanism of testimonial inquiries, the danger of such official usurpation of the grand jury process may not be unreasonably great. Individuals called to testify before the grand jury will have available their Fifth Amendment privilege against self-incrimination. . . .

But when we move beyond the realm of grand jury investigations limited to testimonial inquiries, as the Court does today, the danger increases that law enforcement officials may seek to usurp the grand jury process for the purpose of securing incriminating evidence from a particular suspect through the simple expedient of a subpoena . . . Thus, if the grand jury may summon criminal suspects [to obtain voice exemplars] without complying with the Fourth Amendment, it will obviously present an attractive investigative tool to prosecutor and police. . . .

. . . [B]y holding that the grand jury's power to subpoena these respondents for the purpose of obtaining exemplars is completely outside the purview of the Fourth Amendment, the Court fails to appreciate the essential difference between real and testimonial evidence in the context of these cases, and thereby hastens the reduction of the grand jury into simply another investigative device of law enforcement officials. By contrast, the Court of Appeals, in proper recognition of these dangers, imposed narrow limitations on the subpoena power of the grand jury that are necessary to guard against unreasonable official interference with individual liberty but that would not impair significantly the traditional investigatory powers of that body. . . .

NOTES AND QUESTIONS

1. A grand jury subpoena requires its recipient to appear before the grand jury at a specified place and time to give testimony or, in the case of a subpoena *duces tecum*, to produce evidence demanded in the subpoena. Defiance of the subpoena can result in severe sanctions, including imprisonment. So why doesn't a grand jury subpoena constitute a "seizure" for Fourth Amendment purposes? Doesn't Justice Marshall have a point?

2. In addition to the majority's arguments, some have said it makes a difference that the recipient of a grand jury subpoena has the opportunity to challenge it before a court before being required to comply. A subpoena is thus not like a stop and frisk. But what if the subpoena requires the witness to appear before the grand jury or to produce documentary or other evidence before the grand jury "forthwith" — i.e., immediately? Several courts have upheld the use of such subpoenas (often served when there is a threat that evidence sought by the subpoena will be destroyed) while noting that they may be misused and do not confer on police the authority to seize either the person who is commanded to appear or any items the subpoena may seek. See, e.g., United States v. Lartey, 716 F.2d 955, 961 (2d Cir. 1983).

3. However persuasive (or unpersuasive) its rationale, *Dionisio* plainly states that the Fourth Amendment has little (if any) application to a grand jury subpoena seeking testimony from a witness. The situation is somewhat (but only somewhat) different for a subpoena *duces tecum*. In Hale v. Henkel, 201 U.S. 43 (1906), the Court considered a challenge to a grand jury subpoena demanding the production of corporate documents in connection with an investigation into possible antitrust violations. It observed as follows:

[A]n order for the production of books and papers may constitute an unreasonable search and seizure within the Fourth Amendment. While a search ordinarily implies a quest by an officer of the law, and a seizure contemplates a forcible dispossession of the owner, still, as was held in the *Boyd* case, the substance of the offense is the compulsory production of private papers, whether under a search warrant or a *subpoena duces tecum*, against which the person, be he individual or corporation, is entitled to protection. Applying the test of reasonableness to the present case, we think the *subpoena duces tecum* is far too sweeping in its terms to be regarded as reasonable. It does not require the production of a single contract, or of contracts with a particular corporation, or a limited number of documents, but all understandings, contracts, or correspondence between the MacAndrews & Forbes Company, and no less than six different companies, as well as all reports made, and accounts rendered by such companies from the date of the organization of the MacAndrews & Forbes Company, as well as all letters received by that company since its organization from more than a dozen different companies, situated in seven different States in the Union.

Id. at 76-77.

The Court went on to note that "[d]oubtless many, if not all, of these documents may ultimately be required, but some necessity should be shown . . . or some evidence of their materiality produced, to justify an order for the production of such a mass of papers." Id. at 77.

What is the basis for the Court's holding in *Hale*? If the idea of *Hale*'s overbreadth doctrine is that the demand for a mass of papers is like a physical search, why should it be enough for the government to show that in the circumstances of a particular case its demand is reasonable? Why not require a warrant based on probable cause? If this *isn't* the rationale behind *Hale*, what is? And what is the relevance of *Boyd* (which we first examined in Chapter 4)? Didn't *Boyd* involve an order to produce a *single* invoice that was undeniably germane to the proceeding?

As these questions suggest, *Hale*'s language is at least a little misleading — over the course of the past century, at least on this particular front, the Court's bark has been a good deal worse than its bite. Today, subpoenas are rarely quashed because they are, in the language of the *Hale* Court, "too sweeping . . . to be regarded as reasonable." It would be an exaggeration to say that there is *no* Fourth Amendment regulation of subpoenas. But it would not be much of an exaggeration.

4. In United States v. R. Enterprises, 498 U.S. 292 (1991), the Supreme Court took up the question of what *statutory* standards might apply to federal grand jury subpoenas seeking documentary or other physical evidence. Federal Rule of Criminal Procedure 17(c) governs the issuance of subpoenas *duces tecum* in federal criminal proceedings. It provides that "[o]n motion made promptly, the court may quash or modify [a] subpoena if compliance would be unreasonable or oppressive." In *R. Enterprises*, the Fourth Circuit quashed certain business records subpoenas issued in connection with a grand jury investigation into the interstate transportation of obscene materials. The circuit court cited the subpoena standards of relevancy, admissibility, and specificity set out by the Supreme Court in United States v. Nixon, 418 U.S. 683 (1974). The Fourth Circuit recognized that *Nixon* dealt with a trial subpoena, not a grand jury subpoena, but concluded that its standards were "equally applicable" in the grand jury context. The Supreme Court disagreed:

> The grand jury occupies a unique role in our criminal justice system. It is an investigatory body charged with the responsibility of determining whether or not a crime

has been committed. Unlike this Court, whose jurisdiction is predicated on a specific case or controversy, the grand jury "can investigate merely on suspicion that the law is being violated, or even just because it wants assurance that it is not." United States v. Morton Salt Co., 338 U.S. 632, 642-643 (1950). The function of the grand jury is to inquire into all information that might possibly bear on its investigation until it has identified an offense or has satisfied itself that none has occurred. As a necessary consequence of its investigatory function, the grand jury paints with a broad brush. . . .

A grand jury subpoena is thus much different from a subpoena issued in the context of a prospective criminal trial, where a specific offense has been identified and a particular defendant charged. "[T]he identity of the offender, and the precise nature of the offense, if there be one, normally are developed at the conclusion of the grand jury's labors, not at the beginning." Blair v. United States, 250 U.S. 273, 282 (1919). . . .

This Court has emphasized on numerous occasions that many of the rules and restrictions that apply at a trial do not apply in grand jury proceedings. This is especially true of evidentiary restrictions. . . . In Costello v. United States, 350 U.S. 359 (1956), this Court declined to apply the rule against hearsay to grand jury proceedings. Strict observance of trial rules in the context of a grand jury's preliminary investigation "would result in interminable delay but add nothing to the assurance of a fair trial." Id., at 364. In United States v. Calandra, 414 U.S. 338 (1974), we held that the Fourth Amendment exclusionary rule does not apply to grand jury proceedings. Permitting witnesses to invoke the exclusionary rule would "delay and disrupt grand jury proceedings" by requiring adversary hearings on peripheral matters, id., at 349, and would effectively transform such proceedings into preliminary trials on the merits, id., at 349-350. The teaching of the Court's decisions is clear: A grand jury "may compel the production of evidence or the testimony of witnesses as it considers appropriate, and its operation generally is unrestrained by the technical procedural and evidentiary rules governing the conduct of criminal trials," id., at 343.

This guiding principle renders suspect the Court of Appeals' holding that the standards announced in Nixon as to subpoenas issued in anticipation of trial apply equally in the grand jury context. The multifactor test announced in Nixon would invite procedural delays and detours while courts evaluate the relevancy and admissibility of documents sought by a particular subpoena. We have expressly stated that grand jury proceedings should be free of such delays. . . . Additionally, application of the Nixon test in this context ignores that grand jury proceedings are subject to strict secrecy requirements. Requiring the Government to explain in too much detail the particular reasons underlying a subpoena threatens to compromise "the indispensable secrecy of grand jury proceedings." United States v. Johnson, 319 U.S. 503, 513 (1943). Broad disclosure also affords the targets of investigation far more information about the grand jury's internal workings than the Federal Rules of Criminal Procedure appear to contemplate.

The investigatory powers of the grand jury are nevertheless not unlimited. Grand juries are not licensed to engage in arbitrary fishing expeditions, nor may they select targets of investigation out of malice or an intent to harass. In this case, the focus of our inquiry is the limit imposed on a grand jury by Federal Rule of Criminal Procedure 17(c). . . .

This standard is not self-explanatory. . . . In Nixon, this Court defined what is reasonable in the context of a jury trial. We determined that, in order to require production of information prior to trial, a party must make a reasonably specific request for information that would be both relevant and admissible at trial. But, for the reasons we have explained above, the Nixon standard does not apply in the context of grand jury proceedings. . . .

To the extent that Rule 17(c) imposes some reasonableness limitation on grand jury subpoenas . . . our task is to define it. In doing so, we recognize that a party to whom a grand jury subpoena is issued faces a difficult situation. As a rule, grand juries do not announce publicly the subjects of their investigations. A party who desires to challenge a grand jury subpoena thus may have no conception of the Government's purpose in seeking production of the requested information. Indeed, the party will often not know whether he or she is a primary target of the investigation or merely a peripheral witness. Absent even minimal information, the subpoena recipient is likely to find it exceedingly difficult to persuade a court that "compliance would be unreasonable." As one pair of commentators has summarized it, the challenging party's "unenviable task is to seek to persuade the court that the subpoena that has been served on [him or her] could not possibly serve any investigative purpose that the grand jury could legitimately be pursuing." 1 S. Beale & W. Bryson, Grand Jury Law and Practice §6:28 (1986).

Our task is to fashion an appropriate standard of reasonableness, one that gives due weight to the difficult position of subpoena recipients but does not impair the strong governmental interests in affording grand juries wide latitude, avoiding minitrials on peripheral matters, and preserving a necessary level of secrecy. We begin by reiterating that the law presumes, absent a strong showing to the contrary, that a grand jury acts within the legitimate scope of its authority. Consequently, a grand jury subpoena issued through normal channels is presumed to be reasonable, and the burden of showing unreasonableness must be on the recipient who seeks to avoid compliance. . . . To the extent that the Court of Appeals placed an initial burden on the Government, it committed error. Drawing on the principles articulated above, we conclude that where, as here, a subpoena is challenged on relevancy grounds, the motion to quash must be denied unless the district court determines that there is no reasonable possibility that the category of materials the Government seeks will produce information relevant to the general subject of the grand jury's investigation. . . .

It seems unlikely, of course, that a challenging party who does not know the general subject matter of the grand jury's investigation, no matter how valid that party's claim, will be able to make the necessary showing that compliance would be unreasonable. . . . Consequently, a court may be justified in a case where unreasonableness is alleged in requiring the Government to reveal the general subject of the grand jury's investigation before requiring the challenging party to carry its burden of persuasion. We need not resolve this question in the present case, however, as there is no doubt that respondents knew the subject of the grand jury investigation pursuant to which the business records subpoenas were issued. In cases where the recipient of the subpoena does not know the nature of the investigation, we are confident that district courts will be able to craft appropriate procedures that balance the interests of the subpoena recipient against the strong governmental interests in maintaining secrecy, preserving investigatory flexibility, and avoiding procedural delays. For example, to ensure that subpoenas are not routinely challenged as a form of discovery, a district court may require that the Government reveal the subject of the investigation to the trial court *in camera,* so that the court may determine whether the motion to quash has a reasonable prospect for success before it discloses the subject matter to the challenging party.

Applying these principles in this case demonstrates that the District Court correctly denied respondents' motions to quash. . . .

498 U.S. at 297-302. What is the meaning of *R. Enterprises'* relevance requirement? The Court says that one should start with a fairly strong presumption in favor of the subpoena and then ask whether "there is no reasonable possibility that the

category of materials the Government seeks will produce information relevant to the general subject of the grand jury's investigation." How likely is a "reasonable possibility"? How often would you expect a court to find that none exists?

5. Whatever the "reasonable possibility" standard means, it is plainly *much* less onerous than a probable cause standard. Why should that be so? Why should the standards for obtaining documents by subpoena be so much more lax than the standards that must be met to justify a police search for those same documents?

Two possible answers may be worth considering. The first bears on a good deal of the law of search and seizure; it is laid out in Louis Michael Seidman, The Problems with Privacy's Problem, 93 Mich. L. Rev. 1079 (1993). Seidman's claim is that police searches always involve "collateral damage"—the officer sees things other than the things he is looking for, and the encounter between the officer and citizen often involves substantial coercion—and a large part of what the probable cause requirement protects against is that collateral harm. Subpoenas, he says, are different:

> Subpoenas amount to self-searches. They involve no violence, no disruption, no public humiliation or embarrassment. Like the required completion of tax returns, subpoenas invade informational privacy but impose no collateral damage. For precisely this reason, the Court treats them no differently from tax returns. So long as the subpoena is "reasonable" and not unduly burdensome, a defendant has no . . . right not to comply.

Id. at 1092.

The second reason relates to the historical origins of the grand jury. A probable cause standard and warrant requirement might be necessary means of checking the ability of government officials to use their coercive power improperly, a means of protecting, in the words of the Fourth Amendment, "the right of the people to be secure in their persons, houses, papers, and effects." But the grand jury, in its classical conception, is not allied to government officials; it is *itself* "the people." This view of grand juries fits with a larger view of the original understanding of the Bill of Rights as a whole: not as a series of countermajoritarian rights, but as a series of *majoritarian* protections against official oppression. That understanding might explain the breadth of grand juries' power: Grand juries were a way that the people could check the power of government officials; they were not themselves in need of checking.

6. Are you persuaded by this analysis? Of course, the theory depends heavily on the continuing validity of the image of grand juries as independent decision-makers. If, instead, grand juries have become agents of the prosecution, they are not so much a check on state power as a weapon for the state to wield in its efforts to catch criminals. Consider *R. Enterprises'* statement that a grand jury "is to inquire into all information that might possibly bear on its investigation until it has identified an offense or satisfied itself that none has occurred." In fulfilling such a charge, a grand jury might well require the production of material that could intensely embarrass (not to mention burden) the party required to respond. (One is tempted to recall various subpoenas seeking gifts, books, and other items bearing on the relationship between Monica Lewinsky and former President Clinton. It's also worth pointing out the reams of paper that grand juries may require

both individuals and corporations to produce in the context of an ordinary white collar case.)

7. Indeed, couldn't Professor Seidman's argument be turned on its head? After all, it's one thing when police obtain and look through my appointment book because they have probable cause to believe it will reflect the payment of bribes to a local official. It's quite another, isn't it, when my telephone records, bank records, and credit card receipts are perused by government prosecutors who don't even know whether a crime has been committed? Consider the following analysis:

> [T]he federal subpoena power [is] something akin to a blank check. Prosecutors can go after whomever they like; they can be as intrusive as they choose; they can fight as hard as they want. Federal criminal law covers enough ground that if prosecutors look hard enough, they can find nearly anyone to have violated it. And prosecutors decide how hard to look. . . . Some sort of serious regulation is needed. The real question is, what form should it take? . . .
>
> An analogy to the civil process is useful. The rules for discovery in civil cases invite case-by-case adjustment based on the seriousness and scope of the case. Trial judges can give lawyers and litigants a lot of rope or a little. . . .
>
> If rough judgments about the importance of a case and the need for intrusive investigation are possible in civil cases, they are possible in white-collar criminal investigations as well. Indeed, the idea that unreasonably burdensome subpoenas should be quashed already exists in the law, and on occasion that idea translates into legally enforceable limits. What does not presently exist is the idea that the line between reasonable and unreasonable burdens should track the line between serious and less-than-serious crimes. . . . And that judgment ought to be made by courts, not by the prosecutors conducting the investigation.

William J. Stuntz, O.J. Simpson, Bill Clinton, and the Transsubstantive Fourth Amendment, 114 Harv. L. Rev. 842, 864-868 (2001). Do you agree?

8. When does a grand jury investigation begin? Many criminal investigations become grand jury investigations when potential witnesses either cannot (because they are under legal obligations committing them to secrecy in the absence of legal compulsion) or will not voluntarily provide information to police. In such circumstances, neither the police nor prosecutors can compel disclosure in most cases; it is the grand jury that provides investigators with this authority.

One might ask whether this makes sense — that essentially the only manner in which a reluctant witness may be required to testify or produce evidence during the investigation of a crime is to convene 16 to 23 citizens who have limited time or expertise to audit (much less oversee) a lengthy criminal investigation. If grand juries have indeed become agents of the prosecution, why not admit as much by conferring the grand jury's subpoena power directly on the prosecutor and relying on administrative controls to minimize abuse?

9. At any rate, short of invoking a legitimate Fifth Amendment claim and putting the prosecutor to the choice of whether to seek immunity, most grand jury witnesses have few grounds on which to resist a subpoena. (For a discussion of the Fifth Amendment privilege in this and other contexts, see Chapter 6, pages 751-804.) Depending on the circumstances, such witnesses may therefore deem it very important that their compelled testimony is subject to rules regarding grand jury secrecy — the subject to which we next turn.

2. Grand Jury Secrecy

FEDERAL RULES OF CRIMINAL PROCEDURE

Rule 6. The Grand Jury

(d) Who May Be Present.

(1) While the Grand Jury Is in Session. The following persons may be present while the grand jury is in session: attorneys for the government, the witness being questioned, interpreters when needed, and a court reporter or an operator of a recording device.

(2) During Deliberations and Voting. No person other than the jurors, and any interpreter needed to assist a hearing-impaired or speech-impaired juror, may be present while the grand jury is deliberating or voting.

(e) Recording and Disclosing the Proceedings.

(1) Recording the Proceedings. Except while the grand jury is deliberating or voting, all proceedings must be recorded by a court reporter or by a suitable recording device. But the validity of a prosecution is not affected by the unintentional failure to make a recording. Unless the court orders otherwise, an attorney for the government will retain control of the recording, the reporter's notes, and any transcript prepared from those notes.

(2) Secrecy.

(A) No obligation of secrecy may be imposed on any person except in accordance with Rule 6(e)(2)(B).

(B) Unless these rules provide otherwise, the following persons must not disclose a matter occurring before the grand jury:

(i) a grand juror;

(ii) an interpreter;

(iii) a court reporter;

(iv) an operator of a recording device;

(v) a person who transcribes recorded testimony;

(vi) an attorney for the government; or

(vii) a person to whom disclosure is made under Rule 6(e)(3)(A)(ii) or (iii).

(3) Exceptions.

(A) Disclosure of a grand-jury matter — other than the grand jury's deliberations or any grand juror's vote — may be made to:

(i) an attorney for the government for use in performing that attorney's duty;

(ii) any government personnel — including those of a state or state subdivision or of an Indian tribe — that an attorney for the government considers necessary to assist in performing that attorney's duty to enforce federal criminal law; or

(iii) a person authorized by 18 U.S.C. §3322.[4]

(B) A person to whom information is disclosed under Rule 6(e)(3)(A)(ii) may use that information only to assist an attorney for the government in

---

4. This statute authorizes disclosures to an attorney for the government and banking regulators for the purpose of enforcing civil forfeiture and civil banking laws. — EDS.

performing that attorney's duty to enforce federal criminal law. An attorney for the government must promptly provide the court that impaneled the grand jury with the names of all persons to whom a disclosure has been made, and must certify that the attorney has advised those persons of their obligation of secrecy under this rule.

(C) An attorney for the government may disclose any grand-jury matter to another federal grand jury.

(D) An attorney for the government may disclose any grand-jury matter involving foreign intelligence, counterintelligence (as defined in 50 U.S.C. §401a), or foreign intelligence information (as defined in Rule 6(e)(3)(D)(iii)) to any federal law enforcement, intelligence, protective, immigration, national defense, or national security official to assist the official receiving the information in the performance of that official's duties.

(i) Any federal official who receives information under Rule 6(e)(3)(D) may use the information only as necessary in the conduct of that person's official duties subject to any limitations on the unauthorized disclosure of such information.

(ii) Within a reasonable time after disclosure is made under Rule 6(e)(3)(D), an attorney for the government must file, under seal, a notice with the court in the district where the grand jury convened stating that such information was disclosed and the departments, agencies, or entities to which the disclosure was made.

(iii) As used in Rule 6(e)(3)(D), the term "foreign intelligence information" means:

(a) information, whether or not it concerns a United States person, that relates to the ability of the United States to protect against —

— actual or potential attack or other grave hostile acts of a foreign power or its agent;

— sabotage or international terrorism by a foreign power or its agent; or

— clandestine intelligence activities by an intelligence service or network of a foreign power or by its agent; or

(b) information, whether or not it concerns a United States person, with respect to a foreign power or foreign territory that relates to —

— the national defense or the security of the United States; or

— the conduct of the foreign affairs of the United States.

(E) The court may authorize disclosure — at a time, in a manner, and subject to any other conditions that it directs — of a grand-jury matter:

(i) preliminarily to or in connection with a judicial proceeding;

(ii) at the request of a defendant who shows that a ground may exist to dismiss the indictment because of a matter that occurred before the grand jury;

(iii) at the request of the government if it shows that the matter may disclose a violation of state or Indian tribal criminal law, as long as the disclosure is to an appropriate state, state-subdivision, or Indian tribal official for the purpose of enforcing that law; or

(iv) at the request of the government if it shows that the matter may disclose a violation of military criminal law under the Uniform Code of Military Justice, as long as the disclosure is to an appropriate military official for the purpose of enforcing that law.

(F) A petition to disclose a grand-jury matter under Rule 6(e)(3)(E)(i) must be filed in the district where the grand jury convened. Unless the hearing is ex parte — as it may be when the government is the petitioner — the petitioner must serve the petition on, and the court must afford a reasonable opportunity to appear and be heard to:

(i) an attorney for the government;

(ii) the parties to the judicial proceeding; and

(iii) any other person whom the court may designate.

(G) If the petition to disclose arises out of a judicial proceeding in another district, the petitioned court must transfer the petition to the other court unless the petitioned court can reasonably determine whether disclosure is proper. If the petitioned court decides to transfer, it must send to the transferee court the material sought to be disclosed, if feasible, and a written evaluation of the need for continued grand-jury secrecy. The transferee court must afford those persons identified in Rule 6(e)(3)(F) a reasonable opportunity to appear and be heard.

(4) Sealed Indictment. The magistrate judge to whom an indictment is returned may direct that the indictment be kept secret until the defendant is in custody or has been released pending trial. The clerk must then seal the indictment, and no person may disclose the indictment's existence except as necessary to issue or execute a warrant or summons.

(5) Closed Hearing. Subject to any right to an open hearing in a contempt proceeding, the court must close any hearing to the extent necessary to prevent disclosure of a matter occurring before a grand jury.

(6) Sealed Records. Records, orders, and subpoenas relating to grand-jury proceedings must be kept under seal to the extent and as long as necessary to prevent the unauthorized disclosure of a matter occurring before a grand jury.

(7) Contempt. A knowing violation of Rule 6 may be punished as a contempt of court.

NOTES AND QUESTIONS

1. The proceedings of grand juries are traditionally secret. Note that Rule 6(e), like the law in most states, imposes obligations on everyone but the witness herself not to reveal what happens in the grand jury. There are also strict limits on the people who may be present during grand jury proceedings — to the point that in the federal system and most states, not even the lawyer representing the witness may attend. Absent a Fifth Amendment or other valid legal privilege, a grand jury

witness summoned to testify is required to appear and answer questions; she may be imprisoned for contempt by the court for refusing to do so. Such a witness may know little about the nature of the grand jury's inquiry or the importance of her testimony to this inquiry at the time of appearance. Nevertheless, the witness need not be given the equivalent of *Miranda* warnings before testifying, see United States v. Mandujano, 425 U.S. 564 (1976) (plurality opinion), and need not be informed, at least as a constitutional matter, that she is the target of the investigation. See United States v. Washington, 431 U.S. 181 (1977).

2. In such circumstances, it might be argued that grand jury secrecy is at least one benefit enjoyed by witnesses — helping to preserve their privacy and to minimize any stigma that may attend a grand jury appearance. In Douglas Oil Co. v. Petrol Oil Stops Northwest, 441 U.S. 211, 219 n. 10 (1979) (quotation omitted), however, the Supreme Court's articulation of the traditional rationales for grand jury secrecy mainly emphasized the *investigative* advantages of secrecy:

> (1) To prevent the escape of those whose indictment may be contemplated; (2) to insure the utmost freedom to the grand jury in its deliberations, and to prevent persons subject to indictment or their friends from importuning the grand jurors; (3) to prevent subordination of perjury or tampering with the witness who may testify before the grand jury and later appear at the trial of those indicted by it; (4) to encourage free and untrammeled disclosures by persons who have information with respect to the commission of crimes; (5) to protect the innocent accused who is exonerated from disclosure of the fact that he has been under investigation, and from the expense of standing trial where there was no probability of guilt.

But is secrecy always in the interest of investigators? Or even most of the time? Selective disclosure of some investigative information "can place members of a targeted enterprise in a noncustodial 'prisoner's dilemma,' giving each person reason to fear that one of more of his comrades will race to the prosecutor's office to betray him in exchange for leniency, and therefore giving him reason to get there first." Daniel C. Richman, Grand Jury Secrecy: Plugging the Leaks in an Empty Bucket, 36 Am. Crim. L. Rev. 339, 346 (1999). In some cases, disclosure of grand jury information may stimulate witnesses to come forward; investigators might wish to barter such information to obtain access to evidence they do not have.

The law enforcement personnel participating in a grand jury investigation may thus have reasons to adhere strictly to secrecy norms; they may also have reasons to evade such norms or at least to interpret them quite narrowly. Consider the conflicting incentives operating on such personnel as you read the following case.

IN RE SEALED CASE NO. 99-3091

Appeal to the United States Court of Appeals for the D.C. Circuit
192 F.3d 995 (1999)

PER CURIAM

The Office of Independent Counsel (OIC) seeks summary reversal of the district court's order to show cause why OIC should not be held in contempt for violating the grand jury secrecy rule, and its order appointing the United States Department of Justice as prosecutor of OIC in a criminal contempt proceeding. In the alternative, OIC seeks a stay of those orders pending appeal. We conclude we have jurisdiction to consider the interlocutory appeal and grant the motion for summary reversal.

On January 31, 1999, while the Senate was trying President William J. Clinton on articles of impeachment, the *New York Times* published a front page article captioned "Starr is Weighing Whether to Indict Sitting President." As is relevant here, the article reported:

> Inside the Independent Counsel's Office, a group of prosecutors believes that not long after the Senate trial concludes, Mr. Starr should ask the grand jury of 23 men and women hearing the case against Mr. Clinton to indict him on charges of perjury and obstruction of justice, the associates said. The group wants to charge Mr. Clinton with lying under oath in his Jones deposition in January 1998 and in his grand jury testimony in August, the associates added.

The next day, the Office of the President (the White House) and Mr. Clinton jointly filed in district court a motion for an order to show cause why OIC, or the individuals therein, should not be held in contempt for disclosing grand jury material in violation of Federal Rule of Criminal Procedure 6(e). The White House and Mr. Clinton pointed to several excerpts from the article as evidence of OIC's violations of the grand jury secrecy rule.

OIC responded that the matters disclosed in the article merely rehashed old news reports and, in any event, did not fall within Rule 6(e)'s definition of "matters occurring before the grand jury." OIC also submitted a declaration from Charles G. Bakaly, III, then-Counselor to the Independent Counsel, regarding his communications with the author of the article, Don Van Natta, Jr. Bakaly declared, among other things, that in his conversations with Van Natta about whether the Independent Counsel could indict the President while still in office, "I refused to confirm or comment on what Judge Starr or the OIC was thinking or doing." According to OIC, the declaration was for the purpose of demonstrating that even if the matters disclosed were grand jury material, OIC was not the source of the information in the article.

Notwithstanding the foregoing, Independent Counsel Kenneth W. Starr asked the Federal Bureau of Investigation to provide OIC assistance in conducting an internal leak investigation. The Department of Justice authorized the FBI to do so, and as a result of the investigation, [   ].[2] Consequently, OIC took administrative action against Bakaly and referred the matter to the Department of Justice for a criminal investigation and decision. OIC informed the district court of these developments, withdrew Bakaly's declaration, and abandoned its argument that OIC was not the source of the information disclosed in the *New York Times* article. Although OIC noted that "the article regrettably discloses sensitive and confidential internal OIC information," it continued to maintain that the information was not protected by Rule 6(e).

Troubled by these developments, the district court ordered Bakaly and OIC to show cause why they should not be held in civil contempt for a violation of Rule 6(e), concluding that the portion of the *New York Times* article quoted above revealed grand jury material and constituted a *prima facie* violation of Rule 6(e). [   ] The

---

2. Bold brackets signify sealed material.

district court scheduled a consolidated show cause hearing, ordered the FBI and OIC to produce in camera all their relevant investigative reports, and required the FBI agents involved in the investigation to appear to testify. In accordance with this court's holding in In re Sealed Case No. 98-3077, 151 F.3d 1059, 1075-76 (D.C. Cir. 1998), the district court ordered that the proceedings be closed and *ex parte*.

Convinced that the district court had misinterpreted this court's precedent, OIC and Bakaly asked the district court to certify for interlocutory appeal the question of the proper scope of Rule 6(e). The district court denied the request, referring only to its previous orders. In the meantime, DOJ entered an appearance as counsel for the potential FBI witnesses and sought a stay of the proceedings, including Bakaly's requests for discovery, pending the completion of its criminal investigation. The district court granted the stay, and on July 13, DOJ notified the district court by letter that it had completed its investigation. [ ]

One day later, on July 14th, the district court *sua sponte* issued an order appointing DOJ to serve as prosecutor of the contempt charges against Bakaly *and OIC*. The district court explained its unexpected inclusion of OIC in DOJ's prosecution: "DOJ's letter only refers to the contempt charges lodged against Mr. Bakaly. However, the Court also needs to resolve the closely related allegations against the OIC. The Court believes that these matters are best resolved through a single contempt proceeding involving both Mr. Bakaly and the OIC." Although the district court decided to afford Bakaly and OIC the protections of criminal law, it left open the possibility of civil, or a combination of civil and criminal, contempt sanctions. The district court also scheduled a pre-trial status conference for July 23.

Both DOJ and OIC responded immediately. In another letter to the court, DOJ asked the district court to withdraw its referral of OIC for prosecution. DOJ explained that based on its investigation, there was no factual basis for proceeding with a criminal contempt prosecution against the OIC in connection with the *New York Times* article. In addition, DOJ stated its view that the district court lacked authority to proceed against OIC for criminal contempt because Rule 6(e) only applies to individuals, OIC cannot be held vicariously liable for acts of its staff, and OIC is entitled to sovereign immunity.

OIC filed an emergency motion to vacate the district court's July 14 order, objecting to being named as a criminal defendant and to the entry of an order without affording the parties an opportunity to respond to DOJ's first letter. OIC also argued that there was no factual basis for the order, and raised numerous legal objections, including the argument that OIC is entitled to sovereign immunity from a criminal contempt proceeding.

Faced with having to enter an appearance as a criminal defendant at the status conference scheduled for July 23, and not having obtained a ruling from the district court on the emergency motion, on July 22, OIC noted an *ex parte* appeal from the district court's March 25 and July 14 orders and filed a motion for summary reversal or, in the alternative, stay pending appeal. Because the criminal contempt proceedings were scheduled to commence immediately, we issued an administrative stay of those proceedings so that we would have sufficient opportunity to consider the merits of the motion. To obtain an adversarial viewpoint on what we consider to be the dispositive issue in this case, we ordered Mr. Clinton and the White House, along with DOJ and OIC, to brief the question whether the alleged disclosures in the *New York Times* article relied upon by the district court in ordering a criminal contempt proceeding constitute a *prima facie* violation of Rule 6(e).

[Before reaching the Rule 6(e) issue, the court of appeals determined that by failing to respond to OIC's motion to vacate and allowing to stand its order requiring the OIC to appear as a criminal defendant at a status conference, the district court had conclusively rejected the OIC's claim of sovereign immunity. The court of appeals determined that this ruling was immediately appealable as a collateral order and that, in the circumstances of this case, taking pendent jurisdiction and disposing of the case on the merits of the Rule 6(e) issue was permissible and preferable to resolving the federal sovereign immunity issue.]

Turning . . . to the merits of this case, we conclude that the disclosures made in the *New York Times* article do not constitute a *prima facie* violation of Rule 6(e). A *prima facie* violation based on a news report is established by showing that the report discloses "matters occurring before the grand jury" and indicates that sources of the information include government attorneys. Because OIC has withdrawn its argument that none of its attorneys was the source of the disclosures in the *New York Times* article at issue here, the only remaining issue is whether those disclosures qualify as "matters occurring before the grand jury." Fed.R. Crim. P. 6(e)(2).[8]

The district court concluded that only one excerpt from the *New York Times* article constituted a *prima facie* violation of Rule 6(e). That excerpt . . . disclosed the desire of some OIC prosecutors to seek, not long after the conclusion of the Senate trial, an indictment of Mr. Clinton on perjury and obstruction of justice charges, including lying under oath in his deposition in the Paula Jones matter and in his grand jury testimony. These statements, according to the district court, reveal a specific time frame for seeking an indictment, the details of a likely indictment, and the direction a group of prosecutors within OIC believes the grand jury investigation should take. Not surprisingly, Mr. Clinton and the White House agree with the district court's expansive reading of Rule 6(e). OIC takes a narrow view of the Rule's coverage, arguing that matters occurring outside the physical presence of the grand jury are covered only if they reveal grand jury matters. DOJ generally supports OIC with respect to the Rule's coverage, but emphasizes the importance of the context and concreteness of disclosures.

The key to the district court's reasoning is its reliance on this court's definition of "matters occurring before the grand jury." In In re Motions of Dow Jones & Co., 142 F.3d 496, 500 (D.C. Cir.), *cert. denied*, 525 U.S. 820 (1998), we noted that this phrase encompasses "not only what has occurred and what is occurring, but also what is likely to occur," including "the identities of witnesses or jurors, the substance of testimony as well as actual transcripts, the strategy or direction of the investigation, the deliberations or questions of jurors, and the like." Id. (internal quotation omitted). In the earlier contempt proceeding against Independent Counsel Starr, however, we cautioned the district court about "the problematic nature of applying so broad a definition, especially as it relates to the 'strategy or direction of the investigation,' to the inquiry as to whether a government attorney has made unauthorized disclosures." In re Sealed Case No. 98-3077, 151 F.3d at 1071 n. 12. Despite the seemingly broad nature of the statements in *Dow Jones*, we have never read Rule 6(e) to require that a "veil of secrecy be drawn over all matters occurring in the world

8. OIC contends that as an entity rather than an individual, it is not subject to Rule 6(e). It is unnecessary to decide this issue given our conclusion that there is no *prima facie* violation of Rule 6(e).

that happen to be investigated by a grand jury." Securities & Exch. Commn. v. Dresser Indus., Inc., 628 F.2d 1368, 1382 (D.C. Cir. 1980) (en banc). Indeed, we have said that "[t]he disclosure of information 'coincidentally before the grand jury [which can] be revealed in such a manner that its revelation would not elucidate the inner workings of the grand jury' is not prohibited." Senate of Puerto Rico v. United States Dept. of Justice, 823 F.2d 574, 582 (D.C. Cir. 1987) (quoting Fund for Constitutional Govt. v. National Archives and Records Serv., 656 F.2d 856, 870 (D.C. Cir. 1981)). Thus, the phrases "likely to occur" and "strategy and direction" must be read in light of the text of Rule 6(e) — which limits the Rule's coverage to "matters occurring before the grand jury" — as well as the purposes of the Rule.

As we have recited on many occasions,

> Rule 6(e) . . . protects several interests of the criminal justice system: "First, if pre-indictment proceedings were made public, many prospective witnesses would be hesitant to come forward voluntarily, knowing that those against whom they testify would be aware of that testimony. Moreover, witnesses who appeared before the grand jury would be less likely to testify fully and frankly, as they would be open to retribution as well as to inducements. There also would be the risk that those about to be indicted would flee, or would try to influence individual grand jurors to vote against indictment. Finally, by preserving the secrecy of the proceedings, we assure that persons who are accused but exonerated by the grand jury will not be held up to public ridicule."

In re Sealed Case No. 98-3077, 151 F.3d 1059, 1070 (D.C. Cir. 1998) (quoting Douglas Oil Co. v. Petrol Stops Northwest, 441 U.S. 211, 219 (1979)). These purposes, as well as the text of the Rule itself, reflect the need to preserve the secrecy of the *grand jury* proceedings themselves. It is therefore necessary to differentiate between statements by a prosecutor's office with respect to its own investigation, and statements by a prosecutor's office with respect to a *grand jury*'s investigation, a distinction of the utmost significance. . . .

Information actually presented to the grand jury is core Rule 6(e) material that is afforded the broadest protection from disclosure. Prosecutors' statements about their investigations, however, implicate the Rule only when they directly reveal grand jury matters. To be sure, we have recognized that Rule 6(e) would be easily evaded if a prosecutor could with impunity discuss with the press testimony about to be presented to a grand jury, so long as it had not yet occurred. Accordingly, we have read Rule 6(e) to cover matters "likely to occur." And even a discussion of "strategy and direction of the investigation" could include references to not yet delivered but clearly anticipated testimony. But that does not mean that *any* discussion of an investigation is violative of Rule 6(e). Indeed, the district court's Local Rule 308(b)(2), which governs attorney conduct in grand jury matters, recognizes that prosecutors often have a legitimate interest in revealing aspects of their investigations "to inform the public that the investigation is underway, to describe the general scope of the investigation, to obtain assistance in the apprehension of a suspect, to warn the public of any dangers, or otherwise aid in the investigation."

It may often be the case, however, that disclosures by the prosecution referencing its own investigation should not be made for tactical reasons, or are in fact prohibited by other Rules or ethical guidelines. For instance, prosecutors may be prohibited by internal guidelines, see, e.g., United States Attorney Manual §1-7.530, from discussing the strategy or direction of their investigation before an indictment is sought.[9] This would serve one of the same purposes as Rule 6(e): protecting the reputation of innocent suspects. But a court may not use Rule 6(e) to generally regulate prosecutorial statements to the press. The purpose of the Rule is only to protect the secrecy of grand jury proceedings.

Thus, internal deliberations of prosecutors that do not directly reveal grand jury proceedings are not Rule 6(e) material. As the Fifth Circuit stated in circumstances similar to those presented here,

> [a] discussion of actions taken by government attorneys or officials — e.g., a recommendation by the Justice Department attorneys to department officials that an indictment be sought against an individual — does not reveal any information about matters occurring before the grand jury. Nor does a statement of opinion as to an individual's potential criminal liability violate the dictates of Rule 6(e). This is so even though the opinion might be based on knowledge of the grand jury proceedings, provided, of course, the statement does not reveal the grand jury information on which it is based.

[In re Grand Jury Investigation [*Lance*], 610 F.2d 202, 217 (5th Cir. 1980)]. It may be thought that when such deliberations include a discussion of whether an indictment should be sought, or whether a particular individual is potentially criminally liable, the deliberations have crossed into the realm of Rule 6(e) material. This ignores, however, the requirement that the matter occur before the grand jury. Where the reported deliberations do not reveal that an indictment *has been* sought or *will be* sought, ordinarily they will not reveal anything definite enough to come within the scope of Rule 6(e).

For these reasons, the disclosure that a group of OIC prosecutors "believe" that an indictment should be brought at the end of the impeachment proceedings does not on its face, or in the context of the article as a whole, violate Rule 6(e).[10] We acknowledge, as did OIC, that such statements are troubling, for they have the potential to damage the reputation of innocent suspects. But bare statements that some assistant prosecutors in OIC wish to seek an indictment do not implicate the grand jury; the prosecutors may not even be basing their opinion on information presented to a grand jury.

The fact that the disclosure also reveals a time period for seeking the indictment of "not long after the Senate trial concludes" does not in any way indicate what is "likely to occur" before the grand jury within the meaning of Rule 6(e). That disclosure reflects nothing more than a desire on the part of some OIC prosecutors to seek an indictment at that time, not a decision to do so. The general uncertainty as to whether an indictment would in fact be sought (according to the article, only some prosecutors in OIC thought one should be) leads us to

9. But see Eric H. Holder and Kevin A. Ohlson, Dealing with the Media in High-Profile White Collar Cases: The Prosecutor's Dilemma, in WHITE COLLAR CRIME, at B-1, B-1 to B-2 (1995) ("[I]n cases involving well-known people, the public has a right to be kept reasonably informed about what steps are being taken to pursue allegations of wrongdoing so that they can determine whether prosecutors are applying the law equally to all citizens. This point has become particularly pertinent in recent years because powerful figures increasingly seem to characterize criminal investigations of their alleged illegal conduct as 'political witch hunts.' This type of epithet only serves to unfairly impugn the motives of prosecutors and to undermine our legal system, and should not go unanswered.").

10. Indeed, the article stated that Independent Counsel Starr had not himself made any decision on whether to bring an indictment.

conclude that this portion of the article did not reveal anything that was "occurring before the grand jury."

Nor does it violate the Rule to state the general grounds for such an indictment—here, lying under oath in a deposition and before the grand jury—where no secret grand jury material is revealed. In ordinary circumstances, Rule 6(e) covers the disclosure of the names of grand jury witnesses. Therefore, the statement that members of OIC wished to seek an indictment based on Mr. Clinton's alleged perjury before a grand jury would ordinarily be Rule 6(e) material. In this case, however, we take judicial notice that the President's status as a witness before the grand jury was a matter of widespread public knowledge well before the *New York Times* article at issue in this case was written; the President himself went on national television the day of his testimony to reveal this fact. Where the general public is already aware of the information contained in the prosecutor's statement, there is no additional harm in the prosecutor referring to such information.[11] Therefore, it cannot be said that OIC "disclosed" the name of a grand jury witness, in violation of Rule 6(e), by referring to the President's grand jury testimony.[13]

Similarly, it would ordinarily be a violation of Rule 6(e) to disclose that a grand jury is investigating a particular person. Thus, the statement that a grand jury is "hearing the case against Mr. Clinton" would be covered by Rule 6(e) if it were not for the fact that the *New York Times* article did not reveal any secret, for it was already common knowledge well before January 31, 1999, that a grand jury was investigating alleged perjury and obstruction of justice by the President. Once again, the President's appearance on national television confirmed as much.

In light of our conclusion that the excerpt from the *New York Times* article does not constitute a *prima facie* violation of Rule 6(e), we reverse and remand with instructions to dismiss the Rule 6(e) contempt proceedings against OIC. Because we have granted OIC's request for summary reversal, we dismiss as moot the alternative request for a stay. . . .

NOTES AND QUESTIONS

1. After the Rule 6(e) contempt proceeding against the OIC was dismissed, Bakaly ultimately stood trial and was found not guilty of criminal contempt in connection with the *New York Times* article. Given the ruling in In Re Sealed Case No. 99-3091 that the information in the article did not constitute a prima facie violation of Rule 6(e), the charges against Bakaly did not involve such a violation, but instead the allegation that Bakaly had lied in the court papers initially filed with the district court that explained the extent of his role in providing information for the article. As a *Wall Street Journal* article commented at the time of

---

11. The prosecutor must still be careful, of course, when making such statements not to reveal some aspect of the grand jury investigation which is *itself* still cloaked in secrecy.

13. Of course, a prosecutor is not free to leak grand jury material and than make a self-serving claim that the matter is no longer secret. Cf. In re North, 16 F.3d 1234, 1245 (D.C. Cir. 1994) ("We do not intend to formulate a rule that once a leak of Rule 6(e) has occurred, government attorneys are free to ignore the pre-existing bond of secrecy.").

his acquittal, this created the unusual situation where "Mr. Bakaly was prosecuted for allegedly lying about leaking information that was legal to leak." Gary Fields, Starr Assistant Is Not Guilty of Contempt, Wall Street Journal, Oct. 9, 2000, at A26.

2. Independent Counsel Kenneth Starr's investigation highlighted some confusion in the state of the law regarding grand jury secrecy. Do prosecutors violate Rule 6(e) when they reveal information about what witnesses have told FBI agents outside the grand jury? Are documents produced to the grand jury under compulsion of subpoena "matters occurring before the grand jury" for the purpose of Rule 6(e)? Professor Daniel Richman has proffered one explanation as to why Rule 6(e) doctrine is somewhat unsettled on these basic issues:

> Rule 6(e) does not establish a general regime of investigative secrecy for prosecutors and law enforcement agents. It addresses only what occurs "before the grand jury." As a matter of physical reality, however, the only thing that clearly occurs before a grand jury is testimony by a live witness, and sometimes the introduction of exhibits. Just about everything else generally occurs in a prosecutor's office or out in the field: deliberations about what investigations the grand jury will pursue, and which witnesses and documents will be subpoenaed in its name; interviews of potential witnesses conducted with an eye to deciding whether they will actually be brought before the grand jury; and receipt and review of documents obtained via grand jury subpoena. Particularly when prosecutors simultaneously develop a case in the grand jury and pursue other investigative options without using the grand jury, the language of Rule 6(e) provides all too little guidance as to what the government's secrecy obligations are. . . .

Daniel C. Richman, Grand Jury Secrecy: Plugging the Leaks in an Empty Bucket, 36 Am. Crim. L. Rev. 339, 341 (1999).

3. One could argue that ambiguity over the scope of Rule 6(e) benefits law enforcement personnel who may wish to interpret the reach of the Rule more or less broadly depending on the advantages that secrecy or disclosure may confer in a given case. But this is not to suggest that would-be "leakers" need rely on such ambiguity to evade enforcement. Leak investigations are notoriously difficult to bring to any successful resolution, in large measure because often those most knowledgeable about the source of the leak—people in the media—are not compelled to disclose *their* sources. In addition, because grand jury witnesses are not generally bound by secrecy restrictions, there may be multiple ways in which information about a grand jury investigation has legitimately entered the public domain—making even the identification of a breach of secrecy very difficult. In practice, this means that intentional leaks of grand jury material are virtually impossible to prove. Does this fact draw into question Rule 6(e)'s entire regime for grand jury secrecy? Or does Rule 6(e) serve its purpose by articulating a norm that will be at least partly internalized by investigative personnel?

4. If the articulation of a norm of investigative secrecy through a legal prohibition like Rule 6(e) is important, it's worth asking whether confining that norm to grand jury investigations can be justified. After all, the subject of a traditional FBI investigation certainly suffers reputational injury when that fact becomes widely known—whether or not a grand jury has been convened. Professor Richman has gone even further to note that to the extent Rule 6(e) is about limiting the harms suffered by those who are the subject of a criminal investigation, the Rule may have

the effect of showing special concern for the type of suspect who needs it least — the often well-heeled, white-collar suspect who is implicated in the sort of complex case most likely to be pursued in a grand jury:

> Does it make sense to have a system that in effect shows a special solicitude for targets and witnesses in white collar cases? Aren't these, in fact, the cases where, in the face of efforts by well-financed lawyers to impede information collection, the government is most in need of options that might include the selective dissemination of investigative data? One can also argue that the need for prosecutors to defend an investigation to the public while it is on-going is likely to be greater in white collar than in other contexts. After all, white collar targets are far better able to marshal support in the press and elsewhere than other targets — support that may impede the progress of an investigation and/or sway the potential jury pool.

Daniel C. Richman, Grand Jury Secrecy: Plugging the Leaks in an Empty Bucket, 36 Am. Crim. L. Rev. 339, 355 (1999). Does Rule 6(e) reflect nothing more than the political clout of white-collar defendants? Or are there other reasons for the law's special concern with investigative leaks in the grand jury context?

5. Look again at the text of Rule 6(e). Notice that it does provide for exceptions to the rule prohibiting disclosure of material occurring before the grand jury. Before passage of the USA PATRIOT Act (Uniting and Strengthening America by Providing Appropriate Tools Required to Intercept and Obstruct Terrorism Act) of 2001, Pub. L. No. 107-56, 115 Stat. 272, these exceptions included, inter alia, disclosures directed by a court at the request of a defendant, upon a showing that grounds might exist for a motion to dismiss the indictment because of matters occurring before the grand jury; disclosures made by a government attorney to another federal grand jury; and disclosures permitted by a court to an appropriate state official, upon a showing that grand jury proceedings might disclose a violation of state criminal law. As Sara Sun Beale and James Felman have pointed out, nearly all the exceptions before PATRIOT preserved a role for courts in supervising disclosure. Sara Sun Beale and James E. Felman, The Consequences of Enlisting Federal Grand Juries in the War on Terrorism: Assessing the USA Patriot Act's Changes to Grand Jury Secrecy, 25 Harv. J. L. & Pub. Pol'y 699, 705-705 (2002).

The PATRIOT Act at least partially changed this landscape. It amended Rule 6 to provide that disclosure of matters occurring before the grand jury may also be made to any federal law enforcement, intelligence, protective, immigration, national defense, or national security official when such matters involve foreign intelligence or counterintelligence, in order to assist the official receiving the information in the performance of his official duties. There is no provision for prior court authorization, though notice that the amended rule does provide that "[w]ithin a reasonable time after such disclosure, an attorney for the government must file under seal a notice with the court stating the fact that such information was disclosed and the departments, agencies, or entities to which the disclosure was made."

Are these changes to the traditional regime justifiable? Beale and Felman acknowledge that concerns with grand jury secrecy would not in all cases outweigh the need for broader use of national security-related information that might emerge in the course of a grand jury investigation. They go on to assert, however, that the PATRIOT Act's reforms (particularly to the extent that these reforms downplay the role of the judiciary) raise legitimate concerns:

> The potential for a backdoor expansion of the grand jury's investigative jurisdiction is . . . problematic because it may increase the risk that the national defense and security institutions will be inappropriately involved in domestic affairs. Domestic law enforcement operates in a legal and constitutional culture that gives substantial weight to the rights of individuals. The relation of the government to its citizens is shaped by the constitutional requirement that the government respect each citizen's constitutional rights. The intelligence and military communities operate in a far different context than domestic law enforcement, and their institutional cultures and values have been shaped by their roles. Foreign powers, their agents, and their armies have no constitutional rights comparable to the rights identified by the Fourth, Fifth, and Sixth Amendments. In general, therefore, federal law has precluded the military from taking part in domestic law enforcement, and has drawn a sharp distinction between domestic and foreign intelligence surveillance. These limitations have been intended to reduce the likelihood that the military and foreign intelligence communities will erode the rights of American citizens. Particularly in the absence of judicial review, and in a context where the process operates in secret, arming these communities with the powers of the grand jury is highly problematic.

Id. at 717-718. Do you agree? Is it likely that the military and the intelligence community will find it convenient to draw upon the powers of the grand jury in their counterterrorism work? Doesn't this depend, in part, on what alternative authorities these communities possess?

3.   Lawyers' Role

In most criminal cases, defense lawyers are first drawn into the case when police have made an arrest and a defendant is in need of representation at an initial appearance. By this point, the government may have gathered most of its evidence. The defendant himself may well have confessed. The defense lawyer may find that his options in the representation are already severely constrained by what has gone before — at a time when the lawyer had never even heard of the case.

The lawyer representing the target of a grand jury investigation is often in a considerably different position. The investigation of a complex criminal matter may extend over many months and even years. The lawyer may have been retained very early, by a potential criminal defendant who will put substantial resources into avoiding criminal charges or conviction. At this point, the government may have obtained only a small fraction of the evidence needed fully to investigate the case. In such circumstances, the defense lawyer may have the opportunity to take steps that will keep his client from ever being arrested or indicted.

Lawyers representing targets or potential targets of a grand jury investigation thus have some opportunity to shape the criminal investigation in ways the lawyers representing clients in more routine criminal cases cannot. The defense lawyer retained early may, at a minimum, prevent his client from making damaging admissions by advising her to remain silent. By conducting interviews, examining records, and the like, he may have a very good idea about the nature of the case the government is likely to be able to put together long before the government's investigators have even subpoenaed the relevant evidence. The defense lawyer may follow the course of the grand jury's investigation as it unfolds by debriefing many of the witnesses who testify before the grand jury and are willing to speak with him after the fact. Such an attorney may have substantial information about the nature of the government's inquiry before criminal charges are ever brought. He may use this information to persuade the government that criminal charges are inappropriate; that government prosecutors should confer immunity on his client to obtain valuable evidence against others; that his client should be permitted to plead guilty to lesser charges.

Sociologist Kenneth Mann has argued that the white-collar criminal defense attorney plays a different role in that he is positioned "to prevent the government from obtaining evidence that could be inculpatory of his client and used by the investigator or prosecutor to justify issuance of a formal criminal charge." Kenneth Mann, Defending White-Collar Crime 6 (1985). Based on his empirical examination of white-collar defense attorneys at work (including extensive fieldwork that he performed), Mann describes "information control" as a principal feature of their usual strategy:

> Information control entails keeping documents away from and preventing clients and witnesses from talking to government investigators, prosecutors, and judges. . . . It occurs before the substantive defense and is in some ways a more important defense. If successful, it keeps the raw material of legal argument out of the hands of the government, it obviates argument about the substantive legal implications of facts about crime, and it keeps the government ignorant of evidence it needs in deciding whether to make a formal charge against a person suspected of committing a crime. And, even if a formal charge is made, it keeps facts about a crime out of the arena of plea negotiations and out of the courtroom if a trial takes place. For these reasons, information control lies at the very heart of the defense function, preventing the imposition of a criminal sanction on an accused person who has committed a crime, as well as on the rare one who has not.
>
> Attorneys act in two different ways to control information. First, they oppose their adversaries in quasi-judicial and court settings. In one situation, the attorney argues to a judge in court or to an investigator in an office that a subpoena for documents is improper because, for instance, it is overburdensome or vague. In another situation, the attorney argues that information already seized by the government should not be admissible evidence because of government misbehavior in making the seizure. The essential feature of these information control arguments is their focus on the behavior of the opposing party, directly by convincing that party not to press the request or indirectly through the sanction of a judge or other decisionmaker. . . .
>
> Second, the defense attorney uses an information control strategy that focuses on the potential source of inculpatory information, rather than on the behavior of the adversary seeking to gain access to the source. The defense attorney's aim is to instruct the client or third party holding inculpatory information how to refrain from disclosing it to the government and, if necessary, to persuade or force him to refrain. The legal justification supporting such information control actions is usually not communicated to the adversary. The setting of this action is typically concealed, behind the attorney-client confidentiality privilege or in private attorney-witness meetings, and concealment is often essential to success of the information control action. . . .
>
> When an attorney in a meeting in his office advises a client about to be questioned by a government agent to "avoid answering that question, and if pushed, tell him that you have to examine your books before responding," the target of control is the client

and the aim is information control. The attorney has acted on the client and the information in the client's possession, in a setting concealed from the adversary. If the client handles the situation well, he may successfully avoid prosecution or avoid or delay raising of an issue where this result may be important to other defense efforts. . . .

. . . What is distinctive in the white-collar cases is the centrality of information control strategies to defense work: they are fundamental modus operandi constituting a basic defense plan. . . .

Id. at 7-8.

This obviously raises ethical questions concerning just how far a lawyer may go to keep facts from being revealed in the course of a criminal investigation involving his client. Consider in this connection Mann's discussion of preparing a client for a grand jury appearance in a complex case:

. . . In a federal grand jury appearance, where defense counsel is not allowed, the attorney must educate his client to be ready to assert his right to leave the room and consult with his attorney outside. When this situation is anticipated, some attorneys drill their clients and have them participate in a mock grand jury interrogation in the attorney's office.

An invariable principle of competent defense work is that the attorney prepare his client for questions that will be posed by the interviewer. Here attorneys walk an extremely narrow line between insufficient preparation and improper influence. It is certainly true that highly ethical and competent defense attorneys have clients whom they honestly believe should not be indicted, but who also believe that the clients could fail to demonstrate this through confused and unintelligent explanations. The attorney has to bring such a client to understand how to organize his thoughts and what to emphasize. But it is also true that other attorneys — perhaps committed less to the truth and more to their client's winning the case — improperly influence a client by letting him know, even if only by hinting, what to leave out and what to include and how to shape facts so that an appearance of propriety is created where in fact wrongdoing occurred. . . .

Id. at 137. Mann offers the words of one attorney in a large New York law firm who represents clients in connection with complex grand jury investigations:

Sure I prepare my witnesses before they go into the grand jury. Take for instance now, where we are representing a company and its officers. All the officers — at least ten — have been called before the grand jury. I've prepared them in this sense: with each one I go over the facts of the matter extensively. I let each one know what the other one has said or is going to say. This is not with the intent of suborning perjury or getting them to fabricate anything. If my theory of the case is true, and I believe it is, then I want to have it presented in the strongest way. It's a fascinating process. I love doing this.

There is no better feeling when you are a litigator than coming back from a deposition session in which every question asked by the prosecutor you had asked your client in preparing, and every answer came out as you expected. It gives you a real feeling of triumph.

Id. at 137-138.

Based on his extensive empirical work, Mann concludes that "[o]ne of the main weaknesses of the government position in investigating and prosecuting white-collar crime is created by the attorney's effect on the pool of evidence." Once an attorney is involved, he observes, "evidence that might have been easily accessible and even voluntarily or unknowingly turned over to the government becomes inaccessible." Id. at 248. And he observes that this conclusion is true regardless whether the attorney acted improperly or conducted himself in strict compliance with ethical rules.

Mann's work raises an interesting question. As he notes, the white-collar cases he examined involved relatively less intrusive methods of information acquisition on the part of the government than are often employed in street crime cases. Investigators resorted to "subpoenas, summonses, and interviews in noncustodial circumstances" rather than searches, seizures, and custodial police interrogation. Mann's research suggests that while the grand jury has broad subpoena power, the intervention of lawyers in a situation where targets are "request[ed] . . . to hand over information and allow[ed] . . . substantial time between the request and the requirement of response" permits the concealment of important inculpatory evidence. Id. at 249. Does this mean that the tactics associated with the investigation of street crime should be more freely employed in the investigation of public corruption, securities fraud, and the like? Consider Mann's final remarks:

> The use of the subpoena for documents, the summons for documents, and the grand jury and administrative interview are expressions in the American legal system of the high value given to the individual's right to privacy and freedom from government oppression. These values are central to the large degree of autonomy granted to the individual and the great distrust of official power. Any change in these rules therefore touches on the very heart of the social structure and should be countenanced only with great caution. Notwithstanding this cautionary warning, more intrusiveness into the realm of the corporate entity and the workplace may be justified by the high cost to society of crime that is covered up in these places. Certainly an examination of the costs to privacy and the benefit to law enforcement should be undertaken, and due attention should be given to the investigative procedures of other countries where search and seizure play a greater role in white-collar crime law enforcement, apparently without undermining individual rights and the democratic character of the society. In this way, a remedy may be found for the implications of extensive information control found in white-collar crime cases, without altering the high value of the counselor role held by the defense attorney in the American adversary process.

Id. at 249-250. Do you agree? Should complex criminal investigations look more like street crime cases? Or should the investigation of street crime more closely resemble the typical grand jury investigation in a complex case?

In this regard, you may wish to ponder the increasing invocation of attorney disciplinary rules, particularly by attorneys for organizational clients, to prevent prosecutors (or those acting under a prosecutor's direction) from undertaking investigative steps such as interviewing employees of a suspect organization without the corporate attorney's permission or presence. See United States v. Talao, 222 F.3d 1133 (9th Cir. 2000) (discussing propriety of prosecutor's meeting with a corporation's bookkeeper who had been subpoenaed to testify before the grand jury and was represented by the corporation's attorney, but who had told the prosecutor that corporate principals were pressuring her to testify untruthfully and that she did not wish to be represented by this attorney because she could not speak truthfully in his presence). 28 U.S.C. §530B of the Citizens Protection Act makes state ethics rules applicable to federal prosecutors handling grand jury investigations in a given locality "to the same extent and in the same manner as other attorneys in that State." Often referred to as the "McDade Amendment," Section 530B was the brainchild of Joseph McDade, a Pennsylvania Congressman who in 1992 had been indicted on five counts of bribery-related charges by a federal grand jury. "Even as the indictment was handed down, McDade complained that federal investigators had harassed and hounded him and that they had 'turned his life into "a living nightmare."'" Fred C. Zacharias and Bruce A. Green, The Uniqueness of Federal Prosecutors, 88 Geo. L.J. 207, 212 (2000). Shortly after his acquittal in 1996, Congressman McDade introduced the first version of his ethics legislation. "With the 1998 federal appropriations bill," Section 530B passed as "a remarkable rider regulating federal government attorneys." Id. at 208.

Professor Douglass has closely examined the effects of holding federal prosecutors to the "no-contact" rule providing that lawyers "shall not communicate about the subject of the representation with a person the lawyer knows to be represented by another lawyer in the matter . . . ":

> [T]he Sixth Amendment now provides suspects no protection against investigative contacts until the time charges are brought. The Fifth Amendment and the Due Process Clause may protect them from coercive interrogation, but except for suspects who demand counsel while in police custody, those provisions do not stop police from asking questions in the absence of counsel. Nor do they impose significant restraints on the acquisition of information by deception through the use of informants.
>
> By contrast, the ethical rule forbidding contacts with represented persons prevents a prosecutor from "communicating" with a represented suspect either directly or through government agents or informants, in the absence of counsel. . . .
>
> . . . When a whistleblower inside a represented corporation calls the FBI to report that his boss is shredding documents, a prosecutor may sense an important break in the case. But she should also sense the looming possibility of an ethical violation if she encourages agents to meet privately with the insider, or to offer the insider a recording device for his next conversation with the boss. . . .
>
> The broadest application of the no-contact rule — and accordingly the most troublesome for prosecutors — occurs when a corporation is represented during criminal investigation. The rule prohibits contact with a represented "person," a term that includes corporations. But who within the corporation is protected from contact? . . . In those jurisdictions that . . . adhere to [the] broad version of the rule, a corporation effectively can shield all of its employees from direct contact with investigators simply by hiring an attorney.

John G. Douglass, Jimmy Hoffa's Revenge: White-Collar Rights Under the McDade Amendment, 11 Wm. & Mary Bill Rts. J. 123, 134-135, 138-139 (2002). Professor Douglass concludes that application of the no-contact rule to federal prosecutors has amounted to providing special treatment to white-collar suspects: "[A]s a practical matter, the protection of [the no-contact rule] is enjoyed almost exclusively by individuals and corporations during investigations of white-collar crimes. That protection is not available to most suspects of most police investigations, because most people suspected of a crime do not have lawyers before criminal charges are filed." Id. at 124-125. He continues:

> . . . Proponents of the McDade approach ask simply, "Why shouldn't federal prosecutors be held to the same ethical standards as other attorneys?" When the question is framed in that manner, the "right" answer seems unavoidable.
>
> But when it comes to deciding how — or whether — to apply [the no-contact rule] to forbid investigative contacts with represented persons, the "parity of ethics" question puts the debate in a false light. Applying the no-contact rule to criminal investigators does not result in equal treatment of prosecutors in comparison to other lawyers. To the contrary, in criminal investigations, the rule operates almost exclusively in one direction. As a practical matter, it limits only the conduct of the prosecutor and government agents. With rare exceptions, it does nothing to limit the access of white-collar defense counsel to anyone.
>
> The debate . . . has little to do with insuring parity of ethics among different segments of the bar. It is primarily a struggle over "information control" in white-collar investigations. As Kenneth Mann's study of white-collar practitioners observed, "[t]he defense attorney's first objective is to prevent the government from obtaining evidence that could be inculpatory of his client." Keeping investigators away from suspects and potential witnesses is an effective means of preventing the government from obtaining evidence, and that is the principal function of [the no-contact] rule in white-collar investigations.

Id. at 142-143.

D. Law Enforcement and Counterterrorism

It has become little more than a truism that September 11th "changed everything." But it's well worth thinking about precisely what this means in the context of American criminal procedure. Consider the following discussion:

> Cartographers once drew mythical, menacing beasts to mark the edges of the known world. The mapmakers diagrammed what information they had and then warned prudent travelers about the unfathomable perils of unknowable places — "Here, There be Dragons!" In some ways, American jurisprudence is like those old maps. It, too, divides the world into comfortable spaces and forbidden regions. It, too, has dangerous borders and, one might say, dragons. The known world coincides with the realm of domestic policy. In that domain, courts and legislatures have partnered to articulate a rich lattice of constitutional and statutory rights. Courts have mapped out procedures and rights that restrict police behavior and protect persons accused of heinous crimes. Here, reason rules. But this known, comfortable world ends at the nation's border. Doubtful of their competence and fearful that their errors might jeopardize national interests, judges have traditionally granted Congress and the president almost complete discretion over questions about immigration, the military, espionage, and many other aspects of foreign affairs. To American judges, foreign policy is an unordered wilderness, the domain of realpolitik rather than reason. Here, there are unfathomable perils; here, there be dragons.
>
> The horrible events of September 11, 2001, made hash of these boundaries. Viewed one way, the attacks were in the domestic domain, a terrible crime of unprecedented magnitude. Nineteen people living in the United States hijacked American

airplanes from American airports to destroy buildings and murder thousands of people in the United States. Viewed differently, the tragedy was in the domain of foreign affairs, a gruesome and chilling military strike in a new kind of global war. Enemy agents under the direction of a hostile foreign organization infiltrated the United States by posing as ordinary immigrants and then struck American targets.

The antiterrorism measures developed in response to September 11 reflect these complexities. The new policies blend criminal law enforcement with immigration policy, foreign intelligence operations, and military force. . . .

In many respects, . . . September 11's legacy in the domain of civil liberties is mixed, uncertain, and inchoate. It may take years for the full shape and impact of that legacy to emerge, and its character may depend on whether September 11 turns out to [be] the first of many equally bloody attacks on Americans, or whether it proves to be the worst of a relatively small set. This much, however, seems clear. September 11 has changed the conceptual context for civil liberties in the United States by blurring the boundary between domestic policy and foreign policy. . . .

Christopher L. Eisgruber and Lawrence G. Sager, Civil Liberties in the Dragons' Domain: Negotiating the Blurred Boundary between Domestic Law and Foreign Affairs After 9/11, in Mary L. Dudziak ed., September 11 in History 163, 163-164, 166-167 (2003). Professors Eisgruber and Sager argue that the President and Congress, in the wake of 9/11, "have invoked their discretion over foreign affairs in order to escape restrictions that courts have imposed on domestic police activities." Id. at 164. They argue that in the new world of counterterrorism, courts interested in protecting civil liberties cannot afford to treat the realm of foreign affairs as terra incognita: "Unless judges are willing to scrutinize the government's behavior in the domain of foreign policy, their supervision of the criminal law process will be subject to evasion, as the government reclassifies law enforcement within the categories of foreign affairs." Id. at 167.

Yet we have already glimpsed the profound uncertainty that characterizes much of the law potentially impacting on counterterrorism efforts, post-9/11. Does the Fourth Amendment reach the search or seizure of foreign nationals located here or abroad — particularly foreign nationals whose only prior connection to the United States is their participation in a war against it? And just what, if anything, does Miranda v. Arizona, 384 U.S. 436 (1966), have to do with the interrogation of foreign nationals in military custody and being questioned for purposes unrelated to law enforcement? Are courts in a position to map out this landscape? Or should their efforts be directed at marking out the domain of criminal procedure — separating it from the uncharted realms of international conflict to prevent its doctrines from being diluted by the exigencies of war? It's also worth asking whether we even understand the legal tradeoffs presented by counterterrorism efforts. Professor Heymann, for instance, has argued that we have overemphasized some questions to the neglect of other, potentially more important ones:

> The focus of concern about the tension between liberty and security in dealing with terrorism has centered on . . . the . . . USA PATRIOT Act. But, the issues presented by the statute — involving privacy of space and communications and the reputational risks that arise with a broader sharing of information — are not as important as those within the discretion of the executive branch, before as well as after September 11. . . .
>
> The issues of discretion involve matters of life or death, torture, detention without trial, trial without juries, and basic freedoms to dissent. These discretionary determinations also raise issues of profiling that cut deeply into notions of equal citizenship

and equal protection. Most of these questions involve the human rights of citizens of other countries, but some involve Americans as well.

The critical tradeoffs forced on those living in the United States by the events of September 11 are not those pitting the rights of Americans to be free of intrusive investigative steps against the needs of national security. They are:

— The privacy rights that are involved in the collection and use of information from a wide variety of sources versus the privacy rights compromised by intrusive techniques.
— The costs in terms of privacy and efficiency of investigating all possible suspects versus the discriminatory effects of focusing investigation on groups characterized by ethnic characteristics.
— Internal security measures versus law enforcement measures and the use of intelligence agencies versus the use of law enforcement agencies.
— The difficulty of trials in the United States versus assassination abroad or military tribunals (which are spared the difficulties of open proof and a independent fact finder).
— Greatly increasing the level of intrusiveness of investigative activity in the United States versus encouraging other nations to increase the intrusiveness of their own investigations.

Philip B. Heymann, Civil Liberties and Human Rights in the Aftermath of September 11, 25 Harv. J. L. & Pub. Pol'y 440, 441-442 (2002).

We have touched on some specific issues that have arisen since 9/11 — ethnic profiling, datamining, national identification cards, torture — in earlier chapters. Here, we take up the broader, thematic question of how law should respond when a problem seems to transcend the "normal" concerns of criminal procedure — when it blurs the boundaries between domestic crime and foreign threat, as well as the spheres of operation of the military, the intelligence community, and law enforcement. United States v. United States District Court, 407 U.S. 297 (1972), commonly referred to as *Keith*, for Damon J. Keith, the district court judge who first heard it, would at first blush seem an unlikely case with which to begin this discussion. *Keith*, after all, did not involve terrorism, or even a foreign threat. Yet this is one of only a handful of cases in which the Supreme Court has taken up this distinction between threats to the nation and "ordinary crime." Moreover, *Keith* involves a context already familiar to us — namely, the use of electronic surveillance. We thus begin with *Keith* before turning to more specific legal issues that have arisen in the post-9/11 environment.

UNITED STATES v. UNITED STATES DISTRICT COURT

Certiorari to the United States Court of Appeals for the Sixth Circuit
407 U.S. 297 (1972)

Mr. Justice Powell delivered the opinion of the Court.

The issue before us is an important one for the people of our country and their Government. It involves the delicate question of the President's power, acting through the Attorney General, to authorize electronic surveillance in internal security matters without prior judicial approval. Successive Presidents for more than one-quarter of a century have authorized such surveillance in varying degrees, without guidance from the Congress or a definitive decision of this Court. This case brings the issue here for the first time. Its resolution is a matter of national concern, requiring sensitivity both to the Government's right to protect itself from unlawful subversion and attack and to the citizen's right to be secure in his privacy against unreasonable Government intrusion.

This case arises from a criminal proceeding in the United States District Court for the Eastern District of Michigan, in which the United States charged three defendants with conspiracy to destroy Government property. . . . One of the defendants, Plamondon, was charged with the dynamite bombing of an office of the Central Intelligence Agency in Ann Arbor, Michigan.

During pretrial proceedings, the defendants moved to compel the United States to disclose certain electronic surveillance information and to conduct a hearing to determine whether this information "tainted" the evidence on which the indictment was based or which the Government intended to offer at trial. In response, the Government filed an affidavit of the Attorney General, acknowledging that its agents had overheard conversations in which Plamondon had participated. The affidavit also stated that the Attorney General approved the wiretaps "to gather intelligence information deemed necessary to protect the nation from attempts of domestic organizations to attack and subvert the existing structure of the Government." The logs of the surveillance were filed in a sealed exhibit for *in camera* inspection by the District Court.

On the basis of the Attorney General's affidavit and the sealed exhibit, the Government asserted that the surveillance was lawful, though conducted without prior judicial approval, as a reasonable exercise of the President's power (exercised through the Attorney General) to protect the national security. The District Court held that the surveillance violated the Fourth Amendment, and ordered the Government to make full disclosure to Plamondon of his overheard conversations.

The Government then filed in the Court of Appeals for the Sixth Circuit a petition for a writ of mandamus to set aside the District Court order, which was stayed pending final disposition of the case. After concluding that it had jurisdiction, that court held that the surveillance was unlawful and that the District Court had properly required disclosure of the overheard conversations. We granted certiorari.

Title III of the Omnibus Crime Control and Safe Streets Act, 18 U.S.C. §§2510-2520, authorizes the use of electronic surveillance for classes of crimes carefully specified in 18 U.S.C. §2516. Such surveillance is subject to prior court order. Section 2518 sets forth the detailed and particularized application necessary to obtain such an order as well as carefully circumscribed conditions for its use. The Act represents a comprehensive attempt by Congress to promote more effective control of crime while protecting the privacy of individual thought and expression. Much of Title III was drawn to meet the constitutional requirements for electronic surveillance enunciated by this Court in Berger v. New York, 388 U.S. 41 (1967), and Katz v. United States, 389 U.S. 347 (1967).

Together with the elaborate surveillance requirements in Title III, there is the following proviso, 18 U.S.C. §2511(3):

"Nothing contained in this chapter . . . shall limit the constitutional power of the President to take such measures as he deems necessary to protect the Nation against actual or potential attack or other hostile acts of a foreign power, to obtain foreign intelligence information deemed essential to the security of the United States, or to protect national security information against foreign intelligence activities. *Nor shall anything contained in this chapter be deemed to limit the constitutional power of the President to take such measures as he deems necessary to protect the United States against the overthrow of the Government by force or other unlawful means, or against any other clear and present danger to the structure or existence of the Government.* The contents of any wire or oral communication intercepted by authority of the President in the exercise of the foregoing powers may be received in evidence in any trial hearing, or other proceeding only where such interception was reasonable, and shall not be otherwise used or disclosed except as is necessary to implement that power." (Emphasis supplied.)

The Government relies on §2511(3). It argues that "in excepting national security surveillances from the Act's warrant requirement Congress recognized the President's authority to conduct such surveillances without prior judicial approval." Brief for United States 7, 28. . . .

We think the language of §2511(3), as well as the legislative history of the statute, refutes this interpretation. The relevant language is that:

"Nothing contained in this chapter . . . shall limit the constitutional power of the President to take such measures as he deems necessary to protect . . ."

against the dangers specified. At most, this is an implicit recognition that the President does have certain powers in the specified areas. Few would doubt this, as the section refers — among other things — to protection "against actual or potential attack or other hostile acts of a foreign power." But so far as the use of the President's electronic surveillance power is concerned, the language is essentially neutral.

Section 2511(3) certainly confers no power, as the language is wholly inappropriate for such a purpose. It merely provides that the Act shall not be interpreted to limit or disturb such power as the President may have under the Constitution. In short, Congress simply left presidential powers where it found them. . . .

The legislative history of §2511(3) supports this interpretation. Most relevant is the colloquy between Senators Hart, Holland, and McClellan on the Senate floor:

"Mr. HOLLAND. . . . The section [2511(3)] from which the Senator [Hart] has read does not affirmatively give any power. . . . *We are not affirmatively conferring any power upon the President.* We are simply saying that nothing herein shall limit such power as the President has under the Constitution. . . . We certainly do not grant him a thing.

"There is nothing affirmative in this statement.

"Mr. McCLELLAN. Mr. President, *we make it understood that we are not trying to take anything away from him.*

"Mr. HOLLAND. The Senator is correct.

"Mr. HART. Mr. President, there is no intention here to expand by this language a constitutional power. Clearly we could not do so.

"Mr. McCLELLAND. Even though intended, we could not do so.

"Mr. HART. . . . However, we are agreed that this language should not be regarded as intending to grant any authority, including authority to put a bug on, that the President does not have now.

"In addition, Mr. President, *as I think our exchange makes clear, nothing in section 2511(3) even attempts to define the limits of the President's national security power under present law, which I have always found extremely vague* . . . . *Section 2511(3) merely says*

that if the President has such a power, then its exercise is in no way affected by title III."
(Emphasis supplied.)

One could hardly expect a clearer expression of congressional neutrality. The debate above explicitly indicates that nothing in §2511(3) was intended to *expand* or to *contract* or to *define* whatever presidential surveillance powers existed in matters affecting the national security. If we could accept the Government's characterization of §2511(3) as a congressionally prescribed exception to the general requirement of a warrant, it would be necessary to consider the question of whether the surveillance in this case came within the exception and, if so, whether the statutory exception was itself constitutionally valid. But viewing §2511(3) as a congressional disclaimer and expression of neutrality, we hold that the statute is not the measure of the executive authority asserted in this case. Rather, we must look to the constitutional powers of the President.

It is important at the outset to emphasize the limited nature of the question before the Court. This case raises no constitutional challenge to electronic surveillance as specifically authorized by Title III of the Omnibus Crime Control and Safe Streets Act of 1968. Nor is there any question or doubt as to the necessity of obtaining a warrant in the surveillance of crimes unrelated to the national security interest. Katz v. United States, 389 U.S. 347 (1967); Berger v. New York, 388 U.S. 41(1967). Further, the instant case requires no judgment on the scope of the President's surveillance power with respect to the activities of foreign powers, within or without this country. The Attorney General's affidavit in this case states that the surveillances were "deemed necessary to protect the nation from attempts of *domestic organizations* to attack and subvert the existing structure of Government" (emphasis supplied). There is no evidence of any involvement, directly or indirectly, of a foreign power.[8]

Our present inquiry, though important, is therefore a narrow one. It addresses a question left open by *Katz,* supra, at 358 n. 23:

"Whether safeguards other than prior authorization by a magistrate would satisfy the Fourth Amendment in a situation involving the national security. . . ." . . .

We begin the inquiry by noting that the President of the United States has the fundamental duty, under Art. II, §1, of the Constitution, to "preserve, protect and defend the Constitution of the United States." Implicit in that duty is the power to protect our Government against those who would subvert or overthrow it by unlawful means. In the discharge of this duty, the President—through the Attorney General—may find it necessary to employ electronic surveillance to obtain intelligence information on the plans of those who plot unlawful acts against the Government. The use of such surveillance in internal security cases has been

8. . . . Although we attempt no precise definition, we use the term "domestic organization" in this opinion to mean a group or organization (whether formally or informally constituted) composed of citizens of the United States and which has no significant connection with a foreign power, its agents or agencies. No doubt there are cases where it will be difficult to distinguish between "domestic" and "foreign" unlawful activities directed against the Government of the United States where there is collaboration in varying degrees between domestic groups or organizations and agents or agencies of foreign powers. But this is not such a case.

sanctioned more or less continuously by various Presidents and Attorneys General since July 1946. Herbert Brownell, Attorney General under President Eisenhower, urged the use of electronic surveillance both in internal and international security matters on the grounds that those acting against the Government

> "turn to the telephone to carry on their intrigue. The success of their plans frequently rests upon piecing together shreds of information received from many sources and many nests. The participants in the conspiracy are often dispersed and stationed in various strategic positions in government and industry throughout the country."

Though the Government and respondents debate their seriousness and magnitude, threats and acts of sabotage against the Government exist in sufficient number to justify investigative powers with respect to them. The covertness and complexity of potential unlawful conduct against the Government and the necessary dependency of many conspirators upon the telephone make electronic surveillance an effective investigatory instrument in certain circumstances. The marked acceleration in technological developments and sophistication in their use have resulted in new techniques for the planning, commission, and concealment of criminal activities. It would be contrary to the public interest for Government to deny to itself the prudent and lawful employment of those very techniques which are employed against the Government and its law-abiding citizens.

It has been said that "[t]he most basic function of any government is to provide for the security of the individual and of his property." Miranda v. Arizona, 384 U.S. 436, 539 (1966) (WHITE, J., dissenting). And unless Government safeguards its own capacity to function and to preserve the security of its people, society itself could become so disordered that all rights and liberties would be endangered. As Chief Justice Hughes reminded us in Cox v. New Hampshire, 312 U.S. 569, 574 (1941):

> "Civil liberties, as guaranteed by the Constitution, imply the existence of an organized society maintaining public order without which liberty itself would be lost in the excesses of unrestrained abuses."

But a recognition of these elementary truths does not make the employment by Government of electronic surveillance a welcome development — even when employed with restraint and under judicial supervision. There is, understandably, a deep-seated uneasiness and apprehension that this capability will be used to intrude upon cherished privacy of law-abiding citizens. We look to the Bill of Rights to safeguard this privacy. . . .

National security cases, moreover, often reflect a convergence of First and Fourth Amendment values not present in cases of "ordinary" crime. Though the investigative duty of the executive may be stronger in such cases, so also is there greater jeopardy to constitutionally protected speech. "Historically the struggle for freedom of speech and press in England was bound up with the issue of the scope of the search and seizure power," Marcus v. Search Warrant, 367 U.S. 717, 724 (1961). History abundantly documents the tendency of Government — however benevolent and benign its motives — to view with suspicion those who most fervently dispute its policies. Fourth Amendment protections become the more necessary when the targets of official surveillance may be those suspected of unorthodoxy in their political beliefs. The danger to political dissent is acute where the Government attempts to act under so vague a concept as the power to protect "domestic security." . . . The price of lawful public dissent must not be a dread of subjection to an unchecked surveillance power. Nor must the fear of unauthorized official eavesdropping deter vigorous citizen dissent and discussion of Government action in private conversation. For private dissent, no less than open public discourse, is essential to our free society.

As the Fourth Amendment is not absolute in its terms, our task is to examine and balance the basic values at stake in this case: the duty of Government to protect the domestic security, and the potential danger posed by unreasonable surveillance to individual privacy and free expression. . . .

Though the Fourth Amendment speaks broadly of "unreasonable searches and seizures," the definition of "reasonableness" turns, at least in part, on the more specific commands of the warrant clause. Some have argued that "[t]he relevant test is not whether it is reasonable to procure a search warrant, but whether the search was reasonable," United States v. Rabinowitz, 339 U.S. 56, 66 (1950). This view, however, overlooks the second clause of the Amendment. The warrant clause of the Fourth Amendment is not dead language. Rather, it has been

> "a valued part of our constitutional law for decades, and it has determined the result in scores and scores of cases in courts all over this country. It is not an inconvenience to be somehow 'weighed' against the claims of police efficiency. It is, or should be, an important working part of our machinery of government, operating as a matter of course to check the 'well-intentioned but mistakenly over-zealous executive officers' who are a part of any system of law enforcement." Coolidge v. New Hampshire, 403 U.S., at 481.

See also United States v. Rabinowitz, supra, 339 U.S., at 68 (Frankfurter, J., dissenting); Davis v. United States, 328 U.S. 582, 604 (1946) (Frankfurter, J. dissenting). . . .

. . . Fourth Amendment freedoms cannot properly be guaranteed if domestic security surveillances may be conducted solely within the discretion of the Executive Branch. The Fourth Amendment does not contemplate the executive officers of Government as neutral and disinterested magistrates. Their duty and responsibility are to enforce the laws, to investigate, and to prosecute. Katz v. United States, supra, at 359-360 (DOUGLAS, J., concurring). But those charged with this investigative and prosecutorial duty should not be the sole judges of when to utilize constitutionally sensitive means in pursuing their tasks. . . .

It may well be that, in the instant case, the Government's surveillance of Plamondon's conversations was a reasonable one which readily would have gained prior judicial approval. But this Court "has never sustained a search upon the sole ground that officers reasonably expected to find evidence of a particular crime and voluntarily confined their activities to the least intrusive means consistent with that end." *Katz*, supra, at 356-357. The Fourth Amendment contemplates a prior judicial judgment, not the risk that executive discretion may be reasonably exercised. This judicial role accords with our basic constitutional doctrine that individual freedoms will best be preserved through a separation of powers and division of functions among the different branches and levels of Government. . . .

It is true that there have been some exceptions to the warrant requirement. But those exceptions are few in number and carefully delineated; in general, they serve the legitimate needs of law enforcement officers to protect their own well-being and preserve evidence from destruction. . . .

The Government argues that the special circumstances applicable to domestic security surveillances necessitate a further exception to the warrant requirement. It is urged that the requirement of prior judicial review would obstruct the President in the discharge of his constitutional duty to protect domestic security. We are told further that these surveillances are directed primarily to the collecting and maintaining of intelligence with respect to subversive forces, and are not an attempt to gather evidence for specific criminal prosecutions. It is said that this type of surveillance should not be subject to traditional warrant requirements which were established to govern investigation of criminal activity, not ongoing intelligence gathering.

The Government further insists that courts "as a practical matter would have neither the knowledge nor the techniques necessary to determine whether there was probable cause to believe that surveillance was necessary to protect national security." . . .

As a final reason for exemption from a warrant requirement, the Government believes that disclosure to a magistrate of all or even a significant portion of the information involved in domestic security surveillances "would create serious potential dangers to the national security and to the lives of informants and agents. . . . Secrecy is the essential ingredient in intelligence gathering; requiring prior judicial authorization would create a greater 'danger of leaks . . . , because in addition to the judge, you have the clerk, the stenographer and some other officer like a law assistant or bailiff who may be apprised of the nature' of the surveillance." Brief for United States 24-25.

These contentions in behalf of a complete exemption from the warrant requirement, when urged on behalf of the President and the national security in its domestic implications, merit the most careful consideration. We certainly do not reject them lightly, especially at a time of worldwide ferment and when civil disorders in this country are more prevalent than in the less turbulent periods of our history. . . .

But we do not think a case has been made for the requested departure from Fourth Amendment standards. The circumstances described do not justify complete exemption of domestic security surveillance from prior judicial scrutiny. Official surveillance, whether its purpose be criminal investigation or ongoing intelligence gathering, risks infringement of constitutionally protected privacy of speech. Security surveillances are especially sensitive because of the inherent vagueness of the domestic security concept, the necessarily broad and continuing nature of intelligence gathering, and the temptation to utilize such surveillances to oversee political dissent. We recognize, as we have before, the constitutional basis of the President's domestic security role, but we think it must be exercised in a manner compatible with the Fourth Amendment. In this case we hold that this requires an appropriate prior warrant procedure.

We cannot accept the Government's argument that internal security matters are too subtle and complex for judicial evaluation. Courts regularly deal with the most difficult issues of our society. There is no reason to believe that federal judges will be insensitive to or uncomprehending of the issues involved in domestic security cases. Certainly courts can recognize that domestic security surveillance involves different considerations from the surveillance of "ordinary crime." . . .

Nor do we believe prior judicial approval will fracture the secrecy essential to official intelligence gathering. The investigation of criminal activity has long involved imparting sensitive information to judicial officers who have respected the confidentialities involved. . . . Moreover, a warrant application involves no public or adversary proceedings: it is an *ex parte* request before a magistrate or judge. Whatever security dangers clerical and secretarial personnel may pose can be minimized by proper administrative measures, possibly to the point of allowing the Government itself to provide the necessary clerical assistance.

Thus, we conclude that the Government's concerns do not justify departure in this case from the customary Fourth Amendment requirement of judicial approval prior to initiation of a search or surveillance. Although some added burden will be imposed upon the Attorney General, this inconvenience is justified in a free society to protect constitutional values. Nor do we think the Government's domestic surveillance powers will be impaired to any significant degree. A prior warrant establishes presumptive validity of the surveillance and will minimize the burden of justification in post-surveillance judicial review. By no means of least importance will be the reassurance of the public generally that indiscriminate wiretapping and bugging of law-abiding citizens cannot occur.

We emphasize, before concluding this opinion, the scope of our decision. As stated at the outset, this case involves only the domestic aspects of national security. We have not addressed and express no opinion as to, the issues which may be involved with respect to activities of foreign powers or their agents. . . .

Moreover, we do not hold that the same type of standards and procedures prescribed by Title III are necessarily applicable to this case. We recognize that domestic security surveillance may involve different policy and practical considerations from the surveillance of "ordinary crime." The gathering of security intelligence is often long range and involves the interrelation of various sources and types of information. The exact targets of such surveillance may be more difficult to identify than in surveillance operations against many types of crime specified in Title III. Often, too, the emphasis of domestic intelligence gathering is on the prevention of unlawful activity or the enhancement of the Government's preparedness for some possible future crisis or emergency. Thus, the focus of domestic surveillance may be less precise than that directed against more conventional types of crime.

Given these potential distinctions between Title III criminal surveillances and those involving the domestic security, Congress may wish to consider protective standards for the latter which differ from those already prescribed for specified crimes in Title III. Different standards may be compatible with the Fourth Amendment if they are reasonable both in relation to the legitimate need of Government for intelligence information and the protected rights of our citizens. For the warrant application may vary according to the governmental interest to be enforced and the nature of citizen rights deserving protection. . . .

. . . We do not attempt to detail the precise standards for domestic security warrants any more than our decision in *Katz* sought to set the refined requirements for the specified criminal surveillances which now constitute Title III. We do hold, however, that prior judicial approval is required for the type of domestic security surveillance involved in this case and that such approval may be made in accordance with such reasonable standards as the Congress may prescribe. . . .

The judgment of the Court of Appeals is hereby affirmed.

THE CHIEF JUSTICE concurs in the result.

MR. JUSTICE REHNQUIST took no part in the consideration or decision of this case.

[The concurring opinion of Justice Douglas and Justice White's opinion concurring in the judgment are omitted.]

NOTES AND QUESTIONS

1. What is the difference between a threat to national security and an "ordinary" crime? Does every conspiracy to destroy government property represent a national security case? Is a plot to blow up banks a threat to national security or a conspiracy to damage private property? Does "ordinary" crime become a threat to national security because it poses risks of a certain magnitude? Because it is directed at a particular goal? At a particular target? And what is it about a threat to national security that justifies more relaxed Fourth Amendment standards than in the ordinary criminal case?

2. For that matter, what is intelligence as opposed to, say, evidence? Reconsider the passage in which the Court says that the gathering of security intelligence

is often long range and involves the interrelation of various sources and types of information. The exact targets of such surveillance may be more difficult to identify than in surveillance operations against many types of crime specified in Title III. Often, too, the emphasis of . . . intelligence gathering is on the prevention of unlawful activity or the enhancement of the Government's preparedness for some possible future crisis or emergency. Thus, the focus of . . . surveillance may be less precise than that directed against more conventional types of crime.

Id. at 322. Does this amount to saying that the prevention of substantial (catastrophic?) harm to the nation justifies dispensing with the Fourth Amendment mandate that ". . . no Warrants shall issue, but upon probable cause, . . . particularly describing the place to be searched, and the persons or things to be seized"? Is this position justifiable? You may wish to note that in a portion of the opinion not excerpted here, Justice Powell cites Camara v. Municipal Court, 387 U.S. 523 (1967), which we first saw at page 554 supra, for the proposition that the warrant application "may vary according to the governmental interest to be enforced and the nature of citizen rights deserving protection." 407 U.S. at 323. If health and safety inspection warrants may issue outside of the traditional probable cause formula, why not warrants seeking "security intelligence"?

3. How about the line the Court draws between the domestic aspects of national security and "the issues which may be involved with respect to activities of foreign powers or their agents"—issues about which the Court says nothing? Congress never took up the Court's invitation to fashion rules for domestic security surveillance. But in 1978, in the Foreign Intelligence Surveillance Act ("FISA"), 50 U.S.C. §§1801-1811, it did undertake to regulate the collection of *foreign* intelligence information in the United States. Because FISA surveillance is extremely important in terrorism investigations, it's worth considering some of the principal features of this law.

FISA surveillance is directed at obtaining "foreign intelligence information"—including information that relates to, and if concerning a U.S. person, is necessary to, the ability of the United States to protect against international terrorism. 50 U.S.C. §1801(e). The Act creates a FISA court, the FISC, and an associated FISA Court of Review composed of specially designated Article III judges. Judges on the FISC issue surveillance orders, but on different terms than the ones contained in Title III. FISA orders generally issue on the basis of two principal findings: that there is "probable cause to believe that . . . the target of the electronic surveillance is a foreign power or an agent of a foreign power," and that "each of the facilities or places at which surveillance is directed is being used, or is about to be used, by a foreign power or its agent." 50 U.S.C. §1805(a)(3). (Foreign powers include not only states, but groups "engaged in international terrorism.")

FISA thus differs from Title III in the broad sense that it is status-based, not evidence-based. As you already know, investigators executing a Title III warrant generally listen in on a particular line when there is probable cause to believe that listening in on that line will uncover evidence of a specified crime. Once someone is a proper FISA target, in contrast, FISA authorizes something quite close to status-based surveillance of that person. In many electronic surveillances the FBI may be authorized to conduct, simultaneously, telephone, cell phone, e-mail and computer surveillance of a target's home, workplace, and vehicles. (Similar breadth is accorded in physical searches of a target's residence, office, automobiles, computers, safe deposit boxes, and mail.) Surveillance is authorized for 90 days and may continue for as long as a year when the target is not a U.S. person—meaning, for FISA, a U.S. citizen or lawful permanent resident alien. The Act does not require that notice be provided to the target of such surveillance unless the government intends to use FISA intercepts in the course of judicial or other official proceedings. Minimization relates only to U.S. persons, and is almost invariably done after the fact—in the most usual case, after communications have been recorded. It is also heavily weighted toward the retention of information—so that the communication of or information concerning a U.S. person is generally deleted only if *it could not be* foreign intelligence information or evidence of a crime.

4. In the wake of 9/11, FISA became for a time the centerpiece of ongoing efforts at working out the appropriate relationship between law enforcement and the intelligence community in the context of counterterrorism. But understanding this story requires a little background. You should know that before FISA's enactment, several lower courts had recognized the authority of the President to engage in *warrantless* electronic surveillance to gather foreign intelligence information. In United States v. Truong Dinh Hung, 629 F.2d 908 (4th Cir. 1980), for example, the Fourth Circuit determined (in a case involving an electronic surveillance carried out prior to FISA's passage) that the President has this constitutional authority, but only when the object of the surveillance is a foreign power, its agent, or collaborator, and when the surveillance is conducted "primarily" for foreign intelligence, as opposed to law enforcement reasons. Since FISA's enactment, Presidents have used it to collect foreign intelligence in the United States—but without relinquishing the claim of inherent powers in this area.

Before passage of the PATRIOT Act (Uniting and Strengthening America by Providing Appropriate Tools Required to Intercept and Obstruct Terrorism Act) of 2001, Pub. L. No. 107-56, 115 Stat. 272, FISA required a national security officer in the Executive Branch (typically the FBI Director) to certify in a FISA application that "the purpose" of the contemplated surveillance was to obtain foreign intelligence information. The Justice Department, moreover, had procedures in place that prevented foreign intelligence officers from freely sharing FISA information with criminal investigators, even when these investigators were pursuing the same target, and even though FISA itself expressly contemplates that evidence of crime that results from FISA surveillance may be used in a criminal case. The Justice Department's "wall" procedures were widely condemned in the wake of 9/11 for frustrating coordination between the intelligence and law enforcement communities. Consider the testimony of Stewart Baker, formerly General Counsel of the National Security Agency, before the National Commission on Terrorist Attacks Upon the United States:

> The "wall" between intelligence and law enforcement was put in place to protect against a theoretical risk to civil liberties that could arise if domestic law enforcement and foreign intelligence missions were allowed to mix. . . .
>
> [O]ver the 1990s, the wall grew higher and higher. . . . Indeed, in 2000 and 2001, as Al-Qa'ida was slowly bringing its September 11 plans to fruition, the FBI office that handled Al-Qa'ida wiretaps in the U.S. was thrown into turmoil because of the new heights to which the wall had been raised. The [FISA] Court . . . had ordered strict procedures to ensure that its intelligence wiretaps were not contaminated by a law enforcement purpose. When those procedures were not followed strictly enough, the court barred an FBI agent from the court because his affidavits did not fully list all contacts with law enforcement. In the spring and summer of 2001, with Al-Qa'ida's preparations growing even more intense, the turmoil apparently grew so bad that numerous national security wiretaps were allowed to lapse. . . .
>
> [T]he source of this tragedy was not wicked or uncaring officials. The wall was built by smart, even wise professionals who thought they were acting in the country's and their agency's best interest. They were focused on the theoretical privacy risks that would come if foreign intelligence and domestic law enforcement were allowed to mix, and by a fear that in the end the courts and Congress would not understand if we put aside those theoretical concerns to combat a threat that was both foreign and domestic. They feared, and with good reason, that years of successful collaboration would end in disaster if the results of a single collaboration could be painted in the press and public as a privacy scandal. To protect against that possibility, they drafted ever more demanding rules — created an ever-higher wall — to govern operations at the border between domestic law enforcement and foreign intelligence.

Testimony of Stewart Baker Before the Nat'l Comm. on Terrorist Attacks Upon the United States (Dec. 8, 2003).

Congress sought with the PATRIOT Act to "break[] down barriers between criminal law enforcement and intelligence (or counterintelligence)" and to relax any legal requirement, real or imagined, that government show that its primary purpose in FISA surveillance "was other than criminal prosecution." In re: Sealed Case, 310 F.3d 717, 732-733 (Foreign Int. Surv. Ct. Rev. 2002). The Patriot Act amended FISA to require certification that foreign intelligence is a "significant purpose," rather than "the" purpose, for a FISA request; the Act also encouraged coordination between intelligence and law enforcement officials in counterterrorism efforts and stated explicitly that such coordination is no impediment to a "significant purpose" certification. 50 U.S.C. §§1804(a)(7)(B), 1806(k).

Critics charged that these amendments amounted to authorizing an endrun around the protections of Title III in routine criminal cases. The FISA Court of Review, however, ultimately determined that the amended FISA provisions satisfied the Fourth Amendment. The court concluded that both before and after passage of the PATRIOT Act, FISA's drafters contemplated using FISA to obtain foreign intelligence information about a target's activities, even if the primary purpose of doing so was to prosecute him for his foreign intelligence-related crimes: "[A]rresting and prosecuting terrorist agents of, or spies for, a foreign power may well be the best technique to prevent them from successfully continuing their terrorist or espionage activity." The court then took up the question whether such surveillance — with the primary purpose of prosecuting a target for foreign intelligence-related crimes, rather than gathering foreign intelligence information about him — is constitutional:

> It will be recalled that *Keith* carefully avoided the issue of a warrantless foreign intelligence search: "We have not addressed, and express no opinion as to, the issues which may be involved with respect to activities of foreign powers or their agents." 407 U.S. at 321-322. But in indicating that a somewhat more relaxed warrant could suffice in the domestic intelligence situation, the court drew a distinction between the crime involved in that case, which posed a threat to national security, and "ordinary crime." It pointed out that "the focus of domestic surveillance may be less precise than that directed against more conventional types of crimes."
>
> The main purpose of ordinary criminal law is twofold: to punish the wrongdoer and to deter other persons in society from embarking on the same course. The government's concern with respect to foreign intelligence crimes, on the other hand, is overwhelmingly to stop or frustrate the immediate criminal activity. . . . [T]he criminal process is often used as part of an integrated effort to counter the malign efforts of a foreign power. Punishment of the terrorist or espionage agent is really a secondary objective; indeed, punishment of a terrorist is often a moot point.
>
> The distinction between ordinary criminal prosecutions and extraordinary situations underlies the Supreme Court's approval of entirely warrantless and even suspicionless searches that are designed to serve the government's "special needs, beyond the normal need for law enforcement." Vernonia School Dist. 47J v. Acton, 515 U.S. 646 (1995) (quoting Griffin v. Wisconsin, 483 U.S. 868 (1987) (internal quotation marks omitted)) (random drug-testing of student athletes). Apprehending drunk drivers and securing the border constitute such unique interests beyond ordinary, general law enforcement. Id. at 654 (citing Michigan Dep't of State Police v. Sitz, 496 U.S. 444 (1990), and United States v. Martinez-Fuerte, 428 U.S. 543 (1976)).
>
> A recent case, City of Indianapolis v. Edmond, 531 U.S. 32 (2000), is relied on by both the government and *amici*. In that case, the Court held that a highway check point designed to catch drug dealers did not fit within its special needs exception because the government's "primary purpose" was merely "to uncover evidence of ordinary criminal wrongdoing." Id. at 41-42. The Court rejected the government's argument that the "severe and intractable nature of the drug problem" was sufficient justification for such a dragnet seizure lacking any individualized suspicion. Id. at 42. *Amici* particularly rely on the Court's statement that "the gravity of the threat alone cannot be dispositive of questions concerning what means law enforcement officers may employ to pursue a given purpose." Id.
>
> But by "purpose" the Court makes clear it was referring not to a subjective intent, which is not relevant in ordinary Fourth Amendment probable cause analysis, but rather to a programmatic purpose. The Court distinguished the prior check point cases *Martinez-Fuerte* (involving checkpoints less than 100 miles from the Mexican border) and *Sitz* (checkpoints to detect intoxicated motorists) on the ground that the former involved the government's "longstanding concern for the protection of the

integrity of the border," id. at 38 (quoting United States v. Montoya de Hernandez, 473 U.S. 531 (1985)), and the latter was "aimed at reducing the immediate hazard posed by the presence of drunk drivers on the highways." Id. at 39. The Court emphasized that it was decidedly not drawing a distinction between suspicionless seizures with a "non-law-enforcement primary purpose" and those designed for law enforcement. Rather, the Court distinguished general crime control programs and those that have another particular purpose, such as protection of citizens against special hazards or protection of our borders. The Court specifically acknowledged that an appropriately tailored road block could be used "to thwart an imminent terrorist attack." Id. at 44. The nature of the "emergency," which is simply another word for threat, takes the matter out of the realm of ordinary crime control.

FISA's general programmatic purpose, to protect the nation against terrorists and espionage threats directed by foreign powers, has from its outset been distinguishable from "ordinary crime control." After the events of September 11, 2001, though, it is hard to imagine greater emergencies facing Americans than those experienced on that date.

We acknowledge, however, that the constitutional question presented by this case — whether Congress' disapproval of the primary purpose test is consistent with the Fourth Amendment — has no definitive jurisprudential answer. The Supreme Court's special needs cases involve random stops (seizures) not electronic searches. In one sense, they can be thought of as a greater encroachment into personal privacy because they are not based on any particular suspicion. On the other hand, wiretapping is a good deal more intrusive than an automobile stop accompanied by questioning.

Although the Court in *City of Indianapolis* cautioned that the threat to society is not dispositive in determining whether a search or seizure is reasonable, it certainly remains a crucial factor. Our case may well involve the most serious threat our country faces. Even without taking into account the President's inherent constitutional authority to conduct warrantless foreign intelligence surveillance, we think the procedures and government showings required under FISA, if they do not meet the minimum Fourth Amendment warrant standards, certainly come close. We, therefore, believe firmly, applying the balancing test drawn from *Keith,* that FISA as amended is constitutional because the surveillances it authorizes are reasonable.

310 F.3d at 744-746. Does this clarify where the line is between "ordinary crime" or "ordinary law enforcement" and "extraordinary situations" demanding different Fourth Amendment rules? What if the primary purpose of FISA surveillance is to prosecute a target for a crime wholly unrelated to his activities on behalf of a terrorist group — say, for tax evasion? Provided that the target is otherwise an appropriate subject of foreign intelligence gathering and that foreign intelligence collection is a "significant" purpose of the surveillance, would such surveillance be constitutional? Why or why not?

5. Think again about Mr. Baker's remarks in the preceding note. Just what is the "theoretical risk to civil liberties that could arise if domestic law enforcement and foreign intelligence missions" are allowed to mix? Does the concern stem from marrying the prosecutor's case-creating ingenuity with the broad scope of FISA surveillance — which authorizes him to look in every corner? Or does the concern come instead from the different orientations of the agencies involved in law enforcement and intelligence? It's worth considering this "theoretical risk" fairly closely, given the broad changes since 9/11 in the direction of information sharing and mutual cooperation in counterterrorism efforts.

NOTES ON POST-9/11 LEGAL DEVELOPMENTS

1. *Keith* affirms quite clearly that Fourth Amendment standards in investigations involving the national security may differ from those in more routine criminal cases. What about the law governing interrogation? Consider United States v. Bin Laden, 132 F. Supp. 2d 168 (2001). In this case, two defendants charged with participating in the bombings of the U.S. embassies in Kenya and East Africa moved to suppress statements made to U.S. law enforcement officials while the defendants, each a nonresident alien, were in the custody of the Kenyan and South African police. The district court took up the question what standards should apply to the admission of statements made in such a context:

> Our analysis . . . turns chiefly on the constitutional standard we adopt today, as a matter of first impression, concerning the admissibility of a defendant's admissions at his criminal trial in the United States, where that defendant is a non-resident alien and his statements were the product of an interrogation conducted abroad by U.S. law enforcement representatives. We conclude that such a defendant, insofar as he is the present subject of a domestic criminal proceeding, is indeed protected by the privilege against self-incrimination guaranteed by the Fifth Amendment, notwithstanding the fact that his only connections to the United States are his alleged violations of U.S. law and his subsequent prosecution. Additionally, we hold that courts may and should apply the familiar warning/waiver framework set forth in Miranda v. Arizona, 384 U.S. 436 (1966), to determine whether the government, in its case-in-chief, may introduce against such a defendant evidence of his custodial statements — even if that defendant's interrogation by U.S. agents occurred wholly abroad and while he was in the custody of foreign authorities.

Id. at 181. In another portion of its opinion, the court took up the question of how application of the *Miranda* framework might affect the collection of foreign intelligence:

> To the extent that a suspect's *Miranda* rights allegedly impede foreign intelligence collection, we note that *Miranda* only prevents an unwarned or involuntary statement from being used as evidence in a domestic criminal trial; it does not mean that such statements are never to be elicited in the first place.

Id. at 189. And later:

> It bears reiteration that the issues addressed by this Opinion relate solely to the admissibility of statements in an American court. This is *not* the same question as the ability of American law enforcement or intelligence officials to obtain intelligence information from non-citizens abroad, information which may be vital to national security interests. What we find impermissible is not intelligence gathering by agents of the U.S. government empowered to do so, but rather the use in a domestic criminal trial of statements extracted in violation of the Fifth Amendment.

Id. at 189, n. 19.

But does the court successfully avoid interfering with intelligence collection efforts? Note that the court seems to set down a standard for the admissibility of statements taken "by U.S. law enforcement representatives." Isn't the predictable effect to create another "wall" between intelligence and law enforcement officers? So that FBI criminal investigators will not participate in the interrogation of suspected al-Qaeda members in the hope that if a trial ensues, *Miranda* will be deemed inapplicable as to an interrogation conducted by the CIA? Is this desirable? Why should it matter who conducts the interrogation?

For that matter, is this a context where *Miranda* rules should determine the admissibility of statements at trial—whether or not the interrogated party is a nonresident alien and whether or not the interrogation takes place here or abroad? Recall the case of Jose Padilla, the so-called "dirty bomber." Padilla was arrested on May 8, 2002 pursuant to a material witness warrant issued in the Southern District of New York. He was held in the maximum security wing of the Metropolitian Correctional Center in Manhattan until June 9, when the President issued an order to Secretary of Defense Donald H. Rumsfeld designating Padilla an "enemy combatant" and directing the Secretary to detain him in military custody. The President made factual findings explaining his decision. The President concluded that Padilla

> (1) "is closely associated with al Qaeda, an international terrorist organization with which the United States is at war;" (2) that he "engaged in . . . hostile and war-like acts, including . . . preparation for acts of international terrorism" against the United States; (3) that he "possesses intelligence" about al Qaeda that "would aid U.S. efforts to prevent attacks by al Qaeda on the United States"; and finally, (4) that he "represents a continuing, present and grave danger to the national security of the United States," such that his military detention "is necessary to prevent him from aiding al Qaeda in its efforts to attack the United States."

Rumsfeld v. Padilla, 124 S. Ct. 2711, 2715 (2004). Padilla was thereafter taken into custody by the Defense Department and was transferred to a high-security naval brig in Charleston, South Carolina. Secretary of Defense Donald H. Rumsfeld was quoted at the time: "We're not interested in punishing him at the moment. We're interested in finding out what in the world he knows." Investigation of Man Accused of Dirty Bomb Attack Continues, ABC News (June 11, 2002).

Assume the government had good reason to believe that Padilla was conspiring with others to detonate a bomb containing radioactive material on U.S. soil. Is the *Miranda* framework appropriate in a context where interrogators are primarily interested in obtaining intelligence to prevent such a terrorist attack (and where obtaining evidence against the suspect is, at best, a secondary goal)? The *Bin Laden* court, with its repeated refrain about not interfering with intelligence collection vital to the national security, suggests that the answer to this question is no. But if it is appropriate in such a context for interrogators to continue to press (outside the *Miranda* framework's generous provisions for cutting off interrogation), why should *Miranda* dictate the admissibility of statements in the event of a later trial?

On the other hand, does departure from the *Miranda* framework, with its provisions for cutting off interrogation, set us inevitably on the path to the abuses of Abu Ghraib?

2. Note that such questions seemed to be on the minds of the Justices hearing oral argument in Chavez v. Martinez, 538 U.S. 760 (2003), which we first discussed on page 780. Consider a portion of the oral argument:

> QUESTION: Mr. Paz, let me—let me tell you that I have difficulty with the proposition which you're urging, which is that any coercion that would suffice to require the confession to be excluded from—from trial is also a coercion that violates the Fifth Amendment, not—leaving substantive due process aside.

Suppose you have a situation in which a — a felon has taken a hostage and buried the hostage somewhere, and suppose that it is possible for the police official to use a degree of coercion which would not shock the conscience. It isn't beating the person with a rubber hose, but let's say failing to give a *Miranda* warning, or using a — a sort of trickery that — that would amount to coercion, threatening perhaps, you know, if you don't confess, your brother will be prosecuted or something like that. If would be sufficient to exclude the testimony [of] the confession from the trial, but the policeman doesn't care about that. He wants to save the life of the — of the hostage who's been — who's been buried.

Now, you would say that[,] that — that policeman by extracting that confession has violated the Fifth Amendment.

MR. PAZ: There may be a violation, and — and I would agree that most likely if — if it was in violation of *Miranda*, there would be — there would be no — it would not be admitted into a criminal case. . . .

Oral Arg. Tr. at 30-31. (In a later portion of the argument, another Justice turned explicitly to terrorism: "So let's assume somebody is — you think he's going to blow up the World Trade Center.")

Recall the result in *Chavez*. A plurality of the Justices, in a portion of Justice Thomas's opinion that was joined by Chief Justice Rehnquist and Justices O'Connor and Scalia, concluded that the Fifth Amendment is only violated when compelled statements are used in evidence against a defendant in a criminal case — so that the use of compulsion in police questioning, by itself, cannot ground a civil claim for damages for violating Fifth Amendment rights. The plurality also concluded that the *Miranda* exclusionary rule is "a prophylactic measure to prevent violations of the right protected by the text of the Self-Incrimination Clause" and that, therefore, ". . . Chavez's failure to read *Miranda* warnings to Martinez did not violate Martinez's constitutional rights and cannot be grounds for a §1983 action." 538 U.S. at 772. Justice Souter, joined by Justice Breyer, did not go so far as to say the Fifth Amendment may *only* be violated by the introduction of the compelled statement in a criminal case. But they too rejected Martinez's Fifth Amendment claim for civil redress, citing concerns about its potential reach:

The most obvious drawback inherent in Martinez's purely Fifth Amendment claim to damages is its risk of global application in every instance of interrogation producing a statement inadmissible under Fifth and Fourteenth Amendment principles, or violating one of the complementary rules we have accepted in aid of the privilege against evidentiary use. If obtaining Martinez's statement is to be treated as a stand-alone violation of the privilege subject to compensation, why should the same not be true whenever the police obtain any involuntary self-incriminating statement, or whenever the government so much as threatens a penalty in derogation of the right to immunity, or whenever the police fail to honor *Miranda*? Martinez offers no limiting principle or reason to foresee a stopping place short of liability in all such cases.

Id. at 778-779. The Court remanded Martinez's case on the issue whether Martinez could pursue a substantive due process claim. But note that substantive due process may leave substantial room for coercive methods, at least in appropriate, "ticking bomb" cases. In County of Sacramento v. Lewis, 523 U.S. 833, 849 (1998), the Supreme Court declared that ". . . conduct intended to injure *in some way unjustifiable by any government interest* is the sort of official action most likely to rise to the conscience-shocking level" and thus to violate substantive due process (emphasis added).

The Solicitor General in *Chavez* argued that a holding "that the taking of an involuntary statement constitutes a completed Fifth and Fourteenth Amendment violation — without regard to whether it will be used in a criminal trial, or whether the circumstances of its taking are sufficiently severe to 'shock the conscience' — [would] chill legitimate law enforcement efforts to obtain potentially life-saving information during emergencies." Brief for the United States as *Amicus Curiae* Supporting Petitioner, at 23. The government argued that maintaining the distinction between police conduct that renders a statement inadmissible and police conduct that independently violates the Constitution "provides necessary breathing space that furthers . . . the need for law enforcement to confront imminent threats." Id. at 24. Does the Court's holding in *Chavez* provide this "necessary breathing space"? Should it?

3. Note that the United States has ratified the Convention Against Torture and Other Cruel, Inhuman, or Degrading Treatment or Punishment, opened for signature Dec. 10, 1984, S. Treaty Doc. No. 100-20 (1988), 1465 U.N.T.S. 85. Implementing legislation criminalizes torture by U.S. nationals abroad. (The United States determined that existing federal and state criminal law appeared sufficient to establish jurisdiction for offenses committed within the U.S.) Title 18 defines torture as follows:

(1) "torture" means an act committed by a person acting under the color of law specifically intended to inflict severe physical or mental pain or suffering (other than pain or suffering incidental to lawful sanctions) upon another person within his custody or physical control;

(2) "severe mental pain or suffering" means the prolonged mental harm caused by or resulting from —

(A) the intentional infliction or threatened infliction of severe physical pain or suffering;

(B) the administration or application, or threatened administration or application, of mind-altering substances or other procedures calculated to disrupt profoundly the senses or the personality;

(C) the threat of imminent death; or

(D) the threat that another person will imminently be subjected to death, severe physical pain or suffering, or the administration or application of mind-altering substances or other procedures calculated to disrupt profoundly the senses or personality. . . .

18 U.S.C. §2340.

4. The USA PATRIOT Act (Uniting and Strengthening America by Providing Appropriate Tools Required to Intercept and Obstruct Terrorism Act) of 2001, Pub. L. No. 107-56, 115 Stat. 272, equipped federal law enforcement and intelligence officials with a variety of new or expanded investigative tools — some limited to the counterterrorism context and others applying generally. Section 215 of the Act, the so-called "library" provision, has been among its most controversial provisions. It provides in relevant part as follows:

§1861. Access to certain business records for foreign intelligence and international terrorism investigations

(a)(1) The Director of the Federal Bureau of Investigation or a designee of the Director (whose rank shall be no lower than Assistant Special Agent in Charge) may make an application for an order requiring the production of any tangible things (including books, records, papers, documents, and other items) for an investigation to obtain foreign intelligence information not concerning a United States person or to protect against international terrorism or clandestine intelligence activities, provided that such investigation of a United States person is not conducted solely upon the basis of activities protected by the first amendment to the Constitution. . . .

       (b) Each application under this section

          (1) shall be made to —

             (A) a judge of the [FISA] court . . . or

             (B) a United States Magistrate Judge . . . who is publicly designated . . . to hear applications and grant orders . . . under this section on behalf of a judge of [the FISA] court; and

          (2) shall specify that the records concerned are sought for an authorized investigation . . . to obtain foreign intelligence information not concerning a United States person or to protect against international terrorism or clandestine intelligence activities.

       (c)(1) Upon an application made pursuant to this section, the judge shall enter an ex parte order as requested, or as modified, approving the release of records if the judge finds that the application meets the requirements of this section. . . .

       (d) No person shall disclose to any other person (other than those persons necessary to produce the tangible things under this section) that the Federal Bureau of Investigation has sought or obtained tangible things under this section. . . .

50 U.S.C. §1861. Note that the provision is not about libraries *per se*. It broadly authorizes intelligence officers to seek and obtain orders for the production of business records of any kind — from flight school enrollments to credit card receipts, bank deposits, and chemical supply company purchase records. What is the source of the controversy over this provision? Consider the following observations:

    . . . Section 215 mirrors, in the intelligence-gathering context, the scope of authority that already exists in traditional law enforcement investigations. Obtaining business records is a long-standing law enforcement tactic. Ordinary grand juries for years have issued subpoenas to all manner of businesses, including libraries and bookstores, for records relevant to criminal inquiries. For example, in the 1997 Gianni Versace murder case, a Florida grand jury subpoenaed records from public libraries in Miami Beach and in the 1990 Zodiac gunman investigation, a New York grand jury subpoenaed records from a public library in Manhattan. Investigators believed that the gunman was inspired by a Scottish occult poet, and wanted to learn who had checked out his books. . . .

    Section 215 merely authorizes the FISA court to issue similar orders in national-security investigations. It contains a number of safeguards that protect civil liberties. First, Section 215 requires FBI agents to get a court order. . . . FISA orders are unlike grand jury subpoenas, which are requested without court supervision and are only subject to challenge after they have been issued.

    Second, Section 215 has a narrow scope. It can only be used (1) "to obtain foreign intelligence information not concerning a United States person"; or (2) "to protect against international terrorism or clandestine intelligence activities." It cannot be used to investigate ordinary crimes, or even domestic terrorism. Thus, the scope is substantially narrower than the scope of traditional law enforcement investigations — for in those investigations, the grand jury may seek the production of any business records unless the subpoena recipient can demonstrate that "there is no reasonable possibility that the category of materials the Government seeks will produce information relevant to the general subject of the grand jury's investigation," . . .

In short, critics of Section 215 make a very difficult and, in the end, unpersuasive argument. They offer the view, in effect, that traditional law enforcement powers that have been used in grand juries for years to investigate common law crimes and federal criminal offenses ought not to be used with equal authority to investigate potential terrorist threats. To many, that argument seems to precisely reverse the evaluation — if anything, the powers used to investigate terrorism, espionage and threats to national security ought to be greater than those used to investigate mere criminal behavior. . . .

Paul Rosenzweig, Civil Liberty and the Response to Terrorism, 42 Duq. L. Rev. 663, 693-696 (2004). Is this analysis persuasive? After all, why shouldn't counter-terrorism experts be able to get access to flight school records when they wish to follow a lead about potential terrorist attack? Or are we again concerned about some risk to civil liberties arising from arming the intelligence community with the investigative tools of the law enforcement community — and vice versa? Do differences between intelligence collection and grand jury investigation suggest that the grand jury analogy is unhelpful? Consider Professor Schulhofer's analysis:

> Before 9/11, FISA gave investigators access to the records of a narrow category of travel-industry businesses, provided that the person targeted was a foreign agent. The Patriot Act now permits FBI access to all the records of any business and any non-business entity, apparently including noncommercial entities such as a synagogue or mosque. And the new authority . . . drops the requirement that the records pertain to a suspected foreign agent. Formerly confidential records concerning any American citizen are now available for FBI inspection on a clandestine basis whenever an investigator thinks they may be relevant to a terrorism investigation, whether or not the person concerned is a foreign agent or a suspected criminal offender. . . . [T]his is the antithesis of government restraint: Judicial oversight is allowed no role as a check on the executive branch, and the powers granted extend far beyond the international terrorism suspects that are the legitimate targets of concern.

Stephen J. Schulhofer, No Checks, No Balances: Discarding Bedrock Constitutional Principles, in Richard C. Leone and Greg Anrig, Jr., eds., The War on Our Freedoms 74, 77-78 (2003). Does this fairly characterize Section 215? Does it make a difference to your evaluation of the section that it provides that on a semiannual basis, the Attorney General must "fully inform" the House Permanent Select Committee on Intelligence and the Senate Select Committee on Intelligence concerning all requests for production? That the Attorney General has disclosed that, "at least as of September 2003, the provision had not been used to secure any records"? Rosenzweig, 42 Duq. L. Rev. at 697. Note that Section 215 was drafted to sunset on December 31, 2005. If you were considering its extension, what changes, if any, would you make to the law?

5. It should by now be apparent that the events of 9/11 have resulted in an intense reexamination of the legal authorities to be afforded to law enforcement in its counterterrorism efforts, and of the appropriate role of law enforcement as opposed to the military or the intelligence community. Events *since* 9/11 — most pointedly the indefinite detention of Jose Padilla, an American citizen arrested in May 2002 upon his return from Pakistan and as he stepped off a plane at Chicago's O'Hare International Airport — have also sparked a debate on the questions of preventive detention and detention for the purpose of interrogation.

Hamdi v. Rumsfeld, 124 S. Ct. 2633 (2004), and Rumsfeld v. Padilla, 124 S. Ct. 2711 (2004), posed fundamental questions about the circumstances in which an American citizen may be detained as an enemy combatant in the war on terror — detention that takes place outside the usual context of criminal charge and conviction.[5] The Court in these cases, however, may have sidestepped as many questions as it answered.

Yaser Esam Hamdi was born in Louisiana in 1980 and moved with his family to Saudi Arabia as a child. By 2001, he resided in Afghanistan. During that year, Hamdi was seized by members of the Northern Alliance, a coalition of military groups opposed to the Taliban, and turned over to the United States. He was initially detained and interrogated in Afghanistan before being transferred to the United States Naval Base in Guantanamo Bay and then to the United States, when it was discovered that Hamdi was an American citizen. The government contended before the Court that Hamdi was an "enemy combatant" who could be held in the United States indefinitely without formal charges or proceedings. Hamdi's father, as next friend, filed the petition for a writ of habeas corpus that brought Hamdi's case before the Court. He argued that Hamdi was "an inexperienced aid worker caught in the wrong place at the wrong time." 124 S. Ct. at 2660.

A plurality composed of Justice O'Connor, Chief Justice Rehnquist, Justice Kennedy, and Justice Breyer determined that the Authorization for Use of Military Force ("AUMF") passed by Congress in the immediate aftermath of September 11 constituted explicit congressional authorization to the President for the detention of American citizens who were "part of or supporting forces hostile to the United States or coalition partners in Afghanistan and who engaged in an armed conflict against the United States." Id. at 2639 (internal quotations omitted). The AUMF authorized the President to "use all necessary and appropriate force against those nations, organizations, or persons he determines planned, authorized, committed, or aided the terrorist attacks" or "harbored such organizations or persons, in order to prevent any future acts of international terrorism against the United States by such nations, organizations, or persons." In the words of the plurality,

> The AUMF authorizes the President to use "all necessary and appropriate force" against "nations, organizations, or persons" associated with the September 11, 2001, terrorist attacks. There can be no doubt that individuals who fought against the United States in Afghanistan as part of the Taliban, an organization known to have supported the al Qaeda terrorist network responsible for those attacks, are individuals Congress sought to target in passing the AUMF. We conclude that detention of individuals falling into the limited category we are considering, for the duration of the particular conflict in which they were captured, is so fundamental and accepted an incident to war as to be an exercise of the "necessary and appropriate force" Congress has authorized the President to use.

Id. at 2640. The plurality determined, however, that for those citizens held in continued custody after a battlefield capture, some process is due. Thus, a citizen-detainee

---

5. In yet another related case, Rasul v. Bush, 124 S. Ct. 2686 (2004), the Court determined that federal courts have jurisdiction to determine the legality of the Executive detention of foreign nationals detained at Guantanamo Bay in connection with the "war on terror." The Court, however, did not go beyond the jurisdictional question and declined to address "[w]hether and what further proceedings [might] become necessary" after the United States makes its response to the merits of the detainees' claims. Id. at 2699.

seeking to challenge his classification as an enemy combatant "must receive notice of the factual basis for his classification, and a fair opportunity to rebut the Government's factual assertions before a neutral decisionmaker." Id. at 2648. The plurality went on to note, however, that hearsay might be accepted in such a proceeding; that "the Constitution would not be offended by a presumption in favor of the Government's evidence, so long as that presumption remained a rebuttable one and fair opportunity for rebuttal were provided"; and that "[t]here remains the possibility that the standards . . . could be met by an appropriately authorized and properly constituted military tribunal." Id. at 2649, 2651.

Justice Souter, joined by Justice Ginsburg, concluded that the AUMF did *not* authorize Hamdi's detention and that this detention was forbidden by 18 U.S.C. §4001(a), which states that "[n]o citizen shall be imprisoned or otherwise detained by the United States except pursuant to an Act of Congress." The opinion went on to note:

> Because I find Hamdi's detention forbidden by §4001(a) and unauthorized by the Force Resolution, I would not reach any questions of what process he may be due in litigating disputed issues in a proceeding under the habeas statute or prior to the habeas enquiry itself. For me, it suffices that the Government has failed to justify holding him in the absence of a further Act of Congress, criminal charges, a showing that the detention conforms to the laws of war, or a demonstration that §4001(a) is unconstitutional.

Justices Souter and Ginsburg nevertheless joined with the plurality in ordering remand to give "practical effect" to the conclusion of a majority of the Court that Hamdi's present detention was unlawful:

> . . . Although I think litigation of Hamdi's status as an enemy combatant is unnecessary, the terms of the plurality's remand will allow Hamdi to offer evidence that he is not an enemy combatant, and he should at the least have the benefit of that opportunity.
> It should go without saying that in joining with the plurality to produce a judgment, I do not adopt the plurality's resolution of constitutional issues that I would not reach. It is not that I could disagree with the plurality's determinations (given the plurality's view of the Force Resolution) that someone in Hamdi's position is entitled at a minimum to notice of the Government's claimed factual basis for holding him, and to a fair chance to rebut it before a neutral decision maker. . . . On the other hand, I do not mean to imply agreement that the Government could claim an evidentiary presumption casting the burden of rebuttal on Hamdi, or that an opportunity to litigate before a military tribunal might obviate or truncate enquiry by a court on habeas.

Id. at 2660.

There were two dissenting opinions in *Hamdi*. Justice Scalia, joined by Justice Stevens, argued in dissent that absent a suspension of the writ of habeas corpus, an American citizen accused of being an enemy combatant and detained within the territorial jurisdiction of a federal court is entitled to have this charge adjudicated in a criminal trial:

> Where the Government accuses a citizen of waging war against it, our constitutional tradition has been to prosecute him in federal court for treason or some other crime. Where the exigencies of war prevent that, the Constitution's Suspension Clause, Art. I, §9, cl. 2, allows Congress to relax the usual protections temporarily. Absent suspension,

however, the Executive's assertion of military exigency has not been thought sufficient to permit detention without charge.

Id. Justice Thomas's dissent, in contrast, took the plurality to task for affording *too much* process to Hamdi, not too little:

> I acknowledge that the question whether Hamdi's executive detention is lawful is a question properly resolved by the Judicial Branch, though the question comes to the Court with the strongest presumptions in favor of the Government. The plurality agrees that Hamdi's detention is lawful if he is an enemy combatant. But the question whether Hamdi is actually an enemy combatant is "of a kind for which the Judiciary has neither aptitude, facilities, nor responsibility and which has long been held to belong in the domain of political power not subject to judicial intrusion or inquiry." Chicago & Southern Air Lines [v. Waterman S.S. Corp., 333 U.S. 103, 111 (1948)]. That is, although it is appropriate for the Court to determine the judicial question whether the President has the asserted authority, we lack the information and expertise to question whether Hamdi is actually an enemy combatant, a question the resolution of which is committed to other branches. . . .

Id. at 2678.

The plurality in *Hamdi* declined to consider the legality of any detention of American citizens outside the narrow circumstances presented in that case:

> Here the basis asserted for detention by the military is that Hamdi was carrying a weapon against American troops on a foreign battlefield; that is, that he was an enemy combatant. The legal category of enemy combatant has not been elaborated upon in great detail. The permissible bounds of the category will be defined by the lower courts as subsequent cases are presented to them.

Id. at n. 1, 2642. And in *Padilla*, the Court said nothing at all about the substantive grounds on which an American citizen might be detained as an enemy combatant ruling, instead, that Padilla's habeas petition had been filed in the wrong court. Justice Stevens, joined by Justices Souter, Ginsburg, and Breyer, said, in dissent:

> Whether respondent is entitled to immediate release is a question that reasonable jurists may answer in different ways.[8] There is, however, only one possible answer to the question whether he is entitled to a hearing on the justification for his detention.
>
> At stake in this case is nothing less than the essence of a free society. Even more important than the method of selecting the people's rulers and their successors is the character of the constraints imposed on the Executive by the rule of law. Unconstrained Executive detention for the purpose of investigating and preventing subversive activity is the hallmark of the Star Chamber. Access to counsel for the purpose of protecting the citizen from official mistakes and mistreatment is the hallmark of due process.
>
> Executive detention of subversive citizens, like detention of enemy soldiers to keep them off the battlefield, may sometimes be justified to prevent persons from launching

---

8. Consistent with the judgment of the Court of Appeals, I believe that the Non-Detention Act, 18 U.S.C. §4001(a), prohibits — and the Authorization for Use of Military Force Joint Resolution, 115 Stat. 224, adopted on September 18, 2001, does not authorize — the protracted, incommunicado detention of American citizens arrested in the United States.

or becoming missiles of destruction. It may not, however, be justified by the naked interest in using unlawful procedures to extract information. Incommunicado detention for months on end is such a procedure. Whether the information so procured is more or less reliable than that acquired by more extreme forms of torture is of no consequence. For if this Nation is to remain true to the ideals symbolized by its flag, it must not wield the tools of tyrants even to resist an assault by the forces of tyranny.

124 S. Ct. 2711, 2735 (2004). Does this final excerpt suggest that preventive detention — to keep "subversive citizens" from "launching or becoming missiles of destruction" may sometimes be lawful *outside* the context of criminal charges? Or is it silent on that question? What does it mean to say that "[w]hether [Padilla] is entitled to immediate release is a question that reasonable jurists may answer in different ways"? Could a reasonable jurist find the AUMF to authorize the preventive detention of a citizen bound on launching a missile of destruction — provided that appropriate process is afforded? And what about detention for interrogation? Is it *ever* permissible to detain an American citizen "enemy combatant" for this purpose — provided that detention is not prolonged? Note that the plurality in *Hamdi* at one point took up the question of how long a person in Hamdi's situation might be detained, given the indefinite endpoint of a "war on terror":

> Hamdi contends that the AUMF does not authorize indefinite or perpetual detention. Certainly, we agree that indefinite detention for the purpose of interrogation is not authorized. Further, we understand Congress' grant of authority for the use of "necessary and appropriate force" to include the authority to detain for the duration of the relevant conflict, and our understanding is based on longstanding law-of-war principles. If the practical circumstances of a given conflict are entirely unlike those of the conflicts that informed the development of the law of war, that understanding may unravel. But that is not the situation we face as of this date. Active combat operations against Taliban fighters apparently are ongoing in Afghanistan. . . .

124 S. Ct. at 2641-2642. What does this suggest about the plurality's view of the detention of Padilla?

6. What *is* the appropriate role of law enforcement in counterterrorism? Consider finally the testimony of William P. Barr, former Attorney General, before the National Commission on Terrorist Attacks:

> [T]here is an insurmountable problem in separating domestic intelligence from law enforcement in this country — and that relates to the end game. At the end of the day, the people looking for the terrorists are going to have to take action to incapacitate them. This may have to be done at an instant's notice. . . . We hear a lot of talk about "prevention," but what does that actually entail? Apart from any legal concerns, it is doubtful we will tolerate regular use of domestic hit squads. The fact is that within the United States, the end game will frequently involve using law enforcement powers to take people into custody to prosecute them, if not for terrorism than for some other offense that will still effectively neutralize them without exposing sensitive information.
>
> But this means that intelligence activities must be conducted at every stage in a manner that preserves law enforcement options. This does not require delaying or diminishing intelligence activities. It does mean that intelligence activities must be carried out with an awareness of law enforcement options and in tandem with efforts

to preserve and perfect those options. If law enforcement powers are to be invoked, its standards must be satisfied. As leads are pursued, for example, it may be necessary to preserve evidence that can be used to support future arrest. Or it may be necessary to develop alternative evidence so as to protect sensitive sources and methods. Or it may be necessary to develop potential charges on a technical violation to have a sound basis to hold a suspect. In some cases, military tribunals might be an option, but even then legal standards must be satisfied. All of this requires full integration of intelligence collection with law enforcement activities. . . .

Testimony of William P. Barr Before the Nat'l Comm. on Terrorist Attacks Upon the United States (Dec. 8, 2003). Does this risk a dilution of the legal standards that have governed law enforcement in this country? What are the risks of the alternative to full integration of intelligence collection with law enforcement activities?

United States Constitution (Selected Provisions)

ARTICLE I

Section 9. . . . The Privilege of the Writ of Habeas Corpus shall not be suspended, unless when in Cases of Rebellion or Invasion the public Safety may require it.

No Bill of Attainder or ex post facto Law shall be passed. . . .

ARTICLE III

Section 1. The judicial Power of the United States, shall be vested in one supreme Court, and in such inferior Courts as the Congress may from time to time ordain and establish. . . .

Section 2. The judicial Power shall extend to all Cases, in Law and Equity, arising under this Constitution, the Laws of the United States, and Treaties made, or which shall be made, under their Authority; — to all Cases affecting Ambassadors, other public Ministers and Consuls; — to all Cases of admiralty and maritime Jurisdiction; — to Controversies to which the United States shall be a Party; — to Controversies between two or more States; — between a State and Citizens of another State; — between Citizens of different States; — between Citizens of the same State claiming Lands under Grants of different States, and between a State, or the Citizens thereof, and foreign States, Citizens or Subjects.

In all Cases affecting Ambassadors, other public Ministers and Consuls, and those in which a State shall be Party, the supreme Court shall have original Jurisdiction. In all the other Cases before mentioned, the supreme Court shall have appellate Jurisdiction, both as to Law and Fact, with such Exceptions, and under such Regulations as the Congress shall make.

The Trial of all Crimes, except in Cases of Impeachment, shall be by Jury; and such Trial shall be held in the State where the said Crimes shall have been committed; but when not committed within any State, the Trial shall be at such Place or Places as the Congress may by Law have directed. . . .

ARTICLE IV

Section 2. The Citizens of each State shall be entitled to all Privileges and Immunities of Citizens in the several States.

A Person charged in any State with Treason, Felony, or other Crime, who shall flee from Justice, and be found in another State, shall on Demand of the executive Authority of the State from which he fled, be delivered up, to be removed to the State having Jurisdiction of the Crime. . . .

ARTICLE VI

. . . This Constitution, and the Laws of the United States which shall be made in Pursuance thereof; and all Treaties made, or which shall be made, under the Authority of the United States, shall be the supreme Law of the Land; and the Judges in every State shall be bound thereby, any Thing in the Constitution or Laws of any State to the Contrary notwithstanding. . . .

AMENDMENT I

Congress shall make no law respecting an establishment of religion, or prohibiting the free exercise thereof; or abridging the freedom of speech, or of the press; or the right of the people peaceably to assemble, and to petition the Government for a redress of grievances.

AMENDMENT II

A well regulated Militia, being necessary to the security of a free State, the right of the people to keep and bear Arms, shall not be infringed.

AMENDMENT III

No Soldier shall, in time of peace be quartered in any house, without the consent of the Owner, nor in time of war, but in a manner to be prescribed by law.

AMENDMENT IV

The right of the people to be secure in their persons, houses, papers, and effects, against unreasonable searches and seizures, shall not be violated, and no Warrants shall issue, but upon probable cause, supported by Oath or affirmation, and particularly describing the place to be searched, and the persons or things to be seized.

AMENDMENT V

No person shall be held to answer for a capital, or otherwise infamous crime, unless on a presentment or indictment of a Grand Jury, except in cases arising in the land or naval forces, or in the Militia, when in actual service in time of War or public danger; nor shall any person be subject for the same offence to be twice put in jeopardy of life or limb; nor shall be compelled in any criminal case to be a witness against himself, nor be deprived of life, liberty, or property, without due process of law; nor shall private property be taken for public use, without just compensation.

AMENDMENT VI

In all criminal prosecutions, the accused shall enjoy the right to a speedy and public trial, by an impartial jury of the State and district wherein the crime shall have been committed, which district shall have been previously ascertained by law, and to be informed of the nature and cause of the accusation; to be confronted with the witnesses against him; to have compulsory process for obtaining witnesses in his favor, and to have the Assistance of Counsel for his defence.

AMENDMENT VII

In Suits at common law, where the value in controversy shall exceed twenty dollars, the right of trial by jury shall be preserved, and no fact tried by a jury, shall be otherwise re-examined in any Court of the United States, than according to the rules of the common law.

AMENDMENT VIII

Excessive bail shall not be required, nor excessive fines imposed, nor cruel and unusual punishments inflicted.

AMENDMENT IX

The enumeration in the Constitution, of certain rights, shall not be construed to deny or disparage others retained by the people.

AMENDMENT X

The powers not delegated to the United States by the Constitution, nor prohibited by it to the States, are reserved to the States respectively, or to the people.

AMENDMENT XIII

Section 1. Neither slavery nor involuntary servitude, except as a punishment for crime whereof the party shall have been duly convicted, shall exist within the United States, or any place subject to their jurisdiction.

　　Section 2. Congress shall have power to enforce this article by appropriate legislation.

AMENDMENT XIV

Section 1. All persons born or naturalized in the United States, and subject to the jurisdiction thereof, are citizens of the United States and of the State wherein they reside. No State shall make or enforce any law which shall abridge the privileges or immunities of citizens of the United States; nor shall any State deprive any person of life, liberty, or property, without due process of law; nor deny to any person within its jurisdiction the equal protection of the laws. . . .

　　Section 5. The Congress shall have power to enforce, by appropriate legislation, the provisions of this article.

Table of Cases

Principal cases are indicated by italics.

Table of Authorities

Table of Statutes and Rules

INDEX